COLLECTED WORKS OF JOHN STUART MILL

VOLUME XX

The Collected Edition of the Works of John Stuart Mill has been planned and is being directed by an editorial committee appointed from the Faculty of Arts and Science of the University of Toronto, and from the University of Toronto Press. The primary aim of the edition is to present fully collated texts of those works which exist in a number of versions, both printed and manuscript, and to provide accurate texts of works previously unpublished or which have become relatively inaccessible.

Essays on French History and Historians

by JOHN STUART MILL

Editor of the Text

JOHN M. ROBSON

Professor of English,
Victoria College, University of Toronto

Introduction by

JOHN C. CAIRNS

Professor of History,
University of Toronto

UNIVERSITY OF TORONTO PRESS

ROUTLEDGE & KEGAN PAUL

© University of Toronto Press 1985
Toronto and Buffalo
Printed in Canada

ISBN 0-8020-2490-4

London: Routledge & Kegan Paul
ISBN 0-7100-9475-2

Canadian Cataloguing in Publication Data
Mill, John Stuart, 1806–1873
[Works]
Collected works of John Stuart Mill

Includes bibliographies and indexes.
Partial contents: v. 20.   Essays on French history
and historians.
ISBN 0-8020-2490-4   (v. 20)

1. Philosophy – Collected works.   2. Political
science – Collected works.   3. Economics –
Collected works.   I. Robson, John M., 1927–   .
II. Title.

B1602.A2 1963   192   C64-000188-2

This volume has been published
with the assistance of a grant
from the Social Sciences
and Humanities Research Council
of Canada

Contents

Introduction

JOHN C. CAIRNS

JOHN MILL'S INTEREST IN FRENCH PUBLIC LIFE between the two empires is somewhat flatly proposed in his *Autobiography*. The casual reader of the few and sober pages alluding to his lifelong acquaintance with the land, the people, and the history might not readily grasp what France had been to him: not merely a window on the wider cultural world, but a laboratory of intellectual exploration and political experimentation, and a mirror, the clearest he knew, in which to see what preoccupied him in England. There were times when he thought they did "order this matter better in France," times when he did not; times even when his criticisms of the faults he perceived in the French character approached in severity his denunciations of faults in the English. But sympathetic or censorious, and preoccupied with responsibilities and problems in England, he followed French thought and French public life more closely perhaps than any other Englishman of his time. France offered not only the most exciting intellectual and political spectacle in Europe, but an instructive angle of vision from which to perceive England. France's history, its men of thought and action were as integral a part of Mill's education as the famous tutorship of his father and Bentham had been. Like the early philosophes, he eagerly sought out the stimulating relativity of another society.

The essays in this volume, mostly occasional pieces on revolution and history, span the two decades from youth to middle age, from the embattled liberalism of the opposition under the rule of Charles X (set against the Tory administrations of Canning and Wellington) almost to the eve of the Second Empire. At their centre is the Revolution of 1789, cataclysmic, still mysterious, the ultimate implications of which were far from clear, and about which Mill grew increasingly uncertain. He followed the revived debate of this great affair with intense interest. By no means uncommitted among its protagonists, he tried to weigh the evidence and extract the lessons. Avid for fresh insights, scornful of uncongenial interpretations, he came to see that 1789 could not by itself provide what he wanted. He cast about more broadly for the grand hypothesis that would situate the age of revolution through which he was living and illuminate the whole course of European civilization. Finally he searched for a philosophy and a science of history. Following at the same time the progress of the struggle for liberty and order in France, he commented and judged and published his opinions until the aftermath of the Revolution of 1848 betrayed the high liberal hopes of February. When for the second time he witnessed the collapse of liberalism, Mill fell silent. He had found and absorbed what he sought from French thought; he did not believe that for the foreseeable future French public life had instruction to offer; his radical and democratic enthusiasms were muted. Thereafter he continued to observe; he continued to travel in France; he was led by the accident of his wife's death there to take up his last residence in France. But he did not write publicly about it. Writing publicly about it belonged to an earlier and more hopeful time.

MILL'S EXPERIENCE OF FRANCE AND THE FRENCH

THE FRENCH EDUCATION OF JOHN MILL was, like its English counterpart, precocious, thanks not only to his father's ambition but also to the hospitality of General Sir Samuel Bentham and his wife. Lady Bentham particularly had a clear notion of what was good for her young charge; the boy was willing and the father acquiescent. The long summer season of 1820 in southwest France turned into a year, in which the agreeable pleasure of swimming in the shadow of the Pont du Gard was mixed with attention to serious studies and precise accounts of things seen, done, and learned from Toulouse and Montpellier to Paris and Caen.

John Mill would recollect that he had returned home in July 1821 with "many advantages." He singled out three: "a familiar knowledge of the French language, and acquaintance with the ordinary French literature," the advantage of "having breathed for a whole year the free and genial atmosphere of Continental life," and "a strong and permanent interest in Continental liberalism, of which [he] ever afterwards kept [himself] *au courant*, as much as of English politics."[1] He had arrived observing, comparing, judging; he left doing much the same, but with less concern to memorize the Departmental "chefs lieux by heart so as to be able to repeat them without hesitation," and a superior capacity to comment on the struggle among liberals, conservatives, and reactionaries around Louis XVIII.[2] He said that France had taught him a relativity of values which thereafter kept him "free from the error always prevalent in England, and from which even [his] father with all his superiority to prejudice was not exempt, of

[1]John Stuart Mill, *Autobiography*, in *Autobiography and Literary Essays*, ed. John M. Robson and Jack Stillinger, *Collected Works of John Stuart Mill* [*CW*], I (Toronto: University of Toronto Press, 1981), 59, 63. On the year in France, see *John Mill's Boyhood Visit to France*, ed. Anna J. Mill (Toronto: University of Toronto Press, 1960), and Iris Wessel Mueller, *John Stuart Mill and French Thought* (Urbana: University of Illinois Press, 1956), 2-10.

[2]Journal, 22 June, and Notebook, 27 May, 1820, in *John Mill's Boyhood Visit to France*, 22, 105-6.

judging universal questions by a merely English standard."[3] He had certainly discovered people different from those James Mill had perceived coming up in post-war France ("very quiet & contented slaves" under "a quiet, gentle despotism"),[4] and he took the trouble to jot down his independent view.[5] When fourteen, he had met "many of the chiefs of the Liberal party" at J.B. Say's house in Paris. Afterwards, he recalled having encountered Henri Saint-Simon there, "not yet the founder either of a philosophy or a religion, and considered only as a clever *original*."[6] Considering the fuss Saint-Simon had provoked by the spring of 1820 with his celebrated parable, contrasting two hypothetical losses to France (all its creative and industrious élite, or all its 30,000 dignitaries and high functionaries), which led to his unsuccessful prosecutions and trial on various charges—a scandal compounded by the outrage and uproar over Louvel's almost simultaneous assassination of the duc de Berry—this was the least one could say.[7]

John Mill was addicted to recording facts and figures. Yet it is clear from the reports he shaped to his father's expectation that he was not indifferent to the land. He saw much of it then; later he tramped over large stretches of it, seeking a return to health. His letters reveal the profound impact on him of the magnificent French countryside: "I never saw anything more lovely than the Peyrou & its view this evening just after sunset," he wrote Harriet from Montpellier in December 1854; "everything was pure & the *tone* that of the finest Poussin."[8]

Following his year among the French, Mill's attentions were again absorbed by his father's curriculum and his own "self-education." This included Condillac and a first appreciation of the French Revolution, but it seems to have left no room for broader pursuit of his continental interests. France had stimulated his desire to travel, but, still a lad, he spent holidays with his family in the country; later in the 1820s, with no more than a month off from his responsibility at India House, he settled for walking tours with friends in the English counties. Ten years passed before his return to France. But he constantly followed its public life; as early as April 1824 he sprang to the defence of French liberalism under

---

[3]*Autobiography*, *CW*, I, 63.

[4]Letter of James Mill to Francis Place of 6 Sept., 1815, Place Collection, BL Add. MSS, 35152, f160r.

[5]"It is commonly said that the French are an idle people; this I do not think true . . ." (Notebook, 27 May, 1820, in *John Mill's Boyhood Visit to France*, 105).

[6]*Autobiography*, *CW*, I, 63.

[7]Mueller states that Mill was evidently "unaware of the lasting influence this early experience was to have on him" (*Mill and French Thought*, 8), but it is not clear that merely meeting Saint-Simon had any influence on him at all.

[8]Letter to Harriet Mill, in *The Later Letters of John Stuart Mill* [*LL*], ed. Francis E. Mineka and Dwight N. Lindley, *CW*, XIV-XVII (Toronto: University of Toronto Press, 1972), XIV, 263 (22 Dec., 1854).

attack in the *Edinburgh Review*, protesting the "torrent of mere abuse . . . poured out against the French, for the sole purpose of gratifying [English] national antipathy," and extolling French science and letters.[9] His commitment to France was made long before the first of the intellectual encounters (if we except the brief friendship with the future chemist Antoine Jérôme Balard during his year with the Benthams) that accompanied his reading of the political scene.

Gustave d'Eichthal, a recruit to the rising Saint-Simonian school, first saw Mill at the London Debating Society in May 1828; he was to correspond with him on and off for more than forty years. "Dans une mesure," d'Eichthal recalled, "c'est lui qui m'a ouvert l'Angleterre comme je lui ai ouvert la France. Ce qui nous rapprochait ce n'étaient point des idées abstraites. C'était notre nature et nos désirs d'apôtre."[10] Though he did not convert Mill to the faith in its brief but curious heyday under Prosper Enfantin, directly and indirectly d'Eichthal planted the seeds of alternative visions in Mill's mind shortly after the apparent collapse of the world Mill had made for himself at the *Westminster Review*. Afterwards, Mill said that he and his friends had "really hoped and aspired" to be the new philosophes, and that "No one of the set went to so great excesses in this boyish ambition as I did. . . ." In 1826 he "awakened from this as from a dream."[11] As he arranged all this in retrospect, Weber and Wordsworth then offered the consolations and stimulus of contemplation and inner happiness. But it was the Saint-Simonians who proposed a view of history and human development that plausibly situated the times. It was they who, for Mill, best explained the century's collisions and angularities as characteristic of the transition from an "organic period" of faith to a "critical period" of disputes and uncertainties, the resolution of which, he hoped, would bring a new era of liberty informed by education and "the true exigencies of life."[12]

It is doubtful that Mill in the late 1820s shared such an understanding. And though he may well have read Saint-Simon and Augustin Thierry's address "To the Parliaments of France and England" of 1814, with its appeal for a Franco-British union that could "change the state of Europe" and bring true peace,[13] it is more likely to have been after July 1830 than before. D'Eichthal pressed him in the autumn of 1829 for a statement; Mill was reserved. Sympathetic to his correspondent's exposition of the doctrine, he condemned the

[9]"Periodical Literature: Edinburgh Review" (1824), *CW*, I, 301-2, 304-5, 307-11.

[10]D'Eichthal to Dr. Henry (26 Nov., 1873), quoted in Gustave d'Eichthal, *A French Sociologist Looks at Britain: Gustave d'Eichthal and British Society in 1828*, trans. and ed. Barrie M. Ratcliffe and W.H. Chaloner (Manchester: Manchester University Press, 1977), 3n. On d'Eichthal, see the editors' "Gustave d'Eichthal (1802-1886): An Intellectual Portrait," *ibid.*, 109-61.

[11]*Autobiography*, *CW*, I, 111, 137.

[12]*Ibid.*, 171, 173.

[13]"The Reorganisation of the European Community; or, The Necessity and the Means of Uniting the Peoples of Europe in a Single Body While Preserving for Each of Them Their Independence, by the comte de St. Simon and A. Thierry, His Pupil, Oct. 1814," in Henri de Saint-Simon, *Selected Writings*, ed. and trans. F.M.H. Markham (Oxford: Blackwell, 1952), 30-1, 50-1.

Saint-Simonian books he had read (one such seemed "the production of men who had neither read nor thought, but hastily put down the first crudities that would occur to a boy who had just left school"). Auguste Comte's early outline of a *Système de politique positive* (1824), sent by d'Eichthal the previous year, he found at least plausible, clear, and methodical, but ultimately a clever exercise. Its conception of the ends of government and the constitution of a new ruling class Mill rejected completely.[14] A month after this cold douche, he made amends by saying something favourable about the Saint-Simonians, but it was little enough. He discouraged d'Eichthal from coming to England "with a view to my complete initiation in the St Simonian doctrine." Doubting its applicability in France, he was sure it was unacceptable and undesirable in England.[15] Given the report he had of a meeting, Mill wondered "how you have hitherto escaped the jokers and epigrammatists of the Parisian *salons*."[16]

Nevertheless, the Saint-Simonians had something he wanted. The celebrated "crisis" in his "mental history" was on him. He had come through "the dry heavy dejection of the melancholy winter of 1826-27," was questioning and doubting Bentham and his father, discovering the weak places of his philosophy. He had "only a conviction, that the true system was something much more complex and many sided" than he had imagined. He discovered from acquaintance with European, especially French, thought the logic of the mind's "possible progress," the relativity of historical institutions, and the truth that "any general theory or philosophy of politics supposes a previous theory of human progress, and that this is the same thing with a philosophy of history."[17] On the eve of the July Revolution, he was apparently feeling his way. Closer contact with the

---

[14]This was the revised edition of the essay Comte had first published in 1822, and which contained the germ of his philosophical and historical thought, to which Mill would be infinitely more receptive after 1830. It is reprinted in *Système de politique positive, ou Traité de sociologie, instituant la religion de l'humanité*, 4 vols. (Paris: Carilian-Goeury and Dalmont, *et al.*, 1851-54), IV, Appendice générale, 47-136. Letter to d'Eichthal, in *The Earlier Letters of John Stuart Mill [EL]*, ed. Francis E. Mineka, *CW*, XII-XIII (Toronto: University of Toronto Press, 1963), XII, 34-8 (8 Oct., 1829). On Mill and the Saint-Simonians, see Mueller, *Mill and French Thought*, 48-91, and Richard K.P. Pankhurst, *The Saint-Simonians, Mill and Carlyle: A Preface to Modern Thought* (London: Sidgwick and Jackson, 1957), *passim*. There is no direct evidence, but one may suspect that he found the opening passages of the public lectures unsettling: "C'est au milieu de ces deux armées que nous venons apporter la paix, en annonçant une doctrine qui ne prêche pas *seulement l'horreur du sang*, mais l'horreur de la lutte, sous quelque nom qu'elle se déguise. *Antagonisme*, entre un pouvoir spirituel et un pouvoir temporel, *opposition*, en l'honneur de la liberté, *concurrence*, pour le plus grand bien de tous, nous ne croyons à la nécessité éternelle d'aucune de ces machines de guerre. . . ." (*Doctrine de Saint-Simon. Exposition. Première année, 1829*, new ed., intro. and notes by C. Bouglé and Elie Halévy [Paris: Rivière, 1924], 122.) Cf. Frank E. Manuel, *The Prophets of Paris* (Cambridge, Mass.: Harvard University Press, 1962), 158-9; D.G. Charlton, *Secular Religions in France, 1815-1870* (London: Oxford University Press, 1963), 65-79, and Georg G. Iggers, *The Cult of Authority. The Political Philosophy of the Saint-Simonians: A Chapter in the History of Totalitarianism* (The Hague: Nijhoff, 1958), *passim*.

[15]Letter to d'Eichthal, *EL*, *CW*, XII, 45-9 (9 Feb., 1830).

[16]Letter to d'Eichthal, *ibid.*, 49-50 (6 Mar., 1830).

[17]*Autobiography*, *CW*, I, 137, 143, 169.

Saint-Simonian school in Paris during the summer of 1830 eventuated in the *Examiner* articles, "The Spirit of the Age," which revealed that while he was no convert, as he put it, *"je tiens bureau de St Simonisme chez moi."*[18]

More sympathetic, he remained unconvinced. If in the aftermath of 1830 he placed the Saint-Simonians "decidedly *à la tête de la civilisation*" and imagined their prescription as "likely to be the final and permanent condition of the human race," he guessed mankind would not be ready for it for "many, or at least several, ages."[19] He assisted d'Eichthal and Charles Duveyrier before and during their mission to England, publicly (though also anonymously) criticized the French government for prosecuting the Saint-Simonians, but concluded that that phase of their work, which had transformed political discourse in France, was almost done.[20] His private remarks about the communal life reported from Ménilmontant where, following schism, most of the sect had followed Père Enfantin ("the best man they know, but I wish they had a better still") were cool.[21] After the sensational trial of Enfantin and his disciples on 27-28 August, 1832, resulting in fines, imprisonments and dissolution of the school, Mill remarked to Carlyle that "There was much in the conduct of them all, which really one cannot help suspecting of quackery." In the *Examiner*, however, he condemned the government's heavy hand.[22] The subsequent scattering of the disciples, the notorious journey to Constantinople in search of *la femme libre, la Mère suprême*,[23] left him melancholy that so much creativeness should have succumbed to such madness. Uncharacteristically patronizing, he noted that "St Simon really for a Frenchman was a great man," and the society bearing his name had been "the only spiritual fruit of the Revolution of 1830."[24] He defended it against the ridicule of *The Times*, however, concluding it had had a "highly beneficial influence over the public mind of France."[25] Years later, he

---

[18]Letter to d'Eichthal, *EL, CW*, XII, 71 (1 Mar., 1831); Mill, "The Spirit of the Age," *Examiner*, 9 Jan.-29 May, 1831, 20-1, 50-2, 82-4, 162-3, 210-11, 307, 339-41.

[19]Letter to d'Eichthal, *EL, CW*, XII, 88-9 (30 Nov., 1831).

[20]Summary of French news, *Examiner*, 29 Jan., 1832, 72-3.

[21]Letter to Thomas Carlyle, *EL, CW*, XII, 106 (29 May, 1832); letter to d'Eichthal and Duveyrier, *ibid.*, 107-9 (30 May, 1832). On life at Ménilmontant, see Sébastien Charléty, *Histoire du Saint-Simonisme (1825-1864)* (Paris: Hartmann, 1931), 161-75.

[22]Letter to Carlyle, *EL, CW*, XII, 120 (17 Sept., 1832); summary of French news, *Examiner*, 9 Sept., 1832, 585. On the trial, see Charléty, *Histoire du Saint-Simonisme*, 175-85, and Louis Blanc, *Histoire de dix ans, 1830-1840*, 12th ed., 5 vols. (Paris: Baillière, 1877), III, 319-38.

[23]The empty chair beside Enfantin's, reserved for the *Mère-Messie*, seems to have been offered to George Sand, but, sympathetic as she was to the movement, she had doubts about the place of women in it: "Je n'ai pas encore trouvé une solution aux doutes de tout genre qui remplissent mon esprit, et je ne saurais en accepter aucune que je n'eusse bien examinée" (letter to Marie Talon of 10 Nov., 1834, in George Sand, *Correspondance*, 17 vols. [Paris: Garnier, 1964-83], II, 739-40).

[24]Letter to Carlyle, *EL, CW*, XII, 150-1 (11-12 Apr., 1833).

[25]Review of *St. Simonism in London, Examiner*, 2 Feb., 1834, 68; Mueller, *Mill and French Thought*, 48-91; cf. John M. Robson, *The Improvement of Mankind: The Social and Political Thought of John Stuart Mill* (Toronto: University of Toronto Press, 1968), 76-80.

still referred to "my friends the St Simonians."[26] He could scarcely have imagined the immense influence some of them were to have in the engineering, railway, and banking enterprises of France after 1840.[27]

The Saint-Simonians reinforced Mill's intense interest in the affairs of France; stimulated by them, he developed a progressive view of history working itself out through organic and critical periods. He said they had "much changed" him.[28] Whatever their absurdities, their bold vision of the ideal society, ostensibly democratic and led by an intellectual élite, must help others to move the world toward it. But unlike Saint-Simon, Mill did not think the times were ripe. Hence his own rather Saint-Simonian conclusion that "the mental regeneration of Europe must precede its social regeneration," for all the dogmas, from religion to rationalism, had proved inadequate.[29]

For several years it seemed to Mill that Auguste Comte might prove to be the prophet of this "mental regeneration." Comte had broken with the Saint-Simonians in 1828. Mill's first impression of the short work d'Eichthal sent him, however, was unfavourable. Despite its arresting aspects, he then thought the view of history "warped & distorted by the necessity of proving that civilisation has but one law, & that a law of progressive advancement."[30] Yet it was to this conclusion that the liberal school of French historians, to which Mill soon subscribed, was attached. Moreover, after 1830 he became increasingly sympathetic to the Saint-Simonian world-view. When therefore he read the first two volumes of Comte's *Cours de philosophie positive* in 1837, he was more impressed: "one of the most profound books ever written on the philosophy of the sciences."[31] Further volumes sustained his enthusiasm: "He makes some mistakes, but on the whole, I think it very nearly the grandest work of this age."[32] No one before Comte, Mill was to say thirty years later, "had penetrated to the philosophy of the matter, and placed the necessity of historical studies as the foundation of sociological speculation on the true footing."[33] In the course of

---

[26]Letter to Robert Barclay Fox, *EL, CW*, XIII, 473 (6 May, 1841).

[27]"It is not enough," Emile Péreire, the future banker and railway magnate, is said to have told Armand Carrel when he left the *National* in 1835, "to outline gigantic programs on paper; I must write my idea on the earth" (Rondo E. Cameron, *France and the Economic Development of Europe, 1800-1914: Conquest of Peace and Seeds of War* [Princeton: Princeton University Press, 1961], 134; see Charléty, *Histoire du Saint-Simonisme*, 205-63).

[28]Letter to d'Eichthal, *EL, CW*, XII, 45 (9 Feb., 1830); *Autobiography, CW*, I, 171.

[29]Letter to R.B. Fox, *EL, CW*, XIII, 563-4 (19 Dec., 1842).

[30]Letters to d'Eichthal, *ibid.*, XII, 34, 35-8 (15 May, 8 Oct., 1829); on Comte and Mill, see Walter M. Simon, *European Positivism in the Nineteenth Century: An Essay in Intellectual History* (Ithaca: Cornell University Press, 1963), 172-201; Bruce Mazlish, *James and John Stuart Mill: Father and Son in the Nineteenth Century* (New York: Basic Books, 1975), 255-62.

[31]Letter to John Pringle Nichol, *CW*, XII, 363 (2 Dec., 1837).

[32]Letter to Alexander Bain, *ibid.*, XIII, 487 (Autumn 1841); he read Comte's work, he recalled, "with avidity" (*Autobiography, CW*, I, 217).

[33]"Auguste Comte and Positivism" (1865), *Essays on Ethics, Religion, and Society, CW*, X (Toronto: University of Toronto Press, 1969), 308.

the decade, from about 1828, Mill had been influenced to rethink fundamentally his conception of history and its function. To Comte more than to any other he was indebted for his new insight. The sectarianism, however, to which he had objected earlier, became clearer as Comte's work advanced and even less acceptable to Mill as he came under the influence of the liberal journalists and Tocqueville.

Encouraged by Armand Marrast, former editor of the liberal *Tribune*, who had fled Sainte-Pélagie prison in July 1835 to find refuge in England, Mill wrote Comte directly in 1841. The correspondence flourished, Mill keeping his distance, minimizing their differences, Comte explaining but giving no ground. Comte paraded his persecution by the government; Mill sought to assuage his bitterness, passing on the favourable remarks by Guizot (who had been Ambassador in London, February-October 1840), juggling with the confidences about Comte's marital problems, promising (rashly) that he should not worry about material matters "aussi longtemps que je vivrai et que j'aurai un sou à partager avec vous."[34] Comte's final importunings and intransigences wore the friendship down. The financial generosity Mill had arranged from George Grote, William Molesworth, and Raikes Currie ran out. Grote broke with Comte in 1848. Mill professed a high opinion for "la théorie de la méthode positive," but made clear his disapproval of the manner in which Comte applied it to social questions. Comte put his complaints in print; this did not affect the even estimate Mill gave of him in the *Autobiography*.[35] On the question of equality of women, on the ultimate immovability of Comte regarding his own *pouvoir spirituel*, they parted company. "He is a man," Mill remarked, "one can serve only in his own way."[36]

For all the angular behaviour, Mill had nevertheless remained sympathetic to Comte's distress. Harriet Taylor's tart strictures (Mill had shown her some of the correspondence) on "This dry sort of man" as being "not a worthy coadjutor & scarcely a worthy opponent" he did not share.[37] Year after year he had been responsive, protective, patient. But by 1844 Mill's concern with liberty was so marked that, much as he appreciated Comte's "admirable historical views," "I think and have always thought him in a radically wrong road, and likely to go farther and farther wrong. . . ."[38] The prediction was accurate. Sectarianism was the problem. The final statement in the *Système de politique positive* meant that

---

[34]Letter to Auguste Comte, *CW*, XIII, 585 (15 June, 1843). Mill did not then send him any money; see letter to John Austin, *ibid.*, 714 (13 Apr., 1847). In December, 1848, however, he made a single contribution; see letter to Emile Littré, *ibid.*, 741 (22 Dec., 1848).

[35]*Ibid.*, 742; Simon, *European Positivism*, 186-90; *Autobiography*, *CW*, I, 173, 271-2.

[36]Letter to Sarah Austin, *EL*, *CW*, XIII, 654 (18 Jan., 1845); Simon, *European Positivism*, 186-91.

[37]Harriet Taylor to Mill (c. 1844), in Friedrich A. Hayek, *John Stuart Mill and Harriet Taylor: Their Friendship and Subsequent Marriage* (London: Routledge and Kegan Paul, 1951), 114.

[38]Letter to Nichol, *EL*, *CW*, XIII, 739 (30 Sept., 1844). Cf. David H. Lewisohn, "Mill and Comte on the Methods of Social Science," *Journal of the History of Ideas*, XXXIII (1972), 315-24.

free thought would be coerced by the tyranny of public opinion sanctioned by moral authority.[39] In the guise of a "plan for the regeneration of human society," Comte's imagination had conceived a humourless, ludicrously detailed, anti-intellectual "absolute monarchy." After Comte's death, Mill attributed the work to the "melancholy decadence of a great intellect."[40] The result of such a system would be "a despotism of society over the individual, surpassing anything contemplated in the political ideal of the most rigid disciplinarian among the ancient philosophers."[41] With Comte, as with the Saint-Simonians, however, Mill had undertaken "the task of sifting what is good from what is bad." In neither case had he been able to accept the whole, to join without reservation the "active and enthusiastic adherents, some of them of no inconsiderable personal merit, in England, France, and other countries."[42] Reading a French obituary notice of Comte's death in 1857, he noted ironically, "It seems as if there would be no thinkers left in the world."[43]

By then he had been acquainted with Alexis de Tocqueville for more than two decades. For while Mill was assiduously, even deferentially, corresponding with Comte, he deepened his knowledge of Tocqueville's views, following his early acquaintance with De la démocratie en Amérique. The style of his exchange with Tocqueville differed greatly from that of his relations with Comte or the Saint-Simonians. With the last he had been the pursued, the reserved commentator, to some extent the receptive pupil, the distressed friend and even-handed defender. With Comte, after an initially negative reaction, he had been the admiring convert and interlocutor, the helpful friend, and finally the disenchanted critic, convinced that, though Comte's insight into the nature of the historical process was profound and true, the ultimate meaning of his system was abhorrent. With Tocqueville there were reservations, question marks, but the meeting of minds at first seemed close. If the Saint-Simonians raised doubts about the steadiness of brilliant French thinkers, and Comte illustrated the limitation of the doctrinaire mentality, Tocqueville confirmed that impression of liberality in the "continental" mind Mill said he had taken back to England from his boyhood visit to France. In each case, what first attracted Mill was the broad historical conception they all advanced.

[39]Letter to Célestin de Blignières, *LL*, *CW*, XV, 768-9 (22 Jan., 1862).

[40]"Auguste Comte and Positivism," *CW*, X, 358, 343, 367.

[41]*On Liberty*, in *Essays on Politics and Society*, *CW*, XVIII-XIX (Toronto: University of Toronto Press, 1977), XVIII, 227. See also Mueller, *Mill and French Thought*, 92-133; and cf. Robson, *The Improvement of Mankind*, 95-105, who stresses Mill's slowness, by comparison with Grote, to see the direction Comte had taken.

[42]*Autobiography*, *CW*, I, 271. See also Pankhurst, *The Saint-Simonians: Mill and Carlyle, passim*.

[43]Letter to Harriet Mill, *LL*, *CW*, XV, 537 (16 Sept., 1857). Mill himself has been accused of showing "more than a touch of something resembling moral totalitarianism," aggressively proselytizing to his own "religion of humanity" (Maurice Cowling, *Mill and Liberalism* [Cambridge: Cambridge University Press, 1963], xii, 77-93), and exonerated as forthrightly as "an unqualified liberal" (John Gray, *Mill on Liberty: A Defence* [London: Routledge and Kegan Paul, 1983], 119).

"I have begun to read Tocqueville," he noted in April 1835. "It seems an excellent book: uniting considerable graphic power, with the capacity of generalizing on the history of society, which distinguishes the best French philosophers of the present day. . . ."[44] On Tocqueville's second visit to England in May 1835, Mill's direct overture to him as a possible correspondent for the *London Review* brought the warmest response, and flattery that "peu de Français savent manier leur langue comme vous maniez la nôtre."[45] Their differences about democracy were in the open from the beginning, even if Mill underplayed beforehand his published criticism of the first two volumes of the *Démocratie* ("a shade more favourable to democracy than your book, although in the main I agree, so far as I am competent to judge, in the unfavourable part of your remarks, but without carrying them quite so far"). The review was handsome enough: he pronounced the book to be a work "such as Montesquieu might have written, if to his genius he had superadded good sense."[46] This broad proclamation that the "insular" crowd of English politicians should take it from a Frenchman, "whose impartiality as between aristocracy and democracy is unparalleled in our time," that "the progress of democracy neither can nor ought to be stopped"[47] was the vigorous beginning of his reflection on and dialogue with Tocqueville. Tocqueville reshaped Mill's approach to, acceptance of, and effort to resolve the difficulties and dangers of democracy. Of all his reviewers, he said, Mill was "le seul qui m'ait *entièrement* compris, qui ait su saisir d'une vue générale l'ensemble de mes idées, la tendance finale de mon esprit."[48]

As it turned out, Tocqueville contributed only once to Mill's journal; Mill ventured to convey that "people here" found the article "a little *abstract*."[49] But their relations were good: he once told Tocqueville that he and Armand Carrel (an odd couple) were the only Frenchmen for whom he had "une véritable admiration."[50] Yet Tocqueville was the more solicitous of their friendship, Mill more elusive than Tocqueville's other English friends and correspondents. Again Mill's notice of the third and fourth volumes of *Démocratie*, though it appeared in October 1840 at a moment when Anglo-French relations were strained almost to the point of rupture, was graciously received, and the remark of Royer-Collard

---

[44]Letter to Joseph Blanco White, *EL*, *CW*, XII, 259 (15 Apr., 1835).

[45]Tocqueville to Mill, in *Oeuvres, papiers, et correspondances d'Alexis de Tocqueville*, ed. J.P. Mayer, *et al.* (Paris: Gallimard, 1951-), VI, 293 (June 1835). "I learnt the language in the country itself, and acquired the colloquial part of it in greater perfection than most English do . . . " (letter to Carlyle, *EL*, *CW*, XII, 180 [5 Oct., 1833]).

[46]Letter to Tocqueville, *EL*, *CW*, XII, 272 (Sept. 1835); cf. Tocqueville to Mill, *Oeuvres*, VI, 295-7 (12 Sept., 1835); Mill, "De Tocqueville on Democracy in America [I]" (1835), *CW*, XVIII, 57.

[47]"De Tocqueville on Democracy in America [I]," *CW*, XVIII, 50.

[48]Tocqueville to Mill, *Oeuvres*, VI, 302 (3 Dec., 1835).

[49]Letter to Tocqueville, *EL*, *CW*, XII, 304 (27 Apr., 1836); cf. J.P. Mayer's remarks in Tocqueville, *Oeuvres*, VI, 16.

[50]Letter to Tocqueville, *EL*, *CW*, XII, 309 (9 Nov., 1836).

next year that it was "un ouvrage original" passed on to the reviewer.[51] But Mill told Tocqueville, "you have so far outrun me that I am lost in the distance," and that it would take him time to sort out what he could accept from what would require further explanation. "In any case you have accomplished a great achievement: you have changed the face of political philosophy. . . . I do not think that anything more important than the publication of your book has happened even in this great age of events. . . ." It would be read even "in this stupid island."[52] To others, however, he remarked that French philosophers had created "almost a new French language," that Tocqueville was "really abstruse," and that he found it "tough work reviewing him, much tougher than I expected."[53] Nevertheless, looking back, he decided that his own thought had "moved more and more in the same channel" as Tocqueville's, and that his "practical political creed" over the quarter century had been modified as a result.[54]

In the case of the Saint-Simonians and Comte, Mill had been led through study of their works to reflect more fully on French public policy and the fate of opposition opinion. The correspondence with Tocqueville concentrated on the uncertain Franco-British relationship. In the vanguard of "insular" and "ignorant" English journalism, Mill early distinguished the *Edinburgh Review*, as he later insisted upon *The Times*. He said one could almost count the Englishmen who were "aware that France has produced any great names in prose literature since Voltaire and Rousseau."[55] Seeking his collaboration with the *London Review*, he told Tocqueville that politicians, publicists, and people "know about as much of France as they do of Timbuctoo."[56] The severity of his comparisons of the two nations was sometimes exaggerated. Even as a boy, he claimed, he had felt "the contrast between the frank sociability and amiability of French personal intercourse, and the English mode of existence in which everybody acts as if everybody else (with few, or no, exceptions) was either an enemy or a bore."[57] But this judgment, set down later in life, was much affected by his peculiar situation; close friends had been few and, as in J.A. Roebuck's case, Mill's feeling toward them had been at risk when they presumed to speak of his deepest attachment. Alexander Bain remarked that Mill himself did not show

[51]Mill to Tocqueville, *ibid.*, 316 (7 Jan., 1837); Tocqueville to Mill, *Oeuvres*, VI, 327, 329-30, 334 (3 May, 18 Oct., 1840, 18 Mar., 1841); Mill to Tocqueville, *EL, CW*, XIII, 457 (30 Dec., 1840).

[52]Letter to Tocqueville, *EL, CW*, XIII, 434 (11 May, 1840).

[53]Letter to R.B. Fox, *ibid.*, 441 (3 Aug., 1840).

[54]*Autobiography, CW*, I, 199-201; Mueller, *Mill and French Thought*, 134-69 and the critical discussion of her interpretation in H.O. Pappé, "Mill and Tocqueville," *Journal of the History of Ideas*, XXV (1964), 217-34; Robson, *Improvement of Mankind*, 105-14.

[55]"Periodical Literature: Edinburgh Review," *CW*, I, 307-11; "De Tocqueville on Democracy in America [II]" (1840), *CW*, XVIII, 155.

[56]Letter to Tocqueville, *EL, CW*, XII, 271 (Sept. 1835).

[57]*Autobiography, CW*, I, 59-61.

a "boundless capability of fellowship," and it is clear that Tocqueville, sensitive in his own approaches, registered this reserve. Bain thought Mill dealt partially with France and the French, however, by comparison with England and the English.[58] But if this bias did exist, it did not carry over into all matters; certainly not into foreign affairs. In private he was quite capable of turning the comparison to the advantage of his own people. Of Aristide Guilbert's offer of an article for the *London and Westminster Review*, Mill commented that it "promises fair, but I have never found that a Frenchman's promise to do anything punctually could be depended upon. They promise everything and do nothing. They are not men of business. Guilbert is better, being half an Englishman."[59] Public disputes between the two countries were not so lightly laughed off.

Mill himself was alive to the danger of too great a concentration of interest in another society. "I sometimes think," he observed in his diary, "that those who, like us, keep up with the European movement, are by that very circumstance thrown out of the stream of English opinion and have some chance of mistaking and misjudging it."[60] The intense diplomatic crisis of 1839-41[61] revealed clearly that he had by no means lost his native bearings. It marked the beginning of a profound difference between himself and Tocqueville which never was resolved; it showed a very real limitation to Mill's capacity for evaluating the rights and wrongs of the old Anglo-French antagonism. He said he understood the sense of

---

[58]"He always dealt gently with her faults, and liberally with her virtues," Bain said, adding that "his habitual way of speaking of England, the English people, English society, as compared with other nations, was positively unjust, and served no good end" (Alexander Bain, *John Stuart Mill: A Criticism with Personal Recollections* [London: Longmans, Green, 1882], 150, 78, 161). Cf. Tocqueville to Mill, *Oeuvres*, VI, 291 (June 1835).

[59]Letter to John Robertson, *EL, CW,* XII, 343 (28 July, 1837).

[60]Diary, 14 Jan., 1854, in *The Letters of John Stuart Mill,* ed. Hugh S.R. Elliot, 2 vols. (London: Longmans, Green, 1910), II, 359.

[61]A long struggle and eventual war occurred between Turkey and its Albanian vassal in Egypt, the Pasha Mohammed Ali. France favoured his ambitions in large parts of the Ottoman Empire. Finally, Britain and Russia, backed by Austria and Prussia, concluded the Treaty of London (15 July, 1840), agreeing to force him to disgorge all but southern Syria in return for hereditary possession of Egypt. This convention effectively isolated France and led Mohammed Ali to appeal to the French Prime Minister, Adolphe Thiers. The Foreign Secretary, Palmerston, arranged for the Sultan to depose the Pasha, while Thiers was backed by a violent press outcry in Paris that he support him and France's interests in Egypt by war, if necessary. By autumn, the situation turned against Mohammed Ali: Louis Philippe chose the path of negotiation; François Guizot returned to Paris from the Embassy in London, bent upon a peaceful resolution of the crisis with England; Thiers was isolated, and replaced by Marshal Soult with Guizot as Foreign Minister. But Anglo-French disputes continued on through the decade, with intense anti-English feeling on all sides in France. See Douglas Johnson, *Guizot: Aspects of French History, 1787-1874* (Toronto: University of Toronto Press, 1963), 263-85; R.W. Seton-Watson, *Britain in Europe, 1789-1914* (Cambridge: Cambridge University Press, 1937), 192-222; Charles K. Webster, *The Foreign Policy of Palmerston, 1830-1841: Britain, the Liberal Movement and the Eastern Question,* 2 vols. (London: Bell, 1951), *passim*; Kenneth Bourne, *Palmerston, the Early Years, 1784-1841* (London: Lane, 1982), 550-620; Pierre Renouvin, *Histoire des relations internationales,* V: *Le XIXe siècle. Première partie: de 1815 à 1871* (Paris: Hachette, 1954), 114-26; André Jardin and André Jean Tudesq, *La France des notables,* 2 vols. (Paris: Editions du Seuil, 1973), I, 184-90.

humiliation that created the noisy popular demand for fortification of Paris: "This is foolish, but who can wonder at it in a people whose country has within this generation been twice occupied by foreign armies? If that were our case we should have plenty of the same feeling."[62] He bracketed Adolphe Thiers with Lord Palmerston as "the two most lightheaded men in Europe," who had done "incalculable" evil and "rekindled" the old national antipathies.[63] He was inclined to think that "that shallow & senseless coxcomb Palmerston" had unnecessarily challenged Thiers, that "no harm whatever to Europe would have resulted from French influence with Mehemet Ali, & it would have been easy to *bind* France against any future occupation of [Egypt] for herself." However, the deed was done, and "this mischievous spirit in France" had been raised.[64] And when Tocqueville put it to him that Thiers had had no alternative save to take a high line, and that the British government's actions in isolating France and forcing her to accept war or humiliating retreat had been inexcusable, Mill stood firm. Culpable as the British government had been, he replied, it would not have acted so badly save for "such a lamentable want both of dignity & of common sense on the part of the journalists & public speakers in France," "the signs of rabid eagerness for war, the reckless hurling down of the gauntlet to all Europe, the explosion of Napoleonism and of hatred to England, together with the confession of Thiers & his party that they were playing a double game, a thing which no English statesman could have avowed without entire loss of caste as a politician." Still it was true, too, that he would "walk twenty miles to see [Palmerston] hanged, especially if Thiers were to be strung up with him."[65]

This was not Tocqueville's style. The disagreement here never was resolved. France, he said, was saddened and humiliated. He explained that the worst danger for any nation came when its moral fibre was weakened. After Thiers' defiance, Guizot had been called in to give way; a large part of the middle class cravenly opted for peace and its own selfish interest. The result had been a *sauve*

---

[62]Letter to John Sterling, *EL, CW,* XIII, 446 (1 Oct., 1840).

[63]Letter to R.B. Fox, *ibid.,* 448 (25 Nov., 1840).

[64]Letters to d'Eichthal, *ibid.,* 456 (25 Dec., 1840), and to Sterling, *ibid.,* 451-2 (19 Dec., 1840). The "mischievous spirit" was more intense on the left than on the right. Louis Blanc, the Jacobin-Socialist with whom Mill would strike up a friendship years later, was embittered by what seemed to him the ignoble attitude of the ruling class toward the bullying anti-French policies of England. "Mais dans la politique étrangère comme dans la politique intérieure, la bourgeoisie n'a eu ni prudence voire ni coup d'oeil. Voulant la paix d'une ardeur violente, elle a eu l'étourderie de ne s'en point cacher. Elle a mis à s'humilier une affectation folle. Aussi, les occasions de guerre se sont-elles multipliées à l'excès. Que de provocations! que de mépris! . . . Voire que la France ne peut plus sortir de chez elle sans être exposée à l'outrage. . . . Ce silence est fatal, ce repos est sinistre. . . . Dix ans de paix nous ont plus brisés que n'eût fait un demi-siècle de guerres; et nous ne nous en apercevons seulement pas!" (*Histoire de dix ans,* V, 457-60.) Blanc was to continue preaching this message. See Leo A. Loubère, *Louis Blanc: His Life and Contribution to the Rise of Jacobin Socialism* (Evanston: Northwestern University Press, 1961), 51-3.

[65]Tocqueville to Mill, *Oeuvres,* VI, 330-1 (18 Dec., 1840); Mill to Tocqueville, *EL, CW,* XIII, 459-60 (30 Dec., 1840).

qui peut, peace at any price. "Il faut," he told Mill, "que ceux qui marchent à la tête d'une pareille nation y gardent toujours une attitude fière s'ils ne veulent laisser tomber très bas le niveau des moeurs nationales." No nation could surrender its pride.[66] Mill granted that, but delivered a lecture, too:

The desire to shine in the eyes of foreigners & to be highly esteemed by them must be cultivated and encouraged in France, at all costs. But, in the name of France & civilization, posterity have a right to expect from such men as you, from the nobler & more enlightened spirits of the time, that you should teach to your countrymen better ideas of what it is which constitutes national glory & national importance, than the low & grovelling ones which they seem to have at present—lower & more grovelling than I believe exist in any country in Europe at present except perhaps Spain.

In England, by contrast, "the most stupid & ignorant person" knew that national prestige followed from industry, good government, education, morality. The implication, of course, was that in France they did not. Mill's countrymen, he added, saw French conduct as "simple puerility," judging the French "a nation of sulky schoolboys."

Considering what had happened in the eastern Mediterranean crisis, the sentiment is remarkable. Evidently he permitted himself to deliver this scolding because he prefaced it with a renewed declaration of sympathy for France, a country "to which by tastes & predilections I am more attached than to my own, & on which the civilization of Continental Europe in so great a degree depends."[67] Tocqueville absorbed it quietly. However, his public statement in the Chamber of Deputies, some months later, was no less firm. This in turn brought Lord Brougham to attack him in the House of Lords, and Mill, saddened to see Tocqueville included in the French "war party," defended him in the *Morning Chronicle*.[68] All the same, he thought fit to say to Tocqueville privately, "voyez ce qui est advenu de ce que nous avons eu, un seul instant, un homme à caractère français à notre Foreign Office."[69] Clearly Mill never understood Tocqueville's concept of national prestige, or his fears for the health of the French national spirit; across more than a century thereafter, few Englishmen did: it remained an impenetrable mystery for most of them, and Mill, for all his francophilism, appeared scarcely better equipped to penetrate it. In the autumn of 1843, Tocqueville made one last reference to the continuing Franco-British tension in Europe and around the world, uncompromising but

---

[66]Tocqueville to Mill, *Oeuvres*, VI, 335 (18 Mar., 1841). On the repudiation of war by the *haute bourgeoisie*, see Adeline Daumard, *La bourgeoisie parisienne de 1815 à 1848* (Paris: SEVPEN, 1963), 633-41.

[67]Letter to Tocqueville, *EL, CW*, XIII, 536 (9 Aug., 1842).

[68]"Lord Brougham and M. de Tocqueville," *Morning Chronicle*, 20 Feb., 1843, 3.

[69]Letter to Tocqueville, *EL, CW*, XIII, 571 (20 Feb., 1843). Tocqueville's reply to Brougham is included in Tocqueville, *Oeuvres*, VI, 341-2; Tocqueville to Mill, *ibid.*, 339-40, 343-4 (9 Feb., 12 Mar., 1843); cf. Seymour Drescher, *Tocqueville and England* (Cambridge, Mass.: Harvard University Press, 1964), 159-61.

optimistic: "La trace des fautes commises par votre gouvernement en 1840 s'efface assez sensiblement." He thought both the government and the people of the United Kingdom were seeking to draw closer to France and were having "une heureuse influence sur l'esprit public en France." Mill having sent him his *Logic*, Tocqueville thanked him warmly, asking again whether Mill could not come to visit them. Mill made no further mention of the Mediterranean affair, thanked him, and asked whether Tocqueville would not come to England.[70]

Four years passed before they made contact briefly in 1847. They perceived the Revolution of 1848 very differently. Tocqueville had set his face against social revolution; February brought misgivings, and the insurrection in June seemed to him inevitable. Mill could never have used the words Tocqueville chose to characterize the desperate challenge from the streets flung at the government and the National Assembly.[71] In the parliamentary debate on a constitution for the new Republic, Tocqueville argued for a second chamber. Mill took a contrary view of the matter. Moreover, he favoured inclusion of the *droit au travail* in the constitution, and to this Tocqueville was opposed. Between them still was their disagreement on foreign policy: on 30 November, 1848, Tocqueville indicted Great Britain and Russia for conspiring to bar France from the eastern Mediterranean, saying he preferred war to humiliation.[72] What Mill thought of Tocqueville's brief but pacific tenure as Foreign Minister, June-October 1849, one must guess.

When their nine years' silence was broken by Tocqueville in June 1856, he was graceful, slightly formal: "Voilà bien longtemps, mon cher Monsieur Mill, que nous avons perdu la bonne habitude de correspondre." He reiterated his compliments and his "sentiments de vieille amitié." Mill replied six months later (though he had been on holiday for no more than three months following arrival of the letter), thanking "cher Monsieur de Tocqueville" for sending his *L'ancien régime et la révolution*, praising it ("Envisagé seulement comme un chapitre

---

[70]Tocqueville to Mill, *Oeuvres*, VI, 345 (27 Oct., 1843); Mill to Tocqueville, *EL, CW*, XIII, 612-13 (3 Nov., 1843).

[71]"Elle ne fut pas, à vrai dire, une lutte politique (dans le sens que nous avions donné jusque-là à ce mot) mais un combat de classe, une sorte de guerre servile. Elle caractérisa la révolution de Février, quant aux faits, de même que les théories socialistes avaient caractérisé celle-ci, quant aux idées; ou plutôt elle sortit naturellement de ces idées, comme le fils de la mère; et on ne doit y voir qu'un effort brutal et aveugle, mais puissant des ouvriers pour échapper aux nécessités de leur condition qu'on leur avait dépeinte comme une oppression illégitime et pour s'ouvrir par le fer un chemin vers le bien-être imaginaire qu'on leur avait montré de loin comme un droit." (*Souvenirs, Oeuvres*, XII, 151.) The aftermath left him sorrowful and apprehensive. If the June insurrectionaries had risen against "des droits les plus sacrés," not all were "le rebut de l'humanité"; many were merely misled, believing society to be founded on injustice, wishing to give it "une autre base. C'est cette sorte de religion révolutionnaire que nos baïonnettes et nos canons ne détruiront pas." (Letter from Tocqueville to Eugène Stoeffels of 21 July, 1848, *Oeuvres complètes d'Alexis de Tocqueville*, ed. Mme de Tocqueville [and Gustave de Beaumont], 9 vols. [Paris: Lévy Frères, 1864-66], V, 458-9.)

[72]Drescher, *Tocqueville and England*, 152, 159-61.

d'histoire universelle, il me paraît un des plus beaux qu'on ait jamais fait . . ."),
saying he had not wished to write until he had read it through twice. Of public
affairs Mill noted only that the book's "noble amour de la liberté" was a
permanent reproach to "le triste régime que votre grande patrie, l'oeil droit du
monde, est réduite à subir dans ce moment." By return of post, Tocqueville
replied, barely revealing his slight hurt: "J'avais été un peu chagriné de votre
silence, avant que ses causes ne m'eussent été expliquées," adding that no one
else's opinion was more precious. He would gladly write of politics, but he
feared his letter would be seized. "Ne m'oubliez pas entièrement," he
concluded, "c'est tout ce que je réclame de vous en ce moment."[73] Mill appears
to have been silent. Two years later, he sent Tocqueville his *On Liberty*.
Tocqueville replied at once, warmly addressing him again as "Mon cher Mill,"
as he had used to do years before.[74] There seems to have been no reply.

Critical as Mill was of the English ruling class, he laid the principal blame for
Anglo-French misunderstandings at the French doorstep. The French "character", he told Robert Fox, was "excitable," unstable, "& accordingly alternates
between resentment against England and Anglomania." Palmerston might make
the occasion, but the underlying cause was the "mischievous spirit in France."
D'Eichthal was treated to some home truths: "It is impossible not to love the
French people & at the same time not to admit that they are children—whereas
with us even children are care-hardened men of fifty. It is as I have long thought
a clear case for the *croisement des races*." If the two nations avoided war, it was
thanks to English indifference. "Heureusement," he told Tocqueville in 1843,
"notre public ne s'occupe jamais d'affaires étrangères. Sans cela l'Europe serait
toujours en feu. . . ."[75] However much Mill was drawn to the culture of France,
he reacted to collisions of national sentiment as an Englishman. Nevertheless, if
inevitably he was an outsider, he was also a deeply informed and committed
observer, looking for fresh signs and portents. France remained a mirror: in it he
continued to see much of what he thought best in European civilization.

This was true even during "le triste régime" of Napoleon III. In the summer of
1857, long before the substantial dismantling of the authoritarian Empire began,
Mill discerned stirrings in the general elections that returned eight independents
and five republicans, despite the fact that 84.6% of the vote went to official
government candidates.[76] Over-optimistic after 1860, he exaggerated signs of
the devolution of authority and felt consoled by "the wonderful resurrection of
the spirit of liberty in France, combined with a love of peace which even

[73]Tocqueville to Mill, *Oeuvres*, VI, 348-9, 350-1 (22 June, 19 Dec., 1856); Mill to Tocqueville,
LL, CW, XV, 517-18 (15 Dec., 1856).

[74]Tocqueville to Mill, *Oeuvres*, VI, 351-2 (9 Feb., 1859).

[75]Letters to R.B. Fox, *EL, CW*, XIII, 448 (21 Nov., 1840); to Sterling, *ibid.*, 451-2 (19 Dec.,
1840); to d'Eichthal, *ibid.*, 457 (25 Dec., 1840); and to Tocqueville, *ibid.*, 571 (20 Feb., 1843).

[76]Letter to Pasquale Villari, *LL, CW*, XV, 534 (30 June, 1857); cf. Theodore Zeldin, *The Political
System of Napoleon III* (London: Macmillan, 1958), 66-7.

sympathy with Poland does not prevail over."[77] He was not entirely wrong in this, but he mistook a particular for the general phenomenon. Like most observers, he did not sense on the tranquil eve of the Imperial catastrophe that the republican party, which he favoured, was potentially a great force.[78] The war of 1870 was a surprise.

Believing that Prussia was fighting for her own liberty and for Europe's, Mill called for "many" demonstrations against Bonaparte and advocated preparations for war since England's "turn must come" if the Prussians were defeated. For the French people he expressed sorrow; it was Napoleon's war. All the same, it was time that France drew the consequences of her situation: "elle devra se contenter d'être l'une des grandes puissances de l'Europe, sans prétendre à être la seule, ou même la première. . . ."[79] Like others, he thought Gladstone could have prevented one "of the wickedest acts of aggression in history,"[80] but the specific guilt was clear. If the "ignorant" French people were to be pitied, the "whole writing, thinking, & talking portion of the people" was not.[81] It was of this élite that he thought when he said France had deliberately sought war because "she could not bear to see Germany made powerful by union" and that she should therefore be punished. Admitting after the military disaster that no one had anticipated so swift a collapse, he still insisted that "to those who knew France there was nothing surprising in it when it came. I hope it will tend to dispel the still common delusion that despotism is a vigorous government. There never was a greater mistake."[82] A certain hardness of tone had crept in.

In the aftermath of the Commune, Mill denounced Thiers's savage treatment of Paris: "The crimes of the *parti de l'ordre* are atrocious, even supposing that they are in revenge for those generally attributed to the Commune." He feared

---

[77]"Centralisation" (1862), *CW*, XIX, 579-613; letter to John Elliot Cairnes, *LL*, *CW*, XV, 917 (24 Jan., 1864). On public opinion and the differences between it and press opinion, see Lynn M. Case, *French Public Opinion on War and Diplomacy during the Second Empire* (Philadelphia: University of Pennsylvania Press, 1954), 178-86.

[78]See letter to d'Eichthal, *LL*, *CW*, XVII, 1718 (10 May, 1870).

[79]Letters to Henry Fawcett, *ibid.*, 1753-4 (26 July, 1870), and to d'Eichthal, *ibid.*, 1762 (27 Apr., 1870).

[80]Letters to Charles Wentworth Dilke, *ibid.*, 1766-7 (30 Sept., 1870), and to Fawcett, *ibid.*, 1777 (18 Nov., 1870).

[81]"Stern justice is on the side of the Germans, & it is in the best interests of France itself that a bitter lesson shd now be inflicted upon it, such as it can neither deny nor forget in the future. The whole writing, thinking, & talking portion of the people undoubtedly share the guilt of L. Napoleon, the moral guilt of the war, & feel neither shame nor contrition at anything but the unlucky result to themselves. Undoubtedly the real nation, the whole mass of the people, are perfectly guiltless of it; but then they are so ignorant that they will allow the talkers & writers to lead them into just such corners again if they do not learn by bitter experience what will be the practical consequences of their political indifference. The peasantry of France like the women of England have still to learn that politics concern themselves. The loss of Alsace & Lorraine will perhaps be about as painless a way of learning this lesson as could possibly be devised." (Letter to John Morley, *ibid.*, 1774-5 [16 Nov., 1870].) In all, a rather cold and extraordinary outburst of embitterment and suppressed hostility.

[82]Letter to Charles Loring Brace, *ibid.*, 1799-1800 (19 Jan., 1871).

repression would produce still another explosion, whereas France needed a policy of limited social experimentation.[83] But seeing the strong republican tide coming in from the summer of 1871 on, hoping for a federalist government, he took heart. With his new friend, Louis Blanc, still embittered over the outcome of 1848, Mill disagreed about the new republicanism; he did not think (as Thornton had reported Blanc did) that the peasantry were contributing to it "in the same un-intelligent way in which they were lately imperialists." Rather, he accepted the judgment of his stepdaughter that the key to this phenomenon of growing republican strength was the lay schoolmaster.[84] As for the then fashionable talk about France's decadence, Mill did not venture to pronounce on the matter. He thought moral decadence the only real form. It was true that "le caractère français a de très grands défauts, qui ne [se] sont jamais plus montrés que dans l'année malheureuse qui vient de s'écouler," but he supposed it had been much the same in what were called "les plus beaux jours de la France." What worried him was that the quality of discourse seemed defective; he detected "l'insuffisance intellectuelle de la génération présente pour faire face aux difficiles et redoutables problèmes d'un avenir qui a l'air d'être très prochain."[85]

By then his virtually lifelong French education was drawing to a close. It had accounted for three or four shifts of direction in his intellectual journey. It made him both an enthusiast and a severe critic. Though he knew very well the land he found so dramatic and so consolatory, lived there a fair portion of his life, and chose to lie there forever, he remained what he had always been since the age of fourteen, an observer with his French notebook open, but with a primarily English agenda. It pained him, as it had Saint-Simon long before, that the two peoples should get along so poorly. "There is something exceedingly strange & lamentable," he remarked to his most enduring French friend, "in the utter incapacity of our two nations to understand or believe the real character & springs of action of each other."[86]

---

[83]Letter to Frederic Harrison, *ibid.*, 1816 (May? 1871); see also letter to Charles Dupont-White, *ibid.*, 1863-5 (6 Dec., 1871).

[84]Letter to William Thomas Thornton, *ibid.*, 1913 (5 Oct., 1872), and Thornton's report of Blanc's view, 1913n. On the incoming republican tide, see Jacques Gouault, *Comment la France est devenue républicaine: Les élections générales et partielles de l'assemblée nationale, 1870-1875* (Paris: Colin, 1954). Concerning the lay schoolteacher, to whom Helen Taylor apparently pointed, see Katherine Auspitz, *The Radical Bourgeoisie: The Ligue de l'enseignement and the Origins of the Third Republic, 1866-1885* (Cambridge: Cambridge University Press, 1982), especially 123-60; Eugen J. Weber, *Peasants into Frenchmen: The Modernization of Rural France, 1870-1914* (Stanford: Stanford University Press, 1976), 303-38; and Barnett Singer, *Village Notables in Nineteenth-Century France: Priests, Mayors, Schoolmasters* (Albany: State University of New York Press, 1982), 108-46.

[85]Letter to Dupont-White, *LL, CW*, XVII, 1864-5 (6 Dec., 1871).

[86]Letter to d'Eichthal, *EL, CW*, XIII, 465 (23 Feb., 1841).

MILL AND HISTORY

MILL'S LIFE coincided with the rise of the modern historical profession. The origins of the new history lie in the eighteenth century, in the work of both the "philosophical" historians who sought pattern and meaning, and the "critical" historians who began the search for sources and their collection and evaluation. At Mill's birth, the state of history was far from brilliant. The archives were neglected and disarranged, the libraries were unwelcoming.[87] In 1800, Madame de Staël had noted "la médiocrité des Français comme historiens." On the eve of the Imperial defeat, Chateaubriand remarked how strange it was "comme cette histoire de France est tout à faire, et comme on s'en est jamais douté."[88] Napoleon, of course, had done little to encourage serious historical studies. The Revolution before him had set about the organization of its archives under the direction of the Jansenist politician Armand Camus; Bonaparte in turn appointed the professor, politician, and former cleric Pierre Daunou to continue the work at the national and departmental levels, and although Daunou was no special friend of the Empire, he lent his scholarly abilities to the defence of the régime when Napoleon's purposes and prejudices coincided with his own. The Emperor conceived of written history as a political and social instrument: Pierre Edouard Lemontey was directed to write a history of France from the death of Louis XIV to demonstrate the decadence of the Bourbon monarchy. Historians had to be "trustworthy men who will present the facts in their true light and offer healthy instruction by leading the reader up to the year 8." Those who conceived the task differently would not be "encouraged by the police."[89] The immediate inheritance of the Bourbon Restoration was meagre.

In England the situation, though different, was no better. Mill's reiterated complaints were justified. The universities were, and were to remain until after the mid-century, largely uninterested in modern history. In the uncatalogued depositories, whether Westminster Abbey's chapter-house or the Tower of

[87]Louis Halphen, *L'histoire en France depuis cent ans* (Paris: Colin, 1914), 6-7; Camille Jullian, Introduction, *Extraits des historiens français du XIXe siècle* (Paris: Hachette, 1904), iii-vii; George Peabody Gooch, *History and Historians in the Nineteenth Century*, 2nd ed. (London: Longmans, Green, 1952), 151-6.

[88]Anne Louise de Staël-Holstein, *De la littérature considérée dans ses rapports avec les institutions sociales* (1800), in *Oeuvres complètes*, 3 vols. (Paris: Didot, 1871), I, 232 (Chap. vi); François René de Chateaubriand, Letter to the duchesse de Dura (1813), in *Correspondance générale de Chateaubriand*, 5 vols., ed. Louis Thomas (Paris: Champion, 1912), I, 278.

[89]Memorandum of 1808, quoted in Gooch, *History and Historians*, 153-4. Jacques Godechot, *Les institutions de la France sous la révolution et l'empire*, 2nd ed. (Paris: Presses Universitaires de France, 1968), 756. Ranke said that historical studies in his time had developed "in opposition to the tyranny of Napoleonic ideas" (quoted in H.R. Trevor-Roper, *The Romantic Movement and the Study of History* [London: Athlone Press, 1969], 2).

London, rats and mice went about their casual destruction. Foreign scholars who came calling were appalled. The Society of Antiquaries, founded in 1751, was unconcerned. The Record Commission Gibbon had asked for, established in 1800, was largely made up of Anglican divines and politicians, uninterested, incompetent. Sir James Mackintosh, appointed to it in 1825, was its first historian. Not until Sir Harris Nicolas, a former naval officer and barrister turned antiquarian, revealed the research conditions he had experienced in editing Nelson's letters did anyone pay attention. In 1830, addressing himself to the Home Secretary, Lord Melbourne, Nicolas declared the existing history of England "not merely imperfect and erroneous but a discredit to the country, for almost every new document proves the current histories false. Scarcely a statement will bear the test of truth."[90] His evidence in 1836 before the Select Committee, chaired by Mill's friend Charles Buller, was instrumental in bringing about the replacement of the indolent Record Commission. Then, with the establishment of the Public Record Office in 1838, the work of collecting and preserving the nation's archives seriously began. But the mid-century passed before the kind of collection and publication of sources Guizot directed under the July Monarchy was started in England.

History, often the mere servant of philosophy and policy, was the concern of the very few. All the same, a profound change had set in, outgrowth of the Enlightenment, consequence of the Revolution.[91] A new desire to know the past was abroad, to find a legitimating past to sanction the present. By the time John Mill was choosing his own reading, the French and German historical fields were alive with *érudits* and writers. He classified history as part of his "private reading." He said it had been his "strongest predilection, and most of all ancient history." His father having alerted him to the problem of bias in history, he had read critically from the first. Naturally he had also written histories—of India, of the ancient world, of Holland. At ten he began what he hoped would be a publishable history of Roman government, but he abandoned the project and destroyed the manuscript.[92]

If history had been his strongest "predilection" as a child, its attractions for him weakened. It was never at the centre of his adult activity. Whether it was a hobby[93] is debatable; the evidence is not strong. But Mill read history, reflected on history, principally the history of Europe. History in general he defined as

[90]Quoted in Gooch, *History and Historians* 267-8; cf. Ernest Llewellyn Woodward, *The Age of Reform, 1815-1870* (Oxford: Clarendon Press, 1938), 531-2.

[91]Herbert Butterfield, *Man on His Past: The Study of the History of Historical Scholarship* (Cambridge: Cambridge University Press, 1955), 1-61; Hedva Ben-Israel, *English Historians on the French Revolution* (Cambridge: Cambridge University Press, 1968), 3-62.

[92]*Autobiography, CW*, I, 15-17; see also Appendix C, *CW*, I, 582-4.

[93]This is the view of Michael St. John Packe, *The Life of John Stuart Mill* (London: Secker and Warburg, 1954), 293. "Nothing," Mill once noted, "impresses one with a more vivid feeling of the shortness of life than reading history" (Diary, 1 Feb., 1854, *Letters of John Stuart Mill*, ed. Elliot, II, 365).

"the record of all great things which have been achieved by mankind."[94] The history of Europe was peculiarly instructive because "among the inhabitants of our earth, the European family of nations is the only one which has ever yet shown any capability of spontaneous improvement, beyond a certain low level."[95] After 1826 his interest shifted steadily toward the philosophy of history and discovery of the laws governing human progress. Still severe in criticism of those whose scholarly standards failed his test, he became bent on the subordination of history to philosophy, seeking principles from historical facts, interpreting facts in the light of principles. He was sure all history was in its "infancy." What passed for history "till near the present time," he said in 1836, was "almost entirely useless in fact." But a great change had set in: "intelligent investigation into past ages, and intelligent study of foreign countries" had begun. Almost two decades later, he again remarked on

how new an art that of writing history is; how very recently it is that we possess histories, of events not contemporary with the writer, which, apart from literary merit, have any value otherwise than as materials; how utterly uncritical, until lately, were all historians, even as to the most important facts of history, and how much, even after criticisms had commenced, the later writers merely continued to repeat after the earlier.[96]

The convention that history should be in the narrative form he dismissed with the observation that "it is as much the historian's duty to judge as to narrate, to prove as to assert." Moreover, where the requisite materials were missing, "a continuous stream of narrative" was impossible. Showing some inclination to dismiss narrative as "an amusing story,"[97] he nevertheless remarked of Grote's *History of Greece*, "Wherever the facts, authentically known, allow a consecutive stream of narrative to be kept up, the story is told in a more interesting manner than it has anywhere been told before, except in the finest passages of Thucydides. We are indeed disposed to assign to this history almost as high a rank in narrative as in thought."[98] But it was "thought," not narrative, that concerned Mill. In a system of education, history, "when philosophically studied," would offer "a certain largeness of conception," permitting the student to realize completely "the great principles by which the progress of man and the condition of society are governed."[99] Mill did not unduly prize historiography; at best, for him, it was the first step toward a proper understanding of the past.

[94]"Civilization" (1836), *CW*, XVIII, 145.

[95]"De Tocqueville on Democracy in America [II]," *ibid.*, 197. Mill's view that the history of England was "one of the least interesting" (letter to Harriet Taylor, *LL*, *CW*, XIV, 6 [27 June, 1849]) anticipated the opinion of a twentieth-century English historian who also concerned himself with pattern in history: "a stuffy little closet that had not had an airing for years" (Arnold J. Toynbee, *A Study of History*, 12 vols. [London: Oxford University Press, 1934-61], XII, 630).

[96]"State of Society in America," *CW*, XVIII, 93; "Grote's History of Greece [II]," *Essays on Philosophy and the Classics*, *CW*, XI (Toronto: University of Toronto Press, 1978), 328.

[97]"Grote's History of Greece [I]," *CW*, XI, 303-4.

[98]"Grote's History of Greece [II]," *ibid.*, 330.

[99]"Civilization," *CW*, XVIII, 145.

Niebuhr may have effected "a radical revolution" in Roman history, and Grote may have rescued Greek history from hitherto superficial examination, but Mill's object in studying the past was less historiographical than sociological.[100] The past existed to be made use of. It was the present that concerned him, or the present *in history*, what he called "the most important part of history, and the only part which a man may know and understand, with absolute certainty, by using the proper means." The past itself was no guide to the present: "the present alone affords a fund of materials for judging, richer than the whole stores of the past, and far more accessible."[101] At best, then, history, like travel, was "useful *in aid* of a more searching and accurate experience, not *in lieu* of it. No one learns any thing very valuable from history or from travelling, who does not come prepared with much that history and travelling can never teach." History's value "even to a philosopher" is "not so much positive as negative": it teaches "little" but is "a protection against much error." Conversely, since one could not know other people and other ages as well as one knows one's own, knowledge of the present age could help in interpreting the past and in making "a faithful picture" of earlier people and modes of existence, and in assigning "effects to their right causes."[102]

Mill was concerned with the present in historical context, hence his immediate attraction to the historical periodizations of the Saint-Simonians and Comte. They persuaded him that the early nineteenth century was "an age of transi-

---

[100]"Grote's History of Greece [II]," *CW*, XI, 328. Mill was not more concerned about fundamental historical research than were some of the historians whose work he commented on. Notoriously the Sorbonne offered no leadership in this field. Ernest Lavisse was to say that its chairs were looked on "comme un lieu de repos pour les professeurs fatigués de l'enseignement secondaire" (quoted in Pierre Leguay, *La Sorbonne* [Paris: Grasset, 1910], 11). The small, rather isolated world of the *érudits* in the Ecole des Chartes (perhaps conceived in Napoleon's mind in 1807, but founded by royal ordinance in February 1821), whose *archivistes* were the continuators of the Benedictine tradition, was outside Mill's province of observation. It was this Cinderella of French intellectual life—it is Gabriel Hanotaux's phrase—together with the young men returning from study in German seminars, who would in the second half of the century rescue historical studies from the spent philosophical school and the eloquent orators of the Collège de France and the Faculté. If Guizot was responsible for the pursuit of documents ("des faits, rien que des faits, dûment établis, tel est désormais le mot d'ordre" [Halphen, *L'histoire en France depuis cent ans*, 76]), it was only after 1865 that serious emulation of the German historical method began in France. (See Halphen, 57-9, 118, 143-5; Gabriel Hanotaux, *Sur les chemins de l'histoire*, 2 vols. [Paris: Librairie Ancienne Edouard Champion, 1924], I, 1-18; William R. Keylor, *Academy and Community: The Foundation of the French Historical Profession* [Cambridge, Mass.: Harvard University Press, 1975], 19-89; Guy Bourdé and Hervé Martin, *Les écoles historiques* [Paris: Editions du Seuil, 1983], 83-111, 137-70.)

[101]Mill, "The Spirit of the Age," *Examiner*, 9 and 23 Jan., 1831, 20, 50-2. The view was close to that of Tocqueville: "c'est l'homme politique qu'il faut faire en nous. Et, pour cela, c'est l'histoire des hommes et surtout de ceux qui nous ont précédés le plus immédiatement dans ce monde qu'il faut étudier. L'autre histoire n'est bonne qu'en ce qu'elle donne quelques notions générales sur l'humanité tout entière et en ce qu'elle prépare à celle-là." (Letter to Gustave de Beaumont of 25 Oct., 1829, *Oeuvres*, VIII, 1, 93.)

[102]"State of Society in America," *CW*, XVIII, 93.

tion."[103] In such an age, the old doctrines and institutions no longer responded to current needs; contradictory voices spoke; the old authorities clung to power; the new men struggled to take over in "a moral and social revolution." This process had "been going on for a considerable length of time in modern Europe," but the present moment was crucial. The authority, the legitimacy of the old institutions, lay and religious, had vanished. Change, the "progress" of "civilization," could be resisted temporarily—Bonaparte had done that—but the process was ultimately irresistible: "The revolution which had already taken place in the human mind, is rapidly shaping external things to its own forms and proportions."[104]

As a social scientist, Mill found the intelligible historical unit in the "State of Society," which he defined as "the simultaneous state of all the greater social facts or phenomena." He concluded that such states, or ages, were linked causally. The task was "to find the laws according to which any state of society produces the state which succeeds it and takes its place." He thought the evidence proved that this succession took place not, as Vico had proposed, in "an orbit or cycle," but in "a trajectory or progress." Progress did not necessarily imply "improvement," but the "general tendency" was and would continue to be "towards a better and happier state." French thinkers, he remarked, hoped from mere historical analysis to discover "the law of progress" which would permit prediction of the future. But by such means they could at best discover some rough "empirical law," not "a law of nature." Comte had shown that the principal social phenomena changed from age to age, particularly from generation to generation. He alone had seen that man's condition and actions were increasingly the result of "the qualities produced in [him] by the whole previous history of humanity." Only when generalizations from history were properly linked with "the laws of human nature" would historical study reveal "Empirical Laws of Society."[105]

The key to unlocking the secret of progress was intellect, "the state of the speculative faculties of mankind; including the nature of the beliefs which by any means they have arrived at, concerning themselves and the world by which they are surrounded." Intellect and knowledge made possible both material advances and social unity; each new mode of social thought was the primary agent in shaping the society where it appeared (society itself created that thought only in a secondary manner). Hence Mill's conclusion that human progress depended mainly on "the law of the successive transformation of human opinions." Comte alone had tried to determine that law. Whatever the results to date, Mill believed that historical enquiry covering "the whole of past time, from the first recorded condition of the human race, to the memorable phenomena of the last and present

---

[103]"The Spirit of the Age," *Examiner*, 9 and 23 Jan., 1831, 20, 50.

[104]*Ibid.*, 6 Feb., 15 and 29 May, 1831, 82, 83, 84, 307, 340.

[105]*A System of Logic Ratiocinative and Inductive*, *CW*, VII-VIII (Toronto: University of Toronto Press, 1974), VIII, 911-17 (Bk. VI, Chap. x).

generations" was the method "by which the derivative laws of social order and of social progress must be sought." With this instrument, men could see "far forward into the future history of the human race," determine how and how much "to accelerate the natural progress in so far as it is beneficial," and to fend off those perils that even genuine progress entailed. So history was to serve "the highest branch of speculative sociology" and "the noblest and most beneficial portion of the Political Art." A glittering vista of science and art stretched ahead, united to complete "the circle of human knowledge."[106]

Some twenty years after he had formally stated this view of things (1843), Mill denied the charge that his doctrine implied "overruling fatality." He said that "universal experience" showed that human conduct could be accounted for not only by "general laws" but by "circumstances" and "particular characters" also. The will of "exceptional persons" might be "indispensable links in the chain of causation by which even the general causes produce their effects." Taking issue with Macaulay on the role of the great man, somewhat relaxing his claim for the predictive capability announced in 1843, he proposed in 1862:

The order of human progress . . . may to a certain extent have definite laws assigned to it; while as to its celerity, or even as to its taking place at all, no generalization, extending to the human species generally, can possibly be made; but only some very precarious approximate generalizations, confined to the small portion of mankind in whom there has been anything like consecutive progress within the historical period, and deduced from their special position, or collected from their particular history.

To an extreme degree, ancient Greece showed the extraordinary influence of a single city-state and a few exceptional individuals. The experience would not be repeated. Mill stood by his view, derived from Comte, that with the progress of civilization the influence of chance and character must decline: "the increasing preponderance of the collective agency of the species over all minor causes is constantly bringing the general evolution of the race into something which deviates less from a certain and pre-appointed track."[107] Comte had been "free from the error of those who ascribe all to general causes, and imagine that neither casual circumstances, nor governments by their actions, nor individuals of genius by their thoughts, materially accelerate or retard human progress," but neither he nor Mill committed "the vulgar mistake" of imagining that men of action or of thought could "do with society what they please."[108]

Mill was interested in history for what it could do rather than for what it might be. And what he called "historical science" was becoming more tractable, not only because historians were more inquiring, or more skilful, but because

---

[106]*Ibid.*, 926-30.

[107]*Ibid.*, 932-42 (Bk. VI, Chap. xi).

[108]"Auguste Comte and Positivism" (1865), *CW*, X, 322. On Dilthey's critique of Mill concerning the role of the great man, see Jacques Kornberg, "John Stuart Mill: A View from the Bismarckian Reich," *Mill News Letter*, XII, no. 1 (Winter, 1977), 10-16.

"historical science" itself was changing: "in every generation, it becomes better adapted for study."[109] The past properly understood, as the raw material for the science of society, was taking shape. Helped by "the historical school of politicians" in France (and, he said, in Germany),[110] Mill had moved on to Comte and a serviceable philosophy of history. More than thirty years later he would still say, "We find no fundamental errors in M. Comte's general conception of history."[111]

Mill seems not to have had the temperament to be an historian. After 1830, especially, his interests drew him along another path. John Carlyle rated him "a strange enthusiast with many capabilities but without much constancy of purpose." Thomas Carlyle was breezily patronizing: "a fine clear Enthusiast, who will one day come to something. Yet to nothing Poetical, I think: his fancy is not rich; furthermore he cannot *laugh* with any compass."[112] The estimate appears to cut across his own proposal two years later that Mill should write a history of the French Revolution. This had certainly seemed to be Mill's intention. He had collected materials, made himself expert. He told Carlyle that he had "many times" thought of writing such a history: "it is highly probable that I shall do it sometime if you do not," but he saw two obstacles:

the difficulty of doing so tolerably . . . [and the] far greater difficulty of doing it so as to be read in England, until the time comes when one can speak of Christianity as it may be spoken of in France; as by far the greatest and best thing which has existed on this globe, but which is gone, never to return, only what was best in it to reappear in another and still higher form, some time (heaven knows when). One could not, *now*, say this openly in England, and be read—at least by the many; yet it is perhaps worth trying. Without *saying out* one's whole belief on that point, it is impossible to write about the French Revolution in any way professing to tell the whole truth.[113]

[109]*System of Logic, CW*, VIII, 942 (Bk. VI, Chap. xi). The classic critique of Mill and Comte in this matter is in K.R. Popper, *The Open Society and Its Enemies* (1945), 2 vols., 4th rev. ed. (London: Routledge and Kegan Paul, 1962) and the same author's *The Poverty of Historicism* (1957), rev. ed. (London: Routledge and Kegan Paul, 1961). (On Mill's Benthamite eclecticism, however, see Lewisohn, "Mill and Comte on the Methods of Social Science," 315–24.) Popper holds that the "doctrine of historical laws of succession is . . . little better than a collection of misapplied metaphors" (*Poverty of Historicism*, 119), sees a "close similarity between the historicism of Marx and that of J.S. Mill" (*Open Society*, II, 87), and concludes that all such historicist philosophies, like philosophies from Heraclitus and Plato down through Lamarck and Darwin, "are characteristic products of their time—a time of social change," giving witness to "the tremendous and undoubtedly somewhat terrifying impression made by a changing social environment on the minds of those who live in this environment" (*ibid.*, 212). "It almost looks," he says, "as if historicists were trying to compensate themselves for the loss of an unchanging world by clinging to the faith that change can be foreseen because it is ruled by an unchanging law" (*Poverty of Historicism*, 161).
[110]"Spirit of the Age," *Examiner*, 6 Feb., 1831, 83.
[111]"Auguste Comte and Positivism" (1865), *CW*, X, 322.
[112]John Carlyle to Thomas Carlyle (12 Feb., 1831), in *The Collected Letters of Thomas and Jane Welsh Carlyle*, ed. Charles Richard Sanders, *et al.* (Durham, N.C.: Duke University Press, 1970-), V, 235n; Thomas Carlyle to Jane Carlyle, *ibid.*, 428 (14 Sept., 1831).
[113]Letter to Carlyle, *EL, CW*, XII, 182 (5 Oct., 1833).

The two comments were apposite: Carlyle judged Mill incapable of an empathetic reading of the evidence and an imaginative reconstruction of the explosive and deeply mysterious episode he conceived the Revolution to have been;[114] Mill's own interest in the Revolution had altered: it was no longer the storehouse of wisdom for the radical reform movement, but an integral part of, a critical episode in, the development of civilization toward the understanding of which he and others were only beginning to move. His preoccupation was to say "one's whole belief," "to tell the *whole* truth." The remark that it was "perhaps worth trying" revealed his diminishing purpose to write history.

Mill wanted to write about history, to philosophize about it, to subordinate the facts of history to "principles," to extract instruction from history. Drawn naturally to France from his boyhood experience, he saw clearly that French history offered a potentially rich field for the exploration of the interplay of character, circumstance, thought, and great impersonal forces and tendencies. He would echo Guizot in saying, "A person must need instruction in history very much, who does not know that the history of civilization in France *is* that of civilization in Europe" (230 below).[115] Reading the young French liberal historians, he was impelled not to write like them but to write about them, to make use of them, to extract the moral from them. He would like, as he told Macvey Napier, "to write occasionally on modern French history & historical literature, with which from peculiar causes I am more extensively acquainted than Englishmen usually are."[116] He prided himself on his broad reading in the subject as forthrightly as he disapproved of his fellow countrymen who knew nothing of it. He believed it a scandal that "while modern history has been receiving a new aspect from the labours of men who are not only among the profoundest thinkers, . . . the clearest and most popular writers of their age, even those of their works which are expressly dedicated to the history of our own

[114]Presumably Carlyle meant such a response to the past as even Guizot, a "philosophical historian" whom Mill thought the greatest of the time, showed in a relaxed moment: "J'aime l'histoire. C'est la vie humaine sans fatigue, comme spectacle et non comme affaire. Je m'y intéresse et n'y suis pas intéressé. C'est une émotion mêlée de mouvement et de repos. . . . En tout le passé me plaît et m'attache infiniment. Je le contemple avec respect et compassion. Ils ont fait tout cela, ils ont senti tout cela, et ils sont morts! Ce contraste si frappant, ou plutôt cette union si intense de la vie et de la mort, de l'activité et de l'immobilité, du bruit et du silence, ce sceau irrévocable posé sur ces êtres jusque-là si animés et si mobiles, et l'impénétrable mystère de leur destinée actuelle et définitive, cela m'émeut et m'attendrit jusqu'au fond de l'âme." (Letter to the princesse de Lieven of 4 Sept., 1838, *Lettres de François Guizot et de la princesse de Lieven*, ed. Jacques Naville, 3 vols. [Paris: Mercure de France, 1963-64], I, 186.) Carlyle had given voice to much the same romantic fascination half a dozen years before: "Rough Samuel and sleek wheedling James *were*, and *are not*. . . . Gone! Gone!! . . . The mysterious River of Existence rushes on. . . ." ("Boswell's Life of Johnson," *Fraser's Magazine*, V [Apr. 1832], 387.) If it was not an essential response on the part of an historian, it was nonetheless widely shared, then and later, but it does not appear to have been Mill's.

[115]Page references to material printed in this volume are given in the text.

[116]Letter to Macvey Napier, *EL*, *CW*, XIII, 431 (27 Apr., 1840).

country remain mostly untranslated and in almost all cases unread."[117] Unlike the productions of narrative historians,[118] their histories of revolution, whether of France in 1789 or of England in 1688, were a significant part of the literature of political and social commitment under the Bourbons. Mill had seen this before 1830, and he was as clear about it after. The history of France, he remarked about the mid-century, was "perhaps the most [interesting] & certainly the most instructive in so far as history is ever so."[119]

By then, Mill had long since abandoned whatever intention he had formerly had of contributing to the history of the Revolution. His task was not historiography but commentary and historical speculation: the search for a science of history. The European tendency, he wrote in 1836, "towards the philosophic study of the past and of foreign civilizations, is one of the encouraging features of the present time." A similar tendency was perceptible even in England, "the most insular of all the provinces of the republic of letters."[120]

DULAURE AND SISMONDI

WITH DULAURE AND SISMONDI Mill was reaching back into the pre-Revolutionary generations where the origins of the liberal historical interpretation lay. In 1826, Jacques Antoine Dulaure was seventy-one years old. After 1789, he had quickly turned his pen against the old régime with a volume detailing the crimes and follies of the aristocracy.[121] A sometime member of the Cordelier and Jacobin clubs, he had sat in the Convention with the Girondins, though he was an independent deputy from Puy-de-Dôme. He voted for the death penalty for Louis XVI and defended Madame Roland before fleeing to asylum in Switzerland. Returning in 1795, he became an agent of the Directory in Corrèze and the Dordogne until his opposition to Bonaparte on 18 Brumaire ended his political career. During the Hundred Days, he used his pen against the Emperor. He

---

[117]Mill, "De Tocqueville on Democracy in America [II]," CW, XVIII, 155.

[118]Macaulay was, of course, his exemplar: "He is very characteristic & so is his book, of the English people & of his time." The History of England was readable, it would sell, but it was "without genius," and he found it "exactly au niveau of the ideal of shallow people with a touch of the new ideas." Even as "a work of art" it was wanting. (Letters to Harriet Taylor, LL, CW, XIV, 6 [27 Jan., 1849]; to William George Ward, ibid., 29 [Spring 1849]; and to Arthur Hardy, ibid., XV, 511 [29 Sept., 1856].)

[119]Letter to Harriet Taylor, ibid., XIV, 6 (27 Jan., 1849).

[120]"State of Society in America" (1836), CW, XVIII, 94.

[121]Jacques Antoine Dulaure, Histoire critique de la noblesse depuis le commencement de la monarchie jusqu'à nos jours (Paris: Guillot, 1790), cited in Stanley Mellon, The Political Uses of History: A Study of French Historians in the French Restoration (Stanford: Stanford University Press, 1958), 19-20.

was thus congenial to Mill as an early member of "the historical school of politicians."

By contrast, Charles Simonde (who assumed the additional Italian form de Sismondi), fifty-three years old in 1826, a Protestant pastor's son and a citizen of Geneva, had a more unhappy experience of the Revolution. Apprenticed in Lyon in 1792, he returned home almost immediately, only to be driven to England by the Revolutionary *coup* at the end of the year. Returning home again in 1794, he and his family soon fled to a farm near Lucca. But the ebb and flow of revolution and reaction there put him in prison three times before 1800, when he went back to Geneva.[122] He wrote an *Histoire des républiques italiennes du moyen âge* before determining in May 1818 to write the history of France, an immense enterprise of twenty-nine volumes that occupied him to the eve of his death in 1841. Like Dulaure, Sismondi had not been sorry to see Napoleon humbled in 1814, but his loyalties were confused in the *chassé-croisé* of that uncertain moment (he had been on the government's books in 1810 for a 2000 franc subvention).[123] Nor was he favourable to the Bourbons. But he had returned to Paris in 1813, and had made the acquaintance of the liberal politician Benjamin Constant. An intimate friend of Germaine de Staël, Constant had bitterly attacked the Emperor. Yet on Bonaparte's return from Elba, Constant permitted the infinitely resourceful Fouché to persuade him to take a seat on the Conseil d'état and to produce the *Acte additionnel* of 22 April, 1815, a liberal supplement to and modification of the Imperial system, which pleased few and was accepted by Napoleon (who would have abandoned it had the decision at Waterloo not gone against him) as an exercise in public relations. Sismondi's relations with Constant must explain his defence of the document, for which the Emperor rewarded him with a long interview. Not unreasonably, therefore, the news from Belgium after 18 June led Sismondi to return to Geneva. Madame de Staël remained friendly, but other friends were cool.[124] Mill seems not to have held this Bonapartist flirtation, supposing he knew of it, against Sismondi. The main thing was that the preface of his *Histoire* showed an earnest commitment to social progress: "En rassemblant les souvenirs nationaux, c'est moins à la réputation des morts qu'au salut des vivans que nous devons songer."[125] Liberty was his passion. Perhaps less awkwardly than Dulaure, Sismondi could be made to fit the conception of "philosophical historian" Mill came to hold.

---

[122]Jean Rodolphe de Salis, *Sismondi, 1773-1842: La vie et l'oeuvre d'un cosmopolite philosophe* (Paris: Librairie Ancienne Henri Champion, 1932), 1-41.

[123]Godechot, *Les institutions de la France*, 756.

[124]Salis, *Sismondi*, 1-41; François Mignet, "The Life and Opinions of Sismondi," *North American Review*, LXVI (Jan., 1848), 32-72.

[125]Sismondi, *Histoire des Français*, 31 vols. (Paris: Treuttel and Würtz, 1821-44), I, xv. From a letter of 1835: "I have not given up any of my youthful enthusiasm; I feel, perhaps, more strongly than ever the desire for nations to become free, for the reform of governments, for the progress of morality and happiness in human society" (quoted by Mignet, "The Life and Opinions of Sismondi," 69).

Mill's review of the works of these two men was a vehicle for taking aim at aristocracy, church, monarchy, and the conservative historiography perpetuating the myth of chivalry. Characteristically, he began with an ironical cut at the *Quarterly Review* and his fellow countrymen who had yet to discover the superiority of other nations in certain matters, specifically literature and history. The starkest contrast was drawn between pre- and post-Revolutionary studies: mere ornament and frivolousness, the mark of literature in "every country where there is an aristocracy," having yielded to earnest regard for truth in the flood of important histories since 1821. A cascade of generalized scorn for previous historians of France set off the merits of Dulaure and Sismondi with their scrupulous regard for "facts" (17). Like most historians then and later, Mill did not trouble to consider seriously what a historical fact might be. The unquestioned assumptions of the critical method in historiography are apparent in his magisterial commentaries.

Lest readers mistake his purpose, he laid bare the object and conclusion of his examination at the outset, namely, proof that "the *spirit of chivalry*" was almost unknown in the Middle Ages (20). Rather, it was a set of ideals in the rough and tumble of a time, marked by depravity and misery, whose noble class was the antithesis of civilization. His allusion to the persistence of the knightly state of mind in the nineteenth century was not subtle. Though claiming high regard for objective fact, Mill fell back upon the "hue and cry" of Dulaure's French conservative critics as proof of Dulaure's reliability (21). Almost simultaneously, he attacked defenders of the English status quo. In short, it was quickly apparent that Mill had some trouble keeping his mind on the remote past. He confined himself principally to France, he explained, because "the feudal system never existed in its original purity, in England" and because no English historian had yet, like Dulaure, undertaken "the toilsome and thankless service of dragging into light the vices and crimes of former days" (26). His description of feudal society emphasized the "perpetual civil war," the cruelties visited by kings and aristocrats on the people (28). He noted that in England "it has been the interest of the powerful, that the abominations of the clergy in the middle ages should be known" (32), but also that in reality they had been less heinous than those of the barons. With the aid of Dulaure's and Sismondi's narratives, he challenged the latter-day descendants of what he took to be a barbarous aristocracy *and* the new "romantic" historians. Vigilant against the conservative implications of sentimentalizing the Middle Ages, he hailed the enthusiasm for history of which romanticism was nevertheless a powerful component. He distinguished, in short, between "*nostalgic* historiography and historiography which *restored*,"[126] chiding those who could not or would not do so—"Even Mr. Hallam does not believe in the reality of knights-errant . . ." (34).

[126]Benedetto Croce, *History: Its Theory and Practice*, trans. Douglas Ainslie (London: Harrap, 1921), 264.

Mill's Middle Ages were nearly an unrelieved catalogue of aristocratic and monarchical wrongdoing. The most glamorous actors, such as Richard Coeur de Lion, were brought to book in light of the misdeeds chronicled by Dulaure and Sismondi (34). Only with the appearance of "a sort of *public opinion*" once the national power came into being, he argued, was there any improvement of noble conduct (42). Urban privileges had to be wrung from a perfidious feudal class. The only luminous figure Mill perceived in a dark landscape was Saint Louis, "a perfect specimen of a mind governed by conviction; a mind which has imperfect and wrong ideas of morality, but which adheres to them with a constancy and firmness of principle, in its highest degree perhaps the rarest of all human qualities" (44).

Approaching the subject that subsequently became important to him, he considered the question of gallantry to which he attributed "nine-tenths of the admiration of chivalry" (45). It amounted to mere male vanity; the idolatry of women marked a "low state of civilization" (46). If the few were set on pedestals, the many were disregarded in a world of mistreatment and rape. In time, the aristocracy gave up its independent power, but not its masculine conceits and illusions; it never reformed itself. Thanks to works like Dulaure's and Sismondi's, the French at least would be disabused about the romanticized past. Unhappily, there were no English equivalents. Hallam was granted some measure of "liberality" in his discussion of the Middle Ages (52), but he had been taken in by legend and was without philosophy; if he knew the sources and had something to say about English constitutional history, his work was judged "a sketch of one of the most remarkable states of society ever known, at once uninstructive and tiresome." His volumes were "an utter failure" (52).[127]

The breathtaking judgments the young Mill handed out, founded more on a philosophy of history than on close acquaintance with research, may not seem entirely off the mark. But that his reading was openly inquisitive might be difficult to show. François Mignet, whom he much admired, would, like historians since, point to Sismondi's attention to the effect of economic change in history,[128] an emphasis Mill appears not to have noticed. Nor did he comment on the inflexibility of the moral code Sismondi applied to his thirteen centuries, possibly because he then still shared the assumption. It was revealing that only at the end of his review did Mill draw attention to the lack in Dulaure of a generalizing, that is, of a philosophical mind: he states the facts as he finds them, praises and censures where he sees reason, but does not look out for causes and effects, or parallel instances, or apply the general principles of human nature to the state of society he is describing, to show from what circumstances it became

---

[127]In this, Mill was much more severe than Guizot, who translated and admired Hallam, although he was critical of his lack of historicist empathy for the plight of Strafford (see Stanley Mellon, Editor's Introduction, in François Guizot, *Historical Essays and Lectures* [Chicago: University of Chicago Press, 1972], xxx).

[128]Mignet, "The Life and Opinions of Sismondi," 56; Salis, *Sismondi*, 435-6.

what is was. It is true he does not profess to be a historian, but only to sketch a *tableau moral* (51). Reading this from another pen, Mill might have said, "On croit rêver!" By nearly every test he would normally apply, Dulaure should have failed almost as absolutely as Henry Hallam. The secret, however, was in the point of view.

Sismondi offered more generalizations, if not more philosophical reflection, and sustained the underlying assumption of Mill's review. Showing movement if little colour, his long narrative continued to appear for years after the first volumes Mill surveyed. Its principal value lay in the sources brought together. But the verdict was to be that the first three volumes, the historical event of 1821, Camille Jullian said, were the best of it. They were received by both the philosophic and the romantic schools, welcomed by Augustin Thierry and Guizot. Even Michelet was said to have remarked of Sismondi, "notre père à tous."[129] Mill was not wrong to single him out.

MILL AND THE REVOLUTION OF 1789

MILL ENCOUNTERED the French Revolution shortly after his return from France in 1821. He learned that "the principle of democracy" had triumphed a generation earlier to become "the creed of a nation." This revelation made sense of fragmented melodramatic events, all he had known of the matter, and sustained all his "juvenile aspirations to the character of a democratic champion." He imagined himself caught up in a similar revolution, "a Girondist in an English Convention."[130] If the recollection across three decades was accurate, it might seem unexceptional, were it not that Mill's identification with the Girondins was an assertion of independence from his father, who dismissed the Revolution as "some kind of ruffians in the metropolis [being] allowed to give laws to the whole nation."[131] Lamartine was to colour the confused tragedy of the Girondins in 1847, but their drama was known long before. Their neo-classical poses and search for glory may well have appealed to John Mill. He would have met them in François Toulongeon's *Histoire de France depuis la révolution de 1789*,[132] and learned that they supported a republic only after the abolition of the

---

[129]Jullian, *Extraits des historiens français*, xxiv; Michelet's remark is quoted in Pierre Moreau, *L'histoire en France au XIXe siècle: Etat présent des travaux et esquisse d'un plan d'études* (Paris: Les belles lettres, [1935]), 35.

[130]*Autobiography*, *CW*, I, 65-7; see John Coleman, "John Stuart Mill on the French Revolution," *History of Political Thought*, IV (Spring, 1983), 89-110.

[131]Joseph Hamburger, *James Mill and the Art of Revolution* (New Haven: Yale University Press, 1963), 21.

[132]The indirect evidence is in a letter from Mill to Charles Comte, *EL*, *CW*, XII, 22 (25 Jan., 1828). On this "calm philosophic" historian, see Agnes M. Smith, "François Emmanuel Toulongeon: Contemporary Historian of the French Revolution," in *Bourgeois, Sans-Culottes, and Other Frenchmen: Essays on the French Revolution in Honour of John Hall Stewart*, ed. Morris Slavin and Agnes M. Smith (Waterloo, Ont.: Wilfrid Laurier University Press, 1981), 97-111.

monarchy. In Madame de Staël's *Considérations sur les principaux événemens de la révolution française*, he would have seen them less heroically.[133] What is sure is that the liberal historians of the 1820s took them as champions; the sympathetic treatment by Thiers and Mignet may have confirmed in the mind of the memorialist the germ of the thought held by the boy of fifteen.

There is no evidence that Mill thought before the second half of the 1820s of writing a history of the Revolution. In his review of Mignet in April 1826, he alluded to documentary materials accessible in England, adding, "We purpose to lay some of them before our readers ere long" (5). Almost two years later he protested that "on est ici dans une si crasse ignorance sur la révolution, et tous, jusqu'aux individus les plus instruits, ont des idées tellement ridicules sur la nature de cette crise politique, qu'avec mon peu de lumières et de connaissance des faits j'ai crû pouvoir faire quelque chose pour dessiller les yeux de mes compatriotes." Claiming to know almost everything from the standard histories and the published memoirs, he asked Charles Comte to recommend further materials on royalist intentions before the flight to Varennes. But beyond "quelques articles," he mentioned no larger project, although, he added, "je ne vois guère que moi en angleterre qui rendent justice à la révolution."[134] The collection of books and materials he had, however, suggests that such was his intention. The years immediately preceding the collapse of the Bourbon monarchy showed no progress toward realizing this project, despite his detailed attack on Sir Walter Scott's version of the Revolution. And it may be supposed that his "half formed intention of writing a History of the French Revolution"[135] was steadily weakening as he was drawn toward the broad historical perspectives of the Saint-Simonians. His own explanation was that he was then digesting and maturing his thoughts "without any immediate call for giving them out in print," and that had he "gone on writing" he "would have much disturbed the important transformation in [his] opinions and character, which took place in those years."[136] Perhaps the initial great enthusiasm he felt over the events of July 1830 stimulated his earlier ambitions to write a history, but the increasing disappointment he experienced in closely following the course of the new régime may well have confirmed his growing interest in a much larger view of the historical past, convinced him that the Saint-Simonians had properly seen beneath the surface events of political revolutions, and led once more to his letting 1789 slip away. Moreover, his encounter with Carlyle, whom he first met in September 1831, may also have affected his intent as it became clearer that Carlyle was becoming set on writing a history himself.

---

[133]See Michael J. Sydenham, *The Girondins* (London: Athlone Press, 1961), 1-16.

[134]Letters to Charles Comte, *EL, CW*, XII, 21-2, 25 (25 Jan., and 27 June, 1828). "He is very well informed on the history of the French Revolution," d'Eichthal noted, "and we talked at length about recent events in France whose importance for their own cause the English liberals are well aware of" (d'Eichthal, *A French Sociologist*, 61 [Journal, 21 July, 1828]).

[135]*Autobiography, CW*, I, 135.

[136]*Ibid.*, 137.

To Carlyle's statement that, despite the difficulty of writing, it was one of his "superstitions never to turn back," and that thus one must *"march on, & complain* no more about it," Mill responded in a minor key: he had the same thought. If he was to attempt "a *general* view of any great subject" he wished to say not merely "*something* true, but to omit nothing which is material to the truth." The sole encouragement to undertake such a task was that "imperfect and dim light" was still better than "total darkness." His long rumination betrayed serious doubts about so immense a subject. He spoke of returning to work after a brief holiday, when he hoped to "produce something worthy of the title you give me," but thought he was "rather fitted to be a logical expounder than an artist." Still, there was work to be done in exposing the logical side of "Truth" before the poetic, and that he hoped to do.[137]

He was proposing Carlyle would do the great artistic history, while he could do only the analytical. Despite reservations about Mill's literary capacity, Carlyle nevertheless urged him to set forth his "ideas and acquisitions" about the Revolution at greater length, for "It is properly the grand *work* of our era. . . ."[138] But Carlyle was already moving toward his own *French Revolution.* Mill continued to remark, as he did to Tocqueville, "We have not so much as one readable history of the Revolution . . . ,"[139] but himself made no move to supply it. He may well not have had the time for it. Moreover, his growing attraction to French historical speculation was leading him steadily away from any such specific task. From the summer of 1832, he steadily despatched books from his own library and procured fresh materials for Carlyle. And, although he continued to reflect and comment on the Revolution from time to time, it was clear, long before Carlyle was in print, that Mill had abandoned even the glimmering of his former project.

MIGNET

However halting Mill's resolve to write an analytical history became, he had been sufficiently motivated for the better part of a decade, and sufficiently convinced that such a study could be a vehicle by which to forward his argument in England, that he followed the literature and published four essays on as many of the Revolution's historians. In this connection, Dulaure had been a transitional figure, useful to Mill (like Sismondi) principally for furnishing materials with which to challenge the romanticized version of the past. Not only were the Middle Ages brutal and strife-ridden, Mill concluded, but their feudal survivals in the eighteenth century were preposterous. In the young historians Adolphe Thiers and François Mignet he found the support he was looking for. They could

---

[137]Carlyle to Mill, *Collected Letters*, VI, 174 (16 June, 1832); Mill to Carlyle, *EL*, *CW*, XII, 110-11, 113 (17 July, 1832). See Ben-Israel, *English Historians on the French Revolution*, 58-9.
[138]Carlyle to Mill, *Collected Letters*, VI, 446 (24 Sept., 1833).
[139]Letter to Tocqueville, *EL*, *CW*, XII, 271 (Sept., 1835).

help him make his case against the *ancien régime*, broadly conceived, and on behalf of the liberal reformers of the Revolution's early phase. Unencumbered by personal experience and memory, they did not linger over the reservations and dilemmas of the earlier liberal champions like Madame de Staël. They observed but were not embarrassed by the break between the liberal phase of the Revolution and the Terror. They accepted the challenge of the counter-revolution head-on. "Ecrivez, Messieurs, faites des livres," Royer-Collard, leader of the *doctrinaires*, remarked when the liberal Decazes ministry fell following the duc de Berry's assassination; "il n'y a pas autre chose à faire en ce moment."[140]

In 1821 Thiers and Mignet appeared in Paris from the south. They were just twenty-four; the liberal opposition was warming up. With letters of introduction to Jacques Antoine Manuel, leader of the Chamber opposition, they made the acquaintance of this group, including Talleyrand, and established themselves in the opposition salons and press, Thiers at the *Constitutionnel*, Mignet at the *Courrier Français*. They were lawyers from the Faculté at Aix, attracted by history, Thiers the more politically ambitious, Mignet the more scholarly. Mignet had already obtained the *couronne* of the Académie des Inscriptions et Belles Lettres for his memoir, *Les institutions de saint Louis*. Established as a lecturer at the Athénée, 1822-24, he discussed the Reformation and the English revolutions of the seventeenth century in such a way as left no doubt that he was attacking the Bourbon monarchy. Guizot had been silenced at the Sorbonne in 1822 for just this *lèse-majesté*; Mignet fell under no ban. But reaching for a wider audience, he, like Thiers,[141] determined to write the history of the Revolution.

His two volumes were published in May 1824, offering in a single instalment the whole of the version Thiers served up at greater length over five years. It was less narrative than exposition, an analysis of a great event that worked itself out as it had to. After collecting materials for two years, Mignet had written his book rapidly in November-December 1823. Jules Simon proposed that Mignet might have said "ma révolution" (a boutade concerning 1830 incorrectly ascribed to

---

[140]Pierre Paul Royer-Collard, letter to Amable Guillaume Prosper de Barante of 1 Aug., 1822, in *Souvenirs du baron de Barante*, ed. Claude de Barante, 8 vols. (Paris: Calmann Lévy, 1890-1901), III, 29.

[141]Yvonne Knibiehler, *Naissance des sciences humaines: Mignet et l'histoire philosophique au XIXe siècle* (Paris: Flammarion, 1973), 130-1; Paul de Rémusat, *A. Thiers* (Paris: Hachette, 1889), 34. The later volumes of Thiers' *Histoire de la révolution française*, judged superior to the early ones, owed much to Mignet's shorter work. Carlyle's estimate was unfriendly: "Thiers's *History* in ten volumes foolscap-octavo, contains, if we remember rightly, one reference. . . . A superficial air of order, of clearness, calm candour, is spread over the work; but inwardly it is waste, inorganic: no human head that honestly tries can conceive the French Revolution *so*." ("Parliamentary History of the Revolution," *London and Westminster Review*, V & XXVII [Apr., 1837], 234.) Mill was evidently much less critical, since he passed on to Sarah Austin his father's suggestion that she should translate it, and noted that it "would be sure to sell" (*EL, CW*, XII, 292 [9 Jan., 1836]). He had of course sent it up to Carlyle in the first place, and he recommended it to various people. Thiers, the politician, he despised.

Thiers). Louis Halphen remarked that Mignet, like Thiers and (as would be said later on) Guizot, gave the impression "of having known from the beginning of time what [he] had just learned that morning."[142] The work was marked by the *fatalisme historique* distinguishing the liberal counter-offensive against the Ultra-royalist reaction, almost in response to Sismondi's dictum that "l'étude des faits sans philosophie ne seroit pas moins décevante que celle de la philosophie sans faits."[143] It echoed, as Sainte-Beuve pointed out, Joseph de Maistre's view of the Revolution as a great irresistible force.[144] Accusing the aristocracy of the whole responsibility for the outbreak of the Revolution and all the ensuing violence, Mignet challenged not merely the régime and its supporters but also the old liberals who had agreed with Benjamin Constant that one must distinguish "those measures which [the government] had the right to take, from those crimes which they committed and which they did not have the right to commit."[145] It was the first complete history, "un tableau d'ensemble vivant et rapide, un résumé frappant, théorique, commode." It had a huge success, with translations into five other languages.[146]

Mill's review distinguished a greater degree of popular narrative in Mignet than some were inclined to, while underlining his subordination of history to "philosophy," a characteristic of the "modern" style of historiography. Like Carlyle, he proclaimed Mignet "the highest specimen" of the new school, stated his agreement with the account, and once more berated the old narrative historians in England (4). In contrast to what Carlyle would later say, however, he approved Mignet's skill in the selection and marshalling of details (4). Mill gave so much space to illustrative extracts that one has the feeling he had little to say. He made no comment on the uncritical handling of sources; or upon the use Mignet made of oral evidence; or upon the role of individuals within the controlling conditions of *fatalisme historique*. And he did not mention the

---

[142]Jules Simon, *Mignet, Michelet, Henri Martin* (Paris: Calmann Lévy, 1890), 92; Halphen, *L'histoire en France depuis cent ans*, 38-9.

[143]Sismondi, *Histoire des Français*, IX, 2.

[144]Charles Augustin Sainte-Beuve, "M. Mignet," *Revue des Deux Mondes*, n.s. XIII (15 Mar., 1846), 1097.

[145]In the 1829 revision of his pamphlet of 1797, Constant remarked that "To justify the reign of '93, to picture its crimes and frenzies as a necessity that weighs inevitably upon peoples when they seek freedom, is to harm a sacred cause, to do it more damage than its most avowed enemies" (Benjamin Henri Constant de Rebecque, *Des effets du régime que l'on a nommé* révolutionnaire *relativement au salut et à la liberté de la France* [1797, as revised in 1829], quoted in Mellon, *Political Uses of History*, 22-3).

[146]Sainte-Beuve, "M. Mignet," 1096. Carlyle granted Mignet's history was more honest and thorough than Thiers's, but derided its "philosophical reflections" as "a quantity of mere abstractions and dead logical formulas" which passed for "Thinking." In one of his mixed verdicts, he proclaimed that Mignet had produced an "eminently unsatisfactory" book, without "life, without colour or verdure." The "little book, though abounding too in errors of detail, better deserves what place it has than any other of recent date." Mignet thus "takes his place at the head of that brotherhood of his," since he was "not a *quack* as well!" ("Parliamentary History of the French Revolution," 235-6.)

conception of class struggle as a motor force.[147] But, anticipating Carlyle, Mill was critical of the reflections which principally established the work in Revolutionary historiography and which made it, as Thiers is said to have thought of his own book, *"une arme de guerre"* against the Bourbons.[148] If he was not affronted, as Constant was, by the global explanation of the whole Revolutionary experience, he was unimpressed by Mignet's talent for generalization, an aptitude with which he considered Madame de Staël firmly endowed, even though her taste for dubious epigrams was still more marked (13). The result was a short, schoolmasterly reprimand, separating the *faux brillants* from the *vrais*. An entertaining story well told, the book would reveal to the English "what intelligent Frenchmen think and say on the subject of the French Revolution" (13-14). But this remark did not quite catch the controversial, essentially political nature of Mignet's work.

Years later, in December 1861, Taine, who was no friend of "la vulgate de Thiers et de Mignet,"[149] chanced to have a chat with Mignet whom he had not previously met. "Il y a un fonds de stérilité; on voit qu'il n'a pas vécu dans les idées générales, qu'il y est impropre," he noted. "Il n'est pas artiste non plus, voyez son histoire de Marie Stuart, sa Révolution française; c'est glacé. Il est propre à digérer des matériaux indigestes, à exposer clairement, en bel ordre. Il a le talent français de la classification parfaite et de l'élégance noble académique," but about *les forces profondes*, "il a l'air encore dépaysé."[150] By then, of course, Mignet had long since abandoned the political scene, having settled for the archives of the Foreign Ministry under the July Monarchy, and become *secrétaire perpétuel* of the Académie des Sciences Morales et Politiques. Philosophical history as practised by the opposition literati under the Bourbon monarchy had become an historiographical artifact. But perhaps Mill had caught something of the limitation Taine perceived thirty-five years later.

Still it is true that Mignet's *Revolution* was a youthful tour de force, part of a general movement that finally toppled the Bourbon monarchy. Whatever his criticisms, Mill had recognized its significance as a *pièce d'occasion*; by praising Mignet's skill and achievement, he had early singled out an historian whose total work, some twenty volumes, would win the approval of scholars at home and abroad.[151]

---

[147]See Knibiehler, *Naissance des sciences humaines*, 118-65.

[148]Quoted in James Westfall Thompson, *et al.*, *A History of Historical Writing*, 2 vols. (New York: Macmillan, 1942), II, 247.

[149]The expression is Alice Gérard's, *La révolution française, mythes et interprétations, 1789-1870* (Paris: Flammarion, 1970), 34.

[150]Hippolyte Taine, *H. Taine, sa vie et sa correspondance*, 2nd ed., 4 vols. (Paris: Hachette, 1902-07), II, 223-4.

[151]Knibiehler, *Naissance des sciences humaines*, *passim*. "He is the Ranke of France, and he disputes with Guizot the title of the greatest French historian of the first half of the nineteenth century. . . . No historian has done more to apply the methods and spirit of scientific research to the life of states." (Gooch, *History and Historians*, 188.) Cf. Ben-Israel, *English Historians on the French Revolution*, 59-62.

SCOTT

When Mignet arrived in Paris, the battle over romanticism was at its height, with Walter Scott at its centre. Mignet waited a year before making a statement, but the popular verdict was in: the reading public was entranced. The novels were translated into French beginning in 1816, and 200,000 copies were sold during Louis XVIII's reign, 1.5 million by the end of Charles X's. If Chateaubriand and others had pointed the way,[152] Scott's pre-eminence was established so rapidly that historians (whose audience in those days was the literate general public) greeted this voice with some approval. The earliest was Augustin Thierry, former secretary to Saint-Simon, a journalist, not yet the historian of the Norman Conquest, not quite so cautious as he would be later on. Of Scott's books he said there was more true history in them than in "les compilations philosophiquement fausses" claiming the name of history. He discerned in Scott's reading of the past "cette *seconde vue* que, dans les temps d'ignorance, certains hommes s'attribuent pour l'avenir."[153] He named it "divination historique." Experience and time brought Thierry justifiably to rate his own historical gifts superior to Scott's, but he conceived them as complementary spirits, and years after he was sufficiently secure to admit the fact.[154]

Mignet was initially spellbound: "Il faut le dire, Walter Scott est un des quatre premiers génies anglais: il se montre l'égal de Richardson, de Milton, de Shakespeare," a man who knew how to infuse history with movement and vitality, how to identify the essential characteristics of an epoch. Reflection brought reserve. Scott, he concluded a little later, was more familiar with Scottish chronicles than with French: "Où sont nos villes, leurs corporations, leurs bourgeois, leurs quarteniers, leurs échevins? Où sont nos parlements . . . nos paysans? On connaît la cour de Louis XI, on ne connaît pas son siècle."[155] As the new historians made their way, Scott's reputation with the French historians was qualified but not extinguished. He had shown them something essential; his reputation and influence remained greater with them than with English historians.[156]

---

[152]Halphen, *L'histoire en France depuis cent ans*, 9-10, 17-18; Knibiehler, *Naissance des sciences humaines*, 104.

[153]Quoted in Rulon Nephi Smithson, *Augustin Thierry: Social and Political Consciousness in the Evolution of a Historical Method* (Geneva: Droz, 1973), 81, 297, from Thierry's review of *Ivanhoe* in the *Censeur Européen* of 29 May, 1820.

[154]Smithson, *Augustin Thierry*, 99n, from the Preface to *Dix ans d'études historiques* (1835). Louis Maigron, *Le roman historique à l'époque romantique: Essai sur l'influence de Walter Scott*, new ed. (Paris: Librairie Ancienne Henri Champion, 1912), 213-18. Thierry later transferred some of the admiration he had for Scott to Armand Carrel, his protégé, for whose *Résumé de l'histoire de l'Ecosse* (Paris: Lecointe and Durey, 1825) he provided an introduction.

[155]Quoted in Knibiehler, *Naissance des sciences humaines*, 104-5.

[156]"Ce fut plus d'un succès; ce fut un engouement. Une génération tout entière en demeura éblouie et séduite." (Maigron, *Le roman historique*, 51.)

Mill was familiar with the French reception of Scott. His own experience did not predispose him to share it. As a child he had known "the metrical romances" his father recommended to him and been "intensely delighted" with their "animated narrative." But when still in his teens, he had scathingly criticized Hume's *History* as "really a romance," bearing "nearly the same degree of resemblance to any thing which really happened, as *Old Mortality*, or *Ivanhoe*. . . . Romance is always dangerous, but when romance assumes the garb of history, it is doubly pernicious."[157] He continued to judge the novels harshly, for offering mere amusement. Scott, he declared later, had "no object but to please." He nevertheless granted that "at the height of his popularity" Scott "was breathing the breath of life into the historical literature of France, and, through France, of all Europe."[158] During the 1820s, however, he was not greatly impressed. The publication in June 1827 of Scott's *Life of Napoleon Buonaparte* decided him to make a prolonged statement. His review, the last article he wrote for the *Westminster Review* in the 1820s, cost him "more labour than any previous; but it was a labour of love, being a defence of the early French Revolutionists against the Tory misrepresentations of Sir Walter Scott." He even bought many books "for this purpose," in numbers that "far exceeded the worth of the immediate object"; but, as we have seen, he "had at that time a half formed intention of writing a History of the French Revolution."[159]

The review constitutes the nearest thing to a fully developed statement about the Revolution Mill ever set down. It was also a blistering attack on Scott. After a preliminary bow to his literary talent, Mill said the book "would be admirable as a romance" but was not history (55). Bonaparte's life would require other talents. Mill's subject, of course, was not Napoleon, but rather the nature of history, the distortions of Tory history, and a defence of the Girondins. Whatever his subject, however, a true historian must be "a *philosopher*," able to render the facts of history *useful* by adducing principles from them and applying principles to explain them, a man of broad views and experience, able to weigh and link evidence, "a consummate *judge*" (56). In a word, "the historian" resembled considerably the continental philosophical historian and no other. Scott did not measure up: bland and aristocratic, hard-working, wishing to please all, he was finally judged to be a not entirely illiberal or disingenuous "advocate of the aristocracy against the people" (57). His social and political philosophy was summarized as "whatever is English is best; best, not for England only, but for every country in Christendom, or probably the world" (60). There followed a catalogue of his sins and errors: ignorant of the facts about France and the French, he had read few authorities, failed to understand circumstances, and was

---

[157]*Autobiography*, *CW*, I, 19; Mill, "Brodie's History of the British Empire" (1824), in *Essays on England, Ireland, and the Empire*, *CW*, VI (Toronto: University of Toronto Press, 1982), 3.

[158]"Periodical Literature: Edinburgh Review," *CW*, I, 320; "Writings of Alfred de Vigny" (1838), *CW*, I, 481, 472.

[159]*Autobiography*, *CW*, I, 135.

"not to be trusted" (63). At best, Scott saw "a *part* of the truth" but was "far too slightly acquainted with the monuments of the times, to have the faintest or most distant perception of it as a *whole*" (65). His pre-Revolutionary chapters were prejudiced and misleading; what followed was worse. His skilfully told story, doubtless sincerely intended, manipulated the facts in the cause of a theory that was not true. Still, Mill gave him this: the work was "less malignant" than most other Tory studies of the Revolution (110).

Mill's view of the early Revolution, what he would call its "true history," was in stark contrast to Scott's. The Bonapartist episode he quickly dismissed as a vulgar coda, a familiar exercise of power by an adventurer moved by "the lowest impulses of the lowest description of human beings" (58). The Revolution was something else: a "vast convulsion," originated, heroically defended, and at last ended by "the people" when they awoke from "the frenzy" into which the privileged orders had driven them by opposing "representative government" (58). As an unprecedented manifestation of popular will, it could not be judged by ordinary rules. Where Scott saw ambitious men seeking office, Mill saw patriots seeking liberty. Where Scott proposed the perverse nature of the lower orders running amok, Mill saw ordinary men driven to excess by injustice and oppression. Scott was granted the perceptiveness of glimpsing some part of the truth (for instance, about peasant-landlord ties in the Vendée), but accused of general failure to comprehend social relations under the *ancien régime*. Where Scott saw vicious, irreligious philosophes undermining society, Mill saw benefactors of mankind. Scott's court was weak and ineffectual, Mill's wicked and tyrannical. Mill was amused by the suggestion that the royal government might have forced the election results it needed, a course "so perfectly according to the English model" (72). Against Scott's "conjuring up a republican party" (79), Mill argued there had been no such party, only varieties of constitutional monarchists in the Legislative Assembly until such time as both "the nullity of the Duke of Orleans as a politician" (81) and the perfidy of the King forced them to become republicans. Mill ridiculed Scott's suggestion that the Revolution ought to have adopted something like the British constitution in the circumstances following the States General, when "the struggle was not *for* a revolution, but *against* a counter-revolution" (86). To Scott the Girondins were "philosophical rhapsodists" willing to use force to establish "a pure republic"; Mill exalted them as "the purest and most disinterested body of men, considered as a party, who ever figured in history," statesmen who had war thrust on them, who laboured vainly to save the crown, and who were left with no alternative save a republic (98).

All this was put with passion (Scott was called "childish," accused of "effrontery," supposed to be suffering "mental hallucination" [68n, 69n, 79n]), buttressed by appeal to authorities of all persuasions. It was the liberal version of the early Revolution, stopping short of the Jacobin period that Mill found distasteful. If he had a clear overview, it was close to Mignet's. But it was significant that he did not push on beyond the early years. What concerned him was defence of the liberal champions of constitutional monarchy against an unscrupulous aristocracy, that is, defence of "the honest part of the revolutionists" against "the general opinion" in England that had done them (and, it went without saying, those in England who thought like them) more harm even than Scott (110). If Scott had a didactic purpose, Mill had nothing less. But he must be read in the context of an entrenched conservative historiography, deep-seated national prejudice against the French, and of course the struggle for reform of the House of Commons. He admitted that the *Life* contained "juster views" than those he particularly took issue with (110), though how they appeared in a writer so roundly declared unfit for the historian's task he did not venture to explain.

Notoriously, Scott's book was put together under great pressure, nine volumes in a year, amid many anxieties. He himself acknowledged some part of its limitation.[160] Carlyle's famous tribute was that Scott "taught all men this truth, which looks like a truism, and yet was as good as unknown to writers of history and others, till so taught: that the bygone ages of the world were actually filled with living men, not by protocols, state-papers, controversies and abstractions of men." No doubt this was less true of the *Life of Napoleon* than of the historical novels. Perhaps Mill would, some years after he wrote his devastating review, have been more inclined to grant as much. His own views about the depths and poetry of history were changing. But he never found the words. Whether he could have accepted Carlyle's posthumous verdict that Scott "understood what *history* meant; this was his chief intellectual merit," one must guess.[161]

ALISON

Mill believed that the huge sales Scott enjoyed had a harmful effect on the public mind. But he also knew that Scott had made an important contribution to the

[160]Leslie Stephen, "Sir Walter Scott," *Dictionary of National Biography*, XVII, 1038; cf. Edgar Johnson, *Sir Walter Scott*, 2 vols. (New York: Macmillan, 1970), II, 1064-6; Ben-Israel, *English Historians and the French Revolution*, 56-9. "Superficial it must be," Scott said, "but I do not care for the charge. Better a superficial book which brings well and strikingly together the known and acknowledged facts, than a dull boring narrative pausing to see farther into a mill-stone at every moment than the nature of the mill-stone admits." (Quoted from Scott's Diary, 22 Dec., 1825, in Thomas Preston Peardon, *The Transition in English Historical Writing, 1760-1830* [New York: Columbia University Press, 1933], 216.) But scholars one hundred and fifty years later, however sympathetic and measured in their expression, have echoed something of Mill's severity: "Allowing for the license of the romantic biographer or historian, we are still justified in observing with surprise how Scott tampers with his evidence, distorts his sources, in effect turns perjurer on behalf of some of the wildest forces in Europe" (R. C. Gordon, "Scott Among the Partisans: A Significant Bias in his *Life of Napoleon Buonaparte*," in *Scott Bicentenary Essays: Selected Papers Read at the Sir Walter Scott Bicentenary Conference*, ed. Alan Bell [Edinburgh and London: Scottish Academic Press, 1973], 129).

[161]Carlyle, "Memoirs of the Life of Scott," *London and Westminster Review*, VI & XXVIII (Jan. 1838), 337; Carlyle's Journal, quoted in James Anthony Froude, *Thomas Carlyle: A History of the First Forty Years of His Life, 1795-1835*, 2 vols. (London: Longman, et al., 1882), II, 310.

revival of written history, that he was dealing with not merely a pillar of the Tory establishment but a formidable man of letters. In taking on the work of Alison, however, he was jousting with a writer of more ordinary talents, if also of great industry, whose account of the Revolution was also Tory propaganda. What ultimately justified taking notice of such a study was, again, the immense sales Alison had both at home and, in translation, abroad. Of the whole multi-volume *History of Europe from the Commencement of the French Revolution to the Restoration of the Bourbons*, more than half a million copies were sold before his death, though at the time Mill could hardly have foreseen it would have such success.

A native of Shropshire who had early moved to Edinburgh where he took up the law, Alison became an advocate-deputy for Scotland, wrote books on the criminal law, and was eventually appointed sheriff of Lanarkshire. By the time he visited France in 1814-15, his conservative views were fixed. Leslie Stephen's judgment that he was "intelligent and hard-working, if not brilliant," is borne out by his numerous publications. He had defeated Macaulay in election as Lord Rector of Marischal College, Aberdeen, and Palmerston as Lord Rector of Glasgow. He was a believer in the institution of slavery, and later a strong supporter of the American Confederacy. His literary taste ran to "elevating" romances and against the Dickensian preoccupation with the manners of the middle and lower classes. He refused to "worship the Dagon of Liberalism."[162] He was very nearly everything Mill was not; their views could hardly have been more different, whether of the French Revolution or, late in life, the American Civil War: Alison supported the Confederacy, while Mill, "very retiring and embarrassed in his manner," as Henry Adams noted, was "a mighty weapon of defence for our cause in this country."[163]

Alison began his *History* on New Year's Day 1829, intending to illustrate the corruption of human nature and the divine hand in events; his work was induced, he said, "by the clear perception that affairs were hurrying on to some great social and political convulsion in this country. The passion for innovation which had for many years overspread the nation, the vague ideas afloat in the public mind, the facility with which Government entered into these views—all these had awakened gloomy presentiments in my mind."[164] His first two volumes were published in April 1833.

As Alison had published a year-long series of articles in *Blackwood's* on the French Revolution and the English reform issue in 1831-32, Mill knew what to

---

[162]Quoted in Leslie Stephen, "Sir Archibald Alison," *Dictionary of National Biography*, I, 287-90.

[163]Henry Adams to Charles Francis Adams, Jr., in *The Letters of Henry Adams*, ed. Jacob Clavner Levenson, *et al.* (Cambridge, Mass., and London: Belknap Press of Harvard University Press, 1982-), I, 330.

[164]Quoted in Gooch, *History and Historians*, 304.

expect. But he inquired of Carlyle whether the book "is worth reading, or reviewing—I suppose it is wrong, when one has taken the trouble to accumulate knowledge on a subject, not to work it up if one can into some shape useful to others—and if I am to write about the F.R. it may as well be while my recollections of the original authorities are fresh." Clearly Mill, though now far from sure that he wished to pursue his former intention to write a history and evidently yielding the ground to and actively assisting Carlyle, still wished to make a statement. He wished to pillory the errors, bias, and flaccid lack of philosophy he found in Alison. He wished also to discuss his own conception of history. Alison's work was both an affront to scholarship and an occasion for Mill to reveal something of his recent historical reflection. Carlyle was encouraging: "by all means *review him*, and in the widest vehicle you can get. It is a thing utterly unknown to the English and ought to be known. Speak of it what *you* know. If Alison prove stupid dismiss *him* the sooner, but tell your own story freely without fear or favour."[165]

Mill was eager to take on both Whig and Tory. Having read Alison, he wrote again:

the man is quite inconceivably stupid and twaddling, I think beyond anybody who has attempted to write elaborately on the subject. He has no research; the references with which he loads his margin are chiefly to compilations. I could write something about him or rather about his subject; but I could employ myself better unless there were some widely-circulated periodical that would publish it: the Edinburgh Review perhaps would, were it not that I should wish to shew up Macaulay's ignorance of the subject and assumption of knowledge, as shewn in that very review.[166]

Simultaneously, however, he offered to the *Monthly Repository* "a few pages on a stupid book lately published by a man named Alison, and pretending to be a history of the French Revolution." He then followed this proposal with the tired and dutiful statement, "I am sick of that subject, but I could write something on it which perhaps would be of more use to the M.R. than something better would be. . . ."[167]

Mill could not see how to strike the larger target behind Alison. When done, he called his review "a poor, flimsy, short paper on that book of Alison's, which I undertook in an evil hour, when the subject was as remote as possible from those which were occupying my thoughts and feelings at the time; and which I accordingly performed exceedingly ill, and was obliged to cancel the part which had cost me most labour." What this part was he did not reveal; why he abandoned it is unknown. He told Carlyle the review was "not worth *your*

---

[165]Letter to Carlyle, *EL, CW*, XII, 152 (11-12 Apr., 1833); Carlyle to Mill, *Collected Letters*, VI, 373 (18 Apr., 1833).

[166]Letter to Carlyle, *EL, CW*, XII, 155 (18 May, 1833). The reference is to Macaulay's review of Dumont's *Recollections of Mirabeau, Edinburgh Review*, LV (July, 1832), 552-76. (By compilations Mill means not collections but what are now called secondary sources.)

[167]Letter to W.J. Fox, *EL, CW*, XII, 157 (18 May, 1833).

perusal."[168] Mill seems to have believed that the book was not worth his critique, was too slight to bear the weight of the crushing rejoinder he had in him. Five years earlier, when he had still thought seriously of doing a history, he had dissected Scott's work, using detailed references to the memoirs and histories. Now he was no longer interested in doing that. Neither Alison nor his work justified presentation of what Mill had once thought he had to say about the Revolution as a result of his exacting scrutiny of the published sources, and in the light of his Radical beliefs.

Alison's qualifications were quickly discarded: it was not even a question of measuring him against an ideal historian's talent to create character, summon up the historical setting, establish the play between personality and circumstance. As a Tory, Mill noted, Alison might be expected to disapprove of his actors; instead he offered only indiscriminately charitable judgments. Rather than "that highest impartiality which proceeds from philosophic insight," there was "abundance of that lower kind which flows from milkiness of disposition." Free of cant, he was devoid of originality. If he followed Thiers and Mignet, he rendered the drama of events "flat, cold, and spiritless" (116). If he honestly revealed his sources, their poverty betrayed his slight reading.[169] His memory was defective, his knowledge of the French language flawed. He knew enough about neither the Revolution nor "the universal subject, the nature of man" (122). His reflective capacity was barren, his generalizations were either truisms or "such as a country-gentleman, accustomed to being king of his company, talks after dinner" (116). Alison's "insignificant book" was judged to be empty of knowledge, thought, and philosophy (122). But, as Mill pointed out, if that were all he himself had to say, his article might end.

He had two things to say, the first of which had been slipped in earlier: in praising this not very exceptional writer, Mill had noted that Alison at least "does not join in the ill-informed and rash assertion of the *Edinburgh Review*, reechoed by the *Quarterly*, that the first authors of the French Revolution were mediocre men" (115). This was as close as he got, on this occasion, to assailing Macaulay directly. The second, more important thing he wished to repeat was that the Revolution could never be understood unless as "one turbulent passage in a progressive revolution embracing the whole human race." There was an immense "moral revolution" under way, in which the events in France were "a mere *incident* in a great change in man himself, in his belief, in his principles of conduct, and therefore in the outward arrangements of society; a change which is but half completed, and which is now in a state of more rapid progress here in

---

[168]Letters to W.J. Fox, *ibid.*, 159 [June, 1833], and to Carlyle, *ibid.*, 162 (5 July, 1833).

[169]It may well have been Mill's criticism in the review that caused Alison to include a substantial list of his sources as a preface to the 2nd ed. (1835), and to subsequent editions. Ben-Israel judges that "Alison knew the sources but not how to use them. His bibliographical prefaces . . . are now the best part of the book." (*English Historians and the French Revolution*, 150.)

England, than any where else." All this, which Mill believed to be part of "the *scientific* aspect" of history, escaped Alison (118). Mill's position was that the Revolution had produced "substantial good . . . at the cost of immediate evil of the most tremendous kind." No one could ever know whether more could have been obtained for less, or whether averting revolution (how this might have been achieved he did not explain) would not have halted all progress and reduced the French to "the condition of Russian boors." The Tories had reduced revolution to "a bagatelle," the work of a handful of wilful bloody-minded men; they refused to understand that "rapid progress" and "practical good" might not be achieved by peaceful means. They would not see that it was the French crown and its advisers that had abandoned peaceful means. Crimes were committed, some by "bad men," but all with a single object: to save the Revolution, whatever the cost (120, 121).

When he read the first volume, Mill may have underestimated Alison's work as popular history and propaganda. In reply to Carlyle's note of approval of the review,[170] Mill remarked somewhat evenly, "*I* also am conscious that I write with a greater appearance of *sureness* and strong belief than I did for a year or two before, in that period of *recovery* after the petrification of a narrow philosophy. . . ." This rather mixed and invertebrate review, however, does not make a strong impression. It is uncertainly dependent on three disparate intentions: to rekindle, if only momentarily, the fire of Mill's earlier defence of the Revolution; to strike out at political opponents; to say something about his currently developing philosophy of history. Naturally it did nothing to give Alison pause: if it led him to fatten up his bibliographical prefaces, it by no means discouraged him from pursuing his narrative. He continued to revise his work, which had an immense success as a detailed history of the Revolution in its wider setting. It was translated into many languages and became the best-selling such work for much of the century in England and North America.[171] Mill was unrepentant. Nine years after his review, when Alison had completed the final volume, he told Napier, "You have touched up Alison very well & it was time. My fingers have often itched to be at him. The undeserved reputation into which that book is getting, merely because it is Tory history, & the only connected one of that important time, is very provoking."[172]

CARLYLE

When Mill first mentioned Alison to him, Carlyle already had a copy "lying on a Table." Having "glanced" at it, he was both impressed and dismissive. His

---

[170]"There is not a word in it that I do not subscribe to: it is really a *decided* little utterance, with a quiet emphasis, a conscious incontrovertibility, which (heretic that I am) I rejoice to see growing in you" (Carlyle to Mill, *Collected Letters*, VI, 445 [24 Sept., 1833]).

[171]Ben-Israel, *English Historians and the French Revolution*, 152-3.

[172]Letters to Carlyle, *EL*, *CW*, XII, 181 (5 Oct., 1833), and to M. Napier, *ibid.*, XIII, 551-2 (15 Oct., 1842).

reaction told something about his own scholarship. "He is an Ultra Tory," he told Mill, "and therefore cannot understand the French Revolution; otherwise, they say, a man of considerable ability; his Margin bears marks of great inquiry (*Thiers* and the like I saw quoted almost every page), the man too was in France and published *Travels*. . . ."[173] That Carlyle should have been impressed by Alison's first citation of his references, where Mill was so scathing, illustrated a gap between their conceptions of research that one might not infer from Mill's appreciation of Carlyle's *History* in 1837. At the time of his review of Alison, Mill had of course revised his early estimate of Carlyle's writing as "consummate nonsense."[174] On Carlyle's initiative they had met in September 1831 and begun a correspondence almost at once, and by the next summer Mill was evidently handing over the Revolution: ". . . I am rather fitted to be a logical expounder than an artist. You I look upon as an artist, and perhaps the only genuine one now living in this country: the highest destiny of all, lies in that direction; for it is the artist alone in whose hands Truth becomes impressive, and a living principle of action."[175] With the same forthrightness with which he approved Mill's high opinion of and attachment to him, Carlyle took full advantage of Mill's generosity in sending him books for the history he now thought of writing.[176] In a way, Mill was a collaborator from the outset.

For more than four years they discussed the work, Mill advising and then responding to the steady importuning, Carlyle communicating something of the gestation throes foretelling the strange and awful work he found welling up in him. "What it is to be I cannot yet tell: my doors of utterance are so wonderful, one knows not how to shape thoughts such as to pass thro'." His head "buzzing," he read on and speculated about the literary event "the right *History* (that impossible thing I mean by History) of the French Revolution" would prove to be. Whoever should write "the *truth*" about this "grand Poem of our Time" would be "worth all other writers and singers." Hence the conclusion: "If I were spared alive myself, and had means, why might not I too prepare the way for such a thing?"[177] So Mill continued to oblige with books, Carlyle proclaimed his gratitude, the work took shape. "The French business grows darker and darker upon me: dark as chaos. Ach Gott!"[178] Above all, it should not be like other

[173]Carlyle to Mill, *Collected Letters*, VI, 373 (18 Apr., 1833).

[174]Letter to Sterling, *EL, CW*, XII, 85 (20-22 Oct., 1831).

[175]Letter to Carlyle, *ibid.*, 113 (17 July, 1832). In general, on Carlyle's *History*, see Ben-Israel, *English Historians and the French Revolution*, 127-47; Alfred Cobban, *Aspects of the French Revolution* (New York: Braziller, 1968), 243-55.

[176]Carlyle to J.A. Carlyle, *Collected Letters*, VI, 196 (31 July, 1832); Mill to Carlyle, *EL, CW*, XII, 116-21, 125-30, 132-5 (17 Sept., 22 Oct., 27 Dec., 1832).

[177]Carlyle to Mill, *Collected Letters*, VI, 303, 446 (12 Jan., 24 Sept., 1833).

[178]*Ibid.*, VII, 276 (28 Aug., 1834). The sly complexity of Carlyle's reaction to Mill shows in a letter to his mother of 30 May, 1834: "By far the sensiblest man I see is Mill, who seems almost fonder of me than ever. The class he belongs to has the farther merit of being genuine and honest so far as they go. . . ." (*Ibid.*, 196.) And again to his mother, 25 Oct., 1834: "indeed nothing can exceed the obligingness of Mill . . ." (*ibid.*, 320).

histories, "which are so many 'dead thistles for Pedant chaffinches to peck at and fill their crops with.'"[179] By February 1835 the first volume was written and Mill was given it to read. On March 6 Mill brought the terrible news of its accidental burning. Carlyle's reaction was superb, his consideration of the distracted Mill paternal, his acceptance of the offer of financial compensation spontaneous.[180]

One must imagine the intensity of Mill's commitment to the work after what Carlyle called this "miserablest accident (as we name such things) of my whole life." Seeing it as "purely the hand of Providence," he admitted that the manuscript had "pleased me better than anything I had ever done," acknowledged that "*That* first volume" could not be reproduced, and bravely hoped to produce another that would be "if not better or equal, *all* that I can."[181] But to Mill he wrote courageously: "The thing must be made *better* than it was, or we shall never be able, not to forget it, but to laugh victorious in remembering it." He refused the £200 Mill pressed on him, accepting only £100, the amount he said he had spent, and continued to ask and to receive from Mill "brave cargoes of Books."[182] His recovery was swift, his optimism marked: "I do really believe the Book will be the better for it, and we shall all be the better."[183] If the labour was heavy, the composition was rapid, though by the spring of 1836 the mere thought of the day when "this fatal History" would no longer weigh on him was like "a prophecy of resurrection."[184] Mill again read the manuscript and sent off his annotations and suggestions, removing "anything *merely* quaint in the mode of expression," and saying, "The only general remark I have to make on stile is that I think it would often *tell* better on the reader if what is said in an abrupt, exclamatory & interjectional manner were said in the ordinary grammatical mode of nominative & verb. . . ." Mill's manner was tentative and deferential, Carlyle's response appreciative and slightly mocking: "No Surgeon can touch sore places with a softer hand than you do." His "quarrel with the Nominative-and-verb" caused him "great sorrow," but it was "not a quarrel of my seeking. I mean, that the common English mode of writing has to do with what I call *hearsays* of things; and the great business for me, in which alone I feel any comfort, is recording the *presence*, bodily concrete coloured presence of things;—for which the Nominative-and-verb, as I find it Here and Now, refuses to stand me in due stead." But he would comply "more and more as I grow wiser."[185]

---

[179]Carlyle to J.A. Carlyle, *ibid.*, 325 (28 Oct., 1834).
[180]Letters to Carlyle, *EL*, *CW*, XII, 252-7 (7, 10, 23 Mar., 1835); Carlyle to Mill, *Collected Letters*, VIII, 70-2 (7, 9 Mar., 1835).
[181]Carlyle to James Fraser, *Collected Letters*, VIII, 66-9 (7 Mar., 1835).
[182]Carlyle to Mill, *ibid.*, 72-4 (9, 13, 17 Mar., 1835).
[183]Carlyle to Margaret A. Carlyle, *ibid.*, 84 (25 Mar., 1835).
[184]Carlyle to Mill, *ibid.*, 350 ([late May?], 1836).
[185]Letter to Carlyle, *EL*, *CW*, XII, 307 (20 July?, 1836); Carlyle to Mill, *Collected Letters*, IX, 14-15 (22 July, 1836).

Mill was anxious to publish a review before the book appeared. He had discovered from responses to Carlyle's article on Mirabeau in the *Westminster Review* for January 1837 that some of his friends did not care for the style. Sarah Austin reported that her husband and George Lewis were "clamorous against poor Carlyle's article & say you will ruin the review if you admit any more. I am afraid this is a very general opinion, though I grieve it should be so." Mill told her the Mirabeau had been "the most popular article we ever had in the review," that the only people he met who disliked it were John Arthur Roebuck, George Grote, and William Nassau Senior, "& those three dislike everything, the *style* of which is not humdrum." As for Carlyle's "usual peculiarities," they had in that case fallen "greatly short of the average degree of them."[186] Thus riding the criticism off, he took the warning and determined to pre-empt opinion on the *History*. The book and the review appeared in July 1837.[187]

He took the offensive from high ground: the book was unprecedented and must be judged accordingly. Both history and poetry, with a "peculiar" style "unlike the jog-trot characterless uniformity which distinguishes the English style," it had, he admitted, some "mere mannerisms," German "transcendentalisms" that obscured meaning, but as literature was surpassed "only by the great masters of epic poetry." The narrative was "strictly true"; based on "irrefragable authority," it presented "human beings," rather than the "stuffed figures" other historians served up (134, 135). Hume and Gibbon compared unfavourably with Carlyle in this regard. Mill quoted large extracts to illustrate the poetry and power of the narrative. He judged the theory informing the *History* sound: crown, aristocracy, and clergy had failed in their commissions and so were "hurled . . . into chaos." As for the Revolution's "melancholy turn," "the horrors," "the iron despotism by which it was forced to wind itself up" and the comparative "smallness of its positive results," Mill endorsed Carlyle's opinion that "the French people" were unprepared for the event, did not know what they wished, how they should be governed, in whom they should have faith (159, 160).

His criticisms were gently put: Carlyle was too light on theory. "Without a hypothesis to commence with, we do not even know what end to begin at, what points to enquire into." Mill "fancied" Carlyle undervalued "general principles" and "set too low a value on what constitutions and forms of government can do" (162). But more he did not challenge in this "perfectly true picture of a great historical event, as it actually happened" (158). Aware of the problem of access, he did not fault Carlyle for failing to push his research into Croker's large

---

[186]S. Austin to Mill, quoted in *EL*, *CW*, XII, 334n (n.d.); Mill to S. Austin, *ibid.*, 333-4 (26 Apr., 1837).

[187]Carlyle, his book delayed, had asked whether a later review might not be better, "to have a friend lying back a little, to silence marauders?" (Carlyle to Mill, *Collected Letters*, IX, 129 [28 Jan., 1837].) Obviously Mill thought rather that he could turn the enemy back, and he always believed he had routed them.

collection of contemporary pamphlets;[188] but neither did he fault him for the relatively slight bibliography he had worked from, for accepting legends, for being apparently fixated on the surface drama and neglecting the context, for failing to discuss the origins (Mill said only that the introductory chapters were "the least interesting part of the book" [139]) and the outcome of the Revolution. Indeed, beyond the fundamental agreement between them on the decrepitude of the old order and the virtue of the early Revolutionaries, it is difficult to see what Mill and Carlyle had in common.

Mill, of course, had been fully warned of what Carlyle had had in mind, and had wholeheartedly abetted the enterprise. If the Girondins were less than favourably treated, there was enough philosophy rumbling beneath the vibrant surface of events to redeem such a lapse. Carlyle had broken the political mould completely, "delivered," as Acton was to say, "our fathers from thraldom to Burke."[189] He had asked new questions, written a new history. Moreover, he had done what Mill was convinced he himself could not do: he had created a work of art. Still, a reader may come away from Mill's review, with its curious Carlylean capitalizations, believing that the most rigorous standards he had applied to Scott, and to some extent to Alison, if not Mignet, are absent there. Partly, it is that by 1837 Mill's conception of history and his interest in the Revolution had changed; partly that Mill was now receptive to the imaginative attempt Carlyle had made to portray and understand the Revolution from within, to see it, as historians in the twentieth century would say, from below.

Afterwards, Mill prided himself on three reviewing achievements in the

---

[188]Carlyle had done his best to gain access to the first two instalments of J.W. Croker's large collection of printed materials then still uncatalogued in the British Museum. As a consequence of this situation and of his unsatisfactory relations with Anthony Panizzi ("the respectable sub-librarian," in Carlyle's cutting phrase, then working on the collection), he was able to consult only a few items in a cursory manner (see Ben-Israel, *English Historians and the French Revolution*, 138-9, 198-201). From Panizzi's point of view, however, Carlyle was overbearing and unreasonable. "For all practical purposes," Carlyle was to complain years later to the Royal Commission investigating the Museum's library problems, "this collection of ours might as well have been locked up in water-tight chests and sunk on the Dogger Bank as put in the British Museum" (quoted in Edward Miller, *Prince of Librarians: The Life and Times of Antonio Panizzi of the British Museum* [London: Deutsch, 1967], 178-9, 183). Michelet, from the security of his former privileged access to the Archives Nationales, did not rate Carlyle's loss highly. Criticizing Louis Blanc's history of the Revolution, written in exile in London, he asked: "'Peut-on à Londres écrire l'histoire du Paris révolutionnaire?' Cela ne se peut qu'à Paris. A Londres, il est vrai, il y a une jolie collection de pièces françaises, imprimés, brochures et journaux qu'un amateur, M. Croker, vendait 12,000 francs au musée Britannique, et qu'on étend un peu depuis. Mais une collection d'amateur, des curiosités détachées ne remplacent nullement les grands dépôts officiels où tout se suit, où l'on trouve et les faits et leur liaison, où souvent un événement représenté vingt, trente, quarante fois, en ses versions différentes, peut être étudié, jugé et contrôlé. C'est ce que nous permettent les trois grands corps d'archives révolutionnaires à Paris." (*Histoire de la révolution française* [Paris: Gallimard, 1952], Préface de 1868, 17.) Naturally, the Archives in which Michelet had spent his days thirty years before were not open to Carlyle or anyone else at the time.

[189]John Emerich Edward Dalberg-Acton, *Lectures on the French Revolution*, ed. John Neville Figgis and Reginald Vere Laurence (London: Macmillan, 1910), 358-9.

London and Westminster: preparing the way for acceptance of Lord Durham's Report, accelerating the success of Carlyle's *French Revolution*, and establishing in England Guizot's reputation as an historian. In the *Autobiography* he spoke of pre-empting "the commonplace critics" by hailing Carlyle's book as "one of those productions of genius which are above all rules, and are a law to themselves." He did not think his review had been well executed, but looked on it as "an honest attempt to do immediate service" to a deserving man and his work. He had said much the same thing in a more aggressive manner to R.B. Fox: the article had "greatly accelerated" Carlyle's success, for whether "so strange & incomprehensible" a book would "succeed or fail seemed to depend upon the turn of a die—but I got the first word, blew the trumpet before it at its first coming out & by claiming for it the honours of the highest genius frightened the small fry of critics from pronouncing a hasty condemnation, got fair play for it & then its success was sure."[190] At the time, he had told Carlyle that the review was having "a good effect," though the oral and written opinions on the article itself were "mostly unfavourable."[191] This was not mysterious: whatever the personal commitments that made him champion Carlyle's *Revolution*, he had not applied to it the standards of criticism by which he judged other works. Three years later, alluding to the period of "my Carlylism, a vice of style which I have since carefully striven to correct," he told a correspondent whom he was admonishing for the same affectation, "I think Carlyle's costume should be left to Carlyle whom alone it becomes & in whom it would soon become unpleasant if it were made common. . . ."[192]

MILL AND THE REVOLUTION OF 1830

CARLYLE'S *French Revolution* and Mill's review of it were written in the wake of another Revolution that, from Mill's point of view, had burst gloriously on the scene and subsided ingloriously within a matter of weeks or months. The political void Carlyle envisioned at the centre of the 1789 experience Mill detected in the July Days, as the aftermath revealed the incapacity or self-interest of those who superseded the Bourbon monarchy. He had been excited by the lively press wars of the late 1820s. If the duc de Berry's murder in February 1820 brought a temporary crack-down on the press, the running battle of the opposition parties with the governments of Louis XVIII and Charles X saw at least as many victories as defeats for the liberal press, its proprietors, and its journalists. Neither direct censorship nor regulatory measures weakened its independence. French journals were numerous, variegated, and vigorous. Under

---

[190]*Autobiography*, *CW*, I, 225; Mill to R.B. Fox, *EL*, *CW*, XIII, 427 (16 Apr., 1840).
[191]Letter to Carlyle, *EL*, *CW*, XII, 339 (30 June, 1837).
[192]Letter to George Henry Lewes, *ibid.*, XIII, 449 (probably late 1840).

the moderate ministry of the vicomte de Martignac in 1828-29, the press régime was relaxed, and although he was replaced by the ultra-royalist prince de Polignac in August 1829 it was the latitude of the laws Martignac had permitted that goaded the government into its final assault on the press in July 1830, and so precipitated the Revolution.[193]

How much Mill knew of the close manoeuvring in this long contest that had gone on from the time of his first visit to France can only be surmised. But with the installation of Polignac, both King and minister were daily vilified in the opposition sheets. Mill, who followed the press, was approving. "In France," he wrote d'Eichthal, "the best thinkers & writers of the nation, write in the journals & direct public opinion: but our daily & weekly writers are the lowest hacks of literature. . . ."[194] On the eve of the outbreak, he condemned *The Times* for siding with Polignac, reeled off the despotic acts of Charles X's reign (the notorious Law of Sacrilege, 1826, "worthy of the days of Calas and La Barre," had "persuaded the civilized world that the reign of despotism was assured for another century, and that France was relapsing into the servitude and superstition of the middle ages"), and proposed that in the "most unlikely" event the government did suppress demonstrations, a calamity would ensue for France and Europe.[195] He did not apprehend imminent revolt. One week later the five July Ordinances were published, the journalists reacted fiercely, and the confused and complex politics and violence began which sent the King on his journey into exile and some days later installed Louis Philippe d'Orléans on the throne as King of the French.[196]

Early in August, Mill, with his friends George Graham and John Arthur Roebuck, went off to Paris.[197] He stayed a month. For him it was both a fulfilment and the beginning of a long disenchantment. Years later, Charles Eliot Norton noticed "the sentimental part of [Mill's] intelligence, which is of

[193]Irene Collins, *The Government and the Newspaper Press in France, 1814-1881* (London: Oxford University Press, 1959), 1-59; Charles Ledré, *La presse à l'assaut de la monarchie, 1815-1848* (Paris: Colin, 1960), 5-122; Daniel L. Rader, *The Journalists and the July Revolution in France: The Role of the Political Press in the Overthrow of the Bourbon Restoration, 1827-1830* (The Hague: Nijhoff, 1973), *passim*. On Mill and the July Revolution, see Mueller, *Mill and French Thought*, 17-47.

[194]Letter to d'Eichthal, *EL, CW*, XII, 38-9 (7 Nov., 1829).

[195]Mill, "The French Elections," *Examiner*, 18 July, 1830, 450.

[196]David H. Pinkney, *The French Revolution of 1830* (Princeton: Princeton University Press, 1972), 73-195; Ledré, *La presse à l'assaut de la monarchie*, 105-23; Rader, *The Journalists and the July Revolution*, 208-59.

[197]In Macaulay's dismissive phrase, "on a mission to preach up the Republic and the physical check, I suppose." But Macaulay was bent on a mission similar to Mill's: "I have a plan of which I wish to know your opinion. In ten days or thereabouts I set off for France where I hope to pass six weeks. I shall be in the best society, that of the Duc de Broglie, Guizot, and so on. I think of writing an article on the politics of France since the Restoration, with characters of the principal public men, and a parallel between the present state of France and that of England." (Letter to M. Napier of 19 Aug., 1830, *The Letters of Thomas Babington Macaulay*, ed. Thomas Pinney, 6 vols. [Cambridge: Cambridge University Press, 1974-81], I, 281-2.)

immense force, and has only been kept in due subjection by his respect for his own reason."[198] It was on view in 1830. Mill expected too much. He carried with him an idealized vision of revolution founded on his reading of 1789, too limited a knowledge of the persons and forces in play in France, and a strong sense of his personal goals at the time. He was unprepared for the sharp political game that replaced one monarch with another and brought about a large-scale administrative shuffle, but produced no serious social change. By the laws of March and April 1831, power remained securely with the landowning and professional class, a small *pays légal* attached to the state through the offices it offered them.[199] If the ultra-royalists went home to their estates, the popular element brought into the streets to make the revolution also subsided. The new régime was defensive from the start.

At the time, Mill barely sensed what was happening. Though "the cowardice and imbecility of the existing generation of public men, with scarcely a single exception," promised little, he took hope from "the spirit and intelligence of the young men and of the people, the immense influence of the journals, and the strength of the public voice." Believing, mistakenly, that "there has been an excellent revolution without leaders," he hoped naively that "leaders will not be required in order to establish a good government."[200] Roebuck's story was that he, Mill, and their friends had almost forced the audience at the Opéra (including Louis Philippe) by their shouts of "Debout! debout!" to stand for the Marseillaise.[201] If so, they were only playing games while the tough-minded men who had engineered the new monarchy were establishing themselves in power. Mill's remarks on the goodness of "the common people" were romantic and sentimental: "The inconceivable purity and singleness of purpose, almost amounting to *naïveté*, which they all shew in speaking of these events, has given me a greater love for them than I thought myself capable of feeling for so large a collection of human beings, and the more exhilarating views which it opens of human nature will have a beneficial effect on the whole of my future life."[202] From the beginning, he pictured a Manichean situation: the good people versus

[198]Letter from Norton to Chauncey Wright of 13 Sept., 1870, *Letters of Charles Eliot Norton*, ed. Sarah Norton and M.A. De Wolfe Howe, 2 vols. (Boston and New York: Houghton Mifflin, 1913), I, 400.

[199]Jean Lhomme, *La grande bourgeoisie au pouvoir, 1830-1880* (Paris: Presses Universitaires de France, 1960), 13-123; Jardin and Tudesq, *La France des notables*, I, 122-72; Pinkney, *The Revolution of 1830*, 274-95.

[200]Letter to James Mill, *EL, CW*, XII, 54 (13 Aug., 1830).

[201]*Life and Letters of John Arthur Roebuck*, ed. Robert E. Leader (London: Arnold, 1897), 30.

[202]Letters to James Mill of 13, 20, and 21 Aug., 1830, *EL, CW*, XII, 54-63 (the latter two also published in *Examiner*, 29 Aug., 1830, 547-8). "Never since the beginning of the world was there seen in a people such a heroic, such an unconquerable attachment to justice. The poorest of the populace, with arms in their hands, were absolutely masters of Paris and all that it contains; not a man went richer to his home that night." (Mill, "Attempt to Save the Ex-Ministers," *Examiner*, 24 Oct., 1830, 674.) Cf. Edgar L. Newman, "What the Crowd Wanted in the French Revolution of 1830," in *1830 in France*, ed. John M. Merriman (New York: New Viewpoints, 1975), 17-40.

the wicked monied classes, the virtuous poor versus the scoundrel placehunters. Such a reading could have no happy confirmation.

Until 1834 he contributed observations on the French scene to the *Examiner*, arguing his expertise from "a tolerably familiar acquaintance with the history of France for the last forty years" and his experience in Paris in August-September 1830. Of the revolution outside the capital, of ongoing disturbances among the peasantry, of the struggle for traditional rights in the collision between rural capitalism and the community, Mill made almost no mention. His angle of vision remained political. Early on, he began to see that France had exchanged "a feeble despotism for a strong and durable oligarchy," that the parallel drawn with 1688 was too close. At least the Bourbons (that "stupid race") had been denied the cunning to ally themselves with "the monied class." England showed how the monied aristocracy worked: 150 years after the Glorious Revolution, Englishmen were still fruitlessly demanding parliamentary reform.[203] He expressed hope nevertheless that "the young men who now head the popular party" and "the patriots of more established character and more mature years" would create a liberal régime against the "jobbing oligarchy"; he continued to believe that "the educated classes in France, on all questions of social improvement to which their attention has been directed, are in advance of the majority of the same classes in England"; he attacked the British press, particularly *The Times*, for its "crazy outcries" and the "fund of stupidity and vulgar prejudice in our principal journalists" on the subject of France; he greeted the modest extension of the suffrage as "poor enough" and criticized "M. Guizot and his friends" for their "bigotted and coxcombical devotion to their own ways and their own disciples." He watched, in short, as his romantic enthusiasm for a popular revolution ostensibly led by an intellectual élite of historian journalists (in so far as it had any leaders) was dissipated by the realities of the *situations acquises* and everyday politics.[204] By February 1831, he openly hoped for the fall of Louis Philippe. The Revolution, he said that spring, had "brought forth none but bitter fruits": unemployment, fear of war, political dissension, and oppression.[205]

Mill's intermittent chronicle did not much depart from its constant themes of jobbery, persecution of the press, and the hollowness of the parliamentary process. When the Lyon silkweavers rose in revolt on 21-22 November, 1831, however, he was sympathetic. "It is melancholy," he noted, "to see, that an

[203]Mill, "Prospects of France, No. I," *Examiner*, 19 Sept., 1830, 594-5. See Pamela Pilbeam, "The 'Three Glorious Days': The Revolution of 1830 in Provincial France," *The Historical Journal*, XXVI (Dec., 1983), 831–44.

[204]"Prospects of France, No. IV," "Prospects of France, No. V," "Attempt to Save the Ex-Ministers," "Ignorance of French Affairs by the English Press," *Examiner*, 10, 17, 24 Oct., 14 Nov., 1830, 642-4, 660-1, 673-4, 723-4; summaries of French news, 2 and 9 Jan., 1831, *ibid.*, 8, 24-5.

[205]Summaries of French news, *ibid.*, 13 and 27 Feb., 1831, 105-6, 136; "The Prospects of France," *ibid.*, 10 Apr., 1831, 225-6.

event so pregnant with meaning as the late insurrection of Lyon, should have made no deeper impression upon the men by whom France is now governed, than is indicated by all they do, and by all they fail to do, day after day, and month after month."[206] He accurately assessed the importance of an event that would one day be seen to mark the origin of the modern labour movement. But it was the struggle for free speech that most concerned him, and he was optimistic on grounds that thus far the press had been "more than a match for every government which has defied it to a contest."[207] Parliament gave him less hope, pained as he was to see former liberals, like Casimir Périer who had helped to overthrow the Villèle ministry in 1828, becoming agents of repression.[208] A bloody clash on 5-6 June, 1832, occurred between the army and opponents of the régime on the occasion of the funeral of the opposition deputy, General Lamarque, a Bonapartist and friend of La Fayette; the capital was placed in a state of siege. "The government of the barricades," Mill commented, "has done what Charles X was not permitted to do. It has assumed the power of dispensing with the laws and the courts of justice." What he called "the forty years war" that momentarily had seemed to end in 1830 had now "broken out afresh."[209] Optimism gave way to Cassandra-like intimations of disaster. Of Marshal Soult's ministry of all talents (October 1832-July 1834), Mill remarked that with such men as Thiers, Guizot, and the duc de Broglie, no other government had had such brilliance, "yet none ever was more certain of mis-governing France, and coming to a speedy and disgraceful end." Though Louis Philippe was undeniably the target for repeated attempts on his life, Mill judged the one of 19 November, 1832, likely to be "one of the low tricks with which the French police has long familiarised us."[210]

French events were "paltry," the Revolution of 1830 had turned sour; Mill grew tired: ". . . I am so thoroughly *sick* of the wretched aspect of affairs [in France]," he commented in March 1833, "that I have written little about them in the Examiner for a long time." Only the Saint-Simonians had made good the promise of 1830, and they had "run wild." Apart from them, he told Carlyle, "the excessive avidity & barrenness of the French mind has never been so

[206]Summaries of French news, *ibid.*, 4, 11, 18, 25 Dec., 1831, 776-7, 793, 808-9, 825; summaries of French news, *ibid.*, 1, 8, 29 Jan., 12 Feb., 1832, 9-11, 24-5, 72-3, 104-5. On the revolt, see Blanc, *Histoire de dix ans*, III, 45-80; Fernand Rude, *L'insurrection lyonnaise de novembre 1831: Le mouvement ouvrier de 1827-1832* (Paris: Editions Anthropos, 1969), esp. 233ff.; Robert Bezucha, *The Lyon Uprising of 1834: Social and Political Conflict in the Early July Monarchy* (Cambridge, Mass.: Harvard University Press, 1974), 48-72; Maurice Moissonnier, *La révolte des canuts: Lyon, novembre 1831*, 2nd ed. (Paris: Editions Sociales, 1975), *passim*.

[207]Summary of French news, *Examiner*, 12 Feb., 1832, 104.

[208]Summary of French news, *ibid.*, 29 Apr., 1832, 280; "The Close of the Session in France," *ibid.*, 6 May, 1832, 291-2; summary of French news, *ibid.*, 20 May, 1832, 329-30.

[209]Summaries of French news, *ibid.*, 10, 17, 24 June, 1832, 377, 392-4, 408; cf. Blanc, *Histoire de dix ans*, III, 265-315.

[210]Summaries of French news, *Examiner*, 21 Oct., 25 Nov., 2, 9 Dec., 1832, 680-1, 760, 777, 792; a young man named Bergeron was tried and acquitted for lack of proof.

strikingly displayed: there are such numbers of talkers & writers so full of noise and fury, keeping it up for years and years, and not one new thought, new to *them* I mean, has been struck out by all the collisions since I first began attending to these matters."[211] Guizot's legislation on primary education caught his interest.[212] He thought the question of the unrepresentative character of the Chamber of Deputies was beginning to interest the nation.[213] But the savage crushing of renewed strike activity and the ensuing insurrection in Lyon, followed by the notorious massacre of April 1834 in Paris, led him to conclude that the ministerial record was poor save in the field of repression.[214]

THE MONSTER TRIAL

Mill's autumnal note was struck in the aftermath of strong blows to the opposition. The most formidable force Louis Philippe had to face was the amorphous republican movement, a bewildering variety of men and ideas, each with historical antecedents, loosely grouped around the notion of popular sovereignty and universal suffrage, but divided on means. Legislation against unauthorized associations struck at their organizations, but they grouped and regrouped to escape its severities. The sympathetic press and its journalists endured incessant prosecutions for their attacks on the ministry and vilification of the crown.[215] In the spring of 1834 matters came to a head with the government's decision to strike at the newly formed republican Société des Droits de l'Homme which aimed at political and social revolution. When juries failed to uphold the state in eighty percent of the cases brought against a single newspaper, the *Tribune* of Armand Marrast, the chambers voted for a law that would bring such prosecutions before correctional tribunals.[216]

The Lyon silk workers had struck in February; on 9-12 April there took place the terrible street battle between them and the army for control of the city, in which some three hundred soldiers and workers were killed. This gave the signal to the republicans of the Société des Droits de l'Homme to raise barricades in the Marais district of Paris on 13 April. Though the arrest of 150 leaders led to attempts to abort the rising, a clash took place and the insurgents were crushed by the army in a barbarous exercise of brutality and mutilation, the most celebrated

[211]Summary of French news, *Examiner*, 31 Mar., 1833, 201; letters to William Tait, *EL, CW*, XII, 148 (30 Mar., 1833), and to Carlyle, *ibid*, 150 (11-12 Apr., 1833).

[212]Summaries of French news, *Examiner*, 5, 19 May, 21 July, 1833, 282, 313, 457.

[213]Summary of French news, *ibid*., 12 Jan., 1834, 23; "State of Opinion in France," *ibid*., 30 Mar., 1834, 195-6.

[214]Summaries of French news, *ibid*., 20, 27 Apr., 11 May, 1 June, 1834, 250, 265, 297-8, 345.

[215]J. Tchneroff, *Le parti républicain sous la monarchie de juillet*, 2nd ed. (Paris: Pedone, 1905), 34ff.; Georges Weill, *Histoire du parti républicain en France de 1814 à 1870*, new ed. (Paris: Alcan, 1928), 53ff.; Ledré, *La presse à l'assaut de la monarchie*, 125ff.

[216]The *Tribune* succumbed on 11 May, 1835, after 111 prosecutions and 20 convictions: see Weill, *Histoire du parti républicain*, 115; Ledré, *La presse à l'assaut de la monarchie*, 161-2.

episode of which was the horrifying slaughter of the inhabitants of a house at 12 rue Transnonain.[217] The deputies quickly agreed to increase the size of the army, some 2000 suspects were rounded up, and an ordinance provided for bringing insurgents from both cities to trial before the Chamber of Peers. This was the *procès monstre*, staged at the Luxembourg Palace, May 1835-January 1836, with hundreds of witnesses called, thousands of pages of documents in submission, and 164 leaders on trial. It was designed to destroy the republican and insurrectional movements, and its size underlined the apparent magnitude of the opposition from the left. Its proceedings were marked by tumult, citation of some of the defence lawyers for contempt of court, and the escape of twenty-eight of the principal accused.[218]

Mill's article appeared while the trial was still in progress. It was a frank defence of the Société des Droits de l'Homme, particularly against the charge that it was hostile to private property. He seized the occasion to deliver still another lesson to Whigs and Tories on the meaning of the great events from 1789 to the fall of Robespierre, and to clear the Revolution (save for the Babeuf episode) of this same charge. The trial itself he saw as an attempt to create panic and strike at the opposition, to confuse matters by trying both "the pretended authors of the pretended republican conspiracy of Paris" and "the presumed authors of the real trades' union revolt at Lyon" before the tame placemen in the Chamber of Peers. Full of contempt for this upper chamber, for "the imbecility" of its composition, he predicted that the trial would be "its last throw for political importance"(129).

In fact the prison break-out and flight to England of such important leaders among the accused as Godefroy Cavaignac and Armand Marrast demoralized those remaining in Sainte-Pélagie prison. Moreover, the failed assassination attempt on the King on 22 July by Giuseppe Fieschi, a self-proclaimed republican with two accomplices from the Société des Droits de l'Homme, damaged their cause still more. Public sympathy fell away. By the time the Cour des Pairs pronounced its last sentence of deportation or imprisonment in January 1836, the internal prospects of the régime were much improved. The Société was destroyed, the opposition had divided into a small underground revolutionary movement and a weakened republican group seeking now to elect deputies to the Chamber of Deputies and to survive the new press laws. Mill was appalled by the legislation, which seemed likely to touch even English newspapers critical of the

[217]On the Lyon and Paris risings, see Blanc, *Histoire de dix ans*, IV, 223-85; Edouard Dolléans, *Histoire du mouvement ouvrier*, 3 vols. (Paris: Colin, 1936-53), I, 93-107; Weill, *Histoire du parti républicain*, 101; and the comprehensive study by Bezucha, who presents the confrontation as the *canuts'* (male weavers') attempt "to establish a claim to control over their work in the future" (*The Lyon Uprising of 1834*, ix; see especially, 96-133, 149-74).

[218]On the trial, see Blanc, *Histoire de dix ans*, IV, 355-423; Weill, *Histoire du parti républicain*, 104-8; Bezucha, *The Lyon Uprising of 1834*, 175-92. Armand Carrel was chosen as one counsel for the defence, but the Cour des Pairs refused to recognize such outsiders.

régime. Six years before he had remarked that the Houses of Parliament could not show a single member "who approaches within twenty degrees of M. de Broglie."[219] The duc de Broglie now presided over the government that had brought these things about. "I should much like to know," Mill wrote to Carlyle, "what old Sieyes thinks of the present state of France. . . . What a curious page all this is in the history of the French revolution. France seems to be *désenchanté* for a long time to come—& as the natural consequence of political disenchantment—profoundly demoralized. All the educated youth are becoming mere venal commodities."[220]

Some months later, in January 1837, Mill remarked to Tocqueville that French politics appeared to be "in the same torpid state." Tocqueville said he did not know anyone who could grasp French affairs: "Nous sommes dans cet état douteux de demi-sommeil et de demi-réveil qui échappe à l'analyse." But he thought the nation had survived the threat of revolutionary violence and anarchy, and was returning to its liberal and democratic instincts: "mais que Dieu nous garde des émeutes! elles semblent menacer le gouvernement et par le fait elles ne nuisent qu'à la liberté."[221] Mill would have accepted the conclusion, but not the presumption on which it was based.[222] He abhorred violence, too, but his sympathies were with those who had challenged the small *pays légal* and their "shop-keeper king," and who seemed to have failed.

CARREL

Soon after the great trial, Mill's despondency deepened with the sudden death of the journalist he admired more than any other. Armand Carrel, with Thiers and Mignet, had founded the *National* in January 1830, intending to destroy not only the Polignac ministry but the Bourbon monarchy as well. Being historians, they developed the parallel between their France and England on the eve of 1688. Sovereignty was located in the people, and they called in the final crisis for the "république, déguisée sous la monarchie, au moyen du gouvernement représentatif."[223] In some sense the July Monarchy was their creation. Thiers had

---

[219]Letter to d'Eichthal, *EL*, *CW*, XII, 33 (15 May, 1829).

[220]Letter to Carlyle, *ibid.*, 278-9 (17 Oct., 1835). Sieyès, who was in his eighty-eighth year, evidently thought only that the parliamentarians "talk too much, and don't act enough" (quoted in Glyndon G. Van Deusen, *Sieyès: His Life and His Nationalism* [New York: Columbia University Press, 1932], 142). For the rest, he would say, "Je ne vois plus; je n'entends plus; je ne me souviens plus, je ne parle plus; je suis devenu entièrement négatif" (quoted in Paul Bastid, *Sieyès et sa pensée* [Paris: Hachette, 1970], 284). He died the following June.

[221]Letter to Tocqueville, *EL*, *CW*, XII, 317 (7 Jan., 1837); Tocqueville to Mill, *Oeuvres*, VI, 325-6 (24 June, 1837).

[222]The previous year, Mill noted his reservations about Tocqueville's estimate of democracy and aristocracy, but it may be queried that he discerned in Tocqueville's "historiography which addresses the 'whole future'" an "essentially antilibertarian" bias (Hayden White, *Metahistory: The Historical Imagination in Nineteenth-Century Europe* [Baltimore: Johns Hopkins University Press, 1973], 205).

[223]*National*, 31 July, 1830, quoted in Ledré, *La presse à l'assaut de la monarchie*, 117.

promptly moved into politics; Mignet retired to scholarship and the archives, leaving Carrel, the most effervescent and brilliant of them, at the *National*.

Carrel had given proof of unorthodoxy in 1821 when, though an army officer, he had rashly associated with Carbonari conspirators. He had resigned his commission in 1823 to join a foreign legion helping the Spanish rebels against Ferdinand VII, and thus soon found himself in a war on the opposite side from the French army that had been sent down to put the King back on his throne. For this he was three times court-martialled, escaping with his life only on a legal technicality.[224] A student of history, he thereafter helped Augustin Thierry assemble the materials for his history of the Norman Conquest and began the work which led to his own *Histoire de la contre-révolution en Angleterre*. He was, however, a political journalist, and he was independent. He refused a *préfecture* under the July régime; he joked about what he might have done had he been offered an army division. And he served notice that he was still a democrat.[225] By early 1832, Carrel was moving toward the republican position, though he did not overtly ally himself with the Société des Droits de l'Homme. He attacked the authorities and was repeatedly prosecuted. Juries would not convict him. The government was determined to drive the opposition press out of existence by police harassment, arrests, trials, imprisonments, and fines.[226] Concentrating on Marrast's *Tribune*, they brought it to collapse in May 1835, but Carrel, more *nuancé*, they did not bring down.

Mill was aware of Carrel's intensely nationalist stance in the diplomatic crisis of 1830-31, of his certain Bonapartist sympathy, and of his contempt for Louis Philippe's refusal to launch French forces on the road to the liberation of the Poles and the Belgians. (Scornful of a policy of "la paix à tout prix," Carrel said, "Il y avait plus de fierté sous le jupon de la Pompadour.")[227] It seemed not to disturb him. He was quick to notice Carrel's toast to the Reform Bill at a patriotic banquet, offering France's sympathy and congratulations, despite lingering anti-English feeling in the *National*.[228] When the newspaper attacked English

---

[224]On Carrel, see R.G. Nobécourt, *La vie d'Armand Carrel* (Paris: Gallimard, 1930); for the early adventures characteristic of his impulsive, changeable nature, see *ibid.*, 23-60.

[225]*Ibid.*, 61-126. "Je ne voulais pas d'un gouvernement," he told Jules Simon, "qui prétendait être un minimum de république, et n'était qu'un minimum de royauté" (Simon, *Mignet, Michelet, Henri Martin*, 94). "Le balancement de sa démarche," Louis Blanc noted of him at the height of his powers, "son geste bref, ses habitudes d'élégance virile, son goût pour les exercices du corps, et aussi une certaine âpreté qu'accusaient les lignes heurtées de son visage et l'énergie de son regard, tout cela était plus militaire que de l'écrivain" (*Histoire de dix ans*, III, 128).

[226]Nobécourt, *La vie d'Armand Carrel*, 126-75; Collins, *The Government and the Newspaper Press*, 60-81; Mill, summaries of French news, *Examiner*, 25 Mar., 9 Sept., 1832, 200-1, 585.

[227]Quoted in Ledré, *La presse à l'assaut de la monarchie*, 132. War was the solution for all problems: "Quand la confiance publique est perdue, quand il n'y a plus ni crédit ni commerce possible, quand la détresse, le désespoir, la passion ont mis les armes à la main de la classe qui vit de son travail, il faut la guerre" (quoted in Tchneroff, *Le parti républicain*, 135). On Carrel's strongly nationalist views, see the selections from his articles in R.G. Nobécourt, *Armand Carrel, journaliste: Documents inédits et textes oubliés* (Rouen: Defontaine, [1935]), esp. 93-115, 153-5, and Nobécourt, *La vie d'Armand Carrel*, 126-9, 277-8.

[228]Summary of French news, *Examiner*, 3 June, 1832, 361.

journals for their treatment of France, Mill agreed, saying Carrel should know that "the popular party" thought as ill of Marshal Soult's government as Carrel did himself.[229] Despite Carrel's somewhat turbulent disposition, or perhaps because of it, he had appeal for Mill, who believed he was a wise man, just the same. Carrel could be cautious; he showed this after the disastrous rioting attending Lamarque's funeral.[230] And in the autumn of 1833, on a visit to France, Mill was introduced to Carrel. He communicated the immensely favourable impression he got to Carlyle, and was to incorporate his immediate reactions in his article four years later (201). Carrel's mind struck him as much more refined than that of Godefroy Cavaignac, President of the Société des Droits de l'Homme. He was heartened by the meeting and by the prospect of correspondence: "with Carrel I am to establish an exchange of articles; Carrel is to send some to the Examiner and I am to send some to the National, with liberty to publish them here."[231]

Mill followed the running battle with the régime, in which Carrel, sustaining prosecutions and fines, sought to evade the Cour Royale de Paris and the Cour de Cassation, tirelessly printed court proceedings, hounded the King mercilessly, and predicted "un gouvernement sans rois et sans nobles."[232] He was delighted when Carrel was acquitted by a jury in the Cour d'Assises de la Seine-Inférieure, having argued that if Louis Philippe wished to be his own minister he must expect to be treated like other ministers.[233] But the net tightened. After Fieschi's attempt, the press law of September 1835 limited room for manoeuvre.[234] With the *Tribune* already closed down, and François Raspail's *Réformateur* fallen victim to the new law, the *National* was the last important defender of republicanism. Carrel had accepted republicanism, but he was a moderate, no

---

[229]"French and English Journals," *ibid.*, 2 Dec., 1832, 772-3.

[230]"Nous avons une monarchie à renverser," he wrote to a friend in September 1833; "nous la renverserons, et puis il faudra lutter contre d'autres ennemis" (letter of Carrel to Anselme Petetin of 5 Sept., 1833, quoted in Weill, *Histoire du parti républicain*, 95). See also Nobécourt, *La vie d'Armand Carrel*, 174-5.

[231]Letter to Carlyle, *EL, CW*, XII, 197 (25 Nov., 1833).

[232]Summaries of French news, *Examiner*, 19 Jan., 13 Apr., 31 Aug., 1834, 40-1, 232, 552. Carrel's editorial of 15 June, 1834, is quoted in Ledré, *La presse à l'assaut de la monarchie*, 156.

[233]He was prosecuted and acquitted for "Ouverture de la session de 1834," *Le National de 1834*, 1 Aug., 1834, 1. On Carrel's battles with the regime, 1833-34, see Nobécourt, *La vie d'Armand Carrel*, 155-95. Of 520 press prosecutions in Paris, 1830-34, only 188 resulted in condemnations (Collins, *The Government and the Newspaper Press*, 79). Carrel, however, was condemned and sent to Sainte-Pélagie prison later in the year. He remained there from 5 Oct., 1834, to 2 Apr., 1835, in the rather relaxed conditions of access to visitors and journalistic activity which were permitted to him. From there he launched further thunderbolts against the Cour des Pairs, which was about to stage *le procès monstre* (Ledré, *La presse à l'assaut de la monarchie*, 158, n94). He appeared before the Cour on 15 December, 1834, to argue the case of the *National*'s chief editor, creating a sensation (Blanc, *Histoire de dix ans*, IV, 327-34; Nobécourt, *La vie d'Armand Carrel*, 195-216).

[234]The legislation of September 1835 was so repressive that both opposition and some majority deputies opposed it. Tocqueville believed the full rigour of the law was not applied, but those who tested it could be driven out of business; a new tone of moderation was prudent. See Collins, *The Government and the Newspaper Press*, 82-99; Blanc, *Histoire de dix ans*, IV, 445-8.

revolutionist; he had no use for utopian activists. "Des fous! des brouillons! des envieux! des impuissants!" he had said in 1831. "Que de temps il faudra avant que le pays soit mûr pour la République!"[235] Though he had moved to republicanism, he still favoured manoeuvre. Entering Sainte-Pélagie prison, he had written Chateaubriand, wondering how long it would be before men would sensibly work out their "inévitables transactions" by negotiation rather than death and exhaustion. The prison experience was sinister and embittering, he was personally threatened, and he had no affinity for the rough sort of man. All the same, he recognized the demands of the working class: one must "posséder assez d'intelligence pour le comprendre, assez de coeur pour ne pas s'en effrayer."[236] Sainte-Beuve reckoned him too sensitive, too obstinate, too little able to strike the popular note, though a great and principled journalist. What attracted Mill to Carrel is easy to see.

Carrel was cut off early by misadventure in a duel. The journalist Emile de Girardin brought out a cheap daily, *La Presse*, which he hoped to sustain by advertising on English lines. Carrel, welcoming the possibility of lower cost to the public through increased circulation, doubted Girardin's democratic motives. Saying so, he brought upon himself the riposte that republican editors afforded their comfortable situation at the expense of their readers. When Girardin threatened to back this up with proofs, Carrel believed he was being threatened with revelations about his private life. The quarrel could not be resolved and Carrel issued his challenge, which led to a fatal encounter in the Bois de Vincennes on 22 July, 1836.[237]

Mill took the news hard and sent word to Carlyle, who replied that Godefroy Cavaignac had told him of "*la mort funeste de Carrel.*" He supposed that "such as he was, there is not his like left in France. And to die as a fool dieth!—It seems to me, as I tell you always, that France has pitiful destinies lying before it. . . ."[238] Mill expressed his sense of loss to Tocqueville when he told him that though he had many friends in France, he and Carrel were the two for whom he felt "une véritable admiration."[239] It was a curious confession; it is unlikely that Tocqueville could have appreciated Carrel in the same way. Mill had not known Carrel well, but he had made him a symbol of democratic uprightness and

[235]Quoted in Weill, *Histoire du parti républicain*, 116n. See Nobécourt, *La vie d'Armand Carrel*, 135-54, 269-77.

[236]Letter from Carrel to Chateaubriand of 4 Oct., 1834, in *Mémoires d'outre-tombe*, 4 vols. (Paris: Flammarion, 1964), IV, 536. Chateaubriand's description of Carrel's life in prison is *ibid.*, 537-8. See also Weill, *Histoire du parti républicain*, 116-17; Nobécourt, *La vie d'Armand Carrel*, 195-202, 215-16.

[237]Sainte-Beuve, "Armand Carrel" (17 May, 1852), *Causeries du lundi*, 15 vols. (Paris: Garnier, 1851-62), VI, 144-5; Chateaubriand, *Mémoires*, IV, 538-9; Blanc, *Histoire de dix ans*, V, 54-63; Nobécourt, *La vie d'Armand Carrel*, 282-304; Collins, *The Government and the Newspaper Press*, 88-9.

[238]Carlyle to Mill, *Collected Letters*, IX, 28 (28 July, 1836).

[239]Letter to Tocqueville, *EL, CW*, XII, 309 (9 Nov., 1836).

tenacity in the face of oligarchical evil—"the unapproachable Armand Carrel,"
as he would say, a man with neither legislative nor any other public office,
merely the editorship of a newspaper, who had made himself "the most powerful
political leader of his age and country."[240] In this there was some extravagance;
it showed that, at thirty, Mill was still capable of responding to the romantic
excitement that had taken him to Paris in August 1830 and which had been
rekindled in Carrel's presence three years later.

The long commemorative article appeared fifteen months after Carrel's death,
drawing on studies by Désiré Nisard and Emile Littré. Mill's interpretation
continued to be heightened: "The man whom not only his friends but his
enemies, and all France, would have proclaimed President or Prime Minister
with one voice. . . . Ripened by years and favoured by opportunity, he might
have been the Mirabeau or the Washington of his age, or both in one." (169,
170.) For this there really was no evidence, and others saw him more clearly.[241]
Carrel seemed to Mill unusually practical for a Frenchman. His history of the
English counter-revolution was judged superior to the works of Guizot and
François Mazure. Again, in this article, Mill castigated the betrayers of 1830, the
oligarchy who had fallen on public office "like tigers upon their prey" (192),
against whom Carrel showed so well. Possessing the gifts of Mirabeau, "he
could make men of all sorts, even foreigners, feel that they could have been loyal

---

[240]Mill, "Fonblanque's England under Seven Administrations" (1837), *CW*, VI, 380. Carrel had
visited England from 30 August to early October, 1834, and again from the middle of May to
mid-June, 1836, when (according to his biographer), "il est très recherché par la société et les
honorables gentlemen le reçoivent somptueusement," and saw Louis Napoleon Bonaparte, but there
is no record of his meeting on either occasion with Mill (Nobécourt, *La vie d'Armand Carrel*, 197-9,
238).

[241]Again, Blanc's sketch contains more light and shade: "Quoique plein de douceur et d'abandon
dans l'intimité, il apparaissait, dans la vie publique, dominateur et absolu. . . . Il était né chef de
parti: chef d'école, il n'aurait pu l'être. Il manquait de ce fanatisme froid qui naît des études
opiniâtres et fait les novateurs. Voltairien avant tout, il ne paraissait pas avoir souci de marquer sa
place dans l'histoire par l'initiative de la pensée. . . . Il possédait au plus haut point le
commandement; il passionnait ses amis: c'était du caractère. . . . Il fut longtemps girondin par
sentiment; et il lui en coûta beaucoup pour s'incliner devant la majesté de cette dictature
révolutionnaire, l'effroi, la gloire, le désespoir et le salut de la France. . . . Forcé souvent d'éteindre
dans ses amis le feu dont il était lui-même consumé, il s'exaltait et se décourageait tour à tour dans
cette lutte intérieure. . . ." (*Histoire de dix ans*, III, 128-30.) "Un trouble invincible l'agitait. Car,
tout en le saluant chef de parti, l'opinion ne lui fournissait aucun point d'appui sérieux, et il le sentait
amèrement. . . . Il s'affligeait aussi du perpétuel refoulement de ses désirs. Il lui aurait fallu les
tourments de la gloire, la vie des camps; et il n'avait, pour en employer son énergie, que le
journalisme. . . ." (*Ibid.*, V, 56-7.) It was Carrel's ambivalence concerning the state, his hesitation
as between Gallo-Roman decentralization and Bonapartist centralization, that struck a twentieth-
century commentator. "At the time of his death," Jacques Barzun remarked, "Carrel must be called a
harbinger at once of the Second Republic and of the Second Empire. To which would he have
remained faithful in the end? Mill thought, to the Republic; an acute French critic [Jules Amédée
Barbey d'Aurevilly] thought, to Bonaparte. The speculation is instructive, for it leads us into the
heart of the intellectual *malaise* of the forties, and thence to the final phase of Romantic
historiography." (Jacques Barzun, "Romantic Historiography as a Political Force in France,"
Journal of the History of Ideas, II [June, 1941], 325.)

to him—that they could have served and followed him in life and death" (203). Mill pictured him as a moderate, pacific, single-minded republican who toward the end of his life sensibly came round to "demanding an extension of the suffrage; that vital point, the all-importance of which France has been so slow to recognise, and which it is so much to be regretted that he had not chosen from the first, instead of republicanism, to be the immediate aim of his political life" (209). Thus he was "a martyr to the morality and dignity of public discussion," and a victim of "that low state of our civilisation" that makes a man defend his reputation "sword in hand, as in the barbarous ages" (212-13). His memory, Mill said, would live on with that of the events of 1830, but "the star of hope for France in any new convulsions, was extinguished when Carrel died" (211).

As review and commentary, the article was unusually emotional and lyrical. Mill told Molesworth: "I have written *con amore* & those who have seen it think it the best thing I have yet done. I never admired any man as I did Carrel; he was to my mind the type of a philosophic radical *man of action* in this epoch."[242] The intense personal reaction he had to Carrel enabled him to set aside or rationalize much in his nature and his life that he might well have disapproved in another man. He made of Carrel everything that a young liberal should be, even to coming round at the end to reflect a touch of the English radical. He had almost produced an example of that *croisement des races* he believed would be to the benefit of both peoples.

TWO "GREAT HISTORICAL MINDS"

MICHELET

Carrel had been secretary to Augustin Thierry in the mid-1820s, and it was Thierry who had called for a "historiography of French liberty," documenting the thesis that liberty was old and that the middle class had been the bearer of the nation's interest.[243] What Carrel might have done as historian of this theme, had he returned to his studies as he sometimes suggested he might, remains an open question. Another historian, for whom Thierry also paved the way, showed how uncertainly focused this romantic impulse was. Like Thierry, Jules Michelet wrote history to shape the present and future. As Thierry put it in 1817, "We are constantly being told to model ourselves on our forefathers. Why don't we follow this advice! Our forefathers were the artisans who established the

---

[242]Letter to William Molesworth, *LL*, *CW*, XVII, 1978 (22 Sept., 1837). Twenty-two years later, Mill refused to permit a translation of *On Liberty* to appear with notes and preface by Emile de Girardin because "il me répugne d'être associé de quelque manière que ce soit, avec l'homme qui a tué Carrel" (letter to Dupont-White, *LL*, *CW*, XV, 642 [29 Oct., 1859]).

[243]Mellon, *Political Uses of History*, 8-12; Gossman, "Augustin Thierry," 6-19.

communes of the Middle Ages and who first conceived freedom as we understand it today."[244] For Thierry and Carrel, writing history was a political act. But it is not sure that this was so for Michelet. If he shared Thierry's passion for erudition and critical imagination, Michelet developed a history that was far more personal than the history of his contemporaries. He was to become the greatest of the philosophical and romantic historians. His origins and his trajectory were almost entirely different from theirs.

He had read enormously in literature and philosophy, the classics and contemporary authors, French, English, and German. He read Herder, he ever after claimed Vico as his master. Like the Saint-Simonians, he was in search of a system that would explain the meaning of human experience, and his chosen field finally was history. Between 1825 and 1831, he published three short summaries of European history for secondary instruction, an abridged translation of Vico's *Scienza nuova* with his own commentary, an introduction to "universal history," and a history of the Roman Republic. He was a professor at the Collège Sainte-Barbe from 1822 to 1827, a *maître de conférences* at the Ecole Normale from 1827 to 1837. Indeed, he had taught his budding *normaliens* at 6:30 in the mornings in order to be at the Tuileries by 8 o'clock to instruct the princesse Louise, daughter of the duchesse de Berry, in history. After the July Days he was similarly chosen to tutor Louis Philippe's fifth child, the princesse Clémentine. A rising star after 1831, he lectured for Guizot (Minister of Public Education) at the Sorbonne from 1834 to 1836, and took up the *chaire d'histoire et de morale* at the Collège de France on 23 April, 1837. The most important post he held was as *chef de la section historique* in the Archives du Royaume (later Archives Nationales) from the autumn of 1830 until 1852. Though he had also written earlier on the history of France, from then on his broad concerns in history were narrowed down to the history of his own country. The result was the first six volumes of his *Histoire de France*, from the beginnings to the end of the Middle Ages, published between 1833 and 1844. He believed that a great age of historiography was opening up; he was at the very centre of the collective historical enterprise sponsored by Guizot and supported by the state. Increasingly he came to regard France as the heart of the European experience and himself as the chosen historian of her past.[245]

Unlike his contemporaries, Michelet could not have claimed 1830 as his Revolution. While they were helping to topple the Bourbon monarchy, he was giving his courses. But reflection on the July Days led him to accept the legend of a spontaneous uprising with only one collective, nameless hero: the people.

---

[244]Quoted by Gossman, "Augustin Thierry," 8.

[245]"Vivant esprit de la France, où te saisirai-je, si ce n'est en moi?" (*Histoire de la révolution française*, Préface de 1847, 1). Paul Viallaneix, *La voie royale: Essai sur l'idée de peuple dans l'oeuvre de Michelet* (Paris: Delagrave [1959]), 91ff; Stephen A. Kippur, *Jules Michelet: A Study of Mind and Sensibility* (Albany: State University of New York Press, 1981), 26ff.

The theme of his *Introduction à l'histoire universelle*, published the following year, was the history of the world as the struggle and triumph of liberty. If the *Trois Glorieuses* later assumed in his mind an importance and an impact they had not had at the time, still reflection on them helped him to see the underlying theme of the national history he determined to write, the materials for which surrounded him at the Archives. In all this, he was initially the admirer and the protégé of Guizot. But he grew increasingly outspoken and radical, attacking the Church and the Jesuit Order, celebrating *le peuple* and eventually the French Revolution in a way that was uncongenial to the régime. Thus it was not surprising that, in the growing tension of the winter of 1847-48, Michelet should have been seen as a prophet of some great popular disturbance. In January 1848, his lectures at the Collège de France were suspended.

Mill was well aware of him. Had the *London and Westminster Review* continued, he said, he would have written "more than one article on Michelet, a writer of great & original views, very little known among us."[246] Through d'Eichthal he received a letter from Michelet in April 1840, accompanied by two volumes of the *Histoire de France*, and he thanked him by the same route for his "admirable" work, with which he was "intimately acquainted" and for which he had "long felt the warmest admiration." He hoped to review both these volumes and the earlier *Histoire de la république romaine*.[247] He then received the message that as Volume V of the *Histoire de France* was "si peu favorable aux Anglais," Michelet was hoping that "la haute impartialité" of Mill would assure the volume a good reception in England. To this end he wished Mill to know that (a) where Joan of Arc and other matters were concerned, he had rigorously rejected the chronicles and based himself on the documents, and (b) though reputed to be "un homme d'*imagination*," he was in fact "dominé par la passion de la *vérité*."[248] How well Mill was acquainted with Michelet's personal opinions of England, save as they appeared in his work, and whether he knew Michelet had visited England in the summer of 1834 and found it as little attractive as he might have expected from his studies,[249] one may wonder. But he noted ironically of a letter from Michelet that it "proves to me by the

[246]Letter to M. Napier, *EL, CW,* XIII, 431 (27 Apr., 1840).
[247]Letter to d'Eichthal, *ibid.*, 432 (7 May, 1840).
[248]Quoted *ibid.*, 432n. Michelet's letter appears in his *Journal*, ed. Paul Viallaneix and Claude Digeon, 4 vols. (Paris: Gallimard, 1959-76), I, 814, where it is dated 24 Sept., 1841, i.e., some sixteen months after the letter from Mill to Gustave d'Eichthal, to which Eugène d'Eichthal appended the quotation.
[249]Michelet's chief complaint was of course the patent miseries of the industrial revolution with which he here first became acquainted. Travelling for a month, 5 August to 3 September, in England, Ireland, and Scotland, he was disturbed by the "nouvelle féodalité" with its enslavement of children in the factories: "C'est encore un spectacle de voir, au milieu de cette haute civilisation et chez le peuple où l'instruction est le plus répandue, ces pieds nus, ces jambes sans bas. L'aisance a augmenté; la simplicité, la dureté, la patience n'ont pas diminué." (Michelet, *Journal*, I, 145 [22 Aug., 1834].) See also Viallaneix, *La voie royale*, 40-1; Kippur, *Jules Michelet*, 74-6.

extravagance of its compliments upon the letter I wrote to him, that if one gives a man exactly the sort of praise he wants to receive, one is sure of getting into his good graces."[250] All the same, Michelet judged well in approaching Mill for an impartial review of a work that showed little appreciation of England other than as the anti-France that galvanized the disunited French into closing ranks and becoming one people.[251]

Mill was about to do four things: to make a familiar declaration about "the French school" of history; to proclaim a new star in the field of history; to emphasize again the shared French and English past of the Middle Ages; and to make a personal statement about his view of the past. He promised that his review would cause some of Napier's readers to "stare,"[252] but there was little to surprise them. His opening salvo against the stagnation of historical studies in England (Carlyle's "signal example" apart) was familiar (219). Distinguishing the French as superior even to the Germans, Mill named Thierry, Guizot, and Michelet as "the three great historical minds of France, in our time" (221). All of them avoided "the first stage" of historical inquiry, i.e., judging the past by the standards of the present (222). All of them met the criteria of poetry and imagination characterizing "the second stage," i.e., producing a true "historical romance." Indeed, only the French "school of writers" (Carlyle and Niebuhr apart) passed this test (224, 225). And only Guizot had made "frequent and long incursions" into the "third, and the highest stage of historical investigation," i.e., the construction of "a science of history" to determine the fundamental law of cause and effect (228, 225). What little had been done toward "this greatest achievement" was mostly his contribution (225). Michelet's distinction, then, was something else: he was "the poet" of the "internal life" of the French people. He knew how to reveal "the spirit of an age," distilling it from the documents "by the chemistry of the writer's own mind" (233). He had done this for Rome, where Niebuhr had been silent. He did it for the Middle Ages, not without committing errors, but safeguarded by his "deep erudition, and extensive research" (233).[253] Entranced by his emphasis on geography and his sketches of the French provinces, Mill criticized Michelet only for taking Thierry's redis-

---

[250]Letter to R.B. Fox, *EL, CW*, XIII, 442 (3 Aug., 1840).

[251]This was a stock idea; Michelet firmly lodged it in French historiography. After the *coup d'état* in December 1851, someone close to Louis Napoleon told Harriet Grote that the recipe for securing popular support was simple: "Two passions are predominant in the mass of the people to which a ruler of France can always have recourse; the love of glory and the hatred of England. On these foundations we can build securely." (Quoted in Nassau William Senior, *Journals Kept in France and Italy from 1848 to 1852, with A Sketch of the Revolution of 1848*, ed. M.C.M. Simpson, 2 vols. [London: King, 1871], II, 289-90.)

[252]Letter to Bain, *EL, CW*, XIII, 612 (3 Nov., 1843).

[253]Taine asked the question: "Devons-nous croire M. Michelet? Pour ma part, après expérience faite, je réponds oui: car, lorsqu'on étudie les documents d'une époque qu'il a étudiée, on éprouve une sensation semblable à la sienne. . . ." ("M. Michelet" [1855], *Essais de critique et d'histoire*, 6th ed. [Paris: Hachette, 1892], 107.)

covery of the "race of Gaels" and carrying the influence of race in history too far (235, 236).

Mill admitted that he was more concerned to publicize Michelet than to criticize him (254). Anthony Panizzi had given him a critical review the previous year. Mill had written Michelet to ask whether there was anything he would care to have communicated to the British public,[254] but there appears to have been no reply. The object was to have him read in England, to warn readers of the difficulties he presented and the unfamiliar conceits, "the personification of abstractions, to an almost startling extent" (255). Mill saw his great strengths and at least suspected his weakness.

After this review in 1844, Mill wrote nothing further of Michelet. On the later volumes of the *Histoire de France* he made no comment, and of the *Histoire de la révolution française*, written 1846-53, he said nothing. With its extreme nationalist fervour, almost religious celebration of "the people," and personification of revolution, it could hardly have appealed to him. By then, Michelet had left "the second stage" for some subjective realm of history outside Mill's scheme of things.[255] Mill was by no means unique in not foreseeing the direction Michelet's history was to take. Sponsored by Guizot, approved by Carrel, Michelet had seemed early on to be in sympathy with their views. His purposes, however, became increasingly nationalist, his vision narrowed, his mystic sense of himself embodying the past dithyrambic. What preoccupied him had little to do with the progress of civilization that concerned Mill.

Toward the end of his life, Mill noted that the French made too free with the phrase "the principles of the Revolution." It was the result of "an infirmity of the French mind which has been one main cause of the miscarriage of the French nation in its pursuit of liberty & progess: that of being led by phrases & treating abstractions as if they were realities which have a will & exert active power."[256] Almost certainly he thought Michelet a casualty of this defect. The originality and talent that he had recognized thirty years before in this review were clear. But there was in Michelet and his work a cast of mind profoundly antipathetical to Mill.[257]

---

[254]Letter to Michelet, *EL*, *CW*, XIII, 596 (12 Sept., 1842). Michelet's *Journal* contains only a single reference to Mill by name, at I, 814 (24 Sept., 1841).

[255]Identifying himself with his historical actors in a manner not entirely different from the style affected by Carlyle two decades earlier, Michelet reported his own harrowing revolutionary experiences to correspondents. Hence his celebrated wish that he be remembered for having discerned the goal of history: "Thierry l'appelait *narration*, et M. Guizot, *analyse*. Je l'ai nommé *résurrection*, et ce nom lui restera." ("A M. Edgar Quinet," *Le Peuple* [Paris: Didier, 1946], 25.)

[256]Letter to Thomas Smith, *LL*, *CW*, XVII, 1911 (4 Oct., 1872).

[257]After the shattering of his hopes for the February Revolution, Michelet was still more radicalized. He told his students in 1850 that his chair at the Collège de France was "not only a magistrature but a pontificate." His classroom was the scene of demonstrations; his lectures, reported a colleague, were "deplorable rhapsodies, mostly sheer nonsense . . . attaining a sort of fantastic madness." The faculty and administration wanted him disciplined, the government harassed him, the police attended his course. He was suspended in March 1851, dismissed in April 1852, and deprived

GUIZOT

Michelet owed much to Guizot: his position as royal tutor, his post at the Archives, his early opportunities at the Sorbonne, if not at the Collège de France. It was Guizot who suspended Michelet's lectures in 1847. Not remarkably, the protégé's estimate of his benefactor varied from one period to another: he both admired Guizot's work and dismissed it as grey. They could hardly have been more different. Though they had in common their commitment to written history as having a social purpose, their purposes were diametrically opposed.[258] Despite his clear reservations about the later work, Mill placed Michelet in the triumvirate with Augustin Thierry and Guizot, but he was clear that Guizot was the great historian of the age, "the one best adapted to this country." What raised him to the summit was the grasp he showed for "the main outline of history" (227, 228). Mill thought the framework he had established, showing the interplay of ideas and institutions, weighing the influence of Roman, Germanic, and Christian factors in European civilization, would endure. If history still had no Newton, Guizot was its "Kepler, and something more" (228). He accounted it one of his successes to "have dinned into people's ears that Guizot is a great thinker & writer," and so have been responsible for having him read in England.[259] Mill had not quite taken his measure at first. He seems to have discovered the historian, as distinct from the politician, about 1832. The first discussion of him was so infused with political comment that the exceptional historian Mill was shortly to proclaim was not easily recognized. Granting him "no ordinary knowledge of history" and "no ordinary powers of philosophizing" to analyse and explain, Mill criticized his understanding of the English constitution as "deficient." He had not even troubled to cross the Channel to inform himself. He was bracketed with the *doctrinaire* "speculators" who made 1688 their "*beau idéal*," purporting "to found their political wisdom principally on history, instead of looking to history merely for *suggestions*, to be brought to the test of a larger and surer experience."[260]

Guizot's political reputation with Mill rose and fell several times. Perceived on the eve of 1830 as a champion of liberty, he fell from grace in the first weeks of the new régime. In Mill's view, the brave workmen of Paris had driven Charles X out, only to see him replaced by the jobbers, including Guizot,

---

of his post at the Archives Nationales in June. (Kippur, *Jules Michelet*, 116-37, esp. 131, 133.) On his general development away from his earlier views, see Oscar H. Haac, *Les principes inspirateurs de Michelet* (Paris: Presses Universitaires de France, 1951). On other aspects of his broad intellectual activity, see Linda Orr, *Jules Michelet: Nature, History, and Language* (Ithaca: Cornell University Press, 1976).

[258]Johnson, *Guizot*, 370-4; Mellon, Editor's Introduction to Guizot, *Historical Essays and Lectures*, xxxix-xliv.

[259]Letter to R.B. Fox, *EL*, *CW*, XIII, 427 (16 Apr., 1840).

[260]Summary of French news, *Examiner*, 21 Oct., 1832, 680.

"a favourer of the new Aristocracy."[261] Among the new men providing for themselves and their friends was the Minister of the Interior; none "had so numerous a *coterie* as Monsieur and Madame Guizot."[262] Out of office for two years after 2 November, Guizot and his friends were denounced as trimmers, seeking a middle way between reaction and progress.[263] As Minister of Public Education in Soult's cabinet, Guizot struck Mill as dogmatic, offensive, professorial, and "probably at the moment the most unpopular man in France."[264] Mill did not comment on his education law, but he was aware of the important historical and archival work he had set afoot. His politics then appeared to be less of an issue. Through the later 1830s Mill transferred much of his former disapproval of Guizot to his fellow historian and political rival, Thiers.[265]

When Guizot left Paris to become Ambassador in London in February 1840 (and bide his time until Louis Philippe should summon him back to replace Thiers as Prime Minister), Mill was delighted. If Guizot knew of his caustic commentaries, he chose to overlook them. Visiting him, Mill found his conversation rewarding, up to his expectations, and his being in London "a real *événement*, for it makes our stupid incurious people read his books." He thought one could see the difference between France and England by comparing their respective "Conservative party" leaders, Guizot and Peel.[266] Mill's direct contact was short-lived. The diplomatic crisis with Great Britain that was to destroy Thiers's government ended Guizot's embassy in October 1840; he soon became the dominant figure in Soult's second cabinet until in 1847 he formed his own government that lasted until the Revolution of February 1848. Mill became deeply impressed, judging Guizot to be "the greatest public man living," and he recanted his past opinions. "I cannot think without humiliation," he wrote in 1840,

of some things I have written years ago of such a man as this, when I thought him a dishonest politician. I confounded the prudence of a wise man who lets some of his

---

[261]Letter to James Mill, *EL, CW,* XII, 60-1 (21 Aug., 1830).

[262]"Prospects of France," *Examiner,* 17 Oct., 1830, 660-1.

[263]Summary of French news, *ibid.,* 9 Jan., 1831, 25.

[264]Summary of French news, *ibid.,* 21 Oct., 1832, 680.

[265]"Thiers completely verifies the impression his history makes. Even among French ministers he *stands out,* conspicuously unprincipled." (Letter to Carlyle, *EL, CW,* XII, 220 [2 Mar., 1834].) All the same, Mill was of two minds about the historian: "We dislike M. Thiers' politics much, and his unbounded *suffisance* still more; but nobody [i.e., *The Times*] is entitled to speak scornfully of the author of the best history in the French language, and the best specimen of historical narrative, of any length, perhaps in all modern literature" (summary of French news, *Examiner,* 21 Oct., 1832, 680). Then, twelve years later: "Thiers is inaccurate, but less so than Sir Walter Scott" (221). Of the parliamentary events that brought Thiers and his followers into office in March 1840, he wrote: "It is a great event, & makes me recur to what I have so often thought, *les choses marchent vîte en France* (& in this age, altogether one may add)" (letter to d'Eichthal, *EL, CW,* XIII, 433 [7 May, 1840]). His attacks on "ce petit fripon" (letter to Adolphe Narcisse Thibaudeau, *ibid.,* XII, 291 [1836?]) were to grow again during the eastern crisis that summer of 1840.

[266]Letter to d'Eichthal, *EL, CW,* XIII, 438-9 (17 June, 1840).

maxims go to sleep while the time is unpropitious for asserting them, with the laxity of principle which resigns them for personal advancement. Thank God I did not wait to know him personally in order to do him justice, for in 1838 & 1839 I saw that he had reasserted all his old principles at the first time at which he could do so with success & without compromising what in his view were more important principles still. I ought to have known better than to have imputed dishonourable inconsistency to a man whom I now see to have been consistent beyond any statesman of our time & altogether a model of the consistency of a statesman as distinguished from that of a fanatic.[267]

This extraordinary disavowal of his previous observations was not to be the last word. Even under the spell of immediate contact, Mill said, that though he honoured and venerated him above all contemporary statesmen, "I differ from many of his opinions."[268] Some time later when Comte registered his complaints of mistreatment at the minister's hands, Mill expressed his "impression pénible" that a great scholar should show "l'esprit de secte" toward a blameless philosopher.[269] A renewed reserve showed, whether because of the Comte affair or the unyielding domestic policies of the Soult-Guizot government. Explaining his inability to provide an introduction to Guizot for John Austin, he said his acquaintance with the minister was "so very slight," and received Sarah Austin's report of his "elevated moral character" coolly. Four years after the enthusiastic recognition of Guizot's true distinction, Mill remarked evenly, "A man in such a position as his, acts under so many difficulties, and is mixed up in so many questionable transactions that one's favourable opinion is continually liable to receive shocks, and I have for many years been oscillating in Guizot's case between great esteem and considerable misgivings." Still, he was ready to take the largest view, admitting, "If he was an angel he would be sure to be misunderstood in the place he is in. I do not know whether to wish or to deprecate [the possibility of] his being thrown out of it. . . ."[270]

That same year, 1845, Mill published his lengthy review of Guizot's essays and lectures. Ten years before he had commissioned the Rev. Joseph Blanco White to review the lectures. He had found White's paper "still wanting to give a complete notion of the nature & value of Guizot's historical speculations," and had himself added several pages at the beginning and the end.[271] In these pages Mill had condemned "the profoundly immoral, as well as despotic *régime* which France is now enduring." Calling the July Monarchy "an imitation" of the

---

[267]Letter to R.B. Fox, *ibid.*, 454-5 (23 Dec., 1840). Mill was not alone in succumbing. Jules Simon would say: "On était tout surpris et charmé, quand on pénétrait dans son intimité, de le trouver simple, gai, bienveillant, et même caressant" (Simon, *Thiers, Guizot, Rémusat*, 2nd ed. [Paris: Calmann Lévy, 1855], 20). This was not Daumier's view.
[268]Letter to d'Eichthal, *EL, CW*, XIII, 457 (25 Dec., 1840).
[269]Letter to A. Comte, *ibid.*, 518-19 (6 May, 1842).
[270]Letter to S. Austin, *ibid.*, 653-4 (18 Jan., 1845).
[271]Letters to J.B. White, *ibid.*, XII, 259, 264, 280, 285 (15 Apr., 19 May, 21 Oct., 24 Nov., 1835).

Empire, he had accused it of seducing France's distinguished men by office. He had had harsh words for Guizot:

In the capacity of a tool of this system, though we believe him to be greatly more sincere than most of the other tools, we have nothing to say for M. Guizot. But in the more honourable character which he had earned for himself as a professor and as a literary man, before practical politics assailed him with their temptations and their corrupting influences, he deserves to be regarded with very different feelings. (370.)

The puzzle was that, though deeply attached to his principles, he supported institutions that repressed them; he knew the dangers of power, but did nothing to save himself from them. "Alas! we must say of M. Guizot, what he so feelingly and truly has declared of Italy—'*Il lui manque la foi, la foi dans la vérité!*'" (392.)

Such had been Mill's sentiment at the beginning of 1836. Not quite a decade later, his long essay was free of censure of the politician. Rather, he cleared away the past with a reference to Guizot's work as Foreign Minister in resolving the Anglo-French crisis after 1840: the statesman "to whom perhaps more than to any other it is owing that Europe is now at peace" (259). Mill could then get on with the business of publicizing Guizot as the most significant historian of the age. It was high time: the printed lectures being discussed were first delivered almost a generation before.

After the ritual comparison of the state of historical studies in France, Germany, and England (even "insular England" was, thanks to Coleridge and "the Oxford school of theologians," stirring in the right direction [261]), Mill proposed that Guizot's chief quality was that he asked the right questions. Thus he had been able in the early essays to tell more about the fall of Rome than had Gibbon. The laws, not the chronicles, contained the clue: when despotism destroyed the middle-class *curiales*, it extinguished the Empire's vitality. Seeking the dynamic of civilization, Guizot found it in the "systematic antagonism" of ideas and institutions (269). The mark of Europe had always been complexity and competition. The spirit of liberty emerged not from the ancient world but from the barbarian invaders and was borne through the centuries by the struggles of the middle class. Mill accepted Guizot's organization of European history into "the period of confusion, the feudal period, and the modern period" (274), which became a received view in the nineteenth century. He followed his argument without serious disagreement, save for the explanation of feudalism's fall. This he thought unconvincing; he probably disliked its political implications. The feudal system succumbed, in Mill's view, not because unequal claims and unequal power led to unequal rights and so to the acceptance of royal authority, but because pressure was exerted from the monarch above and the freemen below, and because feudalism "contained within itself a sufficient mixture of authority and liberty, afforded sufficient protection to industry, and encouragement and scope to the development of the human faculties, to enable the natural causes of social improvement to resume their course" (289).

"Writing the history of France," Fustel de Coulanges was to say, "was a way of working for a party and fighting an adversary."[272] If Mill observed as much, he did not comment on it. He could not know that Guizot told Charles de Rémusat that his lectures at the Sorbonne (in 1820) were designed to "multiply 'doctrinaires' under the very fire of the enemy."[273] "On vient de suspendre mon cours," Guizot wrote Barante, after the axe fell two years later. "Je regrette un peu cette petite tribune d'où j'exerçais encore quelque action directe sur des hommes qui se mêleront de l'avenir."[274] Mill appears not to have discerned any narrow political or social purpose in Guizot's interpretation of the contradictions of the past working themselves out: national reconciliation on the terms of those who had borne liberty through the centuries and were best qualified to assure it.[275] Guizot had affected an impartiality of tone unknown in Thierry, let alone Michelet. The essays and lectures appeared to be dispassionate, founded on immense reading, an explanation to a middle-class generation asking in the aftermath of an unprecedented cultural and political upheaval who they were and where they came from. Guizot saw himself engaged in the task of philosophical history, investigating not its "anatomy," or its "physiognomy," but its "physiology." He was showing the interrelatedness of the events that made up the history of civilization. "Au commencement de ce cours," he told the audience that attended his lectures on Saturday mornings, 1828-30:

je n'ai cherché que les résultats généraux, l'enchaînement des causes et des effets, le progrès de la civilisation, caché sous les scènes extérieures de l'histoire; quant aux scènes mêmes, j'ai supposé que vous les connaissiez. . . . L'histoire proprement dite

[272]Translated by Johnson, *Guizot*, 322, from Numa Denis Fustel de Coulanges, "Chronique," *Revue des Deux Mondes*, CI (1 Sept., 1872), 243. On Guizot as historian, see Johnson's balanced appraisal, *Guizot*, 320-76; and the comments in Leonard Krieger's Preface and Mellon's Editor's Introduction to Guizot, *Historical Essays and Lectures*, ix-xlv. On Guizot's historiographical inheritance at the moment of his dismissal from the Conseil d'Etat in 1820, see Shirley M. Gruner, "Political Historiography in Restoration France," *History and Theory*, VIII (1969), 346-65.

[273]Quoted in E.L. Woodward, *Three Studies in European Conservatism: Metternich, Guizot, the Catholic Church in the Nineteenth Century* (London: Constable, 1929), 133, from a letter to Charles de Rémusat (1820).

[274]Letter to Prosper de Barante of 22 Oct., 1822, *Souvenirs du baron de Barante*, III, 50.

[275]Guizot was adamant: "Je n'ai, de ma vie, prostitué l'histoire au service de la politique. Mais quand l'histoire parle, il est bon que la politique écoute." (Quoted in Rut Keiser, *Guizot als Historiker* [n.p.: Saint-Louis, 1925], 38n.) In the 1857 preface to his lectures, Guizot wrote: "C'est la rivalité aveugle des hautes classes sociales qui a fait échouer parmi nous les essais de gouvernement libre. . . . Pour le vulgaire plaisir de rester, les uns impertinents, les autres envieux, nobles et bourgeois ont été infiniment moins libres, moins grands, moins assurés dans leurs biens sociaux qu'ils n'auraient pu l'être avec un peu plus de justice, de prévoyance et de soumission aux lois divines des sociétés humaines. Ils n'ont pas su agir de concert pour être libres et puissants ensemble; ils se sont livrés et ils ont livré la France aux révolutions." (*Mémoires pour servir à l'histoire de mon temps*, 8 vols. in 4 [Paris: Michel Lévy, 1858-70], I, 294-6.) "Guizot," Faguet remarked, "est un penseur réprimé par un homme d'Etat" (Emile Faguet, *Politiques et moralistes du dix-neuvième siècle*, 1st ser. [Paris: Société française d'imprimerie et de librairie, 1901], 367).

enveloppe et couvre l'histoire de la civilisation. Celle-ci ne vous sera pas claire si l'autre ne vous est pas présente; je ne puis vous raconter les événemens et vous avez besoin de les savoir. . . .[276]

Mill noted certain exaggerations; he put them down to the necessities of the lecture. The breadth of Guizot's generalizations seemed to place them above particular pleading. With Guizot's argument that French civilization exemplified better than any other the very essence of civilization ("C'est la plus complète, la plus vraie, la plus civilisée, pour ainsi dire")[277] Mill was in agreement. He did not so much question Guizot's assumptions as share them. He, too, believed that history had a rational structure and so would yield to rational inquiry. He, too, believed that the history of Europe was the history of universal principles working their way through a variety of circumstances. Both of them believed in the phenomenon of the great man who affects the course of history in the service of the tendency of his time, who embodies the dominant principles of the age.

Guizot, however, was a Calvinist: he assumed the existence of God without claiming to know his motives or his precise effect on men's actions. In opposition, deprived of his teaching post by the University, he had been inclined to minimize the latitude left to individuals. No other time, he said somewhat extravagantly, had been so marked by "l'empreinte de la fatalité." Events seemed to happen by themselves: "jamais la conduite des choses humaines n'a plus complètement échappé aux hommes. . . . Ils ne sont aujourd'hui que de vieilles marionnettes effacées, absolument étrangères aux scènes que la Providence leur fait jouer."[278] In office, however, the specific purposes of the Almighty appeared rather more clear. "La mission des gouvernements," Guizot told the Chamber on 3 May, 1837, "n'est pas laissée à leur choix, elle est réglée en haut. C'est la Providence qui détermine dans quelle étendue se passent les affaires d'un grand peuple."[279] And on the eve of assuming the powers of Prime Minister, in the eastern crisis of 1840, with war and peace in the balance, he reflected: "Nous sommes des instruments entre les mains d'une Puissance supérieure qui nous emploie, selon ou contre notre goût, à l'usage pour lequel elle nous a faits. . . ."[280] But Providence was remote, men were responsible, they made their own history. All they had to bear in mind were the natural limits to their presumptions: "La bonne politique consiste à reconnaître d'avance ces nécessités naturelles qui, méconnues, deviendraient plus tard des leçons divines, et à y conformer de bonne grâce sa conduite."[281] Mill would not have put it that

---

[276]François Guizot, *Cours d'histoire moderne: Histoire de la civilisation en France depuis la chute de l'empire romain jusqu'en 1789*, 5 vols. (Paris: Pichon and Didier, 1829-32), II, 267-8.

[277]*Ibid.*, I, 26.

[278]Letter to Barante of 20 Oct., 1822, *Souvenirs du baron de Barante*, III, 49.

[279]Quoted in Agénor Bardoux, *Guizot* (Paris: Hachette, 1894), 180.

[280]Letter to the princesse de Lieven (1 Oct., 1833), *Lettres de François Guizot*, II, 240.

[281]François Guizot, *Monk: Chute de la république et rétablissement de la monarchie en Angleterre en 1660* (Paris: Didier, 1851), ix-xi.

way, of course, but Guizot's faith did not obviously intrude on his history. Despite the philosophy informing his conception of the past, he wrote something approaching what in the next century would be called "technical history."[282]

Mill's disappointment with Guizot's intransigent conservatism may have followed from unwillingness to recognize the implication of the historian's philosophy of history. The Germans, it has been said, conceived of history as "une lutte entre des principes opposées" without necessarily leading to the impasse of the July Monarchy.[283] That may be so, but undeniably there was a spaciousness and a cosmopolitanism in Guizot, an austere parade of certainty and equanimity in this early work that appealed to Mill.[284] He discerned consistency, comprehensiveness, maturity, the "entire absence of haste or crudity" as the hallmark of "a connected body of thought, speculations which, even in their unfinished state, may be ranked with the most valuable contributions yet made to universal history" (259). Possibly the fact that the lectures were incomplete, that the treacherous passages of modern history were not negotiated, averted more serious disagreement between Mill and Guizot. "The rapid sketch which occupies the concluding lectures of the first volume," Mill noted, "does little towards resolving any of the problems in which there is real difficulty" (290).

The "manière 'fataliste' d'envisager l'histoire"[285] that the pre-1830 liberals shared exercised an immense attraction for Mill partly because, to a point, he and they were bound on the same road, partly because they spoke so well and with such assurance. Guizot, as Sainte-Beuve said, put himself "insensiblement en lieu et place de la Providence."[286] A moralist, like Mill, he also saw the social destination in terms of political and constitutional arrangements. What Mill was evidently reluctant to concede—and how could it be proved true?—was the possibility that, in Emile Faguet's formula,

[282]Herbert Butterfield, *Christianity and History* (London: Bell, 1949), 19-25.

[283]Edouard Fueter, *Histoire de l'historiographie moderne* (Paris: Alcan, 1914), 634. Cf.: "L'idéal orléaniste tend à stériliser la curiosité historique. 1830 a donné la solution définitive des conflits séculaires entre les Français et leur dynastie, démontrent A. Thierry et Guizot: une sorte de fin de l'histoire, compensée par l'autosatisfaction et les honneurs officiels. Le finalisme bourgeois, après 1830, prend un caractère tout rétrospectif." (Gérard, *La révolution française*, 38.) Guizot put it more personally and succinctly: "Je suis de ceux que l'élan de 1789 a élevés et qui ne consentiront point à descendre" (*Mémoires pour servir à l'histoire de mon temps*, I, 27).

[284]"Il comprend beaucoup de choses," Charles de Rémusat said, "et se pique de comprendre tout. . . . Il a l'air de tout dominer, d'avoir vu le terme et le faible de tout, approfondi toutes les questions et pris sur toutes des conclusions; mais on voit bientôt ses limites." (*Mémoires de ma vie*, 5 vols. [Paris: Plon, 1958-67], I, 440, 446.)

[285]Halphen, *L'histoire en France depuis cent ans*, 34-5. He adds: "jamais sans doute l'histoire n'a été à un pareil degré infestée de maximes politiques ou de généralités philosophiques. . . . Philosopher était devenu une mode à laquelle presque aucun historien ne croyait pouvoir se soustraire." (*Ibid.*, 38-9.)

[286]Sainte-Beuve, "Discours sur l'histoire de la révolution d'Angleterre par M. Guizot" (4 Feb., 1850), *Causeries du lundi*, I, 317.

Il est bien rare que pour un homme politique l'histoire soit autre chose que de la politique rétrospective. Elle lui sert d'argument, de point de départ pour sa déduction, et de preuve à l'appui de ce qu'il veut lui faire dire. Elle est, à ses yeux, destinée à le justifier, à l'expliquer et à le préparer. Il est bien difficile que pour M. Guizot l'histoire universelle, ou au moins l'histoire moderne, ne soit pas une introduction au gouvernement de M. Guizot.[287]

In Mill, the reformer and the amateur of history were sometimes at odds. Guizot felt no such tension: the nineteenth century was the heir of a long struggle; the *juste milieu* must hold firm against careless new men and upstart ideologies. "L'histoire," he remarked, "abât les prétentions impatientes et soutient les longues espérances."[288] This appeal to something like a *moyenne* if not a *longue durée* was Guizot's principal attraction for Mill.[289] The immediate political and social implications of it for his own time posed a problem. Thus Mill wished always to separate the politician from the historian, save for the moment around 1840 when, suppressing his previous criticisms, he achieved an unstable rationalization of his doubts about the man. In this way he kept his clear and generous view of the historian.[290] Comparing him with Thierry, Mignet, Thiers, even with Vico, Herder and Condorcet, he considered Guizot to be "a man of a greater range of ideas and greater historical impartiality than most of these." For his "immortal Essays and Lectures" posterity would "forgive him the grave faults of his political career" (185, 186). Mill had many contradictory thoughts about Guizot, but there is no reason to think he ever went back on that.

---

[287]Faguet, *Politiques et moralistes*, 328.

[288]Quoted in Bardoux, *Guizot*, 124.

[289]Fernand Braudel, "Histoire et sciences sociales: la longue durée," in his *Ecrits sur l'histoire* (Paris: Flammarion, 1969), 41-83.

[290]He did so even when blaming him for the intrigue surrounding the Spanish marriages in 1846. With Sir Robert Peel as Prime Minister and Lord Aberdeen at the Foreign Office, Guizot had achieved relatively good relations with England. The return of Palmerston in June 1846 altered affairs. For years, Britain and France had jockeyed in Madrid to assert their control and influence the marriage of the Queen. Guizot had backed the suit of the duc de Montpensier, Louis Philippe's son; Aberdeen supported a Coburg prince. Amidst a welter of intrigue, the French ambassador proposed that Isabella marry an effeminate relative and, simultaneously, her sister Luisa marry Montpensier: Isabella would have no children, and the throne would then pass to Louis Philippe's grandson. By late 1845, both Victoria and Louis Philippe and their governments had thought neither the Coburg nor the Orleanist suitors of Isabella would be put forward, but when Palmerston returned to office and clumsily reintroduced Leopold of Coburg's name, Louis Philippe and Guizot concluded they had been duped, the Madrid scheme was approved, and the marriages took place on 10 October, 1846. Naturally, the English also believed they had been duped. Mill judged unfairly that Guizot "is evidently not above low tricks & equivocations, which seem to be quite excused to every Frenchman by their being for the supposed honour & glory of France. Guizot I wished to think better of, but after all this only brings me back, and that not altogether, to my first opinion of him, which some parts of his public conduct from 1839 downwards had modified." (Letter to J. Austin, *EL, CW*, XIII, 714 [13 Apr., 1847].) See Johnson, *Guizot*, 300-9; Seton-Watson, *Britain in Europe*, 242-8; Muriel E. Chamberlain, *Lord Aberdeen: A Political Biography* (London: Longman, 1983), 343-89; Jasper Ridley, *Lord Palmerston* (London: Constable, 1970), 303-20.

MILL AND THE END OF THE JULY MONARCHY

COMING TO TERMS WITH GUIZOT, as he seemed to do from the late 1830s, Mill was trying to come to terms with the July Monarchy. As the years passed and his health became indifferent, it was more difficult to sustain the same concern. The young liberals of the Bourbon restoration had dispersed variously to university chairs, archives, the ministerial bench. Saint-Simonism, imaginative and far-sighted, so clear about what had actually happened in 1830, had quickly burnt itself out in sectarianism and scattered, part of it to pursue bizarre eccentricities, part of it powerfully to influence the national economy. Comte, like the Saint-Simonians, had revealed a strong anti-libertarian streak and been dropped. Carrel was dead. With Tocqueville relations were more distant. The press remained vigorous and combative. Though Marrast had grown more moderate after his period of exile in England, new opposition papers sprang up. The King and his ministers were harried without cease.[291] Still, history was not repeating itself. Mill observed the scene more remotely. He maintained contact with a few friends in France, but he had little to say.

DUVEYRIER

Three years older than Mill, Duveyrier had come into his life with Gustave d'Eichthal as co-leader of the first mission sent by Père Enfantin to bring about the conversion of England. The Saint-Simonians believed that amidst the Reform Bill agitation England was about to pull down the last bastions of feudal power and so offer herself to the new teaching. Without having encouraged their embassy, Mill had been helpful once they arrived and handed them on to people he supposed might hear them out. He had made it plain he was unlikely to become a convert, though he read *Le Globe*, considered them "decidedly *à la tête de la civilisation*," and thought their organization would one day be "the final and permanent condition of the human race." He admired them and wished them well, but he kept his distance; their doctrine was "only *one* among a variety of interesting and important features in the time we live in."[292] Their optimistic reports to Enfantin were belied; England was not ripe. Mill did not make good his promise of articles on them for the *Morning Chronicle*. In the scandal of their prosecution, Duveyrier was specifically charged with outrage for the article "De la femme" he published in *Le Globe* in 1832 shortly before it ceased publication. Mill was cool, perhaps sensing the oddly regimented and ritualistic social

---

[291]Collins, *The Government and the Newspaper Press*, 82-99; Ledré, *La presse à l'assaut de la monarchie*, 125-95.

[292]Letter to d'Eichthal, *EL, CW*, XII, 88-9 (30 Nov., 1831); letter to d'Eichthal and Duveyrier, *ibid.*, 108 (30 May, 1832).

arrangements in the barracks at Ménilmontant (lights out at 9:30 p.m., reveille at 4:30 a.m.).[293] Nearly everything about the dispensation at Ménilmontant must have seemed alien to Mill, not merely the flamboyant dress and liturgy of the sect, but also the untoward scenes its exercises provoked when thousands of Parisians flocked out to observe the public rites of its priesthood.

In the trial, which took place on 27 and 28 August, 1832, Duveyrier had a prominent role. The son of the *premier président* of the Cour Royale at Montpellier, he had studied the Christian mystics and, in observance of the Saint-Simonian rule that each member proclaim his acceptance of responsibility before God and man by bearing his name on his breast, had affected the inscription "Charles, poète de Dieu." At one moment during the proceedings, he caused a sensation by pointing to a group of lawyers in the visitors' section of the courtroom and shouting, "I told them when I came in that I am being charged with saying that everyone was living in a state of prostitution and adultery, but you are in fact all living in that state. Well, have the courage to say so out loud. That is the only way you can defend us."[294] Like Enfantin and Michel Chevalier, Duveyrier was sentenced to a year in prison and a fine of 1000 francs. The organization was ordered dissolved. Duveyrier, however, obtained a pardon through his family, probably, as Mill supposed, by renouncing allegiance to Enfantin.[295] With d'Eichthal, he went off to Naples for a time before returning to Paris and a career in journalism and writing for the theatre. He assured Mill that although he had not changed "a single opinion," he had changed "his whole line of conduct."[296] Mill, however, appeared to be more surprised than pleased by the news of Duveyrier's apparent defection. The report that some of the faithful had set out for the Bosphorus "*pour chercher la femme libre* suggested greater madness than I had imputed to them."[297]

Mill's correspondence contains no further reference to him, but he evidently kept up with Duveyrier's activity. Two books appeared, the first in 1842 and the second in 1843. In the spring of 1844, Mill began his article on the second of them, *Lettres politiques*, a collection of Duveyrier's pamphlets. He told Napier, "It is the last I mean to write, for the present on any French topic—& its subject is, not French history or literature, but present French politics, introducing, however, remarks & speculations of a more general character."[298] This was one

---

[293]Letter to Carlyle, *ibid.*, 105-6 (29 May, 1832). "The poor Saint-Simonians," Carlyle wrote. "Figure Duveyrier, with waiter's apron, emptying slop pails,—for the salvation of a world" (letter to Mill, *Collected Letters*, VI, 174-5 [16 June, 1832]). See also Manuel, *Prophets of Paris*, 308-9.

[294]Manuel, *Prophets of Paris*, 186, citing *Procès en la cour d'assises de la Seine, les 27 et 28 août* (Paris, 1832), 194. See Pankhurst, *The Saint-Simonians, Mill and Carlyle*, 84-100; Mill to Carlyle, *EL, CW*, XII, 119-20 (17 Sept., 1832).

[295]Letter to Carlyle, *EL, CW*, XII, 150 (11-12 Apr., 1833).

[296]Letters to Carlyle, *ibid.*, 133, 139-40, 150 (27 Dec., 1832, 2 Feb., 11-12 Apr., 1833).

[297]Letter to Carlyle, *ibid.*, 150 (11-12 Apr., 1833).

[298]Letter to M. Napier, *ibid.*, XIII, 684 (27 Oct., 1845).

more mirror held up to view the reflection of representative government and its dilemmas in the aftermath of the Revolution and in the presence of democracy.

France remained instructive because it had swept away all the institutions other nations were then only dismantling and had a "passion for equality almost as strong" as that of the United States (297). Disapproving Duveyrier's flattery of the crown and the government, Mill was more open to his acceptance of the existing constitution and his insistence that the question was how to make the system work efficiently, how to free electors, ministers, and people from the burden of corruption. Everywhere, including England, "Sincere Democrats are beginning to doubt whether the *desideratum* is so much an increased influence of popular opinion, as a more enlightened use of the power which it already possesses." But he condemned the narrow suffrage in France, the repressive legislation, "the disgraceful manner" in which the system worked (300). He was receptive to Duveyrier's suggestion that the landed proprietors should be encouraged back into public life alongside the bourgeoisie; that trained functionaries be guaranteed "fixity," responsibility, and adequate salaries; and that the electoral process be permitted to operate absolutely without official meddling. He remarked that this vision of a society presided over by a neo-Saint-Simonian élite was "a favourable specimen" of French thought applied to the practical problems of government (313).

To Duveyrier's parallel argument that, since the old foreign policies were as defunct as the old régimes, France must abandon territorial ambitions and the revanchism dating from 1815 and join with the other great powers to bring about political and economic peace through arbitration and mediation, Mill was not receptive. He thought such interventionism unwise, though superior to war. He gave no hint of anticipating the trend of international co-operation that was to gather strength through the second half of the century.[299] Nor did he show confidence in Duveyrier's suggestions that government arbitrate labour-management disputes, though he approved the programme of "*justice and compromise.*" The tone here was quiet, interested, but faintly disabused. Mill neither accepted the political quiescence of Duveyrier nor suggested the need for drastic change. He believed that the problems of representation were similar in England and France, but more sharply defined and more clearly observed in the French context. Neither Duveyrier nor Mill gave the least hint of an upheaval soon to come. Duveyrier argued specifically against the utility of another such event. It would be more than a dozen years before Mill conceded, not just for England

---

[299]Mill had a "passage controverting the warlike propensity of the French" that Napier removed. He did not complain, but defended his point of view ("a very old & firm one with me") that the French did not necessarily seek prestige through war, saying he thought the *Edinburgh Review* had recently been "very unjust" (letter to M. Napier, *ibid.*, 701 [1 May, 1846]). On Mill's "realistic" views on international relations, see Kenneth E. Miller, "John Stuart Mill's Theory of International Relations," *Journal of the History of Ideas*, XXII, no. 4 (1961), 493-514.

with its tradition of compromise and its history of successful opposition to monarchical absolutism, but for every nation, the rightness of working for improvement within the prevailing arrangements.[300] But it was less Charles Duveyrier, or John Austin, than the events of 1848 that convinced him.

MILL AND THE REVOLUTION OF 1848

TEN MONTHS before Louis Philippe was forced to abdicate, Mill remarked to Austin that while doubtless he, living in France, was "much impressed with the unfavourable side" of France after a number of revolutions, with vulgar lower-class ambition and other "disgusting" manners, he (Mill) often thought England's "torpid mind" would profit from "the general shake-up" of revolution. He gave no hint of thinking that France would profit from a renewal of the experience. In April 1847, the overall prospect there struck him as fair: the people were generally free of tyranny, justice was "easily accessible," and there were "the strongest inducements to personal prudence & forethought." Not even a well-intentioned government, but only revolution (that is, 1830) could have achieved as much.[301] He seemed to be reassessing the July Monarchy again. The remarks were puzzling. Mill made no allusion to the serious depression of 1845-47: an immense fall in French production, large-scale unemployment, a substantial part of the swollen population in the capital on relief, great rural distress and unrest. In three months the first of the electoral reform banquets, devised to circumvent the restrictive law on political associations, was held on 9 July at the Château-Rouge, the famous dancehall in Montmartre, with 1200 constituents and eighty-five deputies in attendance; almost seventy banquets took place outside Paris before the end of the year. Mill of course was by no means exceptional in apprehending no general crisis; others closer to the scene than he were hardly less unaware.[302] But his observations were indicative of the concentration of his thought on the political process. He had never looked very far past the political scene in the capital. Thus he missed the profound movement that was taking place in the country. He followed the press to some extent, a steady diet of scandal and complaint, an endless skirmishing between the government and the opposition. There is no evidence that he noted the near-unity of the varieties of opposition in the banquet campaign as a possible signal that a trial of strength was at hand.

---

[300]Mill, "Recent Writers on Reform" (1859), *CW*, XIX, 352.

[301]Letter to J. Austin, *EL*, *CW*, XIII, 713-14 (13 Apr., 1847).

[302]Benjamin Rush, United States Minister in France, wrote in December 1847: "If I looked to the country, instead of the newspapers or speeches at political banquets, I should have thought I had come to a country abounding in prosperity of every kind and full of contentment" (quoted by Priscilla Robertson, *Revolutions of 1848: A Social History* [Princeton: Princeton University Press, 1952], 13).

The explosion took him by surprise. Guizot was dismissed on 23 February; the King abdicated next day. "I am hardly yet out of breath from reading and thinking about it," Mill reported on 29 February. "Nothing can possibly exceed the importance of it to the world or the immensity of the interests which are at stake on its success." He saw the Revolution in political terms: the King and his ministers had provoked "the people" by forbidding the Paris banquet; the republicans had triumphed "because *at last* they had the good sense to raise the standard not of a republic but of something in which the middle classes could join, viz., electoral reform." Should they succeed in creating "reasonable republican government, all the rest of Europe, except England and Russia, will be republicanised in ten years, and England itself probably before we die." But he saw three problems ahead: the possibility of war, the matter of socialism, the question of leadership. First, Lamartine might be propelled into war with Austria as the result of popular pressure to help the Milanese expel the Habsburg occupant from Lombardy. Second, "Communism," by which he evidently meant everything from Fourierism to Proudhonism,[303] had taken "deep root" in the country and in the republican ranks. How, despite the vague announcement that the Provisional Government would establish *ateliers nationaux*, would the new men make good their promise to provide "work and good wages to the whole labouring class"? Third, Marrast and even the former Orleanist Lamartine ("who would ever have thought it—Lamartine!") were well enough as ministers, but something was missing: "In my meditations and feelings on the whole matter, every second thought has been of Carrel—he who perhaps alone in Europe was qualified to direct such a movement. . . . Without Carrel, or, I fear, any one comparable to him, the futurity of France and of Europe is most doubtful." His words suggested again the excitement of 1830, but muted, infused with only a limited awareness of the enormous social problems, qualified by doubt about the middle-aged men of the Provisional Government. "There never was a time," Mill thought, "when so great a drama was being played out in one generation."[304]

---

[303]Fourierism, like Saint-Simonism, he found "totally free from the objections usually urged against Communism." He admired its "great intellectual power" and its "large and philosophic treatment of some of the fundamental problems of society and morality." It was not in contradiction with "any of the general laws by which human action, even in the present imperfect state of moral and intellectual cultivation, is influenced," and needed "opportunity of trial." (*Principles of Political Economy, CW*, II-III [Toronto: University of Toronto Press, 1965], II, 210, 213.) He thought, however, that "many of the details *are*, & all *appear*, passablement ridicules," and he had doubts about the missing element of "*moral sense*" ("Nobody is ever to be made to do anything but act just as they like. . . ."). Not fancifully, therefore, he asked whether it was "a foundation on which people would be able to live & act together" (letter to Harriet Taylor, *CW*, XIV, 21-2 [c. 31 Mar., 1849]). In the same consideration, however, Mill made short shrift of Proudhon: "I heartily wish Proudhon dead . . . there are few men whose state of mind, taken as a whole, inspires me with so much aversion, & all his influence seems to me mischievous except as a potent *dissolvent* which is good so far, but every single thing which he would substitute seems to me the worst possible in practice & mostly in principle" (*ibid.*, 21).

[304]Letter to Henry S. Chapman, *EL, CW*, XIII, 731-2 (29 Feb., 1848).

After Lamartine had moved to assure Europe that France would not abet a war of Italian liberation,[305] Mill was satisfied the government would act wisely. If there was to be "a good deal of experimental legislation, some of it not very prudent," he noted unenthusiastically, "there cannot be a better place to try such experiments in than France." He was sure that the "regulation of industry in behalf of the labourers" would fail as it had "in behalf of the capitalist," or at least be trimmed to "its proper limits." But he was greatly confident that what would be tried "relating to labour & wages" would "end in good."[306] In early March he made a public defence of the government's action in the *Spectator*.[307] But through the stormy spring of demonstrations, attempted coups, intense debate on the social question, national elections with universal male suffrage, and rising discontent among the swiftly growing army of the urban unemployed, he made no further comment.

As it happened, the drama of the Revolution was reaching its climax with the elections to a National Assembly. The broad tide of rural conservatism that came in was in protest against neglect of the interests of the countryside by an urban leadership. Mill's reaction is not recorded.[308] To judge from Harriet Taylor's remarks, however,[309] he may well have approved of, first, the moderate course pursued against radical opinion, and, second, the conservative Executive Commission selected by the Assembly to replace the Provisional Government. In his view, Lamartine, now out of office, had done no more than repeat the Girondist strategy of calling in provincial France to hold the line against the revolutionary political clubs of Paris. In fact, the Revolution was now bound on a course leading to destruction of the Republic.

Mill followed events distantly. He knew that Marrast was no longer at the *National*, had left the Government, and was Mayor of Paris (he was also the real leader of the majority in the Executive Commission). Mill nevertheless sent him a copy of his *Principles of Political Economy*, published on 25 April, saying he knew Marrast might not have time to read it but might perhaps have others do so, and asked if he could use his influence to have the *National* take his articles, as "lettres d'un Anglais," which would be done in the newspaper's style. The moment was as ill-chosen as Mill's expression of his "sympathie profonde" for

[305]See Lawrence C. Jennings, *France and Europe in 1848: A Study of French Foreign Affairs in Time of Crisis* (Oxford: Clarendon Press, 1973), 1-23.

[306]Letters to S. Austin, *EL, CW*, XIII, 733-4 (7 and ? Mar., 1848).

[307]Letter to the editor of the *Spectator*, XXI, 18 Mar., 1848, 273.

[308]Even professional revolution-watchers could miss the significance; thus Friedrich Engels: "In the National Assembly only one new element is to be added—peasants, who constitute five-sevenths of the French nation and are for the petty-bourgeois party of the *National*" (letter to Emil Blank of 28 Mar., 1848, in Karl Marx and Friedrich Engels, *Selected Correspondence* [Moscow: Foreign Languages Publishing House, n.d.], 55).

[309]The labour question "has been so well placed on the tapis by the noble spectacle of France ('spite of Pol^l Eco^y blunders) that there is no doubt of its continuing *the* great question until the hydra-headed selfishness of the idle classes is crushed by the demands of the lower" (letter from Harriet Taylor to W.J. Fox of 12 May, 1848, in Hayek, *John Stuart Mill and Harriet Taylor*, 123-4).

"l'oeuvre de régénération sociale qui se poursuit maintenant en France" was inappropriate to the reaction then under way in the country, the Assembly, and the Government, and to which Marrast was no stranger.[310] The Mayor was up to his neck in politics and the situation in Paris was extremely volatile. Within a few days, on 15 May, an abortive left-wing *coup d'état* occurred: the Assembly was invaded by a mob and some of the crowd went on to the Hôtel de Ville. There the security chief, an old friend of one of the leaders, Armand Barbès, admitted this rag-tag band. Marrast was evidently not very upset; he temporized, summoned military assistance, and at length sent word through his secretary that the invaders should leave: "Que Barbès fasse au plus tôt cesser cette comédie, il va être arrêté d'un moment à l'autre."[311] It was farce, but it was indicative of what was on Marrast's mind.

Mill could have no knowledge of the extraordinary political manoeuvrings in Paris. When he assured Marrast of his "sympathie profonde," he could not have understood that the tide had turned. Alarmed by the numbers of unemployed men in the city, the government announced its intention of closing the *ateliers nationaux*. With that, a spontaneous working-class insurrection was mounted against it, on 23-26 June. The pitched battles that took place made it the bloodiest fratricidal rising the capital had known. The government was legitimately defending itself, but the repression was severe and the social fears unleashed were exaggerated. A confusion of motives and hostilities were at the origin of this disastrous collision, in the course of which the Executive Commission retired, leaving General Eugène Cavaignac chief of the executive power, for all practical purposes dictator, with a new ministry round him.[312] Mill made no comment, but in August he lashed out publicly against the English enemies of the Republic and the misrepresentation of events. Alluding to the régime's "first difficulties" and the dangers of "an indefinite succession of disorders, repressed only by a succession of illegal violences on the part of the government," he denied (mistakenly) tales of "horrible barbarity" having taken

---

[310]Letter to Marrast, *EL*, *CW*, XIII, 735-6 (May 1848). President of the Assembly from June on, Marrast appeared to enjoy his arrival in power. Tocqueville, who saw him in the constitutional committee that autumn, dismissed him as "un républicain à la façon de Barras et qui a toujours préféré le luxe, la table et les femmes à la démocratie en guenilles." As Secretary of the committee, Marrast "mit fort à découvert la paresse, l'étourderie et l'impudence qui faisaient le fond de son caractère." (Tocqueville, *Souvenirs*, *Oeuvres*, XII, 184, 192.)

[311]Georges Duvau, *1848* (Paris: Gallimard, 1965), 136-7. Such was the confusion and oddity of events this day that Armand Barbès was received in a polite manner and shown by Marrast's secretary to a room on the same floor of the Hôtel de Ville as the mayor himself occupied. Before the guard arrived to take him away, he set to work, drawing up a hypothetical new provisional government. "Tout cela," he said later of the questions and counter-questions, declarations and threats exchanged with the officer who at length burst in on him, "est assez étrange et même un peu burlesque, mais j'affirme que ce fut ainsi" (Henri Guillemin, *La tragédie de quarante-huit* [Geneva: Editions du Milieu du Monde, 1948], 254).

[312]See Frederick A. De Luna, *The French Republic under Cavaignac, 1848* (Princeton: Princeton University Press, 1969), 128-73.

place in the June Days. He had confidence in the "mildness and moderation of the sincere republican party," and in Cavaignac.[313] But he saw the possibility that such troubles would result in the French permitting their Republic "to be filched from them by artifice . . . under the ascendancy of some popular chief, or under the panic caused by insurrection."[314]

Within days, this rough prophecy began to be borne out. Mill was particularly sensitive to the attack on the press, asking whether in such circumstances Socialists and Monarchists could "be reproached for using their arms."[315] His sympathies lay with Lamartine (whose *Histoire des Girondins* he had been reading with approval), the former Provisional Government, "and many of the party who adhere to them." He was favourable also to the Jacobin-Socialist Louis Blanc,[316] a member of the February ministry, author of the *droit au travail* decree ("Le Gouvernement provisoire de la République française s'engage à garantir l'existence de l'ouvrier par le travail . . .") that had been forced on the moderate ministers on 25 February by fear of the street crowds to whom Blanc owed his ministerial post. As President of the ill-starred Commission du Luxembourg that sought unsuccessfully to grapple with unemployment and the whole range of industrial relations until it and the *ateliers nationaux* (more akin, in the event, to *ateliers de charité*) could be shut down in June, Blanc found himself falsely accused of aiding and abetting Armand Barbès and those on the extreme left who had staged the futile *coup d'état manqué* of 15 May. In the immediate aftermath of the June Days, Marrast led the attack on him; he was indicted in the prevailing reaction that had developed steadily following the conservative results of the general election for a Constituent Assembly on 23 April. On 26 August, the Assembly voted to lift Blanc's parliamentary immunity so that he could be tried on charges of having conspired with the crowd that invaded the Assembly on 15 May. Whether or not the confused events of that day were a trap sprung by the right (among the noisy demonstrators was the police-spy Aloysius Huber), Blanc, despite the appeals made to him to join the *émeutiers*, neither instigated nor encouraged the invasion of the Palais Bourbon and was not even present at the Hôtel de Ville. Rather than stand trial in the unpromising climate of opinion, he slipped away and was permitted to take the

---

[313]Mill's confidence was by no means entirely mistaken, despite the bloody repression of the insurrection. Cavaignac failed to prevent or punish the subsequent *fusillades* that horrified and enraged Herzen and others, but he was not, as Maurice Agulhon said, "une sorte de brute guerrière ou—comme on dira cruellement dans les faubourgs—un 'prince du sang.' Ce militaire était le plus authentique et le plus fidèle des républicains de la veille." (*1848, ou L'apprentissage de la république, 1848-1852* [Paris: Editions du Seuil, 1973], 74.) Cf. De Luna's careful appraisal in *The French Republic under Cavaignac*, 161-73.

[314]French Affairs, *Daily News*, 9 Aug., 1848, 3.

[315]The French Law against the Press, *Spectator*, XXI, 19 Aug., 1848, 800; Collins, *The Government and the Newspaper Press*, 104-7.

[316]Letter to Nichol, *EL*, *CW*, XIII, 739-40 (30 Sept., 1848).

train to Ghent; he was arrested there briefly, and then at once crossed over to England.[317]

Blanc's was a singular case: since the publication of his *L'organisation du travail* (1840), he had been peculiarly marked out for retribution by those who feared and hated his proposals for social reform, the popular forces that put him into the Provisional Government in February, and the implications, at least, of the Luxembourg Commission and the workshops. Mill, without the possibility of knowing in detail what had happened during the months since February, considered Blanc and the other former ministers to be exemplary tribunes. But it was too late for them. In the election for the presidency of the Republic that December, Lamartine was swept aside, the radical candidates trailed distantly, and even Cavaignac was handily defeated by Louis Napoleon Bonaparte. The great mass of the electorate, peasants, voted against the republicans they blamed for disregarding their grievances and increasing their taxes; they voted for a legendary name, as did much of the urban population and a majority of the political *notables*. "It is a great deal," Guizot observed, "to be simultaneously a national glory, a revolutionary guarantee, and a principle of authority."[318]

In this situation, Mill's energies were given to defending the defunct February régime against its Tory critics; it was one more skirmish on behalf of reform. Outdistanced by events in France, won over by what he called the "*legitimate* Socialism" of Louis Blanc,[319] he attacked Brougham's version of the Revolution: Brougham's assessment of the Provisional Government was a caricature, and his estimate of Guizot's ministry exaggeratedly favourable; and thus the outbreak of revolution in his account was virtually inexplicable. In Mill's view, the spirit of compromise and justice Duveyrier had proposed France must accept had not been realized; the Republic had come too soon, preceded by too little education for it and too great a fear of 1793. The Lamartine government had done the best they could in the situation with which they had been confronted. His analysis was political; he showed no strong sense of the social dimensions of the upheaval. "Their great task," he said, "was to republicanize the public mind" (335). If there were errors, they were committed less by the government than by the political clubs. If Lamartine had served notice that the treaties of 1814-15

[317]See Loubère, *Louis Blanc*, 74-142; Donald Cope McKay, *The National Workshops: A Study in the French Revolution of 1848* (Cambridge, Mass.: Harvard University Press, 1933), *passim*; for the view that the whole 15 May affair was "une opération de police bien menée" and "une manoeuvre politique aussi, fort intelligente, et signée Marrast," see Guillemin, *La tragédie de quarante-huit*, 231-57. Of Blanc's own account (*Histoire de la révolution de 1848*, 2 vols. [Paris: Librairie Internationale, 1870], II, 66-97, 184-211), which combines his earlier recollections, McKay notes that it is "often inaccurate and occasionally thoroughly unreliable" (*National Workshops*, 177).

[318]De Luna, *The French Republic under Cavaignac*, 395. Mill said it was "one of the most striking instances in history of the power of a name" (letter to H.S. Chapman, *LL, CW*, XIV, 32 [28 May, 1849]).

[319]Letter to Nichol, *EL, CW*, XIII, 739 (30 Sept., 1848).

must be revised and that suppressed nationalities had the right to seek military assistance for their liberation, still the government's foreign policy had been peaceful.

Mill met criticism of the *droit au travail* decree by arguing that such a right was absolute, though practicable only where men gave up the other right "of propagating the species at their own discretion" (350). He asserted the justice of socialism and the need for the state to create "industrial communities on the Socialist principle" (352), if only as an educational experience. Mill knew little of the intrigues about the *ateliers nationaux*, which he defended, as he cleared Blanc of responsibility for their closing. Once again, his point was that the experiment had been made before adequate preparation could take place.[320] It had divided republicans and terrified the bourgeoisie: "These things are lamentable; but the fatality of circumstances, more than the misconduct of individuals is responsible for them" (354). Finally, he took issue with Brougham's insular view that sound political institutions cannot be legislated into existence. His answer was that, ready or not for the Republic, France had to attempt the experiment. He did not regret the Assembly's decision to abandon a second chamber in the new constitution adopted in November 1848. He thought universal suffrage had, if anything, returned too conservative a majority. Far from blindly following Paris, the provinces had too much curbed the city, "almost the sole element of progress which exists, politically speaking, in France" (360). Though he accepted Brougham's view that no legislature should try to exercise executive power, he opposed popular election of the chief of government as being unlikely to select an eminent politician. This, of course, Louis Napoleon had not been. And he predicted accurately that "the appointment of a President by the direct suffrages of the community, will prove to be the most serious mistake which the framers of the French Constitution have made" (362).

Within the limits of what could then be known, Mill's discussion was fair enough. But he perceived the great rural and urban problems dimly; his concern was with representative government. Continental socialism had thrust itself on his attention late in the day: he had been ambivalent about Fourier and hostile to Proudhon, he knew little of Cabet and Blanc until 1848.[321] His vision of the Provisional Government was simplistic; he saw Lamartine somewhat through the haze of his highly coloured *Histoire des Girondins*; he made no comment on Marrast's evolution from radical journalism to the defence of law and order at the

---

[320]Blanc was vague when testifying before the parliamentary *commission d'enquête* after the events, prior to his flight into exile, saying rightly that nothing was "ready for the *immediate solution* of the problem of poverty!" (McKay, *National Workshops*, 150.)

[321]See his defence of Cabet in his letter in the *Daily News*, 30 Oct., 1849, 3. He did not readily see the importance of Proudhon, "a firebrand," "the most mischievous man in Europe, & who has *nothing* whatever of all that I like & respect in the Socialists to whom he in no way belongs" (letter to H.S. Chapman, *LL, CW*, XIV, 34 [28 May, 1849]).

Hôtel de Ville.[322] His implied point of reference seemed to be 1789-91, modified by the appearance of "*legitimate* Socialism." Disappointment was inevitable. He nonetheless discerned warning signs, and was confirmed sooner than he anticipated by Louis Napoleon's progress to dictatorship. Carrel had been tempted by Bonapartism; Mill never was. Louis Napoleon he branded "a stupid, ignorant adventurer who has thrown himself entirely into the hands of the reactionary party, &, but that he is too great a fool, would have some chance by these means of making himself emperor."[323] There, of course, he was wrong. He did not guess that this man could calmly, with little artifice and no panic, "filch" the Republic.[324] He was wrong in imagining that Victor Considérant and the Fourierists (among socialists "much the most sensible and enlightened both in the destructive, & in the constructive parts of their system")[325] could seriously weigh upon the proceedings in the Assembly.

Not least, Mill did not see that the tremendous power of the liberal press, durable and resilient, had almost come to an end. He did not understand what it meant that the *National* had become the unofficial newspaper of the Provisional Government: that men like Marrast had become part of the new establishment. He was disturbed by the repression of the opposition journals, but did not fully grasp that universal suffrage had swept the *petite* and *moyenne* bourgeoisies aside. He did not see what it meant that Bonaparte had been elected President against the majority of the press, that the extraordinary force it had been ever since 1814 was finished.[326] Perhaps the surface indications were misleading. The constitution of 4 November, 1848, was the most democratic France had ever had, with universal manhood suffrage, freedom of the press, freedom of assembly, freedom of petition. Even the *droit au travail* was alluded to in the preamble.[327] A revolution had taken place. But Cavaignac, for one, doubted that the country was republican, and the election of Louis Napoleon suggested he was

---

[322]Cf. Tocqueville's harsh view: "Quant à Marrast, il appartenait à la race ordinaire des révolutionnaires français qui, par liberté du peuple, ont toujours entendu le despotisme exercé au nom du peuple" (*Souvenirs*, *Oeuvres*, XII, 182).

[323]Letter to H.S. Chapman, *LL*, *CW*, XIV, 33 (28 May, 1849).

[324]Mill was not alone in mistaking him. Tocqueville said, "Il était très supérieur à ce que sa vie antérieure et ses folles entreprises avaient pu faire penser à bon droit de lui. Ce fut ma première impression en le pratiquant. Il déçut sur ce point ses adversaires et peut-être plus encore ses amis, si l'on peut donner ce nom aux hommes politiques qui patronnèrent sa candidature." (*Souvenirs*, *Oeuvres*, XII, 211.)

[325]Letter to H.S. Chapman, *LL*, *CW*, XIV, 34 (28 May, 1849). Tocqueville saw Considérant in the constitutional committee, judging him one of the "rêveurs chimériques . . . qui aurait mérité d'être placé aux petites maisons s'il eût été sincère, mais je crains qu'il ne méritât mieux" (*Souvenirs*, *Oeuvres*, XII, 180).

[326]See André Jean Tudesq, *L'élection présidentielle de Louis Napoléon Bonaparte, 10 décembre 1848* (Paris: Colin, 1965), *passim*; Collins, *The Government and the Newspaper Press*, 100-35.

[327]See the debate in Paul Bastid, *Doctrines et institutions politiques de la seconde république*, 2 vols. (Paris: Hachette, 1945), II, 79-85. On the constitution in general, see *ibid.*, 70-149, and the summary account in De Luna, *The French Republic under Cavaignac*, 329-35.

right. Pressed to pre-empt the election results by *coup d'état*, Cavaignac refused: the Republic might succumb, he said, but it would rise again, "whereas the republic would be lost forever if the one who represented it should give the example of revolt against the will of the country."[328] It was left to Mill's friend, Marrast, President of the Assembly, to proclaim Bonaparte President of the Republic. "Tocqueville," the British Ambassador, Lord Normanby, noted in his diary the next day, "rather quaintly, said to me yesterday, 'There only remains now one question, whether it is the Republicans or the Republic itself which the country cannot abide.'"[329]

By the summer of 1851, Mill was "for the first time downhearted about French affairs."[330] When, some time later, Louis Napoleon made himself dictator, then Emperor, and finally the ally of England, he was pained. The Revolution of 1848 faded into the past. The only point of its being recalled in Normanby's memoirs, with their "calomnies ridicules et atroces," Mill wrote, was that they offered Louis Blanc an opportunity to set the record straight.[331] The new Girondins, Lamartine and his colleagues, had tried the experiment; France had not been ready for it. So tyranny once more settled on the country. And if the government of England had progressed so little as barely to restrain itself from co-operating in running Napoleon's enemies to the ground, "such is the state of the world ten years after 1848 that even this must be felt as a great victory."[332]

FOR MORE THAN TWENTY YEARS, Mill had observed and commented on the politics of contemporary France, had studied and sought to explain to Englishmen the constructive nature of the great Revolution in whose name much of the social and political struggle of the nineteenth century was taking place. The young French historians who boldly celebrated the Revolution as prologue to the apparent triumph of liberalism forty or so years later, or who explained the present as the outcome of the liberal impulse working its way through the centuries, he acclaimed as the best of the time. The French scene was animated,

---

[328]De Luna, *The French Republic under Cavaignac*, 395.

[329]Constantine Henry Phipps, Marquis of Normanby, *A Year of Revolution, from a Journal Kept in Paris in 1848*, 2 vols. (London: Longman, *et al.*, 1857), II, 375.

[330]Letter to Bain, *LL*, *CW*, XIV, 76 (Summer 1851).

[331]Letter to Louis Blanc, *ibid.*, XV, 562 (9 July, 1858); Louis Blanc, *1848: Historical Revelations Inscribed to Lord Normanby* (London: Chapman and Hall, 1858), subsequently published as *Révélations historiques en réponse au livre de lord Normanby* (Brussels: Meline, Cans, 1859). Cf. cx n below.

[332]Mill to Giuseppe Mazzini, *LL*, *CW*, XV, 548 (21 Feb., 1858). Palmerston's government was defeated in February 1858 over the Conspiracy to Murder Bill that would have permitted handing over political refugees to the French authorities, closing off "the only impregnable asylum, in Europe," as Louis Blanc put it (*1848: Historical Revelations*, v). Mill saw it as a failed attempt, in the aftermath of French pressure on London following Orsini's bomb attack against Napoleon III, to drag England "dans la boue, en faisant d'elle une succursale de la police française" (letter to Pasquale Villari, *LL*, *CW*, XV, 550 [9 Mar., 1858]).

creative, disputatious, sometimes explosive, but always instructive. It was his self-imposed task to try to make Englishmen see through the haze of their insularities and prejudices the essential lessons that France offered to all who shared in the common civilization. Some part of his special certainty about the relevance of France to English society flowed from his own peculiar acquaintance with the land and the people and their thought; some part was surely no more than the intelligent appraisal of intrinsic fact. But time carried away both the observer and the observed. As the mid-century approached, it was apparent to him that the Revolution was more complex and its meaning more ambiguous than he had thought; it was clear that the young philosophical historians had begun to take their place in the historiographical museum, that their works were after all *pièces d'occasion*; it was evident that the imminent triumph of liberalism had again been delayed and that other struggles must one day be fought; it was obvious that Mill's own interest in history had shifted onto quite another plane of regularities and laws and predictive capacity, leaving the Revolution and its portents not so much diminished as more spaciously situated in a vast ongoing historical process.

Despite his didactic purpose and immediate political and social concerns, Mill was too good a student of the past to permit disappointments and setbacks to break his commitment to France as the touchstone of Europe. He was far from being uncritical, he was by no means unprejudiced, he had his blind-spots. But he never went back on his conviction that, whatever the aberration of the moment, France and its destiny were central to civilization. By 1849, many hopes had foundered, and he felt it keenly that men had failed or been removed prematurely from the scene. He knew that the immense expectations of 1830 would never come again, that the social and political process was infinitely more complex and its desired outcome infinitely less assured in the foreseeable future than he and his young friends had imagined in the excitements of Paris that summer nearly twenty years before. He remained watchful but publicly silent, his former impulse to interpret the news from France now quite gone. For Mill at the mid-century, great swings of hopefulness and despair concerning France and democracy lay ahead, but for the moment that was all.

Textual Introduction

JOHN M. ROBSON

THOUGH MILL is properly celebrated as a political philosopher, logician, and economist, throughout his work one finds evidence of an intense interest in history. Indeed his first childhood writings, prompted by his father's *History of British India*, which was composed at the table across which the child worked at his lessons, were histories of India, Rome, and Holland. He never wrote a history in his adult years, but rather occupied himself with the philosophy of history and with the implications of that philosophy for social theory and practical politics. While he took great interest in British and classical history (see especially Volumes VI and XI of the *Collected Works*), his principal concentration was on French history, particularly in its social and political manifestations. Rich evidence of his fascination with French affairs is to be found throughout his works, especially in his newspaper writings and letters, as well as in the details of his life, from his boyhood visit to Pompignan and Montpellier in 1820-21 to his death in Avignon in 1873.

French history had the immediacy of current politics, for he first read of the Revolution of 1789 in the midst of his apprenticeship in British radicalism, and dreamt of being a British Girondist.[1] Later, when he was seeking an independent role for himself as a radical journalist, the Revolution of 1830 gave him a model in the young republicans, especially Armand Carrel. During and after the struggle for the English Reform Act of 1832, Mill followed and wrote about French politics, always keeping an eye on parallels with and lessons for Britain. The Revolution of 1848 again found an advocate in him, his growing interest in socialism being so stimulated by the experiments during the short-lived republic that he modified crucial passages in his *Principles of Political Economy* for its second edition of 1849 and more thoroughly for the third edition of 1852. One could cite much more evidence of various kinds, but the essays gathered in this volume give proof enough of both his interest and his understanding; reference to other volumes in the edition will further confirm the assertions just made.

The eleven essays in the main text and a twelfth, which appears as Appendix A, were published between April 1826, just before Mill's twentieth birthday, and

[1]*Autobiography, CW,* I, 63-5.

April 1849, just before his forty-third. In provenance they are less diverse than those in other volumes of this edition, seven having appeared in the *Westminster Review*, two in the *Monthly Repository*, and three in the *Edinburgh Review*. Chronology provides apt groupings: (1) of those in the *Westminster*, three were published between 1826 and 1828, during its first period, before the Mills withdrew over disagreement with the editorial policy and practice of John Bowring; indeed the third of these, Mill's review of Scott's *Life of Napoleon*, was his last contribution until his own editorship. (2) The two in the *Monthly Repository* (1832 and 1835) were written during the hiatus between his periods of contribution to the *Westminster*. (3) The next three (1836-37) are again to be located in sets of the *Westminster* (one, Appendix A, during the brief life of the *London Review*, the other two in the *London and Westminster*). (4) When in 1840 he relinquished the *London and Westminster*, he immediately began writing for the *Edinburgh*, where his greatest essays (1844-46) were those on French history.[2] (5) Then, finally so far as this volume is concerned, his defence of the French Revolution of 1848 was assigned to the *Westminster*, in recognition of the essay's radical compatibility with his old periodical ground.

THE EARLY *WESTMINSTER* ESSAYS

NOTHING IS KNOWN about the composition of the first two essays, "Mignet's French Revolution" and "Modern French Historical Works," which appeared in successive issues of the *Westminster* (April and July 1826) during one of Mill's most intensely active periods. He had probably just finished editing Jeremy Bentham's *Rationale of Judicial Evidence*, which appeared in five volumes in 1827; he was contributing long essays both to the *Westminster* and to the *Parliamentary History and Review*; he was very active in the London Debating Society and in the early morning discussion group at George Grote's house; and he was working his way upward in the India Office (his salary was raised to £100 per annum in May 1827 and then he leaped ahead in position and salary to £600 in 1828).[3]

The review of Mignet shows by direct statement and implication the young Mill's awareness of the sources for French history; it also demonstrates his control of the language in that, though he cites the English translation of Mignet in the heading to the article, the quotations (which are extensive, occupying over fifty percent of the text) are not taken from that translation, but are rendered in

---

[2]There also was published in 1840 his second review of Tocqueville's *Democracy in America*, which, with his first review in 1835 (both of which are in *CW*, XVIII, 47-90, 153-204), provides much that is germane to the themes of this volume.

[3]Bain, *John Stuart Mill*, 31. For a fuller account of his activities in these years, see the Introduction to *CW*, I, xii-xiii.

his own words. (This practice of translating extensive passages came to characterize Mill's reviews, in accordance with his purpose of making the historians known; it also made the reviews easier to write for one who translated with such facility.) It is also worth noting that he promises (on behalf of the *Westminster*) to go more generally into the question of the French Revolution in a later number; he kept this promise to some extent in his review of Scott two years later, but one can infer his desire, finally abandoned only when Carlyle took up the task, to write a history of that revolution.

Neither the review of Mignet nor "Modern French Historical Works," the article that appeared in the next number of the *Westminster*, presents any special textual problem. The latter concentrates on an earlier period in European history, the age of chivalry, and Mill uses the opportunity to assert that the English have more need of "monitors than adulators," because French literature (in which category he would, of course, include history) has surpassed English, especially in that the French write not merely to say something, but because they have something to say (17). He manages thus to combine the habitual *Westminster* line on history, politics, and literature with his own bias towards the French. Varied sources, English and French, illustrate Mill's claim to mastery of the issues—at least it seems likely that the review's readers would not infer its author to be a twenty-year-old with no formal academic training.

Impressive as these two articles are, the third in this group, "Scott's Life of Napoleon" (April 1828), is much more mature. Bain calls it a "masterpiece," saying that in execution "it is not unworthy to be compared with the Sedgwick and Whewell articles,"[4] and indeed it would not be out of place in *Dissertations and Discussions* with those better known essays. Given pride of first place in the *Westminster*,[5] its ample scope (sixty-three pages of the *Westminster*) shows that the editor was nothing loath to give the young Mill his head. The article, Mill says,

cost me more labour than any previous; but it was a labour of love, being a defence of the early French Revolutionists against the Tory misrepresentations of Sir Walter Scott, in the introduction to his *Life of Napoleon*. The number of books which I read for this purpose, making notes and extracts—even the number I had to buy (for in those days there was no public or subscription library from which books of reference could be taken home), far exceeded the worth of the immediate object; but I had at that time a half formed intention of writing a History of the French Revolution; and though I never executed it, my collections afterwards were very useful to Carlyle for a similar purpose.[6]

Some evidence of his reading has survived in a letter of 1 January, 1828, to Charles Comte, whom he had met in Paris through J.B. Say some years earlier.

---

[4]*John Stuart Mill*, 37.

[5]Two other of Mill's early *Westminster* articles also lead their numbers: "Law of Libel and Liberty of the Press" in April 1825, and "The Game Laws" in January 1826.

[6]*Autobiography*, *CW*, I, 135. Cf. John Cairns' Introduction, xxxix and li above.

He remarks that he has been working for a long time on the review, and asks
Comte's help with a task beyond his powers and knowledge, one he has taken on
only because—a constant refrain in his writings on France—the English are so
ignorant of their neighbour's history. His reading, he says, has included most of
the memoirs (presumably he refers to the massive *Collection des mémoires
relatifs à la révolution française* that appeared in the 1820s) as well as Mignet,
Toulongeon, "et autres" (later to Carlyle he says he had read the first two
volumes of Montgaillard for the Scott review).[7] The review contains long
extracts in French, taken usually from sources ignored by Scott, who is heavily
criticized for errors, ignorance, and Tory bias, but Mill concludes with a
statement that he feels no hostility towards Scott, "for whom, *politics apart*," he
has "that admiration which is felt by every person possessing a knowledge of the
English language" (110).[8] The words I have italicized reveal the main force of
the account. Mill's particular personal bias shows in the extensive treatment
given to the Gironde (98-109), towards whom, he says, Scott has, not
untypically, been unjust: "of none have the conduct and aims been so miserably
misunderstood, so cruelly perverted" (98). Evidently pleased with the article
himself, he had offprints made, sending some to Charles Comte in Paris;[9] these
are textually identical with the original. And many years later, near the end of his
life, he still clearly remembered the article (though not its date), writing to Emile
Acollas about views he had held since youth: "en 1827 (alors même j'avais
beaucoup étudié la Révolution française) j'ai publié un article dans la revue de
Westminster où j'ai soutenu par des preuves irrécusables précisément votre
thèse, savoir que l'attaque a toujours été du côté de la Contre Révolution et que la
Révolution n'a fait que se défendre."[10]

ESSAYS IN THE *MONTHLY REPOSITORY*

THE FIRST OF THESE, "Alison's History of the French Revolution" (July and
August 1833), shows in its recorded history and text the influence of Mill's new
and overbearing friend, Thomas Carlyle, whose presence will be seen in most of
the essays from the 1830s here reprinted. Their letters early in 1833 deal with a
multitude of personal and intellectual matters, one of which was history (Mill
had been reading, for example, some manuscript pages of Grote's *History of
Greece*, the first volumes of which appeared only in 1846). In the spring, Mill

---

[7]*EL, CW*, XII, 21-2, 217 (2 Mar., 1834). Mill was acquainted with much of the contents of the
Collection des mémoires, ed. Saint-Albin Berville and Jean François Barrière, 68 vols. (Paris:
Baudoin, 1820-28), though even his voracious appetite may have failed before the end.

[8]For praise of Scott's novels as historical *sources*, see 184-5 and 226.

[9]*EL, CW*, XII, 24-5 (27 June, 1828).

[10]*LL, CW*, XVII, 1831 (20 Sept., 1871).

asked Carlyle about the advisability of reading and reviewing Alison's work.[11] Encouraged by Carlyle, he hoped to have an article ready for the June number of the *Monthly Repository*, but completed it only in time for it to appear in two parts, as the conclusion of the July number and the opening piece in that for August. He reported to Carlyle that the review was not worth his perusal and that it would have been better to wait until it could all appear at once. "I shall in future," he adds, "never write on any subject which my mind is not full of when I begin to write; unless the occasion is such that it is better the thing were ill done than not at all, that being the alternative."[12] Perusal of the article, in spite of Mill's warning, must have been ego-warming to Carlyle, for it begins with a long quotation from his "Biography" (identified as to title and provenance, though not as to author), and the same essay is quoted later, as is a passage from a private letter Carlyle wrote to Mill on 13 January, 1833 (the source of which is not identified). Mill continued, as will be shown below, this habit of quoting overtly and covertly from Carlyle until their disagreements came to outweigh their mutual admiration (always more sincere on Mill's side).

The second of Mill's articles in the *Monthly Repository* on French matters appeared in June 1835, at another time of intense activity. He was strenuously occupied in bringing out the first issues of the *London Review*, which he not only edited, but wrote extensively for: in the first number, for April, appeared his "Sedgwick" and "Postscript"; in the second, for July, his "Tennyson," "Rationale of Representation," and "Parliamentary Proceedings of the Session." He was also writing in the *Globe*, was presumably still recovering from the shock of having been responsible for the burning in March of the manuscript of the first volume of Carlyle's *French Revolution*, and was planning a trip in Germany for July and August. It is not surprising, then, that "The Monster Trial," as he entitled his article (after the French *procès monstre*), occupies only four pages of the *Monthly Repository*. Its brevity, however, does not imply insignificance, for he touches on major concerns, especially freedom of the press. He also asserts again that the English are negligent of French affairs; only the *Examiner* has, in the last four years, "placed carefully" before its readers "the passing events . . . with regular explanatory comments" (125)—of course written by Mill himself. He in fact then quotes a long passage from his own article of 26 January, 1834,[13]

---

[11]See the Introduction, pp. xlvi-l above, for a full discussion. Only the first two volumes of Alison's work were reviewed by Mill: *History of Europe during the French Revolution. Embracing the Period from the Assembly of the Notables, in MDCCLXXXIX, to the Establishment of the Directory, in MDCCXCV*, 2 vols. (Edinburgh: Blackwood; London: Cadell, 1833). Eight further volumes were published, III and IV (1835) with a different subtitle, and V-X (1836-42) with the title *History of Europe from the Commencement of the French Revolution in 1789 to the Restoration of the Bourbons*.

[12]*EL, CW*, XII, 158 (20 May, 1833), 159 (June, 1833), and 162 (5 July, 1833).

[13]The variants between the two versions reflect merely the different house styles of the *Examiner* and the *Monthly Repository*.

on the persecution of the French republicans, with whom he had acquaintance (as is indicated by the mention of his having been in Paris when the manifesto of the Société des Droits de l'Homme was issued) and also much sympathy.

ESSAYS IN THE *LONDON AND WESTMINSTER REVIEW*

AFTER 1834, Mill's disillusionment with the course of French politics in the age of the *juste milieu*, as well as his increasing involvement in British politics, where he thought (quite mistakenly) that the time had come for Radical sharing of power if not indeed leadership, led him away from public comment on contemporary French events, though not on the history of France and its historians. So, early in the career of his own journal, the *London Review* (later the *London and Westminster*), Mill requested from Joseph Blanco White a review of Guizot's *Lectures on European Civilization*, which appeared in the number for January 1836. In the event, Mill was a joint author of the article (which we therefore print here as an appendix). Just how much he contributed is not certain, though his extant letters to White are helpful in this respect, showing Mill as an editor supple, if determined, in his relations with contributors. On 21 October, 1835, he wrote to White:

> Your article on Guizot is excellent as far as it goes but something seems still wanting to give a complete notion of the nature & value of Guizot's historical speculations. I will not ask you to take in hand again a subject of which I do not wonder that you should be tired, but if you would permit me, I should like much to add, mostly at the end of the article, a few more observations & specimens—especially that noble analysis of the feudal system in Lecture 4 of the first volume. The whole should then be submitted for your approval, either in MS. or in type. If you consent to this do not trouble yourself to write only on purpose to say so as I shall consider silence as consent.[14]

The comment in a letter to Henry S. Chapman, asking that the article be set and proof sent as soon as possible, indicates a somewhat different judgment. He refers to an essay by John Robertson "and another (the one on Guizot which I have, I think, with tolerable success) manufactured from a so-so article into a good one."[15] The silky tone returns, however, in the next letter to White:

> I have now the pleasure of sending you a proof of the article on Guizot, in which I hope you will point out every, the smallest, thought or expression to which you in the slightest degree object, will make any suggestions for the improvement of the article, & which may occur to you. I think it will be very interesting & instructive & it is a kind of article which the review much wanted.
>
> Perhaps the few remarks which I have inserted near the beginning of the article, respecting M. Guizot's political conduct, are not sufficiently in the tone & spirit of the rest of the article—if you think so, pray cancel them & substitute anything which you prefer—but it strikes me that something on that topic was wanted in that place.

[14]*EL, CW*, XII, 280.
[15]*Ibid.*, 284 (n.d., but certainly November 1835).

I return, at the same time, a few pages of your MS. which I was obliged to omit in order to make room for what I added & to render the general character of the article less discursive.[16]

Since Mill listed the article in his bibliography of published writings, one may assume that White accepted the version given him. On internal evidence and that of these letters, one may speculate that the portions by Mill are those at 369.33-370.16, 384.14-389.15, and 392.4 to the end.

The next article in this volume has a personal character, for it marks the real culmination of Mill's friendly relations with one of the strongest influences on him in the 1830s. In "Carlyle's French Revolution," after praising Carlyle's "creative imagination," Mill lauds also his research, and adds: "We do not say this at random, but from a most extensive acquaintance with his materials, with his subject, and with the mode in which it has been treated by others" (138). He could with justice have gone further, and asserted his intimate knowledge of the author and his writings, for Mill and Carlyle had indeed come to know one another well from the time when Carlyle thought Mill's "The Spirit of the Age" signalled the appearance of a "new mystic" available for discipleship. The most recent manifestation of their friendship had been Mill's soliciting of Carlyle's "Parliamentary History of the French Revolution," for the April 1837 issue of the *London and Westminster*. An editorial note to that article, however, adumbrated differences that were to surface later: Mill indicated that some opinions expressed by Carlyle were not consonant with the review's attitudes, which would likely be developed in the next number.[17] That promise was fulfilled, though not through emphasized disagreement, in Mill's highly laudatory review of Carlyle's *French Revolution*.

That the article appeared so quickly is indicative of Mill's strength of will (surely motivated in part by remorse over the destruction of Carlyle's manuscript), for, though Carlyle had arranged in January that Mill would receive unbound sheets of the book to expedite a review, it seems that only at the end of April did Mill receive the "first copy" the printer could get bound.[18] And if he had been busy before, he must now have been nearly frantic: in addition to running the *London and Westminster*, he had published in it in January his

---

[16]*Ibid.*, 285 (24 Nov., 1835).

[17]"The opinions of this review on the French Revolution not having yet been expressed, the conductors feel it incumbent on them to enter a *caveat* against any presumption respecting those opinions which may be founded on the Newgate Calendar character of the above extracts. Some attempt at a judgment of that great historical event, with its good and its evil, will probably be attempted in the next number." (*CW*, I, 603-4.) The disagreement here intimated, and more than hinted at in Mill's article (see, e.g., 157-8, 160-3), had reached serious proportions when Carlyle's "Memoirs of Mirabeau" in the number of the review for January 1837 had repelled many of Mill's friends and political associates. Though Mill defended his choice of Carlyle as a contributor, the "Parliamentary History" was actually Carlyle's final article in the *London and Westminster*, and while there seems not to have been a break in their personal relations for some years, eventually they came into stark and unrelenting opposition in public over Ireland and the West Indies.

[18]Carlyle to Mill, *Collected Letters*, IX, 113, 197-8 (9 Jan. and 27 Apr., 1837).

review of *Thoughts in the Cloister and the Crowd*, in April his articles on Fonblanque and (with Grote) on Taylor, and in July, along with the Carlyle review, he contributed "The Spanish Question" (with Joseph Blanco White); further, although he was on a walking tour in Wales during part of September and October, the October number contained his "Parties and the Ministry" and "Armand Carrel." Most significantly, he was, especially from June to August, working hard at his *System of Logic*, to that end reading Whewell's *History of the Inductive Sciences*, rereading Herschel's *Discourse*, and becoming excited over the first two volumes of Auguste Comte's *Cours de philosophie positive*. He was also now, after his father's death in mid-1836, the male head of a large family. In the circumstances, it is not surprising that the review of Carlyle shows some signs of haste, most evidently in the length of the quoted extracts.

Mill's not including the essay in *Dissertations and Discussions* may appear somewhat odd, in view of his statements that it was one of few in the *London and Westminster* that achieved their intended goals, in this case to make a strong claim for Carlyle's genius before others had a chance to deny it.[19] The claim is repeated in the part of the *Autobiography* drafted seventeen years later,[20] by which time there was quite enough evidence of the distance between them practically and ideologically; there is not much indication that between 1854 and 1859, when *Dissertations and Discussions* appeared, their relations, already bad, had significantly worsened. It is sure enough, of course, that Harriet Taylor had a part in making the selection for *Dissertations and Discussions*, though she did not live to see its publication, and perhaps she was more strongly offended by Carlyle than Mill was. In any case, it seems a pity that Mill did not at least include parts of the review, as he did in other cases where the article in full appeared outdated or relatively insignificant.

Mill continued for a few years to use Carlyle as an authority in other essays, sometimes openly and sometimes quietly. In "Armand Carrel," which was published in October 1837, the bearing of witness is at its height. In the first paragraph Mill uses a German phrase undoubtedly taken from Carlyle's *French Revolution*; at 182-3 he uses an image found in a letter to him from Carlyle; at 187 the "formulas" attributed by Carlyle to Mirabeau appear again (cf. 161 where Mill cites the *French Revolution*); at 201, in the midst of a long quotation from a letter from himself to Carlyle, he puts in quotation marks "quiet emphasis," a term Carlyle had applied in another letter to Mill's tone in the review of Alison (Carlyle was not in 1837 identified here; see the discussion of textual variants at cxv); and at 215 a common remark of Carlyle's is attributed to "one of the greatest writers of our time" (in 1837 he had been "one of the noblest spirits of our time"). Other places in the present volume also reveal traces of

[19]*EL, CW*, XIII, 427 (16 Apr., 1840).
[20]*CW*, I, 233-5.

their relations: in "Michelet" (1844), the final text at 227 praises Thierry for making "the age tell its own story; not drawing anything from invention, but adhering scrupulously to authentic facts"; as first published, the essay says that Thierry, in this laudable adherence, is "like Mr. Carlyle." Similarly, in "Guizot's Essays and Lectures on History" (1845) at 261 the comment that the "Oxford theologians" have "a theory of the world" originally included the comment, "as Mr. Carlyle would say." By 1859, when the revised version appeared, Mill was happier to keep his prophetic authority veiled.

"Armand Carrel" is, according to the heading in the *London and Westminster* for October 1837, a review of "*Armand Carrel, his Life and Character*. From the French of D. Nisard. Preceded by a Biographical Sketch, abridged from the French of E. Littré." Republished in *Dissertations and Discussions*, it reveals in its history and content a very strong personal as well as political attachment to the subject. Mill followed Carrel's career from the time of the Revolution of 1830, especially in relation to the French government's continued limitation of press freedom. They met in Paris in 1833 (the encounter is outlined in the letter from Mill to Carlyle quoted in the article at 201-2) and perhaps again in London in 1834 and/or 1836; Mill made much of Carrel's speech in the Cour des Pairs in defence of the *National* in December 1834; he tried repeatedly to get contributions from Carrel for the *London and Westminster*, believing that his signature alone would benefit the review, and made sure Carrel got the issues as they appeared.[21] Carrel epitomized for Mill the best features of the young men of the *mouvement*, and provided an ideal, even if an unrealized one, for Mill's own activities as a radical publicist and reformer in the 1830s.

Given the strength of Mill's feeling, it is somewhat surprising that he seems not to have begun his article until a year after Carrel's death, at which time, recalling their first meeting, he wrote to Carlyle (8 August, 1837) to ask for the return of his descriptive letter.[22] By 29 August he had finished the article, or at least was confident that it would be ready for the October number, and a month later, while on a holiday tour, he wrote to his sub-editor, John Robertson, revealing the special significance Carrel had for him: "We want *now* to give a *character* to the Review, as Carrel gave one to the National. . . . I dare not violate my instinct of suitableness, which we must the more strive to keep up the more we are exposed to swerve from it by our attempts to make the Review acceptable to the public."[23] At least part of what he meant is indicated in the article, when he says: "The English idea of a newspaper, as a sort of impersonal thing, coming from nobody knows where, the readers never thinking of the writer, nor caring whether he thinks what he writes, as long as *they* think what he

---

[21]*EL, CW*, XII, 197, 239, 254, 255, 262, and 281.

[22]*Ibid.*, 346. He subsequently returned the letter to Carlyle, the manuscript being in Carlyle House.

[23]*Ibid.*, 349 and 353 (28 Sept., 1837; Mill's italics).

writes;—this would not have done for Carrel, nor been consistent with his objects" (197).

Rather slight changes in the article as republished call attention to otherwise hidden peculiarities. In *Dissertations and Discussions* the title reads "Armand Carrell. Biographical Notices by MM. Nisard and Littré," while the title in 1837, "*Armand Carrel, his Life and Character*," clearly implies that a single work is under review. Also the first words of the original version, "This little work is" are modified in the version of 1859 to "These little works are"; and further on "one distinguished writer" is replaced by "two distinguished writers." In fact no copy has been found of the separate publication (a pamphlet, one would judge) that was apparently under review in 1837, and it appears likely that it never was published. Désiré Nisard's article on Carrel, which is clearly the source of Mill's translations and references, appeared in the *Revue des Deux Mondes* in October 1837, and (given the frequent friendly correspondence between him and Mill about the *London and Westminster*, to which Nisard contributed) a pre-publication copy was probably sent to Mill. Emile Littré's account of Carrel seems not to have appeared in print until it was published in 1854 as an introductory "notice biographique" to Charles Romey's edition of Carrel's *Oeuvres littéraires et économiques*, well after the first appearance of Mill's article, but before its republication; again Mill's quotations and references clearly come from this notice, although seventeen years intervene between Mill's citations from it and its independent publication. Odd as the sequence of events may seem, one may infer that Mill, who was acquainted with Littré, was given the text for translation, it being assumed that it would also appear in French at about the same time.[24] Finally, Hooper, named in 1837 as the publisher of the "not yet published" work, was at that time the publisher of the *London and Westminster*. What seems most likely is that Mill proposed to Hooper a pamphlet consisting of Nisard's and Littré's essays, translated (and likely paid for) by himself; he then reviewed a work (his translation, perhaps unfinished) that existed in manuscript, but was never published.

If this interpretation is correct, it strengthens the already powerful evidence of Mill's extraordinary attachment to Carrel's character and career, an attachment, as is demonstrated by John Cairns in the Introduction above (lxii-lxvii), that was not short-lived. For example, he wrote to Henry Chapman immediately after the French Revolution of February 1848: "In my meditations and feelings on the whole matter, every second thought has been of Carrel—he who perhaps alone in Europe was qualified to direct such a movement, to have perished uselessly, and the very man who killed him, now a prominent reformer. . . ." And, sending a set of *Dissertations and Discussions* to Charles Dupont-White mainly because

---

[24]At one point (196) Mill says, "We will not spoil by translation M. Littré's finely chosen phraseology"—and quotes part of a sentence in French as it appeared seventeen years later.

he had been a friend of Carrel, he comments: "Je me réjouirai toujours de l'avoir, moi aussi, personnellement connu, et je conserve de lui un souvenir des plus vifs."[25]

ESSAYS IN THE *EDINBURGH REVIEW*

MILL'S INTENSE POLITICAL INVOLVEMENT of the 1830s having ended in disillusionment, at least so far as his personal ambitions as editor or actor were concerned, he decided to divest himself of the *London and Westminster* and, though as author mainly concerned in the last stages of composition of his *Logic*, to offer his services as essayist and reviewer to the *Edinburgh*. This connection began with his second review of Tocqueville's *Democracy in America*, but even before that article was written he outlined his further hopes to Macvey Napier, editor of the *Edinburgh*, in a letter partly quoted in the Introduction above:

. . . I should like very much . . . to write occasionally on modern French history & historical literature, with which from peculiar causes I am more extensively acquainted than Englishmen usually are. If I had continued to carry on the London & W. review, I should have written more than one article on Michelet a writer of great & original views, very little known among us. One article on his history of France, & another combining his Roman history with Arnold's, might I think be made very interesting & useful. Even on Guizot there may be something still to be written.[26]

Nothing came of this notion for some time, though in 1842 Mill did much reading on Roman history, consulting the German authorities as well as Michelet and Arnold.[27] Eventually his attention moved from Rome back to France, and in a letter to Alexander Bain (of which unfortunately only part is known) he says: "I am now vigorously at work reviewing Michelet's *History of France* for the *Edinburgh*. I hope to *do* Napier, and get him to insert it before he finds out what a fatal thing he is doing."[28] The reference here is to what he had earlier described to Napier as his "strongly Guelphic" views, and later identified to R.B. Fox as

---

[25]*EL, CW*, XIII, 731-2 (29 Feb., 1848); *LL, CW*, XIV, 644 (5 Nov., 1859). Mill's attachment is hinted at also in his early suggestion to Molesworth that he would "probably publish the article with [his] name hereafter" (*LL, CW*, XVII, 1978 [22 Sept., 1837]). When "Armand Carrel" was published in *Dissertations and Discussions* in 1859, it was already known to be his; even in its first form it had appeared with his habitual signature, "A," and he had distributed some offprints. It is interesting to note that Walter Bagehot (not claiming special knowledge) was aware that Mill was the author of the article in its original form. In the second of his "Letters on the French Coup d'Etat of 1851" he says (and it is likely Mill would have been pleased at the comment): "I remember reading, several years ago, an article in the *Westminster Review*, on the lamented Armand Carrel, in which the author, well known to be one of our most distinguished philosophers, took occasion to observe, that what the French most wanted was '*Un homme de caractère*'" (in *Collected Works*, ed. Norman St. John Stevas, IV [London: The Economist, 1968], 38).

[26]*EL, CW*, XIII, 431 (27 Apr., 1840).

[27]See *ibid.*, 498, 504-5, 529, 543, 548-9, and 551.

[28]*Ibid.*, 595 (Sept. 1843).

his "arrant Hildebrandism," that is, his favouring the popes over the kings,[29] a matter that emerges in a letter to Michelet while the article was in progress, as well, of course, as in the text itself. Reporting to Bain that the essay was in Napier's hands by 3 November, 1843, Mill commented, "If he prints it, he will make some of his readers stare." With the hindsight of a half-century, in some respects dulled but percipient in others, Bain remarks in his biography of Mill: "We have a difficulty, reading it now, to see anything very dreadful in its views. But a philosophic vindication of the Papacy and the celibacy of the clergy, as essential preservatives against barbarism, was not then familiar to the English mind."[30]

The essay, being cogitated and written during the final stages of Mill's work on his *System of Logic*, shows many signs of his matured views on the lessons and methods of history, for instance on the three stages of historical writing and the formation of national character ("Ethology," as he called the new science in his *Logic*). It also introduces a theme more dominant later in his writings, the historical record of women's outstanding contributions to political and social life, and furthermore suggests the instructive role he now saw as more appropriately his than the active one he strove for in the 1830s.

The second notion canvassed by Mill when he wrote to Napier about contributing an historical series to the *Edinburgh* was further comment on Guizot. This came to fruition in "Guizot's Essays and Lectures on History" (1845), a much more comprehensive essay than the jointly written "Guizot's Lectures on European Civilization" in the *London Review* nine years earlier. Like "Michelet's History of France," it was republished in *Dissertations and Discussions* in 1859, where they together make a major contribution to the effect of that collection.

Mill was moving into a new period of activity when this essay was composed, though the themes of the *Logic* were still running through his mind, as one can see especially in the article's discussions of such issues as scientific history as an interpretative tool, the relations between successive states of society, and the constructive, indeed essential, role of antagonism in cultural, intellectual, and social progress. This last theme is of course predictive of Mill's future work as well, being central to *On Liberty* and important in other of his essays; his comment on the "stationary state" in "Guizot" also suggests the development of this idea in his *Principles*; and again there is mention of the role of women in history, one of the principal emphases in his *Subjection of Women*. When beginning work on "Guizot," Mill was also seeing through the press the first edition of his *Essays on Some Unsettled Questions of Political Economy* (1844),

[29]*Ibid.*, 505, 602 (3 Mar., 1842, and 23 Oct., 1843).

[30]*Ibid.*, 612; Bain, *John Stuart Mill*, 78. Here Bain, like most of his contemporaries, including Mill and others of Scottish origin and residence, uses "English" rather than "British," although the *Edinburgh Review* in its origin and continuing force was true to its name.

the questions having remained unsettled since he wrote the essays in the early thirties (and to this day not entirely resolved). He was already planning to develop his ideas on political economy into a treatise,[31] and he published "The Currency Question" in the *Westminster* in June 1844 and "The Claims of Labour" (on which he was working in this period) in the *Edinburgh* in April 1845.

Unlike these two articles, Mill's accounts of the French historians were not occasional, not even in the sense of being responses to recent publications. He therefore was not specially anxious to rush his thoughts into print. So, though Napier was evidently pressing him early in 1844, he indicated that he would not have "Guizot" ready for the spring number, even if there were room for it; and, though he told John Sterling in May that he had been writing it, he remarked to Napier in November that "Guizot of course can wait indefinitely."[32] And wait it did, until after the appearance of the number containing "The Claims of Labour" and the next number in July. When it was published in October it was well received, Francis Jeffrey commenting,

Guizot, on the whole, I think excellent, and, indeed, a very remarkable paper. There are passages worthy of Macaulay, and throughout the traces of a vigorous and discursive intellect. He idolises his author a little too much (though I am among his warmest admirers) and I think under-estimates the knowledge and the relish of him which is now in this country. I cordially agree with most of the doctrine, and the value that is put on it, though I am far from being satisfied with the account of the Feudal system, and the differences between it and clanship, and the patriarchal, or Indian or North American tribes and associations, with which the affinities are curious.

These remarks were made before Jeffrey knew the author's identity; when informed, Jeffrey said: "Your key to the articles has, in some instances, surprised me, as to Neaves especially, and as to Mill also: for though I have long thought highly of his powers as a reasoner, I scarcely gave him credit for such large and sound views of *realities* and practical results as are displayed in that article."[33] One of the reasons for such approval may be the article's echo, noted by Napier, of ideas advanced by the eighteenth-century Scottish school, including Gilbert Stuart and Millar. In any case, the success of the account was understandably pleasing to Mill, who received (without asking for them) reprints, and rather surprisingly agreed that Napier's excision of the conclusion

---

[31]See *EL, CW*, XIII, 629-30 (29 May, 1844); he wrote most of the *Principles* in 1846 (see the Textual Introduction to *CW*, II, lxv-lxvii).

[32]*EL, CW*, XIII, 618, 629-30, 646.

[33]Letters to Macvey Napier of 8 and 13 Oct., 1845, in Macvey Napier (the younger), *Selections from the Correspondence of Macvey Napier* (London: Macmillan, 1897), 507, 509-10. Jeffrey had not entertained the same high view of Mill's "Michelet," commenting to Napier on 27 December, 1843 (and thus indicating that the number appeared—as was common—before its ostensible publication date): "There is thought and some clever suggestions in Mill's *Michelet*, but nothing systematic nor much well made out. I cannot but think, too, that he has made a bad choice of citations, the greater part of which are harsh, self-willed, and affectedly dogmatic." (*Ibid.*, 455.)

of his essay was warranted. Unfortunately, the manuscript (like those of almost all Mill's review articles) has not survived, and so we lack the text of what would undoubtedly be the most interesting variant, for which we must rely on his statement to Napier:

The omission of the concluding paragraph I do not regret: it could be well spared, & though I am fully convinced of the truth of all it contained, I was not satisfied with the manner in which it was expressed. You are of course quite right in not printing what you think would expose you to attack, when you do not yourself agree in it. At the same time, I do not know how a public writer can be more usefully employed than in telling his countrymen their faults, & if that is considered anti-national I am not at all desirous to avoid the charge. Neither do I think that the English, with all their national self-conceit, are now much inclined to resent having their faults pointed out—they will bear a good deal in that respect.[34]

"Duveyrier's Political Views of French Affairs," which appeared in the *Edinburgh* in April 1846, is similarly non-occasional; indeed Mill began writing it in the spring of 1844, thinking it might find a place in the *British and Foreign Review*, then edited by John Mitchell Kemble.[35] On 6 June, disappointed in his hopes that it would be finished (part was completed and the rest in draft), he wrote to Kemble promising that, official work and a holiday intervening, he would finish it in time for the August number; again on 14 August he asked for a stay, being "loaded with occupation."[36] The next surviving evidence leaves us in darkness as to the intermediate history: a letter to Napier on 1 May, 1846, acknowledges a generous remittance for the article, and then refers to what is, for us, yet another not-to-be-retrieved variant:

I cannot complain of your having left out the passage controverting the warlike propensity of the French, though I should have been glad if it had been consistent with your judgment to have retained it. The opinion is a very old & firm one with me, founded on a good deal of personal observation & I do not think you will find that Englishmen or other foreigners *who have lived long in France* & mixed in French society, are, so generally as you seem to think, of a different opinion. I have certainly heard, from such persons, the same opinion which I have expressed, & quite as strongly. And I am sure you will admit that national importance, & consideration among other nations, may be very strongly desired & sought by people who would rather have it in any other way than by war. I venture to say thus much because I think the Edin. has lately been sometimes very unjust to the French. . . .[37]

Here Mill shows less indulgence for a fellow editor's need to maintain a steady colouration in a journal, perhaps because his own editorship was a further two years in the past, but more likely because the subject was of greater contemporary importance, the essay on Duveyrier being much more concerned with

---

[34]*EL, CW*, XIII, 683 (20 Oct., 1845).
[35]*Ibid.*, 627 (May? 1844).
[36]*Ibid.*, 632-3, 634.
[37]*Ibid.*, 701.

current issues than that on Guizot. Mill does not ignore history, but the history that matters is mainly that since 1830, when France embarked on a constitutional course with, as it were, no native roots. The July monarchy was, of course, apparently continuing at the height of its success, with no portents of its downfall in less than two years. Mill was able here to draw on his extensive knowledge of the development of the French constitution in theory and practice during the preceding decade and a half, as well as his acquaintance with Duveyrier and his writings, and draw conclusions about the immediate problems and eventual solutions. His essay indeed typifies those of his writings (see especially the essays in Volume VI of the *Collected Works*) where one finds assessments that combine urgency with measured comment, one of the best of his remarks here being, "It is not the uncontrolled ascendancy of popular power, but of any power, which is formidable" (306).

In recognition, perhaps, of the dual nature of the essay, Mill did not include it in *Dissertations and Discussions*, but extracted the more generalized part for insertion in the revised version of "Tocqueville on Democracy in America [II]" there reprinted.[38] Only this passage then provides variants.

THE *WESTMINSTER* AGAIN

THE FRENCH REVOLUTION OF 1848, with its concomitant upheavals elsewhere in Europe, once again fired Mill's imagination, the idealist heat being heightened by Harriet Taylor's enthusiasm. Though the socialist experiment was short-lived, its lessons, he believed, were of lasting value, as he indicates in the *Autobiography* when discussing the changes made in the *Principles of Political Economy* for the 2nd (1849) and 3rd (1852) editions. The increased value attached to socialism (in his use of the term) was the result, he says, partly of "the change of times, the first edition [1848] having been written and sent to press before the French Revolution of 1848, after which the public mind became more open to the reception of novelties in opinion, and doctrines appeared moderate which would have been thought very startling a short time before." In the next year or two, he adds, he and his wife (as she became in 1851) gave much time "to the study of the best Socialistic writers on the Continent, and to meditation and discussion on the whole range of topics involved in the controversy. . . ."[39]

The reason for these changes may not have been so evident to contemporary readers of the *Principles*, but Mill had responded earlier, if at first anonymously, to the Revolution, choosing for his vehicle the *Westminster*, which was more

---

[38]He explicitly excluded from *Dissertations and Discussions* material of passing interest, carrying the policy so far—if not always immediately intelligibly—as to exclude all the essays gathered in Volume VI of the *Collected Works*.

[39]*Autobiography, CW*, I, 241.

cviii TEXTUAL INTRODUCTION

open to radical views than the *Edinburgh*. In "Vindication of the French Revolution of February 1848," published in April 1849, he takes as opponent the ever-available judgments of Lord Brougham (one of the originators and early mainstays of the *Edinburgh*). Though in this respect occasional, the article had lasting value for Mill as a defence of principles valid for the foreseeable future, and Brougham's pamphlet, *Letter to the Marquess of Lansdowne*, though viciously assailed, merely served as the best available entrée to the subject, which again brought back excited memories. The remark quoted above showing Mill's regret that Carrel was not living at that hour is echoed emphatically in Bain's recollection of their conversations at the time. The "Vindication," Bain says, "like [Mill's] 'Armand Carrel,' is a piece of French political history, and the replies to Brougham are scathing. I remember well, in his excitement at the Revolution, his saying that the one thought that haunted him was—Oh, that Carrel were still alive!"[40] As a glance at the article will show, Mill here engages major constitutional and practical questions in defending the revolutionists, and, in elucidating principles of comparative politics, brings to bear his careful consideration of the development of French institutions.

The essay takes forensic form, and Mill's concern over the basis of his defence is seen in his decisions about the authenticating evidence. This concern appears strongly in a letter to Hickson probably written in March of 1849:

I attach importance to most of the notes, since when I am charging Brougham with misrepresentation of what Lamartine said, it will not do to bid the reader trust to my translations—and the passages from Tocqueville being cited as evidence to matters of fact, ought to be given in the original. You however must judge what is best for your review. You kindly offered me some separate copies—I should not desire more than 50, but in these I would like to have the notes preserved and it would not be necessary for that purpose to set them up in smaller type. If the types are redistributed I would willingly pay the expense of recomposing. I cannot imagine how the printer could commit the stupid blunder of putting those notes with the text. As a heading, "The Revolution of February and its assailants" would do. In the separate copies I should like to have a title page, which might run thus: "A Vindication of the French Revolution of 1848 in reply to Lord Brougham and others."[41]

These "notes," which consist of the original passages that Mill translated, do not

---

[40]Bain, *John Stuart Mill*, 93-4. Mill's correspondence at the time further supports these judgments. His view of Carrel's relevance was not idiosyncratic. In the immediate aftermath of the February Revolution, on 2 March, there was a procession to Carrel's grave in the St. Maur cemetery, as a preliminary to his remains being removed to the Pantheon. Present were many "respectable young men, who walked arm-in-arm, wearing sprigs of everlasting in their hats, and sung in chorus the 'Chant des Girondins.'" Marrast (now editor of the revived *National*, the voice of the Provisional Government) delivered a eulogy. Then Emile de Girardin, editor of *La Presse*, "by whose hand Carrel fell . . . bewailed his own misfortune in having occasioned the death of so illustrious a citizen. . . ." The French were more forgiving of Girardin than was Mill (see the Introduction, lxvii n above), for he "was loudly applauded" and then "embraced" by Marrast. (See "The Republic of France," *Daily News*, 4 Mar., 1848, 4, and 6 Mar., 2.)

[41]*LL, CW,* XIV, 13-14.

appear in the article, but they are attached as an appendix to the pamphlet off-print, and appear in *Dissertations and Discussions* as an appendix to Volume II; here, acknowledging Mill's attachment to them, we include them as Appendix B.

Other indications of the significance of the argument to Mill are seen in his procuring and disposing of offprints (he referred to the article even before publication as a "pamphlet"), and in his reprinting it in *Dissertations and Discussions*, long after what Bain calls his "sanguine belief in the political future of France" had disappeared following the "fatality of December, 1851," when Louis Napoleon engineered his *coup d'état*.[42]

The initial composition is not well documented, although there is no doubt that he and Harriet were highly offended by the British press's revealing through its animosity its ignorance of France. The first extant reference to the article dates from 6 February, 1849, when Mill reported to Hickson that it was finished, except for the revision, which was retarded by difficulties he was having with his eyesight. He will, he says (making a rare and welcome reference to reading Dickens), "'make an effort' (vide chap. 1 of Dombey) and let you have it soon" for the *Westminster*. And less than two weeks later he writes to Harriet: "The pamphlet [*sic*] has gone to Hickson—I had thought of sending one of the separate copies to L. Blanc. Whom else should it go to? To all the members of the Prov[isional] Gov[ernment] I think, & as it will not be published till April I had better take the copies to Paris with me & send them when there as it saves so much uncertainty & delay."[43]

He returned to the matter of the titles in reporting on 14 March to Harriet Taylor on the article's progress:

I have had the proof of the pamphlet, all but the last few pages. There seems very little remaining in it that could be further softened without taking the sting out entirely—which would be a pity. I am rather against giving away *any* copies, at least for the present, in England—except to Louis Blanc to whom I suppose I should acknowledge authorship. . . . As a heading *in the review* I have thought of "The Revolution of February & its assailants"—it does not seem advisable to put Brougham's name at the top of the page—& "the Revolution of February" or anything of that kind itself would be tame, & excite no attention.[44]

In sending a copy to Louis Blanc, Mill expressed strongly his approbation of the revolutionists' behaviour:

permettez-moi de vous faire l'hommage d'un petit écrit destiné à servir de protestation contre les calomnies odieuses dont on cherche à flétrir votre noble révolution de février, et ceux qui l'ont dirigée pendant les premiers jours.

J'ai tâché de rendre justice à la part que vous avez prise personnellement dans le grand

---

[42]*John Stuart Mill*, 93.

[43]*LL, CW*, XIV, 7, 10. He went to France about 20 April, returning about 12 May, and so perhaps this plan was fulfilled.

[44]*Ibid.*, 15.

événement, et vous verrez que j'y parle du socialisme avec une sympathie plus ouverte que celle que j'ai manifestée dans la première édition de mon Econ. politique. Je crois que vous serez plus satisfait de la seconde.[45]

Ten years later the question of attribution arose again when Blanc wished to pay public tribute to Mill's account. Mill responded:

Je n'ai aucune raison pour ne pas vouloir être cité comme l'auteur de la brochure sur la Révolution de Février. Au contraire je me réjouirais d'associer mon nom à cette protestation en faveur de principes qui sont les miens, et d'hommes que je respecte profondément.[46]

As indicated in the editorial headnote to the text, Mill's wishes concerning the titles were acceded to; however, some of the remaining "sting" that he thought could not be spared was extracted in the reprint in *Dissertations and Discussions*, ten years after the letter to his wife quoted above. Indeed, it seems certain that this was one of the two articles (the other probably being "Sedgwick's Discourse") in which he felt the need to remove some of the "asperity of tone" of the original version.[47] The number of "softening" variants helps make this (given its date) one of the most heavily revised essays in *Dissertations and Discussions*.

The accession to imperial power of Louis Napoleon provides much of the explanation of Mill's not writing at length or publicly on France during the remainder of his life. He felt not only abstract revulsion but personal distress during the Second Empire, as his letters show, but no major essays dwell on his concern. Furthermore, his extended comments in essays on history and historians after 1850 are exclusively devoted to the classical period, where his interest in philosophy was intertwined with historical considerations. But his extensive and intensive examinations of the themes developed in this volume, valuable in themselves, may also be seen behind his major political and social writings of the 1850s and 1860s.

TEXTUAL VARIANTS

THE GREAT MAJORITY of textual variants in Mill's periodical essays derive from their revision for the first two volumes of *Dissertations and Discussions* (1859), which contain articles from 1832 to 1853; alterations in the second edition of

---

[45]*Ibid.*, 23-4 (Apr. 1849).

[46]*Ibid.*, XV, 545 (11 Jan., 1858). Consequently Blanc quoted the long passage on the *droit du travail*, prefacing it by saying it was appropriate for him to leave his defence "in the hands of one whose authority the English people have long since learned to respect,—a man highly distinguished for his qualities both of head and heart, and incontestably the first political economist of our day, Mr. John Stuart Mill." And he followed the quotation by describing Mill as "one of the most eminent philosophers and writers of this country." (Blanc, *1848: Historical Revelations*, 83-7. Blanc quoted the passage: "To one class of thinkers . . . the present race of mankind" [348-50 below].)

[47]See *CW*, X, cxix and 494.

those volumes (1867) were infrequent. The articles, dating from 1859 to 1866, that were republished in the third volume of *Dissertations and Discussions* (also 1867), were less thoroughly revised (or, perhaps it is fairer to say, needed less revision). The fourth and final volume (1875), containing materials dating from 1869 to 1873, was prepared for publication after Mill's death by his step-daughter, Helen Taylor; there is no evidence that Mill was responsible for any of the rare changes in it (and in the third edition of Volumes I and II, and the second edition of Volume III, which were published with it in 1875). There is, indeed, a gradual decrease in frequency of changes, substantive and formal, both as the years progress and as the gap between the time of first publication and of republication decreases.

These generalizations, which derive from a study of all the revisions, are borne out by the essays in this volume, six of which appeared in *Dissertations and Discussions*, two in part and four in full, all in Volumes I and II. Because he chose not to include in *Dissertations and Discussions* any of his apprentice essays, the first three essays in this volume were not rewritten; neither, as mentioned above, was the review of Carlyle's *French Revolution*. "The Monster Trial" was not reprinted, undoubtedly because Mill thought it too occasional for long wear, but it reveals variants of some interest in Mill's self-quotation of a passage from an article in the *Examiner*. The results of collation of the texts that Mill could have prepared will be seen in footnotes, which record the substantive variants in accordance with the system outlined on cxiv-cxvi below.

While a full appreciation of the significance of Mill's changes can be gained only by examining each in context, an impracticable goal here, some indications of their general tenor are appropriate. A rough initial classification (used also in the other volumes of this edition) will help in describing the kind and frequency of his revisions: one can distinguish (though there is overlapping) among changes that reveal (1) alterations in opinion or fact, including omissions, amplifications, or corrections; (2) alterations resulting from the time between versions or from their different provenances; (3) alterations that qualify, emphasize, or give technical clarity; and (4) alterations that are purely verbal, or give semantic clarity, or result from shifts in word usage, and alterations in emphasis indicated by changes from italic to roman typeface.

In "The Monster Trial" there are only three substantive changes between the quoted passage as it appeared in the *Examiner* in 1834 and in the *Monthly Repository* in 1835 (see 126[a], [b-b], 128[c]). Of these, the second is a trivial example of the fourth type, but the other two, involving excision of passages having to do with a radical view of the rights of property, illustrate type 1 because they involve important differences in intention and effect. It will be noted, of course, that they could be classed as type 2 because the passages, appropriate in a newspaper, might be thought not to serve the different ends of a periodical, especially after the passage of a year and a half.

More illustrative, of course, are the changes in the six essays reprinted in whole or in part in *Dissertations and Discussions*. In all there are 488 substantive variants, of which 38 may be seen as type 1, 45 as type 2, 152 as type 3, and 253 as type 4. Of the total, only 37 reflect changes resulting from revision in the 1867 edition of *Dissertations and Discussions*, and almost all of these are type 4. In "Alison's History" (a comparatively short essay, it will be recalled, only part of which was reprinted) there are 41 variants, of which over two-thirds are type 4; 15 of these (including the one variant from 1867) result from the removal of italics, a quieting revision found in the essays dating from the early 1830s that in their original forms show Carlyle's influence on Mill's prose. The one change that I have labelled as type 1 is that from "men's" to "people's" (119^{r-r}), an acknowledgment by Mill of the pronominal gender distortion that he tried to alleviate in his writings after the early 1850s.[48] As an illustration of type 2 changes, one may cite 120^{x-x}, in which the "Tories" of 1832 became "Conservatives" in 1859, reflecting the change in terminology (not, of course, that the earlier term disappeared). A type 3 change, typical not only of its kind but also of Mill's ceaseless search for precise categorization, is seen at 120^{a-a}, where "never" was replaced by "has scarcely ever".

General illustrations of the types of alteration may be seen in the most heavily and most interestingly revised essay, "Armand Carrel," which contains 246 changes, more than half of those in this volume as a whole, 23 of them being type 1 and 31 type 2. Of the former, good instances will be found at 173^{j-j}, ^{k} (the motivation here a little mysterious), 177^{e-e}, and ^{g} (cf. the footnote where the fact is corrected). At 185^{j-j} one sees the common qualification of Mill's early enthusiasm for August Comte—but compare 228^{s-s}. At 185^{k-k} there is a reflection of Mill's further reading in the philosophy of history as Vico and Condorcet are listed with Herder, while von Müller is dropped. The type 2 changes reflecting the passage of time are illustrated by 187^t (cf. 187n), where Mill, having referred in 1837 to the hoped-for completion of Guizot's *Histoire de la révolution d'Angleterre* (2 vols., 1826-27), deleted the promissory note, for the work had been completed by four further volumes, two in 1854 and two in 1856; the type 2 changes reflecting the change of provenance are illustrated close by, at 188^{v-v}, where the revision includes deletion of the reference to "this review" (it also includes the type 4 change from "contemporaries" to "cotemporaries," Mill's common form). An interesting series of type 3 changes, close in effect to type 1, will be seen at 192^{n-n} and following, where the proper ways of describing the effects of the Revolution of 1830 are explored. Such changes are related to those counted as type 4 that soften the elegiac tone at 169^h, $^{j-j}$, 173^g, 199^{l-l}, $^{m-m}$, and 212^{e-e}; these have a cumulative effect indicating that individually minor

---

[48]Recurrences after the first such change, which may be taken to derive from it, are like all similarly entailed revisions counted as type 4. For further comment on this particular change, see John M. Robson, "'Joint Authorship' Again: The Evidence of the Third Edition of Mill's *Logic*," *Mill News Letter*, VI (Spring 1971), 15-20.

changes can have an importance going beyond type 3 to type 1. It should be mentioned that only 8 of the variants in "Armand Carrel" date from 1867, but 24 arise from Mill's quotations from one of his letters to Carlyle; these are of unequal significance, but certainly should not be ignored in any close study of Mill's political views in the 1830s.[49] Finally (though one is tempted to continue exhaustively and exhaustingly), material of interest to historians of the language can be found in those variant notes that show a change from italic to roman type for words taken into English from French; Mill was, one may infer, an important source of such loan words, his works providing in this, as in other respects, significant material for philologists.

In "Michelet's History of France," "Guizot's Essays and Lectures," and the small part of "Duveyrier's Political Views" that was republished, the substantive changes bear out the generalizations made above about frequency and importance: "Michelet" reveals 63 variants, 7 of them dating from 1867; only 8 of the total show the characteristics of types 1 and 2. "Guizot" has 44, a surprising proportion (nearly a quarter) from 1867; all but 2 of the total are of types 3 and 4. And "Duveyrier" shows only 4, of which 1 is from 1867, and 3 are type 4. "Vindication of the French Revolution of February 1848" is an exception to the pattern; for reasons stated above, both its subject and its personal attack on Brougham gave matter for thought in the ten years intervening between its first publication and its republication in *Dissertations and Discussions*. In fact it contains 90 revisions (10 of them from 1867),[50] of which 10 may be seen as type 1; once more it may be claimed that students of Mill, in this case especially those interested in the roots of his qualified socialism, should look carefully at these first and second thoughts.

The accidental variants (not reported in detail in this edition), mainly consisting of changes in punctuation and spelling, do not reveal sufficient evidence to justify major generalizations. They of course show, to an indeterminable extent, the preferences of printers, editors, and publishing houses. (The *Edinburgh Review*, for instance, may have revised Mill's manuscripts by removing some hyphenations, judging by the comparative frequency of such changes when revisions in essays from it are compared with those from the *Westminster*.) As usual in Mill's case, the essays show a slight lightening in punctuation in their republication, but "Armand Carrel" reveals in *Dissertations and Discussions* a great preponderance of added over removed commas. As elsewhere, the earlier "any thing" and "every thing [body]" are collapsed into one word, and participles with "s" ("realising," "analysed") tend to take "z"

---

[49]In two cases our reading of the letter to Carlyle differs from that in *Earlier Letters*: at 204^t, a cancelled "at" appears more likely than "on"; and at 204$^{v\text{-}v}$ the manuscript seems to agree with the reading in all versions of "Armand Carrel," i.e., "respect".

[50]One type 4 change, the addition of "de" to Lamartine's name, is noted only on its first appearance (338$^{k\text{-}k}$).

forms, except for "recognize" and its cognates, where the reverse occurs; the forms of "shew" take the "o" spelling, and "enquiry" and its cognates take an initial "i". The addition or removal of initial capital letters (roughly in balance) has not yielded any conclusions, nor are any of these changes suggestive of altered emphasis, as they are in other places, for example in some of the works in Volumes XVIII-XIX of the *Collected Works*.

TEXTUAL PRINCIPLES AND METHODS

AS THROUGHOUT this edition, the copy-text for each item is that of the final version supervised by Mill, unless only a part of an essay was later reprinted, in which case the latest full version is adopted.[51] There are, it is to be regretted, no extant manuscripts for any of the essays here included. Details concerning revisions are given in the headnotes to each item and in the discussion above.

Method of indicating variants. All the substantive variants are governed by the principles enunciated below; "substantive" here means all changes of text except spelling (including initial capitalization), hyphenation, punctuation, demonstrable typographical errors, and such printing-house concerns as type size, etc. All substantive variants are indicated, except the substitution of "on" for "upon" (twenty-two instances) and of "though" for "although" (five instances). The variants are of three kinds: addition of a word or words, substitution of a word or words, deletion of a word or words. The following illustrative examples are drawn, except as indicated, from "Armand Carrel."

Addition of a word or words: see 170^{n-n}. In the text, the passage "or even who can" appears as "or ^{n}even^n who can"; the variant note reads " $^{n-n}+59,67$". Here the plus sign indicates the editions of this particular text in which the addition appears. The editions are always indicated by the last two numbers of the year of publication: here 59 = 1859 (the first edition of Volumes I and II of *Dissertations and Discussions*); 67 = 1867 (the second edition of those volumes). Information explaining the use of these abbreviations is given in each headnote, as required. Any added editorial comment is enclosed in square brackets and italicized.

Placing this example in context, the interpretation is that when first published (1837) the reading was "or who can"; this reading was altered in 1859 to "or even who can" and the latter reading was retained in 1867 (the copy-text).

Substitution of a word or words: see 169^{j-j}. In the text the passage "We can still remember" appears as "^{j}We can still^j remember"; the variant note reads

[51]The argument for this practice is given in my "Principles and Methods in the Collected Edition of John Stuart Mill," in *Editing Nineteenth-Century Texts*, ed. John M. Robson (Toronto: University of Toronto Press, 1967), 96-122.

"[j-j]37[1,2]   It is still given to us, to". Here the words following the edition indicator are those for which "We can still" were substituted; applying the same rules and putting the variant in context, the interpretation is that when first published (in 1837 as article and offprint) the reading was "It is still given to us, to remember"; in 1859 this was altered to "We can still remember"; and the reading of 1859 (as is clear in the text) was retained in 1867.

In this volume there are few examples of passages altered more than once: see 201[a-a]. The text reads " [a]Mr. Carlyle's[a] words"; the variant note reads " [a-a]33 your]   37[1,2]   the". Here the different readings, in chronological order, are separated by a square bracket. The interpretation is that the reading in the earliest version (1833), "your words", was altered in the second version (1837[1] and the identical 1837[2]) to "the words", and in the final versions (1859 and 1867, the copy-text) to "Mr. Carlyle's words". (The circumstances are unusual, for the version of 1833 is from a letter from Mill to Carlyle.) The other cases, all instances of a wording altered and then returned to its original reading, are signalled by the absence of an expected edition indicator. See, e.g., 206[h], where the variant note reads " [h]59   or seemed to present"; the lack of the expected "67" indicates that the words "or seemed to present" were added in 1859 but deleted in 1867 in a return to the original reading.

Deletion of a word or words: see 169[h] and 118[j-j]. The first of these is typical, representing the most convenient way of indicating deletions in a later edition. In the text at 169[h] a *single* superscript appears *centred* between "gone" and "; and"; the variant note reads " [h]37[1,2]   . He is gone". Here the words following the edition indicators are the ones deleted; applying the same rules and putting the variant in context, the interpretation is that when first published (1837) the reading was "gone. He is gone; and"; in 1859 the period and "He is gone" were deleted, and the reading of 1859 (as is clear in the text) was retained in 1867.

The second example (118[j-j]) illustrates the method used in the volume to cover more conveniently deletions when portions of the copy-text were later reprinted, as in the case of "Alison's History of the French Revolution," part of which was republished in *Dissertations and Discussions*, Volume I. That is, there is here, exceptionally, a later version of part of the copy-text, whereas normally the copy-text is the latest version. In the text the words "The hundred political revolutions" appear as "The [j]hundred[j] political revolutions"; the variant note reads " [j-j]−59,67". The minus sign indicates that in the editions signified the word enclosed was deleted; putting the example in context the interpretation is that when first published (1832) the reading was (as is clear in the text) "The hundred political revolutions"; this reading was altered in 1859 to "The political revolutions", and the latter reading was retained in 1867.

Dates of footnotes: see 187n. Here the practice, when a note was added by Mill to a version after the first, is to place immediately after the footnote indicator, in square brackets, the figures indicating the edition in which Mill's footnote first appeared. In the example cited, "[67]" signifies that the note was added in 1867. If no such indication appears, the note is in all versions.

Punctuation and spelling. In general, changes between versions in punctuation and spelling are ignored. Those changes that occur as part of a substantive variant are included in that variant, and the superscript letters in the text are placed exactly with reference to punctuation. Changes between italic and roman type are treated as substantive variants and are therefore shown, except in foreign phrases and titles of works.

Other textual liberties. Some of the titles have been modified or supplied; the full titles in their various forms will be found in the headnotes. The dates added to the titles are those of first publication. When footnotes to the titles gave bibliographic information, these have been deleted, and the information given in the headnotes. Having adapted our practices to composition by word-processor, we have not reproduced digraphs. At 204n-5n quotation marks have been added to what was clearly intended to be recognized as a quotation. In the headnotes the quotations from Mill's bibliography, the manuscript of which is a scribal copy, are also silently corrected; the note below lists them.[52] While the punctuation and spelling of each item are retained, the style has been made uniform: for example, periods are deleted after references to monarchs (e.g., "Louis XIV."), and their numerical designations are regularized as capital roman numerals; dashes are deleted when combined with other punctuation before a quotation or reference; and italic punctuation after italic passages has been made roman. Indications of ellipsis have been normalized to three dots plus, when necessary, terminal punctuation. The positioning of footnote indicators has been normalized so that they always appear after adjacent punctuation marks; in some cases references have been moved from the beginning to the end of quotations for consistency.

Also, in accordance with modern practice, all long quotations have been reduced in type size and the quotation marks removed. In consequence, it has occasionally been necessary to add square brackets around Mill's words in quotations; there is little opportunity for confusion, as there are no editorial insertions except page references. Double quotation marks replace single, and titles of works originally published separately are given in italics. Mill's references to sources, and additional editorial references (in square brackets),

---

[52]In a few cases my reading of the manuscript differs from that in the edition by Ney MacMinn, J.M. McCrimmon, and J.R. Hainds, *Bibliography of the Published Writings of J.S. Mill* (Evanston: Northwestern University Press, 1945), to which page references (as MacMinn) are given in the headnotes. The corrected scribal errors (the erroneous reading first, with the corrected one following in square brackets) are:

168.15   intituled [entitled]
258.14   Lecture on history [Lectures on History]
296.7   Duveyriai's [Duveyrier's]
318.9   Bunghan's [Brougham's]
367.8   articles [article]

have been normalized. When necessary his references have been corrected; a list of the corrections and alterations is given in the note below.[53]

Appendices. Appendix A, the review of Guizot's *Lectures*, is placed here because it was jointly written by Joseph Blanco White and Mill, and the precise contribution of each is not known; otherwise it is treated uniformly with the main text.

Appendix B contains the French texts of the material quoted in Mill's own translation in "Vindication of the French Revolution of February 1848." The importance Mill attached to their being available is explained at cviii-cix above.

---

[53]Following the page and line notation, the first reference is to Mill's identification; the corrected identification (that which appears in the present text) follows in square brackets. There is no indication of the places where a dash has been substituted for a comma to indicate adjacent pages, where "P." or "Pp." replaces "p." or "pp." (or the reverse), or where the volume number has been added to the reference.

7.36   41 [41-5]
10.39   57 [60-6]
12.2   289 [289-92]
12.29   379 [379-81]
14.5   161 [160-1]
21n.1   xx [xx-xxi]
29n.1   142 [142n]
30n.1   10 [10-11]
31n.2   94 [94-5]
31n.4   136 [136-7]
35n.6   36 [36-7]
36n.1   101 [101-2]
36n.2   111 [111-12]
36n.12   114 [114-15]
36n.18   120 [120-2]
44n.1   102 [101-3]
44n.1   203 [201-4]
44n.1   309 [308-9]
44n.2   240 [239-40]
48n.1   318 [318-19]
48n.2   347 [347-8]
48.27   297 [297-8]
50n.1   243 [242-3]
68n.14   xl [xx]
75n.3   215-16 [215n-17n]
75n.13   177 [174-7]
75n.23   127 [126-7]
85n.7   310, 318 [308, 316]
85n.10   236-7 [237-8]
85n.10   481 [482-8]
88.35   130 [130-1]
93n.12   25 [23]
94n.1   278 [277-8]
100n.7   389 [388-91]
104n.3   42 to 47 [46-7] [*moved from text and reference divided to match quotations*]
106n.1   449 [450] [*moved to footnote in this ed.*]
106n.2   455 [454-6] [*moved to footnote in this ed.*]
140n.1   461 [461-2]

Appendix C consists of the textual emendations; its headnote outlines the principles and practices adopted in altering Mill's text.

Appendix D, the Index of Persons and Works Cited, provides a guide to Mill's references and quotations, with notes concerning the separate entries, and a list of substantive variants between his quotations and their sources. The most extensive quotation is, as one would expect, from reviewed works; a large number of the shorter quotations (some of which are indirect) are undoubtedly taken from memory, with no explicit references being given, and the identification of some of these is inescapably inferential. It will be noted that Mill habitually translates from the French; this volume gives the best evidence of his very considerable skill.

Since Appendix D serves as an index to persons, writings, and statutes, references to them do not appear in the general Index, which has been prepared by Dr. Maureen Clarke and Dr. Jean O'Grady.

ACKNOWLEDGMENTS

TO THE MEMBERS OF THE EDITORIAL COMMITTEE, to the editorial and printing staff of the University of Toronto Press, and especially to the copy-editors,

---

141n.17   256 [256-62] [full reference for the document cited]

142n.6   262 [262-76] [full reference for the document cited]

146n.1   324 [324-5]

146n.4   319 [318-20]

147n.3   267-306 [267-400]

148n.12   i [no vol. given, as 1st ed. in fact one volume; same change throughout this essay]

149n.6   149, &c. [149-51]

150n.1   12-48-84, &c. [48, 12, 84, 48]

152n.1   141-166 [141-65]

151n.2   Note, p. 281 [p. 282n]

153n.1   310 [110]

153n.2   161 [160-1]

157n.2   ii, 75-87. [Vol. II, pp. 71-7.] [to conform to the ed. used elsewhere in this volume, and to the events described]

237n.7   171 [171n]

244n.1   343 [343-4]

247n.1   297-302 [297-8, 300-2] [moved from text and reference divided to match quotations]

250n.2   538-543 [537-43]

251n.3   607-8 [606-7]

272n.1   Vol. iv. p. 191 [Vol. III, pp. 191-2]

281n.1   Vol. iii ad fin. [Vol. II, pp. 451-2] [not at the end]

301.30   168 [168-70]

304.35   3-6 [4-6] [earlier reference to 3 added above]

310.35   69-84 [83-4] [the preceding quotations are given specific references; JSM is presumably referring to the whole of the third Letter, which begins on 69, but his first quotation from the Letter is from 71, and the Letter ends on 100]

379n.2   vol. iii. p. 165 [Vol. XIX, p. 239] [the given reference not being verifiable (the passage is in Chap. 16 of Bk. 5, so perhaps the "p. 165" is explicable), the actual reference in the SC ed. is given]

Rosemary Shipton and Margaret Parker, I express my deep appreciation and thanks. I am greatly indebted to the staffs of various libraries, including the British Library, the University of Toronto Library, the Victoria University Library, the University of London Library, the library of the Institute of Historical Research, the British Library of Political and Economic Science, the London Library, and (a repeated but still special thanks for prompt and ever-courteous aid) the library of Somerville College, Oxford. Help of various kinds but always selfless came from these inadequately acknowledged scholars and friends: R.C. Alston, T.D. Barnes, Kathleen Coburn, M.J. Crump, J.L. Dewan, J. and M.L. Friedland, Gregory Hutchinson, André Jardin, Jay Macpherson, J. O'Donnell, David H. Pinkney, Aubrey Rosenberg, H.G. Schogt, C.A. Silber, and William Thomas.

A generous grant in support of editing and publication from the Social Sciences and Humanities Research Council of Canada places us yet again in grateful debt. Its major benefit to me is the rewarding company of the editorial team who have done all the hard work: more easily in writing than speech I thank Marion Filipiuk (our resident expert in French), Jean O'Grady, Rea Wilmshurst, Allison Taylor, Jonathan Cutmore, and Maureen Clarke. Her Huguenot heritage and historical profession make as appropriate as it is pleasant to announce again my enduring obligation to one member of the editorial committee, Ann P. Robson, ma femme qui, en dépit du dicton de François Ier, ne varie point.

MIGNET'S FRENCH REVOLUTION

1826

EDITOR'S NOTE

Westminster Review, V (Apr., 1826), 385-98. Headed: "Art. V.—*Histoire de la Révolution Française, depuis 1789, jusqu'en 1814*. / Par F[rançois] A[uguste] Mignet. Paris [: Firmin Didot], 1824. 2 vols. [*sic for* 2 parts.] 8vo. Pp. 735. / *History of the French Revolution*. By F.A. Mignet, 8vo. 2 vols. / 12mo. 2 vols. 1826. [London:] Hunt and Clarke." Running titles: "French Revolution." Unsigned. Not republished. Identified in Mill's bibliography as "A review of Mignet's History of the French Revolution, in the 10th number of the Westminster Review" (MacMinn, 7). There is no separate copy of this article in Mill's library, Somerville College.

For comment on the essay, see xxxix–xlii and xciv–xcv above.

Mignet's French Revolution

THIS IS A VERY SPRIGHTLY NARRATIVE of the French Revolution, in two small volumes: which is as much as to say, that it is calculated to be most extensively popular. It possesses, indeed, all the requisites for a popular history. It tells an interesting story; it tells it in an interesting manner; it is not too long to be readable; it addresses itself to the reigning sentiment in the nation for which it is written; and there is just philosophy enough in it to persuade common readers that they are deriving instruction, while there is not enough to task their attention or their patience. There is a sort of middle point which it is difficult to hit exactly, between a philosophical history and a mere narrative. M. Mignet seems to have aimed at this point; he has at any rate attained it.

The old mode of writing a history resembled the mode of writing a novel; with only this difference, that the facts were expected to be true. In both cases there was a story to be told, and he who told it best was the best novelist, or the best historian. The poems which preceded the first histories, and which were probably intended, with some qualifications, to pass for histories, were written with the same ends in view as the prose histories which followed them. Greater license of amplification was, indeed, allowed to the poet, but in other respects the standard of excellence was the same: he who raised the most vivid conceptions, and the most intense emotions, was the greatest master of his art. This mode of writing history attained its highest excellence in the hands of the Greek and Roman historians. Livy, perhaps, exemplifies it in its purest state. In what remains of his history we have a surprising instance of the perfection to which the art of narration may be carried, where no other part of the duties of a historian is attended to; and for that very reason. Thucydides, with the exception of his early chapters,[*] which consist chiefly of a comment upon evidence, may be regarded as another variety of the same class. Each stands preeminent among his countrymen in the talent of narrative, each avoids generalization, and when he has any reflections to make, puts them into the mouth of one of the dramatis personae; retaining the character of the story-teller, even when he puts on that of the orator or the politician.

Between this style of historical composition, and the more modern one, which makes history subservient to philosophy, in which the narrative itself is but a

---

[*Thucydides (Greek and English), trans. Charles Forster Smith, 4 vols. (London: Heinemann; Cambridge, Mass.: Harvard University Press, 1969), Vol. I, pp. 3-7 (i-iii).]

secondary object, the illustration of the laws of human nature and human society being the first, there is an intermediate style, which endeavours to unite the characteristic properties of both the others. In this the primary object is still the gratification of that large class, who read only for amusement. With this purpose long inductions of facts or trains of reasoning being inconsistent, they are accordingly avoided, or banished to an appendix. Dramatic interest is with these, as with the first class of historians, the main object; but such general reflections are interspersed, drawn from the surface of the subject, as may be comprehended without any effort of attention, by an ordinary understanding. The common reader is thus provided with such instruction, or supposed instruction, as his habits of mind render him capable of receiving, and is possessed with a high idea of the powers of the writer, who can communicate wisdom in so easy and entertaining a form. Of the popularity which may be acquired by this mode of writing history, the success of Hume is a striking example.[*] Excelling all modern historians in his powers of narrative, he has also obtained credit for the profundity of his reflections. That his reputation for this quality is so widely diffused, is of itself a sufficient proof that it is undeserved. Had his reflections been really profound, we may venture to affirm that they would have been less popular. By a profound reflection, is meant a reflection, the truth of which is not obvious at first sight, and to a cursory reader, but which, in proportion as a man grows wiser, and takes a deeper insight into things, forces itself upon his assent.

When we say, that M. Mignet seems to have formed himself in this school, and that he is the highest specimen of it, among recent writers, which our recollection suggests to us, we have conveyed, we think, a tolerably accurate conception of his character as a historian. Little, therefore, remains to be done beyond the selection of such passages as seem best adapted to exhibit the degree in which he possesses the various attributes of his class: for we do not purpose to enter at present into the general question of the French revolution; it being our intention, at no distant period, to treat of that subject at greater length.[†] In the main, our view of the subject accords with that of M. Mignet; and for this reason, among others, we are anxious that his work should be extensively circulated in this country. There is nothing more disgraceful to Englishmen than their utter ignorance, not only of the causes and effects, but of the very events, the story, of the French revolution. With the majority of them, even of those among them who read and think, the conception they have of that great event is all comprehended in a dim but horrible vision of mobs, and massacres, and revolutionary tribunals, and guillotines, and fishwomen, and heads carried on pikes, and *noyades*, and *fusillades*, and one

---

[*David Hume, *The History of England from the Invasion of Julius Caesar to the Revolution in 1688* (1754-62), 8 vols. (London: Cadell, Rivington, *et al.*, 1823).]

[†Mill treated the subject at length in "Scott's Life of Napoleon," *Westminster Review*, IX (Apr., 1828), 251-313 (reprinted at pp. 53-110 below).]

Robespierre, a most sanguinary monster. What the Tory prints choose to tell them of this most interesting period of modern history, so much they know, and nothing more: that is, enough to raise in their minds an intense yet indefinite horror of French reforms and reformers, and as far as possible of all reforms and reformers. *Now*, however, when they have ceased to tremble for themselves, and to start from their sleep at the terrific idea of a landing of French Jacobins or a rising of English ones to confiscate their property and cut their throats, they can, perhaps, bear to look at the subject without horror; and we exhort them to buy and read M. Mignet's work, that they may know in what light the revolution is regarded by the nation which saw and felt it, which endured its evils, and is now enjoying its benefits.

M. Mignet, in his two volumes, had not space to do more than relate the *story* of the revolution. Proofs, in seven hundred pages, he could give none; his work is not even attended by the *pièces justificatives*, which usually follow in the train of a French history. The revolution has been long *une cause jugée*, in the minds of all disinterested persons in France; and none of M. Mignet's countrymen would have asked him for his proofs, who would have been capable of being convinced by them if offered. To an English reader, this omission will diminish in some degree the value of the book. A writer who opposes the current opinion, has need of all the proofs he can muster. Happily, the proofs are not scanty, and are, even in this country, accessible.[*] We purpose to lay some of them before our readers ere long.

M. Mignet's narrative powers are of a high order. He has mastered the grand difficulty in narration; he is interesting, without being voluminous; concise, without being vague and general. Former writers on the French revolution had either lost themselves in a sea of details, dwelling on circumstance after circumstance with such painful minuteness that he who had patience to read to the end of the story had time before he arrived there to forget the beginning; or had contented themselves with a meagre abstract, describing the most remarkable scenes in terms so general as to have fitted a hundred other scenes almost as well. In narrative, as in description, it is impossible to excite vivid conceptions, in other words it is impossible to be interesting, without entering somewhat into detail. A *particular* event cannot be characterized by a *general* description. But details are endless. Here then is the dilemma. *All* the details it is not possible to give, not only because nobody would read them, but because if read they would defeat their own purpose. If the reader's conception wants vivacity where there are no details, where there is excess of details it wants distinctness. The multitude of the parts injures the *ensemble*. The difficulty is in the apt *selection* of details. It is in judging *which* of the individualizing features it is best to delineate, when there is not room for all: it is in fixing upon those features which are the most strikingly

[*Mill is referring, at least in part, to *Collection des mémoires relatifs à la révolution française*, ed. Saint-Albin Berville and Jean François Barrière, 68 vols. (Paris: Baudouin, 1820-28).]

characteristic, or which, if delineated, will of themselves suggest the remainder, that the rarest quality, perhaps, of the skilful narrator displays itself. M. Mignet possesses this quality in an extraordinary degree. His narrative may be pronounced a model of the apt selection of details. No one has better allied circumstantiality with condensation. We have all heard of *graphic* descriptions. M. Mignet's is a graphic narrative: and whoever looks even at the outside of the voluminous compilations which are called Histories of the Revolution, and then turns to M. Mignet's small volumes, will wonder by what art he can abridge so much, with so little of the appearance of an abridgement.

We quote the following sketch of the state of affairs at the opening of the Etats Généraux, partly for the complete justification which it affords of the early revolutionists, and partly as a specimen of the manner in which M. Mignet has executed one of the most important parts of his task:

The government ought to have been better aware of the importance of the States-general. The re-establishment of that assembly announced of itself a great revolution. Looked forward to by the nation with eager hope, they reappeared at a moment when the ancient monarchy was in a state of decrepitude, and when they alone were capable of reforming the state, and supplying the necessities of the king. The difficulties of the times, the nature of their commission, the choice of their members, every thing announced that they were convoked no longer as the payers of taxes, but as the makers of laws. The public voice and the instructions of their constituents had confided to them the right of regenerating France; and public support, and the enormity of existing abuses, promised them strength to undertake and accomplish this great task.

It was the interest of the monarch to associate himself in their undertaking. By this means he might have re-established his power, and protected himself against the revolution, by being himself the author of it. Had he taken the lead in reforms, settled with firmness but with justice the new order of things; had he realized the wishes of the nation by defining the rights of the citizen, the functions of the States-general and the bounds of the royal authority; had he sacrificed his own arbitrary power, the superiority of the nobles, and the privileges of the corporate bodies; had he, in short, executed all the reforms which were called for by the public voice, and subsequently effected by the Constituent Assembly; he would have prevented the fatal dissensions which afterwards broke out. It is rarely that a prince consents to the diminution of his power, and has the wisdom to concede what he will ultimately be forced to sacrifice. Yet Louis XVI would have done so, if instead of being ruled by those around him, he had obeyed the impulses of his own mind. But utter anarchy prevailed in the royal councils. At the meeting of the States-general, no measures had been adopted, nothing previously settled, to prevent future disputes. Louis wavered irresolute, between his ministry, directed by Necker, and his court, governed by the queen and several princes of his family.

The minister, satisfied with having carried the double representation of the commons, dreaded the king's indecision and the discontent of the court. Insufficiently alive to the magnitude of a crisis which he regarded as financial rather than political, instead of anticipating he waited for the result, and flattered himself that he could guide the course of events which he had done nothing to prepare. He felt that the ancient organization of the states could no longer be maintained, and that the existence of three estates, with each a veto on the other two, was a hindrance to the accomplishment of reforms and to the conduct of administration. He hoped, after the effects of this threefold opposition should be proved by experience, to reduce the number of the orders, and obtain the adoption of the British form of government, including the nobles and clergy in one chamber, and the commons in another. He did not perceive that when once the struggle had begun, his interference would be vain, and half-measures be satisfactory to nobody: that the weaker party from obstinacy, and the stronger from the force of circumstances, would refuse their assent to this system of conciliation. A compromise can only be satisfactory, while the victory is undecided.

The court, far from wishing to give regularity to the States-general, desired to annul them. It preferred the occasional resistance of the great public corporations to a division of authority with a permanent assembly. The separation of the orders favoured its designs: by fomenting their disunion, it sought to prevent them from acting. From the vice of their organization, former States-general had effected nothing; and it the more confidently anticipated a similar result now, as the first two estates seemed less than ever inclined to acquiesce in the reforms demanded by the third. The clergy desired to retain their wealth and privileges, and foresaw that they would have more sacrifices to make than advantages to gain. The nobles were conscious that even in resuming their long-lost political independence, they would have more to concede to the people on the one hand, than to obtain from the monarch on the other. The approaching revolution was about to take place almost exclusively in favour of the commons, and the first two estates were led to coalesce with the court against the commons, as they had previously coalesced with the commons against the court. Interest was the sole motive of this change of side; and they allied themselves to the monarch with no attachment to him, as they had defended the people with no view to the public good.

No means were spared to keep the nobles and clergy in this disposition. Courtship and seducements were lavished upon their leaders. A committee, partly composed of the most illustrious personages, was held at the house of the Comtesse de Polignac, and the principal members of the two orders were admitted to it. It was there that two of the most ardent defenders of liberty in the parliament, and before the convocation of the States-general, d'Epréménil and d'Entragues, were won over, and became its most inveterate enemies. *There* were regulated the costumes of the three orders,[*] and etiquette first, intrigue next, and lastly force, were applied to disunite them. The court was led away by the recollection of the old States-general: and imagined it possible to manage the present like the past; to keep down Paris by the army, and the deputies of the commons by those of the nobles; to control the States, by disuniting the orders, and to disunite the orders by reviving the old usages which elevated the nobility and humiliated the commons. It was thus that after the first sitting of the assembly, they imagined that they had prevented every thing by conceding nothing.*

Of the rapidity and dramatic interest of his narrative, the following passage is an example. He has just been relating the early acts of the Constituent Assembly.

The attempt to prevent the formation of the assembly having failed, nothing remained to the court but to become a party to its proceedings, in order to get the direction of them into its own hands. By prudence and good faith it might yet have repaired its errors and effaced the memory of its hostilities. There are times when we can originate sacrifices; there are others when we can do no more than take the merit of accepting them. At the opening of the States-general the monarch might have made the constitution. It was now only time to receive it from the assembly; if he had accommodated himself to this situation, his situation

[*See *Gazette Nationale, ou Le Moniteur Universel*, 1789, Introduction, p. 235.]
*[Translated from] Mignet, pp. 41-5.

would infallibly have been improved. But the counsellors of Louis, recovered from the first emotion of surprise at their defeat, resolved to have recourse to the bayonet, having had recourse to authority in vain. They intimated to him that the contempt of his commands, the safety of his throne, the maintenance of the laws of the kingdom, and even the happiness of his people, demanded that he should recal the assembly to submission; that the assembly, sitting at Versailles, in the immediate neighbourhood of Paris, and supported by both places, required to be subdued by force; that it must either be removed or dissolved; that this design required immediate execution, to arrest the progress of the assembly, and that to carry it into effect it was necessary to call in the troops without delay, to intimidate the assembly, and keep down Paris and Versailles.

While these schemes were in preparation, the deputies of the nation were commencing their legislatorial labours, and preparing that constitution so impatiently waited for, and which they thought it no longer fitting to delay. Addresses poured in from Paris and the great towns, applauding their wisdom, and encouraging them to carry forward the work of the regeneration of France. In this posture of affairs the troops arrived in great numbers; Versailles assumed the appearance of a camp; the hall of the states was surrounded by guards, and entrance interdicted to the public; Paris was environed by several bodies of troops, which seemed posted to undertake, as need might be, a blockade or a siege. These immense military preparations, the arrival of trains of artillery from the frontiers, the presence of foreign regiments, whose obedience was without limits, every thing gave indication of sinister designs. The people were in agitation; the assembly wished to undeceive the king, and request the removal of the troops. On the motion of Mirabeau, it presented to the king a firm and respectful address, but in vain.[*] Louis declared that he was sole judge of the necessity of calling in or of withdrawing the troops, which he assured them were no more than an army of precaution, to prevent disturbances, and protect the assembly; he likewise offered to remove the assembly to Noyon or Soissons, in other words, to place it between two armies, and deprive it of the support of the people.[†]

Paris was in the most violent fermentation; that immense city was unanimous in its devotion to the assembly: its own danger, that of the national representatives, and the scarcity of subsistence, predisposed it to insurrection. The capitalists, from interest and the fear of a national bankruptcy, enlightened men and all the middle class from patriotism, the populace, oppressed by want, imputing its sufferings to the court and the privileged orders, desirous of agitation and of novelty, had ardently embraced the cause of the revolution. It is difficult to figure to one's self the internal commotion which agitated the capital of France. Awakened from the repose and silence of servitude, it was still, as it were, astonished at the novelty of its situation, and intoxicated with liberty and enthusiasm. The press blew up the flame; the newspapers gave circulation to the deliberations of the assembly, and seemed to make their readers actually present at its meetings: and the questions which were there agitated, were again discussed in the open air, in the public places. It was in the Palais Royal especially that the deliberative assembly of the capital was held. It was thronged by a multitude, which seemed permanent, but which was perpetually changing. A table was the *rostra*, the first comer was the orator; they harangued on the dangers of the country, and exhorted to resistance. Already, on a motion made at the Palais Royal, the prisons of the Abbaye had been forced, and some grenadiers of the French guards carried off in triumph,

[*See Honoré Gabriel Riqueti, comte de Mirabeau, speeches of 8 and 9 July, 1789, in *Oeuvres de Mirabeau*, 9 vols. (Paris: Dupont and Brissot-Thivars, 1825-27), Vol. VII, pp. 148-58 and 158-63.]

[†Louis XVI, "Réponse du roi à l'assemblée nationale" (11 July, 1789), *Gazette Nationale, ou Le Moniteur Universel*, 10-13 July, 1789, p. 74.]

who had been confined there for refusing to fire upon the people. This commotion had led to no result; a deputation had solicited, in favour of the liberated prisoners, the good offices of the assembly, who had appealed to the clemency of the king in their behalf; they had returned to their confinement, and had received their pardon. But this regiment, one of the bravest and fullest in its numbers, had become favourable to the popular cause.[*]

We give the sequel of this passage in the original, despairing to preserve its spirit in a translation.

Telles étaient les dispositions de Paris lorsque Necker fut renvoyé du ministère. La cour, après avoir établi des troupes à Versailles, à Sèvres, au Champ-de-Mars, à Saint-Denis, crut pouvoir exécuter son plan. Elle commença par l'exil de Necker et le renouvellement complet du ministère. Le maréchal de Broglie, Lagallissonnière, le duc de la Vauguyon, le baron de Breteuil et l'intendant Foulon, furent désignés comme remplaçants de Puiségur, de Montmorin, de la Luzerne, de Saint-Priest et de Necker. Celui-ci reçut le samedi, 11 juillet, pendant son dîner, un billet du roi qui lui enjoignait de quitter le royaume sur le champ. Il dîna tranquillement sans faire part de l'ordre qu'il avait reçu, monta ensuite en voiture avec madame Necker, comme pour aller à Saint-Ouen, et prit la route de Bruxelles.

Le lendemain dimanche, 12 juillet, on apprit à Paris, vers les quatre heures du soir, la disgrace de Necker et son départ pour l'exil. Cette mesure y fut considérée comme l'exécution du complot dont on avait aperçu les préparatifs. Dans peu d'instants la ville fut dans la plus grande agitation; des rassemblements se formèrent de toutes parts, plus de dix mille personnes se rendirent au Palais-Royal, émues par cette nouvelle, disposées à tout, mais ne sachant quelle mesure prendre. Un jeune homme plus hardi que les autres, et l'un des harangueurs habituels de la foule, Camille Desmoulins, monte sur une table, un pistolet à la main, et il s'écrie: "Citoyens, il n'y a pas un moment à perdre; le renvoi de M. Necker est le tocsin d'une Saint-Barthélemy de patriotes! ce soir même tous les bataillons suisses et allemands sortiront du Champ-de-Mars pour nous égorger! il ne nous reste qu'une ressource, c'est de courir aux armes." On approuve par de bruyantes acclamations. Il propose de prendre des cocardes pour se reconnaître et pour se défendre.—"Voulez-vous, dit-il, le vert, couleur de l'espérance, ou le rouge, couleur de l'ordre libre de Cincinnatus?"—"Le vert, le vert, répond la multitude." L'orateur descend de la table, attache une feuille d'arbre à son chapeau, tout le monde l'imite, les marronniers du Palais sont presque dépouillés de leurs feuilles, et cette troupe se rend en tumulte chez le sculpteur Curtius.

On prend les bustes de Necker et du duc d'Orléans, car le bruit que ce dernier devait être exilé, s'était aussi répandu; on les entoure d'un crêpe et on les porte en triomphe. Ce cortége traverse les rues Saint-Martin, Saint-Denis, Saint-Honoré, et se grossit à chaque pas. Le peuple fait mettre chapeau bas à tous ceux qu'il rencontre. Le guet à cheval se trouve sur sa route, il le prend pour escorte; le cortége s'avance ainsi jusqu'à la place Vendôme, où l'on promène les deux bustes autour de la statue de Louis XIV. Un détachement de royal allemand arrive, veut disperser le cortége, est mis en fuite à coups de pierres, et la multitude continuant sa route, parvient jusqu'à la place Louis XV. Mais là, elle est assaillie par les dragons du prince de Lambesc; elle résiste quelques moments, est enfoncée, le porteur d'un des bustes et un soldat des gardes-françaises sont tués; le peuple se disperse, une partie fuit vers les quais, une autre se replie en arrière sur les boulevards, le reste se précipite dans les Tuileries par le pont tournant. Le prince de Lambesc les poursuit dans le jardin, le sabre nu, à la tête de ses cavaliers; il charge une multitude sans armes qui n'était point du cortége et

[*Translated from Mignet, pp. 57-60.]

qui se promenait paisiblement. Dans cette charge, un vieillard est blessé d'un coup de sabre; on se défend avec des chaises, on monte sur les terrasses, l'indignation devient générale, et le cri aux armes retentit bientôt partout, aux Tuileries, au Palais-Royal, dans la ville et dans les faubourgs.

Le régiment des gardes-françaises était, comme nous l'avons déjà dit, bien disposé pour le peuple; aussi l'avait-on consigné dans ses casernes. Le prince de Lambesc, craignant malgré cela qu'il ne prît parti, donna ordre à soixante dragons d'aller se poster en face de son dépôt, situé dans la Chaussée-d'Antin. Les soldats des gardes, déjà mécontents d'être retenus comme prisonniers, s'indignèrent à la vue de ces étrangers, avec lesquels ils avaient eu une rixe peu de jours auparavant. Ils voulaient courir aux armes, et leurs officiers eurent beaucoup de peine à les retenir en employant, tour-à-tour, les menaces et les prières. Mais ils ne voulurent plus rien entendre, lorsque quelques-uns des leurs vinrent annoncer la charge faite aux Tuileries et la mort d'un de leurs camarades. Ils saisirent leurs armes, brisèrent les grilles, se rangèrent en bataille, à l'entrée de la caserne, en face des dragons, et leur crièrent: Qui vive?—Royal Allemand.—Etes-vous pour le tiers-état?—Nous sommes pour ceux qui nous donnent des ordres.—Alors les gardes-françaises firent sur eux une décharge qui leur tua deux hommes, leur en blessa trois et les mit en fuite. Elles s'avancèrent ensuite au pas de charge et la baïonnette en avant jusqu'à la place Louis XV, se placèrent entre les Tuileries et les Champs-Elysées, le peuple et les troupes, et gardèrent ce poste pendant toute la nuit. Les soldats du Champ-de-Mars reçurent aussitôt l'ordre de s'avancer. Lorsqu'ils furent arrivés dans les Champs-Elysées, les gardes-françaises les reçurent à coups de fusil. On voulut les faire battre, mais ils refusèrent: les Petits-Suisses furent les premiers à donner cet exemple que les autres régiments suivirent. Les officiers désespérés ordonnèrent la retraite; les troupes rétrogradèrent jusqu'à la grille de Chaillot, d'où elles se rendirent bientôt dans le Champ-de-Mars. La défection des gardes-françaises, et le refus que manifestèrent les troupes, même étrangères, de marcher sur la capitale, firent échouer les projets de la cour.

Pendant cette soirée le peuple s'était transporté à l'Hôtel-de-Ville, et avait demandé qu'on sonnât le tocsin, que les districts fussent réunis et les citoyens armés. Quelques électeurs s'assemblèrent à l'Hôtel-de-Ville, et ils prirent l'autorité en main. Ils rendirent pendant ces jours d'insurrection les plus grands services à leurs concitoyens et à la cause de la liberté par leur courage, leur prudence et leur activité; mais dans la première confusion du soulèvement, il ne leur fut guère possible d'être écoutés. Le tumulte était à son comble; chacun ne recevait d'ordre que de sa passion. A côté des citoyens bien intentionnés étaient des hommes suspects qui ne cherchaient dans l'insurrection qu'un moyen de désordre et de pillage. Des troupes d'ouvriers, employés par le gouvernement à des travaux publics, la plupart sans domicile, sans aveu, brûlèrent les barrières, infestèrent les rues, pillèrent quelques maisons; ce furent eux qu'on appela les brigands. La nuit du 12 au 13 se passa dans le tumulte et dans les alarmes.*

After every allowance is made (and much ought to be made) for the deep interest of the events themselves, great praise is still due to the powers both of narration and description, which the above passage displays.

M. Mignet generally subjoins to each chapter a *résumé* of the progress of events during the period which it embraces. The same sort and degree of talent is manifested in these *résumés* which is conspicuous in the body of the work. We

---

*Mignet, pp. 60-6.

quote the following, though one of the longest, not because it is the best, but because it contains a summary view of the early history of the Revolution:

If one were to describe a nation which had just passed through a great crisis, and to say, There was in this country a despotic government whose authority has been limited, two privileged orders whose supremacy has been abolished, an immense population already enfranchised by the growth of civilization and intelligence, but destitute of political rights, and which, when they were refused to its entreaties, has been compelled to assume them by force; if to this it were added that the government, after resisting for a time, had at length yielded to the revolution, but that the privileged orders stedfastly persevered in their resistance, the following are the conclusions which might be drawn from these data:

The government will feel regret, the people will show distrust, the privileged orders, each in its own way, will make war on the new order of things. The nobles, too feeble at home to make any effectual opposition, will emigrate and stir up foreign powers, who will make preparations for an attack; the clergy, who abroad would be deprived of their means of action, will remain in the interior, and there endeavour to raise up enemies to the revolution. The people, threatened from without, endangered from within, irritated against the emigrants for exciting foreigners to hostilities, against foreigners for attacking its independence, and against the clergy for stirring up insurrections at home, will treat the emigrants, the foreigners, and the clergy as enemies. It will first demand that the refractory priests be placed under surveillance, next that they be banished, that the revenues of the emigrants be confiscated, and finally, that war be made upon confederated Europe, to prevent the disadvantage of having to sustain the attack. The original authors of the revolution will condemn those of its measures which are inconsistent with the law; the continuators of the revolution will see in them, on the contrary, the salvation of their country. A discord will break out between those who prefer the constitution to the state, and those who prefer the state to the constitution; the prince, impelled by his interests as king, his affections, and his conscience, to reject this policy, will pass for an accomplice in the counter-revolutionary conspiracy, because he will appear to protect it. The revolutionists will then attempt, by intimidation, to draw the king to their side, and, failing of success, they will subvert his power.

Such was the history of the Legislative Assembly. The internal tumults led to the decree against the priests; the menaces of foreigners to that against the emigrants; the confederacy of foreign powers, to the war against Europe; the first defeat of our armies, to the formation of the camp of twenty thousand. The suspicions of the Girondists were directed towards Louis, by the refusal of his assent to most of these decrees.[*] The division between that party and the constitutional monarchists, the latter wishing to appear legislators, as in time of peace, the former, enemies, as in time of war, disunited the partisans of the revolution. In the minds of the Girondists, liberty depended upon victory, and victory upon these decrees. The 20th of June was an attempt to compel the acceptance of the decrees; on its failure, they deemed it necessary to renounce the revolution or the throne, and they made the 10th of August. Thus but for the emigration which produced the war, and the schism in the church

[*See "Décret relatif aux troubles excités sous prétexte de religion" (16 Nov., 1791), in *Gazette Nationale, ou Le Moniteur Universel*, 17 Nov., 1791, p. 1338; "Décret concernant les émigrans" (9 Nov., 1791), *ibid.*, 10 Nov., 1791, pp. 1310-11; "Décret d'augmentation de vingt mille hommes pour l'armée" (8 June, 1792), *ibid.*, 9 June, 1792, p. 668; Louis XVI, "Refus de sanction au décret contre les prêtres non assermentés"; "Proclamation du roi" (12 Nov., 1791), and untitled refusal, *ibid.*, 20 Dec., 1791, p. 1481, 14 Nov., 1791, p. 1325, and 20 June, 1792, p. 716, respectively.]

which produced the tumults, the king would probably have been reconciled to the revolution, and the revolutionists would never have thought of a republic.*

We have given this and other extracts in a translation with reluctance. Our only remaining specimen shall be in the original language.

The following is a brief but interesting *résumé* of the decline and fall of the virtuous and unfortunate Gironde:

Ainsi succomba le parti de la Gironde, parti illustre par de grands talents et de grands courages, parti qui honora la république naissante par l'horreur du sang, la haine du crime, le dégoût de l'anarchie, l'amour de l'ordre, de la justice et de la liberté; parti mal placé entre la classe moyenne, dont il avait combattu la révolution, et la multitude dont il repoussait le gouvernement. Condamné à ne pas agir, ce parti ne put qu'illustrer une défaite certaine, par une lutte courageuse et par une belle mort. A cette époque, on pouvait avec certitude prévoir sa fin: il avait été chassé de poste en poste: des Jacobins, par l'envahissement des Montagnards; de la commune, par la sortie de Pétion; du ministère, par la retraite de Roland et de ses collègues; de l'armée, par la défection de Dumouriez. Il ne lui restait plus que la convention; c'est là qu'il se retrancha, qu'il combattit, et qu'il succomba. Ses ennemis essayèrent tour-à-tour, contre lui, et des complots et des insurrections. Les complots firent créer la commission des douze,[*] qui parut donner un avantage momentané à la Gironde, mais qui n'en excita que plus violemment ses adversaires. Ceux-ci mirent le peuple en mouvement, et ils enlevèrent aux Girondins, d'abord leur autorité en détruisant les douze, ensuite leur existence politique en proscrivant leurs chefs.

Les suites de ce désastreux évènement ne furent selon la prévoyance de personne. Les Dantonistes crurent que les dissensions des partis seraient terminées, et la guerre civile éclata. Les modérés du comité de salut public crurent que la convention reprendrait toute la puissance, et elle fut asservie.[†] La commune crut que le 31 mai lui vaudrait la domination, qui échut à Robespierre, et à quelques hommes dévoués à sa fortune ou à l'extrême démocratie. Enfin, il y eut un parti de plus à ajouter aux partis vaincus, et dès-lors aux partis ennemis; et comme on avait fait, après le 10 août, la république contre les constitutionnels, on fit, après le 31 mai, la *terreur* contre les modérés de la république.[†]

Did space permit, we would gladly quote M. Mignet's characters of the leading members of the Constituent Assembly. In general it appears to us that the characters of eminent men, which we read in historians, are very little to be depended upon. It is no easy matter to draw a character at once correct and complete, even of one who is personally known to us, if there be any thing about him more than common; but from hearsay, or from his public acts, it may be pronounced impossible. The troubled period, however, of the French revolution exhibited many of its actors in such varied situations, several of them very trying

---

*[Translated from] Mignet, pp. 289-92.

[*François Bergoing, Antoine Bertrand, Jacques Boileau, Jean Baptiste Boyer-Fonfrède, Jean François Martin Gardien, Jean René Gomaire, Pierre François Joachim Henry-Larivière, Augustin Bernard François Legoazre de Kervélégan, Etienne Mollevault, Jean Paul Rabaut Saint-Etienne, Charles Vaissière de Saint-Martin-Valogne, and Louis François Sébastien Viger.]

[†The "modérés" included Jean Jacques de Bréard-Duplessys, Louis Bernard Guyton-Morveau, and Jean Baptiste Treilhard.]

†Mignet, pp. 379-81.

ones, that the data it affords for judging of their characters, though far from adequate, are less scanty than ordinary. M. Mignet has turned these data to the best account. His portraits *seem* accurate, and they are, at any rate, animated.

Our preliminary observations will have prepared the reader to find that we cannot speak altogether so favourably of M. Mignet's reflections as of his narrative. The prevailing vice of French writers, since Montesquieu, is that of straining at point, at sententiousness, at being striking—we want a word—at producing an effect by mere smartness of expression; and from this vice M. Mignet's work, though one of the best of its kind, is not wholly free. The sort of writers in whom this defect is conspicuous, and of whom, in recent times, Madame de Staël is one of the most favourable specimens, can never communicate a fact without edging in, to account for it, some axiom or principle, wide in its extent and epigrammatic in its form. Generalization in history is so far from being blamable, that history would be of no use without it; but general propositions intended to be of any use, concerning the course of events in matters where large bodies of men are concerned, cannot be compressed into epigrams; for there is not one of them that is true without exception, and an epigram admits not of exceptions. What do these generalizations amount to? Commonly to this: that something which has happened once or twice will happen always.

M. Mignet's generalizations are, in most cases, the generalizations of an acute mind; but in his anxiety to be sententious, he almost always overdoes the generalization; he affirms that to be true in all cases which is only true in some, or enunciates without qualification a proposition which must be qualified to be defensible. He generalizes upon first impressions; and as first impressions are sometimes right, he often, by generalizing on the first impression of a remarkable fact, stumbles upon a valuable and even a recondite truth—a truth which, if it did not stand single among so many *faux brillans*, might be supposed to have emanated from a mind profoundly versed in human nature. When this happens, the point of the expression adds great force to the sentiment, and imprints it in the imagination. Here, however, M. Mignet is far excelled by Madame de Staël, whose chief merit, in our opinion, is the unrivalled felicity with which she has given expression to many important truths suggested to her forcibly by the circumstances of the times in which she lived, which will be remembered long after the brilliant paradoxes and pompous inanities, which she threw out in such abundance along with them, shall be forgotten.

M. Mignet has been occasionally betrayed into dressing up a truism in epigrammatic guise, and bringing it out with the air of an oracle, as a piece of consummate wisdom. The following maxims—"*C'est toujours sur le passé qu'on règle sa conduite et ses espérances*" (p. 458). "*Tout ce qui existe s'étend*" (p. 166), to account for the rapid growth of the Jacobin club. "*Il ne suffit pas d'être grand homme, il faut venir à propos*" (p. 107). "*Dès qu'il y a des partis déplacés dans un état, il y a lutte de leur part,*" &c. (p. 204), and several others, are examples.

The following are obvious cases of incorrect generalization: "Tous les partis sont les mêmes, et se conduisent par les mêmes maximes, ou si l'on veut par les mêmes nécessités" (p. 518), merely because the Girondists and the Montagnards died with equal courage.

"Quand on sait ce qu'on veut, et qu'on le veut vite et bien, on l'emporte toujours" (p. 357). Had he said *souvent*, the proposition would have been true: as it stands, it is extravagant.

"En révolution les hommes sont mûs par deux penchans, l'amour de leurs idées et le goût du commandement" (p. 442). Two very powerful forces, it is true; but that they are far from being the only ones which act upon man, "en temps de révolution," is evident enough. The other principles of human nature are not suspended, during that period, or any other.

"En révolution les hommes sont facilement oubliés, parce que les peuples en voient beaucoup et vivent vite. Si l'on ne veut pas qu'ils soient ingrats, il ne faut pas cesser un instant de les servir à leur manière" (pp. 160-1). A general proposition grounded on one or two instances, and only on the surface of those.

The next two are examples of important truths, or rather of approximations to important truths, spoiled by their epigrammatic form: "On est bientôt, en révolution, ce qu'on est cru être" (p. 311). "Le plus grand tort des partis, après celui d'être injustes, est celui de ne vouloir pas le paraître" (p. 317).

To have expressed accurately what there is of truth in these maxims, in such manner as to be intelligible, would have spoiled all the point of the phrase.

The following remark, with a slight qualification, contains the expression of an important fact: "Dès qu'on est en révolte, le parti dont l'opinion est la plus extrême et le but le plus précis, l'emporte sur ses associés" (p. 388). The party which has the most definite purpose commonly prevails; and this (as it happens) is generally the party which goes to the greatest lengths in matter of opinion. The men who have no fixed set of opinions follow the march of events: those who have, lead it.

The following is a profound remark, happily expressed: "Barrère, qui, comme tous les esprits justes et les caractères faibles, fut pour la modération, tant que la peur ne fit pas de lui un instrument de cruauté et de tyrannie" (p. 363). It is most true, as is hinted in this passage, that the great incentive to cruelty is fear.

The last observation which we shall quote, relates to the formation of a judicial establishment; and, though somewhat loosely expressed, indicates an acute perception of an important principle of legislation: "Ce redoutable pouvoir, lorsqu'il relève du trône, doit être inamovible pour être indépendant; mais il peut être temporaire lorsqu'il relève du peuple, parce qu'en dépendant de tous, il ne dépend de personne" (p. 153).

We shall now take our leave of M. Mignet's work, by recommending the perusal of it to all who desire either to be amused by a most entertaining and well told story, or to learn, by a few hours reading, what intelligent Frenchmen think and say on the subject of the French Revolution.

MODERN FRENCH HISTORICAL WORKS

1826

EDITOR'S NOTE

Westminster Review, VI (July, 1826), 62-103. Headed: "Art. IV.—*Histoire Physique, Civile, et Morale de Paris, depuis les premiers temps historiques jusqu'à nos jours; contenant par ordre chronologique, la description des accroissemens successifs de cette ville et de ses monumens anciens et modernes; la notice de toutes ses institutions, tant civiles que religieuses; et, à chaque période, le tableau des moeurs, des usages, et des progrès de la civilisation. Ornée de gravures représentant divers plans de Paris, ses monumens et ses édifices principaux* [1821-25]. Par J[acques] A[ntoine] Dulaure, de la Société Royale des Antiquaires de France. Seconde édition, considérablement augmentée en texte et en planches. 10 vols. 8vo. Paris [: Guillaume], 1823. / *Histoire des Français.* Par J[ean] C[harles] L[éonard] Simonde de Sismondi. Les neuf premiers volumes. [Ultimately 31 vols.] 8vo. Paris [: Treuttel and Würtz], 1821, 1823, 1826." Running titles: "Modern French Historical Works— / Age of Chivalry." Unsigned. Not republished. Identified in Mill's bibliography as "A review of Dulaure's History of Paris and Sismondi's History of France. In the 11th number of the Westminster Review" (MacMinn, 7). There is no separate copy of this essay in Mill's library, Somerville College.

For comment on the article, see xxxiii–xxxvii and xcv above.

Modern French Historical Works

THOUGH WE HAVE NOT, like so many of our contemporaries, made it our grand occupation, to impress our countrymen with a deep sense of their own wisdom and virtue, and to teach them how proud they ought to be of every thing English, more especially of every thing that is English and bad; we are far from being unconscious how much they have really to be proud of, and in how many respects they might be taken as models by all the nations of the world. If we saw them in any danger of forgetting their own merits, we too might preach them a sermon on that hacknied text. But it is not their failing to underrate themselves, or to overrate other nations. They are more in need of monitors than of adulators; and we cannot but think that it may be of some use to them to know, that if there are some points in which they are superior to their neighbours, there are others in which they are inferior; that they may learn something from other nations, as well as other nations from them.

While the *Quarterly Review* is labouring to convince us that we are a century and a half in advance of our nearest continental neighbours,[*] it is impossible to shut our eyes to the fact, that those neighbours are at present making a much greater figure in the world of literature than ourselves. This is something quite new in the history of the two countries; it certainly was not the case before the French revolution; but it undoubtedly is the case now. While our *littérateurs*, with the usual fate of those who aim at nothing but the merely ornamental, fail of attaining even that; an entirely new class of writers has arisen in France, altogether free from that frivolousness which characterized French literature under the *ancien régime*, and which characterizes the literature of every country where there is an aristocracy. They write as if they were conscious that the reader expects something more valuable from them than mere amusement. Though many of them are highly gifted with the beauties of style, they never seem desirous of shewing off their own eloquence; they seem to write because they have something to say, and not because they desire to say something. In philosophy, they do not sacrifice truth to rhetoric; in history they do not sacrifice truth to romance. This change in the character of French literature is most of all remarkable in their historical compositions. The historians of *ci-devant* France were justly charged with despising facts, and

[*Richard Chenevix, "History and Prospects of English Industry," *Quarterly Review*, XXXIV (June, 1826), 47.]

considering, not what was true, but what would give scenic interest to their narrative; the French historians of the present day are distinguished by almost German research, and by a scrupulousness in producing vouchers for their minutest details, which forbids the idea of their having any thing in view but truth.

In the last five years France has produced many historical works of great importance; more than were ever produced by one nation within the same space of time. Some of these have been already mentioned in this journal;[*] others we may perhaps take a future opportunity of making known to our readers. At the present moment, two of the most important lie before us; and we have derived so much instruction as well as gratification from their perusal, that we purpose giving in the present article some account of their contents.

M. Dulaure has named his work a history of Paris: the title is less attractive than the book. It is a history of Paris, even in the ordinary sense; but if it had been no more, we should have left it to antiquaries, and to the *amateurs* of steeples, columns, and old tomb-stones. M. Dulaure's work, as a topographical history, is admirable; but it has other and far greater merits. Our histories of London are histories of buildings,[†] but his subject is men. His history of Paris is a chapter of the history of mankind. After describing the city of Paris as it existed at each period of its history, he does what is not often done by antiquaries, he condescends to bestow some attention upon the *inhabitants*. This part of his book, which, we are happy to observe, has been detached from the rest, and printed as a separate work in two octavo volumes, is not so much a history of Paris, as a history of civilization in France; which is, to a great degree, the history of civilization in Europe. In it we may read how men were governed, and how they lived and behaved, in the good old times; subjects on which little is said in the vulgar histories, and that little is but little to be relied upon. M. Dulaure has one merit, which is not a common one with historians: he pays great regard to facts, and little to assertions. He has not been satisfied with taking upon trust from one author, what *he* had already taken upon trust from another. His work is not a mere register of the opinions of his predecessors, predecessors who did but register the opinions of their contemporaries. His ideas, such as they are, are his own.

[*E.g., in John Stuart Mill, "Mignet's French Revolution," *Westminster Review*, V (Apr., 1826), 385-98 (reprinted above, pp. 1-14), and in five articles, probably by Henry Southern: "Court of Louis XIV and the Regency," *ibid.*, II (July, 1824), 121-49; "Barante, *Histoire des ducs de Bourgogne*," *ibid.* (Oct., 1824), 442-62; "Montlosier's *French Monarchy*," *ibid.*, III (Jan., 1825), 35-48; "The *Chronicles* of Froissart," *ibid.*, IV (July, 1825), 1-20; and "*Private Memoirs of Madame du Hausset*," *ibid.*, V (Jan., 1826), 249-62.]

[†Mill may have in mind such works as James Peller Malcolm, *London redivivum*, 4 vols. (London: Rivington, *et al.*, 1802-07), and David Pugh ("David Hughson"), *London: Being an Accurate History and Description*, 6 vols. (London: Stratford, 1805-09), but he ignores other works, such as Henry Hunter, *The History of London*, 2 vols. (London: Stockdale, 1811), which is not a history merely "of buildings."]

M. de Sismondi is already known to the public as a historian. His *History of France*, though it has not done every thing which a history of France might have done, may be pronounced worthy of his reputation; and, when completed, will supply an important desideratum in literature. Indeed, when it is considered in what spirit, and with what objects, all former histories of France had been written, it is matter of congratulation that they were as dull in manner as they were dishonest in their purpose, and deceptious in their tendency; and that the sphere of their mischievousness was considerably narrowed, by the happy impossibility of reading them. We have in our own history a standing example how deep a root party lies may take in the public mind, when a writer, in whom the arts of the most consummate advocate are combined with all the graces of style, employs his skill in giving them the colour of truth.[*] It is most fortunate, therefore, that the first readable history of France should be the production of a writer who is of no party, except that of human nature; who has no purpose to serve except that of truth, and whose only bias is towards the happiness of mankind. The chief defect of M. de Sismondi's work, considered as a popular history, is the prolixity of the three first volumes; a space which, we should think, might have been better occupied than in relating how one dull, uninteresting battle or murder was succeeded by another exactly similar, in the reigns of the *rois fainéans*, or of the grandsons of Louis the Debonair. M. de Sismondi, perhaps, may urge in his defence, that his object was, to give a practical feeling of the state of society which he was describing; that, dull as these incidents are, their incessant recurrence was the sole characteristic of the period; a period the most distracted and miserable which is recorded in history: that to have merely related a battle and a murder or two, as a specimen of the rest, would have made but a feeble impression; and that it was necessary to convince the reader by tedious experience, that the history of the times consisted of nothing else. How far this apology might avail M. de Sismondi with ordinary readers, we do not consider ourselves perfectly qualified to judge: for ourselves, we think that our incredulity would have yielded to a less ponderous argument than three mortal volumes. It is but just to state, that these volumes do give, in a high degree, that practical feeling of the times, which they are apparently designed to convey; and that the reader who will have patience to go through them (for without reading them he will not fully understand the history of the subsequent period), will be amply repaid by the never-flagging interest which is kept up throughout the other six volumes.

All that is published of M. de Sismondi's work, and the more novel and interesting part of M. Dulaure's, relate to the middle ages; and to that period we shall, in the present article, confine our remarks; reserving the privilege of making ample use, on future occasions, of the important information which M.

[*The reference is almost certainly to David Hume, whose *History of England* was frequently criticized by Mill on these grounds.]

Dulaure has furnished relative to the later period of the French monarchy. Our purpose at present is, to do something towards forming, if possible, a correct estimate of what is called the age of chivalry. Hitherto, in this country especially, we have judged of that age from two or three of the facts, and no more: and even of those we have looked only at one side. The works before us are almost the first, in which any pains have really been taken to discover the *truth* with regard to the age of chivalry. In these, however, an ample stock of facts has been collected, and the subject is now ripe for a deliberate examination. All these facts lead but to one conclusion; and that conclusion is so directly at variance with the conceptions ordinarily entertained respecting the age of chivalry, that the very enunciation of it will be startling to the majority of readers; and it will not be embraced upon any evidence not absolutely irresistible. We are persuaded, however, that the more narrowly the records of the period are looked into, and the more accurately its real history becomes known, the more strictly conformable this conclusion will appear to historical truth.

The conclusion is, that the compound of noble qualities, called the *spirit of chivalry* (a rare combination in all ages) was almost unknown in the age of chivalry; that the age so called was equally distinguished by moral depravity and by physical wretchedness; that there is no class of society at this day in any civilized country, which has not a greater share of what are called the knightly virtues, than the knights themselves; that, far from civilizing and refining the rest of the world, it was not till very late, and with great difficulty, that the rest of the world could succeed in civilizing them.

If this conclusion be true, it must be obvious that there is not in all history a truth of greater importance. There is scarcely any portion of history the misapprehension of which has done more to rivet the most mischievous errors in the public mind. The age of chivalry was the age of aristocracy, in its most gigantic strength and wide-extending sway; and the illusions of chivalry are to this hour the great stronghold of aristocratic prejudices. All that is aristocratic in European institutions comes to us from those times. In those times lived our ancestors, whose wisdom and virtue are found so eminently serviceable in bearing down any attempt to improve the condition of their descendants. All those whose great grandfathers had names, and who think it more honourable (as it certainly is less troublesome) to have had brave and virtuous ancestors, than to be brave and virtuous themselves; all those who, loving darkness better than light, would have it thought that men have declined in morality in proportion as they have advanced in intelligence; all, in short, whose interest or taste leads them to side with the few in opposition to the many, are interested in upholding the character of the age of chivalry. "On nous a dit," says M. de Sismondi,

que la plus basse superstition, que l'ignorance et la brutalité des manières, que l'asservissement des basses classes, que l'anéantissement de toute justice, de tout frein salutaire pour les plus hautes, n'avaient point empêché cet héroïsme universel que nous avons nommé la chevalerie, et qui n'exista jamais que dans des fictions brillantes. Plutôt que de perdre cette douce illusion, et de détruire ce monde poétique, ferons-nous violence à l'histoire, et nous refuserons-nous à voir qu'un semblable état social n'a jamais produit que l'intolérable souffrance et l'avilissement de la féodalité?*

Before we proceed to indicate, for we can but indicate, the evidence of the important proposition which is the grand result both of M. Dulaure's and of M. de Sismondi's work, we think it proper to exhibit a specimen of what may be termed a mild, candid, and well-bred mode of dealing with unwelcome assertions; for we are not, as yet, entitled to call them truths. It always gives us pleasure to meet with these virtues in a controversialist; and the serviles in France, to do them justice, seem nowise inferior to their English brethren in these points. No sooner did M. Dulaure's work make its appearance than the hue and cry was raised against it. The sort of arguments, with which the book and its author were assailed, are nearly decisive of the great merit of both. Invective in general, and imputation of enmity to religion, royalty, and his country, in particular; these, together with defamation of his private character, are the reply which has been made to M. Dulaure's work.†

We own that we are in general predisposed in favour of a man whom we hear accused by a certain class of politicians of being an *enemy to his country*. We at

---

*Introduction, pp. xx-xxi.
†The following note appended to the preface of the second edition, may serve as a specimen of the frantic rage which the work has kindled in the ultra-royalist writers, and of the dignified calmness with which their reproaches have been met by M. Dulaure.

"La passion de ces écrivains les a poussés fort au-delà des convenances, de la raison et de la vérité.

"M. de Saint-Victor, auteur d'un *Tableau Historique et Pittoresque de Paris* [3 vols. (Paris: Nicolle and Le Normant, 1808)], sans penser que l'espèce de rivalité qui existe entre nous devait rendre son jugement suspect, a publié un *prospectus* où il fait l'éloge de son *Tableau Historique*, et parle ainsi de mon *Histoire de Paris*: *C'est un scandale sans exemple, une longue et furieuse diatribe contre la religion et la monarchie; un amas de mensonges grossiers, de calomnies impudentes*. Il assure que son *Tableau de Paris* servira de *contrepoison aux mensonges et aux infamies de toute espèce accumulées* dans mon ouvrage.

"Je ne crois pas que, parmi tous les prospectus passés et présens, on puisse en trouver un seul qui soit aussi riche en invectives; je ne veux ni ne dois y répondre.

"Qu'opposer à la *Gazette de France*, qui en Octobre 1821, affirme sérieusement, que je suis *un prêtre défroqué échappé à la basilique de Clermont*, que lui opposer, si ce n'est un *démenti*? [The slighting mention of Dulaure's work in the *Gazette de France*, 18 Oct., 1821, p. 3, does not contain the words here cited, nor does the earlier scathing review of 30 Aug., 1821, pp. 3-4.]

"Que dire à cet homme de lettres, qui en 1821, a pris l'engagement public de me convaincre d'imposture, et qui n'a pas encore satisfait à cet engagement? Que lui dire, si ce n'est: *j'attends*?

"Que dire à ces journalistes, qui, pour trouver matière à leurs censures, ont puisé dans mon propre *errata* des fautes que j'y ai moi-même reconnues et corrigées?

"Ces hommes, pour lancer leurs traits sans danger, se rangent bravement sous le bouclier respectable de la puissance." [Dulaure, Vol. I, pp. ii n-iii n.]

once conclude, that he has either actually rendered, or shown himself disposed to render, some signal service to his country. We conclude, either that he has had discernment to see, and courage to point out, something in his own that stands in need of amendment, or something in another country which it would be for the advantage of his own to imitate; or that he has loved his country well enough to wish it free from that greatest of misfortunes, the misfortune of being successful in an unjust cause; or (which is the particular crime of M. Dulaure), that he has given his countrymen to know, that they once had vices or follies which they have since corrected, or (what is worse still), which they have yet to correct. Whoever is guilty of any one of these crimes in this country, is a fortunate man if he escapes being accused of *un-English* feelings. This is the epithet which we observe to be appropriated to those, whose wish is that their country should *deserve* to be thought well of. The man of *English* feelings is the man whose wish is, that his country should *be* thought well of; and, above all, should think well of itself, particularly in those points wherein it deserves the least. The modern English version of the maxim *Spartam nactus es, hanc exorna*,[*] may be given thus—England is your country, be sure to praise it lustily. This sort of patriotism is, it would appear, no less in request with certain persons in France, than with the corresponding description of persons in England. Accordingly, M. Dulaure's bold exposure of the vices and follies of his countrymen in the olden time, has been thought by many persons extremely *un-French*. But he shall speak for himself.

L'histoire, quoique très-instructive, lorsqu'elle est écrite avec une sévère fidélité, a des parties qui peuvent paraître désolantes aux lecteurs peu familiarisés avec ses tableaux austères; aux lecteurs habitués au régime des panégyriques et des complimens; aux lecteurs pénétrés d'un aveugle respect pour les temps passés et pour les personnes revêtues de la puissance; aux lecteurs trompés par des historiens qui, dans la crainte des persécutions, ou dans l'espoir des récompenses, ont altéré les traits les plus caractéristiques des personnages historiques.

Si l'on présente à ces lecteurs mal disposés des vérités qui leur sont inconnues, des vérités contraires à leurs préventions, à leurs idées reçues, ils s'irritent contr'elles; ne pouvant les vérifier, ils les révoquent en doute, ou accusent l'auteur d'être inexact, même infidèle. C'est ce qu'ils ont fait pour mon *Histoire de Paris*.

On m'a, en conséquence de ces préventions, adressé plusieurs reproches, et surtout celui d'avoir écrit en *ennemi de la France*. Je n'ai écrit qu'en ennemi de la barbarie, qu'en ennemi des erreurs et des crimes qui l'accompagnent. J'aime beaucoup mon pays, mais j'aime autant la vérité. [And wherefore should he love truth, but for the sake of his country?]

On m'a encore accusé d'avoir de préférence cité les crimes, et passé sous silence les actes de vertu. Ignore-t-on que, dans les temps malheureux dont j'ai décrit les moeurs, les vices étaient la règle générale, et les actes de vertu les exceptions.

Je devais abondamment décrire le mal, puisque le mal abondait; mais je n'ai pas négligé le peu de bien que les monumens historiques m'ont fourni. . . . Qu'on me cite une action,

[*Cicero, *Epistolarae ad Atticum*, in *Opera*, 10 vols. (Leyden: Elzevir, 1642), Vol. III, p. 111 (IV, vi, 2).]

justement célèbre, justement louable, et non étrangère à mon sujet, que je n'aie mentionnée honorablement?

On s'est permis de dire que la publication de mon *Histoire de Paris* était *un scandale sans exemple*. Ce reproche, qui doit s'adresser plutôt aux personnages historiques qu'à l'historien, prouve que celui qui me l'adresse n'a lu ni Tacite, ni Suétone, ni les monumens de notre histoire, ni Grégoire de Tours, ni nos annales, ni nos chroniques, ni les écrits de l'abbé Suger, ni des milliers de pièces où les actions scandaleuses se reproduisent à chaque page. Il n'a pas lu non plus les Homélies du pape saint Grégoire-le-Grand, qui dit: *Si du récit d'un fait véritable il résulte du scandale, il vaut mieux laisser naître le scandale que de renoncer à la vérité.*[*]

Je pourrais ramener les lecteurs de bonne foi; je ne réussirais jamais à persuader ceux qui ont pris le parti de se refuser à l'évidence.*

The countryman who, being present at a dispute in Latin, discovered which of the disputants was in the wrong, by taking notice which of them it was who lost his temper, would have had little difficulty in deciding between M. Dulaure and his *ultra* antagonists.

The tone of fearless honesty in the above passage, and the beautiful simplicity of its style, are maintained throughout the work, and may serve, once for all, as a specimen of its general character. Our whole remaining space will be far from sufficient to do justice to the more important subject of this article.

We premise, that whatever we may say against the *age* of chivalry, is or is not to be applied to chivalry itself, according to the ideas which the reader may attach to the term. If by chivalry be meant the feelings, habits or actions of an ordinary chevalier, we shall easily shew it to have been not admirable, but detestable. But if by chivalry be meant those virtues, which formed part of the ideal character of a perfect knight, it would be absurd to deny its beneficial tendency, or to doubt that the estimation in which those virtues were held contributed to render them more prevalent than they otherwise would have been, and by that means to elevate the moral condition of man. We propose only to inquire, to what extent any such virtues really were prevalent during the age of chivalry.

A few introductory observations on the feudal system (and on so hacknied a subject we promise that they shall be few) are an indispensable introduction to a view of that state of society of which the feudal system formed so important a feature.

It is now acknowledged, and therefore needs not here be proved, that the feudal system was not the work of contrivance, of skill devising means for the attainment of an end, but arose gradually, and, as it were, spontaneously, out of the

[*St. Gregory I, *Homiliarum in Ezechielem prophetam*, in *Opera omnia*, Vols. LXXV-LXXIX of *Patrologiae cursus completus, series latina*, ed. Jacques Paul Migne (Paris: Migne, 1849), Vol. LXXVI, col. 842.]

*[Dulaure,] Preface to the Second Edition. [Vol. I, pp. ii-vii. Mill's square-bracketed addition.]

pre-existing circumstances of society; and that the notion of its having been introduced into the countries of western Europe by their Gothic and Teutonic conquerors is wholly erroneous. It is now known that those barbarians were very like any other barbarians; and that without any refined notions of feudal or any other sort of polity, they spread themselves over the land and appropriated it. Their kings, like all other kings, had exactly as much power as they could get; that is to say, in a rude nation, more or less according to circumstances. Originally they enjoyed, during good behaviour, a considerable share of voluntary obedience, but had little power of enforcing any obedience which was not voluntary. They became powerful sovereigns, however, when the followers of a single chief, scattered in small parties over a large country, acquired the habit of looking to the king and not to their countrymen in a body, for protection in case of need.

The vigorous monarchs of the second race, from Pépin d'Héristal to Charlemagne, at first under the title of *Maires du Palais*, afterwards under that of kings, extended the Frankish empire over Germany, Italy, and a great part of Spain, as well as over Belgium and France. The military talents of these sovereigns, and the accession of power which they derived from their vast territorial acquisitions, put a finishing hand to the change which had been going on from the time of Clovis downwards, and the government of Charlemagne may be considered a despotic monarchy. As such, it shared the fate of other despotisms. After a few generations, the sceptre fell into the hands of princes entirely destitute of spirit and ability; the reins of government became relaxed; the power of the state became unequal to the protection of its subjects; disorder at first insensibly crept in, but soon advanced with gigantic strides; and the empire, which had spread itself from one end of Europe to the other, became incapable of opposing effectual resistance to the most contemptible aggressor.

In the despotic governments of Asia, this series of events has always been, from the beginning of history, of periodical recurrence. A Pepin founds a great empire, a Charlemagne consolidates it, which it then becomes the occupation of a series of Lothaires to lose. By the time it has reached the condition of Germany and France in the third and fourth generations of the descendants of Charlemagne, internal revolt or foreign invasion subverts the old dynasty, and establishes a new one; which, after a time, degenerates, and is in its turn displaced. Events took another turn among the conquerors of Europe. They had as yet no standing armies; the nurseries of that class of military adventurers who have always so much abounded in Asia, the materials and instruments of revolutions. Nor was a Genghis or a Timour found among the pirates of the north. The enemies whom Europe had to dread were a race who sought, not conquest, but plunder. The Danes or Normans, repelled from our own country by the vigour of Alfred, fell with redoubled fury upon France, and reduced its northern provinces almost to the condition of a desert. The government, which had, by this time, fallen into the last stage of decrepitude, could still less protect its subjects against these invaders, than it could protect them against one another.

A state of anarchy has this advantage over a despotism, that it invariably works its own cure. When the monarch could no longer protect his subjects, they were forced to protect themselves. Protect themselves they could not, except by combination: and they therefore combined. Where all were left to their own resources, it of course happened, that some had resources, and some had not. Those who had, were able to command assistance, and could therefore protect themselves: those who had not, were reduced to seek protection from others. The monarch, to whom they had been accustomed to look for protection, being no longer capable of affording it, their next recourse was to their strongest neighbour. Land was at that time the only source of wealth; the great landholder alone had the means of fortifying a castle, and maintaining a sufficient number of warriors to defend it. To him, therefore, all his neighbours, and among the rest the smaller landholders, had recourse. To induce the superior to extend his protection over their land and its produce, they had no return to offer except their aid in defending his. Here we see the principle of the feudal system. The forms of that system arose gradually; we have not room to show how.

The combination, which to its weaker members had been intended only as a means of defence, gave to its stronger head an accession of strength for purposes of attack. The weaker communities or principalities had often to sustain aggressions from the stronger; which they sometimes found themselves able to resist, and sometimes not. In the latter case, the same motives which had induced individuals to place themselves under the protection of a combination, induced the head of that combination, when in his turn attacked, to place himself under the protection of the head of a stronger combination than his own. And thus arose by degrees the great feudal principalities which we hear of for the first time during the decline of the Carlovingian race, and some of which were large and powerful kingdoms, when the authority of the feeble descendant of Charlemagne did not extend beyond the city of Laon and its vicinity.

In England, during the reign of Edward the Confessor, the formation of the feudal system had already proceeded thus far. Godwin Earl of Wessex, Leofric Earl of Mercia, Siward Earl of Northumberland, and others, were virtually independent princes, any one of them capable of coping single-handed with the acknowledged monarch of their common country. It has been supposed that the feudal system was introduced into England at the Conquest. But this is only so far true, that the great lords had not, until that epoch, become the vassals of the crown. In France and Germany, this last step in the formation of the feudal system was taken at a much earlier date; but in what manner, and when, is left, like every thing that is valuable in the history of that remote period, to inference and conjecture. It appears probable that the chiefs who, under the name of dukes and counts, had already exercised, by the king's appointment, a delegated authority in the municipal towns, and who, in the decline of the royal power, had gradually withdrawn themselves from subjection, became the heads of all the greater combinations: or perhaps that the heads of those combinations found it convenient to obtain, from the petty prince who was still called king of France, a nominal delegation of his nominal authority, to facilitate the establishment of their ascendancy over the fortified towns; for an expiring authority always lingers in the towns for some time after it has lost all footing in the country. The transition was easy (when feudal ideas gained vigour) from this relation to the scarcely less nominal one of lord and vassal; for the paramountcy of the king was for many years almost a nominal privilege.

Thus arose the feudal system: of the workings of which we shall now attempt a rapid sketch. Our examples and proofs will be drawn chiefly from France. This, to an English reader, requires explanation. Our reasons for not selecting our own country as the theatre on which to exhibit feudality and its train of effects, are these:—In the first place, no one has yet been found to perform for England the service which has been performed by M. Dulaure for his own country; the toilsome and thankless service of dragging into light the vices and crimes of former days: and, secondly, the feudal system never existed in its original purity, in England. The kings of England enjoyed, from the Conquest downwards, a degree of power which the kings of continental Europe did not acquire till many generations later. There were no Godwins and Leofrics after the Conquest. The lands having come into the possession of the followers of the Conqueror at different times, as they were successively forfeited by their Saxon proprietors, all the various territorial acquisitions of a great baron were rarely situated in one part of the island: he was never strong enough in any one of his fiefs to establish his independence in that one, while the attempt, even if successful, would have involved the forfeiture of the rest. The king, therefore, was always stronger than any one, or any two or three, of his vassals. They could resist him only when combined. It is difficult to say how much of our present liberty we may not owe to this fortunate vigour of the royal authority, which compelled the barons to have recourse to parliaments, as the single means of effectual opposition to the encroachments of the king. This comparative strength of the general government of the country mitigated many of the worst evils of the feudal system. Great crimes could not be committed with the same impunity in England as in France. Private wars never prevailed to the same extent: it being the interest of the king to make himself the arbiter of all disputes, and his power being in general sufficient to enforce obedience. It was only in times of acknowledged civil war, such as the calamitous period which followed the usurpation of Stephen, that England was subject to those evils from which France never was free.

In Germany, on the other hand, the principal feudatories not only made themselves independent, but remained so. It is in France that we must contemplate the feudal system, if we wish to observe it in both its stages; the feudal aristocracy and the feudal monarchy; the period in which the great vassals were independent princes, and the period in which they were subjects. Each of these periods had its peculiar characteristics: we will begin with the first.

In the year 987, Hugh Capet, one of the chiefs who at that time shared France among them, usurped the throne. We have already stated the narrow limits, within which the possessions of the descendant of Charlemagne were at that time confined. Hugh Capet therefore acquired, as king of France, little territory beyond what he had previously held as count of Paris; a domain greatly inferior to that of the dukes of Burgundy or Normandy, or the counts of Flanders or Poitiers. It extended, in length, from Laon to Orleans, in breadth from Montereau to Pontoise. He and his immediate successors, being princes of no talent, instead of enlarging their territory or extending their influence, allowed what power they had to slip out of their hands; and, in the reign of Philip, third in descent from Hugh Capet, we find their authority bounded by the walls of five towns, Paris, Orleans, Etampes, Melun, and Compiègne.

The combinations which gave birth to the feudal system had, to a certain extent, answered their end. They afforded considerable protection against foreign, and some degree of protection against internal, assailants. The seed was put into the ground with some chance that he who sowed would be enabled to reap: and, from this time, progression in wealth and civilization recommenced. But, though some security to person and property is absolutely necessary to enable wealth to accumulate at all, the feudal system is a decisive experiment how small a portion of security will suffice.

Three classes composed, at this early period, the population of a feudal kingdom: the serfs who produced food, the nobles, or military caste, who consumed it, and a class of freemen who were neither nobles nor serfs: but this class, among the laity at least, soon terminated its short-lived existence. A class of freemen it can scarcely be called. Their freedom, the sort of freedom which they enjoyed, excluded them from protection, without exempting them from tyranny. The slave was at least secure from the oppressions of all masters but his own; the freeman was, like uninclosed land, the common property of all. We learn from the capitularies, or ordinances, of the Carlovingian race, that the *ingenui*, or free-born, were frequently forced to perform menial offices in the houses of the *seigneurs*: if poor, they were compelled to follow the nobles to the wars; if rich, they were amerced in an amount exceeding their property.* They were thus driven to seek subsistence and comparative security by becoming the slaves of their oppressors. As for the serfs, they were, literally, in the condition of domestic cattle; their master considered them as such, and treated them in the same manner; or rather, much more cruelly, because he feared them more. They were liable, at

*Dulaure, Vol. I, p. 460.

his will, to the infliction of any amount of stripes; to the loss of their ears, eyes, nose, feet, or hands, and, finally, of their lives. Power absolutely unchecked, in the hands of such men as the feudal chieftains, men utterly unaccustomed to control any impulse of passion, had its customary effect. We are informed that a hundred and fifty lashes were a frequent punishment for the most trivial fault.*

In order to form some further conception of this state of society, we have to imagine a perpetual civil war: war, not between two great divisions of the nation, which might rage in one district, leaving the others in tranquillity, but between every landed proprietor and his next neighbour.

That the knights of old were very easily affronted, is acknowledged by their panegyrists themselves. Even in these days, when that salutary instrument of moral discipline, the gallows, renders the consequences of an affront offered to an irascible neighbour somewhat less serious than formerly, we are not wont to regard irascible characters with much veneration or esteem. But we invest the irascible characters of former days with all the courage of a captain of dragoons, and so delighted are we with our own romantic conceptions, that we are ready to fall down and worship their imaginary original. When a knight was insulted, or thought fit to consider himself so, our notion is, that with scrupulous regard to all the niceties of modern honour, he sent his squire with a defiance to his enemy, challenging him to single combat. Possibly some knights might have been found who were thus punctilious; but the generality of them had a much less refined notion of the point of honour. Assassination, indeed, though horribly frequent, was but the exception, not the rule; or society must have ceased to exist. It was the labourers, and other cattle, on the offender's estate, who in general paid the penalty of their master's offence. The insulted party sallied out of his castle, and without any previous notice, proceeded to devastate the lands of his enemy; destroying the crops, burning the habitations, and carrying away both the species of live stock above spoken of. This done, he made haste to seek shelter in his castle, before his enemy had time to call together his vassals and pursue him. The other party, if he did not succeed in overtaking the plunderers, retaliated by entering upon the domain of the aggressor, and doing all the mischief he could. If they met, a battle took place; and woe to the vanquished! If unfortunate enough to be taken prisoner, he was subjected to the most excruciating torments, until forced to comply with whatever demands the victor's rapacity might dictate. *Catasta* was the name of the most usual instrument of torture. The prisoner, being placed on an iron cage, or chained down upon an iron bed, was exposed, in that situation, to fire. One of M. Dulaure's anecdotes will serve for illustration. Theobald V, Count of Chartres and Blois, a contemporary of our Henry II, and one of the most powerful feudatories north of the Loire, was engaged in hostilities with Sulpice, Seigneur of Amboise. His enemy fell into his hands, was put in irons, and exposed every day to the

Ibid., p. 461.

catasta. In vain did he offer large sums by way of ransom; the rapacity of the conqueror would be satisfied with nothing less than the possession of the town and castle of Chaumont. The required concession was at length extorted from the agonized captive: but his vassals still held the place, and refused to surrender it. His life speedily fell a sacrifice to this horrible torture.*

The celebrated anecdote of King John and the Jew's teeth,[*] as it has, besides the cruelty, something whimsical in it, fixes itself in the memory; and is perpetually quoted as an extraordinary instance of the cruel treatment to which the Jews were subject in that reign. Yet what is this, compared to what we here see practised by one *seigneur* upon another? Judge what must have been the treatment of the mere knight, and still more that of the burgess and the slave.

The fortresses, in which the terrified cultivators took refuge, were generally strong enough to defy any means of attack which the art of war at that time afforded. But the strongest castle might be taken by treachery or surprise; and, on these occasions, men, women and children were cut to pieces. This, indeed, was in a manner the law of war. On the storming of a place, it was the ordinary course of events. We hear much of the horrible butcheries which were practised in the wars of religion, on the storming of a town. We imagine, few are aware that these butcheries were neither new nor extraordinary; that they were no more than what the barons practised in their most ordinary wars, both foreign and domestic, when they had not even the imaginary dictates of their horrible superstition to plead in excuse.

It was an easy transition from these exploits to highway robbery. This practice, we are accordingly informed, was universal among the poorer nobility. Any honest employment would have been disgraceful: they wanted money: if they had cities to pillage, it was well; if not, they pillaged travellers. An Indian Brahmin, when his profession fails him, is at liberty to engage in the occupations of that caste which is next in rank to his own: on a similar principle, the greatest chieftains of France, princes of the blood, and even kings themselves, when they could no longer support themselves by their respective vocations of governing and fighting, betook themselves to the profession of a highwayman as the next in dignity. Eudes I, Duke of Burgundy; another Eudes, brother to King Henry I; Philip, a son of King Philip I, and that monarch himself, are numbered among the high-born predecessors of Cartouche and Turpin. What was to them only an occasional resource, was to an inferior class of nobles their daily bread. Sometimes they sallied out, and waylaid pedlars on the highway, or pilgrims journeying with valuables to some sacred place: at other times they seized the peasants in the public market, stripped them of what they had, and detained them prisoners, or put them to the torture, to extort the disclosure of hidden treasure.

*Ibid., Vol. II, p. 142n.

[*See Matthew Paris, *Angli historia major*, ed. William Wats (London: Hodgkinson, 1640), p. 229.]

When Louis VI, surnamed le Gros, the fourth descendant of Hugh Capet who filled the throne, and the first who was worthy of it, arrived at the age of manhood, the royal authority was at the lowest ebb. For many years of his life, he found full occupation in reducing his immediate subjects, the petty landholders of the royal domain, to a moderate degree of obedience. A description of the state in which he found that portion of France, may serve as a specimen of what must have been the condition of the remainder.

The rural counts, viscounts, and barons, who held immediately of the king, in the duchy of France, had availed themselves of Philip's weakness to shake off his authority altogether, in the castles in which they had fortified themselves. From these castles they sallied forth and fell upon the travellers and traders (*marchands*) who passed within reach of their retreat, unless the latter consented to redeem themselves with a high ransom: they equally abused their strength against the monasteries, and against all the ecclesiastical lords. Sometimes they went and lodged with them, together with their squires, their soldiers, their horses, and their dogs, and required that the religious establishment whose forced hospitality they were enjoying, should defray the expense of their maintenance for months; sometimes they levied contributions in money or in kind, upon the peasants of the bishops or monks, as a compensation for the protection which these warriors promised to extend towards them. The barons, in particular, who were vassals of any ecclesiastical body, seemed to think that their vassalage itself gave them a title to the spoil of their clerical superiors.*

Louis, who was not only king of France, but the immediate feudal superior of these freebooters, found himself not only no match for their united strength, but scarcely able to cope with the lord of a castle single-handed. He prudently limited his first undertakings to the protection of the monasteries against the extortions of the nobility. By this means he obtained the sanction of the church, and the co-operation of the abbey troops, by whose aid he repressed the disorders of the principal Châtelains, and brought most of them into comparative subjection to his authority.

The names and designations of some of these worthies have been preserved to us. Hugh de Pompone, Seigneur of Crécy, and Châtelain of Gournay, infested with his depredations, not only the highway, but the river Marne, stopping passengers by land and water, and levying contributions. When attacked by Louis, this bandit was defended by his father, Guy, Count of Rochefort, and by Theobald, Count of Champagne. The fortress of Montlhéri, the patrimony and residence of a branch of the Montmorency family, was the retreat of a band of robbers, who desolated the whole country from Corbeil to Châteaufort, and interrupted all communication between Paris and Orleans. Hugh, Seigneur of Puiset, a place situated not far from the road which connects Chartres with Orleans, plundered travellers to the very gates of Chartres. Louis reduced his castle, and retained him for some time in confinement; but on his succeeding, by the death of an uncle, to the county of Corbeil, the relinquishment of this inheritance in favour of Louis was the price of his release. This lesson produced no change in his habits of life. No sooner was

*[Translated from] Sismondi, Vol. V, pp. 10-11.

Louis occupied in another quarter, than he rebuilt, in violation of an express engagement, the fortifications of Puiset, seized the king's peasants in the public market-place, and extorted sums of money by way of ransom.

But these were vulgar trespasses, hardly worthy of mention. It was reserved for Thomas de Marne, a baron of Picardy, to exemplify in its perfection the true greatness of villainy. "This seigneur," says the abbot of Nogent,[*] quoted by M. de Sismondi,

had, from his earliest youth, continually augmented his riches by the pillage of travellers and pilgrims, and extended his domain by incestuous marriages with rich heiresses, his relations. His cruelty was so unheard-of, that even butchers, who nevertheless pass for unfeeling, are more sparing of the sufferings of the cattle which they are slaying, than he was of the sufferings of men: for he was not contented with punishing them by the sword, for determinate faults, as people are accustomed to do: he racked them by the most horrible tortures. When he wished to extort a ransom from his captives, he hung them up by some delicate part of the body; or laid them upon the ground, and, covering them with stones, walked over them; beating them at the same time, until they promised all that he required, or perished under the operation.*

It was not until the twenty-second year of his reign, that Louis could subjugate this demon in human form. For eighteen years at least of this long interval, he continued his execrable mode of life; and might have continued it longer, had he not, when besieged in his castle of Coucy, been mortally wounded and taken prisoner in a *sortie*. "The king," says M. de Sismondi, "tried to induce him, in his last moments, to release the traders whom he had kidnapped on the highway; whom he kept in prison to extort a ransom, or tortured for his amusement: but even in the agonies of death Coucy refused all mercy, and seemed to regret the loss of dominion over his prisoners, much more than the termination of life."[†] Thus perished Thomas de Marne. But his eldest son Enguerrand de Coucy trod faithfully in his steps; and succeeded in making head against the whole power of the king. After being vainly besieged in the castle of la Fère, he was taken into favour, and received in marriage a princess of the blood royal.

In 1109, says M. Dulaure, one of those horrible occurrences, so frequent in the annals of feudality, took place at the castle of la Roche-Guyon on the Seine. The lord of this castle, Guy de la Roche-Guyon, is praised by contemporary writers for renouncing the practices of his father and grandfather: "Il était enclin à se conduire en homme probe et honnête, et s'abstenait de pillage et de vol: 'Peut-être,' adds one author, 'se serait-il laissé aller aux habitudes de ses pères, s'il eût plus longuement vécu.' "[†] This chief, whom the chronicler supposes to have died just

[*Guibert.]
*[Translated from] Sismondi, Vol. V, pp. 94-5.
[†*Ibid.*, pp. 210-11.]
†Dulaure, Vol. II, pp. 136-7. [Dulaure refers to "l'abbé Suger et les grandes Chroniques."]

in time to save his virtue, was assassinated by Guillaume his brother-in-law, who, with the aid of several knights, laid an ambuscade in the chapel of the castle, and murdered Guy, his wife and children, and every other human being in the place. Had this been all, he might have retained the castle to the end of his natural life: but he was suspected by the neighbouring barons of being in an understanding with the English. They resolved to dislodge him. Being besieged in the castle, he opened the gates, stipulating for his life and liberty. It seems that some of the besiegers were not parties to the capitulation. Guillaume was massacred, together with the rest of the besieged: we are not told whether by those who had not engaged for his safety, or by those who had.

In this state was the royal domain, under the fifth of the Capets. But enough of causes; it is time to look at effects. Of the seventy-three years which composed the reigns of Hugh Capet, his son, and grandson, forty-eight were years of famine; being two out of three. Of these famines, pestilence was almost a uniform, cannibalism a frequent, accompaniment.* So much for the feudal system, and the perpetual civil war which was its consequence. In the long reign of Charlemagne we hear only of two famines; and even under the feeble Louis le Débonnaire, whose reign was disgraced by so many rebellions, there is only mention of one.† So much more destructive of security was feudal order, than what elsewhere goes by the name of civil war; and so endurable a thing is even despotism, compared with "liberty," when all the liberty is for a few barons, and the mass of the people are slaves.

In this country, it has been the interest of the powerful, that the abominations of the clergy in the middle ages should be known; and accordingly they are known. But it has not been the interest of the powerful in this country, that the abominations of the barons should be known; and consequently they are not simply unknown, but their authors are believed to have been patterns of the noblest virtues. The clergy were, in reality, by many degrees the less wicked of the two. They at all times administered better justice to their vassals, than the military chiefs; they at all times discouraged depredations and private wars. True it is, that in their eyes these were secondary offences; it was not for such crimes that interdicts and excommunications were sent forth: these were reserved for the man who married his fourth cousin, or who presumed to summon an ecclesiastic before a secular court. Robbery and murder were not, it is true, sins of so black a dye as the foregoing; they *were* sins, however, and, as such, were condemned. To the exertions of the clergy was owing the *truce of God*, one of the most curious traits in the character of the times. In a council composed of laymen and ecclesiastics, held in the diocese of Perpignan, it was resolved that three days and two nights in each week should be allowed to the nobles, to fight, burn, and plunder, under certain

*Dulaure, Vol. II, pp. 154-60.
†*Ibid.*, Vol. I, p. 462.

restrictions; by which concession it was hoped to induce them to suspend those recreations during the remainder of the week. This attempt to compromise with the vices of the times, was not, we are told, at first, altogether unsuccessful. But the compact was not adopted in all the districts of France, nor even in the royal domain; and as there existed no means of enforcing its observance, it fell every where into desuetude. It being thought that the time allowed for pillage was possibly not quite long enough, it was enlarged to four days and three nights, and at length to nearly six days and five nights; but the shortest intermission of mutual devastation was more than could be endured.*

During the succeeding reigns, the power of the crown was gradually on the increase, and that of the great feudatories on the wane. Many of the most powerful fiefs became, by marriage or otherwise, integral parts of the English or French monarchies. The expulsion of the English from the north of France, by Philip Augustus, added their possessions to the royal domain; and the enfranchisement of the large towns, which uniformly allied themselves with the king against their old masters, enabled him to break the power of the feudal aristocracy. While this great change in the frame of society was going on, no improvement took place in the moral habits of the nobility. They continued to rob on the highway, and to quarrel and fight with one another, as before. Nor was it till long after the reign of Saint Louis, that the châtelains of France universally abandoned the profession of a highwayman. "Tels," says M. Dulaure,

étaient les chevaliers du douzième et treizième siècle, dont la loyauté tant exaltée dans les romans, dans les compositions poétiques, et sur notre scène moderne, se trouve constamment démentie par l'histoire. Ces hommes auxquels on attribue tant d'exploits glorieux, tant d'actions généreuses et honorables, n'étaient que des brigands impitoyables, des misérables dignes de figurer dans les bagnes ou les cachots de Bicêtre. Je révèle ici une des nombreuses impostures de nos écrivains.[†]

It is not asserted, that there were no exceptions to this general depravity. All which is contended for is, that the virtuous characters of those days were as much less virtuous than those of our own, as the wicked characters were more wicked, and that they were proportionally much more rare. Such is not the impression conveyed by the romances of chivalry; and it is the misfortune of modern writers, that they have mistaken the romances of chivalry for the history of chivalry. We shall be told, that romances are good evidence of manners. We answer with M. Roederer:[‡] of manners, yes: of the characters of their heroes, not at all. The romances of chivalry did not even profess to represent the knights as they were, but as they ought to be. What would be thought of a writer who should seriously infer,

*Ibid., Vol. II, p. 152.
[†]Ibid., p. 343.
[‡]See a recent work of considerable merit, intituled, Louis XII, et François I, par P.L. Roederer, [2 vols. (Paris: Bossange, 1825),] Vol. II, p. 252.

that in the time of Richardson the character of an English gentleman resembled that of Sir Charles Grandison?[*]

Even Mr. Hallam does not believe in the reality of knights-errant; of persons who travelled about, liberating captives, and redressing wrongs.[†] But a romance must have a hero, and a hero must be a character to be admired. There never was a state of society (howsoever depraved) in which the character of a redresser of wrongs was not admired; on the contrary, it is admired in the direct ratio of the frequency of grievous wrongs. The romances of the east abound with good viziers: when the hero is a vizier, we may be sure he is always a good one: and how often does a good vizier arise? About as often as a good king: once in two hundred years.

One would expect to find the most admirable models of chivalrous virtue among those whose names and actions history has celebrated, and who were most admired by their contemporaries.* In these respects no chevalier ever exceeded Richard Coeur de Lion. A few anecdotes, therefore, of his life, will go far to illustrate, not only the practical morality of the age, but moreover its theoretical standard of moral approbation. This mirror of chivalry is first introduced to our notice in the character of a rebellious and treacherous son, intrusted by his father with the government of a province, and exciting that province to rebel. As Duke of

[*Samuel Richardson, *The History of Sir Charles Grandison* (1753-54), 3rd ed., 7 vols. (London: Richardson, 1754).]

[†Henry Hallam, *View of the State of Europe during the Middle Ages*, 2 vols. (London: Murray, 1818), p. 552.]

*M. Dulaure admits, that there were some estimable men; but he finds them chiefly among the clergy. He mentions only one name among the barons; Charles Count of Flanders, surnamed the Good. [Vol. II, p. 196.] M. de Sismondi has given us some account of this personage; and a few anecdotes concerning the most estimable nobleman of his day, may not be uninteresting, as illustrative of the ideas of the times. He kept, we are told, three doctors of theology in his house, who, every night, after supper, read and expounded the Bible. He enacted severe laws against profane swearing, and was "marvellously severe and rigorous" in executing those which had already been enacted against witches and necromancers. He banished all Jews and usurers from his territories; declaring, in language oddly compounded of feudal and theological ideas, "qu'il ne les voulait souffrir jusqu'à ce qu'ils eussent satisfait et amendé le meurtre par eux commis du fils de leur seigneur." ([Pierre d'] Oudegherst, *Annales et Chroniques de Flandre* [2 vols. (Ghent: de Goesin-Verhaeghe; Paris: Janet, [1789]), Vol. I, p. 360; Mill is quoting from Sismondi, Vol. V, p. 205.]) We are next informed of the precautions of this enlightened prince to obviate famine. These consisted in prohibiting *les cervoises*, (probably beer), destroying all the dogs and calves, and forcing the corn-dealers to open their granaries and sell their corn *at a reasonable price*. This last act of despotism brought on a quarrel between him and van der Strate, a great corn-dealer, and the head of one of the most powerful families in Flanders. In the course of the dispute, insulting doubts having been intimated concerning the title of the van der Strates to be considered of free condition, that family were so incensed at the affront, that they murdered the good count at the foot of the altar. His successor [Guillaume Cliton] revenged his death by causing a hundred and eleven persons to be precipitated from a high tower. (Sismondi, Vol. V, pp. 205-7.)

Aquitaine, we find him carrying off the wives and daughters of his principal vassals; and, after keeping them until he was weary of possession, giving them away in presents to his followers.* When reconciled to his father, he turns round upon his former partizans, invades their territories, captures their towns, and loads them with exactions.† Again and again received into favour, again and again did he rebel. At length his father died, and he succeeded to the throne. His first act, in this new situation, was to place his father's treasurer, Stephen of Tours, seneschal of Anjou, in irons: nor did he release him until (says Roger de Hoveden) he had delivered up all the late king's money, and his own, to the last penny.‡

He appears to no greater advantage as a champion of the cross. It is related of him, that, when walking in the streets of Messina, he heard the cry of a hawk proceeding from the house of a peasant. A hawk, in England, was to plebeians a prohibited bird. Richard, forgetting that he was no longer in England, but in a country where the peasants had knives, and knew how to use them, entered the house, and took possession of the bird; but an assembled crowd speedily put him to flight. The same imperious temper and despotic habits soon after led him to commit a still greater outrage. A monastery, situated on the strait of Messina, appeared to him a convenient place for lodging his magazines: with him, to desire and to seize were one; he turned out the monks, and put a party of soldiers into their place. Disgusted at these and other acts of oppression, the inhabitants of Messina shut the gates upon Richard and his troops; a conflict ensued, and he forced his way into the place.§ Another anecdote, which is related of him while at Messina, is strikingly characteristic of his jealous and vindictive disposition. In the crusading army he had no rival in warlike exercises, except a French knight, named Guillaume des Barres. On one occasion, while the knights were exercising without the walls, an ass passed by loaded with reeds, which then, as now, were used in that country as vine props. They seized the reeds, and commenced a mock fight. Richard and Guillaume des Barres were opposed to one another. Their reeds were shivered at the first shock, but the reed of Guillaume tore Richard's cloak. This insignificant mischance provoked Richard to such a degree of fury, that he rushed upon his adversary, and strove violently to unhorse him. In this endeavour he was defeated, which inflamed his passion still more; he swore that he would be for ever the enemy of Guillaume des Barres, and was mean enough to require that the king of France should withdraw his protection from that knight, and banish him from Messina. Nor was it till long after, that, by the entreaties of Philip, aided by those of all the barons and prelates in the army, who placed themselves on their knees

---

*Sismondi, Vol. VI, p. 36. See also p. 27.

†[Jacques Nicolas Augustin] Thierry, *Histoire de la Conquête de l'Angleterre par les Normands* [(1825), 2nd ed., 4 vols. (Paris: Sautelet, 1826)], Vol. III, p. 337.

‡*Ibid.*, Vol. IV, p. 30. [See Roger (of Hoveden), *Annalium pars prior et posterior*, in *Rerum anglicarum scriptores*, ed. Henry Savile (London: Bishop, *et al.*, 1596), p. 373.]

§Thierry, *Histoire*, Vol. IV, pp. 36-7.

before him, he was prevailed upon to restrain his resentment during such time as he and Guillaume should both wear the badge of the crusade.*

The conduct of Coeur de Lion, after the surrender of Acre, was even in that age remarkable for its ferocity. The garrison and inhabitants were to remain prisoners for forty days, at the expiration of which term, if not previously ransomed, they were to be at the mercy of the conqueror. Not being ransomed, they were, by Richard's order, put to death in cold blood.[†]

On his return to England, having laid siege to Nottingham, he erected a gibbet within sight of the walls, and hanged several men-at-arms whom he had taken prisoners, to strike terror into the besieged.[‡]

At a later period, we find him raising the wind in a manner truly royal, by turning off his chancellor,[*] and declaring all the acts of that functionary null and void; obliging those whose titles were thus invalidated, to purchase valid ones, or forfeit their right.

We soon after find him swearing a truce with the king of France, and violating it immediately.[§] Nor was this his last breach of faith. After resigning, by solemn treaty, the paramountcy of Auvergne to his rival the king of France, and even undertaking to aid him in enforcing the right against the unwilling Auvergnats, he broke the treaty, and made an alliance with the Auvergnats against their new liege lord. He very soon broke his faith with them too, and concluding a separate truce, looked on quietly, and saw them subdued. The truce expired, and hostilities renewed between the two kings. Richard had the assurance to renew his correspondence with the Auvergnats, claim their performance of the engagement which he himself had violated, and exhort them to renew the war. They were too prudent to be again deceived; and the royal troubadour consoled himself by composing satirical verses upon what he termed their breach of faith.[¶]

---

*Sismondi, Vol. VI, pp. 101-2.

[†]Ibid., pp. 111-12. It is worthy of remark, that the other great historical example of royal chivalry, the Black Prince, also caused several thousand persons to be massacred in cold blood at Limoges. The circumstance is related by Froissart, by whom it is disapproved. [Jean Froissart, Chroniques, in Collection des chroniques nationales françaises écrites en langue vulgaire du treizième au seizième siècle, ed. Jean Alexandre Buchon, 48 vols. (Paris: Verdière, 1824-26), Vol. V, p. 220.] In the later period of chivalry, which has never been sufficiently distinguished from the earlier, increasing civilization had mitigated considerably the horrors of knightly vengeance.

[‡]Thierry, Histoire, Vol. IV, p. 84.

[*]Hubert Walter.]

[§]Thierry, Histoire, Vol. IV, pp. 114-15. The words of an old writer [Bertrand de Born] on this occasion, are characteristic: The two kings, says he, after this truce, would no longer occupy themselves in war, but only in hunting, amusements, and doing evil to their men: "E en far tort à lor baros." Choix des Poésies Originales des Troubadours, publié par [François Just Marie] Raynouard [6 vols. (Paris: Didot, 1816-21),] Vol. V, p. 93 (apud Thierry, ibid.).

[¶]Ibid., pp. 120-2.

But the reader has probably had enough of the "glory of chivalry."[*] To be the glory of chivalry, indeed, nothing was necessary but the reputation of military prowess: a reputation founded upon achievements in war, and superiority in jousts and tournaments. The pomp and pageantry which adorned these exhibitions have captivated the imaginations, not only of contemporaries but of posterity; and when the imagination is gained, the reason, as experience shows, very seldom fails to follow. That the characteristics of a knight were undaunted courage and the most ardent desire of glory, is a proposition which has hitherto been taken for granted by the admirers, and hardly denied by the impugners of chivalry; and when we wish to say of any one that he is a pattern of all the military virtues, our expression is, that he is worthy of the age of chivalry. Now this proceeds, as it appears to us, upon a complete misapprehension. That courage and the love of glory were not uncommon among the knights, it would be absurd to doubt; since these are qualities which are never wanting, where there are dangers, and a public opinion. But that either quality was universal among them is the dream of a romancer; and we will venture to affirm, that there is more real courage in a single regiment of the British or French army in the year 1826, than there was in the whole chivalry of France or England five centuries ago.

We must not be misled by the great estimation in which military prowess was held. This is no proof of its universality, but the reverse. When particular examples of any virtue are extravagantly praised, it is a certain sign that the virtue is rare. It is pertinently remarked (we believe, by M. Dulaure), that there are at this day hundreds in the French army who possess all the heroic qualities which immortalized Bayard,* but who are utterly unknown, precisely *because* there are so many. Thus it is that we continue to talk of the continence of Scipio; yet, what mighty matter did this continence amount to? He did not ravish a beautiful woman, whom the fortune of war had thrown into his hands.[†] Now, if this be greatness, what subaltern officer, we were going to say, common soldier, in the British army, is not as great a man as Scipio? As a proof of Scipio's continence, the story is

[*Edmund Burke, *Reflections on the Revolution in France*, in *Works*, 8 vols. (London: Dodsley, *et al.*, 1792-1827), Vol. III, p. 111.]

*It may not be impertinent here to remark, that when Bayard lived, knighthood, in its original character, had long been extinct; that Bayard himself had never received the *accolade*, but was a chevalier by birth, like most of the noblemen of his day; that he was not even called, during his life, the chevalier Bayard, but Captain Bayard, *le capitaine Bayard*: and that the title of *knight without fear and without reproach*, supposed to have been conferred upon him by the suffrage of his contemporaries as the peculiar reward of his eminent virtue, was in reality a common title of courtesy, shared with him by many other warriors of the time. (See the work of M. Roederer, already referred to [*Louis XII et François Ier*, Vol. II, pp. 280-3].)

[†See *Livy* (Latin and English), 14 vols., trans. B.O. Foster, *et al.* (London: Heinemann; New York: Putnam's Sons; and [Vols. VI-XIV] Cambridge, Mass.: Harvard University Press, 1919-59), Vol. VII, pp. 190-4 (xxvi, 50, 1-14).]

ridiculous; but, as a proof of the lawless and brutal incontinence of his contemporaries, this one anecdote, though it be but an anecdote, is worth a thousand volumes.

The ardour of the knights for military enterprises was indeed universal. But this ardour was no proof of exalted courage. Their military enterprises exposed them to hardly any danger. Cased in impenetrable armour, they could in general defy all attempts on life or limb; and the battles of chivalry, how destructive soever to the almost unarmed infantry, were rarely fatal to the men-at-arms. It might be, that a few knights were trampled on by horses, or crushed, in falling, by the weight of their armour. But if unhorsed, and at the victor's mercy, their lives were scarcely ever in any danger, except from private vengeance; it was neither esteemed dishonourable to give, nor to accept, a ransom; it was the law of war. To compare the courage of an average knight, with that of a modern private soldier, would be like drawing a comparison, for endurance of cold, between a man wrapped up in furs, and a barefooted and naked savage.*

Trifling, however, as was the danger of their warlike enterprises, they always courted in preference the least hazardous even of these. In their hostilities with one another, we have already mentioned that it was their great endeavour, after devastating the country, to escape to their strongholds without the risk of an engagement. They always preferred to encounter the inhabitants of the towns, who were destitute of defensive armour, and of whom they might hope to cut down thousands without the loss of a man. If, indeed, we look for real courage in the feudal times, we must seek it among those brave citizens, who did not fear, under such tremendous disadvantages, to face these terrible opponents in the field, in defence of all that they held dear. Among the few pages of the feudal annals which it gives pleasure to read, is that which records the glorious struggle which the burgesses of Flanders, forsaken and sold by their ally Edward I of England, maintained against Philippe le Bel and the whole chivalry of France. Thousands and thousands of them were cut to pieces; but they triumphed!

The taste of the chevaliers for tournaments, and other warlike exercises, may be as easily explained as their love of military adventure. M. de Sismondi treats both merely as the resources of *désoeuvré* savages to expel ennui. They sought excitement in the lists and in the field, as our German ancestors sought it by staking

---

*See an able chapter on chivalry in M. Roederer's work. M. Roederer, after quoting Mr. Hallam for the remark, that the battles of chivalry were an affair of very little danger, reproaches his countrymen with having suffered an Englishman to be the first man to whom this observation occurred. If he had read further, he would have seen that Mr. Hallam, though he made the remark, knew not how to apply it. We believe, that M. Roederer himself is the first writer who has turned it to the proper account. [Roederer, "De l'esprit chevaleresque attribué à François Ier, et de la chevalerie," Sect. 5 in Vol. II of *Louis XII et François Ier*, pp. 238-94; for the reference to Hallam's *View* (Vol. I, pp. 358-60 in the 1st ed.) and Roederer's comment, see pp. 260, 261n.]

their liberty on the throw of a die. "Un esprit inquiet, un vague désir d'aventures, le besoin d'émotions, et l'espoir d'améliorer sa condition par la violence plus que par l'industrie, formaient alors le caractère de la noblesse Française."* The following passage characterizes chivalry with equal vigour and accuracy. We give it in the original, because it is at the same time a specimen of the style of M. de Sismondi's work:

Les paysans, les bourgeois, tous ceux qui travaillaient pour gagner leur misérable vie, qui se trouvaient sans cesse vexés, opprimés, insultés par leurs supérieurs, ne demandaient que le repos, et une sûreté que l'ordre public était loin de leur garantir: mais les nobles étaient, au contraire, dévorés par l'ennui, et souvent aussi aiguillonnés par la cupidité: leur esprit, qui n'avait reçu aucune culture, qui ne soupçonnait pas même les avantages de l'instruction, ne trouvait aucune ressource dans la solitude ou la vie domestique: toute occupation laborieuse ou lucrative leur était interdite, elle dérogeait à la noblesse, elle les assimilait à ces vilains qu'ils faisaient travailler comme des bêtes de somme et qu'ils maltraitaient comme des ennemis. Les cours plénières, les tournois, les pas d'armes se présentent à notre imagination comme les divertissemens de cette noblesse brillante. Nous y voyons les riches récompenses décernées à la valeur, et nous oublions que même pour ceux qui pouvaient en jouir, huit jours de fête étaient achetés par une année de langueur et de solitude. Mais tandis que les serfs de chaque baron lui fournissaient le pain, la viande, peut-être la laine et le lin dont il avait besoin pour sa consommation habituelle, il fallait qu'il achetât les armes, les équipages, les habits somptueux avec lesquels il voulait paraître aux fêtes chevaleresques, et lui qui ne produisait rien, qui ne vendait rien, il n'avait jamais de l'argent, il ne pouvait s'en procurer que par la rapine et par la guerre: la cupidité avait donc bien plus de part que l'amour du danger à cet empressement avec lequel il courait partout où il entendait le bruit des armes. *La cupidité et l'ennui étaient les deux mobiles de la noblesse*; la vanité concourait avec l'ennui pour entretenir cette passion pour les tournois que les excommunications de l'église ne pouvaient modérer; car Grégoire IX avait de nouveau, le 27 Février 1228, frappé d'anathème ceux qui combattaient dans les *jeux de lance* (*hastiludia*) et soumis leurs terres à l'interdit. La cupidité et l'ennui conduisaient les gentilshommes Français partout où la vue du sang ruisselant réveillait l'âme engourdie, et où le pillage livrait au guerrier cet or qu'aucune honnête industrie ne pouvait lui procurer.[†]

M. de Sismondi's two great *stimuli*, cupidity and ennui, were quite capable of leading them into danger, but it required another sort of qualities to bring them successfully out of it. As often as the demand for excitement and the demand for plunder brought a large number of them together in one enterprise, the same passions invariably hurried them into irregularities which put to hazard, if they did not frustrate, the success of the expedition. Their impatience of subordination made them regardless of discipline, and uncontrollable by the authority of their commander; their habitual thoughtlessness rendered them incapable of directing their own conduct, and they would not suffer it to be directed by any one else. Let the admirer of chivalry read the history of any enterprise of *real danger* in which they were ever engaged; of any of the crusades for example, more especially of the

*Sismondi, Vol. VII, p. 108.
[†]*Ibid.*, pp. 122-3.

two last; let him mark, not only the rapine and cruelty, but the stupidity, the supineness, the headlong confidence, the incapacity of foreseeing and providing against the most obvious difficulties, which rendered their whole career one series of blunders and misfortunes. If he weighs all this, and moreover bethinks himself of the peculiar character of their warfare, by which even personal prowess was made to depend almost entirely on the steeds, the armour, and the bodily strength of the combatants,* he must acknowledge that the far-famed knights of the middle ages were nearly as destitute even of the military virtues, in any extended sense of the term, as they were of all other virtues whatsoever.

So much for the "cheap defence of nations." Now for the "nurse of manly sentiment and heroic virtue."[*]

The characteristic virtues of chivalry, according to Mr. Hallam, were loyalty, courtesy, and munificence.[†] Its claim to these qualities has in general been allowed; and it has, on this foundation, been without further question admitted to have been the great refiner of manners, and purifier of morals. Is this notion well grounded, or not? Let us inquire.

If by munificence be meant, according to Mr. Hallam's definition, "disdain of money,"[‡] meaning disdain of wealth, not only this quality did *not* characterize the age of chivalry, but the diametrically opposite qualities *did*. In no age was the thirst for plunder a more all-engrossing passion, nor the source of more numerous or greater crimes. But if it be only meant, that the wealth which was lightly got was lightly squandered; that the feudal chief was profuse in bestowing upon the instruments of his strength, or the ministers of his vanity or his amusement, gifts which cost him nothing but the groans of his bondmen, or the blood of those of his neighbour; the little value set upon wealth thus obtained, is only a proof how lightly the crimes by which it was purchased weighed upon the conscience of the offender. When all that had been got by one crime had been expended, what could be more obvious than, by another crime, to get more?

Loyalty is defined by Mr. Hallam to mean, fidelity to engagements. By courtesy, was meant, not only ceremonious politeness, but good feeling and good conduct towards each other, and particularly towards prisoners.[§] Of both these qualities there were shining examples towards the conclusion of the age of chivalry. There was but little of either in the earlier period; and at no time were these virtues very commonly practised. While the feudal nobility retained their turbulent independence, no perfidy was thought too odious in order to gain an end, nor any abuse of power too flagrant when practised upon the defenceless. The

---

*"Dans toutes les guerres du moyen âge," says M. de Sismondi, "on aurait pu dire que ce qu'on nommait bravoure était en raison inverse du vrai courage; celui qui par ses armes était le plus redoutable, était aussi celui qui risquait le moins." (Vol. VI, p. 364.)

[*For both phrases, see Burke, *Reflections*, p. 111.]

[†*View*, Vol. II, p. 549.]

[‡*Ibid.*, p. 551.]

[§*Ibid.*, p. 549.]

treacherous devices which they employed to entrap one another, the horrid cruelties which they practised upon one another when entrapped, the assassinations which they sometimes perpetrated, sometimes (though more rarely) suborned, and of which the altar was not unfrequently the scene, are topics which we have already in some measure illustrated, and have not room to exhibit further. When one baron took a fancy to the wife of another, it appears, from several instances related by M. de Sismondi, that he made no scruple of carrying off the object of his passion, and marrying her; so much for the loyalty, the courtesy, and we will add, the religion, of the times.*

*The mild and respectful treatment of prisoners, so universal in modern Europe, being in general ascribed to the refining influence of chivalry on modern manners, we quote from M. de Sismondi the following anecdote, which speaks for itself. The event related took place in the reign of our Henry I, and was several years posterior to the first crusade: "Au commencement de l'année 1119, le roi Henri se vit encore abandonné par un autre de ses vassaux, sur la fidélité duquel il n'avait pas cru pouvoir concevoir un doute. C'était Eustache de Breteuil, à qui il avait donné en mariage Juliane, sa fille naturelle. Eustache profitant de l'embarras où il voyait son beau-père, lui avait demandé en don la tour d'Ivry, qui avait appartenu à ses prédécesseurs. Henri ne voulut pas s'en dessaisir; mais afin de donner au comte de Breteuil une garantie que cette tour ne serait jamais employée à lui nuire, il obligea Harenc (c'était le nom de l'homme qui en avait le commandement) à remettre, comme ôtage, son fils au comte de Breteuil, tandis qu'il se fit livrer à lui-même les deux filles que le comte avait eues de sa fille Juliane. Il semblait ainsi avoir établi entr'eux une garantie mutuelle, qui lui aurait répondu de leur fidélité, si la violence des passions, chez ces hommes féroces, avait pu être enchaînée, ou par les liens du sang, ou par le danger de leurs proches. Eustache de Breteuil, qui ne pouvait croire que ses filles courussent aucun danger entre les mains de leur grand-père, somma le gouverneur de la tour d'Ivry de lui ouvrir cette forteresse, s'il ne voulait pas que son fils fût livré sous ses yeux aux plus horribles tourmens; et comme celui-ci se refusait à perdre son château et à violer son serment, Eustache fit à l'instant arracher les yeux du jeune homme, et les envoya au malheureux Raoul de Harenc. Raoul vint se jeter aux pieds de Henri, et lui demander justice de l'outrage qui lui avait été fait sous la foi royale. La pitié pour un brave et fidèle chevalier, le ressentiment contre son gendre, l'emportèrent dans le coeur du roi d'Angleterre sur l'amour de son sang; il abandonna à la vengeance de Raoul ses propres petites-filles, qu'il gardait en ôtage, et auxquelles, par de terribles représailles, Raoul fit arracher les yeux et couper le nez. Le gouverneur d'Ivry annonça ensuite au comte de Breteuil que sa barbarie était retombée sur ses enfans, qu'ils étaient mutilés comme son fils l'avait été, mais que leur vie lui répondait encore de la vie de son fils, et que la tour ne lui serait point livrée. A la nouvelle de cette effroyable vengeance, le comte de Breteuil arbora les drapeaux de France, et commença à faire la guerre à son beau-père. Toutefois les habitans de Breteuil ne voulurent pas le seconder dans sa rébellion; ils ouvrirent la ville à Henri. Juliane, qui s'y trouvait alors, n'eut que le temps de se réfugier dans la citadelle: elle y fut assiégée par le roi son père; les vivres lui manquaient, et elle fut bientôt réduite à offrir de capituler. Son père ne voulut lui accorder que des conditions honteuses: le pont qui unissait la citadelle à la ville, avait été coupé; le roi d'Angleterre ne permit point qu'il fût rétabli pour donner passage à Juliane. Il exigea qu'après avoir relevé ses habits au-dessus de sa ceinture, exposée au froid du mois de Février, à la vue et à la risée de toute l'armée, elle se fit dévaler avec des cordes du haut des murs, jusque dans le fossé plein d'eau, où il la fit reprendre." (Sismondi, Vol. V, pp. 139-41.) This anecdote, as the reader will perceive, illustrates several features of the times at once.

But when the greater barons ceased to be independent sovereigns, and the smaller barons and knights to be subjects and retainers of those sovereigns; when their exploits came to be performed in national armies, and their virtues and vices to be exhibited on a great theatre, exposed to the view of whole nations; they then became, for the first time, amenable to a sort of *public opinion*. It is when individuals come under the influence of public opinion, that they begin to exhibit some glimmerings of virtue. But what kind of virtue? This will depend upon the kind of public to whose opinion they are amenable. The only public to which the knights of chivalry were amenable, was a public composed of one another. The opinion which other classes might form concerning their conduct, was a matter of too little importance to them to be at all regarded.

The consequences of this situation well deserve to be traced. Though it is not true of every individual that his interest makes his morality, it is strictly true of every class of men. When a set of persons are so situated as to be compelled to pay regard to the opinion of one another, but not compelled to pay any regard to the opinion of the rest of the world, they invariably proceed to fabricate two rules of action; one rule for their behaviour to one another, another rule for their behaviour to all persons except themselves. This was literally, strictly, what the chevaliers did. A chevalier was bound by the opinion of the chevaliers to keep his word with another chevalier, and to treat him, when a prisoner, with gentleness and respect. His own interest would prompt him to do so, if a man of common prudence; since he could not know how soon he might be a prisoner, and might have occasion to be released upon parole, or promise of ransom. But we are not to suppose that it was necessary for a knight to fulfil his engagements with any one except a knight. Exactly as the profligate man of fashion of the present day will pay a gaming debt to the last farthing, though it leave him pennyless, while he internally resolves never to pay his tradesmen at all: so would a baron keep his word with another baron, and break his word, and his oath too, with a low-born *bourgeois*.

History, though conversant only with events upon a great scale, affords abundant evidence to bear out this assertion. Notwithstanding the rapacity and avarice of the barons, their profusion rendered them in general needy. The towns, which at first were part of their domain, amenable to their jurisdiction and subject to their arbitrary exactions, took advantage of their wants to purchase, among other privileges, that of having an adminstration of justice and a municipal government of their own. This was a concession which nothing but the most pressing necessities could ever have extorted from those haughty superiors, and which they never afterwards thought of without resentment. No opportunity was missed of resuming the concession, and re-establishing their former supremacy over the town: retaining, however, the purchase-money of freedom. The pages of M. de Sismondi exhibit such numerous examples of this kind of perfidy, that it is impossible to suppose that it could have been considered at all disgraceful. Every privilege, in fact, which a town could succeed in wringing from the penury of its lord, was the commencement of a long struggle between the town and the *seigneur*; the seigneur struggling to get back his power, the townsmen to prevent him. If the lord succeeded, any new attempt to throw off his authority was called rebellion, and treated accordingly; for this also see Sismondi, *passim*.

King John of France, who was taken prisoner at Poitiers, is related to have said, that if truth and good faith had disappeared from the earth, they ought to be found on the lips and in the hearts of monarchs. This John, who was surnamed the Good, and who, if the anecdote be authentic, could talk in such magnifient terms about justice and good faith, had solicited and obtained from the pope, a few years before, for himself and his successors, a curious sort of privilege: it was that of violating all vows made and to be made, all oaths taken and to be taken, which they could not conveniently keep, *quae servare commode non possetis*, commuting them for other pious works.*

This John, who was a contemporary of the Black Prince and of Bertrand du Guesclin, and who lived, therefore, in the halcyon days of chivalrous virtue, had, it seems, but an indifferent opinion of the knights of his day. He accused the French knights of having become insensible to honour and fame: *Honoris et famae, proh dolor! neglectâ pulchritudine.*[†] The same prince, on hearing the song of Roland, observed, *Il y a long-temps qu'on ne voit plus de Roland en France.* An old captain, who was present, did not deny the fact, but threw all the blame of it upon the monarch himself: *On en verrait encore s'ils avaient un Charlemagne à leur tête.*[‡] Deceived, like ourselves, by romances, even the chevaliers of that day looked back, it seems, with admiration, to the imaginary heroism of their forefathers. Yet this was the most shining period of the age of chivalry. It was also the last. A few years after, chivalry silently expired. The use of fire-arms became general. Cuirasses, as it turned out, were not bullet-proof. The chevaliers tried hard to render them so, by making them thicker and thicker, heavier and heavier, till at last (says Lanoue) *Il n'y avait homme de trente ans qui n'en fût estropié.*[§] Finding that all this would not save them from gunpowder, the cowards forsook the field, and abandoned the defence of their country and their liege-lord to hired soldiers—to plebeians.

Such was the age of chivalry. But to all our denunciations of the vices of that age, one glorious exception must be made. Either the whole testimony of history is false, or Saint Louis never violated his word, nor swerved from what he thought the dictates of his conscience. Historians have not done justice to Saint Louis. He has been pictured as a virtuous man, but a slave to priestcraft. Nothing can be more

*Dulaure, Vol. III, p. 184 [citing Clement VI, Letter to King John and Queen Joanna of France, in Luc d'Achery, *Spicilegium* (1655-77), new ed., 3 vols. (Paris: Montalant, 1723), Vol. III, p. 724].

[†]Roederer, *Louis XII et François Ier*, Vol. II, p. 251.

[‡]*Ibid.*, p. 290.

[§]*Ibid.*, p. 268.

unfounded. His mind was strongly tinctured with the superstitions of the age; he conceived the deity not as an indulgent father, but as an irritable and jealous master; all this is true: but it is not true that he was priest-ridden; for he several times resisted not only his clergy, but the pope himself.* He followed the dictates of his own mind. His ideas of religious duty were his own; and every action of his life was governed by them. He thought it his duty to persecute, and he did persecute; he thought it his duty to be an ascetic, and he was an ascetic; but he also thought it his duty to keep his word, and he kept it inviolably; he thought it a sin even to retain what his predecessors had unjustly acquired, and he made restitution with the most scrupulous exactness. He was a perfect specimen of a mind governed by conviction; a mind which has imperfect and wrong ideas of morality, but which adheres to them with a constancy and firmness of principle, in its highest degree perhaps the rarest of all human qualities.

When we contemplate one who in so barbarous an age, and under all the temptations of power, although misled by a bad religion, did not make that religion a substitute for morality, but devoted himself to the fulfilment of his real duties, with the same earnestness as his imaginary ones, we admire even the power over himself which his austerities display; we lament the erroneousness of his opinions, but we venerate the man. Very differently are we affected by the religion which characterized the times. The knights and nobles of the day were as pious, many of them, as Saint Louis himself; but how different a piety! All his intolerance was theirs, without a spark of his virtue. When we read of their crusades, their pilgrimages, and their persecutions, we are apt, by a natural mistake, to speak of their *fanaticism*. But fanaticism is far too respectable a name. Fanaticism supposes principle: the notion of fulfilling a duty. *Their* fires were kindled not to fulfil a duty, but to escape from its fulfilment. They thought to strike a bargain with Omnipotence; to compound for one crime by practising another. It was not from principle, but from mere selfishness, that they burned heretics, slaughtered Saracens, and plundered Jews. They imagined that he who sacrificed hecatombs of unbelievers to the God of mercy, was freed from every moral obligation towards his fellow-men. Never did their religion for a moment stand in the way of their passions. In sacking a town, neither priests, nor nuns, nor crosses, nor relics, were sacred to them.† In their private wars, the church lands, being an easier prey, were even less respected than those of one another; nor were their devastations restrained by that excommunication which encroachments upon that species of property invariably entailed. But they had been taught that by giving way to their darling passions, their avarice and cruelty, against the miscreants who denied the faith, they atoned for the indulgence of the same passions against the true

*See Sismondi, Vol. VIII, pp. 101-3, and Vol. VII, pp. 201-4, 308-9.
†See, among innumerable other examples, the description of the sacking of Strasburg, in Sismondi, Vol. IV, p. 128.

believers. The publication of a crusade, especially against the emperor or the Albigenses, was commonly accompanied by an offer to the champions of the cross, of—what? Remission of all sins, past and future, in the other world, together with permission to rob their creditors in this. They were exempted, during the crusade, from the payment of interest on their debts. The cunning priests, who added this earthly recompense to the heavenly one, knew well the sort of persons with whom they had to deal. That some of the crusading knights were mainly influenced by motives of religion, is as true, as that some were influenced by the desire of military glory; but the great bulk were influenced by nothing but M. de Sismondi's *"deux mobiles de la noblesse,"* cupidity and ennui.

There is one feature in the chivalrous character which has yet to be noticed; we mean, its gallantry. And this we shall think it necessary to examine the more fully, because we are persuaded that nine-tenths of the admiration of chivalry are grounded upon it. We own it is hard to speak ill of men who could make vows to their lady-love that they would wear a scarf over one eye till they should have signalized her charms by some exploit, or who could leave the ranks and challenge one another to single combat, to settle which man of them adored the most beautiful mistress. We trust, however, that without treason to the fair sex, of which we profess ourselves devoted admirers, it may be permitted to doubt whether these fopperies contributed much to the substantial happiness of women, or indicated any real solicitude for their welfare. To us it seems very clear, that such demonstrations of eagerness, not to make a woman happy, but to make the whole world acknowledge the pre-eminence of her charms, had their source in mere vanity, and the love of distinction; and that the knight who fought a duel concerning the beauty of his mistress, because she was *his* mistress, would have done the same thing for his falcon, if it had been the fashion.

If it could be proved that women, in the middle ages, were well treated, it would be so decisive a proof of an advanced stage of civilization, as it would require much evidence to rebut. That they were so treated, however, is not to be believed without proof. That a knight prided himself upon the beauty of his mistress, and deemed his honour concerned in maintaining it at the sword's point, is no proof. In the Asiatic kingdoms, in which, above all countries in the world, women are not only practically ill-treated, but theoretically despised, the whole honour of a family is considered to be bound up in its women. If their seclusion is intruded upon; if the foot of a stranger profanes the zenana, the disgrace is indelible. This is one species of foppery: the gallantry of the middle ages was another: and, like the ceremonious politeness which distingished alike the chevaliers and the orientals, they characterize that period in the progress of society, which may be termed the age of false refinement, and which is situated half way between savage and civilized life.

Good treatment of women, we have already observed, is one of the surest marks of high civilization. But it seems to be very little considered, in what good treatment of women consists. It does not consist in treating them as idols to be worshipped, or as trinkets to be worn for display; any more than in shutting them up like jewels in a case, removed from the light of the sun and the sight of men. In both cases, this treatment is a proof that they are valued; else why are so much pains taken about them? But in both cases they are valued exactly like beautiful trinkets; the value set upon them is quite compatible with perfect indifference to their happiness or misery.

Professor Millar, perhaps the greatest of philosophical inquirers into the civilization of past ages, has observed, with truth, that during the savage state, when the attention of men is wholly engrossed by the pursuit of the necessaries of life, the pleasures of sex are little regarded, and little valued; but as soon as the satisfaction of their more pressing wants gives leisure to cultivate the other enjoyments within their reach, these pleasures are among the first which engage their attention. If the savage state is, of all others, that in which the sexual passion is weakest, the half-savage state, or the state immediately bordering on barbarism, is that in which it is strongest.[*] This remark explains the treatment of women in feudal Europe, as well as in Asia, different as their condition in these two states of society may appear. In Asia, where food could always be obtained with comparatively trifling labour, and where very little clothing and lodging were necessary either to existence or to comfort, the savage or hunting state seems never to have existed; the pleasures of sex were probably cultivated from the beginning, and, man abusing his natural superiority, the women were made slaves. In Europe, on the contrary, as among the North American Indians, women were not valued as sources of pleasure, and were not valuable for the labour of hunting, in that state of society the only kind of hard labour. No motives, therefore, existed for reducing them to bondage; and when these barbarians over-spread the Roman empire, and, possessing themselves of the land, began to lead an idle life instead of a laborious one, this new state of society found the women free. From this circumstance arose the different situation of women in Asia and in feudal Europe. In the latter, where they were free, to obtain the woman who was the object of desire became often a matter of extreme difficulty, and generally could not be effected without her own consent: in the former, where they were slaves, to obtain any number of women independently of their consent, became, to a rich man, a matter of no difficulty at all; and his solicitude was transferred to the means of keeping them.

We thus see that the seclusion of women in Asia, and the idolatry of them in Europe, were both marks of the same low state of civilization. The latter, no doubt, gave to some women for a time more power. But we must not overrate the value of this power to their happiness. The question is not, how much power a knight would give his mistress leave to fancy she exercised over him, in order that she might

[*John Millar, *An Historical View of the English Government* (London: Strahan, Cadell, and Murray, 1787), pp. 36-7, 79-81.]

consent to his obtaining power over her; but in what manner *he* employed his power over her when obtained. Of the domestic lives of the knights, we have hardly any direct information; and in the absence of any, we may proceed upon the general presumption, that men who were brutal towards one another, would not be less brutal towards their wives. Allowing that a woman who had been an object of desire, and who was still a source of vanity from her personal charms, might command tolerable treatment on account of those charms, while they lasted, and on account of her children at a later period; we profess ourselves not to be of the number of those who sympathize exclusively with beautiful women. Although the heroines of romances were somehow always beautiful, it may yet be inferred, from the inherent probabilility of the thing, that there were ugly women in those days as well as in our own; though we are left to conjecture what sort of treatment may peradventure have been undergone by such ill-fated females, if any such there were. A knight who had to maintain at the point of the sword, that his lady was the most beautiful lady in the whole world, would, in common prudence, attach himself to some fair one, whose pretensions to that character might be maintained without subjecting him to any extraordinary degree of ridicule. We know, in point of fact, that a small number of beautiful women engrossed all the admiration and all the vows of all the knights, and that the large and unattractive majority were altogether neglected. It is the treatment of them, however, and not that of their more attractive sisters, which is the test of civilization.

There is positive evidence, how little regard was paid by a warrior of the age of chivalry, to the feelings even of the object of his passion, when he had the power of gratifying that passion independently of her consent. If a baron happened to be smitten by the charms of the daughter of one of his vassals, he demanded of her father, as a matter of course, that she should be yielded up to his embraces.* The frequency of rapes and abductions, even in the case of women of elevated rank, is another important proof how little connection the foppish gallantry of that age had with the real happiness of the sex affected to be adored. We have mentioned in a former page the chivalrous treatment of the Gascon ladies by Coeur de Lion. Matilda, daughter of Malcolm III, King of Scotland, while residing in England previously to her marriage with our Henry I, is well known to have taken the habit of a nun, "not," says Hume, "with a view of entering into a religious life, but merely in consequence of a custom, familiar to the English ladies, who protected their chastity from the brutal violence of the Normans, by taking shelter under that

---

*See, for example, the account of the birth and parentage of William the Conqueror, in Sismondi, Vol. IV, pp. 239-40. The story is curious, and characteristic of the times. It resembles an anecdote related of the Anglo-Saxon King Edgar. [See William of Malmesbury, *Gesta regum anglorum*, ed. Thomas Duffus Hardy, 2 vols. (London: English Historical Society, 1840), Vol. I, p. 236 (Bk. II, Sect. 148); Mill probably (see the next footnote) took the reference from David Hume, *The History of England* (1754-62), 8 vols. (London: Cadell, *et al.*, 1823), Vol. I, pp. 122-3.]

habit, which, amidst the horrible licentiousness of the times, was yet generally revered."*

We reject the giants of romance; why should we continue to believe in the reality of the knights-errant, their antagonists? Yet if both are the representatives of really existing personages, let us remember that the knights who liberated imprisoned damsels were few, while the giants who held these damsels in durance were many; and that the prototypes of the giants were knights and noblemen, though they were not knights-errant.

Though it is almost unnecessary to add, that whatever portion of power or good treatment the women enjoyed, was confined entirely to the women of rank, and that all other women were, like their husbands, slaves; we will, however, conclude our observations on this subject, by a very sensible passage from M. Roederer's work, already alluded to, in which this as well as some other very pertinent observations are forcibly put. The age of chivalry, he says,

Fut pour les femmes, ainsi que les hommes, une période d'abjection et de malheur. Ne regardant pas le bonheur des seigneurs qui opprimaient la nation comme partie du bonheur de la nation, ou comme une compensation de son malheur, je ne compte pas non plus la gloire des *châtelaines* dans le bilan des femmes Françaises du même temps. Celles-ci vivaient dans l'oppression comme leurs pères, leurs maris, leurs enfans. On pourrait même contester à ces dames de château, qui brillaient de tant d'éclat sur les amphithéâtres d'un tournoi, qui étaient pour la confrérie des chevaliers l'objet d'un culte religieux et d'une adoration solennelle; on pourrait leur contester un bonheur correspondant à de si belles apparences, et demander si cette idolâtrie qui leur était vouée, n'était pas une des pompes de la grandeur de ces temps-là, l'ostentation intéressée d'une courtoisie profitable, ou l'exagération d'une servilité réelle sous des apparences passionnées; et si, dans l'intérieur de la société domestique, les grandes dames n'étaient pas exposées comme les autres à toute la rudesse d'une domination sans frein? (*Louis XII et François Ier*, Vol. I, pp. 297-8.)

We have dwelt so long upon the period of the feudal aristocracy, that we have not time to give a detailed character of the feudal monarchy; and perhaps it will be better, before attempting the task, to wait for the additional materials which we may expect to find in the next portion of M. de Sismondi's history. We shall content ourselves with mentioning a few facts, merely to show that the aristocracy did not change its character during the two or three centuries which followed its subjugation by the crown.

Enguerrand de Coucy, having seized two young noblemen, who, with their preceptor, had trespassed on his forests in pursuit of rabbits, hanged them all three. In the reign of any other prince than Saint Louis, he might possibly have come off with impunity. Saint Louis at first intended to put him to death, but at the intercession of all the great barons, he contented himself with imposing a heavy

---

*Hume, Vol. I, pp. 318-19. See, in Dr. [Robert] Henry's *History of Great Britain* (1771-93), [2nd ed., 12 vols. (London: Strahan and Cadell, 1788-95),] Vol. VI, pp. 347-8, the remarkable words of a great council of the clergy on this occasion.

fine, and three years exile in Palestine, with the forfeiture of the seignorial rights of *haute justice*, and *garenne*: of keeping rabbits, and of judging men.*

Guy de Montfort assassinated Henry, son of Richard, Duke of Cornwall, before the altar, at Viterbo.†

Saint Louis besieged the castle of La Roche de Gluy upon the Rhone, to punish its lord for practising robbery on the highway: having made himself master of the castle, he restored it to its owner, first stipulating for the discontinuance of his depredations.‡

The next person of whom we shall make mention is Amalric, Viscount of Narbonne, who, having the *droit de justice*, violated the laws, and, what was of more consequence, offended the monarch, by putting to death two of his own vassals, notwithstanding their appeal to the royal court. Amalric's sovereign was far from being a Saint Louis; he imprisoned the rebellious vassal for a time, then took him from prison and put him at the head of an army.§

Jourdain de l'Isle, *sire* (seigneur) of Casaubon, after receiving the royal pardon eighteen times for different offences, was hanged the nineteenth for rape, rapine, and murder. This happened under Charles IV, in 1323.

Hannot and Pierre de Léans were hanged in 1332, for assassinating la demoiselle Péronne d'Estreville in the church.

Mathieu de Houssaie was condemned to a gibbet in 1333; Jourdan Ferron, a *damoiseau* or page, in the same year. In the following year eleven nobles were executed (*suppliciés*) for the assassination of Emeri Béranger.

Adam de Hordain, another knight, was hanged in 1348, and so on.¶ It was not till the climax of the power of Louis XIV, that the nobles were reduced into perfect obedience to the laws.

As the king's government, however, increased in strength, assassination became too dangerous to be openly practised, and a safer mode of taking vengeance upon an enemy now came into vogue. Accusations of poisoning became frequent, and gained general credit. The imperfection of the courts of justice, and the peculiar nature of this crime, generally prevented the fact from being judicially proved; but the generality of the suspicion is a sufficient proof of the spirit of the times. Another mode of getting rid of an enemy was suggested by the superstitions of the day. The practice of enchantments, for the destruction of particular persons, became very frequent. The efficacy of these operations was imaginary, but the intention was real. Waxen images, says M. Dulaure, play a very conspicuous part in French history. A waxen image was constructed, as nearly as possible resembling the person intended to be destroyed; a priest was

---

*Sismondi, Vol. VIII, p. 98.
†*Ibid.*, p. 219.
‡Dulaure, Vol. III, p. 54.
§Sismondi, Vol. IX, p. 412.
¶Dulaure, Vol. III, p. 260.

employed to baptise the image by the name of the intended victim, and it was then tortured, mutilated, or pierced through and through, with the proper forms of incantation. The effect of the operation thus performed upon the image, was supposed to be felt by its human namesake in his own person.

The gradual disuse of trial by battle, which was abolished by Saint Louis in his own domains, and discouraged every where, both by him and his successors; the substitution of technical procedure in the king's court, and the gradual supercession of the seignorial jurisdictions by the royal ones, gave rise and encouragement to another sort of crime, judicial perjury. This, which is perhaps the most pernicious of offences, because it destroys the efficacy of the remedy against all others, and the frequency of which is, for that and other reasons, one of the most decisive tests of the moral depravity of a nation, became, if we may credit historians, horribly frequent. Corruption in the judges also became a common offence.*

When the nobles no longer enjoyed any power of their own, except over their serfs and domestics, they had no chance for importance but by resorting to the court, and rivalling with one another in magnificence and servility.† The means of magnificence had to be squeezed out of their vassals, whose situation consequently became more miserable than ever.‡ The same cause brought about a considerable change in the manners of the nobility. No longer permitted to seek excitement in private wars, they sought it in the licentiousness of a court. Intrigue took the place of rape, as poisoning had done of assassination. The manners of the later period of the age of chivalry, and of the age which immediately succeeded it, as they are pictured in Brantôme[*] and other works of his day, were dissolute to a degree never since equalled. Nor did their debauchery resemble the refined gallantry of the court of Louis XV; it was coarse and gross to a degree of which even the language of Rabelais is hardly an exaggeration. To sum up all in few words: when the vices of a highwayman ended, the vices of a courtier began.

We had intended to quote some striking anecdotes of the times; such as the expedition of the *pastoureaux*, the destruction of the Templars, the pretended conspiracy of the lepers to poison the fountains and subvert Christianity: and to have sketched the persecutions of the Jews and of the Albigenses, and the still more extraordinary persecution of the mendicant Franciscans, for offending the

---

*See *ibid.*, Vol. III, pp. 242-3, for a remarkable instance. See also Sismondi, Vol. IX, p. 195. "Le siècle," (says he) "dont nous faisons l'histoire, est celui de la plus grande corruption de l'ordre judiciaire; il n'y a pas un des procès intentés sous Philippe le Bel, qui ne porte des marques intrinsèques de faux témoignage."

†See a striking instance of their servility even as early as the reign of Philip Augustus. (Sismondi, Vol. VI, p. 154.)

‡*Ibid.*, Vol. VIII, p. 428. He compares their condition to that of the subjects of Turkey.

[*Pierre de Bourdeille, abbé de Brantôme, *Mémoires*, 6 vols. (Leyden: Sambix, 1665-66).]

pope, by denying that their meat was their own at the moment when they were putting it into their mouths. But these, and innumerable other interesting facts, which M. Dulaure and M. de Sismondi have recorded, we must content ourselves with exhorting the reader to gather from those authors themselves. Both works are as delightful in style, as they are important in matter. The manner of M. Dulaure is characterized by extreme neatness and exquisite simplicity, and carries the reader along with it, by its deep earnestness, and high tone of moral feeling. To one who is daily sickened by the repulsive tone of heartless levity, and recklessness about good and evil, which is one of the besetting sins of our own literature in the present day, this quality of M. Dulaure's work renders it peculiarly attractive.* M. de Sismondi's style is more diffuse, but almost always sprightly, and frequently eloquent. His eloquence, however, flows naturally from him; neither he nor M. Dulaure is infected by that rage for fine writing, which is the bane of all real eloquence; they never declaim, never hunt after common-place metaphors, but speak the plain and unaffected language of men who wish that the reader should think of their ideas more than of themselves.

There is little appearance in M. Dulaure's work of a generalizing, that is, of a philosophical, mind: he states the facts as he finds them, praises and censures where he sees reason, but does not look out for causes and effects, or parallel instances, nor applies the general principles of human nature to the state of society he is describing, to show from what circumstances it became what it was. It is true he does not profess to be a historian, but only to sketch a *tableau moral*. M. de Sismondi aims much more at generalization; and the reflections with which he frequently commences his chapters, exhibit far more of the genuine philosophy of history, than is to be found in any other work on the middle ages (those of Professor Millar excepted)[*] with which we are acquainted.

The badness of those ages will now be thoroughly understood by a large class of readers in France. In this country, we cannot hope that it will be comprehended as yet. There is no popular book on the middle ages in our language; nor any book in which the truth is plainly and fully told concerning chivalry and its times. Millar's *Historical View of the English Government*, though admirable as far as it goes, is rather a history of institutions, than of morals and manners; and when it does touch upon the latter, is not detailed enough to give any thing like a vivid conception of the times. The design of the work, moreover, is confined to our own country. Yet he is almost the only writer we have, who has made the middle ages a subject of philosophical investigation. There is, indeed, Mr. Hallam; but we should be much

*It is a quality, however, by no means peculiar to M. Dulaure; several other French writers of the present day are distinguished by it in an equal, perhaps in a still greater degree. M. Roederer, in the work from which we have had occasion to quote, is a striking example.

[*In addition to Millar's *Historical View*, Mill may have in mind his *Observations Concerning the Distinction of Ranks in Society* (London: Richardson and Murray, 1771).]

surprised if the nation which has produced a Millar, could admire or read the *History and Government of Europe during the Middle Ages*. This work appears to us equally faulty in the design and in the execution. In the first place, the design is fundamentally bad. The work is neither a history of Europe, nor a history of European civilization. Considered as a history of Europe, it is the most meagre of abstracts. Conceive an attempt to write "the history of France from its conquest by Clovis to the invasion of Naples by Charles VIII," in one chapter of ninety-nine quarto pages! It is evident that nothing worth relating of the history of France could be included in that compass: it is not a historical sketch, but a chronological table, or the table of contents to a historical work; and it is long since we remember to have read ninety-nine duller pages. If, on the other hand, the work was intended to be a history, not of Europe, but of its civilization, why encumber it with several hundred pages of tiresome and useless narrative? Even in the dissertations, which compose the remainder of the work, we cannot help seeing much more of pretension than of real merit. Mr. Hallam is not wanting in liberality; his leanings are in general towards the side of the many; his incidental remarks are frequently pointed in expression, and occasionally soar somewhat above the level of common-place. But he has neither discernment enough to see through any reigning error, nor philosophy enough to trace the causes and consequences of the things which he describes; but deals out little criticisms and little reflections, and little scraps of antiquarian lore, which neither throw any light upon the condition of mankind in the middle ages, nor contribute either to support or illustrate any important principle: in fine, he has succeeded in rendering a sketch of one of the most remarkable states of society ever known, at once uninstructive and tiresome. The best part of his work is that which relates to our own country. In this part he must be allowed the merit of having resorted to the original authorities, and established several interesting points of constitutional history. But considering him as a historian of the middle ages, we are compelled to pronounce his work an utter failure. Its want of merit is rendered still more striking, when compared with the merit of other writers. To appreciate Mr. Hallam, it is not even necessary to have read Millar; it is sufficient to have read Sismondi.

SCOTT'S LIFE OF NAPOLEON

1828

EDITOR'S NOTE

Westminster Review, IX (Apr., 1828), 251-313. Headed: "Art. I.—*The Life of Napoleon Buonaparte, Emperor of the French. With a Preliminary View of the French Revolution*. By the Author of 'Waverley,' &c. [Walter Scott.] In Nine Volumes. Edinburgh [: Cadell; London: Longman, Rees, Orme, Brown, and Green], 1827." Running titles: "*French Revolution—* / Scott's *Life of Napoleon*." Unsigned. Pamphlet offprint, with title page reading: "*A* / *Critical Examination* / *of the* / *Preliminary View* / *of the* / *French Revolution,* / *prefixed to* / *Sir Walter Scott's Life of Bonaparte.* / *With Observations on the Work Itself.* / From the Westminster Review, No. XVIII." Printed London: Hansard, 1828. Headed: "Critical Examination, &c. &c. &c." Paginated 1-63; no running titles. Unsigned. Identified in Mill's bibliography as "A review of Sir Walter Scott's Life of Napoleon Bonaparte, in the 18th number of the Westminster Review" (MacMinn, 10). The copies of the offprint in Mill's library, Somerville College, have no corrections or emendations.

For comment on the essay, see xliii–xlvi and xcv–xcvi above.

Scott's Life of Napoleon

SIR WALTER SCOTT cannot write any thing which, as a literary composition, will not be read with pleasure; and if it were possible to consider the work before us merely as a well-told story, we are not sure that it is inferior even to the most perfect of his former productions. Few books, indeed, have ever afforded so much for minute criticism to fasten upon; and that description of critics with whom the substitution of one connecting particle where another would have been more appropriate is a crime for which all the higher excellencies of composition cannot atone, have made so great a noise concerning its small blemishes, that comparatively little has been heard of its uncommon merits.[*] But the extreme of carelessness in the minutiae of style, a fault always more endurable than the opposite one of a too studious and visible attention to them, is pardonable, and almost allowable, in a writer who has merits of so much higher a rank than mere correctness. In Sir Walter Scott, no faults are worth noting except those which impair the effect of beauties. The author who could conceive and execute the admirable narrative of Napoleon's first Italian expedition, in the third volume,[†] could afford to be inelegant, to be even ungrammatical, in every page. His occasional repetitions, and the intermixture of many inappropriate, among many felicitous, similies, will be forgiven by those who know how few writers are capable of unfolding a complicated and intricate train of events so that it shall appear simple and intelligible, and of maintaining, throughout a voluminous work, so lively, rapid, and spirited a style, that the interest never flags, the attention never is wearied; in which qualities this work pre-eminently excels.

But these excellencies do not suffice to constitute a history. From that which is offered to the public as a record of real events, something more is required than that it should be sprightly and entertaining. The *Life of Napoleon* would be admirable as a romance: to have made it any thing higher, would have required far other endowments than had been displayed even in the most finished performances of the Author of *Waverley*.[‡]

If it be any part of the duty of an historian to turn the facts of history to any *use*;

[*See, e.g., Anon., review of Scott, *Life of Napoleon Buonaparte*, *Monthly Review*, n.s. VI (Sept., 1827), 92-5.]

[†Pp. 85ff.]

[‡Walter Scott, *Waverley; or, 'Tis Sixty Years Since*, 3 vols. (Edinburgh: Constable; London: Longman, *et al.*, 1814).]

and if a fact can be of use only by being made subservient either to the confirmation or illustration of a *principle*; the historian who is fit for his office must be well disciplined in the art of connecting facts into principles, and applying principles to the explanation of facts: he must be a man familiar with generalization and general views; a man whose knowledge is systematic, whose mind can embrace classes as well as individuals, who can discriminate between the results of narrow and partial observation, and those of enlarged experience; in short, a *philosopher*. Further, if it be ever the duty of an historian to elicit real facts, from vague, scanty, or conflicting, testimony, it is necessary that he should be profoundly skilled in the difficult art of weighing evidence: he must be capable of combining together a chain of circumstances, each of which proves nothing by itself, but every thing when skilfully combined; he must be practised in striking the balance between opposing testimonies, or between testimony on the one side and probability on the other; he must be, to sum up this also in one word, a consummate *judge*. Sir Walter Scott's title to these high qualifications still remained to be established. It is in the present volumes that we must look for the proof of it, if proof is to be found.

Of the degree in which he possessed those more common qualities, which suffice for giving a correct statement of ordinary events—the qualities of industry, candour, and impartiality—the public had some means of judging from his previous performances. And first, with respect to industry; while his earlier writings had proved how much he is capable of, his later ones had afforded no less conclusive evidence, that any degree of pains employed upon his productions, more than was necessary to their sale, was, in his estimation, superfluous. Applying himself in this frame of mind to the composition of an historical work, it was not very likely that he should have recourse to any other than the vulgar authorities, nor, consequently, that he should take any other than the vulgar view of the events which he relates. And the celerity with which he projected and completed a work which, to execute it tolerably, would have required many years reading, was a satisfactory proof, if there were no other, that, on this point at least, the presumption had not been fallacious.

With respect to his candour: if the studied forbearance towards political adversaries which distinguishes his writings, had flowed from a genuine, passionate, and overpowering love of truth, there would have been room for highly favourable anticipations indeed. But the prevailing tone of his works in every other respect, forbids us to ascribe to any such cause his specious semblance of impartiality. There is sufficient evidence in Sir Walter Scott's writings, that he is a person of a mild and tolerant disposition, constitutionally exempt from acrimony of all kinds, with a decided bias towards aristocratic persons and aristocratic opinions, but not attaching so much importance to the difference between one opinion and another, as to feel, even towards persons of the most opposite principles, much positive dislike. This original liberality, and almost indifference, in matters of opinion, enabled him to fall easily into a practice which he appears to have prescribed to himself from an early period—that of adopting such a mode of writing as should be best calculated to win the good word and good opinion of every body. For this purpose he has laboured, with a skill and success surpassing all previous example; and since to please all is to please persons of all political opinions, the precise degree of compromise conducive to this end, was very accurately calculated, and studiously employed. All the substantial advantage in point of opinion must, indeed, be given to the aristocracy, because they, being accustomed to entire subservience, can ill bear any thing which falls far short of it; while, on the other hand, even democrats and democratic principles must be treated with a certain appearance of respect, because, the object being to please every body, it will not do to make intemperate and offensive attacks either upon men or opinions in which any considerable section of the reading public take an interest. But the democrats, being accustomed to pure abuse, are tolerably well satisfied when they meet with a writer in whom the abuse is a little qualified; and their favour is sufficiently attained by keeping somewhat to the liberal side of high Tory opinions, and allowing a fair share of the common feelings and intellect of men, to persons who, by Tory writers in general, are considered as destitute of them, being addicted to the notion that the House of Commons should represent the people, and similar heterodoxies. By this mark, accordingly, Sir Walter Scott has guided himself; and has taken pains to be, on all occasions, a little more just towards the friends of the people than is usual with their enemies. His *Old Mortality* is a miserable travestie of the Scottish Covenanters, compared with Laing's *History*, or Mr. Galt's *Ringan Gilhaize*;[*] and so is his *View of the French Revolution*, compared with Mignet or Bailleul.[†] But a bigotted Tory can scarcely read either work without some mitigation of his prejudices. Sir Walter Scott is not the man from whom it could be expected that he should be an unbiassed judge between the aristocracy and the people; but considering him as the advocate of the aristocracy against the people, he is not altogether an illiberal or disingenuous one.

The work may be appropriately divided into two parts; the History of the French Revolution, and that of the Reign of Napoleon Bonaparte. This is somewhat more than a merely chronological division. The two subjects are as unlike as those of the *Iliad* and of the *Odyssey*; though, like these, they form a portion of the same series of events, and concern in part the same persons. The former period seems to contain nothing but what is extraordinary; the latter, hardly any thing but what is common-place. The reign of Napoleon affords little or nothing to the historian,

[*Scott, *Old Mortality*, in *Tales of My Landlord*, 4 vols. (Edinburgh: Blackwood; London: Murray, 1816), Vols. II-IV; Malcolm Laing, *The History of Scotland*, 2 vols. (London: Cadell and Davies; Edinburgh: Manners and Miller, 1800); and John Galt, *Ringan Gilhaize; or, The Covenanters*, 3 vols. (Edinburgh: Oliver and Boyd, 1823).]

[†François Auguste Marie Mignet, *Histoire de la révolution française*, 2 pts. (Paris: Didot, 1824); Jacques Charles Bailleul, *Examen critique de l'ouvrage posthume de Mme la baronne de Staël*, 2 vols. (Paris: Bailleul, 1818).]

except ordinary characters and ordinary events. The career which he ran, had been trodden times out of number by successful adventurers; there have never been wanting just such men as he, when such prizes have been attainable by them: the most obvious causes suffice to account for every event in his history: to comprehend it thoroughly, there needed no extraordinary depth of philosophy; the lowest impulses of the lowest description of human beings are the moving principle of the whole, and few men know and understand less of these than they ought. Where one man is the sole disposer of events, history is easily written: it is only to study the character of that one man: if this be vulgar, all is vulgar; if it be peculiar, he who has seized its peculiarities has the key to all which may appear remarkable in the events of the period. The lines of Napoleon's character are few, and strongly marked: to trace them correctly, far inferior powers to those of Sir Walter Scott would have been sufficient. And if his story be inaccurate, as we have no doubt that it is, in many of the details, those details are of such sovereign unimportance for any purpose of utility or instruction, that we, for our share, should have little objection, provided they be amusing, to dispense altogether with their being true.

To write the history of the French Revolution was a task requiring far other powers, involving far other difficulties. To say that, on no occasion, did surprising events succeed one another with such breathless rapidity, that never were effects so extraordinary produced by such a complication of causes, nor in so short a space of time, would be to form a very inadequate idea of the peculiarities of that momentous period, considered as a theme for history. It was marked by a characteristic still more embarrassing to such men as those by whom history is commonly written. The moving forces in this vast convulsion, the springs by which so much complex machinery was now set in motion, now stopt, now swept away, were of a class for the laws of whose action the dictionary of historical common-places does not yet afford one established formula—a class which the routine-historian has not yet been taught by familiarity to fancy that he understands. Heretofore, when a change of government had been effected by force in an extensive and populous country, the revolution had been made always by, and commonly for, a few: the French Revolution was emphatically the work of the people. Commenced by the people, carried on by the people, defended by the people with a heroism and self-devotion unexampled in any other period of modern history, at length terminated by the people when they awoke from the frenzy into which the dogged resistance of the privileged classes against the introduction of any form whatever of representative government, had driven them; the French Revolution will never be more than superficially understood, by the man who is but superficially acquainted with the nature and movements of popular enthusiasm. That mighty power, of which, but for the French Revolution, mankind perhaps would never have known the surpassing strength—that force which converts a whole people into heroes, which binds an entire nation together as one man, was able, not merely to overpower all other forces, but to draw them into its own line, and convert them into auxiliaries to itself. The vulgar politician finds to his confusion (if indeed it is in the power of any vulgar politician to make the discovery), that all the causes which he is in the habit of calling in upon other occasions to account for every thing in history which perplexes him, are powerless here; that party interests, and class interests, and personal interests, and individual depravity, and individual virtue, and even the highest endowments of individual intellect and genius, appear to influence the train of events only when they fall in with it, and add force to the current, which, as often as they are thrown into opposition with it, they are found inadequate to withstand. The rules by which such a period is to be judged of, must not be common rules: generalizations drawn from the events of ordinary times, fail here of affording even that specious appearance of explanation, which is the utmost that such empirical philosophy can ever accomplish. The man who is yet to come, the philosophical historian of the French Revolution, will leave these solemn plausibilities far behind, and will draw his philosophy from the primaeval fountain of human nature itself. Whatever else he may derive from what are called the records of past times, a lesson which he will *not* learn from them is, what is meant by a *people*; or from what causes, and in obedience to what laws, the *thing*, which that name expresses, is accustomed to act, on those rare occasions on which the opportunity of acting is allowed to it: and it is quite possible to be a tolerable poet, and much more than a tolerable novelist, without being able to rise to the comprehension of that one idea, or to know more of those laws and those principles than a child in the cradle.

We have stated but a part of the inherent difficulties of the subject. That the very facts of the French Revolution, from the multitude of conflicting testimonies, are incapable of being elicited but by one who possesses all the endowments of the most sagacious and practised judge, is still but a part, perhaps not the greatest part, of those difficulties. Suppose the facts ascertained—to interpret and account for them would demand, along with the most minute knowledge of the circumstances of France and of the French people for centuries back, a mind profoundly conversant with human nature under all the modifications superinduced by acting upon the extensive theatre of a whole nation; and the deepest insight into the springs of human society, into the causes by the perpetual and often unseen agency of which, a nation is made to be what it is, in respect to civilization, morals, modes of thinking, physical condition, and social relations. Nor is this all. To judge of the French Revolution, is to judge statesmen, and the acts of statesmen, in novel and critical situations. It is to form an estimate of great changes in the government and institutions of a country; of new laws established, of old ones overthrown, and of the manner in which the helm of government was conducted through a course beset with perils and difficulties more trying, perhaps, than were ever before experienced by a great and powerful nation. It is not too much to expect, that the writer, whose judgment is to guide that of his readers in such high concerns, shall himself know as much as philosophy and experience can teach, of the science of government and legislation: that he shall be well skilled both in the theory and in the practice of politics; shall know at the same time what is best in itself, and how to make allowance for the obstacles and counteracting forces, which often render what is not best in itself, necessary either as a precaution or as a compromise.

To this rare combination of qualities, Sir Walter Scott has no claim. In political and social philosophy his principles are all summed up in the orthodox one, that whatever is English is best; best, not for England only, but for every country in Christendom, or probably the world. By starting from this point it must be acknowledged that much trouble is saved, and not a little of what is apt to be thought the duty of a historian, very comfortably abridged. To a mind properly imbued with this axiom, to sit in judgment upon the statesmen or institutions of other countries is an easy task. To inquire patiently into the suitableness of a system of government to the nature of man in general, or to the circumstances of any nation in particular; to examine how far it did or did not provide for the exigencies of that nation; to take account of the degree in which its framers might expect that causes peculiar to that nation would promote, modify, or impede, its action; and, if it be pronounced bad, to consider what means they had by whom it was adopted, of establishing any thing better; all this, to a person of such enlarged views, is unnecessary labour. Sir Walter Scott settles all these questions in a moment, by a summary appeal to that ever-ready standard of comparison, English practice. Whatever he finds here established, or whatever bears the same name with any thing which is here established, is excellent: and if the statesmen of France, unfortunately for themselves, not judging of things by the same comprehensive rule, formed a different opinion, the folly thus evinced accounts for all the subsequent misfortunes of their country. Should an institution happen not to be English, it is condemned: and here something more of thought is required in making out a case against it, though not much; for nobody is ignorant how ridiculously easy it is to find inconveniences and dangers on one side of every political question, sufficient to decide it, if we only take care to keep our eyes well shut to the inconveniences and dangers on the other. Although, too, no other reasons for condemnation should be discoverable, there is one argument against all systems that are not English, which can never be wanting; they are *untried theories*: no free institutions except ours, according to our author, having ever had the sanction of experience; for it never occurs to him that the *principle* of an institution may have been tried successfully any number of times, although the exact *model* may be to be found nowhere.

While Sir Walter Scott's acquirements are of this mean description, in the science of politics, and the philosophy of the social union, he is almost equally deficient in that acquaintance with facts, without which the most philosophical statesman is no better qualified to judge what is fittest for a nation, than the most profound physician to prescribe what is fittest for a patient whom he has not seen. There is no proof, in this work of Sir Walter Scott, that he has taken the trouble to make himself well acquainted with the state of France at the time when the Revolution broke out; with the physical condition and mental peculiarities of the people, the habitual feelings and modes of thinking of the different classes of society, and the working of the great machine of government in the detail. Not only is there no proof that he has made himself well acquainted with these circumstances, but there is conclusive proof that he has not made himself acquainted with them at all; that he has scarcely so much as adverted to them as being among the things which it is necessary for a historian of the Revolution to know; and has therefore committed all the mistakes that are incident to a historian who is thoroughly unacquainted with the spirit of the times which he is describing. His complete ignorance of the position in which individuals and parties were placed, leads him regularly to ascribe their actions to other than the true causes. He blames men who did the best they could, for not doing better; treats men who had only a choice of inconveniences, as if they were the masters of events, and could regulate them as they pleased; reproaches men who were beset by dangers on both sides, because they did not, to avoid the dangers on one side, precipitate themselves into those on the other; goes to search for discreditable motives at an immense distance, when the most creditable ones were obviously afforded by the state of affairs; and judges of the conduct of men in the crisis of a revolution, by the same standard which he would have applied to persons securely in possession of the governing power in peaceable times.

Such and no higher being the qualifications which Sir Walter Scott brings to the task of making an estimate, moral and philosophical, of the French Revolution; the reader may judge what is the value of his opinions on the subject, and how well the conception which his book conveys of the Revolution resembles its real character. The work has, in addition to these, all the defects of a book hastily written: it is utterly without research. The author has been satisfied with resorting to the most hackneyed and obvious authorities: he has read perhaps one or two of the professed histories of the period; some of the more popular of the memoirs he has consulted, but we find it difficult to believe that he has read them: he has left but few references at the bottom of the page to betray to the public in general the superficiality of his reading, but, that some even of these few are made from memory, is demonstrated by his referring, for proof of an assertion, to the very passage which proves the assertion to be false.* The documents which breathe the

*On presenting Louis XVI with the keys of Paris, Bailly said, comparing the entry of Louis with that of Henry IV, "*Il avait reconquis son peuple, aujourd' hui c' est le peuple qui a reconquis son roi.*" Our author places this in Bailly's speech of the 6th October 1789, and moralizes on the insulting irony of such an address on such an occasion. For this he refers to the *Mémoires de Bailly, Choix de ses Lettres et Discours*; and the speech is there, sure enough, but the expressions above alluded to are not in it. Those expressions were used on a different occasion, immediately after the capture of the Bastille, when they were neither insulting nor inappropriate, but well suited, on the contrary, to conciliate the vanquished, and soften the humiliation of defeat. [See Jean Sylvain Bailly, *Mémoires de Bailly*, 3 vols. (Paris: Baudouin, 1821-22), Vol. II, p. 58; Scott, Vol. I, p. 199.]

living spirit of the time, the only monuments of really cotemporary history, (which is the most different thing imaginable from history written by cotemporaries, after they have undergone a thousand changes of opinion and feeling, and when the genuine impression of the present events has faded from their recollection) are the decrees of the national assemblies, the speeches of their members, the papers laid before them, and the immensely numerous books, pamphlets, and periodicals, of the day. These genuine authorities, as neither fame nor profit was to be got by consulting them, our author had not thought it necessary to consult. We doubt whether he has given, to more than two or three of them, even the most cursory perusal.

It may be thought surprising, that a book should be offered to the public, by so distinguished a writer, as the history of so recent and so universally interesting a period, in which so little pains have been taken to ensure that which, all other qualities being put out of the question, is at any rate a *sine quâ non* of history, namely, truth. But our author enjoyed two advantages, either of which would have made it safe for him to deviate from the truth even more widely than he has: he wrote for readers thoroughly ignorant of the subject, and for readers the whole of whose prepossessions were more or less strongly on his side. For being ignorant of the subject, some of his readers have the excuse, that to this very hour there does not exist one tolerable account of this remarkable portion of history, in the English tongue. But the number of Englishmen to whom works written in the French language are accessible, is now so great, that the marvellous extent of their ignorance respecting the French Revolution, must be regarded as a proof, that this reading nation chuses to read dissertations on Aeolic Digammas, or Iron Masks,[*] or any other matter of frivolous and idle curiosity, sooner than any thing which will furnish them with *evidence* upon matters on which their minds have been made up without it. For ignorance has not here had the effect which conscious ignorance in a well-regulated mind ought to have, that of preventing them from forming any opinion. Acted upon as their ignorance has been, from day to day and from year to year, by the torrents of unmeasured and undiscriminating invective which have been poured forth against the Revolution, by men who knew nearly as little about it as the public themselves, but who knew perfectly what mode of treating the subject

[*For the Aeolic digamma, see Alexander Pope, *The Dunciad* (1728), in *Works*, new ed., ed. Joseph Warton, *et al.*, 10 vols. (London: Priestley, and Hearn, 1822-25), Vol. V, p. 253 (Bk. IV, ll. 215-18); Richard Payne Knight, *An Analytical Essay on the Greek Alphabet* (London: Elmsley, 1791); and (closer to the date of Mill's comment) such works as Thomas Burgess, *A Letter to the Lord Bishop of Durham* (Carmarthon: Evans, 1815); Burgess, *Vindication of the Late Bishop of Asaph's Edition of the Lacedaemonian Decree* (Durham: printed Walker, 1816); Herbert Marsh, *Horae Pelasgicae* (London: Murray, 1815); and the edition published in 1820 of Knight's *Carmina Homerica, Ilias et Odyssia* (London: Valpy). For the Iron Mask, see, e.g., Joseph Delort, *Histoire de l'homme au masque de fer* (Paris: Delaforest, 1825); and George Agar Ellis, *The True History of the State-Prisoner Commonly Called "The Iron Mask"* (London: Murray, 1826).]

would be acceptable to those on whom the reputation and the sale of their lucubrations depended; a feeling has been generated, which predisposes men to credit upon any evidence or no evidence, any assertion with respect to the French Revolution or revolutionists, provided only it be sufficiently unfavourable: and he who would seek to refute even the most extravagant of these assertions, finds it difficult to obtain a hearing, and scarcely possible to persuade.

It cannot, however, be deemed of small importance to the best interests of mankind, that the opinions which they form on such a subject as the French Revolution, should be correct opinions. So long as all who hold the lot of mankind to be capable of any material improvement, or conceive that any good can be accomplished by taking the powers of government out of the hands of those who are interested in abusing them, are deemed to be sufficiently answered by pointing to the calamitous issue of that great experiment; so long it will be a duty not to suffer that its history should be rendered the fitter to form the groundwork of these decisive conclusions, by being falsified and garbled. It is not in such an article as the present, that we can pretend to sketch the true history or trace the character of the French Revolution. But we can at least shew that Sir Walter Scott is not to be trusted; which we the more willingly do, as, in refuting his misrepresentations, we are exposing *à fortiori* those of the crowd of hirelings, who with inferior abilities, but with the same purposes, daily essay to fling each his minute and separate portion of dirt upon some of the noblest deeds and brightest characters in history. Such men are not important enough for any other chastisement than they may indirectly suffer, from the blow aimed at a more formidable enemy: and we shall mention them no further in this notice.

The work opens with a sketch of the state of France before the Revolution, and a view of the remote causes of that catastrophe. The whole of this is comprehended in two chapters, which consist of seventy-nine pages: a shorter space, therefore, than is frequently taken up by the dull introductions of our author's novels, is all that he allows for what ought to be the quintessence of the internal history of France during more than a century. To have executed this portion of his task well, would of itself have required more reading and research than he has given to the entire work. It is almost unnecessary to say, therefore, that he has performed it ill; and has not only failed to communicate full and accurate knowledge, but has betrayed the lamentable extent of his own ignorance. This is the more to be regretted, as he has stated the little which he knows, with considerable force, and very tolerable fairness. The influence of such an aristocracy as that of France upon the national literature, is powerfully delineated; the character of the noblesse and clergy, during the fifty years preceding the Revolution, is traced with an indulgent, but with no feeble hand: and the exclusion of the *tiers-état*, that is, of almost the whole of the talent, and much the greater part of the opulence, of France, from all employment or influence in the affairs of the state, is deservedly reprobated. Our author, however, shares the vulgar error, which considers this monopoly of office as the principal, and almost the sole, cause of the Revolution: at least we may gather as much from the fulness with which he developes and expatiates upon it, while all the other causes are lumped together in a short and passing notice. This is by no means a trifling error; on the contrary, few can be named, which have contributed more to prevent the Revolution from being understood, or to lend an apparent sanction to the conclusions which aristocratic logic has drawn from it for aristocratic purposes. We dwell not upon the gross injustice towards the eminent men who originally took the lead in the Revolution, and whom this theory represents as ambitious spirits, struggling for no higher object than the removal of their personal disabilities, instead of patriots striving to free their country from a yoke which weighed it down to the earth. We shall not insist upon this, characteristic though it be—for thus it is that our author always contrives to disguise or throw into the shade whatever is exalted in purpose or generous in sentiment, in those whose principles he disapproves, while he gives credit to the royalists for the most chivalrous disinterestedness and honour, not only without evidence, but in direct contradiction to the testimony of the better members of their own body. But (to say no more upon this point) mark the implied imputation upon the French people, which this theory of the Revolution conveys. If the excesses of the Revolution had no greater provocation than our author tells us of, what must not we think of them? Slur over the fact that every man's liberty was at the mercy of every minister or clerk of a minister, or lacquey of a minister, or mistress of a lacquey of a minister—that every man's property was at the mercy of *intendants* and *subdélégués*, and the whole fry of agents and sub-agents in one of the most odious systems of fiscal tyranny ever known; sink all this, and a hundred things besides, and fix upon non-admissibility to office as the great practical grievance of the *tiers-état*, and what is the inference? For our author certainly will not succeed in persuading anybody, that it was the ineligibility of the merchants and *avocats* of Paris and Bordeaux to public offices, and of their sons to promotion in the army, which caused the peasants of several of the provinces of France to rise in arms and burn the houses of their *seigneurs*:[*] the provocations, therefore, which are assigned, being obviously insufficient, and the real ones having been carelessly overlooked or purposely passed over, the only explanation which seems to offer itself is the perversity of the people: of whose supposed readiness at all times, unless kept down by terror, to rise against their superiors and make war upon person and property, another example is thus manufactured.

Sir Walter Scott may be well assured that the grievances which could excite in the peasantry feelings of such bitter hatred towards the privileged classes, were grievances which affected themselves, and not other people. The Roman tribune understood the nature of the people much better, when he reproached them with being abundantly eager and zealous when their efforts were required to prevent the

[*Scott, Vol. I, pp. 43-4.]

usurpation of their lands, or protect their persons from the rapacity and cruelty of their creditors, but deaf to the call of their leaders when there was nothing to contend for except the privilege of rewarding those leaders with offices and honours.[*] The feelings of the people are not wont to be excited by an abstract principle. It is not a distant or a contingent evil which works upon *them*. The tyranny which excites *them* to resistance must be felt, not conceived; they must discover it by their sensations, not by their reason. The abuses which they resent, are those which bear upon their direct interests; which "come home to their business and bosoms."[†] Never yet did a people hate their superiors, but for some real or imagined wrong; never were they stimulated to such outrages as those which signalized the breaking out of the French Revolution, except by the intolerable pressure of active, grinding oppression. And in no country, pretending to civilization, had the peasantry been so borne down by oppression as in France. "Les jeunes gens et les étrangers," says Madame de Staël,

qui n'ont pas connu la France avant la révolution, et qui voient aujourd'hui le peuple enrichi par la division des propriétés et la suppression des dîmes et du régime féodal, ne peuvent avoir l'idée de la situation de ce pays, lorsque la nation portait le poids de tous les priviléges. Les partisans de l'esclavage dans les colonies ont souvent dit qu'un paysan de France était plus malheureux qu'un nègre. . . . La misère accroît l'ignorance, l'ignorance accroît la misère; et quand on se demande, pourquoi le peuple François a été si cruel dans la révolution, on ne peut en trouver la cause que dans l'absence de bonheur, qui conduit à l'absence de moralité.*

Our author himself observes, that in La Vendée alone had the privileged classes done their duty towards the cultivators of the soil, and that in La Vendée alone was any stand made by those cultivators in their defence.[‡] This observation is an approach to the true theory of the causes of the Revolution, and is conceived in a spirit of which it were to be wished that there were more frequent examples in these volumes. Indications of such a spirit are indeed not rare in his occasional remarks; in which respect he resembles many other writers, who have falsified history in the gross, as thoroughly as himself. He is far too acute not to see a *part* of the truth; far too slightly acquainted with the monuments of the times, to have the faintest or most distant perception of it as a *whole*. We may perhaps take some future opportunity of making known to our readers, what substantial reasons the peasants had for detesting both the government and their seigneurs. In the meantime, we

[*See *Livy* (Latin and English), 14 vols., trans. B.O. Foster, *et al.* (London: Heinemann; New York: Putnam's Sons, 1919-59), Vol. III, p. 334 (vi, 39, 9-10); he records the sentiment as being that of two tribunes, Gaius Licinius and Lucius Sextius.]

[†Francis Bacon, *The Essays or Counsels, Civile and Morall* (1625), in *The Works of Francis Bacon*, ed. James Spedding, *et al.*, 14 vols. (London: Longman, *et al.*, 1857-74), Vol. VI, p. 373.]

*[Anne Louise Germaine Necker, baronne de Staël-Holstein,] *Considérations sur* [*les principaux événemens de*] *la Révolution Françoise*, Pt. I, Chap. vi [Vol. I, p. 79].

[‡Scott, Vol. I, pp. 30-1.]

shall do no more than refer them to a book which is in every man's hands. If, in place of his first two chapters, Sir Walter Scott had merely reprinted the concluding dissertation in the first volume of Arthur Young's excellent work on France,[*] he would have done more to convey a just idea of the causes of the French Revolution than will be done by twenty such productions as his "Preliminary View." We believe, that most men who have read that dissertation, will exclaim with its author, who had himself seen and heard all he describes—that no man of common sense and feeling can lament the fall of such a government, or look with any but a mitigated severity upon the terrible retribution which an oppressed people exacted from their tyrants the moment they were free.

Among the causes which most powerfully promoted, or at least directed, the tendency to change, our author justly assigns a high rank to the increased influence of literature. And here we may be sure that the opportunity is eagerly seized, of recommending himself to our moral public, by an invective against the French philosophers, as they are termed; principally upon the two points of licentiousness and irreligion. In the course of this diatribe, our author manifests no very accurate knowledge of the writings or lives of these objects of his somewhat undiscriminating dislike. As for fairness, it would be too much to expect it from such a writer on such a subject; and accordingly we are not surprised to find the immense benefits which the philosophers conferred upon their country and mankind, altogether overlooked, while whatever either is, or can be made to appear, objectionable in them or in their works, is grossly exaggerated. Thus, they are gravely stated to have been engaged in a sort of "anti-crusade," not only against Christianity, but against "religious principles of every kind;"[†] a description which, if applicable at all, can apply only to one or two of them, and those neither the ablest nor the most influential, perhaps to one only, and him not a Frenchman, the Baron d'Holbach; while on the other hand, how large a portion of the writings of Rousseau, and especially of Voltaire, is taken up in maintaining and enforcing the being and attributes of God, is known to every one who has read them. The ancient fiction of a "league," a "conspiracy,"[‡] is revived; when it is notorious, that the supposed heads of this conspiracy, Voltaire and Rousseau, were at open war with each other, that Condorcet, in like manner, did not disguise his contempt for Mably,[§] that Turgot wrote against Helvétius,[¶] while equal dissensions and differences of opinion existed among the less distingished thinkers and writers of

---

[*Travels during the Years 1787, 1788, and 1789 (1792), 2nd ed., 2 vols. (London and Bury St. Edmunds: Richardson, 1794), Vol. I, pp. 597-629.]

[†Scott, Vol. I, p. 61.]

[‡Ibid., pp. 61, 59.]

[§Marie Jean Antoine Nicolas Caritat, marquis de Condorcet, Vie de Voltaire (1787), in Voltaire, Oeuvres complètes, 66 vols. (Paris: Renouard, 1817-25), Vol. LXIV, p. 169.]

[¶Anne Robert Jacques Turgot, "A Monsieur de C[ondorcet] sur le livre De l'esprit" (1760?), in Oeuvres, 9 vols. (Paris: Delance, et al., 1808-11), Vol. IX, pp. 288-98.]

the class; and that nothing like an organized system of concert or co-operation ever existed among any portion of their number. Our author can know little of French literary history, or he would not talk of the close union and alliance which existed among the philosophers, "and more especially the Encyclopedists"[*]—we presume, between Diderot and d'Alembert—for of these two individuals only was this formidable corps, whose name has so long resounded from every corner of Europe, composed; they having written (with scarcely any exception but that of a small number of articles by Voltaire) the whole of the moral, theological, and metaphysical part of the *Encyclopédie*;[†] and it is worthy of remark, that of this pair of conspirators against religion, d'Alembert never published a single line against it. With respect to licentiousness, our author forgets that what was the vice of their age and of the society in which they moved, cannot with justice be laid at their door; it was not they who made French society what it was; on the contrary, it was through the influence principally of their writings, that it ever became any thing else. It is high time that Sir Walter Scott should be told, if he has not yet found it out, that licentiousness was a quality with which what are termed the philosophers were not more, but, on the contrary, less chargeable, than most writers of their day; that none of the authors peculiarly remarkable for it were to be found in their ranks, while several of those most distinguished by it (among whom it is sufficient to name Piron) were no less characterized by a bitter hostility against the persons and principles of the philosophers: that the virtues most opposite to licentiousness, found in Rousseau, if not always a consistent, at least an enthusiastic, advocate; and that many of the most distinguished among the philosophical writers, as Condillac, Condorcet, and above all, Turgot, were pure on this point, some of them to a degree of scrupulosity. However, it must be admitted, that several of the writers whom our author mentions, have produced works in some degree deserving the character which he assigns to them. Most certainly we do not quarrel with him for expressing his disapprobation of these writings: he should remember, however, that there ought to be bounds even to the most merited censure, and that there is still an immense distance between any licentiousness of which they can be accused, and that libertinism, which he justly characterizes as inconsistent with manly and virtuous patriotism. Because the ideas prevalent in a country allow a certain latitude of speaking, or even of acting, with respect to the branch of morality here concerned, it does not follow that all who in any degree avail themselves of this licence must therefore make the pursuit of sensual gratifications the business of their lives. Such an occupation, like the

[*Scott, Vol. I, p. 53.]

[†*Encyclopédie, ou Dictionnaire raisonné des sciences, des arts et des métiers*, ed. Denis Diderot and Jean Le Rond d'Alembert, 17 vols. (Paris: Briasson, *et al.*, 1751-65). Voltaire in fact contributed more than twenty articles (in the E, F, and G sections), e.g., "Esprit," Vol. V, pp. 973-5; "Franchise," Vol. VII, pp. 283-4; "Gens de lettres," *ibid.*, pp. 599-600; and "Histoire," Vol. VIII, pp. 220-5.]

inordinate pursuit of every other merely individual enjoyment, is incapable of co-existing with any nobler aspirations, and if it does not begin, is sure to terminate, in utter selfishness; but it is false that voluptuousness, in this sense of the word, was, or is, more prevalent in France than in any other nation; and most especially is it false that any portion of the philosophers, either in their own lives, or in the doctrines and principles they inculcated, are chargeable with it.*

*With how much greater discrimination does the editor of Madame Campan's memoirs animadvert upon the same persons, and the same faults, which are the subject of our author's less judicious and less considerate disapprobation. After censuring some of the philosophers, and in particular Diderot by name, for participating practically in the licentiousness of the times, he adds, "Non que je veuille assurément jeter du blâme sur les philosophes: si leur conduite était légère, la plupart de leurs doctrines étaient pures; elles ont passé de leurs écrits dans nos moeurs. Si les liens de la famille se sont resserrés; si nous sommes meilleurs époux, meilleurs pères, et plus hommes de bien; si le vice est méprisé; si la jeunesse, avide d'études sérieuses, repousse avec dégoût les ouvrages licencieux qu'accueillait le libertinage de ses pères, nous le devons à un nouvel ordre de choses. En morale, comme en politique, en législation, en finances, les philosophes ont préparé d'utiles réformes." ([Jean François Barrière, "Notice sur la vie de madame Campan," in Jeanne Louise Henriette Genest Campan, *Mémoires sur la vie privée de Marie Antoinette*, 2 vols. (London: Colburn and Bossange, 1823), Vol. I,] p. xx.)

The tone of this author, who, even while blaming the men, eagerly bears testimony to the admirable moral effect of their writings, suggests, when contrasted with the opposite language of Sir Walter Scott, an acute sense of the difference between a writer who really knows his subject, and one who has only dipped into it to find reasons for opinions which he already held. That author must indeed know little of French literature and history, who can accuse the philosophers of having demoralized the French people! the philosophers, than whom, it may safely be affirmed, no set of writers ever did one tenth part so much to elevate the standard of morals among their countrymen.

For a powerful defence of the philosophers against these vulgar imputations, see pp. 236 to 279 of the first volume of a most valuable work recently published at Paris, and intituled, *Histoire de France depuis la fin du règne de Louis XVI jusqu'à l'année 1825, par l'abbé de Montgaillard*. [9 vols. (Paris: Moutardier, 1827).] The testimony of this author in favour of the philosophers possesses the greater weight, as their most prejudiced enemies may be defied to point out any one well-founded accusation against them which he has disguised or extenuated. Some of them, indeed, are treated by him with unmerited severity. In further illustration of the same subject, see Bailleul's *Examen Critique de l'ouvrage posthume de Madame de Staël*, Vol. I, pp. 153-6.

While we are on a similar subject, we cannot pass unnoticed our author's childish remarks on certain passages in the memoirs of Madame Roland; remarks which are in themselves sufficient to prove his complete unfitness for the office of an historian, if incapacity to estimate the modes of thinking and feeling of another state of society, and inability to distinguish between differences of manners and differences of morals, be a disqualification for writing history. We will appeal to every candid person who has really read the autobiography of this admirable woman, whether any thing can be conceived more opposite to the whole tone and character of her mind, than "habitual impurity of language and ideas," [Scott, Vol. I, p. 56,] and whether the very passages in her memoirs, which our author considers to be proofs of it, are not, on the contrary, conclusive evidence of a more than common purity of disposition? [Scott refers to the portrait of Louvet, in Marie Jeanne

Our author does not, like others of the alarmists, represent the philosophers, with the "licence and infidelity"[*] which they promoted, as the sole causes of, and movers in, the Revolution. He owns that a great political change would have been needed, and would have taken place,

had the French court and her higher orders retained the simple and virtuous manners of Sparta, united with the strong and pure faith of primitive Christians. The difference lay in this, that a simple, virtuous, and religious people, would have rested content with such changes and alterations in the constitution of their government as might remove the evils of which they had just and pressing reason to complain. They would have endeavoured to redress obvious and practical errors in the body politic, without being led into extremes, either by the love of realizing visionary theories, the vanity of enforcing their own particular philosophical or political doctrines, or the selfish arguments of demagogues, who, in the prospect of bettering their own situation by wealth, or obtaining scope for their ambition, aspired, in the words of the dramatic poet, to throw the elements of society into confusion; and thus

—disturb the peace of all the world
To rule it when 'twas wildest.*

Now, inasmuch as the most moral and religious people that ever existed, the English of the reign of Charles I, carried their "changes and alterations" so far as to abolish monarchy and cut off the king's head, we see that our author's ideas of avoiding "extremes" and redressing "obvious and practical errors," are of a tolerably radical extent.

It well becomes *him* to rail at theorists, who can overlook such a fact because it interferes with his theory. But it is ever thus with those who style themselves *par excellence* the men of practice and experience.

Our author takes a juster view of the causes which produced the errors of the Revolution, in the following acute and original remarks on the state of infancy in which the public mind had been kept by the restraints on the press.

An essay on the French monarchy, showing by what means the existing institutions might have been brought more into union with the wishes and wants of the people, must have procured for its author a place in the Bastille; and yet subsequent events have shown, that a system which might have introduced prudently and gradually into the decayed frame of the French government the spirit of liberty, which was originally inherent in every feudal monarchy, would have been the most valuable present which political wisdom could have

---

Phlipon Roland de la Platière, *Mémoires de madame Roland*, 2 vols. (Paris: Baudouin, 1820), Vol. II, pp. 190-2.] Of the private morals of Madame Roland, our author has not the effrontery even to hint a suspicion. With respect to the particulars which offend him in her writings, and which would offend him justly in any woman of a country where the conventional standard of propriety is a more rigorous one, we may advise him to take a lesson of good sense and liberality from Morris Birkbeck, whose observations on an occasion somewhat similar, have been quoted in the sixth number of this journal [Peregrine Bingham (prob.), "On Emigration," *Westminster Review*, III (Apr., 1825)], p. 473.

[*Scott, Vol. I, p. 62.]

*Ibid. [The concluding quotation is from Thomas Otway, *Venice Preserv'd; or, A Plot Discover'd* (London: Hindmarsh, 1682), p. 17 (Act II).]

rendered to the country. The bonds which pressed so heavily on the subject might thus have been gradually slackened, and at length totally removed, without the perilous expedient of casting them all loose at once. But the philosophers, who had certainly talent sufficient for the purpose, were not permitted to apply to the state of the French government the original principles on which it was founded, or to trace the manner in which usurpations and abuses had taken place, and propose a mode, by which, without varying its form, those encroachments might be restrained, and those abuses corrected. An author was indeed at liberty to speculate at any length upon general doctrines of government; he might imagine to himself an Utopia or Atalantis, and argue upon abstract ideas of the rights in which government originates; but on no account was he permitted to render any of his lucubrations practically useful, by adapting them to the municipal regulations of France. The political sage was placed with regard to his country, in the condition of a physician prescribing for the favourite sultana of some jealous despot, whom he is required to cure without seeing his patient, and without obtaining any accurate knowledge of her malady, its symptoms, and its progress. In this manner the theory of government was kept studiously separated from the practice. The political philosopher might, if he pleased, speculate upon the former, but he was prohibited, under severe personal penalties, to illustrate the subject by any allusions to the latter. Thus, the eloquent and profound work of Montesquieu[*] professed, indeed, to explain the general rights of the people, and the principles on which government itself rested, but his pages shew no mode by which these could be resorted to for the reformation of the constitution of his country. He laid before the patient a medical treatise on disease in general, instead of a special prescription, applying to his peculiar habits and distemper.

In consequence of these unhappy restrictions upon open and manly political discussion, the French government in its actual state was never represented as capable of either improvement or regeneration; and while general and abstract doctrines of original freedom were everywhere the subject of eulogy, it was never considered for a moment in what manner these new and more liberal principles could be applied to the improvement of the existing system. The natural conclusion must have been, that the monarchical government in France was either perfection in itself, and consequently stood in need of no reformation, or that it was so utterly inconsistent with the liberties of the people as to be susceptible of none. No one was hardy enough to claim for it the former character, and least of all those who presided in its councils, and seemed to acknowledge the imperfection of the system by prohibiting all discussion on the subject. It seemed, therefore, to follow, as no unfair inference, that to obtain the advantages, which the new elementary doctrines held forth, and which were so desirable and so much desired, a total abolition of the existing government to its very foundation, was an indispensable preliminary; and there is little doubt that this opinion prevailed so generally at the time of the Revolution, as to prevent any firm or resolute stand being made in defence even of such of the actual institutions of France as might have been amalgamated with the proposed reform.*

This is well thought, and well expressed; and the illustration which concludes the first paragraph, has a merit which our author's figurative illustrations do not always possess; it really illustrates.

The reign of Louis XVI previous to the Revolution, is sketched in our author's usual lively manner; the character of that well-meaning, but weak and vacillating prince, is justly estimated, and the series of blunders by which the court not only

[*Charles Louis de Secondat, baron de la Brède et de Montesquieu, *De l'esprit des loix*, 2 vols. (Geneva: Barillot, [1748]).]

*Scott, Vol. I, pp. 69-71.

precipitated the crisis, but threw away the chances of giving it a direction favourable to themselves, are tolerably exposed.[*] But what our author sees and condemns in these proceedings is their weakness only, not their wickedness. The frantic struggles of enraged despotism to put down by force that rising spirit of liberty, which it already hated and feared with as much intensity as now after twenty years of exile—these are to be mildly censured, not for the atrocity of the end, but for the inefficacy of the means, and because the conspirators, being as imbecile as they were base, had the awkwardness to endanger their precious persons and privileges by the consequences of failure. A government, beggared by its profligate expenditure, exhausts every illegal resource, and tries all that can be done by the most desperate and tyrannical expedients to extort money from the people without giving them in return those constitutional reforms to which they were entitled; and this conduct appears to our author highly blameable, because it was *bad policy*, and rendered the crown "odious and contemptible."[†] A government does its utmost to tread out the few sparks which centuries had not extinguished of freedom and constitutional control—it does this not so much as a year before the assembly is convened, which is destined to give to France a representative constitution; and this our author condemns—why? Because it excites "national discontent!"[‡] So liberal and indulgent is Sir Walter Scott towards the royalists: but his liberality and indulgence stop there. When every violence which tyranny prompted and fear would permit, has been tried in vain, this government at length has recourse to the people, and condescends to *ask* for what it has at last found that it no longer has power to seize: the National Assembly meets, and by means of a temporary popular enthusiasm, wrings from the government ten times as many of its unjust privileges, as the parliaments had ever dreamed of questioning; it adds, by its reforms, the parliaments themselves, and the whole of the privileged classes, to the number of its enemies;—and now, if the Assembly is not so silly as to suppose that the power of misrule has been resigned willingly, if it harbours even a suspicion that the fate of the parliaments is in reserve for it, or takes the commonest precaution to secure itself against the hostility of the court, and of the numerous and powerful classes whom it has offended,—not only its conduct is disapproved of, but its motives are misconstrued, and its whole system of action tortured and perverted. "Et voilà justement comme on écrit l'histoire."*

[*Ibid., pp. 84ff.]
[†Ibid., p. 103.]
[‡Ibid., p. 105.]
*[François Marie Arouet Voltaire, *Charlot, ou La comtesse de Gevry* (1767), in *Oeuvres complètes*, Vol. VI, p. 108 (Act I, Scene vii).] There occurs in the same chapter a signal instance of the almost incredible inaccuracy which runs through the details of this work. Our author asserts that the second assembly of Notables, which was called together by Necker, recommended that the *tiers-état* might have a body of representatives equal in number to those of the noblesse and clergy united. [Scott, Vol. I, pp. 113-14.] Now, he would have

There is something amusing in the *naïveté* with which our author lays it down, that the elections ought to have been tampered with, to obtain returns favourable to the court; evidently without the slightest suspicion that a course so perfectly according to the English model, can deserve or incur the disapprobation of any body. He says, with equal gravity, that the public mind ought to have been

---

found in the commonest compilations [see, e.g., Montgaillard's *Histoire*, Vol. I, p. 440], that this measure, commonly called the double representation of the *tiers*, was recommended by one only of the seven *bureaux* into which the Notables were divided, namely that over which Monsieur, afterwards Louis XVIII presided; while the remaining six *bureaux* gave their suffrages against it, and the point was conceded, not in consequence of, but in spite of, the advice of that assembly.

We observe at the distance of a few pages from the above a still more striking inaccuracy, which is the more remarkable, as it makes directly against the partialities of the writer. [Scott, Vol. I, pp. 134ff.] It occurs in his account of the memorable 23rd of June, 1789; the day of the royal sitting, wherein the king annulled the early proceedings of the National Assembly, and in which Mirabeau made that emphatic reply to the satellite of despotism [Henri Evrard, marquis de Dreux-Brézé], which will be remembered so long as the memory of past events shall be preserved among men. [Honoré Gabriel Riqueti, comte de Mirabeau, speech of 23 June, 1789, in *Oeuvres de Mirabeau*, 9 vols. (Paris: Dupont and Brissot-Thivars, 1825-27), Vol. VII, pp. 127-8.] In general, our author is apt to extenuate or pass over in silence the arbitrary proceedings of Louis XVI or his court; but on this occasion, writing as usual from memory, he falls into a directly opposite error; for whereas Louis in reality only cancelled the resolution constituting the Etats Généraux a national assembly, and required them to separate for that day (in order that there might be no deliberation), and to assemble on the morrow in three chambers, as three separate orders, our author accuses him of having gone to the length of dissolving the assembly, an excess of despotism which he certainly did not meditate until the attempt to frustrate their proceedings by milder means had been tried and had failed. [See "Délibération relative à la manière dont l'assemblée doit se constituer" (17 June, 1789), *Gazette Nationale, ou Le Moniteur Universel*, 16-20 June, 1789, pp. 41-2; and "Déclaration du roi, concernant la présente tenue des états-généraux" and "Déclaration des intentions du roi" (both 23 June, 1789), *ibid.*, 20-24 June, 1789, pp. 46-7 and 47-8.] This blunder must relieve our author from the suspicion of bad faith, in the numerous instances in which his inaccuracies of detail might appear to have a political purpose.

Since we are on the subject of his minor errors, we will mention several more, which deserve notice, either from the carelessness which they indicate, or from the support which they lend to some of the reigning prejudices on the Revolution. Speaking of the revision of the constitution in the year 1791, after the king was brought back from his flight, our author says, "The Assembly clogged, however, the future inviolability of the king with new penalties. If the king, after having accepted the constitution, should retract, they decreed he should be considered as abdicated. If he should order his army, or any part of it, to act against the nation, this should in like manner be deemed an act of abdication; and an abdicated monarch, it was farther decreed, should become an ordinary citizen, answerable to the laws for every act he had done *before* or since the act of abdication." (Scott, Vol. I, p. 253.) All that is invidious in the enactments here cited, consists solely in the word *before*, which word is an interpolation of our author. The terms of the decree are, *pour tous les délits postérieurs à son abdication*. [See Constitution française (14 Sept., 1791), *Lois, et actes du gouvernement*, Vol. IV, pp. 188-232; the quotation is from Art. VIII, p. 193.] What is most remarkable in this blunder is the ignorance which it imports of the most universally and

preoccupied with arguments of a sound and virtuous tendency. This is extremely fine; but by whom preoccupied? By the court and aristocracy of France? "Sound and virtuous"[*] arguments from such a quarter would indeed have been something new. By Necker? Does our author suppose that he could have retained his office for an hour, if he had attempted to promulgate among the people, either in his ministerial or in his private capacity, ideas of rational freedom? Necker shewed himself, on more than one occasion during the Revolution, unequal to the

---

dramatically interesting portion of the history of the Revolution. On the king's trial, a great part of the discussion turned upon this very provision of the very decree here referred to: the speakers who contended against his condemnation taking their stand upon that article of the constitution, which *exempted* the king, even after his abdication, from any responsibility for acts committed while he was king. Sir Walter Scott's reading of the decree would entirely exonerate the regicides; since Louis had certainly committed actions which, in any other person than the king, would have amounted to treason.

Our author is wrong in ascribing to the Constituent Assembly (Scott, Vol. I, p. 216) the ridiculous affectation of changing the titles of Monsieur and Madame, for Citoyen and Citoyenne. This piece of fanatical absurdity originated with the commune of Paris, after the 10th of August 1792 (see the *Histoire de la Révolution* [*de France*] *par Deux Amis de la Liberté* [by F.M. Kerverseau, G. Clavelin, *et al.*, new ed., 19 vols. (Paris: Garnery, and Bidault, 1792-1803), subsequently referred to as *Deux amis*], Vol. IX, p. 24), and passed from them to the National Convention.

A more serious misrepresentation is that of the motives of the Constituent Assembly for adopting the *Constitution Civile du Clergé*. [Loi sur la constitution civile du clergé (24 Aug., 1790), *Lois, et actes du gouvernement*, Vol. I, pp. 372-3.] This measure, our author, in the spirit which pervades the whole work, imputes to "the fanaticism of the modern philosophers, who expected by this indirect course to have degraded the Christian religion" (Scott, Vol. I, p. 226). It would become Sir Walter Scott to be more careful of the evidence on which he advances these sweeping charges of irreligion. As is observed by Mignet, "La constitution civile ne fut pas l'ouvrage de philosophes, mais de Chrétiens austères." [Mignet, *Histoire*, p. 145.] The Constituent Assembly, which is accused of pretending to reform the church only in order to destroy it, this very assembly, when Mirabeau laid before them for their adoption a proposed address to the people on the *constitution civile*, which is deservedly ranked as one of the most eloquent productions of that extraordinary man, would not even hear it out, because, though written in a highly religious tone, it contained some expressions reflecting too strongly upon the state and character of the church previously to the reform. [Mirabeau, speech of 14 Jan., 1791, in *Oeuvres*, Vol. IX, pp. 14-46.] Let Sir Walter Scott take the trouble to refer, for his own refutation, to the mere names of those who composed the Ecclesiastical Committee of the Assembly. The constitutional church-establishment was devised by the Jansenists or rigid party, who are in the Catholic church nearly what the Calvinists are among Protestants; and especially by Camus, a leading Jansenist, well known in the revolutionary annals. The influence of this party, as well as of the Protestants, among whom Barnave, Rabaut-Saint-Etienne, and Boissy d'Anglas, were conspicuous, was very powerful in the Revolution, though little known in this country, where the stupidity of party prejudice attributes all to infidels. It was not so in France, where, as we learn from Ferrières, the non-juring priests imputed all the strong measures of the Revolution to the Protestants, in the hope of arming the Catholic peasantry against it by their religious animosities. [Charles Elie Ferrières, *Mémoires* (1821), 2nd ed., 3 vols. (Paris: Baudouin, 1821-22), Vol. II, p. 262.]

[*Scott, Vol. I, p. 114.]

great difficulties of his very trying situation; but a writer who can so little appreciate those difficulties is scarcely entitled to sit in judgment on him, and affect to point out by what means he might have been more successful.

There was a reason, more than Sir Walter Scott dreams of, for doing nothing to gain over the *tiers-état* to the court. Nobody doubted that they would *be* on the side of the court, without prompting. It was not from the commons, but from the privileged orders, that all resistance to the will of the monarch had previously come; it was they who, when called upon for the sacrifice of their pecuniary immunities, had demanded the convocation of the Etats Généraux to sustain them in their refusal. The commons, it was well known, were, and with good reason, inveterately hostile to the privileged orders, but they neither were, nor did any one suppose them to be, disaffected to the king; on the contrary, the privileged classes openly proclaimed that the *tiers-état* would be, as it had ever been, in favour of the king, and against liberty, that is, against aristocratical ascendancy. Accordingly the court party took no trouble to gain the *tiers-état*, while, on the contrary, every man and even every woman about the palace was assiduously engaged in paying court to the deputies of the noblesse, from whom alone any resistance was apprehended; and succeeded in gaining those who had taken the lead in the previous resistance, d'Epréménil and d'Antraigues.*

*Of the eagerness, and we will add, the duplicity and treachery, with which the deputies of the *noblesse de campagne* were caressed and cajoled by the men and women of the court, we have an amusing account from one of those deputies, the marquis de Ferrières (see his *Memoirs*, Vol. I, pp. 34-7), who, though a decided royalist and anti-revolutionist, draws a picture of the courtiers both in respect to head and heart, which, indifferently as we think of courtiers in general, and of the French court in particular, we cannot help believing to be somewhat overcharged. Toulongeon describes these cajoleries in still stronger terms ([François Emmanuel Toulongeon,] *Histoire de France, depuis la Révolution de 1789* [7 vols. (Paris: Treuttel and Würtz, 1801-10)], Vol. I, p. 25), and adds that attempts were made to gain the principal orators of the *tiers-état*, when it was afterwards found that this order was likely to become formidable (p. 57). The court must therefore stand acquitted from the imputation of not having made ample use of those "usual ministerial arts" which our author fancies that they neglected, and thinks they ought to have employed. [Scott, Vol. I, pp. 116-17.] The following anecdote to the same effect, related by the royalist Dampmartin, is amusing. "Je dînai," says he, "chez le duc de Luxembourg. . . . Nous étions trop nombreux pour que l'entretien devînt général; mais on appercevait sans peine les soins consacrés avec peu d'art à séduire les provinciaux nouvellement débarqués. Je reçus en mon particulier des attentions qui ne me parurent pas naturelles. L'énigme se trouva résolue par la demande que me fit la duchesse, de quel bailliage j'étais député." ([Anne Henri Cabet,] vicomte de Dampmartin,] *Evénemens qui se sont passés sous mes yeux pendant la Révolution Française* [2 vols. (Berlin: n.p., 1799)], Vol. I, pp. 33-4.) [The concluding reference is to Adélaïde Geneviève, duchesse de Montmorency-Luxembourg.] The same writer hints that the exertions of Cazalès, the leading church-and-king orator in the Constituent Assembly, were partly the effect of similar allurements. "Cazalès, dont le riche talent a depuis fixé l'admiration générale, ne laissait encore appercevoir qu'une pétulance qui s'exaltait par les égards et les cajoleries que les habitans des cours savent si bien employer vis-à-vis des personnes dont ils pensent avoir besoin. Leurs charmes ont assez de pouvoir pour que les caractères les plus prononcés en soient amollis." (Pp. 34-5.)

That chivalrous loyalty, therefore, which Sir Walter Scott admires in the *noblesse*, only commenced when they discovered that other persons than themselves were about to gain the ascendancy in the Etats Généraux, and that the engine which they had constructed in hopes to wield it against the royal authority, was wrested from them and turned against themselves, by that *people* whom they had scorned. *Then*, they were extremely willing to make a parade of their loyalty; as some of them who had never before mentioned the name of God but in mockery, became patterns of devotion from the moment when they had hopes that the yell of fanaticism might serve them to incite the country-people against the Assembly.*
Then they were ready to die for that king, whom many of them had ridiculed and lampooned; that queen, whose character they had been the first to vilify;[†] and that despotism, against which, for their own purposes, they had struck the first blow.[‡]
Yet, amid all this pretence, still true to their character, they thought merely of their own privileges, and not for one instant of his safety whom they professed to serve. The majority fled to the courts of other despots, there to stir up foreign enemies, to make war upon their country in the name of their king: that king being all the time, as they studiously gave out, a captive in the hands of the very men whom they thus irritated to frenzy. Those who remained proclaimed everywhere the king's insincerity, made his name a pretext for all their liberticide intrigues, and leagued themselves with the worst of the Jacobins to promote every measure which they

*Our authority is the memoirs of the royalist Ferrières, Vol. II, pp. 199, 259.

[†]Our authority is the memoirs of the royalist Madame Campan, *passim*. See also *Deux Amis*, Vol. IX, pp. 215n-17n.

[‡]On this point, we may at least indicate a portion of that evidence which we have not room to exhibit. That the privileged classes commenced the Revolution, by resisting, in the Notables, the proposed new taxes, and by demanding, in the assembly of the clergy and in the parliaments, the convocation of the Etats Généraux, is matter of undisputed fact. That they did so in the hope of getting the powers of government into their hands by means of an aristocratical legislature, is asserted in express terms by three royalists, [François Claude Amour, marquis de] Bouillé (*Mémoires*, ed. 12mo [2 vols. (Paris: Giguet, 1802)], Vol. I, pp. 49, 67, 69), Ferrières (Vol. I, p. 2), and [Jean François] Marmontel (*Mémoires* [1804], London ed. [4 vols. (Peltier, 1805)], Vol. IV, pp. 12-13), as well as by Madame de Staël, in her *Considerations*, &c. (Vol. I, pp. 174-7.) The whole of the introductory portion of the *History of the Revolution* by [Antoine Etienne Nicolas] Fantin Desodoards [*Histoire philosophique de la révolution de France*, new rev. ed., 4 vols. (Paris: Perlet, *et al.*, 1797), Vol. I, esp. pp. 61-2 (Bk. I, Chap. xviii)], and the Memoir of Necker, which M. Boissy d'Anglas has annexed to his *Life of Malesherbes*, are filled with evidence of the same fact. [François Antoine Boissy d'Anglas, "Sur M. Necker," *Essai sur la vie, les écrits et les opinions de M. de Malesherbes, adressé à mes enfans*, 3 pts. (Paris: Treuttel and Würtz, 1819-21), Pt. 2, pp. 239-88.] For proof that the ministers relied upon the *tiers-état*, and its influence in the Etats Généraux, for support against the refractory nobles and parliaments, the reader may refer to Toulongeon (Vol. I, pp. 15, 22), Madame de Staël (Vol. I, pp. 126-7), Bouillé (Vol. I, Chap. iv [esp. p. 61]), Marmontel (Vol. IV, p. 39), Bertrand de Moleville (*Mémoires Particuliers pour servir à l'Histoire de la fin du Règne de Louis XVI* [2 vols. (Paris: Michaud, 1816)], Vol. I, pp. 21-2).

The state of opinion at the opening of the Etats Généraux is well described by the Abbé de Montgaillard (*Histoire*, Vol. I, pp. 235-6).

thought calculated to raise the disorder to its height, in order to ruin those whom they hated bitterest of all, the partisans of an orderly and well-regulated liberty.*

We have now arrived at the opening of the Revolution itself: and from this point we can no longer give to our author's attempt at history, even that qualified praise which we have bestowed upon the introductory chapters. From this point it conveys none but false impressions: it is a story skilfully, and even artfully constructed for a purpose. We have no intention of imputing insincerity to Sir Walter Scott. Though he obviously attempts throughout to impress the reader with a certain view of the facts, he probably is himself persuaded that this view is the true one. But that important branch of the talent of the narrator, which Sir Walter Scott in his character of a romancer pre-eminently possesses, the art of so relating every incident that it shall strike the reader not as an isolated incident, but as a part of the train of events,—of keeping the whole posture of affairs, such as it is supposed to be in the story, constantly present to the reader's conception, and almost to his sight—is a talent most delightful in a novelist, most dangerous when the subject is real history, and the author's view of the posture of affairs happens to be wrong. It is nothing less than the art of so dressing up a fact, as to make it appear to mean more than it does; of so relating and arranging the events to be related, as to make them tell a different story from what would be implied in the mere chronological recital of them. We are far from maintaining that this mode of relating facts is always blameable. We by no means affirm that an historian should be required to state first the naked facts, without any admixture of inference, and then speculate upon causes, motives, and characters, if he pleases. It would often be impossible to find room for all the facts, upon which inferences of this sort may very properly have been founded; and such part of the facts as are related, when the nature of the case does not permit the introduction of the whole, may justifiably be coloured, that is, although not sufficient in themselves to prove the theory, may be so related as to suggest it, *if* the theory be true, and evidence to prove it be produceable on fit occasions. Our quarrel with Sir Walter Scott is, that his theory is *not* true: that his view of the *rationale* of the French Revolution is *not* capable of being proved, but capable, on the contrary, of being disproved by the most cogent

*We had made references to an incredible number of passages, chiefly from Bertrand de Moleville, Ferrières, Bouillé, Madame Campan, and other royalist writers, bearing testimony to the abhorrence in which the royalists held the very idea of a constitution even on the English model, the pertinacity with which they clung to the ancien régime, refusing to hear of the slightest modification or reform, and their inveterate malignity towards all the moderate revolutionists, contrasted with a sort of favour and partiality towards the furious Jacobins, whom, according to Madame Campan, they declared that every true royalist ought to cherish, because they were the enemies of their enemies, and because their excesses tended to the ruin of the Revolution. [See, e.g., Campan, *Mémoires*, Vol. II, pp. 154-5, 182.] But we have not room to insert these extracts entire; while, if abridged, they would lose a great part of their force; and what hope can we entertain of convincing any one, whom the conduct of the royalist party since the restoration has not convinced?

evidence. And if this be so, it undoubtedly is a great additional evil, that what cannot be proved is insinuated almost in every sentence; that the language in which the events are related, invariably implies a particular mode of accounting for them; that every separate fact as it arises, finds the reader artificially prepared to put that interpretation upon it which the author's system requires; that causes are feigned, and the events so managed as to appear the natural consequences of them; that the hypothesis is slid in and gains credence under cover of the facts, because they are so related as seemingly not to allow of any other explanation.

During the Revolution, a variety of shades of opinion manifested themselves, and a variety of distinct and hostile parties grew up, among the defenders of the popular cause. The vulgar mouth-pieces of aristocracy to whom in our own country the office of forming the public sentiment on the Revolution was abandoned, have generally lumped all these parties and opinions together, in order that all of them, and the Revolution itself, might share the opprobrium which is justly due to the terrorists alone. Sir Walter Scott is quite superior to these low artifices: but he has fallen into an error as gross, and far more plausible. He has committed the very common blunder of ascribing to persons what was the effect of circumstances, and to settled design what was the result of immediate impulse. Every one of his characters has a part premeditated and prepared, and is ready to march upon the stage and enact it at the precise moment when his *entrée* will produce the most striking scenic effect. All the parties which gradually arose during the Revolution are represented as already existing from its commencement. At the very opening of the drama, we have already Constitutionalists, Republicans, and Jacobins, all of whom are described as even then entertaining all the opinions, and prosecuting systematically all the designs, which they manifested when they were most conspicuous, and most powerful. The struggle between the people and the court is made to appear, in all its stages, to have arisen solely from the endeavours of these different parties to carry their supposed designs into effect: the events are, with much skill, so presented as on every occasion to make the revolutionists appear the aggressors; they are pictured as omnipotent, having nothing to fear, nothing, for any good purpose, to desire; while the court and the aristocracy are represented from the first in no character but that of helpless unresisting victims, altogether without power even of self-defence, and quite impotent for attack. If any precaution, therefore, is taken, under the idea that any attack from that quarter is possible, it is held up as a studied indignity, intended to prepare the way for the subversion of the throne, and clear the ground for trying quackish political experiments, at the expense of a nation's happiness.

Now there is not a word of all this but what is purely fabulous. There is not a truth in history more firmly established, than the non-existence of any republican party at the commencement of the Revolution. The wishes of all then centered in a constitutional monarchy. There may have been, and probably were, speculative philosophers, at that time as at most others, who preferred in the abstract a republican form of government; but, if such there were, they had not the remotest idea of introducing it into France; and it is not proved that at this early period so much as one member of the Constituent Assembly was even in this speculative sense a republican. If any were so, they were of the number of those whom Sir Walter Scott acknowledges to have been, in their conduct, supporters of monarchy.* The men who formed the extremity of the *côté gauche*, who were esteemed the most *exagérés* among the democrats, were Barnave, Duport, and the Lameths: yet all these, when at length there *was* a republican party, were its most determined opponents, and threw away safety, fortune, popularity, every thing which they most valued, to save the throne. One of the Lameths, even, on the subversion of monarchy, expatriated with La Fayette, and shared with him that memorable captivity which the brutal vengeance of an infuriated despot[*] inflicted, and in which the author of "New Morality," in a spirit worthy of his sarcasm upon Ogden, found matter for savage exultation.[†]

The very name of a French republic was scarcely breathed, never publicly pronounced, until the king's flight from Paris: when two years experience, terminated by that ill-fated attempt, had clearly proved the impossibility of trusting to his good faith, so long as all who surrounded him were inveterately hostile to the new order of things; when the experiment of a free constitution with him at its head, had decidedly failed, and all discerning persons saw the impossibility of arriving at a settled government, or maintaining the authority of the laws, while the executive authority was in hands which could not safely be intrusted with the power necessary to enforce them. It was not till after ample and melancholy experience of this fact, that some of those who afterwards composed the Girondist party became republicans; but even then, by the great majority of that party, nothing more was at first thought of than a change of monarch; and nothing more would have been thought of to the last, if the Duke of Orleans, the only member of the royal family who was not inveterately hostile to the popular cause, had been of a character to possess, or to deserve, the smallest portion of public respect.

It may surprise some readers to find that Sir Walter Scott makes no allusion to the Orleanist party, which used to be employed with so much effect, in the character of a bugbear, by the enemies of liberal principles in France. This party, which was supposed to comprise all the abler and more energetic of the adherents

---

*Lafayette, for example, who in his beautiful letter of thanks to the chevalier d'Archenholz, written in the dungeons of Olmutz, takes credit to himself for having sacrificed republican inclinations to the welfare of his country. ["Lettre du général La Fayette au chevalier d'Archenholz" (Magdebourg, 27 Mar., 1793), in Jean Baptiste Regnault-Warin, *Mémoires pour servir à la vie du général La Fayette*, 2 vols. (Paris: Hesse, 1824), Vol. II, p. 116.]

[*Frederick William II of Prussia.]

[†George Canning and George Ellis, ["New Morality,"] *Anti-Jacobin; or, Weekly Examiner*, II, 36 (9 July, 1798), 282-7; for Canning's sarcasm on William Ogden, see his Speech on the Indemnity Bill (11 Mar., 1818), *PD*, 1st ser., Vol. 37, cols. 1026-8.]

of the popular cause, was represented as compassing the king's destruction as a means, and, as an end, the elevation of the Duke of Orleans either to the regency or to the throne, and of themselves to the principal offices of state. As it is unquestionable that Orleanists, if not an Orleanist party, did at one time exist, the discerning reader, when he finds that Sir Walter Scott is generous enough to forego all the advantages which the impugners of the popular leaders have derived from the connexion of several of them with that unhappy man, is apt to think that a writer with his partialities would hardly have been so unnecessarily candid on this point, without some ulterior object. Sir Walter Scott has sagacity enough to know, that different imputations suit different times, and that attacks upon visionary theorists *take* much better now, in this country at least, than accusations of aiming at personal aggrandizement under the mask of popular principles. This we suspect to be the true reason of his conjuring up a republican party, and putting aside not only what is fictitious, but what is true, in the denunciations of royalist writers against the Orleanists. For it is impossible that he should be ignorant (scanty and careless as his reading on the subject of the Revolution has been), that not Republicanism but Orleanism was the only reproach, connected with designs against the king, which was imputed at the time to any individual member of the Constituent Assembly: not Republicanism but Orleanism was the accusation brought against the only member of it, whom our author singles out by name as one of the republican party;* and, in fact, the only shade of opinion which existed in the

---

*We mean Barnave. For the truth of our assertion, see the furious *Memoirs* of the Abbé Georgel [Jean François Georgel, *Mémoires pour servir à l'histoire des événemens de la fin du dix-huitième siècle*, 6 vols. (Paris: Eymery and Delaunay, 1817-18), Vol. II, e.g., p. 422]; and a still more intemperate production (if that be possible), intituled *Conjuration d'Orléans*, and attributed to the noted royalist writer, Montjoie. [Christophe Félix Louis Montjoie, *Histoire de la conjuration de L.P.J. d'Orléans*, 6 vols. (Paris: Les marchands de nouveautés, 1800), esp. Vol. II, pp. 65-140 (Book V).] See even the work, above cited, of the Abbé de Montgaillard, Vol. II, p. 81.

It is extraordinary that our author, who is so incessantly harping upon a republican party—an organized body, whose leaders were in the Constituent Assembly, and who were perpetually busy in the active prosecution of their designs—should never be able to name more than one of these formidable persons, and that this one, by a *curiosa infelicitas*, should be Barnave [Scott, Vol. I, p. 147n]; Barnave, than whom few men ever gave more solid proofs of his attachment to constitutional monarchy; Barnave, the very man who moved the re-establishment of royalty after the return from Varennes, when, if he had thrown his weight into the other scale, it is extremely probable, that a republican government might have been established without violence or danger. [See his speech of 15 July, 1791, *Gazette Nationale, ou Le Moniteur Universel*, 17 July, 1791, p. 818.]

This blunder of our author can be surpassed by nothing except the strange mental hallucination, for we will give it no harsher name, by which he has accused the same individual of having been betrayed by republican enthusiasm into palliating the massacres of September. We have far too good an opinion of Sir Walter Scott to believe that he has invented a story, which we are certain that he cannot have found in any of the memorials of the times, and we will therefore only suppose that in writing from memory, he has

Assembly beyond what our author terms the party of Bailly and La Fayette, was Orleanism. The difference between the Orleanists and the other section of the popular party did not consist in a greater hostility to royalty; for, on the contrary, their leader Mirabeau was inclined, as his speeches prove, to give a larger share of power to the king than even Necker himself, the largest indeed which was at all consistent with the circumstances of the time, or perhaps with constitutional freedom.[*] The distinction lay in this—that, while both parties desired a monarchical and representative government, La Fayette and the majority felt sufficient confidence in the good intentions of Louis, to be desirous of retaining him at its head, while the other party would have preferred his peaceable deposition, and the elevation of some individual to the constitutional throne, who had never known what it was to be a despot. All the more discerning among the friends of freedom, and especially Mirabeau, perhaps the only true statesman whom the Revolution produced, thoroughly distrusted the king. They knew, what in our times some other persons ought to have learned,—that it is next to an impossibility for a monarch, used to absolute power, to accommodate himself to limitations; and they were convinced that Louis, at least, was not the man who would be an exception to the rule. Incapable of maintaining and abiding by his firmest convictions, if they were in opposition to the will of those by whom he was immediately surrounded, he was formed to be the tool of any person who had the opportunity and the will to use him as such: completely at the beck of his queen and her counter-revolutionary counsellors, he had shewn by his conduct both before and immediately after the meeting of the Etats Généraux, that he was capable of being hurried into every extreme of despotism by such counsellors, although he personally did not share the passions in which their counsels originated: and the patriots thought, not without reason, that the man who, after saying that nobody except Turgot and himself desired the good of the people,[†] could dismiss this same Turgot a few months

---

confounded Barnave with some other and far different person. It would have been strange enough if Barnave had palliated the massacres of September, when, if we believe Mignet [p. 278n], he was himself marked out to be included in them, a fate from which he, as well as Duport and Charles Lameth, were only saved by Danton. Long before this time Barnave had retired from public life in disgust (see the *Memoirs* of Madame Campan, Vol. II, p. 192), and far from considering the public good to center, as our author expresses it, in a pure republic, he had been engaged up to the last moment in a most bitter contest against the supposed partisans of a republic, and indeed (for such are understood to have been the views of the *feuillant* party) for the establishment of a second Chamber. It is even supposed that the letter of the Emperor Leopold, denouncing the Jacobins, which produced so much irritation at Paris, was the composition of Barnave and Duport. [See Leopold II, Letter of 17 Feb., 1792, *Gazette Nationale, ou Le Moniteur Universel*, 2 Mar., 1792, p. 254.]

[*Mirabeau, speeches of 1 and 12 Sept., 1789, in *Oeuvres*, Vol. VII, pp. 244-63 and 266-9.]

[†See Charles Durozoir, biography of Turgot, in *Biographie universelle ancienne et moderne*, ed. Louis Gabriel Michaud, 52 vols. (Paris: Michaud frères, 1811-28), Vol. XLVII, p. 81.]

afterwards, at the persuasion of the very men of whose worthlessness he was so clearly convinced, was a man whose good feelings were no security against the worst conduct. Having this opinion of Louis, these statesmen, though fully aware of all the objections to the Duke of Orleans as a man, still thought, that owing the crown to the new order of things, and being unable to maintain it by any support but that of the friends of freedom, he would be less objectionable as the head of a constitutional monarchy, than a man who thought himself, and was thought by a powerful party, to be a despot by divine right. Our Revolution of 1688 formed at once a precedent for such a settlement of affairs, and an example of its beneficial effects. It is deeply to be regretted that uncontrollable circumstances prevented these views from being realized. As it turned out, the change of dynasty was only thought of for an instant, not by a party, but by scattered individuals, and thought of merely, like the republic at a later period, as a *pis aller*. The nullity of the Duke of Orleans as a politician, which became more clearly manifested by subsequent events, and the complete annihilation of the little character he possessed, detached from him all the more sincere and disinterested of his adherents; and when Louis had so acted that even Sir Walter Scott admits he ought not to have been replaced on the throne,[*] these and many others, being of the same opinion with Sir Walter Scott, became republicans because they had no choice.*

But it is not the republicans alone that have had the misfortune to offend our author: the constitutional royalists come in for nearly an equal share of his displeasure. Much good indignation, and no inconsiderable quantity of what is intended to be wit, is expended upon them, for rejecting the counsels of experience, and attempting to renovate the constitution of France by means of abstract and untried theories. It is with such vulgar weapons, that Sir Walter Scott does not disdain to assail some of the most remarkable men who have ever figured in public affairs. To point out the real faults in the conduct of the early revolutionists—to shew in what respects the means which they employed, were ill-suited to attain the ends which they had in view,—*this*, it is not every body who is capable of; but if to dub them *theorists* be sufficient, then there is not a creature so dull, so ignorant, so thoroughly mean in understanding and void of ideas, who is not perfectly competent to condemn philosophers and statesmen without a hearing, and decide at his ease all the questions which perplexed the most thinking

[*Scott, Vol. I, pp. 255-6.]

*Of the view which has been taken of the Orleanist party in the text, the decisive evidence is of course to be sought for in the lives, the speeches, and the writings of the men themselves. But in order to shew that several of the most intelligent writers on the Revolution have concurred substantially in the opinion above expressed, we may refer the reader to Toulongeon (*Histoire de France depuis la Révolution de 1789*, Vol. I, pp. 118-19), to Madame de Staël (*Considérations sur la Révolution Françoise*, Vol. I, 2nd pt., Chap. vi, near the end [pp. 306-7]), and to a passage in Arthur Young (see, in his work on France, the diary of his third tour in that country, *ad diem* 12th June, 1789 [2nd ed., Vol. I, p. 121]).

men of their day. It seems no more than reasonable to demand, in behalf of conclusions which are the result of thought, that some portion of thought shall also be deemed necessary in order to criticize them; and that a body of men, who comprised in their ranks nearly all the political wisdom which could be found in an age and country abounding in it, shall at least be thought worthy of having their motives and reasons weighed, and of being condemned, if condemned they must be, for the injustice or inexpediency of their course of action, not for its novelty.

It cannot be denied that the early revolutionists did attempt to discover what was the best possible form of government; and, having, in their own opinion, found it, did endeavour to bring the government of their own country as nearly into accordance with it as they could. We shall not seek to defend them against these imputations; but, if our author's objection to their scheme of government be that it was untried, we are entitled to require him to shew that there was any *tried* scheme, which would have afforded better prospects of success.

His opinion on the subject might have been foretold. It is, that they should have adopted the English constitution; or something as nearly resembling it as possible.

Now this, from a writer who is perpetually crying out against visionary projects, is a tolerable specimen of a visionary project; and its author is justly chargeable with the very fault which he imputes to the revolutionists, that of being so wedded to a favourite system, as to insist upon introducing it at all hazards, even when the very circumstances which constitute its excellence at other times, would infallibly work its destruction.

It is not on account of the imperfections of the British constitution, great as we deem these to be, on its native soil, that we blame those who, at this period of the Revolution, sought to introduce it into France. With all its defects, we are well content that foreign nations should look to it as their model; for there is little danger of their copying it in those parts which are the cause of our evils. It is not probable that they should fail of making their Lower House a real representative organ: and as we should be satisfied with this in our own country, so we are of opinion that in any other, the British constitution, with this modification alone, would suffice for good government.

But what may be very true of a settled order of things, it may be altogether absurd to affirm of a revolution. Why do the King and the House of Peers, in this country, never convert the powers which they constitutionally possess, to the overthrow of the constitution and the abolition of the House of Commons? Nobody supposes that it is because they *would* not; for it is the theory of our constitution, that every one who has power seeks its enlargement, and, in times more favourable to them, they have attempted such things. It is because they *could* not; and because, power to effect such schemes being manifestly wanting, the desire never arises in their minds. Nobody, however, will deny that it is in their power to impede and thwart in a hundred ways the operations of the Commons, and even to put a stop to the business of government altogether. They have, therefore, much power, capable of being mischievously employed. Our security against their so employing it is, that they could serve no purpose by doing so, except that of destroying the constitution; and, of success in such a design, they well know that they have no chance. Give them a chance, and you will soon know the mischief which they can still do. Let the time ever come, when by the exercise of their powers in a manner opposed to the end for which those powers were given, the king may hope to erect an absolute monarchy, or the peers to establish themselves in undivided rule as an aristocratical senate, and we are justified in saying that either their powers must be suspended, or the government cannot be carried on. Such was the posture of affairs during the French Revolution; and he who does not carry this conviction along with him through the whole of its history, will never form a rational conception of the Revolution in any of its stages, much less as a whole.

If the attempt to establish a government of two chambers on the English model, had been made, the Upper House must have been formed from among the high noblesse and clergy, either by the king's choice, or by the suffrages of the privileged orders themselves. In whichever way selected, this second chamber would have been, as the high noblesse and the high clergy almost universally were, inveterately hostile to nearly every necessary reform, and (as soon as they saw that they were not about to have absolute control over the legislature) to the representative system itself. Not one of the great objects of the Revolution would, with their consent, have been effected; and either those objects must have been renounced, or it would have been necessary to decide which chamber should turn the other out of doors, or, what is most probable, the court would have taken advantage of their dissensions to discredit them in the public mind, and would have availed itself of the authority of one branch of the legislature to rid itself for ever of both. This is what stamps the conduct and counsels of Mounier (whom our author characterizes as one of the wisest men in France),[*] of Lally Tolendal, and the remainder of the *modérés* (or *monarchiens*, as they were afterwards called), with absurdity; and marks them as altogether unequal to the difficulties of the crisis which they had aided so powerfully in bringing on. That the intentions of these men were good, is not to be denied; but the good intentions of men, who not only give the most unseasonable and ruinous advice, but desert their post and abandon their country because that advice is not listened to, are of little use. The emigration of Mounier and Lally, at the time when, if ever, the presence of wise and moderate men was required, admits of but one excuse; and that is, the supposition that they were conscious of being deficient in all the qualities which could be available in

[*Scott, Vol. I, p. 140.]

troubled times, and felt that the moment was past when such men as they were, could act a part in the Revolution.*

Our author next pronounces that the Assembly erred, by not giving sufficient power to the king.[*] He gets over all the difficulties of this question very summarily. It was surely very foolish in the Assembly to waste so much time and labour in anxious deliberation on points which our author settles so perfectly at his ease. Nothing can be more conclusive than the case he can always make out against them; nothing more completely satisfactory than the reasons he gives, to prove them always in the wrong; and the chief impression which is made upon the reader, is one of astonishment, that a set of persons should have been found so perversely blind to considerations so obviously dictated by sound policy and common sense. But when we examine the original authorities, we find that these considerations were no more unknown or unheeded by the Assembly than by our author himself. The difference in point of knowledge between them and him consisted chiefly in this, that they likewise knew the reasons which made for the *other* side of the question, and might therefore be pardoned if, being thus burthened with arguments on *both* sides, they were slower to decide, and sometimes came to a different decision from that which, as long as we confine ourselves to *one*, appears so eminently reasonable.

The point which Sir Walter Scott so quietly disposes of was, in fact, the great difficulty of their situation. There is no denying, that the king, or whoever else is placed at the head of the executive, ought to have more power than the Constituent Assembly gave him. And most of the popular leaders felt this strongly enough; *all*, after a very short experience of the constitution they had framed. In truth, the executive had not power enough to enforce obedience to the laws, or to prevent, in many places, the most worthless part of the population, often headed and organized by professional robbers, from availing themselves of the universal relaxation of restraint, and perpetrating the most horrid enormities. The popular party knew all this; but they knew also, that every atom of power which they gave to the executive over the military, through whom alone these disorders could have been suppressed, would be employed at the first favourable opportunity to put down the Revolution and restore absolute monarchy. It was this conviction, strong from the first, and continually gaining strength by the conduct of the court from 1789 to 1792, which finally brought on, and rendered imperatively necessary, the subversion of the throne. And it is this conviction which induced even d'Escherny,

---

*We are aware that the ostensible motive for their desertion of their duty, was the horrors of the fifth and sixth of October; but it is difficult to mention such an excuse with a grave face. Without doubt, there was enough in the events of that day to disgust men, such as they were, of feeling and humanity; but, after all, what could become of a nation in troubled times, if the murder of two persons were sufficient to frighten every well-meaning and virtuous man from his post?

[*Scott, Vol. I, pp. 141-2.]

a writer who regards the republicans with horror, and calls the constitution of 1791 *un système monstrueux*, to declare, that the day of the 10th of August decided whether France should be governed by an absolute king, or by demagogues, meaning the republican leaders.*

"Avant d'avoir une monarchie constitutionnelle," says M. Bailleul, "il fallait vaincre les hommes puissans qui n'en voulaient pas. Les erreurs viennent de ce qu'on confond toujours les institutions avec les combats qu'il fallait livrer pour les obtenir."† This is a truth which, as applied to the French Revolution, our author cannot or will not see. In reading him, nobody would ever guess, that France had for the time no choice but between an absolute monarchy and a republic. Of the first we should never learn from him that there was the least danger; and to the latter, France according to him was only brought by the criminal recklessness of a set of hair-brained enthusiasts, wild in their ends and unscrupulous in the choice of their means, who were willing to let murder and rapine loose upon society, to deluge their country with bloodshed, and stain their consciences with guilt, for the mere difference between monarchical and republican forms.

"N'est-il pas bien étrange de voir," says M. Bailleul, "et ceux qui prennent le titre d'historiens, et ceux qui prétendent faire de la morale sur la révolution, en saisir l'esprit, comme Madame de Staël," and we will add, like Sir Walter Scott, *"faire une abstraction entière et complète de l'attaque*, ne s'occuper que de ceux contre qui elle est dirigée, signaler comme des forfaits, non seulement les coups que par erreur ou par esprit de vertige, ils se sont portés entr'eux, mais appeler surtout crimes, forfaits, les combats qu'ils ont livrés aux ennemis de la patrie?"‡ This sentence might be imagined to have been written on purpose to describe the work before us. Our author systematically "makes abstraction of the attack," and treats the defence as a premeditated and unprovoked aggression. This it is to start

---

*[François Louis, comte] D'Escherny, *Philosophie de la Politique* [2 vols. (Paris: n.p., 1796)], quoted at great length in the Appendix to the second volume of the *Memoirs* of Madame Campan [Vol. II, p. 444 (Note P), quoted from d'Escherny, Vol. II, p. 297]. For the strongest and most distinct testimony to the fact, that what appears the unnecessary limitation of the king's power was not occasioned by any fanaticism of democracy, or bigotted attachment to system, but by real dread of the use to which that power would be converted, *vide* Madame de Staël, (Vol. I, pp. 308, 316,) who, being of the party of Mounier, and a perfect idolator of the British constitution, cannot be here suspected of partiality. Ferrières is, if possible, still more positive on the same point; (see Vol. I, pp. 368, 391, Vol. II, pp. 236-7, 481), passages which, although written by a royalist, and one who not only perceives but exaggerates the faults of the constitution of 1791, contain the most entire and honorable vindication of the authors of that constitution, which has ever appeared. The same author says, that the constitutional party were, perhaps, more deeply impressed than even the royalists, with the necessity of giving efficiency to the executive, as well as more sincerely attached to the person of the king. (Vol. III, p. 15.)

†*Examen Critique de l'Ouvrage Posthume de Madame de Staël*, 2me partie, chap. ix [Vol. I, p. 317].

‡*Ibid.*, Vol. II, p. 34.

with false ideas, and read just enough to be confirmed in them—not enough to correct them.

Burke has asserted, in one of his rhapsodies against the French Revolution, that, from the day when the Etats Généraux assembled at Versailles, despotism was no more.[*] We will not take this assertion in the sense in which it was meant; for, in that sense, nothing was ever thrown out even by that author in his wildest moments, more glaringly absurd. But there is a sense in which it is perfectly well founded; that despotism, and the National Assembly, could not subsist together; and that the existence of the one necessarily implied the subversion of the other. The popular party were thoroughly aware of this. So were the royalists. They knew that, not indeed when the Assembly met, but as soon as it shewed itself firmly determined that France should be free, she *was* free, and could not be again enslaved while the Assembly remained, to guard and consolidate her freedom. Accordingly, the dissolution of the Assembly entered into all their plans; and they never, for a single moment, ceased plotting to accomplish it. We agree with Burke, that the Revolution, so far as it was necessary or justifiable, was terminated when the Assembly met. From that time the struggle was not *for* a revolution, but *against* a counter-revolution. To the well-grounded apprehension of such a calamity, and to the precautions necessary to be taken in order to guard against it, ought really to be ascribed all those proceedings, both of the constitutionalists and of the Gironde, which, in the former party, our author imputes to the desire of reducing the royal authority to a name; in the latter, to a fanatical hatred even of the name.[†]

Could the revolutionists forget that the attempt to put down the Revolution had once been made, and had failed only because the military had remembered that they were citizens before they were soldiers? We allude to the events which preceded the insurrection of Paris and the destruction of the Bastille.

Few of our readers, we hope, are ignorant, that in July 1789, when the Constituent Assembly had only sat for a few weeks, when it had done nothing, as yet, of what our author deems blameable in its proceedings; when his friends Lally and Mounier were still predominant in its counsels; when it had scarcely begun to occupy itself with the reform of abuses, or the establishment of a constitution, and had only had time to shew that it would not resign the entire power of legislation to the privileged classes, by giving to each order a separate voice; so early as this, troops from distant parts of the kingdom were marched upon Paris; a large force, under an avowed anti-revolutionist,[‡] was encamped in its immediate vicinity, and artillery was moved upon that city and upon Versailles, sufficient for a siege. At this juncture, Necker, and all the ministers not decidedly hostile to the new

[*Edmund Burke, *Reflections on the Revolution in France*, in *Works*, 8 vols. (London: Dodsley, *et al.*, 1792-1827), Vol. III, pp. 182-3.]

[†Scott, Vol. I, pp. 140-6.]

[‡Victor François, duc de Broglie.]

order of things, received an abrupt dismissal, and Necker was banished from France. They were succeeded by men notoriously inimical to the Revolution;[*] men odious to the people, some of them for their personal corruption, all for their political views, and every thing seemed prepared for dissolving the Assembly and crushing resistance by force of arms. That this purpose was really entertained, none but the most prejudiced and dishonest even among the royalist writers have hitherto been bold enough to deny. The king in person, at the famous *séance royale*, had threatened the Assembly with dissolution if it did, what it had nevertheless done.* The courtiers themselves made no secret of what was intended: with their accustomed fool-hardiness, they openly triumphed in the approaching humiliation of the popular party, and punishment of its leaders; and it is a fact known to many now living, that several members of the minority of the noblesse, who had relatives or friends connected with the court, were warned by them to save themselves, by a timely flight, from the death or captivity which was in store for them.[†] At this crisis the people rose in arms, organized the burgher-milita afterwards called the National Guard, were joined by a portion of the military, took the Bastille, and reduced the court to the necessity of indefinitely postponing the execution of its criminal design. Now let us hear our author speculate, and conjecture, and calculate, probabilities, in opposition to the plain and well-established facts above related.

The successful party may always cast on the loser the blame of commencing the brawl, as the wolf punished the lamb for troubling the course of the water, though he drank lowest down the stream. But when we find one party completely prepared, and ready for action, forming plans boldly, and executing them skilfully, and observe the other uncertain and unprovided, betraying all the imbecility of surprise and indecision, we must necessarily believe the attack was premeditated on the one side, and unexpected on the other. The abandonment of thirty thousand stand of arms at the Hotel des Invalides, which were surrendered without the slightest resistance, though three Swiss regiments lay encamped in the Champs Elysées; the totally unprovided state of the Bastille, garrisoned by about one hundred Swiss and Invalids, and without provisions even for that small number; the absolute inaction of the Baron de Bezenval, who—without entangling his troops in the narrow streets, which was pleaded as his excuse—might, by marching along the Boulevards, a passage so well calculated for the manoeuvres of regular troops, have relieved the siege of that fortress; and finally, that general's bloodless retreat from Paris— shew that the king had, under all these circumstances, not only adopted no measures of a hostile character, but must, on the contrary, have issued such orders as prevented his officers from repelling force by force. We are led, therefore, to believe, that the scheme of assembling the troops round Paris was one of those half-measures, to which, with great

[*For the names of the ministers dismissed and their replacements, see above p. 9 in the quotation from Mignet.]

*His words were, "seul je ferai le bien de mes peuples; seul je me considérerai comme leur véritable représentant; et connaissant vos cahiers, &c. &c." (See the *Mémoires de Bailly*, Vol. I, p. 213.)

†Ferrières also attests the fact, Vol. I, p. 122.

political weakness, Louis resorted more than once—an attempt to intimidate by the demonstration of force, which he was previously resolved not to use.*

And accordingly, the insurrection is ascribed to "dark intrigues,"[*] which had been long formed by the Republican and Jacobin parties for the subversion of the throne. Thus far Sir Walter Scott. Now hear the marquis de Ferrières; himself a member of the Assembly, a deputy of the noblesse, who always voted with the noblesse, and who is so far from being a revolutionist, that there are few of the revolutionists to whom he will allow the common merit of sincerely desiring the public good: "Trente régimens," says he, "marchaient sur Paris. Le prétexte était la tranquillité publique; l'objet réel, la dissolution des états" (Vol. I, p. 71); with much more to the same effect, from which we shall quote only what follows. The circumstances which it relates took place on the very day on which the Bastille was taken, and are the more memorable from the allusion made to them the next day by Mirabeau, in perhaps the most splendid apostrophe recorded in history.[†]

La cour était résolue d'agir cette même nuit. Les régimens de Royal-Allemand et de Royal-Etranger avaient reçu ordre de prendre les armes. Les hussards s'étaient portés sur la place du château; les gardes-du-corps occupaient les cours. A ces préparatifs menaçans la cour joignit un air de fête, qui, dans la circonstance, ajoutait l'insulte à la cruauté. Le comte d'Artois, les Polignac, Mesdames, Madame,[‡] et Madame d'Artois, se rendirent sur la terrasse de l'orangerie. On fit jouer la musique des deux régimens. Les soldats, auxquels on n'avait pas épargné le vin, formèrent des danses: une joie insolente et brutale éclatait de toutes parts: une troupe de femmes, de courtisans, d'hommes vendus au despotisme, regardaient cet étrange spectacle d'un oeil satisfait, et l'animaient par leurs applaudisse-mens. Telle était la légèreté, ou plutôt l'immoralité de ces hommes, qu'assurés, à ce qu'ils croyaient, du succès, ils se livraient à un insultant triomphe. L'assemblée nationale offrait un aspect bien différent, un calme majestueux, une contenance ferme, une activité sage et tranquille, tout annonçait les grands desseins dont elle était occupée, et le danger de la chose publique. Ce n'était point ignorance des desseins de la cour. L'assemblée savait qu'*au moment même de l'attaque de Paris*, les régimens de Royal-Etranger et les hussards devaient environner la salle des états-généraux, *enlever les députés* que leur zèle et leur patriotisme avaient désignés pour victimes, et *en cas de résistance employer la force*. Elle savait que le roi devait venir le lendemain faire accepter la déclaration du 23 Juin, et *dissoudre l'assemblée*;[§] que déjà plus de quarante mille exemplaires de cette déclaration étaient envoyés aux intendans et aux subdélégués, avec ordre de la publier, et de l'afficher dans toute l'étendue du royaume. (Vol. I, pp. 130-1.)

Is this sufficient? We are curious to know what more unexceptionable evidence our author can demand. No doubt he disbelieves Ferrières—though he too can quote Ferrières when it answers his purpose. No doubt he disbelieves Madame de

---

*Scott, Vol. I, pp. 163-5. [For the fable referred to in the quotation, see Jean de La Fontaine, *Fables choisies mises en vers* (Paris: Thierry, 1668), pp. 23-4 (Book I, Fable x).]

[*Scott, Vol. I, p. 154.]

[†Mirabeau, Speech of 15 July, 1789, in *Oeuvres*, Vol. VII, pp. 167-8.]

[‡"Mesdames" refers to Marie Adélaïde and Victoire Louise, the surviving daughters of Louis XV; "Madame" to Louise Marie Joséphine, comtesse de Provence.]

[§See above, p. 72n.]

Staël;[*] he disbelieves Bailly;[†] he disbelieves Dumouriez—a writer to whom, on other occasions, he gives even more credit than is due, and who informs us, that, even at Cherbourg, the royalists were exulting in their anticipated victory, and triumphing in the thought that the minority of the noblesse were, perhaps, already in the Bastille.[‡] But we will make free to inquire, does he disbelieve two persons, who ought to know whether the design existed or not; viz. the person who planned it, and the person who was to have executed it—the minister Breteuil, and the minister and commander of the troops, the Maréchal de Broglie himself? The former boasted, both subsequently and at the time, not only of the conspiracy, but of what were to have been its sanguinary consequences; and named several of the very men who were marked out to pay with their lives the penalty of having wished their country to be free. As for Broglie, the letter is extant in which he offered himself to be the wretched instrument in the perpetration of crimes, compared with which those of the butcher of Porlier and Lacy are innocence itself.[*] "Avec cinquante mille hommes," says he, "je me chargerais volontiers de dissiper tous ces beaux esprits qui calculent sur leurs prétentions, et cette foule d'imbécilles qui écoutent, applaudissent, et encouragent. Une salve de canons, ou une décharge de coups de fusils, aurait bientôt dispersé ces argumentateurs, et remis la puissance absolue qui s'éteint, à la place de cet esprit républicain qui se forme." See the Correspondence published at Paris and London in 1789, and never disavowed; or the *History*, by the abbé de Montgaillard.[§] We shall now adopt the words of the latter author.

Lorsque le maréchal de Broglie eut pris le commandement des troupes destinées à dissoudre l'assemblée des états-généraux, le baron de Breteuil, qu'on pouvait considérer en quelque sorte, comme premier ministre, par l'influence sans bornes qu'il exerçait sur l'esprit de la reine et sur celui du roi; le baron de Breteuil disait, portes ouvertes; "Au surplus, *s'il faut brûler Paris, on brûlera Paris, et l'on décimera ses habitans*: aux grands maux, les grands remèdes." On répète mot pour mot ce qu'on a entendu dire au baron de Breteuil en 1794, ce dont il se glorifiait encore à cette époque.[¶] . . . On tient également de ce ministre, que le duc

---

*Considérations sur la Révolution Françoise, Vol. I, pp. 231-2.

[†]*Mémoires de Bailly*, Vol. I, pp. 191, 299, 313, 342, 361, 391-2. Some of these passages prove more, others less, but all are important.

[‡][Charles François Dumouriez, *La vie et les*] *Mémoires de Dumouriez* [4 vols. (Paris: Baudouin, 1822-23)], Vol. II, p. 35.

[*The Spanish generals Juan Díaz Porlier and Louis de Lacy were put to death by Ferdinand VII.]

§Vol. II, pp. 63-4 [where the letter is given].

[¶]"Et dix ans plus tard," the author indignantly adds, "ce despote de la vieille roche (suivant son expression favorite), était dans les antichambres de Cambacérès, et recevait de Napoléon une pension de douze mille francs sur sa cassette!" There would be matter enough for indignation here, if it were rational to be angry with the beasts of the field for merely following their nature. Any act of baseness is credible in a royalist of 1789. The court of Napoleon was thronged with *émigrés* of the 14th of July. It was the despotism which they had valued, not the despot. No one licked the dust before the *parvenu* emperor with greater *gusto* than the abbé Maury, than whom a more unprincipled *intrigant* never sold his conscience for gain.

d'Orléans, le marquis de la Fayette, le comte de Mirabeau, l'abbé Sieyès, Barnave, Chapelier, Lally-Tolendal, Mounier, et huit ou dix autres membres de l'assemblée nationale étaient désignés comme victimes impérieusement réclamées par le salut du trône et de l'état. Une compagnie de canonniers avait été casernée aux écuries de la reine, et l'on ne cachait pas que cette compagnie était destinée à mitrailler l'assemblée.*

Let no man wonder that Mounier and Lally, men whose love of freedom was sufficiently lukewarm to suit even Sir Walter Scott, were doomed to perish on the same scaffold with Barnave and Mirabeau. To have desired the liberty of France was an offence which nothing could redeem. By being more scrupulous, more moderate, a less envenomed opponent than the rest, all which was ever gained was, to be more bitterly detested. An enemy always hates those most whom he most fears; a criminal ever most abhors those among his pursuers whom he believes to be most inflexibly virtuous.

It is of little use to heap up quotations in order to convince a writer who, by an elaborate argument, concludes that it is most likely a thing is white, when every credible person who has seen it assures him that it is black. Yet we cannot refrain from quoting one passage more; it is from Lacretelle; an author whose principles are those of the most decided royalism, and who has written a History of the Constituent Assembly, in a spirit generally as unfair as that of Sir Walter Scott, but who, on this occasion, pays the following tribute to truth:

Le château était rempli de généraux, de colonels, d'aides-de-camp qui revenaient essoufflés de leurs courses insignifiantes. Tout présentait à la fois un air de mystère et de confiance. Le roi seul laissait lire sur son visage la perplexité de son esprit. La reine semblait jouir avec orgueil de la pensée qu'elle seule dirigeait toute cette noblesse armée pour la défense du trône. Sa figure était empreinte d'une majesté nouvelle. Les adorateurs de la cour lui faisaient oublier les aveugles et atroces malédictions du peuple. *Il n'était plus douteux pour personne qu'un coup d'état ne dût être frappé.* Quelles en devaient être la force et l'étendue? Les mémoires de ce temps sont si stériles et si rares, qu'ils fournissent peu de moyen d'éclaircir ce mystère. Ce qu'il y a de certain, c'est que la reine, ni le comte d'Artois, n'avaient ni conçu ni présenté des projets sévères et cruels, qui, fort éloignés de leurs propres penchans, auraient fait une violence intolérable au coeur du roi. Il s'agissait, si j'en crois et la vraisemblance et les renseignemens particuliers qu'il m'a été possible de recueillir, de faire respecter la déclaration du 23 Juin dans toute son étendue, d'y ajouter encore quelques clauses satisfaisantes pour le parti populaire, et de *dissoudre l'assemblée*, si elle persistait à vouloir, à elle seule, déterminer la constitution du royaume.†

This is the testimony which Sir Walter Scott would refute by a ratiocination: and what a ratiocination! Nothing can be more engaging than the amiable simplicity which it betokens, if the author is himself persuaded by his own reasoning. That want of preparation, or rather of means adequate to the intended purpose, which

*[Montgaillard,] *Histoire de France depuis la fin du règne de Louis XVI*, Vol. II, pp. 62-3.

†[Charles Jean Dominique de Lacretelle, *Histoire de l'assemblée constituante*, 2 vols. (Paris, Strasburg, and London: Treuttel and Würtz, 1821),] Vol. I, pp. 68-9.

was really owing to blind, besotted, headlong confidence, imagining that the troops had only to show themselves and all would be quiet, he, good man, esteems a demonstrative proof that no violence was intended! Truly it is no wonder that they were unprepared, when, on the very day of the capture of the Bastille, at the very instant when a deputation of the Assembly was waiting upon the king, to represent to him the state of Paris, and express their alarms; "l'intendant de Paris était dans la chambre, en bottes et le fouet à la main, assurant que tout était tranquille;"* when, "le soir même du 14 Juillet, on regardait à Versailles dans les cercles des femmes à-la-mode et des petits-maîtres, tous les avis que l'on recevait de Paris comme autant de fables; à les entendre, il ne s'agissait que de quelques misérables, dont la maréchaussée ferait justice."†

Hear Ferrières again: "La cour, habituée à voir Paris trembler sous un lieutenant de police, et sous une garde de huit cents hommes à cheval, ne soupçonna pas même une résistance. Elle ne prévit rien, ne calcula rien, ne songea pas même à s'assurer des soldats dont elle voulait faire l'instrument de ses desseins." (Vol. I, p. 75.) And again, speaking of the ministers, "Ils regardaient la situation de Paris comme l'effet d'une émeute passagère; ils ne doutaient pas qu'à l'approche des troupes le peuple tremblant ne se dispersât, que les chefs consternés ne vinssent implorer la clémence du monarque" (p. 116). He even intimates a suspicion that they allowed the insurrection to proceed, in order that they might have a better excuse for the rigorous measures which they had previously resolved upon (p. 115).‡

No wonder that the king had not given the necessary orders, when he was kept in such profound ignorance of what was passing, that he did not even know of the insurrection, and the capture of the Bastille, until the duc de Liancourt, a member of the popular party in the Assembly, who had access to him by office, as grand master of his wardrobe, awakened him in the night, and apprised him of those events which his counsellors had till then concealed from him: "Mais, dit le roi, après un silence, c'est une révolte.—Sire, c'est une Révolution."§

Our readers must excuse us for dwelling a little longer on this great aera in the history of the Revolution. If the events themselves are important, the manner in

*Toulongeon, Vol. I, p. 18. The vicomte de Toulongeon was himself a distinguished member of the minority of the noblesse, and his *History* is equal in authority to the memoirs of an eye witness. It is by far the most instructive and most philosophical work of its class. [Louis Bénigne François de Bertier de Sauvigny was Intendant of Paris.]

†[Joseph] Lavallée, *Histoire* [*de l'origine, des progrès, et de la décadence*] *des* [*diverses*] *Factions de la Révolution Française*, [3 vols. (London: Murray, 1816),] Vol. I, p. 86.

‡Montgaillard (Vol. II, p. 82) confirms the assertion.

§Toulongeon, Vol. I, p. 78, &c. &c. The cause of the precipitate retreat of the baron de Bezenval is thus stated by Montgaillard, on the authority of the minister Breteuil, as before: "Le baron de Bezenval faisait achever des bains où toutes les recherches du luxe avaient été prodiguées; il craignait leur dévastation, et ce favori, si brave à Versailles, donna aux troupes placées sous ses ordres l'ordre de battre en retraite, *quoique le roi lui eût*

which they are here treated is no less curious, as a specimen of the book. We are presented with a lecture, in a strain of lofty morality, on the duties which were incumbent upon Louis in this great emergency.[*] We are told, that he ought to have marched into Paris at the head of his guards, and put down the insurrection by the strong hand of power: his life itself was not too much to be sacrificed in the performance of this sacred obligation, so exalted is Sir Walter Scott's idea of the duties of kings; but, when the revolt was quelled, our author is pleased to say that Louis would have been infinitely criminal, if he had not given to his subjects a national representation. This is excellent advice, and admirably, no doubt, the latter part of it would have been observed, if the enterprise had succeeded; but we could have suggested something which would have been still better, viz. not to attempt to deprive his subjects of the national representation which they already possessed. This would have been less grand; it would not have called upon the monarch for any exposure of his life; but it would have prevented the insurrection. To tell us that Louis ought to have put down the tumults and to have renounced despotism, when if he had renounced despotism there would have been no tumults to put down, is a very pleasant way of begging the question against the people. Other persons besides kings would have reason to be thankful for a similar lesson of morality. You rob a man of his watch: the man discovering the theft, seizes you by the collar, and insists upon your giving back the stolen property: at this juncture Sir Walter Scott comes up, and lectures you as follows: Knock down the insolent aggressor: when you have done this, I shall then hold you infinitely criminal, if you do not restore to him his watch; but in the mean time, I will gladly assist you in chastising him, his violence deserves it!

We must not pass unnoticed another characteristic trait in our author's narrative of these transactions. When the soldiers, who were intended to overawe Paris, fraternized with the people, and refused to fire upon their fellow citizens, he can find no means of accounting for conduct so extremely un-military, except the influence of debauchery. "They were plied," says he, "with those temptations which are most powerful with soldiers—wine, women, and money, were supplied in abundance—and it was amidst debauchery and undiscipline that the French army renounced their loyalty, which used to be even too much the god of their

---

formellement prescrit d'avancer, coûte qui coûte. M. de Breteuil s'exprimait publiquement de la sorte sur cette particularité, pendant son séjour à Londres." (Vol. II, p. 81.) The reader will recollect, that from this inaction of Bezenval, Sir Walter Scott concludes, not only that Louis had *not* ordered him to attack Paris, but that he had *expressly* ordered him not even to repel force by force. [Scott, Vol. I, pp. 164-5.] No wonder; our author's knowledge of the events of this day being chiefly derived from the *Memoirs* of the veridical baron de Bezenval himself. [Pierre Joseph Victor, baron de Besenval, *Mémoires*, 4 vols. (Paris: Buisson, 1805-06); see, e.g., Vol. III, p. 411.]

[*Scott, Vol. I, pp. 159-60.]

idolatry, and which was now destroyed like the temple of Persepolis, amidst the vapours of wine, and at the instigation of courtezans."*

Does not Sir Walter Scott richly deserve the pointed sarcasm of Madame de Staël, upon the royalist party? "Un des grands malheurs de ceux qui vivent dans les cours, c'est de ne pouvoir se faire une idée de ce que c'est qu'une *nation*."† Once more, does our author really not believe in the possibility of public spirit or patriotism, or if these expressions do not please him, sincere enthusiasm? The alternative was that of being slaves or freemen, of enslaving their countrymen or helping them to be free; and he can find no more creditable motive for preferring freedom, than wine, women, and money! If Sir Walter Scott had one tenth part as much knowledge of the Revolution, as an author who writes its history ought to have, he would have known that the sentiments which, according to him, it required debauchery to excite in the regiments assembled at the metropolis, were shared by the military without the aid of debauchery, all over France. Let him read, for example, the address of the garrison of Strasbourg to the National Assembly on the 16th October, 1789, a perfect model of propriety and good taste:‡ let him read in Dumouriez's *Memoirs*§ the conduct of the garrison of Cherbourg; let him read in Bouillé's *Memoirs*,¶ or in Soulavie's Annals of Louis XVI,[*] or in the Life of Malesherbes,‖ the refusal of the troops in Dauphiné, even before the Revolution, to act against the people:** let him read in the *Histoire de la Révolution par Deux Amis de la Liberté*, numerous instances of the most sublime disinterestedness and self-devotion in these very *gardes-françaises* whom he has so unjustly inculpated, and he will then see whether these were men who needed the "vapours of wine" and the "instigation of courtezans," to impel them to act as citizens and freemen ought.[†]

We make no apology for having detained our readers so long on the first and greatest epoch of the Revolution. Where, from the immensity of the subject, much must necessarily be left undone, it is better to establish one important point thoroughly, than a hundred imperfectly. If the reader is now convinced, that Sir

Ibid., p. 154.
†Staël, *Considerations*, &c., Vol. I, p. 228.
‡In the Appendix to the first volume of Toulongeon. [P. 131; the Appendix is separately paged.]
§Vol. II, p. 48.
¶Chap. iii. [Vol. I, p. 49.]
[*Jean Louis Soulavie, *Mémoirés historiques et politiques du règne de Louis XVI*, 6 vols. (Paris: Treuttel and Würtz, 1801), Vol. VI, pp. 209-11, 268-9.]
‖*Essai sur la Vie, les Ecrits, et les Opinions, de Malesherbes*, par M. le Comte Boissy d'Anglas, Vol. II, p. 191.
**See also, on the sentiments of the army in general Madame de Staël, *Considerations*, &c., Vol. I, pp. 208, 213; and the *Memoirs* of Bertrand de Moleville, Vol. I, p. 23.
[†See *Deux amis*, Vol. I, pp. 346-51, and Vol. II, 308-17, e.g.]

Walter Scott has altogether misunderstood and misrepresented that event upon which all the subsequent history of the Revolution turns (and if he is not, we utterly despair of making any impression upon him), he will be willing to believe without much further proof, that the other great events of the Revolution are similarly dealt with. Yet, in alluding to the plots and aggressions of the royalist party against the order of things established by the Constituent Assembly, we cannot help pausing for a moment at the famous fifth of October, 1789, to give a further specimen of our author's fitness for the office of an accurate and impartial historian.

We need scarcely remind any reader, not thoroughly unacquainted with the facts of the Revolution, that, on the occasion to which we allude, the king was brought from Versailles to the Tuileries, under circumstances of considerable indignity, by a mob of Parisians who sallied out from Paris for this if for any preconcerted purpose, and by a portion of whom, during their stay at Versailles, various excesses were committed, and in particular an attempt was made (there is too much reason to believe) against the life of the queen. In all this, our author is very perfect; but he never hints that a plot existed among the royalists to convey the king to Metz, and placing him under the protection of the anti-revolutionary general Bouillé, to commence a civil war; that a variety of other intrigues were on foot for effecting a counter-revolution, and that the removal of the king from Versailles to Paris, was really on the part of the revolutionists a defensive act. Yet he would have found all this asserted not only by many writers of the constitutional party, but by the royalist Ferrières;* it has been avowed by Breteuil, Bouillé,[*] and the comte de Mercy, then ambassador of Austria at the court of France;† and it may be gathered even from the proceedings before the Châtelet, notwithstanding the strenuous efforts of that tribunal to disguise it. Our author does not scruple to quote Ferrières for an insignificant expression vaguely attributed to Barnave, which he imagines can be turned in some manner to the discredit of that distinguished person.[†] We have seen, however, that Sir Walter Scott can be very incredulous, as well as very easy of belief, when a favourite hypothesis is concerned. Even if he did not give credit to the assertion of Ferrières with respect to the royalist plots, that assertion proves at least, that their reality was generally believed; and might have suggested to our author that there may have been a more creditable motive for wishing to bring the king to Paris, than the desire of placing him and the Assembly "under the influence of popular frenzy."[‡]

But our author had a different theory. We need scarcely say, that in his theory all is ascribed to the manoeuvres of the republican party; his established mode of accounting for all the commotions under the first two national assemblies. The

---

Mémoires, Vol. I, pp. 261, 263, 277-8, Vol. II, p. 177.
[*Bouillé, Chaps. ix-xi; Vol. I, pp. 146-88, Vol. II, pp. 5-90.]
†Montgaillard, Vol. II, p. 154.
[†Scott, Vol. I, p. 206n, quoting Ferrières, Vol. I, p. 307.]
[‡Scott, Vol. I, p. 181.]

imputed object of these agitators, is of course the establishment of a republic; and he insinuates that regicide formed, even at this time, part of their ultimate intentions. Need we repeat, that this pretended republican party is a mere fiction of his own brain; that no such party existed for nearly two years afterwards; and that most of the men who subsequently composed it were, at this time, peaceably following their professions at Bordeaux or Marseilles? Will our author pretend that Mirabeau and the Duke of Orleans were republicans; or will he deny, that, by the universal admission of revolutionists and royalists, this affair was concerted by them, if concerted at all? Sir Walter Scott is not contented with inventing leaders for this popular tumult, he must invent subordinate agents for it too. "The Jacobins were the first to sound the alarm through all their clubs and societies."[*] The reader may form some conception of the accuracy of this history, and of the spirit in which it is written, when we inform him, that at this time the Jacobin club did not exist, much less any of the affiliated societies. The "alarm" was sounded, to use our author's expression, not in any club or society, but in the district assemblies, and in a place tolerably well known in the Revolution, to wit, the gardens of the Palais-Royal; not by Jacobins, but by all the more ardent and enthusiastic partisans of the Revolution, to whom indeed it is sufficiently fashionable to give that now opprobrious name, but who had nothing whatever in common with the party called the Terrorists, to whom alone the appellation of Jacobins is usually given by our author.

The reader must forgive us, if a desire to do justice to the wisest, most honest, and most calumniated, body of legislators, who ever held in their hands the destinies of a nation, induces us to be more prolix than may perhaps suit that class of minds, to whom the truth or falsehood of an historical statement is matter of indifference compared with its liveliness or dulness. It is for the maligner of the Constituent Assembly, it is for the apologist, the panegyrist, of the vindictive and sanguinary satellites of despotism, it is for him to be amusing, he knows that his readers, at least those whom he chiefly cares for, are to the full as eager to believe him, as he to be believed. It is for Sir Walter Scott to assert: *our* part must be to *prove*. Assertion is short, and proof is long: assertion is entertaining, and proof is dull: assertion may be read, as glibly and as cursorily as it is written; proof supposes thought in the writer, and demands it of the reader. Happy the historian who can permit himself to assert, for he will count ten readers to one of him who is compelled to prove!

There was scarcely a month during the first three years of the Revolution, which was not signalized by some plot or counter-revolutionary movement in the interior.* In the south of France, large bodies of armed men were repeatedly collected, for the avowed purpose of restoring the ancient order of things. The

[*Ibid., p. 184.]
*See Volumes II to VI of the *Histoire de la Révolution, par Deux Amis de la Liberté*.

assemblages which took place and the camps which were formed at Jalès and elsewhere, form a highly important, though to most persons almost an unknown, chapter of the history of the Revolution.* Armed bodies of emigrant Frenchmen were constantly hovering over the frontiers, by the connivance, and at length with the open encouragement, of the neighbouring powers: while France might be said to be without an army for her defence, the officers being counter-revolutionists almost to a man, feuds existing in most of the regiments between them and the soldiers, which were fomented even by the royalists, in order to disorganize the army, and disable it from offering any effectual resistance.[†] The ministers of the king were several of them declared anti-revolutionists. The courtiers and the privileged classes were continually giving out, that the emigrants were on the point of returning with a powerful army to dissolve the Assembly, and deliver its leaders to the rigour of the law.[‡] The royalists openly and universally asserted that the king was insincere in his professions of attachment to the new institutions; and nothing contributed more than these reports, to convert the enthusiastic attachment which was universally manifested towards him when he gave in his adhesion to the constitution, into suspicion and hatred. Ferrières has no doubt that, if Louis had put forth his authority, and exerted his personal influence over the troops, he could have crushed the Assembly;[§] and so conscious were the popular leaders of their own insecurity, that the abbé Sieyès said to a person, from whom we have the information, *toutes les nuits je vois ma tête rouler sur le plancher*. Even in 1791, the aristocrats, according to Ferrières, "ne parlaient que de guerre, de sang, et de vengeance."[¶] It was suspected at the time, it is now fully established by the avowals of the minister Bertrand de Moleville (who enters into the minutest details on the subject), that the king was in regular correspondence with the emigrants and with foreign powers, to procure his restoration to absolute authority by Austrian bayonets.[‖] Meanwhile he continued to profess, in language apparently the most feeling and sincere, his adherence to the new order of things. He came spontaneously to the Assembly on the 4th of February, 1790, to associate himself formally (such was his expression) with the plans and proceedings of the Assembly; and professed a devoted attachment to the new constitution, in a really eloquent and affecting speech, if we could suppose it to be sincere, which rendered him for a considerable time the idol of the people.[*] At the federation of July 1790

---

*See, for many interesting particulars, the work of Dampmartin, above referred to. [See, e.g., Vol. I, pp. 187ff.]

[†]Ferrières, Vol. II, p. 99.

[‡]*Ibid.*, p. 100.

[§]*Ibid.*, Vol. I, p. 391.

[¶]*Ibid.*, Vol. II, p. 254.

[‖]*Mémoires particuliers*, &c. par Bertrand de Moleville, Vol. I, pp. 371, 373, 375, 377; Vol. II, pp. 309, 312-13, 317, 323ff., 329, 331-2.

[*"Discours prononcé par le roi à l'assemblée nationale" (4 Feb., 1790), *Gazette Nationale, ou Le Moniteur Universel*, 6 Feb., 1790, pp. 147-8.]

(an event of which, strange to say, our author makes no mention), he solemnly swore adherence to the constitution; he spontaneously renewed his oath but a few weeks before his flight from Paris;* he spontaneously addressed to his ambassadors abroad, for communication to the courts at which they were accredited, a long letter, embodying every thing in sentiment which was constitutional, and revolutionary, and such as La Fayette himself would have dictated, together with the firmest assurances that he highly approved of the Revolution; that France's greatest enemies were the enemies of the new order of things, and that the pretence that he was not free was a calumny:† again and again he solemnly assured La Fayette, Rochambeau, and others, that he had no intention of flying; and this almost up to the very day when he fled to join the allies, leaving behind him a solemn protestation against all which had been done since the 5th of October 1789, from which date, he pretended, his want of liberty had rendered the sanction which he had given to all the decrees of the Assembly, a nullity.[*]

We do not recite these facts for the sake of casting reproach upon the memory of Louis. His faults have been bitterly expiated. But, in bare justice to the men who, after all this, had the generosity to replace him on the throne, it ought to be considered whether they had not reason to be niggardly of power to such a king, so circumstanced; a king, whose word, whose oath, was an empty sound; a king, incapable of adhering to his firmest convictions, and surrounded by persons who, if he formed an honest resolution, never suffered him to keep it.

If we have had any success at all in convincing our readers, we have now made it apparent to them, that the Constituent Assembly understood their own position, and that of their country, far better than Sir Walter Scott imagines; and that if they did not adopt the course which he, judging after the event, imagines would have prevented the ills which befel their country, it was not because they were less wise than he, but because they were wiser. No course which they could have adopted would have been so dangerous, as to establish a vigorous and efficient executive government with Louis at its head. And few will blame them for not having adopted the only third course which was open to them, the deposition and confinement of the king; few will deny that, before proceeding to this last and most painful extremity, such a scheme of limited monarchy as they attempted was an experiment which they would not have been excusable if they had refused to try. It is on the probabilities of success which this scheme held out, that we ground the

*Mémoires de Dumouriez, Vol. II, p. 111, &c. &c.
†This letter may be found entire in the Appendix to the second volume [pp. 419-22] of Dumouriez's Memoirs, forming part of the collection of Memoirs on the Revolution, now publishing at Paris. [Collection des mémoires relatifs à la révolution française, ed. Saint-Albin Berville and Jean François Barrière, 68 vols. (Paris: Baudoin, 1820-28).] It may not be useless to remark, that our references to the pages of any work forming part of this collection, are to be understood of that edition, unless otherwise expressed.
[*"Proclamation du roi à tous les Français à sa sortie de Paris" (20 June, 1791), Gazette Nationale, ou Le Moniteur Universel, 22 June, 1791, p. 718.]

justification of the Constituent Assembly; it is on the failure of the experiment, that we rest our defence of the Gironde, or, as our author terms it, the Republican party, who succeeded them.

None have sustained so much injustice at the hands of our author as this last, and most unfortunate party: of none have the conduct and aims been so miserably misunderstood, so cruelly perverted. The following extract is a very favourable specimen of his mode of treating them.

After saying that the Girondist party was "determined that the Revolution should never stop until the downfal of the monarchy," our author continues:

Its most distinguished champions were men bred as lawyers in the south of France, who had, by mutual flattery, and the habit of living much together, acquired no small portion of that self-conceit and over-weening opinion of each other's talents, which may be frequently found among small provincial associations for political or literary purposes. Many had eloquence, and most of them a high fund of enthusiasm, which a classical education, and their intimate communication with each other, where each idea was caught up, lauded, re-echoed, and enhanced, had exalted into a spirit of republican zeal. They doubtless had personal ambition, but in general it seems not to have been of a low or selfish character. Their aims were often honourable though visionary, and they marched with great courage towards their proposed goal, with the vain purpose of erecting a pure republic in a state so disturbed as that of France, and by hands so polluted as those of their Jacobin associates. It will be recorded, however, to the disgrace of their pretensions to stern republican virtue, that the Girondists were willing to employ, for the accomplishment of their purpose, those base and guilty tools which afterwards effected their own destruction. They were for using the revolutionary means of insurrection and violence, until the republic should be established, and no longer; or, in the words of the satirist,

> For letting Rapine loose, and Murther,
> To rage just so far, but no further;
> And setting all the land on fire,
> To burn to a scantling, but no higher.*

He afterwards terms them, in a spirit of more bitter contempt, "the association of philosophical rhapsodists, who hoped to oppose pikes with syllogisms, and to govern a powerful country by the discipline of an academy."[†]

He derides "the affected and pedantic fanaticism of republican zeal of the Girondists, who were amusing themselves with schemes, to which the country of France, the age and the state of manners were absolutely opposed."[‡]

And elsewhere, he calls them, "the Brissotin, or Girondist faction" (he seldom, if ever, terms the supporters of despotism a faction), "who, though averse to the existence of a monarchy, and desiring a republic instead, had still somewhat more

---

*Scott, Vol. I, pp. 264-6. [The concluding verse is Samuel Butler, *Hudibras* (1678), ed. Zachary Grey, 2 vols. (London: Vernor and Hood, *et al.*, 1801), Vol. II, p. 307 (Pt. III, Canto ii, ll. 1043-6).]

[†]Scott, Vol. I, p. 269.

[‡]*Ibid.*, p. 313.

of principle and morals than the mere Revolutionists and Jacobins, who were altogether destitute of both."*

The utmost which he can find to say in behalf of the purest and most disinterested body of men, considered as a party, who ever figured in history, among whose leaders not so much as one man of even *doubtful* integrity and honour can be found, is, that they had "somewhat more" of principle and morals, than persons who were "altogether destitute of both"!

His commendations of one of their number are less sparingly bestowed.

> In raking up the disgusting history of mean and bloody-minded demagogues, it is impossible not to dwell on the contrast afforded by the generous and self-devoted character of Barbaroux, who young, handsome, generous, noble-minded, and disinterested, sacrificed his family-happiness, his fortune, and finally his life, to an enthusiastic, though mistaken, zeal for the liberty of his country.†

Unquestionably nothing can be better deserved than this panegyric; but why is a particular individual singled out to be the subject of it, when he, although excellent, was only one among many, alike in all the noble qualities which adorned this favourite of our author, and for the misery of France, alike also in their unhappy fate? Justice required that the same measure should be dealt out to them as to Barbaroux, even if it were true that their zeal for the liberty of their country was a "mistaken" zeal, and that they were for using the "revolutionary means of insurrection and violence" to establish a republic. But their zeal was not a mistaken zeal, and they were not for establishing a republic by insurrection and violence; most of them did not contemplate a republic at all, and designed at most nothing further than to depose the king, and elevate the young prince royal, under the direction of a council of regency, to the constitutional throne.

These may be startling assertions to some, who have formed their opinions solely from the indefatigable perseverance with which Sir Walter Scott, almost in every page, assures us of the contrary: but however paradoxical here, on the other side of the channel they are established truths, which few persons indeed of any party think of disputing, and of which nothing but the profound ignorance of our countrymen on the Revolution, could render it necessary to offer any proof: especially as this is not in any degree a question of opinion and reasoning, but one of mere fact and evidence, which every person, who has read the authorities carefully, is competent to decide.

We have already mentioned, that the first germ of a republican party appeared in France, when the king, after a long course of dissimulation and insincerity, fled from the capital, and was brought back by force. Notwithstanding the decisive evidence which he had thus afforded of his undiminished hostility to the constitution, the predominant party in the Constituent Assembly thought fit to

*Ibid., p. 307.
†Ibid., p. 342.

restore him to the throne. We are far from contending that they ought to have acted otherwise, although Sir Walter Scott is of that opinion, and maintains that they were alike wrong in again offering, and Louis in accepting, the constitutional crown.[*] What is now his opinion, was that of many of the more ardent revolutionists at the time; and, among the rest, of a few who subsequently became aggregated to the Gironde party; for the great majority, including those from whom that party derives its distinctive name, were not in Paris until they came thither as members of the second National Assembly. In July 1791, before the resolution had been definitively taken to reinstate the king, a meeting was held in the Champ de Mars to subscribe a petition calling for his dethronement.[†] In this document no change in the monarchical constitution of France, as decreed by the Constituent Assembly, was hinted at: but the acknowledged fact, that the petition was drawn up by Brissot, whose speculative opinions were certainly republican, together with an expression of Brissot and Pétion, about the same time, which is recorded by Madame Roland, "qu'il fallait préparer les esprits à la république,"[‡] and the fact, that a newspaper under the title of *The Republican* was set on foot at this period by Brissot and Condorcet (although it only reached the second number), seem to render it probable, that if they had succeeded in obtaining the deposition of Louis, they would really have made an effort for the establishment of a republican government in preference to a change of monarch.* When the Assembly, however, under the guidance of Barnave and Chapelier, esteemed up to that time the most democratic of the popular leaders, re-established royalty in the person of the former sovereign, the idea of a republic was dropped, and the two or three men who had entertained it became amalgamated with the general body of the Girondist party, who, as we have previously stated, were not republicans.

The difference between the Constitutionalists and the Gironde, at the opening of the second, or Legislative Assembly, is thus expressed by Mignet: "Il [the Gironde party] n'avait alors aucun projet subversif; mais il était disposé à défendre la révolution de toutes les manières, à la différence des constitutionnels, qui ne voulaient la défendre qu'avec la loi."[§] This assertion of Mignet (whom however we do not cite as an authority, since he was not, any more than ourselves, a contemporary and actor in the scene) is borne out by the direct testimony of every credible witness who had any tolerable means of knowing the fact. It is demonstrated as cogently by the recorded acts and speeches of the men themselves.

[*_Ibid._, p. 255.]
[†See _Deux amis_, Vol. VIII, p. 73.]
[‡_Mémoires_, Vol. I, p. 351.]
*We are also assured by Ferrières, Vol. II, p. 347, that Brissot at this time proposed a republican government in the Jacobin club; and a proclamation to the same effect by his friend Achille Duchâtelet, which was placarded in the streets of Paris, is given verbatim by the same author, pp. 388-91.
[§Mignet, _Histoire_, p. 206. Mill's words in square brackets.]

Sir Walter Scott, as we have already observed, has allowed, has asserted indeed, with more confidence than we should venture to do, that the reasons for deposing Louis preponderated, at the time of his return from Varennes, over those for retaining him on the throne.[*] These reasons, which our author considered sufficient, could be no others, than the certainty of the king's insincerity, and the necessity of having a first magistrate sincerely attached to the constitution. Let us reflect how vastly more imminent that necessity had become, in the interval which separated the meeting of the second National Assembly from the memorable 10th of August 1792.

During this period, a new and most formidable element of danger had been introduced into the already perilous and embarrassing state of public affairs. A foreign despot had not only countenanced the emigrants in their warlike preparations, and in assuming a hostile attitude on the frontier, but had presumed to require, as a condition of friendship between the two governments, the re-establishment of the monarchy upon the footing of the royal declaration of the 23rd of June, 1789.[†] War had ensued; its commencement had been disastrous, an invasion was at hand, and the disorganization of the army, from the general relaxation of discipline, the emigration of most of the officers, and the want of military experience in the soldiers, had reached to such a height, that nothing but the most unheard-of efforts, such efforts as were at last made by Dumouriez and Carnot, could give the nation a chance of saving herself from the enemies of her freedom. It was not in such times as these that France could be preserved by men who were only half desirous that she should extricate herself from her difficulties. There were needed other "organizers of victory"[‡] than a chief magistrate who sympathized with the invaders of his country more than with his country itself. It was not from Louis that exertions could be expected for the prosecution of a war against his own brothers, and the assertors of his absolute authority. Yet not so soon did the Gironde renounce the hope of saving at once their country and the king. Louis, who was as vacillating in his choice of counsellors as in his counsels, had changed from a purely royalist to a mixed administration composed of constitutionalists and royalists. The divisions which speedily arose in this motley ministry (our author is here, as usual, most elaborately wrong) had terminated by the dismissal of the leading constitutional minister,[§] which the Assembly soon caused to be succeeded by the forced retirement of his royalist colleagues. Louis selected his next ministers from the ranks of the Gironde; and so far was this party from entertaining any hostility to the king, that Roland and Clavières, as Madame

[*Scott, Vol. I, p. 256.]

[†Leopold II, Letter to Louis XVI (3 Dec., 1791), *Gazette Nationale, ou Le Moniteur Universel*, 26 Dec., 1791, p. 1505.]

[‡Mill is adapting a well-known description of Carnot; see *Mémoires historiques et militaires sur Carnot*, ed. Saint-Albin Berville and Jean François Barrière (Paris: Baudouin, 1824), pp. 69-70.]

[§Louis Marie Jacques Amalric, comte de Narbonne-Lara.]

Roland informs us,[*] were at first completely the dupes of his apparent sincerity. Had he consented to the strong measures which they deemed necessary to secure the constitution against its foreign and internal enemies, they would have continued in office, and Louis probably, had remained constitutional monarch of France. But he refused to sanction the two decrees of the Assembly, for the banishment of the non-juring priests,* and for the formation of a camp of twenty thousand men under the walls of Paris.[†] The discussions consequent on this refusal occasioned the dismissal of the Girondist ministers, and ultimately produced the downfall of the throne: not however until the leading Girondists had made another effort to save the unfortunate and misguided monarch, which we shall relate in the words of their friend and apologist Bailleul.

J'ai déjà dit plusieurs fois dans le cours de cet ouvrage, et je viens de répéter tout à l'heure, que le parti républicain se formait insensiblement, et n'existait pas. En effet, l'autorité royale circonvenue, obsédée par les intrigues et les projets de la conspiration, ne laissait plus même échapper de ces lueurs de bonne volonté qui avaient jusque-là soutenu l'espoir des patriotes. Que faire? Que résoudre dans cet état d'anxiété? L'établissement d'une république se présentait à eux comme une dernière ressource, s'il était impossible de sauver autrement la liberté, contre laquelle toutes les forces étaient dirigées.

Puisque Madame de Staël[†] veut bien accorder quelque valeur aux députés que l'on a désignés sous le nom de Girondins,[‡] a-t-elle pu croire que des hommes de ce talent, tout grand qu'était leur enthousiasme, n'aient pas quelquefois réfléchi sur la position où se trouvait la France, et qu'ils se soient ainsi précipités en aveugles dans les événemens les plus affreux et les plux épouvantables? A-t-elle pu croire même qu'ils n'aient pas prévu les dangers dont cette conflagration les menaçait personnellement? Ce serait une bien grande erreur. Non-seulement ils y avaient pensé, mais ils en étaient occupés, et singulièrement préoccupés: on en jugera par le récit suivant.

Je ne crois pas me tromper, en disant que les trois hommes les plus distingués du parti appelé de la Gironde, étaient Vergniaud, Guadet, et Gensonné. Vergniaud, l'un des orateurs les plus éloquens qui aient jamais parlé aux hommes, avait une âme encore bien au-dessus de son talent. Guadet, d'un caractère emporté, était un homme de beaucoup d'esprit, plein de franchise, et capable de revenir à toutes les idées saines et raisonnables. La gravité de Gensonné eût pû passer en proverbe: esprit méditatif et profond, chacune de ses paroles, même dans la conversation, était pesée et mûrie avant d'être livrée à l'examen et à

[*Mémoires, Vol. I, p. 362.]

*["Décret sur les prêtres non-sermentés" (27 May, 1792), Gazette Nationale, ou Le Moniteur Universel, 4 June, 1792, p. 647; for Louis XVI's refusal to sanction it, see ibid., 20 June, 1792.] Sir Walter Scott cannot refrain from imputing this decree, though purely political in its object, to philosophic intolerance, and an intention of degrading and subverting the national faith. [Scott, Vol. I, p. 300.] But it is useless to expose in further detail these endless instances of blind and obstinate prejudice.

[†"Décret d'augmentation de vingt mille hommes pour l'armée" (8 June, 1792), Gazette Nationale, ou Le Moniteur Universel, 9 June, 1792, p. 668; for Louis XVI's refusal to sanction it, see ibid., 20 June, 1792, p. 716.]

†To understand this allusion, it must be remembered, that Bailleul's work was suggested and occasioned by Madame de Staël's Considerations.

[‡Staël, Considérations, Vol. II, p. 28.]

la réflexion des autres. On fera peut-être bien à des hommes de cette supériorité, la grâce de croire, sans que j'insiste, qu'ils ne se sont pas trouvés environnés de toutes les circonstances extraordinaires et redoutables, sans y donner quelqu'attention. Voici ce que Vergniaud et Gensonné ont répété nombre de fois devant moi, et tous les prisonniers qui se trouvaient alors à la Conciergerie, du côté nommé des *douze*.

Ils avaient cherché à se ménager une entrevue avec Thierry, valet-de-chambre du roi. Cette entrevue eut lieu. Là, Vergniaud, Guadet et Gensonné exposèrent à Thierry les dangers de la patrie et les dangers personnels du roi; ils lui en indiquèrent les causes, et, par suite, ils tracèrent des plans de conduite, au moyen desquels des rapprochemens indispensables, si l'on ne voulait livrer l'état aux plus horribles convulsions, auraient lieu.

Thierry, accoutumé à n'entendre que les choses les plus dégoûtantes sur le compte de ces hommes; qui, comme tout ce qui composait l'entourage du roi, croyait être généreux à leur égard, en pensant qu'ils ne mangeaient pas des petits enfans, fut on ne peut plus ébahi de tant de franchise, de raison et de prévoyance; je dois dire plus, il en fut touché: il leur exprima à quel point il était enchanté de les avoir entendus; il ne leur dissimula point combien cette ouverture lui donnait de consolations et d'espérances, et il les termina en les priant de mettre par écrit tout ce qu'il venait d'entendre, s'ils l'autorisaient à en faire part au roi. La proposition fut acceptée avec empressement. On se sépara, en convenant du jour où l'on se réunirait. Tous furent exacts au rendez-vous. Un mémoire contenant le fond de ce qui avait été dit à Thierry dans la première conférence, lui fut remis. Il promit de le communiquer aussitôt au roi, et de faire connaître sa réponse; ce qui donna lieu à une troisième réunion, dans laquelle Thierry, fondant en larmes, déclara que l'on ne voulait entendre à aucun rapprochement. Vergniaud lui répondit: Dites bien à votre maître que nous ne nous dissimulons pas nos propres dangers, mais qu'à partir de ce moment il n'est plus en notre pouvoir de le sauver. Voilà ce que j'ai entendu dire, répéter, et répéter encore par Vergniaud et par Gensonné. Guadet n'était pas avec nous à la Conciergerie, il était en fuite. Ce mémoire, confié par eux à Thierry, s'est, autant qu'il m'en souvient, retrouvé dans l'armoire de fer, et l'on en fit un des chefs les plus graves de l'accusation de ses auteurs.[*]

This *Mémoire*, admirable for its good sense and good feeling, may be seen in the Appendix to the second volume of the *Memoirs* of Dumouriez, as recently reprinted at Paris.[†] It is with difficulty that we refrain from increasing the length of an already long article, by transcribing this document into our pages. We beseech the reader to refer to it, to read it diligently, and then endure, if he can, to hear these men represented as conspirators, who plotted the destruction of royalty, who watched the king's acts with a desire to find them such as afforded a hold for misrepresentation, and were never so well pleased as when he rendered himself unpopular, and gave pretexts for holding up his office as a nuisance, and himself as an enemy of the people. We cannot deny ourselves the pleasure of employing, for the expression of our own feelings, the affecting words of M. Bailleul.

O vous qui serez grands dans la postérité, vous dont je reçus, avec vos derniers adieux, les protestations d'un amour si sincère, si ardent pour votre patrie, l'expression si pure de vos voeux pour le bonheur de vos concitoyens; vous qui versiez des larmes si amères sur les malheurs de ces temps, et qui en retraciez les causes avec tant de justesse et d'énergie,

[*Bailleul, *Examen critique*, Vol. II, pp. 42-6.]
[†"Copie de la lettre écrite au citoyen Boze, par Guadet, Vergniaud et Gensonné," in Dumouriez, Vol. II, pp. 422-6.]

auriez-vous jamais cru qu'on eût pu vous accuser d'avoir bouleversé la France pour le plaisir d'essayer un systême de gouvernement absolument nouveau pour elle, et qu'une femme aimant la liberté, par conséquent la vérité, écrirait, sous les yeux des témoins de votre courage, de votre sublime dévouement et de vos derniers momens, ces paroles: "Les Girondins voulurent la république, et ne parvinrent qu'à renverser la monarchie?"[*] Ils ne voulaient que la liberté; une monarchie constitutionnelle franchement établie eût fait leur bonheur. M. de Lally, cité par Madame de Staël, en proclamant que *leur existence et leur mort furent également funestes à la patrie*,[†] a commis dans la première partie de son assertion une effroyable injustice; il a prouvé qu'il ne soupçonnait même pas les causes véritables des événemens qui se sont succédés avec tant de rapidité à cette époque.*

Greatly as we have already exceeded the usual limits of an article, we cannot permit ourselves to leave the stain which is attempted to be cast upon men in so many respects admirable, imperfectly washed away. We should feel as if we had violated a duty, if we did not exhibit by ample evidence how unanimously men of all parties have concurred in exculpating the Girondists from the imputations now sought to be fixed upon them by Sir Walter Scott. We shall offer no apology to the reader for heaping up a multitude of attestations; we do not *solicit* his attention to this mass of evidence, we *demand* it. We demand it in the name and in behalf of the whole human race, whom it deeply imports that justice should be done, at least by another age, to the few statesmen who have cared for their happiness. Does the man exist who, having read the accusation brought against such men, will consider it too much trouble to listen to the defence? Let such amuse themselves with romance; it belongs to other men to read history.

Our first quotation shall be drawn from the *Histoire de la Révolution de France, par Deux Amis de la Liberté*, one of the most impartial works which have appeared on the subject of the Revolution, and written, as our quotation will shew, in a spirit very far indeed from being favourable to the Gironde:

La vérité est, que ni les uns ni les autres [the Gironde nor the Montagne] ne pensoient à cette époque à fonder une république en France. Le parti de la Gironde ou de Brissot, fier d'appartenir à une ville qui s'étoit, plus qu'aucune autre, fait remarquer par un ardent amour pour la liberté, comptant d'ailleurs sur le talent de la plupart des individus qui le composoient, vouloit s'illustrer par quelque coup d'éclat, soit en se rendant maître des volontés d'un monarque au moins avili, soit en le faisant descendre d'un trône où il ne pouvoit plus être qu'un objet de dérision, afin d'y placer son fils dont ils auroient dirigé l'enfance, exercé les pouvoirs et distribué les faveurs. S'il n'est pas démontré par des preuves écrites, que ce fussent-là les intentions ultérieures de Brissot et des députés de la Gironde, ou de ceux qui suivoient la même bannière, le projet n'en est pas moins incontestable, pour tous les hommes qui ont un peu observé la conduite des intrigans qui s'agitoient alors, et je dirai à ceux qui peuvent en douter, rappelez-vous les discours des chefs, quelques jours avant que le canon écrasât le château des Tuileries, vous les verrez éperdus, essayant de soutenir, pour quelque tems encore, le colosse ruiné qu'ils avoient

[*Staël, *Considérations*, Vol. II, p. 28.]
[†*Ibid.*, pp. 28-9.]
*Bailleul, *Examen Critique*, Vol. II, pp. 46-7.

eux-mêmes sappé par ses bases; vous les verrez effrayés de l'audace de ceux dont jusqu'alors ils avoient su diriger les mouvemens, qu'ils avoient regardés comme des machines dont ils avoient cru pouvoir disposer à volonté; vous les verrez prévoir les désordres sanglans auxquels cette troupe avide de trésors, avide de pouvoirs dont elle étoit incapable de jouir, devoit nécessairement s'abandonner: mais il n'étoit plus tems, l'abîme qu'ils avoient eux-mêmes ouvert étoit sous leurs pas; il n'y avoit plus d'espoir rétrograde, il fallait suivre le torrent, et s'y précipiter.

Au surplus, leur conduite publique prouvoit assez qu'ils ne vouloient qu'une simple déchéance. Dans toutes les adresses qu'ils se faisoient faire contre le roi, on ne demandoit que la déchéance, on ne parloit que de la déchéance, en maintenant l'acte constitutionnel, jamais on n'y insinua le mot de république.

Mais voici un fait plus positif: lorsque, pour porter le dernier coup de massue à Louis XVI, on fit venir à la barre les prétendues sections de Paris, le maire à leur tête, Pétion, l'intime ami de Brissot, et la plus vigoureuse colonne du parti; Pétion, introduit dans la salle du corps législatif, tout enivré de sa gloire présente, et encore plus de celle qui l'attendoit, dit hautement, et avec une naïveté qui n'étoit qu'à lui, aux députés qui faisoient grouppe à l'entrée de la salle: *Ma foi, Messieurs, je vois que la régence me tombe sur la tête, je ne sais pas comment m'en défendre.* Et ce propos, ou tel autre semblable, il l'a répété plusieurs fois; des personnes qui l'ont entendu, et qui vivent encore, peuvent dire si on en impose. (Vol. VII, pp. 12-15.)

Compare this account of the conduct and designs of the Gironde with that of Sir Walter Scott. Need we say more?

Our next citation shall be from Toulongeon, also a constitutional monarchist, equal to the author last quoted in impartiality, and far superior to him in philosophy. We shall not quote from this writer any of the passages in which he denies the existence of a republican party at the commencement of the Revolution. In his account of the events which followed the king's flight, he says, "La république n'était alors même, ni dans l'opinion de ceux qui réfléchissaient, ni dans le sentiment de ceux qu'il détermine toujours seuls" (Vol. II, p. 49). Of the Gironde at the opening of the second national assembly, he remarks, "Ce parti ne voulait pas la république; mais la marche de ce parti rendit la république nécessaire" (Vol. II, p. 91). Even in June, 1792, "Vergniaud, Isnard, étaient des chefs du parti de la Gironde: ils voulaient mettre l'autorité royale dans leur dépendance; mais ils ne voulaient pas la détruire en l'avilissant" (Vol. II, p. 171). Again, "Vergniaud, Guadet, tout ce qu'on appelait la Gironde, parce que les députés de ce département s'y faisaient le plus remarquer, voulut d'abord gouverner la royauté, plus encore par son influence et par son crédit, que par l'autorité, qu'ils aimaient mieux distribuer qu'exercer; et lorsque la royauté fut abolie, ils voulurent fonder la république par les moyens licites et avec les formes légales" (Vol. III, p. 9). And, finally, of Vergniaud, on the very day of the subversion of the throne, "Au dix Août, il voulait encore une monarchie systématique peut-être, mais tempérée. Dès que le mot république fut proclamé, il fut républicain." (Vol. IV, p. 11.)[*] These are Sir Walter Scott's fanatical

[*Mill's reference is incorrect, and the passage has not been located.]

enthusiasts, who plotted the destruction of royalty for years before, and made no scruple of employing insurrection and bloodshed to realize their visionary projects of a pure republic.

"Quoique la faction des Girondins," says Soulavie, "fût un composé de toute sorte d'opinions, sa majorité a voulu une régence pendant la minorité du fils de Louis XVI, pour gouverner et pour perdre la reine, dont les projets connus de contre-révolution mettaient en péril, non-seulement l'existence politique mais la vie même des Girondins."* If we were disposed to place much dependence upon anecdotes, which are only related by this author, we could transcribe several which he adduces to show that not only down to the subversion of the throne, but almost to the very day when the convention met and the republic was proclaimed, neither the Gironde nor the Montagne had finally decided upon establishing it: we could quote the story which he tells of the almost ludicrous consternation of Condorcet and Sieyès, when this event was reported to them,[†] and the declaration of the minister Montmorin to Soulavie himself, that a republic was then the least bad of all governments which were likely to be established, but that what the Gironde desired was a regency, which would be infinitely worse.[*] As we have less confidence, however, in the testimony of Soulavie, than in that of either of the writers whom we have before quoted, we allude to his evidence only in confirmation of theirs, and shall proceed to show that the royalists themselves, even those among them who have spoken of the Gironde with the most bitter hatred, have by no means accused them of being republicans, but of wishing for a king who should distribute honours and places among themselves, or, at most, of being indifferent to every form of government, provided they themselves were at the head of it. We have no apprehension that these last imputations should be believed, for Sir Walter Scott himself does ample justice to the character of the Girondists, as far as regards personal views; but, that the only accusation brought against them by their bitterest enemies should be that of selfish ambition,[†] proves at least the extreme absurdity of the charge of fanatical republicanism, and the following passages further add the direct testimony of the most decided, and the most trustworthy of the royalist writers, to the fact that most of these statesmen were not republicans.

We shall begin with Ferrières, generally the most candid and impartial of the royalists, but whose moderation entirely deserts him when he touches upon the Girondists. This writer particularly distinguishes the Girondist party from the republicans. Among the latter, he ranks Buzot and Pétion; but of the Girondists, especially the deputies of the Gironde itself, Vergniaud, Guadet, Gensonné,

*Soulavie, *Mémoires*, Vol. VI, p. 450.
†*Ibid.*, pp. 454-6.
[*Ibid.*, pp. 463-5.]
[†See Jean Baptiste Amar's speech in presenting the "acte d'accusation" against the Girondists (3 Oct., 1793), *Procès-verbal de la convention nationale*, Vol. XXII, pp. 55-6.]

Ducos, and Fonfrède, he says, "Les Girondins étaient assez indifférens à la forme du gouvernement pourvu qu'ils gouvernassent et qu'ils pussent disposer de l'argent et des places; mais sentant que les constitutionnels ne lâcheraient pas leur proie, ils se rallièrent aux républicains, attendant à prendre un parti décidé d'après les événemens, et à se vendre à la cour ou à se donner à la république, selon que l'exigeraient leurs intérêts et les circonstances" (Vol. III, pp. 16-17). Assuredly, if these persons had shown the slightest symptom of fanatical attachment to a republican government, and hatred of royalty, such things could not have been said of them. Again, long after the insurrection, or rather tumult, of the 20th June 1792, we are told by Ferrières, "les Girondins ne voulaient qu'effrayer la cour. La déchéance n'entrait pas alors dans leurs vues," (Vol. III, p. 165): that Pétion opposed the insurrection of the 10th of August, because it was the wish of the Gironde that the deposition of Louis should be decreed by the Assembly, and executed without tumult or violence (p. 178); that the Gironde had no concern in that insurrection (p. 180); that they were astonished at it (p. 182); that even at the opening of the convention, "la république n'était point définitivement arrêtée dans l'opinion des Girondins" (p. 245); and was carried independently of them, by what he terms the republican party.

Our next authority shall be Bertrand de Moleville, a royalist far more inveterately prejudiced than Ferrières; a man who avowedly disapproves of the introduction of any form of representative government into France, and cannot quite reconcile himself to its existence in England; and this man, it is important to observe, was a minister of Louis within a few months preceding his deposition. This author always speaks of the Girondists in the bitterest terms, and even accuses them of what we believe was never imputed to them by any other writer (it was scarcely insinuated even in the *acte d'accusation* against them, by the horrible Amar),[*] we mean personal corruption. After speaking of the letter (formerly alluded to) which was addressed to the king by the *trois scélérats* (it is thus that he designates Vergniaud, Guadet, and Gensonné)*—of which letter he seems to confess that he knew the contents only at second-hand (he certainly gives a most incorrect account of them), he next describes a plan of insurrection, which he affirms to have been devised by the Gironde in consequence of the ill success of their attempt to conciliate the king; and hereupon he observes,

Les chefs du parti de la Gironde, qui avaient conçu et dirigé ce plan, n'avaient point alors le projet de détruire le gouvernement monarchique; ils voulaient seulement que la déchéance du roi fût prononcée, pour faire passer la couronne à son fils, et établir un conseil de régence qu'ils auraient composé de leurs créatures, s'ils n'avaient pu s'y placer eux-mêmes, et sur lequel ils auraient eu, dans tous les cas, assez d'influence pour être assurés d'en obtenir tout l'argent et tous les emplois qu'ils auraient demandés; mais, comme il était bien plus aisé d'exciter une insurrection violente, que de la modérer à volonté, et d'en

[*Ibid.]
*Vol. II, p. 111.

obtenir précisément tels ou tels résultats, ils n'auraient pas hésité à abandonner ce plan, si le roi avait voulu consentir à rappeler au ministère trois scélérats [by this polite expression we are here to understand Roland, Servan and Clavières] qui leur étaient trop servilement dévoués, pour oser leur rien refuser. (Vol. II, p. 122.)

The abbé Georgel, a Jesuit, than whom the abbé Barruel himself scarcely regards the Revolution with a more frantic abhorrence, takes precisely the same view of the conduct and designs of the Gironde.* We shall not prolong our article by quoting, in the *ipsissima verba* of this author, any portion of his dull abuse. The substance of it is all contained in the passages which we have already quoted from Bertrand and Ferrières.

It will be thought, probably, that we have rather been too profuse than too sparing of evidence to prove Sir Walter Scott ignorant of his subject, and the story of the reckless enthusiasm and republican zeal of the Girondists a romance. It will amuse the reader to compare the above quotations with the passages which we previously transcribed from Sir Walter Scott. They contradict him point-blank in every particular, whether of praise or of blame. In support of his view of the Gironde we can find only one authority, that of Madame de Staël;[*] the most questionable of all witnesses, when she deposes to any facts but those within her own immediate observation. We have not nearly exhausted the evidence on the other side. We have cited as yet none of the witnesses who may be supposed partial to the Gironde, except Bailleul, from whom, moreover, we have drawn but a small part of the testimony which his highly instructive pages afford. We shall only further direct the attention of the reader to Lavallée, a writer of no very decided political opinions, but friendly to the Gironde, being personally acquainted with their principal leaders, and having been an *employé* of Roland, when minister of the interior. From him we have an interesting statement of what passed at a secret meeting of the leading Girondists and one or two other persons. They were all agreed that France was in a state nearly approximating to anarchy; that it would remain so, until there was a change of government; and that, with a view to this change, it was above all to be desired, that the king should voluntarily abdicate; but they were by no means agreed, supposing that a change could be brought about, what the change should be. Brissot declared strongly for a republic; Gensonné desired time for consideration; Condorcet and Guadet were not indisposed to a proposition which was made, of elevating the prince of Conti to the Regency; and, when the meeting broke up, nothing had been resolved upon.[†] If any decision was subsequently come to, the appointment of the Girondist ministry, which took place

---

*Georgel, *Mémoires*, Vol. III, pp. 361-2, *et passim* [Jean François Georgel and Augustin Barruel, *Mémoires pour servir à l'histoire du jacobinisme*, 4 vols. (London: Boussonnier, 1797-98)].

[*Considérations*, Vol. II, pp. 28-31.]

†[Lavallée,] *Histoire des Factions de la Révolution Française*, Vol. I, pp. 199-213.

subsequently, must naturally have altered it; and what is known of their subsequent plans has been already stated.

We shall here take our leave, both of the Girondists and of Sir Walter Scott. We have left much unsaid, which cannot so properly be said on any other occasion; many misrepresentations unanswered, which it would have been of importance to expose. We would willingly have entered into considerable details respecting the royalist party, whose faults our author has extenuated as much as he has exaggerated those of the revolutionists; respecting the *Montagnards*, some of whom individually he has treated with great injustice, and of whose character and principles of action, as a body, he has no more than the most superficial conception; respecting the *libéraux* of the present day, whom he has treated, in the latter part of his work, with greater asperity and unfairness than is shewn towards the revolutionists themselves.* We could have wished to take notice of his sophisms on the Napoleon Code,[*] and on every subject, without exception, connected with English institutions and English politics; sophisms which are adapted to the state of all these different questions twenty years ago, and which prove that from that time he has kept his eyes closed to all that has been passing around him, and can neither accommodate his mode of defence to the present modes of attack, nor to the existing state of the public mind. But we must forbear all this; and in conclusion, we shall only say, that with all the faults which we have pointed out

---

*Every one who knows what the *libéraux* of the present century are, is aware that they comprise every shade of political opinion from Mounier to Carnot. Our author, however, industriously identifies all of them with the extinct, and now universally detested, sect of Jacobins. As an example of his mode of dealing with individuals, we may instance his treatment of Comte, known to all Europe as the intrepid writer who, at great personal risk, vindicated the principles of constitutional freedom in the *Censeur Européen*, at a time when there were few to aid him in the glorious conflict; and who has suffered five years exile, and the mean-spirited persecution of the Holy Alliance, in consequence of his manly and stedfast adherence to liberal opinions. This individual, of whom Sir Walter Scott is so consummately ignorant as to have discovered the correct orthography of his name only time enough to insert it in the Errata, he does not scruple to accuse of having been "a promoter of Bonaparte's return." [Scott, Vol. VIII, p. 422; Comte's name appears as "Lecompte."] Will it be believed, that when Napoleon was in full march towards Paris, M. Comte published a pamphlet, which went through three editions in as many days, denouncing the imperial government as tyrannical, and calling upon the French people to resist the usurper! [François Charles Louis Comte, *De l'impossibilité d'établir un gouvernement constitutionnel sous un chef militaire, et particulièrement sous Napoléon* (Paris: Les marchands de nouveautés, 1815).] This work (of which we possess a copy) was translated and widely circulated in Germany, as a proof that the enlightened portion of the French people were hostile to Bonaparte. [*Über die Unmöglichkeit einer constitutionellen Regierung unter einem militärischen Oberhaupte, besonders unter Napoleon*, trans. T. von Haupt (Cologne: Dumont, Bachmann, 1815).] Let the reader give credit after this to our author's imputations against men of whom he knows nothing.

[*Code Napoléon (Paris: Imprimerie impériale, 1807); see Scott, Vol. VI, pp. 52-65.]

and all those which we have not pointed out in this book, the lover of truth has reason to rejoice at its appearance. Much as Sir Walter Scott has wronged the honest part of the revolutionists, the general opinion has hitherto wronged them far more; and to have much chance of correcting that opinion, it was perhaps necessary to temporize with it, and at first give into some portion of the prevailing error. The work contains juster views, and above all, breathes a less malignant spirit, than almost any other Tory publication on the Revolution, and will so far work a beneficial effect upon many minds, which would turn from a perfectly true history of the Revolution without examination or inquiry. We have, therefore, pointed out the errors of this work, not with any wish to see its influence diminished, far less with any hostility towards the author, for whom, politics apart, we share that admiration which is felt by every person possessing a knowledge of the English language. We have been influenced solely by the conviction, that if some readers can as yet endure no more than a part of the truth, there are many who are fully prepared to listen to the whole; and that our remarks have a greater chance of being extensively read and attended to, by being connected, however indirectly, with so celebrated a name.

ALISON'S HISTORY OF THE FRENCH REVOLUTION

1833

EDITOR'S NOTE

Monthly Repository, n.s. VII (July, and Aug., 1833), 507-11, and 513-16. Title footnoted: *"History of Europe during the French Revolution; embracing the period from the Assembly of the Notables in 1789, to the establishment of the Directory in 1796. By Archibald Alison, F.R.S.E. Advocate. In 2 vols. 8vo. [Edinburgh: Blackwood; London: Cadell,] 1833."* Running titles: "The French Revolution." Unsigned. Most of the second part (Aug., 1833) republished in *Dissertations and Discussions*, I, 56-62, entitled: "A Few Observations on the French Revolution," with the title footnoted: "From a review of the first two volumes of Alison's *History of Europe*, *Monthly Repository*, August 1833." Running titles: "The French Revolution." Identified in Mill's bibliography as "A review of Alison's History of the French Revolution in the Monthly Repository for July and August 1833" (MacMinn, 32-3). The copy of the article (tear-sheets) in Mill's library, Somerville College, headed in Mill's hand, "From the Monthly Repository for July & August 1833," contains two corrections also in Mill's hand (here adopted): at 116.14 "this" is altered to "his"; at 119.2 "our" is altered to "an".

The following text, taken from the *Monthly Repository* (our usual rule of using the latest version as copy-text here not applying to *D&D* because only part of the text was republished), is collated with those in *D&D*, 1st ed. (1859), and 2nd ed. (1867). In the footnoted variants, "59" indicates *D&D*, 1st ed., and "67" indicates *D&D*, 2nd ed.

For comment on the essay, see xlvi–l and xcvi–xcvii above.

Alison's History of the French Revolution

OF HISTORY, the most honoured, if not honourable species of composition, is not the whole purport *biographic*? History, it has been said, is the essence of innumerable biographies.[*] Such, at least, it should be: whether it is, might admit of question. But, in any case, what hope have we in turning over those old interminable chronicles, with their garrulities and insipidities; or still worse, in patiently examining those modern narrations, of the philosophic kind, where philosophy, teaching by experience, must sit like owl on house-top, *seeing* nothing, *understanding* nothing, uttering only, with solemnity enough, her perpetual most wearisome *hoo, hoo*:—what hope have we, except the for most part fallacious one of gaining some acquaintance with our fellow-creatures, though dead and vanished, yet dear to us; how they got along in those old days, suffering and doing; to what extent, and under what circumstances, they resisted the devil, and triumphed over him, or struck their colours to him, and were trodden under foot by him; how, in short, the perennial battle went, which men name life, which we also in these new days, with indifferent fortune, have to fight, and must bequeath to our sons and grandsons to go on fighting, till the enemy one day be quite vanquished and abolished, or else the great night sink and part the combatants; and thus, either by some Millennium or some new Noah's Deluge, the volume of universal history wind itself up! Other hope, in studying such books, we have none: and that it is a deceitful hope, who that has tried knows not? A feast of widest biographic insight is spread for us; we enter full of hungry anticipation: alas! like so many other feasts, which life invites us to, a mere Ossian's feast of *shells*,[†] the food and liquor being all emptied out and clean gone, and only the vacant dishes and deceitful emblems thereof left! Your modern historical restaurateurs are indeed little better than high-priests of famine; that keep choicest china dinner-sets, only no dinner to serve therein. Yet such is our biographic appetite, we run trying from shop to shop, with ever new hope; and, unless we could eat the wind, with ever new disappointment.*

Thus writes, although in a publication unworthy of him, an author whom the multitude does not yet, and will not soon understand. The *biographic* aspect here so exclusively dwelt upon, is indeed not the only aspect under which history may profitably and pleasantly be contemplated: but if we find ourselves disappointed of what it ought to afford us in *this* kind, most surely our search will be equally vain for all other fruit. If what purports to be the history of any portion of mankind, keep

[*Carlyle is referring to his own remark in "Thoughts on History," *Fraser's Magazine*, II (Nov., 1830), 414.]

[†See Ossian [James Macpherson], *Fingal, an Ancient Epic Poem in Six Books, with Several Other Poems* (London: Becket and Hondt, 1762), p. 78 (Bk. VI).]

*Article [by Thomas Carlyle] on Biography, in *Fraser's Magazine* [V] for April, 1832, [254-5,] introductory to the admirable article [also by Carlyle] on Boswell's Johnson in the Number for the following month [V (May, 1832), 379-413].

not its promise of making us understand and represent to ourselves what manner of men those were whose story it pretends to be, let it undertake what else it may, it will assuredly perform nothing.

To know our fellow-creature, [we still quote from the same author,] to see into him, understand his goings forth, decipher the whole heart of his mystery;[*] nay, not only to see into him, but even to see out of him, to view the world altogether as he views it; so that we can theoretically construe him, and could almost practically personate him; and do now thoroughly discern both what manner of man he is, and what manner of thing he has got to work on and live on.[†]

This is what a perfect biography, could such be obtained, of any single human being, would do for us, or more properly enable us to do for ourselves, and the perfection of a history, considered in its biographic character, would be to accomplish something of the same kind for an entire nation or an entire age. Thus in respect to the French Revolution, though complete insight is not to be had, we should have been thankful for anything that could have aided us in forming for ourselves even an imperfect picture of the manner in which a Frenchman, at the period of the breaking out of the Revolution lived: what his thoughts were habitually occupied with; what feelings were excited in him by the universe, or by any of the things that dwell therein; above all, what things he fixed his desires upon; what he did for his bread; what things he cared for besides bread; with what evils he had to contend, and how he was enabled to bear up against them; what were his joys, what his consolations, and to what extent he was able to attain them. Such clear view of him and of his circumstances, is the basis of all true knowledge and understanding of the Revolution. Having thus learnt to understand a Frenchman of those days, we would next be helped to know, and to bring vividly before our minds, the new circumstances in which the Revolution placed him; how those circumstances painted themselves to *his* eyes, from *his* point of view; what, as a consequence of the conception he formed of them, he thought, felt, and did, not only in the political, but perhaps still more in what may be called "the private biographic phasis; the manner in which individuals demeaned themselves, and social life went on, in so extraordinary an element as that; the most extraordinary, one might say, for the 'thin rind of habit' was utterly rent off, and man stood there with all the powers of civilization, and none of its rules to aid him in guiding these."[‡]

Such things we would willingly learn from a history of the Revolution; but who among its historians teaches the like? or *has* ought of that kind to teach? or has ever

[*Cf. William Shakespeare, *Hamlet*, III, ii, 366 (in *The Riverside Shakespeare*, ed. G. Blakemore Evans [Boston: Houghton Mifflin, 1974], p. 1165).]

[†Carlyle, "Biography," p. 253.]

[‡Taken from a letter of 12 Jan., 1833, from Carlyle to Mill; see *The Collected Letters of Thomas and Jane Carlyle*, ed. Charles Richard Sanders, *et al.*, Vol. VI (Durham, N.C.: Duke University Press, 1977), p. 302.]

had the thought strike him that such things are to be taught or learnt? Not Mr. Alison's predecessors, of whom, nevertheless, there must be some twenty who have written better books than his; far less Mr. Alison himself. How should he? When in the course of ages a man arises who can conceive a *character*, though it be but of *one* being, and can make his readers conceive it too, we call him a *dramatist*, and write down his name in the short list of the world's great minds; are we then entitled to expect from every respectable, quiet, well-meaning Tory gentleman, that he shall be capable of forming within himself, and impressing upon us, a living image of the character and manner of existence, *not* of *one* human being, but of a nation or a century of mankind? To throw our own mind into the mind and into the circumstances of another, is one of the most trying of all exercises of the intellect and imagination, and the very conception how great a thing it is, seems to imply the capacity of at least partially performing it.

Not to judge Mr. Alison by so high a standard, but by the far lower one of what has actually been achieved by previous writers on the subject, let us endeavour to estimate the worth of his book, and his qualifications as a historian.

And first, of his merits. He is evidently what is termed a kind-hearted, or, at the very least, a good-natured man. Though a Tory, and, therefore, one in whom some prejudices against the actors in the Revolution might be excused, he is most unaffectedly candid and charitable in his judgment of them. Though he condemns them as politicians, he is more indulgent to them as men than even we are, who look with much less disapprobation upon many of their *acts*. He has not, indeed, that highest impartiality which proceeds from philosophic insight, but abundance of that lower kind which flows from milkiness of disposition. He can appreciate talent; he does not join in the ill-informed and rash assertion of the *Edinburgh Review*, reechoed by the *Quarterly*, that the first authors of the French Revolution were mediocre men;[*] on the contrary, speaking in his preface of the Constituent Assembly, he talks of its "memorable discussions," and of himself as "most forcibly impressed with the prodigious, though often perverted and mistaken ability, which distinguished them."[†] Mr. Alison has a further merit, and in a man of his quality of mind it is a most positive one—he is no canter. He does not think it necessary to profess to be shocked, or terrified, at opinions or modes of conduct contrary to what are deemed proper and reputable in his own country. He does not guard his own respectability by a saving clause, whenever he has occasion to name or to praise even a Mirabeau. We should never think of this as a quality worthy of particular notice in a mind accustomed to vigorous and independent thought; but in

[*See John Wilson Croker and John Gibson Lockhart, "The Revolutions of 1640 and 1830," *Quarterly Review*, XLVIII (Mar., 1832), 269; echoed in Thomas Babington Macaulay, "Dumont's *Recollections of Mirabeau*," *Edinburgh Review*, LV (July, 1832), 558-9; and re-echoed in Philip Henry Stanhope, "Lord John Russell, *The Causes of the French Revolution*," *Quarterly Review*, XLIX (Apr., 1833), 156 and 171.]

[†Alison, *History*, Vol. I, p. xvi.]

whatever mind it exists, it is evidence of that which is the first condition of all worth, a desire to *be* rather than to *seem*.

Having said thus much on the favourable side, turn we to the other column of the account, and here we have to say simply this, that, after reading both these volumes carefully through, we are quite completely unable to name any one thing that Mr. Alison has done, which had not been far better done before; or to conjecture what could lead him to imagine that such a work as he has produced was any *desideratum* in the existing literature on the subject. It is hard to say of any book that it is altogether useless; that it contains nothing from which man, woman, or child can derive any one particle of benefit, learn any one thing worth knowing; but a *more* useless book than this of Mr. Alison's, one which approaches nearer to the ideal of absolute inutility, we believe we might go far to seek.

We have not often happened to meet with an author of any work of pretension less endowed than Mr. Alison with the faculty of original thought; his negation of genius amounts almost to a positive quality. Notwithstanding, or, perhaps, in consequence of, this deficiency, he deals largely in general reflections; which accordingly are of the barrenest; when true, so true that no one ever thought them false; when false, nowise that kind of false propositions which come from a penetrating but partial or hasty glance at the thing spoken of, and, therefore, though not true, have instructive truth *in* them; but such as a country-gentleman, accustomed to be king of his company, talks after dinner. The same want of power manifests itself in the narrative. Telling his story almost entirely after Mignet and Thiers,[*] he has caught none of their vivacity from those great masters of narration; the most stirring scenes of that mighty world-drama, under his pen turn flat, cold, and spiritless. In his preface he apologizes for the "dramatic air" produced by inserting fragments of speeches into his text:[†] if the fact were so, it would be a subject of praise, not of apology; but if it *were* an offence, we assure Mr. Alison that he never would be found guilty of it; nothing is dramatic which has passed through the strainer of his translations; even the eloquence of Mirabeau cannot rouse within him one spark of kindred energy and fervour. In the humbler duties of a historian he is equally deficient; he has no faculty of historical criticism, and no research; his marginal references point exclusively to the most obvious sources of information; and even among these he refers five times to a compilation, for once to an original authority. In this he evinces a candour worthy of praise, since his crowded margin *betrays* that scantiness of reading which other authors leave theirs blank on purpose to conceal. We suspect he has written his book rather from memory and notes than with the works themselves before him;

[*François Auguste Marie Mignet, *Histoire de la révolution française*, 2 pts. (Paris: Didot, 1824), and Louis Adolphe Thiers, *Histoire de la révolution française*, 10 vols. (Paris: Lecointe and Durey, 1823-27).]
[†Alison, *History*, Vol. I, p. xvi.]

else how happens it that he invariably misspells the name of one of the writers, he oftenest refers to?* why are several of the names which occur in the history, also misspelt, in a manner not to be accounted for by the largest allowance for typographical errors? why are there so many inaccuracies in matter of fact, of minor importance indeed, but which could hardly have been fallen into, by one fresh from the reading of even the common histories of the Revolution? The very first and simplest requisite for a writer of French history, a knowledge of the French language, Mr. Alison does not possess in the necessary perfection. To *feel* the higher excellences of expression and style in any language implies a mastery over the language itself, and a familiarity with its literature, far greater than is sufficent for all inferior purposes. We are sure that any one who can so completely fail to enter into the spirit of Mirabeau's famous *"Dites-lui que ces hordes étrangères dont nous sommes investis,"*[*] of that inspired burst of oratory upon *la hideuse banqueroute*,[†] and of almost everything having any claim to eloquence which he attempts to render, must be either without the smallest real feeling of eloquence, or so inadequately conversant with the French language, that French eloquence has not yet found its way to his soul. We are the more willing to give Mr. Alison the benefit of this excuse, as we find his knowledge of French at fault in far smaller things. He mistakes *l'impôt du timbre* for a tax on *timber*; *fourche*, apparently from not understanding what it is, he translates a *fork*, and *chariot* a chariot. The waggoner Cathelineau he terms a *charioteer*, and the victims of the revolutionary tribunal are carried from the prison to the guillotine in a *chariot*. Mr. Alison might with as much reason call the dead-cart, during the plague of London, by that name.

If our sole object were to declare our opinion of Mr. Alison's book, our observations might stop here. But Mr. Alison's subject seems to require of us some further remarks, applicable to the mode in which that subject is treated by English writers generally, as well as by him.

* * * * *

*a*History is interesting under a two-fold aspect; it has a *b*scientific*b* interest, and a *c*moral*c* or *d*biographic*d* interest. A scientific, inasmuch as it exhibits the general

---

*M. Toulongeon, always spelt Toulangeon by Mr. Alison. [François Emmanuel Toulongeon, *Histoire de France*, 7 vols. (Paris: Treuttel and Würtz, 1801-10).]

[*Honoré Gabriel Riqueti, comte de Mirabeau, speech of 15 July, 1789, in *Oeuvres de Mirabeau*, 9 vols. (Paris: Dupont and Brissot-Thivars, 1825-27), Vol. VIII, p. 166.]

[†Mirabeau, speech of 26 Sept., 1789, *ibid.*, p. 301.]

*a-a*122[*reprinted as* A Few Observations on the French Revolution *in* D&D, 59,67]
*b-b*59,67   scientific
*c-c*59,67   moral
*d-d*59,67   biographic

laws of the moral universe acting in circumstances of complexity, and enables us to trace the connexion between great effects and their causes. A moral or biographic interest, inasmuch as it *represents to us* the characters and lives of human beings, and calls upon us, according to their deservings or to their fortunes, for *our sympathy, our admiration, or our censure*.

Now, without entering at present, more than to the extent of a few words, into the *hscientifich* aspect of the history of the French Revolution, or stopping to define the place which we would assign to it as an event in universal history, we need not fear to declare utterly unqualified for estimating the French Revolution any one who looks upon it as arising from causes peculiarly French, or otherwise than as one turbulent passage in a progressive *revolution* embracing the whole human race. All political revolutions, not effected by foreign conquest, originate in moral revolutions. The subversion of established institutions is merely one consequence of the previous subversion of established opinions. The *hundred* political revolutions of the last three centuries were but a few outward manifestations of a moral revolution, which dates from the great breaking loose of the human faculties commonly described as the "revival of letters," and of which the main instrument and agent was the invention of printing. How much of the course of that moral revolution yet remains to be run, or how many political revolutions it will yet generate before it be exhausted, no one can foretell. But it must be the shallowest view of the French Revolution, which can *know* consider it as any thing but a mere *incident* in a great change in man himself, in his *belief*, in his principles of conduct, and therefore in the outward arrangements of society; a change *which is but half completed, and which is now in a state of more rapid progress here in England, than any where else*.

Now if this view be just *, which we must be content for the present to assume*, surely for an English historian, writing at this particular time concerning the French Revolution, there was something pressing for consideration of greater interest and importance than the degree of praise or blame due to the few individuals who, with more or less *of* consciousness what they were about, happened to be personally implicated in that strife of the elements.

*e-e*59,67   displays
*f-f*59,67   sympathy, admiration, or censure
*g-g*59,67   Without
*h-h*59,67   scientific
*i-i*59,67   transformation
j-j–59,67
*k-k*59,67   now
*l-l*59,67   incident
*m-m*59,67   beliefs
*n-n*59,67   so far from being completed, that it is not yet clear, even to the more advanced spirits, to what ultimate goal it is tending
*o-o*59,67   (which . . . assume)
p-p–59,67

But also, if, feeling his incapacity for treating history from the scientific point of view, an author thinks fit to confine himself to the *qmoralq* aspect, surely some less common-place moral result, some more valuable and more striking practical lesson, might admit of being drawn from this extraordinary passage of history, than merely this, that men should beware how they begin a political convulsion, because they never can tell how or when it will end; which happens to be the one solitary general inference, the entire aggregate of the practical wisdom, deduced therefrom in Mr. Alison's book.

Of such stuff are ordinary *rmen'sr* moralities composed. Be good, be wise, always do right, take heed what you do, for you know not what may come of it. Does Mr. Alison, or any one, really believe that any human thing, from the fall of man to the last bankruptcy, ever went wrong for want of such maxims as these?

A political convulsion is a fearful thing: granted. Nobody can be assured beforehand what course it will take: we grant that too. What then? No one ought ever to do any thing which has any tendency to bring on a convulsion: is that the principle? But there never was an attempt made to reform any abuse in Church or State, never any denunciation uttered, or mention made of any political or social evil, which had not some such tendency. Whatever excites dissatisfaction with any one of the arrangements of society, brings the danger of a forcible subversion of the entire fabric so much the *snearer: doess* it follow that there ought to be no censure of any thing which exists? Or is this abstinence, peradventure, to be observed only when the danger is considerable? But that is whenever the evil complained of is considerable; because the greater the evil, the stronger is the desire excited to be freed from it, and because the greatest evils are always those which it is most difficult to get rid of by ordinary means. It would follow, then, that mankind are at liberty to throw off small evils, but not great ones; that the most deeply-seated and fatal diseases of the social system are those which ought to be left for ever without remedy.

Men are not to make it the sole object of their political lives to avoid a revolution, no more than of their natural lives to avoid death. They are to take reasonable care to avert both those contingencies when there is a present danger, but *tthey aret* not to forbear the pursuit of any worthy object for fear of a mere possibility.

Unquestionably it is possible to do mischief by striving for a larger measure of political reform than the national mind is ripe for; and so forcing on prematurely a struggle between elements, which, by a more gradual progress, might have been brought to harmonize. And every honest and considerate *uman*, before he engages

*q-q*59,67   moral
*r-r*59,67   people's
*s-s*59, 67   nearer. Does
t-t-59,67
*u-u*59,67   person

in the career of a political reformer, will inquire whether the moral state and intellectual culture of the people are such as to render any great improvement in the management of public affairs possible. But he will inquire too, whether the people are likely ever to be made better, morally or intellectually, without a *ᵛprevious*ᵛ change in the government. If not, it may still be his duty to strive for such a change at whatever *ʷrisks*ʷ.

What decision a perfectly wise man, at the opening of the French Revolution, would have come to upon these several points, he who knows most will be most slow to pronounce. By the Revolution, substantial good has been effected of immense value, at the cost of immediate evil of the most tremendous kind. But it is impossible, with all the light which has been, or probably ever will be, obtained on the subject, to do more than conjecture whether France could have purchased improvement cheaper; whether any course which could have averted the Revolution, would not have done so by arresting all improvement, and barbarizing down the people of France into the condition of Russian boors.

A revolution, which is so ugly a thing, certainly cannot be a very formidable thing, if all is true ˣthe Toriesˣ say of it. For, according to them, it has always depended upon the will of some small number of persons, whether there should be a revolution or ʸnoʸ. They invariably begin by assuming that great and decisive immediate improvements, with a certainty of subsequent and rapid progress, and the ultimate attainment of all ᶻpracticalᶻ good, may be had by peaceable means at the option of the leading reformers, and that to this they voluntarily prefer civil war and massacre for the sake of marching somewhat more directly and rapidly towards their ultimate ends. Having thus made out a revolution to be so mere a *bagatelle*, that, except by the extreme of knavery or folly, it may always be kept at a distance; there is little difficulty in proving all revolutionary leaders knaves or fools. But unhappily theirs is no such enviable position; a far other alternative is commonly offered to them. We will hazard the assertion, that there ᵃneverᵃ yet happened a political convulsion, originating in the desire of reform, where the choice did not, in the full persuasion of every person concerned, lie between ᵇallᵇ and ᶜ*nothing*ᶜ; where the actors in the revolution had not thoroughly made up their minds, that, without a revolution, the enemies of all reform would have the entire ascendency, and that not only there would be no present improvement, but the door would for the future be shut against ᵈallᵈ endeavour towards it.

ᵛ⁻ᵛ67   previous
ʷ⁻ʷ59,67   risk
ˣ⁻ˣ59,67   that Conservatives
ʸ⁻ʸ59,67   not
ᶻ⁻ᶻ59,67   practicable
ᵃ⁻ᵃ59,67   has scarcely ever
ᵇ⁻ᵇ59,67   all
ᶜ⁻ᶜ59,67   nothing
ᵈ⁻ᵈ59,67   every

Unquestionably, such was the conviction of those who took part in the French Revolution, during its earlier stages. *They* did *not* choose the way of blood and violence in preference to the way of peace and discussion. Theirs was the cause of law and order. The States General at Versailles were a body, legally assembled, legally and constitutionally sovereign of the country, and had every right which law and opinion could bestow upon them, to do all that they did. But as soon as they did any thing disagreeable to the king's courtiers, (at that time they had not even *begun* to make any alterations in the fundamental institutions of the country,) the king and his advisers took steps for appealing to the bayonet. Then, and not till then, the adverse force of an armed people stood forth in defence of the highest constituted authority—the legislature of their country—menaced with illegal violence. The Bastille fell; the popular party became the stronger; and success, which so often is said to be a justification, has here proved the reverse: men who would have *h* ranked with Hampden and Sidney, if they had quietly waited to have their throats cut, *become* odious monsters because they have been victorious.

We have not now time nor space to discuss the quantum of the guilt which attaches, not to the authors of the Revolution, but to the *subsequent, to the various* revolutionary governments, for the crimes of the Revolution. Much was done which could not have been done except by bad men. But whoever examines faithfully and diligently the records of those times, whoever can conceive the circumstances and look into the minds *k* of the men who planned and *who* perpetrated those enormities, will be the more fully convinced, the more he considers the facts, that all which was done had one sole object. That object was, according to the phraseology of the time, to *save* the Revolution; to *save* it, no matter by what means; to defend it against its irreconcilable enemies, within and without; to prevent the undoing of the whole work, the restoration of all *which* had been demolished, and the extermination of all who had been active in demolishing; to keep down the royalists, and drive back the foreign invaders; as the means to these ends to erect all France into a camp, subject the whole French people to the obligations and the arbitrary discipline of a besieged city; and to inflict death, or suffer it with equal readiness—death or any other evil—for the sake of succeeding in the object.

*e-e*59,67   They
*f-f*59,67   not
*g-g*59,67   begun
*h*59,67   been
*i-i*59,67   passed for
*j-j*59,67   various subsequent
*k*59,67   even
l-l–59,67
*m-m*59,67   save
*n-n*67   that

But nothing of all this is dreamed of in Mr. Alison's philosophy:[*] he knows not enough, [o]neither of his professed subject, nor[o] of the universal subject, the nature of man, to have got even thus far, to have made this first step towards understanding what the French Revolution was. In this he is without excuse, for had he been even moderately read in the French literature, [p]subsequent[p] to the Revolution, he would have found this view of the details of its history familiar to every writer and to every reader.[a]

It was scarcely worth while to touch upon the French Revolution for the sake of saying no more about it than we have now said; yet it is as much, perhaps, as the occasion warrants. Observations entering more deeply into the subject will find a fitter opportunity when it shall not be necessary to mix them up with strictures upon an insignificant book.

[*Cf. *Hamlet*, I, v, 166-7 (in *The Riverside Shakespeare*, p. 1151).]

[o-o]59,67   either . . . or
[p-p]59,67   subsequent

THE MONSTER TRIAL

1835

EDITOR'S NOTE

Monthly Repository, n.s. IX (June, 1835), 393-6. Headed by title. Running titles as title. Signed "A." Not republished. Identified in Mill's bibliography as "An article headed 'The Monster Trial' in the Monthly Repository for June 1835" (MacMinn, 44). The copy (tear-sheets) in Mill's library, Somerville College, headed in Mill's hand, "From the Monthly Repository for June 1835", has no corrections or emendations. In the Somerville College copy of the *Examiner* for 26 Jan., 1834, from which Mill here quotes, there is one correction, "institution" for "constitution" (127.18), which is here accepted.

The long quotation from Mill's own unheaded leader in the *Examiner* is collated with the original. In the footnoted variants, "34" indicates the *Examiner*.

For comment on the essay, see lx–lxii and xcvii–xcviii above.

The Monster Trial

SO LITTLE is the general course of French affairs attended to in this country, that when, as at present, some single event, either from its importance or its strangeness, attracts a certain degree of notice, its causes, and all which could help to explain it, have been forgotten. It is true that the most assiduous reader of only the English newspapers, even if he retained all he had read, would understand little or nothing of the real character of events in France; for the editors of the English newspapers are as ignorant of France as they probably are of Monomotapa; and their Paris correspondents, being mostly Frenchmen, write as if for Frenchmen, and repeat the mere gossip of the day, pre-supposing as already known all which Englishmen would care to know. By being the solitary exception to this rule, the writer who signed "O.P.Q."[*] in the *Morning Chronicle* gained a temporary popularity, merely because, unlike the rest of the fraternity, he assumed that his readers knew nothing, and had to learn everything. In the *Examiner* alone, for the last four years, those who take interest in the fate of that great country, which divides with ourselves the moral dominion of Europe, have had the passing events placed carefully before them with regular explanatory comments.[†]

From that paper we quote part of an article which appeared on the 26th January, 1834, descriptive of the character and objects of that portion of the French republicans against whom the *procès-monstre*[‡] is mainly directed.

The *Société des Droits de l'Homme* is at present the hobgoblin or bugbear of the *juste milieu*. The language and manner of the partisans of Louis Philippe with respect to that association are a curious medley of affected contempt and intense personal hatred, not without an admixture of fear. They are constantly and studiously imputing to the members of the society the absurdest opinions and the most criminal purposes; they are incessantly averring, with a degree of emphasis which betrays a lurking doubt, that those opinions and purposes are abhorred by the French people, and that the society has not, and never will have, the support of any class whatever, even the lowest. Yet, in the very same breath in which they declare it to be harmless by reason of its insignificance, they proclaim it so mischievous and so formidable, that society is certain to perish unless it be put down, by whatever means.

In truth, the alarmists are equally wrong in both feelings, whether the feelings be sincere or affected. This much-talked-of association is not to be despised; neither, on the other

[*Caleb Charles Colton.]
[†Much of that commentary was by Mill himself.]
[‡The term used for the trial in the *National* from 6 to 20 May, 1835.]

hand, is it to be feared. It does not aim at subverting society, and society would be too strong for it if it did. Were we to believe some people, the edifice of society is so tottering, and its foundations so unstable, that a breath is enough to blow it down; nay, there cannot be any stir in the surrounding atmosphere, nor any knocking upon the ground, without its certain destruction. But we have another idea of society than this; for us it is something more steady and solid than a house of cards. The evil we are apprehensive of is stagnation, not movement; we can anticipate nothing in the present age but good, from the severest, from even the most hostile scrutiny of the first principles of the social union. Instead of expecting society to fall to pieces, our fear is lest (the old creeds, which formerly gave to the established order of things a foundation in men's consciences, having become obsolete) the fabric should mechanically hold together by the mere instinctive action of men's immediate personal interests, without any basis of moral conviction at all. Rather than see this we should prefer to see the whole of the working classes speculatively Owenites or Saint Simonians. We are not frightened at anti-property doctrines. We have no fear that they should ever prevail so extensively as to be dangerous. But we have the greatest fear lest the classes possessed of property should degenerate more and more into selfish, unfeeling Sybarites, receiving from society all that society can give, and rendering it no service in return, content to let the numerical majority remain sunk in mental barbarism and physical destitution. . . . [a]

The [b]Society of the Rights of Man[b] some months ago embodied their principles on the subject of property in the form of a manifesto, along with which they republished, as a compendium of their opinions, a Declaration of the Rights of Man,[*] which was proposed by Robespierre to the National Convention to be prefixed to their republican constitution,[†] and was by that body rejected. The name of Robespierre was well calculated to excite a prejudice against this document, but any thing more harmless than its contents can scarcely be conceived. Such, however, was not the impression of the Parisian public. The writer of this was at Paris when the document made its appearance, and he well remembers his

---

[*Déclaration des droits de l'homme et du citoyen ([Paris:] La société des droits de l'homme, [1833]); Robespierre's Déclaration first appeared in 1793 (Paris: Imprimerie nationale).]

[†Acte constitutionnel de la république (24 June, 1793), Gazette Nationale, ou Le Moniteur Universel, 27 June, 1793, pp. 765-6.]

---

[a]34 [ellipsis indicates the following omission]   All experience justifies us in the conviction that unless the ruling few can be made and kept "uneasy," the many need expect no good; and nothing will make the few uneasy but fears for the security of their property. We are well content, therefore, that there should be cause for such fears. We have no anti-property doctrines ourselves, and therefore cannot honestly give such doctrines any encouragement. But we are quite satisfied that their promulgation has a most salutary effect.

The Society of the Rights of Man cannot, however, be said to have put forward any anti-property doctrines; and nothing can be more absurdly calumnious than the accusations of confiscation, agrarian law, &c., &c. If opinions adverse to the present constitution of property are secretly held by any of the able and accomplished men who guide the proceedings of the association, (which is certainly not to be believed on the evidence of their enemies,) they have not put forward any such opinions. They profess, indeed, democratic republicanism in its fullest extent; and are far more impatient, and willing to take more violent means for obtaining the form of government which they desire, than the more moderate of the Republicans would approve. But on the subject of property they have advanced no doctrines but such as, to an Englishman, sound like the merest truisms; and that these should have been considered dangerous in France, only shows how little peril there is lest in that country anti-property doctrines should ever prevail.

[b-b]34   association

astonishment at the nature and intensity of the sentiments it appeared to excite. Those who did not deem it too contemptible to be formidable were filled with consternation. The Government party, the Carlists, the Liberals, were unanimous in crying anarchy and confusion; even Republicans shook their heads and said, "This is going too far." And what does the reader imagine was the proposition which appeared so startling and so alarming to all parties? It was no other than the definition which, in the Robespierrian declaration of rights, was given of the "right of property," and ran as follows:

"The right of property is the right which every one possesses of using and enjoying the portion of wealth which is guaranteed to him by the law." (*La portion de biens qui lui est garantie par la loi.*)[*]

Such is the superstitious, or rather idolatrous, character of the respect for property in France, that this proposition actually appeared an alarming heresy, was denounced with the utmost acrimony by all the enemies of the propounders, and timidly and hesitatingly excused rather than vindicated by their friends. The maxim was evidently too much for all parties; it was a doctrine considerably in advance of them; even republicans required some time to make up their minds. Ardent revolutionists, men who were ready to take up arms at five minutes' notice for the subversion of the existing dynasty, doubted whether they could admit, as a speculative truth, that property is not of natural right, but of human institution, and is the creature of law. Truly, there is little fear for the safety of property in France. We believe that in no country in the world, not even the United States of America, is property so secure; the most violent convulsion would not endanger it; in a country where nearly two-thirds of the male adult population possess property in land, and where the notions entertained of the inviolability of property are so pedantic and (if we may be permitted the expression) so prudish, that there are persons who will gravely maintain that the state has no right to make a road through a piece of land without the owner's consent, even on payment of compensation.

Strange as it may appear, in the declaration of rights, drawn up by Robespierre, and adopted by the *Société des Droits de l'Homme*, there is not, with the one exception which we have mentioned, one single proposition on the subject of property which was considered exceptionable even by those who were so scandalized at the above definition. No limitation of the right of property was hinted at; no new or alarming maxim promulgated; unless such be implied in the recognition of the principle of the English poor laws, that society is bound to provide subsistence and work for its indigent members;[†] and this document was *rejected* by the convention, by the body which put to death Louis XVI, and created the revolutionary tribunal, rejected by that body as *anarchical*. Yet there are people who believe that the principle of the French revolution was spoliation of property! For the thousandth time, we say to the English Tories and Whigs, that they are as utterly ignorant of the French revolution as of the revolutions among the inhabitants of the moon. Acts of injustice were done; rights, which really partook of the nature of property, were not always treated as such; but the respect of the revolutionary assemblies for all that they considered as entitled to the name of property amounted to actual narrowness and bigotry. We do not affirm this solely of the comparatively moderate and enlightened men who composed the constituent assembly, but in even a greater degree of the violent revolutionists of the convention, to whose obtuser and less cultivated intellects such a prejudice was more natural. In the height of the reign of terror anti-property doctrines would have been scouted, even more decidedly than now; no one dared avow them for fear of the guillotine; nor do

[*Déclaration* (1833), p. 3 (Art. VI).]
[†*Ibid.* (Art. IX).]

such doctrines figure in the history of the revolution at all, save in the solitary instance of the conspiracy of Baboeuf, greatly posterior to the fall of Robespierre and the Montagne. *c* [*]

In April, 1834, about three months after the above article was written, the leaders in a general strike of the silk-weavers of Lyons, which had just terminated unsuccessfully, were prosecuted by order of government; and this prosecution, together with the knowledge that the detestable law[†] then in progress through the Chambers for putting down all associations unlicensed by government would be applied to the extinction of trades' unions, provoked the unfortunate insurrection at Lyons, which lasted five days, and was with some difficulty suppressed. This was not a political, but a trades' union insurrection. The government, however, took that base advantage of the alarm excited by it which all French governments have long been accustomed to take of all events exciting a panic among those who have something to lose. They got up an insignificant riot in the streets of Paris, called it an insurrection, took the most violent measures for repressing it, (a house was broken open, and all the inhabitants, twenty or thirty in number, butchered by the troops,) and availed themselves of the excuse for seizing the persons and papers of all the leading members of the *Société des Droits de l'Homme*.[‡] Not one of those leaders was even suspected of being concerned in either of the two insurrections, but the opportunity was thought a good one for laying, under colour of law, the clutches of the government upon the correspondence of the society. It is now a year that these distinguished persons have been kept in prison; and that time has been employed in manufacturing, from the papers which government got into its possession, evidence of a plot. The next desideratum was, to bring the prisoners before a tribunal which would be sure to convict them. Paris juries had been tried,

[*John Stuart Mill, Summary of French News, *Examiner*, 26 Jan., 1834, pp. 56-7.]

[†Loi sur les associations, Bulletin 115, No. 261 (10 Apr., 1834), *Bulletin des lois du royaume de France*, 9th ser., Pt. 1, VI, 25-6.]

[‡Including Godefroy Cavaignac, Auguste Guinard, and Guillard de Kersausie.]

*c*34 [*paragraph*] In so far as the Society of the Rights of Man contends against the narrow and superstitious notions of property which are prevalent in France, and gives currency to more liberal and more rational views, it can do nothing but good; and even if the speculative truths, which it so energetically proclaims, are intended to serve as a foundation for practical corollaries of a more questionable character, we see no cause for alarm; none even for regret. Without infringing the principle of property, much remains to be done, by morality and even by law, to render the practical working of the principle productive of greater good to society at large: much may be done to mitigate the inequalities of wealth which have as pernicious an effect on those whom they seem to benefit, as upon those on whom they apparently press hardest, and to promote all those tendencies in human affairs which cause society to approximate to what, in the literal sense, must always be an unattainable chimera, equality of fortunes. But all this we have little hope to see done, until the rich shall feel that except by making the law of property popular, they will have some difficulty in maintaining it. Society will then only be on the most desirable footing, when the proprietary class shall feel compelled to make a clear case to the world in favour of the existing institutions of society; when they shall act under an habitual sense of the necessity of convincing the non-proprietary multitude, that the existing arrangement of property is a real good to *them* as well as to the rich; and shall feel that the most effectual way to make them *think* it so, is to make it more and more so in *fact*.

and found not sufficiently docile. They had always scouted the miserable attempts to hunt down innocent men on charges of treason and conspiracy; and memorable had been the exposure, on more than one such occasion, of the malignant and fraudulent artifices of the government. There was, however, a resource. In servile imitation of the English constitution, the Chamber of Peers had been, by the French charter, invested with the power of trying *ministers* for treason or malversation on the prosecution of the Chamber of Deputies.[*] This provision Louis Philippe, following a questionable precedent of Louis XVIII's reign, has applied to the case of persons who are not ministers, nor prosecuted by the Chamber of Deputies; and has brought the pretended authors of the pretended republican conspiracy of Paris, along with the presumed authors of the real trades' union revolt at Lyons, before the Chamber of Peers; that is, before a body named by the government, and mostly holding places under it.

Nothing can denote more complete ignorance of France than the daily speculations in our liberal newspapers as to the embarrassments which the Chamber of Peers is supposed to have brought upon itself by consenting to be made the tool of the government in this matter, and the loss it is likely to sustain in public estimation. The Chamber of Peers is so happily situated, that it cannot possibly suffer any loss of public estimation; any change on that score must be to its advantage. It is as completely insignificant as our House of Lords would be if it were a body of mere pensioners, not hereditary, containing as little talent as at present, and scarcely any fortune. The Chamber of Peers, previously to this trial, was heartily despised. It may now attain the more honourable, and, to a Frenchman especially, far more enviable position of being hated. By showing that it has still the power (in spite of the imbecility inherent in its constitution) of making itself formidable as an instrument of tyranny in the hands of the other two branches of the legislature, it may have a chance, which it certainly had not before, of regaining a certain sort of consideration. The Monster Trial is its last throw for political importance.

[*Charte constitutionnelle, Bulletin 17, No. 133 (4 June, 1814), *Bulletin des lois du royaume de France*, 5th ser., I, 205 (Arts. 55 and 56).]

CARLYLE'S FRENCH REVOLUTION

1837

EDITOR'S NOTE

London and Westminster Review, V & XXVII (July, 1837), 17-53. Headed: *"The French Revolution: A History*. In three volumes. By Thomas Carlyle. Small 8vo. [London:] Fraser, 1837." Running titles: "The French Revolution." Signed "A." Not republished. Identified in Mill's bibliography as "A review of Carlyle's History of the French Revolution, in the same review [as 'Taylor's Statesman,' by Mill and George Grote] for July 1837. (No. 10 and 53.)" (MacMinn, 48.) The copy (bound sheets) in Mill's library, Somerville College, has no corrections or emendations.

In the extensive quotations, the footnotes that Mill takes from Carlyle are signalled by "[TC]."

For comment, see l–lv and xcix–c above.

Carlyle's French Revolution

THIS IS NOT SO MUCH A HISTORY, as an epic poem; and notwithstanding, or even in consequence of this, the truest of histories. It is the history of the French Revolution, and the poetry of it, both in one; and on the whole no work of greater genius, either historical or poetical, has been produced in this country for many years.

It is a book on which opinion will be for some time divided; nay, what talk there is about it, while it is still fresh, will probably be oftenest of a disparaging sort; as indeed is usually the case, both with men's works and with men themselves, of distinguished originality. For a thing which is unaccustomed, must be a very small thing indeed, if mankind can at once see into it and be sure that it is good: when, therefore, a considerable thing, which is also an unaccustomed one, appears, those who will hereafter approve, sit silent for a time, making up their minds; and those only to whom the mere novelty is a sufficient reason for disapproval, speak out. We need not fear to prophesy that the suffrages of a large class of the very best qualified judges will be given, even enthusiastically, in favour of the volumes before us; but we will not affect to deny that the sentiment of another large class of readers (among whom are many entitled to the most respectful attention on other subjects) will be far different; a class comprehending all who are repelled by quaintness of manner. For a style more peculiar than that of Mr. Carlyle, more unlike the jog-trot characterless uniformity which distinguishes the English style of this age of Periodicals, does not exist. Nor indeed can this style be wholly defended even by its admirers. Some of its peculiarities are mere mannerisms, arising from some casual association of ideas, or some habit accidentally picked up; and what is worse, many sterling thoughts are so disguised in phraseology borrowed from the spiritualist school of German poets and metaphysicians, as not only to obscure the meaning, but to raise, in the minds of most English readers, a not unnatural nor inexcusable presumption of there being no meaning at all. Nevertheless, the presumption fails in this instance (as in many other instances); there is not only a meaning, but generally a true, and even a profound meaning; and, although a few dicta about the "mystery" and the "infinitude"[*] which are in the universe and in man, and such like topics, are repeated in varied phrases greatly too often for our taste, this must be borne with, proceeding, as one cannot but see,

[*For one passage using these very common Carlylian terms, see Vol. II, pp. 102-4.]

from feelings the most solemn, and the most deeply rooted which can lie in the heart of a human being. These transcendentalisms, and the accidental mannerisms excepted, we pronounce the style of this book to be not only good, but of surpassing excellence; excelled, in its kind, only by the great masters of epic poetry; and a most suitable and glorious vesture for a work which is itself, as we have said, an epic poem.

To any one who is perfectly satisfied with the best of the existing histories, it will be difficult to explain wherein the merit of Mr. Carlyle's book consists. If there be a person who, in reading the histories of Hume, Robertson, and Gibbon (works of extraordinary talent, and the works of great writers)[*] has never felt that this, after all, is not history—and that the lives and deeds of his fellow-creatures must be placed before him in quite another manner, if he is to know them, or feel them to be real beings, who once were alive, beings of his own flesh and blood, not mere shadows and dim abstractions; such a person, for whom plausible talk *about* a thing does as well as an image of the thing itself, feels no need of a book like Mr. Carlyle's; the want, which it is peculiarly fitted to supply, does not yet consciously exist in his mind. That such a want, however, is generally felt, may be inferred from the vast number of historical plays and historical romances, which have been written for no other purpose than to satisfy it. Mr. Carlyle has been the first to shew that all which is done for history by the best historical play, by Schiller's *Wallenstein*,[†] for example, or Vitet's admirable trilogy,* may be done in a strictly true narrative, in which every incident rests on irrefragable authority; may be done, by means merely of an apt selection and a judicious grouping of authentic facts.

It has been noted as a point which distinguishes Shakespeare from ordinary dramatists, that *their* characters are logical abstractions, his are human beings: that their kings are nothing but kings, their lovers nothing but lovers, their patriots,

---

[*David Hume, *The History of England* (1756-62), 8 vols. (London: Cadell, *et al.*, 1823); William Robertson, *The History of America* (1777), *The History of Scotland* (1759), and *The History of the Reign of the Emperor Charles V* (1769), in *Works*, 6 vols. (London: Longman, *et al.*, 1851), Vols. V-VI, I-II, and III-IV, respectively; and Edward Gibbon, *The History of the Decline and Fall of the Roman Empire*, 6 vols. (London: Strahan and Cadell, 1776-88).]

[†Johann Christoph Friedrich von Schiller, *Wallenstein, ein dramatisches Gedicht* (1798-99), in *Sämmtliche Werke*, 12 vols. (Stuttgart and Tübingen: Cotta'schen Buchhandlung, 1818-19), Vol. IX, Pt. 2.]

*[Louis Vitet,] *Les Barricades* [(Paris: Brière, 1826)]; *Les Etats de Blois* [(Paris: Ponthieu, 1827)]; and *La Mort de Henri III* [(Paris: Fournier jeune, 1829)], three prose plays or rather series of dramatic scenes, illustrative of the League and the period of the religious wars in France. A work scarcely heard of in this country, but which well deserves to be so. The author, like so many of the rising literary notabilities of France (from M. Guizot downwards), is now unhappily withdrawn from literature, by place-hunting, and *doctrinaire* politics.

courtiers, villains, cowards, bullies, are each of them that, and that alone; while his are real men and women, who have these qualities, but have them in addition to their full share of all other qualities (not incompatible), which are incident to human nature.[*] In Shakespeare, consequently, we feel we are in a world of realities; we are among such beings as really could exist, as do exist, or have existed, and as we can sympathise with; the faces we see around us are human faces, and not mere rudiments of such, or exaggerations of single features. This quality, so often pointed out as distinctive of Shakespeare's plays, distinguishes Mr. Carlyle's history. Never before did we take up a book calling itself by that name, a book treating of past times, and professing to be true, and find ourselves actually among human beings. We at once felt, that what had hitherto been to us mere abstractions, had become realities; the "forms of things unknown," which we fancied we knew, but knew their names merely, were, for the first time, with most startling effect, "bodied forth" and "turned into shape."[†] Other historians talk to us indeed of human beings; but what do they place before us? Not even stuffed figures of such, but rather their algebraical symbols; a few phrases, which present no image to the fancy, but by adding up the dictionary meanings of which, we may hunt out a few qualities, not enough to form even the merest outline of what the men *were*, or possibly *could* have been; furnishing little but a canvas, which, if we ourselves can paint, we may fill with almost any picture, and if we cannot, it will remain for ever blank.

Take, for example, Hume's history; certainly, in its own way, one of the most skilful specimens of narrative in modern literature, and with some pretensions also to philosophy. Does Hume throw his own mind into the mind of an Anglo-Saxon, or an Anglo-Norman? Does any reader feel, after having read Hume's history, that he can now picture to himself what human life was, among the Anglo-Saxons? how an Anglo-Saxon would have acted in any supposable case? what were his joys, his sorrows, his hopes and fears, his ideas and opinions on any of the great and small matters of human interest? Would not the sight, if it could be had, of a single table or pair of shoes made by an Anglo-Saxon, tell us, directly and by inference, more of his whole way of life, more of how men thought and acted among the Anglo-Saxons, than Hume, with all his narrative skill, has contrived to tell us from all his materials?

Or descending from the history of civilization, which in Hume's case may have been a subordinate object, to the history of political events: did any one ever gain from Hume's history anything like a picture of what may actually have been passing, in the minds, say, of Cavaliers or of Roundheads during the civil wars? Does any one feel that Hume has made him figure to himself with any precision

[*See Samuel Johnson, "Preface to Shakespeare," in *Works*, 13 vols. (London: Buckland, *et al.*, 1787), Vol. IX, pp. 242-6.]

[†William Shakespeare, *A Midsummer Night's Dream*, V, i, 14-16 (in *The Riverside Shakespeare*, ed. G. Blakemore Evans [Boston: Houghton Mifflin, 1974], p. 242).]

what manner of men these were; how far they were like ourselves, how far different; what things they loved and hated, and what sort of conception they had formed of the things they loved and hated? And what kind of a notion can be framed of a period of history, unless we begin with that as a preliminary? Hampden, and Strafford, and Vane, and Cromwell, do these, in Hume's pages, appear to us like beings who actually trod this earth, and spoke with a human voice, and stretched out human hands in fellowship with other human beings; or like the figures in a phantasmagoria, colourless, impalpable, gigantic, and in all varieties of attitude, but all resembling one another in being shadows? And suppose he had done his best to assist us in forming a conception of these leading characters: what would it have availed, unless he had placed us also in the atmosphere which they breathed? What wiser are we for looking out upon the world through Hampden's eyes, unless it be the same world which Hampden looked upon? and what help has Hume afforded us for this? Has he depicted to us, or to himself, what all the multitude of people were about, who surrounded Hampden; what the whole English nation were feeling, thinking, or doing? Does he shew us what impressions from without were coming to Hampden—what materials and what instruments were given him to work with? If not, we are well qualified, truly, from Hume's information, to erect ourselves into judges of any part of Hampden's conduct!

Another very celebrated historian, we mean Gibbon—not a man of mere science and analysis, like Hume, but with some (though not the truest or profoundest) artistic feeling of the picturesque, and from whom, therefore, rather more might have been expected—has with much pains succeeded in producing a tolerably graphic picture of here and there a battle, a tumult, or an insurrection; his book is full of movement and costume, and would make a series of very pretty ballets at the Opera-house, and the ballets would give us fully as distinct an idea of the Roman empire, and how it declined and fell, as the book does. If we want that, we must look for it anywhere but in Gibbon. One touch of M. Guizot removes a portion of the veil which hid from us the recesses of private life under the Roman empire, lets in a ray of light which penetrates as far even as the domestic hearth of a subject of Rome, and shews us the government at work making that desolate;[*] but no similar gleam of light from Gibbon's mind ever reaches the subject; *human life*, in the times he wrote about, is not what he concerned himself with.

On the other hand, there are probably many among our readers who are acquainted (though it is not included in Coleridge's admirable translation) with that extraordinary piece of dramatic writing, termed "Wallenstein's Camp."[†]

[*François Pierre Guillaume Guizot, "Du régime municipal dans l'empire romain, au cinquième siècle de l'ère chrétienne, lors de la grande invasion des Germains en occident," *Essais sur l'histoire de France*, 2nd ed. (Paris: Brière, 1824), pp. 1-51.]

[†"Wallensteins Lager," the first part of Schiller's *Wallenstein*. Samuel Taylor Coleridge translated *The Piccolomini, or The First Part of Wallenstein; and The Death of Wallenstein*, 2 vols. in 1 (London: Longman and Rees, 1800).]

One of the greatest of dramatists, the historian of the Thirty Years' War,[*] aspired to do, in a dramatic fiction, what even *his* genius had not enabled him to do in his history—to delineate the great characters, and, above all, to embody the general spirit of that period. This is done with such life and reality through ten acts, that the reader feels when it is over as if all the prominent personages in the play were people whom he had known from his childhood; but the author did not trust to this alone: he prefixed to the ten acts, one introductory act, intended to exhibit, not the characters, but the element they moved in. It is there, in this preliminary piece, that Schiller really depicts the Thirty Years' War; without that, even the other ten acts, splendid as they are, would not have sufficiently realized it to our conception, nor would the Wallensteins and Piccolominis and Terzskys of that glorious tragedy have been themselves, comparatively speaking, intelligible.

What Schiller must have done, in his own mind, with respect to the age of Wallenstein, to enable him to frame that fictitious delineation of it, Mr. Carlyle, with a mind which looks still more penetratingly into the deeper meanings of things than Schiller's, has done with respect to the French Revolution. And he has communicated his picture of it with equal vividness; but he has done it by means of real, not fictitious incidents. And therefore is his book, as we said, at once the authentic History and the Poetry of the French Revolution.

It is indeed a favourite doctrine of Mr. Carlyle, and one which he has enforced with great strength of reason and eloquence in other places, that all poetry suitable to the present age must be of this kind:[†] that poetry has not naturally any thing to do with fiction, nor is fiction in these days even the most appropriate vehicle and vesture of it; that it should, and will, employ itself more and more, not in inventing unrealities, but in bringing out into ever greater distinctness and impressiveness the poetic aspect of realities. For what is it, in the fictitious subjects which poets usually treat, that makes those subjects poetical? Surely not the dry, mechanical *facts* which compose the story; but the *feelings*—the high and solemn, the tender or mournful, even the gay and mirthful contemplations, which the story, or the manner of relating it, awaken in our minds. But would not all these thoughts and feelings be far more vividly aroused if the facts were *believed*; if the men, and all that is ascribed to them, had actually *been*; if the whole were no play of imagination, but a truth? In every real fact, in which any of the great interests of human beings are implicated, there lie the materials of all poetry; there is, as Mr. Carlyle has said, the fifth act of a tragedy in every peasant's death-bed;[‡] the life of every heroic character is a heroic poem, were but the man of genius found, who could *so* write it! Not falsification of the reality is wanted, not the representation of it as being any thing which it is not; only a deeper understanding of what it is; the

---

[*Geschichte des dreissigjährigen Kriegs (1791-93), Vol. VI of Sämmtliche Werke.]

[†See, e.g., "State of German Literature," *Edinburgh Review*, XLVI (Oct., 1827), 335; "Biography," *Fraser's Magazine*, V (Apr., 1832), 257; and "Boswell's *Life of Johnson*," ibid. (May, 1832), 387.]

[‡"Burns," *Edinburgh Review*, XLVIII (Dec., 1828), 278.]

power to conceive, and to represent, not the mere outside surface and costume of the thing, nor yet the mere logical definition, and *caput mortuum* of it—but an image of the thing itself in the concrete, with all that is loveable or hateable or admirable or pitiable or sad or solemn or pathetic, in it, and in the things which are implied in it. That is, the thing must be presented as it can exist only in the mind of a great poet: of one gifted with the two essential elements of the poetic character—creative imagination, which, from a chaos of scattered hints and confused testimonies, can summon up the Thing to appear before it as a completed whole: and that depth and breadth of feeling which makes all the images that are called up appear arrayed in whatever, of all that belongs to them, is naturally most affecting and impressive to the human soul.

We do not envy the person who can read Mr. Carlyle's three volumes, and not recognize in him both these endowments in a most rare and remarkable degree. What is equally important to be said—he possesses in no less perfection that among the qualities necessary for his task, seemingly the most opposite to these, and in which the man of poetic imagination might be thought likeliest to be deficient; the quality of the historical day-drudge. A more pains-taking or accurate investigator of facts, and sifter of testimonies, never wielded the historical pen. We do not say this at random, but from a most extensive acquaintance with his materials, with his subject, and with the mode in which it has been treated by others.

Thus endowed, and having a theme the most replete with every kind of human interest, epic, tragic, elegiac, even comic and farcical, which history affords, and so near to us withal, that the authentic details of it are still attainable; need it be said, that he has produced a work which deserves to be memorable? a work which, whatever may be its immediate reception, "will not willingly be let die;"[*] whose reputation will be a growing reputation, its influence rapidly felt, for it will be read by the writers; and perhaps every historical work of any note, which shall hereafter be written in this country, will be different from what it would have been if this book were not.

The book commences with the last illness of Louis XV which is introduced as follows:

President Hénault, remarking on royal Surnames of Honour how difficult it often is to ascertain not only why, but even when, they were conferred, takes occasion in his sleek official way to make a philosophical reflection. "The Surname of *Bien-aimé* (Well-beloved)," says he, "which Louis XV bears, will not leave posterity in the same doubt. This Prince, in the year 1744, while hastening from one end of his kingdom to the other, and suspending his conquests in Flanders that he might fly to the assistance of Alsace, was

[*John Milton, *The Reason of Church Government Urged against Prelaty* (1641-42), in *The Prose Works*, ed. Charles Symmons, 7 vols. (London: Johnson, *et al.*, 1806), Vol. I, p. 119.]

arrested at Metz by a malady which threatened to cut short his days. At the news of this, Paris, all in terror, seemed a city taken by storm: the churches resounded with supplications and groans; the prayers of priests and people were every moment interrupted by their sobs; and it was from an interest so dear and tender that this Surname of *Bien-aimé* fashioned itself, a title higher still than all the rest which this great Prince has earned."*

So stands it written; in lasting memorial of that year 1744. Thirty other years have come and gone; and "this great Prince" again lies sick; but in how altered circumstances now! Churches resound not with excessive groanings; Paris is stoically calm: sobs interrupt no prayers, for indeed none are offered, except Priests' Litanies, read or chanted at fixed money-rate per hour, which are not liable to interruption. The shepherd of the people has been carried home from Little Trianon, heavy of heart, and been put to bed in his own Château of Versailles: the flock knows it, and heeds it not. At most, in the immeasurable tide of French Speech (which ceases not day after day, and only ebbs towards the short hours of night), may this of the royal sickness emerge from time to time as an article of news. Bets are doubtless depending; nay some people "express themselves loudly in the streets."† But for the rest, on green field and steepled city, the May sun shines out, the May evening fades; and men ply their useful or useless business as if no Louis lay in danger.[*]

The loathsome deathbed of the royal debauchee becomes, under Mr. Carlyle's pencil, the central figure in an historical picture, including all France; bringing before us, as it were visibly, all the spiritual and physical elements which there existed, and made up the sum of what might be termed the influences of the age. In this picture, and in that of the "Era of Hope" (as Mr. Carlyle calls the first years of Louis XVI,)[†] there is much that we would gladly quote. But on the whole we think these introductory chapters the least interesting part of the book; less distinguished by their intrinsic merit, and more so by all the peculiarities of manner which either are really defects, or appear so. These chapters will only have justice done them on a second reading: once familiarized with the author's characteristic turn of thought and expression, we find many passages full of meaning, which, to unprepared minds, would convey a very small portion, if any, of the sense which they are not only intended, but are in themselves admirably calculated to express: for the finest expression is not always that which is the most readily apprehended. The real character of the book, however, begins only to display itself when the properly narrative portion commences. This, however, is more or less the case with all histories, though seldom to so conspicuous an extent.

The stream of the narrative acquires its full speed about the hundred and sixty-fifth page, and the beginning of the fourth book. The introductory rapid sketch of what may be called the coming-on of the Revolution, is then ended, and

*[TC] [Charles Jean François Hénault, *Nouvel*] *Abrégé Chronologique de l'Histoire de France* [1744, 3 vols.] (Paris [: Prault, *et al.*], 1775), [Vol. II,] p. 701.

†[TC] *Mémoires de M. le Baron Besenval*, [4 vols.] (Paris [: Buisson], 1805-06), Vol. II, pp. 59-90 [the passage quoted in translation is from p. 63].

[*Carlyle, Vol. I, pp. 3-4.]

[†*Ibid.*, p. 48.]

we are arrived at the calling together of the States General. The fourth book, first chapter, opens as follows:

The universal prayer, therefore, is to be fulfilled! Always in days of national perplexity, when wrong abounded and help was not, this remedy of States General was called for; by a Malesherbes, nay by a Fénélon:* even Parlements calling for it were "escorted with blessings."[*] And now behold it is vouchsafed us; States General shall verily be!

To say, let States General be, was easy; to say in what manner they shall be, is not so easy. Since the year 1614, there have no States General met in France; all trace of them has vanished from the living habits of men. Their structure, powers, methods of procedure, which were never in any measure fixed, have now become wholly a vague Possibility. Clay which the potter may shape, this way or that:—say rather, the twenty-five millions of potters; for so many have now, more or less, a vote in it! How to shape the States General? There is a problem. Each Body-corporate, each privileged, each organised Class has secret hopes of its own in that matter; and also secret misgivings of its own,—for, behold, this monstrous twenty-million Class, hitherto the dumb sheep which these others had to agree about the manner of shearing, is now also arising with hopes! It has ceased or is ceasing to be dumb; it speaks through Pamphlets, or at least brays and growls behind them, in unison,—increasing wonderfully their volume of sound.

As for the Parlement of Paris, it has at once declared for the "old form of 1614." Which form had this advantage, that the *Tiers Etat*, Third Estate, or Commons, figured there as a show mainly: whereby the Noblesse and Clergy had but to avoid quarrel between themselves, and decide unobstructed what *they* thought best. Such was the clearly declared opinion of the Paris Parlement. But, being met by a storm of mere hooting and howling from all men, such opinion was blown straightway to the winds; and the popularity of the Parlement along with it,—never to return. The Parlement's part, we said above, was as good as played. Concerning which, however, there is this further to be noted: the proximity of dates. It was on the 22nd of September that the Parlement returned from "vacation" or "exile in its estates;" to be reinstalled amid boundless jubilee from all Paris. Precisely next day, it was that this same Parlement came to its "clearly declared opinion:" and then on the morrow after that, you behold it "covered with outrages;" its outer court, one vast sibilation, and the glory departed from it for evermore.[†] A popularity of twenty-four hours was, in those times, no uncommon allowance.

On the other hand, how superfluous was that invitation of Loménie: the invitation to thinkers! Thinkers and unthinkers, by the million, are spontaneously at their post, doing what is in them. Clubs labour: *Société Publicole*; Breton Club; Enraged Club, *Club des Enragés*. Likewise dinner-parties in the Palais Royal; your Mirabeaus, Talleyrands dining there, in company with Chamforts, Morellets, with Duponts and hot Parlementeers, not without object! For a certain *Necker*ean lion's-provider, whom one could name, assembles them there;[‡]—or even their own private determination to have dinner does it. And then as to pamphlets—in figurative language, "it is a sheer snowing of pamphlets; like to snow up the Government thoroughfares!"[†] Now is the time for friends of freedom; sane, and even insane.

*[TC] Montgaillard, [*Histoire de France*, 9 vols. (Paris: Moutardier, 1827),] Vol. I, pp. 461-2.

[*Alexandre Lameth, *Histoire de l'assemblée constituante*, 2 vols. (Paris: Moutardier, 1828-29), Vol. I, p. lxxiii (as rendered in English by Carlyle).]

†[TC] [Joseph] Weber, [*Mémoires concernant Marie Antoinette*, 3 vols. (London: the Author, 1804-09),] Vol. I, p. 347. [For the concluding clause, see II Samuel, 4:22.]

‡[TC] Weber, Vol. I, p. 360. [The reference is to Jean Baptiste Artaud.]

[†Besenval, *Mémoires*, Vol. III, p. 343.]

Count, or self-styled Count, d'Aintraigues, "the young Languedocian gentleman," with perhaps Chamfort the Cynic to help him, rises into furor almost Pythic; highest, where many are high.* Foolish young Languedocian gentleman; who himself so soon, "emigrating among the foremost," must fly indignant over the marches, with the *Contrat Social*[*] in his pocket,—towards outer darkness, thankless intriguings, *ignis-fatuus* hoverings, and death by the stiletto! Abbé Sieyès has left Chartres Cathedral, and canonry and book-shelves there; has let his tonsure grow, and come to Paris with a secular head, of the most irrefragable sort, to ask three questions, and answer them: *What is the Third Estate? All. What has it hitherto been in our form of government? Nothing. What does it want? To become something.*[†]

D'Orleans, for be sure he, on his way to Chaos, is in the thick of this,—promulgates his *Deliberations;*[†] fathered by him, written by Laclos of the *Liaisons Dangereuses.*[‡] The result of which comes out simply: "The Third Estate is the Nation."[§] On the other hand, Monseigneur d'Artois, with other Princes of the Blood, publishes, in solemn *Memorial* to the King, that, if such things be listened to, Privilege, Nobility, Monarchy, Church, State, and Strongbox are in danger.[‡] In danger truly: and yet if you do not listen, are they out of danger? It is the voice of all France, this sound that rises. Immeasurable, manifold; as the sound of outbreaking waters: wise were he who knew what to do in it,—if not to fly to the mountains, and hide himself!

How an ideal, all-seeing Versailles Government, sitting there on such principles, in such an environment, would have determined to demean itself at this new juncture; may even yet be a question. Such a Government had felt too well that its long task was now drawing to a close; that, under the guise of these States General, at length inevitable, a new omnipotent Unknown of Democracy was coming into being; in presence of which no Versailles Government either could or should, except in a provisory character, continue extant. To enact which provisory character, so unspeakably important, might its whole faculties but have sufficed; and so a peaceable, gradual, well-conducted Abdication and *Domine-dimittas* have been the issue!

This for our ideal, all-seeing Versailles Government. But for the actual irrational Versailles Government? Alas! that is a Government existing there only for its own behoof: without right, except possession; and now also without might. It foresees nothing, sees nothing; has not so much as a purpose, but has only purposes,—and the instinct whereby all that exists will struggle to keep existing. Wholly a vortex: in which vain counsels,

---

*[TC] [Louis Emmanuel de Launay, comte d'Antraigues,] *Mémoire sur les Etats-Généraux*. See Montgaillard, Vol. I, pp. 457-9.

[*Jean Jacques Rousseau, *Du contrat social, ou Principes du droit politique* (Amsterdam: Rey, 1762).]

[†Emmanuel Joseph Sieyès, *Qu'est-ce que le tiers état?*, 3rd ed. ([Paris:] n.p., 1789), p. 3.]

†[TC] "Délibérations à prendre dans les Assemblées des Bailliages" [attributed to Sieyès, not Laclos, published in Louis Philippe Joseph, duc d'Orléans, *Instructions envoyées par M. le duc d'Orléans* ([Paris: n.p., 1788]), pp. 11-66].

[‡Pierre Ambroise François Choderlos de Laclos, *Les liaisons dangereuses*, 4 vols. (Amsterdam and Paris: Durand, 1782).]

[§See, e.g., Sieyès, *Qu'est-ce que le tiers état?*, p. 154.]

‡[TC] *Mémoire présenté au Roi par Monseigneur Comte d'Artois, M. le Prince de Condé, M. le Duc de Bourbon, M. le Duc d'Enghien, et M. le Prince de Conti* (1788). (Given in *Histoire parlementaire* [*de la révolution française* (*HP*), ed. Philippe Joseph Benjamin Buchez and Prosper Charles Roux, 40 vols. (Paris: Paulin, 1834-38)], Vol. I, pp. 256-62.)

hallucinations, falsehoods, intrigues, and imbecilities whirl; like withered rubbish in the meeting of winds! The Oeil-de-Boeuf has its irrational hopes, if also its fears. Since hitherto all States General have done as good as nothing, why should these do more? The Commons indeed look dangerous; but on the whole is not revolt, unknown now for five generations, an impossibility? The Three Estates can, by management, be set against each other; the Third will, as heretofore, join with the King; will, out of mere spite and self-interest, be eager to tax and vex the other two. The other two are thus delivered bound into our hands, that we may fleece them likewise. Whereupon, money being got, and the Three Estates all in quarrel, dismiss them, and let the future go as it can! As good Archbishop Loménie was wont to say: "There are so many accidents; and it needs but one to save us."—How many to destroy us?

Poor Necker in the midst of such an anarchy does what is possible for him. He looks into it with obstinately hopeful face; lauds the known rectitude of the kingly mind; listens indulgent-like to the known perverseness of the queenly and courtly;—emits if any proclamation or regulation, one favouring the *Tiers Etat*; but settling nothing; hovering afar off rather, and advising all things to settle themselves. . . .[*]

But so, at least, by Royal Edict of the 24th of January,* does it finally, to impatient expectant France, become not only indubitable that national deputies *are* to meet, but possible (so far and hardly further has the royal regulation gone) to begin electing them.[†]

The next Chapter is "The Election."

Up then, and be doing! The royal signal-word flies through France, as through vast forests the rushing of a mighty wind. At Parish Churches, in Townhalls, and every House of Convocation; by Bailliages, by Seneschalsies, in whatsoever form men convene; there, with confusion enough, are primary assemblies forming. To elect your electors; such is the form prescribed: then to draw up your "Writ of Plaints and Grievances (*Cahier de plaintes et doléances*)," of which latter there is no lack.

With such virtue works this Royal January Edict; as it rolls rapidly, in its leathern mails, along these frost-bound highways, towards all the four winds. Like some *fiat*, or magic spell-word;—which such things do resemble! For always, as it sounds out "at the market-cross," accompanied with trumpet-blast; presided by Bailli, Seneschal, or other minor functionary, with beefeaters; or, in country churches, is droned forth after sermon, "*au prône des messes paroissiales;*"[‡] and is registered, posted, and let fly over all the world,—you behold how this multitudinous French people, so long simmering and buzzing in eager expectancy, begins heaping and shaping itself into organic groups. Which organic groups, again, hold smaller organic grouplets: the inarticulate buzzing becomes articulate speaking and acting. By Primary Assembly, and then by Secondary; by "successive elections," and infinite elaboration and scrutiny, according to prescribed process,—shall the genuine "Plaints and Grievances" be at length got to paper; shall the fit National Representative be at length laid hold of.

How the whole People shakes itself, as if it had one life; and, in thousand-voiced rumour,

[*See Necker's "Extrait du rapport fait au roi dans son conseil, le 27 décembre 1788," in F.M. Kerverseau, G. Clavelin, *et al.*, *Histoire de la révolution de France, par deux amis de la liberté*, new ed., 19 vols. (Paris: Garnery, and Bidault, 1792-1803), Vol. I, pp. 79-93. Carlyle refers to this work, one of his main sources, as "*Deux Amis.*"]

*[TC] "Réglement du Roi pour la Convocation des Etats-Généraux à Versailles" [24 Jan., 1789] (reprinted, wrong dated, in *HP*, Vol. I, pp. 262-76).

[†Carlyle, Vol. I, pp. 165-70, 172.]

[‡"Réglement," *HP*, Vol. I, p. 266.]

announces that it is awake, suddenly out of long death-sleep, and will thenceforth sleep no more![*] The long looked-for has come at last; wondrous news, of victory, deliverance, enfranchisement, sounds magical through every heart. To the proud strong man it has come; whose strong hands shall no more be gyved; to whom boundless unconquered continents lie disclosed. The weary day-drudge has heard of it; the beggar with his crust moistened in tears. What! To us also has hope reached; down even to us? Hunger and hardship are not to be eternal? The bread we extorted from the rugged glebe, and, with the toil of our sinews, reaped and ground, and kneaded into loaves, was not wholly for another, then; but we also shall eat of it, and be filled? Glorious news (answer the prudent elders), but all too unlikely!—Thus, at any rate, may the lower people, who pay no money taxes and have no right to vote,* assiduously crowd round those that do; and most halls of assembly, within doors and without, seem animated enough.[†]

Has the reader often seen the state of an agitated nation made thus present, thus palpable? How the thing paints itself in all its greatness—the men in all their littleness! and this is not done by reasoning about them, but by showing them. The deep pathos of the last paragraph, grand as it is, is but an average specimen; as, indeed, is the whole passage. In the remaining two volumes and a half there are scarcely five consecutive pages of inferior merit to those we have quoted. The few extracts we can venture to make, will be selected, not for peculiarity of merit, but either as forming wholes in themselves, or as depicting events or situations, with which the reader, it may be hoped, is familiar.† For the more he previously knew of the mere outline of the facts, the more he will admire the writer, whose pictorial and truly poetic genius enables him for the first time to fill up the outline.

Our last extract was an abridged sketch of the State of a Nation: the next shall be a copious narrative of a single event: the far-famed Siege of the Bastille. How much every such passage must suffer by being torn from the context, needs scarcely be said; and nothing that could be said, could, in this case, make it adequately felt. The history of the two previous days occupies twenty-two pages, rising from page to page in interest. We begin at noon on the fourteenth of July:

All morning, since nine, there has been a cry every where: To the Bastille! Repeated "deputations of citizens" have been here, passionate for arms; whom de Launay has got

[*Cf. Shakespeare, *Macbeth*, II, ii, 32 (in *The Riverside Shakespeare*, p. 1320).]

*[TC] "Réglement," *HP*, Vol. I, pp. 267-307.

[†Carlyle, Vol. I, pp. 173-4.]

†It may be hoped; scarcely, we fear, expected. For considering the extraordinary dramatic interest of the story of the Revolution, however imperfectly told, it is really surprising how little, to English readers, even the outline of the facts is known. Mr. Carlyle's book is less fitted for those who know nothing about the subject, than for those who already know a little. We rejoice to see that a translation of Thiers is announced. As a mere piece of narrative, we know nothing in modern historical writing so nearly resembling the ancient models as Thiers' *History*: we hope he has met with a translator who can do him justice. Whoever has read Thiers first, will be the better fitted both to enjoy and to understand Carlyle. [Louis Adolphe Thiers, *Histoire de la révolution française*, 10 vols. (Paris: Lecointe and Durey, 1823-27); trans. Frederick Shoberl, *History of the French Revolution*, 5 vols. (London: Bentley, 1838).]

dismissed by soft speeches through portholes. Towards noon, Elector Thuriot de la Rosière gains admittance; finds de Launay indisposed for surrender; nay disposed for blowing up the place rather. Thuriot mounts with him to the battlements; heaps of paving-stones, old iron and missiles lie piled; cannon all duly levelled; in every embrasure a cannon,—only drawn back a little! But outwards, behold, O Thuriot, how the multitude flows on, welling through every street; tocsin furiously pealing, all drums beating the *générale*; the Suburb Saint-Antoine rolling hitherward wholly, as one man! Such vision (spectral yet real) thou, O Thuriot, as from thy Mount of Vision, beholdest in this moment: prophetic of what other Phantasmagories, and loud-gibbering Spectral Realities, which thou yet beholdest not, but shalt! "*Que voulez-vous?*" said de Launay, turning pale at the sight, with an air of reproach, almost of menace. "Monsieur," said Thuriot, rising into the moral-sublime, "What mean *you*? Consider if I could not precipate *both* of us from this height,"—say only a hundred feet, exclusive of the walled ditch![*] Whereupon de Launay fell silent. Thuriot shews himself from some pinnacle, to comfort the multitude becoming suspicious, fremescent: then descends; departs with protest; with warning addressed also to the Invalides,—on whom, however, it produces but a mixed indistinct impression. The old heads are none of the clearest; besides, it is said, de Launay has been profuse of beverages (*prodigua des boissons*). They think, they will not fire,—if not fired on, if they can help it; but must, on the whole, be ruled considerably by circumstances.

Wo to thee, de Launay, in such an hour, if thou canst not, taking some one firm decision, *rule* circumstances! Soft speeches will not serve; hard grape-shot is questionable; but hovering between the two is *un*questionable. Ever wilder swells the tide of men; their infinite hum waxing ever louder, into imprecations, perhaps into crackle of stray musketry,—which latter, on walls nine feet thick, cannot do execution. The outer drawbridge has been lowered for Thuriot; new *deputation of citizens* (it is the third, and noisiest of all) penetrates that way into the outer court: soft speeches producing no clearance of these, de Launay gives fire; pulls up his drawbridge. A slight sputter;—which has *kindled* the too combustible chaos; made it a roaring fire-chaos! Bursts forth Insurrection, at sight of its own blood (for there were deaths by that sputter of fire), into endless rolling explosion of musketry, distraction, execration;—and over head, from the fortress, let one great gun, with its grape-shot, go booming, to shew what we *could* do. The Bastille is besieged!

On, then, all Frenchmen that have hearts in their bodies! Roar with all your throats, of cartilage and metal, ye Sons of Liberty; stir spasmodically whatsoever of utmost faculty is in you, soul, body or spirit; for it is the hour! Smite, thou Louis Tournay, cartwright of the Marais, old-soldier of the Regiment Dauphine; smite at that outer drawbridge-chain, though the fiery hail whistles round thee! Never, over nave or felloe, did thy axe strike such a stroke. Down with it, man; down with it to Orcus: let the whole accursed Edifice sink thither, and Tyranny be swallowed up for ever! Mounted, some say on the roof of the guard-room, some "on bayonets stuck into joints of the wall," Louis Tournay smites, brave Aubin Bonnemère (also an old soldier) seconding him: the chain yields, breaks; the huge drawbridge slams down, thundering (*avec fracas*).[†] Glorious: and yet, alas, it is still but the outworks. The Eight grim Towers, with their Invalides' musketry, their paving stones and cannon-mouths, still soar aloft intact;—ditch yawning impassable, stone-faced; the inner drawbridge with its *back* towards us: the Bastille is still to take!

To describe this siege of the Bastille (thought to be one of the most important in History) perhaps transcends the talent of mortals. Could one but, after infinite reading, get to understand so much as the plan of the building! But there is open Esplanade, at the end of the

[*Cf. *Deux amis*, Vol. I, p. 315.]
[†Cf. *ibid.*, pp. 317-18.]

Rue Saint-Antoine; there are such Forecourts, *Cour Avancé, Cour de l'Orme*, arched Gateway (where Louis Tournay now fights); then new drawbridges, dormant-bridges, rampart-bastions, and the grim Eight Towers: a labyrinthic mass, high-frowning there, of all ages from twenty years to four hundred and twenty;—beleaguered, in this its last hour, as we said, by mere Chaos come again![*] Ordnance of all calibres; throats of all capacities; men of all plans, every man his own engineer: seldom since the war of Pygmies and Cranes[†] was there seen so anomalous a thing. Half-pay Elie is home for a suit of regimentals; no one would heed him in coloured clothes: half-pay Hulin is haranguing Gardes Françaises in the Place de Grève. Frantic patriots pick up the grape-shots; bear them, still hot (or seemingly so), to the Hôtel-de-Ville:—Paris, you perceive, is to be burnt! Flesselles is "pale to the very lips," for the roar of the multitude grows deep. Paris wholly has got to the acme of its frenzy; whirled, all ways, by panic madness. At every street-barricade, there whirls simmering, a minor whirlpool,—strengthening the barricade, since God knows what is coming: and all minor whirlpools play distractedly into that grand Fire-Mahlstrom which is lashing round the Bastille.

And so it lashes and it roars. Cholat the wine-merchant has become an impromptu cannoneer. See Georget, of the marine service, fresh from Brest, ply the King of Siam's cannon.[‡] Singular (if we were not used to the like): Georget lay, last night, taking his ease at his inn;[§] the King of Siam's cannon also lay, knowing nothing of *him*, for a hundred years. Yet now, at the right instant, they have got together, and discourse eloquent music. For, hearing what was toward, Georget sprang from the Brest Diligence, and ran. Gardes Françaises also will be here, with real artillery: were not the walls so thick!—Upwards from the Esplanade, horizontally from all neighbouring roofs and windows, flashes one irregular deluge of musketry,—without effect. The Invalides lie flat, firing comparatively at their ease from behind stone; hardly through portholes, shew the tip of a nose. We fall, shot; and make no impression!

Let conflagration rage; of whatsoever is combustible! Guard-rooms are burnt, Invalides' mess-rooms. A distracted "Perukemaker with two fiery torches" is for burning "the saltpetres of the Arsenal;"[¶]—had not a woman run screaming; had not a Patriot, with some tincture of Natural Philosophy, instantly struck the wind out of him (butt of musket on pit of stomach), overturned barrels, and stayed the devouring element. A young beautiful lady, seized escaping in these Outer Courts, and thought falsely to be de Launay's daughter, shall be burnt in de Launay's sight; she lies swooned on a paillasse: but again a Patriot, it is brave Aubin Bonnemère the old soldier, dashes in, and rescues her. Straw is burnt; three cartloads of it, hauled thither, go up in white smoke: almost to the choking of Patriotism itself; so that Elie had, with singed brows, to drag back one cart; and Réole the "gigantic haberdasher" another.[ǁ] Smoke as of Tophet;[**] confusion as of Babel;[††] noise as of the Crack of Doom![‡‡]

Blood flows; the aliment of new madness. The wounded are carried into houses of the

---

[*Cf. Shakespeare, *Othello*, III, iii, 93 (in *The Riverside Shakespeare*, p. 1221).]

[†See Homer, *The Iliad* (Greek and English), trans. A.T. Murray, 2 vols. (London: Heinemann; Cambridge, Mass.: Harvard University Press, 1924), Vol. I, p. 116 (III, 1-7).]

[‡The reference is to Phra Narai.]

[§Cf. Shakespeare, *Henry IV, Part I*, III, iii, 80-1 (in *The Riverside Shakespeare*, p. 870).]

[¶Cf. *Deux amis*, Vol. I, p. 331.]

[ǁCf. *ibid.*, pp. 328-30.]

[**See Isaiah, 30:33.]

[††See Genesis, 11:9.]

[‡‡Cf. Shakespeare, *Macbeth*, IV, i, 117 (in *The Riverside Shakespeare*, p. 1330).]

Rue Cerisaie; the dying leave their last mandate not to yield till the accursed Stronghold fall. And yet, alas, how fall? The walls are so thick! Deputations, three in number, arrive from the Hôtel-de-Ville; Abbé Fauchet (who was one) can say, with what almost superhuman courage of benevolence.* These wave their Town-flag in the arched Gateway: and stand, rolling their drum; but to no purpose. In such Crack of Doom, de Launay cannot hear them, dare not believe them: they return, with justified rage, the whew of lead still singing in their ears. What to do? The Firemen are here, squirting with their fire-pumps on the Invalides' cannon, to wet the touchholes; they unfortunately cannot squirt so high; but produce only clouds of spray. Individuals of classical knowledge propose *catapults*. Santerre, the sonorous brewer of the suburb Saint-Antoine, advises rather that the place be fired, by a "mixture of phosphorus and oil-of-turpentine spouted up through forcing pumps:" O Spinola-Santerre,[*] hast thou the mixture *ready*? Every man his own engineer! And still the fire-deluge abates not; even women are firing, and Turks; at least one woman (with her sweetheart), and one Turk.[†] Gardes Françaises have come: real cannon, real cannoneers. Usher Maillard is busy; half-pay Elie, half-pay Hulin rage in the midst of thousands.

How the great Bastille Clock ticks (inaudible) in its Inner Court there, at its ease, hour after hour; as if nothing special, for it or the world, were passing! It tolled One when the firing began; and is now pointing towards Five, and still the firing slakes not.—Far down, in their vaults, the seven Prisoners[†] hear muffled din as of earthquakes; their Turnkeys answer vaguely.

Wo to thee, de Launay, with thy poor hundred Invalides! Broglie is distant, and his ears heavy: Besenval hears, but can send no help. One poor troop of Hussars has crept, reconnoitring, cautiously along the quais, as far as the Pont Neuf. "We are come to join you," said the Captain; for the crowd seems shoreless. A large-headed dwarfish individual, of smoke-bleared aspect, shambles forward, opening his blue lips, for there is sense in him; and croaks: "Alight then, and give up your arms!" The Hussar-Captain is too happy to be escorted to the barriers, and dismissed on parole. Who the squat individual was? Men answer, It is M. Marat, author of the excellent pacific *Avis au Peuple*![‡] Great truly, O thou remarkable Dogleech, is this thy day of emergence and new-birth: and yet this same day come four years—!—But let the curtains of the Future hang.

What shall de Launay do? One thing only de Launay could have done: what he said he would do. Fancy him sitting, from the first, with lighted taper, within arm's length of the powder-magazine; motionless, like old Roman Senator, or bronze Lamp-holder; coldly apprising Thuriot, and all men, by a slight motion of his eye, what his resolution was:— Harmless he sat there, while unharmed; but the King's fortress, meanwhile, could, might, would, or should, in nowise, be surrendered, save to the King's Messenger: one old man's life is worthless, so it be lost with honour; but think, ye brawling *canaille*, how will it be

---

*[TC] Fauchet's Narrative (*Deux Amis*, Vol. I, pp. 324-5).

[*Carlyle is combining the names of Ambrose Spinola, marquis de los Balbases, a general, and Antoine Joseph Santerre, a brewer.]

†[TC] *Deux Amis* (Vol. I, pp. 318-20 [here a Greek, not a Turk, is mentioned]); [Jean Joseph] Dusaulx, [*De l'insurrection parisienne, et de la prise de la Bastille*, in *Mémoires de Linguet, sur la Bastille, et de Dusaulx, sur le 14 juillet*, ed. Saint Albin Berville and Jean François Barrière (Paris: Baudouin, 1821), *passim*, but including pp. 331n, 372n, 407-8,] &c.

[†Jean Béchade, Jean La Corrège, Bernard Laroche, Jean Antoine Pujade, le comte de Solages, Tavernier, and one Whyte (or De Witt).]

[‡Jean Paul Marat, *Avis au peuple, ou Les ministres dévoilés* (1789), in *HP*, Vol. II, pp. 37-8.]

when a whole Bastille springs skyward!—In such statuesque, taper-holding attitude, one fancies de Launay might have left Thuriot, the red Clerks of the Bazoche, Curé of Saint-Stephen and all the tagrag-and-bobtail of the world, to work their will.

And yet, withal, he could not do it. Hast thou considered how each man's heart is so tremulously responsive to the hearts of all men; hast thou noted how omnipotent is the very sound of many men? How their shriek of indignation palsies the strong soul; their howl of contumely withers with unfelt pangs? The Ritter Glück confessed that the ground-tone of the noblest passage, in one of his noblest Operas, was the voice of the populace he had heard at Vienna, crying to their Kaiser: Bread! Bread![*] Great is the combined voice of men; the utterance of their *instincts*, which are truer than their *thoughts*: it is the greatest a man encounters, among the sounds and shadows, which make up this World of Time. He who can resist that, has his footing somewhere *beyond* time. De Launay could not do it. Distracted, he hovers between two; hopes in the middle of despair; surrenders not his fortress; declares that he will blow it up, seizes torches to blow it up, and does not blow it. Unhappy old de Launay, it is the death-agony of thy Bastille and thee! Jail, jailoring and jailor, all three, such as they may have been, must finish.

For four hours now has the World-Bedlam roared: call it the World-Chimaera, blowing fire! The poor Invalides have sunk under their battlements, or rise only with reversed muskets: they have made a white flag of napkins; go beating the *chamade*, or seeming to beat, for one can hear nothing. The very Swiss at the Portcullis look weary of firing; disheartened in the fire-deluge: a porthole at the drawbridge is opened, as by one that would speak. See Huissier Maillard, the shifty man! On his plank, swinging over the abyss of that stone-ditch; plank resting on parapet, balanced by weight of patriots,—he hovers perilous: such a dove towards such an ark! Deftly, thou shifty Usher: one man already fell; and lies smashed, far down there, against the masonry! Usher Maillard falls not: deftly, unerring he walks, with outspread palm. The Swiss holds a paper through his porthole; the shifty Usher snatches it, and returns. Terms of surrender: Pardon, immunity to all! Are they accepted?—"*Foi d'officier*, on the word of an officer," answers half-pay Hulin,—or half-pay Elie, for men do not agree on it, "they are!" Sinks the drawbridge,—Usher Maillard bolting it when down; rushes-in the living deluge: the Bastille is fallen! *Victoire! La Bastille est prise!**

We quote next the passage on the Burning of Châteaux. Mr. Carlyle gives rather a different account from what English people have been used to, of that feature of the Revolution:

Starvation has been known among the French commonalty before this; known and familiar. Did we not see them, in the year 1775, presenting, in sallow faces, in wretchedness and raggedness, their Petition of Grievances; and, for answer, getting a brand-new gallows forty feet high?[†] Hunger and darkness, through long years! For look

[*This anecdote about Christoph Willibald von Glück's *Iphigenia in Aulis* is told by Guillaume Olivier de Corancez, in *Journal de Paris*, 21 Aug., 1788, pp. 1009-10.]

*[Carlyle, Vol. I, pp. 264-73.] [TC] *Deux Amis*, Vol. I, pp. 267-400; Besenval, [*Mémoires*,] Vol. III, pp. 410-34; Dusaulx, "Prise de la Bastille," [in *De l'insurrection parisienne*,] pp. 291-301; Bailly, *Mémoires* (Collection de Berville et Barrière), Vol. I, pp. 322ff.

[†See Charles Durozoir, biography of Turgot, in *Biographie universelle ancienne et moderne*, ed. Louis Gabriel Michaud, 42 vols. (Paris: Michaud frères, 1811-28), Vol. XLVII, p. 78.]

back on that earlier Paris riot, when a great personage, worn out by debauchery, was believed to be in want of blood-baths; and mothers, in worn raiment, yet with living hearts under it, "filled the public places"[*] with their wild Rachel-cries,—stilled also by the gallows. Twenty years ago, The Friend of Men (preaching to the deaf) described the Limousin peasants as wearing a pain-stricken (*souffre-douleur*) look, a look *past* complaint, "as if the oppression of the great were like the hail and the thunder, a thing irremediable, the ordinance of nature."* And now, if in some great hour, the shock of a falling Bastille should awaken you; and it were found to be the ordinance of art merely; and remediable, reversible!

Or has the reader forgotten that "flood of savages," which, in sight of the same Friend of Men, descended from the mountains at Mont d'Or? Lank-haired haggard faces; shapes rawboned, in high sabots; in woollen jupes, with leather girdles studded with copper-nails! They rocked from foot to foot, and beat time with their elbows too, as the quarrel and battle which was not long in beginning went on; shouting fiercely; the lank faces distorted into the similitude of a cruel laugh. For they were darkened and hardened: long had they been the prey of excise-men and tax-men; of "clerks with the cold spurt of their pen." It was the fixed prophecy of our old Marquis, which no man would listen to, that "such Government by Blind-man's-buff, stumbling along too far, would end by the General Overturn, the *Culbute Générale!*"[†]

No man would listen, each went his thoughtless way;—and Time and Destiny also travelled on. The Government by Blind-man's-buff, stumbling along, has reached the precipice inevitable for it. Dull Drudgery, driven on, by clerks with the cold dastard spurt of their pen, has been driven—into a Communion of Drudges! For now, moreover, there have come the strangest confused tidings; by Paris Journals with their paper wings; or still more portentous, where no Journals are,[†] by rumour and conjecture: Oppression *not* inevitable; a Bastille prostrate, and the Constitution fast getting ready! Which Constitution, if it be something and not nothing, what can it be but bread to eat?

The traveller, "walking up hill bridle in hand," overtakes "a poor woman;" the image, as such commonly are, of drudgery and scarcity; "looking sixty years of age, though she is not yet twenty-eight." They have seven children, her poor drudge and she: a farm, with one cow, which helps to make the children soup; also one little horse, or garron. They have rents and quit-rents, Hens to pay to this Seigneur, Oat-sacks to that; King's taxes, Statute-labour, Church-taxes, taxes enough;—and think the times inexpressible. She has heard that some*where*, in some manner, some*thing* is to be done for the poor: "God send it soon; for the dues and taxes crush us down (*nous écrasent*)!"[‡]

Fair prophecies are spoken, but they are not fulfilled. There have been Notables,

---

[*Jean Charles Dominique de Lacretelle, *Histoire de France pendant le dix-huitième siècle* (1808-26), 5th ed., 3 vols. (Paris: Delaunay, 1819), Vol. III, p. 175.]

*[TC] Fils Adoptif, *Mémoires de Mirabeau*, Vol. I, pp. 364-94. [Honoré Gabriel Riqueti de Mirabeau, *Mémoires biographiques, littéraires et politiques de Mirabeau, écrits par lui-même, par son père, son oncle et son fils adoptif*, ed. Gabriel Lucas-Montigny, 8 vols. (Paris: Auffray, *et al.*, 1834-35); the concluding passage is Carlyle's rendering of a sentence on p. 394. The "Friend of Men" is Victor Riqueti, marquis de Mirabeau, father of Honoré Gabriel Riqueti, comte de Mirabeau; Gabriel Lucas-Montigny is the "fils adoptif."]

[†Carlyle is drawing on Victor Riqueti de Mirabeau, "Lettre à la comtesse de Rochefort" (18 Aug., 1777), *ibid.*, Vol. II, pp. 186-8.]

†[TC] See Arthur Young, [*Travels during the Years 1787, 1788, and 1789* (Bury St. Edmunds: Richardson, 1792)], pp. 137-50, &c.

‡[TC] *Ibid.*, p. 134.

Assemblages, turnings out and comings in. Intriguing and manoeuvring; parliamentary eloquence and arguing, Greek meeting Greek in high places,[*] has long gone on; yet still bread comes not. The harvest is reaped and garnered; yet still we have no bread. Urged by despair and by hope, what can Drudgery do, but rise, as predicted, and produce the General Overturn?

Fancy, then, some five full-grown millions of such gaunt figures, with their haggard faces (*figures hâves*); in woollen jupes, with copper-studded leather girths, and high sabots,—starting up to ask, as in forest-roarings, their washed Upper-Classes, after long unreviewed centuries, virtually this question: How have ye treated us; how have ye taught us, fed us, and led us, while we toiled for you? The answer can be read in flames, over the nightly summer-sky. *This* is the feeding and leading we have had of you: EMPTINESS,—of pocket, of stomach, of head, and of heart. Behold there is *nothing in us*; nothing but what nature gives her wild children of the desert: Ferocity and Appetite; Strength grounded on Hunger. Did ye mark among your Rights of Man, that man was not to die of starvation, while there was bread reaped by him? It is among the Mights of Man.

Seventy-two Châteaus have flamed aloft in the Maconnais and Beaujolais alone: this seems the centre of the conflagration; but it has spread over Dauphiné, Alsace, the Lyonnais; the whole south-east is in a blaze. All over the north, from Rouen to Metz, disorder is abroad: smugglers of salt go openly in armed bands: the barriers of towns are burnt; toll-gatherers, tax-gatherers, official persons put to flight. "It was thought," says Young, "the people, from hunger, would revolt;"[†] and we see they have done it. Desperate Lackalls, long prowling aimless, now finding hope in desperation itself, everywhere form a nucleus. They ring the Church bell by way of tocsin: and the Parish turns out to the work.* Ferocity, atrocity; hunger and revenge: such work as we can imagine!

Ill stands it now with the Seigneur, who, for example, "has walled up the only Fountain of the Township;" who has ridden high on his *chartier* and parchment; who has preserved Game not wisely but too well.[‡] Churches also, and Canonries, are sacked, without mercy; which have shorn the flock too close, forgetting to feed it. Wo to the land over which Sansculottism, in its day of vengeance, tramps roughshod,—shod in sabots! Highbred Seigneurs, with their delicate women and littles ones, had to "fly half-naked," under cloud of night; glad to escape the flames, and even worse. You meet them at the *tables-d'hôte* of inns; making wise reflections or foolish that "rank is destroyed;" uncertain whither they shall now wend.[†] The metayer will find it convenient to be slack in paying rent. As for the Tax-gatherer, he, long hunting as a biped of prey, may now get hunted as one; his Majesty's Exchequer will not "fill up the Deficit,"[§] this season: it is the notion of many that a Patriot Majesty, being the Restorer of French Liberty, has abolished most taxes, though, for their private ends, some men make a secret of it.

Where this will end? In the Abyss, one may prophesy; whither all Delusions, are, at all moments, travelling; where this Delusion has now arrived. For if there be a Faith, from of old, it is this, as we often repeat, that no Lie can live for ever. The very Truth has to change its vesture, from time to time; and be born again. But all Lies have sentence of death written down against them, in Heaven's Chancery itself; and, slowly or fast, advance incessantly

---

[*Cf. Nathaniel Lee, *The Rival Queens; or, The Death of Alexander the Great* (London: Magnes and Bentley, 1677), p. 48 (IV).]

[†Young, *Travels*, p. 141.]

*[TC] See *HP*, Vol. II, pp. 243-6.

[‡Cf. Shakespeare, *Othello*, V, ii, 344 (in *The Riverside Shakespeare*, p. 1240).]

†[TC] See Young, pp. 149-51.

[§*Ibid.*, e.g., pp. 66, 198, 275, 511-16, 558-60.]

towards their hour. "The sign of a Grand Seigneur being landlord," says the vehement plain-spoken Arthur Young, "are wastes, *landes*, deserts, ling: go to his residence, you will find it in the middle of a forest, peopled with deer, wild boars and wolves. The fields are scenes of pitiable management, as the houses are of misery. To see so many millions of hands, that would be industrious, all idle and starving: oh, if I were legislator of France, for one day, I would make these great lords skip again!"* O Arthur, thou now actually beholdest them *skip*;—wilt thou grow to grumble at that too?

For long years and generations it lasted, but the time came. Featherbrain, whom no reasoning and no pleading could touch, the glare of the firebrand had to illuminate: there remained but that method. Consider it, look at it! The widow is gathering nettles for her children's dinner; a perfumed Seigneur, delicately lounging in the Oeil-de-Boeuf, has an alchemy whereby he will extract from her the third nettle, and name it Rent and Law: such an arrangement must end. Ought it? But, O most fearful is *such* an ending! Let those, to whom God, in His great mercy, has granted time and space, prepare another and milder one.[*]

We shall now give a still more striking scene: the opening of the "Insurrection of Women."[†]

If Voltaire once, in splenetic humour, asked his countrymen: "But you, *Gualches*, what have you invented?"[‡] they can now answer: the Art of Insurrection. It was an art needed in these last singular times: an art, for which the French nature, so full of vehemence, so free from depth, was perhaps of all others the fittest.

Accordingly, to what a height, one may well say of perfection, has this branch of human industry been carried by France, within the last half century! Insurrection, which, Lafayette thought, might be "the most sacred of duties,"[§] ranks now, for the French people, among the duties which they can perform. Other mobs are dull masses; which roll onwards with a dull fierce tenacity, a dull fierce heat, but emit no light-flashes of genius as they go. The French mob, again, is among the liveliest phenomena of our world. So rapid, audacious; so clear-sighted, inventive, prompt to seize the moment; instinct with life to its finger-ends! That talent, were there no other, of spontaneously standing in queue, distinguishes, as we said, the French People from all Peoples, ancient and modern.

Let the reader confess too that, taking one thing with another, perhaps few terrestrial Appearances are better worth considering than mobs. Your mob is a genuine outburst of Nature; issuing from, or communicating with, the deepest deep of Nature. When so much goes grinning and grimacing as a lifeless Formality, and under the stiff buckram no heart can be felt beating, here once more, if nowhere else, is a Sincerity and Reality. Shudder at it; or even shriek over it, if thou must; nevertheless consider it. Such a Complex of human Forces and Individualities hurled forth, in their transcendental mood, to act and react, on circumstances and on one another; to work out what it is in them to work. The thing they will do is known to no man; least of all to themselves. It is the inflammablest immeasurable

---

*[TC] *Ibid.*, pp. 48, 12, 84, 48.

[*Carlyle, Vol. I, pp. 314-19.]

[†*Ibid.*, p. 133 (the title of Bk. VII); the following quotation is not from the opening of Bk. VII, Chap. i, but from the opening of Bk. VII, Chap. iv, "The Menads," p. 351.]

[‡François Marie Arouet Voltaire, "Discours aux Velches, par Antoine Vadé" (1764), in *Oeuvres complètes*, 66 vols. (Paris: Renouard, 1817-25), Vol. XLI, pp. 214-17, and *passim*.]

[§Carlyle is drawing on Weber, *Mémoires*, Vol. I, p. 381.]

Fire-work, generating, consuming itself. With what phases, to what extent, with what results it will burn off, Philosophy and Perspicacity conjecture in vain.

"Man," as has been written,"is for ever interesting to man; nay, properly there is nothing else interesting."[*] In which light also, may we not discern why most Battles have become so wearisome? Battles, in these ages, are transacted by mechanism; with the slightest possible development of human individuality or spontaneity: men now even die, and kill one another, in an artificial manner. Battles ever since Homer's time, when they were Fighting Mobs, have mostly ceased to be worth looking at, worth reading of, or remembering. How many wearisome bloody Battles does History strive to represent; or even, in a husky way, to sing:—and she would omit or carelessly slur-over this one Insurrection of Women?

A thought, or dim raw-material of a thought, was fermenting all night, universally in the female head, and might explode. In squalid garret, on Monday morning, Maternity awakes, to hear children weeping for bread. Maternity must forth to the streets, to the herb-markets and Bakers'-queues; meets there with hunger-stricken Maternity, sympathetic, exaspera-tive. O we unhappy women! But, instead of Bakers'-queues, why not to Aristocrats' palaces, the root of the matter? *Allons!* Let us assemble. To the Hôtel-de-Ville; to Versailles; to the Lanterne!

In one of the Guardhouses of the Quartier Saint-Eustache, "a young woman" seizes a drum,—for how shall National Guards give fire on women, on a young woman? The young woman seizes the drum; sets forth, beating it, "uttering cries relative to the dearth of grains." Descend, O mothers; descend, ye Judiths, to food and revenge!—All women gather and go; crowds storm all stairs, force out all women: the female Insurrectionary Force, according to Camille, resembles the English Naval one; there is a universal "Press of women."[†] Robust Dames of the Halle, slim mantua-makers, assiduous, risen with the dawn; ancient Virginity tripping to matins; the Housemaid, with early broom; all must go. Rouse ye, O women; the laggard men will not act; they say, we ourselves may act!

And so, like snowbreak from the mountains, for every staircase is a melted brook, it storms; tumultuous, wild-shrilling, towards the Hôtel-de-Ville. Tumultuous; with or without drum-music: for the Faubourg Saint-Antoine also has tucked up its gown; and, with besom-staves, fire-irons, and even rusty pistols (void of ammunition), is flowing on. Sound of it flies, with a velocity of sound, to the utmost Barriers. By seven o'clock, on this raw October morning, fifth of the month, the Townhall will see wonders. Nay, as chance would have it, a male party are already there; clustering tumultuously round some National Patrol, and a Baker who has been seized with short weights. They are there; and have even lowered the rope of the Lanterne. So that the official persons have to smuggle forth the short-weighing Baker by back doors, and even send "to all the Districts" for more force.

Grand it was, says Camille, to see so many Judiths, from eight to ten thousand of them in all, rushing out to search into the root of the matter! Not unfrightful it must have been; ludicro-terrific, and most unmanageable. At such hour the overwatched Three Hundred are not yet stirring: none but some Clerks, a company of National Guards; and M. de Gouvion, the Major-General. Gouvion has fought in America for the cause of civil Liberty; a man of no inconsiderable heart, but deficient in head. He is, for the moment, in his back apartment;

[*See Johann Wolfgang von Goethe, *Wilhelm Meisters Lehrjahre* (1795-96), in *Werke*, 55 vols. in 36 (Stuttgart and Tübingen: Cotta'schen Buchhandlung, 1828-33), Vol. XVIII, p. 158 (II, iv); see also Carlyle, "Biography," p. 253.]

[†See Camille Desmoulin's account in *HP*, Vol. III, pp. 108-10; see also in the Apocrypha, Judith, 13:7-10.]

assuaging Usher Maillard, the Bastille-serjeant, who has come, as too many do, with "representations." The assuagement is still incomplete when our Judiths arrive.

The National Guards form on the outer stairs, with levelled bayonets; the ten thousand Judiths press up, resistless; with obtestations, with outspread hands,—merely to speak to the Mayor. The rear forces them; nay, from male hands in the rear, stones already fly: the National Guard must do one of two things; sweep the Place de Grève with cannon, or else open to right and left. They open; the living deluge rushes in. Through all rooms and cabinets, upwards to the topmost belfry: ravenous; seeking arms, seeking Mayors, seeking justice;—while, again, the better-dressed speak kindly to the Clerks; point out the misery of these poor women; also their ailments, some even of an interesting sort.*

Poor M. de Gouvion is shiftless in this extremity;—a man shiftless, perturbed; who will one day commit suicide. How happy for him that Usher Maillard, the shifty, was there, at the moment, though making representations! Fly back, thou shifty Maillard; seek the Bastille Company; and O return fast with it;_above all, with thy own shifty head! For, behold, the Judiths can find no Mayor or Municipal; scarcely, in the topmost belfry, can they find poor Abbé Lefevre the Powder-distributor. Him, for want of a better, they suspend there; in the pale morning light; over the top of all Paris, which swims in one's failing eyes:—a horrible end? Nay, the rope broke, as French ropes often did; or else an Amazon cut it. Abbé Lefevre falls, some twenty feet, rattling among the leads; and lives long years after, though always with "a *tremblement* in the limbs."†

And now doors fly under hatchets: the Judiths have broken the Armoury; have seized guns and cannons, three money-bags, paper-heaps; torches flare: in few minutes, our brave Hôtel-de-Ville which dates from the Fourth Henry, will, with all that it holds, be in flames![*]

Here opens a new chapter.

In flames, truly,—were it not that Usher Maillard, swift of foot, shifty of head, has returned!

Maillard, of his own motion, for Gouvion or the rest would not even sanction him,—snatches a drum; descends the Porch-stairs, ran-tan, beating sharp, with loud rolls, his Rogues'-march: to Versailles! *Allons; à Versailles!* As men beat on kettle or warming-pan, when angry she-bees, or say, flying desperate wasps, are to be hived; and the desperate insects hear it, and cluster round it,—simply as round *a* guidance, where there was none: so now these Menads round shifty Maillard, Riding-Usher of the Châtelet. The axe pauses uplifted; Abbé Lefevre is left half-hanged; from the belfry downwards all vomits itself. What rub-a-dub is that? Stanislas Maillard, Bastille-hero, will lead us to Versailles? Joy to thee, Maillard; blessed art thou above Riding-Ushers! Away then, away!

The seized cannon are yoked with seized cart-horses: brownlocked Demoiselle Théroigne, with pike and helmet, sits there as gunneress, "with haughty eye and serene fair countenance;" comparable, some think, to the *Maid* of Orleans, or even recalling "the idea of Pallas Athene."‡ Maillard (for his drum still rolls) is, by heaven-rending acclamation, admitted General. Maillard hastens the languid march. Maillard, beating rhythmic, with sharp ran-tan, all along the Quais, leads forward, with difficulty, his Menadic host. Such a host—marched not in silence! The bargeman pauses on the river; all wagoners and

---

*[TC] *Deux Amis*, Vol. III, pp. 141-65.
†[TC] Dusaulx, "Prise de la Bastille" [in *De l'insurrection parisienne*,] p. 282n.
[*Carlyle, Vol. I, pp. 351-5.]
‡[TC] *Deux Amis*, Vol. III, p. 157.

coach-drivers fly; men peer from windows,—not women, lest they be pressed. Sight of sights: Bacchantes, in these ultimate Formalised Ages! Bronze Henri looks on, from his Pont-Neuf; the Monarchic Louvre, Medicean Tuileries see a day not theretofore seen.

And now Maillard has his Menads in the *Champs Elysées* (fields *Tartarean* rather); and the Hôtel-de-Ville has suffered comparatively nothing. Broken doors; an Abbé Lefevre, who shall never more distribute powder; three sacks of money, most part of which (for Sansculottism, though famishing, is not without honour) shall be returned:* this is all the damage. Great Maillard! A small nucleus of order is round his drum; but his outskirts fluctuate like the mad ocean: for rascality male and female is flowing in on him, from the four winds; guidance there is none but in his single head and two drumsticks.

O Maillard, when, since war first was, had General of Force such a task before him, as thou this day? Walter the Penniless still touches the feeling heart: but then Walter had sanction: had space to turn in; and also his Crusaders were of the male sex. Thou, this day, disowned of Heaven and Earth, art General of Menads. Their inarticulate frenzy thou must, on the spur of the instant, render into articulate words, into actions that are not frantic. Fail in it, this way or that! Pragmatical Officiality, with its penalties and law-books, waits before thee; Menads storm behind. If such hewed off the melodious head of Orpheus, and hurled it into the Peneus waters, what may they not make of thee,—thee rhythmic merely, with no music but a sheepskin drum!—Maillard did not fail. Remarkable Maillard, if fame were not an accident, and history a distillation of rumour, how remarkable wert thou! . . .

Scarcely was Maillard gone, when M. de Gouvion's message to all the Districts, and such tocsin and drumming of the *générale*, began to take effect. Armed National Guards from every District; especially the Grenadiers of the Centre, who are our old Gardes Françaises, arrive, in quick sequence, on the Place de Grève. An "immense people" is there; Saint-Antoine, with pike and rusty firelock, is all crowding thither, be it welcome or unwelcome. The Centre Grenadiers are received with cheering: "it is not cheers that we want," answer they gloomily; "the nation has been insulted; to arms, and come with us for orders!" Ha, sits the wind *so*? Patriotism and Patrollotism are now one!

The Three Hundred have assembled; "all the Committees are in activity;" Lafayette is dictating despatches for Versailles, when a Deputation of the Centre Grenadiers introduces itself to him. The Deputation makes military obeisance; and thus speaks, not without a kind of thought in it: "*Mon Général*, we are deputed by the Six Companies of Grenadiers. We do not think you a traitor, but we think the Government betrays you; it is time that this end. We cannot turn our bayonets against women crying to us for bread. The people are miserable, the source of the mischief is at Versailles: we must go seek the King, and bring him to Paris. We must exterminate (*exterminer*) the *Regiment de Flandre* and the *Gardes-du-Corps*, who have dared to trample on the National Cockade. If the King be too weak to wear his crown, let him lay it down. You will crown his Son, you will name a Council of Regency; and all will go better."† Reproachful astonishment paints itself on the face of Lafayette; speaks itself from his eloquent chivalrous lips: in vain. "My General, we would shed the last drop of our blood for you; but the root of the mischief is at Versailles: we must go and bring the King to Paris; all the people wish it, *tout le peuple le veut*."[*]

My General descends to the outer staircase; and harangues; once more in vain. "To Versailles! To Versailles!" Mayor Bailly, sent for through floods of Sansculottism, attempts academic oratory from his gilt state-coach; realises nothing but infinite hoarse cries

*[TC] *HP*, Vol. III, p. 110 [, 72, 121].
†[TC] *Deux Amis*, Vol. III, p. 160-1.
[*Cf. *ibid*., p. 161.]

of: "Bread! To Versailles!"[*]—and gladly shrinks within doors. Lafayette mounts the white charger; and again harangues, and reharangues: with eloquence, with firmness, indignant demonstration; with all things but persuasion. "To Versailles! To Versailles!" So lasts it, hour after hour;—for the space of half a day.

The great Scipio Americanus can do nothing; not so much as escape. "*Morbleu, mon Général*," cry the Grenadiers serrying their ranks as the white charger makes a motion that way, "You will not leave us, you will abide with us!"[†] A perilous juncture: Mayor Bailly and the Municipals sit quaking within doors; My General is prisoner without: the Place de Grève, with its thirty thousand Regulars, its whole irregular Saint-Antoine and Saint-Marceau, is one minatory mass of clear or rusty steel; all hearts set, with a moody fixedness, on one object. Moody, fixed are all hearts: tranquil is no heart,—if it be not that of the white charger, who paws there, with arched neck, composedly champing his bit; as if no World, with its Dynasties and Eras, were now rushing down. The drizzly day tends westward; the cry is still: "To Versailles!"

Nay now, borne from afar, come quite sinister cries; hoarse, reverberating in longdrawn hollow murmurs, with syllables too like those of *Lanterne*! Or else, irregular Sansculottism may be marching off, of itself; with pikes, nay with cannon. The inflexible Scipio does at length, by aide-de-camp, ask of the Municipals: Whether or not he may go? A Letter is handed out to him, over armed heads; sixty thousand faces flash fixedly on his, there is stillness and no bosom breathes, till he have read. By Heaven, he grows suddenly pale! Do the Municipals permit? "Permit and even order,"[‡]—since he can no other. Clangour of approval rends the welkin. To your ranks, then; let us march!

It is, as we compute, towards three in the afternoon. Indignant National Guards may dine for once from their haversack: dined or undined, they march with one heart. Paris flings up her windows, claps hands, as the Avengers, with their shrilling drums and shalms tramp by; she will then sit pensive, apprehensive, and pass rather a sleepless night.* On the white charger, Lafayette, in the slowest possible manner, going and coming, and eloquently haranguing among the ranks, rolls onward with his thirty thousand. Saint-Antoine, with pike and cannon, has preceded him; a mixed multitude, of all and of no arms, hovers on his flanks and skirts; the country once more pauses agape: *Paris marche sur nous.*[§]

We cannot stop here. See the beginning of the next chapter.

For indeed, about this same moment, Maillard has halted his draggled Menads on the last hill-top; and now Versailles, and the Château of Versailles, and far and wide the inheritance of Royalty opens to the wondering eye. From far on the right, over Marly and Saint-Germain-en-Lay; round towards Rambouillet, on the left: beautiful all; softly embosomed; as if in sadness, in the dim moist weather! and near before us is Versailles, New and Old; with that broad frondent *Avenue de Versailles* between,—stately-frondent, broad, 300 feet as men reckon, with four rows of elms; and then the *Château de Versailles*, ending in royal Parks and Pleasances, gleaming lakelets, arbours, Labyrinths, the *Ménagerie*, and Great and Little Trianon. High-towered dwellings, leafy pleasant places; where the gods of this lower world abide: whence, nevertheless, black Care cannot be excluded; whither Menadic Hunger is even now advancing, armed with pike-thyrsi!

[*Cf. *ibid.*, p. 162.]
[†Cf. *ibid.*, p. 163.]
[‡Cf. *ibid.*, p. 164.]
*[TC] *Ibid.*, p. 165.
[§Carlyle, Vol. I, pp. 356-8, 360-3. For the last quotation, see *Deux amis*, Vol. III, p. 176.]

Yes, yonder, Mesdames, where our straight frondent Avenue, joined, as you note, by Two frondent brother Avenues from this hand and from that, spreads out into Place Royale and Palace Forecourt; yonder is the *Salle des Menus*. Yonder an august Assembly sits regenerating France. Forecourt, Grand Court, Court of Marble, Court narrowing into Court you may discern next, or fancy: on the extreme verge of which that glass-dome, visibly glittering like a star of hope, is the—Oeil-de-Boeuf! Yonder, or nowhere in the world, is bread baked for us. But, O Mesdames, were not one thing good: That our cannons, with Demoiselle Théroigne and all show of war, be put to the rear? Submission beseems petitioners of a National Assembly; we are strangers in Versailles,—whence, too audibly, there comes even now sound as of tocsin and *générale*! Also to put on, if possible, a cheerful countenance, hiding our sorrows; and even to sing? Sorrow, pitied of the Heavens, is hateful, suspicious to the Earth.—So counsels shifty Maillard; haranguing his Menads, on the heights near Versailles.

Cunning Maillard's dispositions are obeyed. The draggled Insurrectionists advance up the Avenue, "in three columns" among the four Elm-rows; "singing *Henri Quatre*," with what melody they can; and shouting *Vive le Roi*.[*] Versailles, though the Elm-rows are dripping wet, crowds from both sides, with: "*Vivent nos Parisiennes*, Our Paris ones for ever!"[†]

We skip 20 pages, and pass to a later part of the same incident.

Deep sleep has fallen promiscuously on the high and on the low, suspending most things, even wrath and famine. Darkness covers the Earth.[‡] But, far on the north-east, Paris flings up her great yellow gleam; far into the wet black Night. For all is illuminated there, as in the old July Nights; the streets deserted, for alarm of war; the Municipals all wakeful; patrols hailing, with their hoarse *Who-goes*. There, as we discover, our poor slim Louison Chabray, her poor nerves all fluttered, is arriving about this very hour. There Usher Maillard will arrive, about an hour hence, "towards four in the morning." They report, successively, to a wakeful Hôtel-de-Ville what comfort they can report; which again, with early dawn, large comfortable placards, shall impart to all men.[§]

Lafayette, in the Hôtel de Noailles, not far from the Château, having now finished haranguing, sits with his officers consulting: at five o'clock the unanimous best counsel is, that a man so tost and toiled for twenty-four hours and more, fling himself on a bed, and seek some rest. . . .

The dull dawn of a new morning, drizzly and chill, had but broken over Versailles, when it pleased Destiny that a Bodyguard should look out of window, on the right wing of the Château, to see what prospect there was in Heaven and in Earth. Rascality male and female is prowling in view of him. His fasting stomach is, with good cause, sour; he perhaps cannot forbear a passing malison on them; least of all can he forbear answering such.

Ill words breed worse: till the worst word came; and then the ill deed. Did the maledicent Bodyguard, getting (as was too inevitable) better malediction than he gave, load his musketoon, and threaten to fire; nay, actually fire? Were wise who wist! It stands asserted; to us not credibly. Be this as it may, menaced Rascality, in whinnying scorn, is shaking at all Grates: the fastening of one (some write, it was a chain merely) gives way; Rascality is in the Grand Court, whinnying louder still.

The maledicent Bodyguard, more Bodyguards than he do now give fire; a man's arm is

[*See *Deux amis*, Vol. III, p. 178.]
[†Carlyle, Vol. I, pp. 364-5.]
[‡Cf. Isaiah, 60:2.]
[§See *HP*, Vol. III, pp. 118-19.]

shattered. Lecointre will depose that "the Sieur Cardaine, a National Guard without arms, was stabbed." But see, sure enough, poor Jerôme l'Heritier, an unarmed National Guard he too, "cabinet maker, a saddler's son, of Paris,"* with the down of youthhood still on his chin,—he reels death-stricken; rushes to the pavement, scattering it with his blood and brains!—Allelew! Wilder than Irish wakes, rises the howl: of pity; of infinite revenge. In few moments, the Grate of the inner and inmost Court, which they name Court of Marble, this too is forced, or surprised, and bursts open: the Court of Marble too is overflowed: up the Grand Staircase, up all stairs and entrances rushes the living Deluge! Deshuttes and Varigny, the two sentry Bodyguards, are trodden down, are massacred with a hundred pikes. Women snatch their cutlasses, or any weapon, and storm-in Menadic:—other women lift the corpse of shot Jerôme; lay it down on the marble steps; there shall the livid face and smashed head, dumb for ever, *speak*.

Wo now to all Bodyguards, mercy is none for them! Miomandre de Sainte-Marie pleads with soft words, on the Grand Staircase, "descending four steps:"—to the roaring tornado.[*] His comrades snatch him up, by the skirts and belts; literally, from the jaws of Destruction; and slam-to their Door. This also will stand few instants; the panels shivering in, like potsherds. Barricading serves not: fly fast, ye Bodyguards; rabid Insurrection, like the hellhound Chase, uproaring at your heels!

The terrorstruck Bodyguards fly, bolting and barricading; it follows. Whitherward? Through hall on hall: wo, now! towards the Queen's Suite of Rooms, in the furthest room of which the Queen is now asleep. Five sentinels rush through that long Suite; they are in the Anteroom knocking loud: "Save the Queen!" Trembling women fall at their feet with tears; are answered: "yes, we will die; save ye the Queen!"

Tremble not, women, but haste: for, lo, another voice shouts far through the outermost door, "save the Queen!" and the door is shut. It is brave Miomandre's voice that shouts this second warning. He has stormed across imminent death to do it; fronts imminent death, having done it. Brave Tardivet du Repaire, bent on the same desperate service, was borne down with pikes; his comrades hardly snatched him in again alive.[†] Miomandre and Tardivet: let the names of those two Bodyguards, as the names of brave men should, live long.

Trembling Maids of Honour, one of whom from afar caught glimpse of Miomandre as well as heard him, hastily wrap the Queen; not in robes of state. She flies for her life, across the Oeil-de-Boeuf; against the main door of which too Insurrection batters. She is in the King's Apartment, in the King's arms; she clasps her children amid a faithful few. The Imperial-hearted bursts into mother's tears: "O my friends, save me and my children, *O mes amis, sauvez-moi et mes enfans!*"[‡] The battering of Insurrectionary axes clangs audible across the Oeil-de-Boeuf. What an hour!

Yes, friends: a hideous fearful hour; shameful alike to Governed and Governor; wherein Governed and Governor ignominiously testify that their relation is at an end. Rage, which had brewed itself in twenty thousand hearts, for the last four-and-twenty hours, has taken *fire*: Jerôme's brained corpse lies there as live-coal. It is, as we said, the infinite Element bursting in; wild-surging through all corridors and conduits.

Meanwhile, the poor Bodyguards have got hunted mostly into the Oeil-de-Boeuf. They may die there, at the King's threshold; they can do little to defend it. They are heaping

*[TC] Déposition de [Laurent] Lecointre, *ibid.*, pp. 111-15. [The quotations are on p. 115.]

[*Cf. *Deux amis*, Vol. III, p. 221.]

[†Cf. *ibid.*, p. 222.]

[‡Cf. *ibid.*, p. 225, and Ferrières; Vol. I, p. 324.]

tabourets (stools of honour), benches and all moveables, against the door; at which the axe of Insurrection thunders. But did brave Miomandre perish, then, at the Queen's outer door? No, he was fractured, slashed, lacerated, left for dead; he has nevertheless crawled hither; and shall live, honoured of loyal France. Remark also, in flat contradiction to much which has been said and sung, that Insurrection did *not* burst that door he had defended; but hurried elsewhither, seeking new Bodyguards.*

Poor Bodyguards, with their Thyestes' Opera-Repast! Well for them, that Insurrection has only pikes and axes; no right sieging-tools! It shakes and thunders. Must they all perish miserably, and Royalty with them? Deshuttes and Varigny, massacred at the first inbreak, have been beheaded in the marble court: a sacrifice to Jerôme's *manes*: Jourdan with the tile-beard did that duty willingly; and asked, If there were no more? Another captive they are leading round the corpse, with howl-chauntings: may not Jourdan again tuck up his sleeves?

And louder and louder rages Insurrection within, plundering if it cannot kill; louder and louder it thunders at the Oeil-de-Boeuf: what can now hinder its bursting in?—On a sudden it ceases; the battering has ceased! Wild rushing: the cries grow fainter; there is silence, or the tramp of regular steps; then a friendly knocking: "We are the Centre Grenadiers, old Gardes Françaises: open to us, Messieurs of the Garde-du-Corps; we have not forgotten how you saved us at Fontenoy!"[†] The door is opened; enter Captain Gondran and the Centre Grenadiers: there are military embracings; there is sudden deliverance from death into life.

Strange Sons of Adam! It was to "exterminate" these Gardes-du-Corps that the Centre Grenadiers left home; and now they have rushed to save them from extermination. The memory of common peril, of old help, melts the rough heart; bosom is clasped to bosom, not in war. The King shews himself, one moment, through the door of his apartment, with: "Do not hurt my Guards!"—"*Soyons frères*, let us be brothers!" cries Captain Gondran;[*] and again dashes off, with levelled bayonets, to sweep the Palace clear.

Now too Lafayette, suddenly roused, not from sleep (for his eyes had not yet closed), arrives; with passionate popular eloquence, with prompt military word of command. National Guards, suddenly roused, by sound of trumpet and alarm-drum, are all arriving. The death-knell ceases: the first sky-lambent blaze of Insurrection is got damped down; it burns now, if unextinguished, yet flameless, as charred coals do, and not inextinguish-able.[†]

And what (it may be asked) are Mr. Carlyle's *opinions*?

If this means, whether is he Tory, Whig, or Democrat; is he for things as they are, or for things *nearly* as they are;[‡] or is he one who thinks that subverting things as they are, and setting up Democracy is the main thing needful? we answer, he is none of all these. We should say that he has appropriated and made part of his own frame of thought, nearly all that is good in all these several modes of thinking.

---

*[TC] [Jeanne Louise Henriette Genest] Campan, *Mémoires* [*sur la vie privée de Marie Antoinette*, 2 vols. (London: Colburn and Bossange, 1823)], Vol. II, pp. 71-7.

†[TC] Toulongeon, [*Histoire de France*, 7 vols. (Paris: Treuttel and Würtz, 1801-10),] Vol. I, p. 144.

[*Cf. *Deux amis*, Vol. III, p. 226.]

[†Carlyle, Vol. I, pp. 385-6, 388-93.]

[‡Cf. the title of William Godwin's *Things As They Are; or, The Adventures of Caleb Williams* (1794), 4th ed., 3 vols. (London: Simpkin and Marshall, 1816).]

But it may be asked, what opinion has Mr. Carlyle formed of the French Revolution, as an event in universal history; and this question is entitled to an answer. It should be, however, premised, that in a history upon the plan of Mr. Carlyle's, the opinions of the writer are a matter of secondary importance. In reading an ordinary historian, we want to know his opinions, because it is mainly his *opinions* of things, and not the things themselves, that he sets before us; or if any features of the things themselves, those chiefly, which his *opinions* lead him to consider as of importance. Our readers have seen sufficient in the extracts we have made for them, to be satisfied that this is not Mr. Carlyle's method. Mr. Carlyle brings the thing before us in the *concrete*—clothed, not indeed in *all* its properties and circumstances, since these are infinite, but in as many of them as can be authentically ascertained and imaginatively realized: not prejudging that some of those properties and circumstances will prove instructive and others not, a prejudgment which is the fertile source of misrepresentation and one-sided historical delineation without end. Every one knows, who has attended (for instance) to the sifting of a complicated case by a court of justice, that as long as our image of the fact remains in the slightest degree vague and hazy and undefined, we cannot tell but that what we do *not* yet distinctly see may be precisely that on which all turns. Mr. Carlyle, therefore, brings us *acquainted* with persons, things, and events, before he suggests to us what to think of them: nay, we see that this is the very process by which he arrives at his own thoughts; he paints the thing to himself—he constructs a picture of it in his own mind, and does not, till afterwards, make any logical propositions about it at all. This done, his logical propositions concerning the thing may be true, or may be false; the thing is there, and any reader may find a totally different set of propositions in it if he can; as he might in the reality, if *that* had been before him.

We, for our part, do not always agree in Mr. Carlyle's opinions either on things or on men. But we hold it to be impossible that any person should set before himself a perfectly true picture of a great historical event, as it actually happened, and yet that his judgment of it should be radically wrong. Differing partially from some of Mr. Carlyle's detached views, we hold his theory, or theorem, of the Revolution, to be the true theory; true as far as it goes, and wanting little of being as complete as any theory of so vast and complicated a phenomena can be. Nay, we do not think that any rational creature, now that the thing can be looked at calmly, now that we have nothing to hope or to fear from it, can form any second theory on the matter.

Mr. Carlyle's view of the Revolution is briefly this: That it was the breaking down of a great Imposture: which had not always been an Imposture, but had been becoming such for several centuries.

Two bodies—the King and Feudal Nobility, and the Clergy—held their exalted stations, and received the obedience and allegiance which were paid to them, by virtue solely of their affording *guidance* to the people: the one, directing and keeping order among them in their conjunct operations towards the pursuit of their most important temporal interests; the other, ministering to their spiritual teaching and culture. These are the grounds on which alone any government either claims obedience or finds it: for the obedience of twenty-five millions to a few hundred thousand never yet was yielded to avowed tyranny.

Now, this guidance, the original ground of all obedience, the privileged classes *did* for centuries give. The King and the Nobles led the people in war, and protected and judged them in peace, being the fittest persons to do so who then existed; and the Clergy did teach the best doctrine, did inculcate and impress upon the people the best rule of life then known, and did believe in the doctrine and in the rule of life which they taught, and manifested their belief by their actions, and believed that, in teaching it, they were doing the highest thing appointed to mortals. So far as they did this, both spiritual and temporal rulers deserved and obtained reverence, and willing loyal obedience. But for centuries before the French Revolution, the sincerity which once was in this scheme of society was gradually dying out. The King and the Nobles afforded less and less of any real guidance, of any real protection to the people; and even ceased more and more to fancy that they afforded any. All the important business of society went on without them, nay, mostly in spite of their hindrance. The appointed spiritual teachers ceased to do their duty as teachers, ceased to practise what they taught, ceased to believe it, but alas, not to cant about it, or to receive wages as teachers of it. Thus the whole scheme of society and government in France became one great Lie: the places of honour and power being all occupied by persons whose sole claim to occupy them was the pretence of being what they were not, of doing what they did not, nor even for a single moment attempted to do. All other vileness and profligacy in the rulers of a country were but the inevitable consequences of this inherent vice in the condition of their existence. And, this continuing for centuries, the government growing ever more and more consciously a Lie, the people ever more and more perceiving it to be such, the day of reckoning, which comes for all impostures, came for this: the Good would no longer obey such rulers, the Bad ceased to be in awe of them, and both together rose up and hurled them into chaos.

Such is Mr. Carlyle's idea of what the Revolution was. And now, as to the melancholy turn it took, the horrors which accompanied it, the iron despotism by which it was forced to wind itself up, and the smallness of its positive results, compared with those which were hoped for by the sanguine in its commencement.

Mr. Carlyle's theory of these things is also a simple one: That the men, most of them good, and many of them among the most instructed of their generation, who attempted at that period to regenerate France, failed in what it was impossible that any one should succeed in: namely, in attempting to found a government, to create a new order of society, a new set of institutions and habits, among a people having no convictions to base such order of things upon. That the existing government, habits, state of society, were bad, this the people were thoroughly convinced of, and rose up as one man, to declare, in every language of deed and word, that they would no more endure it. What was, was bad; but what was good, nobody had determined; no *opinion* on that subject had rooted itself in the people's minds; nor was there even any person, or any body of persons, deference for whom was rooted in their minds and whose word they were willing to take for all the rest. Suppose, then, that the twelve hundred members of the Constituent Assembly had even been gifted with perfect knowledge what arrangement of society was best:—how were they to get time to establish it? Or how were they to hold the people in obedience to it when established? A people with no preconceived reverence, either for it or for them; a people like slaves broke from their fetters—with all man's boundless desires let loose in indefinite expectation, and all the influences of habit and imagination which keep mankind patient under the denial of what they crave for, annihilated for the time, never to be restored but in some quite different shape?

Faith, doubtless, in representative institutions, there was, and of the firmest kind; but unhappily this was not enough: for all that representative institutions themselves can do, is to give practical effect to the faith of the people in something else. What is a representative constitution? Simply a set of contrivances for ascertaining the convictions of the people; for enabling them to declare what men they have faith in; or, failing such, what things the majority of them will insist upon having done to them—by what *rule* they are willing to be governed. But what if the majority have not faith in any men, nor know even in the smallest degree what things they wish to have done, in what manner they would be governed? This was the condition of the French people. To have made it otherwise was possible, but required time; and time, unhappily, in a Revolution, is not given. A great man, indeed, may do it, by inspiring at least faith in himself, which may last till the tree he has planted has taken root, and can stand alone; such apparently was Solon,* and such perhaps, had he lived, might have been Mirabeau: nay, in the absence of other greatness, even a great quack may temporarily do it; as Napoleon, himself a mixture of great man and great quack, did in some measure exemplify. Revolutions sweep much away, but if any Revolution since the beginning of the world ever founded anything, towards which the minds of the people had not been growing for generations previous, it has been founded by some individual man.

Much more must be added to what has now been said, to make the statement of Mr. Carlyle's opinions on the French Revolution anything like complete; nor shall

---

*A more definite, as well as, we think, a juster idea of this great man, than we have met with elsewhere, may be found in Mr. Bulwer's *Athens*; a book which, if it be completed as it has been begun, will, by its effect in correcting prejudices which have been most sedulously fostered, and diffusing true notions on one of the most interesting of all parts of the world's history, entitle its author to no humble meed of praise. [Edward Lytton Bulwer, *Athens, Its Rise and Fall, with Views of the Literature, Philosophy, and Social Life of the Athenian People*, 2 vols. (London: Saunders and Otley, 1837); on Solon, Vol. I, pp. 315-73.]

we any further set forth, either such of those opinions as we agree in, or those, far less numerous, from which we disagree. Nevertheless, we will not leave the subject without pointing out what appears to us to be the most prominent defect in our author's general mode of thinking. His own method being that of the artist, not of the man of science—working as he does by figuring things to himself as wholes, not dissecting them into their parts—he appears, though perhaps it is but appearance, to entertain something like a contempt for the opposite method; and to go as much too far in his distrust of analysis and generalization, as others (the Constitutional party, for instance, in the French Revolution) went too far in their reliance upon it.

Doubtless, in the infinite complexities of human affairs, any general theorem which a wise man will form concerning them, must be regarded as a mere approximation to truth; an approximation obtained by striking an average of many cases, and consequently not exactly fitting any one case. No wise man, therefore, will stand upon his theorem only—neglecting to look into the specialties of the case in hand, and see what features *that* may present which may take it out of any theorem, or bring it within the compass of more theorems than one. But the far greater number of people—when they have got a formula by rote, when they can bring the matter in hand within some maxim "in that case made and provided" by the traditions of the vulgar, by the doctrines of their sect or school, or by some generalization of their own—do not think it necessary to let their mind's eye rest upon the thing itself at all; but deliberate and act, not upon knowledge of the thing, but upon a hearsay of it; being (to use a frequent illustration of our author) provided with spectacles, they fancy it not needful to use their eyes.[*] It should be understood that general principles are not intended to dispense with thinking and examining, but to help us to think and examine. When the object itself is out of our reach, and we cannot examine into it, we must follow general principles, because, by doing so, we are not so likely to go wrong, and almost certain not to go so far wrong, as if we floated on the boundless ocean of mere conjecture; but when we are not driven to guess, when we have means and appliances[†] for observing, general principles are nothing more or other than helps towards a better use of those means and appliances.

Thus far we and Mr. Carlyle travel harmoniously together; but here we apparently diverge. For, having admitted that general principles (or *formulae*, as our author calls them, after old Mirabeau, the crabbed *ami des hommes*)[‡] are helps to observation, not substitutes for it, we must add, that they are *necessary*

[*See, e.g., Carlyle's letter to Mill (13 June, 1833), in *The Collected Letters of Thomas and Jane Welsh Carlyle*, ed. Charles Richard Sanders, *et al.*, Vol. VI (Durham, N.C.: Duke University Press, 1977), pp. 402-3.]

[†Cf. Shakespeare, *Henry IV, Part II*, III, i, 29 (in *The Riverside Shakespeare*, p. 902).]

[‡Victor Riqueti de Mirabeau, "Lettre au bailli de Mirabeau" (16 Feb., 1781), in Honoré Gabriel Riqueti de Mirabeau, *Mémoires*, Vol. III, pp. 151-2.]

helps, and that without general principles no one ever observed a particular case to any purpose. For, except by general principles, how do we bring the light of past experience to bear upon the new case? The essence of past experience lies embodied in those logical, abstract propositions, which our author makes so light of:—there, and no where else. From them we learn what has ordinarily been found true, or even recal what we ourselves have found true, in innumerable unnamed and unremembered cases, more or less resembling the present. We are hence taught, at the least, what we shall *probably* find true in the present case; and although this, which is only a probability, may be lazily acquiesced in and acted upon without further inquiry as a certainty, the risk even so is infinitely less than if we began without a theory, or even a probable hypothesis. Granting that all the facts of the particular instance are within the reach of observation, how difficult is the work of observing, how almost impossible that of disentangling a complicated case, if, when we begin, no one view of it appears to us more probable than another. Without a hypothesis to commence with, we do not even know what end to begin at, what points to enquire into. Nearly every thing that has ever been ascertained by scientific observers, was brought to light in the attempt to test and verify some theory. To start from a theory, but not to see the object through the theory; to bring light with us, but also to receive other light from whencesoever it comes; such is the part of the philosopher, of the true practical *seer* or person of insight.

Connected with the tendency which we fancy we perceive in our author, to undervalue general principles, is another tendency which we think is perceptible in him, to set too low a value on what constitutions and forms of government can do. Be it admitted once for all, that no form of government will enable you, as our author has elsewhere said, "given a world of rogues, to produce an honesty by their united action;"[*] nor when a people are wholly without faith either in man or creed, has any representative constitution a charm to render them governable well, or even governable at all. On the other hand, Mr. Carlyle must no less admit, that when a nation *has* faith in any men, or any set of principles, representative institutions furnish the only regular and peaceable mode in which that faith can quietly declare itself, and those men, or those principles, obtain the predominance. It is surely no trifling matter to have a legalized means whereby the guidance will always be in the hands of the Acknowledged Wisest, who, if not always the really wisest, are at least those whose wisdom, such as it may be, is the most available for the purpose. Doubtless it is the natural law of representative governments that the power is shared, in varying proportions, between the really skilfullest and the skilfullest quacks; with a tendency, in easy times, towards the preponderance of

[*"Characteristics," *Edinburgh Review*, LIV (Dec., 1831), 382.]

the quacks, in the "times which try men's souls,"[*] towards that of the true men. Improvements enough may be expected as mankind improve, but that the best and wisest shall always be accounted such, *that* we need not expect; because the quack can always steal, and vend for his own profit, as much of the good ware as is marketable. But is not all this to the full as likely to happen in every other kind of government as in a representative one? with these differences in favour of representative government, which will be found perhaps to be its only real and universal pre-eminence: That it alone is government by consent—government by mutual compromise and compact; while all others are, in one form or another, governments by constraint: That it alone proceeds by quiet muster of opposing strengths, when that which is really weakest sees itself to be such, and peaceably gives way; a benefit never yet realized but in countries inured to a representative government; elsewhere nothing but actual blows can show who is strongest, and every great dissension of opinion must break out into a civil war.

We have thus briefly touched upon the two principal points on which we take exception, not so much to any opinion of the author, as to the tone of sentiment which runs through the book; a tone of sentiment which otherwise, for justness and nobleness, stands almost unrivalled in the writings of our time. A deep catholic sympathy with human nature, with all natural human feelings, looks out from every page of these volumes; justice administered in love, to all kind of human beings, bad and good; the most earnest exalted feeling of moral distinctions, with the most generous allowances for whatever partial confounding of these distinctions, either natural weakness or perverse circumstances can excuse. No greatness, no strength, no goodness or lovingness, passes unrecognized or unhonoured by him. All the sublimity of "the simultaneous death-defiance of twenty-five millions"[†] speaks itself forth in his pages—not the less impressively, because the unspeakable folly and incoherency, which always in real life are not one step from, but actually pervade, the sublimities of so large a body (and did so most notably in this instance) are no less perceptible to his keen sense of the ludicrous. We presume it is this which has caused the book to be accused, even in print, of "flippancy," a term which appears to us singularly misapplied.[‡] For is not this mixture and confused entanglement of the great and the contemptible, precisely what we meet with in nature? and would not a history, which did not make us not only see this, but feel it, be deceptive; and give an impression which would be the more false, the greater the general vivacity and vigour of the delineation? And indeed the capacity to see and feel what is loveable, admirable,

---

[*Thomas Paine, *The American Crisis, No. I* (1776), in *The Political and Miscellaneous Works*, 2 vols. (London: Carlile, 1819), Vol. I, p. 3.]

[†Carlyle, Vol. III, p. 4.]

[‡See Sydney Morgan, "The French Revolution," *Athenaeum*, 20 May, 1837, p. 353.]

in a thing, and what is laughable in it, at the same time, constitutes humour; the quality to which we owe a Falstaff, a Parson Adams, an Uncle Toby, and Mause Headriggs and Barons of Bradwardine without end.[*] You meet in this book with passages of grave drollery (drollery unsought for, arising from the simple statement of facts, and a true natural feeling of them) not inferior to the best in Mr. Peacock's novels; and immediately or soon after comes a soft note as of dirge music, or solemn choral song of old Greek tragedy, which makes the heart too full for endurance, and forces you to close the book and rest for a while.

Again, there are aphorisms which deserve to live for ever; characters drawn with a few touches, and indicating a very remarkable insight into many of the obscurest regions of human nature; much genuine philosophy, disguised though it often be in a poetico-metaphysical vesture of a most questionable kind; and, in short, new and singular but not therefore absurd or unpractical views taken of many important things. A most original book; original not least in its complete sincerity, its disregard of the merely conventional: every idea and sentiment is given out exactly as it is thought and felt, fresh from the soul of the writer, and in such language (conformable to precedent or not) as is most capable of representing it in the form in which it exists there. And hence the critics have begun to call the style "affected;"[†] a term which conventional people, whether in literature or society, invariably bestow upon the unreservedly natural.*

In truth, every book which is eminently original, either in matter or style, has a hard battle to fight before it can obtain even pardon for its originality, much less applause. Well, therefore, may this be the case when a book is original, not in matter only or in style only, but in both; and, moreover, written in prose, with a

---

[*In, respectively, Shakespeare, *Henry IV, Part I* and *Part II*; Henry Fielding, *Joseph Andrews*, in *Works*, 12 vols. (London: Otridge and Rackham, *et al.*, 1824), Vols. V-VI; Laurence Sterne, *The Life and Opinions of Tristram Shandy*, 9 vols. in 5 (London: Tonson and Millar, 1781); and Walter Scott, *Old Mortality*, in *Tales of My Landlord*, 4 vols. (Edinburgh: Blackwood; London: Murray, 1816), Vols. II-IV, and Scott, *Waverley*, 3 vols. (Edinburgh: Constable; London: Longman, *et al.*, 1814).]

[†Morgan, "The French Revolution," p. 353.]

*A curious instance of this occurred lately. Mr. D'Israeli, a writer of considerable literary daring, tried in his novel, *Henrietta Temple*, one of the boldest experiments he had yet ventured upon; that of making his lovers and his other characters speak naturally the language of real talk, not dressed-up talk; such language as all persons talk who are not in the presence of an audience. A questionable experiment—allowable as an experiment, but scarcely otherwise; for the reader does not want pure nature, but nature idealised; nobody wants the verbiage, the repetitions and slovenlinesses, of real conversation, but only the substance of what is interesting in such conversation, divested of these. There was much which might have been said by critics against Mr. D'Israeli's experiment; but what did they say? "Affectation!"—that was their cry. Natural conversation in print looked so unnatural to men of artificiality; it was so unlike all their experience—of books! [For the anonymous criticism of Benjamin Disraeli's *Henrietta Temple* (London: Colburn, 1837), see *Literary Gazette* (3 Dec., 1836), p. 771.]

fervour and exaltation of feeling which is only tolerated in verse, if even there. And when we consider that Wordsworth, Coleridge, and others of their time, whose deviation from the beaten track was but a stone's throw compared with Mr. Carlyle, were ignominiously hooted out of court by the wise tribunals which in those days dispensed justice in such matters, and had to wait for a second generation before the sentence could be reversed, and their names placed among the great names of our literature, we might well imagine that the same or a worse fate awaits Mr. Carlyle; did we not believe that those very writers, aided by circumstances, have made straight the way[*] for Mr. Carlyle and for much else. This very phenomenon, of the different estimation of Wordsworth and Coleridge, now, and thirty years ago, is among the indications of one of the most conspicuous new elements which have sprung up in the European mind during those years: an insatiable demand for realities, come of conventionalities and formalities what may; of which desire the literary phasis is, a large tolerance for every feeling which is natural and not got-up, for every picture taken from the life and not from other pictures, however it may clash with traditionary notions of elegance or congruity. The book before us needs to be read with this catholic spirit; if we read it captiously, we shall never have done finding fault. But no true poet, writing sincerely and following the promptings of his own genius, can fail to be contemptible to any who desire to find him so; and if even Milton's *Areopagitica*,[†] of which now, it would seem, no one dares speak with only moderate praise, were now first to issue from the press, it would be turned from with contempt by every one who will think or speak disparagingly of this work of Mr. Carlyle.

We add one short extract more from near the end of the book; a summing up, as it were, of the morality of the great catastrophe:

The Convention, now grown Anti-Jacobin, did, with an eye to justify and fortify itself, publish lists of what the Reign of Terror had perpetrated—lists of persons guillotined. The lists, cries splenetic Abbé Montgaillard, were not complete. They contain the names of—how many persons thinks the reader?—Two Thousand all but a few. There were above four thousand, cries Montgaillard; so many were guillotined, fusilladed, noyaded, done to dire death; of whom nine hundred were women.[‡] It is a horrible sum of human lives, M. l'Abbé; some ten times as many shot rightly on a field of battle, and one might have had his Glorious-Victory with *Te Deum*. It is not far from the two-hundredth part of what perished in the entire Seven Years' War. By which Seven Years' War, did not the great Fritz wrench Silesia from the great Theresa; and a Pompadour, stung by epigrams, satisfy herself that she could not be an Agnes Sorel? The head of man is a strange vacant sounding-shell, M. l'Abbé, and studies Cocker to small purpose.[§]

[*See Isaiah, 40:3.]
[†(1644); in *The Prose Works*, Vol. I, pp. 286-331.]
[‡*Histoire de France*, Vol. IV, p. 241.]
[§Edward Cocker, *Cocker's Decimal Arithmetick* (London: Richardson and Lacy, 1675); many later eds.]

But what if History, somewhere on this planet, were to hear of a Nation, the third soul of whom had not, for thirty weeks each year, as many third-rate potatoes as would sustain him? History, in that case, feels bound to consider that starvation is starvation; that starvation from age to age presupposes much: History ventures to assert that the French Sansculotte of ninety-three, who, roused from long death-sleep, could rush at once to the frontiers and die fighting for an immortal Hope and Faith of Deliverance for him and his, was but the *second*-miserablest of men! The Irish Sans-potato, had he not senses then; nay, a soul? In his frozen darkness, it was bitter for him to die famishing; bitter to see his children famish. It was bitter for him to be a beggar, a liar, and a knave. Nay, if that dreary Greenland-wind of benighted Want, perennial from sire to son, had frozen him into a kind of torpor and numb callosity, so that he saw not, felt not, was this, for a creature with a soul in it, some assuagement, or the cruellest wretchedness of all?

Such things were—such things are; and they go on in silence peaceably; and Sansculottisms follow them. History, looking back over this France through long times, back to Turgot's time, for instance, when dumb Drudgery staggered up to its King's Palace, and in wide expanse of sallow faces, squalor and winged raggedness, presented, hieroglyphically, its Petition of Grievances, and for answer got hanged on a "new gallows forty feet high,"[*]—confesses, mournfully, that there is no period to be met with, in which the general twenty-five millions of France suffered *less* than in this period which they name Reign of Terror! But it was not the Dumb Millions that suffered here; it was the Speaking Thousands, and Hundreds, and Units, who shrieked, and published, and made the world ring with their wail, as they could and should: that is the grand peculiarity. The frightfullest Births of Time are never the loud speaking ones, for these soon die; they are the silent ones which can live from century to century! Anarchy, hateful as Death, is abhorrent to the whole nature of man; and so must itself soon die.

Wherefore let all men know what of depth and of height is still revealed in man; and, with fear and wonder, with just sympathy and just antipathy, with clear eye and open heart, contemplate it and appropriate it; and draw innumerable inferences from it. This inference, for example, among the first:—That "if the gods of this lower world will sit on their glittering thrones, indolent as Epicurus' gods, with the living Chaos of Ignorance and Hunger weltering uncared for at their feet, and smooth Parasites preaching Peace, peace, when there is no peace," then the dark chaos, it seems, will rise. . . . That there be no second Sansculottism in our earth for a thousand years, let us understand well what the first was; and let Rich and Poor of us go and do *otherwise*.[†]

[*See p. 147n above.]
[†Carlyle, Vol. III, pp. 433-5; the concluding allusion is to Luke, 10:37.]

ARMAND CARREL

1837

EDITOR'S NOTE

Dissertations and Discussions, 2nd ed. (1867), I, 211-83, where the title appears as "Armand Carrel. / Biographical Notices by MM. Nisard and Littré"; the title is footnoted, *"London and Westminster Review*, October 1837." Reprinted from *L&WR*, XXXVIII (Oct., 1837), 66-111, where it is headed: "Art. IV.—*Armand Carrel, his Life and Character*. From the French of D. Nisard. Preceded by a Biographical Sketch, abridged from the French of E. Littré. London: Hooper (not yet published)." (For reasons given in the Textual Introduction, cii above, references in the text are not to this work, but to Jean Marie Napoléon Désiré Nisard, "Armand Carrel," *La Revue des Deux Mondes*, XII [Oct., 1837], 5-54; and Emile Littré, "Notice biographique," in *Oeuvres littéraires et économiques d'Armand Carrel*, ed. Charles Romey [Paris: Guillaumin and Lecou, 1854], 5-66.) Running titles: "Armand Carrel." Signed "A." Also pamphlet offprint, with a title page reading: "*Life and Character / of / Armand Carrel. /* From the 'London and Westminster Review,' No. XI and LIV. / London: / Printed by C. and W. Peynell, / Little Pulteney Street. / MDCCCXXXVII." Repaginated [1]-47, [48] blank. Identified in Mill's bibliography as "An article entitled 'Armand Carrel' in the same number of the same review [as 'Parties and the Ministry']" (MacMinn, 49). A copy of the pamphlet reprint in Mill's library, Somerville College, has no corrections or emendations.

The following text, taken from the 2nd ed. of *D&D* (the last in Mill's lifetime) is collated with that in *D&D*, 1st ed., the pamphlet offprint, and that in the *L&WR*. The two long quotations from Mill's letter of 25 Nov., 1833, are collated with the original as printed in *Earlier Letters*. In the footnoted variants, "33" indicates the letter to Carlyle in *Earlier Letters*, "37[1]" indicates *L&WR*, "37[2]" indicates the pamphlet offprint, "59" indicates *D&D*, 1st ed. (1859), and "67" indicates *D&D*, 2nd ed. (1867).

For comment on the essay, see lxii–lxvii and c–ciii above.

Armand Carrel

[a]THESE LITTLE WORKS ARE[a] the tribute paid by [b]two[b] distinguished [c]writers[c] to one whose memory, though he was but shown to the world, the world will not, and must not be suffered to let die.[*] Cut off at the age of thirty-six by that union of misfortune and fault (*Schicksal und eigene Schuld*)[†] to which it has been asserted that all human miscarriages are imputable, he lived long enough to show that he was one of the few, never [d]so few as in these latter times[d], who seem raised up to turn the balance of events at some trying moment in the history of nations, and to have or to want whom, at critical periods, is the salvation or the destruction of an era.

[e] We seize [f]the[f] opportunity to contribute what we can, as well from our own knowledge as from the materials supplied by MM. Nisard and Littré, towards a true picture of a man, more worthy to be known, and more fit to be imitated, than any who has occupied a position in European politics for many years. It has not been given to those who knew Carrel, to see him in any of those situations of outward power and honour, to which he would certainly have forced his way, and which, instead of being honours to [g]him[g], it was reserved for him perhaps to rescue from ignominy. The man whom not only his friends but his enemies, and all France, would have proclaimed President or Prime Minister with one voice, if any of the changes of this changeable time had again given ascendancy to the people's side, is gone [h] ; and his place is not likely to be again filled in our time. But there [i]are[i] left to us his memory, and his example. [j]We can still[j] remember and meditate

[*Cf. John Milton, *The Reason of Church Government* (1641-42), in *The Prose Works*, ed. Charles Symmons, 7 vols. (London: Johnson, *et al.*, 1806), Vol. I, p. 119.]

[†Thomas Carlyle, *The French Revolution*, 3 vols. (London: Fraser, 1837), Vol. II, p. 220.]

[a-a]37[1,2]   This little work is
[b-b]37[1,2]   a
[c-c]37[1,2]   writer
[d-d]37[1,2]   , alas! so few as in our modern Europe
[e]37[1,2]   We, too, have somewhat to say of Carrel; and since the evil hour to France and to the world in which he perished, we have not ceased to look for an opportunity such as the work of M. Nisard presents to us.
[f-f]37[1,2]   that
[g-g]37[1,2],59   *him*
[h]37[1,2]   . He is gone
[i-i]37[1,2],59   is
[j-j]37[1,2]   It is still given to us, to

on what he was, how much and under how great disadvantages he accomplished, and what he would have been. We can learn from the study of him, what we all, but especially those of kindred principles and aspirations, must be, if we would make those principles effectual for good, those aspirations realities, and not the mere dreams of an idle and self-conceited imagination.

Who, then, and what was Armand Carrel? "An editor of a republican newspaper," exclaims some English Tory, in a voice *by* which it is doubtful whether the word "republican" or "newspaper" is uttered *in* the most scornful intonation. Carrel *was* the editor of a republican newspaper: his glory consists precisely in this, that being that, and *by* being that, he was *the greatest political leader of his time*. And we do not mean by a political leader one who can create and keep together a political party, or who can give it importance in the State, or *even* who can make it deserve importance, but who can do any and every one of all these, and do them with an easy superiority of genius and character, which renders competition hopeless. Such was Carrel. Ripened by years and favoured by opportunity, he might have been the Mirabeau or the Washington of his age, or both in one.

The life of Carrel may be written in a few sentences. "Armand Carrel," says M. Littré,

was a sub-lieutenant and a journalist: in that narrow circle was included the life of a man who, dying in the flower of youth, leaves a name known to all France, and lamented even by his political enemies. His celebrity came not from the favour of governments, nor from those elevated functions which give an easy opportunity of acquiring distinction, or, at the least, notoriety. Implicated in the conspiracies against the Restoration, an officer in the service of the Spanish Constitution, taken prisoner in Catalonia and condemned to death; bold in the opposition before the July Revolution, still bolder after it; he was always left to his own resources, so as never to pass for more than his intrinsic worth: no borrowed lustre was ever shed on him; he had no station but that which he created for himself. Fortune, the inexplicable chance which distributes cannon-balls in a battle, and which has so large a dominion in human affairs, did little or nothing for him; he had no "star," no "run of luck;" and no one ever was less the product of favourable circumstances: he sought them not, and they came not. Force of character in difficult times, admirable talents as a writer at all times, nobleness of soul towards friends and enemies; these were what sustained him, and gave him in all quarters and in all times, not only an elevated place in the esteem of men, but an ascendancy over them.[*]

Thus far M. Littré, a man who does not cast his words at random—a witness, whose opinions indeed are those of Carrel, but whose life is devoted to other pursuits than politics, and whose simplicity and purity of character, esteemed by

---

[*Translated from Littré, "Notice," pp. 5-6.]

*k-k*37[1,2],59   in
*l-l*37[1,2]   with
*m-m*37[1,2]   one of the greatest political leaders in all history
n-n+59,67

men who do not share his opinions, peculiarly qualified him to declare of Carrel that which [o]the best[o] men in France, of whatever party or shade of opinion, feel. M. Nisard, the representative of a much fainter shade of liberalism than M. Littré, does but fill up the same outline with greater richness of detail, with the addition of many interesting traits of personal character, and with a more analytical philosophy. From the two together we have learned the facts of the early life of Carrel, and many particulars of his habits and disposition, which could be known only to familiar companions. On the great features which make up a character, they show us almost nothing in Carrel which we had not ourselves seen in him: but, in what they have communicated, we find all those details which justify our general idea; and their recollections bear to our own the natural relation between likenesses of the same figure taken from different points. We can therefore, with increased confidence, attempt to describe what Carrel was; what the world has lost in him, and in what it may [p] profit by his example.

The circumstance most worthy of commemoration in Carrel is not that he was an unblemished patriot in a time of general political corruption; others have been that, others are so even at present. Nor is it that he was the first political writer of his time: he could not have been this, if he had not been something to which his character as a writer was merely subsidiary. There are no great writers but those whose qualities as writers are built upon their qualities as human beings—are the mere manifestation and expression of those qualities: all besides is hollow and meretricious, and if a writer who assumes a stile for the sake of stile, ever acquires a place in literature, it is in so far as he [q]assumes[q] the stile of those [r]whose stile is not assumed[r]; of those to whom language altogether is but the utterance of [s]their feelings, or the means to their practical ends[s].

Carrel was one of these; and it may even be said that [t] being a writer was to him merely an accident. He was neither by character nor by preference a man of speculation and discussion, for whom the press, if still but a means, is the best and often the sole means of fulfilling his vocation. The career of an administrator or that of a [u]military commander[u] would have been more to Carrel's taste, and in either of them he would [v]probably[v] have excelled. The true idea of Carrel is not that of a literary man, but of a man of action, using the press as his instrument; and in no other aspect does his character deserve more to be studied by those of all countries, who [w] are qualified to resemble him.

[o-o]37[1,2] all good
[p]37[1,2] still
[q-q]37[1,2] gives himself
[r-r]37[1,2] who give themselves no stile
[s-s]37[1,2] a feeling, or the means to an end
[t]37[1,2] the
[u-u]37[1,2] general
[v-v]37[1,2] certainly
[w]37[1,2] aspire and

He was a man called to take an active part in the government of mankind, and needing an engine with which to move them. Had his lot been cast in the cabinet or in the camp, of the cabinet or of the camp he would have made his instrument. Fortune did not give him such a destiny, and his *principles* did not permit him the means by which he could have acquired it. Thus excluded from the region of deeds, he had still that of words; and words are deeds, and the cause of deeds. Carrel was not the first to see, but he was the first practically to realize, the new destination of the political press in modern times. It is now beginning to be felt that journalism is to modern Europe what political oratory was to Athens and Rome, and that, to become what it ought, it should be wielded by the same sort of men: Carrel seized the sceptre of journalism, and with that, as with the *baton* of a general-in-chief, *ruled amidst innumerable difficulties and reverses that "fierce democracy,"[*] which he perhaps alone of all men living, trampled upon and irritated as it has been, could have rendered at once gentle and *powerful*.

Such a position did Carrel occupy, for a few short years in the history of his time. A brief survey of the incidents of his career and the circumstances of his country, will show how he *acquitted* himself in this situation. That he committed no mistakes in it, we are nowise concerned to prove. We may even, with the *modesty* befitting a distant observer, express our opinion as to what his mistakes were. But we have neither known nor read of any man of whom *it could be said* with assurance that, in Carrel's circumstances and at his years, he would have committed fewer; and we are certain that there *have* been none whose achievements would have been greater, *or whose* errors nobler or more nobly redeemed.

Carrel was the son of a merchant of Rouen. He was intended for business, but his early passion for a military career induced his father (a decided royalist) to send him to the Ecole Militaire of St. Cyr. "His literary studies," says M. Nisard,

were much neglected. He himself has told me that, although one of the best scholars in capacity, he was one of the most moderate in attainment. His military predilections showed themselves, even at school, in the choice of his reading. His favourite authors were the

[*John Milton, *Paradise Regained*, in *Poetical Works* (London: Tonson, 1695), p. 55 (Bk. IV, l. 266 [l. 269 in later eds.]).]

*x-x*37[1,2]   conscience
*y-y*37[1,2]   truncheon
*z*37[1,2]   rallied the scattered hosts round him, and
*a-a*37[1,2]   formidable
*b-b*37[1,2]   comported
*c-c*37[1,2]   humility
*d-d*37[1,2]   we could say
*e-e*37[1,2]   has
*f-f*37[1,2]   his

historians, especially where they treated of military events [g] . All other studies he was impatient of, and they profited him little. I have heard him say, however, that Virgil made an impression on him, and he has sometimes repeated verses to me which his memory had retained unforgotten, though never again read. . . . After leaving school, and while preparing for St. Cyr, he directed his studies exclusively to history and the strategic art. At St. Cyr he devoted to the same occupation all the time which the duties of the place allowed him.[*]

On leaving St. Cyr he entered the army as a sub-lieutenant, the grade answering in the French army to that of an ensign in the English.

In this early direction of the tastes and pursuits of Carrel, we may trace the cause of almost his only defects, and of his greatest qualities. From it he doubtless derived the practicalness (if the word may be pardoned) in which the more purely speculative Frenchmen of the present day (constituting a large proportion of the most accomplished minds of our age) it may be said without disrespect to them, are generally deficient; and of which in England we have too much, with but little of the nobler quality which in Carrel it served to temper and rein in. It is easy to be practical, in a society all practical: there is a practicalness which comes by nature, to those who know [h]little[h] and aspire to nothing; exactly this is the sort which the vulgar form of the English mind exemplifies, and which all the English institutions of education, whatever else they may teach, are studiously conservative of: but the atmosphere which kills so much thought, sobers what it spares, and the English who think at all, speculating under the restraining influence of such a medium, are guided more often than the thinkers of other countries into the practicalness which, instead of chaining up the spirit of speculation, lights its path and makes safe its footsteps.

What is done for the best English thinkers by the influences of the society in which they [i]grow up[i], was done for Carrel by the inestimable advantage of an education and pursuits which had for their object not thinking or talking, but doing. [j]He who thinks without any experience in action, or without having action perpetually in view; whose mind has never had anything to do but to form conceptions, without ever measuring itself or them with realities,[j] may be a great man; thoughts may originate with him, for which the world may bless him to the latest generations [k] . There ought to be such men, for they see many things which

[*Translated from Nisard, "Armand Carrel," p. 34.]

[g]37[1,2] ; and those details, so foreign to a school life, delighted him before he could understand them. Never was there an earlier or a more decided vocation

[h-h]37[1,2] nothing

[i-i]37[1,2] move

[j-j]37[1,2] When a man sets himself to thinking, whose business it has never been to act, he

[k]37[1,2] ; but before his thoughts can be acted upon, they must be recast in the mould of other and more business-like intellects. There is no limit to the chimeras which a man may persuade himself of, whose mind has never had anything to do but to form conceptions, without ever measuring itself and them with realities

even wise and strong minds, which are engrossed with active life, never can be the first to see. But the man to lead his age is he who has been familiar with thought directed to the accomplishment of immediate objects, and who has been accustomed to see his theories brought early and promptly to the test of experiment; the man who has seen at the end of every theorem to be investigated, a problem to be solved; who has learned early to weigh the means which can be exerted against the obstacles which are to be overcome, and to make an estimate of means and of obstacles habitually a part of all his theories that have for their object practice, either at the present or at a more distant period. This was essentially Carrel's distinguishing character among [l]the popular party in his own country;[l] and it is a side of his character which, naturally perhaps, has hardly yet been enough appreciated in France. In it he resembled Napoleon, who had learnt it in the same school, and who by it mastered and ruled, as far as so selfish a man could, his country and age. But Napoleon's really narrow and imperfectly cultivated mind, and his peremptory will, turned aside contemptuously from all speculation, and all attempt to stand up for speculation, as *bavardage* [m] . Carrel, born at a more fortunate time, and belonging to a generation whose best heads and hearts war and the guillotine had not swept away, had an intellect capacious enough to appreciate and sympathize with whatever of truth [n]and[n] ultimate value to mankind there might be in all theories, together with a rootedly practical turn of mind, which seized and appropriated to itself such part only of them as might be realized, or at least might be hoped to be realized, in his own day. As with all generous spirits, his hopes sometimes deceived him as to what his country was ripe for; but a short experience always corrected his mistake, and warned him to point his efforts towards some more attainable end.

Carrel entered into life, and into a military life, at a peculiar period. By foreign force, and under circumstances humiliating to the military pride of the nation, the Bourbons had been brought back. With them had returned the emigrants with their feudal prejudices, the ultra-Catholics with their bigotry and pretensions to priestly domination. Louis XVIII, taking the advice of Fouché, though in a different sense from that in which it was given, had lain down in the bed of Napoleon, "*s'était couché dans les draps de Napoléon*"—had preserved that vast net-work of administrative tyranny which did not exist under the old French government, which the Convention created for a temporary purpose, and which Napoleon made permanent;[*] that system of [o]bureaucracy[o], which leaves no free agent in all

[*See Loi sur le mode de gouvernement provisoire et révolutionnaire (14 frimaire an II; 4 Dec., 1793), *Lois, et actes du gouvernement*, VIII, 100-13; and Loi concernant la division du territoire de la république et l'administration, Bulletin 17, No. 115 (28 pluviôse an VIII; 17 Feb., 1800), *Bulletin des lois de la république française*, I, 1-94.]

[l-l]37[1,2]   Frenchmen,
[m]37[1,2]   : nor, indeed, was he far wrong as to such speculations as he chiefly had knowledge of
[n-n]37[1,2]   or
[o-o]37[1,2]   *bureaucracy*

France, except the man at Paris who pulls the wires; which regulates from a distance of several hundred miles, the repairing of a shed or the cutting down of a tree, and allows not the people to stir a finger even in their local affairs, except indeed by such writing and printing as a host of restrictive laws permitted to them, and (if they paid 300 francs or upwards in direct taxes) by electing and sending to Paris the two-hundredth or three-hundredth ^{p}fractional^{p} part of a representative, there to vote such things as the Charter of Louis XVIII placed within the competency of the national council.[*] That Charter, extorted from the prudence of Louis by the necessities of the times, and "broken ere its ink was dried," alone stood between France and a dark, soul-stifling and mind-stifling despotism, combining ^{q}some of^{q} the worst of the evils which the Revolution and Napoleon had cleared away, with the worst of those which they had brought.

By a combination of good sense and ^{r}folly^{r}, of which it is difficult to say which ^{s}was^{s} most profitable to the cause of freedom, the Bourbons saw the necessity of giving a representative constitution, but not that of allying themselves with the class in whose hands that constitution had placed so formidable a power. They would have found them tractable enough; witness the present ruler of France,[†] who has "lain down in the sheets of Napoleon" with considerably more effect. The Constitution of 1814, like that of 1830 which followed it, gave a share of the governing power exclusively to the rich:[‡] if the Bourbons would but have allied themselves with the majority of the rich instead of the minority, they would have been on the throne now, and with as absolute a power as any of their predecessors, so long as they conformed to that condition. But they would not do it: they would not see that the only aristocracy possible in a wealthy community, is an aristocracy of wealth: Louis during the greater part of his reign, and Charles during the whole of his, bestowed exclusively upon the classes which had been powerful once, those favours which, had they been ^{t}shared^{t} with the classes which were powerful ^{u}now^{u}, would have rendered the majority of those classes the most devoted adherents of the throne. For the sake of classes who had no longer ^{v}the principal^{v} weight in the country, and whose power was associated with the recollections of

[**Charte constitutionnelle*, Bulletin 17, No. 133 (4 June, 1814), *Bulletin des lois du royaume de France,* 5th ser., I, 197-207; the electoral qualifications are given in Art. 40, p. 203.]

[†Louis Philippe.]

[‡*Charte constitutionnelle* (1814), Art. 38, p. 203; *Charte constitutionnelle*, Bulletin 5, No. 59 (14 Aug., 1830), *Bulletin des lois du royaume de France*, 9th ser., Pt. 1, I, Art. 32, p. 56.]

$^{p-p}$+59,67
$^{q-q}$+59,67
$^{r-r}$37^{1,2} absurdity
$^{s-s}$37^{1,2} has been
$^{t-t}$37^{1,2} even *shared*
$^{u-u}$37^{1,2} *now*
$^{v-v}$37^{1,2} any real

[w]all[w] which the country [x]most[x] detested, the Bourbons not only slighted the new aristocracy, but kept both them and the people in perpetual alarm, both for [y]whatever[y] was dearest to them in the institutions which the Revolution had given, and which had been cheaply purchased by the sacrifice of a whole generation, and even for the "material interests"[*] (such as those of the possessors of national property) which had grown out of the Revolution, and were identified with it. The Chamber of Deputies, therefore, or, as it might have been called, the new Estate of the Rich, worked like the Comitia Centuriata of the Roman Commonwealth, which, in this respect, it resembled. Like the Comitia Centuriata, it was, from the principle of its constitution, the organ of the rich; and like that, it served as an organ for popular purposes so long as the predominant section of the rich, being excluded from a direct share in the government, had a common interest with the people. This result might have been foreseen; but the Bourbons either did not foresee it, or thought themselves strong enough to prevent it.

At the time, however, when Carrel first entered into life, any one might have been excused for thinking that the Bourbons, if they had made a bad calculation for the ultimate [z]duration[z] of their dynasty, had made a good one for [a]its present interests[a]. They had [b]put down,[b] with triumphant success, a first attempt at resistance by the new aristocracy.

A Chamber of furious royalists, elected immediately after the second restoration (afterwards with affectionate remembrance called the *chambre introuvable*, from the impossibility of ever [c]again[c] getting a similar one), had sanctioned or tolerated excesses against the opposite party, worthy only of the [d]most[d] sanguinary times of the Revolution; and had carried their enterprises in behalf of feudalism and bigotry to a pitch of rashness by which Louis, who was no fanatic, was seriously alarmed: and in September 1817, amidst the applauses of all France, he dissolved the Chamber, and called to his councils a semi-liberal ministry. The indignation and alarm excited by the conduct of the royalists, produced a reaction among the classes possessed of property, in favour of liberalism. By the law as it then stood, a fifth part of the Chamber went out every year:[†] the elections in 1818 produced

---

[*The phrase "intérêts matériels" appears in Nisard, "Armand Carrel," p. 25; Mill had earlier used it in a letter (25 Nov., 1833) to Carlyle (quoted extensively below, pp. 201-2, 204n-5n), in *Earlier Letters*, ed. Francis E. Mineka, *Collected Works*, Vols. XII-XIII (Toronto: University of Toronto Press, 1963), Vol. XII, p. 192.]

[†*Charte constitutionnelle* (1814), Art. 37, p. 203.]

[w-w]37[1,2]   everything
[x-x]+59,67
[y-y]37[1,2]   all that
[z-z]37[1,2]   interests
[a-a]37[1,2]   their own
[b-b]37[1,2]   resisted, and
[c-c]37[1,2]   after
[d-d]+59,67

hardly any but liberals; those in 1819 did the same; and those of 1820, it was evident, would give the liberal party a majority. The electoral body too, as, fortunately, electoral bodies are wont, had not confined its choice to men who represented exactly its own interests and sentiments, but had mingled with them the ablest and most honoured of its temporary allies, the defenders of the "good old cause."[*] The new aristocracy could still hear, and not repudiate, the doctrines of 1789, pronounced with the limitations dictated by experience, from the eloquent lips of Foy, and Benjamin Constant, and Manuel. It could still patronize a newspaper press, *free for the first time since 1792*, which raised its voice for those doctrines, and for an interpretation of the charter in the spirit of them. Even among the monied classes themselves there arose, as in all aristocracies there will, some men whose talents or sympathies make them the organs of a better cause than that of *f* aristocracy. Casimir Périer had not yet sunk the defender of the people in the defender of his counting-house; and Laffitte was then what he is still, and will be to the end of his disinterested and generous career. Among the new members of the legislature there was even found the Abbé Grégoire, one of the worthiest and most respected characters in France, but a *g*conspicuous member of the Montagne party in the Convention*g*.*

This rapid progress of the popular party to ascendancy was not what Louis had intended: he wished to keep the liberals as a counterpoise to the priestly party, but it never entered into his purposes that they should predominate in the legislature. His "*système de bascule*", literally *h*system of see-saw*h*, of playing off one party against another, and maintaining his influence by throwing it always into the scale of the weakest, required that the next move should be to the royalist side. Demonstrations were therefore made towards a modification of the electoral law; to take effect while the anti-popular party had still a majority, before the dreaded period of the next annual elections. At this crisis, when the fate of parties hung trembling in the balance, the Duc de Berri, heir presumptive to the throne, fell by the hand of an assassin. This catastrophe, industriously imputed to the renewed propagation of revolutionary principles, excited general horror and alarm. The new aristocracy recoiled from their alliance with liberalism. The crime of Louvel was as serviceable to the immediate objects of those against whom it was

[*William Wordsworth, Sonnet XIII (1807) of "Sonnets Dedicated to Liberty," in *The Poetical Works*, 5 vols. (London: Longman, *et al.*, 1827), Vol. III, p. 139 (l. 12).]

*[59] He has been called a regicide: had the assertion been true, it was equally true of Carnot and many others of the noblest characters in France; but the fact was otherwise. Grégoire was absent on a mission during the trial of Louis XVI, and associated himself by letter with the verdict, but not with the sentence.

*e-e*37[1,2]   then for the first time free
*f*37[1,2]   an
*g-g*37[1,2]   regicide
*h-h*37[1,2]   *system of see-saw*

perpetrated, as the crime of Fieschi has been since. A change of ministry took place; laws were passed restrictive of the press, and a law which, while it kept within the letter of the charter by not disfranchising any of the electors, created within the electoral body a smaller body returning an additional number of representatives.[*] The elections which took place in consequence, gave a decided majority to the feudal and priestly party; an ultra-royalist ministry was appointed; and the triumph of the *retrogrades*, the party of ancient privileges, seemed assured.

It is incident to a country accustomed to a state of revolution, that the party which is defeated by peaceful means will try violent ones. The popular party in France was now in a similar situation to the popular party in England during the royalist reaction which followed the dissolution of the last parliament of Charles II. Like them, they had recourse to what Carrel afterwards, in his *History of the Counter-Revolution in England*, called "the refuge of weak parties," conspiracy.[†] The military revolutions in Spain, Portugal, and Naples, had *inspired* many ardent spirits in France *with a desire to follow the example*: from 1820 to 1822 *Carbonaro* societies spread themselves over France, and military conspiracies continually broke out and were suppressed. It would have been surprising if Carrel, whose favourite heroes even at school were Hoche, Marceau, and Kléber, whose democratic opinions had attracted the notice of his superiors at St. Cyr, and to whose youthful aspirations no glory attainable to him appeared equal to that of the successful general of a liberating army, had not been implicated in some of these conspiracies. Like almost all the bravest and most patriotic of the young men in his rank of society entertaining liberal opinions, he paid his tribute to the folly of the day; and he had a narrow escape from discovery, of which M. Littré gives the following narrative.

Carrel was a sub-lieutenant in the 29th of the line, in 1821, when conspiracies were forming in every quarter against the Restoration. The 29th was in garrison at Béfort and New Brisach. Carrel was quartered in the latter place. He was engaged in the plot since called the conspiracy of Béfort. The officers at New Brisach who were in the secret, were discouraged by repeated delays, and would not stir until the insurrection should have exploded at Béfort. It was indispensable, however, that they should move as soon as the blow should have been successfully struck in the latter place. The Grand Lodge (of

[*See Loi sur la publication des journaux et écrits périodiques (31 Mar., 1820), Bulletin 356, No. 8494, *Bulletin des lois du royaume de France*, 7th ser., X, 385-7; Loi relative à la censure des journaux (26 July, 1821), Bulletin 464, No. 10,933, *ibid.*, XIII, 33-4; and Loi sur les élections, Bulletin 379, No. 8910 (29 June, 1820), *ibid.*, X, 1001-6.]

[†Carrel, *Histoire de la contre-révolution en Angleterre, sous Charles II et Jacques II* (Paris: Sautelet, 1827), p. 326.]

*i-i*37[1,2]   retrograde party
*j-j*37[1,2]   suggested to
*k-k*37[1,2]   the idea of imitation
*l-l*37[1,2]   *Carbonaro*

Carbonari) had sent from Paris several conspirators; one of them, M. Joubert, had come to New Brisach, to see what was to be done; Carrel offered to go with him to Béfort, to join in the movement, and bring back the news to New Brisach. Both set off, and arrived at Béfort towards midnight. The plot had been discovered, several persons had been arrested, the conspirators were dispersed. Carrel rode back to New Brisach at full gallop, and arrived early in the morning. He had time to return to his quarters, put on his uniform, and attend the morning exercise, without any one's suspecting that he had been out all night. When an inquiry was set on foot to discover the accomplices of the Béfort conspirators, and especially to find who it was that had gone thither from New Brisach, nothing could be discovered, and suspicion rested upon any one rather than Carrel, for his careless levity of manner had made his superiors consider him a man quite unlikely to be engaged in plots.[*]

Nine years later, M. Joubert was heading the party which stormed the Louvre on the 29th of July, and Carrel had signed the protest of the forty-two journalists, and given, by an article in the *National*, the first signal of resistance.[†] This is not the only instance in the recent history of France, when, as during the first French Revolution, names lost sight of for a time, meet us again at the critical moments.

These attempts at insurrection did the Bourbons no damage, but caused them some uneasiness with regard to the fidelity of the army. The counter-revolutionary party, however, was now under the conduct of the only man of judgment and sagacity who has appeared in that party since the Revolution; M. de Villèle. This minister *adopted (though, it is said, with misgiving and reluctance)* the bold idea of conquering the disaffection of the army by sending it to fight against its principles. He knew that with men in the position and in the state of feeling in which it was, all depended on the first step, and that if it could but be induced to fire one shot for the *drapeau blanc* against the *tricolore*, its implicit obedience might be reckoned on for a long time to come. *n* Accordingly, constitutional France took the field against constitutional government in Spain, as constitutional England had done before in France—in order that Ferdinand, save the mark! might be restored to the enjoyment of liberty: and the history of the campaign, by which he was restored to it, *furnishes* a curious picture of a victorious army putting down by force those with whom it sympathized, and protecting them against the vengeance of allies whom it despised and detested.

At this period, political refugees, and other ardent lovers of freedom, especially military men, flocked to the Spanish standard; even England, as it may be remembered, contributing her share, in the persons of Sir Robert Wilson and others. Carrel, already obnoxious by his opinions to his superior officers, and now placed between the dictates of his conscience and those of military discipline,

[*Translated from Littré, pp. 7-8.]
[†Both the protest and the article appeared in the single-sheet edition of the *National* for 27 July, 1830.]

*m-m*37[1,2]   conceived, or if he did not conceive, adopted
*n*37[1,2]   That first shot he judged, and judged truly, that it would not refuse to fire.
*o-o*37[1,2]   would furnish

acted like Major Cartwright at the opening of the American war: he threw up his commission rather than fight in a cause he [P]abhorred[P]. Having done this, he did what Major Cartwright did not: he joined the opposite party, passed over to Barcelona in a Spanish fishing-boat, and took service in the "foreign liberal legion,"[*] commanded by a distinguished officer, Colonel Pachiarotti, an Italian exile.

We shall not trace Carrel through the vicissitudes of this campaign, which was full of hardships, and abounded in incidents honourable to him both as an officer and as a man. It is well known that in Catalonia the invading army experienced from Mina, Milans, and their followers, almost the only vigorous resistance it had to encounter; and in this resistance the foreign legion, in which Carrel served, bore a conspicuous part. Carrel himself has sketched the history of the contest in two articles in the *Revue Française*, [q]much remarked at the time[q] for their impartiality and statesmanlike views, and which first established his reputation as a writer.[†]

In September 1823, the gallant Pachiarotti had already fallen; supported on horseback by Carrel during a long retreat after he was mortally wounded, and recommending with his dying breath to the good offices of the ['persons present'], "ce brave et noble jeune homme." What remained of the legion, after having had, in an attempt to relieve Figueras, two desperate encounters with superior force, at Llado and Llers, in which it lost half its numbers, capitulated,* and Carrel became the prisoner of his former commanding officer, the Baron de Damas. As a condition of the surrender, M. de Damas pledged himself to use his utmost exertions for obtaining the pardon of all the French who were included in the capitulation. Though such a pledge was formally binding only on the officer who gave it, no government could without [s]dishonour[s] have refused to fulfil its conditions; least of all the French cabinet, of which M. de Damas almost immediately afterwards became a member. But the rancour which felt itself restrained from greater acts of vindictiveness, with characteristic littleness took refuge in smaller ones. Contrary to the express promise of M. de Damas (on whose

---

[*See Carrel, "De la guerre d'Espagne en 1823," *Revue Française*, III (May, 1828), 168.]

[†"De l'Espagne et de sa révolution," *Revue Française*, II (Mar., 1828), 261-91, and "De la guerre d'Espagne en 1823," *ibid.*, III (May, 1828), 131-73.]

*M. de Chièvres, aide-de-camp of M. de Damas, was the officer through whose exertions, mainly, terms were granted to the legion; and Carrel, who never forgot generosity in an enemy, was able, by the manner in which he related the circumstance, to do important service to M. de Chièvres at a later period, when on trial for his life upon a charge of conspiracy against the government of Louis Philippe. The particulars are in M. Littré's narrative [pp. 32-5].

[p-p]37[1,2]   detested
[q-q]37[1,2]   remarkable
[r-r]37[1,2]   bystanders
[s-s]37[1,2],59   infamy

individual honour, however, no imputation appears to rest), and in disregard of the fact that Carrel had ceased to be a member of the army before he committed any act contrary to its laws, the prisoners, both officers and soldiers, were thrown into gaol, and Carrel was among the first selected to be tried by military law before a military tribunal. The first court-martial declared itself incompetent. A second was appointed, and ordered to consider itself competent. By this second court-martial he was found guilty, and sentenced to death. He appealed to a superior court, which annulled the sentence, on purely technical grounds. The desire of petty vengeance was now somewhat appeased. After about nine months of rigorous and unwholesome confinement, which he employed in diligent studies, chiefly historical, Carrel was brought a third time to trial before a third court-martial, and acquitted; and was once again, at the age of twenty-four, turned loose upon the world.

After some hesitations, and a struggle between the wishes of his family, which pointed to a counting-house, and his own consciousness of faculties suited for a different sphere, he became secretary to M. Augustin Thierry, one of that remarkable constellation of 'cotemporary' authors who have placed France at the head of modern historical literature. Carrel assisted M. Thierry (whose sight, since totally lost, had already been weakened by his labours) in collecting the materials for the concluding volume of his longest work, *The History of the Conquest of England by the Normans*:[*] and it was by M. Thierry's advice that Carrel determined to make literature his profession. M. Nisard gives an interesting account of the manner in which the doubts and anxieties of Carrel's mother gave way before the authority of M. Thierry's reputation.

During this period, Carrel's mother made a journey to Paris. M. Thierry's letters had not removed her uneasiness; the humble life of a man of letters did not give her confidence, and did not seem to be particularly flattering to her. She needed that M. Thierry should renew his former assurances, and should, in a manner, stand surety for the literary capacity and for the future success of her son. At two different meetings with M. Thierry, she made a direct appeal to him to that effect. *"Vous croyez donc, Monsieur, que mon fils fait bien, et qu'il aura une carrière?" "Je réponds de lui,"* answered M. Thierry, *"comme de moi-même; j'ai quelqu'expérience des vocations littéraires: votre fils a toutes les qualités qui réussissent aujourd'hui."* While he thus spoke, Madame Carrel fixed upon him a penetrating look, as if to distinguish what was the prompting of truth, from what might be the effect of mere politeness, and a desire to encourage. The young man himself listened in respectful silence, submissive, and according to M. Thierry almost timid, before his mother, whose decision and firmness of mind had great sway over him. Carrel, in this, bowed only to his own qualities: what awed him in his mother was the quality by which afterwards, as a public man, he himself overawed others. The first meeting had left Madame Carrel still doubtful. M. Thierry, pressed between two inflexible wills, the mother requiring of him almost to

[*Jacques Nicolas Augustin Thierry, *Histoire de la conquête de l'Angleterre par les Normands* (1825), 2nd ed., 4 vols. (Paris: Sautelet, 1826).]

[*-*]37[1,2]   contemporary

become personally responsible for her son, the son silently but in intelligible language pledging himself that the guarantee should not be forfeited, had doubtless at the second meeting expressed himself still more positively. Madame Carrel returned to Rouen less uneasy and more convinced.[*]

Here then closes the first period of the life of Carrel; and the second, that of his strictly literary life, begins. This lasted till the foundation of the *National*, a few months before the Revolution of July.

The period of six years, of which we have now to speak, formed the culminating point of one of the most brilliant developments of the French national mind: a development which for intensity and rapidity, and if not for duration, for the importance of its durable consequences, has not many parallels in history. A large income not being in France, for persons in a certain rank of society, a necessary of life; and the pursuit of money being therefore not so engrossing an object as it is here, there is nothing to prevent the whole of the most gifted young men of a generation from devoting themselves to literature or science, if favourable circumstances combine to render it fashionable to do so. Such a conjuncture of circumstances was presented by the state of France, at the time when the Spanish war and its results seemed to have riveted on the necks of the French people the yoke of the feudal and sacerdotal party for many years to come. The Chamber was closed to all under the age of forty; and besides, at this particular period, the law of partial renewal had been abrogated, a septennial act had been passed,[†] and a general election, at the height of the Spanish triumph, had left but sixteen Liberals in the whole Chamber of Deputies. The army, in a time of profound peace, officered too by the detested *émigrés*, held out no attraction. Repelled from politics, in which little preferment could be hoped for by a *"roturier"*, and that little at a price which a Frenchman will least of all consent to pay—religious hypocrisy; the *élite* of the educated youth of France precipitated themselves into literature and philosophy, and remarkable results soon became evident.

The national intellect seemed to make a sudden stride, from the stage of adolescence to that of early maturity. It had reached the era corresponding to that in the history of an individual mind, when, after having been taught to think (as every one is) by teachers of some particular school, and having for a time exercised the power only in the path shown to it by its first teachers, it begins, without abandoning that, to tread also in other paths; learns to see with its naked eyes, and

[*Translated from Nisard, pp. 36-7.]

[†*Charte constitutionnelle* (1814), Art. 38, p. 203; Loi relative au renouvellement intégral et septennal de la chambre des députés, Bulletin 672, No. 17,159 (9 June, 1824), *Bulletin des lois du royaume de France*, 7th ser., XVIII, 321-2.]

*u-u*37[1,2]   parvenu

not through the eye-glasses of its teachers,[*] and, from being one-sided, becomes many-sided[†] and of no school. The French nation had had two great epochs of intellectual development. It had been taught to speak by the great writers of the seventeenth century,—to think by the philosophers of the eighteenth. The present became the era of reaction against the ⱽnarrownessesⱽ of the eighteenth century, as well as against those narrownesses of another sort which the eighteenth century had left. The stateliness and conventional decorum of old French poetic and dramatic literature, gave place to a licence which made free scope for genius and also for absurdity, and let in new forms of the beautiful ʷas well as manyʷ of the hideous. Literature shook off its chains, and used its liberty like a galley-slave broke loose; while painting and sculpture passed from one unnatural extreme to ˣanotherˣ, and the stiff school was succeeded by the spasmodic. This insurrection against the old traditions of classicism was called romanticism: and now, when the mass of ʸrubbishʸ to which it had given birth has produced another oscillation in opinion the reverse way, one inestimable result seems to have survived it—that life and human feeling may now, in France, be painted with as much liberty as they may be discussed, and, when painted truly, with approval: as by George Sand, and in the best writings of Balzac. While this revolution was going on in the artistic departments of literature, that in the scientific departments was still more important. There was reaction against the metaphysics of Condillac and Helvetius; and some of the most eloquent men in France imported Kantism from Germany, and Reidism from Scotland, to oppose to it, and listening crowds applauded, and an "eclectic philosophy" was formed. There was reaction against the irreligion of Diderot and d'Holbach; and by the side of their irreligious philosophy there grew up religious philosophies, and philosophies prophesying a religion, and a general vague feeling of religion, and a taste for religious ideas. There was reaction against the premises, rather than against the conclusions, of the political philosophy of the Constituent Assembly: men found out, that underneath all political philosophy there must be a social philosophy—a study of agencies lying deeper than forms of government, which, working through forms of government, produce in the long run most of what these seem to produce, and which sap and destroy all forms of

[*See Carlyle's letter to Mill (13 June, 1833), in *The Collected Letters of Thomas and Jane Welsh Carlyle*, ed. Charles Richard Sanders, *et al.*, Vol. VI (Durham, N.C.: Duke University Press, 1977), pp. 402-3.]

[†See Goethe's remark reported in *Characteristics of Goethe. From the German of Falk, Müller, etc.*, trans. Sarah Austin, 3 vols. (London: Wilson, 1833), Vol. I, pp. 12-13. Cf. John Stuart Mill, *Autobiography*, in *Autobiography and Literary Essays*, ed. John M. Robson and Jack Stillinger, *CW*, Vol. I (Toronto: University of Toronto Press, 1981), p. 171.]

ᵛ⁻ᵛ37¹,²   narrowness
ʷ⁻ʷ37¹,²   and almost all forms
ˣ⁻ˣ37¹,²   the other
ʸ⁻ʸ37¹,²   garbage

government that lie across their path. Thus arose the new political philosophy of the present generation in France; which, considered merely as a portion of science, may be pronounced [z]greatly[z] in advance of all the other political philosophies which [a]had yet existed;[a]—a philosophy rather scattered among many minds than concentrated in one, but furnishing a storehouse of ideas to [b]those[b] who meditate on politics, such as all ages and nations could not furnish previously; and inspiring at the same time more comprehensive, and therefore more cautious views of the past and present, and far bolder aspirations and anticipations for the future. It would be idle to hold up any particular book as a complete specimen of this philosophy: different minds, according to their capacities or their tendencies, have struck out or appropriated to themselves different portions of it, which as yet have only been partially harmonized and fitted into one another. But if we were asked for the book which up to the present time embodies the largest portion of the spirit, and is, in the French phrase, the highest expression, of this new political philosophy, we should point to the *Democracy in America*, by M. de Tocqueville.[*]

It was above all, however, in history, and historical disquisition, that the new tendencies of the national mind made themselves way. And a fact may be remarked, which strikingly illustrates the difference between the French and the English mind, and the rapidity with which an idea, thrown into French soil, takes root, and blossoms, and fructifies. Sir Walter Scott's romances have been read by every educated person in Great Britain who has grown up to manhood or womanhood in the last twenty years; and, except the memory of much pleasure, and a few mediocre imitations, forgotten as soon as read, they have left no traces that we know of in the national mind. But it was otherwise in France. Just as Byron, and the cast-off boyish [c]extravagances[c] of Goethe and Schiller which Byron did but follow, have been the origin of all the sentimental ruffians, the Lacenaires in imagination and in action, with which the Continent swarms, but have produced little fruit of that description, comparatively speaking, in these islands; so, to compare good influences with bad [d] , did Scott's romances, and especially *Ivanhoe*,[†] which in England were only the amusement of an idle hour, give birth [e](or at least nourishment)[e] to one of the principal intellectual products of

---

[*Alexis Henri Charles Maurice Clérel, comte de Tocqueville, *De la démocratie en Amérique*, 2 vols. (Paris: Gosselin, 1835); completed by 2nd pt., 2 vols. (Paris: Gosselin, 1840).]

[†*Ivanhoe, a Romance*, 3 vols. (Edinburgh: Constable, 1820).]

[z-z]37[1,2]   unspeakably
[a-a]37[1,2]   have yet existed in the world:
[b-b]37[1,2]   all
[c-c]37[1,2]   extravagancies
[d]37[1,2]   ones
[e-e]+59,67

our time, the modern French school of history. M. Thierry, whose *Letters on the History of France* gave the first impulse, proclaims the fact.[*] Seeing, in these fictions, past events for the first time brought home to them as realities, not mere abstractions; startled by finding, what they had not dreamed of, Saxons and Normans in the reign of Richard I; [f] thinking men felt flash upon them for the first time the meaning of that philosophical history, that history of human life, and not of kings and battles, which Voltaire talked of,[†] but, writing history for polemical purposes, could not succeed in realizing. Immediately the annals of France, England, and other countries, began to be systematically searched; the characteristic features of society and life at each period were gathered out, and exhibited in histories, and speculations on history, and historical fictions. All works of imagination were now expected to have a *couleur locale*; and the dramatic scenes and romances of Vitet, Mérimée, and Alfred de Vigny, among the best productions of the romantic school [g]in those years[g], are evidences of the degree in which they attained it. M. de Barante wrote the history of two of the most important centuries [h]in[h] his country's annals, [i]from the materials, and often in the words,[i] of Froissart and Comines.[‡] M. Thierry's researches into the early history of the town-communities, brought to light some of the most important facts of the progress of society in France and in all Europe.[§] While Mignet and Thiers, in a style worthy of the ancient models, but with only the common ideas of their time, recounted the recent glories and sufferings of their country, other writers, among whom Auguste Comte [j]in his commencements,[j] and the founders of the St. Simonian school were conspicuous, following in the steps of [k]Vico, Herder, and Condorcet[k], analyzed the facts of universal history, and connected them by generalizations, which, if unsatisfactory in [l]some[l] respects, explained much, and placed much in a new and striking light; and M. Guizot, a man of a greater range of ideas and greater historical impartiality than [m]most of[m] these, gave to the world

[*Jacques Nicolas Augustin Thierry, *Lettres sur l'histoire de France* (1827), 5th ed. (Brussels: Hauman, 1836), pp. 71-2.]

[†See "Histoire" (1784), *Dictionnaire philosophique*, in *Oeuvres complètes*, 66 vols. (Paris: Renouard, 1817-25), Vol. XXXVI, p. 419.]

[‡Amable Guillaume Prosper Brugière, baron de Barante, *Histoire des ducs de Bourgogne de la maison de Valois, 1364-1477*, 13 vols. (Paris: Lavocat, 1824-26).]

[§Thierry, *Lettres*, pp. 223ff. (Letters xiii ff.)]

[f]37[1,2]   all
[g-g]+59,67
[h-h]37[1,2]   of
[i-i]37[1,2]   in the style and from the materials
[j-j]+59,67
[k-k]37[1,2]   Herder and Johannes von Müller
[l-l]37[1,2]   many
[m-m]37[1,2]   all

those immortal Essays and Lectures,[*] for which posterity will forgive him "the grave faults of his" political career.

In the midst of an age thus teeming with valuable products of thought, himself without any more active career to engross his faculties, the mind of Carrel could not remain unproductive. "In a bookseller's back-shop," says M. Nisard (for the young author, in his struggle for subsistence, for a short time entered seriously into the views of his family, and embarked some money supplied by them in an unsuccessful bookselling speculation), "on a desk to which was fastened a great Newfoundland dog, Carrel, one moment absorbed in English memoirs and papers, another moment caressing his favourite animal, conceived and wrote his *History of the Counter-Revolution in England*."[†] It was published in February 1827; and though the age has produced historical works of profounder philosophical investigation, yet in its kind, and for what it aims at, it deserves to be considered one of the most finished productions of that remarkable era.

It is a history of the two last Stuarts; of their attempts to re-establish Popery and arbitrary power, their temporary success, and ultimate overthrow by the Revolution of 1688. Their situation and conduct presented so close a parallel to that which the two last Bourbons at that time exhibited in France, that the subject was a favourite one with the French writers of the period. There could not have been a more natural occasion for violent republicanism, or any kind of revolutionary violence, to display itself, if Carrel had been the fanatic which it is often supposed that all ᵒdemocraticᵒ reformers must be. But we find no republicanism in this book, no partisanship of any kind; the book is almost too favourable to the Stuarts; there is hardly anything in it which might not have been written by a clear-sighted and reflecting person of any of the political parties which divide the present day. But we find instead, in every page, distinct evidence of a thoroughly practical mind: a mind which looks out, in every situation, for the causes which were actually operating, discerns them with sagacity, sees what they must have produced, what could have been done to modify them, and how far they were practically misunderstood: a statesman, judging of statesmen by placing himself in their circumstances, and seeing what they could have done; not by the rule and square of some immutable theory of mutable things, nor by that most fallacious test for estimating men's actions, the rightness or wrongness of their

[*François Pierre Guillaume Guizot, *Essais sur l'histoire de France* (1823), 2nd ed. (Paris: Brière, 1824); *Cours d'histoire moderne: Histoire générale de la civilisation en Europe, depuis la chute de l'empire romain jusqu'à la révolution française* (Paris: Pichon and Didier, 1828); and *Cours d'histoire moderne: Histoire de la civilisation en France, depuis la chute de l'empire romain jusqu'en 1789*, 5 vols. (Paris: Pichon and Didier, 1829-32).]

[†Translated from Nisard, p. 39.]

n-n37¹,²   his despicable
o-o37¹,²   radical

speculative views. If Carrel had done nothing else, he would have shown by this book that [p], like Mirabeau, he was not a slave to[p] formulas;[*] no pre-established doctrine as to how things [q]must be[q], ever prevented him from seeing them as they [r]were[r]. "Everywhere and at all times," says he, "it is the wants of the time which have created the conventions called political principles, and those principles have always been pushed aside by those wants."[†] "All questions as to forms of government," he says in another place, "have their [s]data[s] in the condition of society, and nowhere else."[‡] The whole spirit of the new historical school is in these two sentences. The great character by which Carrel's book differs from all other histories of the time, with which we are acquainted, is, that in it alone are we led to understand and account for all the vicissitudes of the time, from the ebb and flow of public opinion; the causes of which, his own practical sagacity, and a Frenchman's experience of turbulent times, enabled Carrel to perceive and interpret with a truth and power that must strike every competent judge who compares his short book with the long books of other people. And we may here notice, as an example of the superiority of French historical literature to ours, that, of the most interesting period in the English annals, the period of the Stuarts, France has produced, within a very few years too, the best, the second-best, and the third-best history. The best is this of Carrel; the second-best is the unfinished work* of M. Guizot, his *History of the English Revolution* [t] ;[§] the third in merit is M. Mazure's *History of the Revolution of 1688*, a work of [u] greater detail, and less extensive views, but which has brought much new information from Barillon's papers and elsewhere, is unexceptionable as to impartiality, and on the whole a highly valuable accession to the literature of English history.[¶]

The style of the *Histoire de la Contre-Révolution*, according to M. Nisard, did not give Carrel the reputation he afterwards acquired as a master of expression. But

[*See p. 161 above.]

[†Translated from Carrel, *Histoire de la contre-révolution en Angleterre*, p. 65.]

[‡Translated from *ibid.*, p. 3.]

*[67] Since completed. (1866.)

[§François Pierre Guillaume Guizot, *Histoire de la révolution d'Angleterre depuis l'avènement de Charles Ier jusqu'à la restauration de Charles II*, 1st pt., 2 vols. (Paris: Leroux and Chantpie, 1826-27). The work was completed in six volumes by the addition of *Histoire de la république d'Angleterre et de Cromwell (1649-1658)*, 2 vols. (Paris: Didier, 1854), and *Histoire du protectorat de Richard Cromwell et du rétablissement des Stuart (1658-1660)*, 2 vols. (Paris: Didier, 1856).]

[¶François Antoine Jean Mazure, *Histoire de la révolution de 1688, en Angleterre*, 3 vols. (Paris: Gosselin, 1825), using, *inter alia*, the letters of Paul de Barillon.]

[p-p]37[1,2]   he too, like Mirabeau, was not a man of
[q-q]37[1,2]   *must be*
[r-r]37[1,2]   *were*
[s-s]37[1,2]   *data*
[t]37[1,2]   , which, it is said, he is now completing
[u]37[1,2]   much

we agree with M. Nisard, a most competent judge, and a severe critic of his ᵛcotemporariesᵛ, in thinking this judgment of the French public erroneous. We already recognise in this early performance, the pen which was afterwards compared to a sword's point (*il semblait écrire avec une pointe d'acier*).[*] It goes clean and sharp to the very heart of the thing to be said, says it without ornament or periphrasis, or *phrases* of any kind, and in nearly the fewest words in which so much could be told. The style cuts the meaning into the mind as with an edge of steel. It wants the fertility of fancy which Carrel afterwards displayed; an indispensable quality to a writer of the first rank, but one which, in spite of the authority of ʷCicero andʷ Quintilian,[†] we believe to be, oftener than is supposed, the last rather than the first quality which such writers acquire. The grand requisite of good writing is, to have something to say: to attain this, is becoming more and more the grand effort of all minds of any power, which embark in literature; and important truths, at least in human nature and life, seldom reveal themselves but to minds which are found equal to the secondary task of ornamenting those truths, when they have leisure to attend to it. A mind which has all natural human feelings, which draws its ideas fresh from realities, and, like all first-rate minds, varies and multiplies its points of view, gathers as it goes illustrations and analogies from all nature. So was it with Carrel. The fashion of the day, when he began, was picturesqueness of style, and that was what the imitative minds were all straining for. Carrel, who wrote from himself and not from imitation, put into his style first what was in himself first, the intellect of a great writer. The other half of the character, the imaginative ˣpartˣ, came to maturity somewhat later, and was first decidedly recognised in the Essays on the War in Spain, which, as we have already said, were published in the *Revue Française*, a periodical on the plan of the English reviews, to which nearly all the most philosophical minds in France contributed, and which was carried on for several years with first-rate ability.

The editor of this review was M. Guizot. That Guizot and Carrel should for a time be found not only fighting under the same banner, but publishing in the same periodical organ, is a fact characteristic of the fusion of parties and opinions which had by this time taken place to oppose the progress of the counter-revolution.

[*Littré, p. 6.]

[†See Cicero, *De oratore* (Latin and English), 2 vols., trans. E.W. Sutton (London: Heinemann; Cambridge, Mass.: Harvard University Press, 1942), Vol. I, p. 80 (I, xxv, 113-14); Quintilian, *Institutio oratoria* (Latin and English), trans. H.E. Butler, 4 vols. (London: Heinemann; Cambridge, Mass.: Harvard University Press, 1921), Vol. III, p. 211 (VIII, iii, 2).]

ᵛ⁻ᵛ37¹,² contemporaries (witness his criticisms on Victor Hugo and Lamartine, inserted in this Review) ["Victor Hugo," *London Review*, II (*L&WR*, XXXI) (Jan., 1836), 389-417, and "Lamartine," *London and Westminster Review*, IV & XXVI (Jan., 1837), 501-41.]

ʷ⁻ʷ+59,67

ˣ⁻ˣ37¹,² half

The victory in Spain had put the royalists in complete possession of the powers of government. The elections of 1824 had given them, and their septennial act secured to them for a period, their *chambre des trois cents*, so called from the 300 feudalists, or creatures of the feudalists, who, with about 100 more moderate royalists, and sixteen liberals of different shades, made up the whole Chamber. It is for history, already familiar with the frantic follies of this most unteachable party, to relate all they did, or attempted; the forty millions sterling which they voted into their own pockets under the name of compensation to the emigrants; their law of sacrilege, worthy of the bigotry of the middle ages; the re-establishment of the Jesuits, the putting down of the Lancasterian schools, and throwing all the minor institutions of education (they did not yet openly venture upon the *y*University*y*) into the hands of the priests.[*] The madmen thought they could force back Catholicism upon a people, of whom the educated classes, though not, as they are sometimes represented, hostile to religion, but *z*either simply indifferent or*z* decidedly disposed to a religion of some sort or other, had for ever bidden adieu to that form of it, and could as easily have been made Hindoos or Mussulmans as Roman Catholics. All that bribery could do was to make hypocrites, and of these (some act of hypocrisy being a condition of preferment) there were many edifying examples; among others, M. Dupin, *a*since*a* President of the Chamber of Deputies, who, soon after the accession of Charles X, devoutly followed the Host in a procession to St. Acheul.* If our memory deceive us not, Marshal Soult was another of these illustrious converts; he became one of Charles X's peers, and wanted only to have been his minister too, to have made him the Sunderland of the French 1688.

In the meantime, laws were prepared against the remaining liberties of France,

[*See, respectively, Loi concernant l'indemnité à accorder aux anciens propriétaires des biens-fonds confisqués et vendus au profit de l'état en vertu des lois sur les émigrés, les condamnés et les déportés, Bulletin 30, No. 680 (27 Apr., 1825), *Bulletin des lois du royaume de France*, 8th ser., II, 229-38; Loi pour la répression des crimes et des délits commis dans les édifices ou sur les objets consacrés à la religion catholique ou aux autres cultes légalement établis en France, Bulletin 29, No. 665 (20 Apr., 1825), *ibid.*, pp. 221-5; two speeches (26 May and 4 July, 1826) by Denis le comte Frayssinous recognizing the presence of the Jesuits, *Moniteur Universel*, 29 May, 1826, p. 820, and 6 July, 1826, p. 1021 (the Edit du roi, concernant la société des jésuites, of Nov., 1764 [Paris: Simon], by Louis XV, which banished the Jesuits, was still in effect); and Ordonnance du roi relative à l'administration supérieure de l'instruction publique, aux collèges, institutions, pensions, et écoles primaires, Bulletin 664, No. 16,774 (8 Apr., 1824), *Bulletin des lois du royaume de France*, 7th ser., XVIII, 200-3.]

*[59] Also memorable as almost the only man of political distinction who has given in a similar adhesion to the present despotism. *b*(1859.)*b*

*y-y*37[1,2]   Universities
*z-z*37[1,2]   on the contrary
*a-a*37[1,2]   now
b-b+67

and against the institutions dearest to the people, of those which the Revolution had given. Not content with an almost ^cconstant^c censorship on the newspaper press, the faction proposed rigid restraints upon the publication even of books below a certain size. A law also was framed to re-establish primogeniture and entails, among a nation which universally believes that the family affections, on the strength of which it justly values itself, depend upon the observance of equal justice in families, and would not survive the revival of the unnatural preference for the eldest son. These laws passed the Chamber of Deputies amidst the most violent storm of public opinion which had been known in France since the Revolution. The Chamber of Peers, faithful to its mission as the Conservative branch of the Constitution, rejected them.[*] M. de Villèle felt the danger, but a will more impetuous and a judgment weaker than his own, compelled him to advance. He created (or ^d the King created) a batch of sixty-six peers, and dissolved the Chamber.

But affairs had greatly altered since the elections of 1824. By the progress, not only of disgust at the conduct of the faction, but of a presentiment of the terrible crisis to which it was about to lead, the whole of the new aristocracy had now gone over to the people. Not only they, but the more reasonable portion of the old aristocracy, the moderate royalist party, headed by Chateaubriand, and represented by the *Journal des Débats*, had early separated themselves from the counter-revolutionary faction of which M. de Villèle was the unwilling instrument. Both these bodies, and the popular party, now greatly increased in strength even among the electors, knit themselves in one compact mass to overthrow the Villèle Ministry. The ^e*Aide-toi* Society^e, in which even M. Guizot acted a conspicuous part, ^fbut which was mainly composed^f of the most energetic young men of the popular party, conducted the correspondence and organized the machinery for the elections. A large majority was returned hostile to the ministry: they were forced to retire, and the King had to submit to a ministry of moderate royalists, commonly called, from its most influential member, the Martignac Ministry.

The short interval of eighteen months, during which this ministry lasted, was the brightest period which France has known since the Revolution: for a reason which well merits attention; those who had the real power in the country, the men of

---

[*Projet de loi sur les successions et les substitutions (5 Feb., 1826), *Moniteur Universel*, 11 Feb., 1826, p. 168 (rejected by the Peers on 8 Apr.; *ibid.*, 12 Apr.); Projet de loi sur la police de la presse (27 Dec., 1826), *ibid.*, 30 Dec., 1826, p. 1730 (withdrawn by ordinance; *ibid.*, 19 Apr., 1827); see also Ordonnance du roi portant la remise en vigueur des lois des 31 mars 1820 et 26 juillet 1821, Bulletin 170, No. 6439 (24 June, 1827), *Bulletin des lois du royaume de France*, 8th ser., VI, 729.]

^{c-c}37^{1,2}   periodical
^d37^{1,2}   more properly
^{e-e}37^{1,2}   society *Aide-toi*
^{f-f}37^{1,2}   and composed mainly

property and the men of talent, had not the power at the Tuileries, nor any near prospect of having it. It is the grievous misfortune of France, that being still new to constitutional ideas and institutions, she has never known what it [g]is[g] to have a fair government, [h] in which there [i]is[i] not one law for the party in power, and another law for its opponents. The French government is not a constitutional government —it is a despotism limited by a parliament; whatever party can get the executive into its hands, and induce a majority of the Chamber to support it, does practically whatever it pleases; hardly anything that it can be guilty of towards its opponents alienates its supporters, unless they fear that they are themselves marked out to be the next victims; and even the trampled-on minority fixes its hopes not upon limiting arbitrary power, but upon becoming the stronger party and tyrannizing in its turn. It is to the eternal honour of Carrel that he, and he almost alone, in a subsequent period far less favourable than that of which we are speaking, recognised the great principle of which all parties had more than ever lost sight;—saw that this, above all, was what his country wanted; unfurled the banner of equal justice and equal protection to all opinions, bore it bravely aloft in weal and woe over the stormy seas on which he was cast, and when he [j]sank, sank[j] with it flying. It was too late. A revolution had intervened; and even those who suffered from tyranny, had learnt to hope for relief from revolution, and not from law or opinion. But during the Martignac Ministry, all parties were equally afraid of, and would have made equal sacrifices to avert, a convulsion. The idea gained ground, and appeared to be becoming general, of building up in France for the first time a government of law. It was known that the King was wedded to the counter-revolutionary party, and that without a revolution the powers of the executive would never be at the disposal of the new aristocracy of wealth, or of the men of talent who had put themselves at the head of it. But they had the command of the legislature, and they used the power which they had, to reduce within bounds that which [k]by peaceable means[k] they could not hope to have. For the first time it became the object of the first speculative and practical politicians in France, to limit the [l]power[l] of the executive; to erect barriers of opinion, and barriers of law, which it should not be able to overpass, and which should give the citizen that protection which he had never yet had in France, against the tyranny of the magistrate: to form, as it was often expressed, *les moeurs constitutionnelles*, the habits and feelings of a free government, and establish in France, what is the greatest political blessing [m]enjoyed[m] in England, the national feeling of respect and obedience to the law.

[g-g]37[1,2]   was
[h]37[1,2]   one
[i-i]37[1,2]   was
[j-j]37[1,2]   sunk, sunk
[k-k]+59,67
[l-l]37[1,2]   powers
[m-m]37[1,2]   we enjoy

Nothing could seem more hopeful than the progress which France was making, under the Martignac Ministry, towards this great improvement. The discussions of the press, and the teachings of the able men who headed the Opposition, especially the Doctrinaires (as they were called), M. Royer Collard, the Duc de Broglie, M. Guizot, and their followers, who then occupied the front rank of the popular party, were by degrees working the salutary feelings of a constitutional government into the public mind. But they had barely time to penetrate the surface. The same madness which hurled James II from his throne, was now fatal to Charles X. In an evil hour for France, unless England one day repay her the debt which she unquestionably owes her for the Reform Bill,[*] the promise of this auspicious moment was blighted; the Martignac Ministry was dismissed, a set of furious *émigrés* were appointed, and a new general election having brought a majority still more hostile to them, the famous Ordonnances were issued,[†] and the Bourbon Monarchy was swept from the face of the earth.

We have called the event which necessitated the Revolution of July, a misfortune to France. We wish earnestly to think it otherwise. But if in some forms that Revolution has brought *n*considerable*n* good to France, in many it has brought *o*serious*o* ill. Among the evils which it has done we select two of the greatest *p* : it stopped the progress of the French people towards recognising the necessity of equal law, and a strict definition of the powers of the magistrate; and it *q*checked, and for a time almost suspended,*q* the literary and philosophic movement which had commenced.

On the fall of the old aristocracy, the new oligarchy came at once into power. They did not all get places, only because there were not places for all. But there was a large abundance, and they rushed upon them like tigers upon their prey. No precaution was taken by the people against this new enemy. The discussions of the press in the years preceding, confined as they had been both by public opinion and by severe legal penalties, strictly within the limits of the Charter,[‡] had not made familiar to the public mind the necessity of an extended suffrage; and the minds

---

[*2 & 3 William IV, c. 45 (1832).]

[†Ordonnance du roi qui suspend la liberté de la presse périodique et semi-périodique, Ordonnance du roi qui dissout la chambre des députés des départemens, Ordonnance du roi qui réforme, selon les principes de la charte constitutionnelle, les règles d'élection, et prescrit l'exécution de l'article 46 de la charte, Ordonnance du roi qui convoque les colléges électoraux d'arrondissement pour le 6 septembre prochain, les colléges de departement pour le 13, et la chambre des députés pour le 28 du même mois, Bulletin 367, Nos. 15135-8 (25 July, 1830), *Bulletin des lois du royaume de France*, 8th ser., XII, 33-4, 35, 35-9, 39-40.]

[‡*Charte constitutionnelle* (1814), Art. 8, p. 200.]

*n-n*37[1,2]   immense
*o-o*37[1,2]   unspeakable
*p*37[1,2]   and most permanent
*q-q*37[1,2]   put a stop, or nearly so, to

even of enlightened men, as we can 'personally testify', at the time of the formation of the new government, were in a state of the utmost obtuseness on the subject. The eighty thousand electors had hitherto been on the side of the people, and nobody seemed to see any reason why this should not continue to be the case. The oligarchy of wealth was thus allowed quietly to instal itself; its leaders, and the men of literary talent who were its writers and orators, became ministers, or expectant ministers, and no longer sought to limit the power which was henceforth to be their own; by degrees, even, as others attempted to limit it, they violated in its defence, one after another, every salutary principle of freedom which they had themselves laboured to implant in the popular mind. They reckoned, and the event shows that they could safely reckon, upon the King whom they had set up; that he would see his interest in keeping a strict alliance with them. There was no longer any rival power interested in limiting that of the party in office. There were the people; but the people could not make themselves felt in the legislature; and attempts at insurrection, until the resistance becomes thoroughly national, a government is always strong enough to put down. There was the aristocracy of talent: and the course was adopted of buying off ˢthisˢ with a portion of the spoil. One of the most deplorable effects of the new government of France, is the profligate immorality which it is industriously spreading among the ablest and most accomplished of the youth. All the arts of corruption which Napoleon exercised towards the dregs of the Revolution, are put in practice by the present ruler upon the *élite* of France: and few are they that resist. Some rushed headlong from the first, and met the bribers half way; others held out for a time, but their virtue failed them as things grew more desperate, and as they grew more hungry. Every man of literary reputation who will sell himself to the government, is gorged with places and loaded with decorations. Every rising young man, of the least promise, is lured and courted to the same dishonourable distinction. Those who resist the seduction must be proof against every temptation which is strongest on a French mind: for the vanity, which is the bad side of the national sociability and love of sympathy, makes the French, of all others, the people who are the most eager for distinction, and as there is no national respect for birth, and but little for wealth, almost the only adventitious distinctions are those which the government can confer. Accordingly the pursuits of intellect, but lately so ardently engaged in, are almost abandoned; no enthusiastic crowds now throng the lecture-room; M. Guizot has left his professor's chair and his historical speculations, and would fain be the Sir Robert Peel of France; M. Thiers is trying to be the Canning; M. Cousin and M. Villemain have ceased to lecture, have ceased even to publish; M. de Barante is an ambassador; Tanneguy Duchâtel, instead of expounding Ricardo, and making his profound speculations known where they are more needed than in

---

ʳ⁻ʳ37[1,2]   testify from our own knowledge
ˢ⁻ˢ37[1,2],59   these

any other country in Europe, 'became' a Minister of Commerce who dared not act upon his own principles, and is waiting to be so again; the press, which so lately teemed with books of history and philosophy, now scarcely produces one, and the young men who could have written them are either placemen, or gaping place-hunters, disgusting the well-disposed of all parties by their avidity, and their open defiance of even the pretence of principle. "

Carrel was exposed to the same temptations with other young men of talent, but we claim no especial merit for him in having resisted them. Immediately after the Revolution, in which, as already observed, he took a distinguished part, he was sent by the government on an important mission to the West: on his return he found himself gazetted for a prefecture; which at that time he might honestly have accepted, as many others did whom the conduct of the government afterwards forced to retire. Carrel used sportively to say that if he had been offered a regiment, he perhaps could not have found in his heart to refuse. But he declined the prefecture, and took his post as editor and chief writer of the *National*, which he had founded a few months before the Revolution, in conjunction with MM. Mignet and Thiers, but which M. Thiers had conducted until he and M. Mignet got into place. Carrel now assumed the management: and from this time his rise was rapid to that place in the eye of the public, which made him, at one period, the most conspicuous 'private' person in France. Never was there an eminence better merited; and we have now to tell how he acquired it, and how he used it.

It was by no trick, no compliance with any prevailing fashion or prejudice, that Carrel became the leading figure in politics on the popular side. It was by the ascendancy of character and talents, legitimately exercised, in a position for which he was more fitted than any other man of his age, and of which he at once entered into the true character, and applied it to its practical use. From this time we are to consider Carrel not a literary man, but as a politician, and his writings are to be judged by the laws of popular oratory. "Carrel," says M. Nisard,

was a writer, only for want of having an active career fit to occupy all his faculties. He never sought to make himself a name in literature. Writing was to him a means of impressing, under the form of doctrines, his own practical aims upon the minds of those whom he addressed. In his view, the model of a writer was a man of action relating his acts: Caesar in his *Commentaries*, Bonaparte in his *Memoirs*: he held that one ought to write either after having acted, or as a mode of action, when there is no other mode effectual or allowable. At a later period his notion was modified, or rather enlarged;[*]

[*Translated from Nisard, pp. 32, 33. The references are to Gaius Julius Caesar, *Commentariorum de bello gallico*, Vol. I of *C. Julii Caesaris quae exstant opera*, 2 vols. (Paris: Barbou, 1755); and Napoléon I, *Mémoires pour servir à l'histoire de France sous Napoléon*, 7 vols. (Paris: Didot, 1823-24).]

*-r*37[1,2]   was
"37[1,2]   Are we wrong in saying that the July Revolution has been a misfortune to France?
v-v+59,67

and he recognised, that there is not only *action* upon the outward world, there is also action upon the spiritual world of thought and feeling, the action of the artist, the preacher, and the philosopher. "Thus completed," says M. Nisard, "Carrel's idea is the best theory of the art of composition:"[*] as indeed it is; and it was the secret of Carrel's success.

He who has a passion stronger than the love of literary reputation, and who writes only to inspire others with the same; such a man, proceeding upon the simple idea that the pen should be a mere instrument, will write *well* from the commencement; and if he has *instinct*, which only means, a turn of mind conformable to the genius of his nation, he may become a writer of the first rank, without even considering himself to be a writer.[†]

Of his eminence as a writer, there is but one opinion in France, there can be but one among competent judges in any country. Already, from the time of his Essays on the War in Spain, "nothing mediocre had issued from his pen."[‡] In the various papers, literary or political, which he published in different periodical works,

that quality of painting by words, which had been seen almost with surprise in his articles on Spain, shines forth in nearly every sentence. But let there be no mistake. It was not some art or mystery of *effect* in which Carrel had grown more dexterous; his expression had become more graphic, only because his thoughts had become clearer, of a loftier order, and more completely his own. "Like all great writers," he proportions his style to his ideas, and can be simple and unpretending in his language when his thoughts are of a kind which do not require that Reason, to express them, should call in the aid of Imagination. To apply to all things indiscriminately a certain gift of brilliancy which one is conscious of, and for which one has been praised, is not genius, any more than flinging epigrams about on all occasions is wit.

"All the qualities," continues M. Nisard,

which Carrel possessed from his first taking up the pen, with this additional gift, which came the last, only because there had not ˣbefore beenˣ any sufficient occasion to call it out, burst forth in the ʸpolemicsʸ of the *National*, with a splendour which to any candid person it must appear hardly possible to exaggerate. For who can be ungrateful to a talent which even those who feared, admired; whether they really feared it less than they pretended, or that in France, people are never so much afraid of talent as to forego the pleasure of admiring it. I shall not hesitate to affirm that from 1831 to 1834, the *National*, considered merely as a monument of political literature, is the most original production of the nineteenth century.[§]

[*Translated from Nisard, pp. 33-4.]
[†Translated from *ibid.*, p. 33.]
[‡Translated from *ibid.*, p. 49.]
[§Translated from *ibid.*, pp. 49-50.]

ʷ⁻ʷ37¹,² He has this in common with the great writers, that
ˣ⁻ˣ37¹,² been before
ʸ⁻ʸ37¹,² *polémique*

This from so sober a judge, and in an age and country which has produced Paul Louis Courier, is, we may hope, sufficient.

Both M. Littré and M. Nisard[*] compare Carrel's political writings, as literary productions, to the letters of Junius;[†] though M. Nisard gives greatly the superiority to Carrel. But the comparison itself is an injustice to him. There never was anything less like popular oratory, than those polished but stiff and unnatural productions; where every cadence seems pre-determined, and the writer *knew* the place of every subsequent word in the sentence, before he finally *resolved* on the first. The Orations of Demosthenes, though even Demosthenes could not have extemporized them, are but the ideal and unattainable perfection of extemporaneous speaking: but Apollo himself could not have spoken the Letters of Junius, without pausing at the end of every sentence to arrange the next. A piece of mere painting, like any other work of art, may be finished by a succession of touches: but when spirit speaks to spirit, not in order to please but to incite, everything must seem to come from one impulse, from a soul engrossed for the moment with one feeling. It seemed so with Carrel, because it *was* so. "Unlike Paul Louis Courier," says M. Littré, "who hesitated at a word, Carrel never hesitated at a sentence;"[‡] and he could speak, whenever called upon, in the same style in which he wrote. His style has that *breadth*, which, in literature, as in other works of art, shows that the artist has a *character*—that some conceptions and some feelings predominate in his mind over others. Its fundamental quality is that which M. Littré has well characterized, *la sûreté de l'expression*:[§] it goes straight home; the right word is always found, and never seems to be sought: words are never wanting to his thoughts, and never pass before them. "*L'expression*" (we will not spoil by translation M. Littré's finely chosen phraseology) "*arrivait toujours abondante* comme la pensée, si pleine et si abondante elle-même;" "and if one is not conscious of the labour of a writer retouching carefully every passage, one is conscious of a vigorous inspiration, which endows everything with movement, form, and colour, and *casts in one and the same mould the style and the thought*."[¶]

It would have been *in complete contradiction to* Carrel's idea of journalism,

[*Littré, p. 38; Nisard, pp. 50-1.]
[†*Junius: Including Letters by the Same Writer, under Other Signatures, (Now First Collected)*, 3 vols. (London: Rivington, *et al.*, 1812).]
[‡Translated from Littré, p. 37.]
[§*Ibid.*]
[¶*Ibid.* (partly translated.)]

*z-z*37[1,2]   knows
*a-a*37[1,2]   determines
*b-b*37[1,2]   *was*
*c-c*37[1,2]   *breadth*
*d-d*37[1,2]   *character*
*e-e*37[1,2]   a solecism in

for the writer to remain behind a curtain. The English idea of a newspaper, as a sort of impersonal thing, coming from nobody knows where, the readers never thinking of the writer, nor caring whether he thinks what he writes, as long as *they* think what he writes;—this would not have done for Carrel, nor been consistent with his objects. The opposite idea already to some extent prevailed in France; newspapers were often written in, and had occasionally been edited, by political characters, but no political character *f*(since the first Revolution) had*f made* itself by a newspaper. Carrel did so. To say that during the years of his management Carrel *conducted* the *National*, would give an insufficient idea. The *National was* Carrel; it was as much himself as was his conversation, as could have been his speeches in the Chamber, or his acts as a public functionary. "The *National*," says M. Littré, "was a personification of Armand Carrel; and, if the journal gave expression to the thoughts, the impulses, the passions of the writer, the writer in his turn was always on the breach, prepared to defend, at the peril of his life or of his liberty, what he had said in the journal."[*]

He never separated himself from his newspaper. He never considered the newspaper one thing and himself another. What was said by a newspaper to a newspaper, he considered as said by a man to a man, and acted accordingly. He never said anything in his paper, to or of any man, which he would not have both dared, and thought it right, to say personally and in his presence. He insisted upon being treated in the same way; and generally was so; though the necessity in which he thought himself of repelling insult, had involved him in two duels before his last fatal one. Where danger was to be incurred in resisting arbitrary power, he was always the first to seek it: he never hesitated to throw down the gauntlet to the government, challenging it to try upon him any outrage which it was meditating against the liberty or the safety of the citizen. Nor was this a mere bravado; no one will think it so, who knows how unscrupulous are all French governments, how prone to act from irritated vanity more than from calculation, and how likely to commit an imprudence rather than acknowledge a defeat. Carrel thwarted a nefarious attempt of the Périer Ministry to establish the practice of incarcerating writers previously to trial. The thing had been already done in several instances, when Carrel, in a calm and well-reasoned article, which he signed with his name, demonstrated its illegality, and declared that if it was attempted in his own case he would, at the peril of his life, oppose force to force.[†] This produced its effect: the illegality was not repeated; Carrel was prosecuted for his article, pleaded his own cause, and was acquitted; as on every subsequent occasion when the paper was prosecuted and he defended it in person before a jury. The *National*, often

[*Translated from *ibid.*, pp. 37-8.]

[†Carrel, "Du flagrant délit en matière d'impression et publication d'écrits," *National*, 24 Jan., 1832, pp. 1-2.]

*f-f*37[1,2]   had ever yet

prosecuted, was never condemned but once, when, by a miserable quibble, the cause was taken from the jury to be tried by the court alone; and once again before the Chamber of Peers, an occasion which was made memorable by the spirit with which Carrel spoke out in the face of the tribunal which was sitting to judge him, what all France thinks of one of the most celebrated of its proceedings, the trial and condemnation of Marshal Ney.[*] Nothing on this occasion could have saved Carrel from a heavy fine or a long imprisonment, had not a member of the Chamber itself, General Excelmans, hurried away [g] by an irresistible impulse, risen [h] in his place, acknowledged the sentiment, and repeated it.[†]

Without these manifestations of spirit and intrepidity, Carrel, however he might have been admired as a writer, could not have acquired his great influence as a man; nor been enabled without imputation on his courage, to keep aloof from the more violent proceedings of his party, and discountenance, as he steadily did, all premature attempts to carry their point by physical force.

Whatever may have been Carrel's individual opinions, he did not, in the *National*, begin by being a republican; he was willing to give the new chief magistrate a fair trial; nor was it until that personage had quarrelled with Lafayette, driven Dupont de l'Eure and Laffitte from office, and called Casimir Périer to his councils for the avowed purpose of turning back the movement, that Carrel hoisted republican colours. Long before this the symptoms of what was coming had been so evident, as to embitter the last moments of Benjamin Constant, if not, as was generally believed, to shorten his existence. The new oligarchy had declared, both by their words and their deeds, that they had conquered for themselves, and not for the people: and the King had shown his determination that through them he would govern, that he would make himself necessary to them, and be a despot, using them and rewarding them as his tools. It was the position which the King assumed as the head of the oligarchy, which made Carrel a republican. He was no fanatic, to care about a name, and [i] was too essentially practical in his turn of mind to fight for a mere abstract principle. The object of his declaration of republicanism was a thoroughly practical one—to strike at the ringleader of the opposite party; and, if it were impossible to overthrow him, to do what was possible—to deprive him of the support of opinion.

Events have decided against Carrel, and it is easy, judging after the fact, to pronounce that the position he took up was not a wise one. We do not contend that

[*Carrel, Speech in the House of Peers (16 Dec., 1834), reported in *National*, 17 Dec., 1834, pp. 1-4.]

[†Rémi Joseph Isadore Exelmans, Speech in the House of Peers (16 Dec., 1834), reported in *National*, 17 Dec., 1834, p. 2.]

[g]37[1,2]   as
[h]37[1,2]   up
[i]37[1,2]   he

it was so; but we do contend, that he might think it so, with very little disparagement to his judgment.

On what ground is it that some of the best writers and thinkers, in free countries, have recommended kingly government—have stood up for constitutional royalty as the best form of a free constitution, or at least one which, where it exists, no rational person would wish to disturb? On one ground only, and on one condition:—that a constitutional monarch does not himself govern, does not exercise his own will in governing, but confines himself to appointing responsible ministers, and even in that, does but ascertain and give effect to the national will. When this condition is observed—and it is, on the whole, faithfully observed in our own country—it is asked, and very reasonably, what more could be expected from a republic? and where is the benefit which would be gained by opening the highest office in the State, the only place which carries with it the most tempting part ^{j}(to common minds)^j of power, the show of it, as a prize to be scrambled for by every ambitious and turbulent spirit, who is willing to keep the community, for his benefit, in the mean turmoil of a perpetual canvass? These are the arguments used: they are, in the present state of society, unanswerable; and we should not say a word for Carrel, if the French government bore, or ever had borne, the most distant resemblance to this idea of constitutional royalty. But it never did: no French king ever confined himself within the limits which the best friends of constitutional monarchy allow to be indispensable to its innocuousness: it is always the king, and not his ministers, that governs; and the power of an English king would appear to Louis Philippe a mere mockery of royalty. Now, if the ^{k}chief functionary^k was to be his own minister, it appeared to Carrel absolutely necessary that he should be a responsible one. The principle of a responsible executive appeared to him too all-important to be sacrificed. As the king would not content himself with being king, there must, instead of a king, be a removable and accountable magistrate.

As for the *dangers* of a republic, we should carry back our minds to the period which followed the Three Days, and to the impression made on all Europe by the ^{l}bravery^l, the ^{m}integrity^m, the gentleness and chivalrous generosity, displayed at that time by the populace of Paris—and ask ourselves whether it was inexcusable to have hoped everything from a people, of whom the very lowest ranks could thus act? a people, too, among whom, out of a few large towns, there is little indigence; where almost every ^{n}peasant^n has his piece of land, where ^{o}the number of landed proprietors is more than half the number of^o grown-up men in the country, and where, by a natural consequence, the respect for the right of property amounts to a

$^{j-j}$+59,67
$^{k-k}$37^{1,2} king
$^{l-l}$37^{1,2} heroism
$^{m-m}$37^{1,2} purity
$^{n-n}$37^{1,2} one
$^{o-o}$37^{1,2} there are more landed properties than there are

superstition? If among such a people there could be danger in republicanism, Carrel saw greater dangers, which could only be averted by republicanism. He saw the whole Continent armed, and ready at a moment's notice to pour into France from all sides. He thought, and it was the principal mistake which he committed, that this collision could not be averted; and he thought, which was no mistake, that if it came, nothing would enable France to bear the brunt of it but that which had carried her through it before, intense popular enthusiasm. This was impossible with Louis Philippe: and if a levy *en masse* was to be again required of all citizens, it must be in a cause which should be worth fighting for, a cause in which all should feel that they had an equal stake.

These were the reasons which made Carrel declare for a republic. *P*They*P* are, no doubt, refuted by the fact, that the public mind was not ripe for a republic, and would not have it. It would have been better, *q*probably*q*, instead of the republican standard, to have raised, as Carrel afterwards did, that of a large parliamentary reform. But the public as yet were still less prepared to join in this demand than in the other. A republic would have brought this among other things, and although, by professing republicanism, there was danger of alarming the timid, there was the advantage of being able to appeal to a feeling already general and deeply rooted, the national aversion to the principle of hereditary privileges. The force of this aversion was clearly seen, when it extorted even from Louis Philippe the abolition of the hereditary peerage: and in choosing a point of attack which put this feeling on his side, Carrel did not show himself a bad tactician.

Nor was it so clear at that time that the public mind was not ripe. Opinion advances quickly in times of revolution; at the time of which we speak, it had set in rapidly in the direction of what was called "the movement;" and the manifestation of public feeling at the funeral of General Lamarque, in June 1832, was such, that many competent judges think it must have been yielded to, and the King must have changed his policy, but for the unfortunate collision which occurred on that day between the people and the troops, which produced a conflict that lasted two days, and led to the memorable ordonnance placing Paris under martial law.[*] On this occasion the responsible editor of the *National*[†] was tried on a capital charge for an article of Carrel's,[‡] published just before the conflict, and construed as an instigation to rebellion. He was acquitted not only of the capital, but of the minor offence; and it was proved on the trial, from an official report of General Pajol,[§]

[*Ordonnance du roi qui met la ville de Paris en état de siège, Bulletin 161, No. 4204 (6 June, 1832), *Bulletin des lois du royaume de France*, 9th ser., Pt. 2, Sect. 1, IV, 662.]
[†J.B. Alexandre Paulin.]
[‡"Qu'il faut craindre de rendre les modérés violens en se moquant de la modération," *National*, 31 May, 1832, p. 1.]
[§See the report of Claude Pierre Pajol, *National*, 30 Aug., 1832, p. 2.]

*p-p*37[1,2]   All of them
*q-q*37[1,2]   doubtless

the officer in command, that the conflict began on the side of the military, who attacked the people because '(as at the funeral of our Queen Caroline)' an attempt was made to change the course of the procession, and carry Lamarque's remains to the Pantheon. But, the battle once begun, many known republicans had joined in it; they had fought with desperation, and the blame was generally thrown upon them; from this time the fear of *émeutes* spread among the trading classes, and they rallied round the throne of Louis Philippe.

Though the tide now decidedly turned in favour of the party of resistance, and the moderate opposition headed by M. Odilon Barrot and M. Mauguin lost ʳthe greater part ofˢ its supporters, the republican opposition continued for some time longer to increase in strength: and Carrel, becoming more and more indisputably at the head of it, rose in influence, and became more and more an object of popular attention.

It was in the autumn of 1833 that we first saw Carrel. He was then at the height of his reputation, and prosperity had shed upon him, as it oftenest does upon the strongest minds, only its best influences. An extract from a letter written ʳnot longʳ after will convey in its freshness the impression which he then communicated to an English observer.

I knew Carrel as the most powerful journalist in France, sole manager of a paper which, while it keeps aloof from all ᵘcoterieᵘ influence, and from the actively revolutionary part of the republican body, has for some time been avowedly republican; and I knew that he was considered a vigorous, energetic man of action, who would always have courage and conduct in an emergency. Knowing thus much of him, I was ushered into the *National* office, where I found six or seven of the innumerable *rédacteurs* who belong to a French paper, tall, dark-haired men, with formidable ᵛmoustachesᵛ, and looking fiercely republican. Carrel was not there; and after waiting some time, I was introduced to a slight young man, with extremely polished manners, no ʷmoustachesʷ at all, and apparently fitter for a drawing-room than a camp; this was the commander-in-chief of those formidable-looking champions. But it was impossible to be five minutes in his company without perceiving that he was accustomed to ˣascendancyˣ, and so accustomed as not to feel ʸit. Insteadʸof ᶻtheᶻ eagerness and impetuosity which one finds in most Frenchmen, his manner is extremely deliberate: without any affectation, he speaks in a sort of measured cadence, and in a manner of which ᵃMr. Carlyle'sᵃ words, "quiet emphasis,"[*] are more

[*Carlyle, letter to Mill (24 Sept., 1833), in *Collected Letters*, Vol. VI, p. 445; Carlyle is referring to Mill's tone in his review of Alison's *History of the French Revolution*, p. 111-22 above.]

ʳ⁻ʳ+59,67
ˢ⁻ˢ37¹,² almost all
ᵗ⁻ᵗ37¹,² soon
ᵘ⁻ᵘ33,37¹,² *coterie*
ᵛ⁻ᵛ33,37¹,² *moustaches* (which many of the republicans have taken to wearing)
ʷ⁻ʷ33,37¹,² *moustaches*
ˣ⁻ˣ33 *ascendancy*
ʸ⁻ʸ33 it; instead
ᶻ⁻ᶻ33,37¹,² that
ᵃ⁻ᵃ33 your] 37¹,² the

characteristic than of any man I know; there is the same quiet emphasis in his writings:—a man singularly free, if we may trust appearances, from self-consciousness; simple, graceful, *b*at times*b* almost *c*infantinely*c* playful *d* ; and combining perfect self-reliance with the most unaffected modesty; always pursuing a path of his own ("*Je n'aime pas*," said he to me one day, "*à marcher en troupeau*"), occupying a midway position, facing one way towards the supporters of monarchy and an aristocratic limitation of the suffrage, with whom he will have no compromise, on the other towards the extreme republicans, who have anti-property doctrines, and instead of his United States republic, want a republic *e*after the fashion of the Convention*e*, with something like a dictatorship in their own *f*hands. He*f* calls himself a Conservative Republican (*l'opinion républicaine conservatrice*); not but that he sees plainly that the present constitution of *g*society*g* admits of many improvements, but he thinks they can only take place gradually, or at least that philosophy has not yet matured them; and he would rather hold back than accelerate the *h*political*h* revolution which he thinks inevitable, in order to leave time for ripening those great questions, chiefly affecting the constitution of property and the condition of the working classes, which would press for a solution if a revolution were to take place. As for himself, he says that he is not *un homme spécial*, that his *métier de journaliste* engrosses him too much to enable him to study, and that he is profoundly ignorant of much upon which he would have to decide if he were in power; and could do nothing but bring together a body *i*genuinely*i* representative of the people, and assist in carrying into execution the dictates of their united wisdom. This is modest enough in the man who would certainly be President of the Republic, if there were a republic within five years, and the extreme party did not get the upper hand. He seems to know well what he does know: I have met with no such views of the French Revolution in any book, as *j* I have heard from him.[*]

This is a first impression, but it *k*was*k* confirmed by all that we afterwards saw and learnt. Of all distinguished Frenchmen whom we have known, Carrel, in manner, answered most to Coleridge's definition of the manner of a gentleman, that which shows respect to others in such a way as implies an equally habitual and secure reliance on their respect to *l*himself*l*.[†] Carrel's manner was not of the self-asserting kind, like that of many of the most high-bred Frenchmen, who succeed perfectly in producing the effect they desire, but who seem to be desiring it: Carrel seemed never to concern himself about it, but to trust to what he was, for what he would appear to be. This had not always been the case; and we learn from M. Nisard, that in the time of his youth and obscurity he was sensitive as to the

---

[*John Stuart Mill, letter to Carlyle (25 Nov., 1833), pp. 194-6.]
[†Samuel Taylor Coleridge, *The Friend* (London: Gale and Curtis, 1812), p. 243.]

b-b+59,67
*c-c*33 *infantinely*
*d*33,37[1,2] , as they all say, when he is among his intimates, and indeed I could see that myself
*e-e*33,37[1,2] *de la façon de la Convention*
*f-f*33 hands; he
*g-g*33 property
h-h+37[1,2],59,67
*i-i*33 generally
*j*33 those
*k-k*37[1,2] has been
*l-l*37[1,2] yourself

consideration shown him, and susceptible of offence. It was not in this only that he was made better by being better appreciated. Unlike vulgar minds, whose faults, says M. Nisard, "augment in proportion as their talents obtain them indulgence, it was evident to all his friends that his faults diminished, in proportion as his brilliant qualities, and the celebrity they gave him, increased."[*]

One of the qualities which we were most struck with in Carrel was his modesty. It was not that common modesty, which is but the negation of arrogance and overweening pretension. It was the higher *quality*, of which that is but a small part. It was the modesty of one who knows accurately what he is, and what he is equal to, never attempts anything which requires qualities that he has not, and admires and values no less, and more if it be reasonable to do so, the things which he cannot do, than those which he can. It was most unaffectedly that he disclaimed all mastery of the details of politics. I understand, he said, the principles of a representative government. But he said, and we believe him to have sincerely thought, that when once a genuinely representative legislature should have been assembled, his function would be at an end. It would belong to more instructed men, he thought, to make laws for France; he could at most be of use in defending her from attack, and in making her laws obeyed. In this Carrel did himself less than justice, for though he was not, as he truly said, *un homme spécial*, though he had not *profoundly* studied political economy or jurisprudence, no man ever had a greater gift of attaching to himself men of special acquirements, or could discern more surely what man was fit for what thing. And that is the exact quality wanted in the head of an administration. Like Mirabeau, Carrel had a natural gift for being Prime Minister; like Mirabeau, he could make men of all sorts, even foreigners, and men who did not think themselves inferior to him but only different, feel that they could have been loyal to him—that they could have served *o* and followed him in life and death, and marched under his orders wherever he chose to lead: sure, with him, of being held worth whatever they were worth, of having their counsels listened to by an ear capable of appreciating them, of having the post assigned to them for which they were fittest, and a commander to whom they could trust for bringing them off in any embarrassment in which he could ever engage them.

Shortly after we first knew Carrel, we had an opportunity of judging him in one of the most trying situations in which the leading organ of a movement party could be placed; and the manner in which he conducted himself in it, gave us the exalted idea which we never afterwards lost, both of his nobleness of character, and of his eminent talents as a political leader.

A small and extreme section of the republican body, composed of men, some of

[*Translated from Nisard, pp. 22, 23.]

*m-m*37[1,2]   modesty
*n-n*37[1,2]   systematically
*o*37[1,2]   him

them highly accomplished, many of them pure in purpose and full of courage and enthusiasm, but without that practicalness which distinguished Carrel,—more highly endowed with talent for action, than with judgment for it,—had formed themselves into a society, which placed itself in communication with the discontented of the labouring classes, and got under their command the greater part of the insurrectionary strength of the party.* These men raised the cry of social

*The following extract from the letter already quoted, contains a picture of one of the most remarkable of these men. We have no reason to believe that he is a specimen of the rest, for he is as completely an individual as Carrel: "A *P* man whose name is energy; who cannot ask you the commonest question but in so decided a manner that he makes you start: *q* who impresses you with a sense of irresistible power and indomitable will; you might fancy him an incarnation of Satan, if he were your enemy or the enemy of your party, and if you had not associated with him and seen how full of sweetness and amiableness and gentleness he is *r*. . . . His*r* notion of duty is that of a Stoic; he conceives it as something quite infinite*,* and having nothing whatever to do with happiness, something immeasurably above it: a kind of half Manichean in his views of the universe: according to him, man's life consists of one perennial and intense struggle against the principle of evil, which but for that struggle would wholly overwhelm him: generation after generation carries on this battle, with little success as yet; he believes in perfectibility and progressiveness, but thinks that hitherto *s*progress*s* has consisted only in removing some of the impediments to good, not in realizing the good itself: that, nevertheless, the only satisfaction which man can realize for himself is in battling with this evil principle, and overpowering it; that after evils have accumulated for centuries, there sometimes comes one great clearing-off, *t* one day of reckoning called a revolution: that it is only on *u*such*u* rare occasions, very rarely indeed on any others, that good men get into power, and then they ought to seize the opportunity for doing all they can: that any government which is boldly attacked, by ever so small a minority, may be overthrown, and that is his hope with *v*respect*v* to the present government. *w* He is *x*much more accomplished*x* than most of the political men I *y*have seen*y*; has a wider range of ideas,

*P*33   very different man from Carrel is Cavaignac; he is president of the *Société des Droits de l'Homme*, who are the active stirring revolutionary party, who look up to *Robespierre*, and aim at *l'égalité absolue*: he is for taking the first opportunity for overthrowing the government by force, and thinks the opportunity must come in a few months, or a year at farthest: a

*q*33,37[1,2]   a man

*r-r*33   : intense in everything, he is the intensest of atheists, and says, "je n'aime pas ceux qui croient en Dieu" because "it is generally a reason for doing nothing for Man": but his

*s-s*33   *progress*

*t*33   [EL *reads* on]

*u-u*33   *such*

*v-v*33   [EL *reads* regard]

*w*33   His notion of *égalité absolue* is rather speculative than practical: he says he does not know whether it should be by an equal division of the *means* of production (land and capital) or by an equal division of the produce: when I stated to him the difficulties of both he felt and acknowledged them; all he had to propose were but a variety of measures *tending towards* an equalisation of property: and he seems to have a strange reliance on *events*, thinking that when the end is clearly conceived, the circumstances of the case would when power is in the right hands, suggest the most appropriate means. Cavaignac is the son of a Conventionalist and regicide.

*x-x*33,37[1,2]   a much more accomplished man

*y-y*33   saw there

reform, and a modification of the constitution of property,—ideas which the St. Simonians had set afloat, in connexion with a definite scheme, and with speculative views the most *enlarged, and in several respects the most just,* that had ever been connected with Utopianism *b*. But*b* these republicans had no definite plan; the ideas were comparatively vague and indeterminate in their minds, yet were sincerely entertained, and did not, whatever ignorant or cowardly persons might suppose, mean plunder for themselves and their associates. The Society published a manifesto, in which these aspirations were dimly visible, and in which they reprinted, with their adhesion, a Declaration of the Rights of Man, proposed by Robespierre in the National Convention,[*] and by that body rejected. This document was harmless enough, and we could not see in it any of the anti-property doctrines that appeared to be seen by everybody else, for Paris was convulsed with apprehension on the subject. But whether it was the name of Robespierre, or the kind of superstition which attaches to the idea of property in France, or that the manifesto was considered a preliminary to worse things supposed to be meditated by its authors, the alarm of the middle classes was now thoroughly excited: they became willing to join with any men and any measures, in order to put down not only this, but every other kind of republicanism; and from this time, in reality, dates the passionate resistance to the democratic movement, which, with the assistance of Fieschi, was *improved* into the laws of September 1835,[†] by which laws, and by the imprisonment and exile of its most active members, the republican party has been for the present silenced.

The conduct by which the prospects of the popular party were thus compromised, Carrel had from the first disapproved. The constitution of property appeared to him a subject for speculative philosophers, *c* not for the mass: he did not think that the present idea of property, and the present arrangements of it, would last for ever unchanged, through the progressive changes of society and civilization; but he believed that any improvement of them would be the work of a generation, and

---

converses on art, and most subjects of general interest: always throwing all he has to say into a few brief energetic sentences, as if it was contrary to his nature to expend one superfluous word." [Mill to Carlyle (25 Nov., 1833), pp. 196-7.]

*z*There can be no indelicacy in now saying, that the original of this picture was Godefroi Cavaignac.*z*

[*See p. 126 above.]

[†Loi sur les crimes, délits et contraventions de la presse et des autres moyens de publication, Bulletin 155, No. 356 (9 Sept., 1835), *Bulletin des lois du royaume de France*, 9th ser., Pt. 1, VII, 247-56; Loi sur les cours d'assises, Bulletin 155, No. 357, *ibid.*, pp. 256-9; and Loi qui rectifie les articles 341, 345, 346, 347 et 352 du code d'instruction criminelle, et l'article 17 du code pénal, Bulletin 155, No. 358, *ibid.*, pp. 259-62.]

z-z+59,67
*a-a*37[1,2]   just and enlarged
*b-b*37[1,2]   , and having no fault whatever except that they were impracticable: but
*c*37[1,2]   and

not of an hour. Against the other peculiar views of this revolutionary party he had combated both in private and in the *National*. He had taken no part in their projects for arriving at a republic by an insurrection. He had set his face against their notion of governing by an active minority, for the good of the majority, but if necessary in opposition to ^{d}its^d will, and by a provisional despotism that was to terminate some day in a free government. A free, full, and fair representation of the people was his object; full opportunity to the nation to declare its will—the perfect submission of individual crotchets to that will. And without condemning the Republic of the Convention ^{e}under the extraordinary circumstances which accompanied its brief career^e, he preferred to cite as an example the Republic of the United States; not that he thought it perfect, nor even ^{f}a^f model which France ought ^{g}in all respects^g to imitate, but because it presented ^{h} to France an example of what she most wanted—protection to all parties alike, limitation of the power of the magistrate, and fairness as between the majority and the minority.

In the newspaper warfare, of an unusually vehement character, stirred up by the manifesto of the revolutionary republicans, Carrel was the last of the journalists to declare himself. He took some days to consider what position it most became him to assume. He did not agree in the conclusions of this party, while he had just enough of their premises in common with them, to expose him to misrepresentation. It was incumbent on him to rescue himself, and the great majority of the popular party, from responsibility for opinions which they did not share, and the imputation of which was calculated to do them so much injury. On the other hand, the party could not afford to lose these able and ^{i}energetic^i men, and the support of that portion of the working classes who had given their confidence to them. The men, too, were many of them his friends; he knew them to be good men, superior men, men who were an honour to their opinions, and he could not brook the cowardice of letting them be run down by a popular cry. After mature deliberation, he published in the *National* a series of articles, admirable for their nobleness of feeling and delicacy and dexterity in expression: in which, without a single subterfuge, without deviating in a word from the most open and straightforward sincerity, he probed the question to the bottom, and contrived with the most ^{j}exquisite^j address, completely to separate himself from all that was objectionable in the opinions of the manifesto, and at the same time to present both the opinions and the men in the most advantageous light, in which, without disguising his

---

$^{d\text{-}d}$37^{1,2} their
$^{e\text{-}e}$+59,67
$^{f\text{-}f}$37^{1,2} the
$^{g\text{-}g}$+59,67
^{h}59   or seemed to present
$^{i\text{-}i}$37^{1,2} active
$^{j\text{-}j}$37^{1,2} consummate

disagreement, it was possible to place them.[*] These were triumphs which belonged only to Carrel; it was on such occasions that he showed, though in a bloodless field, the qualities of a consummate general.

In the deliberations of the republican party among themselves, Carrel was more explicit. The society which issued the manifesto, and which was called the Society of the Rights of Man, made an overture to a larger society, that for the Protection of the Liberty of the Press, which represented all the shades of republicanism, and invited them to adopt the manifesto. The committee or council of the association *k*was*k* convened to take the proposal into consideration: and Carrel, though on ordinary occasions he absented himself from the proceedings of such bodies, attended. At this deliberation we had the good fortune to be present, and we shall never forget the impression we received of the talents both of Carrel and of the leader of the more extreme party, M. Cavaignac. Carrel displayed the same powerful good sense, and the same spirit of conciliation, in discussing with that party his differences from them, which he had shown in his apology for them to the public. With the superiority of a really comprehensive mind, he placed himself at their point of view; laid down in more express and bolder terms than they had done themselves, and in a manner which startled men who were esteemed to go much *l*farther*l* than Carrel, the portion of *m*philosophic*m* truth which there was in the premises from which they had drawn their erroneous conclusions; and left them less dissatisfied than pleased, that one who differed from them so widely, agreed with them in so much more than they expected, and could so powerfully advocate a portion of their views. The result was that Carrel was chosen to draw up a report to the society, on the manifesto, and on the invitation to adopt it. His report, in which he utters his whole mind on the new ideas of social reform considered in reference to practice, remained unpublished: Carrel did not proclaim unnecessarily to the world the differences in his own party, but preferred the prudent maxim of Napoleon, *il faut laver notre linge sale chez nous*.[†] But at a later period, when the chiefs of the extreme party were in prison or in banishment, the republican cause for the present manifestly lost, himself publicly calumniated (for from what calumny is he sacred whom a government *n*detests?*n*) as having indirectly

[*Carrel, "Du nouveau procès entre la république et le tiers-parti," *National*, 27 Oct., 1833, pp. 2-3; "La révolution et le tiers-parti," *ibid.*, 29 Oct., 1833, p. 1; and unheaded article, *ibid.*, 30 Oct., 1833, p. 2.]

[†"Allocution de l'empereur aux membres du corps législatif présens à l'audience du 1er janvier 1814," in *Histoire parlementaire de la révolution française*, ed. Philippe Joseph Benjamin Buchez and Prosper Charles Roux, 40 vols. (Paris: Paulin, 1834-38), Vol. XXXIX, p. 460.]

*k-k*37[1,2] were
*l-l*37[1,2] further
*m-m*37[1,2] eternal
*n-n*37[1,2],59 detests!

instigated the Fieschi atrocity, and his house searched for papers on pretence of ascertaining if he was concerned in it, which the cowardly hypocrites who sought to involve him in the odium never themselves even in imagination conceived to be possible; at this time, when no one could any longer be injured by setting his past conduct in its true light, Carrel published his Report on the Robespierre Manifesto: and under the title of *Extrait du dossier d'un prévenu de complicité morale dans l'attentat du 28 Juillet*,[*] it subsists for any one to read, a monument at once of the far-sighted intellect of Carrel, and of his admirable skill in expression.

During the rapid decline of the republican party, we know little of what passed in Carrel's mind; but our knowledge of him would have °led us to surmise° what M. Nisard states to be the fact, that he became sensible of the hopelessness of the cause, and only did not abandon the advocacy of it as an immediate object, from a sense of what was due to the consistency which a public man is bound to maintain before the public, when it is the sacrifice of his interest only, and not of his honesty, that it requires of him; and of what was due to the simple-minded men whom he had helped to compromise, and whose whole stay and support, the faith which kept them honest men, and which saved them from despair, would have expired within them if Carrel had deserted them. As is beautifully said by M. Nisard,

to resist your better judgment; never to give way, nor allow your misgivings to become visible; to stand firm to principles proclaimed at some critical moment, though they were no more than sudden impressions or rash hopes which impatience converted into principles; not to abandon simple and ardent minds in the path in which you have yourself engaged them, and to whom it is all in all; purposely to repress your doubts and hesitations, and coldly to call down upon your own head fruitless and premature perils, in a cause in which you are no longer enthusiastic, in order to keep up the confidence of your followers: such is the price which must be paid for being the acknowledged chief of an opinion at war with an established government:—to do this, and to do it so gracefully and *p*unostentatiously*p*, that those who recognise you as their chief shall pardon you your superiority to them; and with a talent so out of comparison, that no self-love in the party you represent, can conceive *q*the*q* idea of equalling you. During more than four years, such was the task Carrel had to fulfil—and he fulfilled it: never for a single moment did he fall below his position. He never incited those whom he was not resolved to follow; and in many cases where the impulse had been given not by him, but against his judgment, he placed himself at the head of those whom he had not instigated. The same man whose modesty in ordinary circumstances allowed the title of chief of the republican opinion to be disputed to him, seized upon it in time of danger as a sign by which the stroke of the enemy might be directed to him. He was like a general who, having by his courage and talents advanced to the first rank of the army, allows his merits to be contested in the jealousies and gossipings of the barrack, but in a

[*Paris: Paulin, 1835.]

°-°37[1,2]   enabled us to predict
*p-p*37[1,2]   so without ostentation
*q-q*37[1,2]   an

desperate affair assumes the command in chief by the right of the bravest and *r* most able.[*]

*s*The doubts and misgivings, however, which Carrel is stated to have so painfully experienced, never affected the truth of his republican principles, but at most their immediate applicability. The very foundation of Carrel's character was sincerity and singleness of purpose; and nothing would have induced him to continue professing to others, convictions which he had ceased to entertain.

*t*While*t* Carrel never abandoned republicanism, it necessarily, after the laws of September, ceased to be so prominent as before in his journal. He felt the necessity of rallying under one standard all who were agreed in the essential point, opposition to the oligarchy; and he was one of the most earnest in demanding an extension of the suffrage; that vital point, the all-importance of which France has been so slow to recognise, and which it is so much to be regretted that he had not chosen from the first, instead of republicanism, to be the *u*immediate*u* aim of his political life.*s*

But the greatest disappointment which Carrel suffered was the defeat not of republicanism, but of what M. Nisard calls his *"théorie du droit commun;"*[†] those ideas of moderation in victory, of respect for the law, and for the rights of the weaker party, so much more wanted in France than any political improvements which are possible where those ideas are not.

"I affirm," says M. Nisard,

that I have never seen him in real bitterness of heart, but for what he had to suffer on this point; and on this subject alone his disenchantment was distressing. His good sense, the years he had before him, the chapter of accidents, would have given him patience as to his own prospects, but nothing could console him for seeing that noble scheme of reciprocal forbearance compromised, and thrown back into the class of doctrines for ever disputable—by all parties equally; by the government, by the country, and by his own friends. *There*, in fact, was the highest and truest inspiration of his good sense, the most genuine instinct of his generous nature. All Carrel was in that doctrine. Never would he have proved false to that noble emanation of his intellect and of his heart. *v* . . . The Revolution of July, so extraordinary among revolutions from the spectacle of a people leaving the vanquished at full liberty to inveigh against and even to ridicule the victory, gave ground to hope for a striking and definitive return to the principle of equal law. Carrel made

[*Translated from Nisard, pp. 8-9.]
[†*Ibid.*, p. 14.]

*r*37[1,2] the
*s-s*37[1,2] [*paragraphs in reverse order*]
*t-t*37[1,2] But while
u-u+59,67
*v*37[1,2] If sometimes vague menaces escaped from him in the excitement of controversy, they made no one doubt him who was not interested in doubting him, and in ruining his noblest claim to the confidence of his country. . . .

himself the organ of this hope, and the theorist of this doctrine. He treated the question with the vigour and clearness which were usual with him. He opposed to the examples, so numerous in the last fifty years, of governments which successively perished by overstraining their powers, the idea of a government offering securities to all parties against its own lawful and necessary instinct of self-preservation. He invoked practical reasons exclusively, denying himself rigidly the innocent aid of all the language of passion, not to expose his noble theory to the ironical designation of Utopianism. It was these views which ^wgave^w Carrel so many friends in all parts of France, and in all places where the *National* penetrated. There is, apart from all political parties, a party composed of all those who are either kept by circumstances out of the active sphere of politics, or who are too enlightened to fling themselves into it in the train of a leader who is only recommended by successes in parliament or in the press. How many men, weary of disputes about forms of government—incredulous even to Carrel's admirable apologies for the American system —quitting the shadow for the substance, ranged themselves under that banner of equal justice which Carrel had raised, and to which he would have adhered at the expense, if necessary, even of his individual opinions. Testimonies of adhesion came in to him from all quarters, which for a moment satisfied his utmost wishes: and I saw him resigning himself to be, for an indeterminate period, the first speculative writer of his country. But errors in which all parties had their share, soon cooled him. It was a severe shock. Carrel had faith in these generous views; he had adopted them with stronger conviction perhaps than his republican theories, to which he had committed himself hastily, and under the influence of temporary events rather than of quiet and deliberate meditations. ^x . . . It is more painful surely to a generous mind to doubt the possibility of a generous policy, than to the leader of a party to doubt that his opinions have a chance of prevailing: Carrel had both disappointments at once.

The affliction of Carrel was irreparable from the moment when he remained the sole defender of the common rights of all, between the nation which from fear made a sacrifice of them to the government, and his own party, which cherished secretly thoughts inconsistent with them. We had a long conversation on the subject a few months before his death, in a walk in the Bois de Boulogne. I perceived that he had almost renounced his doctrine as a principle capable of present application: he at most adhered to it as a Utopia, from pure generosity, and perhaps also from the feeling of his own strength. Carrel believed that if his party came into power, he would have the force to resist the temptation of arbitrary authority, and not to accept it even from the hands of a majority offering it to him in the name of his country. But a cause deferred was to him a lost cause. His doubts were equivalent to a defeat. Though this principle was the most disinterested conviction of his mind and the best impulse of his heart, the theories of men of action always imply in their own minds the hope of a prompt reduction to practice. From the moment when his doctrine failed as a practicable policy, it could no longer be a doctrine for him. Towards the end of his life he spoke of it only as a result of the progress of improvement, which it would not be his fate to live to see, and which perhaps would never be arrived at.[*]

We can conceive few things more melancholy than the spectacle of one of the noblest men in France, if not the noblest, dying convinced against his will, that his

[*Translated from *ibid.*, pp. 14-15, 16.]

^{w-w}37^{1,2}   made
^x37^{1,2}   Sustained in these by a point of honour against doubts growing ever stronger, must he doubt of the others too?

country is incapable of freedom; and under whatsoever institutions, has only the choice, what man or what party it will be under the despotism of. But we have not Carrel's deliberate opinion; we have but his feelings in the first agony of his disenchantment. That multitude of impartial men in all quarters of France, who responded for a short time so cordially to his voice, will again claim the liberties which, in a moment of panic, they have surrendered to a government they neither love nor respect, and which they submit to and even support against its enemies, solely in despair of a better.

But Carrel was not one of those whom disappointment paralyzes; unsuccessful in one worthy object, he always found another. The newspaper press, gagged by the September laws, no longer afforded him the same instrument of power, and he meditated a total or partial retirement from it, either to recruit himself by study, *se retremper par l'étude*, for which, even at an earlier period, he had expressed to us an earnest longing, or to write what he had for some time had in view, the History of Napoleon. But he would have been called from these pursuits into a more active life; at the impending general election, he would have been chosen a deputy; having already been once put up without his knowledge, and defeated only by one vote. What course he would have struck out for himself in the Chamber, we shall never know, but it is not possible to doubt that it would have been an original one, and that it would have been brilliant, and most beneficial to his country. So immensely the superior of all his rivals in the qualities which create influence, he would probably have drawn round him by degrees all the sections of the popular party; would have given, if any one could, unity, decision, and definiteness to their vague plans and divided counsels; and the destiny which he could not *y*conquer*y* for himself as President of a Republic, he might one day have gloriously fulfilled as minister under a reformed legislature, if any such reform could in France (which he regarded as impossible) render royalty compatible with the prevalence of the popular interest. These are vain dreams now; but the time was, when it was not foolish to indulge in them. Such dreams were the comfort of those who knew him, and who knew how ill his country can supply his place. *z*He was at once the Achilles and the Ulysses of the democratic party*z*: and the star of hope for France in any new convulsions, was extinguished when Carrel died.

It is bitter to lose such a man; bitterest of all to lose him in a miserable duel *a* . But ill shall it fare with the government which *b*can rejoice in the death of such an enemy*b*, and the time may come when it would give its *c*most precious treasures*c* to recal from the grave the victim whom, whether intentionally on its part or not, its

---

*y-y*37[1,2]   have conquered
*z-z*37[1,2]   Deprived of him, French politics are now a blank
*a*37[1,2]   with such an adversary [Emile de Girardin]
*b-b*37[1,2]   deems such services worthy of reward
*c-c*37[1,2]   dearest blood

enmity has sent thither. The heir to the French throne[*] is reported [d] to have said of Carrel's death, that it was a loss to all parties; he, at least, will probably live to find it so. Such a government as that now existing in France cannot last; and whether it end peacefully or violently, whether the return tide of public opinion shall bear the present reigning family aloft on its surface, or whelm them in its depths, bitterly will that man be missed, who alone, perhaps, would have been capable of saying to that tremendous power, Thus far shalt thou go, and no [e]farther[e].[†] There are in France philosophers superior to Carrel, but no man known by such past services, equal like him to the great practical questions which are coming, and whose whole nature and character speak out like his, to the best qualities and noblest sympathies of the French mind. He had all that was necessary to give him an advocate in every French breast, and to make all young and ardent Frenchmen see in him the ideal of their own aspirations, the expression of what in their best moments they would wish to be.

His death is not to be confounded with the vulgar deaths of those who, hemmed in between two cowardices, can resist the fear of death, but not the [f] meaner fear of the tongues of their fellow-creatures. His duel was a consequence of the system which he adopted for repelling the insults to which, as a journalist identifying himself with his journal, he was peculiarly exposed; and which, not only for his influence as a public man, but for the respectablility of the press, and for preserving that high tone of public discussion from which he himself never swerved, he thought it necessary not to pass unpunished. His system, alas! is sufficiently refuted by its having cost so precious a life: but it *was* his system. "He often repeated," says M. Littré,

that the *National* had no *procureur du roi* to defend it, and that it must be its own defender. He was persuaded, too, that nothing gives more food to political [g]enmities[g], or renders them more capable of reaching the last excesses, than the impunity of calumny: he contended that the men of the Revolution had prepared their own scaffold by not imposing silence on their defamers: and had it been necessary for him to expose himself even more than he did, he never would have suffered, in whatever situation he might have been placed, that his name and character should with impunity be trifled with. This was his answer when he was blamed for risking his life too readily; and now, when he has fallen, it is fit, in defending his memory from a reproach which grief has wrung from persons who loved him, to recal the words he uttered on his death-bed: "The standard-bearer of the regiment is always the most exposed."[‡]

He died a martyr to the morality and dignity of public discussion: and though

[*Ferdinand, duc d'Orléans.]
[†See Job, 38:11.]
[‡Translated from Littré, pp. 58-9.]

[d]37[1,2]   by M. Nisard [p. 54]
[e-e]37[1,2]   further, here shall thy proud waves be stayed
[f]37[1,2]   still
[g-g]37[1,2]   hatreds

even that cause would have been far better served by his life than by such a death, he was the victim of his virtues, and of that low state of our civilization, after all our boasting, which has not yet [h]contrived[h] the means of giving [i]to[i] a man whose reputation is important to him, [j]protection[j] against insult, but [k]leaves[k] him to seek reparation sword in hand, as in the barbarous ages. While he lived, he did keep up in the press generally, something of that elevation of tone which distinguished it under the Restoration, but which in the *débordement* of political and literary profligacy since the Revolution [l]of 1830[l], it had become difficult to preserve: and all we [m]know[m] of the state of newspaper discussion since his death, exalts our sense of the moral influence which Carrel exercised over the press of France.

Carrel was of middle height, slightly made, and very graceful. Like [n]most[n] persons of really fine faculties, he carried those faculties with him into the smallest things; and did not disdain to excel, being qualified to do so, in [o] things which are great only to little men. Even in the details of personal equipments, his taste was watched for and followed by the amateurs of such matters. He was fond of all bodily exercises, and had, says M. Nisard, *un peu de tous les goûts vifs*,[*] more or less of all strong and natural inclinations; as might be expected from his large and vigorous human nature, the foundation of strength of will, and which, combined with intellect and with goodness, constitutes greatness. He was a human being complete at all points, not a fraction or *frustum* of one.

"The distinctive feature of his character," says M. Nisard,

was his unbounded generosity. In whatever sense we understand that word, [p] whether it mean the impulse of a man who devotes himself, or merely pecuniary liberality, the life of Carrel gives occasion for applying it in all its meanings. All the actions of his public life are marked with the former kind of generosity. His errors were generally acts of generosity ill-calculated. As for pecuniary generosity, no one had it more, or of a better sort. Carrel could neither refuse, nor give little. [q] [†]

[*Nisard, p. 31.]
[†Translated from *ibid.*, p. 21.]

[h-h]37[1,2]   found out
[i-i]+59,67
[j-j]37[1,2]   redress
[k-k]37[1,2]   obliges
[l-l]+59,67
[m-m]37[1,2]   hear
[n-n]37[1,2]   all
[o]37[1,2]   those
[p]37[1,2]   the vagueness of which is its beauty;
[q]37[1,2]   I do not diminish the merit of his generosity, by saying that there was in it a certain improvidence, which was but his confidence in the future. He drew upon the future to meet the demands of his liberality. Exposed by his position to incessant applications, he often had recourse to the purses of his friends to relieve sufferings, perhaps not of the most authentic kind, and ran into debt to give alms. [*Ibid.*]

There are stories told of him like those told of Goldsmith, or any other person of thoughtless generosity. [r] As is often the case with persons of strong impulses, he was of a careless character when not under excitement, and his inattention sometimes caused inconvenience to himself, and made him give unintentional offence to others. But on occasions which called into action his strong will, he had the eye of an eagle: "he seized with a glance, as on a field of battle, the whole *terrain* on which he was placed; and astonished above all by the sureness of the instinct with which he divined the significance of small things. Small things," continues M. Littré, "are those which the vulgar do not perceive; but when such things have produced serious effects, pause, quite disconcerted, before the irrevocable event which might so easily have been prevented." [s] [*]

His conversation, especially on political subjects, M. Nisard, comparing him with the best conversers in a country where the art of conversation is [t]far[t] more cultivated than it is here, declares to be the most perfect he ever heard: and we can add our testimony to his, that Carrel's writings in the *National* seemed but the continuation of his conversation. He was fond of showing that he could do equal justice to all sides of a question: and he would

take up a government newspaper, or one of a more moderate opposition than his own, and reading the article of the day, he would adopt its idea, and complete it or develop it in the spirit of the opinions which had inspired it. At other times he would in the same way recompose the speeches in the Chamber. "They have not given," he would say, "the best reasons for their opinions; *this* would have been more specious, and would have embarrassed us more." His facility was prodigious. And the reasons he gave were not rhetorical fallacies, but just arguments. They embodied all that could be said truly and honourably on that side of the question. "By this he demonstrated[u] two of his qualities, vastly superior to mere facility in arguing for the sake of argument: on the one hand, his knowledge of the interests of all parties; on the other, his real esteem for what was just in the views [v] most opposite to his own.

We have marked [w] these traits of character, because they help to complete the picture of what Carrel was, and, while they give reality to our conception of him, and bring him home to the feelings as a being of our own flesh and blood, they all give additional insight into those great qualities which it is the object of this paper to commemorate. The mind needs such examples, to keep alive in it that faith in

[*Translated from Littré, p. 62.]

[r]37[1,2] M. Nisard tells of his pawning his watch to relieve a person not in extreme necessity, and of his taking the cloth off his horse on a winter evening, to throw it over a poor man whom he saw in the streets, shivering with cold. [P. 22.]
[s]37[1,2] Carrel was never reduced to say "who'd have thought it." "Everybody," says M. Littré, "thinks of great things; superior minds alone take proper account of small ones." [Translated from Littré, p. 62.]
[t-t]+59,67
[u-u]37[1,2] He wished by this to demonstrate
[v]37[1,2] the
[w]37[1,2] all

good, without which nothing worthy the name of good can ever be realized: it needs to be reminded by them that (as [x] is often repeated by one of the [y]greatest writers[y] of our time) man is still man.[*] Whatever man has been, man may be; whatever of heroic the heroic ages, whatever of chivalrous the romantic ages have produced, is still possible, nay, still *is*, and a hero of Plutarch may exist amidst all the pettinesses of modern civilization, and with all the cultivation and refinement, and [z] the analyzing and questioning spirit of the modern European mind. The lives of those are not lost, who have lived [a] enough to be an example to the world; and though his country will not reap the blessings his life might have conferred upon it, yet while the six years following the Revolution of 1830 shall have a place in history, the memory of Armand Carrel will not [b]utterly perish[b].

Si quis piorum manibus locus; si, ut sapientibus placet, non cum corpore extinguuntur magnae animae; placidè quiescas, nosque ab infirmo desiderio et mulieribus lamentis ad contemplationem virtutum tuarum voces, quas neque lugeri, neque plangi fas est: admiratione te potiùs, et immortalibus laudibus, et si natura suppeditet, similitudine decorabimus.[†]

[*Thomas Carlyle; see, e.g., *Sartor Resartus* (1833-34), 2nd ed. (Boston: Munroe, 1837), p. 299 (Bk. III, Chap. xii); "Characteristics," *Edinburgh Review*, LIV (Dec., 1831), 383.]
[†Tacitus, *Agricola*, in *Dialogus, Agricola, Germania* (Latin and English), trans. Maurice Hutton (London: Heinemann; New York: Macmillan, 1914), p. 250 (46).]

[x]37[1,2]   it
[y-y]37[1,2]   noblest spirits
[z]37[1,2]   all
[a]37[1,2]   long
[b-b]37[1,2]   perish utterly from among men

MICHELET'S HISTORY OF FRANCE

1844

EDITOR'S NOTE

Dissertations and Discussions, 2nd ed. (1867), II, 120-80. Headed as title; title footnoted, "*Edinburgh Review*, January 1844." Running titles as title. Reprinted from *Edinburgh Review*, LXXIX (Jan., 1844), 1-39, where it is headed: "Art. I.—Histoire de France. Par M. [Jules] Michelet, Membre de l'Institut, Professeur d'Histoire au Collège Royal de France, Chef de la Section Historique aux Archives du Royaume. 8vo. Vols. 1, 2, 3, 4, 5. Paris: [Hachette,] 1833-42"; running titles: "*Recent French Historians*— / Michelet's *History of France*." Unsigned. Identified in Mill's bibliography as "A review of Michelet's History of France in the Edinburgh Review for January 1844 (No 159)" (MacMinn, 56). The copy in Mill's library, Somerville College (tear-sheets of *ER*), has, in Mill's hand, "(Edinburgh Review, January 1844)"; there are no corrections or emendations in it.

The following text, taken from the 2nd ed. of *D&D* (the last in Mill's lifetime) is collated with that in *D&D*, 1st ed. (1859), and that in *ER*. In the footnoted variants, "44" indicates *ER*, "59" indicates *D&D*, 1st ed., and "67" indicates *D&D*, 2nd ed. (1867).

For comment on the essay, see lxvii–lxxi and ciii–civ above.

Michelet's History of France

IT HAS OF LATE been a frequent remark among Continental thinkers, that the tendencies of the age set strongly in the direction of historical inquiry, and that history is destined to assume a new aspect from the genius and labours of the minds now devoted to its improvement. The anticipation must appear at least premature to an observer in England, confining his observation to his own country. Whatever may be the merits, in some subordinate respects, of such histories as the last twenty years have produced among us, they are in general distinguished by no essential character from the historical writings of the last century. No signs of a new school have been manifested in them; they will be affirmed by no one to constitute an era, or even prefigure the era which is to come: save that the "shadow of its coming"[*] rested for an instant on the lamented Dr. Arnold at the close of his career; while Mr. Carlyle has shown a signal example, in his *French Revolution*,[†] of the epic tone and pictorial colouring which may be given to literal truth, when materials are copious, and when the writer combines the laborious accuracy of a chronicler with the vivid imagination of a poet.

But whoever desires to know either the best which has been accomplished, or what the most advanced minds think it possible to accomplish, for the renovation of historical studies, must look to the Continent; and by the Continent we mean, of course, in an intellectual sense, Germany and France. That there are historians in Germany, our countrymen have at last discovered. The first two volumes of Niebuhr's unfinished work, though the least attractive part to ordinary tastes, are said to have had more readers, or at least more purchasers, in English than in their native language. Of the remaining volume a translation has lately appeared, by a different, but a highly competent hand.[‡] Schlosser, if not read, has at least been

---

[*Cf. Thomas Carlyle, "The Nibelungen Lied," *Westminster Review*, XV (July, 1831), 17, and Colossians, 2:17.]

[†Carlyle, *The French Revolution*, 3 vols. (London: Fraser, 1837).]

[‡Barthold Georg Niebuhr, *The History of Rome*, 3 vols., trans. Julius Charles Hare and Connop Thirlwall (Vols. I and II), William Smith and Leonhard Schmitz (Vol. III) (London: Taylor, 1828 [Vol. I], 1832 [Vol. II], and Taylor and Walton, 1842 [Vol. III]). Niebuhr's work was "completed" by Schmitz's edition of his *Lectures on the History of Rome*, 2 vols. (London: Taylor and Walton, 1844).]

heard of in England;[*] and one of Ranke's works has been twice translated:[†] we would rather that two of them had been translated once. But, though French books are supposed to be sufficiently legible in England without translation, the English public is not aware, that both in historical speculations, and in the importance of her historical writings, France, in the present day, far surpasses Germany. What reason induces the educated part of our countrymen to *ignore*, in so determined a manner, the more solid productions of the most active national mind in Europe, and to limit their French readings to M. de Balzac and M. Eugène Sue, there would be some difficulty in precisely determining. Perhaps it is the ancient dread of French infidelity; perhaps the ancient contempt of French frivolity and superficiality. If it be the former, we can assure them that there is no longer ground for such a feeling; if the latter, we must be permitted to doubt that there ever was. It is unnecessary to discuss whether, as some affirm, a strong religious "revival" is taking place in France, and whether such a phenomenon, if real, is likely to be permanent. There is at least a decided reaction against the *irreligion* of the last age. The Voltairian philosophy is looked upon as a thing of the past; one of its most celebrated assailants has been heard to lament that it has no living representative sufficiently considerable to perform the functions of a "constitutional opposition" against the reigning philosophic doctrines. The present French thinkers, whether receiving Christianity or not as a divine revelation, in no way feel themselves called upon to be unjust to it as a fact in history. There are men who, not disguising their own unbelief, have written deeper and finer things in vindication of what religion has done for mankind, than have sufficed to found the reputation of some of its most admired defenders. If they have any historical prejudice on the subject, it is in favour of the priesthood. They leave the opinions of David Hume on ecclesiastical history[‡] to the exclusive patronage (we are sorry to say) of Protestant writers in Great Britain.

With respect to the charge so often made against French historians, of superficiality and want of research, it is a strange accusation against the country which produced the Benedictines. France has at all times possessed a class of

[*Friedrich Christoph Schlosser, *Universalhistorische Uebersicht der Geschichte der alten Welt und ihrer Kultur*, 9 vols. (Frankfurt: Varrentrapp, 1826-34); *Geschichte des achtzehnten Jahrhunderts und des neunzehnten bis zum Sturz des französicher Kaiserreichs*, 7 vols. (Heidelberg: Mohr, 1836-49).]

[†Leopold von Ranke, *Die römischen Päpste, ihre Kirche und ihr Staat im 16 und 17 Jahrhundert*, 3 vols. (Berlin: Duncker and Humblot, 1834-36); trans. Sarah Austin as *The Ecclesiastical and Political History of the Popes of Rome during the Sixteenth and Seventeenth Centuries*, 3 vols. (London: Murray, 1840); and trans. Walter Keating Kelly as *The History of the Popes, Their Church and State in the Sixteenth and Seventeenth Centuries* (London: Whittaker, 1843).]

[‡In his *History of England, passim.*]

*a-a*44   ignore
*b-b*44   infidelity

studious and accurate *érudits*, as numerous as any other country except Germany; and her popular writers are not more superficial than our own. Voltaire gave false views of history in many respects, but not falser than Hume's; Thiers is inaccurate, but less so than Sir Walter Scott. France has done more for even English history than England has. The very first complete history of England, and to this day not wholly superseded by any other, was the production of a French emigrant, Rapin de Thoyras.[*] *c* The histories and historical memoirs of the Commonwealth period, never yet collected in our own country, have been translated and published at Paris in an assembled form, under the superintendence of M. Guizot;[†] to whom also we owe the best history, both in thought and in composition, of the times of Charles I.[‡] The reigns of the last two Stuarts have been written, with the mind of a statesman and the hand of a vigorous writer, by Armand Carrel, in his *Histoire de la Contre-révolution en Angleterre*;[§] and at greater length, with much research and many new facts, by M. Mazure.[¶] To call these writings, and numerous others which have lately appeared in France, superficial, would only prove an entire unacquaintance with them.

Among the French writers now labouring in the historical field, we must at present confine ourselves to those who have narrated as well as philosophized; who have written history, as well as written *about* history. Were we to include in our survey those general speculations which aim at connecting together the facts of universal history, we could point to some which we deem even more instructive, because of a more comprehensive and far-reaching character, than any which will now fall under our notice. Restricting ourselves, however, to historians in the received sense of the word, and among them to those who have done enough to be regarded as the chiefs and representatives of the new tendency, we should say that the three great historical minds of France, in our time, are Thierry, Guizot, and the

[*Paul de Rapin de Thoyras, *L'histoire d'Angleterre*, 8 vols. (The Hague: Rogissart, 1724).]

[†*Collection des mémoires relatifs à la révolution d'Angleterre*, ed. François Pierre Guillaume Guizot, 25 vols. (Paris and Rouen: Béchet, 1823-25).]

[‡*Histoire de la révolution d'Angleterre*, 1st pt., 2 vols. (Paris: Leroux and Chantpie, 1826-27).]

[§Paris: Sautelet, 1827.]

[¶François Antoine Jean Mazure, *Histoire de la révolution de 1688 en Angleterre*, 3 vols. (Paris: Gosselin, 1825).]

*c*44   Of Mr. Turner's really learned works on our early ages—works standing almost alone among us in extent of original research—it is, after all, the greatest merit to have served as preparatory studies for the *Norman Conquest* of Augustin Thierry.* [*footnote:*] *And (we may add) for the *Histoire de France* of M. Michelet, who has derived important aid from Mr. Turner's review of the Lancastrian period of our history. [Mill is probably referring to both Sharon Turner's *The History of the Anglo-Saxons*, 4 vols. (London: Cadell and Davies, 1799-1805), and his *History of England*, 3 vols. (London: Longman, *et al.*, 1814-23); in Vols. II and III of the latter the Lancastrians are covered. For Thierry's work, see p. 35n above.]

writer whose name, along with that of his most important production, stands at the beginning of the present article.

To assist our appreciation of these writers, and of the improved ideas on the use and study of history, which their writings exemplify and diffuse, we may observe that there are three distinct stages in historical inquiry.

The type of the first stage is Larcher, the translator of Herodotus,[*] who, as remarked by Paul Louis Courier, carries with him to the durbar of Darius the phraseology of the Court of Louis Quatorze;* and, nowise behind him, an English translator of the *Anabasis*, who renders ἄνδρες στρατιῶται by "gentleman of the

[*Histoire d'Hérodote, trans. Pierre Henri Larcher, 7 vols. (Paris: Musier and Nyon, 1786).]

*"Figurez-vous un truchement qui, parlant au sénat de Rome pour le paysan du Danube, au lieu de ce début,

Romains, et vous Sénat, assis pour m'écouter,

commencerait: Messieurs, puisque vous me faites l'honneur de vouloir bien entendre votre humble serviteur, j'aurai celui de vous dire. . . . Voilà exactement ce que font les interprètes d'Hérodote. La version de Larcher, pour ne parler que de celle qui est la plus connue, ne s'écarte jamais de cette civilité: on ne saurait dire que ce soit le laquais de Madame de Sévigné, auquel elle compare les traducteurs d'alors: car celui-là rendait dans son langage bas, le style de la cour, tandis que Larcher, au contraire, met en style de la cour ce qu'a dit l'homme d'Halicarnasse. Hérodote, dans Larcher, ne parle que de princes, de princesses, de seigneurs, et de gens de qualité; ces princes montent sur le trône, s'emparent de la couronne, ont une cour, des ministres et de grands officiers, faisant, comme on peut croire, le bonheur des sujets; pendant que les princesses, les dames de la cour, accordent leurs faveurs à ces jeunes seigneurs. Or est-il qu'Hérodote ne se doute jamais de ce que nous appelons princes, trône et couronne, ni de ce qu'à l'académie on nomme faveurs des dames et bonheur des sujets. Chez lui, les dames, les princesses mènent boire leurs vaches, ou celles du roi leur père, à la fontaine voisine, trouvent là des jeunes gens, et font quelque sottise, toujours exprimée dans l'auteur avec le mot propre: on est esclave ou libre, mais on n'est point sujet dans Hérodote. . . . Larcher ne nommera pas le boulanger de Crésus, le palefrenier de Cyrus, le chaudronnier Macistos; il dit grand panetier, écuyer, armurier, avertissant en note que cela est plus noble." ([Paul Louis Courier de Méré,] *Prospectus d'une Traduction Nouvelle d'Hérodote* (1822), *Oeuvres [complètes] de P. L. Courier* [4 vols. (Brussels: La librairie parisienne, française et étrangère, 1828),] Vol. III, pp. 262-3.) [The account of Mme de Sévigné and the translators of Herodotus comes from Voltaire, "Traductions" (1761), *Mélanges littéraires*, in *Oeuvres complètes*, 66 vols. (Paris: Raynouard, 1817-25), Vol. XLIII, pp. 117-18.]

For another specimen, we may instance the Abbé Velly, the most popular writer of French history in the last century. We quote from M. Thierry's third letter on the History of France:

"S'agit-il d'exprimer la distinction que la conquête des barbares établissait entre eux et les vaincus, distinction grave et triste, par laquelle la vie d'un indigène n'était estimée, d'après le taux des amendes, qu'à la moitié du prix mis à celle de l'étranger, ce sont de pures préférences de cour, *les faveurs de nos rois* s'adressent surtout aux vainqueurs. S'agit-il de présenter le tableau de ces grandes assemblées, où tous les hommes de race Germanique se rendaient en armes, où chacun était consulté depuis le premier jusqu'au dernier; l'Abbé

army."[*] The character of this school is to transport present feelings and notions back into the past, and refer all ages and forms of human life to the standard of that in which the writer himself lives. Whatever cannot be translated into the language of their own time, whatever they cannot represent to themselves by some fancied modern equivalent, is nothing to them, calls up no ideas in their minds at all. They cannot imagine anything different from their own everyday experience. They assume that words mean the same thing to a monkish chronicler as to a modern member of parliament. If they find the term *rex* applied to Clovis or Clotaire, they already talk of "the French monarchy," or "the kingdom of France." If among a tribe of savages newly escaped from the woods, they find mention of a council of leading men, or an assembled multitude giving its sanction to some matter of general concernment, their imagination jumps to a system of free institutions, and a wise contrivance of constitutional balances and checks. If, at other times, they find the chief killing and plundering without this sanction, they just as promptly figure to themselves an acknowledged despotism. In this manner they antedate not only modern ideas, but the essential characters of the modern mind; and imagine their ancestors to be very like their next neighbours, saving a few eccentricities, occasioned by being still Pagans or Catholics, by having no *habeas corpus* act, and no Sunday schools. If an historian of this stamp takes a side in controversy, and

---

Velly nous parle d'une espèce de *parlement ambulatoire* et des *cours plénières*, qui étaient (après la chasse) *une partie des amusemens de nos rois*. 'Nos rois,' ajoute l'aimable abbé, 'ne se trouvèrent bientôt plus en état de donner ces superbes fêtes. On peut dire que le règne des Carlovingiens fut celui des cours plénières. . . . Il y eut cependant toujours des fêtes à la cour; mais, avec plus de galanterie, plus de politesse, plus de goût, on n'y retrouva ni cette grandeur ni cette richesse.'

"'Hilderic,' dit Grégoire de Tours, 'régnant sur la nation des Franks et se livrant à une extrême dissolution, se prit à abuser de leurs filles: et eux, indignés de cela, le destituèrent de la royauté. Informé, en outre, qu'ils voulaient le mettre à mort, il partit et s'en alla en Thuringe.' Ce récit est d'un écrivain qui vivait un siècle après l'événement. Voici maintenant les paroles de l'Abbé Velly, qui se vante, dans sa préface, de puiser aux sources anciennes, et de peindre exactement les moeurs, les usages, et les coutumes: 'Childéric fut un prince à grandes aventures; . . . c'était l'homme le mieux fait de son royaume. Il avait de l'esprit, du courage: mais, né avec un coeur tendre, il s'abandonnait trop à l'amour: ce fut la cause de sa perte. Les seigneurs Français, aussi sensibles à l'outrage que leurs femmes l'avaient été aux charmes de ce prince, se liguèrent pour le détrôner. Contraint de céder à leur fureur, il se retira en Allemagne.'" [Jacques Nicolas Augustin Thierry, *Lettres sur l'histoire de France* (1827), 5th ed. (Brussels: Hauman, 1836), pp. 32-3, and 30, quoting Paul François Velly, *Histoire de France*, and Gregory of Tours, *Histoire des Francs*.]

[*Ἀναβασις Κυρου Χενοφοντος; or, The Expedition of Cyrus into Persia, and the Retreat of the Ten Thousand Greeks*, trans. N.S. Smith (London: Longman, *et al.*, 1824), p. 20. Cf. Xenophon, *The Anabasis of Cyrus*, in *Hellenica, Anabasis, Symposium, and Apology* (Greek and English), trans. Carleton L. Brownson and O.J. Todd, 3 vols. (London: Heinemann; New York: Putnam's Sons, 1918), Vol. II, p. 265 (I, iii, 3), where the term is translated as "Fellow-soldiers."]

passes judgment upon actions or personages that have figured in history, he applies to them in the crudest form the canons of some modern party or creed. If he is a Tory, and his subject is Greece, everything Athenian must be cried down, and Philip and Dionysius must be washed white as snow, lest Pericles and Demosthenes should not be sufficiently black. If he be a Liberal, Caesar and Cromwell, and all usurpers similar to them, are "damned to everlasting fame."[*] Is he *a disbeliever of revelation? a short-sighted,* narrow-minded Julian becomes his pattern of a prince, and the heroes and martyrs of Christianity objects of scornful pity. If he is of the Church of England, Gregory VII must be an ambitious impostor, because Leo X was a self-indulgent voluptuary; John Knox nothing but a coarse-minded fanatic, because the historian does not like John Wesley. Humble as our estimate must be of this kind of writers, it would be unjust to forget that even *their* mode of treating history is an improvement upon the uninquiring credulity which contented itself with copying or translating the ancient authorities, without ever bringing the writer's own mind in contact with the subject. It is better to conceive Demosthenes even under the image of Anacharsis Clootz, than not as a living being at all, but a figure in a puppet-show, of which Plutarch is the showman; and Mitford, so far, is a better historian than Rollin. He does give a sort of reality to historical personages: he ascribes to them passions and purposes, which, though not those of their age or position, are still human; and enables us to form a tolerably distinct, though in general an exceedingly false notion of their qualities and circumstances. This is a first step; and, that step made, the reader, once in motion, is not likely to stop there.

Accordingly, the second stage of historical study attempts to regard former ages not with the eye of a modern, but, as far as possible, with that of a *cotemporary*; to realize a true and living picture of the past time, clothed in its circumstances and peculiarities. This is not an easy task: the knowledge of any amount of dry generalities, or even of the practical life and business of his own time, goes a very little way to qualify a writer for it. He needs some of the characteristics of the poet. He has to "body forth the forms of things unknown."[†] He must have the faculty to see, in the ends and fragments which are preserved of some element of the past, the consistent whole to which they once belonged; to discern, in the individual fact which some monument hands down or to which some chronicler testifies, the general, and for that very reason unrecorded, facts which it presupposes. Such gifts of imagination he must possess; and, what is rarer still, he must forbear to

[*Alexander Pope, *An Essay on Man* (1733-34), in *Works*, ed. Joseph Warton, *et al.*, 10 vols. (London: Priestley, and Hearne, 1822-25), Vol. III, p. 146 (Ep. IV, l. 284).]
[†William Shakespeare, *A Midsummer Night's Dream*, V, i, 14-15 (in *The Riverside Shakespeare*, ed. G. Blakemore Evans [Boston: Houghton Mifflin, 1974], p. 242).]

*d-d*44   an unbeliever? a pedantic
*e-e*44   contemporary

abuse them. He must have the conscience and self-command to ^{f}affirm^f no more than can be vouched for, or deduced by legitimate inference from what is vouched for. With the genius for producing a great historical romance, he must have the virtue to add nothing to what can be proved to be true. What wonder if so rare a combination is not often realized?

Realized, of course, in its ideal perfection, it never is; but many now aim at it, and some approach it, according to the measure of their faculties. Of the sagacity which detects the meaning of small things, and drags to light the forgotten elements of a gone-by state of society, from scattered evidences which the writers themselves who recorded them did not understand, the world has now, in Niebuhr, an imperishable model. The reproduction of past events in the colours of life, and with all the complexity and bustle of a real scene, can hardly be carried to a higher pitch than by Mr. Carlyle. But to find a school of writers, and among them several of the first rank, who systematically direct their aims towards this ideal of history, we must look to the French historians of the present day.

There is yet a third, and the highest stage of historical investigation, in which the aim is not simply to compose histories, but to construct a science of history. In this view, the whole of the events which have befallen the human race, and the states through which it has passed, are regarded as a series of phenomena, produced by causes, and susceptible of explanation. All history is conceived as a progressive chain of causes and effects; or (by an apter metaphor) as a gradually unfolding web, in which every fresh part that comes to view is a prolongation of the part previously unrolled, whether we can trace the separate threads from the one into the other, or not. The facts of each generation are looked upon as one complex phenomenon, caused by those of the generation preceding, and causing, in its turn, those of the next in order. That these states must follow one another according to some law, is considered certain: how to read that law, is deemed the fundamental problem of the science of history. To find on what principles, derived from the nature of man and the ^{g}laws of the outward world^g, each state of society and of the human mind produced that which came after it; and whether there can be traced any order of production sufficiently definite, to show what future states of society may be expected to emanate from the circumstances which exist at present—is the aim of historical philosophy in its third stage.

This ultimate and highest attempt, must, in the order of nature, follow, not precede, that last described; for before we can trace the filiation of states of society one from another, we must rightly understand and clearly conceive them, each apart from the rest. Accordingly, this greatest achievement is rather a possibility to be one day realized, than an enterprise in which any great progress has yet been made. But of the little yet done in ^{h}this^h direction, by far the greater part has

$^{f\text{-}f}$44   assert
$^{g\text{-}g}$44   system of the universe
$^{h\text{-}h}$44   that

hitherto been done by French writers. They have made more hopeful attempts than any one else, and have more clearly pointed out the path: they are the real harbingers of the dawn of historical science.

Dr. Arnold, in his *Historical Lectures*[*]—which, (it should not be forgotten,) though the latest production of his life, were the earliest of his systematic meditations on *general* history—showed few and faint symptoms of having conceived, with any distinctness, this third step in historical study. But he had, as far as the nature of the work admitted, completely realized the second stage; and to those who have not yet attained that stage, there can scarcely be more instructive reading than his *Lectures*. The same praise must be given, in an even higher sense, to the earliest of the three great modern French historians, M. Augustin Thierry.

It was from historical romances that M. Thierry learned to recognise the worthlessness of what in those days were called histories; [i] Chateaubriand and Sir Walter Scott were his early teachers. He has himself described the effect produced upon him and others, by finding, in *Ivanhoe*,[†] Saxons and Normans in the reign of Richard I.[‡] Why, he asked himself, should the professed historians have left such a fact as this to be brought to light by a novelist? and what else were such men likely to have understood of the age, when so important and distinctive a feature of it had escaped them? The study of the original sources of French history, completed his conviction of the senselessness of the modern compilers. He resolved "to plant the standard of historical reform;"[§] and to this undertaking all his subsequent life has been consecrated. His *History of the Norman Conquest*, though justly chargeable with riding a favourite idea too hard, forms an era in English history. In another of his works, the *Lettres sur l'Histoire de France*, in which profound learning is combined with that clear practical insight into the realities of life, which in France, more than in any other country except Italy, accompanies speculative eminence, M. Thierry gives a *piquant* exposure of the incapacity of historians to enter into the spirit of the middle ages, and the ludicrously false impressions they communicate of human life as it was in early times. Exemplifying the right method as well as censuring the wrong, he, in the same work, extracted from the records of the middle ages some portions, not large but valuable, of the neglected facts which constitute the real history of European society.[¶] Nowhere, however, is M. Thierry's genius so pleasingly displayed, as in his most recent publication, the work of his premature old age, written under

[*Thomas Arnold, *Introductory Lectures on Modern History* (Oxford: Parker, 1842).]
[†Scott, *Ivanhoe, a Romance*, 3 vols. (Edinburgh: Constable, 1820).]
[‡Thierry, *Lettres*, pp. 71-2 (Letter vi).]
[§Thierry, *Dix ans d'études historiques* (Brussels: Hauman, 1835), p. xv.]
[¶See *Lettres*, pp. 29-49 (Letters iii-iv).]

[i]44 M. de

the double affliction of blindness and paralysis—the *Récits des Temps Mérovin-*
giens.[*] This book, the first series of which is all that has [j] been published, was
destined to paint—what till that time he had only discussed and described—that
chaos of primitive barbarism and enervated civilization, from which the present
nations of Europe had their origin, and which forms the transition from ancient to
modern history. He makes the age tell its own story; not drawing anything from
invention, but [k] adhering scrupulously to authentic facts. As [l] the history of the
three centuries preceding Charlemagne was not worth writing throughout in [m]
fulness of detail [n] , he contents himself with portions of it, selecting such as, while
they are illustrative of the times, are also in themselves complete stories, furnished
with characters and personal interest. The experiment is completely successful.
The grace and beauty of the narration makes these true histories as pleasant reading
as if they were a charming collection of fictitious tales; while the practical feeling
they impart of the form of human life from which they are drawn—the familiar
understanding they communicate of "la vie barbare,"—is unexampled even in
fiction, and unthought of heretofore in any writing professedly historical. The
narratives are preceded by an improved *résumé* of the author's previous labours in
the theoretical department of his subject, under the title of a *Dissertation on the*
Progress of Historical Studies in France.[†]

M. Guizot has a mind of a different cast from M. Thierry: the one is especially a
man of speculation and science, as the other is, more emphatically, in the high
European sense of the term, an artist; though this is not to be understood of either in
an exclusive sense, each possessing a fair share of the qualities characteristic of the
other. Of all Continental historians of whom we are aware, M. Guizot is the one
best adapted to this country, and a familiarity with whose writings would do most
to train [o] and ripen among us the growing spirit of historical speculation.

M. Guizot's only narrative work is the [p] history, already referred to, of what is
called in France the English Revolution. His [q]other[q] principal productions are the
Essais sur l'Histoire de France, published in 1822, and the *Lectures*,[‡] which the

---

[*Thierry, *Récits des temps mérovingiens précédés de considérations sur l'histoire de*
France, 2 vols. (Paris: Tessier, 1840).]
[†Actually entitled "Considérations sur l'histoire de France" (see the preceding note).]
[‡For the full titles, see p. 186 above.]

[j]44   yet
[k]44   , like Mr. Carlyle,
[l]44   , however,
[m]44   the same
[n]44   as the French Revolution
[o]44   up
[p]44,59   unfinished
[q-q]+67

whole literary public of Paris thronged to hear, from 1828 to 1830, and to which [r] the political events of the last of those years put an abrupt termination. The immense popularity of these writings in their own country—a country not more patient of the "genre ennuyeux"[*] than its neighbours—is a sufficient guarantee that their wearing the form of dissertation, and not of narrative, is, in this instance, no detriment to their attractiveness. Even the light reader will find in them no resemblance to the chapters on "manners and customs," which, with pardonable impatience, he is accustomed to skip when turning over any of the historians of the old school. For in them we find only that dullest and most useless of all things, mere facts without ideas: M. Guizot creates within those dry bones a living soul.[†]

M. Guizot does not, as in the main must be said of M. Thierry, remain in what we have called the second region of historical inquiry: he makes frequent and long incursions into the third. He not only inquires what our ancestors were, but what made them so; what gave rise to the peculiar state of society of the middle ages, and by what causes this state was progressively transformed into what we see around us. His success in this respect could not, in the almost nascent state of the science of history, be perfect; but it is as great as was perhaps compatible with the limits of his design. For ([s]as M. Comte has[s] well remarked) in the study of history, we must proceed from the *ensemble* to the details, and not conversely.[‡] We cannot explain the facts of any age or nation, unless we have first traced out some connected view of the main outline of history. The great universal results must be first accounted for, not only because they are the most important, but because they depend on the simplest laws. Taking place on so large a scale as to neutralize the operation of local and partial agents, it is in them alone that we see in undisguised action the inherent tendencies of the human race. Those great results, therefore, may admit of a complete theory; while it would be impossible to give a full analysis of the innumerable causes which influenced the local or temporary development of some section of mankind; and even a distant approximation to it supposes a previous understanding of the general laws, to which these local causes stand in the relation of modifying circumstances.

But before astronomy had its Newton, there was a place, and an honourable one, for not only the observer Tycho, but the theorizer, Kepler. M. Guizot is the Kepler, and something more, of his particular subject. He has a real talent for the explanation and generalization of historical facts. He unfolds at least the proximate

[*Voltaire, *L'enfant prodigue* (1736), in *Oeuvres complètes*, Vol. II, p. 401.]
[†Cf. Ezekiel, 37:3-5.]
[‡Auguste Comte, *Cours de philosophie positive*, 6 vols. (Paris: Bachelier, 1830-42), Vol. IV, p. 362 (Lecture 48).]

[r]44,59   , as well as to his English history,
[s-s]44   it has been

causes of social phenomena, with rare discernment, and much knowledge of human nature. We recognise, moreover, in all his theories, not only a solidity of acquirements, but a sobriety and impartiality, which neither his countrymen, nor speculative thinkers in general, have often manifested in so high a degree. He does not exaggerate the influence of some one cause or agency, sacrificing all others to it. He neither writes as if human affairs were absolutely moulded by the wisdom and virtue or the vices and follies of rulers; nor as if the general circumstances of society did all, and accident or eminent individuals could do nothing. He neither attributes everything to political institutions, nor everything to the ideas and convictions in men's minds; but shows how they both co-operate, and react upon one another. He sees in European civilization the complex product of many conflicting influences, Germanic, Roman, and Christian; and of the peculiar position in which these different forces were brought to act upon one another. He ascribes to each of them its share of influence. Whatever may be added to his speculations in a more advanced state of historical science, little that he has done, will, we think, require to be undone; his conclusions are seldom likely to be found in contradiction with the deeper or more extensive results that may, perhaps, hereafter be obtained.

It speaks little for the intellectual tastes and the liberal curiosity of our countrymen, that they remain ignorant or neglectful of such writings. The *Essays* we have 'seldom' met with an Englishman who had read. Of the *Lectures*, one volume has been twice translated,[*] and has had some readers, especially when M. Guizot's arrival in England as the representative of his country, obtruded (as Dr. Chalmers would say)[†] a knowledge of his existence and character upon London society. But the other five volumes are untranslated and unread, although they are the work itself, to which the first volume is, in truth, only the introduction. When the Villèle Ministry was overthrown, and the interdict removed by which the Government of the Restoration had chained up all independent speculation, M. Guizot reopened his lecture-room, after a suspension of near ten years. Half the academic season having then expired, he was compelled, not only to restrict his view of modern history to the merest outline, but to leave out half the subject altogether; treating only of the progress of Society, and reserving for the more extended labours of subsequent years, the development of the individual human being. Yet critics have been found in England, who, in entire ignorance that the volume before them was a mere preface, visited upon the author, as shortcomings

[*General History of Civilisation in Europe, from the Fall of the Roman Empire to the French Revolution, trans. D.A. Talboys (Oxford: Talboys, 1837); and Lectures on European Civilization, trans. P.M. Beckwith (London: Macrone, 1837).]

[†Thomas Chalmers, Considerations on the System of Parochial Schools in Scotland (Glasgow: Hedderwick, 1819), p. 6.]

ᵗ⁻ᵗ44 scarcely ever

in his own "doctrines", the *lacunae* unavoidably left in his first year's lectures, and amply filled up in those of the succeeding seasons;—charging upon him as a grave philosophical error, that he saw in history only institutions and social relations, and altogether overlooked human beings.[*]

What has obtained for the introductory volume the share of attention with which it (and not the others) has been treated by the English public, is perhaps that it bears as its second title, *History of Civilization in Europe*; while the other volumes, after the words *Cours d'Histoire Moderne*, bear the designation of "Histoire de la Civilisation en *France*," and as such may have been deemed not specially interesting to England. But though this may avail in explanation, it is inadmissible as an excuse. A person must need instruction in history very much, who does not know that the history of civilization in France *is* that of civilization in Europe. The main course of the stream of civilization is identical in all the western nations; their origin was essentially similar—they went through the same phases—and society in all of them, at least until after the Reformation, consisted fundamentally of the same elements. Any one country, therefore, may, in some measure, stand for all the rest. But France is the best type, as representing best the average circumstances of Europe. There is no country in which the general tendencies of modern society have been so little interfered with by secondary and modifying agencies. In England, for example, much is to be ascribed to the peculiarity of a double conquest. While elsewhere *v*one*v* race of barbarians overran an extensive region, and settled down amidst a subject population greatly more numerous, as well as more civilized, than themselves; the first invaders of England, instead of enslaving, exterminated or expelled the former inhabitants; and after growing up into a nation, were in their turn subdued by a race almost exactly on a level with them in civilization. The Scandinavian countries, on the other hand, and a great part of Germany, had never been conquered at all; and in the latter, much depended upon the elective character of the head of the empire, which prevented the consolidation of a powerful central government. In Italy, the early predominance of towns and town life; in Spain, the Moorish occupation and its consequences, coexisted as modifying causes with the general circumstances common to all. But in France, no disturbing forces, of anything like equal potency, can be traced; and the universal tendencies, having prevailed more completely, are more obviously discernible.

To any European, therefore, the history of France is not a foreign subject, but *w* part of his national history. Nor is there anything partial or local in M. Guizot's

---

[*See, e.g., Anon., "Guizot's *Lectures on European Civilization*, Translated by Priscilla Beckwith," *The Times*, 21 Aug., 1837, p. 6.]

*u-u*44 views
*v-v*44 *one*
*w*44 a

treatment of it. He draws his details and exemplifications from France; but his principles are universal. The social conditions and changes which he delineates, were not French, but European. The intellectual progress which he retraces, was the progress of the European mind. [x]

A similar remark applies to the *History of France*, by M. Michelet, the third great French historian of the present era—a work which, even in its unfinished state, is the most important that he has produced, and of which it is now time that we should begin to give an account.

M. Michelet has, among the writers of European history, a position peculiarly his own.

Were we to say that M. Michelet is altogether as safe a writer as M. Thierry or M. Guizot—that his interpretations of history may be accepted as actual history—that those who dislike to think or explore for themselves, may sleep peacefully in the faith that M. Michelet has thought and explored for them—we should give him a different kind of praise from that which we consider his due. M. Michelet's are not books to save a reader the trouble of thinking, but to make him boil over with thought. Their effect on the mind is not acquiescence, but stir and ferment.

M. Michelet has opened a new vein in the history of the middle ages. A pupil of M. Guizot, or at least an admiring auditor, who has learned from him most of what he had to teach, M. Michelet, for this very reason, has not followed in his wake, but consulted the bent of his own faculties, which prompted him to undertake precisely what M. Guizot had left undone. Of him it would be very unlikely to be said, even falsely, that he thought only of society. Without overlooking society, man is his especial subject. M. Guizot has neglected neither, but has treated them both conformably to the character of his own mind. He is himself two things—a statesman and a speculative thinker; and in his *Lectures*, when he leaves the province of the statesman, it is for that of the metaphysician. His history of the human mind is principally the history of speculation. It is otherwise with M. Michelet. His peculiar element is that of the poet, as his countrymen would say—of the religious man, as would be said in a religious age—in reality, of both. Not the intellectual life of intellectual men, not the social life of the people, but their internal life; their thoughts and feelings in relation to themselves and their destination; the habitual temper of their minds—not overlooking, of course, their external circumstances. He concerns himself more with masses than with literary individuals, except as specimens, on a larger scale, of what was in the general heart of their age. His chief interest is for the collective mind, the everyday plebeian mind of humanity—its enthusiasms, its collapses, its strivings, its

---

[x]44 [*footnote:*] *We hope to be able, erelong, to give a fuller view of the principal work of this eminent writer. [See "Guizot's Essays and Lectures in History," *Edinburgh Review*, LXXXII (Oct., 1845), 381-421 (reprinted below, pp. 257-94).]

attainments and failures. He makes us feel with its sufferings, rejoice in its *y*hopes. He*y* makes us identify ourselves with the varying fortunes and feelings of human nature, as if mankind or Christendom were one being, the single and indivisible hero of a tale.

M. Michelet had afforded an earnest of these qualities in his former writings. He has written a history of the Roman Republic,[*] in which he availed himself largely, as all writers on Roman history now do, of the new views opened by the profound sagacity of Niebuhr. One thing, however, he has not drawn from Niebuhr; for Niebuhr had it not to bestow. We have no right to require that an author, who has done in his department great things which no one before him had done, or could do, should have done all other good things likewise. But without meaning disparagement to Niebuhr, it has always struck us as remarkable, that a mind so fitted to throw light upon the dark places in the Roman manner of existence, should have exhausted its efforts in clearing up and rendering intelligible the merely civic life of the Roman people. By the aid of Niebuhr, we now know, better than we had ever reckoned upon knowing, what the Roman republic was. But what the Romans themselves were, we scarcely know better than we did before. It is true that citizenship, its ideas, feelings, and active duties, filled a larger space in ancient, than in any form of modern life; but they did not constitute the whole. A Roman citizen had a religion and gods, had a religious morality, had domestic relations; there were women in Rome as well as men; there were children, who were brought up and educated in a certain manner; there were, even in the earliest period of the Roman commonwealth, slaves. Of all this, one perceives hardly anything in Niebuhr's voluminous work. The central idea of the Roman religion and polity, the family, scarcely shows itself, except in connexion with the classification of the citizens; nor are we made to perceive in what the beliefs and modes of conduct of the Romans, respecting things in general, agreed, and in what disagreed, with those of the rest of the ancient world. Yet the mystery of the Romans and of their fortunes must lie there. Now, of many of these things, one does learn something from the much smaller work of M. Michelet. In imaging to ourselves the relation in which a Roman stood, not to his fellow-citizens as such, but to the universe, we gain some help from Michelet—next to none from Niebuhr. The work before us has, in a still greater degree, a similar merit. Without neglecting the outward condition of mankind, but on the contrary throwing much new light upon it, he tells us mainly *z* their inward mental workings. Others have taught us as much of how mankind acted at each period, but no one makes us so well comprehend how they felt. He is the subjective historian of the middle ages. For his book, at least in the earlier volumes, is a history of the middle ages, quite

[*Histoire romaine: république, lst pt., 3 vols. (Brussels: Hauman, 1835).]

*y-y*44   hopes; he
*z*44   of

as much as of France; and he has aimed at giving us, not the dry husk, but the spirit of those ages. This had never been done before in the same degree, not even by his eminent precursor, Thierry, except for the period of the Germanic invasions. The great value of the book is, that it does, to some extent, make us understand what was really passing in the collective mind of each generation. For, in assuming distinctness, the life of the past assumes also variety under M. Michelet's hands. With him, each period has a physiognomy and a character of its own. It is in reading him that we are made to feel distinctly, how many successive conditions of humanity, and states of the human mind, are habitually confounded under the appellation of the Middle Ages. To common perception, those times are like a distant range of mountains, all melted together into one cloudlike barrier. To M. Michelet, they are like the same range on a nearer approach, resolved into its separate mountain masses, with sloping sides overlapping one another, and gorges opening between them.

The spirit of an age is a part of its history which cannot be extracted literally from ancient records, but must be distilled from those arid materials by the chemistry of the writer's own mind; and whoever attempts this, will expose himself to the imputation of substituting *a*imagination*a* for facts, writing history by divination, *b*and the like*b*. These accusations have been often brought against M. Michelet, and we will not take upon ourselves to say that they are never just; we think he is not seldom the dupe of his own ingenuity. But it is a mistake to suppose that a man of genius will be oftener wrong, in his views of history, than a dull unimaginative proser. Not only are the very errors of the one more instructive than the commonplaces of the other, but he commits fewer of them. It by no means follows, that he who cannot see so far as another, must, therefore, see more correctly. To be incapable of discerning what is, gives no exemption from believing what is not; and there is no perversion of history by persons who think, equal to those daily committed by writers who never rise to the height of an original idea.

It is true, a person of lively apprehension and fertile invention, relying on his sagacity, may neglect the careful study of original documents. But M. Michelet is a man of deep erudition, and extensive research. He has a high reputation among the French learned for his industry; while his official position, which connects him with the archives of the kingdom, has given him access to a rich source of unexplored authorities, of which he has made abundant use in his later volumes, and which promise to be of still greater importance in those yet to come. Even in its mere facts, therefore, this history is considerably in advance of all previously written. That his accuracy is not vulnerable in any material point, may be believed on the authority of the sober and right-minded Thierry, who, in the

---

*a-a*44 imaginations
*b-b*44 &c.

preface to the *Récits*, in a passage where, though Michelet is not named, he is evidently pointed at, blames his method as a dangerous one, but acquits M. Michelet himself as having been saved by "conscientious studies" from the errors into which his example is likely to betray young writers.[*] The carefulness of his investigations has been impugned on minor points. An English Review has made a violent attack upon his account of Boniface VIII;[†] and, from his references (which are always copious) it does not appear that he had consulted the Italian authorities on *c*whom*c* the reviewer relies.[‡] But it is hard to try an historian by the correctness of his details *d*on*d* incidents only collaterally connected with his subject. We ourselves perceive that he sometimes trusts to memory, and is inaccurate in trifles; but the true question is—Has he falsified the essential character of any of the greater events of the time about which he writes? If he has not, but on the contrary, has placed many of *e*those*e* events in a truer light, and rendered their character more intelligible, than any former historian, to rectify his small mistakes will be a very fitting employment for those who have the necessary information, and nothing more important to do.

The *History*, though a real narrative, not a dissertation, is, in all its earlier parts, a greatly abridged one. The writer dwells only on the great facts which paint their period, or on things which it appears *f*to him*f* necessary to present in a new light. As, in his progress, however, he came into contact with his new materials, his design has extended; and the fourth and fifth volumes, embracing the confused period of the wars of Edward III and Henry V, contain, though in a most condensed style, a tolerably minute recital of events. It is impossible for us to make any approach to an abstract of the contents of so large a work. We must be satisfied with touching cursorily upon some of the passages of history, on which M. Michelet's views are the most original, or otherwise most deserving of notice.

In the first volume, he is on ground which had already been broken and well turned over by M. Thierry. But some one was still wanting who should write the history of the time, in a connected narrative, from M. Thierry's point of view. M. Michelet has done this, and more. He has not only understood, like his predecessor, the character of the age of transition, in which the various races, conquered and conquering, were mixed on French soil without being blended; but

---

[*Thierry, *Récits*, Vol. I, p. 213.]

[†Anthony Panizzi, "Michelet's *Histoire de France*: Boniface VIII," *British and Foreign Review*, XIII (June, 1842), 415-41.]

[‡Panizzi cites Lodovico Antonio Muratori, *Annali d'Italia, dal principio dell'era volgare sino all'anno 1500*, 12 vols. (Milan: Pasquali, 1744-49), and Odorico Rinaldi, *Annales ecclesiastici ab anno ubi desinit cardinalis Baronius*, ed. Giovanni Domenico Mansi, 15 vols. (Lucca: Venturini, 1747-56).]

*c-c*44   which
*d-d*44,59   in
*e-e*44   these
f-f+59,67

he has endeavoured to assign to the several elements of that confused mixture, the share of influence which belongs to them over the subsequent destinies of his country.

It was natural that a subjective historian, one who looks, above all, to the internal moving forces of human affairs, should attach great historical importance to the consideration of Races. This subject, on British soil, has usually fallen into hands little competent to treat it soberly, or on true principles of induction; but of the great influence of Race in the production of national character, no reasonable inquirer can now doubt. As far as history, and social circumstances generally, are concerned, how little resemblance can be traced between the French and the Irish—in national character, how much! The same ready excitability; the same impetuosity when excited, yet the same readiness under excitement to submit to the severest discipline—a quality which at first might seem to contradict impetuosity, but which arises from that very vehemence of character with which it appears to conflict, and is equally conspicuous in Revolutions of Three Days, temperance movements, and meetings on the Hill of Tara. The same sociability and demonstrativeness—the same natural refinement of manners, down to the lowest rank—in both, the characteristic weakness an inordinate vanity, their more serious moral deficiency the absence of a sensitive regard for truth. Their ready susceptibility to influences, while it makes them less steady in right, makes them also less pertinacious in wrong, and renders them, under favourable circumstances of culture, reclaimable and improvable (especially through their more generous feelings) in a degree to which the more obstinate races are strangers. To what, except their Gaelic blood, can we ascribe all this similarity between populations, the whole course of whose national history has been so different? We say Gaelic, not Celtic, because the Kymri of Wales and *Bretagne*, though also called Celts, and notwithstanding a close affinity in language, have evinced throughout history, in many respects, an opposite type of character; more like the Spanish Iberians than either the French or Irish: individual instead of gregarious, tough and obstinate instead of impressible—instead of the most disciplinable, one of the most intractable Races among mankind.

Historians who preceded M. Michelet had seen chiefly the Frankish, or the Roman element, in the formation of modern France. M. Michelet calls attention to the Gaelic element. "The foundation of the French people," he says, "is the youthful, soft, and mobile race of the Gaels, *bruyante*, sensual, and *légère*; prompt to learn, prompt to despise, greedy of new things."* To the ready impressibility of this race, and the easy reception it gave to foreign influences, he attributes the progress made by France. "Such children require severe preceptors. They will meet with such, both from the south and from the north. Their mobility will be

*[Translated from] Michelet, Vol. I, p. 129.

*-*44   Brittany

fixed, their softness hardened and strengthened. Reason must be added to instinct, reflection to impulse."[*]

It is certain that no people, in a semi-barbarous state, ever received a foreign civilization more rapidly than the French Celts. In a century after Julius Caesar, not only the south, the *Gallia Narbonensis*, but the whole east of Gaul, from Treves and Cologne southwards, were already almost as Roman as Italy itself. The Roman institutions and ideas took a deeper root in Gaul than in any other province of the Roman empire, and remained long predominant, wherever no great change was effected in the population by the ravages of the invaders. But, along with this capacity of improvement, M. Michelet does not find in the Gauls that voluntary loyalty of man to man, that free adherence, founded on confiding attachment, which was characteristic of the Germanic tribes, and of which, in his *h*opinion*h*, the feudal relation was the natural result. It is to these qualities, to personal devotedness and faith in one another, that he ascribes the universal success of the Germanic tribes in overpowering the Celtic. He finds already in the latter the root of that passion for equality which distinguishes modern France; and which, when unbalanced by a strong principle of sympathetic union, has always, he says, prevented the pure Celts from becoming a nation. Everywhere among the Celts, he finds equal division of inheritances, while in the Germanic races primogeniture easily established itself—an institution which, in a rude state of society, he justly interprets as equivalent to the permanence of the household, the non-separation of families.

We think that M. Michelet has here carried the influence of Race too far, and that the difference is better explained by diversity of position, than by diversity of character in the Races. The conquerors, a small body scattered over a large territory, could not sever their interests, could not relax the bonds which held them together. They were for many generations encamped in the country, rather than settled in it; they were a military band, requiring a military discipline, and the separate members could not *i*venture*i* to detach themselves from each other, or from their chief. Similar circumstances would have produced similar results among the Gauls themselves. They were by no means without something analogous to the German *comitatus* (as the voluntary bond of adherence, of the most sacred kind, between followers and a leader of their choice, is called by the Roman historians). The *devoti* of the Gauls and Aquitanians, mentioned by M. Michelet himself, on the authority of Caesar* and

---

[* Translated from *ibid*.]

*"Aducantanus, qui summam imperii tenebat, cum DC devotis, quos illi soldurios appellant: quorum haec est conditio, uti omnibus in vita commodis una cum his fruantur quorum se amicitiae dediderint: si quid iis per vim accidat, aut eundem casum una ferant, aut sibi mortem consciscant: neque adhuc hominum memoria repertus est quisquam, qui, eo

*h-h*44   view
*i-i*44   afford

Athenaeus,[*] were evidently not clansmen. Some such relation may be traced in many other warlike tribes. We find it even among the most obstinately personal of all the races of antiquity, the Iberians of Spain; witness the Roman Sertorius and his Spanish body-guard, who slew themselves, to the last man, before his funeral pile. "Ce principe d'attachement à un chef, ce dévouement personnel, cette religion de l'homme envers l'homme,"* is thus by no means peculiar to the Teutonic races. And our author's favourite idea of the "profonde impersonnalité"† inherent in the Germanic genius, though we are far from saying that there is no foundation for it, surely requires some limitation. It will hardly, for example, be held true of the English, yet the English are a Germanic people. They, indeed, have rather (or at least had) the characteristic which M. Michelet predicates of the Celts (thinking apparently rather of the Kymri than of the Gaels), "le génie de la personnalité libre;"[†] a tendency to revolt against compulsion, to hold fast to their own, and assert the claims of individuality against those of society and authority. But though many of M. Michelet's speculations on the characteristics of Races appear to us contestable, they are always suggestive of thought. The next thing to having a question solved, is to have it well raised. M. Michelet's are views by which a thinker, even if he rejects them, seldom fails to profit.

From the Races, our author passes to the provinces, which, by their successive aggregation, composed the French monarchy. France is, in the main, peopled by a mixed race; but it contains several populations of pure race at its remoter extremities. It includes several distinct languages, and above all a great variety of climate, soil, and situation. Next to hereditary organization *j*(if not beyond it)*j*, geographical peculiarities have a more powerful influence than any other natural agency, in the formation of national character. Any one, capable of such speculations, will read with strong interest the review of the various provinces of France, which occupies the first hundred and thirty pages of our author's second volume. In this brilliant sketch, he surveys the local circumstances and national peculiarities of each province, and compares them with the type of character which belongs to its inhabitants, as shown in the history of each province, in the eminent individuals who have sprung from it, and in the results of intelligent personal observation even in the present day. We say *even*, because M. Michelet is not

---

interfecto cujus se amicitiae devovisset, mori recusaret." (*De Bello Gallico* [Vol. I of *C. Julii Caesaris quae exstant opera*, 2 vols. (Paris: Barbou, 1755),] Bk. III, cap. xxii [Vol. I, p. 97].)

[*The Deipnosophists* (Greek and English), trans. Charles Burton Gulick, 7 vols. (London: Heinemann; New York: Putnam's Sons; and Cambridge, Mass.: Harvard University Press, 1927-41), Vol. III, p. 122 (VI, liv; 249[b]).]

*Michelet, Vol. I, p. 168.

†*Ibid.*, p. 171n.

[†*Ibid.*, p. 171.]

j-j+59,67

unaware of the tendency of provincial and local peculiarities to disappear. A strenuous asserter of the power of mind over matter, of will over spontaneous propensities, culture over nature, he holds that local characteristics lose their importance as history advances. In a rude age the "fatalities" of race and geographical position are absolute. In the progress of society, human forethought and purpose, acting by means of uniform institutions and modes of culture, tend more and more to efface the pristine differences. And he attributes, in no small degree, the greatness of France to the absence of any marked local peculiarities in the predominant part of her population. Paris, and an extensive region all round—from the borders of Brittany to *the eastern limits* of Champagne, from the northern extremity of Picardy to the mountains of Auvergne—is distinguished by no marked natural features; and its inhabitants—a more mixed population than any other in France—have no distinct, well-defined individuality of character. This very deficiency, or what might seem so, makes them the ready recipients of ideas and modes of action from all sides, and qualifies them to bind together heterogeneous populations in harmonious union, by receiving the influence and assuming the character of each, as far as may be, without exclusion of the rest. In those different populations (on the other hand), M. Michelet finds an abundant variety of provincial characteristics, of all shades and degrees, up to those obstinate individualities which cling with the tenacity of iron to their own usages, and yield only after a long and dogged resistance to the general movement of humanity. In these portraits of the provinces there is much to admire, and occasionally something to startle. The form and vesture are more poetical than philosophical; the sketch of Brittany wants only verse to be a fine poem. But, though fancifully expressed, there is in this survey of France much more which seems, than which is, fanciful. There is, as we believe, for much, if not most of it, a foundation of sober reason; and out of its poetry we could extract an excellent treatise in unexceptionable prose, did not our limits admonish us to hurry to those parts of the work which are of more universal interest.

From this place the book becomes a picture of the middle ages, in a series of *Tableaux*. The facts are not delivered in the dry form of chronological annals, but are grouped round a certain number of central figures or leading events, selected so that each half century has at least one *Tableau* belonging to it. The groups, we need scarcely add, represent the mind of the age, not its mere outward physiognomy and costume. The successive titles of the chapters will form an appropriate catalogue to this new kind of historical picture gallery:

Chap. I. The year 1000—The French King and the French Pope, Robert and Gerbert—Feudal France.—II. Eleventh Century—Gregory VII—Alliance between the Normans and the Church—Conquests of Naples and England.—III. The Crusade.—IV. Consequences of the Crusade—The Communes—Abailard—First half of the Twelfth

---

*k-k*44   those

Century.—V. The King of France and the King of England, Louis-le-Jeune and Henry Plantagenet—Second Crusade—Humiliation of Louis—Thomas Becket—Humiliation of Henry.—VI. The year 1200—Innocent III—The Pope, by the arms of the Northern French, prevails over the King of England and the Emperor of Germany, the Greek Empire and the Albigeois—Greatness of the King of France.—VII. The last Chapter continued—Ruin of John—Defeat of the Emperor—War of the Albigeois.—VIII. First half of the Thirteenth Century—Mysticism—Louis IX—Sanctity of the King of France.—IX. Struggle between the Mendicant Orders and the University—St. Thomas—Doubts of St. Louis—The Passion as a principle of Art in the Middle Ages.

The next chapter, being the first of the third volume, is headed, "The Sicilian Vespers;" the second, "Philippe le Bel and Boniface VIII."

This arrangement of topics promises much; and the promise is well redeemed. Every one of the chapters we have cited is full of interesting *aperçus*, and fruitful in suggestions of thought.

Forced to make a selection, we shall choose among the features of the middle age as here presented, one or two of the most interesting, and the most imperfectly understood. Of the individual figures in our author's canvass, none is more impressive than Hildebrand. Of the moral and social phenomena which he depicts, the greatest is the Papacy.

Respecting the Papal Church, and that, its greatest Pontiff, the *ᶦopinionsᶦ* of our author are such as, from the greater number of English readers, can scarcely hope for ready acceptance. They are far removed from those either of our Protestant or of our sceptical historians. They are so unlike Hume, that they stand a chance of being confounded with Lingard. Such, however, as they are, we think them well worth knowing and considering. They are, in substance, the opinions of almost every historical inquirer in France, who has any pretensions to thought or research, be he Catholic, Protestant, or Infidel. The time is past when any French thinker, worthy the name, looked upon the Catholic Hierarchy as having *ᵐalwaysᵐ* been the base and tyrannical thing which, to a great extent, it ultimately became. No one now confounds what the Church was, when its prelates and clergy universally believed what they taught, with what it was when they had ceased to believe. No one argues—from the conduct which they even conscientiously pursued when the human intellect, having got beyond the Church, became its most formidable foe—that it must therefore have been equally an enemy to improvement when it was at the head, instead of the rear, of civilization; when all that was instructed in Europe was comprised within its pale, and it was the authorized champion of intelligence and self-control, against military and predatory violence. Even the fraud and craft by which it often aided itself in its struggles with brute force; even the ambition and selfishness by which, in its very best days, its nobler aims, like those of all other classes or bodies, were continually tarnished—do not disguise

*ᶦ⁻ᶦ*44   views
*ᵐ⁻ᵐ*44   *always*

from impartial thinkers on the Continent, the fact that it was the great improver and civilizer of Europe.

That the clergy were the preservers of all letters and all culture, of the writings and even the traditions of literary antiquity, is too evident to have been ever disputed. But for them, there would have been a complete break, in Western Europe, between the ancient and modern world. Books would have disappeared, and even Christianity, if it survived at all, would have existed merely as another form of the old barbarous superstitions. Some, too, are aware of the services rendered even to material civilization by the monastic associations of Italy and France, after the great reform by St. Benedict. Unlike the useless communities of contemplative ascetics in the East, they were diligent in tilling the earth and fabricating useful products; they knew and taught that temporal work may also be a spiritual exercise; and, protected by their sacred character from depredation, they set the first example to Europe of industry conducted on a large scale by free labour. But these things are commonly regarded as good which came out of evil; incidental benefits, arising casually, or providentially, from an institution radically vicious. It would do many English thinkers much good to acquaint themselves with the grounds on which the best Continental minds, without disguising one particle of the evil which existed, openly or latently, in the Romish Church, are on the whole convinced that it was not only a beneficent institution, but the only means capable of being now assigned, by which Europe could have been reclaimed from barbarism.

It is, no doubt, the characteristic evil incident to a corporation of priests, that the exaltation of their order becomes, in and for itself, a primary object, to which the ends of the institution are often sacrificed. That exaltation is the strongest interest of all its members, the bad equally with the good; for it is the means by which both hope to attain their ends. The maintenance of their influence is to them what the maintenance of its revenue is to a temporal government—the condition of its existence. The Romish Church, being more powerfully organized and more thoroughly disciplined than any other, pursued this end with inflexible energy and perseverance, and often by the most culpable means. False miracles, forged donations, "persecution of heretics"—these things we have no desire to extenuate; but he must be wretchedly ignorant of human nature, who believes that any great or durable edifice of moral power was ever raised chiefly by such means. It is in the decline, in the decrepitude of religious systems, that force and artifice come into the first rank as expedients for maintaining a little longer what is left of their dominion. Deep sincerity, entire absorption of themselves in their task, were assuredly as indispensable conditions, in the more eminent of the Popes, of the success which they met with, as in the heroes of the Reformation. In such men the power of the hierarchy might well become a passion; but the extension of that

$^{n-n}$44   religious persecution

power was a legitimate object, for the sake of the great things which they had to accomplish by it.

Who, in the middle ages, were worthier of power, than the clergy? Did they not need all, and more than all the influence they could acquire, when they could not be kings or emperors, and when kings and emperors were among those whose passion and arrogance they had to admonish and govern? The great Ambrose, refusing absolution to Theodosius until he performed penance for a massacre,[*] was a type of what these men had to do. In an age of violence and *brigandage*, who but the Church could insist on justice, and forbearance, and reconciliation? In an age when the weak were prostrate at the feet of the strong, who was there but the Church to plead to the strong for the weak? They were the depositaries of the only moral power to which the great were amenable; they alone had a right to remind kings and potentates of responsibility; to speak to them of humility, charity, and peace. Even in the times of the first ferocious invaders, the *Récits* of M. Thierry (though the least favourable of the modern French historians to the Romish clergy) show, at what peril to themselves, the prelates of the Church continually stepped between the oppressor and his victim. Almost all the great social improvements which took place, were accomplished under their influence. They at all times took part with the kings against the feudal anarchy. The enfranchisement of the mass of the people from personal servitude, they not only favoured, but inculcated as a Christian duty. They were the authors of the "Truce of God," that well-known attempt to mitigate the prevailing brutalities, by a forced suspension of acts of vengeance and private war during four days and five nights of every week. They could not succeed in enforcing this periodical armistice, which was too much in advance of the time. Their worst offence was, that they connived at acts of unjust acquisition by friends and supporters of the Pope; and encouraged unprovoked aggressions, by orthodox princes, against less obedient sons of the Church. We may add, that they were seldom favourable to civil liberty; which, indeed, in the rude form in which its first germs grew up, not as an institution, but as a principle of resistance to institutions, found little favour with speculative men in the middle ages, to whom, by a not unnatural prejudice at such a time, peace and obedience seemed the °primary° ᵖconditionsᵖ of good. But, in another sense, the Church was eminently a democratic institution. To a temporal society in which all rank depended on birth, it opposed a spiritual society in which the source of rank was personal qualities; in which the distinctions of people and aristocracy, freeman and bondman, disappeared—which recruited itself from all ranks—in which a serf

[*St. Ambrose, *Epistola LI*, in *Opera omnia*, Vols. XIV-XVII of *Patrologiae cursus completus, series latina*, ed. Jacques Paul Migne (Paris: Migne, 1845), Vol. XVI, cols. 1161-2.]

°-°44   one
ᵖ-ᵖ44,59   condition

might rise to be a cardinal, or even a pope; while to rise at all to any eminence, almost always required talents, and at least a reputation for virtue. In one of the earliest combinations made by the feudal nobles against the clergy, the league of the French Seigneurs in 1246, it stands in the foremost rank of accusation against them, that they were the "sons of serfs."*

Now we say that the priesthood never could have stood their ground, in such an age, against kings and their powerful vassals, as an independent moral authority, entitled to advise, to reprimand, and, if need were, to denounce, if they had not been bound together into an European body, under a government of their own. They must otherwise have grovelled from the first in that slavish subservience into which they sank at last. No local, no merely national organization, would have sufficed. The State has too strong a hold upon an exclusively national corporation. Nothing but an authority recognised by many nations, and not essentially dependent upon any one, could, in that age, have been adequate to the post. It required a Pope to speak with authority to Kings and Emperors. Had an individual priest [q]or prelate[q] had the courage to tell them that they had violated the law of God, his voice, not being the voice of the Church, would not have been heeded. That the Pope, when he pretended to depose Kings, or made war upon them with temporal arms, went beyond his province, needs hardly, in the present day, be insisted on. But when he claimed the right of censuring and denouncing them, with whatever degree of solemnity, in the name of the moral law which all recognised, he assumed a function necessary at all times, and which, in those days, no one except the Church could assume, or was in any degree qualified to exercise. Time must show if the organ we now have for the performance of this office—if the censure by newspapers and public meetings, which has succeeded to censure by the Church—will be found in the end less liable to perversion and abuse than that was. However this may be, the latter form was the only one possible in those days.

Were the Popes, then, so entirely in the wrong, as historians have deemed them, in their disputes with the Emperors, and with the Kings of England and France? Doubtless they, no more than their antagonists, knew where to stop short. Doubtless, in the ardour of the conflict, they laid claim to powers not compatible with a purely spiritual authority, and occasionally put forth pretensions, which, if completely successful, would have plunged Europe into the torpor of an Egyptian hierarchy. But there never was any danger lest they should succeed too far. The Church was always the weaker party, and occupied essentially a defensive position.

We cannot feel any doubt that Gregory VII, whatever errors he may have committed, was right in the great objects which he proposed to himself. His life is memorable by two things—his contest with the State, and the reform in the Church

*[Translated from] Michelet, Vol. II, p. 615n.

[q-q]44 even

itself, which preceded it. The Church was rapidly becoming secularized. He checked the evil, by enforcing the celibacy of the clergy. Protestant writers have looked upon this ordinance of the Catholic Church, as the joint product of pontifical ambition and popular fanaticism. We would not deny that fanaticism, or rather religious asceticism, had much to do with the popular feeling on the subject, and was perhaps the only lever by which the work could possibly have been accomplished. But we believe that in that age, without the institution of celibacy, the efficiency of the Church as an instrument of human culture was gone. In the early vigorous youth of the feudal system, when everything tended to become hereditary, when every temporal function had already become so, the clerical office was rapidly becoming hereditary too. The clergy were becoming a Braminical caste; or worse—a mere appendage of the caste of soldiery. Already the prelacies and abbacies were filled by the younger brothers of the feudal nobility, who, like their elder brethren, spent the greater part of their time in hunting and war. These had begun to transmit their benefices to their sons, and give them in marriage with their daughters. The smaller preferments would have become the prey of their smaller retainers. Against this evil, what other remedy than that which Gregory adopted did the age afford? Could it remain unremedied?

And what, when impartially considered, is the protracted dispute about investitures, except a prolongation of the same struggle? For what end did the princes of the middle ages desire the appointment of prelates? To make their profit of the revenues by keeping the sees vacant; to purchase tools, and reward adherents; at best, to keep the office in a state of complete subservience. It was no immoderate pretension in the spiritual authority to claim the free choice of its own instruments. The emperors had previously asserted a right to nominate the Pope himself, and had exercised that right in many instances. Had they succeeded, the spiritual power would have become that mere instrument of despotism which it became at Constantinople—which it is in Russia—which the Popes of Avignon became in the hands of the French kings. And even had the Pope maintained his own personal independence, the nomination of the national clergy by their respective monarchs, with no effectual concurrence of his, would have made the national clergy take part with the kings against their own order; as a large section of them always did, and as the whole clergy of France and England ended by doing, because in those countries the kings, in the main, succeeded in keeping possession of the appointment to benefices.

Even for what seems in the abstract a still more objectionable pretension, the claim to the exemption of ecclesiastics from secular jurisdiction, which has scandalized so grievously most of our English historians, there is much more to be said than those historians were aware of. What was it, after all, but the assertion, in behalf of the clergy, of the received English principle of being tried by their peers? The secular tribunals were the courts of a rival power, often in actual conflict with the clergy, always jealous of them, always ready to make use of its jurisdiction as a means of wreaking its vengeance, or serving its ambition; and were stained besides with the grossest corruption and tyranny. "These rights," says M. Michelet,

gave rise, no doubt, to great abuses; many crimes were committed by priests, and committed with impunity; but when one reflects on the frightful barbarity, the execrable fiscality, of the lay tribunals in the twelfth century, one is forced to admit that the ecclesiastical jurisdiction was then an anchor of safety. It spared, perhaps, the guilty, but how often it saved the innocent! The Church was almost the only road by which the despised races were able to recover any ascendancy. We see this by the example of the two Saxons, Breakspear (Adrian IV) and Becket. The liberties of the Church in that age were those of mankind.*

On the other hand, Henry II, by the Constitutions of Clarendon, assumed to himself and his great justiciary a veto on the purely spiritual act of excommunication—the last resort of the Church—the ultimate sanction on which she depended for her moral jurisdiction.[*] No one of the king's tenants was to be excommunicated without his consent. On which side was here the usurpation? And in this pretension Henry was supported by the great majority of his own ʳbishops. Soʳ little cause was there really to dread any undue preponderance of popes over kings.

The Papacy was in the end defeated, even in its reasonable claims. It had to give up, in the main, all the contested points. As the monarchies of Europe were consolidated, and the Kings grew more powerful, the Church became more dependent. The last Pope who dared to defy a bad king, was made a prisoner in his palace, insulted and struck by the emissary of the tyrant.[†] That Pope died broken-hearted; his immediate successor died poisoned.[‡] The next was Clement V, in whom, for the first time, the Church sank into the abject tool of secular tyranny. With him commenced that new era of the Papacy, which made it the horror and disgust of the then rapidly improving European mind, until the Reformation and its consequences closed the period which we commonly call the middle age.

We know it may be said that long before this time venality was a current and merited accusation against the Papal court. We often find Rome denounced, by the indignation of ˢcotemporariesˢ, as a market in which everything might be bought. All periods of supposed purity in the ᶠpastᶠ administration of human affairs are the

*[Translated from] ibid., pp. 343-4.

[*For the Constitutions of Clarendon, see Select Charters and Other Illustrations of English Constitutional History, ed. William Stubbs (Oxford: Clarendon Press, 1870), pp. 131-4.]

[†The references are to Pope Boniface VIII, King Philippe IV, and Guillaume de Nogaret.]

[‡Benedict XI.]

ʳ⁻ʳ44   bishops; so
ˢ⁻ˢ44   contemporaries
ᶠ⁻ᶠ+59,67

dreams of a golden age. We well know that there was only occasionally a Pope who acted consistently on any high ideal of the pontifical character; that many were sordid and vicious, and those who were not, had often sordid and vicious persons around them. Who can estimate the extent to which the power of the Church, for realizing the noble aims of its more illustrious ornaments, was crippled and made infirm by these shortcomings? But, to the time of Innocent III, if not of Boniface VIII, we are unable to doubt that it was on the whole a source of good, and of such good as could not have been provided, for that age, by any other means with which we can conceive such an age to be compatible.

Among the Epochs in the progressive movement of middle-age history, which M. Michelet has been the first to bring clearly and vividly before us, there is none more interesting than the great awakening of the human mind which immediately followed the period of the First Crusade. Others before him had pointed out the influence of the Crusade in generating the feeling of a common Christendom; in counteracting the localizing influence of the feudal institutions, and raising up a kind of republic of chivalry and Christianity; in drawing closer the ties between chiefs and vassals, or even serfs, by the need which they mutually experienced of each other's "voluntary" services; in giving to the rude barons of Western Europe a more varied range of ideas, and a taste for at least the material civilization, which they beheld for the first time in the dominions of the Greek Emperors and the Saracen Soldans. M. Michelet remarks that the effect even upon the religion of the time, was to soften its antipathies and weaken its superstitions. The hatred of Mussulmans was far less intense after the Crusade than at the beginning of it. The notion of a peculiar sanctity inherent in places, was greatly weakened when Christians had become the masters of the Holy Sepulchre, and found themselves neither better nor happier in consequence.

But these special results bear no proportion to the general start which was taken, about this time, by the human mind, and which, though it cannot be ascribed to the Crusade, was without doubt greatly favoured by it. That remarkable expedition was the first great event of modern times, which had an European and a Christian interest—an interest not of nation, or place, or rank, but which the lowest serfs had in common, and more than in common, with the loftiest barons. When the soil is moved, all sorts of seeds fructify. The serfs now began to think themselves human beings. The beginning of the great popular political movement of the middle ages—the formation of the *Communes*—is almost coincident with the First Crusade. Some fragments of the eminently dramatic history of this movement are related in the concluding portion of M. Thierry's *Letters on the History of France*.[*] Contemporaneously with this temporal enfranchisement, began the emancipation of the human mind. Formidable heresies broke out: it was the era of

[*See esp. pp. 242ff. (Letters xiv ff.)]

u-u+59,67

Berengarius, who ^vdenied^v Transubstantiation—of Roscelinus, the founder of Nominalism, and questioner of the received doctrine respecting the Trinity.[*] The very answers of the orthodox to these heretical writings, as may be seen in M. Michelet,* were lessons of free-thinking. The principle of free speculation found a still more remarkable representative, though clear of actual heresy, in the most celebrated of the schoolmen, Abailard. The popularity and European influence of his rationalizing metaphysics, as described by ^wcotemporary^w authorities, must surprise those who conceive the age as one of rare and difficult communications, and without interest in letters. To silence this one man, required the eminent religious ascendancy of the most illustrious churchman of the age, Bernard of Clairvaux. The acquirements and talents of the noble-minded woman, whose name is linked for all time with that of Abailard—a man, so far as we have the means of judging, not her superior even in intellect, and in every other respect unworthy of her—are illustrative of M. Michelet's views on the change which was taking place in the social condition and estimation of women:

The restoration of woman, which had commenced with Christianity, took place chiefly in the twelfth century. A slave in the East, even in the Greek gynaeceum a recluse, emancipated by the jurisprudence of the Roman Empire, she was recognised by the new religion as the equal of man. Still, Christianity, but just escaped from the sensuality of Paganism, dreaded woman, and distrusted her; or rather, men were conscious of weakness, and endeavoured by hardness and scornfulness to fortify themselves against their strongest temptation. . . . When Gregory VII aimed at detaching the clergy from the ties of a worldly life, there was a new outburst of feeling against that dangerous Eve, whose seductions had ruined Adam, and still pursued him in his sons.

A movement in the contrary direction commenced in the twelfth century. Free mysticism undertook to upraise what sacerdotal severity had dragged in the mire. It was especially a Breton, Robert d'Arbrissel, who fulfilled this mission of love. He re-opened to women the bosom of Christ; he founded asylums for them; he built Fontevrault; and there were soon other Fontevraults throughout Christendom. . . . There took place insensibly a great religious revolution. The Virgin became the deity of the world: she usurped almost all the temples and ^x altars. Piety turned itself into an enthusiasm of chivalrous gallantry. The mother of God was proclaimed pure and without taint. The Church of Lyons, always mystical in its tendencies, celebrated, in 1134, the feast of the Immaculate Conception—thus exalting woman in the character of divine maternity, at the precise time when Heloïse was giving expression, in her letters, to the pure disinterestedness of love. Woman reigned

---

[*See Berengarius, *De sacra coena adversus Lanfrancum liber posterior*, ed. A.F. and F.T. Vischer (Berlin: Haude and Spener, 1834), and Roscelinus, "Roscelini nominalistarum in philosophia quondam choragi, ad Petrum Abaelardum epistola hactenus inedita," in *Petri Abaelardi opera omnia*, Vol. CLXXVIII of *Patrologiae cursus completus, series latina*, ed. Jacques Paul Migne (Paris: Garnier, 1849), cols. 357-72.]

*Michelet, Vol. II, pp. 279-80.

^{v-v}44   doubted
^{w-w}44   contemporary
^x44   the

in heaven, and reigned on earth. We see her taking a part, and a leading part, in the affairs of the world. . . . Louis VII dates his acts from the coronation of his wife Adela. Women sat as judges not only in poetical contests and courts of love, but, with and on a par with their husbands, in serious affairs: the King of France expressly recognised it as their right. . . . Excluded up to that time from successions by the feudal barbarism, they everywhere became admitted to them in the first half of the twelfth century: in England, in Castile, in Aragon, at Jerusalem, in Burgundy, Flanders, Hainault, Vermandois, Aquitaine, Provence, and the Lower Languedoc. The rapid extinction of males, the softening of manners, and the progress of equity, re-opened inheritances to women. They transported sovereignties into foreign houses, accelerated the agglomeration of states, and prepared the consolidation of great monarchies.*

Half a century further on, the scene is changed. A new act of the great drama is now transacting. The seeds scattered fifty years before, have grown up and overshadow the world. We are no longer in the childhood, but in the stormy youth of free speculation.

The face of the world was sombre at the close of the twelfth century. The old order was in peril, and the new had not yet begun. It was no longer the mere material struggle of the Pope and the Emperor, chasing each other alternately from Rome, as in the days of Henry IV and Gregory VII. In the eleventh century the evil was on the surface; in 1200, at the core. A deep and terrible malady had seized upon Christendom. Gladly would it have consented to return to the quarrel of investitures, and have had to combat only on the question of the ring and crosier. In Gregory's time, the cause of the Church was the cause of liberty; it had maintained that character to the time of Alexander III, the chief of the Lombard league. But Alexander himself had not dared to support Thomas Becket; he had defended the liberties of Italy, and betrayed those of England. The Church was about to detach herself from the great movement of the world. Instead of preceding and guiding it, as she had done hitherto, she strove to fix it, to arrest time on its passage, to stop the earth which was revolving under her feet. Innocent III seemed to succeed in the attempt; Boniface VIII perished in it.

A solemn moment, and of infinite sadness. The hopes which inspired the Crusade had abandoned the earth. Authority no longer seemed unassailable; it had promised, and had deceived. Liberty began to dawn, but in a hundred fantastical and repulsive shapes, confused and convulsive, multiform, deformed. . . .

In this spiritual anarchy of the twelfth century, which the irritated and trembling Church had to attempt to govern, one thing shone forth above others—a prodigiously audacious sentiment of the moral power and greatness of man. The hardy expression of the Pelagians—"Christ had nothing more than I; I, too, by virtue, can raise myself to divinity"[*]—is reproduced in the twelfth century in barbarous and mystical forms. . . . Messiahs everywhere arise. . . . A Messiah appears in Antwerp, and all the populace follow him; another, in Bretagne, seems to revive the ancient gnosticism of Ireland. Amaury of Chartres, and his Breton disciple, David of Dinan, teach that every Christian is materially a member of Christ; in other words, that God is perpetually incarnated in the human race. The Son, say they, has reigned long enough; let the Holy Ghost now reign. . . . Nothing equals

*[Translated from] *ibid.*, pp. 297-8, 300-2.
[*Cf. Alexander of Hales, *Glossa in quatuor libros sententiarum Petri Lombardi*, Vols. XII-XV of *Bibliotheca Franciscana Scholastica* (Quarrachi: Ex Typographia Colegii S. Bonaventurae, 1951-57), Vol. XIV, p. 121.]

the audacity of these doctors, who mostly teach in the University of Paris (authorized by Philippe-Auguste in 1200). Abailard, supposed to be crushed, lives and speaks in his disciple Peter Lombard, who from Paris gives the law to European philosophy; they reckon nearly five hundred commentators on this schoolman. The spirit of innovation has now acquired two powerful auxiliaries. Jurisprudence is growing up by the side of theology, which it undermines; the Popes forbid the clergy to be professors of law, and, by so doing, merely open public teaching to laymen. The metaphysics of Aristotle are brought from Constantinople, while his commentators,[*] imported from Spain, will presently be translated from the Arabic by order of the kings of Castile, and the Italian princes of the house of Suabia, Frederic II, and Manfred. This is no less than the invasion of Greece and the East into Christian philosophy. Aristotle takes his place almost beside the Saviour. At first prohibited by the Popes, afterwards tolerated, he reigns in the professorial chairs; Aristotle publicly, secretly the Arabs and the Jews, with the pantheism of Averroës and the subtleties of the Cabala. Dialectics enters into possession of all subjects, and stirs up all the boldest questions. Simon of Tournai teaches at pleasure the *pour* and the *contre*. One day when he had delighted the school of Paris, by proving marvellously the truth of the Christian religion, he suddenly exclaimed, "O little Jesus, little Jesus! how I have glorified thy law! If I chose, I could still more easily depreciate it."*

He then vigorously sketches the religious enthusiasts of Flanders and the Rhine, the Vaudois of the Alps, and the Albigeois of Southern France, and proceeds:

What must not have been, in this danger of the Church, the trouble and inquietude of its visible head! . . .

The Pope at that time was a Roman, Innocent III: a man fitted to the time. A great lawyer, accustomed on all questions to consult established right, he examined himself, and believed that the right was on his side. And, in truth, the Church had still in her favour the immense majority—the voice of the people, which is that of God.[†] She had actual possession, *y* so ancient that it might be deemed prescriptive. The Church was the defendant in the cause, the recognised proprietor, who was in present occupancy, and had the title-deeds; the written law seemed to speak for her. The plaintiff was human intellect; but it came too late, and, in its inexperience, took the wrong road, chicaning on texts instead of invoking principles. If asked what it would have, it could make no intelligible answer. All sorts of confused voices called for different things, and most of the assailants wished to retrograde rather than to advance. In politics, their ideas were modelled on the ancient republics; that is, town liberties, to the exclusion of the country. In religion, some wished to suppress the externals of worship, and revert, as they said, to the Apostles; others went further back, and returned to the Asiatic spirit, contending for two gods, or preferring the strict unity of Islamism.[†]

And, after describing the popular detestation which pursued these heretics:

[*Avempace, Averroës, and Avicenna.]
*[Translated from] Michelet, Vol. II, pp. 392-6. [The quotation of Simon of Tournai derives from Matthew Paris, *Angli historia major*, ed. William Wats (London: Hodgkinson, 1640), p. 206.]
[†See Alcuin, Letter to Charlemagne, in *Opera omnia*, Vols. C-CI of *Patrologiae cursus completus, series latina*, ed. Jacques Paul Migne (Paris: Migne, 1851), Vol. C, col. 438.]
†[Translated from] Michelet, Vol. II, pp. 419-21.

*y*44   ancient,

Such appeared at that time the enemies of the Church—and the Church was people —[*l'église était peuple*]. The prejudices of the people, the sanguinary intoxication of their hatred and their terror, ascended through all ranks of the clergy to the Pope himself. It would be too unjust to human nature to deem that egoism or class interest alone animated the chiefs of the Church. No—all indicates that in the thirteenth century they were still convinced of their right. That right admitted, all means seemed good to them for defending it. Not for a mere human interest did St. Dominic traverse the regions of the south, alone and unarmed, in the midst of a sectarian population whom he doomed to death, courting martyrdom with the same avidity with which he inflicted it; and, whatever may have been in the great and terrible Innocent III the temptations of pride and vengeance, other motives animated him in the crusade against the Albigeois and the foundation of the Dominican Inquisition.*

The temporal means by which the Church obtained a brief respite from the dangers which beset it, consisted in letting loose against the rich and heretical South, the fanaticism and rapacity of the North. The spiritual expedient, far the more potent of the two, was the foundation of the Mendicant Orders.

We are too much accustomed to figure to ourselves what are called religious revivals, as a feature peculiar to Protestantism and to recent times. The phenomenon is universal. In no Christian church has the religious spirit flowed like a perennial fountain; it had ever its flux and reflux, like the tide. Its history is a series of alternations between religious laxity and religious earnestness. Monkery itself, in the organized form impressed upon it by St. Benedict, was one of the incidents of a religious revival. We have already spoken of the great revival under Hildebrand. Ranke has made us understand the religious revival within the pale of Romanism itself, which turned back the advancing torrent of the Reformation. As this was characterized by the foundation of the order of Jesuits, so were the Franciscans and Dominicans the result of a similar revival, and became its powerful instrument.

The mendicant orders—especially the most popular of them, the Franciscans —were the offspring of the freethinking which had already taken strong root in the European mind; but the freedom which they represented was freedom in alliance with the Church, rising up against the freedom which was at enmity with the Church, and anathematizing it. What is called, in France, mysticism—in England, religious enthusiasm—consists essentially in looking within instead of without; in relying on an internal revelation from God to the individual believer, and receiving its principal inspirations from that, rather than from the authority of priests and teachers. St. Francis of Assisi was such a man. Disowned by the Church, he might have been a heresiarch instead of a saint; but the Church needed men like him, and had the skill to make its instrument of the spirit which was preparing its destruction. "In proportion to the decline of authority," says M. Michelet, "and the diminution of the priestly influence on the popular mind,

*[Translated from] *ibid.*, pp. 422-3.

religious feeling, being no longer under the restraint of forms, expanded itself into mysticism."* Making room for these mystics in the ecclesiastical system itself, directing their enthusiasm into the path for which it peculiarly qualified them, that of popular preaching, and never parting with the power of repressing any dangerous excess in those whom it retained in its allegiance, the Papacy could afford to give them the rein, and indulge, within certain limits, their most unsacerdotal preference of grace to the law.

The career and character of St. Francis and his early followers are graphically delineated by M. Michelet.[†] As usual with devotees of his class, his great practical precept was the love of God; love which sought all means of demonstrating itself—now by ecstasies, now by austerities like those of an Indian fakeer—but also by love and charity to all creatures. In all things which had life, and in many which had not, he recognised children of God: he invoked the birds to join in gratitude and praise; he parted with his cloak to redeem a lamb from the slaughter. His followers "wandered barefooted over Europe, always run after by the crowd: in their sermons, they brought the sacred mysteries, as it were, on the stage; laughing *in* Christmas, weeping on Good Friday, developing, without reserve, all that Christianity possesses of dramatic elements."[*] The effect of such a band of missionaries must have been great in rousing and feeding dormant devotional feelings *. They* were not less influential in regulating those feelings, and turning into the established Catholic channels those vagaries of private enthusiasm, which might well endanger the Church, since they already threatened society itself. The spirit of religious independence had descended to the miserable, and was teaching them that God had not commanded them to endure their misery. It was a lesson for which they were not yet ripe. "Mysticism," says our author, "had already produced its most terrible fruit, hatred of the law; the wild enthusiasm of religious and political liberty. This demagogic character of mysticism, which so clearly manifested itself in the *Jacqueries* of the subsequent ages, especially in the revolt of the Swabian peasants in 1525, and of the Anabaptists in 1538, appeared already in the insurrection of the *Pastoureaux*," during the reign of St. Louis.[‡] These unhappy people, who were peasantry of the lowest class, and, like all other insurgents of that class, perished miserably—*dispersi sunt, et quasi canes rabidi passim detruncati*, are the words of Matthew Paris[†]—were avowed enemies of the priests, whom they are said to have massacred, and administered the sacraments themselves. They recognised as their chief, a man whom they called

*[Translated from] *ibid.*, Vol. III, p. 195.
[†]*Ibid.*, Vol. II, pp. 537-43.
[*Translated from *ibid.*, pp. 540-1.]
[‡][Translated from] *ibid.*, p. 579.
[†*Angli historia major*, p. 824.]

*z-z*44   at
*a-a*44   ; they

the grand master of Hungary, and who pretended to hold in his hand, which he kept constantly closed, a written commission from the Virgin Mary. So contradictory to history is that superficial notion of the middle ages, which looks upon the popular mind as strictly orthodox, and implicitly obedient to the Pope.

Though the Papacy survived, in apparently undiminished splendour, the crisis of which we have now spoken, the mental ascendancy of the priesthood was never again what it had been before. The most orthodox of the laity, even men whom the Church has canonized, were now comparatively emancipated; they thought *with* the Church, but they no longer let the Church think *for* them. This change in the times is exemplified in the character of St. Louis—himself a lay brother of the Franciscan order; perhaps of all kings the one whose religious conscience was the most scrupulous, yet who learned his religious duty from his own strong and upright judgment, not from his confessor, nor from the Pope. He never shrank from resisting the Church when he had right on his side; and was himself a better sample than any Pope *b*cotemporary*b* with him, of the religious character of his age. The influences of the mystical spirit are easily discernible in his remarkable freedom, so rare in that age, from the slavery of the letter; which, as many anecdotes prove, he was always capable of sacrificing to the spirit, when any conflict arose between them.*

We are obliged to pass rapidly over some other topics, which justice to M. Michelet forbids us entirely to omit. We could extract many passages more illustrative than those we have quoted of his powers as a writer and an artist; such as the highly-finished sketch of the greatness and ruin of the unfortunate house of Hohenstaufen.† We prefer to quote the remarks of greater philosophical interest, with which he winds up one great period of history, and introduces another.

The Crusade of St. Louis was the last Crusade. The middle age had produced its ideal, its flower, and its fruit: the time was come for it to perish. In Philippe-le-Bel, grandson of St. Louis, modern times commence: the middle age is insulted in Boniface VIII, the Crusade burned at the stake in the persons of the Templars.

Crusades will be talked about for some time longer; the word will be often repeated; it is a *c*well-sounding*c* word, good for levying tenths and taxes. But princes, nobles, and popes know well, among themselves, what to think of it. In 1327, we find the Venetian, Sanuto, proposing to the Pope a commercial crusade. "It is not enough," he said, "to invade Egypt," he proposed "to ruin it." The means he urged was to re-open to the Indian trade the channel of Persia, so that merchandize might no longer pass through Alexandria and Damietta. Thus does the modern spirit announce its approach: trade, not religion, will soon become the moving principle of great expeditions.‡

*Michelet, Vol. II, p. 612.
†*Ibid.*, pp. 587-9.
‡[Translated from] *ibid.*, pp. 606-7.

*b-b*44 contemporary
*c-c*44 sounding

And further on, after quoting the bitter denunciation of Dante[*] against the ^dreigning^d family of France—

This furious Ghibelline invective, full of truth and of calumny, is the protest of the old perishing world against the ugly new world which succeeds it. This new world begins towards 1300; it opens with France, and with the odious figure of Philippe-le-Bel.

When the French monarchy, founded by Philippe-Auguste, became extinguished in Louis XVI, at least it perished in the immense glory of a young republic, which, at its first onset, vanquished and revolutionized Europe. But the poor middle age, its Papacy, its chivalry, its feudality, under what hands did they perish? Under those of the attorney, the fraudulent bankrupt, the false coiner.

The bitterness of the poet is excusable; this new world is a repulsive one. If it is more legitimate than that which it replaces, what eye, even that of a Dante, could see this at the time? It is the offspring of the decrepit Roman law, of the old imperial fiscality. It is born a lawyer, a usurer; it is a born Gascon, Lombard, and Jew.

What is most revolting in this modern system, represented especially by France, is its perpetual self-contradiction, its instinctive duplicity, the naïve hypocrisy, so to speak, with which it ^einvokes^e by turns its two sets of principles, Roman and feudal. France looks like a lawyer in a cuirass, an attorney clad in mail; she employs the feudal power to execute the sentences of the Roman and canon law. If this obedient daughter of the Church seizes upon Italy and chastises the Church, she chastises her as a daughter, obliged in conscience to correct her mother's misconduct.*

Yet this revolting exterior is but the mask of a great and necessary transformation; the substitution of legal authority, in the room of feudal violence and the *arbitrium* of the seigneur; the formation, in short, for the first time, of a government. This government could not be carried on without money. The feudal jurisdictions, the feudal armies, cost nothing to the treasury; the wages of all feudal services were the land: but the king's judges and administrators, of whom he has now a host, must ^f be paid.

It is not the fault of this government if it is greedy and ravenous. Ravenousness is its nature, its necessity, the foundation of its temperament. To satisfy this, it must alternately make use of cunning and force: the prince must be at once the Reynard and Isegrim of the old satire. To do him justice, he is not a lover of war: he prefers any other means of acquisition— purchase, for instance, or usury. He traffics, he buys, he exchanges; these are means by which the strong man can honourably plunder his weaker friends.†

This need of money was, for several centuries, the *primum mobile* of European history. In England, it is the hinge on which our constitutional history has wholly turned: in France and elsewhere, it was the source, from this time forward, of all

---

[*Dante Alighieri, "Del purgatorio," in *La divina commedia* (1472), 3 vols. (Florence: Ciardetti, 1821), Vol. II, pp. 243-50 (Canto XX, ll. 43-93).]

*[Translated from] Michelet, Vol. III, pp. 31-2.

†[Translated from] *ibid.*, p. 42.

^{d-d}44   royal
^{e-e}44,59   attests
^f44   all

quarrels between the Kings and the Church. The clergy alone were rich, and money must be had.

The confiscation of Church property was the idea of kings from the thirteenth century. The only difference is, that the Protestants took, and the Catholics made the Church give. Henry VIII had recourse to schism—Francis I to the ⁸Concordat⁸. Who, in the fourteenth century, the King or the Church, was thenceforth to prey upon France?—that was the question.*

To get money was the purpose of Philip's quarrel with Boniface; to get money, he destroyed the Templars.

The proceedings against this celebrated Society occupy two most interesting chapters of M. Michelet's work. His view of the subject seems just and reasonable.

The suppression of the Order, if this had been all, was both inevitable and justifiable. Since the Crusades had ceased, and the crusading spirit died out, their existence and their vast wealth were grounded on false pretences. Among the mass of calumnies which, in order to make out a case for their destruction, their oppressor accumulated against them, there were probably some truths. It is not in the members of rich and powerful bodies which have outlived the ostensible purposes of their existence, that high examples of virtue need be sought. But it was not their private misconduct, real or imputed, that gave most aid to royal rapacity in effecting their ruin. What roused opinion against them—what gave something like a popular sanction to that atrocious trial in its early stages, before the sufferings and constancy of the victims had excited a general sympathy, was, according to our author, a mere mistake—a *mal-entendu*, arising from a change in the spirit of the times.

The forms of reception into the Order were borrowed from the whimsical dramatic rites, the *mysteries*, which the ancient Church did not dread to connect with the most sacred doctrines and objects. The candidate for admission was presented in the character of a sinner, a bad Christian, a renegade. In imitation of St. Peter, he denied Christ;[*] the denial was pantomimically represented by spitting on the cross. The Order undertook to restore this renegade—to lift him to a height as great as the depth to which he had fallen. Thus, in the Feast of Fools, man offered to the Church which was to regenerate him, the homage even of his imbecility, of his infamy. These religious comedies, every day less understood, became more and more dangerous, more capable of scandalizing a prosaic age, which saw only the letter, and lost the meaning of the symbol.[†]

This is not a mere fanciful hypothesis. M. Michelet has elsewhere shown that the initiation into the Guilds of Artificers, in the middle ages, was of this very character. The acolyte affected to be the most worthless character upon earth, and was usually made to perform some act symbolical of worthlessness: after which,

*[Translated from] *ibid.*, p. 50.
[*See Matthew, 26:69-75.]
†[Translated from] Michelet, Vol. III, pp. 127-8.

⁸⁻⁸44 *Concordat*

his admission into the fraternity was to have the merit and honour of his reformation. Such forms were in complete harmony with the genius of an age, in which a transfer of land was not binding without the delivery of a clod—in which all things tended to express themselves in mute symbols, rather than by the conventional expedient of verbal language. It is the nature of all forms used on important occasions, to outlast, for an indefinite period, the state of manners and society in which they originated. The childlike character of the religious sentiment in a rude people, who know terror but not awe, and are often on the most intimate terms of familiarity with the objects of their adoration, makes it easily conceivable that the ceremonies used on admission into the Order were established without any irreverent feeling, in the purely symbolical acceptation which some of the witnesses affirmed. The time, however, had past, when such an explanation would be understood or listened to.

What arrayed the whole people against them—what left them not a single defender among so many noble families to which they were related—was this monstrous accusation of denying and spitting on the cross. This was precisely the accusation which was admitted by the greatest number of the accused. The simple statement of the fact turned every one against them; everybody *h*crossed*h* himself, and refused to hear another word. Thus the Order, which had represented in the most eminent degree the symbolical genius of the middle age, died of a symbol misunderstood.*

From this time the history of France is not, except in a *i*much*i* more indirect manner, the history of Europe and of civilization. The subordination of the Church to the State once fully established, the next period was mainly characterized by the struggles between the king and the barons, and *j*the*j* final victory of the crown. On this subject France cannot represent English history, where the crown was ultimately the defeated instead of the victorious party; and the incidents of the contest are necessarily national, not European incidents. Here, therefore, having regard also to our necessary limits, our extracts from M. Michelet's work may suitably close; although the succeeding volumes, which come down nearly to Louis XI, are not inferior in merit to those from which we have quoted; and are even, as we before remarked, superior in the value of their materials—being grounded, in a great measure, on the public documents of the period, and not, like previous histories, almost exclusively on the chronicles.

In what we have said, we have been far more desirous to make the work known, and recommend it to notice, than to criticise it. The latter could only become a needful service after the former had been accomplished. The faults, whether of matter or manner, of which M. Michelet can be accused, are not such as require

*[Translated from] *ibid.*, p. 206.

*h-h*44   signed
*i-i*44   far
j-j+67

being pointed out to English readers. There is much more danger lest they should judge too strictly the speculations of such a man; and turn impatiently from the germs of truth which often lurk even in the errors of a man of genius. This is, indeed, the more to be apprehended, as M. Michelet, apparently, has by no means the fear of an unsympathizing audience before his eyes. Where we require thoughts, he often gives us only allusions to thoughts. We continually come upon sentences, and even single expressions, which take for granted a whole train of previous speculation—often perfectly just, and perhaps familiar to French readers; but which in England would certainly have required to be set forth in terms, and cleared up by explanations.

His style cannot be fairly judged from the specimens we have exhibited. Our extracts were selected as specimens of his ideas, not of his literary merits; and none have been taken from the narrative part, which is, of course, the principal part of the work, and the most decisive test of powers of composition in a writer of history. We should say, however, of the style generally, that it is sparkling rather than flowing; full of expressiveness, but too continuously epigrammatic to carry the reader easily along with it; and pushing that ordinary artifice of modern French composition, the personification of abstractions, to an almost startling extent. It is not, however, though it is very likely to be taken for, an affected style; for affectation cannot be justly imputed, where the words are chosen, as is evidently the case here, for no purpose but to express ideas; and where, consequently, the mode of expression, however peculiar, grows from, and corresponds to, the peculiarities of the mode of thought.

GUIZOT'S ESSAYS AND LECTURES ON HISTORY

1845

EDITOR'S NOTE

Dissertations and Discussions, 2nd ed. (1867), II, 218-82. Headed by title; title footnoted, "*Edinburgh Review*, October 1845." Running titles as title. Reprinted from *Edinburgh Review*, LXXXII (Oct., 1845), 381-42⊦, where it is headed: "Art. IV.—*Essais sur l'Histoire de France*. Par M. [François Pierre Guillaume] Guizot, Professeur d'Histoire Moderne à l'Académie de Paris. Pour servir de complément aux Observations sur *Histoire de France* de Abbé de Mably. 8vo. Paris [: Brière, 1823]. [Used for reference in this essay is the 2nd ed. (Paris: Brière; Leipzig: Bossange, 1824), which is in Mill's library, Somerville College.] / *Cours d'Histoire Moderne*. Containing, 1. *Histoire Générale de la Civilisation en Europe, depuis la chute de l'Empire Romain jusqu'à la Révolution Française*. [Paris: Pichon and Dider, 1828.] 2. *Histoire de la Civilisation en France, depuis la chute de l'Empire Romain jusqu'en 1789*. [5 vols. Paris: Pichon and Didier, 1829-32.] Par M. Guizot. 6 vols. 8vo." Running titles: "M. Guizot's *Essays and Lectures in History*." Unsigned. Offprinted without title page but repaginated. Identified in Mill's bibliography as "An article on Guizot's Essays and Lectures on History, in the Edinburgh Review for October 1845" (MacMinn, 58). The copy of the offprint in Mill's library, Somerville College, is headed by Mill, "(Edinburgh Review, October 1845)", and contains the following emendations: "*Justificatifs*" is changed to "*Justificatives*" (275.4), "damist" to "amidst" (291.4), and "principal of all government" to "principle of all government" (292.38); also, at 290.25 "events" is underlined in pencil, and "qu?" written in the margin (perhaps in Harriet Taylor's hand); the three changes were made in *D&D*, and "events" was changed to "its wants" (see 290[n-n]).

The following text, taken from *D&D*, 2nd ed. (the last in Mill's lifetime), is collated with that in *D&D*, 1st ed., that of the offprint, and that in *ER*. In the footnoted variants, "45[1]" indicates *ER*, "45[2]" indicates the offprint, "59" indicates *D&D*, 1st ed. (1859), and "67" indicates *D&D*, 2nd ed. (1867).

For comment on the essay, see lxxii–lxxix and civ–cvi above.

Guizot's Essays and Lectures on History

THESE TWO WORKS are the contributions which the present Minister for Foreign Affairs in France has hitherto made to the philosophy of general history. They are but fragments: the earlier of the two is a collection of detached Essays, and [a] therefore of necessity fragmentary; while the later is all that the public possesses, or perhaps is destined to possess, of a systematic work cut short in an early stage of its progress. It would be unreasonable to lament that the exigencies or the temptations of politics have called from authorship and the Professor's chair to the Chamber of Deputies and the Cabinet, the man to whom perhaps more than to any other it is owing that Europe is now at peace. Yet we cannot forbear wishing that this great service to the civilized world had been the achievement of some other, and that M. Guizot had been allowed to complete his *Cours d'Histoire Moderne*. For this a very moderate amount of leisure would probably suffice. For though M. Guizot has written only on a portion of his subject, he has done it in the manner of one to whom the whole is familiar. There is a consistency, a coherence, a comprehensiveness, and what the Germans would term many-sidedness,[*] in his view of European history; together with a full possession of the facts which have any important bearing upon his conclusions; and a deliberateness, a matureness, an entire absence of haste or crudity, in his explanations of historical phenomena; which we never see in writers who form their theories as they go on—which give evidence of a general scheme, so well wrought out and digested beforehand, that the labours both of research and of thought necessary for the whole work, seem to have been performed before any part was committed to paper. Little beyond the mere operation of composition seems to be requisite, to place before us, as a connected body of thought, speculations which, even in their unfinished state, may be ranked with the most valuable contributions yet made to universal history.

Of these speculations no account, having any pretensions to completeness, has ever, so far as we are aware, appeared in the English language. We shall attempt to do something towards supplying the deficiency. To suppose that this is no longer needful would be to presume too much on the supposed universality of the French language among our reading public; and on the acquaintance even of those to

[*Cf. p. 183 above.]

[a]45   is

whom the language opposes no difficulty, with the names and reputation of the standard works of contemporaneous French thought. We believe that a knowledge of M. Guizot's writings is even now not a common possession in this country, and that it is by no means a superfluous service to inform English readers of what they may expect to find there.

For it is not with speculations of this kind as it is with those for which there exists in this country a confirmed and long-established taste. What is done in France or elsewhere for the advancement of Chemistry or of Mathematics, is immediately known and justly appreciated by the mathematicians and chemists of Great Britain. For these are recognised sciences, the chosen occupation of many instructed minds, ever on the watch for any accession of facts or ideas in the department which they cultivate. But the interest which historical studies in this country inspire, is not as yet of a scientific character. History with us has not passed that stage in which its cultivation is an affair of mere literature or of erudition, not of science. It is studied for the facts, not for the explanation of facts. It excites an imaginative, or a biographical, or an antiquarian, but not a philosophical interest. Historical facts are hardly yet felt to be, like other natural phenomena, amenable to scientific laws. The characteristic distrust of our countrymen for all ambitious efforts of intellect, of which the success does not admit of being instantly tested by a decisive application to practice, causes all widely extended views on the explanation of history to be looked upon with a suspicion surpassing the bounds of reasonable caution, and of which the natural result is indifference [b]. And[b] hence we remain in contented ignorance of the best writings which the nations of the Continent have in our time produced; because we have no faith in, and no curiosity about, the kind of speculations to which the most philosophic minds of those nations have lately devoted themselves; even when distinguished, as in the case before us, by a sobriety and a judicious reserve, borrowed from the safest and most cautious school of inductive inquirers.

In this particular, the difference between the English and the Continental mind forces itself upon us in every province of their respective literatures. Certain conceptions of history considered as a whole, some notions of a progressive unfolding of the capabilities of humanity—of a tendency of man and society towards some distant result—of a *destination*, as it were, of humanity—pervade, in its whole extent, the popular literature of France. Every newspaper, every literary review or magazine, bears witness of such notions. They are always turning up accidentally, when the writer is ostensibly engaged with something else; or showing themselves as a background behind the opinions which he is immediately maintaining. When the writer's mind is not of a high order, these notions are crude and vague; but they are evidentiary of a tone of thought which has prevailed so long among the superior intellects, as to have spread from them to

[b-b]45   ;—and

others, and become the general property of the nation. Nor is this true only of France, and of the nations of Southern Europe which take their tone from France, but almost equally, though under somewhat different forms, of the Germanic nations. It was Lessing by whom *the course of* history was styled "the education of the human race."[*] Among the earliest of those by whom the succession of historical events was conceived as a subject of science, were Herder and Kant.[†] The latest school of German metaphysicians, the Hegelians, are well known to treat of it as a science which might even be constructed *à priori*. And as on other subjects, so on this, the general literature of Germany borrows both its ideas and its tone from the schools of the highest philosophy. We need hardly say that in our own country nothing of all this is true. The speculations of our thinkers, and the commonplaces of our mere writers and talkers, are of quite another description.

Even insular England belongs, however, to the commonwealth of Europe, and yields, though slowly and in a way of her own, to the general impulse of the European mind. There are signs of a nascent tendency in English thought to turn itself towards speculations on history. The tendency first showed itself in some of the minds which had received their earliest impulse from Mr. Coleridge; and an example has been given in a quarter where many, perhaps, would have least expected it—by the Oxford school of theologians. However little ambitious these writers may be of the title of philosophers; however anxious to sink the character of science in that of religion—they yet have, after their own fashion, a philosophy of history. They have *d* a theory of the world[‡]—in our opinion an erroneous one, but of which they recognise as an essential condition that it shall explain history; and they do attempt to explain history by it, and have constituted, on the basis of it, a kind of historical system. By this we cannot but think that they have done much good, if only in contributing to impose a similar necessity upon all *e* theorizers of like pretensions. We believe the time must come when all systems which aspire to direct either the consciences of mankind, or their political and social arrangements, will be required to show not only that they are consistent with universal history, but that they afford a more reasonable *explanation* of it than any other

[*Gotthold Ephraim Lessing, *Die Erziehung des Menschengeschlechts* (Berlin: Voss, 1780).]

[†Johann Gottfried von Herder, *Ideen zur Philosophie der Geschichte der Menschheit*, 4 vols. (Riga and Leipzig: Hartknoch, 1784-91); Immanuel Kant, *Idee zu einer allgemeinen Geschichte in weltbürgerlicher Absicht* (1784), in *Sämmtliche Werke*, ed. Karl Rosenkrantz and Friedrich Schubert, 14 vols. in 12 (Leipzig: Voss, 1838-40), Vol. VII, pp. 332-5.]

[‡Mill is using one of Carlyle's favourite terms; see, e.g., "Characteristics," *Edinburgh Review*, LIV (Dec., 1831), 371; and *The French Revolution*, 3 vols. (London: Fraser, 1837), Vol. I, p. 205.]

c-c+59,67
*d*45 , as Mr. Carlyle would say,
*e*45 other
*f-f*45 solution

system. In the philosophy of society, more especially, we look upon history as an indispensable test and verifier of all doctrines and creeds; and we regard with proportionate interest all explanations, however partial, of any important part of the series of historical phenomena—all attempts, which are in any measure successful, to disentangle the complications of those phenomena, to detect the order of their causation, and exhibit any portion of them in an unbroken series, each link cemented by natural laws with those which precede and follow it.

M. Guizot's is one of the most successful of these partial efforts. His subject is not history at large, but modern European history; the formation and progress of the existing nations of Europe. Embracing, therefore, only a part of the succession of historical events, he is precluded from attempting to determine the law or laws which preside over the entire evolution. If there be such laws; if the series of states through which human nature and society are *g*destined*g* to pass, have been determined more or less precisely by the original constitution of mankind, and by the circumstances of the planet on which we live; the order of their succession cannot be *h*discovered*h* by modern or by European experience alone: it must be ascertained by a conjunct analysis, so far as possible, of the whole of history, and the whole of human nature. M. Guizot stops short of this ambitious enterprise; but, considered as preparatory studies for promoting and facilitating it, his writings are most valuable. He seeks, not the ultimate, but the proximate causes of the facts of modern history; he inquires in what manner each successive condition of modern Europe grew out of that which next preceded it; and how modern society altogether, and the modern mind, shaped themselves from the elements which had been transmitted to them from the ancient world. To have done this with any degree of success, is no trifling achievement.

The Lectures, which are the principal foundation of M. Guizot's literary fame, were delivered by him in the years 1828, 1829, and 1830, at the old Sorbonne, now the seat of the *Faculté des Lettres* of Paris, on alternate days with MM. Cousin and Villemain; a triad of lecturers, whose brilliant exhibitions, the crowds which thronged their lecture-rooms, and the stir they excited in the active and aspiring minds so numerous among the French youth, the future historian will commemorate as among the remarkable appearances of that important era. The *Essays on the History of France* are the substance of Lectures delivered by M. Guizot many years earlier; before the Bourbons, in their jealousy of all free speculation, had shut up his class-room and abolished his professorship; which was re-established after seven years' interval by the Martignac Ministry. In this earlier production some topics are discussed at length, which, in the subsequent Lectures, are either not touched upon, or much more summarily disposed of. Among these is the highly interesting subject of the first Essay. The wide difference between M.

*g-g*45   appointed
*h-h*45   determined

Guizot and preceding historians is marked in the first words of his first book. A real thinker is shown in nothing more certainly, than in the questions which he asks. The fact which stands at the commencement of M. Guizot's subject—which is the origin and foundation of all subsequent history—the fall of the Roman Empire—he found an unexplained phenomenon; unless a few generalities about despotism and immorality and luxury can be called explanation. His Essay opens as follows:

The fall of the Roman Empire of the West offers a singular phenomenon. Not only the people fail to support the government in its struggle against the Barbarians; but the nation, abandoned to itself, does not attempt, even on its own account, any resistance. More than this—nothing discloses that a nation exists; scarcely even is our attention called to what it suffers: it undergoes all the horrors of war, pillage, famine, a total change of its condition and destiny, without giving, either by word or deed, any sign of life.

This phenomenon is not only singular, but unexampled. Despotism has existed elsewhere than in the Roman Empire: more than once, after countries had been long oppressed by it, foreign invasion and conquest have spread destruction over them. Even when the nation has not resisted, its existence is manifested in history; it suffers, complains, and, in spite of its degradation, maintains some struggle against its misery: narratives and monuments attest what it underwent, what became of it, and if not its own acts, the acts of others in regard to it.

In the fifth century, the remnant of the Roman legions disputes with hordes of barbarians the immense territory of the Empire; but it seems as if that territory was a desert. The Imperial troops once driven out or defeated, all seems over: one barbarous tribe wrests the province from another; these excepted, the only existence which shows itself is that of the bishops and clergy. If we had not the laws to testify to us that a Roman population still occupied the soil, history would leave us doubtful of it.

This total disappearance of the people is more especially observable in the provinces most advanced in civilization, and longest subject to Rome. The Letter called "The Groans of the Britons," addressed to Aetius,[*] and imploring, with bitter lamentations, the aid of a legion, has been looked upon as a monument of the helplessness and meanness of spirit into which the subjects of the Empire had fallen. This is unjust. The Britons, less civilized, less Romanized than the other subjects of Rome, did resist the Saxons; and their resistance has a history. At the same epoch, in the same situation, the Italians, the Gauls, the Spaniards, have none. The Empire withdrew from those countries, the Barbarians occupied them, and the mass of the inhabitants took not the slightest part, nor marked their place in any manner in the events which gave them up to so great calamities.

And yet, Gaul, Italy, and Spain, were covered with towns, which but lately had been rich and populous. Roads, aqueducts, amphitheatres, schools, they possessed in abundance; they were wanting in nothing which gives evidence of wealth, and procures for a people a brilliant and animated existence. The Barbarians came to plunder these riches, disperse these aggregations, destroy these pleasures. Never was the existence of a nation more utterly subverted; never had individuals to endure more evils in the present, more terrors for the future. Whence came it that these nations were mute and lifeless? Why have so many towns sacked, so many fortunes reversed, so many plans of life overthrown, so many

[*In Gildas, *Opus novum. Gildas britannus monachus cui sapientis cognometu est inditum, de calamitate excidio, & conquestu britanniae, quam angliam nunc vocant, author vetustus a multis diu desyderatus, & nuper in gratiam* (London: Tonstall, 1525), f. B3^v.]

proprietors dispossessed, left so few traces, not merely of the active resistance of the people, but even of their sufferings?

The causes assigned are, the despotism of the Imperial government, the degradation of the people, the profound apathy which had seized upon all the governed. And this is true; such was really the main cause of so extraordinary an effect. But it is not enough to enunciate, in these general terms, a cause which has existed elsewhere without producing the same results. We must penetrate deeper into the condition of Roman society, such as despotism had made it. We must examine by what means despotism had so completely stripped society of all coherence and all life. Despotism has various forms and modes of proceeding, which give very various degrees of energy to its action, and of extensiveness to its consequences.[*]

Such a problem M. Guizot proposes to himself; and is it not remarkable that this question not only was not *i*answered*i*, but was not so much as raised, by the celebrated writers who had treated this period of history before him—one of those writers being Gibbon?[†] The difference between what we learn from Gibbon on this subject, and what we learn from Guizot, is a measure of the progress of historical inquiry in the intervening period. Even the true sources of history, of all that is most important in it, have never until the present generation been really understood and freely resorted to. It is not in the chronicles, but in the laws, that M. Guizot finds the clue to the immediate agency in the "decline and fall" of the Roman empire. In the legislation of the period M. Guizot discovers, under the name of *curiales*, the middle class of the Empire, and the recorded evidences of its progressive annihilation.[‡]

It is known that the free inhabitants of Roman Europe were almost exclusively a town population: it is *j*, then,*j* in the institutions and condition of the municipalities that the real state of the inhabitants of the Roman empire must be studied.

k In semblance, the constitution of the town communities was of a highly popular character. The *curiales*, or the class liable to serve municipal offices, consisted of all the inhabitants (not specially exempted) who possessed landed property amounting to twenty-five *jugera*. *l* This class formed a corporation for the management of local affairs. They discharged their functions, partly as a collective body, partly by electing, and filling in rotation, the various municipal magistracies. Notwithstanding the apparent dignity and authority with which this body was invested, the list of exemptions consisted of all the classes who possessed any influence in the State, any real participation in the governing power. It comprised,

[*Translated from *Essais*, pp. 1-4.]

[†In his *History of the Decline and Fall of the Roman Empire*, 6 vols. (London: Strahan and Cadell, 1776-88).]

[‡Guizot, *Essais*, pp. 11ff.]

*i-i*45   solved
j-j+59,67
*k*45   [*no paragraph*]
*l*45   [*paragraph*]

first, all senatorial families, and all persons whom the Emperor had honoured with the title of *clarissimi*: then, all the clergy, all the military, from the *praefectus praetorii* down to the common legionary, and all the civil functionaries of the State. When we look further, indications still more significant make their appearance. We find that there was an unceasing struggle between the government and the *curiales*—on their part to escape from their condition, on the part of the government to retain them in it. It was found necessary to circumscribe them by every species of artificial restriction. They were interdicted from living *m*out of the town*m*, from serving in the army, or holding any civil employment which conferred exemption from municipal offices, until they had first served all those offices, from the lowest to what was called the highest. Even then, their emancipation was only personal, not extending to their children. If they entered the Church, they must abandon their possessions, either to the *curia* (the municipality), or to some individual who would become a *curialis* in their room. Laws after laws were enacted for detecting, and bringing back to the *curia*, those who had secretly quitted it and entered surreptitiously into the army, the clergy, or some public office. They could not absent themselves, even for a time, without the permission of superior authority; and if they succeeded in escaping, their property was forfeit to the *curia*. No *curialis*, without leave from the governor of the province, could sell the property which constituted him such. If his heirs were not members of the *curia*, or if his widow or daughter married any one not a *curialis*, one-fourth of their property must be relinquished. If he had no children, only one-fourth could be bequeathed by will, the remainder passing to the *curia*. The law looked forward to the case of properties abandoned by the possessor, and made provision that they should devolve upon the *curia*; and that the taxes to which they were liable should be rateably charged upon the property of the other *curiales*.

What was it, in the situation of a *curialis*, which made his condition so irksome, that nothing could keep men in it unless caged up as in a dungeon—unless every hole or cranny by which they could creep out of it, was tightly closed by the provident ingenuity of the legislator?

The explanation is this. Not only were the *curiales* burdened with all the expenses of the local administration, beyond what could be defrayed from the property of the *curia* itself—property continually encroached upon, and often confiscated, by the general government; but they had also to collect the revenue of the State; and their own property was responsible for making up its amount. This it was which rendered the condition of a *curialis* an object of dread; which progressively impoverished and finally extinguished the class. In their fate, we see what disease the Roman empire really died of; and how its destruction had been consummated even before the occupation by the Barbarians. The invasions were no new fact, unheard-of until the fifth century; such attempts had been repeatedly

*m-m*45   in the country

made, and never succeeded until the powers of resistance were destroyed by inward decay. The Empire perished of misgovernment, in the form of over-taxation. The burden, ever increasing through the necessities occasioned by the impoverishment it had already produced, at last reached this point, that none but those whom a legal exemption had removed out of the class on which the weight principally fell, had anything remaining to lose. The senatorial houses possessed that privilege, and accordingly we still find, at the period of the successful invasions, a certain number of families which had escaped the general wreck of private fortunes;—opulent families, with large landed possessions and numerous slaves. Between these and the mass of the population there existed no tie of affection, no community of interest. With this exception, and that of the Church, all was poverty. The middle class had sunk under its burdens. "Hence," says M. Guizot, "in the fifth century, so much land lying waste, so many towns almost depopulated, or filled only with a hungry and unoccupied rabble. The system of government which I have described, contributed much more to this result than the ravages of the Barbarians."[*]

In this situation the northern invaders found the Roman empire. What they made of it, is the next subject of M. Guizot's investigations. The Essays which follow are, "On the origin and establishment of the Franks in Gaul"—"Causes of the fall of the Merovingians and Carlovingians"—"Social state and political institutions of France, under the Merovingians and Carlovingians"—"Political character of the feudal *régime*."[†] But on these subjects our author's later and more mature thoughts are found in his Lectures; and we shall therefore pass at once to the more recent work, returning afterwards to the concluding Essay in the earlier volume, which bears this interesting title: "Causes of the establishment of a representative system in England."[‡]

The subject of the Lectures being the history of European Civilization, M. Guizot begins with a dissertation on the different meanings of that indefinite term; and announces that he intends to use it as "an" equivalent to a state of improvement and progression, in the physical condition and social relations of mankind, on the one hand, and in their inward spiritual development on the other. We have not space to follow him into this discussion, with which, were we disposed to criticize, we might find some fault; but which ought, assuredly, to have exempted him from the imputation of looking upon the improvement of mankind as consisting in the progress of social institutions alone. We shall quote a passage near the conclusion

[*Translated from *ibid.*, p. 42.]
[†Translated from the *Table des matières* of *Essais.*]
[‡Translated from *ibid*. Mill returns to the essay at p. 290 below.]

n-n+59,67

of the same Lecture, as a specimen of the moral and philosophical spirit which pervades the work, and because it contains a truth for which we are glad to cite M. Guizot as an authority:

I think that in the course of our survey we shall speedily become convinced that civilization is still very young; that the world is very far from having measured the extent of the career which is before it. Assuredly, human conception is far from being, as yet, all that it is capable of becoming; we are far from being able to embrace in imagination the whole future of humanity. Nevertheless, let each of us descend into his own thoughts, let him question himself as to the possible good which he comprehends and hopes for, and then confront his idea with what is realized in the world; he will be satisfied that society and civilization are in a very early stage of their progress; that in spite of all they have accomplished, they have incomparably more still to achieve.[*]

The second Lecture is devoted to a general speculation, which is very characteristic of M. Guizot's mode of thought, and, in our opinion, worthy to be attentively weighed both by the philosophers and the practical politicians of the age.

He observes, that one of the points of difference by which modern civilization is most distinguished from ancient, is the complication, the multiplicity, which characterizes it. In all previous forms of society, Oriental, Greek, or Roman, there is a remarkable character of unity and simplicity. Some one idea seems to have presided over the construction of the social framework, and to have been carried out into all its consequences, without encountering on the way any counterbalancing or limiting principle. Some one element, some one power in society, seems to have early attained predominance, and extinguished all other agencies which could exercise an influence over society capable of conflicting with its own. In Egypt, for example, the theocratic principle absorbed everything. The temporal government was grounded on the uncontrolled rule of a caste of priests; and the moral life of the people was built upon the idea, that it belonged to the interpreters of religion to direct the whole detail of human actions. The dominion of an exclusive class, at once the ministers of religion and the sole possessors of letters and secular learning, has impressed its character on all which survives of Egyptian monuments—on all we know of Egyptian life. Elsewhere, the dominant fact was the supremacy of a military caste, or race of conquerors: the institutions and habits of society were principally modelled by the necessity of maintaining this supremacy. In other places, again, society was mainly the expression of the democratic principle. The sovereignty of the majority, and the equal participation of all male citizens in the administration of the State, were the leading facts by which the aspect of those societies was determined. This singleness in the governing principle had not, indeed, always prevailed in those states. Their early history often presented a conflict of forces.

[*Translated from *Civilisation en Europe*, Lecture 1, pp. 30-1.]

Among the Egyptians, the Etruscans, even among the Greeks, the caste of warriors, for example, maintained a struggle with that of priests; elsewhere [in ancient Gaul, for example] the spirit of clanship against that of voluntary association; or the aristocratic against the popular principle. But these contests were nearly confined to ante-historical periods; a vague remembrance was all that survived of them. If at a later period the struggle was renewed, it was almost always promptly terminated; one of the rival powers achieved an early victory, and took exclusive possession of society.[*]

This remarkable simplicity of most of the ancient civilizations, had, in different places, different results. Sometimes, as in Greece, it produced a most rapid development: never did any people unfold itself so brilliantly in so short a time. But after this wonderful outburst, Greece appeared to have become suddenly exhausted. Her decline, if not so rapid as her elevation, was yet strangely prompt. It seemed as though the creative force of the principle of Greek civilization had spent itself, and no other principle came to its assistance.

Elsewhere, in Egypt and India for example, the unity of the dominant principle had a different effect; society fell into a stationary state. Simplicity produced monotony: the State did not fall into dissolution; society continued to subsist, but immovable, and as it were congealed.[†]

It was otherwise, says M. Guizot, with modern Europe.

Her civilization, [he continues,] is confused, diversified, stormy: all forms, all principles of social organization co-exist; spiritual and temporal authority, theocratic, monarchic, aristocratic, democratic elements, every variety of classes and social conditions, are mixed and crowded together; there are innumerable gradations of liberty, wealth, and influence. And these forces are in a state of perpetual conflict, nor has any of them ever been able to stifle the others, and establish its own exclusive authority. Modern Europe offers examples of all systems, of all attempts at social organization; monarchies pure and mixed, theocracies, republics more or less aristocratic, have existed simultaneously one beside another; and, in spite of their diversity, they have all a certain homogeneity, a family likeness, not to be mistaken.

In ideas and sentiments, the same variety, the same struggle. Theocratic, monarchic, aristocratic, popular creeds, check, limit, and modify one another. Even in the most audacious writings of the middle ages, an idea is never followed to its ultimate consequences. The partisans of absolute power unconsciously shrink from the results of their doctrine; democrats are under similar restraints. One sees that there are ideas and influences encompassing them, which do not suffer them to go all lengths. There is none of that imperturbable hardihood, that blindness of logic, which we find in the ancient world. In the feelings of mankind, the same contrasts, the same multiplicity: a most energetic love of independence, along with a great facility of submission; a rare fidelity of man to man, and at the same time an imperious impulse to follow each his own will, to resist restraint, to live for himself, without taking account of others. A similar character shows itself in modern literatures. In perfection of form and artistic beauty, they are far inferior to the ancient; but richer and more copious in respect of sentiments and ideas. One perceives that human nature has been stirred up to a greater depth, and at a greater number of points. The imperfections of form are an effect of this very cause. The more abundant the materials, the more difficult it is to marshal them into a symmetrical and harmonious shape.*

[*Translated from *ibid.*, Lecture 2, pp. 4-5; Mill's words in square brackets.]
[†Translated from *ibid.*, p. 5.]
*[Translated from] *ibid.*, pp. 6-9.

Hence, he continues, the modern world, while inferior to many of the ancient forms of human life in the characteristic excellence of each, yet in all things taken together, is richer and more developed than any of them. From the multitude of elements to be reconciled, each of which during long ages spent the greater part of its strength in combating the rest, the progress of modern civilization has necessarily been slower; but it has lasted, and remained steadily progressive, through fifteen centuries; which no other civilization has ever done.

There are some to whom this will appear a fanciful theory, a cobweb spun from the brain of a *doctrinaire*. We are of a different opinion. There is doubtless, in the historical statement, some of that pardonable exaggeration, which in the exposition of large and commanding views, the necessities of language render it so difficult entirely to avoid. The assertion that the civilizations of the ancient world were each under the complete ascendancy of some one exclusive principle, is not admissible in the unqualified sense in which M. Guizot enunciates it; the limitations which that assertion would require, on a nearer view, are neither few nor inconsiderable. Still less is it maintainable, that different societies, under different dominant principles, did not at each epoch co-exist in the closest contact; as Athens, Sparta, and Persia or Macedonia; Rome, Carthage, and the East. But after allowance for over-statement, the substantial truth of the doctrine appears unimpeachable. No one of the ancient forms of society contained in itself that systematic antagonism, which we believe to be the only condition under which stability and progressiveness can be permanently reconciled to one another.

There are in society a number of distinct forces—of separate and independent sources of power. There is the general power of knowledge and cultivated intelligence. There is the power of religion; by which, speaking politically, is to be understood that of religious teachers. There is the power of military skill and discipline. There is the power of wealth; the power of numbers and physical force; and several others might be added. Each of these, by the influence it exercises over society, is fruitful of certain kinds of beneficial results; none of them is favourable to all kinds. There is no one of these powers which, if it could make itself absolute, and deprive the others of all influence except in aid of, and in subordination to, its own, would not show itself the enemy of some of the essential constituents of human well-being. Certain good results would be doubtless obtained, at least for a time; some of the interests of society would be adequately cared for; because, with certain of them, the natural tendency of each of these powers spontaneously coincides. But there would be other interests, in greater number, which the complete ascendancy of any one of these social elements would leave unprovided for; and which must depend for their protection on the influence which can be exercised by other elements.

We believe with M. Guizot, that modern Europe presents the only example in history, of the maintenance, through many ages, of this co-ordinate action among rival powers naturally tending in different directions. And, with him, we ascribe chiefly to this cause the spirit of improvement, which has never ceased to exist, and still makes progress, in the European nations. At no time has Europe been free from a contest of rival powers for dominion over society. If the clergy had succeeded, as *o*is supposed to have been the case*o* in Egypt, in making the kings subservient to them; if, as among the Mussulmans of old, or the Russians now, the supreme religious authority had merged in the attributes of the temporal ruler; if the military and feudal nobility had reduced the clergy to be their tools, and retained the burgesses as their serfs; if a commercial aristocracy, as at Tyre, Carthage, and Venice, had got rid of kings, and governed by a military force composed of foreign mercenaries; Europe would have arrived much more rapidly at such kinds and degrees of national greatness and well-being as those influences severally tended to promote; but from that time would either have stagnated, like the great stationary despotisms of the East, or have perished for lack of such other elements of civilization as could sufficiently unfold themselves only under some other patronage. Nor is this a danger existing only in the past; but one which may be yet impending over the future. If the perpetual antagonism which has kept the human mind alive, were to give place to the complete preponderance of any, even the most salutary, element, we might yet find that we have counted too confidently upon the progressiveness which we are so often told is an inherent property of our species. Education, for example—mental culture—would seem to have a better title than could be derived from anything else, to rule the world with exclusive authority; yet if the lettered and cultivated class, embodied and disciplined under a central organ, could become in Europe, what it is in China, the Government—unchecked by any power residing in the mass of citizens, and permitted to assume a parental tutelage over all the operations of life—the result would probably be a darker despotism, one more opposed to improvement, than even the military monarchies and aristocracies have in fact proved. And in like manner, if what *p*is thought*p* to be the tendency of things in the United States should proceed for some generations unrestrained; if the power of numbers—of the opinions and instincts of the mass—should acquire and retain the absolute government of society, and impose silence upon all voices which dissent from its decisions or dispute its authority; we should expect that, in such countries, the condition of human nature would become as stationary as in China, and perhaps at *q*as low a*q* point of elevation in the scale.

However these things may be, and imperfectly as many of the elements have yet unfolded themselves which are hereafter to compose the civilization of the modern world; there is no doubt that it *r*has always possessed*r*, in comparison with the older forms of life and society, that complex and manifold character which M. Guizot ascribes to it.

o-o+67
*p-p*45,59   seems
*q-q*45,59   a still lower
*r-r*45   already possesses

He proceeds to inquire whether any explanation of this peculiarity of the European nations can be traced in their origin; and he finds, in fact, that origin to be extremely multifarious. The European world shaped itself from a chaos, in which Roman, Christian, and Barbarian ingredients were commingled. M. Guizot attempts to determine what portion of the elements of modern life derived their beginning from each of these sources.

From the Roman Empire, he finds that Europe derived both the fact and the idea of municipal institutions; a thing unknown to the Germanic conquerors. The Roman Empire was originally an aggregation of towns; the life of the people, especially in *the Western Empire*, was a town life; their institutions and social arrangements, except the system of functionaries destined to maintain the authority of the sovereign, were all grounded upon the towns. When the central power retired from the Western Empire, town life and town institutions, though in an enfeebled condition, were what remained. In Italy, where they were less enfeebled than elsewhere, civilization revived not only earlier than in the rest of Europe, but in forms more similar to those of the ancient world. The South of France had, next to Italy, partaken most in the fruits of Roman civilization; its towns had been the richest and most flourishing on this side the Alps; and having, therefore, held out longer than those farther north against the fiscal tyranny of the Empire, were not so competely ruined when the conquest took place. Accordingly, their municipal institutions were transmitted unbroken from the Roman period to recent times. This, then, was one legacy which the Empire left to the nations which were shaped out of its ruins. But it left also, though not a central authority, the habit of requiring and looking for such an authority. It left "the idea of the empire, the name of the emperor, the conception of the imperial majesty, of a sacred power inherent in the imperial name."[*] This idea, at no time becoming extinct, resumed, as society became more settled, a portion of its pristine power: towards the close of the middle ages, we find it once more a really influential element. Finally, Rome left a body of written law, constructed by and for a wealthy and cultivated society; this served as a pattern of civilization to the rude invaders, and assumed an ever-increasing importance as they became more civilized.

In the field of intellect and purely mental development, Rome, and through Rome, her predecessor Greece, left a still richer inheritance, but one which did not come much into play until a later period.

Liberty of thought—reason taking herself for her own starting-point and her own guide—is an idea essentially sprung from antiquity, an idea which modern society owes to Greece and Rome. We evidently did not receive it either from Christianity or from Germany, for in neither of these elements of our civilization was it included. It was powerful on the contrary, it predominated, in the Graeco-Roman civilization. That was its

[*Translated from *ibid*., pp. 21-2.]

*-*45   western Europe

true origin. It is the most precious legacy which antiquity left to the modern world: a legacy which was never quite suspended and valueless; for we see the fundamental principle of all philosophy, the right of human reason to explore for itself, animating the writings and the life of Scotus Erigena, and the doctrine of freedom of thought still erect in the ninth century, in the face of the principle of authority.*

Such, then, are the benefits which Europe has derived from the relics of the ancient Imperial civilization. But along with this perishing society, the barbarians found another and a rising society, in all the freshness and vigour of youth—the Christian Church. In the debt which modern society owes to this great institution, is 'first to be' included, in M. Guizot's opinion, all which it owes to Christianity.

At that time none of the means were in existence by which, in our own days, moral influences establish and maintain themselves independently of institutions; none of the instruments whereby a pure truth, a mere idea, acquires an empire over minds, governs actions, determines events. In the fourth century nothing existed which could give to ideas, to mere personal sentiments, such an authority. To make head against the disasters, to come victoriously out of the tempests, of such a period, there was needed a strongly organized and energetically governed society. It is not too much to affirm that at the period in question, the Christian Church saved Christianity. It was the Church, with its institutions, its magistrates, its authority, which maintained itself against the decay of the empire from within, and against barbarism from without; which won over the barbarians, and became the civilizing principle, the principle of fusion between the Roman and the barbaric world.[*]

That, without its compact organization, the Christian hierarchy could have so rapidly taken possession of the uncultivated minds of the barbarians; that, before the conquest was completed, the conquerors would have universally adopted the religion of the vanquished, if that religion had been recommended to them by nothing but its intrinsic superiority—we agree with M. Guizot in thinking incredible. We do not find that other savages, at other eras, have yielded with similar readiness to the same influences; nor did the minds or lives of the invaders, for some centuries "after" their conversion, give evidence that the real merits of Christianity had made any deep impression upon them. The true explanation is to be found in the power of intellectual superiority. As the condition of secular society became more discouraging, the Church had more and more engrossed to itself whatever of real talents, as well as of sincere philanthropy, existed in the Roman world.

Among the Christians of that epoch, [says M. Guizot,] there were men who had thought of everything—to whom all moral and political questions were familiar; men who had on all subjects well-defined opinions, energetic feelings, and an ardent desire to propagate them and make them predominant. Never did any body of men make such efforts to act upon the world and assimilate it to themselves, as did the Christian Church from the fifth to the

*[Translated from] *Civilisation en France*, Vol. III, pp. 191-2.
[*Translated from *Civilisation en Europe*, Lecture 2, pp. 23-4.]

ʳ⁻ʳ45   to be first
ᵘ⁻ᵘ45   from

tenth century. She attacked Barbarism at almost all points, striving to civilize it by her ascendancy.[*]

In this, the Church was aided by the important temporal position, which, in the general decay of other elements of society, it had assumed in the Roman empire. Alone strong in the midst of weakness, alone possessing natural sources of power within itself, it was the prop to which all things clung which felt themselves in need of support. The clergy, and especially the Prelacy, had become the most influential members of temporal society. All that remained of the former wealth of the Empire had for some time tended more and more in the direction of the Church. At the time of the invasions, we find the bishops very generally invested, under the title of *defensor civitatis*, with a high public character—as the patrons, and towards all strangers the representatives, of the town communities. It was they who treated with the invaders in the name of the natives; it was their adhesion which guaranteed the general obedience; and after the conversion of the conquerors, it was to their sacred character that the conquered were indebted for whatever mitigation they experienced of the fury of conquest.

Thus salutary, and even indispensable, was the influence of the Christian clergy during the confused period of the invasions. M. Guizot has not overlooked, but impartially analysed, the mixed character of good and evil which belonged even in that age, and still more in the succeeding ages, to the power of the Church. One beneficial consequence which he ascribes to it is worthy of especial notice; the separation (unknown to antiquity) between temporal and spiritual authority. He, in common with the best thinkers of our time, attributes to this fact the happiest influence on European civilization. It was the parent, he says, of liberty of conscience. "The separation of temporal and spiritual is founded on the idea, that material force has no right, no hold, over the mind, over conviction, over truth."[†] Enormous as have been the sins of the Catholic Church in the way of religious intolerance, her assertion of this principle has done more for human freedom, than all the fires she ever kindled have done to destroy it. Toleration cannot exist, or exists only as a consequence of contempt, where, Church and State being virtually the same body, disaffection to the national worship is treason to the State; as is sufficiently evidenced by Grecian and Roman history, notwithstanding the fallacious appearance of liberality inherent in Polytheism, which did not prevent, as long as the national religion continued in vigour, almost every really free thinker of any ability in the freest city of Greece, from being either banished or put to death for blasphemy.* In more recent times, where the chief of the State has been also the supreme pontiff, not, as in England, only nominally, but substantially (as in the case of China, Russia, the Caliphs, and the Sultans of

[*Translated from *ibid.*, Lecture 3, pp. 22-3.]
[†Translated from *ibid.*, Lecture 2, p. 30.]
*Anaxagoras, Protagoras, Socrates, Aristotle, &c.

Constantinople,) the result has been a perfection of despotism, and a voluntary abasement under its yoke, which have no parallel elsewhere except among the most besotted barbarians.

It remains to assign, in the elemental chaos from which the modern nations arose, the Germanic or barbaric element. What has Europe derived from the barbarian invaders? M. Guizot answers—the spirit of liberty. That spirit, as it exists in the modern world, is something which had never before been found in company with civilization. The liberty of the ancient commonwealths did not mean individual freedom of action; it meant a certain form of political organization; and instead of asserting the private freedom of each citizen, it was compatible with a more ᵛcompleteᵛ subjection of every individual to the State, and a more active interference of the ruling powers with private conduct, than is the practice of what are now deemed the most despotic governments. The modern spirit of liberty, on the contrary, is the love of individual independence; the claim for freedom of action, with as little interference as is compatible with the necessities of society, from any authority other than the conscience of the individual. It is in fact the self-will of the savage, moderated and limited by the demands of civilized life; and M. Guizot is not mistaken in believing that it came to us, not from ancient civilization, but from the savage element infused into that enervated civilization by its barbarous conquerors. He adds, that together with this spirit of liberty, the invaders brought also the spirit of voluntary association; the institution of military patronage, the bond between followers and a leader of their own choice, which afterwards ripened into feudality. This voluntary dependence of man upon man, this relation of protection and service, this spontaneous loyalty to a superior not deriving his authority from law or from the constitution of society, but from the voluntary election of the dependent himself, was unknown to the civilized nations of antiquity; though frequent among savages, and so customary in the Germanic race, as to have been deemed, though erroneously, characteristic of it.

To reconcile, in any moderate degree, these jarring elements; to produce even an endurable state of society, not to say a prosperous and improving one, by the amalgamation of savages and slaves, was a work of many centuries. M. Guizot's Lectures are chiefly occupied in tracing the progress of this work, and showing by what agencies it was accomplished. The history of the European nations consists of three periods; the period of confusion, the feudal period, and the modern period. The Lectures of 1828 include, though on a very compressed scale, all the three; but only in relation to the history of society, omitting that of thought, and of the human mind. In the following year, the Professor took a wider range. The three volumes which contain the Lectures of 1829, are a complete historical analysis of the period of confusion; expounding, with sufficient fulness of detail, both the state of political society in each successive stage of that prolonged anarchy, and the state of

ᵛ⁻ᵛ45   unbounded

intellect, as evidenced by literature and speculation. In these volumes, M. Guizot is the philosopher of the period of which M. Augustin Thierry is the painter. In the Lectures of 1830—which, having been prematurely broken off by the political events of that year, occupy (with the *Pièces Justificatives*) only two volumes—he commenced a similar analysis of the feudal period; but did not quite complete the political and social part of the subject: the examination of the intellectual products of the period was not even commenced. In this state this great unfinished monument still remains. Imperfect, however, as it is, it contains much more than we can attempt to bring under even the most cursory review within our narrow limits. We can only pause and dwell upon the important epochs, and upon speculations which involve some great and fertile idea, or throw a strong light upon some interesting portion of the history. Among these last we must include the passage in which M. Guizot describes the manner in which the civilization of the conquered impressed the imagination of the victors.

We have just passed in review the closing age of the Roman civilization, and we found it in full *décadence*, without force, without fecundity, incapable almost of keeping itself alive. We now behold it vanquished and ruined by the barbarians; when on a sudden it reappears fruitful and powerful: it assumes over the institutions and manners which are brought newly into contact with it, a prodigious empire; it impresses on them more and more its own character; it governs and metamorphoses its conquerors.

Among many causes, there were two which principally contributed to this result: the power of a systematic and comprehensive body of civil law; and the natural ascendancy of civilization over barbarism.

In fixing themselves to a single abode, and becoming landed proprietors, the barbarians contracted, both with the Roman population and with each other, relations more various and durable than any they had previously known; their civil existence assumed greater breadth and stability. The Roman law was alone fit to regulate this new existence; it alone could deal adequately with such a multitude of relations. The barbarians, however they might strive to preserve their own customs, were caught, as it were, in the "meshes" of this scientific legislation, and were obliged to bring the new social order, in a great measure, into subjection to it, not politically indeed, but civilly.

Further, the spectacle itself of Roman civilization exercised a great empire over their minds. What strikes our modern fancy, what we greedily seek for in history, in poems, travels, romances, is the picture of a state of society unlike the regularity of our own; savage life, with its independence, its novelty, and its adventure. Quite different were the impressions of the barbarians. What to them was striking, what appeared to them great and wonderful, was civilization; the monuments of Roman industry, the cities, roads, aqueducts, amphitheatres; that society so orderly, so provident, so full of variety in its fixity—this was the object of their admiration and their astonishment. Though conquerors, they were sensible of inferiority to the conquered. The barbarian might despise the Roman as an individual being, but the Roman world in its *ensemble* appeared to him something above his level; and all the great men of the age of the conquests, Alaric, Ataulph, Theodoric, and so many others, while destroying and trampling upon Roman society, used all their efforts to copy it.*

*[Translated from] *Civilisation en France*, Vol. I, pp. 386-8.

w-w45   nets

But their attempt was fruitless. It was not by merely seating themselves in the throne of the Emperors, that the chiefs of the barbarians could reinfuse life into a social order to which, when already perishing by its own infirmities, they had dealt the final blow. Nor was it in that old form that peaceful and regular government could be restored to Europe. The confusion was too chaotic to admit of so easy a disentanglement. Before fixed institutions could become possible, it was necessary to have a fixed population; and this primary condition was long unattained. Bands of barbarians, of various races, with no bond of national union, overran the Empire, without mutual concert, and occupied the country as much as a people so migratory and vagabond could be said to occupy it; but even the loose ties which held together each tribe or band, became relaxed by the consequences of spreading themselves over an extensive territory; fresh hordes, too, were ever pressing on *from* behind; and the very first requisite of order, permanent territorial limits, could not establish itself, either between properties or sovereignties, for nearly three centuries. The annals of the conquered countries during the intermediate period, but chronicle the desultory warfare of the invaders with one another; the effect of which, to the conquered, was a perpetual renewal of suffering, and increase of impoverishment.

M. Guizot dates the termination of this downward period from the reign of Charlemagne; others (for example, M. de Sismondi)[*] have placed it later. We are inclined to agree with M. Guizot; no part of whose work seems to us more admirable than that in which he fixes the place in history of that remarkable man.*

The name of Charlemagne, says M. Guizot, has come down to us as one of the greatest in history. Though not the founder of his dynasty, he has given his name both to his race and to the age.

The homage paid to him is often blind and undistinguishing; his genius and glory are extolled without discrimination or measure; yet at the same time, persons repeat, one after another, that he founded nothing, accomplished nothing; that his empire, his laws, all his works, perished with him. And this historical commonplace introduces a crowd of moral commonplaces, on the ineffectualness and uselessness of great men, the vanity of their projects, the little trace which they leave in the world after having troubled it in all directions. Is this true? Is it the destiny of great men to be merely a burden and a useless wonder to mankind? . . .

At the first glance, the commonplace might be supposed to be a truth. The victories, conquests, institutions, reforms, projects, all the greatness and glory of Charlemagne, vanished with him; he seemed a meteor suddenly emerging from the darkness of barbarism, to be as suddenly lost and extinguished in the shadow of feudality. There are other such examples in history. . . .

But we must beware of trusting these appearances. To understand the meaning of great

[*Jean Charles Léonard Simonde de Sismondi, *Histoire des Français*, 31 vols. (Paris: Treuttel and Würtz, 1821-44), e.g., Vol. III, pp. 274-5.]

Civilisation en France, Vol. II, Lecture 20 [pp. 262-308].

^{x-x}+67

events, and measure the agency and influence of great men, we need to look far deeper into the matter.

The activity of a great man is of two kinds; he performs two parts; two epochs may generally be distinguished in his career. First, he understands better than other people the wants of his time; its real, present exigencies; what, in the age he lives in, society needs, to enable it to subsist, and attain its natural development. He understands these wants better than any other person of the time, and knows better than any other how to wield the powers of society, and direct them skilfully towards the realization of this end. Hence proceed his power and glory; it is in virtue of this, that as soon as he appears, he is understood, accepted, followed—that all give their willing aid to the work, which he is performing for the benefit of all.

But he does not stop here. When the real wants of his time are in some degree satisfied, the ideas and the will of the great man proceed further. He quits the region of present facts and exigencies; he gives himself up to views in some measure personal to himself; he indulges in combinations more or less vast and specious, but which are not, like his previous labours, founded on the actual state, the common instincts, the determinate wishes of society, but are remote and arbitrary. He aspires to extend his activity and influence indefinitely, and to possess the future as he has possessed the present.

Here egoism and illusion commence. For some time, on the faith of what he has already done, the great man is followed in this new career; he is believed in, and obeyed; men lend themselves to his fancies; his flatterers and his dupes even admire and vaunt them as his sublimest conceptions. The public, however, in whom a mere delusion is never of any long continuance, soon discovers that it is impelled in a direction in which it has no desire to move. At first the great man had enlisted his high intelligence and powerful will in the service of the general feeling and wish: he now seeks to employ the public force in the service of his individual ideas and desires; he is attempting things which he alone wishes or understands. Hence disquietude first, and then uneasiness; for a time he is still followed, but sluggishly and reluctantly; next he is censured and complained of; finally, he is abandoned, and falls; and all which he alone had planned and desired, all the merely personal and arbitrary part of his works, perishes with him.[*]

After briefly illustrating his remarks by the example of Napoleon—so often, by his flatterers, represented as another Charlemagne, a comparison which is the height of injustice to the earlier conqueror—M. Guizot observes, that the wars of Charlemagne were of a totally different character from those of the previous dynasty. "They were not dissensions between tribe and tribe, or chief and chief, nor expeditions engaged in for the purpose of settlement or of pillage; they were systematic wars, inspired by a political purpose, and commanded by a public necessity."[†] Their purpose was no other than that of putting an end to the invasions. He repelled the Saracens: the Saxons and Sclavonians, against whom merely defensive arrangements were not sufficient, he attacked and subjugated in their native forests.

At the death of Charlemagne, the conquests cease, the unity disappears, the empire is dismembered and falls to pieces; but is it true that nothing remained, that the warlike

[*Translated from *ibid.*, pp. 262-5.]
[†Translated from *ibid.*, p. 273.]

exploits of Charlemagne were absolutely sterile, that he achieved nothing, founded nothing?

There is but one way to resolve this question: it is, to ask ourselves if, after Charlemagne, the countries which he had governed found themselves in the same situation as before; if the twofold invasions which, on the north and on the south, menaced their territory, their religion, and their race, recommenced after being thus suspended; if the Saxons, Sclavonians, Avars, Arabs, still kept the possessors of the Roman empire in perpetual disturbance and anxiety. Evidently it was not so. True, the empire of Charlemagne was broken up, but into separate states, which arose as so many barriers at all points where there was still danger. To the time of Charlemagne, the frontiers of Germany, Spain, and Italy were in continual fluctuation; no constituted public force had attained a permanent shape; he was compelled to be constantly transporting himself from one end to the other of his dominions, in order to oppose to the invaders the moveable and temporary force of his armies. After him, the scene is changed; real political barriers, states more or less organized, but real and durable, arose; the kingdoms of Lorraine, of Germany, Italy, the two Burgundies, Navarre, date from that time; and in spite of the vicissitudes of their destiny, they subsist, and suffice to oppose effectual resistance to the invading movement. Accordingly that movement ceases, or continues only in the form of maritime expeditions, most desolating at the points which they reach, but which cannot be made with great masses of men, nor produce great results.

Although, therefore, the vast dominion of Charlemagne perished with him, it is not true that he founded nothing; he founded all the states which sprung from the dismemberment of his empire. His conquests entered into new combinations, but his wars attained their end. The foundation of the work subsisted, though its form was changed.[*]

In the character of an administrator and a legislator, the career of Charlemagne is still more remarkable than as a conqueror. His long reign was one struggle against the universal insecurity and disorder. He was one of the sort of men described by M. Guizot, "whom the spectacle of anarchy or of social immobility strikes and revolts; whom it shocks intellectually, as a fact which ought not to exist; and who are possessed with the desire to correct it, to introduce some rule, some principle of regularity and permanence, into the world which is before ᵞthemᵞ."[†] Gifted with an unresting activity unequalled perhaps by any other sovereign, Charlemagne passed his life in attempting to convert a chaos into an orderly and regular government; to create a general system of administration, under an efficient central authority. In this attempt he was very imperfectly successful. The government of an extensive country from a central point was too complicated, too difficult; it required the co-operation of too many agents, and of intelligences too much developed, to be capable of being carried on by barbarians. "The disorder around him was immense, invincible; he repressed it for a moment on a single point, but the evil reigned wherever his terrible will had not penetrated; and even where he had passed, it recommenced as soon as he had departed."[‡]

[*Translated from *ibid.*, pp. 276-8.]
[†Translated from *Civilisation en Europe*, Lecture 3, p. 23.]
[‡Translated from *Civilisation en France*, Vol. II, pp. 278-9.]

ᵞ⁻ᵞ45   their view

Nevertheless, his efforts were not lost—not wholly unfruitful. His instrument of government was composed of two sets of functionaries, local and central. The local portion consisted of the resident governors, the dukes, counts, &c., together with the vassals or *beneficiarii*, afterwards called feudatories, to whom when lands had been granted, a more or less indefinite share had been delegated of the authority and jurisdiction of the sovereign. The central machinery consisted of *missi dominici*—temporary agents sent into the provinces, and from one province to another, as the sovereign's own representatives; to inspect, control, report, and even reform what was amiss, either in act or negligence, on the part of the local functionaries. Over all these the prince held, with a firm hand, the reins of government; aided by a national assembly or convocation of chiefs, when he chose to summon it, either because he desired their counsel or needed their moral support.

Is it possible that of this government, so active and vigorous, nothing remained—that all disappeared with Charlemagne, that he founded nothing for the internal consolidation of society?

What fell with Charlemagne, what rested upon him alone, and could not survive him, was the central government. After continuing some time under Louis le Débonnaire and Charles le Chauve, but with less and less energy and influence, the general assemblies, the *missi dominici*, the whole machinery of the central and sovereign administration, disappeared. Not so the local government, the dukes, counts, *vicaires*, *centeniers*, *beneficiarii*, vassals who held authority in their several neighbourhoods under the rule of Charlemagne. Before his time, the disorder had been as great in each locality as in the commonwealth generally; landed properties, magistracies, were incessantly changing hands; no local positions or influences possessed any steadiness or permanence. During the forty-six years of his government, these influences had time to become rooted in the same soil, in the same families; they had acquired stability, the first condition of the progress which was destined to render them independent and hereditary, and make them the elements of the feudal *régime*. Nothing, certainly, less resembles feudalism than the sovereign unity which Charlemagne aspired to establish; yet he is the true founder of feudal society: it was he who, by arresting the external invasions, and repressing to a certain extent the intestine disorders, gave to situations, to fortunes, to local influences, sufficient time to take real possession of the country. After him, his general government perished like his conquests, his unity of authority like his extended empire; but as the empire was broken into separate states, which acquired a vigorous and durable life, so the central sovereignty of Charlemagne resolved itself into a multitude of local sovereignties, to which a portion of the strength of his government had been imparted, and which had acquired under its shelter the conditions requisite for reality and durability. So that in this second point of view, in his civil as well as military capacity, if we look beyond first appearances, he accomplished and founded much.[*]

Thus does a more accurate knowledge correct the two contrary errors, one or other of which is next to universal among superficial thinkers, respecting the influence of great men upon society. A great ruler cannot shape the world after his own pattern; he is condemned to work in the direction of existing and spontaneous tendencies, and has only the discretion of singling out the most beneficial of these.

[*Translated from *ibid.*, pp. 293-5.]

Yet the difference is great between a skilful pilot and none at all, though a pilot cannot steer *in opposition* to wind and tide. Improvements of the very first order, and for which society is completely prepared, which lie in the natural course and tendency of human events, and are the next stage through which mankind will pass, may be retarded indefinitely for want of a great man, to throw the weight of his individual will and faculties into the trembling scale. Without Charlemagne, who can say for how many centuries longer the period of confusion might have been protracted? Yet in this same example it equally appears what a great ruler can *not* do. Like Ataulph, Theodoric, Clovis, all the ablest chiefs of the invaders, Charlemagne dreamed of restoring the Roman Empire.

This was, in him, the portion of egoism and illusion; and in this it was that he failed. The Roman *imperium*, and its unity, were invincibly repugnant to the new distribution of the population, the new relations, the new moral condition of mankind. Roman civilization could only enter as a transformed element into the new world which was preparing. This idea, this aspiration of Charlemagne, was not a public idea, nor a public want: all that he did for its accomplishment perished with him.

Yet even of this vain endeavour, something remained. The name of the Western Empire, revived by him, and the rights which were thought to be attached to the title of Emperor, resumed their place among the elements of history, and were for several centuries longer an object of ambition, an influencing principle of events. Even, therefore, in the purely egotistical and ephemeral portion of his operations, it cannot be said that the ideas of Charlemagne were absolutely sterile, nor totally devoid of duration.[*]

M. Guizot, we think, is scarcely just to Charlemagne in this implied censure upon his attempt to reconstruct civilized society on the only model familiar to him. The most intelligent *cotemporaries* shared his error, and saw in the dismemberment of his Empire, and the fall of his despotic authority, a return to chaos. Though it is easy for us to see, it was difficult for them to foresee, that European society, such as the invasions had made it, admitted of no return to order but through something resembling the feudal system. By the writers who have come down to us from the age in which that system arose, it was looked upon as nothing less than universal anarchy and dissolution. "Consult the poets of the time, consult the chroniclers; they all thought that the world was coming to an end."[†] M. Guizot quotes one of the monuments of the time, a poem by Florus, a deacon of the church at Lyons, which displays with equal *naïveté* the chagrin of the instructed few at the breaking up of the great unsolid structure which Charlemagne had raised, and the satisfaction which the same fact caused to the people at large;[‡] not the only

[*Translated from *ibid.*, pp. 306-7.]

[†Translated from *Civilisation en Europe*, Lecture 4, p. 7.]

[‡Drepanius Florus, "Querela de divisione imperii post mortem Ludovici Pii," in *Recueil des historiens des Gaules et de la France*, ed. Martin Bouquet, *et al.*, 24 vols. (Paris: aux dépens des libraires associés, *et al.*, 1738-1904), Vol. VII (1749), pp. 301-4; quoted by Guizot, *Civilisation en France*, Vol. II, pp. 438-40.]

*z-z*45   save in obedience
*a-a*45   contemporaries

instance in history in which the instinct of the people has been nearer the truth than the considerate judgment of *b*those who clung to historical precedent*b*. That renewal of the onward movement, which even a Charlemagne could not effect by means repugnant to the natural tendencies of the times, took place through the operation of ordinary causes, as soon as society had assumed the form which alone could give rise to fixed expectations and positions, and produce a sort of security.

The moral and the social state of the people at this epoch equally resisted all association, all government of a single and extended character. Mankind had few ideas, and did not look far around. Social relations were rare and restricted. The horizon of thought and of life was exceedingly limited. Under such conditions, a great society is impossible. What are the natural and necessary bonds of political union? On the one hand, the number and extent of the social relations; on the other, of the ideas, whereby men communicate and are held together. Where neither of these are numerous or extensive, the bonds of a great society or state are non-existent. Such were the times of which we now speak. Small societies, local governments, cut, as it were, to the measure of existing ideas and relations, were alone possible; and these alone succeeded in establishing themselves. The elements of these little societies and little governments were ready-made. The possessors of benefices by grant from the king, or of domains occupied by conquest, the counts, dukes, governors of provinces, were disseminated throughout the country. These became the natural centres of associations co-extensive with them. Round these was agglomerated, voluntarily or by force, the neighbouring population, whether free or in bondage. Thus were formed the petty states called fiefs; and this was the real cause of the dissolution of the empire of Charlemagne.*

We have now, therefore, arrived at the opening of the feudal period; and have to attempt to appreciate what the feudal society was, and what was the influence of that society and of its institutions, on the fortunes of the human race; what new elements it introduced; what new tendencies it impressed upon human nature; or to which of the existing tendencies it imparted additional strength.

M. Guizot's estimate of feudalism is among the most interesting, and *c*on the whole, the most*c* satisfactory, of his speculations. He observes, that sufficient importance is seldom attached to the effects produced upon the mental nature of mankind by mere changes in their outward mode of living:

Every one is aware of the notice which has been taken of the influence of climate, and the importance attached to it by Montesquieu.[*] If we confine ourselves to the direct influence of diversity of climate upon mankind, it is perhaps less than has been supposed; the appreciation of it is, at all events, difficult and vague. But the indirect effects, those for instance which result from the fact, that in a warm climate *d*people live in the open air, while in cold countries they shut themselves up in their houses—that they subsist upon different kinds of food, and the like—are highly important, and, merely by their influence on the

*[Translated from] *Civilisation en France*, Vol. II, pp. 451-2.

[*Charles Louis de Secondat, baron de la Brède et de Montesquieu, *De l'esprit des loix*, 2 vols. (Geneva: Barillot, 1748), Vol. I, pp. 360-443 (Bks. XIV-XVII).]

*b-b*45   the instructed
*c-c*45   most completely
*d*45,59   the

details of material existence, act powerfully on civilization. Every great revolution produces in the state of society some changes of this sort, and these ought to be carefully observed.

The introduction of the feudal *régime* occasioned one such change, of which the importance cannot be overlooked; it altered the distribution of the population over the face of the country. Till that time, the masters of the soil, the sovereign class, lived collected in masses more or less numerous—either sedentary in the towns, or wandering in bands over the country. In the feudal state these same persons lived insulated, each in his own habitation, at great distances from one another. It is obvious how great an influence this change must have exercised over the character and progress of civilization. Social preponderance and political power passed from the towns to the country; private property and private life assumed pre-eminence over public. This first effect of the triumph of the feudal principle, appears more fruitful in consequences, the longer we consider it.

Let us examine feudal society as it is in its own nature, looking at it first of all in its simple and fundamental element. Let us figure to ourselves a single possessor of a fief in his own domain; and consider what will be the character of the little association which groups itself around him.

He establishes himself in a retired and defensible place, which he takes care to render safe and strong; he there erects what he terms his castle. With whom does he establish himself there? With his wife and his children: probably also some few freemen who have not become landed proprietors, have attached themselves to his person, and remain domesticated with him. These are all the inmates of the castle itself. Around it, and under its protection, collects a small population of labourers—of serfs, who cultivate the domain of the seigneur. Amidst this inferior population religion comes, builds a church and establishes a priest. In the early times of feudality, this priest is at once the chaplain of the castle and the parish clergyman of the village; at a later period the two characters are separated. This, then, is the organic molecule, the unit, if we may so speak, of feudal society. This we have to summon before us, and demand an answer to the two questions which should be addressed to every fact in history—what was it calculated to do towards the development, first of man, and next of society?*

The first of its peculiarities, he continues, is the prodigious importance which the head of this little association must assume in his own eyes, and ᵉinᵉ those of all around him. To the liberty of the man and the warrior, the sentiment of personality and individual independence, which predominated in savage life, is now added the importance of the master, the landed proprietor, the head of a family. No feeling of self-importance comparable to this, is habitually generated in any other known form of civilization. A Roman patrician, for example, "was the head of a family, was a master, a superior; he was, besides, a religious magistrate, a pontiff in the interior of his family." But the importance of a religious magistrate is not personal; it is borrowed from the divinity whom he serves. In civil life the patrician

was a member of the senate—of a corporation which lived united in one place. This again was an importance derived from without; borrowed and reflected from that of his corporation. The grandeur of the ancient aristocracies was associated with religious and

*[Translated from] *Civilisation en Europe*, Lecture 4 [pp. 9-12].

ᵉ⁻ᵉ+67

political functions; it belonged to the situation, to the corporation at large, more than to the individual. That of the possessor of a fief is, on the contrary, purely personal. He receives nothing from any one; his rights, his powers, come from himself alone. He is not a religious magistrate, nor a member of a senate; all his importance centres in his own person; whatever he is, he is by his own right, and in his own name. Above him, no superior of whom he is the representative and the interpreter; around him, no equals; no rigorous universal law to curb him; no external force habitually controlling his will; he knows no restraint but the limits of his strength, or the presence of an immediate danger. With what intensity must not such a situation act upon the mind of the man who occupies ^{f}it!^{f} What boundless pride, what haughtiness—to speak plainly, what insolence—must arise in his ^{g}soul!$^{g[*]}$

We pass to the influence of this new state of society upon the development of domestic feelings and family life.

History exhibits to us the family in several different shapes. First, the patriarchal family, as seen in the Bible and ^{h}in^h the various monuments of the East. The family is here numerous, and amounts to a tribe. The chief, or patriarch, lives in a state of community with his children, his kindred (of whom all the various generations are grouped around him), and his domestics. Not only does he live with them, but his interests and occupations are the same with theirs; he leads the same life. This is the situation of Abraham, of the patriarchs, of the chiefs of Arab tribes, who are in our own days a faithful image of patriarchal society.

Another form of the family is the clan—that little association, the type of which must be sought in Scotland and Ireland, and through which, probably a great part of the European world has at some time passed. This is no longer ^{i}a^i patriarchal family. Between the chief and the rest of the people there is now a great difference of condition. He does not lead the same life with his followers: they mostly cultivate and serve; he takes his ease, and has no occupation save that of a warrior. But he and they have a common origin; they bear the same name; their relationship, their ancient traditions, and their community of affections and recollections establish among all the members of the clan a moral union, a kind of equality.

Does the feudal family resemble either of these types? Evidently not. At first sight it has some apparent resemblance to the clan; but the difference is immense. The population which surrounds the possessor of the fief are perfect strangers to him; they do not bear his name; they have no relationship to him, are connected with him by no tie, historical or moral. Neither does he, as in the patriarchal family, lead the same life and carry on the same labour as those about him: he has no occupation but war; they are tillers of the ground. The feudal family is not numerous; it does not constitute a tribe; it is confined to the family in the most restricted sense, the wife and children; it lives apart from the rest of the people, in the interior of the castle. Five or six persons, in a position at once alien from, and superior to, all others, constitute the feudal family. . . . Internal life, domestic society, are certain here to acquire a great preponderance. I grant that the rudeness and violent passions of the chief, and his habit of passing his time in war and in the chase, must obstruct and retard the formation of domestic habits; but that obstacle will be overcome. The chief must return habitually to his own home; there he always finds his wife, his children, and them alone, or almost alone; they, and no others, compose his permanent society—they alone always

[*Translated from *ibid.*, pp. 13-14.]

$^{f-f}$45   it? [Source *has*!]
$^{g-g}$45   soul? [Source *has*!]
$^{h-h}$+67
$^{i-i}$45,59   the

partake his interest, his destiny. It is impossible that domestic life should not acquire a great ascendancy. The proofs are abundant. Was it not in the feudal family that the importance of women took its rise? In all the societies of antiquity, not only where no family spirit existed, but where that spirit was powerful, for instance in the patriarchal societies, women did not occupy anything like the place which they acquired in Europe under the feudal polity. The cause of this has been looked for in the peculiar manners of the ancient Germans; in a characteristic respect which it is affirmed that, in the midst of their forests, they paid to women. German patriotism has built upon one sentence of Tacitus a fancied superiority, a primitive and ineffaceable purity of German manners in the relations of the sexes to each other.[*] Mere chimeras! Expressions similar to those of Tacitus, sentiments and usages analogous to those of the ancient Germans, are found in the recitals of many observers of barbarous tribes. There is nothing peculiar in the matter, nothing characteristic of any particular race. The importance of women in Europe arose from the progress and preponderance of domestic manners; and that preponderance became, at an early period, an essential character of feudal life.[†]

In corroboration of these remarks, he observes in another place, that in the feudal form of society (unlike all those which preceded it) the representative of the chief's person and the delegate of his authority, during his frequent absences, was the *châtelaine*. In his warlike expeditions and hunting excursions, his crusadings and his captivities, she directed his affairs, and governed his people with a power equal to his own.[‡] No importance comparable to this, no position equally calculated to call forth the human faculties, had fallen to the lot of women, before, nor, it may be added, since. And the fruits are seen in the many examples of heroic women which the feudal annals present to us; women who fully equalled, in every masculine virtue, the bravest of the men with whom they were associated; often greatly surpassed them in prudence, and fell short of them only in ferocity.

M. Guizot now turns from the seigneurial abode to the dependent population surrounding it. Here all things present a far worse aspect.

In any social situation which lasts a certain length of time, there inevitably arises between those whom it brings into contact, under whatever conditions, a certain moral tie—certain feelings of protection, of benevolence, of affection. It was thus in the feudal society: one cannot doubt, that in process of time there were formed between the cultivators and their seigneur some moral relations, some habits of sympathy. But this happened in spite of their relative position, and nowise from its influence. Considered in itself, the situation was radically vicious. There was nothing morally in common between the feudal superior and the cultivators; they were part of his domain, they were his property. . . . Between the seigneur and those who tilled the ground which belonged to him, there were (as far as this can ever be said when human beings are brought together) no laws, no protection, no society. Hence, I conceive, that truly prodigious and invincible detestation which the rural population has entertained in all ages for the feudal *régime*. . . . Theocratic and monarchical despotism have more than once obtained the acquiescence, and almost the affection, of the

[*Tacitus, *Germania*, in *Dialogus, Agricola, Germania* (Latin and English), trans. Maurice Hutton (London: Heinemann; New York: Macmillan, 1914), pp. 268-70.]

[†Translated from *Civilisation en Europe*, Lecture 4, pp. 14-18.]

[‡*Civilisation en France*, Vol. IV, p. 171.]

population subject to them. The reason is, theocracy and monarchy exercise their dominion in virtue of some belief common to the master with his subjects; he is the representative and minister of another power, superior to all human powers; he speaks and acts in the name of the Deity, or of some general idea, not in the name of the man himself, of a mere man. Feudal despotism is a different thing; it is the mere power of one individual over another, the domination and capricious will of a human being. . . . Such was the real, the distinctive character of the feudal dominion, and such the origin of the antipathy it never ceased to inspire.[*]

Leaving the contemplation of the elementary molecule (as M. Guizot calls it) of feudal society—a single possessor of a fief with his family and dependents—and proceeding to consider the nature of the larger society, or state, which was formed by the aggregation of these small societies, we find the feudal *régime* to be absolutely incompatible with any real national existence. No doubt, the obligations of service on the one hand, and protection on the other, theoretically attached to the concession of a fief, kept alive some faint notions of a general government, some feelings of social duty. But, in the whole duration of the system, it was never found practicable to attach to these rights and obligations any efficient sanction. A central government, with power adequate to enforce even the recognised duties of the feudal relation, or to keep the peace between the different members of the confederacy, did not and could not exist consistently with feudalism. The very essence of feudality was (to borrow M. Guizot's definition) the fusion of property and sovereignty. The lord of the soil was not only the master of all who dwelt upon it, but he was their only superior, their sovereign. Taxation, military protection, judicial administration, were his alone; for all offices of a ruler, the people looked to him, and could look to no other. The king was absolute, like all other feudal lords, within his own domain, and only there. He could neither compel obedience from his feudatories, nor impose his mediation as an arbitrator between them. Among such petty potentates, the only union compatible with the nature of the case was a federal union—the most difficult to maintain of all political organizations; one which, resting almost entirely on moral sanctions, and an enlightened sense of distant interests, requires, more than any other social system, an advanced state of civilization. The middle age was nowise ripe for it; the sword, therefore, remained the universal umpire; all questions were decided either by private war, or by that judicial combat which was the first attempt of society (as the modern duel is the last) to subject the prosecution of a quarrel by force of arms to the moderating influence of fixed customs and ordinances.

The following is M. Guizot's summary of the influences of feudalism on the progress of the European nations.

Feudality must have exercised a considerable, and on the whole a salutary, influence on the internal development of the individual; it raised up in the human mind some moral

[*Translated from *Civilisation en Europe*, Lecture 4, pp. 18-20.]

notions and moral wants, some energetic sentiments; it produced some noble developments of character and passion. Considered in a social point of view, it was not capable of establishing legal order or political securities; but it was indispensable as a recommencement of European society, which had been so broken up by barbarism as to be unable to assume any more enlarged or more regular form. But the feudal form, radically bad in itself, admitted neither of being expanded nor regularized. The only political right which feudalism has planted deeply in European society, is the right of resistance. I do not mean legal resistance; that was out of the question in a society so little advanced. The right of resistance which feudal society asserted and exercised, was the right of personal resistance—a fearful, an anti-social right, since it is an appeal to force, to war, the direct antithesis of society; but a right which never ought to perish from the breast of man, since its abrogation is simply equivalent to submission to slavery. The sentiment of this right had been lost in the degeneracy of Roman society, from the ruins of which it could not again arise; as little, in my opinion, was it a natural emanation from the principles of Christian society. Feudality re-introduced it into European life. It is the glory of civilization to render this right for ever useless and inactive; it is the glory of the feudal society to have constantly asserted and held fast to it.[*]

There is yet another aspect, and far from an unimportant one, in which feudal life has bequeathed, to the times which followed, a lesson worthy to be studied. Imperfect as the world still remains in justice and humanity, the feudal world was far inferior to it in those attributes, but greatly superior in individual strength of will, and decision of character.

No reasonable person will deny the immensity of the social reform which has been accomplished in our times. Never have human relations been regulated with more justice, nor produced a more general well-being as the result. Not only this, but, I am convinced, a corresponding moral reform has also been accomplished; at no epoch perhaps has there been, all things considered, so much honesty in human life, so many human beings living in an orderly manner; never has so small an amount of public force been necessary to repress individual wrong-doing. But in another respect we have, I think, much to gain. We have lived for half a century under the empire of general ideas, more and more accredited and powerful; under the pressure of formidable, almost irresistible events. There has resulted a certain weakness, a certain effeminacy, in our minds and characters. Individual convictions and will are wanting in energy and confidence in themselves. Men assent to a prevailing opinion, obey a general impulse, yield to an external necessity. Whether for resistance or for action, each has but a mean idea of his own strength, a feeble reliance on his own judgment. Individuality, the inward and personal energy of man, is weak and timid. Amidst the progress of public liberty, many seem to have lost the proud and invigorating sentiment of their own personal liberty.

Such was not the Middle Age. The condition of society was deplorable, the morality of mankind much inferior to what is often asserted, much inferior to that of our own time. But in many persons, individuality was strong, will was energetic. There were then few ideas which ruled all minds, few outward forces which, in all situations and in all places, weighed upon men's characters. The individual unfolded himself in his own way, with an irregular freedom: the moral nature of man shone forth here and there in all its ambitious aspirations, with all its energy. A contemplation not only dramatic and attaching, but instructive and

[*Translated from *ibid.*, pp. 30-2.]

useful; which offers us nothing to regret, nothing to imitate, but much to learn; were it only by awakening our attention to what is wanting in ourselves—by showing to us of what a human being is capable when he will.*

The third period of modern history, which is emphatically the modern period, is more complex and more difficult to interpret than the two preceding. Of this period, M. Guizot had only begun to treat; and we must not expect to find his explanations as satisfactory as in the earlier portions of his subject. The origin of feudalism, its character, its place in the history of civilization, he has discussed, as has been seen, in a manner which leaves little to be desired: but we cannot extend the same praise to his account of its decline, which (it is but fair to consider) is not completed; but which, so far as it has gone, appears to us to bear few marks of that piercing insight into the heart of a question, that determination not to be paid with a mere show of explanation, which are the characteristic ʲexcellenciesʲ of the speculations thus far brought to notice.

M. Guizot ascribes the fall of feudality mainly to its imperfections. It did not, he says, contain in itself the elements of durability. It was a first step out of barbarism, but too near the verge of the former anarchy to admit of becoming a permanent social organization. The independence of the possessors of fiefs was evidently excessive, and too little removed from the savage state. "Accordingly, independently of all foreign causes, feudal society, by its own nature and tendencies, was always in question, always on the brink of dissolution; incapable at least of subsisting regularly or of developing itself, without altering its nature."†

He then sets forth how, in the absence of any common superior, of any central authority capable of protecting the feudal chiefs against one another, they were content to seek protection where they could find it—namely, from the most powerful among themselves; how, from this natural tendency, those who were already strong, ever became stronger; the larger fiefs went on aggrandizing themselves at the expense of the weaker. "A prodigious inequality soon arose among the possessors of fiefs,"[*] and inequality of strength led, as it usually does, to inequality of claims, and at last, of recognised rights.

Thus, from the mere fact that social ties were wanting to feudality, the feudal liberties themselves rapidly perished; the excesses of individual independence were perpetually compromising society itself; it found in the relations of the possessors of fiefs, neither the means of regular maintenance, nor of ulterior development; it sought in other institutions the conditions which were needful to it for becoming permanent, regular, and progressive. The tendency towards centralization, towards the formation of a power superior to the local powers, was rapid. Long before the royal government had begun to intervene at every point of the country, there had grown up, under the name of duchies, counties, viscounties, &c.

*[Translated from] *Civilisation en France*, Vol. IV, pp. 29-31.
†*Ibid.*, pp. 364-6. [The translated quotation is on p. 366.]
[*Translated from *ibid.*, p. 366.]

ʲ⁻ʲ45,59 excellences

many smaller royalties, invested with the central government of this or that province, and to whom the rights of the possessors of fiefs, that is, of the local sovereignties, became more and more subordinate.*

This sketch of the progressive decomposition of the feudal organization, is, no doubt, historically correct; but we desiderate in it any approach to a scientific explanation of the phenomenon. That is an easy solution which accounts for the destruction of institutions from their own defects; but experience proves, that forms of government and social arrangements do not fall, merely because they deserve to fall. The more backward and the more degraded any form of society is, the stronger is the tendency to remain stagnating in that state, simply because it is an existing state. We are unable to recognise in this theory of the decay of feudality, the philosopher who so clearly demonstrated its origin; who pointed out that the feudal polity established itself not because it was a good form of society, but because society was incapable of a better; because the rarity of communications, the limited range of men's ideas and of their social relations, and their want of skill to work political machinery of a delicate or complicated construction, disqualified them from being either chiefs or members of ^{k}an^k organized association extending beyond their immediate neighbourhood. If feudality was a product of this condition of the human mind, and the only form of polity which it admitted of, no evils inherent in feudality could have hindered it from continuing so long as that cause subsisted. The anarchy which existed as between one feudal chief and another—the inequality of their talents, and the accidents of their perpetual warfare—would have led to continual changes in the state of territorial possession, and large governments would have been often formed by the agglomeration of smaller ones, occasionally perhaps a great empire like that of Charlemagne: but both the one and the other would have crumbled again to fragments as that did, if the general situation of society had continued to be what it was when the feudal system originated. Is not this the very history of society in a great part of the East, from the earliest record of events? Between the time when masses could not help dissolving into particles, and the time when those particles spontaneously reassembled themselves into masses, a great change must have taken place in the molecular properties of the atoms. Inasmuch as the petty district sovereignties of the first age of feudality coalesced into larger provincial sovereignties, which, instead of obeying the original tendency to decomposition, tended in the very contrary direction, towards ultimate aggregation into one national government; it is clear that the state of society had become compatible with extensive governments ^{l}. The^l unfavourable circumstances which M. Guizot commemorated in the former period, had in some manner ceased to exist; a great

*[Translated from] *ibid.*, pp. 370-1.

$^{k-k}$45   any
$^{l-l}$45   ; the

progress in civilization had been accomplished, under the dominion and auspices of the feudal system; and the fall of the system was not really owing to its vices, but to its good qualities—to the improvement which had been found possible under it, and by which mankind had become desirous of obtaining, and capable of realizing, a better form of society than it afforded.

What this change was, and how it came to pass, M. Guizot has left us to seek. Considerable light is, no doubt, incidentally thrown upon it by the course of his investigations, and the sequel of his work would probably have illustrated it still more. At present, the philosophic interpreter of historical phenomena is indebted to him, on this portion of the subject, for little besides materials.

It was under the combined assaults of two powers—royalty from above, the emancipated commons from below—that the independence of the great vassals finally succumbed. M. Guizot has delineated with great force and perspicuity the rise of both these powers. His review of the origin and emancipation of the communes, and the growth of the *tiers-état*, is one of the best executed portions of the book; and should be read with M. Thierry's *Letters on the History of France*,[*] as the moral of the tale. In his fifth volume, M. Guizot traces, with considerable minuteness, the progress of the royal authority, from its slumbering infancy in the time of the earlier Capetians, through its successive stages of growth—now by the energy and craft of Philippe Auguste, now by the justice and enlightened policy of Saint Louis—to its attainment, not indeed of recognised despotism, but of almost unlimited power of actual tyranny, in the reign of Philippe le Bel. But on all these imputed causes of the fall of feudalism, the question recurs, what caused the causes themselves? Why was that possible to the successors of Capet, which had been impossible to those of Charlemagne? How, under the detested feudal tyranny, had a set of fugitive serfs, who congregated for mutual protection at a few scattered points, and called them towns, become industrious, rich, and powerful? There can be but one answer; the feudal system, with all its deficiencies, was sufficiently a government, contained within itself a sufficient mixture of authority and liberty, afforded sufficient protection to industry, and encouragement and scope to the development of the human faculties, to enable the natural causes of social improvement to resume their course. What these causes were, and why they have been so much more active in Europe than in parts of the earth which were much earlier civilized, is far too difficult an inquiry to be entered upon in this place. We have already seen what M. Guizot has contributed to its elucidation in the way of general reflection. About the matter of fact, in respect to the feudal period, there can be no doubt. When the history of what are called the dark ages, because they had not yet a vernacular literature, and did not write a correct Latin style, shall be written as it deserves to be, that will be

[*Jacques Nicolas Augustin Thierry, *Lettres sur l'histoire de France* (1827), 5th ed. (Brussels: Hauman, 1836).]

seen by all, which is already recognised by the great historical inquirers of the present time—that at no period of history was human intellect more active, or society more unmistakably in a state of rapid advance *m*, than during a great part of the so much vilified feudal period.*m*

M. Guizot's detailed analysis of the history of European life, is, as we before remarked, only completed for the period preceding the feudal. For the five centuries which extended from Clovis to the last of the Carlovingians,[*] he has given a finished delineation, not only of outward life and political society, but of the progress and vicissitudes of what was then the chief refuge and hope of oppressed humanity, the religious society—the Church. He makes his readers acquainted with the legislation of the period, with the little it possessed of literature or philosophy, and with that which formed, as ought to be remembered, the real and serious occupation of its speculative faculties—its religious labours, whether in the elaboration or in the propagation of the Christian doctrine. His analysis and historical exposition of the Pelagian controversy—his examination of the religious literature of the period, its sermons and legends—are models of their kind; and he does not, like the old school of historians, treat these things as matters insulated and abstract, of no interest save what belongs to them intrinsically, but invariably looks at them as component parts of the general life of the age.

Of the feudal period, M. Guizot had not time to complete a similar delineation. His analysis even of the political society of the period is not concluded; and we are entirely without that review of its ecclesiastical history, and its intellectual and moral life, whereby the deficiency of explanation would probably have been in some degree supplied, which we have complained of in regard to the remarkable progress of human nature and *n*its wants*n* during *o*those*o* ages. For the strictly modern period of history he has done still less. The rapid sketch which occupies the concluding lectures of the first volume, does little towards resolving any of the problems in which there is real difficulty.

We shall therefore pass over the many topics on which he has touched cursorily, and without doing justice to his own powers of thought; and shall only further advert to one question, which is the subject of a detailed examination in the Essay in his earlier volume, "the origin of representative institutions in England"—a question not only of special interest to an English reader, but of much moment in the estimation of M. Guizot's general theory of modern history. For if the natural course of European events was such as that theory represents it, the history of England is an anomalous deviation from that course; and the exception must either

[*Louis V.]

*m-m*45   . From the very commencement of the so much vilified period, every generation overflows with evidences of increasing security, growing industry, and expanding intelligence. But to dwell further on this topic, would be inappropriate to the nature and limits of the present article.
*n-n*45   events
*o-o*45   these

prove, or go far to subvert, the rule. In England as in other European countries, the basis of the social arrangements was, for several centuries, the feudal system; in England as elsewhere, that system perished by the growth of the Crown, and of the emancipated commonalty. Whence came it, that amidst general circumstances so similar, the immediate and apparent consequences were so strikingly contrasted? How happened it, that in the Continental nations absolute monarchy was at least the proximate result, while in England representative institutions, and an aristocratic government with an admixture of democratic elements, were the consequence?

M. Guizot's explanation of the anomaly is just and conclusive. The feudal polity in England was from the first a less barbarous thing—had more in it of the elements from which a government might in time be constructed—than in the other countries of Europe. We have seen M. Guizot's lively picture of the isolated position and solitary existence of the seigneur, ruling from his inaccessible height, with sovereign power, over a scanty population; having no superior above him, no equals around him, no communion or co-operation with any, save his family and dependents; absolute master within a small circle, and with hardly a social tie, or any action or influence, beyond; everything, in short, in one narrow spot, and nothing in any other place. Now, of this picture, we look in vain for the original in our own history. English feudalism knew nothing of this independence and isolation of the individual feudatory in his fief. It could show no single vassal exempt from the habitual control of government, no one so strong that the king's arm could not reach him. Early English history is made up of the acts of the barons, not the acts of this and that and the other baron. The cause of this is to be found in the circumstances of the Conquest. The Normans did not, like the Goths and Franks, overrun and subdue an *almost* unresisting population. They encamped in the midst of a people of spirit and energy, many times more numerous, and almost as warlike as themselves. That they prevailed over them at all was but the result of superior union. That union once broken, they would have been lost. They could not parcel out the country among them, spread themselves over it, and be each king in his own little domain, with nothing to fear save from the other petty kings who surrounded him. They were an army, and in an enemy's country; and an army supposes a commander, and military discipline. Organization of any kind implies power in the chief who presides over it and holds it together. Add to this, what various writers have remarked—that the dispossession of the Saxon proprietors being effected not at once, but gradually, and the spoils not being seized upon by unconnected bands, but systematically portioned out by the head of the conquering expedition among his followers—the territorial possessions of even the most powerful Norman chief were not concentrated in one place, but dispersed in various parts of the kingdom; and, whatever might be their total extent, he was

p-p+59,67

never powerful enough in any given locality to make head against the king. From these causes, royalty was from the beginning much more powerful among the Anglo-Normans than it ever became in France while feudality remained in vigour. But the same circumstances which rendered it impossible for the barons to hold their ground against regal encroachments except by combination, had kept up the power and the habit of combination among them. In French history we never, until a late period, hear of confederacies among the nobles; English history is full of them. Instead of numerous unconnected petty potentates, one of whom was called the King, there are two great figures in English history—a powerful King, and a powerful body of Nobles. To give the needful authority to any act of general government, the concurrence of both was essential: and hence Parliaments, elsewhere only occasional, were in England habitual. But the natural state of these rival powers was one of conflict; and the weaker side, which was usually that of the barons, soon found that it stood in need of assistance. Although the feudatory class, to use M. Guizot's expression, "had converted itself into a real aristocratic corporation,"* the barons were not strong enough "to impose at the same time on the king their liberty, and on the people their tyranny. As they had been obliged to combine for the sake of their own defence, so they found themselves under the necessity of calling in the people in aid of their coalition."†

The people, in England, were the Saxons—a vanquished race, but whose spirit had never, like that of the other conquered populations, been completely broken. Being a German, not a Latin people, they retained the traditions, and some portion of the habits, of popular institutions and personal liberty. When called, therefore, to aid the barons in moderating the power of the Crown, they claimed those ancient liberties as their part of the compact. French history abounds with charters of incorporation, which the kings granted, generally for a pecuniary consideration, to town communities which had cast off their *seigneurs*. The charters which English history is full of, are concessions of general liberties to the whole body of the nation; liberties which the nobility and the commons either wrung from the king by their united strength, or obtained from his voluntary policy as the purchase-money of their obedience. The series of these treaties, for such they in reality were, between the Crown and the nation, beginning with the first Henry, and ending with the last renewal by Edward I of the Great Charter of King John, are the principal incidents of English history during the feudal period. And thus, as M. Guizot observes in his concluding summary—

In France, from the foundation of the monarchy to the fourteenth century, everything was individual—powers, liberties, oppression, and the resistance to oppression. Unity, the principle of all government—association of equals, the principle of all checks—were only found in the narrow sphere of each *seigneurie*, or each city. Royalty was nominal; the

---

*[Translated from] *Essais*, p. 419.
†[Translated from] *ibid*., p. 424.

aristocracy did not form a body; there were burgesses in the towns, but no commons in the State. In England, on the contrary, from the Norman Conquest downwards, everything was collective; similar powers, analogous situations, were compelled to approach one another, to coalesce, to associate. From its origin, royalty was real, while feudality ultimately grouped itself into two masses, one of which became the high aristocracy, the other the body of the commons. Who can mistake, in this first travail of the formation of the two societies, in these so different characteristics of their early age, the true origin of the prolonged difference in their institutions and in their destinies?[*]

M. Guizot returns to this subject in a remarkable passage in the first volume of his Lectures, which presents the different character of the progress of civilization in England and in Continental Europe, in so new and peculiar a light, that we cannot better conclude this article than by quoting it.

When I endeavoured to define the peculiar character of European civilization, compared with those of Asia and of antiquity, I showed that it was superior in variety, richness, and complication; that it never fell under the dominion of any exclusive principle; that the different elements of society co-existed and modified one another, and were always compelled to compromises and mutual toleration. This, which is the general character of European, has been above all that of English civilization. In England, civil and spiritual powers, aristocracy, democracy, and royalty, local and central institutions, moral and political development, have advanced together, if not always with equal rapidity, yet at no great distance after one another. Under the Tudors, for example, at the time of the most conspicuous advances of pure monarchy, the democratic principle, the power of the people, was also rising and gaining strength. The revolution of the seventeenth century breaks out; it is at once a religious and a political one. The feudal aristocracy appears in it, much weakened indeed, and with the signs of *q*decline*q*, but still in a condition to take a part, to occupy a position, and have its share in the results. It is thus with English history throughout: no old element ever perishes entirely, nor is any new one wholly triumphant— no partial principle ever obtains exclusive ascendancy. There is always simultaneous development of the different social powers, and a compromise among their pretensions and interests.

The march of Continental civilization has been less complex and less complete. The several elements of society, religious and civil, monarchical, aristocratic, and democratic, grew up and came to maturity not simultaneously, but successively. Each system, each principle, has in some degree had its turn. One age belongs, it would be too much to say exclusively, but with a very marked predominance, to feudal aristocracy, for example; another to the monarchical principle; another to the democratic. Compare the middle age in France and in England, the eleventh, twelfth, and thirteenth centuries of our history, with the corresponding centuries north of the Channel. In France, you find, at that epoch, feudality nearly absolute—the Crown and the democratic principle almost null. In England, the feudal aristocracy no doubt predominates, but the Crown and the democracy are not without strength and importance. Royalty triumphs in England under Elizabeth, as in France under Louis XIV, but how many *ménagements* it is compelled to observe! How many restrictions, aristocratic and democratic, it has to submit to! In England also, each system, each principle, has had its turn of predominance, but never so completely, never so

[*Translated from *ibid.*, p. 516.]

*q-q*45,59   *décadence*

exclusively, as on the Continent. The victorious principle has always been constrained to tolerate the presence of its rivals, and to concede to each a certain share of influence.*

The advantageous side of the effect of this more equable development is evident enough.

There can be no doubt that this simultaneous unfolding of the different social elements, has greatly contributed to make England attain earlier than any of the Continental nations to the establishment of a government at once orderly and free. It is the very business of government to negotiate with all interests and all powers, to reconcile them with each other, and make them live and prosper together ⌐. Now⌐ this, from a multitude of causes, was already in a peculiar degree the disposition, and even the actual state, of the different elements of English society: a general, and tolerably regular government had therefore less difficulty in constituting itself. So, again, the essence of liberty is the simultaneous manifestation and action of all interests, all rights, all social elements and forces. England, therefore, was already nearer to it than most other States. From the same causes, national good sense, and intelligence of public affairs, formed itself at an earlier period. Good sense in politics consists in taking account of all facts, appreciating them, and giving to each its place: this, in England, was a necessity of her social condition, a natural result of the course of her civilization.[*]

But to a nation, as to an individual, the consequences of doing everything by halves, of adopting compromise as the universal rule, of never following out a general idea or principle to its utmost results, are by no means exclusively favourable. Hear again M. Guizot.

In the Continental States, each system or principle having had its turn of a more complete and exclusive predominance, they unfolded themselves on a larger scale, with more grandeur and *éclat*. Royalty and feudal aristocracy, for example, made their appearance on the Continental scene of action with more boldness, more expansion, more freedom. All political experiments, so to speak, have been fuller and more complete. [This is still more strikingly true of the present age, and its great popular revolutions.] And hence it has happened that political ideas and doctrines (I mean those of an extended character, and not simple good sense applied to the conduct of affairs,) have assumed a loftier character, and unfolded themselves with greater intellectual vigour. Each system having presented itself to observation in some sort alone, and having remained long on the scene, it has been possible to survey it as a whole; to ascend to its first principles, descend to its remotest consequences; in short, fully to complete its theory. Whoever observes attentively the genius of the English nation, will be struck with two facts—the sureness of its common sense and practical ability; its deficiency of general ideas and commanding intellect, as applied to theoretical questions. If we open an English book of history, jurisprudence, or any similar subject, we seldom find in it the real foundation, the ultimate reason of things. In all matters, and especially in politics, pure doctrine and philosophy—science properly so called—have prospered far more on the Continent than in England; they have at least soared higher, with greater vigour and boldness. Nor does it admit of doubt, that the different character of the development of the two civilizations has greatly contributed to this result.[†]

*[Translated from] *Civilisation en Europe*, Lecture 14 [pp. 4-7].
[*Translated from *ibid.*, pp. 7-8.]
[†Translated from *ibid.*, pp. 8-10. The words in square brackets are Mill's.]

⌐⌐45   : now

DUVEYRIER'S POLITICAL VIEWS OF FRENCH AFFAIRS

1846

EDITOR'S NOTE

Edinburgh Review, LXXXIII (Apr., 1846), 453-74. Headed: "Art. VII.—1. *La Pairie dans ses Rapports avec la Situation Politique, son Principe, ses Ressources, son Avenir*. Par M. Charles Duveyrier. 8vo. Paris: [Guyot,] 1842. / 2. *Lettres Politiques*. Par. M. Charles Duveyrier. [2 vols.] 8vo. Paris: [Beck and Amyot,] 1843." Running titles as title. Unsigned. Not republished, but a substantial portion (305-8) quoted in the version of "Tocqueville on Democracy in America [II]" in *Dissertations and Discussions*, II. Identified in Mill's bibliography as "A review of Duveyrier's political pamphlets in the Edinburgh Review for April 1846" (MacMinn, 59). The copy (tear-sheets) in Mill's library, Somerville College, is headed by Mill, "(Edinburgh Review, April 1846)"; it contains no corrections or emendations.

The portion of the text quoted in the *D&D* version of "Tocqueville on Democracy in America [II]" is collated with *D&D*, 1st ed. (1859), and 2nd ed. (1867). In the footnoted variants, "59" indicates *D&D*, 1st ed., and "67" indicates *D&D*, 2nd ed.

For comment on the text, see lxxx–lxxxiii and cvi–cvii above.

Duveyrier's Political Views of French Affairs

THERE ARE SEVERAL CAUSES which make the Political Writings produced at the present time in France, an instructive study to intelligent observers in all countries of Europe.

In the first place, there is much truth in the boast of French writers, that France marches in the van of the European movement. The fact is not necessarily of the highly complimentary character with which those writers generally choose to invest it. Movement is not always progress; and progress itself may be in a downward, as well as in an upward direction. To be foremost in the road which all are travelling, is not of necessity the most honourable position; but it is a position pre-eminently interesting to those who follow. And such, in the present period of the world's history, is the situation of France. The two strongest tendencies of the world in these times are towards Democracy and Revolution; meaning by Democracy—social equality, under whatever form of government; and by Revolution—a general demolition of old institutions and opinions, without reference to its being effected peaceably or violently. In this twofold career, France is the furthest advanced of the European nations. The feelings of her people are nearly as democratic as in the United States; the passion for equality almost as strong. Her institutions indeed infringe upon that equality, by limiting to a narrow class the privilege of electing, or being elected to the Chamber of Deputies. But even these privileges are not hereditary, and carry with them no direct accession of personal rank. In the eye of the law, and in that of private society, there is less difference between man and man than in any other country in Europe. The other European nations are steadily following in the direction of that social equality which, as far as regards the male sex, France has in a great measure realized. That England is undergoing this change as rapidly as the rest, has long been clear to every Englishman who knows any thing more of the world he lives in than the forms of it. Those forms, indeed, subsist with less alteration than in some other countries; but where are the feelings which gave meaning to them? Not the intelligent mechanic only, but the stupidest clown, at heart thinks himself as good as a nobleman; or rather (what is not exactly equivalent) thinks that a nobleman is no better than he; and there are a good many things which indicate, that the nobleman himself secretly thinks much the same.

Not less is France ahead of the rest of Europe, in what may properly, and independently of the specific consequences flowing from it, be called Revolution. Other nations are gradually taking down their old institutions: France, by the sacrifice of a generation, made a clean sweep of hers; and left herself a fair stage, clear of rubbish, for beginning to build anew. France has had her Revolution; has cleansed her Augean stable. She has completed the business of mere destruction; and has come into direct contact with the positive, practical question of the Art of Politics—what is to be done for the governed? Other nations, and England more than any, are in the middle of *their* Revolution. The most energetic minds are still occupied in thinking, less of benefits to be attained, than of nuisances to be abated; and every question of things to be done, is entangled with questions of things which have first to be undone; or of things which must *not* be undone, lest worse should follow.

It would be absurd to deny, that a nation whose institutions have no historical basis, and are not surrounded by that reverential attachment which mankind so much more easily accord to what is made for them, than to what they themselves have made, lies under some serious practical disadvantages; on which this is not the occasion to expatiate, no more than on the advantages by which they are more or less completely compensated. But whatever may be the inconvenience, in point of practical working, of what has been called a "geometrical polity,"[*] in political discussion its effects are wholly beneficial. It makes disputation turn on the real merits of the matter in dispute. Under it, measures are attacked and defended much less on the ground of precedent and practice, or of analogy to the institutions, and conformity to the traditions of the particular nation; and much more on adaptation to the exigencies of human nature and life, either generally, or at the particular time and place. The discussion, therefore, has an interest reaching beyond those who are immediately affected by its result; and French writers say, hitherto not unjustly, that while the voice of the English Journals and Legislative Assemblies has little echo beyond the bounds of the British Empire, the controversies of *their* Tribune, and of their Periodical Press, are watched for and studied all over Europe.

The writings, then, in which intelligent and instructed Frenchmen promulgate their opinions, on the principal topics of public discussion in France, have a twofold interest to foreigners; because the questions discussed are such as either already are, or will soon become, to them also, of great practical moment; and because the principles and premises appealed to are not peculiarly French, but universal.

In both these points of view, the *Lettres Politiques*, named at the head of this article, have a claim to attention. Originally published as a series of Weekly Pamphlets, and since reprinted in two octavo volumes, they form a collection of Dissertations on the topics, present or probable future, of French Politics, to which recent English discussion has produced nothing in its kind comparable. Not, certainly, that among our public writers there are not several with abilities fully

[*See Mill, "Of the Geometrical, or Abstract Method," Bk. VI, Chap. viii, of *A System of Logic* (1843), *CW*, Vols. VII-VIII (Toronto: University of Toronto Press, 1974), Vol. VIII, pp. 887-94.]

equal to M. Duveyrier, but because their abilities are otherwise employed; because they have not yet turned to consider systematically how the institutions of the country may be worked for the benefit of the country; because in England there is still too much to be undone, for the question, "what is to be done," to assume its due importance; and the ablest thinkers, when they descend from the height of purely abstract science, find sufficient scope for their practical energies, in the war still raging around the shattered bulwarks of the great practical abuses; and small chance of followers, or even of spectators, for any other enterprise.

Among many things in these volumes, significant of the character which French political discussion of the higher order has of late assumed, two are specially remarkable to an English reader. One is, the total absence, through the twenty-five Letters, of discussion on any constitutional subject. There are no disquisitions in favour of, or even in deprecation of, organic changes. All such questions are assumed to be settled, and treated as not requiring notice. The other is, that with the most passive acquiescence in the structure of the government, as circumstances have made it, is combined the strongest and most active spirit of political reform. This is a conjunction which of late has occasionally been heard of in England, but we cannot say we ever saw it realized. We are promised indeed a "new generation"[*] of Church-and-King philanthropists, by whom every institution grounded upon contempt of the people, is to be worked for every purpose of kindness to them. But we see no very brilliant embodiment of this vision in half a dozen dreaming young men, whose ideal is Laud. For England the day of Conservative reformers is yet to come.

We know not whether M. Duveyrier is expressing his sincere opinion, or adapting his tone to the audience whom he desires to influence; but he professes himself satisfied with the existing constitution of France. He designates all discussions of its defects as old quarrels, "which divert the public mind from the real business of the country, and statesmen from the transaction of that business."* Short-sighted as this view of things would be, if applied to such questions considered generally, there must be something in it which adapts itself well to the existing state of feeling in France.[†] It is certain that this avowed contentment with "things as they are,"[†] in respect to the distribution of power, is connected with no optimism as to the mode in which power is employed. The question, who shall

[*Benjamin Disraeli, *Coningsby; or, The New Generation*, 3 vols. (London: Colburn, 1844).]

*[Translated from] *La Pairie*, p. 2.

†"Study the masses and you will see that there is something passing in their minds, not unlike the disposition which preceded Louis XIV's majority after the *Fronde*, and the establishment of the Consulate at the end of the last century. The same lassitude, the same disgust with bustle and agitation, the same abatement of the spirit of distrust, the same indifference to the political rights which that spirit had created." ([Translated from] *La Pairie*, pp. 36-7.)

[†Cf. the title of William Godwin's *Things As They Are; or, The Adventures of Caleb Williams* (1794), 4th ed, 3 vols. (London: Simpkin and Marshall, 1816).]

govern? may be for the present in abeyance; but there is the liveliest interest in the question, how?—not by what hands, but for what purposes, and according to what maxims and rules, the powers of government shall be wielded.

In England also, it has been easy to perceive, for some years past, especially since the advent of the Peel Ministry, that a similar change of feeling and tone is in progress, both in the public and in the more thinking minds; though it has not reached by any means so advanced a stage. The interest in constitutional questions has much abated,—in part, from the hopelessness, for the present, of any further organic changes; and, partly, from a growing scepticism, even among ardent supporters of popular institutions, as to their being, after all, the *panacea* which they were supposed to be for the evils that beset our social system. Sincere Democrats are beginning to doubt whether the *desideratum* is so much an increased influence of popular opinion, as a more enlightened use of the power which it already possesses. But in this new tendency of opinion, France is as much ahead of England as she was in the previous democratic movement. We do not hesitate to express our conviction, that in France at least this change has taken place prematurely. Not that opinion could be too soon, or too earnestly, directed to the ends of government; but it may be, and we think has been, too soon averted from the means. The theory of Representative Government and Constitutional rights, which guided the public mind during the fifteen years' struggle against the Bourbons, has been discarded before it had finished its work. France is still a country where twenty persons cannot form an association, or hold a meeting, without permission from the Police;[*] where the personal freedom of the citizen is hardly better secured than in the most despotic monarchies of the Continent; where no agent of government can be legally prosecuted for the most enormous offence, without permission from the government by whose directions that offence may have been committed; and where the election of the representative branch of the Legislature, for a population of thirty-four millions, resides in about two hundred thousand persons,—distributed mostly in bodies of from one to three hundred each; enabling the separate interests of particular localities and of influential electors to decide the fortunes of Cabinets and the course of Legislation. In these things, however, France has for the present acquiesced. In what manner her government should be constituted, and in what manner checked, are not the questions which just now interest her. But it is not because she is blind to the disgraceful manner in which her constitution works, and which throughout these volumes is incessantly adverted to, as the most undeniable and the most familiar of daily phenomena.

Constitutional Government—Government in which the support of a majority in a representative assembly is necessary to office—has only had a real existence in

[*Loi sur les associations, Bulletin 115, No. 261 (10 Apr., 1834), *Bulletin des lois du royaume de France*, 9th ser., Pt. 1, VI, 25-6.]

France since 1830; and in this short period it has rivalled the worst corruptions of the English rotten boroughs. Bribery, indeed, in its coarser forms is comparatively unknown; because the electors are in a rank of life which commands hypocrisy. But a majority of the electors in a majority of the electoral colleges, is not too numerous a body to be bought; and bought it is, by distributing all public employments among the electors and their *protégés*; and by succumbing to the pretensions of every locally influential class interest; or, rather, the nominal government is but their instrument—they are not so much bought, as they are themselves the governing body, and claim to themselves in this shape the profits of power. Their position is not that of the voters in our small boroughs; it more resembles that of the borough holders. The gratification of their cupidity is the condition they are able to impose on any set of men whom they permit to be a Ministry.

When a place, great or small, becomes vacant, what happens? Of the four hundred and fifty deputies who are *au courant* of every thing, because they have the right to penetrate each day and every hour into the *bureaux* of the ministry, there are twenty or thirty who begin the siege. Their tactics are simple: They say to the Minister, "You will appoint such and such a relation or an elector of mine, or I withdraw my support." What can the Minister do? He temporizes; opposes one set of pretensions and demands to another; gives hopes to all, and puts off his decision until some new vacancy occurs, to give the hope of an equivalent to the unsuccessful applicants. Happy the Departments, like that of the navy, of *l'enregistrement et les domaines*, of the army, where the modes of admission and of promotion have been fixed beforehand by general rules! And even there, what latitude is allowed to favour; and in the Execution, too often, what contempt of justice! Favour is the moral ulcer, the chronic malady of the government. The delegates of the *bourgeoisie* finding the privileged class swept away, instead of abolishing privileges, seized on them for themselves; and the electors, instead of being indignant and finding fault with their deputies for usurping the privilege of the greater offices, found it simpler and more advantageous to possess themselves of the smaller. ([Translated from] *Lettres Politiques*, Vol. I, pp. 168-70.)

What else could be expected? There are but 200,000 electors, and 130,000 places* (without reckoning the army) in the gift of the government. Again:

The grand distributor of favours now-a-days, is the electoral body; which takes up the attention of its representatives solely with interests of locality and relationship, and circumscribes their hopes of re-election in an infinity of circles so different one from another, so changing, so personal, that there is no Minister who can take in hand a great enterprise of public utility with assurance of success; witness M. Molé with the question of railways; M. Guizot with the customs union; M. Cunin-Gridaine with the sugar laws,[*] &c. &c. [Translated from *ibid.*, pp. 170-1.]

With the keen sense which the author every where shows of this great evil, by

Lettres Politiques, Vol. I, p. 431.
[*Loi sur les sucres, Bulletin 1019, No. 10,728 (2 July, 1843), *Bulletin des lois du royaume de France*, 9th ser., XXVII, 549-51.]

which the sacrifices that France has made to obtain good government, are to so great a degree stultified and rendered abortive, it may appear strange that he should not contend for a change in the constitution of the legislature. Such, however, is not his expedient. We know not whether it is conviction or policy which prevents him from being a Parliamentary Reformer; whether an enlargement of the basis of the representative system appears to him, in the present condition of France, not desirable, or merely not attainable. For whatever reason, he affirms that agitation for this purpose does no good, and only interferes mischievously with what he upholds as the true corrective of the present vicious mode of government;—the formation of an enlightened public opinion. He maintains that petty and selfish interests predominate in the government only because there are no recognised principles on which it can be conducted in any other manner: That the public mind is uninformed, and has no fixed opinion on any subject connected with government, except the constitution of it: That without clear and definite views, diffused and rooted among the public, on the chief practical questions of government, there is nothing to restrain petty intrigues and cabals, or to support an honest Minister in resistance to the unjustifiable pretensions of classes and coteries. That the men at the head of the government would be glad to have such a support; that they are better than the system they administer, and that it is not willingly that they succumb to it—he assumes as a thing of course. We cannot doubt that he has reason to do so. It is not credible, that men who are among the most instructed and enlightened in France, who have enlarged the domain of thought, as well as contributed largely to the diffusion of its results; that philosophers like Guizot, Villemain, Duchatel, would not gladly wash their hands of *turpitudes* as lowering to the personal dignity, as discreditable to the integrity of those involved in them. They are men with convictions, and who wish their convictions to prevail; and it cannot be agreeable to them to be dependent, not on the steady adherence of a powerful party pledged to their opinions, but on their success in bargaining for the local influence of *notabilités de clocher*,—the oracles of this and that distant and backward *arrondissement*. From this position M. Duveyrier seeks to relieve them. It is ideas, he says, that are wanted;—principles of government capable of inspiring attachment, and stirring the imagination; principles sufficiently practical, and at the same time sufficienty commanding and generous, to rally a large mass of opinion around them. "Vous n'avez," he says to M. Guizot—

Vous n'avez devant vous aucun de ces événemens irrémédiables, aucune de ces positions fatales, qu'il ne soit pas dans la volonté de l'homme de transformer. . . . Redoutez les petites choses, les petits moyens, ennoblissez les débats, posez des principes dont la France soit fière, et toutes ces questions dont on vous menace, loin d'augmenter vos embarras, viendront à votre aide, et vous offriront, pour la consolidation du cabinet, un appui inespéré.

Mais je prévois votre réponse; ce que vous me demandez, c'est une politique grande, généreuse, Française! Eh! que deviendrait-elle, mon Dieu! au milieu des intérêts ardens des localités, de l'égoïsme individuel, des intrigues, des cabales de l'amour propre?

Je le reconnais; ces exigences secondaires sont aujourd'hui toutes puissantes; elles frappent les regards! Ce sont les étoiles qui brillent au ciel, la nuit, quand elles y règnent seules. Mais n'oubliez pas que leur éclat pâlit aux approches du jour, et qu'à la place où elles sont encore, l'oeil les cherche vainement quand le soleil a jeté dans l'espace sa chaleur et sa clarté. (*Ibid.*, pp. 66-7.)

This doctrine, that the moral evils of the present political system of France arise from an intellectual cause—from the absence of convictions in the public mind—is dwelt upon by the author with a persistency and iteration for which the periodical form of the *Letters* afforded great advantages. In a letter to M. Chambolle, an opposition deputy, and editor of a leading opposition Journal,[*] he combats the idea, that any peculiar baseness is imputable to the electoral class. The press and the public, he says, are not at all more immaculate. The very men who job their electoral influence for places for their sons, are men of honour in their private concerns.

Politics, say they, have changed their aspect; men's minds are calmed; affairs are no longer in the critical state in which grand principles, strong passions, great public interests, come into play—of what consequence is it that the candidate is a trifle more or a trifle less with the opposition? it makes but the difference of a few words more or less on one or the other side. Frankly, when one finds the statesmen most opposed to each other declaring that they would govern in very much the same manner, has not the elector a right to treat questions of persons with indifference, and to transfer to his own private interest the degree of solicitude which he would otherwise have granted to those questions?

But this is terrible! the constitution is perverted in its first principles; the very meaning of a representative government is one in which the sincere opinions of the country are, above all, represented.—Most true. But what if the country has no opinions? That is an incident which the constitution has not provided for. . . . Do not wonder, then, if numbers of people are led away by this *naïf* calculation:—Here is one candidate who is for the good of the country, and another who is for the good of the country and for mine also; I should be a fool to hesitate. ([Translated from] *Lettres Politiques*, Vol. II, pp. 171-2.)

Accordingly, so far as a determinate public opinion does exist, questions are decided, and the government conducted not by this shameful appeal to personal and local interests, but on grounds which, right or wrong, are at least of a public character.

There have existed, since 1830, two different kinds of politics.

The one, which may be termed constitutional politics, [la politique constituante,] was directed to founding the constitution, developing it, and defending it against the attacks of parties and the repugnances of Europe.

The other, which may be called the politics of business, [la politique des affaires,] aimed at protecting and encouraging the interests and labours of society, in the arts, the sciences,

[*Le Siècle.*]

religion, military and diplomatic organization, internal administration, commerce, agriculture, and manufactures. [Translated from *La pairie*, p. 3.]

In the former branch, in constitutional or organic politics, the government has proceeded on fixed and determinate principles; and has accordingly been able to carry the Chambers with it, by large and certain majorities.

Unhappily it is not so with the politics of business. Statesmen have not yet any programme for *that* department, any system of government specially applicable to it. Accordingly, as soon as the existence of the monarchy is no longer threatened, the fundamental principles of the constitution no longer in question, what do we behold? The government becomes feeble, uncertain, embarrassed; its majority breaks up into an infinity of minute fractions. . . . Time has resolved most of the questions of constitutional politics which were stirred up internally and externally by the establishment of the new government; and the politics of business have now, in France and in Europe, assumed the ascendant. But there is not yet in France any system of government in matters of business. The opposition, in this respect, is not more advanced than the majority. . . . Were the cabinet overthrown, its successors would encounter the same attacks and the same embarrassments, and would have even less strength to overcome them; for they would not (like the present ministry) come into office to repair faults, and save the country from a dangerous *entraînement*; no important situation would connect itself with *their* ministerial existence.

Once suppose any general principles of government in the business department, and the situation is changed. If the principles are accepted by the most eminent minds of all sections of the majority, one of two things must happen; either the ministry will adopt them, and will, in that case, owe its safety to them; or it will disdain them, and the system will become an instrument of opposition, from which will issue sooner or later a durable cabinet.

Such, at bottom, is the true political situation of the country; its difficulties, and its exigencies. The greatest service which could now be rendered to the nation, would be to introduce into the midst of its affairs, so languid, thorny, and complex, a general system of government, capable of overmastering the intrigues and petty passions of the coteries which have succeeded the factions of former days; and of introducing into discussions a new public interest, sufficiently considerable to impose on rival industries and rival localities, union and agreement.

Twelve years of parliamentary omnipotence have proved this task to be above the strength of the Chamber of Deputies. The greatest of the embarrassments arise from its own composition. It is not from that Chamber that we can expect a remedy. ([Translated from] *ibid.*, pp. 4-6.)

M. Duveyrier's first pamphlet (from which this extract is taken) was on the Chamber of Peers; being an attempt to persuade that body to consider as theirs the task which the Chamber of Deputies appeared to have abandoned. The circumstances which, in his opinion, mark out the less popular branch of the French legislature, for the office of introducing matured and systematic principles of government into the public affairs of France, are, first, its independence of the partial and local interests of constituencies, and secondly, the composition of its *personnel*.

The Chamber of Peers, even when hereditary, was a body of a very different character from the House of Lords. It consisted indeed, for the most part, like that assembly, of the wealthiest landed proprietors; but, in England, to represent these is to represent the principal power in the state; while, in France, "the monarchy of the middle class"—wealth, as such, has but little political power, and landed wealth rather less than even Commercial: the Chamber of Peers, therefore, was a body of exceedingly small importance. Once and once only, for a short period, the accidental coincidence between its tendencies and those of public opinion, invested it with a popularity not its own; when, with the caution inherent in a body of old and rich men, it withstood the counter-revolutionary madness of Charles X, which at last cost him his throne. He swamped it by a large creation, and it relapsed into insignificance. In 1831, its destruction, in its pristine character, was completed by the abolition of its hereditary privilege.[*] But, in losing this, it received what in our author's view was far more than an equivalent. In ceasing to represent the remains of what had once been powerful, the *noblesse* and *la grande propriété*, it became the representative of an existing power—of one of the leading influences in society as at present constituted.

The King names the Peers for life; but he is only empowered to name them from certain enumerated classes or "categories;" consisting chiefly (members of the Institute being almost the sole exception) of persons who have served the state for a certain number of years; either in the Chamber of Deputies, or as functionaries in the different departments of the government. The peerage, therefore, is naturally composed of the most eminent public servants—those who combine talents with experience; and it represents a class of great importance in existing society—the administrative body.

*a*Every people *b* comprises, and probably will always comprise, two societies, an *administration* and a *public*; the one, of which the general interest is the supreme law, where positions are not hereditary, but the principle is that of classing its members according to their merit, and rewarding them according to their works; and where the moderation of salaries is compensated by their fixity, and especially by honour and consideration. The other, composed of landed proprietors, of capitalists, of masters and workmen, among whom the supreme law is that of inheritance, the principal rule of conduct is personal interest, competition and struggle the favourite elements.

These two societies serve mutually as a counterpoise; they continually act and react upon one another. The public tends to introduce into the administration the stimulus naturally wanting to it, the principle of emulation. The administration, conformably to its appointed purpose, tends to introduce more and more into the mass of the public, elements of order and forethought. In this twofold direction, the administration and the public have rendered, and do render daily to each other, reciprocal services. ([Translated from] *La Pairie*, p. 12.)

[*Loi contenant l'article qui remplace l'article 23 de la charte, Bulletin 54, No. 130 (29 Dec., 1831), *Bulletin des lois du royaume de France*, 9th ser., Pt. 1, III, 61-4.]

*a-a*308[*quoted in* "Tocqueville on Democracy in America [II]," D&D, II, 78–83; *in* CW, XVIII, 201-4]

*b*59,67   ,' says M. Duveyrier, '

The Chamber of Deputies, (he proceeds to say,) represents the public and its tendencies. The Chamber of Peers represents, or from its constitution is fitted to represent, those who are or have been public functionaries: whose appointed duty and occupation it has been to look at questions from the point of view not of any mere local or sectional, but of the general interest; and who have the judgment and knowledge resulting from labour and experience. To a body like this, it naturally belongs to take the initiative in all legislation, not of a constitutional or organic character. If, in the natural course of things, well-considered views of policy are any where to be looked for, it must be among such a body. To no other acceptance can such views, when originating elsewhere, be so appropriately submitted— through no other organ so fitly introduced into the laws.

We shall not enter into the considerations by which the author attempts to impress upon the Peers this elevated view of their function in the commonwealth. On a new body, starting fresh as a senate, those considerations might have influence. But the senate of France is not a new body. It set out on the discredited foundation of the old hereditary chamber; and its change of character only takes place gradually, as the members die off. To redeem a lost position is more difficult than to create a new one. The new members, joining a body of no weight, become accustomed to political insignificance; they have mostly passed the age of enterprise; and the Peerage is considered little else than an honourable retirement for the invalids of the public service. M. Duveyrier's suggestion has made some impression upon the public; it has gained him the public ear, and launched his doctrines into discussion; but we do not find that the conduct of the Peers has been at all affected by it. Energy is precisely that quality which, if men have it not of themselves, cannot be breathed into them by other people's advice and exhortations. There are involved, however, in this speculation, some ideas of a more general character; not unworthy of the attention of those who concern themselves about the social changes which the future must produce.

There are, we believe, few real thinkers, of whatever party, who have not reflected with some anxiety upon the views which have become current of late, respecting the irresistible tendency of modern society towards democracy. The sure, and now no longer slow, advance, by which the classes hitherto in the ascendant are merging into the common mass, and all other forces ^{c} giving way before the power of mere numbers, is well calculated to inspire uneasiness, even in those to whom democracy *per se* presents nothing alarming. It is not the uncontrolled ascendency of popular power, but of any power, which is formidable. There is no one power in society, or capable of being constituted in it, of which the influences do not become mischievous as soon as it reigns uncontrolled—as soon as it becomes exempted from any necessity of being in the right, by being able to make its mere will prevail, without the condition of a

^{c}67   are

previous struggle. To render its ascendency safe, it must be fitted with correctives and counteractives, possessing the qualities opposite to its characteristic defects. Now, the defects to which the government of numbers, whether in the pure American, or in the mixed English form, is most liable, are precisely those of a public, as compared with an administration. Want of appreciation of distant objects and remote consequences; where an object is desired, want both of an adequate sense of practical difficulties, and of the sagacity necessary for eluding them; disregard of traditions, and of maxims sanctioned by experience; an undervaluing of the importance of fixed rules, when immediate purposes require a departure from them—these are among the acknowledged dangers of popular government; and there is the still greater, though less recognised, danger, of being ruled by a spirit of suspicious and intolerant mediocrity. Taking these things into consideration, and also the progressive decline of the existing checks and counterpoises, and the little probability there is that the influence of mere wealth, still less of birth, will be sufficient hereafter to restrain the tendencies of the growing power, by mere passive resistance; we do not think that a nation whose historical ^dantécédens^d give it any choice, could select a fitter basis upon which to ground the counterbalancing power in the State, than the principle of the French Upper House. The defects of Representative Assemblies are, in substance, those of unskilled politicians. The mode of raising a power most competent to their correction, would be an organization and combination of the skilled. History affords the example of a government carried on for centuries with the greatest consistency of purpose, and the highest skill and talent, ever realized in public affairs; and it was constituted on this very principle. The Roman Senate was a Senate for life, composed of all who had filled high offices in the State, and were not disqualified by a public note of disgrace. The faults of the Roman policy were in its ends; which, however, were those of all the States of the ancient world. Its choice of means was consummate. This government, and others distantly approaching to it, have given to aristocracy all the credit which it has obtained for constancy and wisdom. A Senate of some such description, composed of persons no longer young, and whose reputation is already gained, will necessarily lean to the Conservative side; but not with the blind, merely instinctive, spirit of conservatism, generated by mere wealth or social importance, unearned by previous labour. Such a body would secure a due hearing and a reasonable regard for precedent and established rule. It would disarm jealousy by its freedom from any class interest; and while it never could become the really predominant power in the State, still, since its position would be the consequence of recognised merit and actual services to the public, it would have as much personal influence, and excite as little hostility, as is compatible with resisting in any degree the tendencies of the really strongest power.

^{d-d}59,67   antecedents

There is another class of considerations connected with Representative Governments, to which we shall also briefly advert. In proportion as it has been better understood what legislation is, and the unity of plan as well as maturity of deliberation which are essential to it, thinking persons have asked themselves the question—Whether a popular body of 658 or 459 members, not specially educated for the purpose, having served no apprenticeship, and undergone no examination, and who transact business in the forms and very much in the spirit of a debating society, can have as its peculiarly appropriate office to make laws? Whether that is not a work certain to be spoiled by putting such a superfluous number of hands upon it? Whether it is not essentially a business for one, or a very small number, of most carefully prepared and selected individuals? And whether the proper office of a Representative Body, (in addition to controlling the public expenditure, and deciding who shall hold office,) be not that of *discussing* all national interests; of giving expression to the wishes and feelings of the country; and granting or withholding its consent to the laws which others make, rather than *of* themselves framing, or even altering them? The law of this and most other nations is already such a chaos, that the quality of what is yearly added, does not materially affect the general mass; but in a country possessed of a real Code or Digest, and desirous of retaining that advantage, who could think without dismay of its being tampered with at the will of a body like the House of Commons, or the Chamber of Deputies? Imperfect as is the French Code, the inconveniences arising from this cause are already strongly felt; and they afford an additional inducement for associating with the popular body a skilled Senate, or Council of Legislation, which, whatever might be its special constitution, must be grounded upon some form of the principle which we have now considered.[a]

M. Duveyrier does not often return, except in the way of incidental allusion, to his idea respecting the Peers; but the conception of the administration, or corps of public functionaries, as the social element to which France must look for improvements in her political system, is carried through the whole series of Pamphlets; and he attempts to avail himself of every side-current of opinion to steer into this harbour. This is especially seen in his Letter to the Duke de Nemours, on *The State and Prospects of Aristocracy in France*.[*] According to this Letter, there is now a distinct acknowledged tendency in the French mind towards aristocracy; a tendency hailed by some, dreaded and rejected by others, but denied by no one. "The best and sincerest thinkers cannot see without alarm the narrow interval which separates the two forces between which the government is divided." [Translated from *Lettres politiques*, Vol. I, pp. 71-2.] Experience proves, that

when the popular and the royal power stand singly opposed to one another, a struggle commences, and one inevitably overpowers the other. Men ask themselves, were some

[*The third letter in *Lettres politiques*, Vol. I, pp. 69-100.]

[e-e]+59,67

unforeseen circumstance to rekindle the conflict, on which side would be the victory, and whether a Republic or an Absolute Monarchy is most to be dreaded? And a Republic is not considered as the most imminent nor the most formidable danger. The wisdom of the King, men say, has fortified the regal power; but the precautions by which the popular power has attempted to ensure its control, have turned to its confusion. The *bourgeoisie* only uses its influence to break up, by intrigue, cabinets which only maintain themselves by the distribution of favours. Thus lowered in its own esteem, and in that of others, what salutary restraint can it impose upon the executive power, which the interest of the ministers lies in extending perpetually? France, therefore, marches by a sort of fatality towards Despotism. But after Despotism come revolutions, and in revolutions dynasties disappear. [Translated from *ibid.*, pp. 72, 71.]

Not only on these political, but also on moral grounds, M. Duveyrier contends for the necessity of intermediate ranks, and a third power interposed between the Royal and the Popular. We give these passages in his own words:

La plaie que tout le monde signale, dont tout le monde souffre, n'est-elle pas ce nivellement hors de nature, qui prétend s'imposer à toutes les situations, à toutes les intelligences, à tous les intérêts; cette personnalité brutale, ce démon de l'envie, cet amour effréné de soi-même, qui s'empare de tout—familles, cités, industries? [*Ibid.*, p. 74.]

No degree of jealousy of natural superiorities, he continues, can prevent them from existing; talents, riches, even historical descent, are still instruments of power; but the social arrangements not being such as to make these powers available for public uses, they work only for the personal ends of the possessors.

Et pourquoi s'en étonner? Quand la grandeur et l'utilité des oeuvres ne suffisent plus pour enrichir, pour ennoblir celui qui les produit, quand on refuse les égards les plus légitimes aux dévoûmens, à la gloire, aux services publics, pourquoi s'étonner que le talent se rende à lui-même l'hommage qu'on lui refuse, et qu'il tourne en vil métier les plus sublimes professions?

On a cru fonder le règne de l'égalité; vaine erreur! L'aristocratie n'est plus, mais le monde est plein d'aristocrates. Toute la difference, c'est que les privilégiés sont désunis; qu'ils ne forment plus corps; qu'il n'existe plus entre eux de point d'honneur. Ils sont toujours au-dessus de la foule; ils peuvent plus qu'elle; mais à cette supériorité d'influence n'est attachée la pratique d'aucune vertu, ni désintéressement, ni bravoure, ni magnificence, aucune obligation morale, aucun service patriotique. La conscience d'une supériorité de nature et de droits est toujours la même; le niveau n'a passé que sur les devoirs. [*Ibid.*, pp. 75-6.]

These arguments for an Aristocracy have not so much novelty or originality, as the views which our author promulgates respecting the mode of supplying the desideratum. An aristocracy, he says, can never be constituted but on the basis of a public function. Even the feudal nobility

originated in the diversity of certain military functions, and in the relations of subordination which arose between them. Dukes were commanders of armies; Marquises were guardians of the frontiers; Counts, governors of provinces; the Barons were the principal officers attached to the person of the Monarch; Chevaliers were inferior officers. Most of these functions were originally personal, and the nobility which they conferred was so too. [Translated from *ibid.*, pp. 76-7.]

Nor was the title ever, during the vigour of the institution, dissevered in the minds of men from the duties which it imposed.

Noblesse oblige! Such was the first lesson inculcated upon the heir of the title. He was considered to be under the obligation of all generous sentiments, of magnificence, of intrepidity; so universal was the opinion that the title was only the sign of a function, and the privileges conferred by it the just reward of public services, of duties from which the *titulaire* could not withdraw himself without meanness and dishonour. [Translated from *ibid.*, pp. 77-8.]

But although feudal dignities, as he justly says, were originally symbols of services, he treats with deserved contempt the idea, that any useful end could be answered by merely creating from the ranks of personal merit, after the foolish example of Napoleon, Dukes, Counts, and Barons.

The question is not about ennobling men by distributing among them the titles of public functions which for the last eight or ten centuries have ceased to exist. The question is of ennobling the functions and public employments of modern times; of raising them gradually to such a degree of honour, that their denominations may become, for future ages, real titles of nobility.

The nobility, then, which we have now to create, is *la noblesse gouvernementale*; and, to say the truth, there has never existed any other. If there be understood by aristocracy a body of individuals distinguished by titles and designations to which are not attached any attributes of government, be assured that the nobility meant is a nobility in its decline. At its origin, or in the time of its greatest eminence, every aristocracy governs. What requires to be ennobled now, is office, power, public trusts. We should desire to see the idea become general, that every one who takes a share in the government of his country is bound to show more virtue, more patriotism, more greatness of soul than the vulgar. This was already the spirit of the old noblesse. In the time of its splendour, there was one sort of people who might postpone the interest of the state to that of their families; there were others for whom it was a perpetual duty to sacrifice their families to the state. The former, when the enemy invaded their native soil, might without dishonour avoid the danger, shut themselves up in their houses, preserve themselves for their wives and children—these were the *bourgeois* and the "vilains, taillables et corvéables;" but the others were obliged to quit every thing, wives, children, lands and manors, and rush to meet the enemy—these were the nobles, who owed to their country the impost of blood. ([Translated from] *ibid.*, pp. 83-4.)

We are thus brought back, by a rather circuitous course, to our author's idea respecting the class of public functionaries, as the only material from which a distinguished class,—a new Aristocracy,—can arise. Does he propose, then, to make them an aristocracy? An aristocracy, according to him, cannot be made. It must make itself. The Judicial Order, the *noblesse de robe*, made itself an aristocracy by its own conduct. The new aristocracy must do the same. He asks no privileges for it; least of all, any hereditary privilege. He aims at investing the class with the various conditions necessary to make them deserve, and, by deserving, obtain, the respect and consideration of the public.

Fixity, in the first place. Nothing is more adverse to the influence which the administrator should possess over his *administrés*, than those frequent changes of residence, which permit only a very small number to familiarize themselves with the special wants of their localities, and to acquire the confidence of the public.

Responsibility, in the second place. The excessive centralization which keeps in the hands of the Ministers (who alone are responsible) the decision of even the simplest questions, and the distribution of even the most trifling employments, takes away from official station its consideration and its authority. The influence which every *employé* in the lower grades is able to exercise through some deputy, so as to frustrate the just *surveillance* of his superiors, relaxes the ties of offical connexion, and is a discouragement to zeal. How can you expect earnestness and self-devotion from a functionary who can neither protect talent, nor repress insolence, nor cashier laziness and incapacity? ([Translated from] *ibid.*, p. 85.)

As a third condition, he insists on the necessity of increasing the salaries of public offices; and doubtless not without reason. It is well known that French governments are as parsimonious in remunerating their *employés*, as prodigal in augmenting the number.

To this, and other considerations connected with the same subject, our author returns in the first letter of the second volume; one of those in which he expresses his opinion with greatest freedom on the system of government now prevailing in France. The principle established by the Revolution, the equal admissibility of all to public employment, has become, he says, merely nominal; for

since the revolution of July two important classes have ceased to furnish their quota to public offices; the great proprietors and the non-proprietors.

On the one hand, the political services required from most of the functionaries of the administration, the extra-official aid expected from them in the management of elections and the formation of majorities, have gradually diminished the consideration attached to public employments; and have driven away from them the *grands propriétaires*, the inheritors of illustrious names or considerable fortunes.

On the other hand, the excessive reduction of salaries has rendered it more and more impossible for persons who have no patrimony, to hold any public function of importance. The absence of any examination or *concours* for admission into most civil offices, and the influence exercised over the Ministers (the distributors of place) by the deputies and the electoral colleges, have banished, even from the smallest and obscurest public employment, that numerous class from which the Republic and the Empire had drawn so many of their most brilliant ornaments. ([Translated from] *ibid.*, Vol. II, pp. 4-5.)

What is now remaining of the great effort of Napoleon to honour genius and public services, and to create for them positions equal to the loftiest stations of the European noblesse? Where is now that national proverb, which then prevailed as a truth, through every branch of the public administration—that the lowest conscript carried in his knapsack the Baton of a Marshal of France? . . . The great positions created by the Empire exist merely in memory. The class which the Restoration did not create, but which it encouraged—to which it gave the greatest share in the management of public affairs—the class of great proprietors, lives isolated, dissatisfied, mistaking its own interests, and allying itself, from mere pettishness, with its most dangerous enemies. The agricultural and labouring classes are relegated to their farms and workshops; and no solicitude, no effort of the government, is exerted to recruit from their ranks, as in the great days of the Republic and Empire, the most ardent and gifted minds. The *bourgeoisie* alone governs; and, by a new form of levelling and equality, claims to reduce every thing to *mesquin* proportions, and to concentrate all rights in the middle regions of the *petite propriété*. ([Translated from] *ibid.*, pp. 41-2.)

It has been said with truth, that the American does not believe in poverty. The Frenchman does. . . . Every petty elector is inveterately conservative of his patrimony; and, not choosing to risk any thing for the establishment of his children, he is invincibly prompted to swell the eternal overflow of the small places inscribed in the budget. ([Translated from] *ibid.*, p. 170.)

For these several inconveniences he proposes remedies. In the first place, the Government must cease to require from its agents degrading services. All interference in elections by the official agents of Government, must be peremptorily abolished. This might or might not affect injuriously the interests of any existing Ministry. It might or might not render the opposition triumphant, and produce parliamentary reform. If these consequences happen, they must be submitted to. They are not for a moment to be considered in comparison with the object. But,

The Executive, interdicting all its agents from any official interference, from any interference whatever, in the operations of the electoral body, would immediately restore to public functions their honour and their dignity. The real ability, intelligence, experience, patriotism, and integrity of the servants of the state, would no longer be at each instant brought into suspicion. ([Translated from] *ibid.*, p. 34.)

And the greater respectability thus given to office, would again, he says, attract to it the opulent classes;—a thing not in itself undesirable, and indispensably necessary so long as a mistaken economy keeps the salaries low.

But, while preventing placemen from jobbing in elections, it is also needful to prevent electors from jobbing in places. For this and other important purposes, the author's expedient is, to make the conferring of public employments not a matter of favour, but, as far as possible, a Judicial Act. Admission into the public service should be granted only to the candidates who are pronounced on a public competition the best qualified. A certain proportion of all promotions should be given to seniority. The remainder must be, and (incompetence having been provided against by the initial arrangements) might safely be, dependent upon choice. To secure an abundance of highly qualified candidates, he proposes that there should be a public system of Education for each leading department of the public service. There is already the Polytechnic school, or College, as we should call it: English readers often forget that *Ecole*, in French, means a College, and *Collège* a School. There are the military and naval schools, the school of engineers, and the school of mines. To these should be added schools of administration, of judicature, of diplomacy, and of finance. These various suggestions, supported at considerable length and in much detail, are the chief practical topic of the book. From a system of arrangements thus combined, he anticipates that the administrative body would be the *élite* of the practical talent and wisdom of the country; and that not only the business of Government in every department would be conducted with a skill and a purity beyond all present experience, but that the class thus formed, surmounted by its natural representatives, the Peerage for life, would become an Aristocracy in the best sense of the word—an aristocracy unprivileged, but real, and the only one with which the circumstances and social elements of a country similar to France are, in the author's opinion, compatible.

In this speculation the reader has seen, we hope, not without interest, a sample of the manner in which the ever active French intellect is applying itself to the new questions, or old questions in new forms, which the changed aspect of modern society is constantly bringing before it; and of the abundant vein of far from worthless thought, portions of which it is at all times throwing up. The present is no doubt a favourable specimen of such speculations. But they almost all exemplify in their degree, that combination of the theoretical and the practical points of view, which is so happily characteristic of the better order of French thinkers. In England the two modes of thought are kept too much apart; the theories of political philosophers are too purely *a priori*; the suggestions of practical reformers too empirical. In France a foundation in general principles, the result of large views and a philosophic mode of thought, is never dispensed with; but the choice of principles for present application is guided by a systematic appreciation of the state and exigencies of existing society. The appreciation may be more or less successful, and is often, no doubt, a total failure; but some such attempt is invariably made.

As is natural to a French political writer, M. Duveyrier devotes a large part of his attention to external affairs. But he does so in a different spirit from that of the writers and orators whose tone has lately rekindled in foreign nations, against France, much of the jealousy and suspicion of former years. Those who best know France, have been most inclined to believe, that the spirit of these orators and writers was far less widely diffused than superficial appearances indicated; and that even in the assailants themselves it was of a less inveterate character than it seemed to be.

M. Duveyrier has no notion of suppressing the national *amour-propre*; nor would he deem himself at all complimented by being supposed exempt from it. But he endeavours to divert it into a rational and a pacific channel. It is not war, he says, it is not territorial extension, by which national greatness and glory are now acquired. By the arts of peace France must henceforth render herself famous. The sufferings and struggles of half a century, and the social and mental advantages which she has bought at so dear a price, have made it her part to assume the initiative in perfecting the machinery and the principles of civil government.

Elle forme à cet égard comme un atelier d'essai au profit du globe entier. . . . L'oeuvre caractéristique de la nation Française est le perfectionnement, au profit d'elle-même et de toutes les autres, non seulement des rouages adminstratifs et politiques, mais des bases mêmes de la société et de la civilisation. (*Ibid.*, Vol. I, pp. 127, 129.)

The author is faithful to his Programme. He advises France to renounce, once for all, the popular object of the Rhenish frontier. He calls it a "misérable intérêt de vanité," and tells her besides, that she cannot have Algiers and the Rhine too. He exhorts her to set an example to Turkey how to govern its Christian subjects, by the manner in which she, in Algeria, can govern her Mussulmans. He recommends an alliance with Germany for peaceful, rather than with Russia, for warlike purposes. To acquire the respect of Europe, her Foreign policy, he says, must be not war and aggrandizement, nor propagandism, but Arbitration and mediation. He would have her combine with Prussia and Austria for the protection of the secondary Powers. He would have international differences decided, not by the coarse expedient of fighting, but by the impartial intervention of friendly powers; nor does he despair of seeing the war of Tariffs, which has succeeded to the war of Armies, terminated in a similar manner; and the adjustment of commercial relations made a matter of general arrangement by Congresses or Conferences among all the powers of Europe. In none of these things does he see insuperable difficulties, if a great nation, like France, would identify herself with them, and make them the leading aim of her external policy.

These are worthy objects; but it may be doubted whether a nation, to which it is necessary to recommend them as means of regaining that importance in the world, which can no longer be successfully sought by war and conquest, is the most likely to render them acceptable to other nations. Plato says, that a people ought to search out and impress as its Governors the persons who most dislike and avoid the office.[*] It is certain, that those who eagerly thrust themselves into other people's disputes, though it be only as arbitrators, are seldom very cordially welcomed; and that those are rarely the best managers of other people's affairs, who have most taste for the bustle and self-importance of management. If, however, men have a taste for meddling, it is better that they should meddle to befriend others, than to oppress and domineer over them; and M. Duveyrier is doing a useful thing, in inculcating upon his countrymen the superiority of the more philanthropic mode of indulging the propensity.

In domestic policy he proclaims the same principle, of peaceful arbitration; the adjustment of conflicting interests, with the least possible hardship and disturbance to any one. His watchwords are, *justice* and *compromise*. To postpone all partial interests to the general interest, but to compensate liberally all from whom sacrifices of their private interest are demanded; and to make up, as far as

[*Republic (Greek and English), trans. Paul Shorey, 2 vols. (London: Heinemann; Cambridge, Mass.: Harvard University Press, 1946), Vol. I, p. 80 (I, i, 19).]

circumstances permit, to the weaker and less fortunate members of society, for whatever disadvantages they lie under in their relations with the strong:—these are his maxims.

Under these different heads, he opens various subjects of discussion; some of which are by no means ripe for a final opinion, and to which we can only cursorily allude. That he is for a progressive reduction of protecting duties, is a matter of course. He has, at the same time, much to say in favour of alleviating the losses of those who suffer by reforms in legislation; or even by improvements in production. These, however, are minor topics compared with one from which no political thinker of any importance can now avert his thoughts;—the improvement of the existing relations between what is designated as the labouring portion of the community, and their employers: the question known to Continental thinkers under the technical appellation of the Organization of Labour.

This is not a subject upon which to enter at the conclusion of an article, nor is it in any sense a principal topic of M. Duveyrier's book. He contents himself with pointing to it in the distance, as a problem waiting for a solution in the depths of futurity. It is possible that, like most French philanthropists, he has in view, as an ultimate possibility, a greater degree of authoritative intervention in contracts relating to labour, than would conduce to the desired end; or be consistent with the proper limits of the functions of government. But he proposes for present adoption, nothing but what is reasonable and useful. He bids the government encourage and favour what is voluntarily done by employers of labour, to raise their labourers from the situation of hired servants, to that of partners in the concern, having a pecuniary interest in the profits. He recommends to honour and imitation the example of M. Leclaire, (mentioned in a former number of this Review,)[*] who has organized his business on the plan of allowing to himself, as well as to each of his *employés*, a fixed salary; and sharing the surplus among the whole body in rateable proportion to the salaries; and who, it appears, has found this system even lucrative to himself, as well as highly advantageous to his labourers.

We have exhibited, we think, enough of the contents of these volumes to justify our favourable opinion of them. On the unfavourable side there is little that we think it important to notice, except a degree of flattery to some of the Chiefs of the ruling party, and especially to the present King of the French;[†]—probably, however, in the author's eyes, not exceeding the courtesy due to persons in high

---

[*Duveyrier, *Lettres politiques*, Vol. II, pp. 258-65, refers to Edmé Jean Leclaire, *Des améliorations qu'il serait possible d'apporter dans le sort des ouvriers peintres en bâtiments* (Paris: Bouchard-Huzard, Carilian-Goeury, n.d.), which is cited by Mill, "The Claims of Labour," *Edinburgh Review*, LXXXI (Apr., 1845), 498-525 (in *Essays on Economics and Society*, CW, Vols. IV-V [Toronto: University of Toronto Press, 1967], Vol. IV, pp. 363-89).]

[†Louis Philippe.]

authority, from one of their own supporters, when he volunteers important, and not always agreeable advice. The style is easy and spirited, occasionally rising into eloquence; and not more diffuse than belongs to the nature of modern periodical writing.

VINDICATION OF THE
FRENCH REVOLUTION OF FEBRUARY 1848

1849

EDITOR'S NOTE

Dissertations and Discussions, 2nd ed. (1867), II, 335-410. Headed: "Vindication of the French Revolution of February 1848, / In Reply to Lord Brougham and others"; title footnoted: "*Letter to the Marquess of Lansdowne, K.G., Lord President of the Council, on the late Revolution in France.* By [Henry Peter,] Lord Brougham, F.R.S., Member of the National Institute. London: Ridgway, 1848.—*Westminster Review*, April 1849." Running titles: "The French Revolution of 1848 / and Its Assailants." Reprinted from *Westminster Review*, LI (Apr., 1849), 1-47, where it appears as the lead article, headed with the same information as in the footnote to the *D&D* title, and the same running titles. Unsigned. Identified in Mill's bibliography as "A review of Lord Brougham's pamphlet on the French revolution, in the Westminster Review for April 1849" (MacMinn, 71). Also offprinted with a title page: "*Defence of the French Revolution of February, 1848, in Reply to Lord Brougham and Others. From the 'Westminster and Foreign Quarterly Review' for April, 1849.* London: Waterlow and Sons, 1849." The first page of the offprint has the same title as the *D&D* version (i.e., the first word is "Vindication" not "Defence"), and the heading from the *Westminster* is repeated; the running titles are again the same. The offprint includes (50-4) an Appendix giving the French versions of the passages from Tocqueville and Lamartine translated by Mill in his text; the Appendix is also given in *D&D*, II, 555-63, and is reprinted below as Appendix B. Unsigned. There is no copy of the original article in Mill's library, Somerville College; the copy of the offprint contains two corrections in ink, both of which were made in *D&D*: at 330.29 "Dourlens" is altered to "Doullens"; and at 357.5 a comma is added after "presbyterianism".

The following text, taken from *D&D*, 2nd ed. (the last in Mill's lifetime), is collated with that in *D&D*, 1st ed., that of the offprint, and that in *WR*. In the footnoted variants, "49[1]" indicates *WR*, "49[2]" indicates the offprint, "59" indicates *D&D*, 1st ed. (1859), and "67" indicates *D&D*, 2nd ed. (1867).

For comment on the essay, see lxxxiii–xci and cvii–cx above.

Vindication of the

French Revolution of February 1848

THAT THE TRANSACTIONS AND THE MEN of the late French Revolution should find small favour in the eyes of the vulgar and selfish part of the upper and middle classes, can surprise no one: and that the newspaper press, which is the echo, or, as far as it is able, the anticipation, of the opinions and prejudices of those classes, should endeavour to recommend itself by malicious disparagement of that great event, is but in the natural order of things. Justice to the men, and a due appreciation of the event, demand that these unmerited attacks should not remain unprotested against. But it is difficult to grapple with so slippery an antagonist as the writer in a newspaper, and impossible to follow the stream of calumny as it swells by a perpetual succession of infinitesimal infusions from incessant newspaper articles. Unless through some similar medium, in which the day's falsehood can be immediately met by the day's contradiction, such assailants are fought at too great a disadvantage. It is fortunate, therefore, when some one, embodying the whole mass of accusation in one general bill of indictment, puts the case upon the issue of a single battle, instead of a multitude of skirmishes. It is an immense advantage to the defenders of truth and justice, when all that falsehood and injustice have got to say is brought together in a moderate compass, and in a form convenient for exposure.

Such an advantage Lord Brougham has afforded by his outpouring of desultory invective against the Revolution and its authors. Among the multitude of performances, similar in intention and often superior in skill, which have issued from the English press since February 1848, *a*his pamphlet*a* is the only one which affects to embrace the whole subject, and the only one which bears a known name. *b*Should*b* it seem to any one that more importance is attached to such a performance, than properly belongs to a thing so slight and trivial, let it be considered that the importance of a numerical amount does not so much depend upon the unit which heads it, as upon the number of the figures which follow.

Lord Brougham

Thinks it a duty incumbent on him, as one who has at various times been a leader in political movements, and had some hand in bringing about the greatest constitutional

*a-a*49[1,2]   the pamphlet before us
*b-b*49[1,2]   In itself, indeed, this production displays considerably more of the will than of the power to injure. In style, it is a determined attempt at rhetoric, but rhetoric of the tritest kind, with no real command of rhetorical resources. It has all the faults without any of the impressiveness of declamation. Its worth in point of matter will be seen presently. And should

change that ever was effected without actual violence,[*] to enter calmly but fully upon the consideration of the most extraordinary Revolution which ever altered the face of affairs in a civilized country.[†]

It is very natural and commendable in any one (even though he may not have had the advantage which Lord Brougham so often reminds the reader that he once enjoyed, of being a fellow-minister with the Marquis of Lansdowne)[‡] to endeavour to understand the remarkable event which is the theme of his vituperation. Remarkable, it may justly be called; though the commonplace hyperbole of "the most extraordinary Revolution which ever altered the face of affairs in a civilized country" will scarcely pass muster, even as a rhetorical flourish. In one respect, indeed, the Revolution of February must be allowed to be extraordinary, if not unexampled. It stands almost alone among revolutions, in having placed power in the hands of men who neither expected nor sought it, nor used it for any personal purpose—not even for that of maintaining, otherwise than by opinion and discussion, the ascendancy of their own party; men whose every act proclaimed them to be that almost unheard-of phenomenon—unselfish politicians; who did not, like the common run of those who fancy themselves sincere, aim at doing a little for their opinions and much for themselves, but, with a disinterested zeal, strove to make their tenure of power produce as much good as their countrymen were capable of receiving, and more than their countrymen had yet learnt to desire. It was not, perhaps, to be expected that men of this stamp should command much of Lord Brougham's sympathy. Lord Brougham has fought, [c]both frequently and effectively[c], on the people's side; but few will assert that he [d]often was much[d] in advance of them, or [e]fought any up-hill battle in their behalf. Even in the days of his [f]greatest[f] glory, it was remarked that he [g]seldom[g] joined any cause until its [h]first[h] difficulties were over, and it had been brought near to the point of success, by labourers [i]of deeper earnestness[i], and more willing to content themselves without indiscriminate applause. If sympathy, therefore, depends on similarity of character, it was not likely that his lordship should feel any warm admiration for the members of the Provisional Government. But he is probably the only man in Europe, of his reputation and standing, who would have been capable of speaking of them in such a strain as the following:

[*The first Reform Act, 2 & 3 William IV, c. 45 (1832).]
[†Brougham, *Letter*, p. 1.]
[‡See, e.g., *ibid.*, pp. 1-2, 5-6, 153-4.]

[c-c]49[1,2]   not unfrequently
[d-d]49[1,2]   ever was
[e]49[1,2]   ever
[f-f]+59,67
[g-g]49[1,2]   never
[h-h]49[1,2]   chief
[i-i]49[1,2]   more in earnest

The instantaneous disappearance of virtues, dominions, princedoms, powers—of all the men who by their station, or their capacity, or their habits of government, or even their habits of business, had a claim to rule the affairs of their country, was succeeded by the sudden lifting up to supreme power of men who, with the single exception of my illustrious friend M. Arago, were either wholly unknown before in any way, even to their very names and existence; or who were known as authors of no great fame; or who were known as of so indifferent reputation, that they had better have not been known at all; and M. Arago, the solitary exception to this actual or desirable obscurity, himself known in the world of science alone.[*]

Remembering that, of the body of men thus spoken of, M. de Lamartine is one, it is difficult not to be amazed at so unbounded a reliance on the ignorance of the public. The literary fame of M. de Lamartine in France and in Europe, can afford to be ignored by Lord Brougham. There was not a single obscure person among the Provisional Government. The seven originally named were all distinguished members of the Chamber of Deputies.[†] Their venerable President, one of the most honoured characters in France, had even held office, if that be a recommendation; he was a member of the first cabinet appointed in 1830, and left the Government when Louis Philippe parted company with popular principles. The "illustrious friend" known only "in the world of science," had been an active and influential politician for twenty years. Three others were leading members of the Paris bar.[‡] The four whom ^{j}, in obedience to the popular voice,^{j} these seven ^{k}accepted^k as their colleagues, were the acknowledged leaders of the republican press;[§] and who that had paid the smallest attention to French affairs, was not familiar with the names and reputation of Marrast and of Louis Blanc?

The first sin of the Revolution in the eyes of the pamphleteer is its singularity. "The like of it never was before witnessed among men." It has "no parallel in the history of nations." It is "wholly at variance with every principle, as well as all experience." If it could possibly last, he would "feel bound to make the addition of a new head or chapter" to "a very elaborate work, the Political Philosophy" of "our Useful Knowledge Society."[¶] If his account of it were true, one would be unable to understand how the Revolution could possibly have happened. It was "the sudden

[*Ibid., p. 2.]
[†Jacques Charles Dupont de l'Eure (President), Dominique François Arago, Isaac Adolphe Crémieux, Louis Antoine Garnier-Pagès, Alphonse Marie Louis de Prat de Lamartine, Alexandre Auguste Ledru-Rollin, and Alexandre Pierre Thomas Amable Marie de Saint-Georges.]
[‡Crémieux, Ledru-Rollin, and Marie de Saint-Georges.]
[§Louis Blanc, Ferdinand Flocon, Armand Marrast, and Alexandre Martin ("Albert").]
[¶I.e., Brougham, Political Philosophy, 3 pts. (London: Society for the Diffusion of Useful Knowledge, and Chapman and Hall, 1842-43).]

$^{j-j}$+59,67
$^{k-k}$49^{1,2} afterwards selected

work of a moment—a change prepared by no preceding plan—prompted by no felt inconvenience—announced by no complaint;" "without ground, without pretext, without one circumstance to justify or even to account for it, except familiarity with change" and "proneness to violence." It was the "work of some half-dozen artisans, met in a printing-office;" "a handful of armed ruffians, headed by a shoemaker and a sub-editor."[*] Who is meant by the sub-editor, his lordship best knows; the shoemaker, it must be presumed, is M. Adolphe Chenu, whose word Lord Brougham takes for the share he had in the transaction, though a bare reading of his deposition[†] is enough to prove that he was already known to be, what he is now admitted to have been, a police spy. To this "handful," be it of "artisans" or "ruffians," everybody submitted, though everybody disapproved. Half-a-dozen obscure men overthrew a government which nobody disliked, and established one which nobody desired. This singular incident, of a government which, so to speak, falls down of itself, does not suggest to the writer that there must have been something faulty in its foundations. It merely proves to him that foundations are of no use. It reveals the "terrible truth," that it is natural to buildings to fall without a cause, and that henceforth none can be expected to stand. It "for ever destroys our confidence in any system of political power which may be reared," not only in France, but on the face of the earth. "All sense of security in any existing government" is gone. "None can now be held safe for an hour."[‡]

The explanation of the Revolution is, in short, that it is entirely inexplicable; and this is intended, not as a confession of ignorance, but as a sufficient theory.

Common sense, however little informed concerning the Revolution, has been unable, from the first, to accept this notion of it. It appears to Lord Brougham very unaccountable that the English journals did not at once declare a determined enmity to the Revolution, but waited a few weeks before assuming their present attitude of hostility.[§] It was because they did not believe, as he professes to do, that the best and wisest of governments had been overthrown by a touch—the mature opinion of the whole country being in its favour. That, too, is the reason why even now, while the grossest misrepresentations of the state of things which the Revolution has produced are universally propagated and very generally believed, hardly any one except the pamphleteer expresses regret for what it swept away. "The illustrious prince, who, with extraordinary ability and complete success, had, in times of foreign and domestic difficulty, steered the vessel of the State in safety and in peace during a period of seventeen years," and who had invited Lord Brougham to the Tuileries, and listened with apparent resignation to

---

[*Brougham, *Letter*, pp. 14, 5, 5, 5, 5, 4, 15, 22, 22, 14, 14, respectively.]
[†In *Rapport de la commission d'enquête sur l'insurrection qui a éclaté dans la journée du 23 juin et sur les événements du 15 mai*, 3 vols. (Paris: n.p., 1848), Vol. I, pp. 182-90.]
[‡Brougham, *Letter*, pp. 14, 15, 31, 31, respectively.]
[§*Ibid.*, pp. 3-4.]

his "earnest and zealous" counsels[*]—has now Lord Brougham for his only, or almost only, regretter and admirer. Why is this? Because everybody, whether acquainted with the facts or not, is able to see that a government which, after seventeen years of almost absolute power over a great country, can be overthrown in a day—which, during that long period, a period too of peace and prosperity, undisturbed by any public calamity, has so entirely failed of creating anywhere a wish for its preservation, that "a capital of one million souls', and a nation of five-and-thirty," including an army of several hundred thousand, look on quietly while "a shoemaker and a sub-editor," followed by "an armed mob of two or three thousand,"[†] turn out the Chambers, and proclaim a totally different set of institutions—that such a government, unless it was so ʲmuchʲ in advance of the public intelligence as to be out of the reach of appreciation by it, was so greatly in arrear of it as to deserve to fall.

This government, Lord Brougham ᵐ confesses, was not without its foibles. The ministry had committed some blunders and indiscretions, and the institutions of the country had a few remaining defects, which the government showed no willingness to remove. There were too many placemen in parliament, and the elective franchise was "too limited,"[‡] being confined, in a nation of thirty-four millions, to about a quarter of a million; distributed, it might have been added, so unequally, that a majority of the constituencies did not exceed 200 or 300 voters. The government should have looked to this. They should have given "votes to all who were liable to serve on juries;" and also "enfranchised, without regard to property, the classes connected with science, letters, and the arts;"[§] which is the same thing twice over, for the jury-list consisted precisely of the electors and of those classes. By this they would have added to the 250,000 electors, and to the large constituencies almost exclusively, some twenty or thirty thousand voters more. The other improvements of which, in Lord Brougham's judgment, the French Constitution stood in need, were to make the peerage hereditary, and allow land to be entailed.[¶] It would have been treating his friends very hardly, to be severe upon them for not effecting these last specimens of constitutional improvement, since they might, with as much chance of success, have attempted to alter the solar system. Hereditary legislation and entails are not things which a nation takes back, when once it has rid itself of them. It certainly was not for this that the government of Louis Philippe, in the moment of trial, was found to be

[*Ibid., pp. 24, 10.]
[†Ibid., p. 14.]
[‡Ibid., e.g., p. 10.]
[§Ibid., p. 49.]
[¶Ibid., pp. 9, 11-12. The reference is to the *Charte constitutionnelle*, Bulletin 5, No. 59 (14 Aug., 1830), *Bulletin des lois du royaume de France*, 9th ser., Pt. 1, I, 51-64.]

ˡ⁻ˡ491,2   greatly
ᵐ491,2   frankly

deserted by all mankind. Accordingly, Lord Brougham can find no mode of accounting for the fact but the selfishness and indifference of the National Guard, who "think only of their shops and their brittle wares; and avoid acting, provided they see no risk of pillage following the outbreak."[*]

This specimen of philosophizing is not at all Baconian, and does no credit to the political philosopher of the Useful Knowledge Society. The National Guard acted vigorously enough in 1832, and again in 1834, when they assisted the troops in putting down much more formidable insurrections than that of 1848. Their conduct in June last was not, as the pamphlet represents,[†] the exception, but the rule. Their horror of *l'émeute* amounted to a passion: it was that, and not any attachment to the throne of Louis Philippe, which made them tolerate him for seventeen years. Why, then, in February, did they, for the first and only time, not only not resist, but openly countenance the insurrection? Because the time had come when disgust with the government had become a stronger feeling than even that passionate horror. The ruler of France had made the terror of the bourgeois at the idea of a new revolution, his sole instrument of government, except personal corruption; and that support now gave way under him.

The explanation of this result of seventeen years of power—the reason why a government which, in the first years following its establishment, the most determined and violent attacks had failed to shake, found itself, in 1848, so feeble, that it fell at the first onset, and not a hand was raised to stay its fall—will be found, we believe, principally in two things.

First—it was a government wholly without the spirit of improvement. Not only did it make an obstinate resistance to all and every organic reform, even the most moderate; to [n] merely legislative or merely administrative improvements it was, in practice, equally inimical: it originated [o]scarcely any[o] itself, and successfully resisted all which were proposed by others. [p] This had not always been, in the same degree, its character: in its earlier years it gave to France two of the most important legislative gifts she ever received—the law of Primary Instruction and that of Vicinal (or local) Roads.[‡] But its love of improvement, never strong, had long given place to a conservatism of the worst sort.[p] There are few instances of a government, in a country calling itself free, so completely sold to the support of all abuses: it rested on a coalition of all the sinister interests[§] in France. Among

[*Brougham, *Letter*, p. 32.]
[†*Ibid.*]
[‡Loi sur l'instruction primaire, Bulletin 105, No. 236 (28 June, 1833), *Bulletin des lois du royaume de France*, 9th ser., Pt. 1, V, 251-62; and Loi sur les chemins vicinaux, Bulletin 422, No. 6293 (21 May, 1836), *ibid.*, XII, 193-200.]
[§The term "sinister interests" derives from Jeremy Bentham; see, e.g., *Plan of Parliamentary Reform* (1817), in *Works*, ed. John Bowring, 11 vols. (Edinburgh: Tait; London: Simpkin, Marshall; Dublin: Cumming, 1843), Vol. III, pp. 440, 446.]

[n]49[1,2],59 all
[o-o]49[1,2],59 none
[p-p]+67

those who influenced the suffrages of the bodies of 200 or 300 electors who returned the ministerial majority, there were always some to whose interests improvement, be it in what it might, would have been adverse. It made things worse, not better, that the most conspicuous instruments of the system were men of knowledge and cultivation, who had gained the greater part of their reputation as the advocates of improvement. In some of these men it might be personal interest, in others hatred of democracy; but neither scrupled, for the sake of keeping their party together, to make themselves subservient to the purposes of their worst supporters. In order to bind these together in an united band to oppose democracy, they were allowed to have their own way in resisting all other change. This was of itself fatal to the durability of a government, in the present condition of the world. No government can now expect to be permanent, unless it guarantees progress as well as order; nor can it continue really to secure order, unless it promotes progress. It can go on, as yet, with only a little of the spirit of improvement *q*. While*q* reformers have even a remote hope of effecting their objects through the existing system, they are generally willing to bear with it. But when there is no hope at all; when the institutions themselves seem to oppose an unyielding barrier to the progress of improvement, the advancing tide heaps itself up behind them till it bears them down.

This was one great characteristic of the government of Louis Philippe. The other, equally discreditable, was the more fatal to that government, because identified, still more than the first, in public opinion, with the personal character and agency of the King himself. It wrought almost exclusively through the meaner and more selfish impulses of mankind. Its sole instrument of government consisted in a direct appeal to men's immediate personal interests or interested fears. It never appealed to, or endeavoured to put on its side, any noble, elevated, or generous principle of action. It repressed and discouraged all such, as being dangerous to it. In the same manner in which Napoleon cultivated the love of military distinction as his one means of action upon the multitude, so did Louis Philippe strive to immerse all France in the *culte des intérêts matériels*,[*] in the worship of the cash-box and of the ledger. It is not, or *r* it has not hitherto been, in the character of Frenchmen to be content with being thus governed. Some idea of grandeur, at least some feeling of national self-importance, must be associated with that which they will voluntarily follow and obey. The one inducement by which Louis Philippe's government recommended itself to the middle classes, was that revolutions and riots *s*are*s* bad for trade. They are so, but that is a very small part of the considerations which ought to determine our estimation of them. While classes were thus appealed to through their class interest, every individual who, either

[*See p. 176n above.]

*q-q*49[1,2]   ; while
*r*49[1,2]   at least
*s-s*49[1,2]   were

from station, reputation, or talent, appeared worth gaining, was addressed through whatever personal interest, either of money or vanity, he was thought most likely to be accessible to. Many were attempted unsuccessfully, many successfully. Corruption was carried to the utmost pitch that the resources at the disposal of the government admitted of.

Accordingly, the best spirits in France had long felt, and felt each year more and more, that the government of Louis Philippe was a demoralizing government; that under its baneful influence all public principle, or public spirit, or regard for political opinions, was giving way more and more to selfish indifference in the propertied classes generally, and, in many of the more conspicuous individuals, to the shameless pursuit of personal gain.

It is almost superfluous to adduce testimonies to facts of such universal notoriety; but it is worth while to refer to two documents, which demonstrate, after all that has been said of the unexpectedness of the events of February, how clearly it was seen by competent judges that, from the principles on which the government had long been carried on, such a termination of its career was almost certain to happen at some time, and might happen at any time.

One of these documents is a speech of M. de Tocqueville, delivered in the Chamber of Deputies on the 27th of January 1848, exactly four weeks before the Revolution.[*] In this remarkable and almost prophetic discourse, M. de Tocqueville said that in the class which possessed and exercised political rights, "political morality is declining; it is already deeply tainted, it becomes more deeply so from day to day. More and more, opinions, sentiments, and ideas of a public character are supplanted by personal interests, personal aims, points of view borrowed from private interest and private life."[†] He called the members of the hostile majority themselves to witness, whether in the five, ten, or fifteen years last elapsed, the number of those who voted for them from private motives was not perpetually increasing, the number who did so from political opinion constantly diminishing?

Let them tell me if around them, under their eyes, there is not gradually establishing itself in public opinion a singular species of tolerance for the facts I have been speaking of,—if, by little and little, there is not forming itself a vulgar and low morality, according to which the man who possesses political rights owes it to himself, owes it to his children, to his wife, to his relations, to make a personal use of those rights for their benefit—if this is not gradually raising itself into a sort of duty of the father of a family?—if this new morality, unknown in the great times of our history, unknown at the commencement of our Revolution, is not developing itself more and more, and making daily progress in the public mind.

[*See "Discours prononcé à la chambre des députés, le 27 janvier 1848," in *Oeuvres complètes*, ed. Mme de Tocqueville [and Gustave de Beaumont], 9 vols. (Paris: Lévy frères, 1864-66), Vol. IX, pp. 520-35.]
[†See App. B below, p. 394.]

He described the acts by which the government of Louis Philippe had made itself accessary to this decline of public spirit. In the first place, by the gigantic strides which it was making towards despotism:

> The government has re-possessed itself, especially in these last years, of greater powers, a larger measure of influence, prerogatives more manifold and more considerable, than it had possessed at any other epoch. It has become infinitely more powerful than could have been imagined, not only by those who conferred, but by those who accepted, the reins of government in 1830.

The mischief was aggravated by the indirect and crafty manner in which it was brought about.

> It was by reclaiming old powers, which were thought to have been abolished in *1830*; by reviving old rights, which were supposed to have been annulled; by bringing again into activity old laws, which were believed to have been abrogated, and applying new ones in a different meaning from that in which they had been enacted. . . . Do you suppose that this crooked and surreptitious manner of gradually regaining ascendancy, as it were by surprise, through other means than those granted by the constitution,—think you that this strange spectacle of address and *savoir-faire,* publicly exhibited for several years on so vast a theatre, to a whole nation looking on,—that this spectacle was of a nature to improve public morals?

And supposing, by a great concession, that the men who wrought this evil were themselves persuaded that it was good—

> They have not the less effected it by means which morality disavows. They have achieved it by taking men not by their honourable side, but by their bad side—by their passions, their weaknesses, their personal interests, often their vices. . . . And to accomplish these things, it has been necessary for them to call to their assistance, to honour with their favour, to introduce into their daily intercourse, men who wished neither for honest ends nor honest means; who desired but the gross satisfaction of their private interests, by the aid of the power confided to them.

After citing one scandalous instance of a high office of trust conferred on a person notoriously corrupt, M. de Tocqueville added: "I do not regard this fact as a solitary one; I consider it the symptom of a general evil, the most salient trait of an entire course of policy. *In the paths which you "have" chosen for yourselves, you had need of such men.*"

As a consequence of these things, he appealed to the whole body of his hearers, whether it was not true that—

> The sentiment, the instinct of instability, that sentiment, the precursor of revolutions, which often presages them, and sometimes causes them to take place—already exists to a most serious degree in the country. . . . Is there not a breeze of revolution in the air? This breeze, no one knows where it rises, whence it comes, nor (believe me) whom it sweeps away. . . . It is my deep and deliberate conviction, that public morals are degenerating, and

---

[t-t]49[1,2]   July
[u-u]49[1,2]   had [aviez *in* Source]

that the degeneracy of public morals will lead you in a short, perhaps a very short time, to
new revolutions. . . . Have you at this very hour the certainty of a to-morrow? Do you know
what may happen in France in a year, in a month, perhaps even in a day? You do not; but this
you know, that the tempest is in the horizon, that it is marching towards you; will you suffer
yourselves to be overtaken by it?

Several changes in legislation have been talked of. I am much inclined to believe that
such changes are not only useful, but necessary. I believe in the utility of electoral reform, in
the urgency of excluding placemen from parliament. But I am not so senseless as to be
unaware, that it is not the laws, in themselves, which make the destiny of peoples; no, it is
not the mechanism of the laws, which produces the great events of the world; it is the spirit
of the government. Keep your laws if you will, though I think it a great error; keep
them—keep even the men, if you like, I for my part will be no obstacle; but, in Heaven's
name, change the spirit of the government, for, I say it again, that spirit is hurrying you to
the abyss.[*]

The other document which shall be cited in proof that the natural consequences
of Louis Philippe's system of government were foreseen by near observers, is the
evidence of M. Goudchaux, banker at Paris, and for some months Minister of
Finance to the Republic; delivered before the Commission d'Enquête on the events
of May and June last. M. Goudchaux, who said in his place in the Assembly that
the Revolution had come too soon, nevertheless declared in his evidence, that he
and some of his political friends felt so convinced that it was impending, that, a
few days before it broke out, they held a meeting at his house, to arrange a list of
names for a Provisional Government; but disagreed on the question whether to
admit or to exclude from the number M. Louis Blanc.[†]

The Revolution, therefore, which appears to Lord Brougham in the singular
character of an event without a cause, was so much the natural result of known
causes, as to be capable of being foreseen. And when what had been foreseen by
the more discerning, actually came to pass, even the undiscerning recognised in it
the legitimate consequence of a just popular indignation. M. Garnier-Pagès was
justified in his apostrophe, in the National Assembly, on the 24th of last October:

I ask it of everybody:—Did not every one, in the first days, agree that the Revolution
which had been accomplished was moral, still more than political? Did not every one agree
that this great renovation had been preceded by a real and terrible reaction against
corruption, and emanated from all that was honest and honourable in the hearts of the
French nation?*

[*Ibid., pp. 395-7.]

[†Michel Goudchaux, "Déposition," in Rapport de la commission d'enquête, Vol. I,
p. 288.]

*"Je le demande à tous: 'Est-ce que tout le monde, dans les premiers jours, ne convenait
pas que la Révolution qui venait de s'accomplir était politique et morale, morale surtout?
Est-ce que tout le monde ne convenait pas que cette grande rénovation avait été précédée par
une réaction réelle et terrible contre la corruption, et faite par tout ce qu'il y avait d'honnête
dans le coeur de la France?'" [Louis Antoine Garnier-Pagès, Speech in the National
Assembly (24 Oct., 1848), Le Moniteur Universel, 25 Oct., 1848, p. 2966.] v

v49[1,2] [paragraph] M. Guizot, in his little tract on Democracy in France [(Paris: Masson, 1849)],
vainly attempts to divert attention from the profligate system of government of which he made himself

Contrast these representations of the state of the national mind preceding the Revolution, by persons really acquainted with it, with the following specimen from Lord Brougham's pamphlet: "The lesson is taught by the experience of February 1848, that to change" the form of government of France "requires no long series of complaints, no suffering from oppression, whether chronic or acute, no indignation at abuses, no combination of parties to effect a change, no preparation for converting the opposition to a ministry into a war with a dynasty."[*] The writer has not the most ordinary knowledge of the public events of his own time. The war with the dynasty began as early as 1831, and was first compelled to mask itself under opposition to a ministry, when the laws of September had made it impossible to attack, through the press, either the King or the monarchy, without the certainty of being ruined and reduced to silence.[†] But public feeling, once sufficiently roused, will force a way through all obstacles; and in spite of the gagging laws, much of the opposition to the Government had latterly become almost avowedly a war against the King. "There was little personal disrespect shown," says the pamphlet, "towards the illustrious Prince."[‡] The main political feature of the six months preceding February was the reform banquets, and the most marked circumstance attending these was the premeditated omission, in most of them, to drink the King's health. Lord Brougham reproaches the reformers with not trusting to "repeated discussion and the exertion of the popular influence"[§] for effecting a reform of the constitution by a vote of parliament. They had little encouragement to rely on such means. The very corruption which was ruining the government in the general opinion, was strengthening it with the narrow and jobbing class who returned a majority of the Chamber. A general election had occurred the summer previous, and the ministerial majority had gained, not lost, in numbers by it. Lord Brougham boasts, through many pages, of the feat performed by Lord Grey's ministry in effecting a great change in the constitution (the first such change in history which was so accomplished) without an insurrection.[¶] But was it without the *fear* of an

[*Brougham, *Letter*, p. 31.]

[†Loi sur les crimes, délits et contraventions de la presse et des autres moyens de publication, Bulletin 155, No. 356 (9 Sept., 1835), *Bulletin des lois du royaume de France*, 9th ser., Pt. 1, VII, 247-56; Loi sur les cours d'assises, Bulletin 155, No. 357 (9 Sept., 1835), *ibid.*, pp. 256-9; and Loi qui rectifie les articles 341, 345, 346, 347 and 352 du code d'instruction criminelle, et l'article 17 du code pénal, Bulletin 155, No. 358 (9 Sept., 1835), *ibid.*, pp. 259-62.]

[‡Brougham, *Letter*, p. 24.]

[§*Ibid.*, pp. 48-9.]

[¶Pp. 52-6; cf. p. 320 above.]

---

the agent, by throwing the whole blame of the catastrophe upon "the idolatry of democracy" [p. 2]. We think this tract the weakest performance to which he ever attached his name, and quite unworthy of his reputation. Its denunciation of democracy is made up of vague and declamatory generalities, which, we should think, even those who agree with him in opinion cannot imagine to be the thing now wanted on so hacknied a subject.

insurrection? If there had been no chance of a rising, would the House of Lords have waved their opposition, or the Duke of Wellington have thrown up the game in despair? If, in England, the mere demonstration of popular force sufficed to effect what elsewhere required its actual exertion, it was because the majority of even the unreformed House of Commons was elected by constituencies sufficiently large for a really powerful and unanimous popular determination to reach it; and because the political usages and long-standing liberties of England allowed of popular meetings and political unions without limit or stint. To the French reformers these means of peaceful demonstration were denied. The nearest approach to them allowed by French law, was the reform dinners; and these, as soon as they began to produce an effect, the government forbade; reviving for that purpose a decree passed in the stormiest period of the first Revolution.[*] It was when this last resource was denied, that popular indignation burst forth, and the monarchy was destroyed.

There never was a greater blunder than to speak of the French Republic as an "improvised government"—"struck out at a heat"—"the result of a sudden thought"—"span new, untried, and even unthought of."[†] The Revolution, indeed, was unpremeditated, spontaneous; the republican leaders had no more to do with effecting it, than the socialist leaders had with the insurrection of June last. But the republicans, immediately after the crisis, became the directors of the movement, because they alone, of the various sections of the French people, had not to improvise a political creed, but already possessed one. It would require a degree of ignorance of French political discussion from 1830 to 1848, which one would not willingly impute even to the author of the *Letter to the Marquess of Lansdowne*, not to know that during those years, republicanism, instead of being "unthought of," had "both been" thought of and talked of, in every variety of tone, by friends and enemies, in all corners of France; that several formidable insurrections had broken out in its name; that many well-known chiefs had been, *and some* still were, in the prisons of Ham, Doullens, and Mont St. Michel, for acts done in its behalf; and that, except the remaining adherents of the elder branch, a republic entered into the calculations of all who speculated either on the dethronement of Louis Philippe, or on the minority of his successor.[‡] If William III had been dethroned for following the example of James II, would the people of this country have put a child on the throne, or sent for some other Prince of Orange

[*For the proclamation issued 21 Feb., 1848, see *The Times*, 23 Feb., 1848, p. 6; for the original decree, see *Gazette Nationale, ou Le Moniteur Universel*, 1 June, 1792, p. 635, and 14 Aug., 1792, p. 953.]

[†Brougham, *Letter*, pp. 30, 15, 29, 15, 15, respectively.]

[‡Louis Philippe d'Orléans, comte de Paris.]

$^{w-w}49^{1,2}$ been both
$^{x-x}49^{1,2}$ or

from beyond sea? Would they not, almost certainly, have fallen back on the Commonwealth? What the English of the seventeenth century would assuredly have done, the French might do in the nineteenth without exciting surprise. And it was the more to be expected that they would do so, since constitutional royalty is in itself a thing as uncongenial to the character and habits of the French, or any other people of the European Continent, as it is suited to the tone of thought and feeling characteristic of England.

From causes which might be traced in the history and development of English society and government, the general habit and practice of the English mind is compromise. No idea is carried out to more than a small portion of its legitimate consequences. Neither by the generality of our speculative thinkers, nor in the practice of the nation, are the principles which are professed ever thoroughly acted upon; something always stops the application half way. This national habit has consequences of very various character, of which the following is one. It is natural to minds governed by habit (which is the character of the English more than of any other civilized people) that their tastes and inclinations become accommodated to their habitual practice; and as in England no principle is ever fully carried out, discordance between principles and practice has come to be regarded, not only as the natural, but as the desirable state. This is not an epigram, or a paradox, but a sober description of the tone of sentiment commonly found in Englishmen. They never feel themselves safe unless they are living under the shadow of some conventional fiction—[y] some agreement to say one thing and mean another. Now, constitutional royalty is precisely an arrangement of this description. The very essence of it is, that the so-called sovereign does not govern, ought not to govern, is not intended to govern; but yet must be held up to the nation, be addressed by the nation, and even address the nation, as if he or she did govern. This, which was originally a compromise between the friends of popular liberty and those of absolute monarchy, has established itself as a sincere feeling in the mind of the nation; who would be offended, and think their liberties endangered, if a king or [z]a[z] queen meddled any further in the government than to give a formal sanction to all acts of parliament, and to appoint as ministry, or rather as minister, the person whom the majority in parliament pointed out; and yet would be unaffectedly shocked, if every considerable act of government did not profess and pretend to be the act and mandate of the person on the throne. The English are fond of boasting that they do not regard the theory, but only the practice of institutions; but their boast stops short of the truth; they actually prefer that their theory should be at variance with their practice. If any one proposed to them to convert their practice into a theory, he would be scouted. It appears to them unnatural and unsafe, either to do the thing which they profess, or to profess the thing which they do. A theory

[y]49[1,2]   of
[z-z]+59,67

which purports to be the very thing intended to be acted upon, fills them with alarm; it seems to carry with it a boundless extent of unforeseeable consequences. This disagreeable feeling they are only free from, when the principles laid down are obviously matters of convention, which, it is agreed on all parts, are not to be pressed home.

It is otherwise in France: so much so, that few Frenchmen can understand this singular characteristic of the English mind; which, seen imperfectly and by glimpses, is the origin of those accusations of profound hypocrisy, mistakenly brought by many foreigners against the English nation. Englishmen, on their part, can in general as little understand the comparative simplicity and directness of Continental notions. The French impatience of discrepancy between theory and practice, seems to them fancifulness, and want of good sense. It was a Frenchman, not an Englishman, who erected the English practice of constitutional monarchy into a theory: but his maxim, "*le roi règne et ne gouverne pas*,"[*] took no root on the other side of the Channel. The French had no relish for a system, the forms of which were intended to simulate something at variance with acknowledged *fact*[a]. Those who were for a king at all, wanted one who was a substantial power in the State, and not a cipher: while, if the will of the nation was to be the government—if the king was to do nothing but register the nation's decrees—both the reason and the feelings of the French were in favour of having those decrees pronounced directly by the people's own delegates.

A constitutional monarchy, therefore, was likely in France, as it is likely in every other country [b]in[b] Continental Europe, to be but a brief halt on the road from a despotism to a republic. But though a republic, for France, was the most natural and congenial of all the forms of free government, it had two great hindrances to contend with. One was, the political indifference of the majority—the result of want of education, and of the absence of habits of discussion and participation in public business. The other was the dread inspired by the remembrance of 1793 and 1794; a dread which, though much weakened since 1830, did and does in some measure subsist, notwithstanding what was so promptly done by the Provisional Government to disconnect the new republic from whatever was sanguinary in the recollections of the old. These two causes prevented the French nation in general from demanding or wishing for a republican government; and as long as those causes continue, they will render its existence, even now when it is established, more or less precarious.

The Provisional Government knew this. They had no illusions. They were not blind to any of their difficulties. The generation of which they were a part, has neither the ardent faith nor the boundless hope which belonged to the era of its predecessors, and which made it easy for an entire people to be transformed into

[*See Louis Adolphe Thiers, leading article, *National*, 4 Feb., 1830, p. 1.]

[a]-[a]49[1,2]   facts
[b]-[b]49[1,2]   of

heroes. It has been publicly stated, that of the eleven members of the Provisional Government, though all or nearly all were republicans, M. Ledru-Rollin alone, before the 24th of February, thought that the time had yet come for a republic: and even he, it would appear, in reliance less on what the public sentiment already was, than on what it might in his opinion be made. It will be the immortal glory of these men with posterity, that they did not need the illusions of political inexperience to make them heroes; that they could act out their opinions with calm determination, without exaggerating to their own minds the measure of success, the amount of valuable result, which probably awaited them. They might regret that the nation was not better prepared for the new régime; but when the old had perished, it was not for them to decide that the institutions of their own preference were too good for their countrymen, but to try whether a republican government, administered by sincere republicans, if it did not find the French people republicans, could make them so.

With this noble hope the members of the Provisional Government, if intentions can be judged from acts, accepted the power which was thrust upon them:[*] and whoever passes judgment on their proceedings according to any other idea of the problem which lay before them, is an incapable appreciator of the situation and its exigency, and grossly unjust to the men.

Never had any man or set of men, suddenly raised to power, a more complicated task before them. It was a more difficult achievement in their case to govern at all, than in the case of almost any other government to govern well. They were nominal dictators, without either soldiers or police whom they could call to their assistance, without even any organized body of adherents. They were absolute rulers, with no means of enforcing obedience. And they actually did rule Paris, for two whole months succeeding a revolution, by means of such obedience only as was given voluntarily. This is the part of their conduct which, to a certain extent, has had least injustice done to it, since it has commonly been admitted to have been a difficult and a meritorious achievement: but the unwilling acknowledgment of merit has stopped in generals; there is hardly one of the acts by which this great feat was accomplished, that has not since been made a subject of reproach to them; though not until the emergency had passed away, and conduct of which the whole benefit had been reaped, could now be criticised at leisure. Lord Brougham, among others, cannot tolerate the speeches by which they calmed the popular effervescence—speeches for which, at the time when they were made, the speakers were worshipped almost as gods by the frightened Parisian bourgeoisie.[†] One would have thought that men whose almost sole engine of

[*Cf. Shakespeare, *Twelfth Night*, II, v, 146 (in *The Riverside Shakespeare*, ed. G. Blakemore Evans [Boston: Houghton Mifflin, 1974], p. 422).]

[†Brougham, *Letter*, e.g., pp. 3, 15. See, e.g., Lamartine's two "Discours au peuple" (25 Feb., 1848), in his *Trois mois au pouvoir* (Paris: Lévy, 1848), pp. 64-6. See also *Le Moniteur Universel*, 28 Feb., 1848, p. 511, for an account of speeches by Arago, Dupont de l'Eure, and Crémieux, on 27 Feb., 1848.]

government, for months, which in times of revolution are ages, was the effect which they could produce by haranguing an armed populace—who had daily to persuade that populace to forego its demands, at the peril of their lives if it persisted in them—and who succeeded in that object, and kept the frame of government in existence until things became quiet, and authority resumed its course—might claim some indulgence as to the means by which this truly wonderful success was attained. One hardly expected to hear them taunted with fulsome flattery and mob-sycophancy, because they gave fair words to those whose good-will was all they had to depend on for preventing confusion. One would have thought, too, that a people, or a populace if the term is preferred, who actually were induced, by fair words alone, to make themselves a voluntary police, and preserve such order in a great capital that the offences committed were fewer than in ordinary times, deserved some praise from their temporary rulers, and might receive it without subjecting these to any imputation of time-serving. But Lord Brougham cannot admit that any praise can be due to a people who make barricades, and turn out a government. One of the most unworthy points in his pamphlet, is the abusive tone and language into which he breaks out, every time that he has occasion to speak of the working classes; of those among them at least who meddle in insurrections, or think they have anything to do with the government except to obey it.[*] "Rabble," "dregs of the populace," "armed ruffians,"[†] are his expressions for the most intelligent and ᶜbest-conductedᶜ labouring class, take it for all in all, to be found on the earth's surface—the artisans of Paris. His determination to refuse them every particle of honour must be inveterate indeed, since he will not allow them even courage; he will not so much as admit that they actually fought!—the many hundreds of killed and wounded being, it must be supposed, the product of accident.

Even fairer opponents than the pamphleteer, while giving deserved credit to the Provisional Government for having overcome the tremendous difficulty of governing and preserving order, have passed a severe judgment upon the measures of legislation and administration which were adopted by this temporary authority. Some of their acts are censured as exceeding the legitimate powers of a Provisional Government, and deciding questions which ought to have been reserved for the appointed representatives of the nation. Others are condemned as ill-judged and pernicious in themselves.[‡]

[*See Samuel Horsley, *The Speeches in Parliament of Samuel Horsley*, ed. H. Horsley (Dundee: Chalmers, 1813), pp. 167-8.]

[†Brougham, *Letter*, pp. 88, 88, 14, respectively.]

[‡See, e.g., Anon., "News of the Week," *Spectator*, 11 Mar., 1848, p. 237; Archibald Alison, "Fall of the Throne of the Barricades," *Blackwood's Edinburgh Magazine*, LXIII (Apr., 1848), 401, 410; John Wilson Croker, "The French Revolution—February 1848," *Quarterly Review*, LXXXII (Mar., 1848), 583-7; and William Edward Hickson, "The French Republic," *Westminster Review*, L (Oct., 1848), 195-7.]

ᶜ⁻ᶜ49¹,²   most well-conducted

How far these charges are merited it will be easier to judge, if we place ourselves in the situation of these men, and endeavour to realize, in imagination, the demands which their position made upon them.

What would have been the proper conduct of men who, believing a democratic republic to be not only in itself the sole form of government which secures due attention to the interests of the great body of the community, but also calculated to work well in their own country—believing, however, that the majority of their countrymen were indifferent, and a great ^dportion^d averse to it—found themselves unexpectedly placed, by an insurrection of their own supporters, in a position in which it seemed in their power to direct, for some time to come, the current of events? Were they to attempt nothing in favour of their own opinions? Were they to assume no initiative? Were they merely to keep things quiet and *in statu quo*, until the apathetic majority could come together and spontaneously determine whether they would have what these, the leaders, thought the best institutions, or what they regarded as the worst? Were the noblest spirits and most enlightened minds in the country to employ an opportunity such as scarcely occurs once in a thousand years, in simply waiting on the whims and prejudices of the many? Were they who, even on the showing of this pamphlet, formed the only party which had fixed principles and a strong public spirit, to leave all to the decision of those who either had only mean and selfish objects, or had not yet acquired any opinions? Had they done so, they would have deserved to be stigmatized in history as the veriest cravens who ever marred by irresolution the opening prospects of a people.

The democratic principles of these men forbade them to impose despotically, even if they had the power, their political opinions upon an unwilling majority; and compelled them to refer all their acts to the ultimate ratification of a freely and fairly elected representative assembly. But the sovereignty of the whole people does not mean the passiveness of individuals—the negation of all impulse, of all guidance, of all initiative, on the part of the better and wiser few. The more firmly resolved were these men to stand by the government of the majority even if it did not adopt their opinions, the more incumbent was it on them to spare no pains for bringing over the majority to them. Their great task was to republicanize the public mind; to strive by all means, apart from coercion or deception, that the coming election should produce an assembly of sincere republicans. And since this could not but, at the best, be regarded as doubtful, they were bound, as far as prudence permitted, to adopt provisionally as many valuable measures as possible; such measures as the future assembly, though it might have hesitated to pass, would not perhaps venture to abrogate. These two things the Provisional Government did in some measure attempt; and though the enemies of popular institutions have clamoured against them as if they had carried both these courses of action to the most abominable extremities, posterity will have more reason, not for censure, but for regret, that they did not venture far enough in either.

^{d-d}49^{1,2}   proportion

Among their proceedings which aimed at the first object, that of republicanizing the nation, those which have been most commented on were the sending of the much-talked-of commissioners to the departments, and M. Ledru-Rollin's and M. Carnot's famous bulletins and circulars.[*]

The deputation of commissioners into all parts of France, to explain what had taken place, to represent the new government, and supersede the authorities appointed under the previous régime, seems so natural and indispensable a proceeding, that the storm of disapprobation which it encountered is only a proof of the blind suspicion and distrust with which the provinces received all they did, and which was one of the greatest difficulties of their situation. Much scandal was given by an expression in M. Ledru-Rollin's instructions to the commissioners, telling them that their powers were unlimited.[†] Was it not the very necessity of the case, that the authority of the Provisional Government was for the time unlimited, that is, unfettered by any constitutional restraints? and could they have gone on without imparting to their sole representatives in the provinces, subject to responsibility to themselves, the fulness of their own power? Not the power assumed, but the use made of it, is, in a time of revolution, the criterion of right or wrong. The Provisional Government knew that these commissioners, so ridiculously compared to the terrible proconsuls of the Convention, were in small danger of being tempted to any over-exertion of power. They knew that their delegates, like themselves, depended on voluntary obedience for being able to exercise any power at all. These formidable despots, who are painted in as frightful colours as if they had carried with them a guillotine *en ambulance*, were, more than once, simply taken by the hand and led out of the town on their way back to Paris. The selection of persons for these appointments has also been much cavilled at. Lord Brougham revives the almost forgotten calumny, that "one of his [M. Ledru-Rollin's] commissioners had been a felon, condemned to the galleys, and had undergone the punishment."[‡] Any one who has taken as much pains to be informed as is implied in merely reading the French newspapers, knows that the person alluded to was not a delegate of the government, or of M. Ledru-Rollin, but of the clubs. Mistakes no doubt were made in the rapid selection of so great a number of persons, in whom zeal for the principles of the Republic, being the most essential requisite, excluded many persons in other respects eligible. But the maligners of the Provisional Government may be challenged to deny, that the great majority of the selections did honour both to the choosers and to the chosen; that a

---

[*Alexandre Auguste Ledru-Rollin, *Bulletins de la république, ministère de l'intérieur*, in *Recueil complet des actes du gouvernement provisoire*, ed. Emile Carrey, 2 pts. (Paris: Durand, 1848), Pt. II, pp. 617-79; and Lazare Hippolyte Carnot, *Le ministère de l'instruction publique et des cultes, depuis le 24 février jusqu'au 5 juillet 1848* (Paris: Pagnerre, 1848); the "circulaire" is on pp. 23-6.]

[†Ledru-Rollin, Bulletin No. 13 (8 Apr., 1848), in *Recueil*, Pt. II, p. 658.]

[‡Brougham, *Letter*, p.113n. The allusion is to Joseph Calixte Martin, alias Riancourt.]

large proportion acquired, in the districts to which they were sent, great and well-merited popularity, and contributed largely to rally those parts of France to the cause of the Republic; that many are now (or were, up to M. Léon Faucher's recent ejection *en masse*) prefects, with general approval, of the departments to which they were delegated; and that where errors had been committed, they were at once corrected, as soon as *e* brought to light.

As little ground is there for the embittered denunciations *f* against the circulars and proclamations. Two only of these documents gave cause for just criticism: the famous sixteenth bulletin,[*] and M. Carnot's circular. The former was withdrawn on the very day of its appearance, and was afterwards declared to have been published by the mistake of a clerk, the draft never having been seen or approved by the minister or by his secretary. M. Carnot, in his celebrated circular, though he expressed himself unguardedly, could never, by any candid reader, be supposed to mean anything but what he has always declared that he did mean: to impress on those to whom the document was addressed, that it was more important, at that particular juncture, that the assembly to be selected should consist of sincere republicans, than that it should contain the greatest possible number of lettered and instructed men;[†] he knowing, as he had good reason to *g*know*g*, that in the greater part of France, most of those who had gained a reputation as men of letters and acquirements under the old régime, like most others who had thriven under that corrupt system, were not to be relied on by the new. It is false that M. Carnot disparaged knowledge, or panegyrized ignorance. He declared, on the contrary, that to make laws and a constitution was a task for the intellectual *élite* of France.[‡] But were nine hundred men of talent, nine hundred talkers, needed, or capable of being made useful, for such a task? While thinking only of the exigencies of the moment, M. Carnot gave expression, perhaps unwittingly, to a great general truth. It is not the business of a numerous representative assembly to make laws. Laws are never well made but by a few—often best by only one. The office of a representative body is not to make the laws, but to see that they are made by the right persons, and to be the organ of the nation for giving or withholding its ratification of them. For these functions, good sense, good intentions, and attachment to the principles of free government, are the most important requisites. Highly cultivated intellect is not *h*essential*h*, even if we could expect to find it, in more than a select few; and as for that superficial cleverness—that command of words and skilful management of commonplaces,

---

[*Ledru-Rollin, Bulletin No. 16 (15 Apr., 1848), in *Recueil*, Pt. II, pp. 663-4.]
[†Carnot, *Le ministère de l'instruction publique*, p. 24.]
[‡*Ibid.*]

*e*49[1,2]   they were
*f*49[1,2]   made
*g-g*49[1,2]   do
*h-h*49[1,2]   needed

which pass for talent and instruction on the hustings, at public meetings, and in society—most really cultivated persons, we believe, are agreed in opinion, that of this all legislative assemblies have, and are likely to have, a much greater abundance than at all conduces to the ends for which they purport to exist.

[i]When[i] such are the worst things that can be charged against the Provisional Government, their conduct must indeed be free from serious reproach. In this particular matter, the management of the elections, their behaviour, in all that is known of it, will bear comparison with that of any government in any country. Probably no government that ever existed, certainly no French government, practised so entire an abstinence from illegitimate influence—from any employment whatever of government influence to procure elections in their own favour. It is not intended to claim merit for them on this account. Their principles required it: but let it be said, that under great temptations they were true to their principles. It is an unfortunate fact, that in many things besides this, had they been less disinterested, less upright, less determined to rely solely on the power of honesty, they would probably have effected more both for themselves and for their cause. It is because they persisted in their resolve to owe nothing to any other than fair means, that they have been precipitated from power; and among many varieties of calumny, have not escaped even those charges from which their whole conduct had borne the stamp of the most evident determination to keep free.

It would be astonishing (if the impudence of party calumny could astonish any one) to observe what are the crimes of which the detractors of this noble body of men have accused, and are not ashamed still to continue accusing them. They are even now spoken of in newspapers, as if their management of the elections had been something almost unexampled in tyranny and turpitude; and all this time neither a bribe nor a threat, either to an elector or to a body of electors, has been proved, or it may almost be said alleged, against them. If the verdict of history [j]was[j] gathered from the assertions of cotemporaries, what contempt would it inspire for the judgment of posterity on eminent characters, when we find that these men have been charged individually with embezzling money from the Treasury; that even M. [k]de[k] Lamartine has thought it necessary to lay before the public the details of his private fortune and pecuniary transactions, in order to extinguish the slander beyond possibility of revival![*] Not without cause; for though malignity itself is not shameless enough any longer to repeat the charge against him personally, his exculpation has not liberated his colleagues; and there have appeared within these few weeks, in more than one English newspaper,

[*See Lamartine, "Lettre aux dix départements" (25 Aug., 1848), in *Trois mois au pouvoir*, pp. 35-9.]

[i-i]49[1,2] Where
[j-j]49[1,2] were
[k-k]+59,67 [*the addition in 59,67 of* de *to Lamartine's name is not henceforth noted; no reason has been discovered for Mill's inconsistency in sometimes including it and sometimes not in 49[1,2]*]

articles in which the financial administration of the Provisional Government has been spoken of as one mass of profligate malversation. There is nothing which the spirit that pursues these men would not dare to assert, when it can venture on this. One member of the Provisional Government has been made a mark for greater inveteracy of assault than the rest—M. Ledru-Rollin. Everybody has heard scandalous stories concerning him; and in his case, some of these were specific, and accompanied with names and circumstances. If those which did not enter into particulars, had no better foundation than those which did, M. Ledru-Rollin, as to pecuniary integrity, is the statesman of most unimpeachable character in Europe; for every accusation of the kind that we are acquainted with, which had any tangible character, was investigated by the Commission d'Enquête,[*] and disproved by the evidence of the persons alleged to have been connected with it. In England, his assailants, and those of his colleagues, seized the opportunity of the appearance of a mass of evidence which they knew nobody would read,[†] to affirm (it must in charity be supposed, without having read it themselves) that it substantiated all the floating rumours of misconduct, and covered the members of the government with indelible disgrace. In France, it was felt even by their enemies to have entirely failed of eliciting the disclosures which had been expected from it. M. Ledru-Rollin instantly rose many degrees in public estimation, and has occupied, since those documents appeared, a position of greater political importance than before.

To speak now of those measures of the Provisional Government which partook of a legislative character; for none of which Lord Brougham can find any other purpose, than "to retain the people's favour."[‡] Assuredly to retain that favour, at such a time, was as virtuous an object, considering what depended on it, as any of those which influence the *course* of legislation in ordinary times. Yet, if it is meant to be said that for the sake of the people's favour they performed one act, issued one single edict, which did not, in and for itself, commend itself to them as a thing fit to be done, the assertion is gratuitous, and in opposition to all that is known of the case. Many things were done hastily, to make sure of their being done at all: some were done, which it has since been necessary to undo; but *no* one thing can they be shown to have done, which was not such as, in their deliberate opinion, ought to have been done.

Lord Brougham regards the immediate abolition of colonial slavery as a hasty measure, and beyond the powers of a Provisional Government.[§] Considering

[*See its *Rapport*, 3 vols. (Paris: n.p., 1848), to which Mill refers for the evidence of Chenu, Goudchaux, and Blanc, at 322, 328, and 353.]

[†Mill is presumably referring to the *Rapport*.]

[‡Brougham, *Letter*, p. 120.]

[§*Ibid.* For the abolition of colonial slavery, see Décret and Arrêtés, Bulletin 5, Nos. 67-9 (4 Mar., 1848), *Bulletin des lois de la république française*, 10th ser., I, 53-4.]

*l-l*49[1,2]   cause [*printer's error?*]
*m-m*49[1,2]   not

what proved to be the character of the National Assembly, who can say, if this great act of justice had been left for it to do, how long "a" time would have passed before it would have found the leisure or the will to perform it? Financial difficulties, which have gathered so heavily round the infant Republic, would have been enough of themselves to have caused the postponement of emancipation, if it was to be preceded, not followed, by compensation. The Government did at once what required to be so done; they struck off the fetters of the slave, knowing, and because they knew, that the act, once done, was irrevocable. By thus acting, they not only made sure from the first, that, whatever else might happen, some hundreds of thousands of human beings should have permanent cause to bless the Revolution, but averted the chances of civil war and massacre consequent on the indefinite withholding, in such circumstances, of so clear a °moral° right. The indemnification of the owners they left to the future Assembly; but committed the French nation, as far as it was in the power of a government to commit them, to that act of justice.

Lord Brougham talks also of "their incredible decree making all judges hold office during pleasure, and by popular election;" thus placing "the administration of justice in the hands of the populace."[*] After this positive assertion, some persons may be surprised to be told that no such decree ever existed. What the writer was confusedly thinking about, must have been the act which removed about half-a-dozen judicial functionaries from office, declaring in the preamble that the inamovability of judges was inconsistent with republican principles.[†] They may have been *p*, and we think they were,*p* wrong in this; but the opinion is one held by a large portion of the republican party; and several of the best writers on judicial establishments, both in France and in England, have sanctioned it by their authority.

A more important subject than this is M. de Lamartine's circular to the diplomatic agents of the French government, otherwise known as his "Manifeste aux Puissances," declaratory of the foreign policy of the new Republic.[‡] This has been made by Lord Brougham the occasion of an attack on M. de Lamartine, which surpasses, in its defiance of fact, almost every other specimen of mis-statement in this most uncandid pamphlet.

The Provisional Government, he alleges, by this manifesto—

Held out the hand of fellowship to the insurgents of all nations. . . . M. Lamartine does not, and he cannot deny, that he assured the people of all other countries of assistance from France in case they should fail to work out by force their own emancipation; in other words,

[*Brougham, *Letter*, p. 120.]
[†See *Le Moniteur Universel*, 18 Apr., 1848, p. 853.]
[‡In *Trois mois au pouvoir*, pp. 69-78.]

n-n+59,67   [*printer's error?*]
o-o+67
*p-p*49[1,2]   right or

he promised that France would help all insurgents who might be defeated by their lawful rulers in their rebellion against established authority. Beyond all question this is the very worst thing that France has done; the most sinning against all principle, the most hurtful to herself and to the world.[*]

In this style he continues for several pages, with the volume before him, or (as the context proves) fresh in his recollection, which, together with M. de Lamartine's defence of his administration, contains a reprint of every speech and every public document which proceeded from him during his "three months in power."[†] Not one of these contains anything resembling what M. de Lamartine, as the organ of the French government, is here charged with having said.

The "Manifeste aux Puissances" is, both in spirit and in letter, a declaration of the intention of the French Republic to remain at peace. The only passages which admit of any other construction shall be quoted at length, to leave no excuse for those who may imagine that what is so positively asserted, and if false may be so easily confuted, must be true.

The treaties of 1815 no longer exist as obligatory, in the opinion of the French Republic; but the territorial boundaries fixed by those treaties are an existing fact, which the Republic admits as a basis and a starting point in its relations with other countries.

But, while the treaties of 1815 no longer exist except as a fact, to be modified by common agreement, and while the Republic openly declares that it has a right and a mission to arrive regularly and pacifically at such modifications—the good sense, the moderation, the conscience, the prudence of the Republic exist, and are for Europe a better and more honourable guarantee than the letter of those treaties which she herself has so often violated or modified.

Apply yourself, sir, to make this emancipation of the Republic from the treaties of 1815 understood and admitted, and to point out that this liberation is in no respect irreconcileable with the repose of Europe.

We avow openly, that *if the hour of reconstruction for certain oppressed nationalities in Europe or elsewhere, appeared to us to have sounded in the decrees of Providence*; if Switzerland, our faithful ally since Francis I, were constrained or menaced in the movement which is taking place within her to lend an additional force to her band of democratic governments; if the independent states of Italy were invaded; if the attempt were made to impose limits or obstacles to their internal transformations, or to contest by force of arms their right of allying themselves with each other to consolidate a common country; the French Republic would consider itself at liberty to take arms for the protection of these legitimate movements of growth and of nationality.[‡]

Does this promise "that France would help all insurgents who might be defeated by their lawful rulers?"[§] Can the most perverse ingenuity find in the preceding words one vestige of a suggestion of such an intention? M. de Lamartine claimed

[*Brougham, *Letter*, pp. 120-2.]
[†Lamartine, *Trois mois au pouvoir, passim.* See Brougham, *Letter*, e.g., pp. 30, 146.]
[‡Translated from Lamartine, *Manifeste aux puissances*, in *Trois mois au pouvoir*, pp. 75-6. Cf. App. B, pp. 397-8 below.]
[§Brougham, *Letter*, p. 121.]

for his country the right, according to its own discretion and judgment, to assist any nation which might be struggling to free itself from the yoke of foreign conquerors. Assistance against foreigners, not against native rulers, was the only assistance of which the smallest mention was made; and the first of the supposed cases, that of an extinguished nationality, was the only one which had anything to do with "insurrection,"[*] even against foreigners. And in that there was not only no promise, but an express reservation to the French government to judge for itself whether the "hour of reconstruction" had arrived or not.

But it is not necessary to rely solely on the words of the manifesto. M. de Lamartine had the advantage, in this case, of being his own commentator. The manifesto was issued on the 4th of March. On the 19th of that month M. de Lamartine received a deputation of Poles, and a deputation of Irish on the 3rd of the month following. Both these deputations asked for the succour, which it is pretended that he had promised to all who might be defeated in a "rebellion" against "their lawful rulers." To both all succour was refused. It is an abuse of the privilege of short memory to have already forgotten declarations which made no little sensation when delivered, and had no slight influence on the subsequent course of events in Europe.

To the Poles, he said—

The Republic is not at war, either open or disguised, with any existing governments, so long as those governments do not declare themselves at war with France. The Republic will neither commit, nor voluntarily suffer to be committed, any act of aggression and violence against the Germanic nations. . . . The Provisional Government will not allow its policy to be altered by a foreign nation, however greatly we sympathize with it. We love Poland, Italy, all oppressed peoples; but above all we love France, and we are responsible for its destinies, and perhaps for those of Europe at the present moment. This responsibility we will resign to no one but to the nation itself. The Republic must not, and will not, act in contradiction to its professions; the credit of its word is at stake, and shall never be forfeited. What have we said in our *manifeste aux puissances*? We said, thinking particularly of you—Whenever it shall appear to us that the time fixed by Providence for the resurrection of a nationality unjustly blotted out from the map has arrived, we shall fly to its assistance. But we have, with good right, reserved to France what belongs to her alone,—the appreciation of the hour, the moment, the justice, the cause, and the means by which it would be fitting for us to intervene. The means which up to this time we have chosen and resolved on, are pacific.[†]

To the Irish, after expressing a warm sympathy with Ireland as identified with "liberty courageously defended against privilege," that is, with the conquests of peaceful agitation, he said,

Any other encouragements it would be improper for us to give, or for you to receive. I have already said it *à propos* of Switzerland, of Germany, of Belgium, and Italy. I repeat it

[*Ibid., e.g., p. 128.]
[†Translated from Lamartine, *Réponse à une députation des Polonais*, in *Trois mois au pouvoir*, pp. 131, 133, 135. Cf. App. B, p. 398 below.]

in the case of every nation which has disputes to adjust, either within itself or with its government. Those whose own blood is not concerned in the affairs of a people, are not free to intervene in its affairs. We are of no party, in Ireland or elsewhere, except the party of justice, of liberty, and of the people's welfare.

We are at peace, and we desire to remain in friendly and equal relations, not with this or the other portion of Great Britain, but with Great Britain itself. We think this peace useful and honourable, not only for Great Britain and the French Republic, but for the human race. We will do no act, speak no word, utter no insinuation contradictory to the principles of the reciprocal inviolability of nations, which we have proclaimed, and of which the Continent is already reaping the fruits. The monarchy had its treaties and its diplomatists; our diplomatists are peoples, and their sympathies are our treaties. We must be senseless to exchange this diplomacy in open daylight, for underhand and separate alliances with parties, even the most legitimate, in the countries which surround us. We have no title to judge them, nor to prefer one of them to another. Declaring ourselves friends of one, would be proclaiming ourselves enemies of another. We do not desire to be enemies of any of your countrymen; we desire, on the contrary, to dissipate by the loyalty of our republican word, the prepossessions and prejudices which may exist between our neighbours and ourselves.[*]

Many will recollect (for much notice was taken of it at the time) the passage which followed these last words: declaring that he never would imitate the conduct of Pitt, when, even during an acknowledged war, he abetted Frenchmen in carrying on in La Vendée an armed contest against their own countrymen.

This contrast between what M. de Lamartine really said, on the subject of affording aid to foreign insurrection, and what it suits the author of the pamphlet to make him say, speaks for itself without further comment.

What was really new and peculiar in M. de Lamartine's manifesto, consisted, as has been seen by the extracts, in two things. He repudiated the treaties of 1815; and he asserted a right, though without admitting an obligation, to afford military aid to nations attempting to free themselves from a foreign yoke.

To discuss these fundamental points of M. de Lamartine's declaration in the manner which they deserve, would require much more space than can be afforded to it. The topics are among the most delicate in political ethics; they are concerned with that nice question, the line which separates the highest right from the commencement of wrong; where one person regards as heroic virtue, what another looks upon as breach of faith, and criminal aggression. To one like Lord Brougham, who is [q] ostentatiously and to his inmost core a man of the last century, M. de Lamartine's principles must naturally appear extremely scandalous.

M. de Lamartine repudiated certain treaties. He declared them no longer binding on France. Treaties are national engagements; and engagements, when in themselves allowable, and made by persons who have a right to make them, should

[*Translated from Lamartine, *Réponse à une députation des citoyens irlandais*, in *Trois mois au pouvoir*, pp. 150-1. Cf. App. B, pp. 398-9 below.]

[q]49[1,2]   avowedly,

be kept: who ever denied it? But another thing must be admitted also, and always has been admitted by the morality and common sense of mankind. This is, that engagements extorted by a certain kind and measure of external force, are not binding. This doctrine is peculiarly applicable to national engagements imposed by foreign armies. If a nation has, under compulsion, surrendered its independence to a conqueror, or even submitted to sacrifices of territory or dignity, greater than according to general opinion could reasonably be imposed, the moral sentiment of mankind has never held engagements of this sort to preclude the nation from re-asserting its independence, or from again resorting to arms, in order that what had been lost by force might be recovered by force. ʳOn what other principle were Prussia and Austria justified in breaking their treaties with Napoleon after his disasters in Russia?ʳ This was the situation of France with respect to the treaties of 1815. They were imposed by conquest, and were agreed to and signed by an intrusive government, while the territory of the nation was occupied by foreign armies. The nation did not consent to them, for an equivalent advantage, but submitted to them, because it was prostrate at the feet of the invaders, and had no power to refuse anything which they might think fit to demand. Such treaties are never understood to bind nations any longer than they find it their interest to acquiesce in them. M. de Lamartine had no need to rest on the fact that these same treaties have been repeatedly remodelled, and in some cases actually violated, by others of the contracting powers; as in the whole treatment of Poland, and remarkably in the very recent instance of Cracow. Nor is it even necessary to consider what the conditions of the treaties were, and to what extent they were dishonourable or injurious to France. Into this question M. de Lamartine did not profess to enter. He simply claimed the right of deciding it, as inherent in, and never foregone by, France. He denied any moral obligation to keep the treaties; but he disavowed any intention of breaking them. He accepted their territorial and other arrangements as existing facts, to be modified only by mutual consent, or by any of those contingencies which in themselves he deemed legitimate causes of war. If it was possible to have assumed any attitude towards those treaties more just and legitimate, more moderate and dignified, more wisely uniting the re-assertion of the nation's own proper freedom of action with the regard due to the just rights and security of its neighbours, the world will be obliged to any one who will point it out.

But the doctrine, that one government may make war upon another to assist an oppressed nationality in delivering itself from the yoke! This offends Lord Brougham more than everything else. Such a breach of received principles, such defiance of the law of nations, he finds no words too strong to designate. He can hardly think of anything bad enough to compare it with. And it would be vain to deny, that in this he is backed by a large body of English opinion. Men who profess

ʳ⁻ʳ+59,67

to be liberal, are shocked at the idea that the King of Sardinia[*] should assist the Milanese in effecting their emancipation. That they should assert their own liberty might be endured; but that any one should help them to do it, is insupportable. It is classed with any unprovoked invasion of a foreign country: the Piedmontese, it would seem, not being fellow-countrymen of the people of Venice and Milan, while the Croats and the Bohemians are.

May we venture, once for all, to deny the whole basis of this edifying moral argumentation? To assist a people struggling for liberty is contrary to the law of nations: Puffendorf perhaps does not approve of it; Burlamaqui says nothing about it; it is not a *casus belli* set down in Vattel.[†] So be it. But what is the law of nations? Something, which to call a law at all, is a misapplication of terms. The law of nations is simply the custom of nations. It is a set of international usages, which have grown up like other usages, partly from a sense of justice, partly from common interest or convenience, partly from mere opinion and prejudice. Now, are international usages the only kind of customs which, in an age of progress, are to be subject to no improvement? Are they alone to continue fixed, while all around them is changeable? The circumstances of Europe have so altered during the last century, that the constitutions, the laws, the arrangements of property, the distinctions of ranks, the modes of education, the opinions, the manners— everything which affects the European nations separately and within themselves, has changed so much, and is likely to change so much more, than in no great lapse of time they will be scarcely recognisable; and is it in their collective concerns, their modes of dealing with one another, that their circumstances, their exigencies, their duties and interests, are absolutely unchanged? What is called the law of nations is as open to alteration, as properly and even necessarily subject to it when circumstances change or opinions alter, as any other thing of human institution.

And, mark, in the case of a real law, of anything properly called a law, it is possible to maintain (however erroneous may be the opinion) that there is never any necessity for disobeying it; that it should be conformed to while it exists, the alternative being open of endeavouring to get it altered. But in regard to that falsely-called law, the law of nations, there is no such alternative; there is no ordinance or statute to repeal; there is only a custom, and the sole way of altering that, is to act in opposition to it. A legislature can repeal laws, but there is no Congress of nations to set aside international customs, and no common force by which to make the decisions of such a Congress binding. The improvement of international morality can only take place by a series of violations of existing rules;

[*Victor Emmanuel II.]

[†Samuel von Pufendorf, *Le droit de la nature et des gens* (1672), trans. Jean Barbeyrac, 5th ed., 2 vols. (Amsterdam: De Coup, 1734); Jean Jacques Burlamaqui, *Principes du droit naturel* (Geneva: Barillot, 1747) and *Principes du droit politique* (Geneva: Barillot, 1751); and Emerich von Vattel, *Le droit des gens*, 2 vols. (Leyden: Dépens de la compagnie, 1758).]

by a course of conduct grounded on new principles, and tending to erect these into customs in their turn.

Accordingly, new principles and practices are, and have been, continually introduced into the conduct of nations towards one another. To omit other instances, one entirely new principle was for the first time established in Europe, amidst general approbation, within the last thirty years. It is, that whenever two countries, or two parts of the same country, are engaged in war, and the war either continues long undecided, or threatens to be decided in a way involving consequences repugnant to humanity or to the general interest, other countries have a right to step in; to settle among themselves what they consider reasonable terms of accommodation, and if these are not accepted, to interfere by force, and compel the recusant party to submit to the mandate. This new doctrine has been acted on by a combination of the great powers of Europe, in three celebrated instances: the interference between Greece and Turkey at Navarino; between Holland and Belgium at Antwerp; and between Turkey and Egypt at St. Jean d'Acre. It is too late in the day, after these precedents, to tell us that nations may not forcibly interfere with one another for the sole purpose of stopping mischief and benefiting humanity.

Can any exigency of this sort be stronger—is any motive to such interference of a more binding character—than that of preventing the liberty of a nation, which cares sufficiently for liberty to have risen in arms for its assertion, from being crushed and trampled out by tyrannical oppressors, and these not even of its own name and blood, but foreign conquerors? The customs, or falsely called laws of nations, laid down in the books, were made for an age like that of Louis XIV to prevent powerful and ambitious despots from swallowing up the smaller states. For this purpose they were well adapted. But the great interests of civilized nations in the present age are not those of territorial attack and defence, but of liberty, just government, and sympathy of opinion. For this state of things what is called the law of nations was not made; and in no state of things at all analogous to this, has that so-called law ever been, in the smallest degree, attended to. There was once in Europe a time when, as much as at present, the most important interests of nations, both in their domestic and in their foreign concerns, were interests of opinion: it was the era of the Reformation. Did any one then pay the least regard to the pretended principle of non-interference? Was not sympathy of religion held to be a perfectly sufficient warrant for assisting anybody? Did not Protestants aid Protestants, wherever they were in danger from their own governments? Did not Catholics support all other Catholics in suppressing heresy? What religious sympathies were then, political ones are now; and every liberal government or people has a right to assist struggling liberalism, by mediation, by money, or by arms, wherever it can prudently do so; as every despotic government, when its aid is needed or asked for, never scruples to aid despotic governments.

A few observations may be permitted on the extreme contempt with which Lord Brougham denounces what he calls

That new-fangled principle, that new speculation in the rights of independent states, the security of neighbouring governments, and indeed the happiness of all nations, which is termed *Nationality*, adopted as a kind of rule for the distribution of dominion. It seems, [he says,] to be the notion preached by the Paris school of the Law of Nations and their foreign disciples, that one state has a right to attack another, provided upon statistically or ethnologically examining the classes and races of its subjects, these are found to vary. These sages of the international law do not, like their predecessor Robespierre (of whom they compose panegyrics), hold exactly that France may legally assail any sovereign who refuses to abdicate, and bestow upon his people the blessings of republican anarchy. But they hold that if any sovereign has two dominions inhabited by different races, France has a right to assist either in casting off his authority. She may intimate to him that he can only continue to rule over the people who are his countrymen; or, if he was born in neither territory, that he must be put to his election, and choose which he will give up, but cannot be suffered to keep both.[*]

It is far from our intention to defend or apologise for the feelings which make men reckless of, or at least indifferent to, the rights and interests of any portion of the human species, save that which is called by the same name and speaks the same language as themselves. These feelings are characteristic of barbarians; in proportion as a nation is nearer to barbarism it has them in a greater degree: and no one has seen with deeper regret, not to say disgust, than ourselves, the evidence which recent events have afforded, that in the backward parts of Europe, and even (where better things might have been expected) in Germany, the sentiment of nationality so far outweighs the love of liberty, that the people are willing to abet their rulers in crushing the liberty and independence of any people not of their own race and language. But grievous as are these things, yet *so long as they exist*, the question of nationality is practically of the very first importance. When portions of mankind, living under the same government, cherish these barbarous feelings— when they feel 'towards' each other " as enemies, or as strangers, v indifferent to each other—they are scarcely capable of merging into one and the same free people. They have not the fellow-feeling which would enable them to unite in maintaining their liberties, or in forming a paramount public opinion. The separation of feeling which mere difference of language creates, is already a serious hindrance to the establishment of a common freedom. When to this are added national or provincial antipathies, the obstacle becomes almost insuperable. The Government, being the only real link of union, is able, by playing off one race

[*Brougham, *Letter*, p. 126.]

*s-s*49[1,2]   assuming their existence
*t-t*59   toward
*u*49[1,2]   either
*v*49[1,2],59   and

and people against another, to suppress the liberties of *"all"*. How can a free constitution establish itself in the Austrian empire, when Bohemians are ready to join in putting down the liberties of Viennese—when Croats and *ˣSerbsˣ* are eager to crush Hungarians—and all unite in retaining Italy in slavery to their common despot? Nationality is desirable, as a means to the attainment of liberty; and this is reason enough for sympathizing in the attempts of Italians to re-constitute an Italy, and in those of the people of Posen to become a Poland. So long, indeed, as a people are *ʸincapable ofʸ* self-government, it is often better for them to be under the despotism of foreigners than of natives, when those foreigners are more advanced in civilization and cultivation than themselves. But when their hour of freedom, to use M. de Lamartine's metaphor,[*] has struck, without their having become merged and blended in the nationality of their conquerors, the re-conquest of their own is often an indispensable condition either to obtaining free institutions, or to the possibility, were they even obtained, of working them in the spirit of freedom.

There remains another measure of the Provisional Government, which opens a still wider field of difficult and important discussion than the preceding: the recognition of the *droit au travail*; of an obligation on society to find work and wages for all persons willing and able to work, who cannot procure employment for themselves.[†]

This conduct of the Provisional Government will be judged differently, according to the opinions of the person judging, on one of the most controverted questions of the time. To one class of thinkers, the acknowledgment of the *droit au travail* may very naturally appear a portentous blunder; but it is curious to see who those are that most loudly profess this opinion. It is singular that this act of the Provisional Government should find its bitterest critics in the journalists who dilate on the excellence of the Poor-law of Elizabeth;[‡] and that the same thing should be so bad *ᶻinᶻ* France, which is perfectly right, in the opinion of the same persons, for England and Ireland. For the "*droit au travail*" is the Poor-law of Elizabeth, and nothing more. Aid guaranteed to those who cannot work, employment to those who can: this is the Act of Elizabeth, and this the promise, which it is so inexcusable in the Provisional Government to have made to France.

The Provisional Government not only offered no more than the promise made by the Act of Elizabeth, but offered it in a manner, and on conditions, far less objectionable. On the English parochial system, the law gives to every pauper a

[**Manifeste*, p. 76; cf. App. B, p. 398 below.]
[†See *Le Moniteur Universel*, 26 Feb., 1848, p. 503.]
[‡43 Elizabeth, c. 2 (1601).]

*ʷ⁻ʷ*49¹,² both
*ˣ⁻ˣ*49¹,²,59 Servians
*ʸ⁻ʸ*49¹,² unfit for
*ᶻ⁻ᶻ*49¹,² for

right to demand work, or support without work, for himself individually. The French Government contemplated no such right. It contemplated action on the general labour market, not alms to the individual. Its scheme was, that when there was notoriously a deficiency of employment, the State should disburse sufficient funds to create the amount of productive employment which was wanting. But it gave no pledge that the State should find work for A or B. It reserved in its own hands the choice of its workpeople. It relieved no individual from the responsibility of finding an employer, and proving his willingness to exert himself. What it undertook was, that there should always be employment to be found. It is needless to enlarge on the incomparably less injurious influence of this intervention of the government in favour of the labourers collectively, than of the intervention of the parish to find employment individually for every able-bodied man who has not honesty or activity to seek and find it for himself.

The *droit au travail*, as intended by the Provisional Government, is not amenable to the commoner objections against a Poor-law. It is amenable to the most fundamental of the objections; that which is grounded on the principle of population. Except on that ground, no one is entitled to find fault with it. From the point of view of every one who disregards the principle of population, the *droit au travail* is the most manifest of moral truths, the most imperative of political obligations.

It appeared to the Provisional Government, as it must appear to every unselfish and open-minded person, that the earth belongs, first *ᵃ, toᵃ* all, to the inhabitants of it; that every person alive ought to have a subsistence, before any one has more; that whosoever works at any useful thing, ought to be properly fed and clothed before any one able to work is allowed to receive the bread of idleness. These are moral axioms. But it is impossible to steer by the light of any single principle, without taking into account other principles by which it is hemmed in. The Provisional Government did not consider, what hardly any of their critics have considered—that although every one of the living brotherhood of humankind has a moral claim to a place at the table provided by the collective exertions of the race, no one of them has a right to invite additional strangers thither without the consent of the rest. If they do, what is consumed by these strangers should be subtracted from their own share. There is enough and to spare for all who *are* born; but there is not and cannot be enough for all who *might* be born; and if every person born is to have *ᵇan indefeasibleᵇ* claim to a subsistence from the common fund, there will presently be no more than a bare subsistence for anybody, and a little later there will not be even that. The *droit au travail*, therefore, carried out according to the meaning of the promise, would be a fatal gift even to those for whose *ᶜespecialᶜ*

*ᵃ⁻ᵃ*49[1,2],59   of [*printer's error?*]
*ᵇ⁻ᵇ*49[1,2]   a first
*ᶜ⁻ᶜ*49[1,2]   special

benefit it is intended, unless some new restraint were placed upon the capacity of increase, equivalent to that which would be taken away.

The Provisional Government then were in the right; but those are also in the right who condemn this act of the Provisional Government. Both have truth on their side. A time will come when these two portions of truth will meet together in harmony. The practical result of the whole truth might possibly be, that all persons living should guarantee to each other, through their organ the State, the ability to earn by labour an adequate subsistence, but that they should abdicate the right of propagating the species at their own discretion and without limit: that all classes alike, and not the poor alone, should consent to exercise that power in such measure only, and under such regulations, as society might prescribe with a view to the common good. But before this solution of the problem can cease to be visionary, an almost complete renovation must take place in some of the most rooted opinions and feelings of the present race of mankind. The majority both of the upholders of old things and of the apostles of new, seem at present to agree in the opinion, that one of the most important and responsible of moral acts, that of giving existence to human beings, is a thing respecting which there scarcely exists any moral obligation, and in which no person's discretion ought on any pretence to be interfered with: a superstition which will one day be regarded with as much contempt, as any of the idiotic notions and practices of savages.

The declaration of the *droit au travail* was followed by the creation of *ateliers nationaux*;[*] which, indeed, was its necessary consequence; since, in the great falling-off of employment through the industrial stagnation consequent on the Revolution, it would neither have been honourable nor safe to make no commencement of fulfilling the promise given, and circumstances did not allow of improvising any better mode of temporary employment for the destitute. Some such measure would have been necessary after any revolution. In 1830, large sums were expended in setting the unemployed to work. It was the misfortune, not the fault, of the Provisional Government, that the numbers requiring employment were so much greater than at any former period, and that the other circumstances of the case were such as to render the creation of these *ateliers* eventually the greatest calamity of the time; since it soon became impossible to provide funds for continuing them, while the first attempt to dissolve them was likely to produce, and did in fact produce, the outbreak *d*in*d* June.

It was not the fall of the monarchy, or the foundation of the republic, that caused the complete temporary paralysis of industry and commerce; it was the appearance on the stage, of the unexpected and indefinitely dreaded phenomenon of Socialism. And it was owing to the diffusion of Socialism among a portion of the labouring classes, that the first step towards the abolition of the *ateliers nationaux*

[*For the latter, see *Le Moniteur Universel*, 27 Feb., 1848, p. 507.]

*d-d*49[1,2] of

became the signal for a determined attempt, by a large section of the workmen of Paris, to follow up the republican revolution by a Socialist one.

Let us here stop to consider what this new phenomenon termed Socialism is, in itself, and in its consequences.

Socialism is the modern form of the protest, which has been raised, more or less, in all ages of any mental activity, against the unjust distribution of social advantages.

No rational person will maintain it to be abstractedly just, that a small minority of mankind should be born to the enjoyment of all the external advantages which life can give, without earning them by any merit or acquiring them by any exertion of their own, while the immense majority are condemned from their birth, to a life of never-ending, never-intermitting toil, requited by a bare, and in general a precarious, subsistence. It is impossible to contend that this is in itself just. It is possible to contend that it is expedient; since, unless persons were allowed, not only to retain for themselves, but to transmit to their posterity, the accumulated fruits of their exertions and of their favourable chances, they would not, it may be said, produce; or if they did, they would not preserve and accumulate their productions. It may also be said that to [e]deny to people the control of what they have[e] thus produced and accumulated, and [f]compel them to share it with[f] those who, either through their fault or their misfortune, [g]have[g] produced and accumulated nothing, would be a still greater injustice than that of which the levellers complain; and that the path of least injustice, is to recognise individual property and individual rights of inheritance.

This is, in few words, the case which the existing order of society can make out against levellers. The levellers of the present day, with few exceptions, acknowledge the force of these arguments; and are by this distinguished from all former opponents of the law of property, and constituted, not levellers in the original sense of the word, but what they term themselves—Socialists.

We grant (they say) that it would be unjust to take from individual capitalists the fruits of their labour and of their frugality. Neither do we propose to do so. But capital is useless without labour, and if capital belongs to the capitalists, labour belongs, by at least as sacred a right, to the labourers. We, the labourers, are at liberty to refuse to work except on such terms as we please. Now, by a system of co-operation among ourselves, we can do without capitalists. We could also, if we had fair play from laws and institutions, carry on productive operations with so much advantage, to our joint benefit, as to make it the interest of capitalists to leave their capital in our hands; because we could offer them a sufficient interest for its use; and because, once able to work for themselves, no labourers of any worth or efficiency would labour for a master, and capitalists would have no means of

---

[e-e]49[1,2]   take from people by force what they had
[f-f]49[1,2]   bestow it on
[g-g]49[1,2]   had

deriving an income from their capitals except by entrusting them to the associated workpeople.

The system of co-operative production, thus established, would cut up by the root the present partial distribution of social advantages, and would enable the produce of industry to be shared on whatever principle, whether of equality or inequality (for on this point different schools of Socialists have different opinions), might appear to the various communities to be just and expedient. Such a plan would, in the opinion of Socialists, be so vast an improvement on the present order of society, that the government, which exists for the good of society, and especially for that of the suffering majority, ought to favour its introduction by every expedient in its power; ought, in particular, to raise funds by taxation, and contribute them in aid of the formation of industrial communities on the co-operative principle: which funds it is not doubted that the success of the scheme would enable, in a few years, to be paid back with interest.

This is Socialism; and it is not obvious what there is in this system of thought, to [h]justify[h] the frantic terror with which everything bearing that ominous name is usually received on both sides of the British Channel.

It really seems a perfectly just demand [i], in the present circumstances of France,[i] that the government should aid with its funds, to a reasonable extent, in bringing into operation industrial communities on the Socialist principle. It ought to do so, even if it could be certain beforehand that the attempt would fail; because the operatives themselves cannot possibly be persuaded of this except by trial; because they will not be persuaded of it until everything possible has been done to make the trial successful; and because a national experiment of the kind, by the high moral qualities that would be elicited in the endeavour to make it succeed, and by the instruction that would radiate from its failure, would be an equivalent for the expenditure of many millions on any of the things which are commonly called popular education.

At all events, this view of the subject was the only one which could be practically taken by the Provisional Government. They had been made a government, chiefly by the working classes of Paris. A majority of the active members of those classes, including most of their leaders, were deeply imbued with Socialist principles and feelings: to them a republican revolution, which neither did nor attempted anything for Socialism, would have been a disappointment and a deception, which they would have resented with arms in their hands. The Provisional Government, therefore, did what any government, situated as they were, must have done. They associated with themselves, in the supreme authority, two of the Socialist chiefs, M. Louis Blanc and M. Albert. And, things not being ripe for the adoption of practical measures of a Socialist character, they did the only thing which could be

[h-h]49[1,2]   account for
[i-i]+59,67

done—they opened an arena for the public discussion of the problem, and invited all competent persons, under the auspices of the government, to contribute their ideas and suggestions towards its solution.

This was the origin of the conferences at the Luxembourg; which, both in themselves, and in respect of the connexion of the Provisional Government with them, have been the subject of such boundless misrepresentation. The prominent feature of those conferences consisted of the Socialist speeches of M. Louis Blanc;[*] of whom Lord Brougham asserts that he has fled to England "to avoid being judged by enlightened freemen, for endeavouring to make his Republic more bloody than it has been since 1794."[†] The accusation is as devoid of truth as his charge against the Montagne party *in the Assembly*, of "panting for the guillotine as an instrument of government."[‡] M. Louis Blanc is not even accused, officially, of being concerned in the insurrection of June; the prosecution against him having reference solely to the affair of May, in which, though the National Assembly was turbulently invaded, "blood," at all events, was neither shed nor thought of; and even as to this, his defence before the Commission d'Enquête appears conclusive.[§] But with regard to his speeches at the Luxembourg, so far as these have been published (and *it has never been pretended* that anything has been kept back which would make a contrary impression), nothing could be less inflammatory and provocative than his tone, nor more sober and reasonable than every suggestion which he propounded for immediate adoption. In fact, he proposed nothing more than that degree of aid by government to the experimental establishment of the co-operative system of industry, which, even if the failure were total, would be a cheap price for setting the question at rest. Far from stirring up the people to a Socialist insurrection, everything proves him to have felt that, of all things that could happen, an insurrection like that of June would be the most ruinous to the immediate prospects of his cause.

It was from no inherent tendency in the principles or teaching of the Socialist chiefs, that this insurrection broke out. It arose from the suddenness and unexpectedness of the Revolution of February, which, being effected mainly by Socialists, brought Socialist opinions into a position of apparent power, before the minds of the community generally were prepared for the situation, or had begun seriously to consider this great problem. Hence hopes were excited of an immediate practical realization, when nothing was yet ripe—when discussion and

[*Printed in Louis Blanc, *La révolution de février au Luxembourg* (Paris: Lévy, 1849), *passim.*]

[†Brougham, *Letter*, p. 57.]

[‡*Ibid.*, p. 80.]

[§In *Rapport de la commission d'enquête*, Vol. I, pp. 103-13, 238-41.]

j-j+59,67

*k-k*49[1,2]   there is no evidence

explanation had nearly all their work to do; and as soon as the first inevitable retrograde steps were taken, the frustration of premature hopes provoked a fatal collision.

If the Revolution of February should yet disappoint the glorious expectations which it raised, this collision will be the cause. It has divided the sincere Republicans, already a small minority, into two parties at enmity with one another. It has alienated from the only Republican party which has any elements of stability, the greater part of the effective strength of the democracy; and it has filled the bourgeoisie with such insane terror at the bare thought of great social changes, that the most beneficent projects share the discredit of the most perilous, and they are ready to throw themselves into the arms of any government which will free them from the fear of a second Socialist insurrection. These things are lamentable; but the fatality of circumstances, more than the misconduct of individuals, is responsible for them.

If we are now asked whether we agree in the anticipations of the Socialists; whether we believe that their co-operative associations [l], at all events in the present state of education,[l] would maintain their ground against individual competition, and secure an adequate amount of the fruits of industry, combined with a just repartition of them—our answer must be, that we do not. It is highly probable that, among a great number of such experiments, some would succeed, while under the influence of the zeal and enthusiasm of the first founders. And, in the face of the evidence which experience affords that mankind may be made capable of almost anything by a persevering application of the power of education in one direction, it would be too much to affirm that a time can never come when the scheme of Owen and of Louis Blanc, of a world governed by public spirit, without needing the vulgar incentives of individual interest, [m]will[m] possess a feasibility which cannot be accorded to it now.

But, in proportion to our distrust of the means which Socialists propose for correcting the unjust inequalities in the lot of mankind, do we deem it incumbent on philosophers and politicians to use their utmost endeavours for bringing about the same end by an adaptation of the existing machinery of society. We hold with Bentham, that equality, though not the sole end, is one of the ends of good social arrangements; and that a system of institutions which does not make the scale turn in favour of equality, whenever this can be done without impairing the security of the property which is the product and reward of personal exertion, is essentially a bad government—a government for the few, to the injury of the many.[*] And the admiration and sympathy which we feel for the glorious band who composed the Provisional Government, and for the party which supported them, is grounded,

[*See, e.g., Bentham, *Principles of the Civil Code* (1838), in *Works*, Vol. I, pp. 302-3, 311-13.]

[l-l]+59,67
[m-m]49[1,2]   may

above all, on the fact that they stand openly identified with this principle, and have in all ways proved their sincere devotion to it. As an exemplification, we extract a few paragraphs from M. de Lamartine's *History of the Girondists*, written before the February Revolution was thought of; paragraphs worthy of the noble conduct which has immortalized their illustrious writer, and [n] to be taken as the creed of an earnest and rational Social Reformer, on the questions connected with property and the distribution of wealth:

An equal repartition of instruction, of faculties, and of the things given by nature, is evidently the legitimate tendency of the human mind. Founders of revealed religions, poets and sages, have eternally revolved this idea in their souls, and have held it up in their Paradise, in their dreams, or in their laws, as the ultimate prospect of humanity. It is, then, an instinct of justice in the human mind. . . . Whatever tends to constitute inequalities of instruction, of rank, of condition, of fortune among mankind, is impious; whatever tends gradually to level these inequalities, which are often injustices, and to share more equitably the common heritage among mankind, is religious. All policy may be judged by this test, as a tree by its fruits. The ideal is but [o]truth at[o] a distance.

But the sublimer an [p]ideal[p], the more difficult it is to realize in institutions on the earth. The difficulty up to this time has been, to reconcile with equality of goods the inequalities of virtues, of faculties, and of exertions, which distinguish mankind from one another. Between the active and the inert, equality of goods is an injustice, for the one produces and the other merely consumes. In order that this community of goods may be just, we must suppose in all mankind the same conscience, the same application to labour, the same virtue. This supposition is chimerical. What social order can rest solidly upon such a falsehood? Of two things, one: society, everywhere present and everywhere infallible, must be able to compel every individual to the same labour and the same virtue; but then, what becomes of liberty? Society, on this footing, would be universal slavery. Or else, society must distribute daily with its own hands, to each according to his works, a share exactly proportioned to the labour and the services of each in the general association. But in that case, who is to be the judge?

Imperfect human wisdom has found it easier, wiser, and more just to say to every one, "Be thy own judge; take to thyself thy own recompense by thy riches or thy indigence." Society has established property, has proclaimed the freedom of labour, and has legalized competition.

But property, when established, does not feed those who possess nothing. But freedom of labour does not give the same means of labour to him who has only his hands, and to him who possesses millions of acres of the earth's surface. But competition is the code of [q]egoism[q]; a war to the death between those who work and those who give work; those who sell, and those who buy; those who revel in abundance, and those who starve. Injustice on all hands! Incorrigible inequalities of nature and of law! The wisdom of the legislator seems to lie in palliating them one by one, generation by generation, law by law. He who seeks to correct everything by one stroke, shatters everything. Possibility is the [r]necessary[r] condition of [s]poor human wisdom[s]. Without pretending to resolve complicated iniquities by

[n]49[1,2]   fit
[o-o]49[1,2]   the truth seen from
[p-p]49[1,2]   idea [*printer's error?*]
[q-q]49[1,2]   egotism
[r-r]+59,67
[s-s]49[1,2]   the miserable wisdom of man

a single solution—to correct without intermission, to be always ameliorating, is the justice of imperfect beings like us. . . . Time seems to be one of the elements even of truth itself: to demand the ultimate truth from one moment of time, is to demand from the nature of things more than it can give. Impatience creates illusions and ruins instead of truths. Delusions are truths gathered before their time. The Christian and philosophic community of the good things of the earth, is the ultimate social truth; the delusions are the violences and the systems by which hitherto men have vainly imagined that they could establish this truth, and organize it into institutions.[*]

Although not necessary for the main purpose of the present article—the vindication of the Revolution of February and of its leading characters against systematic misjudgment and misrepresentation—it is not irrelevant to offer a few pages of comment on the advice tendered to France in Lord Brougham's pamphlet, respecting the formation of a Constitution.

This advice is prefaced by a very plain intimation that it is useless—grounded on the commonplace of essayists and reviewers, that a Constitution cannot be made.[†] "Laws are made; codes and constitutions grow. Those that grow have roots; they bear, they ripen, they endure. Those that are fashioned are like painted sticks planted in the ground, as I have seen trees of liberty: they strike no root, bear no fruit, and swiftly decay."[‡]

We have never been able to see in this trite dictum, anything more than a truism exaggerated into a paradox. Stripped of its metaphorical language, it amounts to this—that political institutions cannot work well, or subsist durably, unless they have existed as customs before they were enacted as laws. No one can be insensible to the advantage in point of security for stability, possessed by laws which merely annex positive sanctions to usages which the people had already adopted, before the legislature recognised them; such as our mercantile law, grounded on the customs of merchants, to which the courts of justice gradually gave legal validity. But this, so far as it is true at all, is as true of any other laws as of political institutions, and as true of a single law as of a code. Why then confine it to codes and Constitutions? Of codes and Constitutions, no more than of single laws, is this pre-existence as custom, however advantageous to stability, a necessary condition of it. What is necessary is, that they should not violently shock the pre-existing habits and sentiments of the people; and that they should not demand and presuppose qualities in the popular mind, and a degree of interest in, and attachment to, the institutions themselves, which the character of the people, and their state of civilization, render unlikely to be really found in them. These two are the rocks on which those usually split, who by means of a temporary

[*Translated from Lamartine, *Histoire des Girondins*, 8 vols. (Paris: Coquebert, 1847), Vol. V, pp. 407-10. Cf. App. pp. 399-400 below.]

[†See James Mackintosh, *The History of England*, 10 vols. (London: Longman, *et al.*, 1830-40), Vol. I, p. 72.]

[‡Brougham, *Letter*, pp. 41-2.]

ascendancy establish institutions alien 'from', or too much in advance of, the condition of the public mind. The founders of the English Commonwealth failed for the first reason. Their republicanism offended the taste for kingship and old institutions, their religious freedom and equality shocked the attachment to prelacy or presbyterianism, which then were pervading principles in the majority of the nation. Charlemagne's attempt to construct a centralized monarchy amidst the distraction and anarchy of the eighth century, failed for the other of the two reasons specified. Its success would have required, both in the governors and the governed, a more cultivated intelligence, a greater comprehension of large views and extended interests, than existed or was attainable in that age, save by eminently exceptional individuals like Charlemagne himself. If the establishment of republicanism in France should turn out to be premature, it will be for the latter reason. Although no popular sentiment is shocked by it, the event may prove that there is no sufficient attachment to it, or desire to promote its success; but a readiness to sacrifice it to any trivial convenience, personal *engouement*, or dream of increased security.

Lord Brougham cannot enter on the subject of the French Constitution, without rebuking the Assembly for the indifference they have shown to this their appointed work.

They seem only able to consider, with any interest, personal questions, or party questions; or (if they deviate into more general views) social questions, as the language of the day terms them. Such are the only discussions in which the National Assembly appears to have taken a deep interest. With the work of framing a Constitution they have as yet troubled themselves but little, although their sittings have lasted well nigh six months, at the cost to the people of a pound a-day to each of the 900 members.[*]

These sentences "were of course" written before the public discussions on the Constitution had commenced; but that does not excuse omission to take notice of the fact, that the work of framing the Constitution was going on uninterruptedly, and with still greater activity, in the five months which preceded, than in the two ^{v} which were occupied by, those public discussions. One of the earliest acts of the Assembly was the nomination of a Committee of thirty of its ablest members, to frame the draft of a Constitution. The draft, when framed, was the subject of ^{w} minute examination and discussion, with closed doors—but of which reports reached the newspapers—in every one of the fifteen *bureaux* of the Assembly; after which the *bureaux* elected another Committee, to be associated with the first Committee in revising the original scheme, and framing a second draft, with the lights derived from the discussion; so that when the day arrived for taking this

[*Ibid., pp. 56, 59.]

$^{t\text{-}t}$49[1,2] to
$^{u\text{-}u}$49[1,2] of course were
^{v}49[1,2] months
^{w}49[1,2] a

second draft publicly into consideration, the work of framing the Constitution was, in reality, finished. It had received the benefit of the best light, of the best wisdom of the Assembly; it was well known how the votes of the Assembly would go, on all disputable points of considerable moment; and little remained for the public discussion to do, except to send forth the arguments of the majority, and the objections and protests of the minority, to their constituents and to the world. Is not this the way in which a Constitution should be made? Are not all Constitutions, and all laws of any value, the work of a few select minds in the first instance, then discussed and canvassed with a greater number, and finally ratified by the many?

The Constitution thus made, and now solemnly proclaimed and adopted,[*] is such as the ideas and the degree of instruction of the age and nation permitted it to be. Of all charges, that to which it is the least obnoxious is the trivial one of introducing new "theoretical" principles.[†] There is in it a remarkable absence of what, in Lord Brougham's eyes, is so great a fault in a political Constitution—original ideas. There is not a principle or a provision in it that is not familiar to the public mind. It is, in fact, a digest of the elementary doctrines of representative democracy. To those who disapprove of democracy, it is, of course, unacceptable: but, that being granted as the indispensable datum, from which the framers of the Constitution were not at liberty to depart—any fault which can be found with their work, on the ground of a deficiency of checks to the preponderance of popular will, must be set down to the account not of new theories, but of the want of them. The presence of such checks, not their absence, would have been the novelty in constitution-making. That would really have been the introduction of a principle new in democratic constitutions, and for which no foundation was laid in the national mind.

Lord Brougham has condescended to bestow upon these unapt scholars, his view of some of the essential requisites of a popular Constitution. First among these, is the ancient device, or rather accident, of two Legislative Chambers.[‡] How unsuited this contrivance would be to the state of the French mind, may be known from the fact, that although supported by some of the most individually influential of French orators and politicans, it has been rejected by a larger majority than any of the other conservative amendments that have been proposed; and has numbered among its opponents the greater part of that large party in the Assembly which calls itself Moderate, and is called by others Anti-republican.

The arguments for a second Chamber, when looked at from one point of view, are of great force; being no other than the irresistible arguments for the necessity or expediency of a principle of antagonism in society—of a counterpoise somewhere to the preponderant power in the State. It seems hardly possible that there should

[*Constitution de la république française, Bulletin 87, No. 825 (4 Nov., 1848), Bulletin des lois de la république française, 10th ser., II, 575-605.]
[†Brougham, Letter, pp. 40ff.]
[‡Ibid., pp. 59ff.]

be permanently good government, or enlightened progress, without such a counterpoise. *It may, however, be maintained, with considerable appearance of reason,* that the antagonism may be more beneficially placed in society itself, than in the legislative organ which gives effect to the will of society; that it should have its place in the powers which form public opinion, rather than in that whose proper function is to execute it; that, for example, in a democratic State, the desired counterbalance to the impulses and will of the comparatively uninstructed many, lies in a strong and independent organization of the class whose special business is the cultivation of knowledge; and will better embody itself in Universities, than in Senates or Houses of Lords.

A second Chamber, howsoever composed, is a serious hindrance to improvement. Suppose it constituted in the manner, of all others, least calculated to render it an obstructive body; suppose that an Assembly of *(say)* 600 persons, is elected by universal suffrage, and when elected divides itself, as under the French Directorial Constitution,[*] into two bodies, say of 300 each. Now, whereas if the whole body sat as one Chamber, the opposition of 300 persons, or one-half of the representatives of the people, would be required to throw out an improvement; on the system of separate deliberation, 150, or one-fourth only, would suffice. Without doubt, the division into two sections, which would be a hindrance to useful changes, would be a hindrance also to hurtful ones; and the arrangement therefore must be regarded as beneficial, by those who think that a democratic Assembly is more likely to make hurtful than useful changes. But this opinion, both historical and daily experience contradicts. There cannot be a case more in point than this very instance of France. The National Assembly was chosen in the crisis of a revolution, by a suffrage including all the labouring men of the community; the doctrines of a subversive character which were afloat, were peculiarly favourable to the apparent interests of labouring men; yet the Assembly elected was essentially a conservative body; and it is the general opinion that the legislature now about to be elected will be still more so. The great majority of mankind are, as a general rule, tenacious of things existing: habit and custom predominate with them, in almost all cases, over remote prospects of advantage; and however popular may be the constitution, in the ordinary course of its working the difficulty is not to prevent considerable changes, but to accomplish them even when most essentially needful. Any systematic provision in the Constitution to render changes difficult, is therefore worse than superfluous—it is injurious.

It is true, that in the times which accompany or immediately follow a revolution, this tendency of the human mind may be temporarily and partially reversed;

[*Constitution de la république française, proposée au peuple français par la convention nationale (Paris: Imprimerie de la république, an III [1795]).]

x-x49[1,2]   We, however, incline to believe
y-y49[1,2]   , say,

partially, we say—for a people are as tenacious of old customs and ways of thinking in the crisis of a revolution as at any other time, on all points except those on which they have become strongly excited by a perception of evils or grievances; those, in fact, on which the revolution itself turns. On such points, indeed, there may easily arise, at those periods, an ardour of ill-considered change; and it is at such times, if ever, that the check afforded by a second or conservative Chamber might be beneficial. But these are the times when the resistance of such a body is practically null. The very arguments used by the supporters of the institution, to make it endurable, assume that it cannot prolong its resistance in excited times. A second Chamber which, during a revolution, should resolutely oppose itself to the branch of the legislature more directly representing the excited state of popular feeling, would be infallibly swept away. It is the destiny of a second Chamber to become inoperative in the [z]very[z] cases, in which its effective operation [a]would have the best[a] chance of producing less harm than good.

If these observations are correct [b](and we give them only for what they are worth)[b], there is no reason to regret the decision by which the Constituent Assembly of the French Republic has rejected the principle of a double legislature. The same considerations serve to justify their adoption of what is termed universal suffrage. Lord Brougham himself [c]admits[c] that the operation of universal suffrage has hitherto proved very different from what its enemies had anticipated.[*] If a suffrage extending to every adult male of the community produces, and is likely to produce, a legislature more justly chargeable with too conservative than with too innovative a spirit, what would it have been if, by a taxpaying or other property qualification, the democracy of Paris, Lyons, and other large towns, had been excluded from its share of influence? Lord Brougham repeats, along with other trite and gone-by observations on the social condition of France, that very commonplace one, that Paris is France.[†] It is true that, from the political passiveness of the majority of the French people, and the habit of looking to the government as the sole arbiter of all political interests, the provinces of France usually submit readily to any existing government; but it is not now true, whatever it may have been formerly, that the provinces follow blindly the *opinion* of Paris; they might more truly be said to be unreasonably jealous of Parisian influences. Paris, with a few of the larger towns, is almost the sole element of progress which exists, politically speaking, in France; instead of having too much power, it has far less than in proportion to its immense superiority in political education and intelligence. Its power is never preponderant but when its insurrectionary element

[*Brougham, *Letter*, pp. 75-6.]
[†*Ibid.*, pp. 109ff.]

[z-z]49[1,2],59   only
[a-a]49[1,2],59   might have a
[b-b]+59,67
[c-c]49[1,2]   is forced to admit,

is brought into play; and this received a blow in June last, which has laid it prostrate for some time at least.

The remainder of Lord Brougham's advice to the French people on constitutional subjects is, that they should have an efficient executive, with power promptly to suppress any attempt at disturbance—a point in which, in the present temper of the French, they are not likely to be found deficient; and lastly, that the legislature should be nothing but a legislature, and should not, by itself attempting to administer, usurp the functions of the executive. On this last topic, Lord Brougham's observations, ^{d}as^d far as they go, are just, and to the point.

The legislative body, [he observes,] should be strictly confined to its proper functions, of making the laws, and superintending the administration both of the executive and of all other departments; but excluded from all share in any of those branches. The office of discussing legislative measures or of controlling the conduct of public functionaries, may well be entrusted to a senate, however constituted, as the imposition of public burthens upon the community may not only with equal safety be placed in its hands, but ought almost exclusively to rest there. A representative body, necessarily numerous, because elected by a great people, can well and safely debate such matters; it is peculiarly fitted for their discussion. Such a body is wholly unfit to handle matters merely of an administrative kind, or of a judicial. Its numbers at once pronounce this disqualification: its responsibility to constituents confirms the sentence: its want of individual responsibility precludes all appeal and all doubt. How can an assembly of six or seven hundred persons conduct foreign negotiations, decide questions of peace and war, or dispose of the national force, whether with a view to internal police or foreign operations, offensive or defensive? How can such a body be entrusted with the appointment to places, civil or military, when each man will be quick to help his fellow-member's job, and none ever feel afraid of constituents who can know little, and care less, about such nominations? Above everything, the judicial office must never be exercised by an assembly like this; and of all appointments from which it should be shut out, those connected with judicial powers fall most certainly under the rule of exclusion.[*]

The principle here contended for is of so much importance, that it deserves to be carried ^{e}farther^e than is done in this passage, or by any existing school of politicians. ^{f}In general,^{f} if a public function is to be discharged with honesty and skill, some one person, or a very small number, should, if possible, be specifically entrusted with it. A few persons, and still more, one person, will feel a moral responsibility, an amenability to the bar of public opinion, which, even when they cannot be made more directly responsible, will be a far stronger security for fidelity and attention to their trust than can be provided in the case of a numerous body. We dissent altogether from the common opinion of democratic republicans, which tends to multiply the conferring of offices by popular election. The sovereign Assembly, which is the organ of the people for superintending and

[*$Ibid.$, pp. 71-2.]

$^{d-d}$49^{1,2} so
$^{e-e}$49^{1,2} further
$^{f-f}$49^{1,2} We regard it as one of the most fundamental of all practical principles of government, that

controlling the government, must of necessity be so elected. But with this exception, it appears to us certain (what even Bentham, though in his earlier speculations he maintained a different opinion, ultimately acknowledged),[*] that judges, administrators, functionaries of all sorts, will be selected with a much more careful eye to their qualifications, if some conspicuous public officer, a President or a minister, has the choice of them imposed on him as part of his peculiar business, and feels his official character and the *g*tenure*g* of his own power to depend, not on what the people may now think of the choice made, but on what they will think of it after trial. It seems equally certain that the President, or prime minister, will be better selected by the people's representatives, than by the people themselves directly. The example of the United States is a strong argument for this opinion. If the President were elected by Congress, he would generally be the leader, and acknowledged ablest man, of his party: elected by the people, he is now always either an unknown mediocrity, or a man whose reputation has been acquired in some other field than that of politics. Nor is this likely to alter; for every politician who has attained *h* eminence has made a multitude of, at least political, enemies, which renders him a less available candidate for his party to put forward, than somebody of the same professed principles who is comparatively obscure. It is to be feared that the appointment of a President by the direct suffrages of the community, will prove to be the most serious mistake which the framers of the French Constitution have made. They have introduced by it into the still more fermentable elements of French society, what even in America is felt to be so great an evil—the turmoil of a perpetual canvass, and the baneful habit of making the decision of all great public questions depend less upon their merits, than upon their probable influence on the next presidential election. And, in addition to this, it will probably be found, if their present institutions last, that they have subjected themselves to a series of much worse selections, and will have their Republic presided over by a less able and less creditable succession of men, than if the chief magistrate had been chosen by the legislature.

It is but just to acknowledge, that this very questionable provision was introduced in obedience to the important principle of preventing the legislature from encroaching on the province of the executive. The object was, to make the President independent of the legislature. It was feared that if he were appointed and could be turned out by them, he would be their mere clerk—would exercise no judgment and assume no responsibility of his own, but simply register the decrees of a body unfit to conduct the business of government in detail. There was,

[*For Bentham's early opinion, see *Bentham's Draught for the Organization of the Judicial Establishment in France* (1790), in *Works*, Vol. IV, pp. 307-9, 354; for his later view, see *The Constitutional Code* (1827, 1841), *ibid.*, Vol. IX, pp. 529-31.]

*g-g*49[1,2]   permanence
*h*49[1,2]   to

however, a means of avoiding this, which would have been perfectly effectual. They might have given to the chief of the executive the power of dissolving the legislature, and appealing afresh to the people. With this safeguard, they might have left to the Assembly the uncontrolled choice of the head of the executive, and the power, by a vote of dismissal, of reducing him to the alternative of either retiring or dissolving the Chamber. The check which, under this arrangement, the legislature and the executive would exercise reciprocally over one another, and the reluctance which each would feel to proceed to an extremity which might end in their own downfall instead of their rival's, would in [i] ordinary cases be [j] sufficient to restrain each within the constitutional limits of its own authority. Instead of this, it is to be feared that by placing face to face an Assembly and a first magistrate—each emanating directly from popular suffrage, and each elected for a term fixed, only capable of being abridged by death or resignation—the Assembly have organized a perpetual hostility between the two powers, replete with dangers to the stability of the Constitution. For if the President and the National Assembly should hereafter quarrel, there may for three whole years be no means by which either can relieve itself from the hostility of the other, except a *coup d'état*.

In addition to these considerations, an executive chosen by a select body, and armed with the power of dissolving the legislature, would probably be a more effectual check than any second Chamber upon the conduct of an Assembly engaged in a course of hasty or unjust legislation. An eminent politician, the leader of a great party, and surrounded by the *élite* of that party as his ministers and advisers, would have more at stake in the good conduct of public affairs, would be more practised and skilful in judging of exigencies, would apply himself to his task with a much deeper sense of permanent responsibility, and, as a consequence of all this, would be likely to carry with him a greater weight of opinion, than an assembly of two or three hundred persons, whether composed of English lords, or of the elective representatives of French or American democracy.

[k] To correct misstatements is so much more tedious a process than to commit them, that space fails us for pointing out, or even alluding to, a tenth part of those which compose the main bulk of Lord Brougham's pamphlet. But we have exhibited a sample, and what we have exhibited is a fair specimen of what remains behind. Let us hope that something has been done towards the more important purpose of vindicating the Revolution, and the Provisional Government, from as unjust aspersions as ever clouded the reputation of great actions and eminent characters.

[i]49[1,2]   all
[j]49[1,2]   amply
[k]49[1,2]   It is time to conclude, though much still remains unsaid.

APPENDICES

Appendix A

Guizot's Lectures on European Civilization (1836)

London Review, II (equivalent to *Westminster Review*, XXXI) (Jan., 1836), 306-36. Headed: "Art. II. *Cours d'Histoire Moderne*, par M. [François Pierre Guillaume] Guizot, Professeur d'Histoire à la Faculté des Lettres de Paris—(consisting of) *Histoire Générale de la Civilisation en Europe, depuis la Chute de l'Empire Romain jusqu'à la Révolution Française*, 1 vol. [Paris: Pichon and Didier, 1828.] *Histoire de la Civilisation Française depuis la Chute de l'Empire Romain jusqu'en 1789*, only 5 vols. published. [Paris: Pichon and Didier, 1829-32.]" Running titles as title. Signed "W. and E."; i.e., Joseph Blanco White and Editor. Identified in Mill's bibliography as "Part of the article on Guizot's Lectures on European Civilization, in the same number of the same work [as 'State of Society in America']" (MacMinn, 46). No copy in Mill's library, Somerville College.

For comment, see lxxiv-lxxv and xcviii-xcix above.

IT IS NOT MANY YEARS since an English nobleman, who long performed his duties of hereditary legislator, under no apprehension of unfitness, on his part, or distrust of his abilities, on that of the public, declared to a brother Peer that he knew no more of the history of England than what he had learnt in Shakspeare.[*] Since the period to which this fact belongs there has been a considerable improvement in the education of all classes. Yet if we could obtain equally unreserved confessions, it is probable that the increase of historical knowledge, in any valuable sense of the term, would be found still to be a rare acquirement among our public men. Few indeed, who have been at a tolerably good school, will not be able to repeat the list of English Sovereigns, with the dates of their accession, and the principal events of their reigns, as they are given in Goldsmith's history,[†] or some more recent abridgment. Most of our legislators will, besides, be found to have, at some period, been moved by a certain degree of secret shame, to make their way through the pages of Hume.[‡] But the

---

[*John Churchill, Duke of Marlborough. For the story, see Mark Noble, *A Biographical History of England from the Revolution to the End of George I's Reign*, 2 vols. (London: Richardson, *et al.*, 1806), Vol. II, p. 189.]

[†Oliver Goldsmith, *The History of England, from the Earliest Times to the Death of George II*, 4 vols. (London: Davies, *et al.*, 1771).]

[‡David Hume, *The History of England* (1756-62).]

number of those who may have made a serious study of history, as an indispensable preparation for an enlightened discharge of their parliamentary duties, will, we fear, be found very small.

Statements of this kind are certainly difficult to be proved; but the present is one not likely to be questioned. When, as it happens with the regular branches of public education, the average of knowledge acquired by the mass of those who have been trained under the system is in value far below the expenditure of time and property which it occasions, though there may exist a strong general conviction of the fact, the assertion of that conviction is invidious, and exposed to a flat denial. It is obvious indeed, but, when denied, not easily substantiated, that, out of ten who have passed between twelve and thirteen years in the study of Latin and Greek, nine can make scarcely any use of those two languages for any purpose of utility or rational amusement. The case is, however, very different in regard to the knowledge of which we are now lamenting the scarcity. The difficulty here would be to prove the existence: for it will not easily be supposed that men will generally become well acquainted with any thing which is slightly thought of, if not totally neglected, in the system of public education; and so it unfortunately happens in regard to history.

The accidental connexion of ancient history with the study of Latin and Greek, which makes up the main *literary* department cultivated in our universities, gives an opportunity to some of the more zealous tutors to oblige a few of their pupils to become acquainted with the historical periods described by Herodotus and Thucydides. Roman history fares generally worse; for very few undergraduates can take up the whole of Livy for their examination, much less fill up the chasms of the narrative from other sources.* The second Decad is the portion most usually read. But even such an imperfect acquaintance with ancient history as

*Two class-books have been for some years published in Germany, which might be used with advantage at the universities, if (what we cannot help calling) an affectation of extreme classical purity, besides other objections arising from want of uniformity in the studies carried on privately by the different colleges, did not preclude the use of such books. The titles of these works are *Antiqua Historia ex ipsis veterum Scriptorum Latinorum narrationibus contexta*, 2 vols., 8vo. [(Leipzig: Hahn, 1811)]—*Antiqua Historia ex ipsis veterum Scriptorum Graecorum narrationibus contexta*, 4 vols., 8vo. [(Leipzig: Weidmann, 1811-12).] Both are compiled by Jo. Godofr. Eichhorn. The latter work is printed on very bad paper, and abounds in typographical errors. But if ancient history should, at any future period, be made a regular and serious study, under a *public* professor, we conceive that no better text-books than these could be adopted. It is true that, as the various portions of the narrative are taken from different writers, the style is very unequal. But the passages from each writer are commonly very long, and all with references to the originals; so that this very circumstance might give occasion to appropriate remarks on the authors themselves, the periods to which they belong, and the peculiarities of their styles.—These observations are made in reference to the system of education at Oxford; but we have reason to believe that they are substantially applicable to Cambridge.

this *incidental* study (for *language* is the immediate object) of two fragments of that history is likely to produce is by no means a necessary condition for taking a degree. From the circumstance that Herodotus presents little difficulty to the student, though a portion of his work is very frequently chosen for the examination required to obtain a common certificate from the examiners, he is not among the Greek writers preferred for the display of scholarship demanded from the young men who aim at *honours*. As the being able to translate Livy cannot be considered a great feat of scholarship—and as accurate knowledge of the historical narrative makes no remarkable show in the schools (the place of examination), the diligent and able students are disinclined to historical books, and take the poets in preference. It may therefore be truly said that, in general, ancient history forms no important part of the university education. Dr. Cardwell, the public professor of ancient history at Oxford, has for some years attracted a numerous audience to his terminal lectures,* by the transient interest produced by the taste and talent with which he treats detached subjects of classical antiquities. The professor of modern history,[*] after having several times attempted, in vain, to collect a class, was obliged to be silent. The truth is, that no kind of knowledge whatever will be attended to at any place of education, unless it is a means of distinction at the examinations; and no kind of knowledge will be made a subject of examination in which the examiners (who, during the time of our intimate acquaintance with Oxford, were frequently not much older or much higher in the ranks of literature than the *examinees*) cannot also distinguish themselves. Hence the almost impossibility of enlarging the circle of studies which limits the ground-work of education in a place which ought to compete with the first universities of Europe. Some men of higher standing have of late been appointed examiners at Oxford;[†] but though a few among these able and learned individuals have contributed to raise the standard of public honours, they have it not in their power to multiply the subjects of examination. That could only be done if the university professors were the regular instructors as well as examiners; enjoying, of course, the privilege of appointing, at the beginning of every scholastic year, a course of study for the whole body of undergraduates.

The general disregard of historical studies in English education becomes a melancholy topic of reflection in the presence of the work which is the subject of this article. But before we say a word on the book itself, we must endeavour to

---

*By *terminal* lectures those are understood which the public professors are, in some cases, expected, in others obliged (according to the foundation statute), to deliver every *term*.

[*Edward Nares.]

[†The reference presumably is to such scholars as William Hayward Cox, Edmund Walker Head, Richard Michell, George Moberly, Frederick Oakeley, and Travers Twiss.]

obviate a just prejudice which attaches itself to the name of M. Guizot. He is known in England chiefly as one of the principal instruments of the profoundly immoral, as well as despotic *régime* which France is now enduring. One of the detestable arts of that system, as of the system of Napoleon, of which it is an imitation, is to seek out, and place in stations of eminence, all the most distinguished abilities in the nation, provided they are willing to prostitute themselves to its service. In the capacity of a tool of this system, though we believe him to be greatly more sincere than most of the other tools, we have nothing to say for M. Guizot. But in the more honourable character which he had earned for himself as a professor and as a literary man, before practical politics assailed him with their temptations and their corrupting influences, he deserves to be regarded with very different feelings. He is among the first, if not the very first, of a school of writers on history, and the philosophy of history, which has arisen within the last twenty years, and which, though to the infinite discredit of our country it has scarcely been heard of here, is, in all the other countries of civilised Europe, known and estimated as it deserves.

The *Histoire de la Civilisation en Europe* (a work complete in itself), and the five volumes which have appeared of the *Histoire de la Civilisation en France*, may be cited as models of the manner in which history should be studied—its facts made to elucidate one another, and the workings of the great determining causes traced through the complication of their multifarious effects. The character of M. Guizot's writings is besides so popular and attractive, that they may be said to be addressed to every one who, being previously acquainted with a mere outline of the history of Europe, from the decline of the Roman empire to the end of the sixteenth century, has also the still more necessary preparation of what might be called an *ethical* taste—that is, an interest in the workings of external events upon man, and the reaction of man's mind upon the world that surrounds him. The applause with which the lectures, which make up these two works, were heard at Paris, proves that among the educated classes of that capital there exists far more of the taste just mentioned than in the corresponding ranks of society among us. Were any such taste alive in England, the works of M. Guizot—(nay, the works of a constellation of French historical writers, which may well excite the emulation of even the most advanced and refined nations)*—would not be generally unknown on this side of the Channel. Even a recent writer, who, though he began to print his work on the English Commonwealth one year before the publication of M. Guizot's *Civilization in Europe*, seems to

---

*We need only allude to Thierry, Barante, Cousin, Villemain, and their numerous pupils and successors—together with the many writers who, without participating in its extravagances, have issued from the St. Simonian school. We confine our examples to those writers who may be considered to represent the new historical method of the present age in France: omitting those, however eminent, who might have been produced at any other period in the development of the national intellect.

have kept it on the anvil till 1832, takes no further notice of his illustrious contemporary and fellow-labourer upon a much ampler scale, than a dry controversy with him in a note near the end of his first volume, and a "See Mably and Guizot" in the more interesting one, which contains his "Proofs and Documents."[*] One can easily understand why a writer who chiefly cultivates the valuable but not very attractive erudition of the mere antiquarian, should turn away from the pages of a more philosophical historian. But that the mass of the reading public, among whom few persons would not be ashamed to be found ignorant of the French language, should remain unacquainted with Guizot's historical Lectures, betrays an evident misdirection in the process of their instruction. It shows that French is cultivated as a mere accomplishment—for show; and that for any of the more essential purposes of a liberal education, it is not cultivated at all. Few, very few of the vast numbers who are taught French at school, acquire the habit of reading that language with ease; and this may account for the general ignorance of modern French literature in England.* Yet, if the young mind were properly trained, through English reading, so that among the multitude of purchasers in the book-market there were but one-fourth who either wished for instruction, or could derive amusement from anything requiring the slightest expense of intellect or thought, the English booksellers would not have omitted the publication of, at least, Guizot's *Civilization in Europe*, in English. That volume by itself is not only invaluable to the philosopher, and

[*Francis Palgrave, *The Rise and Progress of the English Commonwealth. Anglo-Saxon Period*, 2 pts. (London: Murray, 1832), Pt. I, p. 519n (presumably), and Pt. II ("Proofs and Illustrations"), p. ccclxxxix n. But there is a full acknowledgment to Guizot's *Essais*, Pt. I, pp. 528n-9n, and other references to Guizot in the text and notes (usually finding slight fault), e.g., Pt. I, pp. 514n, 542-3 (and note), and 545-6 (and note). Palgrave's reference is to Gabriel Bonnot de Mably, *Observations sur l'histoire de France* (1765), new ed., rev. Guizot, 3 vols. (Paris: Brière, 1823), with which was published the 1st ed. of Guizot's *Essais*.]

*Of the universality and density of this ignorance, striking instances are continually offering themselves. In the present year, 1835, a new Review, calling itself the *British and Foreign*, and professing to devote peculiar attention to foreign literature and philosophy—in an introductory address, written generally in a liberal spirit, speaks of the obligations of the human mind to France in the present era as limited to "what we owe to the modern chemists, natural historians, mathematicians, and astronomers of France." [Christopher Bird, "Introduction," *British and Foreign Review*, I (July–Oct., 1835), 9.] The writer was evidently unaware that France had, since the Revolution, produced a single distinguished name in any other department. And it is our firm conviction, that most of the literary men of celebrity in Great Britain at the present time are ignorant of the very existence of any French writers of eminence (except, indeed, Madame de Staël) posterior to Voltaire and Rousseau: although it is a fact, recognised by all the rest of Europe, that the last twenty years are the most brilliant period in the literary history of France—a period in which she has not only produced her very greatest writer (Paul-Louis Courier), and a host of first-rate works in the most various departments, but in which the tone and character of French intellect has undergone a complete transformation.

most interesting to every reader of cultivated intelligence, but is admirably suited
to be put into the hands of young people near the close of their pupillary
instruction, immediately after they have read Koch's *Tableau des Révolutions de
l'Europe*.[*] Guizot's lectures would unite and arrange in the mind the dry facts
of the *Tableau*;—would not only fix them in the memory, but transform them
into that practical wisdom which the ancients expected from history, and which,
considering the increased experience of ages, and our greater wealth in historical
documents, our own age has an infinitely higher right to demand. It would,
lastly, perform what, in regard to Koch's *Abridgment*,[†] as we have it, is of the
highest importance—for it would help a sensible teacher, and still more a
sensible learner, to correct the false and mischievous views which the French
continuator,[‡] one of the conservative sages (if we do not mistake) of the
restored Bourbons, has attached to the original work.

M. Guizot's manner of treating history will be best exhibited by specimens.
Could we venture to give extracts in the author's own language, we should feel
more sure of interesting our readers; but the conviction which we have already
expressed, that the number of those who in this country can freely take in the
meaning of philosophical French writing is comparatively very small, absolutely
prevents our indulging ourselves in quotations. We cannot, on the other hand,
feel satisfied that we are able to do full justice to our author in our translations of
detached passages. He who, with a sufficient command of the two languages,
should undertake a version of these works, would be able gradually to lead the
English reader into a familiarity with a certain phraseology—with a peculiar set
of figurative or allusive expressions, the philosophic significance of which is
clear and determinate in the author's mind, and is seized at once by all educated
Frenchmen, but which imply combinations of ideas not equally familiar to the
English reader. The national mind of no two countries advances in exactly the
same track: every nation, which is rapidly progressive in intellect, has innumerable meanings to express, which have not yet arisen in the national mind of
any other country; and possesses phrases which at once summon up those
meanings, and which other countries can only gradually learn to understand.
There is a way to translate, not words, but *style*, by means of which, without
destroying individuality, the translator should render such works as have an
European interest into an *European style*. We are quite opposed to the abolition

[*Christophe Guillaume de Koch, *Tableau des révolutions de l'Europe, depuis le
bouleversement de l'empire d'occident jusqu'à nos jours* (Lausanne and Strasbourg:
Bauer, 1771).]

[†*Abrégé de l'histoire des traités de paix entre les puissances de l'Europe depuis la
paix de Westphalie*, 4 vols. (Basle: Decker, 1796-97).]

[‡Maximilian Samson Friedrich Schoell, who reissued Koch's work as *Histoire
abrégée des traités de paix. . . . Ouvrage entièrement refondu, augmenté et continué
jusqu'au Congrès de Vienne et aux Traités de Paris de 1815*, 15 vols. (Paris: Gide,
1817-18).]

of national forms of thought, which necessarily produce peculiar forms of expression; but, like national dress, these should be allowed to prevail at home, and when engaged in our domestic concerns. For the concerns of the human mind, for the great interests of European civilization, we should, by mutual consent, endeavour to modify such forms of thought and expression as produce a feeling of strangeness; and, whilst we carefully avoided all corruptions or distortions of individual languages, we should strive after a general assimilation of tone and manner. This may be done by means of able translations of eminent works—such as those with which we are at present concerned; but it is impracticable in the version of detached passages. A metaphor, a sentiment, for instance, too French (we might say, too Continental) to be verbally translated into English, must in such a case be omitted, or something so different be substituted as must destroy the character of the passage. In the translation of a long work, however, the *outlandish* phrase may be half suppressed the first time it occurs, in the hope that, by means of an imperfect version, the reader may on the next occasion be ready to approach nearer to the original: in fact, the translator of a long work has a constant opportunity to gain over the *national* ear by means of the *universal* understanding. For let it be observed, that what people object chiefly against are not words, but combinations, figures, forms of thought;—and that, whilst they imagine they dislike such expressions because they are not national, the true source of the objection is their not understanding the meaning—or even mistaking it.

In spite of the difficulty which we have attempted to describe, we will introduce detached passages in English, begging the indulgence of our readers, if in general we content ourselves with very imperfect *imitations*. We have also to apologize for not attempting to give a general abstract of the works before us, on the obvious ground that they themselves are a very compressed abstract. Our purpose is to invite readers to M. Guizot's works, and encourage a taste for his manner of treating history.

The subject of M. Guizot's Lectures, as the titles of the two collections express it, is *Civilization*. The course of 1828 comprehends the history of European Civilization in general. In the subsequent courses, the series of which was interrupted by the political events which in an evil hour engaged the Professor in the vulgar career of politics, he commenced filling up that general outline with facts and illustrations taken from the history of his own country. The sources of civilization being the same among the whole European family, the philosophical historian may choose any of the nations where the growth of civilization has been continuous and vigorous, as an example, applicable to all the rest, under certain modifications which must be learnt from the detailed history of each. It was natural that M. Guizot should prefer France; yet it must be acknowledged that his reasons for that choice justify it, independently of his national predilections, and the peculiar interest of the subject to the audience he was addressing. He considers the general progress of European civilization to be more faithfully imaged in the history of France than in that of any other country.

Two things (says M. Guizot) present themselves to the mind, when we assert that a country is highly civilized: an organization of the national body, which makes the advantages of union greatly preponderate over the inconveniences and necessary evils of social restraints; and a free and vigorous development of the mental powers and moral faculties in individuals.[*]

When we say that a country advances in civilization, we may mean that external life is becoming more secure and more agreeable—that mankind are improving their physical condition, subduing the powers of nature more and more to their use, and so improving their social arrangements, that all the conjunct operations which constitute social life are better performed than before: Or we may mean that the mental faculties of mankind are unfolding themselves—that a higher spiritual culture is introducing itself—that the individuals of whom society is made up, are advancing more and more towards the perfection of their nature—that the national mind is becoming wiser, nobler, more humane, or more refined, and that more numerous or more admirable individual examples of genius, talent, or heroism are manifesting themselves. When we use the word civilization in its largest sense, we, according to M. Guizot, include in it both these requisites: the improvement of society and outward life, and that of the inward nature of man. If either improves, and the other does not improve along with it, we have no confidence in the reality, or in the durability of the improvement; we do not consider it as a permanent advance in civilization. The two elements do not always keep pace with each other; but when either of them advances, it surely paves the way for the other. When either gets the start, it is soon arrested till the other has overtaken it; and for the healthy and rapid advancement of both, it is of great importance that their development should take place *pari passu*.

M. Guizot is of opinion, that though other countries may have for a time outstripped France in one or other of these two constituents of civilization, there is no country in which the two have accompanied each other so closely, and been developed so harmoniously together. This opinion he substantiates by a critical survey of the civilization of all the principal nations of Europe: the substance of which we will extract, because, though it does not exemplify M. Guizot's historical method, it is a specimen of his general tone of thought, and is ingenious, and much of it eminently just and important.

He begins with England. English civilization (we adopt M. Guizot's ideas, but do not bind ourselves by the laws of translation) has been mainly directed to the improvement of the social arrangements, and of everything relating to external life: its physical comfort—its freedom—and even its morality; but still, external

[*Civilisation en Europe, pp. 15-19.]

well-being, and such inward culture only as has a direct and evident bearing on external well-being, have engaged the greatest part of the attention of the English national mind. Society, in England, has developed itself more nobly and more brilliantly than *man*: immediate and narrow applications have been more thought of than principles: the *nation* makes a greater figure in history, than the individuals who compose it. This eagerness for outward results—this comparative indifference to truth for itself, and to the development and exercise of the human faculties for themselves, M. Guizot considers to be perceptible even in our most purely speculative philosophers—for instance, our metaphysicians. With less questionable accuracy, he affirms the absence of interest in general and commanding views, to have been, at all periods, characteristic of the nation at large.

I turn my eyes to the period of the greatest intellectual activity of England; to the epochs when ideas, when the workings of the national intellect, have occupied the greatest place in her history—the political and religious convulsions of the sixteenth and seventeenth centuries. Every one knows what a prodigious commotion took place at that period in the English mind. Can any one tell me what great philosophical system, what general doctrines, that have since spread themselves over Europe, this commotion gave birth to? It produced immense and admirable consequences; it created new and better institutions and manners; nor did it act only upon the social life, but also upon the spiritual condition of man; it gave rise to sects, and enthusiasts; but it did little, directly at least, to enlarge the horizon of the human mind—it did not kindle one of those great intellectual torches which illuminate an epoch.[*]

The power of religion has been greater in England than in any country whatever. The earnestness and concentration of the convictions which have impelled the English religious parties have hardly a parallel in history; and their convictions have acted largely on their outward lives. But all their zeal has been spent practically. Leading and luminous views have seldom, if ever, issued from among them. The speculations of English divines have generally been confined by some political aim—have been limited to the removal of some definite and local evil, or to the mere refitting and patching up of old doctrines. The spirit of England is *practical*. The nation has had, and still possesses, great minds; but neither in number nor power (though the latter is unquestionably great) do they bear a due proportion to the colossal growth of the external, the social civilization of the country.

Germany presents a contrast to this picture. The social or external progress has there been difficult and slow: the coarseness of German manners has been proverbial till our own days. But how infinitely beyond this progress of the social body has been that of the individual intellect in that country! Compare the mental powers displayed by the German reformers, Luther, Melancthon, Bucer, with the semi-barbarous manners which they themselves betray, and which, con-

[*Translated from *Civilisation en France*, Vol. I, p. 12.]

sidering their circumstances, may be taken as samples of those which prevailed in the nation. The existence of such minds, in such a state of society, appears a paradox. If we pass on to the seventeenth century, we find Leibnitz and the German Universities in the first rank among the leaders of the mental progress of mankind; while the Courts of Brandenburg and Bavaria, described as we find them in the memoirs of the same period,[*] present the most shocking picture of coarseness and sensuality. Even at this moment, when the good sense and personal virtues of some of the German despots have made *external* Germany advance, its social improvement bears only a very small proportion to the dimensions of its collective mind.

No one is ignorant how great has been, for the last fifty years, in Germany, the activity of the human mind: in all departments—in philosophy, in history, in elegant literature, in poetry—it has made great strides. The road which it has followed may not always have been the best; some of the results which it has arrived at may be contested; but the energy and universality of the development itself are incontestable. Unquestionably, the arrangements of society, the improvement of the outward condition of the people, have not kept pace with it.[†]

Perhaps it is to this circumstance that we might trace the peculiarites of German literature. The German mind appears to have grown without communication with things external. Unsatisfied with the social structure, which always confines, and not unfrequently galls it, if not sufficiently aloof from it, the German mind has created a world for itself, into which the possessors of power have generally had the good sense not to intrude.

The country to which Beauty was given as a curse*—Italy—wants the two characters just mentioned; its civilization is not essentially practical like the English, nor almost exclusively speculative like the German. It is most certain that individual Italians have reached to the highest eminence of pure intelligence, and that the nation has exhibited a degree of social activity and life not inferior *in kind* to that of any other people. Man and society have there displayed themselves with considerable lustre: the Italians have excelled, at once, in science, arts, philosophy, and in the practical concerns of government and life. Italy seems indeed to have now for a long time stood still: she advances on neither of the two paths of civilization; both her social energies and those of her

[*See, e.g., Pierre Philippe Emmanuel, marquis de Coulanges, "Extrait d'un manuscrit de M. de Coulanges, intitulé: Relation de mon voyage d'Allemagne et d'Italie ez années 1657 et 1658," in *Mémoires* (Paris: Blaise, 1820), pp. 13-16, and Antoine, duc de Gramont, *Mémoires du maréchal de Gramont*, in *Collections des mémoires relatifs à l'histoire de France*, ed. Claude Bernard Petitot, 2nd ser., 78 vols. (Paris: Foucault, 1820-29), Vol. LVI, pp. 463-4, 477, Vol. LVII, pp. 4-5.]

[†Translated from *Civilisation en France*, Vol. I, p. 15.]

*"Dono infelice di bellezza." [Vincenzio da] Filicaja ["All'Italia, Sonnetto 1," *Poesie toscane* (Florence: Matini, 1707), p. 320 (l. 2)].

individual minds seem to have become enervated and paralyzed. But if we observe Italy more closely, we shall find that this debility and faintness are not the effect of her own incapacity, but of a foreign yoke; she suffers like a flower struggling to expand its petals under the pressure of a callous, cold hand. The intellectual and political capabilities of Italy are undestroyed: what she wants, what she has ever wanted, is *faith in truth*. It is not enough to have intellect for speculation and talent for conduct; there must be a link to connect the two; there must be a deep conviction that they who know, can and ought to act according to what they know: that the truths which are known do not exist solely for speculation, but have the power and the right to prevail in the government of the outward world. To this faith Italy has always been a stranger. She has been fertile in great minds, and has opened grand and noble views to the intellect: she has also swarmed with practical statesmen of the most surprising talents: but the two classes, and the two pursuits, have always been strangers to each other. The philosophers, the men of general ideas, have never conceived themselves authorized to act; and strong as their conviction of the abstract truth of some great principles may have been, they could never persuade themselves that one atom of the external world might be moved out of its place by the power of such principles. The practical men, on the other hand, the arbiters of society, despised general notions, (the pen which reports M. Guizot's thoughts is irresistibly moved to add—*except generalized principles of deception,*) and have never felt the least desire to regulate the facts under their control, in conformity with any great and comprehensive views. Both classes have acted as if truth was only fit to be known, but not to be acted upon. This, even in the fifteenth century, the principal period of Italian social activity, as well as in subsequent times, has smitten with a kind of sterility both the speculative genius and the practical talent of Italy, and must be assigned as the principal cause of her present hopeless condition.

There is still a great country [says M. Guizot, in a noble passage] which I certainly would not name, were it not out of respect for a generous but unhappy people; else, in connexion with our subject, there would be no necessity to make mention of Spain. Neither great minds, nor great events, are wanting in her history; human intelligence and human society show themselves now and then, in that history, in noble and striking shapes. But they appear scattered and single, like the tall palms of a sandy desert. That chief character of civilization—general, continuous progress, has been denied in Spain both to intellect and society. If the solemn stillness is ever broken, our roused attention is sure to be disappointed. In Spain nothing has a result. In vain should we look for some great idea, some social improvement, some philosophical system, some actively benevolent institution, for which Europe has to thank Spain. She seems quite detached from Europe; she has accepted little at its hands, and has returned still less. I should have reproached myself [concludes M. Guizot] if I had passed the name of Spain in silence; but she is certainly of little consequence in the history of European civilization.[*]

[*Translated from *Civilisation en France*, Vol. I, pp. 18-19.]

From these facts, compared with the general progress of civilization in France, our author concludes in favour of that country as the best suited to illustrate the general character and growth of European civilization. In justice to M. Guizot, we are bound to repeat that this preference is not the effect of national vanity. Highly as he estimates French civilization (and who that is himself free from national partialities will not agree with him?) he does not choose France on account of *absolute* superiority above the three nations which might illustrate the subject in hand; but because, in that remarkable country, the advance of the two elements of civilization—the internal and the external development—has always been more parallel and harmonious than either in England, Germany, or Italy. Though inferior to England in every thing relating to the organization, activity, and freedom of action of the social body; though unable, in the development of the individual mind, to contend with Germany or Italy, the combination and mutual support of theory and practice is better seen in the progress of French civilization, than in the more irregular, though partially more vigorous and extensive growth of other countries.

Man, and Society, in France, have always moved forward, I will not say simultaneously, but separated by a short interval. Side by side with every great event, every revolution, every public improvement, we always find in our history some idea, some general doctrine, corresponding to them. No change has taken place in outward life, which intellect has not promptly seized upon and converted into a source of new riches for her own use; nor has any thing happened in the world of intellect which has not made its influence felt, and generally very speedily, in the world without. For the most part, indeed, the improvements in the social order have been preceded, and in some degree caused, by general ideas; they have been prepared in theory before they have been accomplished in practice, and the intellectual progress has been a-head of the social one. This twofold character, compounded of intellectual activity and practical ability, of meditation and of application, is impressed upon all the great events of French history, upon all the leading classes in French society, and gives them a character and aspect which is found nowhere else.[*]

This description, which, as applied to the present French character, is strikingly just, M. Guizot proves to have been true in all former periods, by a most able general view of his country's history. The historical sketch to which we allude cannot be further reduced than it is in the original, and in that state it is too long for insertion: it is contained in the first lecture on the civilization of France. The whole course of lectures affords ample confirmation of M. Guizot's conclusion.

But whatever may have been the amount of benefit obtained by France herself from the co-ordinate growth of the two civilizations within her territory—the impulse which, evidently from the same cause, she has imparted during the last two centuries to the rest of the European family, both in the old and the new

[*Translated from *ibid.*, pp. 20-1.]

world, is too manifest to be questioned. The spread of French speculations on government, and on moral questions intimately connected with the organization of society, was quite prodigious during the last century. It is common to attribute the diffusive power of French ideas to a peculiar power of the language. But whoever examines the subject with a competent knowledge, will easily perceive that the charm of the French writings does not belong to the language itself, but to the mental habits which have fashioned it into its highly attractive forms. German stands higher above French, as a language, than Greek above Latin. Yet the great master of German poetry and eloquence was, in spite of his anti-Gallican prejudices, obliged to confess that every educated mind must owe a great and most important portion of its education to the instrumentality of the French language.* This peculiar power has, in our opinion, its source in the circumstance, that all French writers above mediocrity have the peculiar art of imparting their speculative principles in a manner which makes the reader feel that by means of them he has acquired a command over a multitude of scattered details, and increased not only his theoretical knowledge but his practical power. They bring the speculative reader into contact with the external world, and accustom the practical one to look to the light of principle for guidance in the concerns of life. They, in fact, unite the two characters which, according to M. Guizot, have always been equally balanced in French civilization: their theory has a constant reference to practice, and their practical maxims are the realization of their theories. It is a common observation that French is a *clear* language; though, as a language, its structure is by no means superior to its sister-languages, Italian and Spanish, which are by no means celebrated for clearness. But the clearness wrongly attributed to the French *language*, belongs to the French habits of thinking: it arises from the happy combination of theory and detail, which has existed in France as a national habit. Thus, while the wants and concerns of life have, as they must in all countries, moulded the language to express easily and clearly the conceptions which relate to material objects, the taste for generalization upon every subject has established and popularized modes of expression well suited to convey the most abstract notions. Such is the real foundation of that perspicuity, which has already established French as the common language of the civilized world.

That the decided tendency of the present period of mankind is to establish a similar alliance, and mutual interchange of beneficial influence, between pure reason and experience, among the leading nations of the world, must be evident to every unclouded mind. The natural right of *principles* to direct human affairs is already perceived by such a majority, even in this *practical* country, that its universal recognition cannot be distant among us; and the blemish which M.

---

*See Goethe's *Wilhelm Meister*, [in *Werke*, 55 vols.] (Stuttgart and Tübingen [: Cotta'schen Buchhandlung, 1828-33]), Vol. XIX, p. 239.

Guizot notices in our national habits of mind has, we venture to hope, a tendency rapidly to disappear.

Modern civilization, (according to M. Guizot,) as compared with the various civilizations of antiquity, is distinguished by one remarkable characteristic,—the multiplicity of the elements of which it is compounded.[*] The European family of nations have grown up to their present condition amidst the conflict of several influences struggling for ascendency, none of which was ever able completely to subdue the others. These warring elements, from which European society has been moulded into shape, may be classed under three heads:—1st. Notions, habits, and institutions, derived from the imperial sway of Rome: 2nd. The sentiments and customs which the northern nations brought with them when they overran the Roman empire: 3rd. The teaching and influence of the Christian clergy—of the hierarchical association called the Church. From each of these three sources some important feature of our modern civilization has been derived; and that civilization would have been wanting in some valuable quality which distinguishes it, if any one of these three sets of influences had been completely put down and annihilated.

All other civilizations, on the contrary, have been comparatively one-sided. The various nations of antiquity, especially in the East, grew up to maturity under the predominant influence of some one civilizing principle, which opposed all tendencies, mental and social, except such as might be made subservient to its exclusive end.

This *unity* must strike every philosophical reader of ancient history. In Egypt, for instance, every thing proceeded from the notion of a *theocracy*. A priesthood enjoyed supreme power in the name of the deity; the king himself was a priest, and the extent of his power, supported by the hierarchy, cannot be better expressed than in the words of one of the Pharaohs, at the moment of appointing Joseph his vizier. "I am Pharaoh, and without thee shall no man lift up his hand or foot in all the land of Egypt." (Genesis, 41 [:44].) Not the smallest fraction of Egyptian knowledge, or Egyptian polity, could be traced to any other source but its priesthood. When that body of men had imparted as much civilization as, in their opinion, might be given to the people with safety to their hereditary power, Egyptian civilization stood still, and acquired a permanency which might well be compared to that of the mummies. The still older civilization of India may, at this moment, be observed as possessing the same *unity* of character. In other cases, the principle which was in the ascendant was the dominion of a conquering race; and the sole end of society and education was to enable that race to maintain its superiority. In other and most memorable instances, every thing yielded to the democratic principle; or, in other words, (for that was the meaning and purpose

[*Civilisation en Europe, pp. 6-8.]

of the ancient democracies,) the passion for political equality among the free citizens of the state, was the influence which shaped all things after its own guise. M. Guizot does not overlook the fact that, in periods previous to that in which the civilization of these various countries began regularly to advance, fierce struggles took place for mastery, between the powers which represented the various principles, theocracy, military aristocracy, and democracy. The warrior-race, for instance, contended for ascendency with the priesthood among the Egyptians, the Etruscans, and the Greeks: the *clan* or family system had also its contests with that of purely democratical union. But when these contests were decided, the conquering principle became completely preponderant, if not entirely exclusive. This simplicity in the civilizing principle naturally produced, in favourable circumstances, a much more rapid progress than is observable in modern Europe. In Greece, the democratic principle produced the most astonishing growth of civilization which was ever recorded, or even conceived. But the unity and simplicity of the animating force, which caused the rapid development of Greece, seems to have been the cause of its quick exhaustion. When the only source of Greek social life happened to be dried up, the moral and civil death of that wonderful people was inevitable. The unity of the civilizing principle had an opposite result in Egypt and India. The civilizing influence spent itself; it did all that its nature admitted, and then civilization stood still. To use our author's expressive language, in those two countries "unity produced monotony: society continued to exist, but motionless, and, as it were, frozen."[*] Another result of this ancient unity was the intolerant and jealous tyranny of each of the exclusive principles which happened to gain the ascendency. The whole of every society of that kind was under the sway of an active principle which could not endure the least approach of any other. This exclusiveness and intolerance extended itself to literature and the arts, especially among the Indian nations. The monuments of Indian genius which, within a few years, have become known among us, present the most surprising uniformity of spirit, of views, of taste.

Let us compare with this unity the almost bewildering variety which appears in our modern civilization. The history of Europe is the picture of a stormy chaos, where the most opposite elements have been for ages fermenting into a life ever new and varied.

All forms, all principles of social organization co-exist: spiritual power and temporal power, theocracy, monarchy, aristocracy, democracy, all contend for mastery. The classes and conditions of men are infinitely varied, and every one is seen pressing upon the next: there is an infinite number of *degrees* of liberty, of wealth, of influence; and while all these various forces are in a constant struggle with one another, no one of them has been able to establish its ascendency by the complete suppression of the rest. Modern Europe offers examples of every system—of every attempt at social organization:

[*Translated from *ibid.*, Lecture 2, p. 5.]

monarchies pure and mixed, theocracies, republics more or less aristocratic, have existed simultaneously side by side; and in spite of their diversity, all of them have a certain resemblance, a kind of family likeness which it is impossible to mistake.

The same variety is apparent in ideas and sentiments. Theocratic, monarchical, aristocratic, and popular opinions have constantly co-existed, in a state of mutual conflict, and of mutual limitation and modification. Even in the boldest writings of the middle ages, you never find an idea followed out to its ultimate consequences. The partisans of absolute power unconsciously shrink from the conclusions to which their doctrine properly leads; we see that they were surrounded by ideas and influences which overawed them, and would not let them carry out their opinions consistently. Democratic writers are forced to be equally guarded. No where do we see that imperturbable hardihood, that reckless consistency, which are so striking in ancient times. The same variety and the same contrasts offer themselves in feelings and characters: a most energetic passion for independence, along with great readiness of submission; a rare fidelity beween man and man, and at the same time an imperious self-will—a *besoin* of shaking off all control, and having no guide but one's own breast. The minds of mankind are as various and as unsettled as the state of society.[*]

A civilization produced by the mutual action of so many principles in a state of constant warfare, both in society and in the human breast, must necessarily be of slow growth: it can only emerge very gradually from chaos. Each of the contending powers is long and greatly counteracted in the good which it has a tendency to produce, as well as in the evil. A great part of the strength of each is exhausted in warring with the others; and hence the slow progress of the modern, compared with the best of the ancient civilizations. Long indeed was the period during which the strongest faith in perfectibility might be shaken at the view of the events which were daily taking place over the face of our portion of the globe. The progress which Europe was making resembled that of a ship in a storm, that threatens destruction at every movement. But the same cause which made the development of our civilization slower, has made it also richer—has introduced into it a great number and variety of beneficent principles, and promises a grander and better ultimate result.

If space permitted, we would transfer to our pages, in nearly its original extent, that portion of the second lecture on the Civilization of Europe, in which M. Guizot assigns to each of the three sets of causes which were at work when modern European society issued from chaos, the portion of influence which has actually belonged to it.[†]

The degenerate and perishing civilization of Rome, left, according to him, three legacies to modern Europe. The first was, municipal institutions, and the spirit of local association and local self-government. The Roman empire was originally compounded of city-communities, managing their own affairs: Rome itself was such a community; and again in its decay the empire gradually resolved itself into such communities—the municipalities being the only portion of

[*Translated from *ibid.*, pp. 6-8.]
[†*Ibid.*, pp. 12-39.]

Roman institutions and Roman society which had any vitality left, when the northern nations overran the western world.

The second gift of ancient Rome to modern Europe was her written laws. These laws had great imperfections; but they were a *system*, and therefore could not have been formed by mere barbarians; they were fashioned by a series of cultivated minds, with the assistance of the experience of ages; they presented to the northern invaders an image of a much higher state of civilization than existed among themselves—of a state of established order and regular government, in which rights were recognised and protected, and much consideration paid to the dictates of justice and the feelings of humanity.

Finally, one great idea, originating in the Roman empire, survived its dissolution, and exercised, as M. Guizot shows, a great influence in modern history, by the aid it afforded to the consolidation of the regal power. This was, the idea of unity in the sovereign authority;—that notion of the majesty of the empire, round which such a host of associations clustered in the mind of a Roman, and which alone could have kept the empire together for ages after the imperial dignity had become the prize of the most able or fortunate military leader of a province.

To the Church, Europe is indebted for whatever it owes to Christianity; and all its moral and religious convictions have bodied themselves forth under that influence. M. Guizot is persuaded that, humanly speaking, Christianity could not have maintained itself against the inroad of Pagan barbarians merely by its intrinsic merits, and by the energy of individual convictions. But its interests were under the special care of a body of men, the most cultivated whom the age afforded, and the only body who, in the general dissolution of all things round them, remained compactly knit together, powerfully organized for a common object. The influence which this body acquired over the barbarian invaders, and which was so early manifested in their outward conversion to Christianity, introduced among them the belief in an authority superior to that of the sword, and in a law binding on the conscience, even in the absence of any temporal sanction. The power of the Church—a power exerted through men's convictions, and by their voluntary concurrence—was for ages the only counterpoise to the mere law of the strongest. From this peculiar position arose the separation of spiritual and temporal power: a fact peculiar to modern Europe, and to which M. Guizot attributes a most salutary influence upon her civilization. It is certain that wherever spiritual and temporal authority have been concentrated in the same hands, civilization has stopped at an early stage. And it is difficult to estimate in how much worse a condition we should now have been, if the great struggle of the middle ages, between the feudal monarchy and aristocracy, and the Romish hierarchy, had terminated in the complete victory of either.

Lastly, to the northern invaders we are indebted for one of our greatest peculiarities—the spirit of liberty, in the peculiar sense attached to the term in

modern times: the spirit of personal independence, which repels the interference
of the state with the private concerns of the individual: as distinguished from the
spirit of liberty as understood in the ancient republics, which may be characterized as the successive sacrifice of *each* to *all*. Greek and Roman liberty did not
mean that the power exercised by the community over the persons composing it,
should be no greater than was conducive to their well-being; it meant that each of
those persons should have an equal chance with any other person, of exercising a
share of that power. The love of liberty, in the modern sense of the phrase, was
repudiated by the notions prevalent in those commonwealths respecting the
duties of a citizen. The imaginary being, the *civitas*, the πόλις, demanded the
annihilation of every individuality. Every citizen was a perfect slave of the
domineering principle, and of those who, for the time being, were its living
representatives.

It is manifestly impossible, in an article like the present, to convey any but a
most imperfect notion of the general character of M. Guizot's historical
speculations. We cannot follow him through the various periods of European
history. At each period, his method is one and the same—the only method which
a philosopher will ever use. He begins by familiarizing himself with the literature
of the period, and any other evidences which it has left of its state of society.
From these, when he has sufficiently imbued himself with their spirit, he learns
what were at each period the causes actually at work, and within what limits each
of those causes was operating. This being known, the general laws of human
nature suffice to show of what kind must have been the influence exercised by
each; and the conclusion is then tested by the history of the succeeding ages.
Unless studied in this way, history is indeed nothing but an "old almanac," and
has neither any meaning of its own, nor throws light upon anything else.

We shall extract one specimen—a part of the observations on the feudal
times, in the fourth lecture on the Civilization of Europe. Even when abridged,
those observations exceed the ordinary dimensions of an extract; but the great
interest of the subject, and the striking and original manner in which it is treated,
are an ample justification for the space which our quotation occupies:

Sufficient importance has seldom been attached to the changes which a new historical
fact, a revolution, a change in the state of society, occasion in the *material* condition of
mankind—the physical state, and outward mode of living, of the people. This class of
considerations have more influence than is commonly supposed over the general state of
civilization. Every one is aware of the notice that has been taken of the influence of
climate, and the importance attached to it by Montesquieu.[*] If we confine ourselves to
the *direct* influence of diversity of climate upon mankind, it is perhaps less than has been
supposed; the appreciation of it is, at all events, difficult and vague. But the indirect
effects of climate—those, for instance, which result from the fact, that in a warm climate

[*De l'esprit des loix, Vol. I, pp. 360-443 (Bks. XIV-XVII).]

mankind live in the open air, while in cold countries they shut themselves up in their houses—that they subsist upon different kinds of food, and the like—are facts of great importance, and which, merely by their influence on the details of material existence, act powerfully on civilization. Every great revolution produces in the state of society some changes of this sort, and these ought to be carefully attended to.

The introduction of the feudal *régime* occasioned one such change, of which the importance cannot be overlooked: it altered the distribution of the population over the face of the country. Till that time, the masters of the country, the sovereign class, lived collected in masses more or less numerous—either sedentary in the towns, or wandering in bands over the country. In the feudal state, these same persons lived insulated, each in his own habitation, at great distances from one another. You perceive at once what an influence this change must have exercised over the character and the progress of civilization. Social preponderance and political power passed at once from the towns to the country; private property, and private life, assumed the pre-eminence over public. This first effect of the triumph of the feudal principle appears more fruitful in consequences, the more we consider it.

Let us examine feudal society as it is in its own nature, looking at it first of all in its simple and fundamental element. Let us figure to ourselves a single possessor of a fief in his own domain, and consider what will be the character of the little association which forms itself round him.

He establishes himself in a retired and defensible place, which he takes care to render safe and strong: he erects there what he terms his castle. With whom does he establish himself there? With his wife and his children: perhaps, too, some few freemen, who have not become landed proprietors, have attached themselves to his person, and continue domesticated with him. These are all the inmates of the castle itself. Around it, and under its protection, collects a small population of labourers—of serfs, who cultivate the domain of the *seigneur*. Amidst this inferior population, Religion comes, builds a church, and establishes a priest. In the early times of feudality, this priest is at once the chaplain of the castle and the parish clergyman of the village: at a later period, the two characters are separated. Here then is the elementary particle—the unit, if I may so speak, of feudal society. We have now to call this element before us, and put the two questions to it which should be addressed to every historical fact: What was it calculated to do towards the development—first, of man; and next, of society?

The first circumstance which strikes us, is the prodigious importance which the possessor of the fief could not but asssume, in his own eyes, and in those of all who surround him. The sentiment of personality and individual independence was the predominant feeling in savage life; but the feeling now generated goes beyond this: it is not merely the liberty of the man and of the warrior, but the importance of the landed proprietor, the head of a family, the master. From this position must arise a sentiment of immense superiority—a superiority quite peculiar, and unlike that which is found in any other civilization. Take, for instance, in the ancient world, the position of a great aristocrat—a Roman patrician, for example. Like the feudal lord, the Roman patrician was the head of a family—was a master, a superior: he was, besides, a religious magistrate, a pontiff in the interior of his family. But the importance of a religious magistrate comes to him from without: it is not an importance purely personal and individual; he receives it from above; he is the delegate of the Divinity—the interpreter of the religious belief which is connected with his office. In civil life, again, the patrician was a member of the senate—of a corporation, which lived united together in one place. This, again, was an importance derived from without, borrowed and reflected from that of his corporation. The grandeur of the ancient aristocrats was associated with religious and political functions: it belonged to the situation, to the corporation at large, more than to the individual. That of the possessor of a fief is, on the contrary, purely individual. He receives nothing from any one: all his rights, all his powers, come from himself alone. He is not a religious magistrate; he is not a member of a senate; his importance is all in his own person; whatever he is, he is by his own right, and in his own name. With what force must not such a situation act upon the mind of him who holds it! What personal pride, what haughtiness—to speak plainly, what insolence—must arise in his soul! Above him no superior of whom he is the representative and the interpreter; around him no equals; no vigorous, universal law to curb him; no external force habitually controlling his will; he knows no restraint but the limits of his strength, or the presence of an immediate danger. Such is the moral result of the situation upon the character of the individual.

I pass to a second consequence, also important, and too little remarked: the peculiar turn given to the family-spirit, by the feudal state of society.

History exhibits to us the family in several distinct shapes. First, the patriarchal family, as seen in the Bible, and the various monuments of the East. The family, there, is numerous, and amounts to a tribe. The chief, the patriarch, lives in a state of community with his children, his kindred (all the various generations of whom are grouped round him), and his servants. Not only does he live with them, but he has the same interests and occupations with them, he leads the same life. Is not this the situation of Abraham, of the patriarchs, of the chiefs of Arab tribes, who are in our own days a faithful image of patriarchal life?

Another form of the family is the *clan*, that little association, the type of which must be sought in Scotland and Ireland, and through which, probably, a great part of the European world has passed. This is no longer the patriarchal family. There is now a great difference of condition between the chief and the rest of the population: he does not lead the same life with his followers; they mostly cultivate and serve: he takes his ease, and has no occupation but that of a warrior. But he and they have a common origin; they bear the same name; their relationship, their ancient traditions, and their community of affections and of recollections, establish among all the members of the clan a moral union, a kind of equality.

Does the feudal family resemble either of these types? Evidently not. At first sight it has some apparent resemblance to the clan; but the difference is immense. The population which surrounds the possessor of the fief are perfect strangers to him: they do not bear his name: they have no relationship to him, are connected with him by no tie, historical or moral. Neither does he, as in the patriarchal family, lead the same life, and carry on the same labours as those about him; he has no occupation but war, they are tillers of the ground. The feudal family is not numerous; it does not constitute a tribe; it is confined to the family in the narrowest sense, the wife and children; it lives separated from the rest of the people, in the interior of the castle. The labourers, the serfs, are no part of it; their origin is different, their inferiority of condition is profound. Five or six persons, in a position at once alien from, and superior to, all others, constitute the feudal family. Its character must therefore become peculiar. It lives retired, concentrated within itself, constantly obliged to defend itself, to distrust, or at least to keep aloof from all, even its servants. Internal life, domestic society, are therefore certain to acquire a great preponderance. I know that the rudeness and violence of the chief's passions, and his habit of passing his time in war or in the chase, must obstruct and retard the formation of domestic habits. But that obstacle will be overcome. It must necessarily happen that the chief will return habitually to his own home: there he will always find his wife, his children, and them alone, or nearly alone; they only will compose his permanent society; they only will always partake his interests, his destiny. It is impossible that domestic life should not acquire a great ascendency. The proofs are abundant. Was it not in the feudal family that the importance of women at length arose? In all the societies of antiquity, not only where no family-spirit existed, but where that spirit was powerful, for instance in the patriarchal societies, women did not occupy any thing like the place which they acquired in Europe under the feudal *régime*. The cause of this has been looked for in the peculiar manners of the ancient Germans, in a characteristic respect which it is affirmed that in the midst of their forests they paid to women. German patriotism has built upon a single sentence of Tacitus[*] a fancied superiority, a primitive and ineffaceable purity of German manners in the relations of the sexes to one another. Mere chimeras! Expressions similar to those of Tacitus, sentiments and usages analogous to those of the ancient Germans, are found in the recitals of many observers of barbarous tribes. There is nothing peculiar in the matter, nothing characteristic of a particular race. The importance of women in Europe arose from the progress and preponderance of domestic manners; and that preponderance became, at an early period, an essential character of feudal life.

A second fact, and another proof of the increased importance of domestic life, is the spirit of hereditary succession, of perpetuity, which evidently predominates in the feudal society. The hereditary spirit is inherent in the spirit of family; but it has nowhere been so largely developed as in feudal life. This arises from the nature of the property with which the family was bound up. A fief was not like any other property: it perpetually needed a possessor to defend it, to fulfil the obligations inherent in it, and maintain its rank in the general association of the rulers of the country. Hence a kind of identification of the actual possessor of the fief with the fief itself, and with the whole series of its future possessors. This circumstance did much to strengthen and draw closer the family ties, already so powerful from the nature of the feudal family.

Let us now quit the seignorial abode, and descend amongst the little population surrounding it. Here all things present a different aspect. Human nature is so fertile in good, that in any social situation which lasts a certain length of time, there inevitably arises between those whom it brings into contact, under whatever conditions, a certain moral tie—certain feelings of protection, of benevolence, of affection. It was thus in the feudal society: one cannot doubt that, after some time, there were formed between the cultivators and their *seigneur*, some moral relations, some habits of sympathy. But this happened *in spite* of their relative position, and nowise from its influence. Considered in itself, the situation was radically vicious. There was nothing morally in common between the feudal superior and the cultivators; they were part of his domain; they were his property; and in that word *property* were included all the rights now deemed to appertain to political sovereignty, as well as those of private property; the right to give laws, to tax, to punish, as well as to use and to sell. Between the *seigneur* and those who tilled the ground which belonged to him, there were (as far as that can ever be said, when human beings are brought together) no laws, no protection, no society.

Hence, I conceive, that truly prodigious and invincible detestation which the rural population have entertained in all ages for the feudal *régime*, for its very name, and for every remembrance of it. Mankind have endured and been reconciled to oppressive despotisms; they have even voluntarily submitted to them. Theocratic and monarchical despotism have more than once obtained the acquiescence, and almost the affection, of the population subjected to them. Feudal despotism, on the contrary, was always rejected, always odious: it weighed upon men's destinies without ever reigning over their souls. The reason is, that theocracy and monarchy exercise their dominion in virtue of some belief, common to the master with his subjects; he is the representative and minister of

[*See p. 284 above.]

another power, superior to all human powers; he speaks and acts in the name of the Deity, or of some general idea, not in the name of the man himself, of a mere man. Feudal despotism is quite different: it is the power of one individual over another, the domination of the personal and capricious will of a human being. This is perhaps the only tyranny, which (to his honour be it said) man never voluntarily resigns himself to. Wherever, in his master, he sees nothing but a man—wherever the hand which presses him down is but a human hand like his own, he is indignant, and if he bears the yoke, bears it with resentment. Such was the real, the distinctive character of the feudal dominion, and such the origin of the antipathy it never ceased to inspire.

The religious element which was joined with it had little power to alleviate its weight. I do not believe that the influence of the priest, in the little society which I have described, was considerable, nor that it had much success in infusing a moral character into the relations between the subject population and their lord. The church has exercised over European civilization a very great influence, but it was by proceeding on a large scale, by changing the general dispositions of mankind. In the details of the little feudal societies, properly so called, the influence of the priest, as between the *seigneur* and the cultivators, was next to nothing. He was generally himself rudely and meanly educated, like a serf, and neither inclined nor in a condition to contend against the arrogance of the lord. No doubt, being the only person called upon to keep up and develop in the subject population something of moral vitality, he was valuable and dear to them on that account; he diffused among them some consolation, and some little instruction; but he neither did, nor could do, I conceive, any thing considerable to improve their condition.[*]

M. Guizot then examines the situation of the feudal landholders, relatively to one another. He observes, that from their mutual relations to each other, and to their liege lord, there naturally grew up in their minds some notions of mutual obligation, of fidelity, of adherence to engagements, of devotion to a common interest; but that the attempt to convert these moral sentiments into legal obligations, and to create national institutions and a regular government, always failed; and failed inevitably: for it was an attempt to establish, in a rude state of society, that kind of government, the existence of which is only possible in high civilization,—a federal government. He then sums up the general results of the feudal system as follows:

Feudality must have exercised a considerable, and, take it for all in all, a salutary influence on the internal development of the individual: it raised up in the human mind some moral notions and moral wants, some energetic sentiments: it produced some noble developments of character and of passion. Considered in the social point of view, it was not capable of establishing legal order or political securities; but it was indispensable as a recommencement of European society, which had been so broken up by barbarism, that it was unable to assume any more enlarged or more regular forms. But the feudal form, radically bad in itself, admitted neither of being enlarged nor regularized. The only political right which feudality has implanted strongly in European society, is the right of resistance. I do not mean *legal* resistance; that was out of the question in a society so little advanced. The right of resistance which the feudal society asserted and exercised is the right of *personal* resistance; a fearful, an unsocial right, since it is an appeal to force, to war, the direct antithesis of society; but a right which ought never to perish from the heart

[*Translated from *Civilisation en Europe*, Lecture 4, pp. 9-21.]

of man, since its abrogation is simply submission to slavery. The sentiment of a right of resistance had perished in the degeneracy of Roman societies, from the ruins of which it could not again rise: as little, in my opinion, was it a natural emanation from the principles of Christian society. Feudality re-introduced it into European manners. It is the glory of civilization to render this right for ever useless and inactive; it is the glory of the feudal society to have constantly maintained it and stood up for it.[*]

This is followed by further remarks, showing that the history of the times confirms the view here taken of the influences of feudality.

Every one who reads these quotations must, if we mistake not, experience the twofold sentiment most complimentary to a philosophic writer: conviction that here is at length the true and commanding view of a great subject; and astonishment that truths so simple and apparently obvious should not have been as distinctly perceived and as prominently brought forward by former writers. It is scarcely exaggeration to say that M. Guizot's work excites these feelings continually.

It ought not, however, to be suppressed, that while the work abounds in such luminous views as those which we have been following up with delight, the attentive reader will nevertheless perceive here and there something like a half-suppressed or gently-breathed sigh of the author for that very *unity* of society which he himself has so ably demonstrated to be both injurious to the true interests of civilization in general, and particularly opposed to the essential character of our own.

In the masterly picture which M. Guizot draws of the Church and its civilizing influence, from the fourth to the thirteenth century, he dwells with particular pleasure on the *unity* of that body. He calls that unity *a glorious and powerful fact.** The unity of the Church alone (he proceeds) was the bond which kept together the various nations, which lay like unconnected fragments of the fallen Roman empire. The notion of this union contained the rudiments (though confused and greatly distorted) not only of a vast and comprehensive sympathy, but (he says) of the grandest and most enlarged conception which ever rallied human beings round it—that of a *spiritual human society*: *i.e.*, mankind reduced to one vast family, united by means of the moral and intellectual faculties. From the fifth to the thirteenth century (says M. Guizot) this idea of the Church rendered great services to mankind:

What sense did the men of that period attach to the expression *unity* of the church? How was it conceived and practised? Community of sentiment, community of belief— whatsoever the sentiment or belief may be—constitute the basis of a social state. It is only upon the truth, or what men conceive to be the truth, that they can ground a society. It has been truly said, that there is no society but between minds; in other words, that an intellectual union is the only true society, and the basis of all others; or, what is the same

[*Translated from *ibid.*, pp. 30-2.]
*[Translated from] *Civilisation en France*, Lecture 12 [Vol. I, p. 424].

thing, men cannot act together unless they have a clearly understood end in view; and they cannot live together unless they all partake of one and the same feeling, arising from one or more facts, so that the single fact, or if there be many, each of them, may be agreed upon as *truth* by all. As there is but *one* universal truth, so a society which has that truth for its basis must be *one*. There cannot be two *true* spiritual societies. This is the abstract notion of Church Unity. But how can men's minds be united in the truth, unless they themselves recognise it as truth? This was sadly overlooked by Christians at all times.[*]

Were it not for a few of the concluding lines, the passage just quoted might be supposed to be from the pen of the most mystical and puzzle-headed divine on this side of the Channel. What could M. Guizot mean by the assertion that "an intellectual union is the only true society;" that "men cannot live together unless they all partake of one and the same feeling, arising from one or more facts, so that the single fact, or if there be many, each of them may be agreed upon as *truth* by all?" Of what *facts* does he assert all this? Are they physical, political, or historical facts? Does he maintain the notion of the Church of Rome, and indeed of the Protestant churches which still cherish an essential part of its spirit—the notion that Christianity, as an historical belief, is the basis of *true* society? Does he forget the testimony of universal history to the fact that the social nature of man will avail itself of the merest trifles to form and maintain associations for power and defence? There is an inaccuracy of language, a confusion of ideas in all this, which betrays a mind under a paroxysm of that weakness which is often occasioned by a temporary ascendency of early habits and feelings over the convictions of the mind. It is a curious fact, that our author was here inspired—will our readers believe it?—by M. de la Mennais, from whom he borrows one of the mystical principles asserted in the passage.* This was certainly not accidental. There are other portions of M. Guizot's lectures which have not a little perplexed us during the considerable period which we have devoted to the study of that excellent work; but which his political conduct, and, above all, his share in the recent attempt to put down the freedom of the press, has painfully explained.[†] M. Guizot is evidently one of those men who, to a clear view of the soundest principles, join an unconquerable attachment to institutions and practices which militate against them. No writer ever pleaded the cause of intellectual freedom with more power of argument; and yet, having done this, he can turn a wistful eye to some of those nebulous spots which float in the

---

[*Translated from *ibid.*, pp. 424-7.]

Ibid., p. 425. [See Hugues Félicité Robert de La Mennais, *Essai sur l'indifférence en matière de religion*, 4 vols. (Paris: Tournach-Molin, *et al.*, 1817-23), Vol. I, pp. 321-4.]

[†Loi sur les crimes, délits et contraventions de la presse et des autres moyens de publication, Bulletin 155, No. 356 (9 Sept., 1835), *Bulletin des lois du royaume de France*, 9th ser., Pt. 1, VII, 247-56; Loi sur les cours d'assises, Bulletin 155, No. 357, *ibid.*, pp. 256-9; and Loi qui rectifie les articles 341, 345, 346, 347 et 352 du code d'instruction criminelle, et l'article 17 du code pénal, Bulletin 155, No. 358, *ibid.*, pp. 259-62.]

full light that surrounds us at the present day: he can speak of the "limits and rights of authority in the intellectual and spiritual world" . . . "a purely moral authority, whose whole power lies in persuasion and example." He complains that "in almost all Protestant countries there is something wanting—something imperfect in the organization of the intellectual society, so that the regular action of the established and ancient opinions is impeded. The rights of tradition have not been reconciled with those of liberty."* What, in the name of wonder, are the Rights of Tradition? How is *the regular action of established and ancient opinions* to be encouraged by any *organization*, without encouraging the mischievous activity of *established* errors? Such indeed are the contradictory wishes of men who see the truth, but cannot make it part and parcel of their souls. This is what some men call *moderation*—namely, the assertion of a principle, combined with practical views and conduct in direct opposition to it. In this manner are the people lulled from year to year, and made to wait for a period when there shall be a constant succession of virtuous despots—a wealthy and pampered hierarchy, exempt from intolerance and pride—and perhaps a series of popes who will publish a jubilee with plenary indulgence, to encourage the philosophers of Europe to hold a public meeting in the Capitol. M. Guizot's inconsistencies, admiring his works as we do, raise more of regret than anger in our heart. He seems to have been fully aware of the temptations to which he was exposed. We remember a passage, which we shall lay before our readers in the original language, lest it should lose part of its force in a translation: it is to be found at the very opening of his first course of published lectures. In a most eloquent conclusion to the first lecture he observes, that people indulge an unlimited ambition in thought, demanding instantaneous wonders, and neverthe-less, when it comes to practice, content themselves with the most imperfect means: fluctuating between the most exaggerated sense of existing evils, and the most easy acquiescence in any supposed remedy which first occurs.[*] Then he adds:

> Nous nous rebutons avec une facilité qui égale presque l'impatience avec laquelle nous désirons. . . . *Nous semblons quelquefois tentés de nous rattacher à des principes que nous attaquons, que nous méprisons, aux principes et aux moyens de l'Europe barbare, la force, la violence, le mensonge, pratiques habituelles il y a quatre ou cinq siècles.*[†]

How lamentable that a man who has this clear view of his mental danger should forget to apply this wise caution to himself when he most wanted it! How unfortunate that he did not stumble on this passage when the practice of stopping men's mouths—when the laws for the suppression of free thought on public concerns—when the principles of the deposed Bourbons—when the policy of

*[Translated from] *Civilisation en Europe*, Lecture 12 [pp. 29-30].
[*Ibid.*, Lecture 1, pp. 32-3.]
†*Ibid.*, p. 33.

the most abominable tyrants, were courting his support and official sanction! Alas! we must say of M. Guizot, what he so feelingly and truly has declared of Italy—*"Il lui manque la foi, la foi dans la vérité!"**

We had prepared not a few observations on the civilizing power of the Church, to which so large a part of M. Guizot's lectures relate; but we are obliged to put them aside until a better opportunity. In the present state of things, when not only history, but facts which are taking place before our eyes, are constantly distorted to serve the interest of the hierarchy—a call to rectify the many false notions which the pious fraud of some, and the pious ignorance of others, industriously propagate and keep alive, for the honour of that imaginary being the *Church*, and the substantial benefit of the party which the law makes its representative, cannot fail to come upon us at no great distance of time. We shall conclude, therefore, by the mere statement of one or two remarks, with the truth of which we have been forcibly struck, in surveying, under the guidance of M. Guizot, European civilization in the successive stages of its development.

One truth, of which M. Guizot manifests a strong sense, and which cannot be too often enforced, is, that civilization (in the extended meaning in which he uses the word, to denote all kinds of improvement) is at present almost in its infancy. "I am persuaded," says M. Guizot in his very first lecture,

that when we shall have fairly entered into this study, we shall soon perceive that civilization is still very young—that the world as yet is far from seeing the end and limits of it. Most certainly, the conceptions of the human mind are not yet all that they are capable of becoming; our imagination is far from being able to embrace all that human nature may attain to; and yet, let each of us interrogate his own mind—let him place before himself all the good which he sees to be possible, and which he hopes for; let him then compare this conception with what now exists in the world, and he will be convinced that society and civilization are yet in a very early stage of their progress, and that, after all they have done, they have incomparably more remaining to do.[*]

Imperfect, however, as is our present state, a comparison of it with all those which have preceded leaves in M. Guizot's mind no doubt of its superiority to them on the whole; and proves, too, that during all the time which has succeeded the destruction of the Roman empire, both society and human nature have been steadily, though slowly advancing. This progressive improvement has been attended with two circumstances sufficiently remarkable to deserve notice.

One is, that those changes which have proved most salutary in the end,—which, when we now look back to them, seem to have been the only means by which some great good could have been achieved, or some insuperable obstacle to further progress removed,—were mostly, in their origin, viewed with the utmost alarm and aversion; and were often considered even by the wisest and best men of the time, as pregnant with the most direful results. Thus, the feudal

Civilisation en France, Vol. I, p. 17.
[*Translated from *Civilisation en Europe*, Lecture 1, pp. 30-1.]

régime, the first step out of anarchy on the only road which could possibly lead to the reconstruction of a regular government, was looked upon by the most enlightened contemporaries with a kind of horror, as a breaking-up of society into fragments,[*] and the final blow to that *unity of the empire* with which all their notions of security and of the social union were associated, and which even the vigorous hand of Charlemagne had vainly attempted to revive.[†] So slow are mankind to perceive when the traditional ideas of their forefathers have ceased to be applicable, and when the time has come for pursuing old ends by new means.

The other remark is of a more encouraging kind: That no sincere and honestly intended effort for the good of mankind, aiming at right objects in the right spirit, even when it entirely failed of its meditated purpose, was ever entirely thrown away. Though the benefits which were intended were not at the time realized, every such attempt is fruitful in unforeseen good tendencies, which often meet with better fortune.[‡] What, for example, could have appeared more utterly lost, than the efforts and sufferings of the heroic men who at various periods, from the commencement of the dark ages, asserted, even to the death, the independence of individual intellect against the pretended infallibility of popes and priesthoods? They perished—their bodies were torn limb from limb—the car of the idol to whom they were immolated passed over them; all voices which responded to them or bewailed them were reduced to silence; and the tyranny which they had made war upon, waxed in compactness and intensity for generations after their names had passed from the minds of all save those who remembered them to abhor them. Yet, even these men, who suffered so cruelly for what they had hoped and ventured in behalf of injured humanity, did not labour and suffer in vain. For though they could not avert from mankind the bondage they were not strong enough to break, they at least recorded on the archives of the human race their solemn and indignant protest against it. That protest did not perish, though they did. For in the lapse of ages, when more favourable times had at length arrived, and human nature was now ripe to free itself from its shackles, new and more fortunate inquirers searched into theological antiquity to verify the pretensions of spiritual despotism, and found there these men, and the memory of what they had done. That discovery broke the spell of the pretended universality on which the Romish hierarchy rested the very foundation of their empire. And no small share in the honour of the ultimate emancipation of the human mind belongs to those who perished obscurely, and as it seemed for ages afterwards, altogether unavailingly, in its cause.

[*Ibid., Lecture 4, p. 7.]
[†Ibid., Lecture 3, pp. 27-9.]
[‡Ibid., Lecture 6, pp. 7-9.]

Appendix B

French Texts of Material Quoted in
Vindication of the French Revolution of February 1848 (1849)

Dissertations and Discussions, 2nd ed. (1867), II, 555-63. Headed: "Appendix to the Paper entitled 'Vindication of the French Revolution of February 1848.'" Running titles: "Appendix." Not mentioned in Mill's bibliography. For comment, see cviii-cix above.

Mill here gives more of the text of Tocqueville's speech of 27 Jan., 1848, than he quotes (in translation) in the "Vindication." The passages he quotes are given in square brackets, with footnotes locating the translations in the text on 326-8 above.

THE FOLLOWING are the passages, translations of which are given in the text.

From the Speech of M. de Tocqueville

Pour parler d'abord de ce que j'ai appelé la classe qui gouverne (remarquez que je prends ces mots dans leur acception la plus générale: je ne parle pas seulement de la classe moyenne, mais de tous les citoyens, dans quelque position qu'ils soient, [qui possèdent et exercent des droits politiques]);[*] je dis donc que ce qui existe dans la classe qui gouverne m'inquiète et m'effraye. Ce que j'y vois, messieurs, je puis l'exprimer par un mot: [les moeurs publiques s'y altèrent, elles y sont déjà profondément altérées; elles s'y altèrent de plus en plus tous les jours; de plus en plus aux opinions, aux sentiments, aux idées communes, succèdent des intérêts particuliers, des visées particulières, des points de vue empruntés à la vie et à l'intérêt privés.][†]

Mon intention n'est point de forcer la chambre à s'appesantir plus qu'il n'est nécessaire, sur ces tristes détails; je me bornerai à m'adresser à mes adversaires eux-mêmes, à mes collègues de la majorité ministérielle. Je les prie de faire pour leur propre usage une sorte de revue statistique des collèges électoraux qui les ont envoyés dans cette chambre; qu'ils composent une première catégorie de ceux

[*See p. 326.21 above.]
[†See p. 326.22-5 above.]

qui ne votent pour eux que par suite, non pas d'opinions politiques, mais de sentiments d'amitié particulière, ou de bon voisinage. Dans une seconde catégorie, qu'ils mettent ceux qui votent pour eux, non pas dans un point de vue d'intérêt public ou d'intérêt général, mais dans un point de vue d'intérêt purement local. A cette seconde catégorie, qu'ils en ajoutent enfin une troisième, composée de ceux qui votent pour eux pour des motifs d'intérêt purement individuels, et je leur demande si ce qui reste est très nombreux; je leur demande si ceux qui votent par un sentiment public désintéressé, par suite d'opinions, de passions publiques, si ceux-là forment la majorité des électeurs qui leur ont conféré le mandat de député; je m'assure qu'ils découvriront aisément le contraire. Je me permettrai encore de leur demander si, à leur connaissance, depuis cinq ans, dix ans, quinze ans, le nombre de ceux qui votent pour eux par suite d'intérêts personnels et particuliers ne croît pas sans cesse; si le nombre de ceux qui votent pour eux par opinion politique ne décroît pas sans cesse? [Qu'ils me disent enfin si autour d'eux, sous leurs yeux, il ne s'établit pas peu à peu, dans l'opinion publique, une sorte de tolérance singulière pour les faits dont je parle, si peu à peu il ne se fait pas une sorte de morale vulgaire et basse, suivant laquelle l'homme qui possède des droits politiques se doit à lui-même, doit à ses enfans, à sa femme, à ses parents, de faire un usage personnel de ces droits dans leur intérêt; si cela ne s'élève pas graduellement jusqu'à devenir une espèce de devoir de père de famille? Si cette morale nouvelle, inconnue dans les grands temps de notre histoire, inconnue au commencement de notre Révolution, ne se développe pas de plus en plus, et n'envahit pas chaque jour les esprits.][*] Je le leur demande?[†]

Je crois, messieurs, qu'on peut, sans blesser personne, dire que [le gouvernement a ressaisi, dans ces dernières années surtout, des droits plus grands, une influence plus grande, des prérogatives plus considérables, plus multiples, que celles qu'il avait possédées à aucune autre époque. Il est devenu infiniment plus grand que n'auraient jamais pu se l'imaginer, non seulement ceux qui l'ont donné, mais même ceux qui l'ont reçu en 1830.][‡] . . . [C'est en ressaisissant de vieux pouvoirs qu'on croyait avoir abolis en Juillet, en faisant revivre d'anciens droits qui semblaient annulés, en remettant en vigueur d'anciennes lois qu'on jugeait abrogées, en appliquant les lois nouvelles dans un autre sens que celui dans lequel elles avaient été faites,][§] c'est par tous ces moyens détournés, par cette savante et patiente industrie, que le gouvernement a enfin repris plus

---

[*See p. 326.30-8 above.]
[†"Discours prononcé à la chambre des députés, le 27 janvier 1848," in *Oeuvres complètes*, ed. Mme de Tocqueville [and Gustave de Beaumont], 9 vols. (Paris: Lévy frères, 1864-66), Vol. IX, pp. 521-3.]
[‡See p. 327.4-8 above.]
[§See p. 327.11-14 above.]

d'action, plus d'activité et d'influence, qu'il n'en avait peut-être jamais eu en France en aucun temps. . . . [Et pensez-vous, messieurs, que cette manière que j'ai appelée tout à l'heure détournée et subreptice, de regagner peu à peu la puissance, de la prendre en quelque sorte par surprise, en se servant d'autres moyens que ceux que la constitution lui avait donnés; croyez-vous que ce spectacle étrange de l'adresse et du savoir-faire donné publiquement pendant plusieurs années, sur un si vaste théâtre, à toute une nation qui le regarde, croyez-vous qu'un tel spectacle ait été de nature à améliorer les moeurs publiques?][*] . . . Ils croient que la révolution qui s'est opérée depuis quinze ans dans les droits du pouvoir était nécessaire, soit; et ils ne l'ont pas fait par un intérêt particulier; je le veux croire; mais [il n'est pas moins vrai qu'ils l'ont opérée par des moyens que la moralité publique désavoue; il n'est pas moins vrai qu'ils l'ont opérée en prenant les hommes, non par leur côté honnête, mais par leur mauvais côté—par leurs passions, par leur faiblesse, par leur intérêt, souvent par leurs vices.][†] C'est ainsi que tout en voulant peut-être un but honnête, ils ont fait des choses qui ne l'étaient pas. [Et pour faire ces choses il leur a fallu appeler à leur aide, honorer de leur faveur, introduire dans leur compagnie journalière, des hommes qui ne voulaient ni d'un but honnête, ni de moyens honnêtes, qui ne voulaient que la satisfaction grossière de leurs intérêts privés, à l'aide de la puissance qu'on leur confiait.][‡] . . . [Je ne regarde pas ce fait comme un fait isolé; je le considère comme le symptôme d'un mal général, le trait le plus saillant de toute une politique: en marchant dans les voies que vous aviez choisies, vous aviez besoin de tels hommes.][§] . . .

Pour la première fois depuis quinze ans, j'éprouve une certaine crainte pour l'avenir; et ce qui me prouve que j'ai raison, c'est que cette impression ne m'est pas particulière: je crois que je puis en appeler à tous ceux qui m'écoutent, et que tous me répondront que dans les pays qu'ils représentent, une impression analogue subsiste; qu'un certain malaise, une certaine crainte a envahi les esprits; que, pour la première fois peut-être depuis seize ans, [le sentiment, l'instinct de l'instabilité, ce sentiment précurseur des révolutions, qui souvent les annonce, qui quelquefois les fait naître, que ce sentiment existe à un degré très grave dans le pays.][¶] . . . Est-ce que vous ne ressentez pas, par une sorte d'intuition instinctive qui ne peut pas s'analyser, mais qui est certaine, que le sol tremble de nouveau en Europe? [Est-ce que vous ne sentez pas—que dirai-je? un vent de révolutions qui est dans l'air? Ce vent, on ne sait où il naît, d'où il vient, ni, croyez-le bien, qui il enlève.][‖] . . .

[*See p. 327.14-19 above.]
[†See p. 327.22-4 above.]
[‡See p. 327.24-8 above.]
[§"Discours," pp. 527-9. See p. 327.30-3 above.]
[¶"Discours," pp. 520-1. See p. 327.36-8 above.]
[‖See p. 327.38-40 above.]

[Ma conviction profonde et arrêtée, c'est que les moeurs publiques se dégradent, c'est que la dégradation des moeurs publiques vous amènera, dans un temps court, prochain peut-être, à des révolutions nouvelles. . . . Est-ce que vous avez à l'heure où nous sommes, la certitude d'un lendemain? Est-ce que vous savez ce qui peut arriver en France d'ici à un an, à un mois, à un jour peut-être? Vous l'ignorez; mais ce que vous savez, c'est que la tempête est à l'horizon, c'est qu'elle marche sur vous; vous laisserez-vous prévenir par elle?][*]

Messieurs, je vous supplie de ne pas le faire; je ne vous le demande pas, je vous en supplie: je me mettrais volontiers à genoux devant vous, tant je crois le danger réel et sérieux, tant je pense que le signaler n'est pas recourir à une vaine forme de rhétorique. Oui, le danger est grand! conjurez-le quand il en est temps encore: corrigez le mal par des moyens efficaces, non en l'attaquant dans ses symptômes, mais en lui-même.

[On a parlé de changements dans la législation. Je suis très porté à croire que ces changements sont non-seulement utiles, mais nécessaires: ainsi je crois à l'utilité de la réforme électorale, à l'urgence de la réforme parlementaire; mais je ne suis pas assez insensé, messieurs, pour ne pas savoir que ce ne sont pas les lois elles-mêmes qui font la destinée des peuples; non, ce n'est pas le mécanisme des lois qui produit les grands événements de ce monde: ce qui fait les événements, messieurs, c'est l'esprit même du gouvernement. Gardez les lois si vous voulez; quoique je pense que vous ayez grand tort de le faire, gardez-les; gardez même les hommes, si cela vous fait plaisir, je n'y fais, pour mon compte, aucun obstacle; mais, pour Dieu, changez l'esprit du gouvernement, car, je vous le répète, cet esprit-là vous conduit à l'abîme.][†]

From the Manifesto of M. de Lamartine

Les traités de 1815 n'existent plus en droit aux yeux de la République Française; toutefois, les circonscriptions territoriales de ces traités sont un fait, qu'elle admet comme base et comme point de départ dans ses rapports avec les autres nations.

Mais, si les traités de 1815 n'existent plus que comme fait à modifier d'un accord commun, et si la République déclare hautement qu'elle a pour droit et pour mission d'arriver régulièrement et pacifiquement à ces modifications, le bon sens, la modération, la conscience, la prudence de la République existent, et sont pour l'Europe une meilleure et plus honorable garantie que les lettres de ces traités, si souvent violés ou modifiés par elle.

Attachez-vous, monsieur, à faire comprendre et admettre de bonne foi cette émancipation de la République des traités de 1815, et à montrer que cette franchise n'a rien d'inconciliable avec le repos de l'Europe.

[*See pp. 327.40-328.5 above.]
[†"Discours," pp. 534-5. See p. 328.6-14 above.]

Ainsi, nous le disons hautement, si l'heure de la reconstruction de quelques nationalités opprimées en Europe ou ailleurs, nous paraît avoir sonné dans les décrets de la Providence; si la Suisse, notre fidèle alliée depuis François 1er, était contrainte ou menacée dans le mouvement de croissance qu'elle opère chez elle pour prêter une force de plus au faisceau des gouvernements démocratiques; si les états indépendants de l'Italie étaient envahis; si l'on imposait des limites ou des obstacles à leurs transformations intérieures; si on leur contestait à main armée le droit de s'allier entre eux pour consolider une patrie Italienne, la République Française se croirait en droit d'armer elle-même pour protéger ces mouvements légitimes de croissance et de nationalité des peuples.[*]

From the Answer of M. de Lamartine to the Polish Refugees

La République n'est en guerre ouverte ni sourde avec aucune des nations, avec aucun des gouvernements existants, tant que ces nations et ces gouvernements ne se déclarent pas eux-mêmes en guerre avec elle. Elle ne fera donc, elle ne permettra volontairement aucun acte d'agression et de violence contre les nations Germaniques. . . . Le Gouvernement Provisoire ne se laissera pas changer sa politique dans la main par une nation étrangère, quelque sympathique qu'elle soit à nos coeurs. Nous aimons la Pologne, nous aimons l'Italie, nous aimons tous les peuples opprimés; mais nous aimons avant tout la France, et nous avons la responsabilité de ses destinées, et peut-être de celles de l'Europe, en ce moment. Cette responsabilité nous ne la remettrons à personne qu'à la nation elle-même. . . . La République ne doit pas et ne veut pas avoir des actes en contradiction avec ses paroles; le respect de sa parole est à ce prix; elle ne la décréditera jamais en y manquant. Qu'a-t-elle dit dans son manifeste aux puissances? Elle a dit, en pensant à vous: Le jour où il nous paraîtrait que l'heure providentielle aurait sonné pour la résurrection d'une nationalité injustement effacée de la carte, nous volerions à son secours. Mais nous nous sommes justement réservé ce qui appartient à la France seule, l'appréciation de l'heure, du moment, de la justice, de la cause et des moyens par lesquels il nous conviendrait d'intervenir. Eh bien, ces moyens, jusqu'ici nous les avons choisis et résolus pacifiques.[†]

From the Answer of M. de Lamartine to the Irish Deputation

Quant à d'autres encouragements, il ne serait pas convenable à nous de vous les donner, à vous de les recevoir. Je l'ai déjà dit à propos de la Suisse, à propos

[*Manifeste aux puissances, in Trois mois au pouvoir (Paris: Lévy frères, 1848), pp. 75-6. See p. 341 above.]

[†Réponse à une députation des Polonais, ibid., pp. 131, 133, 135. See p. 342 above.]

de l'Allemagne, à propos de la Belgique et de l'Italie. Je le répète à propos de toute nation qui a des débats intérieurs à vider avec elle-même ou avec son gouvernement. Quand on n'a pas son sang dans les affaires d'un peuple, il n'est pas permis d'y avoir son intervention ni sa main. Nous ne sommes d'aucun parti en Irlande ou ailleurs, que du parti de la justice, de la liberté, et du bonheur des peuples. Aucun autre rôle ne nous serait acceptable, en temps de paix, dans les intérêts et dans les passions des nations étrangères. La France veut se réserver libre pour tous ses droits.

Nous sommes en paix, et nous désirons rester en bons rapports d'égalité, non avec telle ou telle partie de la Grande Bretagne, mais avec la Grande Bretagne tout entière. Nous croyons cette paix utile et honorable, non seulement pour la Grande Bretagne et la République Française, mais pour le genre humain. Nous ne ferons aucun acte, nous ne dirons aucune parole, nous n'adresserons aucune insinuation en contradiction avec les principes d'inviolabilité réciproque des peuples, que nous avons proclamés, et dont le Continent recueille déjà les fruits. La monarchie déchue avait des traités et des diplomates; nous avons des peuples pour diplomates, et des sympathies pour traités. Nous serions insensés de changer une telle diplomatie au grand jour contre des alliances sourdes et partielles avec les partis même les plus légitimes dans les pays qui nous environnent. Nous n'avons qualité ni pour les juger, ni pour les préférer les uns aux autres. En nous déclarant amis de ceux-ci, nous nous déclarerions ennemis de ceux-là. Nous ne voulons être ennemis d'aucuns de vos compatriotes; nous voulons faire tomber, au contraire, par la loyauté de la parole républicaine, les préventions et les préjugés qui existeraient entre nos voisins et nous.[*]

From the "History of the Girondists"

Le partage égal des lumières, des facultés, et des dons de la nature est évidemment la tendance légitime du coeur humain. Les révélateurs, les poëtes, et les sages ont roulé éternellement cette pensée dans leur âme, et l'ont perpétuellement montrée dans leur ciel, dans leurs rêves, ou dans leurs lois, comme la perspective de l'humanité. C'est donc un instinct de la justice dans l'homme. . . . Tout ce qui tend à constituer des inégalités de lumières, de rang, de conditions, de fortune, parmi les hommes, est impie. Tout ce qui tend à niveler graduellement ces inégalités, qui sont souvent des injustices, et à répartir le plus équitablement l'héritage commun entre tous les hommes, est divin. Toute politique peut être jugée à ce signe, comme tout arbre est jugé à ses fruits: l'idéal n'est que la vérité à distance.

[*Réponse à une députation des citoyens irlandais, ibid., pp. 150-1. See pp. 342-3 above.]

Mais plus un idéal est sublime, plus il est difficile à réaliser en institutions sur la terre. La difficulté jusqu'ici a été de concilier avec l'égalité des biens les inégalités de vertus, de facultés, et de travail, qui différencient les hommes entre eux. Entre l'homme actif et l'homme inerte, l'égalité de biens devient une injustice; car l'un crée, et l'autre dépense. Pour que cette communauté des biens soit juste, il faut supposer à tous les hommes la même conscience, la même application au travail, la même vertu. Cette supposition est une chimère. Or quel ordre social pourrait reposer solidement sur un tel mensonge? De deux choses l'une. Ou bien il faudrait que la société, partout présente et partout infaillible, pût contraindre chaque individu au même travail et à la même vertu; mais alors que devient la liberté? La société n'est plus qu'un universel esclavage. Ou bien il faudrait que la société distribuât de ses propres mains, tous les jours, à chacun selon ses oeuvres, la part exactement proportionnée à l'oeuvre et au service de chacun dans l'association générale; mais alors quel sera le juge?

La sagesse humaine imparfaite a trouvé plus facile, plus sage, et plus juste de dire à l'homme: "Sois toi-même ton propre juge, rétribue-toi toi-même par la richesse ou par la misère." La société a institué la propriété, proclamé la liberté du travail, et légalisé la concurrence.

Mais la propriété instituée ne nourrit pas celui qui ne possède rien. Mais la liberté du travail ne donne pas les mêmes éléments de travail à celui qui n'a que ses bras, et à celui qui possède des milliers d'arpents sur la surface du sol. Mais la concurrence n'est que le code de l'égoïsme, et la guerre à mort entre celui qui travaille et celui qui fait travailler, entre celui qui achète et celui qui vend, entre celui qui nage dans le superflu et celui qui a faim. Iniquité de toutes parts! Incorrigibles inégalités de la nature et de la loi! La sagesse du législateur paraît être de les pallier une à une, siècle par siècle, loi par loi. Celui qui veut tout corriger d'un coup, brise tout. Le possible est la condition de la misérable sagesse humaine. Sans prétendre résoudre par une seule solution des iniquités complexes, corriger sans cesse, améliorer toujours, c'est la justice d'êtres imparfaits comme nous. . . . Le temps paraît être un élément de la vérité elle-même; demander la vérité définitive à un seul jour, c'est demander à la nature des choses plus qu'elle ne peut donner. L'impatience crée des illusions et des ruines au lieu de vérités. Les déceptions sont des vérités cueillies avant le temps. La vérité est évidemment la communauté chrétienne et philosophique des biens de la terre. Les déceptions, ce sont les violences et les systèmes par lesquels on a cru vainement pouvoir établir cette vérité et l'organiser jusqu'ici. (Lamartine, *Histoire des Girondins*, [8 vols. (Paris: Coquebert, 1847),] livre 39, ad finem [Vol. V, pp. 407-10].)[*]

[*See pp. 355-6 above.]

Appendix C

Textual Emendations

IN THIS LIST, following the page and line numbers, the reading of the copy-text is given first, and then the emended reading in square brackets, with explanation if required. "SC" indicates Mill's library, Somerville College. Typographical errors in versions other than the copy-text are ignored.

7.28   d'Eprémenil [d'Eprémenil] [*as at* 74.19]
9.15   dina [dîna] [*accent missing also in* Source]
9.31   maronniers [marronniers] [*as in* Source]
9.34   dévait [devait] [*as in* Source]
10.5   gardes-françoises [gardes-françaises] [*as in* Source *and elsewhere in passage*]
10.9   comme retenus [retenus comme] [*error also in* Source]
10.10   leur [leurs] [*as in* Source]
13.11   Stael [Staël]
13.30   Stael [Staël]
13.40   club: [club.] [*as elsewhere in paragraph*]
13.41   *parties* [*partis*] [*as in* Source]
13.41   *deplacés* [*déplacés*] [*as in* Source]
14.5   vîte [vite] [Source *also reads* vîte]
14.8   mûs [mus] [Source *also reads* mûs]
14.13   parceque [parce que] [*as in* Source]
14.14   vîte [vite] [*as in* Source]
14.19   crû [cru] [*as in* Source]
14.24   revolte [révolte] [*as in* Source]
14.38   depend [dépend] [*as in* Source]
16.8   edition [édition]
16.8   considerablement [considérablement]
20.42   héroisme [héroïsme] [*as in* Source]
21n.5   ecrivains [écrivains] [*as in* Source]
22.31   verifier [vérifier] [*as in* Source]
22.31   revoquent [révoquent] [*as in* Source]
22.32   histoire [Histoire] [*as in* Source *and elsewhere in quotations; italicized in this ed.*]
22.37   préference [préférence] [*as in* Source]
22.39   génerale [générale] [*as in* Source]
22.40   negligé [négligé] [*as in* Source]
23.1   celèbre [célèbre] [*as in* Source]
24.13   l'Héristal [d'Héristal]

27.16   Compiegne [Compiègne]
30.38   Orleans [Orleans,] [*for sense*]
31.8   had ["had] [*restyled in this ed.*]
31n.2   94 [94.] [*page reference corrected in this ed.*]
31.35-7 vol:" "Peut-être," . . ., "se . . . vécu." [vol: 'Peut-être,' . . ., 'se . . . vécu.'"
        [*to conform to* Source]
32.17   Debonnaire [Débonnaire] [*as in* Source]
33.26   revèle [révèle] [*as in* Source]
35n.2   *d'Angleterre* [*de l'Angleterre*] [*as in* Source]
36.22   kings, [kings.]
38.32   *desoeuvré* [*désoeuvré*]
39.2   d'emotions [d'émotions] [*as in* Source]
39.3   Francaise [Française] [*as in* Source]
39.10   devorés [dévorés] [*as in* Source]
39.13   derogeait [dérogeait] [*as in* Source]
39.16   moderer [modérer] [*as in* Source]
39.32   *Sismondi* [Sismondi] [*restyled in this ed.*]
41n.6   fidelité [fidélité] [*as in* Source]
41n.9   prédecesseurs [prédécesseurs] [*as in* Source]
41n.15 enchainée [enchaînée] [*as in* Source]
41n.31 voulèrent [voulurent] [*as in* Source]
41n.31 rebellion [rébellion] [*as in* Source]
41n.32 refugier [réfugier] [*as in* Source]
41n.32 assiègée [assiégée] [*as in* Source]
41n.35 retabli [rétabli] [*as in* Source]
41n.38 fît [fit] [*as in* Source]
41n.39 iillustrates [illustrates]
43.12   *possitis* [*possetis*] [*as in* Source]
43.19   *long temps* [*long-temps*] [*as in* Source]
48.15   periode [période] [*as in* Source]
48.18   glorie [gloire]
48.20   amphithéatres [amphithéâtres] [*as in* Source]
48.21   object [objet]
48.23   vouée, [vouée] [*as in* Source]
48.24   intéressee [intéressée] [*as in* Source]
48.25   l'exageration [l'exagération] [*as in* Source]
49.8   depredations [depredations.]
51n.3   in which [from which]
65n.8   Chap [Chap.]
68n.6   plûpart [plupart] [*as in* Source]
68n.9   jeûnesse [jeunesse] [*as in* Source]
73n.11 *Revolution* [*Révolution*]
74n.20 *Evènemens* [*Evénemens*] [*as in* Source]
74n.20 *à* [*sous*] [*as in* Source]
75n.14 *History* of [*History of*]
75n.24 XVI. [XVI,]
81n.6   *Revolution* [*Révolution*]
81n.7   *Française* [*Françoise*] [*as elsewhere and in fact for this title*]
87n.3   considérérai [considérerai]
87n.4   &c. &c. [&c. &c."]

87.32   steeets [streets]
88.16   étaient [s'étaient] [*as in* Source]
88.21   formérent [formèrent] [*as in* Source]
88.30   *deputés* [*députés*] [*as in* Source]
88.31   avoient [avaient] [*as in* Source]
88.32   *resistance* [*résistance*] [*as in* Source]
88.35   subdélegués [subdélégués] [*as in* Source]
88.35   de les [de la] [*as in* Source]
89.6   viz [viz.]
89.16   d'imbécilles [d'imbéciles] [Source *also reads* imbécilles]
89.26   Baron [baron] [*as in* Source]
89n.1   *Française* [*Françoise*] [*as elsewhere and in fact for this title*]
90.1   d'Orleans [d'Orléans] [*as in* Source]
90.1   Sièyes [Sieyès]
90.3   désignes [désignés] [*as in* Source]
90n.1   XVI. [XVI,]
91.28   revolte [révolte] [*as in* Source]
91.28   Revolution [Révolution] [révolution *in* Source]
92n.1   *qui* [*que*] [Source *also reads* qui]
93.4   que [qui] [*as in* Source]
93n.4   &c. [&c.,]
96.20   Sièyes [Sieyès]
96.24   Molleville [Moleville] [*as elsewhere in article*]
96n.7   Molleville [Moleville] [*as elsewhere in article*]
98.26   "'For ['"For] [*restyled in this ed.*]
98.30-99.2   [*wrong font; restyled in this ed.*]
99.7   both!' [both"!]
102.34 reflexion [réflexion] [*as in* Source]
104.29 cet epoque [cette époque] [*as in* Source]
104.30 s'était [s'étoit] [*as in* Source]
104.30 aucun [aucune] [*as in* Source]
104.32 voulait [vouloit] [*as in* Source]
105.4   était [étoit] [*as in* Source]
105.5   était [étoit] [*as in* Source]
105.6   était [étoit] [*as in* Source]
105.15 énivré [enivré] [Source *also reads* énivré]
105.16 était [étoit] [*as in* Source]
105.16 faisaient [faisoient] [*as in* Source]
105.18 dèfendre [défendre] [*as in* Source]
105.28 réflechissaient [réfléchissaient] [*as in* Source]
105.29 seul [seuls] [*as in* Source]
105.35 parceque [parce que] [*as in* Source]
105.42 systematique [systématique]
106.4   Soulavie [Soulavie,]
106.4   fût ["fût]
106.14 Sieyes [Sieyès]
107.39 démandés [demandés]
108.1   precisément [précisément] [*as in* Source]
116.14 this [his] [*corrected by JSM in SC copy*]
117.1   mispels [misspells]

117.3   mispelt [misspelt]
117.13   investés [investis] [*as in* Source]
119.2   our [an] [*as in* 59,67; *corrected by JSM in SC copy*]
119.4   lesson [lesson,] [*as in* 67]
119.15   revolution [Revolution] [*as in* 59,67, *and elsewhere in passage*]
127.10   loi.) [loi.)]
127.18   constitution [institution] [*corrected by JSM in SC copy of* Source]
135.14   'bodied forth' ["bodied forth"] [*as elsewhere in the sentence*]
138.13   in a a [in a]
141.6   Sièyes [Sieyès]
141n.2   i 457-9 [i. 457-9] [*restyled in this ed.*]
141n.14   d'Enghein [d'Enghien]
142.32   *paroissales* [*paroissiales*] [*as in* Source]
144.10   '*Que voulez-vous?*' ["*Que voulez-vous?*"] [*as elsewhere in passage*]
144.18   *boissons.*) [*boissons*).]
144.11   'What ["What] [*as elsewhere in passage*]
145.4   beleagured [beleaguered]
145.39   Blood ["Blood] [*restyled in this ed.*]
146.4   benevolenee [benevolence]
146.30   ——— [—!—] [*as in* Source]
148.5   *souffredouleur* [*souffre-douleur*] [*as in* Source]
149.22   Laekalls [Lackalls] [*as in* Source]
149n.4   *Parlemantaire* [*Parlementaire*]
151.15   wtth [with]
152.37   Démoiselle [Demoiselle]
152.39   countenance;" [countenance;'] [*restyled in this ed.*]
153.39   better." [better.'] [*restyled in this ed.*]
155.17   no [nos]
155.18   ever!" [ever!'"] [*restyled in this ed.*]
156n.1   *Part.* [*Parl.*] [*restyled in this ed.*]
156.2   Jerôme [Jerôme]
156.19   The ["The] [*restyled in this ed.*]
156.36   *sauvez moi* [*sauvez-moi*]
157.23   extermination, [extermination.]
159.14   obedienee [obedience]
159.22   become [became]
160n.1   we we [we]
176.7   Duputies [Deputies] [*correct in* 37,59,75]
176.22   imposibility [impossibility] [*correct in* 37,59,75]
181.20-1   the History . . . Normans [*The History . . . Normans*] [*as in* 37 *and to regularize*]
191.3   is have [is to have] [*correct in* 37,59,75]
198.18   andcalled [and called] [*correct in* 37,59,75]
198.26   king [King] [*as in* 37,59, *and elsewhere in passage*]
201.24   *redacteurs* [*rédacteurs*]
203.2   Nizard [Nisard] [*correct in* 37,59,75]
215.16   muliebribus [mulieribus]
218.6   1835 [1833] [*as on title page*]
222n.33   une indigène [un indigène] [*as in* Source]
222n.35   s'addressent [s'adressent] [*as in* Source]

239.3   1100 [1200] [*as in* Source *and fact*]
242.37   VII. [VII.,] [*as in* 44; *restyled in this ed.*]
246.14   M [M.] [*correct in* 44,59,75]
247.6   Arragon [Aragon] [*as in* Source]
247.29   nnassailable [unassailable] [*correct in* 44,59,75]
251.6   spoken; the [spoken, the] [*as in* 44 *and for sense*]
268.6   society. [society.'] [*restyled in this ed.*]
276.32   directions. . . . Is [directions. Is] [*see next entry*]
276.33   mankind? [*paragraph*] At [mankind? . . . [*paragraph*] At] [*JSM's ellipsis
         inserted in wrong place; cf. previous entry*]
282.43   corporation.' [*paragraph; reduced type*] 'The [corporation. The] [*the quotation
         is continuous; restyled in this ed.*]
289.17   sixth volume [fifth volume] [*altered to conform to the actual numbering of the
         vols., as explained in the Textual Introduction above*]
303.1   interêts [intérêts] [*as in* Source]
303.4   ciel [ciel,] [*as* Source]
303.6   encore [encore,]
303.6   jété [jeté] [*as in* Source]
305.14   proprieté [propriété]
306.30   late; [late,] [*as in* 59,67]
306.34   uneasiness; [uneasiness,] [*as in* 59,67]
307.25   life; [life,] [*as in* 59,67]
309.18   personalité [personnalité] [*as in* Source]
309.27   réfuse [refuse] [*as in* Source]
311.12   incapacity? [incapacity?'] [*restyled in this ed.*]
312.37   (or . . . it:) [or . . . it:] [*for sense*]
328n.7   France?' [France?'"]
368n.7   *collecta* [*contexta*] [*as on title page*]
371.20   *Civilization of Europe* [*Civilization in Europe*] [*as elsewhere and in fact*]
375.40   Luther [Luther,]
379n.1   Stuttgard [Stuttgart]
379n.1   Tübingeu [Tübingen]
383.15   Empire [empire] [*as elsewhere in passage*]
391.7   liberty.' [liberty.'†] [*footnote on previous page; restyled in this ed.*]
395.11   permettai [permettrai] [*as in* Source]
396.8   que [qu'un] [*as in* Source]
396.31   dégré [degré] [*as in* Source]
397.11   conjurez le [conjurez-le] [*as in* Source]
397.22   gardez-même [gardez même] [*as in* Source]
398.1   réconstruction [reconstruction] [*as in* Source]
398.2   paraissent [paraît] [*typographical error in* Source; *corrected in later ed.*]
398.7   leur [leurs] [*as in* Source]
398.10   de la nationalité [de nationalité] [*as in* Source]
399.21   declarant [déclarant] [*as in* Source]
399.21   ennemi [ennemis] [*as in* Source]
400.4   des [de] [*as in* Source]
400.16   retribue-toi [rétribue-toi] [*as in* Source]

Appendix D

Index of Persons and Works Cited, with Variants and Notes

LIKE MOST NINETEENTH-CENTURY AUTHORS, Mill is cavalier in his approach to sources, sometimes identifying them with insufficient care, and occasionally quoting them inaccurately. This Appendix is intended to help correct these deficiencies, and to serve as an index of names and titles (which are consequently omitted in the general Index). Included here also, at the end of the appendix, are references to British Statutes and French Bills and Statutes, entered by country in order of date. The material otherwise is arranged in alphabetical order, with an entry for each person or work quoted or referred to. References to mythical and fictional characters are excluded. The following abbreviation is used: *HP* for *Histoire parlementaire*, ed. Buchez and Roux. References to Appendices are in italics; when the same quotation or reference in a quotation appears both in the main text and an appendix, the latter is also in parentheses.

The entries take the following form:

1. Identification: author, title, etc. in the usual bibliographic form. When only a surname is given, no other identification has been found.

2. Notes (if required) giving information about JSM's use of the source, indication if the work is in his library, Somerville College, Oxford (referred to as SC), and any other relevant information.

3. Lists of the pages where works are reviewed, quoted, and referred to.

4. In the case of quotations, a list of substantive variants between Mill's text and his source, in this form: Page and line reference to the present text. Reading in the present text] Reading in the source (page reference in the source).

The list of substantive variants also attempts to place quoted passages in their contexts by giving the beginnings and endings of sentences. The original wording is supplied where Mill has omitted two sentences or less; only the length of other omissions is given. There being uncertainty about the actual Classical texts used by Mill, the Loeb editions are cited when possible.

ABAILARD. See Abelard.

ABELARD, PETER.
  NOTE: the references at 238 and 247 are in quotations from Michelet.
  REFERRED TO: 238, 246, 248

ABRAHAM.
  NOTE: the references are in the same quotation from Guizot.
  REFERRED TO: 283 (*386*)

ADELA (of France).
NOTE: wife of Louis VII. The reference is in a quotation from Michelet.
REFERRED TO: 247

ADRIAN IV (Pope).
NOTE: Nicholas Breakspear. The reference is in a quotation from Michelet.
REFERRED TO: 244

AETIUS.
NOTE: the reference is in a quotation from Guizot.
REFERRED TO: 263

AINTRAIGUES. See Antraigues.

ALARIC I.
NOTE: the reference is in a quotation from Guizot.
REFERRED TO: 275

ALBERT. See Martin.

ALCUIN. Letter to Charlemagne. In *Opera omnia*. Vols. C-CI of *Patrologiae cursus completus, series latina*. Ed. Jacques Paul Migne. Paris: Migne, 1851, Vol. C, col. 438.
NOTE: the quotation is indirect.
QUOTED: 248

ALEMBERT, JEAN LE ROND D'.
NOTE: see also Diderot and d'Alembert, *Encyclopédie*.
REFERRED TO: 67

ALEXANDER III (Pope).
NOTE: the reference is in a quotation from Michelet.
REFERRED TO: 247

ALEXANDER OF HALES. *Glossa in quatuor libros sententiarum Petri Lombardi*. Vols. XII-XV of *Bibliotheca Franciscana Scholastica*. Quarrachi: Ex Typographia Colegii S. Bonaventurae, 1951-57.
NOTE: this ed. used for ease of reference.
REFERRED TO: 247

ALFRED THE GREAT (of England). Referred to: 24

ALISON, ARCHIBALD. "Fall of the Throne of the Barricades," *Blackwood's Edinburgh Magazine*, XLIII (Apr., 1848), 393-418.
REFERRED TO: 334

―――― History of Europe during the French Revolution, Embracing the Period from the Assembly of the Notables, in MDCCLXXXIX, to the Establishment of the Directory, in MDCCXCV. 2 vols. Edinburgh: Blackwood; London: Cadell, 1833.
NOTE: eight further volumes were published, III and IV (1835) with a different subtitle, and V-X (1836-42) with the title *History of Europe from the Commencement of the French Revolution in 1789 to the Restoration of the Bourbons*.
REVIEWED: 111-22
QUOTED: 115, 116
115.28-30 "memorable discussions," . . . "most . . . distinguished them."] This [attempt at verbatim quotation] is more particularly the case in all the debates of the National Assembly of France; and in effecting the selection, the author has been most . . . distinguished those memorable discussions. (I, xvi)
116.25 "dramatic air"] There can be no doubt, that in thus presenting the speeches in the words of the real actors on the political stage, the work has assumed in the first volumes a dramatic air, unusual at least in modern histories; but it is the only method by which the spirit and feelings of

the moment can be faithfully transmitted to posterity, or justice done to the motives, on either side, which influenced mankind; and a modern author need not hesitate to follow an example which has been set by Thucydides, Sallust, Livy, and Tacitus. (I, xvi)

AMALRIC, VICOMTE DE NARBONNE. Referred to: 49

AMAR, JEAN BAPTISTE ANDRÉ. Speech in presenting the "acte d'accusation" against the Girondists (3 Oct., 1793), *Procès-verbal de la convention nationale*, XXII, 55-6.
NOTE: the décret is given *ibid.*, 56-60; cf. the shorter account in the *Gazette Nationale, ou Le Moniteur Universel*, 4 Oct., 1793, 1174.
REFERRED TO: 106

AMAURY OF CHARTRES.
NOTE: the reference is in a quotation from Michelet.
REFERRED TO: 247

AMBROSE. See St. Ambrose.

ANAXAGORAS. Referred to: 273n

ANON. "Guizot's Lectures on European Civilization, Translated by Priscilla Beckwith," *The Times*, 21 Aug., 1837, 6.
REFERRED TO: 230

ANON. "News of the Week," *Spectator*, 11 Mar., 1848, 237.
REFERRED TO: 334n

ANON. Review of Benjamin Disraeli's *Henrietta Temple*, *The Literary Gazette, and Journal of the Belles Lettres* (3 Dec., 1836), 771-2.
QUOTED: 164n
64n.17 "Affectation!"] There is a great mixture of talent and of affectation in these volumes. (771)

ANON. Review of Walter Scott's *Life of Napoleon Buonaparte*, *Monthly Review*. n.s. VI (Sept., 1827), 89-105.
REFERRED TO: 55

ANTRAIGUES, LOUIS EMMANUEL HENRI ALEXANDRE DE LAUNAY, COMTE D'.
NOTE: also spelled Aintraigues and Entragues. The reference at 7 is in a quotation from Mignet; that at 141 is in a quotation from Carlyle.
REFERRED TO: 7, 74, 141

———— *Mémoire sur les états-généraux, leurs droits et la manière de les convoquer*. [Paris:] n.p., 1788.
REFERRED TO: 141n

ARAGO, DOMINIQUE FRANÇOIS.
NOTE: the first reference at 321 is in a quotation from Brougham; the second at 321 and those at 332, 333 are to the members of the Provisional Government of 1848.
REFERRED TO: 321, 332, 333

ARBRISSEL, ROBERT D'.
NOTE: the reference is in a quotation from Michelet.
REFERRED TO: 246

ARCHENHOLZ, JOHANN WILHELM VON. Referred to: 78n

ARISTOTLE.
NOTE: the reference at 248 is in a quotation from Michelet.
REFERRED TO: 248, 273n

ARNOLD, THOMAS. Referred to: 217

———— *Introductory Lectures on Modern History*. Oxford: Parker, 1842.
REFERRED TO: 226

ARTAUD, JEAN BAPTISTE.
NOTE: the reference, to "a certain *Necker*ean lion's provider," in a quotation from Carlyle, derives from Weber.
REFERRED TO: 140

ARTOIS, COMTE D'. See Charles X (of France).

ARTOIS, MARIE THÉRÈSE, COMTESSE D'.
NOTE: wife of Charles X. The reference is in a quotation from Ferrières.
REFERRED TO: 88

ATAULF.
NOTE: JSM uses the spelling Ataulph. The reference at 275 is in a quotation from Guizot.
REFERRED TO: 275, 280

ATHENAEUS. *The Deipnosophists* (Greek and English). Trans. Charles Burton Gulick. 7 vols. London: Heinemann; New York: Putnam's Sons (Vols. I-V), and Cambridge, Mass.: Harvard University Press (Vols. VI-VII), 1927-41.
NOTE: the reference derives from Michelet.
REFERRED TO: 237

AUSTIN, SARAH. See Leopold von Ranke, *The Ecclesiastical and Political History*.

—— *Characteristics of Goethe. From the German of Falk, Müller, etc.* 3 vols. London: Wilson, 1833.
NOTE: the reference is to the term "many-sided," which JSM took from Goethe via Austin (see *CW*, I, 171 and 635).
REFERRED TO: 183, 259

AVEMPACE.
NOTE: the reference, in a quotation from Michelet, is to the Arabic commentators on Aristotle.
REFERRED TO: 248

AVERROËS.
NOTE: one of the two references, in a quotation from Michelet, is to the Arabic commentators on Aristotle.
REFERRED TO: 248

AVICENNA.
NOTE: the reference, in a quotation from Michelet, is to the Arabic commentators on Aristotle.
REFERRED TO: 248

BABEUF, FRANÇOIS NOËL.
NOTE: JSM uses the spelling Baboeuf.
REFERRED TO: 128

BACON, FRANCIS.
NOTE: the reference is to "Baconian" philosophizing.
REFERRED TO: 324

—— *The Essays or Counsels, Civill and Morall* (1625). In *The Works of Francis Bacon*. Ed. James Spedding, *et al*. 14 vols. London: Longman, *et al*., 1857-74, VI, 365-604.
NOTE: this ed., which is in SC, is used for ease of reference, though the reference antedates it.
QUOTED: 65
65.8-9 "come . . . their business and bosoms."] I do now publish my Essays; which, of all my other works, have been most current; for that, as it seems, they come . . . men's business and bosoms. (VI, 373; The Epistle Dedicatory, 1625)

BAILLEUL, JACQUES CHARLES. *Examen critique de l'ouvrage posthume de Mme la baronne de Staël, ayant pour titre: Considérations sur les principaux événemens de la révolution française*. 2 vols. Paris: Bailleul, 1818.

BARRUEL, AUGUSTIN. *Mémoires pour servir à l'histoire du jacobinisme.* 4 vols. London: Boussonnier, 1797-98.
REFERRED TO: 108

BAYARD, PIERRE TERRAIL DE.
NOTE: the reference derives from Roederer.
REFERRED TO: 37, 37n

BÉCHADE, JEAN.
NOTE: the reference, in a quotation from Carlyle, is to him as one of seven prisoners in the Bastille.
REFERRED TO: 146

BECKET. See St. Thomas à Becket.

BENEDICT XI (Pope). Referred to: 244

BENTHAM, JEREMY. *Bentham's Draught for the Organization of the Judicial Establishment in France, Compared with That of the National Assembly* (1790). In *Works.* Ed. John Bowring. 11 vols. Edinburgh: Tait; London: Simpkin, Marshall; Dublin: Cumming, 1843, IV, 305-406.
REFERRED TO: 362

———— *The Constitutional Code* (1827, 1841). In *Works*, IX.
REFERRED TO: 362

———— *Plan of Parliamentary Reform, in the Form of a Catechism: with an Introduction, Showing the Necessity of Radical, and the Inadequacy of Moderate Reform* (1817). In *Works*, III, 433-557.
REFERRED TO: 324

———— *Principles of the Civil Code* (1838). In *Works*, I, 297-364.
REFERRED TO: 354

BÉRANGER, EMERI.
NOTE: the reference derives from Dulaure.
REFERRED TO: 49

BERENGARIUS. *De sacra coena adversus Lanfrancum liber posterior.* Ed. A.F. and F.T. Vischer. Berlin: Haude and Spener, 1834.
REFERRED TO: 246

BERGOING, FRANÇOIS.
NOTE: the reference, in a quotation from Mignet, is to the members of the Commission of Twelve.
REFERRED TO: 12

BERNARD OF CLAIRVAUX. See St. Bernard.

BERRY, CHARLES FERDINAND, DUC DE.
NOTE: JSM uses the spelling Berri.
REFERRED TO: 177

BERTIER DE SAUVIGNY, LOUIS BÉNIGNE FRANÇOIS DE.
NOTE: the Intendant of Paris. The reference is in a quotation from Toulongeon.
REFERRED TO: 91

BERTRAND, ANTOINE.
NOTE: the reference, in a quotation from Mignet, is to the members of the Commission of Twelve.
REFERRED TO: 12

BERTRAND DE BORN.
NOTE: referred to by JSM as "an old writer."
REFERRED TO: 36n

BERTRAND DE MOLEVILLE, ANTOINE FRANÇOIS, MARQUIS DE. Referred to: 107

———— *Mémoires particuliers, pour servir à l'histoire de la fin du règne de Louis XVI.* 2 vols. Paris: Michaud, 1816.

QUOTED: 107-8
REFERRED TO: 76n, 93n, 96, 107

BERVILLE, SAINT-ALBIN, and JEAN FRANÇOIS BARRIÈRE, eds. *Collection des mémoires relatifs à la révolution française.* 68 vols. Paris: Baudouin, 1820-28.
REFERRED TO: 5, 97n

—— *Mémoires historiques et militaires sur Carnot, rédigés d'après ses manuscrits, sa correspondance inédite et ses écrits.* Paris: Baudouin, 1824.
NOTE: JSM almost certainly is adapting the famous phrase, "Carnot a organisé la victoire," for which this work provides a convenient reference.
REFERRED TO: 101

BESENVAL, PIERRE JOSEPH VICTOR, BARON DE.
NOTE: the reference at 87 is in a quotation from Scott; that at 91n is in a quotation from Montgaillard (both use the spelling Bezenval); that at 146 is in a quotation from Carlyle.
REFERRED TO: 87, 91n, 146

—— *Mémoires de M. le baron de Besenval.* 4 vols. Paris: Buisson, 1805-06.
NOTE: at 92n JSM uses the spelling Bezenval. The quotations (the first a translation of "s'en expliquoit hautement dans les rues"; the second an English adaptation of "une tourbe soudoyée qui inondoit les avenues et les salles du palais. La société regorgeoit de brochures, de pamphlets") are in quotations from Carlyle, as is the reference at 147.
QUOTED: 139, 140
REFERRED TO: 92n, 147

BIBLE.
NOTE: the reference at 34n derives from Sismondi; those at 283 and *386* are in the same quotation from Guizot.
REFERRED TO: 34n, 283 (*386*)

—— Colossians.
NOTE: see also Carlyle, "The Nibelungen Lied."
QUOTED: 219
219.10   "shadow of its coming"] Let no man therefore judge you in meat, or in drink, or in respect of an holyday, or of the new moon, or of the sabbath days:/Which are a shadow of things to come; but the body is of Christ. (2:16-17)

—— Ezekiel.
REFERRED TO: 228

—— Genesis.
NOTE: the reference is in a quotation from Carlyle.
QUOTED: *380*
REFERRED TO: 145
380.28   "I] And Pharaoh said unto Joseph, I (41:44)

—— Isaiah.
NOTE: the indirect quotation is in a quotation from Carlyle, as is the references at 145.
QUOTED: 155
REFERRED TO: 145, 165

—— Job.
NOTE: the quotations are indirect.
QUOTED: 212, 212n
212n.5   Thus far shalt thou go, and no farther.] When I made the cloud the garment thereof, and thick darkness a swaddlingband for it,/And brake up for it my decreed place, and set bars and doors,/And said, Hitherto shalt thou come, but no further: and here shall thy proud waves be stayed? (38:9-11)
212n.7-8   further, here . . . stayed] [*see preceding entry*]

—— Judith (Apocrypha).
NOTE: the reference is in a quotation from Carlyle.
REFERRED TO: 151

—— Luke.

NOTE: the quotation, which is indirect and adapted, is in a quotation from Carlyle.

QUOTED: 166

166.34   go and do *otherwise*.] And Jesus said to him, "Go and do likewise." (10:37)

—— Matthew.

NOTE: the reference is in a quotation from Michelet.

REFERRED TO: 253

—— II Samuel.

NOTE: the indirect quotation is in a quotation from Carlyle.

QUOTED: 140

140.31   the glory departed from it for evermore.] The glory is departed from Israel: for the ark of God is taken. (4:22)

BINGHAM, PEREGRINE (prob.). "On Emigration," *Westminster Review*, III (Apr., 1825), 448-87.

NOTE: the reference is to a remark quoted from Birkbeck, *q.v.* For evidence of Bingham's authorship, see *Wellesley Index*, III, 562.

REFERRED TO: 69n

BINS DE SAINT-VICTOR, JACQUES MAXIMILIEN BENJAMIN. *Tableau historique et pittoresque de Paris, depuis les Gaulois jusqu'à nos jours.* 3 vols. Paris: Nicolle, and Le Normant, 1808.

NOTE: the quotations at 21n are quoted by Dulaure from an unlocated "prospectus" by Bins de Saint-Victor.

QUOTED: 21n

BIRD, CHRISTOPHER. "Introduction," *British and Foreign Review*, I (July, 1835), 5-16.

QUOTED: *371n*

371n.13-14   "what . . . France."] Yet should we be ungrateful not to acknowledge what . . . France; and should be blind with prejudice, not to see how much more may be derived from the same sources. (9)

BIRKBECK, MORRIS.

NOTE: see also Bingham.

REFERRED TO: 69n

BLANC, JEAN JOSEPH LOUIS.

NOTE: one of the references at 321 is to him as one of the four accepted into the Provisional Government of 1848; that at 332 is to him as one of its members.

REFERRED TO: 321, 328, 332, 353, 354

—— "Déposition de M. Louis Blanc, représentant du peuple (29 mai 1848)." In *Rapport de la commission d'enquête* (*q.v.*), I, 103-13.

REFERRED TO: 353

—— "Déposition de M. Louis Blanc—15 juillet." *Ibid.*, 238-41.

REFERRED TO: 353

—— *La révolution de février au Luxembourg.* Paris: Lévy, 1849.

NOTE: the reference is to Blanc's speeches at the Luxembourg, which are included in this volume, to which JSM seems to refer.

REFERRED TO: 353

BODIN, FÉLIX. See Thiers, *Histoire*.

BOILEAU, JACQUES.

NOTE: the reference, in a quotation from Mignet, is to the members of the Commission of Twelve.

REFERRED TO: 12

BOISSY D'ANGLAS, FRANÇOIS ANTOINE, COMTE DE. Referred to: 73n

—— *Essai sur la vie, les écrits et les opinions de M. de Malesherbes, adressé à mes enfans.* 3 pts. Paris: Treuttel and Würtz, 1819-21.

NOTE: the reference at 75n is to "Sur M. Necker," appended to the second part, 239-88.
REFERRED TO: 75n, 93

BONIFACE VIII (Pope).
NOTE: the references at 239, 247, 251 are in quotations from Michelet.
REFERRED TO: 234, 239, 245, 247, 251, 253

BONNEMER, AUBIN.
NOTE: the references are in a quotation from Carlyle, who uses the spelling Bonnemère.
REFERRED TO: 144, 145

BOUILLÉ, FRANÇOIS CLAUDE AMOUR, MARQUIS DE. Referred to: 94

——— Mémoires de M. de Bouillé, sur la révolution française, depuis son origine jusqu'à la retraite du duc de Brunswick. 2 vols. Paris: Giguet, 1802.
REFERRED TO: 75n, 76n, 93, 94

BOURBON, LOUIS HENRI JOSEPH, DUC DE. See Charles X, Mémoire.

BOYER-FONFRÈDE, JEAN BAPTISTE.
NOTE: the reference, in a quotation from Mignet, is to the Members of the Commission of Twelve.
REFERRED TO: 12

BRAHE, TYCHO. Referred to: 228

BRANTÔME, PIERRE DE BOURDEILLE, ABBÉ DE. Mémoires de Messire Pierre de Bourdeille. 6 vols. Leyden: Sambix, 1665-66.
REFERRED TO: 50

BREAKSPEAR, NICHOLAS. See Adrian IV.

BRÉARD-DUPLESSYS, JEAN JACQUES DE.
NOTE: the reference, in a quotation from Mignet, is to the moderates on the Committee of Public Safety.
REFERRED TO: 12

BRETEUIL, EUSTACHE DE PACY, COMTE DE.
NOTE: the reference is in a quotation from Sismondi.
REFERRED TO: 41n

BRETEUIL, LOUIS CHARLES AUGUSTE LE TONNELIER, BARON DE.
NOTE: the reference at 9 is in a quotation from Mignet; the quotation at 89 and the references at 89n and 91n are in quotations from or derive from, Montgaillard (q.v. for the collation); the reference at 87 is to him as a member of the new ministry following Necker's dismissal.
QUOTED: 89
REFERRED TO: 9, 87, 89, 89n, 91n, 94

BRISSOT, JACQUES PIERRE.
NOTE: the reference at 98 is to the "Brissotin" faction; that at 104 is in a quotation from Kerverseau.
REFERRED TO: 98, 100, 100n, 104, 108

British and Foreign Review; or, European Quarterly Journal. Referred to: 371n

BROGLIE, ACHILLE LÉONCE VICTOR CHARLES, DUC DE. Referred to: 192

BROGLIE, VICTOR FRANÇOIS, DUC DE.
NOTE: maréchal de France. The quotation is in a quotation from Montgaillard (q.v. for the collation); the reference at 12 is in a quotation from Mignet; that at 144 is in a quotation from Carlyle; one at 86 is to him as "an avowed anti-revolutionist" in command of forces near Paris, the second is to him as a member of the new ministry after Necker's dismissal.
QUOTED: 89
REFERRED TO: 12, 86, 89, 144

BROUGHAM, HENRY PETER. Referred to: 319, 320, 322, 323, 324, 329, 330, 333, 334, 343, 344-5

——— Letter to the Marquess of Lansdowne, K.G., Lord President of the Council, on the Late Revolution in France. London: Ridgway, 1848.

NOTE: the third quotation on 323 and the first on 341, being summary, are not collated.
REVIEWED: 317-63
QUOTED: 319, 320, 321, 321-2, 322, 323, 324, 329, 330, 334, 336, 339, 340, 340-1, 341, 342, 347, 353, 356, 357, 361

319.29   Thinks it . . . on him, as one] I think it . . . on one (1)
321.3   The] [*no paragraph*] The (2)
321.3   virtues . . . powers] "virtues . . . powers," (2)
321.28   of it] of this (14)
321.28   men."] men—I will not say men living in a state of civil society, but among any collection of rational beings, connected by the slightest tie, and joined together for the common purposes of their joint defence, or their joint operations of any kind whatever. (14-15)
321.28-9 "no . . . nations."] To changes more or less rapidly brought about every institution of human power or wisdom must always be liable; but so sudden a change as that which in a few hours has, without the very least preparation, destroyed an established Monarchy, and created off-hand a Republic in its stead, having no . . . nations, and being wholly at variance with every principle as well as all experience, I should feel bound to make the addition of a new head or chapter to the work of the Society, did I believe that things could last of their present fashion in France. (5)
321.29-30 "wholly . . . experience."] [*see entry for* 321.28-9 *above*]
321.30-1 "feel . . . chapter"] [*see entry for* 321.28-9 *above*]
321.32   "a very] At the desire of our Useful Knowledge Society, and in constant communication with our lamented friend and colleague, Althorp, I prepared a very (4-5)
321.32   Philosophy"] Philosophy,* [*footnote:*] *The publication was begun in 1840, finished 1846. [*text:*] in which the principles of Government are fully explained, and the theory as well as the history and the practice of the various constitutions that have flourished in ancient or in modern times is minutely described. (5)
321.32-3 "our . . . Society."] [*see entry for* 321.32 *above*]
322.1-3   "the . . . complaint;"] That a total change in their social condition should be the . . . complaint—that all which had before been adopted by the approval, more or less general of the nation, at any rate submitted to in peace by all, should be instantaneously renounced, rejected, cast off, and every vestige be swept away of what had existed with unusual acquiescence, and an entirely new order of things—an order in all particulars new, devised without the least deliberation, struck out at a heat, created off-hand as quick as a ready speaker can off-hand utter half a dozen sentences unpremeditated—that a few minutes by the clock should intervene between the old, obsolete, annihilated, and the span new, untried and even unthought of,—truly this is a convulsion to which no former revolution ever known in the world offers the least parallel. (15)
322.3   "without] [*paragraph*] It would be difficult to imagine a more striking contrast than the late Revolution points to that which we have been briefly contemplating, and the whole comparison is decidedly against the more recent alternation, shewing it to have been without (22)
322.4-5   it, except familiarity with change" and "proneness to violence."] it, if we make a single exception, the familiarity with change, the proneness to violence, the habit of undergoing morbid convulsive movement instead of the healthy natural action of the politic body, a habit superinduced by the disasters of the times, and the use of powerful stimulants. (22)
322.5-6   "work . . . printing-office;"] Then this work . . . printing-office, and leading on to two or three thousand in a capital of one million souls, and a nation of five and thirty, is at once perceived to have the very probable consequence of uniting the ten or twelve thousand felons, chiefly discharged galley-slaves, who are always under the watch of the police, but always hovering about, ready for any mischief; a national alarm is excited, that the Monarchy having been destroyed in one contest, all Paris may be subjected in another to fire, pillage, massacre. (14)
322.6-7   "a handful . . . sub-editor."] So by universal consent, the inhabitants of that great capital submit to the absolute dominion of the dictators thus suddenly appointed by a handful . . . sub-editor, and adopt, as if it had been their own work, the new Government thus proclaimed by that most insignificant band, without even affecting to ask the consent of any human being, or even to apprize any one beforehand of what they intended to do—nay, very possibly without having five minutes before formed any precise intention at all. (14)

322.17 "terrible truth,"] [*paragraph*] Yes! yes! this is the truth—the terrible truth! (14)

322.18-19 "for . . . may be reared,"] The marvellous sight of such a change having been wrought by a handful of men in Paris, and tamely submitted to by all France, for . . . may in that country be reared. (15)

322.20-l "All . . . government"] [*paragraph*] The inevitable result of this experiment is the destruction of all confidence—all . . . Government. (30-1)

322.34-6 "The . . . of seventeen years,"] Far less did any one breathe a whisper of enmity to the dynasty; indeed, generally speaking, there was little personal disrespect shewn towards the . . . of above seventeen years, and whose private conduct was as unimpeachable as his capacity for affairs was renowned. (24)

323.1 "earnest and zealous"] It was earnestly urged upon the late Government by their real and zealous friends—of whom I certainly accounted myself one—that the franchise should be extended considerably. (10)

323.7-8 "A . . . five-and-thirty,"] [*see entry for* 322.5-6 *above*]

323.9 "an armed mob] Instead of attempting to reform the system by lawful means, or to change the Ministers who had just given offence, or to exact punishment by the course of justice for that offence, the indignation of the multitude in Paris suddenly bursts forth, because the police threaten to stop a dinner and a procession; an armed mob resists the authorities; an accident renews the conflict, after it had of itself died away; another accident occasions unnecessary shedding of blood; the populace, further exasperated, march to the National Assembly, and without the assent of any regular body whatever, proclaims a Republic, of which no one had dreamt an hour before, and names as its chiefs some half-dozen men, of whom no one had dreamt at any time, as rulers of the State! (13-14)

323.9-10 of two or three thousand,"] [*see entry for* 322.5-6 *above*]

323.21-3 "votes . . . juries;" and also "enfranchised, without . . . arts;"] Nor would as ample an extension of the electoral lists have been given as many might have deemed desirable and safe; but in all likelihood the rational and important measure would soon have been carried, of giving votes . . . juries, and of enfranchising without . . . arts; an extension most consonant in itself to the soundest principles, most fit to be adopted even by ourselves, and most desirable in France as tending to keep those important classes away from the vile trade of agitation. (49)

324.3-4 "think . . . outbreak."] The National Guards will think . . . outbreak; the bulk of the inhabitants will yield implicit obedience to save their lives; Paris will be conquered, and all France will take the law from Paris. (32)

329.3 is taught] is now taught (31)

329.4 change" . . . "requires] change its form of Government requires (31)

329.15-16 "There . . . shown," . . . "towards . . . Prince."] [*see entry for* 322.34 *above*]

329.20-1 "repeated . . . influence"] But repeated . . . influence would have made it impossible to hold out long. (48-9)

330.16 "improvised government"] My objection is to the manner in which the change was brought about—to the sudden, unpremeditated revolt, and as sudden unpremeditated displacing one system and establishing another,—to Revolutions made with the magic wand of an enchanter,—Monarchies destroyed at a blow,—Republics founded in a trice,—Constitutions made extempore—*improvised*—I must use a foreign word—we have none to express the thing—our sober English habits with difficulty allow us to utter a few sentences in this unpremeditated fashion; we have neither the wish nor the power to make anything but a speech off-hand, and hence are without the means of describing so fantastic an operation. (30)

330.16 "struck . . . heat"] [*see entry for* 322.1-3 *above*]

330.16-17 "the result of a sudden thought"] The mob, led by a few agitators, got the upper hand; the National Guards, afraid of having their shops attacked, their windows and toys broken, declined to do their duty; no sufficient number of troops was assembled, and these were ill distributed; some hundreds of young men, eager to distinguish themselves, headed the multitude; a number of boys from schools took part in the fray; a more powerful body of banditti, discharged from the galleys and the prisons, and always congregated in the capital from whencesoever they come, joined in the disorder which is so congenial to them, eager for the pillage which they surely foresaw; the Abdication took place, the Regency was proposed and accepted both in the streets and in the Chamber of Deputies; when all of a sudden an armed mob rushed in, overpowering the sentinels, terrifying the members, who fled in all directions; and some one, apparently giving vent to the emotion that filled his bosom, exclaimed, like the woman in the German play, "A sudden thought strikes me! Let us swear an eternal Republic; and let us vow to live together under it." (28-9)

330.17   "span . . . of."] [*see entry for* 322.1-3 *above*]

330.17   "unthought of,"] [*see entry for* 322.1-3 *above*]

334.20   "Rabble,"] But nothing can less deserve the praise of humanity than the silly half-measures which would make a Government parley with an armed rabble. (88)

334.20   "dregs of the populace."] See the dregs of the populace for a season triumphant over the police and the law! (88)

334.20-1   "armed ruffians,"] [*see* 322.4-5 *above*]

336.26   "one of his" . . . "commissioners] One of his Commissioners (113n)

339.24   "to retain] Hence all their proceedings were, as might have been foreseen, directed to these two ends; their administrative acts to prevent insurrection—their legislative edicts to retain (120)

340.16-17   "their . . . election;" . . . "the] Their . . . election, was their worst act of internal administration; it placed the (120)

340.34   Held] [*no paragraph*] They held (120)

340.34   nations. . . . M. Lamartine does] nations. It is in vain that M. Lamartine, in the able defence by which he so triumphantly refutes the vile slanders against his personal honour, and shews demonstrably that his hands are clean, attempts to gloss over this the most pernicious act of his short administration. He does (121)

341.2   authority. Beyond] authority. [*6-sentence omission*] [*paragraph*] Beyond (121-2)

347.3   That new-fangled principle, that] [*no paragraph*] But having protested against the propagandist doctrines of the Republic, as openly avowed now as by the Convention, though without the same excuse, I must once more lift up my voice against that (126)

347.4-5   is termed] is somewhat the mode among political reasoners of our day, in other places as well as Paris; I allude to what is termed (126)

347.5-6   seems," . . . "to] seems to (126)

347.8   These] Those (126)

353.8-10   "to . . . 1794."] Some of these economic doctors hold it the absolute right of all men living in a Republic to have so much a day for their support—five francs for eight hours labour, according to the doctrine of M. Louis Blanc, [*3-sentence footnote omitted*] who has shewn his confidence in his principles, and in the Republic that he helped to form in order to propagate them, by flying from his trial, and seeking shelter among us poor benighted creatures, slaves of a Monarchy (and who have hitherto resisted the attempts of his English disciples at organizing our labour), to . . . 1794, and the domination of the mob over the legislature more absolute than it was under the guidance of those famous political economists, Robespierre and St. Just. (56-7)

353.11-12   "panting for . . . government."] But when the dread of a Red Republic began to haunt them, even the National Guard, passive in February, was ready to act in June, and the voices which at one moment had seemed to lift M. Lamartine above all his rivals, left him, with a singular accord, as soon as he formed his most inconceivable, or most suspicious junction with the party that panted for . . . government, and the assignats as a resource of finance. (80)

357.20   They] [*no paragraph*] They (56)

357.22   them. Such are] them—that is, how the impossible problem may be solved by legislation, of finding profitable employment—that is, wages with moderate work—for the whole community, without any regard to the gains of capital, or the investment of capital, or, indeed, the existence of capital. [*2½-page omission*] [*paragraph*] Such, however, are (56-9)

361.10   The legislative body . . . should] 2. The second principle which I would propose as quite essential for obtaining even a possibility of good government, and of a stable system, is that the legislative body, whether consisting of one or of two chambers, and in whatever way both or either may be composed, should (71)

361.19   judicial. Its] judicial. [*paragraph*] Its (72)

———— *Political Philosophy.* 3 pts. London: Society for the Diffusion of Useful Knowledge, and Chapman and Hall, 1842-43.
REFERRED TO: 321, 324

BUCER, MARTIN. Referred to: *375*

BUCHEZ, PHILIPPE JOSEPH BENJAMIN, and PROSPER CHARLES ROUX, eds. *L'histoire parlementaire de la révolution française, ou Journal des assemblées nationales, depuis 1789 jusqu'en 1815*. 40 vols. Paris: Paulin, 1834-38.
NOTE: the references and quotations from 142-55 are in quotations from Carlyle, *French Revolution, q.v.*
QUOTED: 142, 151, 155, 156
REFERRED TO: 141, 143, 146, 149, 151, 153

BULWER (later BULWER-LYTTON), EDWARD GEORGE EARLE LYTTON. *Athens, Its Rise and Fall, with Views of the Literature, Philosophy, and Social Life of the Athenian People*. 2 vols. London: Saunders and Otley, 1837.
REFERRED TO: 160

BURGESS, THOMAS. *A Letter to the Honourable and Right Reverend The Lord Bishop of Durham, on the Origin of the Pelasgi, and on the Original Name and Pronunciation of the Aeolic Digamma: in Answer to Professor Marsh's Horae Pelasgicae*. Carmarthon: Evans, 1815.
NOTE: successively Bishop of St. David's and of Salisbury. Another ed. was published in 1821.
REFERRED TO: 62

———— *Vindication of the Late Bishop of St. Asaph's Edition of the Lacedaemonian Decree, and of His List of Books for the Use of the Younger Clergy, from the Strictures of R.P. Knight, Esq. and the Rev. H. Marsh, D.D*. Durham: printed Walker, 1816.
NOTE: republished (London: printed Nichols, [1821]), as *A Vindication of Bishop Cleaver's Edition of the Decretum Lacedaemoniorum contra Timotheum, from the Strictures of R.P. Knight, Esq*.
REFERRED TO: 62

BURKE, EDMUND. *Reflections on the Revolution in France, and on the Proceedings in Certain Societies in London Relative to That Event. In a Letter Intended to Have Been Sent to a Gentleman in Paris* (1790). In *The Works of the Right Honourable Edmund Burke*. 8 vols. London: Dodsley (Vols. I-III), Rivington (Vols. IV-VIII), 1792-1827, III, 19-321.
NOTE: Vols. III-V of this ed. formerly in SC.
QUOTED: 35, 40
REFERRED TO: 86
35.1 "glory of chivalry."] But the age of chivalry is gone. That of sophisters, economists, and calculators, has succeeded; and the glory of Europe is extinguished for ever. (III, 111)
40.10-11 "cheap . . . nations." . . . "nurse . . . heroic virtue."] The unbought grace of life, the cheap . . . nations, the nurse . . . heroic enterprise is gone! (III, 111)

BURLAMAQUI, JEAN JACQUES. *Principes du droit naturel*. Geneva: Barillot, 1747.
REFERRED TO: 345

———— *Principes du droit politique*. Geneva: Barillot, 1751.
REFERRED TO: 345

BUTLER, SAMUEL. *Hudibras* (1678). Ed. Zachary Grey. 2 vols. London: Vernor and Hood, *et al.*, 1801.
NOTE: Vol. I in SC, with Vol. II of 1806 ed. (Vernor, Hood, and Sharpe). The quotation is in a quotation from Scott.
QUOTED: 98
98.29 higher."] higher:/For venturing to assassinate / And cut the throats of church and state:/ And not be allow'd the fittest men / To take the charge of both again: [*the sentence continues for 28 more lines*] (II, 307; III, ii, 1046-50)

BUZOT, FRANÇOIS NICOLAS LÉONARD. Referred to: 106

BYRON, GEORGE GORDON, LORD. Referred to: 183

CABALA. See Kabbalah.

CAESAR, CAIUS JULIUS. Referred to: 224, 236

———— *Commentariorum de bello gallico.* Vol. I of *C. Julii Caesaris quae exstant opera.* 2 vols. Paris: Barbou, 1755.

NOTE: this ed. formerly in SC. The reference is in a quotation from Nisard.

QUOTED: 236n-7n

REFERRED TO: 194

236n.1   Aducantanus] Adcantuannus (I, 97)

236n.1-237n.1   quos . . . appellant: quorum . . . recusaret.] (quos . . . appellant; *quorum . . . recusaret*) cum iis Adcantuannus eruptionem facere conatus, clamore ab ea parte munitionis sublato, cum ad arma milites concurrissent, vehementerque ibi pugnatum esset, repulsus in oppidum est: uti tamen eadem deditionis conditione uteretur, a Crasso impetravit. (I, 97)

CALONNE, CHARLES ALEXANDRE DE. Referred to: 74

CAMBACÉRÈS, JEAN JACQUES RÉGIS DE, DUC DE PARME.

NOTE: the reference is in a quotation from Montgaillard.

REFERRED TO: 89n

CAMPAN, JEANNE LOUISE HENRIETTE GENEST. *Mémoires sur la vie privée de Marie Antoinette, reine de France et de Navarre; suivis de souvenirs et anecdotes historiques sur les règnes de Louis XIV, de Louis XV, et de Louis XVI.* 2 vols. London: Colburn and Bossange, 1823.

NOTE: the first quotation is from the introductory "Notice sur la vie de madame Campan" by Jean François Barrière; the second, from d'Escherny, is taken by JSM from Campan. The reference at 157, which derives from Carlyle, who was using the 3-vol. ed. of 1822, has been altered to conform to this ed. (and to the events described).

QUOTED: 68n-9n, 85

REFERRED TO: 75n, 76n, 80n, 85n, 157

68n.5   "Non] [*paragraph*] Non (I, xl)

85.2   *un système monstrueux*] Ce système monstrueux fut appelé *constitution*, et ce que la postérité aura peine à croire, c'est que tous les partis vinrent s'y rallier. (II, 444)

CAMUS, ARMAND GASTON. Referred to: 73n

CANNING, GEORGE. Referred to: 193

———— Speech on the Indemnity Bill (11 Mar., 1818; Commons), *PD,* 1st ser., Vol. 37, cols. 1022-40.

REFERRED TO: 78

———— and GEORGE ELLIS. ["New Morality,"] *The Anti-Jacobin; or, Weekly Examiner,* II, 36 (9 July, 1798), 282-7.

NOTE: republished, with title, as Canning's; in Canning's copy (British Library), he indicates that he wrote ll. 81-159, 168-286, and 354-463 (the end); Ellis wrote 1-80, 160-7, and 318-27; together they wrote 328-53 (287-317 are not attributed).

REFERRED TO: 78

CARDAINE.

NOTE: not otherwise identified; the reference is in a quotation from Carlyle.

REFERRED TO: 156

CARDWELL, EDWARD. Referred to: *369*

CARLOMAN.

NOTE: one of the grandsons of Louis I, son of Charles I (the Bald).

REFERRED TO: 19

CARLOMAN.

NOTE: one of the grandsons of Louis I, son of Louis II.

REFERRED TO: 19

CARLYLE, THOMAS. Referred to: 113-14, 133-66 *passim*, 215, 225, 227n

———— "Biography," *Fraser's Magazine*, V (Apr., 1832), 253-60.
NOTE: the quotation at 137 is indirect; that at 162 is in a quotation from Carlyle.
QUOTED: 113, 114, 137, 162
113.1   Of history, the] Of History, for example, the (254-5)
114.4   To] [*no paragraph*] How inexpressibly comfortable to (253)
151.3   "Man," as has been written, "is for ever interesting to man; nay, properly there] "Man is
perennially interesting to man; nay, if we look strictly to it, there (253)

———— "Boswell's Life of Johnson," *Fraser's Magazine*, V (May, 1832), 379-413.
NOTE: the quotation is indirect.
QUOTED: 137
REFERRED TO: 113n

———— "Burns," *Edinburgh Review*, XLVIII (Dec., 1828), 267-312.
NOTE: the quotation is indirect.
QUOTED: 137

———— "Characteristics," *Edinburgh Review*, LIV (Dec., 1831), 351-83.
NOTE: the quotation at 215 is indirect.
QUOTED: 162, 215, 261n
162.26-7   "given a world of rogues, to produce an honesty by their united action,"] What sound
mind among the French, for example, now fancies that men can be governed by 'Constitutions;'
by the never so cunning mechanizing of Self-interests, and all conceivable adjustments of
checking and balancing; in a word, by the best possible solution of this quite insoluble and
impossible problem, *Given a world of Knaves, to produce an Honesty from their united action?*
(382)

———— *The Collected Letters of Thomas and Jane Welsh Carlyle*. Ed. Charles Richard
Sanders, *et al*. Durham, N.C.: Duke University Press, 1970- .
NOTE: the quotation at 114 is in a letter from Carlyle to Mill dated 12 Jan., 1833; that at 201 is in a
letter dated 24 Sept., 1833; the references at 161 and 182-3 are to a letter dated 13 June, 1833.
QUOTED: 114, 201
REFERRED TO: 161, 182-3
114.30   "the] What chiefly attracts me, however, is a face of the matter in which M. Thiers is
unfortunately rather uncommunicative: what I might call the (VI, 302)
201.33   "quiet emphasis"] There is not a word in it [JSM's review of Alison's *History of the
French Revolution*] that I do not subscribe to: it is really a *decided* little utterance, with a quiet
emphasis, a conscious incontrovertibility, which (heretic that I am) I rejoice to see growing in
you. (VI, 445)

———— *The French Revolution: A History*. 3 vols. London: Fraser, 1837.
NOTE: the terms used in the quotation at 133 are so common in Carlyle that no collation is given; the
quotation at 261 is indirect.
REVIEWED: 131-66
QUOTED: 133, 138-9, 139, 140-2, 142-3, 143-7, 147-50, 150, 150-2, 152-4, 154-5, 155-7, 163,
165-6, 169, 261
REFERRED TO: 219
139.22   "Era of Hope"] For them [the masses], in this world, rises no Era of Hope; hardly now in
the other,—if it be not hope in the gloomy rest of Death, for their faith too is failing. (I, 48)
[Earlier Carlyle refers to the age as a "New Era," and capitalizes "Hope" as its characteristic, but
does not actually use the term.]
142.16   themselves. . . . [*paragraph*] But] themselves. [*ellipsis indicates 4½-paragraph omission*] [*paragraph*] But (I, 170-2)
146.3   was one] was of one (I, 269)
148n.12   137-50] 137, 150 (I, 315n)
150.16-17   "Insurrection of Women."] [The title of Vol. I, Bk. VII.] (I, 333)
153.20-1   thou! . . . [*paragraph*] Scarcely] thou! [*ellipsis indicates 3-paragraph omission*]
[*paragraph*] Yes, Paris is marching on us; and more than the women of Paris! Scarcely (I,
358-60)

155.13   Versailles.] Versailles.* [*footnote:*] *See* Histoire Parlementaire, iii. (70-117); Deux Amis (166-177), &c. (I, 365n)
155.32-3 rest. . . . [*paragraph*] The] [*ellipsis indicates 2-page omission*] (I, 366-8)
156.29   those] these (I, 390)
157.31   death-knell] death-melly (I, 392)
163.25-6 "the . . . twenty-five millions"] Whatsoever is cruel in the panic frenzy of Twenty-five million men, whatsoever is great in the . . . Twenty-five million men, stand here in abrupt contrast, near by one another. (III, 4)
165.27   The Convention] [*no paragraph*] It was the frightfullest thing ever born of Time? One of the frightfullest. This Convention (III, 433)
165.32   women.] women.* [*footnote:*] *Montgaillard, iv. 241. (III, 433)
166.2   him?] him?* [*footnote:*] *Report of the Irish Poor-Law Commission, 1836. (III, 433)
166.32   it seems] it would seem (III, 435)
166.32   rise. . . . That] rise; has risen, and O Heavens! has it not tanned their skins into breeches for itself? That (III, 435)
261.22   a theory of the world—] Alone of all Frenchmen he [Lafayette] has a theory of the world, and right mind to conform thereto; he can become a hero and perfect-character, were it but the hero of one idea. (I, 205)

———— "The Nibelungen Lied," *Westminster Review*, XV (July, 1831), 1-45.
NOTE: see also Bible, Colossians.
QUOTED: 219
219.10   "shadow of its coming"] A shadow of coming Fate, as it were, a low inarticulate voice of Doom falls, from the first, out of that charmed Nibelungen-land: the discord of two women, is as a little spark of evil passion, that ere long enlarges itself into a crime; foul murder is done; and now the Sin rolls on like a devouring fire, till the guilty and the innocent are alike encircled with it, and a whole land is ashes, and a whole race is swept away. (17)

———— *Sartor Resartus*. 2nd ed. Boston: Munroe, 1837.
NOTE: in SC. The quotation is indirect.
QUOTED: 215
215.6   man is still man.] 'Here also [said Teufelsdröckh] are men [the Saint-Simonians] who have discovered, not without amazement, that man is still man; of which high, long-forgotten truth you already see them make a false application.' (299)

———— "State of German Literature," *Edinburgh Review*, XLVI (Oct., 1827), 304-51.
REFERRED TO: 137

———— "Thoughts on History," *Fraser's Magazine*, II (Nov., 1830), 413-18.
NOTE: Carlyle's self-quotation is indirect.
QUOTED: 113

CARNOT, LAZARE NICOLAS MARGUERITE. Referred to: 101, 109n, 177

———— *Le ministère de l'instruction publique et des cultes, depuis le 24 février jusqu'au 5 juillet 1848*. Paris: Pagnerre, 1848.
NOTE: Carnot's "circulaire" appears on 23-6 of this pamphlet.
REFERRED TO: 335, 337

CARNOT, SADI, trans. *La révolution de 1848 et ses détracteurs*. Paris: Baillière, 1875.
NOTE: this translation of JSM's "Vindication of the Revolution of February 1848" is in SC.

CAROLINE (of England). Referred to: 201

CARREL, JEAN BAPTISTE NICOLAS ARMAND.
NOTE: the quotations at 202 and 214 are in quotations from Nisard; that at 212 is in a quotation from Littré.
QUOTED: 202, 212, 214
REFERRED TO: 169-215 *passim*

———— "De la guerre d'Espagne en 1823," *Revue Française*, III (May, 1828), 131-73.
NOTE: at 145 the running heads change to "De la guerre de 1823 en Espagne."
QUOTED: 180

REFERRED TO: 180, 188, 195

180.4-5 "foreign liberal legion,"] [*translated in part from:*] Cinq cents environ dans toute la catalogue, restèrent sous les armes et formèrent, sous le nom de légion libérale étrangère, un petit bataillon d'infanterie et un faible escadron de lanciers. (168)

———— "De l'Espagne et de sa révolution," *Revue Française*, II (Mar., 1828), 261-91.
REFERRED TO: 180, 188, 195

———— "Du flagrant délit en matière d'impression et publication d'écrits," *National*, 24 Jan., 1832, 1-2.
REFERRED TO: 197

———— "Du nouveau procès entre la république et le tiers-parti," *National*, 27 Oct., 1833, 1, 2-3.
REFERRED TO: 206-7

———— *Extrait du dossier d'un prévenu de complicité morale dans l'attentat du 28 juillet.* Paris: Paulin, 1835.
REFERRED TO: 207, 208

———— *Histoire de la contre-révolution en Angleterre, sous Charles II et Jacques II.* Paris: Sautelet, 1827.
NOTE: the reference at 187 is in a quotation from Nisard.
QUOTED: 178, 187
REFERRED TO: 187, 221

178.14 "the refuge of weak parties,"] [*translated in part from:*] Elles n'éclataient point par des complots, signes toujours certains de la faiblesse des partis. (326)

187.4-6 "Everywhere . . . times," . . . "it . . . wants."] [*translated from:*] Partout et dans tous les temps ce sont les besoins qui ont fait les conventions appelées principes, et toujours les principes se sont tus devant les besoins. (65)

187.6-8 "All . . . government," . . . "have . . . else."] [*translated from:*] [*paragraph*] Car toute question de forme politique a ses données dans l'état de la société, nullement ailleurs; et, pour cela, la courte existence républicaine de l'Angleterre n'avait été qu'une excursion forcée en dehors des voies constitutionnelles que la nation s'était frayées depuis long-temps. (3)

———— "La révolution et le tiers-parti," *National*, 29 Oct., 1833, 1.
REFERRED TO: 207

———— "Qu'il faut craindre de rendre les modérés violens en se moquant de la modération," *National*, 31 May, 1832, 1.
REFERRED TO: 200

———— Speech in the Chamber of Peers (16 Dec., 1834), *National*, 17 Dec., 1834, 1-4.
REFERRED TO: 198

———— Unheaded article, *National*, 30 Oct., 1833, 2.
REFERRED TO: 207

CARREL, MARIE MADELEINE (née DUBUISSON).
NOTE: mother of Armand Carrel. The quotation is in a quotation from Nisard.
QUOTED: 181
REFERRED TO: 181-2

CARREL, NICOLAS ARMAND.
NOTE: father of Armand Carrel.
REFERRED TO: 172

CARTOUCHE, LOUIS DOMINIQUE.
NOTE: his name became a synonym for brigandage.
REFERRED TO: 29

CARTWRIGHT, JOHN. Referred to: 180

CATHELINEAU, JACQUES. Referred to: 117

Condé, M. le duc de Bourbon, M. le duc d'Enghien et M. le prince de Conti (1788). In *HP*, I, 256-62.
NOTE: the reference is in a quotation from Carlyle.
REFERRED TO: 141

CHARLES, COMTE DE FLANDRE.
NOTE: known as Charles le Bon.
REFERRED TO: 24n

CHARLES DE PROVENCE.
NOTE: one of the grandsons of Louis I.
REFERRED TO: 19

CHATEAUBRIAND, FRANÇOIS RENÉ, VICOMTE DE. Referred to: 190, 226

CHENEVIX, RICHARD. "History and Prospects of English Industry," *Quarterly Review*, XXXIV (June, 1826), 45-99.
REFERRED TO: 17

CHENU, JACQUES ETIENNE ADOLPHE. Referred to: 322

———— Déposition. In *Rapport de la commission d'enquête (q.v.)*, I, 182-90.
NOTE: the "déposition" consists of extracts from his interrogation before the Premier conseil de guerre permanent de la 1re division militaire.
REFERRED TO: 322

CHIÈVRES, PIERRE JACQUES AUGUSTE NICOLAS GASPARD DE. Referred to: 180n

CHILDEBERT III.
NOTE: one of the *rois fainéants*.
REFERRED TO: 19

CHILDÉRIC I.
NOTE: the reference is in a quotation from Velly quoted by Thierry.
REFERRED TO: 223n

CHILDÉRIC III.
NOTE: one of the *rois fainéants*.
REFERRED TO: 19

CHILPERIC II.
NOTE: one of the *rois fainéants*.
REFERRED TO: 19

CHURCHILL, JOHN (Duke of Marlborough).
NOTE: the story is told in Mark Noble, *A Biographical History of England from the Revolution to the End of George I's Reign*. 2 vols. London: Richardson, *et al.*, 1806, II, 189.
REFERRED TO: *367*

CHODERLOS DE LACLOS, PIERRE AMBROISE FRANÇOIS. *Les liaisons dangereuses, ou Lettres recueillies dans une société, et publiées pour l'instruction de quelques autres.* 4 vols. Amsterdam and Paris: Durand, 1782.
NOTE: the reference is in a quotation from Carlyle.
REFERRED TO: 141

CHOLAT.
NOTE: not further identified; the reference is in a quotation from Carlyle.
REFERRED TO: 145

CHRIST. See Jesus.

CICERO, MARCUS TULLIUS. *De oratore* (Latin and English). Trans. E.W. Sutton. 2 vols. London: Heinemann; Cambridge, Mass.: Harvard University Press, 1942.
NOTE: this ed. cited for ease of reference.
REFERRED TO: 188

———— *Epistolarae ad Atticum, aliosque.* In *Opera cum optimis exemplaribus accurate collata.* 10 vols. Leyden: Elzevir, 1642, III.
NOTE: in SC. As the original phrase is in Greek, no collation is given.
QUOTED: 22

CINCINNATUS, LUCIUS QUINCTIUS.
NOTE: the reference, to "l'ordre libre de Cincinnatus," is in a quotation from Mignet.
REFERRED TO: 9

CLAVELIN. See Kerverseau.

CLAVIÈRE, ETIENNE.
NOTE: JSM uses the spelling Clavières.
REFERRED TO: 101, 108

CLEMENT V (Pope). Referred to: 244

CLEMENT VI (Pope). Letter to King John and Queen Joanna of France. In Luc d'Achery, *Spicilegium; sive collectio veterum aliquot scriptorum qui in Galliae bibliothecis delituerant* (1655-77). New ed. 3 vols. Paris: Montalart, 1723, III, 724.
NOTE: this ed. cited by Dulaure.
QUOTED: 43

43.12   *quae servare commode non possetis*] Votis vestris liberter annuimus, iis praecipue per quae, sicut pie desideratis, pacem, et salutem animae, Deo propitio consequi valeatis, Hinc est quod nos vestris supplicationibus inclinati, vobis, et successoribus vestris Regibus et Reginis Franciae, qui pro tempore fuerint, ac vestrum et eorum cuilibet, auctoritate Apostolica, tenore praesentium in perpetuum indulgemus; ut Confessor Religiosus, vel saecularis, quem vestrum et eorum quilibet duxerit eligendum, vota per vos forsitan jam emissa, ac per vos, et successores vestros in posterum emittenda, ultramarino, ac beatorum Petri et Pauli Apostolorum, ac castitatis et continentiae votis dumtaxat exceptis; necnon juramenta per vos praestita, et per vos et eos praestanda in posterum, quae vos et illi servare commodè non possetis, vobis et eis commutare valeat in alia opera pietatis, prout secundum Deum, et animarum vestrarum, et eorum saluti viderit expedire. (III, 724)

CLITON, GUILLAUME.
NOTE: of Normandy. The reference, which derives from Sismondi, is to him as the successor of Charles, comte de Flandre.
REFERRED TO: 34n

CLOOTS, JEAN BAPTISTE DU VAL DE GRÂCE, BARON VON.
NOTE: known as Anacharsis Cloots. JSM uses the spelling Clootz.
REFERRED TO: 224

CLOTAIRE I (of France). Referred to: 223

CLOVIS I (OF FRANCE).
NOTE: the reference at 52 is in a quotation from Hallam.
REFERRED TO: 24, 52, 223, 280, 290

CLOVIS III.
NOTE: of Neustria and Burgundy; one of the *rois fainéants.*
REFERRED TO: 19

COCKER, EDWARD. *Cocker's Decimal Arithmetick: Wherein Is Shewed the Nature and Use of Decimal Fractions . . . Whereunto Is Added His Artificial Arithmetic . . . Also His Algebraic Arithmetic.* London: Richardson and Lacy, 1675.
NOTE: the reference is in a quotation from Carlyle.
REFERRED TO: 165

Code Napoléon. Paris: Imprimerie impériale, 1807.
REFERRED TO: 109

COLERIDGE, SAMUEL TAYLOR.
NOTE: see also Schiller, *The Piccolomini . . .*, trans. Coleridge.
REFERRED TO: 165, 261

———— *The Friend: A Series of Essays*. London: Gale and Curtis, 1812.

NOTE: the quotation is indirect. The passage occurs in "Satyrane's Letters," was reprinted in *Biographia Literaria*, 2 vols. in 1 (London: Rest Fenner, 1817), II, 208 (in SC), and thus omitted in *The Friend*, 3 vols. (London: Rest Fenner, 1818) (in SC).

QUOTED: 202

202.27-9   the manner of a gentleman, that which shows respect to others in such a way as implies an equally habitual and secure reliance on their respect to himself.] The secret of the matter, I believe to be this—we feel the gentlemanly character present to us, whenever under all the circumstances of social intercourse, the trivial not less than the important, through the whole *detail* of his manners and deportment, and with the ease of a habit, a Person shews respect to others in *such a way*, as at the same time implies in his own feelings an habitual and assured anticipation of reciprocal respect from them to himself. (243)

COLTON, CALEB CHARLES.
NOTE: "O.P.Q." of the *Morning Chronicle*.
REFERRED TO: 125

COMINES, PHILIPPE DE. Referred to: 185

COMTE, AUGUSTE. Referred to: 185

———— *Cours de philosophie positive*. 6 vols. Paris: Bachelier, 1830-42.
NOTE: in SC.
REFERRED TO: 228

COMTE, FRANÇOIS CHARLES LOUIS.
NOTE: the founder of *Le Censeur Européen*.
REFERRED TO: 109n

———— *De l'impossibilité d'établir un gouvernement constitutionnel sous un chef militaire, et particulièrement sous Napoléon*. Paris: Les marchands de nouveautés, 1815.
REFERRED TO: 109n

———— *Über die Unmöglichkeit einer konstitutionellen Regierung unter einem militärischen Oberhaupte, besonders unter Napoleon*. Trans. T. von Haupt. Cologne: Dumont, Bachmann, 1815.
REFERRED TO: 109n

CONDÉ, LOUIS JOSEPH DE BOURBON, PRINCE DE. See Charles X, *Mémoire*.

CONDILLAC, ETIENNE BONNOT DE. Referred to: 67, 183

CONDORCET, MARIE JEAN ANTOINE NICOLAS CARITAT, MARQUIS DE. Referred to: 67, 100, 106, 108, 185

———— *Vie de Voltaire* (1787). In Voltaire. *Oeuvres complètes*. 66 vols. Paris: Renouard, 1817-25, LXIV, 1-172.
REFERRED TO: 66

CONSTANT DE REBECQUE, HENRI BENJAMIN. Referred to: 177, 198

CONSTITUTIONS OF CLARENDON. See *Select Charters*, ed. William Stubbs.

CONTI, LOUIS FRANÇOIS JOSEPH DE BOURBON, PRINCE DE.
NOTE: see also Charles X, *Mémoire*.
REFERRED TO: 108

CORANCEZ, GUILLAUME OLIVIER DE. See Glück.

COUCY, ENGUERRAND DE. Referred to: 31, 48

COULANGES, PIERRE PHILIPPE EMMANUEL, MARQUIS DE. "Extrait d'un manuscrit de M. de Coulanges, intitulé: Relation de mon voyage d'Allemagne et d'Italie ez années 1657 et 1658." In *Mémoires*. Paris: Blaise, 1820, 13-16.
REFERRED TO: *376*

74n.15   Luxembourg. . . . Nous] Luxembourg, qui devoit pour le moins autant à son mérite qu'au nom illustre de Montmorenci, l'honneur d'être président de la Noblesse. Nous (I, 33-4)

74n.26   égards et les] égards et par les (I, 35)

DANTE ALIGHIERI.
NOTE: the first reference at 252 derives from, the second is in a quotation from, Michelet.
REFERRED TO: 252

———— "Del purgatorio." In *La divina commedia di Dante Alighieri* (1472). 3 vols. Florence: Ciardetti, 1821, II.
NOTE: this ed. used as contemporary. The second reference is in a quotation from Michelet.
REFERRED TO: 252

DANTON, GEORGES JACQUES.
NOTE: the reference at 12, in a quotation from Mignet, is to the "Dantonistes."
REFERRED TO: 12, 80n

DARIUS I (of Persia). Referred to: 222

DAVID OF DINAN.
NOTE: the reference is in a quotation from Michelet.
REFERRED TO: 247

Déclaration des droits de l'homme et du citoyen, avec des commentaires par le citoyen Laponneraye. [Paris:] La société des droits de l'homme, [1833].
NOTE: the references at 126, 127 are in a self-quotation. See also Robespierre, *Déclaration.*
QUOTED: 127
REFERRED TO: 126, 127, 205, 206
127.9-10   *La portion de biens qui . . . loi.*] VI. La propriété est le droit qu'a chaque citoyen de jouir et de disposer à son gré de la portion de bien qui . . . loi. (3)

DELORT, JOSEPH. *Histoire de l'homme au masque de fer, accompagnée des pièces authentiques et de fac-simile.* Paris: Delaforest, 1825.
NOTE: an example of "Iron Mask" mania; reviewed, with Ellis, by Francis Palgrave, *Quarterly Review*, XXXIV (June, 1826), 19-35.
REFERRED TO: 62

DEMOSTHENES. Referred to: 224

———— *Orations.*
NOTE: as the reference is general, no ed. is cited.
REFERRED TO: 196

DES BARRES, GUILLAUME. Referred to: 35

DESHUTTES.
NOTE: not otherwise identified; the references are in a quotation from Carlyle.
REFERRED TO: 156, 157

DESMOULINS, LUCIE SIMPLICE CAMILLE BENOIST.
NOTE: the quotation at 9 is in a quotation from Mignet; that at 151 is in a quotation from Carlyle.
QUOTED: 9, 151

DESODOARDS. See Fantin Des Odoards.

Deux amis. See Kerverseau.

DIDEROT, DENIS. Referred to: 67, 68n, 183

———— and JEAN LE ROND D'ALEMBERT, eds. *Encyclopédie, ou Dictionnaire raisonné des sciences, des arts et des métiers, par une société de gens de lettres.* 17 vols. Paris: Briasson, *et al.*, 1751-65.
REFERRED TO: 67n

DIONYSIUS OF SYRACUSE. Referred to: 224

DISRAELI, BENJAMIN. *Coningsby; or, The New Generation.* 3 vols. London: Colburn, 1844.
QUOTED: 299

———— *Henrietta Temple.* London: Colburn, 1837.
REFERRED TO: 164n

DOMINIC. See St. Dominic.

DREUX-BRÉZÉ, HENRI EVRARD, MARQUIS DE.
NOTE: the reference is to him as "the satellite of despotism."
REFERRED TO: 72n

DUCHATEL, CHARLES MARIE TANNEGUY. Referred to: 193, 302

DU CHÂTELET, ACHILLE.
NOTE: JSM uses the spelling Duchâtelet.
REFERRED TO: 100n

DUCOS, JEAN FRANÇOIS. Referred to: 106

DU GUESCLIN, BERTRAND. Referred to: 43

DULAURE, JACQUES ANTOINE. *Histoire physique, civile et morale de Paris, depuis les premiers temps historiques jusqu'à nos jours; contenant par ordre chronologique, la description des accroissemens successifs de cette ville, et de ses monumens anciens et modernes; la notice de toutes ses institutions, tant civiles que religieuses; et, à chaque période, le tableau des moeurs, des usages, et des progrès de la civilisation. Ornée de gravures représentant divers plans de Paris, ses monumens et ses édifices principaux* (1821-25). 2nd ed. 10 vols. Paris: Guillaume, 1823-24.
NOTE: the 2-vol. ed. of part of the work, referred to by JSM at 18, has not been located. The ed. begun in 1821 was not completed until 1825.
REVIEWED: 15-52
QUOTED: 21n, 22-3, 31, 33
21n.10-12 *C'est . . . impudentes.*] "*C'est . . . impudentes.*" (I, ii)
22.34 *ennemi de la France*] [*not in italics*] (I, iv)
22.41 fourni. . . . Qu'on] fourni; [*ellipsis indicates 2½-sentence omission*] [*paragraph*] Qu'on (I, v)
23.9-10 *Si . . . vérité.*] "*Si . . . vérité* (1)." [*footnote omitted*] (I, vi)
31.35 s'abstenait . . . vol] [*in italics*] (II, 136)
31.35-6 vol:"] "Peut-être," adds one author, "se] *vol*: peut-être, disent les grandes chroniques, se (II, 136)
33.21-2 "Tels," . . . "étaient] [*paragraph*] Tels étaient (II, 343)
33.22 du] des (II, 343)
33.22 siècle] siècles (II, 343)

DUMOURIEZ, CHARLES FRANÇOIS DU PÉRIER.
NOTE: the reference at 12 is in a quotation from Mignet.
REFERRED TO: 12, 101

———— *La vie et les mémoires du général Dumouriez, avec des notes et des éclaircissemens historiques.* 4 vols. Paris: Baudouin, 1822-23.
NOTE: part of the *Collection des mémoires,* ed. Berville and Barrière, *q.v.*
REFERRED TO: 89, 93, 97, 97n, 103

DUPIN, AMANDINE AURORE LUCIE, BARONNE DUDEVANT ("George Sand").
REFERRED TO: 183

DUPIN, ANDRÉ MARIE JEAN JACQUES. Referred to: 189

DUPONT DE L'EURE, JACQUES CHARLES.
NOTE: the references at 320 and 321 are to him as the President of, and that at 332 as one of the members of, the Provisional Government of 1848.
REFERRED TO: 198, 320, 321, 332, 333n

DUPONT DE NEMOURS, PIERRE SAMUEL.
NOTE: the reference is in a quotation from Carlyle.
REFERRED TO: 140

DUPORT, ADRIEN JEAN FRANÇOIS. Referred to: 78, 80n

DUROZOIR, CHARLES. Biography of Turgot. In *Biographie universelle ancienne et moderne*. Ed. Louis Gabriel Michaud. 52 vols. Paris: Michaud frères, 1811-28, XLVII, 63-84.
NOTE: the quotations of the same passage are in quotations from Carlyle; the first is indirect.
QUOTED: 147, 166
REFERRED TO: 80

DUSAULX, JEAN JOSEPH. *De l'insurrection parisienne, et de la prise de la Bastille*. In *Mémoires de Linguet, sur la Bastille, et de Dusaulx, sur le 14 juillet*. Ed. Saint Albin Berville and Jean François Barrière. Paris: Baudouin, 1821.
NOTE: the quotation (for collation see Carlyle, *French Revolution*) and references are in quotations from Carlyle, who appears to have used this edition, which is part of *Collection des mémoires*, ed. Berville and Barrière *q.v.* Carlyle so conflates and modifies his sources that precise identification is usually impossible.
QUOTED: 152
REFERRED TO: 143-7

DU VAL D'EPRÉMESNIL, JEAN JACQUES.
NOTE: the reference at 7 is in a quotation from Mignet. Mignet and JSM use the spelling Epréménil.
REFERRED TO: 7, 74

DUVEYRIER, CHARLES. *Lettres politiques*. 2 vols. Paris: Beck and Amyot, 1843.
REVIEWED: 295-316
QUOTED: 301, 302, 303, 308, 308-9, 309, 309-10, 310, 311, 311-12, 312, 314
301.14-29   When . . . smaller.] [*translated from:*] Quand une place vient à vaquer, grande ou petite, que se passe-t-il? Sur les quatre cent cinquante députés qui sont au courant de tout, parce qu'ils ont le droit de pénétrer chaque jour et à toute heure dans les bureaux du ministère, il y en a vingt ou trente qui commencent le siége. La tactique est simple. On dit au ministre: vous nommerez tel ou tel parent de tel de mes électeurs, ou je vous retire mon appui. Que peut faire le ministre? Louvoyer, opposer les prétentions et les exigences, donner de l'espoir à tous, et attendre, pour prendre un parti, que de nouvelles vacances viennent offrir l'expectative d'un dédommagement aux solliciteurs éconduits. Heureuses les administrations comme celles de la marine, de l'enregistrement et des domaines, de l'armée, où des règles ont d'avance fixé le mode d'admission et d'avancement. Et encore, quelle latitude offerte à la faveur! et dans l'exécution, trop souvent, quel mépris de la justice! La faveur, voilà la plaie morale, la maladie chronique du gouvernement. [*4½-paragraph omission*] Les mandataires de la bourgeoisie, ne trouvant plus de privilégiés, au lieu d'abolir les priviléges s'en emparèrent, et les électeurs, au lieu de s'indigner et de gourmander leurs députés pour avoir usurpé les priviléges des gros emplois, trouvèrent plus simple et plus avantageux de s'attribuer les petits. (I, 168-70)
301.33-8   The . . . laws,] [*translated from:*] [*no paragraph*] Il ne faut pas se faire illusion; le plus grand distributeur des graces aujourd'hui, c'est le corps électoral, qui n'entretient ses mandataires que d'intérêts de localité et de parenté, et qui circonscrit leurs espérances de réélection dans une infinité de cercles si différens les uns des autres, si changeans, si personnels, qu'il n'y a pas de ministre qui puisse aborder une grande entreprise d'intérêt public avec la certitude du succès, témoin M. Molé avec les chemins de fer, M. Guizot avec l'union douanière, M. Cunin-Gridaine avec la loi des sucres. (I, 170-1)
302.37   Vous n'avez] En résumé, Monsieur [Guizot], vous n'avez (I, 66)
302.38   transformer. . . . Redoutez les] transformer. Soyez franchement national dans le droit de visite; dans la politique intérieure redoutez les (I, 66)
303.7   clarté.] clarté! (I, 67)
303.17-31   Politics . . . hesitate.] [*translated from:*] [*no paragraph*] La politique, se disent-ils, a changé d'aspect; les esprits se sont calmés; il n'y a plus de situation violente où de grands principes, de grandes passions, de grands intérêts publics soient mis en question; dès-lors,

qu'importe que le candidat soit un peu plus ou un peu moins de l'opposition, ce sera un peu plus ou un peu moins de paroles dans un sens ou dans un autre. Franchement, quand on voit les hommes d'Etat les plus opposés déclarer qu'ils ne gouverneraient pas différemment les uns des autres, l'électeur n'est-il pas en droit de traiter les questions de personnes avec indifférence, et de porter sur son intérêt personnel le degré de sollicitude qu'il leur eût accordé? [*paragraph*] Mais c'est horrible! la constitution alors est faussée dans son principe; qui dit gouvernement représentatif dit un gouvernement où l'opinion sincère du pays est avant tout représentée!—Eh! sans doute! mais si le pays n'a pas d'opinion? Voilà un incident que la constitution n'a pas prévu; et, croyez-moi, c'est le cas de beaucoup d'électeurs, l'enquête l'a suffisamment prouvé. Ne vous étonnez donc pas que nombre de gens soient séduits par ce calcul naïf: "Voici un candidat qui fera le bonheur du pays; en voici un autre qui fera le bonheur du pays et le mien; je serais un sot d'hésiter." (II, 171-2)

308.35-7   "The . . . divided."] [*translated from:*] [*paragraph*] Les meilleurs esprits, les coeurs les plus dévoués à la royauté nouvelle ne peuvent considérer aujourd'hui sans effroi le mince intervalle qui sépare les deux forces entre lesquelles se partage désormais le gouvernement; et les voyant armées pour l'attaque bien plus que pour la défense, sans barrières, sans remparts qui les mettent à l'abri d'un coup de main, les hommes d'Etat se demandent, si quelque circonstance imprévue rallumait les hostilités, de quel côté serait la victoire. (I, 71-2)

308.39-309.11   when . . . disappear.] [*translated from:*] [*paragraph*] Les événemens enfantés par la première révolution avaient déjà prouvé que lorsque le pouvoir populaire et le pouvoir royal sont seuls en face l'un de l'autre, la lutte commence et que l'un des deux doit inévitablement dominer l'autre. Il est vrai qu'un principe nouveau a réglé leurs rapports depuis l'établissement du 9 août; et peut-être n'a-t-on pas suffisamment apprécié jusqu'à ce jour l'heureuse influence que doit exercer sur nos destinées futures ce dernier compromis. Sous la préoccupation des périls qui menaçaient la jeune monarchie, il était naturel qu'elle frappât davantage les esprits par ses lacunes que par ses élémens d'ordre et de stabilité; c'est ce qui est arrivé. [*preceding entry immediately follows*] De la république ou de la monarchie absolue, ils se demandent laquelle doit inspirer le plus de crainte. Et c'est un devoir d'instruire votre Altesse Royale que dans l'état des esprits, la république n'est pas considérée comme le danger le plus imminent ni le plus redoutable. "La sagesse du Roi, dit-on, a fortifié la royauté; mais les précautions par lesquelles le pouvoir populaire avait prétendu assurer son contrôle ont tourné à sa confusion; la bourgeoisie ne fait usage de ses droits que pour décomposer par l'intrigue des Cabinets qui ne se maintiennent que par les faveurs. Perdant ainsi sa propre estime par l'intrigue et l'estime des autres par les faveurs, quel frein salutaire pourrait-elle opposer au pouvoir exécutif que l'intérêt des ministres est d'étendre incessamment? Sous cette double déconsidération qui paralyse l'action de ses mandataires, la France, dans un avenir plus ou moins lointain, marche fatalement au despotisme. Mais après le despotisme viennent les révolutions, et dans les révolutions les dynasties disparaissent." (I, 71-2)

309.16   La] [*no paragraph*] La (I, 74)

309.16   n'est-elle] n'est-ce (I, 74)

309.41-310.1   originated . . . too.] [*translated from:*] [*paragraph*] Si je remonte à son origine, j'observe que la noblesse, dont nos pères ont vu les derniers instans, avait pris naissance dans la diversité de certaines fonctions militaires et dans les rapports hiérarchiques qui s'étaient établis entr'elles. Les ducs commandaient les armées; les marquis veillaient sur les frontières; les comtes gouvernaient les provinces; les barons étaient les principaux officiers attachés à la personne du monarque; les chevaliers, des officiers inférieurs. La plupart de ces fonctions furent d'abord personnelles et la noblesse qu'elles conféraient l'était aussi. (I, 76-7)

310.5-9   *Noblesse . . . dishonour.*] [*translated from:*] [*no paragraph*] *Noblesse oblige!* Tel était le premier enseignement que recevait l'héritier du nom. Il avait l'obligation de tous les sentimens généreux, de la magnificence, de l'intrépidité, tant était universelle l'opinion que le titre était seulement le signe d'une fonction, et les priviléges qu'il conférait, la juste récompense de services publics, de devoirs auxquels le titulaire n'aurait pu se soustraire sans lâcheté et sans déshonneur. (I, 77-8)

310.15-35   The . . . blood.] [*translated from:*] La question n'est pas d'ennoblir les hommes en leur distribuant les titres de fonctions publiques qui ont cessé d'exister depuis huit ou dix siècles. La question aujourd'hui est d'ennoblir les fonctions modernes et les emplois publics, et de les élever peu à peu à un tel degré d'honneur que leurs qualifications deviennent, pour les races futures, de véritables titres de noblesse. [*paragraph*] Ainsi, la noblesse qu'il s'agit de créer c'est la noblesse gouvernementale, et, à vrai dire, il n'en a jamais existé d'autre. Si l'on entend par aristocratie, un corps d'individus distingués par des titres, par des qualités auxquelles ne sont attachées aucunes des attributions du Gouvernement, soyez assuré, Monseigneur, qu'il s'agit d'une noblesse à son déclin; mais l'histoire nous l'a prouvé: à son origine, ou à son apogée, toute aristocratie gouverne. Ce qu'il faut donc ennoblir aujourd'hui, c'est la fonction, c'est le pouvoir, ce sont les charges publiques. Il faut désirer voir se répandre cette idée que tout homme qui prend part au gouvernement de son pays, doit montrer plus de vertu, plus de patriotisme, plus de grandeur d'âme que le vulgaire. C'était déjà l'esprit de l'ancienne noblesse; au temps de sa splendeur, il existait des gens qui pouvaient subordonner l'intérêt de l'Etat à leurs intérêts de famille; il y en avait d'autres pour qui c'était un devoir constant de sacrifier la famille à l'Etat. Les premiers, lorsque l'ennemi foulait le sol français, pouvaient sans déshonneur éviter le danger, s'enfermer dans leurs maisons, se conserver pour leurs femmes et leurs enfans; c'étaient les bourgeois, les vilains, taillables et corvéables; mais les autres étaient obligés de tout quitter, femmes, enfans, terres et manoir, pour voler à l'ennemi; c'étaient les nobles qui devaient au Pays l'impôt du sang. (I, 83-4)

311.1-12   Fixity . . . incapacity.] [*translated from:*] La fixité d'abord; rien de plus contraire à l'influence que doit exercer l'administrateur sur ses administrés que ces fréquens changemens de résidence qui permettent à un bien petit nombre de se familiariser avec les besoins particuliers à leurs localités, et d'attirer la confiance publique. [*paragraph*] La responsabilité ensuite; la centralisation excessive, qui place dans la main des ministres, seuls responsables, la décision des plus simples questions et la distribution des plus petits emplois, enlève à l'exercice du pouvoir sa considération en son autorité. Le crédit que tout employé inférieur peut opposer, par la personne des députés, à la juste surveillance de ses supérieurs, détruit les liens de la hiérarchie, décourage bien vite le zèle. Quel dévoûment attendre d'un fonctionnaire qui ne peut ni protéger le talent, ni réprimer l'insolence, ni congédier la paresse ou l'incapacité? (I, 85)

311.25-36   On . . . ornaments.] [*translated from:*] D'un côté, le rôle politique imposé à la plupart des fonctionnaires administratifs, tous les services relatifs aux élections et à la formation des majorités, services qu'ils ont dû rendre à l'autorité supérieure en dehors de leurs fonctions, ont diminué peu à peu la considération attachée à la carrière des emplois publics et en ont éloigné les grands propriétaires, les héritiers des noms illustres et des fortunes considérables. [*paragraph*] De l'autre côté, la réduction excessive des traitemens a rendu de plus en plus impossible l'exercice des fonctions administratives aux personnes qui ne jouissent pas d'une fortune patrimoniale. L'absence de concours et d'examens pour l'admission à la plupart des emplois civils, la haute influence exercée sur les ministres, sur les distributeurs des fonctions par les députés et les collèges électoraux ont éloigné, même des places les plus minimes et les plus obscures, la classe nombreuse d'où la république et l'empire avaient fait surgir tant de dévouemens et tant d'illustrations. (II, 4-5)

311.37-312.4   What . . . France? . . . The . . . *propriété*.]   [*translated from:*] [*no paragraph*] Qu'est-il resté de cette grande tentative impériale qui honorait le génie et les services publics et savait leur créer des positions égales aux plus grandes positions de la noblesse européenne? Qu'est devenu aujourd'hui ce proverbe national qui était alors une vérité dans toutes les branches de l'activité administrative, que le dernier conscrit portait dans sa giberne le bâton de maréchal de France? [*ellipsis indicates 4-sentence omission*] [*paragraph*] Aujourd'hui, les grandes existences créées par l'empire ne sont plus qu'un souvenir; celle que la restauration n'avait pas créée, mais qu'elle avait satisfaite, à qui elle avait donné la première part dans le gouvernement des affaires communes, la grande propriété vit isolée, mécontente, égarée sur ses propres intérêts, faisant alliance, par dépit, avec ses ennemis les plus dangereux. La classe agricole et ouvrière est reléguée dans ses fermes, dans ses ateliers, et aucune sollicitude, aucun effort du gouvernement ne vient recruter dans son sein les grands dévouemens, les grands génies, comme aux beaux jours de la république et de l'empire. La bourgeoisie seule gouverne; nouvelle égalité, nouveau nivellement qui prétend tout abaisser à de mesquines proportions et concentrer tous les droits dans les régions moyennes de la petite propriété. (II, 41-2)

312.6-9   It . . . does. . . . Every . . . budget.] [*translated from:*] On dit avec raison que l'Américain ne croit pas à la misère; ce qui le rend très entreprenant en industrie. Le Français y croit. [*ellipsis indicates 6-sentence omission*] Tout petit électeur est conservateur-né de son patrimoine, et ne voulant rien hasarder pour l'établissement de ses enfans, il est invinciblement entraîné à grossir l'éternel surnumérariat des petits emplois inscrits au budget. (II, 170)

312.19-23 The . . . suspicion.] [*translated from:*] Le pouvoir exécutif, interdisant à ses agens toute démarche, toute influence officielle dans les opérations du corps électoral, rendrait immédiatement aux fonctions publiques leur honneur et leur dignité. L'habileté véritable, l'intelligence, l'expérience, le dévoûment, le patriotisme des serviteurs de l'Etat ne seraient plus à tout instant mis en suspicion. (II, 34)

314.1-4 Elle forme . . . entier. . . . L'oeuvre . . . civilisation.] On reconnaîtra, ce qui est la conséquence du caractère, des moeurs, de l'histoire du peuple français, que sa part dans le grand travail des nations, c'est le perfectionnement des institutions publiques, de l'égalité civile, de la sociabilité humaine et qu'elle forme . . . entier. [*ellipsis indicates 2-page omission*] [*paragraph*] Quand la France aura une intelligence nette de sa destinée sur le globe; quand un Cabinet tout entier aura le courage de proclamer hautement que l'oeuvre . . . civilisation, alors seulement les masses pourront comprendre toute la grandeur du règne de Louis-Philippe. (II, 127, 129)

———— *La pairie dans ses rapports avec la situation politique; son principe, ses ressources, son avenir.* Paris: Guyot, 1842.
REVIEWED: 297-316
QUOTED: 299, 299n, 303, 304, 305

299.27-8 "which . . . business."] [*translated in part from:*] [*paragraph*] Si la Pairie considérait ce mode comme son arche de salut, comme l'unique moyen de conquérir le rang et le pouvoir auxquels elle a droit, elle s'épuiserait en efforts impuissans, et sa tactique ne serait pas sans danger; car prétendre introduire dans l'institution un nouveau principe, quand la loi qui la constitue compte à peine dix années d'existence, n'est-ce pas remettre en question la Charte tout entière, offrir une arme puissante aux partisans de la réforme, ranimer enfin de vieilles querelles qui détournent l'esprit public des véritables affaires du pays, et les hommes d'Etat de leur gestion? (2)

299n.4-8 "Study . . . created."] [*translated from:*] "Etudiez les masses, et vous verrez qu'il s'y passe quelque chose de semblable à la disposition qui a précédé la majorité de Louis XIV après la Fronde, et l'établissement du Consulat à la fin du siècle dernier. Même lassitude, même dégoût du bruit et de l'agitation, même affaiblissement de l'esprit de défiance, même indifférence pour les droits qu'il avait créés. (36-7)

303.36-304.2 There . . . manufactures.] [*translated from:*] Il a existé depuis 1830 deux politiques distinctes: [*paragraph*] L'une, que l'on peut appeler *politique constituante*, s'est appliquée à fonder la constitution, à la développer, à la défendre contre les attaques des partis et les répugnances de l'Europe. [*paragraph*] L'autre, que l'on peut nommer *politique des affaires*, s'est appliquée à protéger, à favoriser les intérêts, les travaux de la société dans les arts, les sciences, la religion, l'organisation militaire et diplomatique, l'administration intérieure, le commerce, l'agriculture, l'industrie. (3)

304.6-34 Unhappily . . . fractions. . . . Time . . . majority. . . . Were . . . remedy.] [*translated from:*] Malheureusement il n'en est pas ainsi pour la *politique des affaires*, qui n'a pas encore inspiré aux hommes d'Etat un programme, un systême de gouvernement spécial à cette politique. Aussi, dès que l'existence de la monarchie n'est plus menacée, dès que les principes fondamentaux des constitutions ne sont plus mis en question, que voyons-nous? [*paragraph*] Le pouvoir devient faible, incertain, embarrassé. La majorité se décompose en nuances infinies, l'accord entre les Chambres semble compromis. [*ellipsis indicates omission of previous clause plus a page*] Le temps a résolu la plupart des questions de politique constituante soulevées au dedans et au dehors par l'établissement du régime nouveau, et il donne aujourd'hui la prépondérance en France et en Europe à la politique des affaires. Or, il n'y a pas encore en France de systême de gouvernement dans les affaires. L'opposition, à cet égard, n'est pas plus avancée que la majorité. Nous croyons donc qu'au-dessus de la lutte des opinions et des partis il y a, au moment où nous écrivons, un intérêt supérieur, une nécessité urgente qui domine tout, même la question de cabinet. [*ellipsis indicates omission of preceding sentence*] [*paragraph*] Le cabinet serait renversé, que celui qui lui succéderait rencontrerait bientôt les mêmes attaques et les mêmes embarras, et il aurait moins de force pour en triompher, car il n'arriverait pas pour réparer des fautes, pour sauver le pays d'un dangereux entraînement. Aucune grande situation ne se rattacherait à son existence. Ce serait recommencer la carrière funeste des hésitations et des tâtonnemens dont la dissolution du ministère Molé fut le prélude. [*preceding sentence omitted in translation*] [*paragraph*] Avec un système général de gouvernement dans les affaires, la situation change. [*paragraph*] S'il produit au grand jour et s'il rallie à lui les esprits éminens de toutes les nuances de la majorité, de deux choses l'une: ou le ministère l'adoptera, et il lui devra, dans ce cas, son salut, ou il le dédaignera, et le système alors deviendra un instrument d'opposition d'où sortira tôt ou tard un cabinet durable. [*paragraph*] Telle est, au fond, la véritable situation politique avec ses difficultés et ses exigences. Le plus grand service que l'on puisse rendre aujourd'hui au pays, c'est d'introduire au milieu de ses affaires si languissantes, si épineuses, si complexes un système général de gouvernement qui domine les intrigues, les petites passions des coteries qui ont remplacé les factions, et qui fasse intervenir dans les discussions un nouvel intérêt public assez considérable pour imposer aux industries et aux localités rivales l'union et l'accord. [*paragraph*] Douze années d'omnipotence parlementaire ont prouvé que cette tâche était au-dessus des forces de la Chambre des députés. Les embarras les plus grands viennent de sa propre composition. Ce n'est pas d'elle qu'on doit attendre le remède. (4-6)

305.24-37 Every . . . services.] [*translated from:*] En réalité, chaque peuple renferme et renfermera toujours probablement une administration et un public, c'est-à-dire deux sociétés: l'une dont l'intérêt commun est la loi suprême, où le principe de l'hérédité ne distribue pas les positions, qui classe les travailleurs d'après leur mérite, et les rétribue d'après leurs oeuvres, et qui compense la modicité des salaires par leur fixité et surtout par l'honneur et la considération; l'autre, composée de propriétaires, de capitalistes, de maîtres et d'ouvriers, dont la loi suprême est celle de l'héritage, dont la règle principale de conduite est l'intérêt personnel, dont la concurrence et la lutte sont les éléments favoris. [*paragraph*] Ces deux société [*sic*] se servent mutuellement de contre-poids; elles agissent et réagissent continuellement l'une sur l'autre. La tendance du public est d'introduire dans l'administration le principe d'émulation qui lui manque; le penchant de l'administration, conforme à sa mission, est d'introduire de plus en plus dans la grande masse du public des élémens d'ordre et de prévoyance. Dans cette double direction, l'administration et le public se sont rendus et se rendent journellement des services réciproques. (12)

EDGAR (of England). Referred to: 47n

EDWARD I (of England). Referred to: 38, 292

EDWARD III (of England). Referred to: 234

EDWARD (Prince of Wales).
NOTE: known as the Black Prince.
REFERRED TO: 36n, 43

EDWARD THE CONFESSOR (of England). Referred to: 25

EICHHORN, JOHANN GOTTFRIED. *Antiqua historia ex ipsis veterum scriptorum grae-corum narrationibus contexta*. 4 vols. Leipzig: Weidmann, 1811-12.
REFERRED TO: *368n*

—— *Antiqua historia ex ipsis veterum scriptorum latinorum narrationibus contexta*. 2 vols. Leipzig: Hahn, 1811.
REFERRED TO: *368n*

ELIE, JACOB JOB.
NOTE: the references are in a quotation from Carlyle.
REFERRED TO: 145, 146, 147

ELIZABETH I (of England).
NOTE: the reference at 293 is in a quotation from Guizot.
REFERRED TO: 293, 348

ELLIS, GEORGE. See George Canning, "New Morality."

ELLIS, GEORGE JAMES WELBORE AGAR. *The True History of the State-Prisoner*

Commonly Called "The Iron Mask;" Extracted from Documents in the French Archives. London: Murray, 1826.
NOTE: reviewed, with Delort, by Francis Palgrave, *Quarterly Review*, XXXIV (June, 1826), 19-35.
REFERRED TO: 62

ENGHIEN, LOUIS ANTOINE HENRI DE BOURBON CONDÉ, DUC D'. See Charles X, *Mémoire*.

ENTRAGUES. See Antraigues.

EPICURUS.
NOTE: the reference is in a quotation from Carlyle.
REFERRED TO: 166

EPRÉMÉNIL. See Du Val d'Eprémesnil.

ESCHERNY, FRANÇOIS LOUIS, COMTE D'. *La philosophie de la politique, ou Principes généraux sur les institutions civiles, politiques et religieuses*. 2 vols. Paris: n.p., 1796.
NOTE: the quotation is taken from an Appendix to Vol. II of Campan's *Mémoires* (*q.v.* for the collation).
QUOTED: 284-5
REFERRED TO: 285n

ESTREVILLE, PÉRONNE D'.
NOTE: the reference derives from Dulaure.
REFERRED TO: 49

EUDES I, DUC DE BOURGOGNE. Referred to: 29

EUDES, COMTE DE BLOIS ET DE CHAMPAGNE.
NOTE: Eudes II of Blois; Eudes I of Champagne; JSM is mistaken in referring to him as brother of Henry I.
REFERRED TO: 29

The Examiner.
NOTE: the reference is to the *Examiner*'s articles on France, 1830-34, most of which were written by JSM himself.
REFERRED TO: 125

EXELMANS, RÉMI JOSEPH ISADORE, COMTE. Speech in the French Chamber of Peers (16 Dec., 1834), *National*, 17 Dec., 1834, 2.
NOTE: JSM uses the spelling Excelmans.
REFERRED TO: 198

FANTIN DES ODOARDS, ANTOINE ETIENNE NICOLAS. *Histoire philosophique de la révolution de France* (1796). New rev. ed. 4 vols. Paris: Perlet, *et al.*, 1797.
NOTE: JSM uses the spelling Desodoards.
REFERRED TO: 75n

FAUCHER, LÉONARD JOSEPH. Referred to: 337

FAUCHET, CLAUDE, ABBÉ.
NOTE: the reference is in a quotation from Carlyle.
REFERRED TO: 146

FÉNELON, FRANÇOIS SALIGNAC DE LA MOTHE.
NOTE: the reference, in a quotation from Carlyle, derives from Montgaillard.
REFERRED TO: 140

FERDINAND VII (of Spain). Referred to: 89, 179

FERRIÈRES, CHARLES ELIE, MARQUIS DE. *Mémoires du marquis de Ferrières, avec une notice sur sa vie, des notes et des éclaircissemens historiques* (1821). 2nd ed. 3 vols. Paris: Baudouin, 1821-22.

NOTE: part of *Collection des mémoires*, ed. Berville and Barrière, *q.v.*
QUOTED: 88, 91, 96, 107
REFERRED TO: 73n, 74n, 75n, 76n, 85n, 87n, 88, 94, 96, 100n, 108
88.9-10 "Trente régimens," . . . "marchaient . . . états";] [*paragraph*] Cependant trente régimens marchaient . . . états. (I, 71)
88.16 étaient] s'étaient [*treated as typographical error in this ed.*] (I, 130)
88.27 desseins] intérêts (I, 131)
88.28-9 *au . . . Paris*] [*not in italics*] (I, 131)
88.30 états-généraux] états (I, 131)
88.30 *enlever les députés*] [*not in italics*] (I, 131)
88.31 *en . . . force*] [*not in italics*] (I, 131)
88.32 *dissoudre l'assemblée*] [*not in italics*] (I, 131)
88.33 les] la [*treated as typographical error in this ed.*] (I, 131)
91.13-14 pas même une] pas une (I, 75)
91.16 "Ils] On eût dit que les nouveaux ministres, assurés du succès, laissaient marcher l'insurrection, et voulaient autoriser le déploiement des mesures de rigueur qu'ils étaient résolus d'employer; ils (I, 115-16)
96.22-3 "ne . . . guerre, de sang, et de vengeance."] La plupart, indiscrets, bouffis d'orgueil, irrités de la moindre résistance, ne . . . guerre, que de sang, que de vengeance. (II, 254)
107.10-11 "les Girondins . . . vues,"] [*paragraph*] Les Girondins . . . vues; c'était une mesure extrême qui avait ses dangers: ils résolurent de hasarder encore une démarche, et de tenter le rétablissement des trois ministres disgraciés. (III, 165)
107.19-20 "la république . . . Girondins";] La république . . . girondins, ni dans celle de la grande majorité de la nation. (III, 242)

FERRON, JOURDAN. Referred to: 49

FIELDING, HENRY. *Joseph Andrews* (1742). In *Works with a Life of the Author*. 12 vols. London: Otridge and Rackham, *et al.*, 1824, V-VI.
NOTE: in SC. The reference is to Parson Adams.
REFERRED TO: 164

FIESCHI, GIUSEPPE. Referred to: 178, 205, 208

FILICAJA, VINCENZIO DA. "All'Italia, Sonnetto 1." In *Poesie toscane*. Florence: Matini, 1707.
QUOTED: *376n*
376n.8 Dono . . . bellezza.] Italia, Italia, o tu, cui feo la Sorte / Dono . . . bellezza, onde hai / Funesta dote d'infiniti guai, / Che in fronte scritti per gran doglia porte. (320; ll. 1-4)

FLESSELLES, JACQUES DE.
NOTE: the reference is in a quotation from Carlyle.
REFERRED TO: 145

FLOCON, FERDINAND.
NOTE: the reference at 321 is to him as one of four accepted into the Provisional Government of 1848; that at 332 is to him as one of its members.
REFERRED TO: 321, 332

FLORUS, DREPANIUS. "Querela de divisione imperii post mortem Ludovici Pii." In *Recueil des historiens des Gaules et de la France*. Ed. Martin Bouquet, *et al.* 24 vols. Paris: Aux dépens des libraires associés, *et al.*, 1738-1904, VII, 301-4.
NOTE: the reference derives from Guizot.
REFERRED TO: 280

FONFRÈDE, JEAN BAPTISTE BOYER. Referred to: 107

FOUCHÉ, JOSEPH.
NOTE: the quotation (repeated) has not been located in a primary source.
QUOTED: 174, 175
REFERRED TO: 174

morale? est-ce qu'il n'était pas évident aux yeux de tous que cette grande révolution avait été précédée par une réaction réelle, irrésistible, contre la corruption, dans tout ce qu'il y avait d'honnête et de généreux dans le coeur de la France? (2966)

Gazette de France.
NOTE: the reference, an indirect quotation in a quotation from Dulaure, is to criticism of Dulaure's *Histoire* (*q.v.*) in Oct., 1821; the specific terms do not occur in the mention of the work on 18 Oct., or in the review of it on 30 Aug.
REFERRED TO: 21n

GENGHIS KHAN. Referred to: 24

GENSONNÉ, ARMAND.
NOTE: the references at 102-3 are in a quotation from Bailleul. See also Guadet, "Copie."
REFERRED TO: 102-3, 106, 107, 108

GEORGEL, JEAN FRANÇOIS. *Mémoires pour servir à l'histoire des événemens de la fin du dix-huitième siècle depuis 1760 jusqu'en 1806-1810, par un contemporain impartial.* 6 vols. Paris: Eymery and Delaunay, 1817-18.
REFERRED TO: 79n, 108

GEORGET.
NOTE: not otherwise identified; the reference is in a quotation from Carlyle.
REFERRED TO: 145

GERBERT. See Sylvester II.

GIBBON, EDWARD. *The History of the Decline and Fall of the Roman Empire.* 6 vols. London: Strahan and Cadell, 1776-88.
REFERRED TO: 134, 136, 264

GILDAS. *Opus novum. Gildas britannus monachus cui sapientis cognomatu est inditum, de calamitate excidio, & conquestu britanniae, quam angliam nunc vocant, author vetustus a multis diu desyderatus, & nuper in gratiam.* Ed. Polydore Vergil and Robert Ridley. London: Tonstall, 1525.
NOTE: Gildas is the source for the story that Aetius, a Roman consul, received in 446 A.D. a letter entitled "The Groans of the Britons." The reference is in a quotation from Guizot.
REFERRED TO: 263

GIRARDIN, EMILE DE. Referred to: 212n

GLÜCK, CHRISTOPH WILLIBALD VON. *Iphegenia in Aulis* (1774).
NOTE: the reference, in a quotation from Carlyle, is to an anecdote told by Guillaume Olivier de Corancez in the *Journal de Paris*, 21 Aug., 1788, 1009-10.
REFERRED TO: 147

GODWIN (Earl of Wessex). Referred to: 25, 26

GODWIN, WILLIAM. *Things As They Are; or, The Adventures of Caleb Williams* (1794). 4th ed. 3 vols. London: Simpkin and Marshall, 1816.
NOTE: in SC.
REFERRED TO: 157, 299

GOETHE, JOHANN WOLFGANG VON.
NOTE: see also Sarah Austin, *Characteristics.*
REFERRED TO: 184

——— *Wilhelm Meisters Lehrjahre* (1795-96). In *Werke.* 55 vols. in 36. Stuttgart and Tübingen: Cotta'schen Buchhandlung, 1828-33, XVIII-XX.
NOTE: in SC. The quotation is in a quotation from Carlyle.
QUOTED: 151
REFERRED TO: *379*
151.3-4 "Man," . . . "is for ever interesting to man; nay, properly there is nothing else interesting."] [*translated from:*] Sie haben Recht, versetzte er mit einiger Verlegenheit, der

GUINARD, AUGUSTE.
NOTE: the reference is to the leading members of the Société des Droits de l'Homme.
REFERRED TO: 128

GUIZOT, FRANÇOIS PIERRE GUILLAUME.
NOTE: the reference at 301 is in a quotation from Duveyrier.
REFERRED TO: 134n, 185, 188, 190, 192, 193, 227-30, 231, 259-94 *passim*, 301, 302, *367-93*

———— *Cours d'histoire moderne: histoire de la civilisation en France, depuis la chute de l'empire romain jusqu'en 1789.* 5 vols. Paris: Pichon and Didier, 1829-32.
NOTE: in SC, with "I" to "V" on spines; cf. the next entry, which has the same general title. We have adopted the short title JSM uses, i.e., *Civilisation en France*.
REVIEWED: 257-94, *367-93*
QUOTED: 271-2, 275, 276, 276-7, 277, 277-8, 278, 279, 280, 281, 286-7, 287, 287-8, *375, 376, 377, 378, 389, 389-90, 392*
REFERRED TO: 186, 228, 229, 230, 231

271.36-272.41 Liberty . . . authority.] [*translated from:*] Un fait immense, et beaucoup trop peu remarqué, à mon avis, me frappe d'abord; c'est que le principe de la liberté de penser, le principe de toute philosophie, la raison se prenant elle-même pour point de départ et pour guide, est une idée essentiellement fille de l'antiquité, une idée que la société moderne tient de la Grèce et de Rome. Nous ne l'avons évidemment reçue ni du Christianisme, ni de la Germanie, car elle n'était contenue ni dans l'un ni dans l'autre de ces élémens de notre civilisation. Elle était puissante au contraire, dominante dans la civilisation gréco-romaine: c'est là sa véritable origine; c'est là le legs le plus précieux qu'ait fait l'antiquité au monde moderne; legs qui n'a jamais été absolument suspendu et sans valeur, car vous avez vu l'idée mère de la philosophie, le droit de la raison à partir d'elle-même, animant les ouvrages et la vie de Jean-le-Scot, et le principe de la liberté de la pensée debout encore, au IXe siècle, en face du principe de l'autorité. (III, 191-2)

275.15-44 We . . . it.] [*translated from:*] [*no paragraph*] Tout à l'heure, nous assistions au dernier âge de la civilisation romaine, et nous la trouvions en pleine décadence, sans force, sans fécondité, sans éclat, incapable, pour ainsi dire, de subsister. La voilà vaincue, ruinée par les barbares; et tout à coup elle reparaît, puissante, féconde; elle exerce sur les institutions et les moeurs qui s'y viennent associer, un prodigieux empire; elle leur imprime de plus en plus son caractère; elle domine, elle métamorphose ses vainqueurs. [*paragraph*] Deux causes, entre beaucoup d'autres, ont produit ce résultat: la puissance d'une législation civile, forte et bien liée; l'ascendant naturel de la civilisation sur la barbarie. [*paragraph*] En se fixant, en devenant propriétaires, les barbares contractèrent, soit entre eux, soit avec les Romains, des relations beaucoup plus variées et plus durables que celles qu'ils avaient connues jusqu'alors; leur existence civile prit plus d'étendue et de permanence. La loi romaine pouvait seule la régler; elle seule était en mesure de suffire à tant de rapports. Les barbares, tout en conservant leurs coutumes, tout en demeurant les maîtres du pays, se trouvèrent pris, pour ainsi dire, dans les filets de cette législation savante, et obligés de lui soumettre, en grande partie, non sans doute sous le point de vue politique, mais en matière civile, le nouvel ordre social. [*paragraph*] Le spectacle seul de la civilisation romaine exerçait d'ailleurs sur leur imagination un grand empire. Ce qui émeut aujourd'hui notre imagination, ce qu'elle cherche avec avidité dans l'histoire, les poèmes, les voyages, les romans, c'est le spectacle d'une société étrangère à la régularité de la nôtre; c'est la vie sauvage, son indépendance, sa nouveauté, ses aventures. Autres étaient les impressions des barbares; c'est la civilisation qui les frappait, qui leur semblait grande et merveilleuse: les monumens de l'activité romaine, ces cités, ces routes, ces aqueducs, ces arènes, toute cette société si régulière, si prévoyante, si variée dans sa fixité, c'était là le sujet de leur étonnement, de leur admiration. Vainqueurs, ils se sentaient inférieurs aux vaincus; le barbare pouvait mépriser individuellement le romain; mais le monde romain, dans son ensemble, lui apparaissait comme quelque chose de supérieur; et tous les grands hommes de l'âge de la conquête, les Alaric, les Ataulphe, les Théodoric et tant d'autres, en détruisant et foulant aux pieds la société romaine, faisaient tous leurs efforts pour l'imiter. (I, 386-8)

276.26-33 The . . . mankind? . . .] [*translated from:*] [*no paragraph*] On lui rend même souvent des hommages aveugles; on lui prodigue, pour ainsi dire, au hasard le génie et la gloire. Et en même temps, on répète qu'il n'a rien fait, rien fondé, que son empire, ses lois, toutes ses oeuvres ont péri avec lui. Et ce lieu commun historique amène une foule de lieux communs moraux sur l'impuissance des grands hommes, leur inutilité, la vanité de leurs desseins, et le peu de traces réelles qu'ils laissent dans le monde, après l'avoir sillonné en tous sens. [*paragraph*] Tout cela serait-il vrai, Messieurs? La destinée des grands hommes ne serait-elle en effet que de peser sur le genre humain et de l'étonner? [*final ellipsis indicates 3-sentence omission*] (II, 262-3)

276.34-277.30   At . . . him.] [*translated from:*] Au premier aspect, il semble qu'il en soit ainsi, et que le lieu commun ait raison. Ces victoires, ces conquêtes, ces institutions, ces réformes, ces desseins, toute cette grandeur, toute cette gloire de Charlemagne se sont évanouies avec lui; on dirait un météore sorti tout à coup des ténèbres de la barbarie pour s'aller perdre et éteindre aussitôt dans les ténèbres de la féodalité. Et l'exemple n'est pas unique dans l'histoire; le monde a vu plus d'une fois, nous avons vu nous-mêmes un empire semblable, un empire qui prenait plaisir à se comparer à celui de Charlemagne, et en avait le droit, nous l'avons vu tomber également avec un homme. [*paragraph*] Gardez-vous cependant, Messieurs, d'en croire ici les apparences: pour comprendre le sens des grands évènemens et mesurer l'action des grands hommes, il faut pénétrer plus avant. [*paragraph*] Il y a dans l'activité d'un grand homme deux parts; il joue deux rôles: on peut marquer deux époques dans sa carrière. Il comprend mieux que tout autre les besoins de son temps, les besoins réels, actuels, ce qu'il faut à la société contemporaine pour vivre et se développer régulièrement. Il le comprend, dis-je, mieux que tout autre, et il sait aussi mieux que tout autre s'emparer de toutes les forces sociales et les diriger vers ce but. De là son pouvoir et sa gloire: c'est là ce qui fait qu'il est, dès qu'il paraît, compris, accepté, suivi, que tous se prêtent et concourent à l'action qu'il exerce au profit de tous. [*paragraph*] Il ne s'en tient point là: les besoins réels et généraux de son temps à peu près satisfaits, la pensée et la volonté du grand homme vont plus loin. Il s'élance hors des faits actuels; il se livre à des vues qui lui sont personnelles; il se complaît à des combinaisons plus ou moins vastes, plus ou moins spécieuses, mais qui ne se fondent point, comme ses premiers travaux, sur l'état positif, les instincts communs, les voeux déterminés de la société, en combinaisons lointaines et arbitraires; il veut, en un mot, étendre indéfiniment son action, posséder l'avenir comme il a possédé le présent. [*paragraph*] Ici commencent l'égoïsme et le rêve: pendant quelque temps, et sur la foi de ce qu'il a déjà fait, on suit le grand homme dans cette nouvelle carrière; on croit en lui, on lui obéit; on se prête, pour ainsi dire, à ses fantaisies, que ses flatteurs et ses dupes admirent même et vantent comme ses plus sublimes conceptions. Cependant le public, qui ne saurait demeurer long-temps hors du vrai, s'aperçoit bientôt qu'on l'entraîne où il n'a nulle envie d'aller, qu'on l'abuse et qu'on abuse de lui. Tout à l'heure le grand homme avait mis sa haute intelligence, sa puissante volonté au service de la pensée générale, du voeu commun; maintenant il veut employer la force publique au service de sa propre pensée, de son propre désir; lui seul sait et veut ce qu'il fait. On s'en inquiète d'abord; bientôt on s'en lasse; on le suit quelque temps mollement, à contre-coeur; puis on se récrie, on se plaint; puis enfin on se sépare; et le grand homme reste seul, et il tombe; et tout ce qu'il avait pensé et voulu seul, toute la partie purement personnelle et arbitraire de ses oeuvres tombe avec lui. (II, 263-5)

277.35-8   "They . . . necessity."] [*translated from:*] [*paragraph*] De ce tableau seul il résulte clairement que ces guerres ne ressemblent point à celles de la première race: ce ne sont point des dissensions de tribu à tribu, de chef à chef, des expéditions entreprises dans un but d'établissement ou de pillage; ce sont des guerres systématiques, politiques, inspirées par une intention de gouvernement, commandées par une certaine nécessité. (II, 273)

277.42-278.24   At . . . changed] [*translated from:*] A la mort de Charlemagne, la conquête cesse, l'unité s'évanouit; l'empire se démembre et tombe en tous sens; mais est-il vrai que rien n'en reste, que toute l'oeuvre guerrière de Charlemagne disparaisse, qu'il n'ait rien fait, rien fondé? [*paragraph*] Il n'y a qu'un moyen de répondre à cette question: il faut se demander si, après Charlemagne, les peuples qu'il avait gouvernés se sont retrouvés dans le même état; si cette double invasion qui, au nord et au midi, menaçait leur territoire, leur religion et leur race, a repris son cours; si les Saxons, les Slaves, les Avares, les Arabes ont continué de tenir dans un état d'ébranlement et d'angoisse les possesseurs du sol romain. Evidemment, il n'en est rien. Sans doute l'empire de Charlemagne se dissout; mais il se dissout en Etats particuliers qui s'élèvent comme autant de barrières sur tous les points où subsiste encore le danger. Avant Charlemagne, les frontières de Germanie, d'Italie, d'Espagne, étaient dans une fluctuation continuelle; aucune force politique, constituée, n'y était en permanence; aussi était-il contraint de se transporter sans cesse d'une frontière à l'autre, pour opposer aux envahisseurs la force mobile et passagère de ses armées. Après lui, de vraies barrières politiques, des Etats plus ou moins bien organisés, mais réels et durables, s'élèvent: les royaumes de Lorraine, d'Allemagne, d'Italie, des deux Bourgognes, de Navarre, datent de cette époque; et malgré les vicissitudes de leur destinée, ils subsistent et suffisent pour opposer au mouvement d'invasion une résistance efficace. Aussi ce mouvement cesse, ou ne se reproduit plus que par la voie des expéditions maritimes, désolantes pour les points qu'elles atteignent, mais qui ne peuvent se faire avec de grandes masses d'hommes, ni amener de grands résultats. [paragraph] Quoique la vaste domination de Charlemagne ait disparu avec lui, il n'est donc pas vrai de dire qu'il n'ait rien fondé; il a fondé tous les Etats qui sont nés du démembrement de son Empire. Ses conquêtes sont entrées dans des combinaisons nouvelles, mais ses guerres ont atteint leur but. La forme a changé, mais au fond l'oeuvre est restée. (II, 276-8)

278.39-41   "The . . . departed."] [translated from:] Je crois en effet qu'il l'avait essayé, mais qu'il y avait très-peu réussi; malgré l'unité, malgré l'activité de sa pensée et de son pouvoir, le désordre était autour de lui immense, invincible; il le réprimait un moment, sur un point; mais le mal régnait partout où ne parvenait pas sa terrible volonté; et là où elle avait passé, il recommençait dès qu'elle s'était éloignée. (II, 278-9)

279.14-40   Is . . . much] [translated from:] [no paragraph] Maintenant je reproduis ici la question que j'élevais tout à l'heure sur les guerres de Charlemagne: est-il vrai, est-il possible que, de ce gouvernement si actif, si puissant, rien ne soit resté, que tout ait disparu avec Charlemagne, qu'il n'ait rien fondé au dedans et pour l'état social? [paragraph] Ce qui est tombé avec Charlemagne, ce qui tenait à lui seul et ne pouvait lui survivre, c'est le gouvernement central. Après s'être prolongées quelque temps sous Louis le débonnaire et Charles le chauve, mais de plus en plus sans force et sans effet, les assemblées générales, les missi dominici, toute l'administration centrale et souveraine ont disparu; mais il n'en a pas été ainsi du gouvernement local, de ces ducs, comtes, vicaires, centeniers, bénéficiers, vassaux, qui, sous Charlemagne, en exerçaient les pouvoirs. Avant lui, le désordre n'était pas moindre dans chaque localité que dans l'Etat en général: les propriétés, les magistratures changeaient sans cesse de main; aucune régularité, aucune permanence dans les situations et les influences locales. Pendant les quarante-six années de son gouvernement, elles eurent le temps de s'affermir sur le même sol, dans les mêmes familles; elles devinrent stables, première condition du progrès qui devait les rendre indépendantes, héréditaires, c'est-à-dire en faire les élémens du régime féodal. Rien à coup sûr ne ressemble moins à la féodalité que l'unité souveraine à laquelle aspirait Charlemagne; et pourtant c'est lui qui en a été le véritable fondateur: c'est lui qui, en arrêtant le mouvement extérieur de l'invasion, en réprimant jusqu'à un certain point le désordre intérieur, a donné aux situations, aux fortunes, aux influences locales, le temps de prendre vraiment possession du territoire et de ses habitans. Après lui, son gouvernement général a péri comme ses conquêtes, la souveraineté unique comme l'empire; mais de même que l'empire s'est dissous en Etats particuliers qui ont vécu d'une vie forte et durable, de même, la souveraineté centrale de Charlemagne s'est dissoute en une multitude de souverainetés locales qui avaient puisé dans sa force et acquis, pour ainsi dire, sous son ombre, les conditions de la réalité et de la durée. En sorte que sous ce second point de vue, et en pénétrant au delà des apparences, il a beaucoup fait et beaucoup fondé. (II, 293-5)

280.11-22   This . . . duration.] [translated from:] C'était là, en lui, la part de l'égoïsme et du rêve; ce fut en cela aussi qu'il échoua. L'empire romain et son unité répugnaient invinciblement à la nouvelle distribution de la population, aux relations nouvelles, au nouvel état moral des hommes; la civilisation romaine ne pouvait plus entrer que comme un élément transformé dans le monde nouveau qui se préparait. Cette pensée, ce voeu de Charlemagne n'étaient point une pensée, un besoin public. Ce qu'il avait fait pour l'accomplir périt avec lui. De cela même, cependant, quelque chose resta; ce nom d'empire d'occident qu'il avait relevé, et les droits qu'on croyait attachés au titre d'empereur, rentrèrent, si je puis ainsi parler, au nombre des élémens de l'histoire, et furent encore, pendant plusieurs siècles, un objet d'ambition, un principe d'évènemens. En sorte que, même dans la portion purement égoïste et éphémère de ses oeuvres, on ne peut pas dire que la pensée de Charlemagne ait été absolument stérile, ni que toute durée lui ait manqué. (II, 306-7)

281.7-23 The . . . Charlemagne.] [*translated from:*] Or, l'état moral et l'état social des peuples, à cette époque, répugnaient également à toute association, à tout gouvernement unique et étendu. Les hommes avaient peu d'idées et des idées fort courtes. Les relations sociales étaient rares et étroites. L'horizon de la pensée et celui de la vie étaient extrêmement bornés. A de telles conditions, une grande société est impossible. Quels en sont les liens naturels, nécessaires? d'une part le nombre et l'étendue des relations, de l'autre le nombre et l'étendue des idées par lesquelles les hommes communiquent et se tiennent. Dans un pays et un temps où il n'y a ni relations ni idées nombreuses et étendues, évidemment les liens d'une grande société, d'un grand Etat, sont impossibles. C'était-là précisément le caractère de l'époque dont nous nous occupons. Les conditions fondamentales d'une grande société n'y existaient donc pas. De petites sociétés, des gouvernemens locaux, des sociétés et des gouvernemens taillés en quelque sorte là à mesure des idées et des relations humaines, cela seul était possible. Cela seul en effet réussit à se fonder. [*paragraph*] Les élémens de ces petites sociétés, de ces petits gouvernmens locaux, étaient tout trouvés. Les possesseurs de bénéfices tenus du roi ou de domaines occupés par la conquête, les comtes, les ducs, les gouverneurs de provinces étaient semés çà et là sur le territoire. Ils devinrent les centres naturels d'associations correspondantes. Autour d'eux s'agglomérèrent, de gré ou de force, les habitans, libres ou esclaves, des environs; et ainsi se formèrent ces petits Etats, ces fiefs dont je parlais tout à l'heure, et une multitude d'autres moins importans, et qui n'ont pas eu la même existence historique. C'est-là, Messieurs, la cause dominante, la vraie cause de la dissolution de l'empire de Charlemagne. (II, 451-2)

286.23-287.3 No . . . will.] [*translated from:*] Que la réforme sociale qui s'est accomplie de notre temps, sous nos yeux, soit immense, nul homme de sens ne le peut contester. Jamais les relations humaines n'ont été réglées avec plus de justice; jamais il n'en est résulté un bien-être plus général. [*paragraph*] Non-seulement la réforme sociale est grande, mais je suis convaincu qu'une réforme morale correspondante s'est aussi accomplie; qu'à aucune époque peut-être il n'y a eu, à tout prendre, autant d'honnêteté dans la vie humaine, autant d'hommes vivant régulièrement; que jamais une moindre somme de force publique n'a été nécessaire pour réprimer les volontés individuelles. La moralité pratique a fait, j'en suis convaincu, presque les mêmes progrès que le bien-être et la prospérité du pays. [*paragraph*] Mais sous un autre point de vue, nous avons, je crois, beaucoup à gagner, et nous sommes justement reprochables. Nous avons vécu, depuis cinquante ans, sous l'empire d'idées générales de plus en plus accréditées et puissantes; sous le poids d'événemens redoutables, presque irrésistibles. Il en est résulté une certaine faiblesse, une certaine mollesse dans les esprits et dans les caractères. Les convictions et les volontés individuelles manquent d'énergie et de confiance en elles-mêmes. On croit à une opinion commune, on obéit à une impulsion générale, on cède à une nécessité extérieure. Soit pour résister, soit pour agir, chacun a peu d'idée de sa propre force, peu de confiance dans sa propre pensée. L'individualité, en un mot, l'énergie intime et personnelle de l'homme est faible et timide. Au milieu des progrès de la liberté générale, beaucoup d'hommes semblent avoir perdu le sentiment fier et puissant de leur propre liberté. [*paragraph*] Messieurs, tel n'était pas le moyen âge. La condition sociale y était déplorable; la moralité humaine fort inférieure à ce qu'on en a dit, fort inférieure à celle de nos jours. Mais dans beaucoup d'hommes, l'individualité était forte, la volonté énergique. Il y avait alors peu d'idées générales qui dominassent tous les esprits, peu d'événemens qui, dans toutes les parties du territoire, dans toutes les situations, pesassent sur les caractères. L'individu se déployait pour son compte, selon son penchant, irrégulièrement et avec confiance; la nature morale de l'homme apparaissait çà et là dans toute son ambition, avec toute son énergie. Spectacle non-seulement dramatique, attachant, mais instructif et utile; qui ne nous offre rien à regretter, rien à imiter, mais beaucoup à apprendre; ne fût-ce qu'en éveillant sans cesse notre attention sur ce qui nous manque, en nous montrant ce que peut un homme quand il sait croire et vouloir. (IV, 29-31)

287.19-22 "Accordingly . . . nature."] [*translated from:*] Aussi, indépendamment de toute cause étrangère, par sa seule nature, par sa tendance propre, la société féodale était-elle toujours en question, toujours sur le point de se dissoudre; incapable du moins de subsister régulièrement et de se développer sans se dénaturer. (IV, 366)

287.28-9 "A . . . fiefs,"] [*translated from:*] [*paragraph*] Et d'abord une prodigieuse inégalité s'introduisit très-vite entre les possesseurs de fiefs. (IV, 366)

287.30-288.3 Thus . . . subordinate.] [*translated from:*] Ainsi, Messieurs, par cela seul que le lien social manquait à la féodalité, les libertés féodales périssaient rapidement; les excès de l'indépendance individuelle compromettaient perpétuellement la société; elle ne trouvait, dans les relations des possesseurs de fiefs, ni de quoi se maintenir régulièrement, ni de quoi se développer; elle eut recours à d'autres principes, à des principes contraires à ceux de la féodalité; elle chercha dans d'autres institutions les moyens dont elle avait besoin pour devenir permanente, régulière, progressive. La tendance vers la centralisation, vers la formation d'un pouvoir supérieur aux pouvoirs locaux, fut rapide. Bien avant que la royauté générale, la royauté qui est devenue la royauté française, intervînt sur tous les points du territoire, il s'y était formé, sous les noms de *duché*, de *comté*, de *vicomté*, etc., plusieurs petites royautés, investies du gouvernement central, dans telle ou telle province, et sous la main desquelles les droits des possesseurs de fiefs, c'est-à-dire les souverainetés locales, s'abaissaient de plus en plus. (IV, 370-1)

375.13-23 I . . . epoch.] [*translated from:*] Je porte mes regards sur les temps de la plus grande activité intellectuelle de l'Angleterre, sur les époques où il semble que les idées, le mouvement des esprits aient tenu le plus de place dans son histoire; je prends la crise politique et religieuse des XVIe et XVIIe siècles. Personne n'ignore quel prodigieux mouvement a travaillé alors l'Angleterre. Quelqu'un pourrait-il me dire quel grand système philosophique, quelles grandes doctrines générales, et devenues européennes, ce mouvement a enfantés? Il a eu d'immenses et admirables résultats; il a fondé des droits, des moeurs; il a non-seulement puissamment agi sur les relations sociales, mais sur les âmes; il a fait des sectes, des enthousiastes; il n'a guère élevé ni agrandi, directement du moins, l'horizon de l'esprit humain; il n'a point allumé un de ces grands flambeaux intellectuels qui éclairent toute une époque. (I, 12)

376.11-17 No . . . it.] [*translated from:*] Il n'y a personne qui ne sache quelle a été depuis cinquante ans l'activité de l'esprit en Allemagne; dans tous les genres, en philosophie, en histoire, en littérature, en poésie, il s'est avancé très-loin; on peut dire qu'il n'a pas toujours suivi les meilleures voies; on peut contester une partie des résultats auxquels il est arrivé; mais quant à l'énergie, à l'étendue du développement même, il est impossible de les contester. A coup sûr, l'état social, la condition publique, n'a point marché du même pied. (I, 15)

377.29-42 There . . . country . . . which . . . myself . . . if . . . civilization.] [*translated from:*] Il y a un autre grand pays dont en vérité je parle par égard, par respect pour un peuple noble et malheureux, plutôt que par nécessité; je veux dire l'Espagne. Ni les grands esprits, ni les grands évènemens n'ont manqué à l'Espagne; l'intelligence et la société humaine y ont apparu quelquefois dans toute leur gloire; mais ce sont des faits isolés, jetés çà et là dans l'histoire Espagnole, comme des palmiers sur les sables. Le caractère fondamental de la civilisation, le progrès, le progrès général, continu, semble refusé, en Espagne, tant à l'esprit humain qu'à la société. C'est une immobilité solennelle, ou des vicissitudes sans fruit. Cherchez une grande idée ou une grande amélioration sociale, un système philosophique ou une institution féconde, que l'Europe tienne de l'Espagne; il n'y en a point: ce peuple a été isolé en Europe; il en a peu reçu et lui a peu donné. Je me serais reproché d'omettre son nom; mais sa civilisation est de peu d'importance dans l'histoire de la civilisation europénne. (I, 18-19)

378.17-30 Man . . . else.] [*translated from:*] [*no paragraph*] L'homme et la société y ont toujours marché et grandi, je ne dirai pas de front et également, mais à peu de distance l'un de l'autre. A côté des grands évènemens, des révolutions, des améliorations publiques, on aperçoit toujours, dans notre histoire, des idées générales, des doctrines qui leur correspondent. Rien ne s'est passé dans le monde réel, dont l'intelligence ne se soit à l'instant saisie, et n'ait tiré pour son propre compte une nouvelle richesse; rien dans le domaine de l'intelligence, qui n'ait eu dans le monde réel, et presque toujours assez vite, son retentissement et son résultat. En général même, les idées en France ont précédé et provoqué les progrès de l'ordre social; ils se sont préparés dans les doctrines avant de s'accomplir dans les choses, et l'esprit a marché le premier dans la route de la civilisation. Ce double caractère d'activité intellectuelle et d'habileté pratique, de méditation et d'application, est empreint dans tous les grands évènemens de l'histoire de France, dans toutes les grandes classes de la société française, et leur donne une physionomie qui ne se retrouve point ailleurs. (I, 20-1)

389.25-6 *a glorious and powerful fact.*] [*translated from:*] [*paragraph*] Fait glorieux et puissant, Messieurs, qui a rendu, du Ve au XIIIe siècle, d'immenses services à l'humanité. (I, 424)

389.35-390.7 What . . . times.] [*translated from:*] Quel sens attachaient à ces mots [l'unité de l'Eglise], Messieurs, les hommes de cette époque, et quels progrès avaient-ils déjà faits dans cette voie? Qu'était vraiment, dans les esprits et dans les faits, cette société spirituelle, objet de leur ambition et de leur respect? Comment était-elle conçue et pratiquée? Il faut répondre à ces questions pour savoir ce qu'on dit quand on parle de l'unité de l'Eglise, et ce qu'on doit penser de ses principes comme de ses résultats. [*paragraph*] Une conviction commune, c'est-à-dire, une même idée reconnue et acceptée comme vraie, telle est la base fondamentale, le lien caché de la société humaine. On peut s'arrêter aux associations les plus bornées et les plus simples, ou s'élever aux plus compliquées, aux plus étendues; on peut examiner ce qui se passe entre trois ou quatre Barbares réunis pour une expédition de chasse, ou dans le sein d'une assemblée appelée à traiter des affaires d'un grand peuple; partout et dans tous les cas, c'est dans l'adhésion des individus à une même pensée que consiste essentiellement le fait de l'association: tant qu'ils ne se sont pas compris et entendus, ils ne sont que des êtres isolés, placés les uns à côté des autres, mais qui ne se pénètrent et ne se tiennent point. Un même sentiment, une même croyance, quels qu'en soient la nature ou l'objet, telle est la condition première de l'état social; c'est dans le sein de la vérité seulement, ou de ce qu'ils prennent pour la vérité, que les hommes s'unissent et que naît la société. Et en ce sens, un philosophe moderne[1] [*footnote:*] [1]M. l'abbé de la Mennais. [*text:*] a eu grande raison de dire qu'il n'y a de société qu'entre les intelligences, que la société ne subsiste que sur les points et dans les limites où s'accomplit l'union des intelligences; que là où les intelligences n'ont rien de commun, la société n'est pas; en d'autres termes, que la société intellectuelle est la seule société, l'élément nécessaire et comme le fond de toutes les associations extérieures et apparentes. [*paragraph*] Or, le caractère essentiel de la vérité, Messieurs, et précisément ce qui en fait le lien social par excellence, c'est l'unité. La vérité est une, c'est pourquoi les hommes qui l'ont reconnue et acceptée sont unis; union qui n'a rien d'accidentel ni d'arbitraire, car la vérité ne dépend ni des accidens des choses, ni de l'incertitude des hommes; rien de passager, car la vérité est éternelle; rien de borné, car la vérité est complète et infinie. Comme de la vérité, l'unité sera donc le caractère essentiel de la société qui n'aura que la vérité pour objet, c'est-à-dire de la société purement spirituelle. Il n'y a pas, il ne peut y avoir deux sociétés spirituelles; elle est, de sa nature, unique et universelle. [*paragraph*] Ainsi est née l'Eglise; de là cette unité qu'elle a proclamé comme son principe, cette universalité qui a toujours été son ambition. [*4-sentence omission*] Or, à quelle condition s'unissent les esprits dans la vérité? A cette condition qu'ils la connaissent et acceptent son empire: quiconque obéit sans connaître la vérité, par ignorance et non par lumière, ou quiconque, ayant connaissance de la vérité, refuse de lui obéir, n'est pas entré dans la société spirituelle: nul n'en fait partie s'il ne voit et ne veut; elle exclut d'une part l'ignorance, de l'autre la contrainte; elle exige de tous ses membres l'intime et personnelle adhésion de l'intelligence et de la liberté. [*paragraph*] Or, à l'époque qui nous occupe, Messieurs, ce second principe, ce second caractère de la société spirituelle manquait à l'Eglise. (I, 424-7)

392.3 "*Il lui*] Ni la capacité intellectuelle ni la capacité politique n'ont péri en Italie; il lui manque ce qui lui a toujours manqué, ce qui est partout une des conditions vitales de la civilisation; il lui (I, 17)

———— *Cours d'histoire moderne: histoire générale de la civilisation en Europe, depuis la chute de l'empire romain jusqu'à la révolution française*. Paris: Pichon and Didier, 1828.

NOTE: in SC, without bookplate, but probably JSM's, with "I" on the spine. See the preceding entry, which has the same general title. See also Guizot, *General History. . .* , and *Lectures. . .* , which are translations of this volume. The Lectures are separately paged. We have adopted the short title JSM uses, i.e., *Civilisation en Europe*.

REVIEWED: 257-94, *367-93*

QUOTED: 267 (*392*), 267-8, 268 (*381-2*), 271, 272, 272-3, 273, 278, 280, 281-2 (*384-5*), 282 (*385-6*), 283-4 (*386-7*), 284-5 (*387-8*), 285-6 (*388-9*), 293-4, 294, *381, 384-8, 391*

REFERRED TO: 186, 228, 229, 230, 231

267.3-11 I . . . achieve.] [*translated from:*] Je crois, Messieurs, que quand nous serons un peu entrés dans cette étude, nous acquerrons bien vite la conviction que la civilisation est très-jeune, qu'il s'en faut bien que le monde en ait encore mesuré la carrière. A coup sûr, la pensée humaine est fort loin d'être aujourd'hui tout ce qu'elle peut devenir, nous sommes fort loin d'embrasser l'avenir tout entier de l'humanité; cependant, que chacun de nous descende dans sa pensée, qu'il s'interroge sur le bien possible qu'il conçoit, qu'il espère; qu'il mette ensuite son idée en regard de ce qui existe aujourd'hui dans le monde; il se convaincra que la société et la civilisation sont bien jeunes; que, malgré tout le chemin qu'elles ont fait, elles en ont incomparablement davantage à faire. (Lecture 1, 30-1)

267.40-268.6   Among . . . elsewhere . . . the . . . society.] [*translated from:*] Chez les Egyptiens, les Etrusques, les Grecs même, etc., la caste des guerriers, par exemple, a lutté contre celle des prêtres; ailleurs, l'esprit de clan contre l'esprit d'association libre, le système aristocratique contre le système populaire, etc. Mais c'est à des époques anté-historiques que se sont passées, en général, de telles luttes; il n'en est resté qu'un vague souvenir. [*paragraph*] La lutte s'est reproduite quelquefois dans le cours de la vie des peuples; mais, presque toujours, elle a été promptement terminée; l'une des forces qui se disputaient l'empire l'a promptement emporté, et a pris seule possession de la société. (Lecture 2, 4-5)

268.7-16   This . . . congealed.] [*translated from:*] De là est résultée, dans la plupart des civilisations antiques, une simplicité remarquable. Elle a eu des résultats très-différents. Tantôt, comme dans la Grèce, la simplicité du principe social a amené un développement prodigieusement rapide; jamais aucun peuple ne s'est déployé en aussi peu de temps, avec autant d'éclat. Mais après cet admirable élan, tout à coup la Grèce a paru épuisée; sa décadence, si elle n'a pas été aussi rapide que son progrès, n'en a pas moins été étrangement prompte. Il semble que la force créatrice du principe de la civilisation grecque fût épuisée. Aucun autre n'est venu la réparer. [*paragraph*] Ailleurs, dans l'Egypte et dans l'Inde, par exemple, l'unité du principe de la civilisation a eu un autre effet; la société est tombée dans un état stationnaire. La simplicité a amené la monotonie; le pays ne s'est pas détruit, la société a continué d'y subsister, mais immobile et comme glacée. (Lecture 2, 5)

268.18-43   Her civilization . . . is . . . shape.] [*translated from:*] Il en a été tout autrement de la civilisation de l'Europe moderne. Sans entrer dans aucun détail, regardez-y, recueillez vos souvenirs; elle vous apparaîtra sur-le-champ variée, confuse, orageuse; toutes les formes, tous les principes d'organisation sociale y coexistent; les pouvoirs spirituel et temporel, les éléments théocratique, monarchique, aristocratique, démocratique, toutes les classes, toutes les situations sociales se mêlent, se pressent; il y a des degrés infinis dans la liberté, la richesse, l'influence. Et ces forces diverses sont entr'elles dans un état de lutte continuelle, sans qu'aucune parvienne à étouffer les autres et à prendre seule possession de la société. Dans les temps anciens, à chaque grande époque, toutes les sociétés semblent jetées dans le même moule: c'est tantôt la monarchie pure, tantôt la théocratie ou la démocratie qui prévaut; mais chacune prévaut à son tour complétement. L'Europe moderne offre des exemples de tous les systèmes, de tous les essais d'organisation sociale; les monarchies pures ou mixtes, les théocraties, les républiques plus ou moins aristocratiques y ont vécu simultanément, à côté les unes des autres; et malgré leur diversité, elles ont toutes une certaine ressemblance, un certain air de famille qu'il est impossible de méconnaître. [*paragraph*] Dans les idées et les sentimens de l'Europe, même variété, même lutte. Les croyances théocratiques, monarchiques, aristocratiques, populaires, se croisent, se combattent, se limitent, se modifient. Ouvrez les plus hardis écrits du moyen-âge: jamais une idée n'y est suivie jusqu'à ses dernières conséquences. Les partisans du pouvoir absolu reculent tout à coup et à leur insçu devant les résultats de leur doctrine; on sent qu'autour d'eux, il y a des idées, des influences qui les arrêtent et les empêchent de pousser jusqu'au bout. Les démocrates subissent la même loi. Nulle part cette imperturbable hardiesse, cet aveuglement de la logique qui éclatent dans les civilisations anciennes. Les sentimens offrent les mêmes contrastes, la même variété; un goût d'indépendance très-énergique à côté d'une grande facilité de soumission; une rare fidélité d'homme à homme, et en même temps un besoin impérieux de faire sa volonté, de secouer tout frein, de vivre seul, sans s'inquiéter d'autrui. Les âmes sont aussi diverses, aussi agitées que la société. [*paragraph*] Le même caractère se retrouve dans les littératures. On ne saurait disconvenir que, sous le point de vue de la forme et de la beauté de l'art, elles sont très-inférieures à la littérature ancienne; mais sous le point de vue du fond des sentimens, des idées, elles sont plus fortes et plus riches. On voit que l'âme humaine a été remuée sur un plus grand nombre de points, à une plus grande profondeur. L'imperfection de la forme provient de cette cause même. Plus les matériaux sont riches, nombreux, plus il est difficile de les ramener à une forme simple. (Lecture 2, 6-9)

271.24-6 "the . . . name."] [*translated from:*] Un autre fait, une autre idée survécut également; c'est l'idée de l'Empire, le nom de l'Empereur, l'idée de la Majesté impériale, d'un pouvoir absolu, sacré, attaché au nom de l'empereur. (Lecture 2, 21-2)

272.11-21 At . . . world.] [*translated from:*] [*no paragraph*] Il n'y avait alors aucun des moyens par lesquels aujourd'hui les influences morales s'établissent ou résistent indépendamment des institutions, aucun des moyens par lesquels une pure vérité, une pure idée acquiert un grand empire sur les esprits, gouverne les actions, détermine des événemens. Rien de semblable n'existait au quatrième siècle, pour donner aux idées, aux sentimens personnels, une pareille autorité. Il est clair qu'il fallait une société fortement organisée, fortement gouvernée, pour lutter contre un pareil désastre, pour sortir victorieuse d'un tel ouragan. Je ne crois pas trop dire en affirmant qu'à la fin du quatrième, et au commencement du cinquième siècle, c'est l'Eglise chrétienne qui a sauvé le christianisme; c'est l'Eglise avec ses institutions, ses magistrats, son pouvoir, qui s'est défendue vigoureusement contre la dissolution intérieure de l'Empire, contre la Barbarie, qui a conquis les Barbares, qui est devenue le lien, le moyen, le principe de civilisation entre le monde romain et le monde barbare. (Lecture 2, 23-4)

272.35-273.2 Among . . . epoch, . . . there . . . ascendancy.] [*translated from:*] Parmi les chrétiens de cette époque, Messieurs, dans le clergé chrétien, il y avait des hommes qui avaient pensé à tout, à toutes les questions morales, politiques, qui avaient sur toutes choses des opinions arrêtées, des sentimens énergiques, et un vif désir de les propager, de les faire régner. Jamais société n'a fait, pour agir autour d'elle et s'assimiler le monde extérieur, de tels efforts que l'Eglise chrétienne du cinquième au dixième siècle. Quand nous étudierons en particulier son histoire, nous verrons tout ce qu'elle a tenté. Elle a en quelque sorte attaqué la barbarie par tous les bouts, pour la civiliser en la dominant. (Lecture 3, 22-3)

273.25-7 "The . . . truth."] [*translated from:*] La séparation du temporel et du spirituel se fonde sur cette idée que la force matérielle n'a ni droit ni prise sur les esprits, sur la conviction, sur la vérité. (Lecture 2, 30)

278.28-32 "whom . . . them."] [*translated from:*] Il y a des hommes que le spectacle de l'anarchie ou de l'immobilité sociale frappe et révolte, qui en sont choqués intellectuellement comme d'un fait qui ne doit pas être, et sont invinciblement possédés du besoin de le changer, du besoin de mettre quelque règle, quelque chose de général, de régulier, de permanent, dans le monde soumis à leurs regards. (Lecture 3, 23)

280.31-2 "Consult . . . end."] [*translated from:*] Consultez soit les poëtes du temps, soit les chroniqueurs; ils se croient tous à la fin du monde. (Lecture 4, 7)

281.33-282.30 Every . . . society?] [*translated from:*] [*no paragraph*] Qui ne sait combien on a étudié la question de l'influence des climats, et toute l'importance qu'y a attachée Montesquieu? Si l'on considère l'influence directe du climat sur les hommes, peut-être n'est-elle pas aussi étendue qu'on l'a supposé; elle est du moins d'une appréciation vague et difficile. Mais l'influence indirecte du climat, ce qui résulte, par exemple, de ce fait que, dans un pays chaud, les hommes vivent en plein air, tandis que, dans les pays froids, ils s'enferment dans l'intérieur des habitations, qu'ils se nourrissent ici d'une manière, là d'une autre, ce sont là des faits d'une extrême importance, et qui, par le simple changement de la vie matérielle, agissent puissamment sur la civilisation. Toute grande révolution amène dans l'état social des modifications de ce genre, et dont il faut tenir grand compte. [*paragraph*] L'établissement du régime féodal en produisit une dont la gravité ne saurait être méconnue; il changea la distribution de la population sur la face du territoire. Jusques-là les maîtres du territoire, la population souveraine, vivaient réunis en masses d'hommes plus ou moins nombreuses, soit sédentaires dans l'intérieur des villes, soit errant par bandes dans le pays. Par la féodalité, ces mêmes hommes vécurent isolés, chacun dans son habitation, à de grandes distances les uns des autres. Vous entrevoyez à l'instant quelle influence ce changement dut exercer sur le caractère et le cours de la civilisation. La prépondérance sociale, le gouvernement de la société passa tout à coup des villes aux campagnes; la propriété privée dut prendre le pas sur la propriété publique, la vie privée sur la vie publique. Tel fut le premier effet, un effet purement matériel, du triomphe de la société féodale. Plus nous y pénétrerons, plus les conséquences de ce seul fait se dévoileront à nos yeux. [*paragraph*] Examinons cette société en elle-même, et voyons quel rôle elle a dû jouer dans l'histoire de la civilisation. Prenons d'abord la féodalité dans son élément le plus simple, dans son élément primitif, fondamental; considérons un seul possesseur de fief dans son domaine; voyons ce que sera, ce que doit faire, de tous ceux qui la composent, la petite société qui se forme autour de lui. [*paragraph*] Il s'établit dans un lieu isolé, élevé, qu'il prend soin de rendre sûr, fort; il y construit ce qu'il appellera son château. Avec qui s'y établit-il? Avec sa femme, ses enfans; peut-être quelques hommes libres qui ne sont pas devenus propriétaires, se sont attachés à sa personne, et continuent à vivre avec lui, à sa table. C'est là ce qui habite dans l'intérieur du château. Tout autour, au pied, se groupe une petite population de colons, de serfs qui cultivent les domaines du possesseur du fief. Au milieu de cette population inférieure, la religion vient planter une église; elle y amène un prêtre. D'ordinaire, dans les premiers temps du régime féodal, ce prêtre est à la fois le chapelain du château et le curé du village; un jour les deux caractères se sépareront; le village aura son curé qui y habitera, à côté de son église. Voilà la société féodale élémentaire, la molécule féodale, pour ainsi dire. C'est cet élément que nous avons d'abord à examiner; nous lui ferons la double question qu'il faut adresser à tous les faits: qu'en a-t-il dû résulter pour le développement 1° de l'homme même 2° de la société? (Lecture 4, 9-12)

282.37-9 "was . . . family."] [*translated from:*] Je prends dans le monde ancien une grande situation aristocratique, un patricien romain, par exemple: comme le seigneur féodal, le patricien romain était chef de famile, maître, supérieur. Il était de plus magistrat religieux, pontife, dans l'intérieur de sa famille. (Lecture 4, 13)

282.41-3 "was . . . corporation."] [*translated from:*] Le patricien romain était en outre membre d'une corporation qui vivait réunie dans un même lieu, membre du sénat; encore une importance qui lui venait du dehors, de sa corporation, une importance reçue, empruntée. (Lecture 4, 13)

282.43-283.10 The . . . Soul!] [*translated from:*] [*no paragraph*] La grandeur des aristocrates anciens, associée à un caractère religieux et politique, appartenait à la situation, à la corporation en général, plutôt qu'à l'individu. Celle du possesseur de fief est purement individuelle; il ne tient rien de personne; tous ses droits, tout son pouvoir lui viennent de lui seul. Il n'est point magistrat religieux; il ne fait point partie d'un sénat; c'est dans sa personne, dans son individu que toute son importance réside; tout ce qu'il est, il l'est par lui-même, en son propre nom. Quelle influence ne doit pas exercer une telle situation sur celui qui l'occupe! Quelle fierté individuelle, quel prodigieux orgueil, tranchons le mot, quelle insolence, doivent naître dans son âme! Au-dessus de lui, point de supérieur dont il soit le représentant et l'interprète; auprès de lui, point d'égaux; nulle loi puissante et commune qui pèse sur lui; nul empire extérieur qui ait action sur sa volonté; il ne connaît de frein que les limites de sa force et la présence du danger. Tel est, sur le caractère de l'homme, le résultat moral de la situation. (Lecture 4, 13-14)

283.13-284.15 History . . . life.] [*translated from:*] Jetons un coup-d'oeil sur les divers systèmes de famille; prenons d'abord la famille patriarcale, dont la Bible et les monumens orientaux offrent le modèle. Elle est très-nombreuse; c'est la tribu. Le chef, le patriarche, y vit en commun avec ses enfans, ses proches, les diverses générations qui se sont réunies autour de lui, toute sa parenté, ses serviteurs; et non-seulement il vit avec eux tous, mais il a les mêmes intérêts, les mêmes occupations; il mène la même vie. N'est-ce pas là la situation d'Abraham, des patriarches, des chefs de tribus arabes qui reproduisent encore l'image de la vie patriarcale? [*paragraph*] Un autre système de famille se présente, le *clan*, petite société dont il faut chercher le type en Ecosse, en Irlande, et par laquelle probablement une grande portion du monde européen a passé. Ceci n'est plus la famille patriarcale. Il y a une grande diversité de situation entre le chef et le reste de la population; il ne mène point la même vie; la plupart cultivent et servent; lui, il est oisif et guerrier. Mais leur origine est commune; ils portent tous le même nom; des rapports de parenté, d'anciennes traditions, les mêmes souvenirs, des affections pareilles établissent entre tous les membres du clan un lien moral, une sorte d'égalité. [*paragraph*] Voilà les deux principaux types de la société de famille que présente l'histoire. Est-ce là, je vous le demande, la famille féodale? Evidemment non. Il semble, au premier moment, qu'elle ait quelque rapport avec le clan; mais la différence est bien plus grande. La population qui entoure le possesseur de fief lui est parfaitement étrangère; elle ne porte pas son nom; il n'y a, entre elle et lui, point de parenté, point de lien historique ni moral. Ce n'est pas non plus la famille patriarcale. Le possesseur de fief ne mène pas la même vie, ne se livre point aux mêmes travaux que ceux qui l'entourent; il est oisif et guerrier, tandis que les autres sont laboureurs. La famille féodale n'est pas nombreuse; ce n'est point la tribu; elle se réduit à la famille proprement dite, à la femme, aux enfans; elle vit séparée du reste de la population, dans l'intérieur du château. Les colons, les serfs, n'en font point partie; l'origine est diverse, l'inégalité de condition prodigieuse. Cinq ou six individus, dans une situation à la fois supérieure et étrangère, voilà la famille féodale. Elle doit évidemment revêtir un caractère particulier. Elle est étroite, concentrée, sans cesse appelée à se défendre, à se méfier, à s'isoler du moins, même de ses serviteurs. La vie intérieure, les moeurs domestiques y prendront, à coup sûr, une grande prépondérance. Je sais que la brutalité des passions, l'habitude du chef de passer son temps, à la guerre ou à la chasse, apporteront au développement des moeurs domestiques un assez grand obstacle. Mais cet obstacle sera vaincu; il faudra bien que le chef revienne habituellement chez lui; il y retrouvera toujours sa femme, ses enfans et eux presque seuls; seuls, ils seront sa société permanente; seuls, ils partageront toujours ses intérêts, sa destinée. Il est impossible que l'existence domestique n'acquière pas un grand empire. Les preuves abondent. N'est-ce pas dans le sein de la famille féodale que l'importance des femmes s'est enfin développée? Dans toutes les sociétés anciennes, je ne parle pas de celles où l'esprit de famille n'existait pas, mais dans celles-là même où il était puissant, dans la vie patriarchale, par exemple, les femmes ne tenaient pas à beaucoup près la place qu'elles ont acquise en Europe sous le régime féodal. C'est au développement, à la prépondérance nécessaire des moeurs domestiques dans la féodalité, qu'elles ont dû surtout ce changement, ce progrès de leur situation. On en a voulu chercher la cause dans les moeurs particulières des anciens Germains, dans un respect national qu'au milieu des forêts, ils portaient, a-t-on dit, aux femmes. Sur une phrase de Tacite, le patriotisme germanique a élevé je ne sais quelle supériorité, quelle pureté primitive et ineffaçable des moeurs germaines dans les rapports des deux sexes. Pures chimères! Des phrases pareilles à celles de Tacite, des sentimens, des usages analogues à ceux des anciens Germains, se rencontrent dans les récits d'une foule d'observateurs des peuples sauvages ou barbares. Il n'y a rien là de primitif, rien de propre à une certaine race. C'est dans les effets d'une situation sociale fortement déterminée, c'est dans les progrès, dans la prépondérance des moeurs domestiques que l'importance des femmes en Europe a pris sa source, et la prépondérance des moeurs domestiques est devenue, de très-bonne heure, un caractère essentiel du régime féodal. (Lecture 4, 14-18)

284.29-285.8 In . . . inspire.] [*translated from:*] [*no paragraph*] La nature de l'homme est si bonne, si féconde, que, lorsqu'une situation sociale dure quelque temps, il s'établit inévitablement entre ceux qu'elle rapproche, et quelles que soient les conditions du rapprochement, un certain lien moral, des sentimens de protection, de bienveillance, d'affection. Ainsi il est arrivé dans la féodalité. Nul doute qu'au bout d'un certain temps, ne se soient formées, entre les colons et le possesseur de fief, quelques relations morales, quelques habitudes affectueuses. Mais cela est arrivé en dépit de leur situation réciproque, et nullement par son influence. Considérée en elle-même, la situation était radicalement vicieuse. Rien de moralement commun entre le possesseur du fief et les colons; ils font partie de son domaine; ils sont sa propriété; et sous ce mot de propriété sont compris tous les droits que nous appelons aujourd'hui droits de souveraineté publique, aussi bien que les droits de propriété privée, le droit de donner des lois, de taxer, de punir, comme celui de disposer et de vendre. Il n'y a, entre le seigneur et les cultivateurs de ses domaines, autant du moins que cela peut se dire toutes les fois que des hommes sont en présence, point de droits, point de garanties, point de société. [*paragraph*] De là, je crois, cette haine vraiment prodigieuse, invincible, que le peuple des campagnes a portée de tout temps au régime féodal, à ses souvenirs, à son nom. Il n'est pas sans exemple que les hommes aient subi de pesans despotismes et s'y soient accoutumés, bien plus, qu'ils les aient acceptés. Le despotisme théocratique, le despotisme monarchique ont plus d'une fois obtenu l'aveu, presque l'affection de la population qui les subissait. Le despotisme féodal a toujours été repoussé, odieux; il a pesé sur les destinées, sans jamais régner sur les âmes. C'est que, dans la théocratie, dans la monarchie, le pouvoir s'exerce en vertu de certaines croyances communes au maître et aux sujets; il est le représentant, le ministre d'un autre pouvoir, supérieur à tous les pouvoirs humains; il parle et agit au nom de la Divinité ou d'une idée générale, point au nom de l'homme lui-même, de l'homme seul. Le despotisme féodal est tout autre; c'est le pouvoir de l'individu sur l'individu, la domination de la volonté personnelle et capricieuse d'un homme. C'est là peut-être la seule tyrannie qu'à son éternel honneur, l'homme ne veuille jamais accepter. Partout où, dans un maître, il ne voit qu'un homme, dès que la volonté qui pèse sur lui n'est qu'une volonté humaine, individuelle comme la sienne, il s'indigne et ne supporte le joug qu'avec courroux. Tel était le véritable caractère, le caractère distinctif du pouvoir féodal; et telle est aussi l'origine de l'antipathie qu'il n'a cessé d'inspirer. (Lecture 4, 18-20)

285.39-286.2 Feudality . . . passion.] [*translated from:*] 1°. La féodalité a dû exercer une assez grande influence, et, à tout prendre, une influence salutaire sur le développement intérieur de l'individu; elle a suscité dans les âmes des idées, des sentimens énergiques, des besoins moraux, de beaux développemens de caractère, de passion. (Lecture 4, 30-1)

286.2-17 Considered . . . advanced. The . . . it.] [*translated from:*] [*paragraph*] 2°. Sous le point de vue social, elle n'a pu fonder ni ordre légal, ni garanties politiques; elle était indispensable pour recommencer en Europe la société tellement dissoute par la barbarie, qu'elle n'était pas capable d'une forme plus régulière ni plus étendue; mais la forme féodale, radicalement mauvaise en soi, ne pouvait ni se régulariser, ni s'étendre. Le seul droit politique que le régime féodal ait su faire valoir dans la société européenne, c'est le droit de résistance: je ne dis pas de la résistance légale; il ne pouvait être question de résistance légale dans une société si peu avancée. [*4-sentence omission*] Le droit de résistance qu'a soutenu et pratiqué le régime féodal, c'est le droit de résistance personnelle; droit terrible, insociable, puisqu'il en appelle à la force, à la guerre, ce qui est la destruction de la société même; droit qui cependant ne doit jamais être aboli au fond du coeur des hommes, car, son abolition, c'est l'acceptation de la servitude. Le sentiment du droit de résistance avait péri dans l'opprobre de la société romaine, et ne pouvait renaître de ses débris; il ne sortait pas non plus naturellement, à mon avis, des principes de la société chrétienne. La féodalité l'a fait rentrer dans les moeurs de l'Europe. C'est l'honneur de la civilisation de le rendre à jamais inactif et inutile; c'est l'honneur du régime féodale de l'avoir constamment professé et défendu. (Lecture 4, 31-2)

293.13-294.2 When . . . influence.] [*translated from:*] [*no paragraph*] Lorsque j'ai tenté de déterminer la physionomie propre de la civilisation européenne comparée aux civilisations anciennes et asiatiques, j'ai fait voir que la première était variée, riche, complexe; qu'elle n'était jamais tombée sous la domination d'aucun principe exclusif; que les divers élémens de l'état social s'y étaient combinés, combattus, modifiés, avaient été continuellement obligés de transiger et de vivre en commun. Ce fait, Messieurs, caractère général de la civilisation européenne, a été surtout celui de la civilisation anglaise: c'est en Angleterre qu'il s'est produit avec le plus de suite et d'évidence; c'est là que l'ordre civil et l'ordre religieux, l'aristocratie, la démocratie, la royauté, les institutions locales et centrales, le développement moral et politique ont marché et grandi ensemble, pêle-mêle pour ainsi dire, sinon avec une égale rapidité, du moins toujours à peu de distance les uns des autres. Sous le règne des Tudor, par exemple, au milieu des plus éclatans progrès de la monarchie pure, on voit le principe démocratique, le pouvoir populaire percer et se fortifier presque en même temps. La révolution du dix-septième siècle éclate; elle est à la fois religieuse et politique. L'aristocratie féodale n'y paraît que fort affaiblie et avec tous les symptômes de la décadence: cependant elle est encore en état d'y conserver une place, d'y jouer un rôle important et de se faire sa part dans les résultats. Il en est de même dans tout le cours de l'histoire d'Angleterre; jamais aucun élément ancien ne périt complétement, jamais aucun élément nouveau ne triomphe tout-à-fait; jamais aucun principe spécial ne s'empare d'une domination exclusive. Il y a toujours développement simultané des différentes forces, transaction entre leurs prétentions et leurs intérêts. [*paragraph*] Sur le continent la marche de la civilisation a été beaucoup moins complexe et moins complète. Les divers élémens de la société, l'ordre religieux, l'ordre civil, la monarchie, l'aristocratie, la démocratie, se sont développés non pas ensemble et de front, mais successivement. Chaque principe, chaque système a eu en quelque sorte son tour. Il y a tel siècle qui appartient, je ne voudrais pas dire exclusivement, ce serait trop, mais avec une prédominance très marquée, à l'aristocratie féodale, par exemple; tel autre au principe monarchique; tel autre au principe démocratique. Comparez le moyen âge français avec le moyen âge anglais, les onzième, douzième et treizième siècles de notre histoire, avec les siècles correspondans au delà de la Manche; vous trouverez en France à cette époque la féodalité presque absolument souveraine, la royauté et le principe démocratique à peu près nuls. Allez en Angleterre, c'est bien l'aristocratie féodale qui domine; mais la royauté et la démocratie ne laissent pas d'être fortes et importantes. La royauté triomphe en Angleterre sous Elisabeth, comme en France sous Louis XIV; mais que de ménagemens elle est contrainte de garder! que de restrictions, tantôt aristocratiques, tantôt démocratiques, elle a à subir! En Angleterre aussi chaque système, chaque principe a eu son temps de force et de succès; jamais aussi complétement, aussi exclusivement que sur le continent: le vainqueur a toujours été contraint de tolérer la présence de ses rivaux et de leur faire à chacun sa part. (Lecture 14, 4-7)

294.5-18   There . . . civilization.] [*translated from:*] [*no paragraph*] Nul doute, par exemple, que ce développement simultané des divers élémens sociaux n'ait beaucoup contribué à faire arriver l'Angleterre, plus vite qu'aucun des Etats du continent, au but de toute société, c'est-à-dire à l'établissement d'un gouvernement à la fois régulier et libre. C'est précisément la nature d'un gouvernement de ménager tous les intérêts, toutes les forces, de les concilier, de les faire vivre et prospérer en commun: or, telle était d'avance, par le concours d'une multitude de causes, la disposition, la relation des divers élémens de la société anglaise: un gouvernement général et un peu régulier a donc eu là moins de peine à se constituer. De même l'essence de la liberté, c'est la manifestation et l'action simultanées de tous les intérêts, de tous les droits, de toutes les forces, de tous les élémens sociaux. L'Angleterre en était donc plus près que la plupart des autres Etats. Par les mêmes causes, le bon sens national, l'intelligence des affaires publiques ont dû s'y former plus vite; le bon sens politique consiste à savoir tenir compte de tous les faits, les apprécier et faire à chacun sa part; il a été en Angleterre une nécessité de l'état social, un résultat naturel du cours de la civilisation. (Lecture 14, 7-8)

294.23-42   In . . . result.] [*translated from:*] Dans les Etats du continent, en revanche, chaque système, chaque principe ayant eu son tour, ayant dominé d'une façon plus complète, plus exclusive, le développement s'est fait sur une plus grande échelle, avec plus de grandeur et d'éclat. La royauté et l'aristocratie féodale, par exemple, se sont produites sur la scène continentale avec bien plus de hardiesse, d'étendue, de liberté. Toutes les expériences politiques, pour ainsi dire, ont été plus larges et plus achevées. Il en est résulté que les idées politiques, je parle des idées générales, et non du bon sens appliqué à la conduite des affaires; que les idées, dis-je, les doctrines politiques se sont élevées bien plus haut et déployées avec bien plus de vigueur rationnelle. Chaque système s'étant en quelque sorte présenté seul, étant resté long-temps sur la scène, on a pu le considérer dans son ensemble, remonter à ses premiers principes, descendre à ses dernières conséquences, en démêler pleinement la théorie. Quiconque observera un peu attentivement le génie anglais sera frappé d'un double fait: d'une part, de la sûreté du bon sens, de l'habileté pratique; d'autre part, de l'absence d'idées générales et de hauteur d'esprit dans les questions théoriques. Soit qu'on ouvre un ouvrage anglais d'histoire, ou de jurisprudence, ou sur toute autre matière, il est rare qu'on y trouve la grande raison des choses, la raison fondamentale. En toutes choses, et notamment dans les sciences politiques, la doctrine pure, la philosophie, la science proprement dite, ont beaucoup plus prospéré sur le continent qu'en Angleterre; leurs élans du moins ont été beaucoup plus puissans et hardis. Et l'on ne peut douter que le caractère différent du développement de la civilisation dans les deux pays n'ait grandement contribué à ce résultat. (Lecture 14, 8-10)

381.21-3   "unity . . . frozen."] [*translated from:*] La simplicité a amené la monotonie; le pays ne s'est pas détruit, la société a continué d'y subsister, mais immobile et comme glacée. (Lecture 2, 5)

381.35-382.17   All . . . society.] [*see entry for* 268.18-43 *minus the first sentence and the concluding paragraph*] (Lecture 2, 6-8)

384.32-6   Sufficient . . . civilization.] [*translated from:*] [*no paragraph*] Il y a un autre ordre de considérations, tout opposé à celui-là, et qu'on a en général trop négligé; je veux parler de la condition matérielle de la société, des changemens matériels introduits dans la manière d'être et de vivre des hommes, par un fait nouveau, par une révolution, par un nouvel état social. On n'en a pas toujours assez tenu compte; on ne s'est pas assez demandé quelles modifications ces grandes crises du monde apportaient dans l'existence matérielle des hommes, dans le côté matériel de leurs relations. Ces modifications ont, sur l'ensemble de la société, plus d'influence qu'on ne le croit. (Lecture 4, 9)

384.36-385.33   Every . . . society?] [*see entry for* 281.33-282.30]

385.34-41   The . . . civilization.] [*translated from:*] Le premier fait qui me frappe en considérant cette petite société, c'est la prodigieuse importance que doit prendre le possesseur du fief, à ses propres yeux et aux yeux de ceux qui l'entourent. le [*sic*] sentiment de la personnalité, de la liberté individuelle, était le sentiment dominant dans la vie barbare. Il s'agit ici de tout autre chose; ce n'est plus seulement la liberté de l'homme, du guerrier; c'est l'importance du propriétaire, du chef de famille, du maître. De cette situation doit naître une impression de supériorité immense; supériorité toute particulière, et bien différente de ce qui se rencontre dans le cours des autres civilisations. (Lecture 4, 13)

385.41-50 Take . . . corporation.] [*translated from:*] Je prends dans le monde ancien une grande situation aristocratique, un patricien romain, par exemple: comme le seigneur féodal, le patricien romain était chef de famille, maître, supérieur. Il était de plus magistrat religieux, pontif dans l'intérieur de sa famille. Or, l'importance du magistrat religieux lui vient du dehors; ce n'est pas une importance purement personnelle, individuelle; il la reçoit d'en haut; il est le délégué de la Divinité, l'interprète des croyances religieuses qui s'y rattachent. Le patricien romain était en outre membre d'une corporation qui vivait réunie dans un même lieu, membre du sénat; encore une importance qui lui venait du dehors, de sa corporation, une importance reçue, empruntée. (Lecture 4, 13)

385.50-386.11 The grandeur . . . individual.] [*see entry for 282.43-283.10*]

386.12-13 I . . . society.] [*translated from:*] Je passe à une seconde conséquence, grave aussi, et trop peu remarquée, le tour particulier de l'esprit de famille féodal. (Lecture 4, 14)

386.14-387.14 History . . . life.] [*see entry for 283.13-284.15*]

387.15-24 A . . . family.] [*translated from:*] Un second fait, nouvelle preuve de l'empire de l'existence domestique, caractérise également la famille féodale, c'est l'esprit d'hérédité, de perpétuité qui y domine évidemment. L'esprit d'hérédité est inhérent à l'esprit de famille; mais il n'a pris nulle part un aussi grand développement que dans la féodalité. Cela tient à la nature de la propriété à laquelle la famille était incorporée. Le fief n'était pas une propriété comme une autre; il avait constamment besoin d'un possesseur qui le défendît, qui le servît, qui s'acquittât des obligations inhérentes au domaine, et le maintînt ainsi à son rang dans l'association générale des maîtres du pays. De là, une sorte d'identification entre le possesseur actuel du fief et le fief même, et toute la série de possesseurs futurs. [*paragraph*] Cette circonstance a beaucoup contribué à fortifier, à resserrer les liens de famille, déjà si puissans par la nature de la famille féodale. (Lecture 4, 18)

387.25-6 Let . . . aspect.] [*translated from:*] Je sors maintenant de la demeure seigneuriale; je descends au milieu de cette petite population qui l'entoure. Ici toutes choses ont un autre aspect. (Lecture 4, 18)

387.26-388.9 Human . . . inspire.] [*see the entry for 284.29-285.8*]

388.10-22 The religious . . . condition.] [*translated from:*] L'élément religieux qui s'y associait était peu propre à en adoucir le poids. Je ne crois pas que l'influence du prêtre, dans la petite société que je viens de décrire, fût grande, ni qu'il réussît beaucoup à légitimer les rapports de la population inférieure avec le seigneur. L'Eglise a exercé sur la civilisation européenne une très-grande action, mais en procédant d'une manière générale, en changeant les dispositions générales des hommes. Quand on entre de près dans la petite société féodale proprement dite, l'influence du prêtre, entre le seigneur et les colons, est presque nulle. Le plus souvent, il était lui-même grossier et subalterne comme un serf, et très-peu en état ou en disposition de lutter contre l'arrogance du seigneur. Sans doute, appelé seul à entretenir, à développer dans la population inférieure quelque vie morale, il lui était cher et utile à ce titre; il y répandait quelque consolation et quelque lumière; mais il pouvait et faisait, je crois, très-peu de chose pour sa destinée. (Lecture 4, 21)

388.33-389.6 Feudality . . . it.] [*see the entries for 285.39-286.2 and 286.2-17*]

391.1-7 "limits . . . world" . . . "a . . . example." . . . "in . . . liberty."] [*translated from:*] Aussi est-elle tombée dans une double faute: d'une part elle n'a pas connu ni respecté tous les droits de la pensée humaine; au moment où elle les réclamait pour son propre compte, elle les violait ailleurs; d'autre part, elle n'a pas su mesurer, dans l'ordre intellectuel, les droits de l'autorité; je ne dis pas de l'autorité coactive qui n'en saurait posséder aucun en pareille matière, mais de l'autorité purement morale, agissant sur les esprits seuls et par la seule voie de l'influence. Quelque chose manque, dans la plupart des pays réformés, à la bonne organisation de la société intellectuelle, à l'action régulière des opinions anciennes, générales. On n'a pas su concilier les droits et les besoins de la tradition avec ceux de la liberté; et la cause en a été sans aucun doute dans cette circonstance que la Réforme n'a pleinement compris et accepté ni ses principes ni ses effets. (Lecture 12, 29-30)

391.30-3 Nous . . . désirons. . . . *Nous . . . siècles.*] [*no paragraph*] Nous . . . désirons. Il faut prendre garde, Messieurs, à ne pas nous laisser envahir par l'un ou l'autre de ces deux défauts. Accoutumons-nous à mesurer ce que nous pouvons légitimement avec nos forces, notre science, notre puissance; et ne prétendons à rien de plus qu'à ce qui se peut acquérir légitimement, justement, régulièrement, en respectant les principes sur lesquels repose notre civilisation même. Nous . . . siècles. (Lecture 1, 33)

392.20-1 "I am persuaded," . . . that . . . do.] [*paragraph; see entry for* 267.3-11]

———— *De la démocratie en France. (Janvier 1849).* Paris: Masson, 1849.

QUOTED: 328n-9n

329n.1 "the idolatry of democracy."] [*translated in part from:*] Plus j'y pense, plus je demeure convaincu que son grand mal, le mal qui est au fond de tous ses maux, qui mine et détruit ses gouvernements et ses libertés, sa dignité et son bonheur, c'est le mal que j'attaque, l'idolâtrie démocratique. (2)

———— *Essais sur l'histoire de France* (1823). 2nd ed. Paris: Brière; Leipzig: Bossange, 1824.

NOTE: in SC. The reference at 136 is to the first essay, "Du régime municipal dans l'empire romain, au cinquième siècle de l'ère chrétienne, lors de la grande invasion des Germains en occident," 1-51. The 1st ed. (Paris: Brière, 1823), to which the reference at *371* presumably applies, was published as a complement to Mably's *Observations, q.v.* At 227 JSM dates the 1st ed. to 1822.

REVIEWED: 257-94

QUOTED: 263-4, 266, 291, 292, 292-3,

REFERRED TO: 136, 186, 227, 229, *371*

263.7-264.11 The . . . consequences.] [*translated from:*] La chute de l'Empire romain en Occident offre un phénomène singulier. Non seulement la nation ne soutient pas le gouvernement dans sa lutte contre les Barbares; mais la nation, abandonnée à elle-même, ne tente, pour son propre compte, aucune résistance. Il y a plus; rien, dans ce long débat, ne révèle qu'une nation existe; à peine est-il question de ce qu'elle souffre; elle subit tous les fléaux de la guerre, du pillage, de la famine, un changement complet de destinée et d'état, sans agir, sans parler, sans paraître. [*paragraph*] Ce phénomène n'est pas seulement singulier; il est sans exemple. Le despotisme a régné ailleurs que dans l'Empire romain; plus d'une fois l'invasion étrangère et la conquête ont dévasté des pays qu'avait opprimés un long despotisme. Là même où la nation n'a pas résisté, son existence se manifeste de quelque façon dans l'histoire; elle souffre, se plaint, et, malgré son avilissement, se débat contre son malheur; des récits, des monuments attestent ce qu'elle a éprouvé, ce qu'elle est devenue, et sinon ce qu'elle a fait, du moins ce qu'on a fait d'elle. [*paragraph*] Au Ve siècle, les débris des légions romaines disputent à des hordes de Barbares l'immense territoire de l'Empire; mais il semble que ce territoire fût un désert. Les soldats de l'Empire éloignés ou vaincus, il n'est plus question de personne ni de rien. Les peuplades Barbares s'arrachent successivement les provinces. A côté d'elles, une seule existence se révèle dans les faits, celle des évêques et du clergé. Si les lois n'étaient là pour nous apprendre qu'une population romaine couvrait encore le sol, l'histoire nous en laisserait douter. [*paragraph*] C'est surtout dans les provinces soumises depuis long-temps à Rome, et où la civilisation est plus avancée, que le peuple a ainsi disparu. On regarde comme un monument de la mollesse des sujets de l'Empire, la lettre des Bretons (*gemitus Brittonum*) implorant avec larmes l'assistance d'Aetius et l'envoi d'une légion.[1] [*footnote omitted*] Cela est injuste. Les Bretons, moins civilisés, moins romains que les autres sujets de Rome, ont résisté aux Saxons, et leur résistance a une histoire. A la même époque, dans la même situation, les Italiens, les Gaulois, les Espagnols n'en ont point. L'Empire s'est retiré de leur pays, les Barbares l'ont occupé, sans que la masse des habitants ait joué le moindre rôle, ait marqué en rien sa place dans les événements qui la livraient à tant de fléaux. [*paragraph*] Cependant la Gaule, l'Italie, l'Espagne étaient couvertes de villes naguère riches et peuplées. La civilisation s'y était développée avec éclat. Les routes, les aqueducs, les cirques, les écoles y abondaient. Rien n'y manquait de ce qui atteste la richesse et procure aux peuples une existence brillante et animée. Les invasions des Barbares venaient piller toutes ces richesses, disperser toutes ces réunions, détruire tous ces plaisirs. Jamais l'existence d'une nation ne fut plus complètement bouleversée; jamais les individus n'eurent plus de maux à endurer et de craintes à concevoir. D'où vient que ces nations sont muettes et mortes? Pourquoi tant de villes saccagées, tant de situations changées, tant de carrières interrompues, tant de propriétaires dépossédés ont-ils laissé si peu de traces, je ne dis pas de leur résistance active, mais seulement de leurs douleurs? [*paragraph*] On allègue le despotisme du gouvernement impérial, l'avilissement des peuples, l'apathie profonde qui s'était emparée de tous les sujets. On a raison. C'est là en effet la grande cause d'un fait si étrange. Mais c'est peu d'énoncer ainsi, d'une façon générale, une cause qui ailleurs, la même en apparence, n'a pas produit les mêmes résultats. Il faut pénétrer plus avant dans l'état de la société romaine, telle que le despotisme l'avait faite. Il faut rechercher par quels moyens il lui avait enlevé à ce point toute consistance et toute vie. Le despotisme peut revêtir des formes très-diverses et s'exercer par des procédés qui donnent à son action une toute autre énergie, à ses conséquences une bien plus grande portée. (1-4)

266.12-16   "Hence," . . . "in . . . Barbarians."] [*translated from:*] De là, au Ve siècle, tant de campagnes en friche et de villes presque désertes ou pleines seulement d'une populace affamée et oisive. Le régime que je viens de décrire y contribua beaucoup plus que les dévastations des Barbares. (42)

266.19-22   "On . . . Gaul"—"Causes . . . Carlovingians"—"Social . . . Carlovingians"—"Political . . . *régime.*"] [*translated from:*] De l'origine et de l'établissement des Francs dans les Gaules. Des causes de la chute des Mérovingiens et des Carlovingiens. De l'état social et des institutions politiques en France du cinquième au dixième siècle. Du caractère politique du Régime féodal. (519)

266.25-6   "Causes . . . England."] [*translated from:*] Des causes de l'établissement du Gouvernement représentatif en Angleterre. (520)

292.15-16   "had . . . corporation,"] [*translated from:*] Il est clair que la hiérarchie féodale s'est convertie en une corporation vraiment aristocratique, que cette corporation se sent obligée de prendre en main la cause nationale, d'agir dans un intérêt public. (419)

292.15-18   "to . . . coalition."] [*translated from:*] Les barons n'étaient pas assez forts pour imposer en même temps au roi leur liberté, au peuple leur tyrannie; et de même qu'ils avaient été obligés de se coaliser pour se défendre, de même ils se sentaient dans la nécessité d'appeler le peuple à l'appui de leur coalition. (424)

292.36-293.8   In . . . destinies.] [*translated from:*] [*paragraph*] Ainsi en France, depuis la fondation de la monarchie jusqu'au XIVe siècle, tout a été individuel, les forces, les libertés, la résistance comme l'oppression: l'unité, principe de tout gouvernement, l'association entre égaux, principe de toutes les garanties, ne se sont rencontrées que dans l'étroite sphère de chaque seigneurie ou de chaque cité; la royauté a été nominale; l'aristocratie n'a point formé un corps; il y a eu des bourgeois dans les villes, et point de bourgeoisie dans l'Etat. En Angleterre, au contraire, depuis la conquête des Normands, tout a été collectif; les forces de même nature, les situations analogues ont été contraintes de se rapprocher, de se coaliser, d'arriver à l'unité par l'association. Dès son origine, la royauté a été réelle; cent cinquante ans après son établissement la féodalité s'est brisée en deux parts, dont l'une est devenue la haute aristocratie, l'autre le corps des communes du pays. Qui pourrait méconnaître, dans ce premier travail de la formation des deux sociétés, dans ces caractères si divers de leur premier âge, les vraies causes de la longue différence de leurs institutions et de leurs destinées? (516)

——— *General History of Civilisation in Europe, from the Fall of the Roman Empire to the French Revolution.* Trans. D.A. Talboys. Oxford: Talboys, 1837.
NOTE: a translation of *Cours d'histoire moderne . . . Civilisation en Europe.*
REFERRED TO: 229

——— *Histoire de la république d'Angleterre et de Cromwell (1649-1658).* 2 vols. Paris: Didier, 1854.
NOTE: Vols. III and IV of *Histoire de la révolution d'Angleterre, q.v.*
REFERRED TO: 187n

——— *Histoire de la révolution d'Angleterre depuis l'avènement de Charles Ier jusqu'à la restauration de Charles II.* 1st pt. 2 vols. Paris: Leroux and Chantpie, 1826-27.
NOTE: no further volumes of this ed. appeared.
REFERRED TO: 187, 221, 227

—— *Histoire du protectorat de Richard Cromwell et du rétablissement des Stuart (1658-1660)*. 2 vols. Paris: Didier, 1856.
NOTE: Vols. V and VI of *Histoire de la révolution d'Angleterre, q.v.*
REFERRED TO: 187n

—— *Lectures on European Civilization*. Trans. P.M. Beckwith. London: Macrone, 1837.
NOTE: a translation of *Cours d'histoire moderne . . . Civilisation en Europe.*
REFERRED TO: 229

——, ed. *Collection des mémoires relatifs à la révolution d'Angleterre, accompagnée de notices et d'éclaircissemens historiques*. 25 vols. Paris and Rouen: Béchet, 1823-25.
REFERRED TO: 221

GUY, COMTE DE ROCHEFORT. Referred to: 30

GUYTON-MORVEAU, LOUIS BERNARD.
NOTE: the reference, in a quotation from Mignet, is to the moderates on the Committee of Public Safety.
REFERRED TO: 12

HALLAM, HENRY. *View of the State of Europe during the Middle Ages*. 2 vols. London: Murray, 1818.
NOTE: the title JSM gives at 51, "History and Government of Europe during the Middle Ages," derives from that which appears at the head of Chap. i in Vol. I and Chap. vii in Vol. II, "View of the History and Governments of Europe during the Middle Ages," and the running titles throughout, "History and Governments of Europe during the Middle Ages."
QUOTED: 40
REFERRED TO: 34, 38n, 40, 51-2
40.17-18 "disdain of money,"] Liberality indeed, and disdain of money, might be reckoned, as I have said, among the essential virtues of chivalry. (II, 551)

HAMPDEN, JOHN. Referred to: 121, 136

HARENC.
NOTE: son of Raoul de Harenc; not otherwise identified. The reference is in a quotation from Sismondi.
REFERRED TO: 41n

HARENC, RAOUL DE.
NOTE: the reference is in a quotation from Sismondi.
REFERRED TO: 41n

HEAD, EDMUND WALKER.
NOTE: the reference is to recently appointed qualified examiners at Oxford.
REFERRED TO: *369*

HEGEL, GEORG WILHELM FRIEDRICH.
NOTE: the reference is to the Hegelians.
REFERRED TO: 261

HÉLOÏSE.
NOTE: the second reference is in a quotation from Michelet.
REFERRED TO: 246

HELVÉTIUS, CLAUDE ADRIEN. Referred to: 66, 183

HÉNAULT, CHARLES JEAN FRANÇOIS. *Nouvel abrégé chronologique de l'histoire de France; contenant les événemens de notre histoire depuis Clovis jusqu'à la mort de Louis XIV* (1744). New ed. 3 vols. Paris: Prault, *et al.*, 1775-74.
NOTE: continuously paginated. The quotation is in a quotation from Carlyle.
QUOTED: 139

HENRI I (of France).
NOTE: grandson of Hugh Capet.
REFERRED TO: 32

HENRI IV (of France).
NOTE: the reference at 152 is in a quotation from Carlyle.
REFERRED TO: 61n, 152

HENRY I (of England).
NOTE: the reference at 41n is in a quotation from Sismondi.
REFERRED TO: 41n, 47, 292

HENRY II (of England).
NOTE: the reference at 239 is in a quotation from Michelet.
REFERRED TO: 28, 35, 239, 244

HENRY IV (Holy Roman Emperor).
NOTE: the reference is in a quotation from Michelet.
REFERRED TO: 247

HENRY IV (of France). See Henri IV.

HENRY V (of England). Referred to: 234

HENRY VIII (of England).
NOTE: the reference is in a quotation from Michelet.
REFERRED TO: 253

HENRY OF ALMAIN.
NOTE: son of Richard, Duke of Cornwall.
REFERRED TO: 49

HENRY, ROBERT. *The History of Great Britain, from the First Invasion of It by the Romans under Julius Caesar* (1771-93). 2nd ed. 12 vols. London: Strahan and Cadell, 1788-95.
NOTE: JSM's reference conforms to this ed.
REFERRED TO: 48n

HENRY-LARIVIÈRE, PIERRE FRANÇOIS JOACHIM.
NOTE: the reference, in a quotation from Mignet, is to the members of the Commission of Twelve.
REFERRED TO: 12

HERDER, JOHANN GOTTFRIED VON. Referred to: 185, 185n

———— *Ideen zur Philosophie der Geschichte der Menschheit.* 4 vols. Riga and Leipzig: Hartknoch, 1784-91.
REFERRED TO: 261

HERODOTUS. *History.*
NOTE: the references at 222 and 222n (the second of which is in a quotation from Courier) derive from the translation by Larcher (*q.v.*); that at *368-9* is general, so no ed. is cited. Two Greek and Latin eds. formerly in SC.
REFERRED TO: 222, 222n, *368-9*

HICKSON, WILLIAM EDWARD. "The French Republic," *Westminster Review*, L (Oct., 1848), 188-236.
REFERRED TO: 334

HILDEBRAND. See St. Gregory VII.

HILDERIC. See Childéric I.

Histoire de la révolution par deux amis de la liberté. See Kerverseau.

Histoire parlementaire. See Buchez.

HOCHE, LAZARE. Referred to: 178

HOLBACH, PAUL HENRI, BARON D'. Referred to: 66, 183

JEANNE D'ARC.
NOTE: the reference, in a quotation from Carlyle, is to the Maid of Orleans.
REFERRED TO: 152

JESUS.
NOTE: the first reference is in a quotation from Simon of Tournai quoted by Michelet; the second is in a quotation from Michelet.
REFERRED TO: 248, 253

JOANNES SCOTUS (Erigena).
NOTE: the reference is in a quotation from Guizot.
REFERRED TO: 272

JOHN (of England).
NOTE: the reference at 239 is in a quotation from Michelet.
REFERRED TO: 29, 239, 292

JOHN (of France). See Jean II.

JOHNSON, SAMUEL. "Preface to Shakespeare. Published in the Year 1768." In *The Works of Samuel Johnson, LL.D.* 13 vols. London: Buckland, *et al.*, 1787, IX, 239-302.
REFERRED TO: 135

JOSEPH (son of Jacob). Referred to: *380*

JOUBERT, CHARLES.
NOTE: the reference is in a quotation from Littré.
REFERRED TO: 179

JOURDAN, MATHIEU JOUVE.
NOTE: the reference is in a quotation from Carlyle.
REFERRED TO: 157

Journal des Débats. Referred to: 190

JULIAN THE APOSTATE.Referred to: 224

JULIANE.
NOTE: the reference is in a quotation from Sismondi.
REFERRED TO: 41n

"JUNIUS." *Junius: Including Letters by the Same Writer, under Other Signatures (Now First Collected). To Which Are Added, His Confidential Correspondence with Mr. Wilkes, and His Private Letters Addressed to Mr. H.S. Woodfall. With a Preliminary Essay, Notes, Fac-similes, &c.* 3 vols. London: Rivington, *et al.*, 1812.
NOTE: in SC.
REFERRED TO: 196

KABBALAH.
NOTE: the reference is in a quotation from Michelet.
REFERRED TO: 248

KANT, IMMANUEL.
NOTE: the reference is to "Kantism."
REFERRED TO: 183

———— *Idee zu einer allgemeinen Geschichte in weltbürgerlicher Absicht* (1784). In *Sämmtliche Werke*. Ed. Karl Rosenkrantz and Friedrich Schubert. 14 vols. in 12. Leipzig: Voss, 1838-40, VII, 315-35.
REFERRED TO: 261

KELLY, WALTER KEATING. See Leopold von Ranke, *The History of the Popes*.

KEPLER, JOHANN. Referred to: 228

NOTE: in SC; the work was completed in 14 vols. (Paris: Buisson) in 1826. The quotation, in a quotation from Carlyle, is summary.
QUOTED: 146

—————— *Histoire de l'assemblée constituante*. 2 vols. Paris, Strasbourg, and London: Treuttel and Würtz, 1821.
NOTE: part, eventually, of his *Histoire de la révolution française*, 8 vols. (Paris: Treuttel and Würtz, 1821-26).
QUOTED: 90

90.21 Le] [*no paragraph*] Le (I, 68)
90.25 adorateurs] adorations (I, 69)
90.26-7 *Il . . . frappé.*] [*not in italics*] (I, 69)
90.34 *dissoudre l'assemblée*] [*not in italics*] (I, 69)

LACY, LOUIS DE.
NOTE: the reference is to the Spanish general butchered by Ferdinand VII.
REFERRED TO: 89

LA FAYETTE, MARIE JOSEPH PAUL ROCH YVES GILBERT DU MOTIER, MARQUIS DE.
NOTE: JSM sometimes uses the spelling Lafayette. The reference at 90 is in a quotation from Montgaillard; the quotation and references at 150, 154, 155, 157 are in quotations from Carlyle.
QUOTED: 150
REFERRED TO: 78, 80, 90, 97, 154, 155, 157, 198

—————— "Lettre du général La Fayette au chevalier d'Archenholz" (Magdebourg, 27 Mar., 1793). In Jean Baptiste Regnault-Warin. *Mémoires pour servir à la vie du général La Fayette, et à l'histoire de l'assemblée constituante*. 2 vols. Paris: Hesse, 1824, II, 116-22.
NOTE: part of *Collection des mémoires*, ed. Berville and Barrière, *q.v.*
REFERRED TO: 78n

LAFFITTE, JACQUES. Referred to: 177, 198

LA FONTAINE, JEAN DE. *Fables choisies mises en vers*. Paris: Thierry, 1668.
NOTE: the reference, to "Le loup et l'agneau," Book I, Fable x, is in a quotation from Scott.
REFERRED TO: 87

LA GALLISSONNIÈRE, AUGUSTIN FÉLIX ELISABETH BARRIN, COMTE DE.
NOTE: the reference at 9 is in a quotation from Mignet; that at 87 is to him as a member of the new ministry following Necker's dismissal.
REFERRED TO: 9, 87

LAING, MALCOLM. *The History of Scotland, from the Union of the Crowns on the Accession of James VI to the Throne of England, to the Union of the Kingdoms in the Reign of Queen Anne*. 2 vols. London: Cadell and Davies; Edinburgh: Manners and Miller, 1800.
REFERRED TO: 57

LALLY-TOLENDAL, TROPHIME GÉRARD, MARQUIS DE.
NOTE: the quotation, which originates with Mme de Staël (*q.v.* for the collation), is in a quotation from Bailleul. The reference at 90 is in a quotation from Montgaillard.
QUOTED: 104
REFERRED TO: 83, 86, 90

LA LUZERNE, CÉSAR HENRI, COMTE DE.
NOTE: the reference at 9 is in a quotation from Mignet; that at 86-7 is to him as one of the ministers dismissed with Necker.
REFERRED TO: 9, 86-7

LAMARQUE, JEAN MAXIMILIEN. Referred to: 200

LAMARTINE, ALPHONSE MARIE LOUIS DE PRAT DE.
NOTE: the references at 321, 332 are to him as one of the members of the Provisional Government of 1848; that at 340-1 is in a quotation from Brougham.
REFERRED TO: 188n, 321, 332, 339, 340-1, 343

————— "Discours au peuple envahissant l'intérieur de l'hôtel de ville, accusant le gouvernement provisoire de trahison, et voulant le forcer à proclamer immédiatement, sans réserver les droits de la nation, la forme du gouvernement républicain" (25 Feb., 1848). In *Trois mois au pouvoir* (*q.v.*), 64-5.
REFERRED TO: 333

————— "Discours au peuple rassemblé en armes dans la salle du trône, et voulant forcer le gouvernement provisoire à arborer le drapeau rouge" (25 Feb., 1848). *Ibid.*, 66.
REFERRED TO: 333

————— *Histoire des Girondins*. 8 vols. Paris: Coquebert, 1847.
NOTE: the quotations are of the same passage; that at 355-6 is JSM's translation of the original, given at *399-400*, which is collated.
QUOTED: 355-6 (*399-400*)
399.26 Le] Ce (V, 407)
399.30-31 l'homme. . . . Tout] l'homme, par conséquent un plan divin que Dieu fait entrevoir à ses créatures. Tout ce qui contrarie ce plan, c'est-à-dire tout (V, 407)
400.11 esclavage. Ou] esclavage. [*paragraph*] Ou (V, 408)
400.14 générale; mais] générale. Mais (V, 408)
400.16-17 par la . . . par la] par ta . . . par ta (V, 408)
400.24 faim.] faim! (V, 409)
400.30 nous. . . . Le temps] nous. Dans les desseins de Dieu, le temps (V, 409)
400.34 temps. La] temps./ XXI./ [*paragraph*] La (V, 409-10)
400.35 terre. Les déceptions] terre; les déceptions (V, 410)

————— *Lettre aux dix départements* (25 Aug., 1848). In *Trois mois au pouvoir* (*q.v.*), 5-60.
REFERRED TO: 338, 341

————— *Manifeste aux puissances. Circulaire du ministre des affaires étrangères aux agents diplomatiques de la république française* (4 Mar., 1848). *Ibid.*, 69-78.
NOTE: the quotation is collated with the French version in App. B. The reference at 342 is in a quotation from Lamartine.
QUOTED: 341 (*397-8*), 342
REFERRED TO: 340, 342, 343-4, 348 (*398*)
398.10 de la nationalité] de nationalité (76) [*treated as printer's error in this ed.*]

————— *Réponse à une députation des citoyens irlandais habitant Dublin, Manchester et Liverpool, demandant la sympathie de la France pour l'indépendance de l'Irlande* (3 Apr., 1848). *Ibid.*, 148-52.
NOTE: the second quotation is collated with the French version in App. B.
QUOTED: 342, 342-3 (*398-9*)
342.37 "liberty . . . privilege,"] [*translated from:*] Dites à vos concitoyens que le nom de l'Irlande et le nom de la liberté courageusement défendue contre le privilége est un même nom pour tout citoyen français! (149)
399.6 peuples. Aucun] peuples! aucun (150)
399.7 étrangères. La] étrangères. la (150)
399.11 entière.] entière! (150)
399.12 humain. Nous] humain! nous (150)
399.15 fruits.] fruits! (150)
399.16 diplomates;] diplomates! (151)
399.17 traités. Nous] traités! nous (151)
399.20 environnent. Nous] environnent! nous (151)

—— *Réponse à une députation des Polonais, demandant l'appui du gouvernement pour le rétablissement de la nationalité polonaise* (19 Mar., 1848). *Ibid.*, 130-6.
NOTE: the quotation is collated with the French version in App.B.
QUOTED: 342 (*398*)
398.12 La République] La République est républicaine sans doute; elle le dit à haute voix au monde; mais la République (131)
398.14 elle.] elle! (131)
398.16 Germaniques. . . . Le Gouvernement] germaniques. [*ellipsis indicates 1½-page omission*] Le Gouvernment (131-2)
398.20 moment.] moment! (133)
398.21-2 elle-même. . . . La République] elle-même! [*ellipsis indicates 1½-page omission*] [*paragraph*] La République (135)
398.29 d'intervenir. Eh] d'intervenir. [*paragraph*] Eh (135)
398.30 pacifiques.] pacifiques! (135)

—— *Trois mois au pouvoir*. Paris: Lévy, 1848.
NOTE: the references are given under separate texts above.

LAMBESC. See Lorraine.

LA MENNAIS, HUGUES FÉLICITÉ ROBERT DE. *Essai sur l'indifférence en matière de religion*. 4 vols. Paris: Tournachon-Molin and Sequin (Vols. I-II); Librairie Classique-Elémentaire (Vols. III-IV), 1817-23.
NOTE: the reference is in a quotation from Guizot.
REFERRED TO: *390*

LAMETH, ALEXANDRE THÉODORE VICTOR, BARON DE. Referred to: 78

—— *Histoire de l'assemblée constituante*. 2 vols. Paris: Moutardier, 1828-29.
NOTE: the quotation (Carlyle's English recension of a French passage) is in a quotation from Carlyle, who gives the reference.
QUOTED: 140

LAMETH, CHARLES MALO FRANÇOIS, COMTE DE. Referred to: 78, 80n

LA NOUE, FRANÇOIS DE.
NOTE: the quotation is taken from Roederer (*q.v.* for the collation).
QUOTED: 43

LANSDOWNE, MARQUIS OF. See Petty-Fitzmaurice.

LARCHER, PIERRE HENRI, trans. *Histoire d'Hérodote traduite du grec, avec des remarques historiques et critiques, un essai sur la chronologie d'Hérodote, et une table géographique*. 7 vols. Paris: Musier and Nyon, 1786.
NOTE: Courier is the source of the references (the second of which is in a quotation from him).
REFERRED TO: 222, 222n

LA ROCHE DE GLUY (Lord of). Referred to: 49

LAROCHE, BERNARD.
NOTE: the reference, in a quotation from Carlyle, is to him as one of seven prisoners in the Bastille.
REFERRED TO: 146

LA ROCHEFOUCAULD-LIANCOURT, FRANÇOIS ALEXANDRE FRÉDÉRIC, DUC DE.
NOTE: the quotation is in a quotation from Toulongeon.
QUOTED: 91

LAUD, WILLIAM. Referred to: 299

LAUNAY, BERNARD RENÉ JOURDAN DE.
NOTE: the quotation, which derives from Dusaulx (*q.v.*), and the references are in a quotation from Carlyle.
QUOTED: 144
REFERRED TO: 143-4, 145, 146, 147

LAVALLÉ, JOSEPH, MARQUIS DE BOIS-ROBERT. *Histoire de l'origine, des progrès, et de la*

décadence des diverses factions qui ont agité la France depuis le 14 juillet, 1789, jusqu'à l'abdication de Napoléon. 3 vols. London: Murray, 1816.
QUOTED: 91
REFERRED TO: 108
91.8 "le soir] Le soir (I, 86)

LA VAUGUYON, PAUL FRANÇOIS, DUC DE.
NOTE: the reference at 9 is in a quotation from Mignet; that at 87 is to him as a member of the new ministry following Necker's dismissal.
REFERRED TO: 9, 87

LÉANS, HANNOT DE. Referred to: 49

LÉANS, PIERRE DE. Referred to: 49

LECLAIRE, EDMÉ JEAN. *Des améliorations qu'il serait possible d'apporter dans le sort des ouvriers peintres en bâtiments, suivies des règlements d'administration et de répartition des bénéfices que produit le travail, par Leclaire et mis en pratique dans sa maison . . . 1842.* Paris: Bouchard-Huzard, Carilian-Goeury, n.d.
REFERRED TO: 315

LECOINTRE, LAURENT. "Dépositions du lieutenant-colonel commandant la première division de la garde nationale de Versailles." In *HP* (*q.v.*), III, 111-15.
NOTE: the quotation is in a quotation from Carlyle.
QUOTED: 156

LEDRU-ROLLIN, ALEXANDRE AUGUSTE.
NOTE: the references at 321, 332 are to him as one of the members of the Provisional Government of 1848; one at 321 is to him as a leading member of the Paris bar.
REFERRED TO: 321, 332, 336, 339

——— *Bulletins de la république, ministère de l'intérieur.* In *Recueil complet des actes du gouvernement provisoire.* Ed. Emile Carrey. 2 pts. Paris: Durand, 1848, II, 617-79.
REFERRED TO: 336

LEE, NATHANIEL. *The Rival Queens; or, The Death of Alexander the Great.* London: Magnes and Bentley, 1677.
NOTE: the reference is in a quotation from Carlyle.
REFERRED TO: 149

LEFÈBRE-LAROCHE, PIERRE LOUIS, ABBÉ.
NOTE: the references are in quotations from Carlyle.
REFERRED TO: 152, 153

LEIBNIZ, GOTTFRIED WILHELM. Referred to: *376*

LEO X (Pope). Referred to: 224

LEOFRIC (Earl of Mercia). Referred to: 25, 26

LEOPOLD II (of Austria).
NOTE: the reference is to him as "a foreign despot."
REFERRED TO: 101

——— Letter to Louis XVI (3 Dec., 1791), *Gazette Nationale, ou Le Moniteur Universel*, 26 Dec., 1791, 1505.
REFERRED TO: 101

——— Letter of 17 Feb., 1792, *ibid.*, 2 Mar., 1792, 254.
REFERRED TO: 80n

LESSING, GOTTHOLD EPHRAIM. *Die Erziehung des Menschengeschlechts.* Berlin: Voss, 1780.
REFERRED TO: 261

L'HÉRITIER, JÉRÔME HONORÉ.
NOTE: the references are in a quotation from Carlyle.
REFERRED TO: 156, 157

LIANCOURT, DUC DE. See La Rochefoucauld-Liancourt.

LICINIUS, GAIUS.
NOTE: the reference derives from Livy.
REFERRED TO: 64-5

LINGARD, JOHN. Referred to: 239

L'ISLE, JOURDAIN DE, SIRE DE CASAUBON. Referred to: 49

LITTRÉ, EMILE. "Notice biographique." In *Oeuvres littéraires et économiques d'Armand Carrel.* Ed. Charles Romey. Paris: Guillaumin and Lecou, 1854, 5-66.
NOTE: JSM is ostensibly reviewing a work still to be published, which combines a translation of an abridged form of an article by Littré on Carrel with the translation of an article on Carrel, by Nisard, *q.v.* The reasons for our using the work cited here are given in the Textual Introduction, cii above.
REVIEWED: 167-215
QUOTED: 170, 178-9, 188, 196, 197, 212, 214, 214n
170.18-35 "Armand Carrel" . . . was . . . them.] [*translated from:*] Armand Carrel a été sous-lieutenant et journaliste; c'est dans ce cercle qu'a été renfermée la vie d'un homme qui, mort à la fleur de l'âge, laisse un nom connu de la France entière, et des regrets même à ses ennemis politiques. Sa renommée ne lui vint pas de la faveur des gouvernements ni de ces fonctions élevées où l'on trouve toujours l'occasion de se distinguer ou, au moins, de faire parler de soi. Impliqué dans les conspirations contre la Restauration, officier au service de la Constitution espagnole, prisonnier en Catalogne, condamné à mort, hardi dans l'opposition avant la révolution de Juillet, plus hardi encore après, il a toujours été laissé à ses propres forces, de manière à ne valoir jamais que sa vraie valeur, à ne recevoir aucun éclat emprunté, et à n'avoir d'autre rang que celui qu'il se créait lui-même. La fortune, cet inexplicable hasard qui distribue les balles dans une bataille, et qu'il faut bien admettre dans les choses humaines, ne se plut pas à le favoriser; il n'eut pas d'étoile qu'il pût invoquer dans les mauvais jours et qui lui jetât un rayon inattendu; et, moins que personne, Armand Carrel a été l'ouvrage des circonstances: il ne les a pas cherchées, elles ne sont pas venues. Force de caractère dans les temps difficiles, admirable talent d'écrivain dans tous les temps, noblesse d'âme envers amis et ennemis, c'est là ce qui le soutint et ce qui lui assurait, partout et à toute époque, non-seulement une place élevée dans l'estime des hommes, mais encore de l'ascendant. (5-6)
178.27-179.11 Carrel . . . plots.] [*translated from:*] Carrel était sous-lieutenant dans le 29e de ligne en 1821, au moment où les conspirations se tramaient de toutes parts contre la Restauration. Le 29e tenait garnison dans Béfort et Neuf-Brissach. Carrel se trouvait dans la dernière de ces deux villes. Il était engagé dans le complot qu'on a appelé depuis conspiration de Béfort; les officiers de Neuf-Brissach qui en faisaient partie avaient été découragés par les lenteurs apportées dans cette affaire, et ils ne voulaient plus marcher que le mouvement n'eût éclaté à Béfort. Il était urgent que, du moins, ils enlevassent leurs soldats dès que le coup aurait réussi dans cette dernière ville. La haute vente avait envoyé de Paris plusieurs conjurés; l'un d'eux, M. Joubert, était à Neuf-Brissach pour juger de ce qu'il y avait à faire. Carrel offrit de l'accompagner à Béfort, d'assister au mouvement et de rapporter la nouvelle à Neuf-Brissach: il s'habilla en bourgeois. Tous deux partirent et arrivèrent à Béfort vers minuit. Le complot avait été découvert, des arrestations avaient été faites, tout le monde était en fuite. Carrel reprit à franc-étrier la route de Neuf-Brissach, où il arriva de grand matin. Il eut le temps de rentrer chez lui, de se mettre en uniforme, et put assister à l'exercice du matin sans qu'on se doutât qu'il avait passé la nuit sur la grand'route. Lorsque l'on fit une instruction pour rechercher les complices des officiers de Béfort, et surtout pour savoir quel était celui qui s'était rendu de Neuf-Brissach dans cette ville, on ne put rien découvrir, et les soupçons se portèrent sur tout autre que sur Carrel; car ses manières légères et insouciantes l'avaient fait regarder, par ses chefs, comme tout à fait en dehors des menées. (7-8)

188.4 (*il . . . d'acier*).] Sa modeste épée de sous-lieutenant fut brisée par le sort entre ses mains; mais la plume qui la remplaça devint redoutable, et il a été dit souvent, et avec raison, qu'il . . . d'acier. (6)

196.16-18 "Unlike . . . Courier," . . . "who . . . sentence;"] [*translated from:*] Au contraire de Paul-Louis Courier, qui hésitait sur un mot, Carrel n'hésitait jamais sur une phrase. (37)

196.22 *la sûreté de l'expression:*] Son style, sans artifice et sans recherche, était un chef-d'oeuvre pour la sûreté de l'expression, qui arrivait toujours abondante comme la pensée, si pleine et si abondante elle-même; et si on ne sentait pas le travail de l'écrivain qui retouche avec soin chaque passage, on sentait une inspiration vigoureuse qui donnait à toute chose le mouvement, la forme et la couleur, et jetait dans un même moule le style et la pensée. (37)

196.24-30 "*L'expression*" . . . "*arrivait . . . thought.*"] [*see preceding entry*]

197.11-15 "The *National*," . . . "was . . . journal."] Le *National*, en effet, n'a pas été pour Carrel un fiord théâtre où il venait jouer le rôle que le hasard lui imposait; ce fut pour lui une arène où il luttait, une tribune du haut de laquelle il parlait, un champ clos où il se serait cru malheureux de ne pouvoir descendre en personne: le *National* fut une personnification d'Armand Carrel; et, si le journal exprima ses pensées, les entraînements, les passions de l'écrivain, l'écrivain, à son tour, était toujours sur la brèche, prêt à défendre, au péril de sa vie ou de sa liberté, ce qu'il venait de dire dans le journal. (37-8)

212.23-35 "He . . . repeated," . . . "that . . . exposed."] [*translated from:*] Il a répété souvent que le *National* n'avait point de procureur du roi pour le défendre, et qu'il fallait qu'il se défendît lui-même. Il était persuadé aussi que rien n'alimente plus les haines politiques et ne les rend plus capables de se porter aux derniers excès que l'impunité des diffamations odieuses: il prétendait que les hommes de la révolution avaient préparé eux-mêmes leur échafaud en n'imposant pas le silence au dénigrement; et, eût-il dû s'exposer bien plus qu'il ne l'a fait, il n'aurait jamais souffert, dans quelque situation où il se fût trouvé, qu'on se jouât impunément de son nom et de sa personne. C'était là ce qu'il répondait quand on le blâmait de risquer sa vie légèrement; et, aujourd'hui qu'il a succombé, il faut, en défendant sa mémoire d'un reproche que la douleur a arraché à des voix amies, se rappeler ce qu'il disait sur son lit de mort: "Le porte-drapeau du régiment est le plus exposé." (58-9)

214.6-11 "he . . . things," . . . "are . . . prevented."] [*translated from:*] Mais, quand une impression venait le saisir, quand son esprit était obligé de déployer ses hautes facultés, endormies souvent devant d'insignifiants détails, alors nul regard mieux que le sien n'embrassait le présent et l'avenir; il reconnaissait d'un coup d'oeil, comme il aurait fait sur le champ de bataille, tout le terrain où il se trouvait placé; et, ce qui étonnait surtout en lui, c'était la sûreté de l'instinct qui lui faisait deviner la portée des petites choses. Les petites choses sont celles que le vulgaire n'aperçoit pas; puis, quand elles ont produit de graves résultats, on s'arrête, tout déconcerté, devant l'irrévocable événement, qu'il aurait été si facile de prévenir. (62)

214n.8-9 "Every body," . . . "thinks . . . ones."] [*translated from:*] Tout le monde songe aux grandes choses; seuls, les esprits supérieurs songent aux petites. (62)

LIVY (Titus Livius). *Livy* (Latin and English). Trans. B.O. Foster, *et al.* 14 vols. London: Heinemann; New York: Putnam's Sons; and (Vols. VI-XIV) Cambridge, Mass.: Harvard University Press, 1919-59.
NOTE: this ed. used for ease of reference.
REFERRED TO: 3, 37, 65, *368-9*

LOMBARD, PETER.
NOTE: the reference is in a quotation from Michelet.
REFERRED TO: 248

LOMÉNIE DE BRIENNE, ETIENNE CHARLES DE, CARDINAL.
NOTE: the reference and quotation are in a quotation from Carlyle.
QUOTED: 142
REFERRED TO: 140

LORRAINE, CHARLES EUGÈNE DE, PRINCE DE LAMBESC.
NOTE: the references are in a quotation from Mignet.
REFERRED TO: 9, 10

LOTHAIRE I, EMPEREUR D'OCCIDENT.
NOTE: the first of the "series of Lothaires."
REFERRED TO: 24

LOTHAIRE II.
NOTE: of Lorraine; one of the grandsons of Louis I.
REFERRED TO: 19

LOUIS I (of France; Roman Emperor).
NOTE: known as le Débonnaire or le Pieux. The reference at 279 is in a quotation from Guizot.
REFERRED TO: 32, 279

LOUIS II (Roman Emperor).
NOTE: known as le Jeune; one of the grandsons of Louis I.
REFERRED TO: 19

LOUIS II (of France).
NOTE: known as le Bègue; one of the grandsons of Louis I.
REFERRED TO: 19

LOUIS III (of France).
NOTE: one of the grandsons of Louis I.
REFERRED TO: 19

LOUIS V (of France).
NOTE: "the last of the Carlovingians."
REFERRED TO: 290

LOUIS VI (of France).
NOTE: known as le Gros.
REFERRED TO: 30, 31

LOUIS VII (of France).
NOTE: known as le Jeune. The references are in quotations from Michelet.
REFERRED TO: 239, 247

LOUIS IX (of France).
NOTE: St. Louis. The reference at 239 and the second at 251 are in quotations from Michelet.
REFERRED TO: 33, 44, 48, 49, 50, 239, 250, 251, 289

LOUIS XI (of France). Referred to: 254

LOUIS XIV (of France).
NOTE: the reference at 293 is in a quotation from Guizot.
REFERRED TO: 49, 222, 293, 299n, 346

LOUIS XV (of France).
NOTE: the first reference at 138 derives from, the second is in a quotation from, Carlyle.
REFERRED TO: 50, 138

—————— *Edit du roi, concernant la société des jésuites.* Paris: Simon, 1764.
NOTE: this edict, of Nov., 1764, banishing the Jesuits, was still in effect at the period of which JSM is writing.
REFERRED TO: 189

LOUIS XVI (of France).
NOTE: the quotation at 87n derives from Bailly (*q.v.* for the collation); that at 91 is from Toulongeon; that at 157 has not been located. The references at 6-7, 7-9, 12, are in quotations from Mignet; that at 80 derives from the *Histoire parlementaire*; the first at 88 is in a quotation from Scott; the second is in a quotation from Ferrières; that at 90 is from Lacretelle; one at 97 derives from Dumouriez; that at 103 is in a quotation from Bailleul; that at 105 is from Kerverseau; that at 106 is in a quotation from Soulavie; one at 107 is in a quotation from Bertrand de Moleville; those at 142, 153, 155, 156, 166 are in quotations from Carlyle; that at 252 is in a quotation from Michelet.

LUCAS-MONTIGNY, GABRIEL.
NOTE: see also Mirabeau, *Mémoires*.
REFERRED TO: 148n

LUTHER, MARTIN. Referred to: *375*

LUXEMBOURG. See Montmorency-Luxembourg.

MABLY, GABRIEL BONNOT DE, ABBÉ. Referred to: 66

—— *Observations sur l'histoire de France* (1765). New ed. Rev. F.P.G. Guizot. 3 vols. Paris: Brière, 1823.
NOTE: this ed. was accompanied by the 1st ed. of Guizot's *Essais*, *q.v.*
REFERRED TO: *371*

MACAULAY, THOMAS BABINGTON. "Dumont's *Recollections of Mirabeau*," *Edinburgh Review*, LV (July, 1832), 552-76.
REFERRED TO: 115

MACKINTOSH, JAMES. *The History of England*. 10 vols. London: Longman, *et al.*, 1830-40.
NOTE: the reference is not overt, but JSM elsewhere (see *CW*, VII, 151-2) attributes the comment to Mackintosh.
REFERRED TO: 356

MACPHERSON, JAMES. See Ossian.

MAILLARD, MARIE JULIEN STANISLAS.
NOTE: the references are in quotations from Carlyle.
REFERRED TO: 146, 147, 152, 153, 154, 155

MALCOLM III (of Scotland). Referred to: 47

MALCOLM, JAMES PELLER. *Londinium redivivum; or, An Antient History and Modern Description*. 4 vols. London: Rivington, *et al.*, 1802-07.
NOTE: cited as an illustration of histories of London, on which JSM comments.
REFERRED TO: 18

MALESHERBES, CHRÉTIEN GUILLAUME DE LAMOIGNON.
NOTE: the reference, in a quotation from Carlyle, derives from Montgaillard.
REFERRED TO: 140

MANFRED (of Sicily).
NOTE: the reference is in a quotation from Michelet.
REFERRED TO: 248

MANUEL, JACQUES ANTOINE. Referred to: 177

MARAT, JEAN PAUL. *Avis au peuple, ou Les ministres dévoilés* (1789). In *HP*, II, 37-8.
NOTE: the reference is in a quotation from Carlyle.
REFERRED TO: 146

MARCEAU, FRANÇOIS SÉVERIN. Referred to: 178

MARIA THERESA (of Austria).
NOTE: the reference is in a quotation from Carlyle.
REFERRED TO: 165

MARIE-ADÉLAÏDE.
NOTE: known as Madame, the elder daughter of Louis XV. The reference is in a quotation from Ferrières.
REFERRED TO: 88

MARIE ANTOINETTE (of France).
NOTE: the quotation, which derives from Ferrières (*q.v.*), is in a quotation from Carlyle; the reference at 6 is in a quotation from Mignet; that at 90 is from Lacretelle; that at 106 is from Soulavie; that at 142 is from Carlyle.

MÉRIMÉE, PROSPER. Referred to: 185

MICHELET, JULES. *Histoire de France*. 5 vols. Paris: Hachette, 1833-42.
NOTE: five further vols. published 1844-67.
REVIEWED: 217-55
QUOTED: 235, 235-6, 237, 238, 238-9, 239, 242, 244, 246, 246-7, 247, 247-8, 248, 248-9, 249, 249-50, 250, 251, 252, 253

235.34-6 "The . . . people," . . . "is . . . things."][*translated from:*] [*paragraph*] La base originaire, celle qui a tout reçu, tout accepté, c'est cette jeune, molle et mobile race des Gaëls, bruyante, sensuelle et légère, prompte à apprendre, prompte à dédaigner, avide de choses nouvelles. (I, 129)

235.38-236.2 "Such . . . impulse."] [*translated from:*] [*paragraph*] Il faut à de tels enfans des précepteurs sévères. Ils en recevront et du midi et du nord. La mobilité sera fixée, la mollesse durcie et fortifiée; il faut que la raison s'ajoute à l'instinct, à l'élan la réflexion. (I, 129)

237.4-6 "Ce . . . l'homme,"] [*paragraph*] Ce . . . l'homme, qui plus tard devint le principe de l'organisation féodale, ne paraît pas de bonne heure chez l'autre branche des tribus odiniques. (I, 168)

237.7 "profonde impersonnalité"] J'ai parlé dans un autre ouvrage de la profonde impersonnalité du génie germanique, et j'y reviendrai ailleurs. (I, 171n)

237.12-13 "le génie . . . libre;"] Ce génie . . . libre, de l'orgueil effréné du moi, n'est-il pas éminent dans la philosophie celtique, dans Pélage, Abailard et Descartes, tandis que le mysticisme et l'idéalisme ont fait le caractère presque invariable de la philosophie et de la théologie allemandes[1]? [*footnote begins with sentence quoted in preceding entry*] (I, 171)

238.37-8 Chap. I. . . . France.] [*translated from:*] Livre IV. Chapitre Ier. *L'an 1000. Le roi de France et le pape français. Robert et Gerbert.—France féodale.* (II, 708)

238.38-9 II. . . . England.] [*translated from:*] Chapitre II. *Onzième siècle.—Grégoire VII.—Alliance des Normands et l'Eglise.—Conquêtes des Deux-Siciles et de l'Angleterre.* (II, 709)

238.39 III. The Crusade.] [*translated from:*] Chapitre III. *La Croisade.* 1195-1199 [*sic for* 1095-1099]. (II, 710)

238.40-239.1 IV. Consequences . . . Century.] [*translated from:*] Chapitre IV. *Suites de la croisade. Les Communes. Abailard. Première moitié du douzième siècle.* (II, 711)

239.1-3 V. . . . Henry.] [*translated from:*] Chapitre V. *Le roi de France et le roi d'Angleterre. Louis-le-Jeune, Henri II (Plantagenet).—Seconde croisade, humiliation de Louis.—Thomas Becket, humiliation d'Henri (seconde moitié du douzième siècle).* (II, 712)

239.3-5 VI. . . . France.] [*translated from:*] Chapitre VI. *1200. Innocent III.—Le pape prévaut, par les armes des Français du Nord, sur le roi d'Angleterre et l'empereur d'Allemagne, sur l'empire grec et sur les Albigeois. Grandeur du roi de France.* (II, 713-14)

239.5-6 VII. . . . Albigeois.] [*translated from:*] Suite du Chapitre VII [*sic*].—*Ruine de Jean. Défaite de l'Empereur. Guerre des Albigeois. Grandeur du roi de France 1204-1222.* (II, 715)

239.6-7 VIII. . . . France.] [*translated from:*] Chapitre VIII. *Première moitié du treizième siècle. Mysticisme. Louis IX. Sainteté du roi de France.* (II, 716)

239.7-9 IX. . . . Ages.] [*translated from:*] Chapitre dernier. *Lutte des Mendians et de l'Université. Saint Thomas. Doutes de saint Louis. La Passion comme principe d'art au moyen-âge.* (II, 718)

239.10-11 "The Sicilian Vespers;"] [*translated from:*] Livre V. Chapitre Ier. *Vêpres siciliennes.* (III, 520)

239.11 "Philippe le Bel and Boniface VIII."] [*translated from:*] Chapitre II. *Philippe-le-Bel,—Boniface VIII. 1285-1304.* (III, 520)

242.5 "sons of serfs."] [*relevant words translated from:*] [*paragraph*] Attendu que la superstition des clercs (oubliant que c'est par la guerre et le sang répandu, sous Charlemagne et d'autres, que le royaume de France a été converti de l'erreur des gentils à la foi catholique), absorbe tellement la juridiction des princes séculiers, que ces fils de serfs jugent selon leur loi les libres et fils de libres, bien que, suivant la loi des premiers conquérans, ce soient eux plutôt que nous devrions juger. (II, 615n)

244.2-9 "These rights," . . . gave . . . mankind.] [*translated from:*] Ces droits donnaient lieu à de grands abus sans doute; bien des crimes étaient impunément commis par des prêtres; mais quand on songe à l'épouvantable barbarie, à la fiscalité exécrable des tribunaux laïques au douzième siècle, on est obligé d'avouer que la juridiction ecclésiastique était alors une ancre de salut. Elle pouvait épargner des coupables; mais combien elle sauvait d'innocens! L'église était presque la seule voie par où les races méprisées pussent reprendre quelque ascendant. On le voit par l'exemple des deux saxons Breakspear (Adrien IV) et Becket. Les libertés de l'église étaient alors celles du monde. (II, 343-4)

246.16-29 The . . . Christendom. . . .] [*translated from:*] La restauration de la femme qui avait commencé avec le christianisme, eut lieu principalement au douzième siècle. Esclave dans l'Orient, enfermée encore dans le gynécée grec, émancipée par la jurisprudence impériale, elle fut reconnue par la nouvelle religion pour l'égale de l'homme. Toutefois le Christianisme, à peine affranchi de la sensualité payenne, craignait toujours la femme et s'en défiait. Il se connaissait faible et tendre. Il la repoussait d'autant plus qu'il sympathisait de coeur avec elle. De là, ces expressions dures, méprisantes même, par lesquelles il s'efforce de se prémunir. La femme est communément désignée dans les écrivains ecclésiastiques et dans les capitulaires par ce mot dégradant, mais profond: *Vas infirmius*. Quand Grégoire VII voulut affranchir le clergé de son double lien, la femme et la terre, il y eut un nouveau déchaînement contre cette dangereuse Eve, dont la séduction a perdu Adam, et qui le poursuit toujours dans ses fils. [*paragraph*] Un mouvement tout contraire commença au douzième siècle. Le libre mysticisme entreprit de relever ce que la dureté sacerdotale avait traîné dans la boue. Ce fut surtout un Breton, Robert d'Arbrissel, qui remplit cette mission d'amour. Il rouvrit aux femmes le sein du Christ, fonda pour elles des asiles, leur bâtit Fontevrault, et il y eut bientôt des Fontevrault par toute la chrétienté.[1] [*footnote omitted; second ellipsis indicates 11-sentence omission*] (II, 297-8)

246.29-247.10 There . . . monarchies.] [*translated from:*] [*paragraph*] La grâce prévalant sur la loi, il se fit insensiblement une grande révolution religieuse. Dieu changea de sexe, pour ainsi dire. La Vierge devint le dieu du monde; elle envahit presque tous les temples et tous les autels. La piété se tourna en enthousiasme de galanterie chevaleresque. La mère de Dieu fut proclamée pure et sans tache. L'église mystique de Lyon célébra la fête de l'immaculée conception [1134][1], exaltant ainsi l'idéal de la pureté maternelle, précisément à l'époque où Héloïse exprimait dans ses fameuses lettres le pur désintéressement de l'amour. [*paragraph*] La femme régna dans le ciel, elle régna sur la terre. Nous la voyons intervenir dans les choses de ce monde et les diriger. Bertrade de Montfort gouverne à la fois son premier époux Foulques d'Anjou, et le second Philippe Ier, roi de France. Le premier, exclus de son lit, se trouve trop heureux, de s'asseoir sur l'escabeau de ses pieds[2]. Louis VII date ses actes du couronnement de sa femme Adèle. Les femmes, juges naturels des combats de poésie et des cours d'amour, siégent aussi comme juges, à l'égal de leurs maris, dans les affaires sérieuses. Le roi de France reconnaît expressément ce droit[1]. Nous verrons Alix de Montmorency conduire une armée à son époux, le fameux Simon de Montfort. [*paragraph*] Exclues jusque-là des successions par la barbarie féodale, les femmes y rentrent partout dans la première moitié du douzième siècle: en Angleterre, en Castille, en Aragon, à Jérusalem, en Bourgogne, en Flandre, Hainaut, Vermandois, en Aquitaine, Provence et bas Languedoc. La rapide extinction des mâles, l'adoucissement des moeurs et le progrès de l'équité, rouvrent les héritages aux femmes. Elles portent avec elles les souverainetés dans des maisons étrangères; elles mêlent le monde, elles accélèrent l'agglomération des états, et préparent la centralisation des grandes monarchies. [*footnotes omitted*] (II, 300-2)

247.15-37 The . . . arise. . . .] [*translated from:*] La face du monde était sombre à la fin du douzième siècle. L'ordre ancien était en péril, et le nouveau n'avait pas commencé. Ce n'était plus la lutte matérielle du pape et de l'Empereur, se chassant alternativement de Rome, comme au temps d'Henri IV et de Grégoire VII. Au onzième siècle, le mal était à la superficie, en 1200 au coeur. Un mal profond, terrible, travaillait le christianisme. Qu'il eût voulu revenir à la querelle des investitures, et n'avoir à combattre que sur la question du bâton droit ou courbé! Au temps de Grégoire VII, l'église c'était la liberté; elle avait soutenu ce caractère jusqu'au temps d'Alexandre III, le chef de la ligue lombarde. Mais Alexandre lui-même n'avait osé appuyer Thomas Becket; il avait défendu les libertés italiennes, et trahi celles d'Angleterre. Ainsi l'église allait s'isoler du grand mouvement du monde. Au lieu de le guider et le devancer, comme elle avait fait jusqu'alors, elle s'efforçait de l'immobiliser, ce mouvement, d'arrêter le temps au passage, de fixer la terre qui tournait sous elle et qui l'emportait. Innocent III parut y réussir;

Boniface VIII périt dans l'effort. [*paragraph*] Moment solennel, et d'une tristesse infinie. L'espoir de la Croisade avait manqué au monde. L'autorité ne semblait plus inattaquable; elle avait promis, elle avait trompé. La liberté commençait à poindre, mais sous vingt aspects fantastiques et choquans, confuse et convulsive, multiforme, difforme. La volonté humaine enfantait chaque jour, et reculait devant ses enfans. C'était comme dans les jours séculaires de la grande semaine de la création: la nature s'essayant, jeta d'abord des produits bizarres, gigantesques, éphémères, monstrueux avortons dont les restes inspirent l'horreur. [*paragraph*] Une chose perçait dans cette mystérieuse anarchie du douzième siècle, qui se produisait sous la main de l'église irritée et tremblante, c'était un sentiment prodigieusement audacieux de la puissance morale et de la grandeur de l'homme. Ce mot hardi des Pélagiens: *Christ n'a rien eu de plus que moi, je puis me diviniser par la vertu*; il est reproduit au douzième siècle sous forme barbare et mystique. L'homme déclare que la fin est venue, qu'en lui-même est cette fin; il croit à soi, et se sent Dieu; partout surgissent des Messies. [*last ellipsis indicates 4-sentence omission*] (II, 392-4)

247.37-248.16   A . . . reign. . . . Nothing . . . it.] [*translated from:*] En Europe, un messie paraît dans Anvers, et toute la populace le suit. Un autre, en Bretagne, semble ressusciter le vieux gnosticisme d'Irlande[2]. Amaury de Chartres, et son disciple, le breton David de Dinan, enseignent que tout chrétien est matériellement un membre du Christ, autrement dit, que Dieu est perpétuellement incarné dans le genre humain. Le fils a régné assez, disent-ils; règne maintenant le Saint-Esprit. C'est sous quelque rapport l'idée de Lessing sur l'éducation du genre humain. [*paragraph*] Rien n'égale l'audace de ces docteurs, qui pour la plupart professent a l'université de Paris (autorisée par Philippe-Auguste en 1200). On a cru étouffer Abailard, mais il vit et parle dans son disciple Pierre-le-Lombard, qui de Paris régente toute la philosophie européenne; on compte près de cinq cents commentateurs de ce scholastique. L'esprit d'innovation a reçu deux auxiliaires. La jurisprudence grandit à côté de la théologie qu'elle ébranle; les papes défendent aux prêtres de professer le droit, et ne font qu'ouvrir l'enseignement aux laïques. La métaphysique d'Aristote arrive de Constantinople, tandis que ses commentateurs, apportés d'Espagne, vont être traduits de l'arabe par ordre des rois de Castille et des princes italiens de la maison de Souabe (Frédéric II et Manfred). Ce n'est pas moins que l'invasion de la Grèce et de l'Orient dans la philosophie chrétienne. Aristote prend place presque au niveau de Jésus-Christ[1]. Défendu d'abord par les papes, puis toléré, il règne dans les chaires. Aristote tout haut, tout bas les Arabes et les Juifs, avec le panthéisme d'Averrhoès et les subtilités de la Cabale. La dialectique entre en possession de tous les sujets, et se pose toutes les questions hardies. Simon de Tournai enseigne à volonté le pour et le contre. Un jour qu'il avait ravi l'Ecole de Paris et prouvé merveilleusement la vérité de la religion chrétienne, il s'écria tout à coup: "O petit Jésus, petit Jésus, comme j'ai élevé ta loi! Si je voulais, je pourrais encore mieux la rabaisser[2]." [*footnotes omitted*] (II, 394-6)

248.19-34   What . . . head! . . . [*paragraph*] The . . . Islamism.] [*translated from:*] Quels devaient être dans ce danger de l'église le trouble et l'inquiétude de son chef visible. [*ellipsis indicates 8-sentence omission*] [*paragraph*] Le pape était alors un Romain, Innocent III[1]. Tel péril, tel homme. Grand légiste[2], habitué à consulter le droit sur toute question, il s'examina lui-même, et crut à son droit. Dans la réalité, l'église avait certainement alors pour elle l'immense majorité, la voix du peuple, qui est celle de Dieu. Elle avait partout, en tout, *la possession actuelle*; possession ancienne, si ancienne qu'on pouvait croire à la prescription. L'église dans ce grand procès, était le défendeur, propriétaire reconnu, établi sur le fond disputé; elle en avait les titres: le droit écrit semblait pour elle. Le demandeur, c'était l'esprit humain, il venait un peu tard. Puis il semblait s'y prendre mal, dans son inexpérience, chicanant sur des textes, au lieu d'invoquer l'équité. Qui lui eût demandé ce qu'il voulait, il était impossible de l'entendre; des voix confuses s'élevaient pour répondre. Tous demandaient choses différentes, la plupart voulaient moins avancer que rétrograder. En politique, ils attestaient la république antique, c'est-à-dire les libertés urbaines, à l'exclusion des campagnes. En religion, les uns voulaient supprimer le culte, et revenir, disaient-ils, aux apôtres. Les autres remontaient plus haut, et rentraient dans l'esprit de l'Asie; ils voulaient deux dieux; ou bien préféraient la stricte unité de l'islamisme. [*footnotes omitted*] (II, 419-21)

248.36-249.11   Such . . . Inquisition.] [*translated from:*] Tels apparaissaient alors les ennemis de l'église; et l'église était peuple. Les préjugés du peuple, l'ivresse sanguinaire des haines et des terreurs, tout cela remontait par tous les rangs du clergé jusqu'au pape. Ce serait aussi faire trop grande injure à la nature humaine que de croire que l'égoïsme ou l'intérêt de corps anima seul les chefs de l'église. Non, tout indique qu'au treizième siècle ils étaient encore convaincus de leur droit. Ce droit admis, tous les moyens leur furent bons pour le défendre. Ce n'était pas pour un intérêt humain que saint Dominique parcourait les campagnes du midi, seul et sans arme, au milieu des sectaires, qu'il envoyait à la mort, cherchant et donnant le martyre, avec la même avidité[1]. [footnote omitted] Et quelle qu'ait été dans ce grand et terrible Innocent III la tentation de l'orgueil et de la vengeance, d'autres motifs encore l'animèrent dans la croisade des Albigeois et la fondation de l'inquisition dominicaine. (II, 422-3)

249.38-250.1 "In . . . authority," . . . "and . . . mysticism."] [translated from:] [paragraph] A mesure que l'autorité s'en allait, que le prêtre tombait dans l'esprit des peuples, la religion, n'étant plus contenue dans les formes, se répandait en mysticisme[1]. [footnote omitted] (III, 195)

250.14-17 "wandered . . . elements."] [translated from:] Ces apôtres effrénés de la grâce, couraient partout pieds nus, jouant tous les Mystères dans leurs sermons, traînant après eux les femmes et les enfans, riant à Noël, pleurant le Vendredi-Saint, développant sans retenue tout ce que le christianisme a d'élémens dramatiques. (II, 540-1)

250.24-9 "Mysticism," . . . "had . . . Pastoureaux,"] [translated from:] Le mysticisme, répandu dans le peuple par l'esprit des croisades, avait déjà porté son fruit le plus effrayant, la haine de la loi[1], l'enthousiasme sauvage de la liberté politique et religieuse. Ce caractère démagogique du mysticisme, qui devait se produire nettement dans les jacqueries des siècles suivans, particulièrement dans la révolte des paysans de Souabe, en 1525, et des anabaptistes, en 1538, il apparut déjà dans l'insurrection des Pastoureaux[2], qui éclata pendant l'absence de saint Louis. [footnotes omitted] (II, 579)

251.26-37 The . . . expeditions.] [translated from:] La croisade de saint Louis fut la dernière croisade. Le moyen-âge avait donné son idéal, sa fleur et son fruit: il devait mourir. En Philippe-le-Bel, petit-fils de saint Louis, commencent les temps modernes; le moyen-âge est souffleté en Boniface VIII, la croisade brûlée dans la personne des Templiers. [paragraph] L'on parlera long-temps encore de croisade, ce mot sera souvent répété: c'est un mot sonore, efficace, pour lever des décimes et des impôts. Mais les grands et les papes savent bien entre eux ce qu'ils doivent en penser[1]. Quelque temps après [1327], nous voyons le vénitien Sanuto proposer au pape une croisade commerciale: "Il ne suffisait pas, disait-il, d'envahir l'Egypte, il fallait la ruiner." Le moyen qu'il proposait, c'était de rouvrir au commerce de l'Inde la route de la Perse, de sorte que les marchandises ne passassent plus par Alexandrie et Damiette[2]. Ainsi s'annonce de loin l'esprit moderne; le commerce, et non la religion, va devenir le mobile des expéditions lointaines. [footnotes omitted] (II, 606-7)

252.3-21 This . . . misconduct.] [translated from:] Cette furieuse invective gibeline, toute pleine de vérités et de calomnies, c'est la plainte du vieux monde mourant, contre ce laid jeune monde qui lui succède. Celui-ci commence vers 1300; il s'ouvre par la France, par l'odieuse figure de Philippe-le-Bel. [paragraph] Au moins quand la monarchie française, fondée par Philippe-Auguste et Philippe-le-Bel, finit en Louis XVI, elle eut dans sa mort une consolation. Elle périt dans la gloire immense d'une jeune république qui, pour son coup d'essai, vainquit l'Europe et la renouvela. Mais ce pauvre moyen âge, papauté, chevalerie, féodalité, sous quelle main périssent-ils? Sous la main du procureur, du banqueroutier, du faux-monnayeur. [paragraph] La plainte est excusable; ce nouveau monde est laid. S'il est plus légitime que celui qu'il remplace, quel oeil, fût-ce celui de Dante, pourrait le découvrir à cette époque? Il naît sous les rides du vieux droit romain, de la vieille fiscalité impériale. Il naît avocat, usurier; il naît gascon, lombard et juif. [paragraph] Ce qui irrite le plus contre ce système moderne, contre la France, son premier représentant, c'est sa contradiction perpétuelle, sa duplicité d'instinct, l'hypocrisie naïve, si je puis dire, avec laquelle il va attestant tour à tour, et alternant ses deux principes, romain et féodal. La France est alors un légiste en cuirasse, un procureur bardé de fer; elle emploie la force féodale à exécuter les sentences du droit romain et canonique. [paragraph] Fille obéissante de l'Eglise, elle s'empare de l'Italie et de l'Eglise même; si elle bat l'Eglise, c'est comme sa fille, comme obligée en conscience de corriger sa mère. (III, 31-2)

252.29-34 It . . . friends.] [translated from:] [paragraph] Ce n'est donc pas la faute de ce gouvernement s'il est avide et affamé. La faim est sa nature, sa nécessité, le fond même de son tempérament. Pour y satisfaire, il faut qu'il emploie tour à tour la ruse et la force. Il y a ici en un seul prince, comme dans le vieux roman, maître Renard et maître Isengrin. [*paragraph*] Ce roi, de sa nature, n'aime pas la guerre, il est juste de le reconnaître; il préfère tout autre moyen de prendre, l'achat, l'usure. D'abord, il trafique, il échange, il achète; le fort peut dépouiller ainsi honnêtement des amis faibles. (III, 42)

253.3-6 The . . . question.] [*translated from:*] [*paragraph*] La confiscation de l'Eglise fut la pensée des rois depuis le treizième siècle, la cause principale de leurs luttes contre les papes; toute la différence, c'est que les protestants prirent, et que les catholiques se firent donner. Henri VIII employa le schisme, François Ier le Concordat. [*paragraph*] Qui donc, au quatorzième siècle, du roi ou de l'Eglise, devait désormais exploiter la France? telle était la question. (III, 50)

253.24-33 The . . . symbol.] [*translated from:*] La forme de réception était empruntée aux rites dramatiques et bizarres, aux *mystères* dont l'église antique ne craignait pas d'entourer les choses saintes. Le récipiendaire était présenté d'abord comme un pécheur, un mauvais chrétien, un renégat. Il reniait, à l'exemple de saint Pierre; le reniement dans cette pantomime, s'exprimait par un acte[1],[*footnote omitted*] cracher sur la croix. L'ordre se chargeait de réhabiliter ce renégat, de l'élever d'autant plus haut, que sa chûte était plus profonde. Ainsi dans la Fête des fols ou idiots (*fatuorum*), l'homme offrait l'hommage même de son imbécillité, de son infamie, à l'Eglise qui devait le régénérer. Ces comédies sacrées, chaque jour moins comprises, étaient de plus en plus dangereuses, plus capables de scandaliser un âge prosaïque, qui ne voyait que la lettre et perdait le sens du symbole. (III, 127-8)

254.14-20 What . . . misunderstood.] [*translated from:*] La vraie cause de leur ruine, celle qui mit tout le peuple contre eux, qui ne leur laissa pas un défenseur parmi tant de familles nobles auxquelles ils appartenaient, ce fut cette monstrueuse accusation d'avoir renié et craché sur la croix. Cette accusation est justement celle qui fut avouée du plus grand nombre. La simple énonciation du fait éloignait d'eux tout le monde; chacun se signait et ne voulait plus rien entendre. [*paragraph*] Ainsi l'ordre qui avait représenté au plus haut degré le génie symbolique du moyen âge, mourut d'un symbole non compris. (III, 206)

———— *Histoire romaine: république*. 1st pt. 3 vols. Brussels: Hauman, 1835.
NOTE: in SC. No more published.
REFERRED TO: 232

MICHELL, RICHARD.
NOTE: the reference is to recently appointed qualified examiners at Oxford.
REFERRED TO: *369*

MIGNET, FRANÇOIS AUGUSTE MARIE. Referred to: 185, 194

———— *Histoire de la révolution française, depuis 1789 jusqu'en 1814*. 2 pts. Paris: Firmin Didot, 1824.
NOTE: JSM in his headnote and at 6 says the work is in two vols. (as the English translation actually is); there are two parts continuously paged.
REVIEWED: 1-14
QUOTED: 6-7, 7-9, 8-10, 11-12, 12, 13, 14, 73n, 100
REFERRED TO: 57, 80n, 116

6.14-7.36 The . . . nothing.] [*translated from:*] Le gouvernement aurait dû mieux comprendre l'importance des états-généraux. Le retour de cette assemblée annonçait seul une grande révolution. Attendus avec espérance par la nation, ils reparaissaient à une époque où l'ancienne monarchie était affaissée, et où ils étaient seuls capables de réformer l'état, de pourvoir aux besoins de la royauté. La difficulté des temps, la nature de leur mandat, le choix de leurs membres, tout annonçait qu'ils n'étaient plus convoqués comme contribuables, mais comme législateurs. Le droit de régénérer la France leur était accordé par l'opinion, dévolu par leurs cahiers, et ils devaient trouver dans l'énormité des abus et dans les encouragements publics, la force d'entreprendre et d'accomplir cette grande tâche. [*paragraph*] Il importait au monarque de s'associer à leurs travaux. Il aurait pu de cette manière restaurer son pouvoir, et se garantir d'une révolution en l'opérant lui-même. Si, prenant l'initiative des changements, il avait fixé avec fermeté mais avec justice le nouvel ordre des choses; si, réalisant les voeux de la France, il eût déterminé les droits des citoyens, les attributions des états-généraux, les limites de la royauté; s'il eût renoncé à l'arbitraire pour lui, à l'inégalité pour la noblesse, aux priviléges pour les corps;

enfin, s'il eût accompli toutes les réformes qui étaient réclamées par l'opinion et qui furent exécutées par l'assemblée constituante, cette résolution aurait prévenu les funestes dissensions qui éclatèrent plus tard. Il est rare de trouver un prince qui consente au partage de son pouvoir et qui soit assez éclairé pour céder ce qu'il sera réduit à perdre. Cependant Louis XVI l'aurait fait, s'il avait été moins dominé par ses alentours, et s'il eût suivi ses inspirations personnelles. Mais l'anarchie la plus grande régnait dans les conseils du roi. Lorsque les états-généraux s'assemblèrent, aucune mesure n'avait été prise; on n'avait rien décidé de ce qui pouvait prévenir les contestations. Louis XVI flottait irrésolu entre son ministère, dirigé par Necker, et sa cour dirigée par la reine et par quelques princes de sa famille. [*paragraph*] Le ministre, satisfait d'avoir obtenu la double représentation du tiers-état, craignait l'indécision du roi et le mécontentement de la cour. N'appréciant pas assez l'importance d'une crise qu'il considérait plus comme financière que comme sociale, il attendait les évènements pour agir, et se flattait de les conduire sans avoir rien fait pour les préparer. Il sentait que l'ancienne organisation des états ne pouvait plus être maintenue, que l'existence des trois ordres, ayant chacun le droit de refus, s'opposait à l'exécution des réformes et à la marche de l'administration. Il espérait, après l'épreuve de cette triple opposition, réduire le nombre des ordres, et faire adopter le gouvernement anglais, en réunissant le clergé et la noblesse dans une seule chambre, et le tiers-état dans une autre. Il ne voyait pas que, la lutte une fois engagée, son intervention serait vaine, que les demi-mesures ne conviendraient à personne; que les plus faibles par opiniâtreté, et les plus forts par entraînement, refuseraient ce système modérateur. Les concessions ne satisfont qu'avant la victoire. [*paragraph*] La cour, loin de vouloir régulariser les états-généraux, désirait les annuler. Elle préférait la résistance accidentelle des grands corps du royaume au partage de l'autorité avec une assemblée permanente. La séparation des ordres favorisait ses vues; elle comptait fomenter leur désaccord, et les empêcher d'agir. Autrefois ils n'avaient jamais eu aucun résultat à cause du vice de leur organisation; elle espérait d'autant plus qu'il en serait de même aujourd'hui, que les deux premiers ordres seraient moins disposés à condescendre aux réformes sollicitées par le dernier. Le clergé voulait conserver ses priviléges et son opulence; il prévoyait bien qu'il aurait plus de sacrifices à faire que d'avantages à acquérir. La noblesse, de son côté, tout en reprenant une indépendance politique depuis long-temps perdue, n'ignorait point qu'elle aurait plus à céder au peuple qu'à obtenir de la royauté. C'était presque uniquement en faveur du tiers-état que la nouvelle révolution allait s'opérer, et les deux premiers ordres étaient portés à se coaliser avec la cour contre lui, comme naguère ils s'étaient coalisés avec lui contre la cour. L'intérêt seul motivait ce changement de parti; et ils se réunissaient au monarque sans attachement, comme ils avaient défendu le peuple, sans vue de bien public. [*paragraph*] Rien ne fut épargné pour maintenir la noblesse et le clergé dans ces dispositions. Les députés de ces deux ordres furent l'objet des prévenances et des séductions. Un comité dont les plus illustres personnages faisaient partie, se tenait chez la comtesse de Polignac; leurs principaux membres y furent admis. C'est là qu'on gagna d'Eprémenil et d'Entragues, deux des plus ardents défenseurs de la liberté dans le parlement ou avant les états-généraux, et qui devinrent depuis ses antagonistes les plus déclarés. C'est là que fut réglé le costume des députés des divers ordres, et qu'on chercha à les séparer d'abord par l'étiquette, ensuite par l'intrigue, et en dernier lieu par la force. Le souvenir des anciens états-généraux dominait la cour: elle croyait pouvoir régler le présent sur le passé, contenir Paris par l'armée, les députés du tiers par ceux de la noblesse, maîtriser les états en divisant les ordres, et pour séparer les ordres faire revivre les anciens usages qui relevaient la noblesse et abaissaient les communes. C'est ainsi qu'après la première séance, on crut avoir tout empêché en n'accordant rien. (41-5)

7.39-9.5 The . . . cause.] [*translated from:*] La cour, après avoir inutilement tenté d'empêcher la formation de l'assemblée, n'avait plus qu'à s'associer à elle pour diriger ses travaux. Elle pouvait encore, avec de la prudence et de la bonne foi, réparer ses fautes et faire oublier ses attaques. Il est des moments où l'on a l'initiative des sacrifices, il en est d'autres où il ne reste plus qu'à se donner le mérite de leur acceptation. Le monarque aurait pu, à l'ouverture des états-généraux, faire lui-même la constitution. Il fallait aujourd'hui la recevoir de l'assemblée: s'il se fût soumis à cette position, il l'eût infailliblement améliorée. Mais, revenus de la première surprise de la défaite, les conseillers de Louis XVI résolurent de recourir à l'emploi des baïonnettes, après avoir échoué dans celui de l'autorité. Ils lui firent entendre que le mépris de ses ordres, la sûreté de son trône, le maintien des lois du royaume, la félicité même de son peuple, exigeaient qu'il rappelât l'assemblée à la soumission; que cette dernière, placée à Versailles, voisine de Paris, deux villes déclarées en sa faveur, devait être domptée par la force; qu'il fallait la transférer ou la dissoudre; que cette résolution était urgente afin de l'arrêter dans sa marche, et qu'il était nécessaire, pour l'exécuter, d'appeler en toute hâte des troupes qui intimidassent l'assemblée et qui continssent Versailles et Paris. [*paragraph*] Pendant que ces trames s'ourdissaient, les députés de la nation ouvraient leurs travaux législatifs, et préparaient cette constitution si impatiemment attendue, et qu'ils croyaient ne devoir plus être retardée. Des adresses leur arrivaient de Paris, et des principales villes du royaume; on les félicitait de leur sagesse, et on les encourageait à poursuivre l'oeuvre de la régénération française. Sur ces entrefaites les troupes arrivaient en grand nombre: Versailles prenait l'aspect d'un camp; la salle des états était environnée de gardes, l'entrée en était interdite aux citoyens; Paris était cerné par divers corps d'armée, qui semblaient postés pour en faire, suivant le besoin, le blocus ou le siége. Ces immenses préparatifs militaires, des trains d'artillerie venus des frontières, la présence des régiments étrangers, dont l'obéissance était sans bornes, tout annonçait des projets sinistres. Le peuple était agité, l'assemblée voulut éclairer le trône et lui demander le renvoi des troupes. Sur la proposition de Mirabeau, elle fit une adresse au roi, respectueuse et ferme, mais qui fut inutile. Louis XVI déclara qu'il était seul juge de la nécessité de faire venir ou de renvoyer les troupes, assura que ce n'était là qu'une armée de précaution pour empêcher les troubles et garder l'assemblée; il lui offrit d'ailleurs de la transférer à Noyon ou à Soissons, c'est-à-dire de la placer entre deux armées, et de la priver de l'appui du peuple. [*paragraph*] Paris était dans la plus grande fermentation; cette ville immense était unanime dans son dévouement à l'assemblée. Les périls dont les représentants de la nation étaient menacés, les siens propres, et le défaut de subsistances, la disposaient à un soulèvement. Les capitalistes, par intérêt, et dans la crainte de la banqueroute; les hommes éclairés, et toute la classe moyenne, l'étaient par patriotisme; le peuple, pressé par ses besoins, rejetant ses souffrances sur les privilégiés et sur la cour, désireux d'agitation et de nouveautés, avait embrassé avec chaleur la cause de la révolution. Il est difficile de se figurer le mouvement qui agitait cette capitale de la France; elle sortait du repos et du silence de la servitude, elle était comme surprise de la nouveauté de sa situation, et s'enivrait de liberté et d'enthousiasme. La presse échauffait les esprits, les journaux répandaient les délibérations de l'assemblée, et faisaient assister en quelque sorte à ses séances; on discutait en plein air, sur les places publiques, les questions qui étaient agitées dans son sein. C'était au Palais-Royal surtout que se tenait l'assemblée de la capitale. Il était toujours rempli d'une foule qui semblait permanente, et qui se renouvelait sans cesse. Une table servait de tribune, le premier citoyen d'orateur; là on haranguait sur les dangers de la patrie, et on s'excitait à la résistance. Déjà, sur une motion faite au Palais-Royal, les prisons de l'Abbaye avaient été forcées, et des grenadiers des gardes-françaises, qui avaient été renfermés pour avoir refusé de tirer sur le peuple, en avaient été ramenés en triomphe. Cette émeute n'avait pas eu de suite; une députation avait sollicité, en faveur des prisonniers délivrés, l'intérêt de l'assemblée, qui les avait recommandés à la clémence du roi; ils s'étaient remis en prison et ils avaient reçu leur grâce. Mais ce régiment, l'un des plus complets et des plus braves, était devenu favorable à la cause populaire. (57-60)

11.3-12.2 If . . . republic.] [*translated from:*] Si l'on présentait le tableau d'un état qui sort d'une grande crise, et qu'on dît: Il y avait dans cet état un gouvernement absolu dont l'autorité a été restreinte; deux classes privilégiées qui ont perdu leur suprématie; un peuple immense, déjà affranchi par l'effet de la civilisation et des lumières, mais sans droits politiques, et qui a été obligé, à cause des refus essuyés, de les conquérir lui-même: si l'on ajoutait, Le gouvernement, après s'être opposé à cette révolution, s'y est soumis, mais les classes privilégiées l'on constamment combattue, voici ce que l'on pourrait conclure de ces données: [*paragraph*] Le gouvernement aura des regrets, le peuple montrera de la défiance, et les classes privilégiées attaqueront l'ordre nouveau chacune à sa manière. La noblesse ne le pouvant pas au-dedans, où elle serait trop faible, émigrera, afin d'exciter les puissances étrangères, qui feront les préparatifs d'une attaque; le clergé, qui perdrait au-dehors ses moyens d'action, restera dans l'intérieur, où il cherchera des ennemis à la révolution. Le peuple, menacé au-dehors, compromis au-dedans, irrité contre l'émigration qui armera les étrangers, contre les étrangers qui attaqueront son indépendance, contre le clergé qui insurgera son pays, traitera en ennemis le clergé, l'émigration et les étrangers. Il demandera d'abord la surveillance, puis le bannissement des prêtres réfractaires; la confiscation du revenu des émigrés; enfin, la guerre contre l'Europe coalisée, pour la prévenir de sa part. Les premiers auteurs de la révolution condamneront celles de ces mesures qui violeront la loi; les continuateurs de la révolution y verront, au contraire, le salut de la patrie, et le désaccord éclatera entre ceux qui préféreront la constitution à l'état et ceux qui préféreront l'état à la constituton. Le prince, porté par ses intérêts de roi, ses affections et sa conscience à rejeter une pareille politique, passera pour complice de la contre-révolution, parce qu'il paraîtra la protéger. Les révolutionnaires tenteront alors de gagner le roi en l'intimidant, et, ne pouvant pas y réussir, ils renverseront son pouvoir. [*paragraph*] Telle fut l'histoire de l'assemblée législative. Les troubles intérieurs amenèrent le décret contre les prêtres; les menaces extérieures, celui contre les émigrés; le concert des puissances étrangères, la guerre contre l'Europe; la première défaite de nos armées, celui du camp de vingt mille hommes. Le refus d'adhésion à la plupart de ces décrets fit suspecter Louis XVI par les Girondins; les divisions de ces derniers et des constitutionnels, qui voulaient se montrer les uns législateurs comme en temps de paix, les autres ennemis comme en temps de guerre, désunirent les partisans de la révolution. Pour les Girondins, la question de la liberté était dans la victoire, la victoire dans les décrets. Le 20 juin fut une tentative pour la faire accepter; mais, ayant manqué son effet, ils crurent qu'il fallait renoncer à la révolution ou au trône, et ils firent le 10 août. Ainsi, sans l'émigration qui amena la guerre, sans le schisme qui amena les troubles, le roi se serait probablement fait à la constitution, et les révolutionnaires n'auraient pas pu songer à la république. (289-92)

13.38-9 "*C'est . . . espérances.*"] [*not in italics*] (458)

13.39 "*Tout ce . . . s'étend*"] Elle ne cessa pas d'abord d'être une assemblée préparatoire: mais, comme tout ce . . . s'étend, le club jacobin ne se contenta pas d'influencer l'assemblée; il voulut encore agir sur la municipalité et sur la multitude, et il admit comme sociétaires des membres de la commune et de simples citoyens. (166)

13.40-1 "*Il ne . . . propos.*"] Sans la révolution, Mirabeau eût manqué sa destinée, car il ne . . . propos. (107)

13.41-2 "*Dès . . . part,*"] Dès . . . part, et ils forcent à prendre contre eux des mesures de guerre. (204)

14.1-3 "Tous les . . . nécessités"] Les uns et les autres moururent avec le même courage, ce qui fait voir que tous les . . . nécessités. (518)

14.5 "Quand] [*no paragraph*] Quand (357)

14.6 toujours"] toujours; c'est ce qui manquait à Dumouriez, ce qui arrêta son audace, et ébranla ses partisans. (357)

14.8-9 "En révolution . . . commandement"] Il ne faut jamais oublier qu'en révolution . . . commandement. (442)

14.15 manière"] manière. (161)

14.19 être"] être; et le parti montagnard le prit pour son chef, parce que les Girondins le poursuivirent comme tel. (311)

14.20 ne vouloir pas] ne pas vouloir (317)

14.29 "Barrère] Ce parti composait les comités de sûreté générale et de salut public; il était dirigé par Barrère (363)

14.35 "Ce redoutable] Mais les juges furent élus et temporaires: ce redoutable (153)

73n.21-2 "La constitution civile ne fut pas l'ouvrage de philosophes . . . austères."] Ce projet dont l'adoption à fait tant de mal, tendait à reconstituer l'église sur ses antiques bases, et à ramener la pureté des croyances: il n'était point l'oeuvre des philosophes . . . austères, qui voulaient appuyer le culte sur la constitution, et les faire concourir l'un et l'autre au bonheur de l'état. (145)

———— *History of the French Revolution, from 1789 to 1814.* 2 vols. London: Hunt and Clarke, 1826.

NOTE: for quotations and references, see the preceding entry; JSM made his own translation, rather than using this version, for the passages in English.

REVIEWED: 1-14

MILANS DEL BOSCH, FRANCISCO. Referred to: 180

MILL, JOHN STUART. "The Claims of Labour," *Edinburgh Review*, LXXXI (Apr., 1845), 498-525. In *CW*, IV, 363-89.
REFERRED TO: 315

―――― "Guizot's Essays and Lectures in History," *Edinburgh Review*, LXXXII (Oct., 1845), 381-421.
NOTE: the reference is prospective to the essay printed at 257-94 above.
REFERRED TO: 231n

―――― "De Tocqueville on Democracy in America [II]," *Edinburgh Review*, LXXII (Oct., 1840), 1-47. In *CW*, XVIII, 153-204.
QUOTED: 305-8

―――― Letter to Thomas Carlyle (25 Nov., 1833). In *Earlier Letters*. Ed. Francis E. Mineka. Vols. XII-XIII of *Collected Works*. Toronto: University of Toronto Press, 1963, XII, 190-7.
NOTE: the collations are given in variant notes at 201-2 and 204n-5n above.
QUOTED: 201-2, 204n-5n
REFERRED TO: 176n

―――― "Mignet's French Revolution," *Westminster Review*, V (Apr., 1826), 385-98.
NOTE: one of the *Westminster* articles on French historical works; reprinted at 3-14 above.
REFERRED TO: 18

―――― "Scott's Life of Napoleon," *Westminster Review*, IX (Apr., 1828), 251-313.
NOTE: reprinted at 53-110 above; the reference (of 1826) is to JSM's plan to write at length in the *Westminster* about the French Revolution.
REFERRED TO: 4

―――― Summary of French news, *Examiner*, 26 Jan., 1834, 56-7.
NOTE: the collations are given as variant notes at 125-8 above.
QUOTED: 125-8

―――― A *System of Logic, Ratiocinative and Inductive* (1843). *Collected Works*, Vols. VII-VIII. Toronto: University of Toronto Press, 1974.
REFERRED TO: 298

MILLAR, JOHN. *An Historical View of the English Government, from the Settlement of the Saxons in Britain to the Accession of the House of Stewart*. London: Strahan, *et al.*, 1787.
NOTE: formerly in SC.
REFERRED TO: 46, 51, 52

―――― *Observations Concerning the Distinction of Ranks in Society*. London: Richardson and Murray, 1771.
NOTE: the reference is inferential.
REFERRED TO: 51

MILTON, JOHN. *Areopagitica: A Speech for the Liberty of Unlicensed Printing, to the Parliament of England* (1644). In *The Prose Works of John Milton; with a Life of the Author, Interspersed with Translations and Critical Remarks*. Ed. Charles Symmons. 7 vols. London: Johnson, *et al.*, 1806, I, 286-331.
NOTE: in SC, now lacking Vol. I.
REFERRED TO: 165

―――― *Paradise Regained* (1671). In *The Poetical Works of Mr. John Milton*. London: Tonson, 1695, 1-66.
NOTE: the works are separately paginated.
QUOTED: 172
172.12-13 "fierce democracy,"] Thence to the famous Orators repair, / Those ancient, whose resistless eloquence / Wielded at will that fierce Democratie, / Shook the Arsenal and fulmined over *Greece*, / To *Macedon*, and *Artaxerxes* Throne. . . . (55; Bk. IV, ll. 264-8)

———— *The Reason of Church Government Urged against Prelaty. In Two Books* (1641-42). In *The Prose Works*, I, 78-151.

QUOTED: 138

138.26 "will not willingly be let die;"] But much latelier in the private academies of Italy, whither I was favoured to resort, perceiving that some trifles which I had in memory, composed at under twenty or thereabout, (for the manner is, that every one must give some proof of his wit and reading there) met with acceptance above what was looked for; and other things, which I had shifted in scarcity of books and conveniences to patch up amongst them, were received with written encomiums, which the Italian is not forward to bestow on men of this side the Alps; I began thus far to assent both to them and divers of my friends here at home, and not less to an inward prompting which now grew daily upon me, that by labour and intense study, (which I take to be my portion in this life) joined with the strong propensity of nature, I might perhaps leave something so written to after times, as they should not willingly let it die. (I, 119)

MINA, FRANCISCO ESPOZ Y. Referred to: 180

MIOMANDRE DE SAINTE-MARIE.

NOTE: not otherwise identified. The quotation is in a quotation from Carlyle.

QUOTED: 157

MIRABEAU, HONORÉ GABRIEL RIQUETI, COMTE DE.

NOTE: the reference at 8 is in a quotation from Mignet; that at 90 is in a quotation from Montgaillard; that at 140 is in a quotation from Carlyle.

REFERRED TO: 8, 73n, 80, 90, 95, 116, 140, 160, 170, 187, 187n, 203

———— *Mémoires biographiques, littéraires et politiques de Mirabeau, écrits par lui-même, par son père, son oncle et son fils adoptif.* Ed. Gabriel Lucas-Montigny. 8 vols. Paris: Auffray, *et al.*, 1834-35.

NOTE: the quotations are in a quotation from Carlyle, and are, therefore, not collated.

QUOTED: 148

REFERRED TO: 161

———— *Oeuvres de Mirabeau.* 9 vols. Paris: Dupont and Brissot-Thivars, 1825-27.

QUOTED: 117

REFERRED TO: 8, 72n, 73n, 80, 88

117.12-13 "*Dites-lui . . . investis,*"] [*paragraph*] Dites-lui que les hordes étrangères dont nous sommes investis, ont reçu hier la visite des princes, des princesses, des favoris, des favorites, et leurs caresses, et leurs exhortations, et leurs présents; dites-lui que toute la nuit ces satellites étrangers, gorgés d'or et de vin, ont prédit dans leurs chants impies l'asservissement de la France, et que leurs voeux brutaux invoquaient la destruction de l'assemblée nationale; dites-lui que, dans son palais même, les courtesans ont mêlé leurs danses au son de cette musique barbare, et que telle fut l'avant-scène de la Saint-Barthélemy. (VII, 166)

117.13-14 *la hideuse banqueroute,*] Mais aujourd'hui la banqueroute, la hideuse banqueroute est là; elle menace de consumer vous, vos propriétés, votre honneur . . . , et vous délibérez! (VII, 301)

MIRABEAU, VICTOR RIQUETI, MARQUIS DE.

NOTE: the quotations at 148, in a quotation from Carlyle, are from Honoré Gabriel de Mirabeau's *Mémoires*, *q.v.*

QUOTED: 148

REFERRED TO: 161

MITFORD, WILLIAM. Referred to: 224

MOBERLY, GEORGE.

NOTE: the reference is to recently appointed qualified examiners at Oxford.

REFERRED TO: *369*

MOLÉ, LOUIS MATHIEU, COMTE.

NOTE: the reference is in a quotation from Duveyrier.

REFERRED TO: 301

MOLLEVAULT, ETIENNE.
NOTE: the reference, in a quotation from Mignet, is to the members of the Commission of Twelve.
REFERRED TO: 12

MONTESQUIEU, CHARLES LOUIS DE SECONDAT, BARON DE LA BRÈDE ET DE. Referred to: 13

——— De l'esprit des loix, ou Du rapport que les loix doivent avoir avec la constitution de chaque gouvernement, les moeurs, le climat, la religion, le commerce, etc. A quoi l'auteur a ajouté des recherches nouvelles sur les loix romaines touchant les successions, sur les loix françoises, et sur les loix féodales. 2 vols. Geneva: Barillot, [1748].
NOTE: the reference at 70 is in a quotation from Scott; that at 281 (384) is in a quotation (repeated) from Guizot.
REFERRED TO: 70, 281 (384)

MONTFORT, GUY DE. Referred to: 49

MONTGAILLARD, GUILLAUME HONORÉ ROCQUES, ABBÉ DE. Histoire de France, depuis la fin du règne de Louis XVI jusqu'à l'année 1825. 9 vols. Paris: Moutardier, 1827.
NOTE: the references at 140 and 141 derive from quotations from Carlyle; that at 165 is in a quotation from Carlyle.
QUOTED: 89, 89n, 89-90, 91n
REFERRED TO: 68n, 72n, 75n, 79n, 89, 91n, 94, 140, 141, 165
89.15   hommes," . . . "je] hommes, je (II, 63)
89.23   Lorsque] [paragraph] Lorsque (II, 63)
89.26-7   s'il . . . habitans] [not in italics] (II, 63)
89.29   époque.* [footnote:] *"Et . . . tard," . . . "ce] époque: et . . . tard, ce (II, 63)
89.29   époque.* . . . On] [ellipsis indicates that JSM has jumped back to middle of preceding paragraph] (II, 62)
91n.13-92n.1   quoique . . . coûte.] [not in italics] (II, 81)

MONTJOIE, CHRISTOPHE FÉLIX LOUIS VENTRE DE LA TOULOUBRE. Histoire de la conjuration de L.P.J. d'Orléans, surnommé Egalité. 6 vols. Paris: Les marchands de nouveautés, 1800.
REFERRED TO: 79n

MONTMORENCY-LUXEMBOURG, ADÉLAÏDE GENEVIÈVE, DUCHESSE DE.
NOTE: the reference is in a quotation from Dampmartin.
REFERRED TO: 74n

MONTMORENCY-LUXEMBOURG, ANNE CHARLES SIGISMOND, DUC DE.
NOTE: the reference is in a quotation from Dampmartin.
REFERRED TO: 74n

MONTMORIN, ARMAND MARC DE, COMTE DE ST. HÉREM.
NOTE: the reference at 9 is in a quotation from Mignet; that at 86-7 is to him as one of the ministers dismissed with Necker; that at 106 derives from Soulavie.
REFERRED TO: 9, 86-7, 106

MORELLET, ANDRÉ, ABBÉ.
NOTE: the reference is in a quotation from Carlyle.
REFERRED TO: 140

MORGAN, SYDNEY (Lady). "The French Revolution," Athenaeum, 20 May, 1837, 353-5.
NOTE: the quotations merely indicate the gravamen of Lady Morgan's criticism of Carlyle's work.
QUOTED: 163, 164
163.31   "flippancy"] But it is one thing to put forth a few pages of quaintness, neologism, and a whimsical coxcombry; and another, to carry such questionable qualities through three long volumes of misplaced persiflage and flippant pseudo-philosophy. (353)
164.19   "affected;"] Originality, without justness of thought, is but novelty of error; and originality of style, without sound taste and discretion, is sheer affectation. (353)

NOTE: a German ed., 3 vols. (Berlin: Reimer, 1827-32 [Vol. II is of the 1836 ed.]), is in SC, as are the two vols. of lectures, ed. Schmitz (London: Taylor and Walton, 1844) that complete Niebuhr's *History*.

REFERRED TO: 219, 232

NISARD, JEAN MARIE NAPOLÉON DÉSIRÉ. "Armand Carrel," *La Revue des Deux Mondes*, XII (Oct., 1837), 5-54.

NOTE: the article is dated July, 1837, by Nisard. JSM is ostensibly reviewing a work still to be published, which combines a translation of Nisard on Carrel with the translation of an abridged article on Carrel by Littré (*q.v.*). The reasons for our using the work cited here are given in the Textual Introduction, cii above.

REVIEWED: 167-215

QUOTED: 172-3, 181-2, 186, 194, 195, 203, 208-9, 209, 209-10, 211, 213, 213n, 214

172.27-173.7 "His literary studies," . . . were . . . him.] [*translated from:*] [*paragraph*] Les études littéraires de Carrel avaient été fort négligées. Il nous racontait que tout en étant dans les meilleurs élèves de son collége par les *dispositions*, il était dans les médiocres par les résultats. Ses penchans militaires se montraient dès le collége par le choix même de ses lectures. Il lisait les historiens, surtout à l'endroit des opérations militaires, et il aimait, avant de les comprendre, ces détails si étrangers à la vic de collége. Jamais vocation ne fut plus précoce et plus décidée. Pour le reste des études, il y assistait avec impatience, plutôt qu'il n'y prenait part. Toutefois, nous disait-il, Virgile l'avait frappé. Il m'en récitait quelquefois des vers appris dans sa tendre jeunesse, et qu'il n'avait ni relus ni oubliés. Regardez comme la destinée d'un homme supérieur se prépare de loin. Cet enfant qui, après avoir dévoré une mauvaise traduction de Xénophon ou de César, est sensible à l'art divin de Virgile, un jour le goût et la volonté en feront un homme d'action; l'instinct en fera un admirable écrivain. [*paragraph*] Au sortir du collége, et pendant la préparation pour entrer à l'école militaire de Saint-Cyr, Carrel se livra exclusivement aux études historiques et de stratégie. A l'école, il y employa tout le temps que lui laissaient les occupations spéciales. (34)

181.25-182.4 During . . . convinced.] [*translated from:*] Dans l'intervalle, la mère de Carrel avait fait un voyage à Paris. Les lettres de M. Thierry ne l'avaient pas rassurée. Cette modeste existence d'homme de lettres ne la tranquillisait point, et paraissait la flatter médiocrement. Elle avait besoin que M. Thierry lui renouvelât ses premières assurances, et se portât en quelque façon garant de l'aptitude littéraire et de l'avenir de son fils. Dans deux dîners qu'elle offrit à M. Thierry, elle l'interpella vivement sur ce sujet. "Vous croyez donc, monsieur, que mon fils réussira, et qu'il aura une carrière?"—"Je réponds de lui comme de moi-même, dit M. Thierry; j'ai quelque expérience des vocations littéraires: votre fils a toutes les qualités qui font le succès aujourd'hui." Pendant qu'il parlait, Mme Carrel fixait sur lui un regard pénétrant, comme pour distinguer ce qui était vrai, dans ses paroles, de ce qui pouvait n'être que politesse ou encouragement. Quant au jeune homme, il écoutait sans rien dire, respectueux, soumis, et, à ce que raconte M. Thierry, presque craintif devant sa mère, dont la fermeté d'esprit et la décision avaient sur lui beaucoup d'empire. Carrel ne fléchissait que devant ses propres qualités, car ce qu'il respectait dans sa mère n'était autre chose que ce qui devait, plus tard, le faire respecter lui-même comme homme public. [*paragraph*] La première réunion avait laissé des doutes à Mme Carrel. Au sortir de la seconde, où, pressé entre ces deux volontés inflexibles, l'une qui lui demandait presque de s'engager pour son fils, l'autre, discrète et silencieuse, qui lui promettait de ne pas lui faire défaut, M. Thierry s'était sans doute montré plus affirmatif, Mme Carrel partit pour Rouen, plus convaincue et plus tranquille. (36-7)

186.5-11 "In . . . back-shop," . . . "on . . . England."] [*translated from:*] C'est dans l'arrière-boutique de cette librairie, sur un comptoir auquel était attaché un gros chien de Terre-Neuve, que Carrel, tantôt plongé dans les recueils politiques anglais, tantôt caressant son chien favori, médita et écrivit l'*Histoire de la contre-révolution en Angleterre*. (39)

194.28-35 "Carrel," . . . was . . . enlarged;] [*translated from:*] [*paragraph*] Carrel n'a été écrivain que faute d'un rôle où il pût agir plus directement. [*12-sentence omission*] Quoiqu'il ait beaucoup écrit, et dès l'école militaire, il n'a jamais pensé à se faire un nom dans les lettres. Ecrire a été pour lui, dans le commencement, un moyen de fixer dans sa mémoire des connaissances dont il pouvait avoir besoin pour un but encore vague, mais nullement littéraire.

Plus tard, ç'a été un moyen d'imposer, sous la forme de doctrines, sa passion d'agir aux consciences et aux évènemens, ou au moins de la soulager. Pour lui, le modèle de l'écrivain était l'homme d'action racontant ce qu'il a fait. C'était César dans ses commentaires, Bonaparte dans ses mémoires. Carrel voulait qu'on écrivît soit après avoir agi, soit pour agir, quand c'était le seul mode d'action opportun ou possible. Plus tard ses idées se modifièrent là-dessus, ou plutôt se complétèrent. (32-3)

195.3-10   "thus completed," . . . "Carrel's . . . composition:" . . . He . . .writer] [*translated from:*] Ainsi complétée, l'idée de Carrel est excellente en soi. Cela équivaut à dire que l'action étant la manifestation la plus franche et la plus naturelle de l'homme, pour bien écrire, il faut être mu par une force aussi impérieuse que celle qui nous fait agir. Or, on n'est dans cette condition-là qu'autant qu'on a une forte et noble passion à satisfaire, quelque grande vérité à défendre, un idéal à atteindre. [*JSM moves back to preceding page*] Mais celui qui n'écrit que pour agir, et qui écrit comme on agit, de toute sa personne, celui-là pourra exceller dès l'abord sans passer par toutes ces transformations où il reste toujours des vestiges de l'imitation dans le naturel. S'il a de l'instinct, c'est-à-dire un tour d'esprit parfaitement conforme au génie de son pays, il pourra devenir un écrivain supérieur sans même se douter qu'il soit écrivain. (33-4)

195.13   "nothing . . . pen."] [*translated from:*] [*paragraph*] Entre les deux articles sur la guerre de 1823 et la polémique à jamais mémorable du *National*, Carrel publia quelques écrits politiques et littéraires. On les compte, car, de ce jour-là, rien de médiocre ne sortit de sa plume. (49)

195.16-25   that . . . wit. [*paragraph*] "All the qualities," . . . which . . . century.] [*translated from:*] Dans ces divers écrits, cette qualité de peindre par l'expression qu'on avait rencontrée avec quelque surprise dans les articles sur L'Espagne, éclate presque à chaque phrase. Mais prenez garde, ce n'est pas une certaine science d'effet où Carrel s'est perfectionné; son expression ne s'illumine et ne se colore que parce que ses pensées sont devenues plus nettes, plus hautes et plus à lui. Il a encore ce trait de ressemblance avec les grands écrivains, qu'il proportionne son style à ses pensées, et qu'il sait être simple et humble quand les pensées sont d'un ordre où il n'est pas besoin, pour les rendre, que la raison s'aide de l'imagination. Appliquer à toutes choses uniformément une certain qualité brillante qu'on se sait, et dont on a été souvent loué, n'est pas plus du génie, que faire des traits à tout propos n'est de l'esprit. [*paragraph*] Toutes les qualités qu'avait Carrel le premier jour qu'il tint une plume, relevées de ce don venu ce dernier, se déployèrent à la fois dans la polémique du *National*, avec une grandeur qui laissera de longs souvenirs. Cette polémique a été admirée de ceux même qui la craignaient, soit qu'on la craignît moins qu'on n'affectait de le dire, soit qu'en France on n'ait jamais assez peur du talent pour se priver de l'admirer! Il est certain qu'entre les mains de Carrel, *le National*, à ne le considérer que comme monument de littérature politique, a été l'oeuvre la plus originale du XIXe siècle. (49-50)

203.2-4   "augment . . . increased."] [*translated from:*] Leurs défauts, au lieu de diminuer, augmentent en proportion de ce que leur talent leur acquiert d'excuses. [*7-sentence omission*] Il a été évident pour tous ses amis que ses défauts diminuaient en proportion de ce que gagnaient ses qualités, et avec elles sa belle renommée. (22, 23)

208.20-209.2   to . . . able.] [*translated from:*] Résister à ses propres lumières, ne pas fléchir, ne pas laisser voir ses doutes, ne pas délaisser les principes arborés dans certaines crises, même si ces principes n'ont été au commencement que des impressions ou des espérances téméraires que l'impatience a converties en doctrines de gouvernement; ne pas manquer aux ames simples qu'on y a engagées et qui y persévèrent et s'y exaltent; étouffer son bon sens de ses propres mains, et, au besoin, appeler froidement sur sa vie ou sur sa liberté des périls inutiles et prématurés, pour ne pas faire douter de soi; voilà à quel prix on est le chef agréé d'une opinion en guerre ouverte avec un gouvernement établi; voilà ce qu'il faut savoir faire à toute heure, et avec beaucoup de bonne grace, en outre, pour que ceux qui le reconnaissent pour chefs [*sic*] le lui pardonnent, et avec un talent si hors de toute portée que nul amour-propre, dans le parti qu'il représente, n'ose s'y égaler. Pendant plus de quatre années, sauf quelque relâchement vers la fin, soit par lassitude, soit dégoût de ces discordes intérieures par lesquelles les partis font scandale de leur défaite, Carrel ne manqua pas un moment à ce rôle. Il n'entraîna jamais que ceux qu'il était résolu à suivre, et, en certaines occasions où l'impulsion n'avait pas été donnée par lui, mais malgré lui, il se mit à la tête de ceux qu'il n'avait pas commandés. Le même homme qui, dans les circonstances ordinaires, souffrait modestement qu'on lui disputât le titre de chef de l'opinion républicaine, s'en emparait dans le danger, comme d'un signe où les coups pussent le reconnaître de loin. Il faisait comme un général porté rapidement, par son courage et ses talens, au premier grade de l'armée: il se laissait contester dans les chuchottemens jaloux de la caserne, sauf à prendre, dans une affaire désespérée, le commandement en chef, du droit du plus courageux et du plus habile. (8-9)

209.17   *"Théorie . . . commun;"*] [*paragraph*] Le coup le plus sensible que reçut Carrel des évènemens, et ceci soit dit à son éternel honneur! ce ne fut pas dans son ambition, mais dans sa plus chère pensée, dans son plus glorieux titre d'écrivain politique, dans sa théorie du droit commun. (14)

209.21-210.41   "I affirm," . . . that . . . at.] [*translated from:*] [*no paragraph*] J'affirme ne lui avoir vu de tristesses vraiment amères que pour les blessures qu'elle eut à souffrir; et, sur ce point seulement, ses désenchantemens furent douloureux. Son bon sens, encore des années de jeunesse et d'âge viril devant lui, l'inattendu, l'inconnu, pouvaient lui faire prendre patience sur ses espérances; mais rien ne le consola de voir cette noble politique de garanties réciproques, compromise et rejetée au rang des choses à jamais controversables par tout le monde, et, comme à l'envi, par le gouvernement, par le pays, par son propre parti. C'était en effet la vue la plus haute et la plus droite de sa raison, l'instinct le plus vrai de sa nature généreuse; Carrel était là tout entier. Jamais il ne se fût retourné contre ce noble enfant de son intelligence et de son coeur. Si quelquefois il le fit craindre par des menaces vagues qui lui échappèrent dans le feu de la polémique, ce ne fut qu'à ceux qui étaient intéressés à avoir cette crainte, et à ruiner par elle son plus noble titre à l'estime publique. Toutefois, les doutes qui purent lui venir en certaines occasions sur l'excellence de cette idée, furent, je le répète, la plus douloureuse de ses épreuves. La révolution de juillet, si extraordinaire entre toutes les révolutions par le spectacle d'un peuple laissant au vaincu la liberté de se plaindre et de se railler de la victoire, avait permis d'espérer un retour éclatant et définitif au droit commun. Carrel se fit l'organe de ces espérances et le théoricien de cette doctrine. Il traita la question avec sa rigueur et sa netteté accoutumées. Il opposa aux exemples, si nombreux depuis cinquante ans, de gouvernemens périssant tous par l'arbitraire, le modèle d'un gouvernement offrant à tous les partis des garanties contre son légitime et nécessaire instinct de conservation. Il n'invoquait que des raisons exclusivement pratiques, se refusant le secours innocent de toute forme passionnée, pour ne pas exposer sa belle théorie à l'ironique qualification d'utopie. C'est cette politique qui fit tant d'amis à Carrel sur tous les points de la France, et partout où pénétrait *le National.* Il eut, en dehors de tous les partis, un parti composé de tous les hommes, soit placés hors des voies de l'activité politique, soit trop éclairés pour s'y jeter à la suite de quelque chef ne se recommandant que par des succès de plume ou de tribune. Que de gens, lassés des querelles sur la forme du gouvernement, incrédules même aux admirables apologies de la forme américaine, quittant l'ombre pour la chose, se rangèrent sous cette bannière du droit commun, que Carrel avait levée sur toutes les fautes et sur toutes les ruines, même sur celles de ses théories républicaines! Il lui en venait de toutes parts des témoignages d'adhésion qui parurent un moment lui suffire, et je le vis se résignant à être, pour un temps indéterminé, le premier écrivain spéculatif de son pays. Mais des fautes où tout le monde eut sa part l'eurent bientôt refroidi. Ce fut un rude coup. Carrel avait foi dans la politique du droit commun: il y avait cru plus fortement peut-être qu'à ses théories républicaines précipitamment arborées, et dans un accès d'inquiétude plutôt qu'après un sûr et paisible regard jeté sur les choses. Après celles-ci, où l'honneur le soutenait contre les doutes croissans, il fallait donc encore douter de celle-là! Carrel eut les deux douleurs à la fois. [*2-paragraph omission*] [*paragraph*] L'affliction de Carrel fut irréparable le jour qu'il se vit resté seul défenseur du droit commun entre la nation, qui, par peur, en faisait le sacrifice au gouvernement, et un parti, son propre parti, qui le menaçait de ses arrière-pensées. Nous eûmes à ce sujet, lui et moi, une longue conversation, quelques mois avant sa mort, dans une promenade au bois de Boulogne. Je vis qu'il y avait presque renoncé comme principe de politique applicable: tout au plus y tenait-il encore comme théorie, par pure générosité, et peut-être aussi par le sentiment de sa force. Carrel pensait que, les choses venant à son parti, il serait de force à résister à la tentation de l'arbitraire, et à ne le prendre pas même des mains d'une majorité qui le lui offrirait au nom du pays. Mais une politique ajournée était pour lui une politique vaincue. Ses doutes sur le droit commun furent une dernière défaite. Quoique ce principe eût été la vue la plus désintéressée de son esprit et le meilleur mouvement de son coeur, les théories des hommes d'action impliquent toujours l'espoir d'une application prochaine. Du moment donc que le droit commun avait échoué comme politique d'application, Carrel devait en abandonner la doctrine. Dans les derniers jours de sa vie, il n'en parlait plus que comme d'un progrès qu'il ne lui serait pas donné de voir de son vivant, et auquel ne devaient peut-être jamais arriver les sociétés humaines. (14-16)

211.12-13 *se retremper par l'étude,*] Carrel sentait le besoin de se renouveler par l'étude. (12)

213.17 *un . . . vifs,*] Comme tous les hommes d'une nature excellente, il avait un . . . vifs, outre que ses impressions, par leur extrême force et par la manière dont il s'y abandonnait, avaient l'air d'être des goûts. (31)

213.22-8 "the . . . character," . . . was . . . little.] [*translated from:*] [*paragraph*] Le trait distinctif du caractère de Carrel était la générosité. De quelque manière qu'on entende ce mot, dont le vague même fait la beauté, la vie de Carrel offre de quoi en appliquer toutes les nuances. Soit qu'il signifie l'entraînement d'un homme qui se dévoue, soit qu'il veuille dire simplement la libéralité, il ne convient à personne mieux qu'à lui. Toutes les actions de sa vie sont marquées de la première sorte de générosité. La plupart de ses fautes ne sont que de la générosité où il manquait du calcul. C'est par là qu'il était populaire en France, où son courage, mieux compris que son talent, lui avait fait plus de partisans que ses écrits. C'est par trop de générosité qu'il joua sa vie une première fois dans le duel légitimiste; c'est par trop de générosité qu'il est mort. [*paragraph*] Quant à la libéralité, personne n'en est plus que lui, et je n'ose en cela lui donner une meilleure sorte. Je n'en diminuerai pas le mérite en disant qu'il y entrait je ne sais quelle imprévoyance qui n'était que de la foi dans sa fortune. On eût dit qu'il chargeait l'avenir de liquider sa générosité. Il ne savait ni refuser ni donner peu. (21)

213n.12-15 I . . . alms.] [*translated from:*] [*see 2nd last sentence of preceding entry, followed by:*] Exposé par sa position à d'incessantes demandes, il puisait souvent dans la bourse de ses amis pour soulager des malheurs qu'il ne suspectait ni ne recherchait jamais. [*paragraph*] On m'a raconté ce trait touchant de sa manière d'obliger. Une personne, dont les nécessités n'étaient pas extrêmes, a recours à lui. Carrel lui offre la somme dont elle a besoin. Il rentre chez lui, et trouve sa bourse vide; il avait promis plus qu'il ne possédait. Sa montre représente à peu près la somme demandée; il la fait mettre au Mont-de-Piété. (21-2)

214.18-29 take . . . own.] [*translated from:*] Il prenait un journal, soit du gouvernement, soit d'une opposition moins prononcée que la sienne, et, lisant l'article du jour, il en adoptait la pensée, et la complétait ou la développait dans le sens des opinions qui l'avaient inspirée. Quelquefois c'était un discours de tribune qu'il refaisait: "Ils n'ont pas donné les meilleures raisons de leur opinion, disait-il; ceci eût été plus spécieux, et nous eût plus embarrassés." J'admirais d'autant plus cette flexibilité d'esprit que ces raisons de gymnastique étaient les meilleures et les plus sincères. C'était tout ce qu'il y a de vrai et d'honorable dans chaque opinion. Carrel voulait me montrer par là deux qualités fort supérieures à une certaine facilité capricieuse et paradoxale, d'une part sa connaissance des intérêts des partis, et d'autre part, l'estime réelle qu'il faisait, à beaucoup d'égards, des plus opposés à ses idées. (10)

———— "Lamartine," *London and Westminster Review*, IV & XXVI (Jan., 1837), 501-41.
REFERRED TO: 188n

———— "Victor Hugo," *London Review*, II (*L&WR*, XXXI) (Jan., 1836), 389-417.
REFERRED TO: 188n

"O.P.Q." See Colton.

OAKELEY, FREDERICK.
NOTE: the reference is to the recently appointed qualified examiners at Oxford.
REFERRED TO: *369*

OGDEN, WILLIAM. Referred to: 78

ORLÉANS, FERDINAND, DUC D'.
NOTE: referred to as heir to the French throne; the indirect quotation of his opinion derives from Nisard.
QUOTED: 78

ORLÉANS, LOUIS PHILIPPE D', COMTE DE PARIS.
NOTE: the reference is to him as the heir presumptive of King Louis Philippe.
REFERRED TO: 330

ORLÉANS, LOUIS PHILIPPE JOSEPH, DUC D'.
NOTE: known as Philippe Egalité. The reference at 9 is in a quotation from Mignet; those at 78-81n include references to Orleanists and Orleanism; that at 90 is in a quotation from Montgaillard; that at 141 is in a quotation from Carlyle. See also Sieyès, "Délibérations."
REFERRED TO: 9, 78, 79, 80, 81, 81n, 90, 95, 141

—— Instructions. See Sieyès.

OSSIAN. Fingal, an Ancient Epic Poem in Six Books: Together with Several Other Poems, Composed by Ossian, the Son of Fingal. Trans. from the Galic Language by James Macpherson. London: Becket and Hondt, 1762.
NOTE: the reference is in a quotation from Carlyle.
REFERRED TO: 113

OTTO IV (Holy Roman Emperor).
NOTE: the reference is in a quotation from Michelet.
REFERRED TO: 239

OTWAY, THOMAS. Venice Preserv'd; or, A Plot Discover'd. London: Hindmarsh, 1682.
NOTE: the quotation is in a quotation from Scott.
QUOTED: 69
69.16-17   —disturb . . . world / To rule it when 'twas wildest.] A Councel's held hard by, where the destruction / Of this great Empire's hatching: There I'l [sic] lead thee! / But be a Man, for thou art to mix with Men / Fit to disturb . . . World, / And rule it when it's wildest— (17; II)

OUDEGHERST, PIERRE D'. Annales de Flandre de P. d'Oudegherst. Ed. Jean Baptiste Lesbroussart. 2 vols. Ghent: de Goesin-Verhaeghe; Paris: Janet, [1789].
NOTE: the quotation derives from Sismondi (q.v. for the collation); this ed., which omits "et chroniques" from the title, cited merely for identification.
QUOTED: 34n

OWEN, ROBERT.
NOTE: the reference at 126, in a self-quotation, is to Owenites.
REFERRED TO: 126, 354

PACCHIAROTTI, GUISEPPE.
NOTE: JSM, like Nisard, whose account he follows, uses the spelling Pachiarotti. The source of the quotation has not been located.
QUOTED: 180
REFERRED TO: 180

PAINE, THOMAS. The American Crisis, No. I (1776). In The Political and Miscellaneous Works of Thomas Paine. 2 vols. London: Carlile, 1819, I, 1-10.
NOTE: in SC; the items are separately paginated.
QUOTED: 163
163.1   "times which try men's souls,"] THESE ARE THE TIMES THAT TRY MEN'S SOULS. (3)

PAJOL, CLAUDE PIERRE. Referred to: 200-1

PALGRAVE, FRANCIS. The Rise and Progress of the English Commonwealth: Anglo-Saxon Period. 2 pts. London: Murray, 1832.
NOTE: the allegation that Palgrave refers to Guizot twice and slightingly is not true; see 371n above.
REFERRED TO: 370-1

PANIZZI, ANTHONY. "Michelet's Histoire de France: Boniface VIII," British and Foreign Review, XIII (June, 1842), 415-41.
REFERRED TO: 234

PITT, WILLIAM (the younger). Referred to: 343

PLATO. *Republic* (Greek and English). Trans. Paul Shorey. 2 vols. London: Heinemann; Cambridge, Mass.: Harvard University Press, 1946.
NOTE: this ed. cited for ease of reference.
REFERRED TO: 314

PLUTARCH. *Lives.*
NOTE: as the references are general, no ed. is cited.
REFERRED TO: 215, 224

POLIGNAC, JULES, DUC DE.
NOTE: the reference is in a quotation from Ferrières.
REFERRED TO: 88

POLIGNAC, YOLANDE MARTINE GABRIELLE DE POLASTRON, DUCHESSE DE.
NOTE: the reference at 7 is in a quotation from Mignet, who refers to her as comtesse; that at 88 is in a quotation from Ferrières.
REFERRED TO: 7, 88

POMPADOUR, JEANNE ANTOINETTE POISSON LE NORMANT D'ETOILES, MARQUISE DE.
NOTE: the reference is in a quotation from Carlyle.
REFERRED TO: 165

POMPONE, HUGH DE (seigneur de Crécy). Referred to: 30

Poor Laws. See 43 Elizabeth, c. 2 (1601).

POPE, ALEXANDER. *The Dunciad* (1728). In *The Works of Alexander Pope: with Notes and Illustrations by Joseph Warton and Others.* Ed. Joseph Warton, *et al.* 9 vols. and Supplementary Vol. London: Priestley, 1822 (Supp. Vol., London: Hearne, 1825), V.
NOTE: in SC.
REFERRED TO: 62

———— *An Essay on Man* (1733-34). *Ibid.*, III, 1-160.
QUOTED: 224
224.6 "damned . . . fame."] If Parts allure thee, think how Bacon shin'd, / The wisest, brightest, meanest, of mankind: / Or ravish'd with the whistling of a Name, / See Cromwell, damn'd to everlasting fame! (III, 146; IV, 281-4)

PORLIER, JUAN DÍAZ.
NOTE: the reference is to the Spanish general butchered by Ferdinand VII.
REFERRED TO: 89

PROTAGORAS. Referred to: 273n

PROVENCE, LOUISE MARIE JOSÉPHINE, COMTESSE DE.
NOTE: the reference to "Madame," wife of "Monsieur" (later Louis XVIII), is in a quotation from Ferrières.
REFERRED TO: 88

PUFENDORF, SAMUEL VON. *Le droit de la nature et des gens, ou Système général des principes les plus importans de la morale, de la jurisprudence, et de la politique.* Trans. Jean Barbeyrac. 5th ed. 2 vols. Amsterdam: De Coup, 1734.
NOTE: in SC. Original Latin ed. (*De jure naturae et gentium*), 1672. JSM uses the spelling Puffendorf.
REFERRED TO: 345

PUGH, DAVID. ("David Hughson"). *London: Being an Accurate History and Description of the British Metropolis and Its Neighbourhood, to Thirty Miles Extent, from an Actual Perambulation.* 6 vols. London: Stratford, 1805-09.
NOTE: cited as an illustration of histories of London, on which JSM comments.
REFERRED TO: 18

Le Républicain. Referred to: 100

RIANCOURT. See Joseph Calixte Martin.

RICHARD (Earl of Cornwall).
NOTE: JSM refers to him as Duke of Cornwall.
REFERRED TO: 49

RICHARD I (of England).
NOTE: known as Coeur de Lion. The second reference at 36 is to him as the royal troubadour.
REFERRED TO: 34, 35, 36, 36n, 47, 185, 226

RICARDO, DAVID. Referred to: 193

RICHARDSON, SAMUEL. *The History of Sir Charles Grandison* (1753-54). 3rd ed. 7 vols.
London: Richardson, 1754.
NOTE: in SC.
REFERRED TO: 22

RINALDI, ODORICO. *Annales ecclesiastici ab anno ubi desinit cardinalis Baronius*. Ed.
Giovanni Domenico Mansi. 15 vols. Lucca: Venturini, 1747-56.
REFERRED TO: 234

ROBERT II (of France).
NOTE: known as le Pieux; son of Hugues Capet. The reference at 238 is in a quotation from
Michelet.
REFERRED TO: 32, 238

ROBERTSON, WILLIAM. *The History of America with a Disquisition on Ancient India*
(1777). In *Works*. 6 vols. London: Longman, *et al.*, 1851, V-VI.
NOTE: in SC.
REFERRED TO: 134

———— *The History of Scotland under Mary and James VI* (1759). *Ibid.*, I-II.
REFERRED TO: 134

———— *The History of the Reign of the Emperor Charles V* (1769). *Ibid.*, III-IV.
REFERRED TO: 134

ROBESPIERRE, MAXIMILIEN FRANÇOIS MARIE ISIDORE DE.
NOTE: the reference at 12 is in a quotation from Mignet; those at 126-7 are in a self-quotation; that
at 347 is in a quotation from Brougham.
REFERRED TO: 5, 12, 126-7, 347

———— *Déclaration des droits de l'homme et du citoyen proposée par Maximilien
Robespierre 24 avril, 1793*. Paris: Imprimerie nationale, 1793.
NOTE: for the collation, see *Déclaration des droits de l'homme*.
QUOTED: 126
REFERRED TO: 127, 205

ROCHAMBEAU, JEAN BAPTISTE DONATIEN DE VIMEUR, COMTE DE. Referred to: 97

ROCHE-GUYON, GUY DE LA. Referred to: 31

ROEDERER, PIERRE LOUIS, COMTE. *Louis XII et François Ier, ou Mémoires pour servir à
une nouvelle histoire de leur règne; suivis d'appendices comprenant une discussion
entre M. le comte Daru et l'auteur, concernant la réunion de la Bretagne à la France*.
2 vols. in 1. Paris: Bossange, 1825.
QUOTED: 43, 48
REFERRED TO: 33, 37n, 38n, 51n
43.17-18 *Honoris . . . pulchritudine*.] [*paragraph*] Dans ce même siècle, le roi Jean déclara
douloureusement que la chevalerie était devenue insensible à la gloire et à l'honneur même:
Honoris . . . pulchritudine; et, pour *rétablir l'honneur et l'ordre de la chevalerie*, il créa une
nouvelle chevalerie dans l'ancienne, afin d'en rassembler l'élite. (II, 251)

43.19-20 *Il . . . Roland en France.*] Le roi Jean n'y croyait-il pas quand, entendant chanter la chanson de Roland, il dit: Il . . . [*not in italics*] Roland en France. (II, 290)

43.21-2 *On . . . tête.*] Et ce vieux capitaine qui lui répondit, On . . . tête, ce vieux capitaine n'y croyait-il pas aussi, et avec lui tous les historiens qui ont rapporté cette anecdote? (II, 290)

43.28-9 *Il n'y . . . ans qui . . . estropié.*] Mais, ô contrariété déplorable! les cuirasses deviennent si lourdes *qu'il n'y . . . ans,* dit Lanoue, *qui . . . estropié,* c'est-à-dire qu'il n'y avait chevalier de trente ans qui ne s'estropiât lui-même pour éviter d'être estropié par un autre. (II, 268)

48.15 Fut pour] Le temps de la première fut pour (I, 297)

ROGER OF HOVEDEN. *Annalium pars prior et posterior.* In *Rerum anglicarum scriptores post Bedam praecipui, ex vetustissimis codicibus manuscriptis nunc primum in lucem editi.* Ed. Henry Savile. London: Bishop, *et al.*, 1596, 228-472.
NOTE: the reference derives from Thierry.
REFERRED TO: 35

ROLAND DE LA PLATIÈRE, JEAN MARIE.
NOTE: the reference at 12 is in a quotation from Mignet; that at 108 is in a quotation from Moleville.
REFERRED TO: 12, 101-2, 108

ROLAND DE LA PLATIÈRE, MARIE JEANNE PHLIPON. Referred to: 68n-9n

———— *Mémoires de Madame Roland.* 2 vols. Paris: Baudouin, 1820.
NOTE: part of the *Collection des mémoires,* ed. Berville and Barrière, *q.v.* This ed. cited because it restored her portrait of Louvet to which Scott objected (see 68n-9n).
QUOTED: 100
REFERRED TO: 68n-9n, 102

100.15 "qu'il . . . république,"] Pétion et Brissot disaient, au contraire, que cette fuite du roi était sa perte, et qu'il fallait en profiter; que les dispositions du peuple étaient excellentes; qu'il serait mieux éclairé sur la perfidie de la cour par cette démarche, que n'auraient pu faire les plus sages écrits; qu'il était évident pour chacun, par ce seul fait, que le roi ne voulait pas de la constitution qu'il avait jurée; que c'était le moment de s'en assurer une plus homogène, et qu'il . . . république. (I, 351)

ROLLIN, CHARLES. Referred to: 224

ROSCELINUS. "Roscelini nominalistarum in philosophia quondam choragi, ad Petrum Abaelardum epistola hactenus inedita." In *Petri Abaelardi . . . opera omnia.* Vol. CLXXVIII of *Patrologiae cursus completus, series latina.* Ed. Jacques Paul Migne. Paris: Garnier, 1849, cols. 357-72.
NOTE: this ed. cited for ease of reference.
REFERRED TO: 246

ROUSSEAU, JEAN JACQUES. Referred to: 66, 67, *371n*

———— *Du contrat social, ou Principes du droit politique.* Amsterdam: Rey, 1762.
NOTE: the reference is in a quotation from Carlyle.
REFERRED TO: 141

ROYER-COLLARD, PIERRE PAUL. Referred to: 192

ST. AMBROSE. *Epistola LI.* In *Opera omnia.* Vols. XIV-XVII of *Patrologiae cursus completus, series latina.* Ed. Jacques Paul Migne. Paris: Migne, 1845, Vol. XVI, cols. 1160-4.
NOTE: this ed. used for ease of reference.
REFERRED TO: 241

ST. BENEDICT. Referred to: 240, 249

ST. BERNARD OF CLAIRVAUX. Referred to: 246

ST. DOMINIC.
NOTE: the reference is in a quotation from Michelet.
REFERRED TO: 249

St. Francis of Assisi. Referred to: 249

St. Gregory I (the Great). *Homiliarum in Ezechielem prophetam.* In *Opera omnia.* Vols. LXXV-LXXIX of *Patrologiae cursus completus, series latina.* Ed. Jacques Paul Migne. Paris: Migne, 1849, Vol. LXXVI, cols. 785-1072.
NOTE: this ed. used for ease of reference. The quotation is in a quotation from Dulaure.
QUOTED: 23

St. Gregory VII.
NOTE: known as Hildebrand. The references at 238, 246, 247 are in quotations from Michelet.
REFERRED TO: 224, 238, 239, 242-3, 246, 247, 249

St. Gregory of Tours.
NOTE: the quotation is in a quotation from Thierry (*q.v.*), who cites *Gregorii Turonensis historia Francorum,* ed. Martin Bouquet; the reference is in a quotation from Dulaure.
QUOTED: 223
REFERRED TO: 23

St. Louis. See Louis IX.

Saint-Martin-Valogne, Charles Vaissière de.
NOTE: the reference, in a quotation from Mignet, is to the members of the Commission of Twelve.
REFERRED TO: 12

St. Peter.
NOTE: the reference is in a quotation from Michelet.
REFERRED TO: 253

Saint-Priest, François Emmanuel Guignard, comte de.
NOTE: the reference at 9 is in a quotation from Mignet; that at 86-7 is to him as one of the ministers dismissed with Necker.
REFERRED TO: 9, 86-7

Saint-Simon, Claude Henri de Rouvroy, comte de.
NOTE: the reference at 126, in a self-quotation, is to Saint-Simonians; those at 185, 203, and *370n* are to the Saint-Simonian school.
REFERRED TO: 126, 185, 203, *370n*

St. Thomas Aquinas.
NOTE: the reference is in a quotation from Michelet.
REFERRED TO: 239

St. Thomas à Becket.
NOTE: the references are in quotations from Michelet.
REFERRED TO: 239, 244, 247

Saint-Victor. See Bins de Saint-Victor.

Sand, George. See Amandine Dupin.

Santerre, Antoine Joseph.
NOTE: the reference is in a quotation from Carlyle.
REFERRED TO: 146

Sanuto, Marino.
NOTE: the quotation derives from Michelet (*q.v.* for the collation).
QUOTED: 251

Schiller, Johann Christoph Friedrich von. Referred to: 184

———— *Geschichte des dreissigjährigen Kriegs* (1791-93). In *Sämmtliche Werke.* 12 vols. Stuttgart and Tübingen: Cotta'schen Buchhandlung, 1818-19, VI.
NOTE: in SC.
REFERRED TO: 137

———— *The Piccolomini; or, The First Part of Wallenstein; and The Death of*

Wallenstein. Trans. Samuel Taylor Coleridge. 2 vols. in 1. London: Longman and Rees, 1800.
REFERRED TO: 136

——— *Wallenstein, ein dramatisches Gedicht* (1798-99). In *Sämmtliche Werke*, IX, Pt. 2.
NOTE: the reference at 136 is to "Wallenstein's Camp" ("Wallensteins Lager"); those at 137 are to Wallenstein, the Piccolomini ("Die Piccolomini"), and to Count Terzsky ("Die Piccolomini" and "Wallensteins Tod"), all parts of *Wallenstein*.
REFERRED TO: 134, 136, 137

SCHLOSSER, FRIEDRICH CHRISTOPH. *Geschichte des achtzehnten Jahrhunderts und des neunzehnten bis zum Sturz des französischen Kaiserreichs*. 7 vols. Heidelberg: Mohr, 1836-49.
REFERRED TO: 220

——— *Universalhistorische Uebersicht der Geschichte der alten Welt und ihrer Kultur*. 9 vols. Frankfurt: Varrentrapp, 1826-34.
REFERRED TO: 220

SCHOELL, MAXIMILIAN SAMSON FRIEDRICH. *Histoire abregée des traités de paix, entre les puissances de l'Europe, depuis la paix de Westphalie. Ouvrage entièrement refondu, augmenté et continué jusqu'au Congrès de Vienne et aux Traités de Paris de 1815*. Ed. Christophe Guillaume de Koch. 15 vols. Paris: Gide, 1817-18.
NOTE: continuation of the work by Koch, *q.v.*
REFERRED TO: *372n*

SCIPIO AFRICANUS, PUBLIUS CORNELIUS. Referred to: 37-8

SCOTT, WALTER.
NOTE: the reference at 184 is to Scott's romances.
REFERRED TO: 184, 221, 226

——— *Ivanhoe, a Romance*. 3 vols. Edinburgh: Constable, 1820.
REFERRED TO: 184, 226

——— *The Life of Napoleon Buonaparte, Emperor of the French. With a Preliminary View of the French Revolution*. 9 vols. Edinburgh: Cadell; London: Longman, *et al.*, 1827.
REVIEWED: 53-110
QUOTED: 66, 67, 68n, 69, 69-70, 70, 71, 72n, 73, 73n, 74n, 87, 88, 92, 94, 95, 98, 99, 109n
66.23 "anti-crusade," . . . "religious . . . kind;"] Unhappily blinded by self-conceit, heated with the ardour of controversy, gratifying their literary pride by becoming members of a league, in which kings and princes were included, and procuring followers by flattering the vanity of some, and stimulating the cupidity of others, the men of the most distinguished parts in France became allied in a sort of anti-crusade against Christianity, and indeed against religious principles of every kind. (I, 61)
66.30 "league,"] [*see preceding entry*]
66.30 "conspiracy,"] An envenomed fury against religion and all its doctrines; a promptitude to avail themselves of every circumstance by which Christianity could be misrepresented; an ingenuity in mixing up their opinions in works, which seemed the least fitting to involve such discussions; above all, a pertinacity in slandering, ridiculing, and vilifying all who ventured to oppose their principles, distinguished the correspondents in this celebrated conspiracy against a religion, which, however it may be defaced by human inventions, breathes only that peace on earth, and good will to the children of men, which was proclaimed by Heaven at its divine origin. (I, 58-9)
67.4 "and . . . Encyclopedists"] In France they had discovered the command which they had acquired over the public mind, and united as they were, (and . . . Encyclopedists,) they augmented and secured that impression, by never permitting the doctrines which they wished to propagate to die away upon the public ear. (I, 53)

68n.39-40 "habitual . . . ideas,"] So far had an indifference to delicacy influenced the society of France, and so widely spread was this habitual . . . ideas, especially among those who pretended to philosophy, that Madame Roland, a woman admirable for courage and talents, and not, so far as appears, vicious in her private morals, not only mentions the profligate novels of Louvet as replete with the graces of imagination, the salt of criticism, and the tone of philosophy, but affords the public, in her own persons, details with which a courtezan of the higher class should be unwilling to season her private conversation. (I, 56-7)

69.2 "licence and infidelity"] We do not tax the whole nation of France with being infirm in religious faith, and relaxed in morals; still less do we aver that the Revolution, which broke forth in that country, owed its rise exclusively to the licence and infidelity, which were but too current there. (I, 62)

69.5 had] These would have existed had (I, 62)

70.3 talent] talents (I, 69)

71.14 "odious and contemptible."] After dismission of the Notables, the minister adopted or recommended a line of conduct so fluctuating and indecisive, so violent at one time in support of the royal prerogative, and so pusillanimous when he encountered resistance from the newly-awakened spirit of liberty, that had he been bribed to render the Crown at once odious and contemptible, or to engage his master in a line of conduct which should irritate the courageous, and encourage the timid, among his dissatisfied subjects, the Archbishop of Sens could hardly, after the deepest thought, have adopted measures better adapted for such a purpose. (I, 103-4)

71.19 "national discontent!"] In punishment of their undaunted defence of the popular cause, the Parliament was banished to Troyes; the government thus increasing the national discontent by the removal of the principal court of the kingdom, and by all the evils incident to a delay of public justice. (I, 105)

72n.35 the king, after having] the King, having (I, 253)

72n.39 before] before (I, 253)

73.2-3 "Sound and virtuous"] Necker, a minister of an honest and candid disposition, a republican also, and therefore on principle a respecter of public opinion, unhappily did not recollect, that to be well-formed and accurate, public opinion should be founded on the authority of men of talents and integrity, and that the popular mind must be pre-occupied by arguments of a sound and virtuous tendency, else the enemy will sow tares, and the public will receive it in the absence of more wholesome grain. (I, 114)

73n.18-19 "the . . . religion"] It can only be imputed, on the one hand, to the . . . religion; and, on the other, to the preconcerted determination of the Revolutionists, that no consideration should interfere with the plan of new-modelling the nation through all its institutions, as well of church as of state. (I, 226-7)

74n.12 "usual ministerial arts"] This might doubtless have been done by the usual ministerial arts of influencing elections, or gaining over to the crown-interests some of the many men of talents, who, determined to raise themselves in this new world, had not yet settled to which side they were to give their support. (I, 116-17)

87.21 The successful] The answer to this is, that the successful (I, 163)

88.3 "dark intrigues,"] Meanwhile, the dark intrigues which had been long formed for accomplishing a general insurrection in Paris, were now ready to be brought into action. (I, 154)

92.29 plied," . . . "with] plied with (I, 154)

94.34 "under . . . of popular frenzy."] For this purpose, all those who desired to carry the Revolution to extremity, became desirous to bring the sittings of the National Assembly and the residence of the King within the precincts of Paris, and to place them under . . . of that popular frenzy which they had so many ways of exciting, and which might exercise the authority of terror over the body of representatives, fill their galleries with a wild and tumultuous band of partizans, surround their gates with an infuriated populace, and thus dictate the issue of each deliberation. (I, 180-1)

95.11 societies."] societies, and the hundreds of hundreds of popular orators whom they had at their command, excited the citizens by descriptions of the most dreadful plots, fraught with massacres and proscriptions. (I, 184)

98.8-9 "determined . . . monarchy,"] In stern opposition to those admirers of the Constitution, stood two bodies of unequal numbers, strength, and efficacy; of which the first was determined

... monarchy, while the second entertained the equally resolved purpose of urging these changes still farther onwards, to the total destruction of all civil order, and the establishment of a government in which terror and violence should be the ruling principles, to be wielded by the hands of the demagogues who dared to nourish a scheme so nefarious. (I, 264-5)

98.30 "the association] The beauty, talents, courage, and accomplishments of this remarkable woman, pushed forward into public notice a husband of very middling abilities, and preserved a high influence over the association (I, 269)

98.33-4 "the affected . . . who were] He has never been supposed to possess any great firmness of principle, whether public or private; but a soldier's honour, and a soldier's frankness, together with the habits of good society, led him to contemn and hate the sordid treachery, cruelty, and cynicism of the Jacobins; while his wit and common sense enabled him to see through and deride the affected . . . who, he plainly saw, were (I, 313)

98.36-7 "the Brissotin . . . faction" (he . . . faction), "who] Their claims to share the spoils of the displaced ministry were passed over with contempt, and the King was compelled, in order to have the least chance of obtaining a hearing from the Assembly, to select his ministers from the Brissotin . . . faction, who (I, 306-7)

109n.11-12 "a . . . return."] This Monsieur Lecompte was a loud, and probably a sincere advocate of freedom, and had been a . . . return, as likely to advance the good cause. (VIII, 422)

———— *Old Mortality.* In *Tales of My Landlord, Collected and Arranged by Jedediah Cleishbotham.* 4 vols. Edinburgh: Blackwood; London: Murray, 1816, II-IV.
NOTE: the reference at 164 is to Mause Headriggs.
REFERRED TO: 57, 164

———— *Waverley; or, 'Tis Sixty Years Since.* 3 vols. Edinburgh: Constable; London: Longman, *et al.,* 1814.
NOTE: the reference at 164 is to the Baron of Bradwardine.
REFERRED TO: 55, 164

SCOTUS ERIGENA. See Johannes Scotus.

SERTORIUS, QUINTUS. Referred to: 237

SERVAN, JOSEPH MICHEL ANTOINE.
NOTE: the reference is in a quotation from Moleville.
REFERRED TO: 108

SÉVIGNÉ, MARIE DE RABUTIN CHANTAL, MARQUISE DE.
NOTE: the reference is in a quotation from Courier. See also Voltaire.
REFERRED TO: 222n

SEXTIUS, LUCIUS.
NOTE: the reference derives from Livy.
REFERRED TO: 64-5

SHAKESPEARE, WILLIAM. Referred to: 134, 135, *367*

———— *Hamlet.* In *The Riverside Shakespeare.* Ed. G. Blakemore Evans. Boston: Houghton Mifflin, 1974, 1135-97.
NOTE: this ed. used for ease of reference. The reference at 114 is in a quotation from Carlyle.
REFERRED TO: 114, 122

———— *Henry IV, Part I. Ibid.,* 842-85.
NOTE: the reference is in a quotation from Carlyle.
REFERRED TO: 145, 164

———— *Henry IV, Part II. Ibid.,* 886-929.
REFERRED TO: 161, 164

———— *Macbeth. Ibid.,* 1306-42.
NOTE: the references are in quotations from Carlyle.
REFERRED TO: 143, 145

———— *A Midsummer Night's Dream. Ibid.*, 217-49.
NOTE: the same passage is quoted in both places.
QUOTED: 135, 224
135.12-14 "forms of things unknown," . . . "bodied forth" . . . "turned into shape."] The poet's
eye, in a fine frenzy rolling, / Doth glance from heaven to earth, from earth to heaven; / And as
imagination bodies forth / The forms of things unknown, the poet's pen / Turns them to shapes,
and gives to aery nothing / A local habitation and a name. (242; V, i, 12-17)
224.30 "body forth the forms of things unknown"] [*see preceding collation*]

———— *Othello. Ibid.*, 1198-1248.
NOTE: the references are in quotations from Carlyle.
REFERRED TO: 145, 149

———— *Twelfth Night. Ibid.*, 403-41.
NOTE: the quotation is an indirect echo.
QUOTED: 333

SIDNEY, ALGERNON. Referred to: 121

Le Siècle. Referred to: 303

SIEYÈS, EMMANUEL JOSEPH.
NOTE: the remark quoted was reported to JSM in a private conversation; the reference at 90 is in a
quotation from Montgaillard; that at 141 is in a quotation from Carlyle.
QUOTED: 96
REFERRED TO: 90, 106, 141

———— "Délibérations à prendre dans les assemblées de bailliages." In Louis Philippe
Joseph, duc d'Orléans, *Instructions envoyées par M. le duc d'Orléans*. [Paris: n.p.,
1788,] 11-66.
NOTE: the reference is in a quotation from Carlyle, who attributes the "Délibérations" to Laclos.
REFERRED TO: 141

———— *Qu'est-ce que le tiers état?* 3rd ed. [Paris:] n.p., 1789.
NOTE: the quotations (both indirect) are in a quotation from Carlyle; the sense of the second appears
in several places.
QUOTED: 141
141.9-10 *What . . . something.*] [*translated from:*] [*paragraph*] 1°. Qu'est-ce que le Tiers-
Etat?—TOUT. [*paragraph*] 2°. Qu'a-t-il été jusqu'à présent dans l'ordre politique?—RIEN.
[*paragraph*] 3°. Que demande-t-il?—A ÊTRE QUELQUE CHOSE. (3)
141.13 "The Third Estate is the Nation."] [*translated from:*] [*paragraph*] Sous le second
rapport, il [Le Tiers] est la *Nation.* (154)

SIMON OF TOURNAI.
NOTE: the quotation, in a quotation from Michelet, derives from Matthew Paris, *q.v.*
QUOTED: 248

SISMONDI, JEAN CHARLES LÉONARD SIMONDE DE. *Histoire des Français*. Vols. I-IX.
Paris: Treuttel and Würtz, 1821-26.
NOTE: ultimately 31 vols. (1821-44).
REVIEWED: 15-52
QUOTED: 20-1, 30, 31, 34n, 39, 40n, 41n, 45, 49, 50n
REFERRED TO: 276
20.39-40 dit," . . . "que] dit que (I, xx)
21.1 brillantes. Plutôt] brillantes; plutôt (I, xxi)
21.4 féodalité?] féodalité. (I, xxi)
30.8-20 The . . . superiors.] [*translated from:*] [*no paragraph*] Les comtes ruraux, les vicomtes
et les barons, qui relevoient immédiatement du roi, dans le duché de France, avoient profité de la
foiblesse de Philippe pour secouer absolument son autorité, dans les châteaux où ils s'étoient
fortifiés. Ils en sortoient pour fondre sur les voyageurs et les marchands qui passoient à portée de
leur retraite, lorsque ceux-ci ne consentoient pas à se racheter par une grosse rançon: ils

abusoient également de leur force contre les couvens et contre tous les seigneurs ecclésiastiques. Tantôt ils venoient loger chez eux avec leurs écuyers, leurs soldats, leurs chevaux et leurs chiens, et ils exigeoient que la maison religieuse où ils prenoient de force l'hospitalité les défrayât pendant des mois entiers; tantôt ils forçoient les paysans des moines ou des évêques à leur payer des redevances, ou en argent ou en denrées, pour la protection que les hommes de guerre promettoient de leur accorder. Les barons en particulier, qui étoient vassaux de quelque église, sembloient se faire un titre de leur vasselage même pour dépouiller leurs seigneurs ecclésiastiques. (V, 10-11)

31.6-17 "This seigneur," . . . had . . . operation.] [*translated from:*] "Ce seigneur, dit l'abbé de Nogent, fils d'Engherrand de Coucy, avoit, dès sa première jeunesse, augmenté incessamment ses richesses par le pillage des voyageurs et des pèlerins, et il avoit étendu sa domination par des mariages incestueux avec de riches héritières ses parentes. Sa cruauté étoit tellement inouïe, que les bouchers, qui cependant passent pour insensibles, épargnent plus de douleurs au bétail, en l'égorgeant, qu'il n'en épargnoit aux hommes; car il ne se contentoit point de les punir par le glaive, pour des fautes déterminées, comme on a coutume de faire; il les déchiroit par les plus horribles supplices. Lorsqu'il vouloit arracher une rançon à ses captifs, il les suspendoit par quelque partie plus délicate de leur corps, ou bien il les couchoit par terre; et les couvrant de pierres, il marchoit dessus, les frappant en même temps jusqu'à ce qu'ils eussent promis tout ce qu'il demandoit, ou qu'ils fussent morts à la peine."[1] [*footnote omitted*] (V, 94-5)

31.22-6 "The king," . . . "tried . . . life."] [*translated from:*] Le roi voulut l'engager à remettre en liberté, dans ses derniers momens, les marchands qu'il avoit enlevés sur les grands chemins; il les retenoit dans ses cachots, pour les forcer à lui payer une rançon, où il les faisoit torturer pour son divertissement; mais même dans les agonies de la mort, Coucy se refusoit à toute miséricorde, et il sembloit regretter sa domination sur ses captifs, bien plus que sa propre vie. (V, 210-11)

34n.11-12 "marvellously severe and rigorous"] [*translated from:*] Il étoit merveilleusement sévère et rigoureux contre les sorcières, enchanteurs, négromanciens et autres, qui s'aidoient de semblables et indues arts. [*Sismondi is quoting Oudegherst*] (V, 205)

34n.14-15 "qu'il] Il chassit et bannit de Flandre tous juifs et usuriers; lesquels avoient auparavant illec vécu sans tribu, disant qu'il [*Sismondi is quoting Oudegherst*] (V, 205)

34n.19 *les cervoises*] Pour à la famine obvier, et afin que les vivres fussent de tant meilleur prix, il fit par tout le pays de Flandre défendre les cervoises, et tuer les chiens et les veaux, ordonnant que tous les greniers des marchands de blés fussent ouverts, et que lesdits blés fussent vendus et distribués à prix raisonnable. [*Sismondi is quoting Oudegherst*] (V, 206)

34n.21 *at a reasonable price.*] [*see preceding entry*]

39n.3 Française."] française: aussi n'y avoit-il jamais des combats à livrer, et des dangers à braver, d'un bout de la chrétienté à l'autre, sans que cette noblesse vînt comme volontaire en réclamer sa part. (VII, 108)

39.7 Les] [*no paragraph*] Les (VII, 122)

39.22 jamais de l'argent] jamais d'argent (VII, 123)

39.25 *La . . . noblesse*] [*not in italics*] (VII, 123)

39.25 vanité] cupidité (VII, 123)

39.29 interdit. La] interdit.[1] [*footnote omitted*] La (VII, 123)

40n.1 "Dans . . . âge," . . . "on] En effet dans . . . âge on (VI, 364)

41n.4 "Au] [*paragraph*] Au (V, 139)

41n.19 tourmens] traitemens (V, 140)

41n.5 sa] la (V, 141)

45.10 *"deux . . . noblesse,"*] [*see entry for 39.25 above*]

49.2 *haute justice, . . . garenne*] Enfin il se laissa fléchir, et il accorda la vie à Enguerrand; mais il lui imposa une amende très-considérable, un exil de trois ans à la Terre-Sainte, et il le priva du droit de haute justice et du droit de garenne dans toutes ses terres.[1] [*footnote omitted*] (VIII, 98)

50n.2 "Le siècle," . . . "dont] Le siècle dont (IX, 195)

50n.4 témoignage."] témoignage; on y trouve sans cesse des attestations solennelles de choses évidemment controuvées, et le sens commun se révolte contre la preuve écrite qu'on lui présente. (IX, 195-6)

SIWARD (Earl of Northumberland). Referred to: 24

SOCRATES. Referred to: 273n

SOLAGES, COMTE DE.
NOTE: no other information available; the reference, in a quotation from Carlyle, is to him as one of seven prisoners in the Bastille.
REFERRED TO: 146

SOLON. Referred to: 160

SOREL, AGNES.
NOTE: the reference is in a quotation from Carlyle.
REFERRED TO: 165

SOULAVIE, JEAN LOUIS. *Mémoires historiques et politiques du règne de Louis XVI, depuis son mariage, jusqu'à sa mort.* 6 vols. Paris: Treuttel and Würtz, 1801.
QUOTED: 106
REFERRED TO: 93, 106
106.4 "Quoique . . . Girondins," . . . "fût] Les girondins et tous les partis effrayés de leur férocité respective, ont été obligés de mentir et de tenir le langage du tems; et quoique . . . girondins fût (VI, 450)

SOULT, NICOLAS JEAN DE DIEU, DUC DE DALMATIE.
NOTE: maréchal de France.
REFERRED TO: 189

SOUTHERN, HENRY (prob.). "Barante, *Histoire des ducs de Bourgogne*," *Westminster Review*, II (Oct., 1824), 442-62.
NOTE: one of the *Westminster* articles on French historical works.
REFERRED TO: 18

——— "The *Chronicles* of Froissart," *Westminster Review*, IV (July, 1825), 1-20.
NOTE: one of the *Westminster* articles on French historical works.
REFERRED TO: 18

——— "Court of Louis XIV and the Regency," *Westminster Review*, II (July, 1824), 121-49.
NOTE: one of the *Westminster* articles on French historical works.
REFERRED TO: 18

——— "Montlosier's *French Monarchy*," *Westminster Review*, III (Jan., 1825), 35-48.
NOTE: one of the *Westminster* articles on French historical works.
REFERRED TO: 18

——— "*Private Memoirs of Madame du Hausset*," *Westminster Review*, V (Jan., 1826), 249-62.
NOTE: one of the *Westminster* articles on French historical works.
REFERRED TO: 18

SPENCER, ROBERT (Earl of Sunderland). Referred to: 189

SPINOLA, AMBROSE, MARQUIS DE LOS BALBASES.
NOTE: the reference is in a quotation from Carlyle.
REFERRED TO: 146

STAËL-HOLSTEIN, ANNE LOUISE GERMAINE NECKER, BARONNE DE.
NOTE: the references at 68n and 85n are in the title of a work by Bailleul.
REFERRED TO: 13, 68n, 85n, *371n*

——— *Considérations sur les principaux événemens de la révolution françoise.* 3 vols. Paris: Delaunay, and Bossange and Masson, 1818.
NOTE: the quotation at 104, and the references at 85 and 102 are in quotations from Bailleul.
QUOTED: 65, 93, 104
REFERRED TO: 72n, 75n, 81n, 85, 85n, 88-9, 93n, 102, 102n, 108

65.14-19   "Les . . . étrangers," . . . qui . . . nègre. . . . La] *[paragraph]* Les . . . étrangers qui . . . nègre. C'étoit un argument pour soulager les blancs, mais non pour s'endurcir contre les noirs. La (I, 79)

93.4-5   "Un . . . faire une idée . . . *nation.*"] Mais un . . . faire l'idée . . . nation. (I, 228)

104.5   monarchie?"] monarchie; ils périrent peu de temps après, en essayant de sauver la France et son roi. (II, 28)

104.7-8   *leur . . . patrie,*] Aussi M. de Lalli a-t-il dit, avec son éloquence accoutumée, que *leur . . . patrie.* (II, 28-9)

STANHOPE, PHILIP HENRY. "Lord John Russell, *The Causes of the French Revolution,*" *Quarterly Review,* XLIX (Apr., 1833), 152-74.
REFERRED TO: 115

STEPHEN (of England). Referred to: 26

STEPHEN OF TOURS. Referred to: 35

STERNE, LAURENCE. *The Life and Opinions of Tristram Shandy, Gentleman* (1760-67). 9 vols. in 5. London: Tonson and Millar, 1781.
NOTE: in SC. The reference is to Uncle Toby.
REFERRED TO: 164

STRAFFORD. See Wentworth.

STUBBS, WILLIAM, ed. "Constitutions of Clarendon." In *Select Charters and Other Illustrations of English Constitutional History from the Earliest Times to the Reign of Edward the First.* Oxford: Clarendon Press, 1870, 129-34.
NOTE: this ed., which postdates the reference, used for ease of reference; the text is on 131-4.
REFERRED TO: 244

SUE, EUGÈNE. Referred to: 220

SUETONIUS TRANQUILLUS, GAIUS.
NOTE: the reference is in a quotation from Dulaure.
REFERRED TO: 23

SUGER, ABBÉ.
NOTE: the reference is in a quotation from Dulaure.
REFERRED TO: 23

SULPICE, SEIGNEUR D'AMBOISE ET DE CHAUMONT.
NOTE: not otherwise identified.
REFERRED TO: 28

SUNDERLAND. See Spencer.

SYLVESTER II (Pope).
NOTE: Gerbert. The reference is in a quotation from Michelet.
REFERRED TO: 239

TACITUS, CORNELIUS.
NOTE: the reference is in a quotation from Dulaure.
REFERRED TO: 23

——— *Agricola.* In *Dialogus, Agricola, Germania* (Latin and English). Trans. Maurice Hutton. London: Heinemann; New York: Macmillan, 1914, 168-252.
NOTE: this ed. used for ease of reference. Two eds. (Leyden: Elzevir, 1640, and Amsterdam: Elzevir, 1672-73) formerly in SC.
QUOTED: 215
215.16-19   nosque ab . . . et immortalibus laudibus . . . decorabimus.] nosque domum tuam ab . . . et laudibus . . . colamus: is verus honos, ea coniunctissimi cuiusque pietas. (250; 46)

——— *Germania. Ibid.,* 264-333.
NOTE: the references at 284 and *387* are in a (repeated) quotation from Guizot.
REFERRED TO: 284 (*387*)

TALLEYRAND-PÉRIGORD, CHARLES MAURICE DE.
NOTE: the reference is in a quotation from Carlyle.
REFERRED TO: 140

TARDIVET DU REPAIRE.
NOTE: not otherwise identified; the reference is in a quotation from Carlyle.
REFERRED TO: 156

TAVERNIER.
NOTE: no other information available; the reference, in a quotation from Carlyle, is to him as one of seven prisoners in the Bastille.
REFERRED TO: 146

THEOBALD II, COMTE DE CHAMPAGNE.
NOTE: known as le Grand.
REFERRED TO: 30

THEOBALD V, COMTE DE CHARTRES ET DE BLOIS.
NOTE: known as le Bon.
REFERRED TO: 28

THÉODORIC.
NOTE: King of the Ostrogoths. The reference at 275 is in a quotation from Guizot.
REFERRED TO: 275, 280

THEODOSIUS I. Referred to: 241

THÉROIGNE DE MÉRICOURT, ANNE JOSÈPHE.
NOTE: the references are in a quotation from Carlyle.
REFERRED TO: 152, 155

THIERRY.
NOTE: the reference, to the servant of Louis XVI, is in a quotation from Bailleul.
REFERRED TO: 103

THIERRY III.
NOTE: of Neustria and Burgundy; one of the rois fainéants.
REFERRED TO: 19

THIERRY IV.
NOTE: of Neustria; one of the rois fainéants.
REFERRED TO: 19

THIERRY, JACQUES NICOLAS AUGUSTIN.
NOTE: the quotation and references at 181 are in a quotation from Nisard.
QUOTED: 181
REFERRED TO: 181, 221, 226-7, 228, 231, 233, 234, 275, *370n*

——— Dix ans d'études historiques. Brussels: Hauman, 1835.
NOTE: in SC.
QUOTED: 226
226.21 "to plant the standard of historical reform;"] [*translated from:*] Cette vocation que j'embrassai dès lors avec toute l'ardeur de la jeunesse, c'était, non de ramener isolément un peu de vrai dans quelque coin mal connu du moyen-âge, mais de planter, pour la France du dix-neuvième siècle, le drapeau de la réforme historique. (xv)

——— Histoire de la conquête de l'Angleterre par les Normands, de ses causes, et de ses suites jusqu'à nos jours, en Angleterre, en Ecosse, en Irlande et sur le continent (1825). 2nd ed. 4 vols. Paris: Sautelet, 1826.
NOTE: JSM's references conform to this ed.
REFERRED TO: 35, 36, 181, 221n, 226

——— Lettres sur l'histoire de France pour servir d'introduction à l'étude de cette histoire (1827). 5th ed. Brussels: Hauman, 1836.

NOTE: in SC.
QUOTED: 222n-3n
REFERRED TO: 185, 226, 245, 289
222n.32 S'agit-il] [*no paragraph*] S'agit-il (32)
222n.34 étranger] étranger[1] [*footnote omitted*] (33)
223n.6 richesse] richesse. . . .[2] [*footnote:*] [2][Velly,] *Histoire de France*, tome I, page 381 et 382. (33)
223n.6-7 richesse. [*paragraph*] "'Hilderic] richesse. . . .[2] [*footnote above*] [*JSM moves back 3 pages; no paragraph*] "Hilderik (30)
223n.10 Thuringe.] Thuringe. . . .[1] [*footnote omitted*] (30)
223n.17 Allemagne."] Allemagne. . . .[2] [*footnote:*] [2][Velly,] *Histoire de France*, tome I, page 41. (30)

———— *Récits des temps mérovingiens précédés de considérations sur l'histoire de France*. 2 vols. Paris: Tessier, 1840.
QUOTED: 234
REFERRED TO: 227, 241
234.3 "conscientious studies"] [*translated from:*] Il peut se rencontrer, je le sais, un homme que l'originalité de son talent absolve du reproche de s'être fait des règles exceptionnelles, et qui, par des études consciencieuses et de rares qualités d'intelligence, ait le privilége de contribuer à l'agrandissement de la science, quelque procédé qu'il emploie pour y parvenir; mais cela ne prouve pas qu'en histoire toute méthode soit légitime. (I, 213-14)

THIERS, LOUIS ADOLPHE. Referred to: 185, 193, 221

———— *Histoire de la révolution française*. 10 vols. Paris: Lecointe and Durey, 1823-27.
NOTE: the title page of I and II has the sub-title, "*accompagnée d'une histoire de la révolution de 1355, ou Des états-généraux sous le roi Jean*," and authorship is assigned to Thiers and Félix Bodin; this joint scheme was abandoned with the publication of III.
REFERRED TO: 116, 143n, 185

———— *History of the French Revolution*. Trans. Frederick Shoberl. 5 vols. London: Bentley, 1838.
NOTE: the reference (1837) anticipates the publication.
REFERRED TO: 143n

———— Leading article in *Le National*, 4 Feb., 1830, 1-2.
NOTE: the notion did not originate with Thiers (it is attributed to Jan Zamoyski), but JSM evidently has him in mind. Thiers made a similar comment, *ibid.*, 20 Jan., 1830, 2.
QUOTED: 332
332.14 "le roi règne et ne gouverne pas."] Le roi n'administre pas, ne gouverne pas, il règne. (1)

THUCYDIDES. *Thucydides* (Greek and English). Trans. Charles Forster Smith. 4 vols. London: Heinemann; Cambridge, Mass.: Harvard University Press, 1969.
NOTE: this ed. cited for ease of reference. Formerly two Greek and Latin eds. in SC.
REFERRED TO: 3, *368*

THURIOT DE LA ROZIÈRE, JACQUES ALEXIS.
NOTE: the quotation and references are in a quotation from Carlyle.
QUOTED: 144
REFERRED TO: 144, 146, 147

TIMUR (Tamurlane).
NOTE: JSM uses the spelling Timour.
REFERRED TO: 24

TOCQUEVILLE, ALEXIS HENRI CHARLES MAURICE CLÉREL, COMTE DE. *De la démocratie en Amérique*. [1st pt.] 2 vols. Paris: Gosselin, 1835. 2nd pt. 2 vols. Paris: Gosselin, 1840.
NOTE: the reference antedates the publication of the final two volumes.
REFERRED TO: 184

—— "Discours prononcé à la chambre des députés, le 27 janvier 1848, dans la discussion du projet d'adresse en réponse au discours de la couronne." In *Oeuvres complètes*. Ed. Mme de Tocqueville [and Gustave de Beaumont]. 9 vols. Paris: Lévy frères, 1864-66, IX, 520-35.

NOTE: the quotations at 326-8 are translations of part of the speech quoted at *394-7*. This ed. postdates JSM's quotations, but the wording he uses is not that in the *Moniteur* of 28 Jan., 1848; this ed. reproduces the text that Tocqueville prepared himself, copies of which (none apparently now extant) he evidently had printed, and perhaps one of which he sent to JSM.

QUOTED: 326-8 (*394-7*)

394.3   Pour parler] [*no paragraph*] Et pour parler (521)

395.24-5   demande? [*paragraph*] Je] demande? [*3½-page omission*] Je (523-7)

395.30   1830. . . . C'est] 1830 [*ellipsis indicates 4-sentence omission*] C'est (527)

396.2   temps. . . . Et] temps. [*paragraph*] Voilà, messieurs, ce que le gouvernement a fait, ce qu'en particulier le ministère actuel a fait. Et (528)

396.9   publiques? . . . Ils] publiques? [*paragraph*] Pour moi, je suis profondément convaincu du contraire; je ne veux pas prêter à mes adversaires des motifs déshonnêtes qu'ils n'auraient pas eus; j'admettrai, si l'on veut, qu'en se servant des moyens que je blâme, ils ont cru se livrer à un mal nécessaire; que la grandeur du but leur a caché le danger et l'immoralité du moyen. Je veux croire cela; mais les moyens en ont-ils été moins dangereux? Ils (528)

396.15   vices. C'est] vices. (Mouvement.) C'est (528)

396.20   confiait. . . . Je ne] confiait; ils ont ainsi accordé une sorte de prime à l'immoralité et au vice. [*paragraph*] Je ne veux citer qu'un exemple, pour montrer ce que je veux dire, c'est celui de ce ministre, dont je ne rappellerai pas le nom, qui a été appelé dans le sein du cabinet, quoique toute la France, ainsi que ses collègues, sussent déjà qu'il était indigne d'y siéger; qui est sorti du cabinet parce que cette indignité devenait trop notoire, et qu'on a placé alors où? sur le siége le plus élevé de la justice, d'où il a dû bientôt descendre pour venir s'asseoir sur la sellette de l'accusé. [*paragraph*] Et bien! messieurs, quant à moi, je ne (529)

396.23-4   hommes. . . . [*paragraph*] Pour la] hommes. [*JSM moves back 8½ pages*] [*no paragraph*] Pour mon compte, je déclare sincèrement à la Chambre que, pour la (529, 520)

396.32   pays. . . . Est-ce que] pays. [*JSM moves ahead 13 pages*] Est-ce que (521, 534)

396.32   ressentez] sentez (534)

396.36-397.1   enlève. . . . [*paragraph*] Ma conviction] enlève: et c'est dans de pareils temps que vous restez calmes en présence de la dégradation des moeurs publiques, car le mot n'est pas trop fort. [*paragraph*] Je parle ici sans amertume, je vous parle, je crois, même sans esprit de parti; j'attaque des hommes contre lesquels je n'ai pas de colère; mais enfin je suis obligé de dire à mon pays ce qui est ma conviction profonde at arrêtée. Eh bien! ma conviction (534)

397.3   nouvelles. . . . Est-ce que] nouvelles. Est-ce donc que la vie des rois tient à des fils plus fermes et plus difficiles à briser que celle des autres hommes? est-ce que (535)

397.7-8   elle? [*paragraph*] Messieurs] elle? (Interruption au centre.) [*paragraph*] Messieurs (535)

TOULONGEON, FRANÇOIS EMMANUEL D'EMSKERQUE, VICOMTE DE. Referred to: 91, 105

—— *Histoire de France, depuis la révolution de 1789, écrite d'après les mémoires et manuscrits contemporains, recueillis dans les dépôts civils et militaires*. 7 vols. Paris: Treuttel and Würtz, 1801-10.

NOTE: the quotation at 157 is in a quotation from Carlyle.

QUOTED: 91, 105, 157

REFERRED TO: 74n, 75n, 81n, 91n, 93, 117

91.7-8   "l'intendant . . . tranquille;"] Le jour même où la Bastille fut assaillie et prise, tandis qu'une députation des états-généraux venait agiter le repos du monarque, l'intendant . . . tranquille. (I, 17-18)

105.27-9   "La république . . . seuls."] Dans les circonstances où elle se trouvait, un changement de dynastie (car la république . . . seuls), un changement de dynastie était donc le seul parti qui pût balancer celui que prit l'assemblée, et la branche d'Orléans était la seule qui eût pu attirer les

TURPIN, RICHARD (DICK).
NOTE: his name became proverbial for highwaymen.
REFERRED TO: 29

TWISS, TRAVERS.
NOTE: the reference is to recently appointed qualified examiners at Oxford.
REFERRED TO: *369*

TYCHO. See Brahe.

VAN DER STRATE, BERTHOLF.
NOTE: the reference derives from Sismondi.
REFERRED TO: 34n

VANE, HENRY. Referred to: 136

VARICOURT, ROUPH DE.
NOTE: the reference is in a quotation from Carlyle, who refers to him as Varigny.
REFERRED TO: 156, 157

VARIGNY. See Varicourt.

VATTEL, EMERICH DE. *Le droit des gens, ou Principes de la loi naturelle appliqués à la conduite et aux affaires des nations et des souverains.* 2 vols. Leyden: Dépens de la compagnie, 1758.
NOTE: also published in Neuchâtel in 1758.
REFERRED TO: 345

VELLY, PAUL FRANÇOIS.
NOTE: the quotations are not collated, because they derive from Thierry, who is citing Velly's *Histoire de France, depuis l'établissement de la monarchie, jusqu'au règne de Louis XIV,* 15 vols. (Paris: Saillant and Nym, Desaint, 1770-86.)
QUOTED: 223n
REFERRED TO: 222n

VERGNIAUD, PIERRE VICTURNIEN.
NOTE: the quotation and the references at 102, and 103 are in a quotation from Bailleul; the reference at 105 is in a quotation from Toulongeon. See also Guadet, "Copie."
QUOTED: 103
REFERRED TO: 102, 103, 105, 106, 107

VICO, GIOVANNI BATISTA. Referred to: 185

VICTOIRE-LOUISE.
NOTE: known as Madame, the younger daughter of Louis XV. The reference is in a quotation from Ferrières.
REFERRED TO: 88

VICTOR EMMANUEL II (of Sardinia). Referred to: 345

VIGER, LOUIS FRANÇOIS SÉBASTIEN.
NOTE: the reference, in a quotation from Mignet, is to the members of the Commission of Twelve.
REFERRED TO: 12

VIGNY, VICTOR ALFRED, COMTE DE. Referred to: 185

VILLÈLE, JEAN BAPTISTE SÉRAPHIN JOSEPH, COMTE DE.
NOTE: the reference at 190 is to the Villèle ministry.
REFERRED TO: 179, 190, 229

VILLEMAIN, ABEL FRANÇOIS. Referred to: 193, 262, 302, *370n*

VIRGIL (Publius Virgilius Maro).
NOTE: the reference is in a quotation from Nisard.
REFERRED TO: 173

WENTWORTH, THOMAS (Earl of Strafford). Referred to: 136

WESLEY, JOHN. Referred to: 224

WHYTE (or De Witt).
NOTE: no other information available; the reference, in a quotation from Carlyle, is to him as one of seven prisoners in the Bastille.
REFERRED TO: 146

WILLIAM I (of England).
NOTE: known as the Conqueror.
REFERRED TO: 26, 47n

WILLIAM III (of England). Referred to: 330

WILLIAM OF MALMESBURY. *Gesta regum anglorum, atque historia novella.* Ed. Thomas Duffus Hardy. 2 vols. London: English Historical Society, 1840.
NOTE: this ed. cited for ease of reference.
REFERRED TO: 47n

WILSON, ROBERT THOMAS. Referred to: 179

WORDSWORTH, WILLIAM. Referred to: 165

———— Sonnet XIII ("O Friend! I know not which way I must look") (1807) of "Sonnets Dedicated to Liberty." In *The Poetical Works.* 5 vols. London: Longman, *et al.,* 1827, III, 139.
NOTE: in SC.
QUOTED: 177
177.5-6 "good old cause"] Rapine, avarice, expense, / This is idolatry; and these we adore: / Plain living and high thinking are no more: / The homely beauty of the good old cause / Is gone; our peace, our fearful innocence, / And pure religion breathing household laws. (III, 139; 9-14)

XENOPHON. *Αναβασις Κυρου Χενοφωντος; or, The Expedition of Cyrus into Persia, and the Retreat of the Ten Thousand Greeks.* Trans. N.S. Smith. London: Longman, *et al.,* 1824.
NOTE: the translated phrase to which JSM calls attention ("gentlemen of the army"—most translations give "soldiers") is footnoted by Smith: "literally, 'Armed Men,' smartly translated, 'Gentlemen of the Army.'"
QUOTED: 222-3

———— *The Anabasis of Cyrus.* In *Hellenica, Anabasis, Symposium, and Apology.* Trans. Carleton L. Brownson and O.J. Todd. 3 vols. London: Heinemann; New York: Putnam's Sons, 1918, 1921, 1922, II, 229-43, III, 1-371.
NOTE: this ed. used for ease of reference.
QUOTED: 223

YOUNG, ARTHUR. *Travels, during the Years 1787, 1788, and 1789. Undertaken More Particularly with a View of Ascertaining the Cultivation, Wealth, Resources, and Natural Prosperity, of the Kingdom of France.* Bury St. Edmunds: Richardson, 1792.
NOTE: the quotations, which are in quotations from Carlyle, are not collated because Carlyle's adaptation is loose. See also 2nd ed., next entry.
QUOTED: 148, 149, 150
REFERRED TO: 148

———— 2nd ed. 2 vols. London and Bury St. Edmunds: Richardson, 1794.
NOTE: the references are to this ed.; see also 1st ed., preceding entry.
REFERRED TO: 66, 81n

BRITISH STATUTES

43 Elizabeth, c. 2. An Act for the Reliefe of the Poore (1601).
REFERRED TO: 127, 348

2 & 3 William IV, c. 45. An Act to Amend the Representation of the People in England and Wales (7 June, 1832).
REFERRED TO: 192, 320, 329

FRENCH BILLS AND STATUTES

Loi sur la constitution civile du clergé, et la fixation de son traitement (24 Aug., 1790). *Lois, et actes du gouvernement*, I, 372-3.
REFERRED TO: 73n

Loi. Constitution française (14 Sept., 1791). *Ibid.*, IV, 188-232.
NOTE: "Déclaration des droits de l'homme et du citoyen" appears on 188-91.
REFERRED TO: 72n

Décret concernant les émigrans (9 Nov., 1791), *Gazette Nationale, ou Le Moniteur Universel*, 10 Nov., 1791, 1310-11.
NOTE: the reference is in a quotation from Mignet; the décret is unheaded in the *Gazette*.
REFERRED TO: 11

Décret relatif aux troubles excités sous prétexte de religion (16 Nov., 1791), *ibid.*, 17 Nov., 1791, 1338.
NOTE: the reference is in a quotation from Mignet. The text of the décret (unheaded in the *Gazette*) appeared on 17 Nov.; voting ended on 12 Nov. (*ibid.*, 24 Nov., 1368-9).
REFERRED TO: 11

Décret sur les prêtres non-sermentés (27 May, 1792), *ibid.*, 4 June, 1792, 647.
REFERRED TO: 102

Décret d'augmentation de vingt mille hommes pour l'armée, et du mode de cette levée (8 June, 1792), *ibid.*, 9 June, 1792, 668.
NOTE: the décret is not entitled in the *Gazette*, nor is the text given. For Louis XVI's refusal to sanction it, see *ibid.*, 20 June, 1792, 716.
REFERRED TO: 11, 102

Acte constitutionnel de la république (24 June, 1793), *ibid.*, 27 June, 1793, 765-6.
NOTE: the reference, to the French Constitution of 1793, is in a self-quotation. The Constitution was not presented for approval by the National Convention (and so does not appear in the *Lois, et actes du gouvernement*), but was approved by "the people of France" at a fête on 10 Aug., 1793. The "Acte" is preceded by a "Déclaration des droits de l'homme et du citoyen."
REFERRED TO: 126

Loi sur le mode de gouvernement provisoire et révolutionnaire (14 frimaire an II; 4 Dec., 1793). *Lois, et actes du gouvernement*, VIII, 100-13.
REFERRED TO: 174

Constitution de la république française, proposée au peuple français par la convention nationale. Paris: Imprimerie de la république, an III [1795].
NOTE: the Directorial Constitution.
REFERRED TO: 359

Loi concernant la division du territoire de la république et l'administration. Bulletin 17, No. 115 (28 pluviôse an VIII; 17 Feb., 1800). *Bulletin des lois de la république française*, I, 1-94.

NOTE: at this time the Bulletins were separately paginated (this is the whole of Bulletin 17).
REFERRED TO: 174

Charte constitutionnelle. Bulletin 17, No. 133 (14 June, 1814). *Bulletin des lois du royaume de France*, 5th ser., I, 197-207.
REFERRED TO: 128, 175, 176, 192

Loi sur la publication des journaux et écrits périodiques. Bulletin 356, No. 8494 (31 March, 1820). *Ibid.*, 7th ser., X, 386-7.
REFERRED TO: 178

Loi sur les élections. Bulletin 379, No. 8910 (29 June, 1820). *Ibid.*, 1001-6.
REFERRED TO: 178

Loi relative à la censure des journaux. Bulletin 464, No. 10,933 (26 July, 1821). *Ibid.*, XIII, 33-4.
REFERRED TO: 178

Ordonnance du roi relative à l'administration supérieure de l'instruction publique, aux collèges, institutions, pensions, et écoles primaires. Bulletin 664, No. 16,774 (8 Apr., 1824). *Ibid.*, XVIII, 200-3.
REFERRED TO: 189

Loi relative au renouvellement intégral et septennal de la chambre des députés. Bulletin 672, No. 17,159 (9 June, 1824). *Ibid.*, XVIII, 321-2.
REFERRED TO: 182, 189

Loi pour la répression des crimes et des délits commis dans les édifices ou sur les objets consacrés à la religion catholique ou aux autres cultes légalement établis en France. Bulletin 29, No. 665 (20 Apr., 1825). *Ibid.*, 8th ser., I, 221-5.
REFERRED TO: 189

Loi concernant l'indemnité à accorder aux anciens propriétaires des biens-fonds confisqués et vendus au profit de l'état en vertu des lois sur les émigrés, les condamnés et les déportés. Bulletin 30, No. 680 (27 Apr., 1825). *Ibid.*, II, 229-38.
REFERRED TO: 189

Projet de loi sur les successions et les substitutions (5 Feb., 1826), *Le Moniteur Universel*, 11 Feb., 1826, 168.
NOTE: concerning primogeniture, the bill was presented to the Chamber of Peers on 10 Feb., and finally rejected on 8 Apr. (*ibid.*, 12 Apr.).
REFERRED TO: 190

Projet de loi sur la police de la presse (27 Dec., 1826), *ibid.*, 30 Dec., 1826, 1730.
NOTE: presented to the Chamber of Deputies on 29 Dec., 1826. Withdrawn by an ordonnance, 17 Apr., 1827 (*ibid.*, 19 Apr., 1827, 615).
REFERRED TO: 190

Ordonnance du roi portant la remise en vigueur des lois des 3l mars 1820 et 26 juillet 1821. Bulletin 170, No. 6439 (24 June, 1827). *Bulletin des lois du royaume de France*, 8th ser., VI, 729.
NOTE: the laws referred to are Loi sur la publication des journaux et écrits périodiques (31 Mar., 1820), *q.v.*; and Loi relative à la censure des journaux (26 July, 1821), *q.v.*
REFERRED TO: 190

Ordonnance du roi qui suspend la liberté de la presse périodique et semi-périodique. Bulletin 367, No. 15,135 (25 July, 1830). *Ibid.*, 8th ser., XII, 33-4.
REFERRED TO: 192

Ordonnance du roi qui dissout la chambre des députés des départemens. Bulletin 367, No. 15,136 (25 July, 1830). *Ibid.*, XII, 35.
REFERRED TO: 192

Ordonnance du roi qui réforme, selon les principes de la charte constitutionnelle, les règles d'élection, et prescrit l'exécution de l'article 46 de la charte. Bulletin 367, No. 15,137 (25 July, 1830). *Ibid.*, 35-9.
REFERRED TO: 192

Ordonnance du roi qui convoque les colléges électoraux d'arrondissement pour le 6 septembre prochain, les colléges de département pour le 13, et la chambre des députés pour le 28 du même mois. Bulletin 367, No. 15,138 (25 July, 1830). *Ibid.*, 39-40.
REFERRED TO: 192

Charte constitutionnelle. Bulletin 5, No. 59 (14 Aug., 1830). *Ibid.*, 9th ser., Pt. 1, I, 51-64.
REFERRED TO: 175, 323

Loi contenant l'article qui remplace l'article 23 de la charte. Bulletin 54, No. 130 (29 Dec., 1831). *Ibid.*, Pt. 1, III, 61-4.
REFERRED TO: 305

Ordonnance du roi qui met la ville de Paris en état de siège. Bulletin 161, No. 4204 (6 June, 1832). *Ibid.*, Pt. 2, Sect. 1, IV, 662.
REFERRED TO: 200

Loi sur l'instruction primaire. Bulletin 105, No. 236 (28 June, 1833). *Ibid.*, Pt. 1, V, 251-62.
REFERRED TO: 324

Loi sur les associations. Bulletin 115, No. 261 (10 Apr., 1834). *Ibid.*, Pt. 1, VI, 25-6.
NOTE: the reference at 128 is to its passing through the Chambers.
REFERRED TO: 128, 300

Loi sur les crimes, délits et contraventions de la presse et des autres moyens de publication. Bulletin l55, No. 356 (9 Sept., 1835). *Ibid.*, Pt. 1, VII, 247-56.
REFERRED TO: 205, 209, 211, 329, *390n*

Loi sur les cours d'assises. Bulletin 155, No. 357 (9 Sept., 1835). *Ibid.*, Pt. 1, VII, 256-9.
REFERRED TO: 205, 209, 211, 329, *390n*

Loi qui rectifie les articles 341, 345, 346, 347 et 352 du code d'instruction criminelle, et l'article 17 du code pénal. Bulletin 155, No. 358 (9 Sept., 1835). *Ibid.*, Pt. 1, VII, 259-62.
REFERRED TO: 205, 209, 211, 329, *390n*

Loi sur les chemins vicinaux. Bulletin 422, No. 6293 (21 May, 1836). *Ibid.*, XII, 193-200.
REFERRED TO: 324

Loi sur les sucres. Bulletin 1019, No. 10,728 (2 July, 1843). *Ibid.*, XXVII, 549-51.
REFERRED TO: 301

Décret and Arrêtés. Bulletin 5, Nos. 67-9 (4 Mar., 1848). *Bulletin des lois de la république française*, 10th ser., I, 53-4.
NOTE: these set up and named the members of the commission to abolish slavery immediately in the French colonies.
REFERRED TO: 339

Constitution de la république française. Bulletin 87, No. 825 (4 Nov., 1848). *Ibid.*, II, 575-605.
REFERRED TO : 358

Index

References to Appendix A are in italic type; Appendix B is not indexed.